DATE DUE

D0713216

INSIDE

WINDOWS NT® SERVER 4

CERTIFIED ADMINISTRATOR'S RESOURCE EDITION

Drew Heywood
Darin Camp
Michael Hayes
Howard Hilliker
Kathy Ivens
Brad McGehee
Barrie Sosinsky

New Riders

New Riders Publishing, Indianapolis, Indiana

...ertified
Administrator's Resource Edition

By Drew Heywood, et al.

Published by:
New Riders Publishing
201 West 103rd Street
Indianapolis, IN 46290 USA

Copyright © 1997 by New Riders Publishing

Printed in the United States of America 1 2 3 4 5 6 7 8 9 0

Library of Congress Cataloging-in-Publication Data

CIP information furnished upon request

Warning and Disclaimer

This book is designed to provide information about the Windows NT Server 4 computer program. Every effort has been made to make this book as complete and as accurate as possible, but no warranty or fitness is implied.

The information is provided on an "as is" basis. The authors and New Riders Publishing shall have neither liability nor responsibility to any person or entity with respect to any loss or damages arising from the information contained in this book or from the use of the discs or programs that may accompany it.

Associate Publisher	*David Dwyer*
Publishing Manager	*Julie Fairweather*
Marketing Manager	*Mary Foote*
Managing Editor	*Sarah Kearns*
Director of Development	*Kezia Endsley*

Product Development Specialist
Sean Angus

Developmental Editors
Ami Frank, Stacia Mellinger

Senior Editor
Suzanne Snyder

Lead Editors
Gina Brown, Jenny Clark,
Suzanne Snyder

Copy Editors
Margo Catts, Larry Frey, Charles
Gose, Dayna Isley, Greg Pearson,
Cliff Shubs, Paul Worthington

Technical Editors
Alain Guilbault

Software Product Developer
Steve Flatt

Assistant Marketing Manager
Gretchen Schlesinger

Acquisitions Coordinator
Amy Lewis

Editorial Assistant
Karen Opal

Manufacturing Coordinator
Brook Farling

Cover Designer
Dan Armstrong

Cover Illustration
©Theo Rudnak-SIS

Cover Production
Nathan Clement

Book Designer
Glenn Larsen

Director of Production
Larry Klein

Production Team Supervisors
Laurie Casey, Joe Millay

Graphics Image Specialists
Clint Lahnen
Laura Robbins

Production Analysts
Dan Harris
Erich J. Richter

Production Team
Kim Cofer, Tricia Flodder,
Mary Hunt, Malinda Kuhn,
Christy Wagner

Indexer
Tim Wright

About the Author

Drew Heywood has been involved in the microcomputer industry since he purchased an Apple II in 1978. For the past 10 years, he has focused on networking. From 1991 to 1995, Drew was a product line manager at New Riders Publishing, where he launched NRP's networking book line and expanded the line to include some of the most successful book titles in the industry. In early 1995, Drew left NRP and with his wife, Blythe, founded InfoWorks Inc. to support their interests as computer consultants. Drew has authored several NRP titles, including *Networking with Microsoft TCP/IP Certified Administrator's Resource Edition*, and all editions of the national bestseller, *Inside Windows NT Server*. In 1996, Drew added public speaking to his activities and was invited to be a guest presenter at Novell's BrainShare conference where he gave two workshops on TCP/IP.

Dedication

For Blythe.

Acknowledgments

My sincere thanks go out to:

Blythe, for her patience, support, and business expertise that support me every day.

My mother, for always helping out in a crisis.

New Riders Publishing for giving me yet another opportunity. To everyone at New Riders, many thanks.

Rob Tidrow, who gave me the chance to do the first edition of this book.

Karanjit Siyan for being a good friend, an example of professionalism, and an outstanding technical resource.

Microsoft for their persistence that has enabled Windows NT Server to become a success.

Contents at a Glance

Table of Contents

3   Your Job as a Windows NT Administrator   49

4   Planning and Installing Network Media   59

Part IV: Management

17 Managing Disk Storage   701

21   Using the Remote Access Server   897

Part V: Exploring the BackOffice Suite

26 Introducing BackOffice   1051

Objectives Matrix

A Planning

Objective	Page Reference
A.1 Plan the disk drive configuration for various requirements. Requirements include: Choosing a file system, Choosing a fault-tolerance method	*Chapter 2, "Introducing Windows NT Server,"* pages **37** *and* **42** *Chapter 7, "Installing Windows NT Server,"* page **181** *Chapter 16, "Using TCP/IP,"* page **579** *Chapter 17, "Managing Disk Storage,"* page **721**
A.2 Choose a protocol for various situations. Protocols include: TCP/IP, NWLink, IPX/SPX Compatible, Transport, NetBEUI	*Chapter 7, "Installing Windows NT Server,"* page **182** *Chapter 8, "Managing the Network Configuration,"* page **238**

B Installation and Configuration

Objective	Page Reference
B.1 Install Windows NT Server on Intel-based platforms.	*Chapter 7, "Installing Windows NT Server,"* page **184**
B.2 Install Windows NT Server to perform various server roles. Server roles include: Primary domain controller, Backup domain controller, Member server	*Chapter 7, "Installing Windows NT Server,"* page **183** *Chapter 9, "Understanding User Accounts, Groups, Domains, and Trust Relationships,"* pages **262–264** *Chapter 10, "Managing Domains and Trust Relationships,"* page **300**

continues

C Managing Resources

continued

D Connectivity

Objective	Page Reference
D.1 Configure Windows NT Server for interoperability with NetWare servers by using various tools. Tools include: Gateway Service for NetWare, Migration Tool for NetWare	*Chapter 23, "Windows NT Server and NetWare,"* pages **975** *and* **983**
D.2 Install and configure Remote Access Service (RAS). Configuration options include: Configuring RAS communications, Configuring RAS protocols Configuring RAS security, Configuring Dial-Up Networking clients	*Chapter 21, "Using the Remote Access Server,"* pages **901–902**, **906**, **916**, **920**, **923**, **928**, *and* **936**

E Monitoring and Optimization

Objective	Page Reference
E.1 Monitor performance of various functions by using Performance Monitor. Functions include: Processor, Disk, Network	*Chapter 20, "Monitoring and Managing the Network,"* pages **862–863**
E.2 Identify performance bottlenecks.	*Chapter 20, "Monitoring and Managing the Network,"* page **862**

F Troubleshooting

Objective	Page Reference
F.1 Choose the appropriate course of action to take to resolve installation failures.	*Chapter 7, "Installing Windows NT Server,"* pages **200** *and* **231**

Objective		Page Reference
F.2	Choose the appropriate course of action to take to resolve boot failures.	*Chapter 7, "Installing Windows NT Server,"* page **231**
F.3	Choose the appropriate course of action to take to resolve configuration errors.	*Chapter 7, "Installing Windows NT Server,"* page **231**
F.4	Choose the appropriate course of action to take to resolve printer problems.	*Chapter 13, "Managing Printing Services,"* pages **478** *and* **483**
F.5	Choose the appropriate course of action to take to resolve RAS problems.	*Chapter 21, "Using the Remote Access Server,"* page **945**
F.6	Choose the appropriate course of action to take to resolve connectivity problems.	*Chapter 8, "Managing the Network Configuration,"* page **249**
F.7	Choose the appropriate course of action to take to resolve resource access problems and permission problems.	*Chapter 12, "Sharing Drives, Directories and Files,"* page **437**
F.8	Choose the appropriate course of action to take to resolve fault-tolerance failures. Fault-tolerance methods include: Tape backup, Mirroring, Stripe set with parity, Disk duplexing	*Chapter 17, "Managing Disk Space,"* pages **726** *and* **729** *Chapter 18, "Backing Up Files,"* page **773**

Introduction

Welcome to the newest edition of this national bestseller, *Inside Windows NT Server 4, Certified Administrator's Resource Edition.* Why the alteration? Three reasons: so this resource can function as an extensive study aide for the Microsoft Certified System Engineers exam #70-67, to make sure information that readers find valuable is constantly being improved upon, and to always work hard to keep you up to date with the ever-changing technology. In an effort to make improvements and add value, a section dedicated to Microsoft's BackOffice Suite has been added near the end of the book. Microsoft BackOffice is a suite of client/server network applications sold as a bundle, or application suite, that runs on Windows NT Server. Components of BackOffice enable you to create a rich range of network applications, for companies as small as the smallest workgroup using a single server, up to worldwide enterprises using hundreds of servers and more than 100,000 clients. Support of networked applications is a particular strength of NT Server, and the range of application services, scalability, and low cost relative to other client/server technologies makes BackOffice a unique product offering. Part V, "Exploring the BackOffice Suite," opens with an overview chapter that provides background information on the suite. The next four chapters break down and explore four different BackOffice applications:

- ◆ Chapter 27, "Systems Management Server"

- ◆ Chapter 28, "Internet Information Server"

- ◆ Chapter 29, "Exchange Server"

- ◆ Chapter 30, "SQL Server"

In addition to this new section, I have gone through each of the other chapters and updated the information therein wherever necessary. I hope these improvements prove valuable to you.

Now, how has the technology changed? A great deal has happened. Windows NT has matured and gained considerably in market acceptance. Windows NT Workstation is being viewed by many as the operating system of choice for high-end desktop computers and is giving Unix a run for the money in many venues. Windows NT Server has penetrated the network server market as previous Microsoft network products have not, and is now a serious competitor.

So, Microsoft's persistence has paid off, and Windows NT is no longer a niche product. You can confidently select it in a wide variety of situations knowing that it is robust, performs well, and has a good mix of features.

Windows NT 4 is deceptive. The primary feature you notice when you first encounter the product is that version 4 has inherited the Windows 95 desktop. That will take some relearning for users familiar with Windows NT 3.5x, but the majority of users prefer the new desktop, and you will probably decide the transition is worth it.

The desktop isn't the only change; new features are scattered throughout the product. Here are a few of the big changes of particular interest to network managers:

- ◆ User profiles have been reorganized and made more powerful.

- ◆ System Policy Editor gives you more control over user's network environments.

- ◆ The new Point-to-Point Tunneling Protocol enables you to send non-TCP/IP data through TCP/IP networks.

- ◆ The NetWare Gateway now supports connections to NetWare Directory Services (NDS), enabling you to work with NetWare 4 servers in NDS mode.

- ◆ A Domain Name Service (DNS) server makes it easy to add a DNS server to your TCP/IP network.

- ◆ The Internet Information Server can turn any Windows NT Server into an Internet server offering World Wide Web, FTP, and Gopher services.

Windows NT Workstation users haven't been left out either, and version 4 has improved support for multimedia, hardware profiles, better compatibility with laptop portables, and a host of other features that users will appreciate.

Windows NT is an eclectic grab bag of good ideas from lots of products with some great homegrown ideas thrown in. It looks like Windows and is used like Windows, so lots of people already know quite a bit about using it, but underneath, Windows NT is completely new. Windows NT works a lot like Unix, and its design will satisfy most critical administrators, but most will find it a lot friendlier than Unix. Finally, Windows NT incorporates some of the best reliability features available, such as a roll-back capability that practically bulletproofs the Registry that is used to store configuration data for the server.

In many ways, however, Windows has burst the bounds of previous products, and Windows NT Server builds in features that are often add-ons. Among features that leap to mind are the ability to automatically replicate directories among servers and the ability to configure RAID level 5 drives using only conventional hardware and software built into the Windows NT operating system.

Because Windows NT can be a desktop platform, a network file server, and an application server, many organizations regard Windows NT as an opportunity to consolidate their networks around a single operating system that is friendly, versatile, and powerful.

Who Should Read This Book

This book targets three groups of readers:

◆ New network administrators. If Windows NT Server is your first encounter with network software, you will find all the help you need, both to get started and to succeed.

◆ Experienced administrators who are making the transition to Windows NT Server. If you are already comfortable with networks, the organization of this book will help you become productive efficiently.

◆ Experienced Windows NT Server administrators who want to make the transition to version 4 as smoothly as possible.

◆ Computer professionals who need to pass the *Implementing and Supporting Microsoft Windows NT Server 4.0* certification exam as they move toward Microsoft Certified Systems Engineer (MCSE) certification or Microsoft Certified Product Specialist (MCPS) certification.

  ◆ MCSE is the Microsoft Certified Professional category for computer professionals who work with Microsoft networks.

◆ MCPS is the Microsoft Certified Professional category for computer professionals who want to be certified specifically for a particular Microsoft product.

This book is a comprehensive volume for the knowledge base required for the NT Server exam, which is a core exam for both certification programs.

If you are interested in the certification exam, I offer the following assistance:

◆ Throughout the book, I'll cover the information needed to pass the *Implementing and Supporting Microsoft Windows NT Server 4.0* exam as part of our discussion of any topic that is related to the exam.

◆ An icon appears before every topic that includes information you'll need for the exam.

◆ Hands-on, step-by-step instructions on performing tasks will help you gain practical knowledge about the skills required for the exam.

◆ Questions and answers at the end of each chapter provide an opportunity to test your understanding of the material in the chapter.

◆ A matrix of test topics and where they are covered within this book is located before the title page of the book. This matrix makes it easy to find exactly what you need, and will help you make sure you've covered all the knowledge bases you need.

I assume that readers come to this book with some working familiarity with Windows. With more than 100 million copies of Windows in use, that seems like a safe bet. I realize, however, that the Windows 95 interface will be new to many.

Beyond a basic knowledge of Windows, I have supplied everything you should need. For beginners, I've included some background information in the appendices, along with some theory about networking. The book is organized in a logical sequence that takes you from equipment and software in boxes to a working network.

Experienced network administrators might want to skip or skim the introductory material in the appendices and cut to the chase. You should still find the chapter sequence helpful, but I've carefully concentrated related material into chapters that focus on specific topics. This approach is designed to make the book a useful reference that enables you to locate answers to your questions efficiently.

How This Book Is Organized

When I was planning the outline for this book, I noticed that the Microsoft manuals, as well as other Windows NT books, were organized around the utilities. You will see a chapter that tells you everything about the User Manager for Domains, for example. The problem with this approach, however, is that most of the Windows NT Server utilities perform a wide variety of tasks. Yes, User Manager for Domains is responsible for managing user accounts, but it is also used to establish domain trust relationships, which logically belong in a separate chapter from user accounts. A simple utility for managing server properties is responsible for tasks as diverse as monitoring user sessions, maintaining shares, replicating directories, and handling alerts.

As a result, I chose to organize this book around topics and tasks. If a utility performs tasks in several areas, a given chapter focuses on features of the utility that are related to the chapter's focus. You might see material on a given utility, such as Server Manager, in several chapters, but I think the topic focus will make it much easier for you to learn about Windows NT Server, to get your network up and running, and to answer your questions as they arise.

Unless you have some experience with Windows NT Server, I recommend that you approach the chapters in this book in sequence. In general, the chapters follow each other logically, and you will often need some understanding of previous chapters to comprehend the current chapter.

You need, for example, a good understanding of domains and groups before you can understand how privileges are assigned to users. So don't skip the chapters on domains with the intent of quickly adding some user accounts so that users are up and running. If you stick to the chapter outline, you will build your knowledge of Windows NT Server on a firm foundation.

After you have gained some experience, however, you should be able to skip around the book as required to isolate the specific information you need.

Finally, a word about what I had to leave out. Windows NT Server is a really big product. Microsoft's documentation exceeds 4,000 pages, so it wasn't possible for me to cover everything there is to know about Windows NT Server. In fact, I doubt that any one book could exhaust the topic. This book is intended to be a first book on Windows NT Server for new and experienced network administrators. My focus is to give you the information you need most and to make the information as accessible as possible.

For some readers, however, there can never be enough detail. If you finish this book and still crave more information about the nuts and bolts of Windows NT Server, look for New Riders Publishing's *Windows NT Server 4, Professional Reference*. Written by Karanjit Siyan, this book will provide the same detailed coverage of Windows NT Server that NetWare administrators have come to expect from his *NetWare, Professional Reference*, which is now in its fourth edition and sets the standard for NetWare references.

Additionally, if you have access to the Internet, you can always get up-to-the-minute information about Windows NT Server and Windows NT Workstation direct from Microsoft at the following locations:

```
http://www.microsoft.com/ntserver
http://www.microsoft.com/ntworkstation
```

New Riders Publishing

The staff of New Riders Publishing is committed to bringing you the very best in computer reference material. Each New Riders book is the result of months of work by authors and staff who research and refine the information contained within its covers.

As part of this commitment to you, New Riders invites your input. Please let us know if you enjoy this book, if you have trouble with the information and examples presented, or if you have a suggestion for the next edition.

Please note, however: New Riders staff cannot serve as a technical resource for Windows NT Server 4 or for questions about software- or hardware-related problems. Please refer to the documentation that accompanies your software or to the applications' Help systems.

If you have a question or comment about any New Riders book, there are several ways to contact New Riders Publishing. We will respond to as many readers as we can. Your name, address, or phone number will never become part of a mailing list or be used for any purpose other than to help us continue to bring you the best books possible.

You can write us at the following address:

New Riders Publishing
Attn: Publisher
201 W. 103rd Street
Indianapolis, IN 46290

If you prefer, you can fax New Riders Publishing at:

317-817-7448

You can also send electronic mail to New Riders at the following Internet address:

sangus@newriders.mcp.com

New Riders Publishing is an imprint of Macmillan Computer Publishing. To obtain a catalog or information, or to purchase any Macmillan Computer Publishing book, call 800-428-5331 or visit our web site at http://www.mcp.com.

Thank you for selecting *Inside Windows NT Server 4, Certified Administrator's Resource Edition!*

Pre-installation and Information Checklist

Use this checklist to help organize your information and ensure a smooth installation:

- Do you have Windows NT Server 4 compact disc or network access to the Windows NT Server files?

- Have you read the Windows NT Server readme files (Setup.txt)?

- Have you backed up all of the files currently on your computer to network share or a media storage device?

- Have you checked all of your hardware against the Windows NT Hardware Compatibility List?

  The most current Hardware Compatibility List is available at:

      http://www.microsoft.com/ntserver/hcl/hclintro.htm

- Have you made an Emergency Repair Disk (ERD)? (See Chapter 1.) This should be a 3.5-inch 1.44 megabyte disk labeled Emergency Repair Disk.

  The ERD is strictly optional for running Windows NT, but it is strongly recommended that you create one during installation and update it every time you make changes to your configuration.

- Have you documented all of the device driver disks and configuration settings for your third-party hardware?

- Have you sent notice to all users of server downtime?

- Record the following information prior to installation:

  Product ID Number: _____

  Name of this computer: _____

  Name of Domain: _____

  Administrator's name: _____

  I/P address: _____

System Requirements

The following describes the system requirements for Windows NT Server 4.

You will need the following hardware:

- 32-bit x86-based microprocessor (such as Intel 80486/25 or higher), Intel Pentium, or supported RISC-based microprocessor such as the MIPS R4x00, Digital Alpha, or PowerPC

- VGA, or higher resolution, monitor

- One or more hard disks, with 90 MB minimum free disk space on the partition that will contain the Windows NT Server systems files (110 MB minimum for RISC-based computers)

- For x86-based computer, a high-density 3.5-inch disk drive, plus a CD-ROM drive (for computers with solely a 5.25-inch drive, you can only install Windows NT Server over the network)

- For any computer not installing over a network, a CD-ROM drive

- One or more network adapter cards, if you want to use Windows NT Server with a network

- Mouse or other pointing device (optional)

The memory requirements are as follows:

- 12 MB RAM minimum for x86-based systems; 16 MB recommended
- 16 MB RAM minimum for RISC-based systems

Windows NT Server supports computers with up to four microprocessors. Support for additional microprocessors is available from your computer manufacturer.

PART I

Getting Ready for Windows NT Server

CHAPTER 1

Understanding Networks

If you have never managed a network before, this chapter is written especially for you. Don't skip it, however, just because you have some experience. Although nothing in this chapter is essential to understanding the rest of the book, it does serve a purpose—to get you in the right frame of mind. Local area network (LAN) administration is a challenging profession, and the right mindset will help you succeed.

Every experienced LAN administrator has been exposed to the highs and lows of a crazy business. One day you can be a hero for helping a critical project meet its deadline; the next you're a goat because someone lost an important file. Never mind whether or not it's the network's fault; you'll be blamed. I know of an organization that typically operates with better than 99.5 percent uptime—seven days a week, 24 hours a day—with users who complain vehemently that the LAN isn't reliable enough. In other words, the pressure on a LAN administrator can be severe.

This book's goal is to make you a hero, but it will take some effort. The goal of this book is to help you succeed in each of the following areas:

◆ Know everything you can about your LAN

◆ Design your LAN for reliability

◆ Make your LAN easy to use

◆ Anticipate problems before they become serious

◆ Fix problems promptly when they occur

◆ Have a disaster plan

Task by task, section by section, *Inside Windows NT Server 4 Certified Administrator's Resource Edition* shows you how to succeed as a LAN administrator.

This chapter starts with a general discussion of LANs to give you an understanding of the technologies you will encounter as an administrator of a Windows NT Server LAN. Armed with this information, you will be better prepared to learn the many job skills that are presented in later chapters.

What Is a Network?

A *network* consists of hardware (servers, workstations, cables, printers, and so on) and software (such as operating systems and applications). The following chapters tackle these hardware and software components. Before digging into the details, however, you should look at networking in more general terms.

Even if you have never used a PC on a network, you have experience with networking. Every time you make a telephone call, you use a network with some amazing properties. By pressing a few buttons, you can connect your telephone to virtually any other telephone in the world. Because this remarkable capability happens behind the scenes, we usually take it for granted. Do you ever think about the steps required to place a long-distance call between California and New York?

It seems simple, but the process is quite complicated. Automated systems at a central office in California must connect the wire from your phone to a long-distance service, which routes your call to the correct central office in New York through a combination of cables, microwave links, or communication satellites. In New York, the central office must connect the call to the wires running to the telephone you are calling. Each of these steps must happen quickly, reliably, and invisibly millions of times a day.

Telephone users are fortunate because teams of highly trained communication technicians and engineers keep the entire process running smoothly. If you were responsible for running the public telephone network, you would need to know a great deal about media, signaling, switching hardware, and so on. As a user, however, you do not see these details.

As a LAN administrator, however, you will become responsible for such details. You will be managing the cabling system that enables your LAN to communicate. You will probably be required to install the hardware that enables your users' PCs to connect to the network. Your servers will require frequent attention. Like it or not, you will need to learn the skills of network engineering.

Fortunately, a LAN isn't as complicated as a worldwide telephone network. In fact, network administration has become progressively easier over the years. Windows NT Server makes it possible to build powerful networks that are easy to administer.

Chapter 3, "Your Job as a Windows NT Administrator," gets you started. Before rushing into the actual tasks of running a LAN, however, you should be familiar with basic LAN theory.

What Are the Components of a Network?

All networks—even the most complicated—contain the same three basic types of building blocks:

- ◆ Devices that provide network services
- ◆ Devices that use network services
- ◆ Something that enables the devices to communicate

You will now look at each item with regard to the public telephone network. A good example of a telephone service is the time and temperature service. Another example is the service provided by many banks that enables you to call in and obtain your account balances by keying in the account number and a pass code. Whenever you call one of these services, you become a service user.

To enable you, a service user, to communicate with a service provider, the telephone company provides a network of cables and switches. These cables and switches connect your telephone to the service and carry information between the two.

The remainder of this section examines these network components in the context of a computer network. In the process, the section explores the types of devices that function as service providers, service users, and communications facilitators.

Servers Provide Services

For a long time, the most common types of service providers on networks were called *file servers*, although they typically provide at least the following two basic types of service:

◆ Sharing access to files

◆ Sharing access to networked printers

Historically, these services were the first to attract users to LANs. Because low-end printers were expensive, users felt a strong incentive to share them. Although various types of printer-sharing devices are available, a network server remains the most effective means of sharing printers. Network servers have many advantages which are discussed in greater detail in Chapter 13, "Managing Printing Services."

File services were also significant incentives for setting up LANs. Until LANs became affordable, sharing files meant swapping media. A few files could be exchanged on floppy disks. Large numbers of files required the use of tape data cartridges. *Sneakernet,* my favorite network pseudo-technical term, describes the process of literally running around to exchange files on floppy disks. File services enable computers on the networks to share their files with other computers by transferring them through the network media.

File and print services can be provided by running special software on users' PCs. This software enables users to share files on their hard drives, as well as any printers attached to their PCs. This approach is called *peer-to-peer networking* because all PCs on the LAN are basically equal.

A contrasting approach uses a special centralized server to provide file and print services. The centralized server is usually called a *dedicated server* because it is devoted entirely to providing file and print services.

Centralized servers generally are based on fairly powerful hardware—high-end Intel PCs or RISC systems are commonly used. These systems have to be fast because they must service the needs of many users. Dedicated servers typically have a great deal of memory and hard drive capacity (often tens of gigabytes).

Dedicated servers usually have features that improve their reliability. Fault-tolerant features enable the server to continue functioning, even when a component fails. Extra hard disks that mirror primary disks are common fault-tolerant features. When the primary disk fails, the mirror disk takes over without interruption of service.

Figure 1.1 illustrates a typical centralized server. Starting with this figure, you can begin to build a picture of a complete LAN.

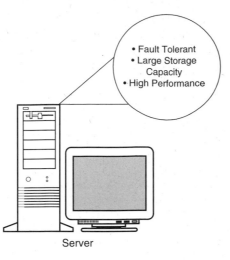

Server

Figure 1.1

A network starts with a server.

Clients Use Services

A *client* is anything on a network that uses the services a server provides. The terms client and server come from a metaphor based on restaurants. The servers provide food services that are consumed by the restaurant clients. Because so much of networking is based on service providers and clients, this model of networking is typically called *client/server computing.*

The most common clients are user workstations; virtually any PC can be turned into a network client. Many PCs are now factory-equipped with network interface boards. All Macintosh computers are network-ready, as are virtually all Unix workstations. Manufacturers have made it increasingly easy to network computers because the majority of computers now being purchased end up attached to a network.

It is important to understand the difference between client/server computing and the older terminal/host computing, which is typically employed with mainframe computers. A terminal is a dumb device with no computing capability. In a terminal/host environment, the terminal accepts user input and displays data to users, but all computing is performed by the central mainframe.

In client/server computing, the client is a powerful computer in its own right. The client may request data from the server, but most of the actual computing is performed by the client computer. Although the client uses the network to share files, printers, and other resources, it can perform most functions quite well without the network.

This book introduces several types of clients. In Microsoft networking environments, the most common clients probably run some version of Microsoft Windows; this book, therefore, focuses on Windows clients. DOS clients, however, are also supported and are covered in Chapter 14, "Using Windows and DOS Clients."

Clients are typically highly individualized, configured for the needs of diverse users. Figure 1.2 illustrates the network you are constructing, which now consists of a server and a client.

Figure 1.2

Network with a server and client.

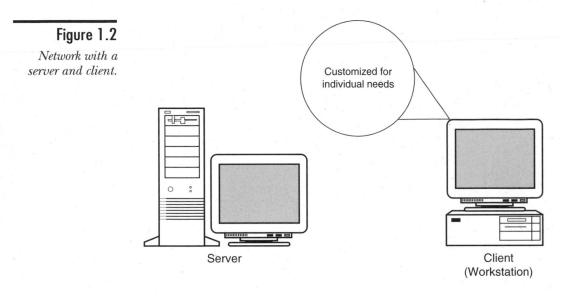

Customized for individual needs

Server

Client
(Workstation)

Note The distinction between peer-to-peer networks and centralized server networks is significant. Both network types are supported by Microsoft products, and you want to choose the correct approach for the needs of your organization.

Centralized server networks are based on specialization. The server is often over-designed to provide fast, reliable service. Critical data stored in a centralized location can be easily protected. Security is easier to maintain if the operating system (OS) is designed with tight security in mind, and it is easier to administer security if data has been stored in one place. Many desktop operating systems have no provisions for security. Others provide some security, but not enough for critical data.

Peer-to-peer networks enable every PC on the network to function as both a server and a client. This type of network eliminates the need for an expensive server, but does have several drawbacks. Files are spread out over many workstations, making it difficult to back them up. Security is difficult to maintain. Desktop PCs are seldom as reliable as a centralized server. Do you have an uninterruptible power supply on your desktop PC so that you won't lose data during a power outage?

continues

Peer-to-peer networks can be cumbersome to administer as well. When users share files on their PCs, they must maintain a list of who in the organization can access the files. Each PC has its own access control list. When staff changes occur, users must update the access control list on their PCs (which can add up to a great many changes).

For informal sharing of files and services, a peer-to-peer approach might work fine. When networking is a mission-critical activity for your organization, however, opt for a centralized server.

Communications Media Interconnect Servers and Clients

Something must be present to enable servers and clients to communicate. That something is called the network *medium*. The range of available media is extremely broad; copper cable, fiber-optic cable, and microwave links represent just a few examples. Leave the more exotic media—such as satellite microwave links—to the experts. On the other hand, you probably will become very familiar with the cables and other media located within the walls of your organization. Because different media are associated with different types of networks, this section marks a good place to discuss network types.

LANs typically are confined to a single building or suite of buildings, although LANs can grow to a size of several square miles. Because LANs typically include large numbers of computers, media are often selected for low cost. The most common media used with LANs are copper cables, which offer excellent performance at moderate cost. Fiber-optic cabling can be used on LANs, particularly for longer cable runs or for high speed connections. Fiber-optic cable costs considerably more than copper, however; few organizations choose to run fiber to users' workstations.

The most important characteristics of LANs for you to remember are high performance and low cost. Local area networks tend to be inherently reliable, so little extra emphasis is placed on reliability.

When networks grow larger than a few square miles, they typically are called wide area networks (WANs). A WAN can cover a city, a country, or even the world. The media used for WANs are generally quite different from the media used for LANs.

WANs must cope with the problems of communicating across public streets and crossing international borders; only large organizations with deep pockets can create private WANs. For most of us, wide area networking involves purchasing communication services from a service provider. Options include leasing a dedicated circuit from a public telephone service, renting communication capability on a satellite link, or subscribing to a public data network. Figure 1.3 illustrates a network that incorporates several types of LAN and WAN media.

Figure 1.3

A network with LAN and WAN components.

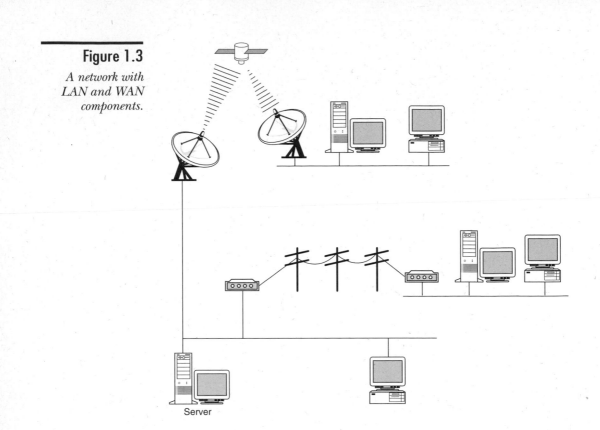

Server

Compared to LANs, WANs are quite costly. You generally pay based on the data-carrying capacity your organization requires. Most services require you to reserve a specific capacity, which you pay for whether you use it or not. Services are emerging, however, that enable you to pay a basic rate and access higher levels of service as needed.

With WANs, you don't have to worry about the actual media being used; the service provider supplies it. A wide variety of service types is available, however. If you are setting up a WAN, familiarize yourself with the options so that you can choose the most cost-effective service for your organization's needs.

Compared to LANs, WANs tend to offer lower performance and to cost much more. The costs of running a WAN directly relate to the amount of network traffic the WAN must support. Long-distance networks tend to be less reliable than LANs, and special effort goes into ensuring network reliability.

Chapter 4, "Planning and Installing Network Media," expands on this basic discussion of media.

Network Operating Systems Run Servers

A computer is nothing without an operating system (OS). The OS is the software that gives the computer its basic capability to communicate, store data, and run programs. You are almost certainly experienced at using one or more workstation operating systems, such as DOS, Windows, Windows NT, or Unix.

Because it might potentially service the needs of tens or hundreds of users, a file/print server is typically a fairly heavy-duty computer. A server, therefore, requires a heavy-duty operating system. A network operating system (NOS) must be powerful enough to service many users simultaneously. A NOS also must be reliable because those users are dependent on it to perform their work. You probably have to reboot your PC occasionally when it hangs up. Would you be as comfortable rebooting a network server supporting hundreds of users?

Microsoft Windows NT Server is the NOS used in this book. Windows NT Server is actually the fourth generation of Microsoft network operating systems. The evolution is as follows:

◆ **MS-NET.** Microsoft developed and licensed it to other vendors but never distributed it directly.

◆ **LAN Manager.** A NOS based on OS/2 version 1.3.

◆ **Windows NT Advanced Server.** Based on Windows NT version 3.1.

◆ **Windows NT Server.** The current product, which derives from the latest version of Windows NT, version 4.

With each generation, Microsoft has improved performance and reliability. Windows NT Server is a world-class NOS that competes effectively in the network marketplace with other products, such as Novell NetWare, IBM LAN Server, and Banyan VINES.

In addition to providing file, print, and other services, a NOS must be capable of maintaining network security. Businesses appreciate LANs because they offer dependable and inexpensive computing services. Business managers, however, need to know that critical information cannot be accessed by competitors or unauthorized staff. (The majority of computer crimes are inside jobs, regardless of all the media coverage of hackers breaking into computers.) Windows NT Server is capable of establishing a high level of network security. Maintaining security is one of the network administrator's most critical jobs. Several chapters in this book explore security concerns, including Chapter 10, "Managing Domains and Trust Relationships," and Chapter 11, "Managing Users and Groups."

Figure 1.4 adds the Windows NT Server NOS to the file server.

Figure 1.4

The network server requires a network operating system.

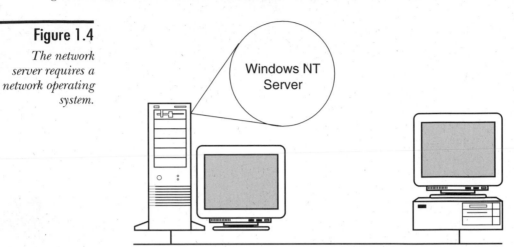

Workstation Operating Systems Run Workstations

Network workstations, or clients, also require operating systems. The needs for a workstation OS are less stringent than for a network OS. Operating systems have become increasingly sophisticated, however; some offer capabilities that make them nearly as powerful as a NOS.

Although DOS has long been the dominant desktop operating system, it is gradually diminishing in popularity. Some users have come to appreciate graphical user environments. Others require higher levels of reliability than DOS provides. Still others need operating systems that can support large amounts of memory or that can multitask. The latest generations of workstation operating systems offer each of these advantages over DOS. A modern networking strategy must be capable of supporting most, if not all, of these more advanced operating systems.

As workstation OSes have evolved, they have taken on many of the features of network OSes. You can, in fact, create complete networks using nothing but Windows for Workgroups, Windows NT Workstation, Macintoshes, or Unix. In most cases, however, these networks are based on peer-to-peer resource sharing, so the need for a dedicated network operating system remains.

Figure 1.5 illustrates a network supporting several different types of client workstations.

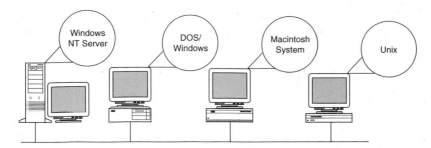

Figure 1.5

A server supporting several types of clients.

Other Servers Enhance Network Services

File and print services aren't the only kinds of services a network can provide. There are many types of communication servers, for example:

◆ **Mail servers.** Enable users to exchange electronic mail with users in the same building or in offices throughout the world.

◆ **Modem servers.** Enable users to share a pool of modems for dialing in to or out of the network. Having a separate modem for each person in your office is not necessary.

◆ **Fax servers.** Enable users to send and receive faxes through the network. Users can send faxes electronically without having to print copies. Incoming faxes can be routed to users much like e-mail, without a single paper document.

◆ **Gateways.** Enable users to communicate with mainframe or minicomputers, or with outside networks such as the Internet.

Figure 1.6 illustrates some of the possibilities a network has in offering users a wide variety of services.

Figure 1.6

A modern LAN offers a wide variety of services.

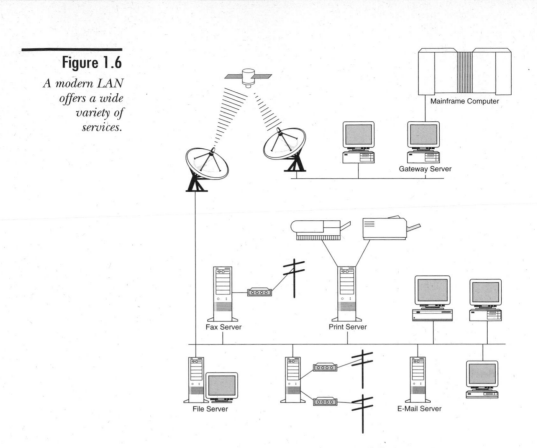

So, How Hard Is This Stuff?

Fortunately, LANs are built from relatively small building blocks. You can begin networking with little more than a server and a couple of workstations. You then can expand your understanding by adding other types of workstations and by providing more types of services.

Windows NT Server is one of the easiest ways yet invented to build a powerful network; it's easy to install and to administer. If you have used Windows, you are already familiar with much you need to know about networking with Windows NT Server.

If you are new to networking, Chapter 3 should be your next step. Chapter 3 examines your job description as a LAN administrator. It explains that the difficulty lies in the number of challenges you're faced with. You need to learn about hardware, software, servers, workstations, printers, utilities, and operating systems. You must learn a great deal, but this book will help you.

Note Chapter 4 explains each area of networking thoroughly. This is the key to learning—take on one challenge at a time, master it, and move on. If you try to understand the entire process at once, it will overwhelm you.

A Formal Approach to Defining a Network

Up to this point, this book has described network concepts in pretty general terms. As you work through it, however, a more formal set of definitions that can be used to organize your knowledge becomes necessary.

Because the Open Systems Integration (OSI) reference model provides a common framework for depicting the organization of network components, practically every book about networking discusses it. The OSI reference model was originally intended to serve as a blueprint for a complete set of network protocols. The protocols have not taken root, but the reference model has.

The OSI reference model works on the premise that a complex task is most easily performed by breaking that task down into subtasks. If you were an engineer designing a car, would you take on the entire challenge at once (body, engine, chassis, suspension, electronics, and so on), or would you start with one part (the body style, for example) and then design the other systems to work with the body you have selected? Some designers start with one task, some others, but few start by trying to plan every nut and bolt at once.

When the task of network communication is broken down into subtasks, solutions for the subtasks are easier to design. This building-block concept offers another benefit as well. If properly implemented, the various subtask solutions can be treated as building blocks to solve large communication problems one piece at a time.

The following is an example of a communication process encountered in everyday life: mailing a business letter. This process requires several steps:

1. You print the letter at your computer.

2. You insert the letter in an envelope and address the envelope according to a standard address format that includes the recipient's company mail stop code. You also might indicate whether the letter is to be routed by standard mail or overnight.

3. You drop the letter in a pickup box.

4. A mail clerk picks up your letter and puts it in a clearly marked box for pickup by the desired carrier.

5. The appropriate carrier picks up the box, which contains dozens of letters, and transports the box to the carrier's depot.

6. At the depot, machines and people sort the items into containers to be sent to the desired destination. The carrier probably has evolved elaborate procedures to ensure that this process happens efficiently and reliably.

7. Another mail carrier picks up the box and transports it to the recipient's office.

8. A mail clerk sorts the items and delivers each one to the appropriate recipient.

9. The recipient retrieves the envelope, opens it, and receives your message.

This example emphasizes that even the everyday process of delivering mail is, in fact, quite complex.

If you had to reinvent the entire process each time you sent a letter, would you bother? Imagine if each letter you sent had to include complete instructions on what would happen to it every step of the way. Would you bother sending much mail? Fortunately, because each subprocess has clearly established procedures, one simple address is all your letter needs to get through the system and to the correct receiver.

The key to making the mail system work is a layered approach. Each layer in the process concentrates on its relationship with adjacent layers, and does not worry about the entire process. The postal service does not need to understand your company's internal mail distribution system and can ignore your internal zip code. Each layer focuses on its specific job and assumes that other layers do the same.

Also note that some of the steps in the process can change without affecting others. If the mail clerk wants to send the letter by overnight express rather than the postal service, a simple modification to step 4 can redirect the letter and substitute a different service in steps 5, 6, and 7. None of these changes has any significant effect on the procedures in steps 1, 2, 3, 8, or 9.

The OSI Reference Model

Figure 1.7 illustrates the layered approach taken by the OSI reference model. The process of network communication is divided into seven layers. You will work more closely with some of these layers than with others. This section examines each of the layers so that you can understand the relevance of the model to your activities as a LAN administrator.

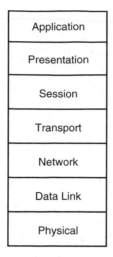

Figure 1.7

The seven layers of the OSI reference model.

| Note | You never know when you and your fellow LAN administrators will want to sit around and recite the layers of the OSI model while seeking cosmic truth in an infinite universe. It's kind of a LAN administrator's mantra that shows you've arrived at a higher level of understanding. To help you on the path of enlightenment, here's a catch phrase that lists the first letters of the layer names in order: |

All

People

Seem

To

Need

Data

Processing

It's an easy phrase to remember, and helps LAN administrators feel indispensable.

The Physical Layer

The *physical layer* is concerned with the way data signals are transmitted on the network medium. At this level, the network transmits and receives individual bits. Higher layers break messages into bits prior to transmission, and then reassemble these bits into messages as they are received.

The OSI physical layer does not define the medium itself, just the signaling methods to be used. Designers of physical layer protocols, however, must be aware of the characteristics of the signaling medium to some degree.

> **Note**   The OSI reference model ignores media; it is concerned with *protocols* (the rules that govern network communication).
>
> The data communication industry borrowed the term protocol from the process of diplomatic communication. Government ambassadors obey complex protocols to ensure that communications are clear and inoffensive.
>
> Each layer of the model is associated with one or more protocols, which are carefully defined standards for carrying out the functions assigned to that layer. Physical layer protocols define the way signals are to be transmitted and received, but they do not describe the cabling or other media.
>
> Although the OSI model ignores media, LAN administrators cannot. Occasionally, media is described as an unofficial "layer zero" of the OSI reference model.

The Data Link Layer

The *data link layer* performs the following tasks:

◆ Fragments messages into bits for transmission by the physical layer.

◆ Reassembles bits received by the physical layer into messages.

◆ Establishes node-to-node communication and manages the flow of data between nodes. (Every device that communicates on the network is a *node.*) This process is called logical link control (LLC).

◆ Checks for errors in transmission. This is also a logical link control function.

◆ Controls access to the communication medium. Most networks can support only one transmission at a time. The data link layer implements media access control (MAC) protocols to ensure that nodes have the opportunity to transmit but do not conflict.

◆ Assigns a *node address* to each device on the network and uses the node addresses to enable devices to receive messages that are intended for them.

The data link layer is typically divided into two sublayers: LLC and MAC (see fig. 1.8). The MAC sublayer works very closely with the physical layer. The MAC and physical layers, in fact, are frequently defined by the same standards. Ethernet (IEEE 802.3) and Token-Ring (IEEE 802.5) are standards that define MAC and physical layer functions. Chapter 4 discusses both of these standards.

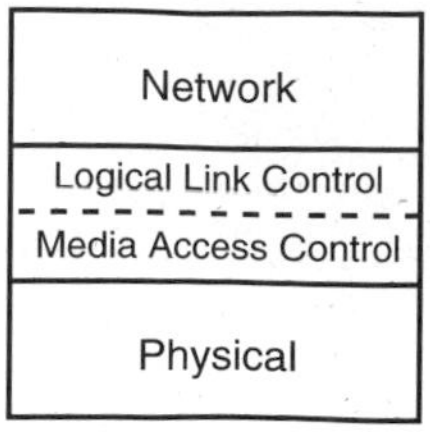

Network
Logical Link Control
Media Access Control
Physical

Figure 1.8

The data link layer consists of two sublayers: MAC and LLC.

Note | Together, the physical and MAC layers work much like an old-time telegraph operator and a telegraph line. The sending telegraph operator is given a message to be transmitted in the form of words and phrases. He converts the text into a series of dots and dashes. The receiving operator must reverse the process and reassemble the dots and dashes into letters, words, and finally phrases.

Computer networks use encoding schemes that are similar in many ways to the Morse dot-and-dash code. Data is converted into strings of ones and zeroes for transmission on the network medium and is reassembled into data frames at the receiving node. A common code for converting character data to bits is ASCII, which assigns a number to each letter and symbol. The capital letter A has an ASCII value of 65, which can be represented by the binary number 01000001.

The messaging unit at the data link layer is usually called a *frame*. Each frame consists of a string of bits that are grouped into fields. Figure 1.9 illustrates the fields in a generic MAC frame. The fields are as follows:

◆ Two address fields identify the physical addresses of the source and destination nodes of the frame. Physical addresses—also called MAC addresses because they are used at the MAC layer—are typically programmed into network cards when they are manufactured and provide a unique means of identifying each node on the network.

◆ A data field includes all data that has been sent down from the upper layers.

◆ An error control field enables the receiving node to determine whether errors occurred in transmission of the frame.

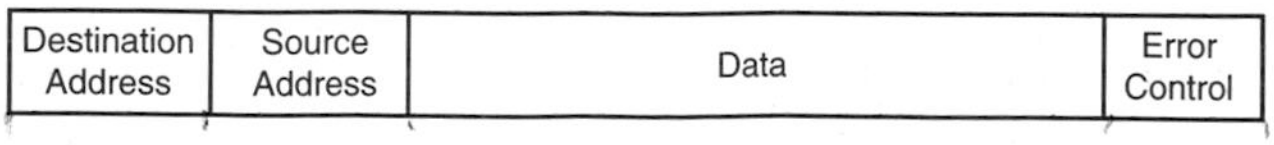

Destination Address	Source Address	Data	Error Control

Figure 1.9

The structure of a generic data link frame.

The Network Layer

The *data link layer* performs communication in a fairly simplistic manner, by transmitting a frame on the media. Each node on the network examines all frames that are transmitted and receives only those frames that identify that node in the frame destination address.

This approach to communication works fine on simple networks, but networks seldom remain simple. Consider the network shown in figure 1.10. If every message were transmitted through every possible path, the network would quickly become saturated with redundant message units. The *network layer* routes messages efficiently and reliably through a complex network.

> **Note**   Complex networks, such as the one shown in figure 1.10, are frequently called *internetworks* to distinguish them from simple networks.

Figure 1.10

The network layer routes messages through complex networks.

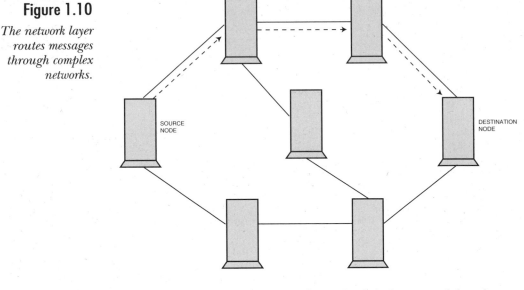

SOURCE NODE

DESTINATION NODE

The unit of information at the network layer is the *packet*. It is the network layer's responsibility to transmit packets through the internetwork. The process of delivering packets through an internetwork is called *routing*.

Windows NT Server supports two primary network protocols: IPX, the standard protocol for NetWare; and IP, a protocol in the TCP/IP protocol suite. Since TCP/IP is the most widely used network protocol, you probably will internetwork your Windows NT Servers with IP, which is discussed in Chapter 16, "Using TCP/IP."

Windows NT Server also supports the NetBEUI protocol, the *NetBIOS Extended User Interface*. NetBEUI is a protocol that was designed to support networking on small, simple networks, and performs very well in that role. NetBEUI, however, cannot be routed through an internetwork. Because of this, Microsoft is de-emphasizing NetBEUI as support for IPX and TCP/IP improves.

Other protocols supported by Windows NT Server are Data Link Control and AppleTalk. Data Link Control (DLC) is a protocol used to communicate with printers that attach directly to the network. AppleTalk is the protocol used by Macintosh computers, and is supported by the Windows NT Server Services for Macintosh.

The Transport Layer

The network layer does not check for errors. It transmits a packet and assumes that the packet will arrive at the chosen destination. Because LANs are generally highly reliable, this assumption can be fairly safe. In many cases, however, errors cannot be tolerated. Suppose you transfer $5,000 from your savings to your checking account. Would you be satisfied if a network error enabled the withdrawal but prevented the deposit?

Service as provided by the network layer is called *unreliable service.* The word unreliable doesn't mean that errors occur frequently, only that errors are not detected.

The *transport layer* adds *reliable service* to the network. Reliable service detects errors and, when detected, retransmits messages.

To provide reliable service, Windows NT Server supports two transport protocols. One is SPX, which is a companion protocol to IPX in the NetWare protocol suite. Also supported is the TCP protocol in the TCP/IP protocol suite. TCP is an extremely robust protocol that can cope with a wide variety of network difficulties.

The Session Layer

The layers discussed so far are concerned with the delivery of single messages. The *session layer* deals with dialogs between nodes and adds a lot of new rules to the basic rules established by the network layer.

When two nodes begin a dialog, they are establishing a *session.* They negotiate to establish the rules of communication and the protocols to be used. They might go through a security procedure where the nodes establish their identities and grant each other access. In the process, the nodes establish what each is permitted to do. When a user establishes a session with a file server, for example, the server probably restricts the user's access to specific server resources.

When a workstation connects to a Windows NT Server, it undergoes a login process in which the user's identity is verified and a session is established. Once the user is recognized by the security procedures, the workstation is permitted to become a network client and to access server resources.

The Presentation Layer

The *presentation layer* is frequently defined incorrectly, in part because the name is somewhat confusing. The presentation layer presents data from the session layer to the application layer. In doing so, the presentation layer might need to convert data from one format to a format required by the application layer.

The presentation layer does not present data to the user and has nothing to do with displaying information on the computer screen.

Several types of data format conversion can be performed at the presentation layer, including data encryption, data compression, and format conversion.

The Application Layer

The *application layer* is also often a source of confusion. This layer does not correspond to end-user applications such as word processors. Rather, the application layer enables user applications to interface smoothly with the network.

The following is a list of some of the functions performed at the application layer:

- ◆ Remote file access
- ◆ File transfer
- ◆ Remote program access
- ◆ Directory services that catalog network resources
- ◆ Remote job execution

Often, the application layer functions are performed by workstation and server operating systems. Windows NT Server can be regarded as providing application layer services.

Comments on the OSI Reference Model

Although the OSI reference model is a useful tool for understanding network protocols, none of the protocols you will encounter exactly fit the model. This discrepancy is particularly true of the TCP/IP protocol suite, which was developed prior to the OSI reference model and consists of four layers.

The lack of an exact fit, however, does not diminish the usefulness of the reference model. It is a useful tool for organizing your knowledge as you dig deeper into the details of networking.

Testing Your Knowledge

1. What are the components of a network?

    A. Mail servers, Modem servers, Fax servers

    B. The layers within the OSI model

    C. Unix, Macintosh System, Windows NT Server

    D. Devices that provide network services, devices that use network services, something that enables the devices to communicate

2. What are the seven layers of the OSI reference model, and what is the correct order?

    A. Presentation, Application, Transport, Session, Network, Data Link, Physical

    B. Application, Preview, Session, Transport, Data Link, Network, Physical

    C. Application, Presentation, Session, Transport, Network, Data Link, Physical

    D. Presentation, Session, Application, Preview, Transport, Network, Physical, Data Link

3. What is the popular phrase used to remember the OSI layer names in the correct order?

    A. People Seem To Need All Data Processed

    B. All People Seem To Need Data Processing

    C. All People Seem To Need Data Preview

    D. People Seem To Need All Data Previewed

4. Which protocol would be ideal for an NT network that has only a small number of workstations, and does not require Internet connectivity?

    A. DLC

    B. IPX/SPX

    C. TCP/IP

    D. NetBEUI

Review Answers

1. D

2. C

3. B

4. D

CHAPTER 2

Introducing Windows NT Server

Windows NT Server version 4 is the latest in a long line of Microsoft networking products. In Windows NT Server, you can see echoes of numerous products coming together in a robust, feature-rich network operating system.

With version 4, Windows NT has acquired the new user interface that was first seen in Windows 95. This user interface is a considerable departure from the old interface popularized by Windows 3.x, and it takes some getting used to. Is the learning curve worth it? Consider that Windows 95 users have the option of choosing the old Windows 3.x interface or the new interface. Take a poll among the Windows 95 users you know to see how many have stuck with the old interface. My guess is that the proportion of Windows 95 users who have chosen to keep the old interface hovers at close to 0 percent.

The networking model for Windows NT Server evolved out of two product lines: LAN Manager and Windows for Workgroups. From LAN Manager came the approach of administering multiserver networks in domains, making it unnecessary to manage each server independently. From Windows for Workgroups came an intuitive approach of sharing network resources that users browse for and connect with. Any user who has shared a printer with Windows for Workgroups will find it easy to work on a Windows NT network.

The robust character of Windows NT arises from lots of experience at designing operating systems. Some of this experience was internal. Microsoft had, after all, developed the XENIX implementation of Unix during the 1980s. They had also worked with IBM on the first two generations of OS/2. When it came time to design a full-featured, multitasking OS, however, Microsoft went one step further and hired David Cutler, who had gained considerable experience with multi-user operating systems while at Digital. These influences came together into an OS that many feel rivals Unix for power and features while retaining the ease of use of Microsoft Windows.

This chapter serves as a brief tour of the features of Windows NT. Here you will gain an understanding of the architecture of Windows NT, which will help you understand the capabilities of the product. Many of the features receive lengthy treatment within this book.

Windows NT Workstation and Server

Windows NT is available in two versions: Windows NT Workstation version 4 and Windows NT Server version 4. The server version is essentially the same as the workstation with the addition of features that enable it to perform as a versatile network operating system.

Microsoft's approach has significant advantages. With Windows NT, you can buy workstation and server products that are nearly identical, run the same programs, and use the same software drivers. You buy only the capability you need for a given computer. The prices are quite reasonable. Windows NT Server lists for about $700, and Windows NT Workstation lists for a bit over $300. Since the closest comparable operating system, Unix, typically sells for about $1,500 per computer, Windows NT stacks up as a bargain.

Another advantage of Windows NT Server is that network clients are packaged separately at a per-client price of $39. With some network servers, if you want two servers, both of which will be used by the same 100 users, you need to purchase two 100-client server licenses. Using per-seat licensing with Windows NT Server, you buy the client licenses once and use them with as many servers as you require.

The workstation and server products are highly synergistic. In fact, Windows NT Workstation serves a number of networking roles. For example, any Windows NT computer can function as a network print server, and any Windows NT computer can serve as a TCP/IP router.

Windows NT computers also make the best clients for Windows NT Server. The first time you print to a network printer from Windows NT, you might not believe how easy it is to set up network printing. A single copy of the printer driver on a Windows NT print server is enough to take care of all Windows NT clients; they just connect to the shared printer and print.

All Windows NT computers can take advantage of *profiles*, which are files that store detailed information about a user's working environment from session to session.

Windows NT Operating System Features

Windows NT has many features that place it in the upper ranks of operating systems for microcomputers and workstations. Many of these features are highly desirable on a workstation and essential on a network server.

Portability

The majority of operating systems are written for a specific hardware platform. MS-DOS, for example, was written for the Intel 8086/8088 series of microprocessors. To this day, MS-DOS applications are limited by the features of microprocessors you can no longer buy. The 8086 and 8088 could address only one megabyte of memory, and that limitation affects DOS applications over a decade after the birth of MS-DOS.

If you're planning the computing strategy for an organization, having operating systems and applications tied to specific hardware should remind you of the days of proprietary mainframe computers. Once you bought a mainframe, you were locked into that vendor's hardware, software, and support. Suppose that a new computer architecture offers more bang for the buck. Wouldn't you like to have the freedom of changing your hardware without the need to upgrade your operating systems and applications?

Windows NT might be the most portable OS on the market, thanks to two design decisions. First, the operating system was written in C, a language that enables programs to be ported easily to other hardware. Second, all of the parts of Windows NT that must be written for specific hardware were isolated in an area called the Hardware Abstraction Layer (HAL). To move Windows NT to a different hardware platform, developers need to do little more than recompile the C code for the new hardware and create a new HAL.

As a result, you can select the hardware platform that provides you with the cost and performance features you want. Windows NT is already available for several platforms, and more are on the way. The standard product includes installation files for the following:

◆ Intel x86 architecture computers

◆ MIPS RISC architecture computers

◆ Digital Alpha AXP RISC architecture computers

◆ PowerPC RISC architecture computers

Multiprocessor computers are available for all of these hardware platforms.

Memory Capacity

Windows NT was designed to take full advantage of 80386 and later Intel processors. As a result, Windows NT can support as much as 4 gigabytes of RAM.

Multitasking and Multithreading

Multitasking is computer sleight of hand. The computer's central processing unit (CPU) isn't really performing several things at once, since it can only do one thing at a time. Instead, the operating system quickly switches several tasks in and out of the CPU, doing a bit of task A, a bit of task B, a bit of task C, and then a bit of A again. Properly executed on a sufficiently fast system, multitasking presents the illusion that A, B, and C are running at the same time.

Multitasking can be a blessing or a curse. Implemented well, multitasking enables an operating system to perform several tasks, more or less at the same time, almost as though each task were running on its own processor. The quality of a multitasking system depends on how well the designers have isolated the various tasks.

It is possible, for example, to implement a sort of multitasking with MS-DOS, which is not, by nature, a multitasking OS. Add-ons, such as Windows, can expand the capabilities of MS-DOS to embrace a sort of multitasking. The problem is that the tasks aren't isolated; one hung task can ruin everything.

Windows NT doesn't have that problem. Tasks are well-isolated and can't hurt each other. Moreover, if a given task hangs, you can kill it without needing to reboot the entire computer.

Each task is given arbitrated access to system resources, such as the CPU and memory, and is allocated at least one thread of execution. A *thread* is a discrete unit of execution that is handled independently by the CPU. Many multitasking operating systems associate processes with threads on a one-to-one basis. Windows NT, on the other hand, has multithreading capability. A given thread can spawn additional threads to perform other discrete tasks. These multiple threads independently perform their tasks. At some point, threads might come back together to produce a collective result. When programs are written to take advantage of Windows NT's multithreading capability, a new significantly higher level of sophistication can be achieved.

Multiprocessor Support

Windows NT has the potential to use more than one processor. The quality this brings to a computer is called scalability. If you buy a multiprocessor network server, you might get along for a while with a single CPU. As your network grows, however, the server might start to choke on the extra work. When that happens, you can scale the server up by installing additional CPUs.

The two styles of multiprocessing are as follows:

◆ Asymmetrical multiprocessing assigns different types of tasks to different processors. This approach is relatively easy to implement, but can result in some processors being busier than others.

◆ Symmetrical multiprocessing has the capability of running any task on any processor. It's a lot more difficult to design an OS for symmetrical multiprocessing, but the payoff is that you are sure of using each processor more fully.

Unfortunately, doubling the processor count doesn't double processing capability. Some overhead is required to manage the process of assigning tasks to processors and coordinating the results of various tasks. As a result, you will encounter diminishing returns as you add processors.

Standard versions of Windows NT Server 4 support symmetrical multiprocessing with up to four processors, while Windows NT Workstation 4 supports two processors. Versions of Windows NT Server written for specialized hardware can support up to 255 processors.

NT File System

Objective A.1

Windows NT introduced the NTFS file system that improves network performance, reliability, and security. The FAT file system used with MS-DOS and the HPFS file system developed for OS/2 are not well-suited to network servers. They cannot dynamically compensate for disk flaws and cannot secure files against intruders who have access to the server.

NTFS compensates for disk flaws by using a hot-fix feature that automatically redirects data in a bad disk sector to a substitute sector.

Objective B.8

Caution NTFS builds security into the file system. You can't simply boot a computer from MS-DOS and bypass NTFS security. Nothing stays secure forever though. A freely available utility called NTFSDOS can be used under DOS to view NTFS volumes as though they are FAT. NTFSDOS understands NTFS long file names and can read compressed files. NTFSDOS remaps NTFS partitions to FAT, making the entire volume visible to the user. A bootable MS-DOS floppy that includes NTFSDOS can be used to access any NTFS file system.

Consequently, in situations that require high security, there is no substitute for physically securing the computer. Servers should be placed in a locked room and access should be restricted. If the computer has the required feature, disable the ability to boot from a floppy disk.

NTFS has other advantages as well:

◆ File names can extend up to 255 characters, including the extension. No longer are you limited to the 8.3 format file names associated with DOS.

◆ File names can include upper- and lowercase letters and a variety of characters prohibited under MS-DOS.

◆ Partitions and files can be extremely large, up to 16 exabytes (that's 1064 gigabytes). That's a lot of data.

◆ File- and directory-level compression can greatly improve file storage capacity. Text-oriented files can be reduced in size by as much as 50 percent, executable files only by 40 percent.

Note Windows NT file systems are discussed in detail in Chapter 17, "Managing Disk Storage."

RAID Support

Redundant Arrays of Inexpensive Disks (RAID) is a technology for improving the performance and fault tolerance of hard drives. Ordinarily, to have the benefits of RAID, you need to purchase special RAID hardware. Windows NT enables you to configure RAID drives using only standard drives and SCSI hardware.

Security

Windows NT can be configured to maintain a very high level of security. Using the proper procedures, it is possible to configure Windows NT computers for Class C2 security, defined by the U.S. Department of Defense as providing "discretionary (need-to-know) protection and, through the inclusion of audit capabilities, for accountability of subjects and the actions they initiate."

Windows NT Workstation security is based on securing shared network directories. Entire directory structures are assigned the same set of access restrictions.

Under NTFS Security on Windows NT Server is much more detailed. Administrators of Windows NT Server determine who will access the network and what resources they are permitted to access, right down to the file level.

Windows NT Server includes several security classes that solve old LAN administrator headaches. Consider the problem of the nightly tape backup. To be any good, the backup should include every file on the server. Ordinarily, that requires full administrator privileges, something you really don't want to give to night operators who will probably be performing the backups. Windows NT Server provides a special set of user privileges that enable tape backup operators to archive files without having the run of the network.

Windows NT design incorporates some clever security features. You will notice, for example, that you log on to a Windows NT computer by typing Ctrl+Alt+Del. This is a protection against programs that attempt to intercept passwords by substituting themselves for the normal logon program. The Ctrl+Alt+Del sequence always directly invokes the logon routine in the Windows NT operating system, an area of Windows NT that cannot be modified by users or intruders.

Another aspect of Windows NT security is that computers as well as users must be permitted access to the network. Even though a user has a valid user account, he can't log on from any Windows NT computer. The computer itself must have been added to the network. If the network consists only of Windows NT computers, it can be made very secure indeed.

Compatibility

Windows NT supports a wide variety of programs, including programs written for the following operating system standards:

◆ MS-DOS

◆ 16-bit Windows applications

◆ 32-bit Windows applications

◆ OS/2 (version 1.x only)

◆ POSIX, a Unix-style interface that enables applications to be easily ported among systems

Unfortunately, support for MS-DOS applications is limited, but it is limited for a very good reason. Windows NT does not permit applications to directly twiddle the hardware. All hardware is controlled by Windows NT; applications that want to access hardware must do so using Windows NT as an intermediary. Programmers of MS-DOS and Windows 3.x applications, however, routinely improve program performance by bypassing the operating system to issue direct calls to the system hardware. Programs that circumvent the operating system to get to the hardware will not run under Windows NT.

Ease of Administration

Over 90 percent of Windows NT administration tasks are performed with graphic utilities. As a result, the user interface is consistent, and there are few commands to remember. The GUI interface, however, is not the only feature that makes an administrator's life easier.

Objective C.2

Centralized User Profiles

Windows NT computers can utilize profiles that describe a user's working environment in great detail. Profiles fall into the following two categories:

◆ User profiles can be modified by individual users. An advantage of a centralized user profile is that users can access their profiles from any Windows NT computer on the network, effectively making their working environment portable. For this reason, Microsoft refers to these centralized user profiles as roaming profiles.

◆ Server-based mandatory profiles. Users cannot modify their settings. They enable an administrator to define a fixed environment for use by individuals or by large groups. A mandatory profile is a great means of ensuring that all users in a particular area have a common working environment. Support is greatly simplified.

Domain-Based Administration

Without some form of enterprise-based server administration, multiserver LANs are nightmares for an administrator. In some LAN environments, when you create a user account on one server, you need to create an identical account on every other server on the LAN. Two accounts are more than double the work because you need to cross-check everything, and problems inevitably arise.

Windows NT Server supports an administration approach that organizes multiple servers into commonly managed groups called domains. Users are not given logon privileges for an individual computer. Their account gives them permission to log on to the domain and gain access to all computers in the domain based on their security permissions. Domain-based administration significantly reduces the effort required to manage user accounts.

Domains also work fine in conjunction with workgroups, so Windows NT Workstation and Windows for Workgroups users can continue to use peer-to-peer resource sharing even as they access central resources on Windows NT Servers.

Directory Replication

If you ever want to distribute files to several servers, you will appreciate the directory replication feature of Windows NT Server. Directory replication enables you to designate an export directory on one server and import directories on other servers. The directory replication service takes responsibility for ensuring that any changes made to files in the export directory are copied to all import directories, without any further intervention from the administrator. Directory replication is a great way to distribute newsletters, phone lists, and commonly used files.

Task Scheduling

You will almost certainly have a need to schedule tasks to happen at particular times. The most common example of a timed task is kicking off the nightly tape backup job, which usually happens in the wee hours of the morning when your users have gone home. Windows NT has a built-in task scheduler that can execute batch and EXE files at any time you designate, on a daily, weekly, or monthly basis.

Remote Administration

All network management functions can be performed remotely, enabling you to manage all of your network servers from a central location.

Auditing

The more critical your LAN becomes, the more you will want to keep track of who is using and abusing it. Windows NT Server has a powerful, but easy-to-use auditing feature that can track all sorts of file access and printing activities. This data can be exported in formats that can be used by spreadsheet and database programs, enabling you to track events and statistics on your network.

API Support

Application program interfaces (APIs) are the commands programmers use to enable their applications to access services provided by operating systems and other applications. In the world of Windows applications, two major APIs are commonly employed, NetBIOS and Windows Sockets, both of which are supported on Windows NT.

NetBIOS

The Network Basic Input Output System (NetBIOS) has long been the standard API for Microsoft network products. Windows applications access the network through the NetBIOS interface. With Windows NT version 4, Microsoft has ensured that NetBIOS applications can network with all three of the transport protocols that are included. NetBIOS applications can participate in a wide area network using the NetBIOS over TCP/IP feature of Windows NT Server 4, for example.

Windows Sockets

Windows Sockets (WinSock) is a Windows-based implementation of the sockets API that is commonly used with Unix. Windows applications written to the Windows Sockets API are ready to network over TCP/IP.

Objective A.2

Transport Protocol Support

As you learned in Chapter 1, "Understanding Networks," protocols are the languages that enable computers to communicate. The computer industry has failed to gravitate toward a single protocol, although TCP/IP is winning many hearts and minds. Fortunately, Windows NT includes support for the three most common protocol suites on LANs: NetBEUI, Novell's IPX/SPX, and TCP/IP.

Figure 2.1 shows how NDIS supports multiple protocol stacks. It also shows another layer that enhances the versatility and simplicity of Windows NT. The Transport Driver Interface (TDI) layer insulates upper-layer applications from protocols, and technically resides between the OSI session and transport layers.

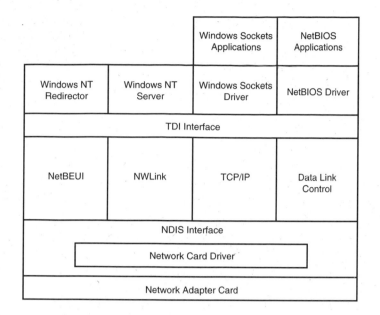

Figure 2.1

Protocol support on Windows NT.

The Network Driver Interface Specification (NDIS) is a key component in Windows protocol support. NDIS enables a computer to run multiple protocol stacks over the same network adapter card. NDIS effectively enables a computer to speak three network protocol languages at the same time.

NetBEUI

NetBIOS extended user interface (NetBEUI) was designed for running NetBIOS applications on local area networks. NetBEUI is a simple, efficient protocol that provides high performance on small networks. Prior to Windows NT version 3.5, NetBEUI was the standard protocol for Microsoft networking products. NetBEUI is a great fit for Windows networking because it is essentially a plug-and-play protocol that requires no configuration other than a simple installation procedure. NetBEUI is, therefore, well-suited to networks that will be administered by end-users, such as Windows for Workgroups.

NetBEUI has a significant problem: it cannot be routed and cannot, therefore, be used as the transport protocol on larger, multisegment networks. Windows NT 3.51 and later versions use TCP/IP as a standard protocol.

NWLink

NWLink is an NDIS-compliant transport that is network-compatible with Novell's IPX/SPX protocols. The IPX/SPX protocols offer high-performance and good functionality on wide area networks while requiring little setup. NWLink conforms to TDI and can support applications written to the NetBEUI and Windows Sockets APIs.

Another benefit of NWLink is that it simplifies the interface between Windows NT and NetWare networks. Windows NT includes NetWare client software and a NetWare gateway, both of which enable Windows network users to access resources on NetWare LANs.

TCP/IP

TCP/IP is named after the two primary protocols in the suite: Transmission Control Protocol (TCP) and Internet Protocol (IP). TCP/IP is a robust, versatile protocol suite that is the most widely used protocol suite in terms of the number of devices networked and the variety of supported computers. TCP/IP is particularly well-suited to wide area networks where reliable delivery is essential.

The downside of TCP/IP is that considerable and expert work is required to install and maintain TCP/IP networks. There is no such thing as a plug-and-play TCP/IP network.

That said, Microsoft has made great strides in simplifying TCP/IP installation and support. Administrators are burdened with relatively little manual editing of configuration files, which is a significant consumer of labor on TCP/IP networks. The Domain Host Configuration Protocol (DHCP) can be used to assign addresses dynamically to network computers. The Windows Internet Naming Service (WINS) adds a relatively low-effort name resolution service to Windows NT networks using TCP/IP.

You will want to install TCP/IP on a network in several situations:

◆ Your network needs to interface with a TCP/IP network, such as the Internet.

◆ TCP/IP is your corporate standard.

◆ TCP/IP is required to connect some devices on your network.

◆ Your network includes two or more network segments, possibly in a wide area network, and it requires a protocol that can be routed among the segments.

> **Note** TCP/IP is discussed in detail in Chapter 16, "Using TCP/IP."

DLC

Data Link Control (DLC) is used in two situations: connecting to IBM mainframes and printing to a DLC-compliant printer. DLC printers can attach directly to the network, eliminating the need for print servers.

| Note | DLC is discussed in Chapter 13, "Managing Printing Services." |

NetWare Interoperability

NetWare dominates the local area network world. Approximately 66 percent of all network computers are networked with NetWare. It is highly desirable for other LAN products to enable users to access resources on NetWare LANs.

Windows NT Server provides the following two means of connecting users to NetWare servers:

◆ Client software that can access NetWare servers. Prior to Windows NT version 4, only bindery-mode servers were supported, such as NetWare 3.12. Starting with Windows NT version 4, support has been added for NetWare Directory Services as well.

◆ A NetWare gateway that enables users to access NetWare services as if they resided on the Windows network.

Both of these features are discussed in Chapter 23, "Windows NT Server and NetWare."

Remote Access Services

Users rely on their LANs, and most LAN administrators have received requests from users who want to log on to the LAN from their homes or while they are traveling. Remote Access Services (RAS) is built into Windows NT and Windows for Workgroups. A Windows NT RAS server provides an inexpensive, easy-to-manage capability that enables users to dial into a LAN. As an added benefit, a RAS server can provide local users with a pool of shared modems, enabling local users who do not own modems to dial out to remote services.

RAS supports modem connections and enables you to configure modem pools. RAS also enables you to connect to a wide area network using X.25 or to access high-speed digital services with ISDN. See Chapter 21, "Using the Remote Access Server," for more information.

Internet Services

Windows NT Server has become a popular platform for providing services on TCP/IP Internets. That popularity is likely to increase because Windows NT Server 4 includes the Internet Information Server. This bundled software makes it extremely easy to add three services to your TCP/IP network:

◆ World Wide Web

◆ FTP server

◆ Gopher server

> **Note** Before I leave the topic of Windows NT features, let me mention some resources you really should have if you plan to work with Windows NT Workstation or Server.
>
> The *Windows NT Resource Kit* is the official reference on Windows NT. It consists of four fat volumes, and, although there is some overlap with the product manuals, the *Resource Kit* contains material that is unavailable anywhere else. It also contains a CD-ROM and several floppy disks of programs and data, some of which I make reference to in this book.
>
> Another important resource is Microsoft's *TechNet*. A subscription to *TechNet* costs only $295 a year, a profound bargain in the computer support industry. Each month you receive two or more CDs containing product and troubleshooting databases, program patches, and information about Microsoft programs.

Testing Your Knowledge

1. Microsoft Windows NT 4 currently supports which of the following architectures out of the box?

   A. Intel x86, MIPS RISC, Digital Alpha AXP RISC, PowerPC RISC

   B. Intel x86, MIPS RISC, Digital Alpha AXP RISC

   C. Intel 386, MIPS RISC, Digital Alpha AXP RISC, PowerPC RISC

   D. CISC, RISC, Asymmetric multiprocessors

2. Which type of multiprocessing does Windows NT support?

   A. Asymmetric multiprocessing

   B. Metric multiprocessing

   C. Symmetric multiprocessing

3. Windows NT supports a wide variety of programs, including programs written for which of the following operating system?

    A. MS-DOS, 16-bit Windows, 32-bit Windows, OS/2 version 1.x, POSIX

    B. Windows NT, NetWare, Lantastic, Banyan Vines

    C. MS-DOS, Windows 3.x, Windows NT, OS/2, Unix

    D. Real Mode, Privileged Mode, Virtual Mode

4. In order to distribute files to several servers using an import and export directory, Windows NT uses _____.

5. Windows NT provides support for the three most common protocol suites. What are these protocol suites?

    A. TAPI, MAPI, TDI

    B. NetBEUI, IPX/SPX, TCP/IP

    C. TCP/IP, NDIS, IPX/SPX

    D. NetBEUI, IPX/SPX, NetBIOS

Review Answers

1. A

2. C

3. A

4. Directory Replication

5. **B**

CHAPTER 3

Your Job as a Windows NT Administrator

L AN administration can be one of the most challenging careers you can imagine. Getting the LAN up and running might be the easy part because after your users' PCs are connected to the LAN, every problem they have suddenly will be the fault of the LAN. Be prepared for many complaints, such as "I never had any problems until you hooked me up to the LAN!" or "Your LAN's losing my files." You'll need all of your technical and interpersonal skills to do a good job.

Okay, so being a LAN administrator "looks like a job for Superman," right? Well, relax. The perfect LAN administrator doesn't exist. Although dozens of job skills appear on a LAN administrator's job description, each person fills the job in different ways. As a rule, the best technicians are weak on people skills, whereas the staff psychologist, who is an expert at soothing shattered nerves, probably will not know his way around a TCP/IP router. You probably will find your niche somewhere between Thomas Edison and Sigmund Freud.

Because the job is so complex, the best way to run a LAN is with a team of complementary personalities. If you must do the job alone, however, read on. This chapter introduces you to the various skills you will need on the job, and gives you some tips on how to succeed in each job that you will perform.

Installing and Managing Servers

Your server probably will be the most complex piece of computing equipment you will have on your LAN. On early LANs, servers were little more than well-equipped PCs, and many LANs continue to function well with PC-class servers. The increasingly critical nature of LANs in business operations, however, has lead to the purchase of more sophisticated hardware for network servers.

Windows NT Server can function on Intel PCs based on the IBM PC architecture (PC compatibles). Many vendors have improved the capabilities of the Intel PC architecture until their server products bear little resemblance to standard desktop PCs. The most powerful of these systems often are classified as *superservers*. Here are some of the features found in more powerful LAN servers:

◆ **Support for massive amounts of memory.** 256 MB and greater system RAM capacities are becoming increasingly common, and gigabyte capabilities exist. Most desktop PC architectures are limited to 64 MB or 128 MB.

◆ **Large hard drive subsystems.** These often are based on RAID technology and are designed for large capacity, high performance, and reliability. See Chapter 17, "Managing Disk Storage," for a full discussion of how Windows NT Server supports RAID.

◆ **Support for multiple processors.** Windows NT Server is capable of utilizing multiple processors by employing a feature called *symmetric multiprocessing* (this term is explained in Chapter 2, "Introducing Windows NT Server"). Multiprocessing can increase server performance.

◆ **Fault tolerance.** A server's resistance to hardware failures can be improved in many ways. Several of the techniques are too expensive to be practical with most desktop PCs. Some of the possibilities follow:

> Uninterruptible power supplies.

> Fault-tolerant disk subsystems that prevent a single hard drive failure from causing data or service loss.

> Error-correcting memory (ECM) that can detect and correct damaged data in memory. When an ordinary PC detects a memory error, it simply shuts down. ECM enables a system to continue functioning despite an occasional memory error.

◆ **Management.** When server operation is critical, it is desirable to know when problems are developing. The best servers can generate network-management alerts that can anticipate problems before they cause a server failure.

Many of the servers used with Windows NT Server will not be based on the Intel PC architecture at all. Many high-performance servers are based on Reduced Instruction Set Computing (RISC) processors such as the MIPS and the Digital Alpha AXP.

If you will be a network administrator, you should become as familiar as possible with your servers. After all, you are the person on the scene. Even if you have purchased technical support from a vendor, that support might be hours away, and hours of downtime are costly. Many organizations that use LANs to support critical systems invest in hardware training for their LAN support staff to ensure a large pool of on-site expertise.

Although you should become familiar with your server, don't feel that you must install and configure it. When dealing with more sophisticated servers, you often will be wise to pay your vendor to set it up for you. Just be sure to ask a great deal of questions during the process.

Managing the Server

After the server is up and running, it is your responsibility to manage it on a daily basis. One of your goals is to develop a feel for how the server is operating. Make notes of the performance statistics you observe under normal operations so that you have a sense of the standard performance of the server. Statistics gathered under normal operation describe the baseline operation of your network. These statistics have several values:

◆ If a statistic changes gradually or suddenly, it will tip you off on a trend, which may be a change in usage patterns or an impending problem.

◆ When problems arise, you can compare current statistics to your baseline. Doing so often tips you off to the cause of the problem, or at least to the area in which you should look first.

◆ Statistics supply you with ammunition when the time comes to upgrade your server or network.

That last point illuminates one of the ongoing problems you face as a LAN administrator: user demand for services always increases faster than you planned. Gigabytes of hard drive space can be filled in days, and you won't believe how quickly a server can outgrow 32 MB of memory. Frequent monitoring of disk storage and memory gives you time to control usage or to order more hardware before your server runs out of a critical resource.

You will be in a constant battle to use your current hardware to the best of its capabilities. Before you tell your boss that you need to upgrade to a multiprocessor RISC server, be sure that you have done the best job possible with your current hardware. Also, be sure when you request an upgrade that it will serve for a reasonable period of time. There are few things managers have less patience with than LAN administrators who frequently request additional server capacity.

Installing and Managing the Network

Networks can be simple or incredibly complicated. The level of complexity has much to do with your involvement in installing the cabling and network hardware. As with the server, the rule is this: the more you know, the better. You are responsible for monitoring the network on a day-to-day basis, and you are the person on-site when a problem arises.

Small networks are easy to install. Premade cables eliminate the need to buy expensive tools. If your network requires cables to pass through walls or over ceilings, however, you often are better off hiring a cable installer. The installer knows the wiring codes and can ensure that you are within the law. The installer also has the equipment and expertise to do the job efficiently and correctly. High-performance cables, such as fiber-optic cable and Level 5 UTP, never should be installed except by trained personnel (see Chapter 4, "Planning and Installing Network Media"). Few organizations can justify the costs of training in-house staff for these jobs. Pay for the expertise of a professional LAN installer so that the job is done right the first time.

Your network will change, and it is your job to know it intimately, to make minor changes, and to hire contractors when the modifications become major. Therefore, you should work with your installer to ensure that the system will be easy to reconfigure. You also should be involved in the cabling of your network so you know how it is configured, and so you can make maintenance changes.

Maintaining Network Security

PC users tend to have a cavalier attitude toward security. DOS (or OS/2 or Macintoshes, for that matter) cannot be secured to any great degree, except with sophisticated and tricky security software that few organizations want. Many companies have suffered critical data losses simply because of the amount of unsecured data that is sitting around on users' desktop PCs.

After users start sharing data on a LAN, the need for security can no longer be ignored. Allowing free-and-easy access by everyone to everything is a recipe for disaster, especially when your LAN is equipped with dial-in capabilities or attachments to outside networks, such as the Internet.

Windows NT Server can be made very secure, but be prepared to work hard to achieve a proper security level. Also, be prepared to take some heat from users who don't understand the need for security and complain every time they are forced to change their passwords.

Security is a sensitive topic because it inconveniences users. Part of your job is to coordinate with management to establish security policies for your organization. Explain to management the risks of not defining and enforcing a solid policy, assist them in creating a policy, and get them to buy in on enforcing the policy. There is nothing more frustrating than trying to enforce security without a partnership with management.

Protecting Data

I'm feeling repetitious, but I'll say it again: The data on your LAN is important. Besides ensuring that proper access security is maintained, you need to ensure against disasters that could jeopardize your data.

Your most important duty in this area is to back up data on a regular basis. If you do nothing else in a day, make sure that last night's backup ran properly and that tonight's will run. Make periodic checks to ensure that the files you are backing up actually can be restored.

Unfortunately, performing backups is only a rewarding activity when disaster strikes. If everything goes well, your safeguards are invisible, and this can make it difficult to sell management on the necessity of backups and to justify equipment that is up to the job. Remember, users and management are viewing the situation from the perspective of desktop PCs; because they have only one hard drive, and that hard drive isn't working all that hard, users seldom experience hard drive failures. Although LAN hard drives are extremely reliable, they do fail, and many users lose their data. More important, critical shared data is present on the LAN. Loss of some of this data could cost your company thousands or millions of dollars.

Make your backup plans carefully and do your duty daily. Eventually, you will be rewarded. When a user "accidentally" erases a critical file, your ability to restore the file from yesterday's backup tape will make you a hero. After this happens a few times, the invisible activity of file backup will have much more visibility and respect in your organization.

Viruses have become a significant threat to computer data. LANs enable viruses to reproduce like rabbits. Make it a point to identify and obtain anti-virus software for your network. Because such software is expensive, management often is reluctant to make the purchase. A virus on a LAN, however, can mean days of downtime, and once bitten, few organizations will hesitate any further.

Documenting the Network

If you're like most computer specialists, you carry a great deal of information in your head that isn't written down. Even if you are the only person in your organization who needs that information, failure to document your LAN is a recipe for disaster.

Considerable time might elapse between when you first do something and when you need to do it again or fix it when it breaks, for example. There are few small problems on a LAN; when something breaks, you will be under pressure to fix it immediately. Proper documentation can compensate for a memory that has gone flat in the heat of the moment.

Also, because you will not be your organization's LAN administrator forever, you should plan for the time you move on or you get some help. Documentation produced during an event is much more useful than documentation produced during a hurried, training, hands-off period.

Few organizations have a good handle on their computer-equipment inventories. As a LAN administrator, you might get involved in determining what equipment and software is on hand, as well as any changes that might occur. Fortunately, several commercial LAN inventory-software packages are available to help you perform this task.

Supporting Network Applications

Installing an application on a network can be much more involved than installing an application on a stand-alone PC. By now, most vendors have made installation of stand-alone applications as simple as typing **A:SETUP**. Installation of a networked application, on the other hand, can take hours or even days to plan and complete.

When you select an application for network installation, you need to check for its compatibility with your type of network server. You also need to confirm that it will work with the various workstation configurations that are present on your network. If workstation upgrades or changes are required, the equipment and labor costs should be part of your planning.

Whenever you install software on a network, you need to be aware of licensing issues. Some software packages incorporate licensing mechanisms. Others require you to use a separate usage-metering system to ensure that your network is operating within license restrictions.

Networks introduce new considerations into running applications. When many users are sharing an application, you need to take special steps to ensure that the users' application setup files remain separate. This can mean that some application files are located on the network, while others are located on the users' workstations—certainly more complicated than the normal situation in which all files are on the users' local hard drives. When users need to share certain files, you might need to spend extra time ensuring that the files are available, but that users cannot interfere with each other's files.

Supporting Users' Workstations

It all starts when you stuff a network board into a user's PC and show the user how to log in and use the network. The minute a workstation is attached to the LAN, it becomes the LAN administrator's problem. Users who "never had any trouble until this PC went on the LAN" come out of the woodwork. Your LAN suddenly is the cause of everything from lost files to global warming.

Add to this the fact that users' PCs are always changing. The evolution of software requires that older computers be upgraded or discarded. The computers might get more memory, a bigger hard drive, a processor upgrade, or new peripherals. As the LAN administrator, you are regarded as the resident PC expert, and you are called for everything PC-related.

Accept it: As a LAN administrator, you probably know more about computers than anyone else in your organization. Expect to receive many phone calls.

Planning the User Environment

By the time you finish this book, you will be pretty comfortable with Windows NT Server and LANs in general. Don't expect your users to read this book or invest the time you spend to become LAN-literate, however. Your users will want the LAN to be as invisible as possible.

One of your jobs is to make the LAN as easy to use as a local PC, and that takes much more work than simply hooking up your users. This might involve using menus, standardizing Windows interfaces, or providing documentation and training for your users.

Training Users

Even after the LAN is as easy to use as you can make it, something will be left over that your users will not understand. If a LAN is new to your users, or if they simply are being introduced to new services, your users probably will require some training.

Training is an ongoing activity in any organization with a LAN. Users need training on LAN-related topics such as logging on, printing to the LAN, sharing files, or sending electronic mail. They're also likely to call you with questions about WordPerfect or 1-2-3, however. Remember, you're the expert!

Training is often the LAN skill in which the top technicians are the weakest. If you're lucky, you will be part of a team that includes an ace technician and an ace trainer. If you fall into one category and have any influence on hiring your teammate, lobby for a coworker who complements your skills. Technicians often don't appreciate trainers, but training is at least as tough a job as running a LAN, and not all people are up to the job. Although a good trainer should be a skilled technician, a trainer's patience and psychology skills might be more important than technical competence.

Solving Problems

LANs will always have problems. Frankly, ordinary server problems might not be the worst you will encounter. User problems often are more troublesome because they always occur when the users are on deadline, and it always seems to be your LAN's fault for causing the projects to fail! Make it your goal to solve the users' problems as efficiently and sympathetically as possible. Even though it's not the fault of your LAN, bail your users out as calmly as possible. You're going to find that users approach LANs with a high level of anxiety that can backfire on you if you lose your cool.

Remember, many users are nervous around PCs and especially around LANs. Your behavior can calm or enhance that nervousness, and much of your performance is gauged on the impact you have on users' comfort levels. In the end, it matters less how well your LAN is running than how your users *perceive* the LAN and you. A LAN that runs perfectly will not win you any points if users don't respect you!

There are some things you can do to improve your problem-solving skills:

- ◆ **Learn, learn, learn.** LAN administration is an extremely challenging job. Devote some time each day to improving your skills.

- ◆ **Understand how LANs work.** Don't just know *how* to do something. Know *why* you are doing it. Good technicians possess a solid mix of theoretical and practical knowledge.

- ◆ **Know your LAN.** Get a feel for how your LAN runs. Then, like an auto mechanic who can tell you when an engine is misfiring, you will know when your LAN isn't working up to its normal level.

- ◆ **Develop a rapport with your users.** Make their concerns your concerns. Let them have a voice in LAN policy. Get them involved in training. Make it their LAN.

◆ **Plan for success.** Document your LAN and keep the documentation up-to-date. Record the problems you encounter and the solutions you find. Whenever you anticipate a change, overplan to ensure a smooth transition.

◆ **Expect problems.** Files are going to be lost, so be sure that your backups happen. Equipment is going to break, so have spares or be prepared to obtain replacements quickly.

◆ **Change things gradually.** Make one change at a time and test it thoroughly. Then it's easy to determine the cause of a new problem.

Testing Your Knowledge

1. Name at least two types of fault tolerance technologies used with server hardware.

2. What type of memory does the abbreviation ECM stand for?

3. What are the reasons why documenting your Network is important?

    A. Memory loss in a heated situation

    B. To keep yourself busy

    C. Maintain LAN inventory records

4. What are some of the things you can do to improve your problem-solving skills?

Review Answers

1. Uninterruptible power supplies; hard drive (RAID); memory (ECM)

2. error-correcting memory

3. A, C

4. Learn and understand how LANs work; Know your LAN; Develop a rapport with your users; Plan for success; Expect and prepare for problems; Change things gradually

CHAPTER 4

Planning and Installing Network Media

The network media marketplace traditionally has been a free-for-all of technologies competing for your equipment-purchasing dollars. You can readily find a wide variety of products ranging from tried-and-true to flaky to leading-edge (typically called *bleeding edge* by those who have been wounded by adopting a new technology too early).

This chapter introduces you to various network media that you might encounter and emphasizes technologies that are well-accepted and work well.

Characteristics of Media

You can make more intelligent media selections if you are aware of a few general media characteristics. No single medium excels in all the characteristics you will examine, and your decisions always will be based on the medium that makes the best compromise for your requirements.

EMI Sensitivity

Electrical signals and magnetic waves are inextricably linked. Changing electrical signals in wires creates magnetic fields around the wires, and changing magnetic fields around wires creates electrical signals in the wires. As a result, any source of changing magnetic fields can produce electrical noise in your LAN cables. Your LAN cables can create magnetic fields that can interfere with nearby electrical devices and with signals in nearby wires.

The noise produced in cables by magnetic fields is called *electro-magnetic interference* (EMI). Sources of EMI include radio transmissions, electric motors, fluorescent lights, and environmental phenomena such as lightning. You probably have heard EMI on the telephone or in AM radio broadcasts.

Most of the buildings LANs run in are filled with EMI noise sources. If your LAN includes cables that are pulled across ceilings, the cables probably are running near fluorescent lights. Because all copper cables are sensitive to EMI, you should be sure that your cable installer is aware of the need to run cables properly to avoid noise sources.

Cables that are sensitive to EMI have another problem: they all produce electro-magnetic fields that broadcast radio signals. These radio signals are a potential security risk because electronic eavesdropping equipment can receive the signals and intercept the network transmissions. If your network is carrying highly critical information, you have two choices: use fiber-optic cable, which is not electrical and cannot broadcast electrical signals; or encrypt the signals on your LAN. Few organizations need to be this concerned about security, but you should evaluate the risk for your organization.

Bandwidth

Bandwidth is a measure of the data rates that a given medium can support. The cables used in LANs typically can support data rates up to about 20 megabits-per-second (Mbps). This rate limit is adequate for many LANs, but some newer LAN-based services are demanding higher performance.

Increasingly, LANs are being used to deliver high volumes of data—including large files and graphic, audio, and video data. These applications are extremely demanding, and 20 Mbps of bandwidth is insufficient when it is shared among several users on a LAN. Network designers are expending considerable effort to bring down the cost of high-bandwidth LANs, and several media choices now can provide 100-Mbps bandwidths at reasonable costs.

Bandwidth in a medium can be used in two ways. When the entire bandwidth is devoted to a single data signal, the cable is operating in *baseband* mode. Most LANs use baseband signaling modes.

When the bandwidth of a medium is used to carry several independent signals, the medium is operating in *broadband* mode. You are familiar with one example of broadband signaling. The cable that brings television signals into your home is carrying several dozen independent television channels. You select a particular channel by setting the tuner on your TV. Network media can operate in much the same way, enabling a high-bandwidth medium to carry multiple lower-bandwidth signals.

Cost

Cost is always relative. At present, the cost of connecting a computer to a network can range from less than $100 to more than $1,000. If your network needs the best performance available, $1,000 per computer might be the only way to go. Remember that a low-cost solution you quickly outgrow is not a bargain.

There are many strategies for improving the performance of a basic network, each with advantages and disadvantages. In this chapter, you will examine high-speed networks, along with other strategies, such as switching hubs and full-duplex connections, that might provide you with the added performance you need at a lower cost.

Performance is not the only factor to consider when examining cost. Particularly with larger LANs, you should be willing to pay for features that make your LAN more reliable and manageable. Managed network components are more costly than basic components, but the extra cost can be justified if just one major network failure is prevented.

Cable Media

The vast majority of LANs utilize media consisting of copper or fiber-optic cable. Copper is inexpensive and an excellent conductor of electricity, and copper cable is by far the more popular LAN media choice. The performance potential of copper cable has been pushed up year by year until it has edged into applications that once were reserved for fiber-optic cable.

The cost of fiber-optic cable, however, has edged downward, and many organizations that have long avoided fiber now are selecting it for its virtually unlimited performance potential. Although the performance of copper cable has improved steadily, fiber-optic cable always will be the medium of choice for the highest performing networks.

This section examines four broad categories of cable:

◆ Coaxial

◆ Shielded twisted-pair (STP)

◆ Unshielded twisted-pair (UTP)

◆ Fiber-optic

The goal in this section is to introduce you to the most common cables used in LANs and to enable you to choose appropriate cables for specific circumstances.

Coaxial Cable

If you examine the structure of a coaxial cable, you can see that the name *coaxial* comes about because the two conductors—the center conductor and the outer shield conductor—share a common axis (see fig. 4.1).

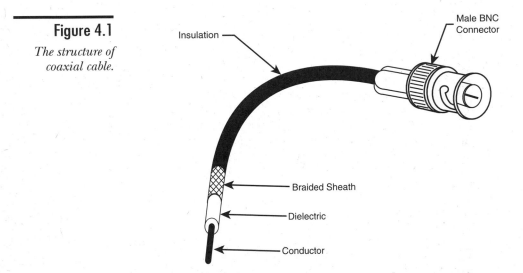

Figure 4.1

The structure of coaxial cable.

Insulation

Male BNC Connector

Braided Sheath

Dielectric

Conductor

The components of coaxial cable follow:

◆ **Center conductor.** In most coaxial cables, the center conductor is a fairly thick solid-copper wire. Stranded center conductors can be used when cables need to be flexible, but stranded conductors reduce the cable lengths that can be used. Solid conductors are preferable for permanent installations.

◆ **Insulation layer.** This layer serves two purposes. It electrically insulates the center conductor from the shield conductor, and it ensures that the center conductor remains centered. A precise physical relationship between the center conductor and the shield is required for peak performance.

◆ **Shield.** The shield is a conductor that completely surrounds the center conductor. The shield serves as the second conductor of the cable, and it protects the center conductor from outside EMI. The shield also reduces electro-magnetic signals that otherwise might radiate from the cable. For many years, shields were required for LAN cables.

◆ **Jacket.** A plastic or Teflon coating protects the outside of the cable. The jacket insulates the shield electrically from the outside and protects it from abrasion and other damage.

Figure 4.1 also shows a common connector used with coaxial cable. This connector is called a BNC connector (for BayoNet Connector) because you install it by twisting angled slots in one connector over pins in the matching connector.

Coaxial cable was used in the first LANs and has many characteristics that make it ideal for high-performance data transmission. Coax can support very high bandwidths, but this capability has not been exploited in most LAN implementations.

The performance of coax is closely related to the diameter of the cable and the thickness of the conductors. To improve the distance characteristics of coax LANs, early designers used thick coax that was expensive, bulky, and difficult to work with. More recent designs have resorted to thinner cable.

Coax cable types are not interchangeable. Besides the diameter of the cable and the nature of the conductors, another important characteristic of a coaxial cable is *impedance*. The impedance of a cable is a measure of the cable's resistance to the flow of alternating current such as data signals; impedance is measured in *ohms*. The following network types require cable with a specific impedance:

◆ RG-8 and RG-11 are 50-ohm coaxial cables with a diameter of approximately one-half inch. These cables are used with the oldest form of Ethernet, commonly called thick Ethernet or simply thicknet. Because these cables are stiff and difficult to work with, you sometimes hear them called "frozen, yellow garden hose."

◆ RG-58 is a thinner 50-ohm cable used with an Ethernet type commonly called thin Ethernet or thinnet. RG-58 is approximately one-quarter inch in diameter and is much easier to work with than RG-8 and RG-11. The thicker cables can carry signals much farther, however, and often are used when longer cable runs are required.

◆ RG-59 is a 75-ohm cable; it is the same cable that is used to wire cable television networks. RG-59 is inexpensive and is used to implement a broadband version of Ethernet.

Coaxial cable has several advantages:

◆ The shielding makes coax highly resistant to EMI.

◆ Networks that use coax have been in use for a considerable time (20 years, in the case of Ethernet) and are well understood, inexpensive, and reliable.

◆ The cables are durable.

Coax does have some disadvantages you should consider:

◆ Coaxial cable is not totally invulnerable to EMI, and it should be avoided in electrically noisy environments.

◆ Coax can be fairly expensive—particularly the thicker types, which can approach fiber-optic cable in cost.

◆ Coax cable is bulky—particularly the thicker varieties.

Shielded Twisted Pair

After coax, the next cable type to be used in LANs was shielded twisted pair (STP), as shown in figure 4.2. A twisted pair consists of two insulated wires that are twisted together. The twists do much more than simply hold the wires together. They cause the wires to alternate positions, causing EMI noises in the wires to cancel out. The twists also reduce the tendency of the cable to radiate electrical signals. Without the twists, the cable would tend to function as an antenna, readily absorbing signals from the environment and emitting its own signals to cause interference in other devices.

Figure 4.2

Shielded twisted-pair cable.

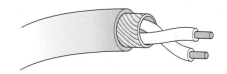

The cable shown in figure 4.2 uses a shield to further improve the cable's noise characteristics. Like the shield in coaxial cable, this shield absorbs outside signals that could cause interference and also absorbs signals that would otherwise be radiated from the wires.

In most implementations, STP cables include more than one pair of twisted wires. Figure 4.3 illustrates a common twisted-pair cable configuration that is used in token-ring networks. IBM created the specifications for the cables that generally are used to wire a token ring; figure 4.3 shows a cable type that is designated as IBM Type 1. This cable consists of two twisted-pair wire pairs enclosed in a common shield.

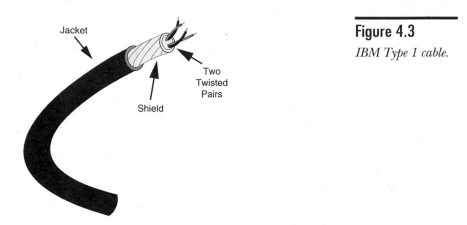

Figure 4.3

IBM Type 1 cable.

Shielded twisted-pair cables are comparable to coaxial cables in many ways. Costs are similar, as are bandwidths and cable diameters. Both perform well for the networks designed around them.

Some advantages of shielded twisted-pair cables are as follows:

◆ **EMI resistance.** STP is highly insensitive to electromagnetic interference.

◆ **High bandwidth.** Until recently, shields were required to achieve high bandwidths with twisted-pair cables. Bandwidths as high as 16 Mbps were achieved in the 1980s.

◆ **Durability.** STP cables generally include large-gauge conductors and are built for sturdiness.

STP cables have some significant disadvantages as well:

◆ STP cable is not totally invulnerable to EMI; it should be avoided in electrically noisy environments.

◆ The cost of STP is comparable to thin coax, although less in general than fiber-optic cable.

◆ STP cable can be particularly bulky.

STP cable remains in use but, like coax, it has grown less popular. Shielded cables have fallen into disfavor due to their fairly high costs and their bulk, which often fills up wiring paths far too quickly. The emphasis these days is on unshielded twisted-pair cable.

Unshielded Twisted Pair

Unshielded twisted pair (UTP) uses twisted pairs of wire, but it does not incorporate a shield. Removal of the shield reduces the cost and bulk of the cable, but makes it more sensitive to EMI and more likely to emit electronic noise. The bulk of UTP cable is reduced even more because most UTP cables use relatively small wire gauges—significantly smaller than gauges commonly used with coax and STP. Figure 4.4 shows an example of a two-pair UTP cable, along with the RJ-45 connector that typically is used. UTP cable was used first for telephone systems; in fact, many of the connecting devices used on UTP LANs are borrowed from telephone technology.

UTP cable has been used for many years for the premise wiring for telephone systems, and many organizations are wired with extra pairs of voice-grade wires. Consequently, customers have long sought to use their leftover telephone pairs to support LAN traffic. Telephone voice cable, however, is designed only for audio frequencies, and voice-grade cable cannot be adapted easily to data requirements. Businesses have come to expect more from telephone cabling than voice-grade service, and it is now universal practice to cable new commercial properties with data-grade UTP. Many business desktop phones are digital and require data-grade cable.

In the 1980s, work started on adapting higher grade UTP cable for data. Several LAN designs were introduced, but they were restricted by fairly low data rates. IBM's original specification for their token-ring network restricted the use of UTP cable to 4-Mbps data rates, while STP was sanctioned for 16-Mbps rates. At higher data rates, cables have a greater tendency to radiate electrical noise that can interfere with nearby cables or electrical devices.

Figure 4.4

UTP cable with an RJ-45 connector.

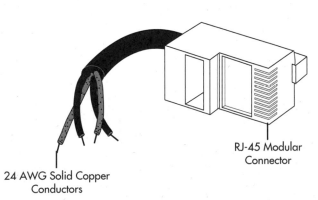

RJ-45 Modular
Connector

24 AWG Solid Copper
Conductors

Note You will see the terms token ring and Token-Ring in this chapter. Token-Ring originated as an IBM technology, and IBM capitalizes Token-Ring and includes a hyphen in the name. Since Token-Ring is an IBM trademark, other vendors generally use lowercase and omit the hyphen. This book will use lowercase unless it is specifically referring to the IBM brand of Token-Ring.

Customer demand for higher data rates over UTP has driven vendors to push the limits upward; several types of networks now can use UTP cable at data rates as high as 100 Mbps. To achieve these data rates, however, it has been necessary to define higher grades of UTP cable. Here are the five grades or categories of UTP cable:

◆ **Category 1.** Voice-grade only. Not usable for data.

◆ **Category 2.** Low-speed data transmissions such as PBX and alarm systems. Not usable at LAN data rates.

◆ **Category 3.** Usable for data transmissions at rates up to 16 Mbps. Used for UTP Ethernet and token ring.

◆ **Category 4.** Usable for data transmissions at rates up to 20 Mbps. Generally used in the same situations as Category 3.

◆ **Category 5.** Usable for data transmissions at rates up to 100 Mbps. Most of the newer 100-Mbps network designs are based on Category 5 cable.

Amazing progress has been made at raising the performance levels possible with UTP. Customers want UTP, which is perceived as being more cost-effective than shielded cables or fiber-optic cables. "Cat 5" cable does indeed deliver on the promise of high LAN speeds, but it is a mixed blessing.

Proper installation of Category 5 cable is considerably more costly than is installation of lower grades of UTP. When pulling Category 5 cable, the standard specifies that a maximum force of 25 Newton meters should be applied. Don't ask me how much 25 Newton meters is. Suffice it to say that most cable installations consist of pulling cable through openings, over ceilings, and through walls; and pulling as hard as it takes to get the cable moving. Cable installers do not use force gauges to ensure that cables are not stretched. Keep in mind, however, that stretching Cat 5 cable does lower its performance potential.

UTP data cables frequently are installed using connection devices similar to those used with telephone cables. UTP connectors resemble the RJ-45 connectors used with telephones, and cable interconnections often are made with punchdown blocks. A *punchdown block* is a plastic block that is studded with metal fingers. Wires are pushed between these fingers to make electrical connections between two cables.

In order for a network to perform at Category 5 levels, all components in the network must be designed to Category 5 specifications. Prior to about 1992, however, Category 5 punchdown blocks were unavailable, so many networks cabled with Category 5 cable prior to that time cannot be expected to perform at top speeds.

Installers need to be more careful in other ways when installing Category 5 cable. With lower grades of UTP, it is common to untwist two or three inches of wire prior to attaching the wires to a punchdown block. The Category 5 specification states that no more than one-half inch of the twisted pair should be untwisted prior to punching it down.

Installation of Category 5 cable systems is costly in several areas:

◆ The cable itself is more costly.

◆ The connection devices cost extra.

◆ Installers require more training.

◆ The procedure is slower.

As a result, properly installed Category 5 cable is not always a bargain. One vendor estimates that the cost difference between Category 5 cable and fiber-optic cable is only about $50 per station. (The electronic components required for fiber-optic cable, however, are considerably more expensive than the components used with UTP.) In summary, select Category 5 cable for solid technical reasons—not because you are looking for a bargain.

Some advantages of unshielded twisted-pair cable follow:

◆ UTP is the most inexpensive of all cable types.

◆ UTP has a low bulk. Because many pairs can be enclosed in a single cable jacket, a given cable path can accommodate more UTP pairs than STP or coax cables.

◆ Installation methods are similar to those used with telephone cabling. The required skills are easy to obtain.

Care should be taken when selecting UTP, however, due to some significant disadvantages:

◆ UTP is potentially very vulnerable to EMI.

◆ At present, 100 Mbps is about the limit of bandwidth for UTP. It's risky to predict, but 100 Mbps might be about the most that UTP can support.

◆ Thin-gauge cables are more vulnerable to damage.

Fiber-Optic Cable

Fiber-optic cable is a nearly perfect medium for the transmission of data signals. Maximum data rates exceed 1,000 gigabits-per-second, and new cable types promise to extend signal ranges to several thousand kilometers. Unfortunately, the performance of fiber-optic cable comes at a high cost, and few organizations choose to use 100 percent fiber-optic cable.

Fiber-optic cable consists of a glass or plastic core that carries data signals in the form of light pulses. Figure 4.5 shows an example of a fiber-optic cable, along with a typical connector.

The components of the cable follow:

◆ **Core.** Silicon glass generally is used because of its high transparency, but some cables with plastic cores have been tried. Glass cables can carry signals for several kilometers without needing to refresh the signals, but the range of plastic cables is limited to about 100 meters.

◆ **Cladding.** A glass coating surrounds the core. The characteristics of the cladding are chosen carefully so that light will be reflected back into the cable, reducing signal loss.

◆ **Sheath.** A tough covering, usually made of Kevlar, protects the cable. Multiple fibers can be bound together in the same sheath.

The light source for fiber-optic cable is generally a solid-state laser called an *injection laser diode* (ILD). The laser light produced by ILDs has several desirable characteristics. It is monochromatic, consisting entirely of a single light wavelength. Laser light also is *coherent*, meaning that all light waves are traveling in the same direction.

Although fiber-optic cable is only slightly more costly than copper cable, the transmitter and receiver devices required are considerably more expensive than comparable devices used with copper cable. Although the cost of a fiber-optic connection gradually has fallen below the $1,000 mark, a 100-Mbps, fiber-optic connection costs several times as much as a 100-Mbps connection based on Category 5 UTP.

The advantage of installing fiber-optic cable is that it has virtually unlimited performance potential. Many organizations already are forced to contemplate the day when 100-Mbps bandwidths are insufficient. Although miracles have been performed in pushing the bandwidth of UTP upward, 100 Mbps might represent a performance limit for UTP cable. Although copper cable is running out of steam at 100 Mbps, fiber-optic cable is just getting started. Using fiber-optic cabling, therefore, is an excellent long-term investment.

Figure 4.5

Fiber-optic cable and a typical connector.

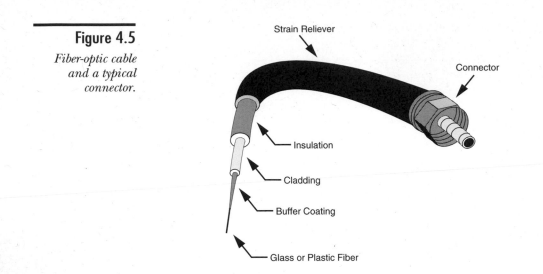

Fiber-optic cable is superior to copper cable in several ways:

◆ The fibers are small, and large numbers of fibers can be bundled to fit through the same space as a single copper cable.

◆ Because light is used for signaling, fiber-optic cable is immune to EMI and cannot radiate electrical noise. Therefore, fiber-optic cable is the only LAN medium that is virtually immune to electronic eavesdropping.

◆ Fiber-optic cables are durable. Glass cannot corrode and connections seldom go bad.

◆ The bandwidth of fiber-optic cable is, for all intents and purposes, unlimited. Your organization can outgrow copper, but fiber is forever.

The cost of installing fiber-optic cable has crept downward as improved installation methods have been devised. You can install fiber with a few hundred dollar's worth of tools and a couple day's of training. Fiber-optic cable's reputation for being expensive to install, therefore, is somewhat outmoded.

Summary of Cable Characteristics

Table 4.1 compares the virtues and liabilities of several types of cable.

TABLE 4.1
Characteristics of Cable Types

Cable Type	Bandwidth	EMI Sensitivity	Cable Cost	Installation Cost
Coax	High	Medium	Low	Medium
STP	Medium	Low	Medium	Medium
UTP	5–100 Mbps	Highest	Lowest	Low to Medium
Fiber-optic	Highest	None	Highest	Highest

Wireless Media

Many people think that LANs shouldn't be cabled at all. Cables clutter up the office and make it difficult to move equipment. Even if you have no objection to cables, you might find occasions when they are impossible to install. Consequently, a variety of network media vendors have attempted to market practical, wireless media.

Here are some situations when cable might be undesirable:

◆ If you are installing a LAN in an old building, it can be difficult to identify cable paths without incurring high costs. In historic buildings, you might be prohibited from running cables. A church, for example, might not want you drilling holes in its marble walls to run network cables.

◆ When LAN signals must cross a public street, you have two choices: lease a line from a telephone provider (expensive) or use wireless media.

◆ If users move frequently, wireless media gives them greater mobility.

◆ If an organization frequently modernizes and remodels, wireless media might be less expensive than the cost of periodically re-cabling.

◆ Now that most executives have portable PCs, you might simply have a boss who wants, and has the authority to demand, the capability to move PCs anywhere without changing cables.

Two types of wireless media are available: optical and radio frequency.

Optical LAN media use a technology similar to a modern television remote control. Pulses of infrared light are transmitted between devices. Optical LANs operate primarily within buildings, but some types can transmit several hundred yards between buildings.

Radio LAN media use a wide variety of radio techniques. Some use low-power transmissions and a technology similar to cellular telephone networks. Others use high-power transmissions and can transmit signals for considerable distances. Because installing high-power, long-distance radio transmissions, such as microwave, requires skilled and licensed specialists, this chapter focuses on the shorter-range solutions.

Optical LANs

Optical LANs can be implemented in two ways:

◆ By broadcasting signals to several receivers

◆ By relaying signals from node to node using point-to-point transmissions

Figure 4.6 illustrates a network that broadcasts infrared signals throughout a room. Signals are transmitted toward a reflective surface on the ceiling that disperses the signals to all receivers in the room. This method does not require careful alignment of transmission and receivers, as does the point-to-point approach. Receivers must be capable, however, of functioning with fairly weak light signals. This system, therefore, can be sensitive to excess ambient light.

Figure 4.6

Operation of a broadcast optical LAN.

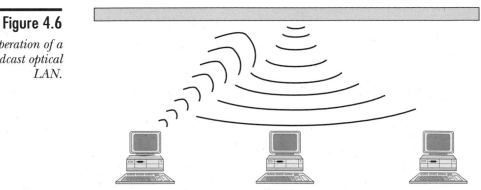

The point-to-point approach is shown in figure 4.7. Because a tight beam is used, receivers can depend on working with a fairly strong light signal. Of course, the transmitters and receivers must be situated so that they will not be obstructed as people walk through the office. That can be a significant challenge that can work against the theoretical advantage of wireless media: that they should be easy to install.

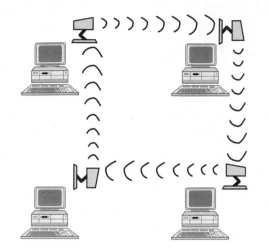

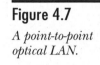

Figure 4.7

A point-to-point optical LAN.

Point-to-point optical LANs are not limited to short-range operation. If you need to connect two buildings that are separated by a few hundred yards, you might consider an optical connection that is based on laser transmitters. Gas lasers can generate very high signal levels that can travel reliably for a considerable distance. Of course, rain or fog can disrupt all such optical communication links.

Although infrared light has the potential for supporting high bandwidths, current infrared LAN technologies typically support bandwidths below 5 Mbps.

Radio Frequency LANs

The majority of wireless LANs use radio frequencies. Two LAN technologies are available:

◆ **Spread spectrum.** This is based on a technology developed by the military to transmit secure signals that are highly resistant to noise.

◆ **18 GHz LANs.** These use a low-power radio technology similar to cellular telephone networks.

Spread Spectrum

Spread spectrum transmissions use several frequencies to transmit a given message. In one scheme, the transmitter hops among the various frequencies, depending on which channel has the least noise at a given time. The transmitter informs the receiver which frequencies it will use so that transmitter and receiver can remain synchronized.

Another scheme divides the message into parts, transmitting different parts over different frequencies. To make the data more secure, dummy data can be transmitted over a separate channel. The intended receiver knows which frequencies carry legitimate data, but eavesdroppers will have difficulty isolating the original message from the many possible frequency channels.

Spread spectrum LAN designers rely primarily on unlicensed frequencies—frequencies that can be used without acquiring a permit from the Federal Communications Commission (FCC). Three unlicensed frequency ranges that can be used for radio LANs are 902–928 MHz, 2.4–2.483 GHz, and 5.725–5.85 GHz. (*Hz,* or *Hertz,* is a measure of radio frequencies in cycles per second.)

Unlicensed frequencies can be used freely with few limitations. This sounds convenient, but you might find yourself sharing a frequency with a radio-controlled model airplane enthusiast or an alarm system. Without the added reliability provided by spread spectrum technology, use of unlicensed frequencies would be impractical.

Spread spectrum transmissions can be powerful enough to penetrate many types of walls. Therefore, spread spectrum is a media option in older construction areas where cables cannot be installed.

Note   Spread spectrum is the way to go if your users want to operate free of cables. One vendor even provides a radio transceiver that installs in the PCMCIA slot of a laptop portable. Although this product has extremely short range, it does make it easy for users of portable computers to hook into the network or move around the office.

18 GHz

The engineers at Motorola have capitalized on their experience with cellular telephones to build a LAN product that operates on similar lines. The key to cellular networks is to use low-power radio transmissions that cover a very limited area called a *cell.*

Devices within a cell communicate with a hub that functions as a transmitter/receiver for the cell. When a message is directed to another device in the same cell as the message's originator, the hub retransmits the message to the cell. When a message is directed to a device in another cell, the hub forwards the message through a cable to the appropriate hub. The organization of a Motorola 18-GHz network is shown in figure 4.8.

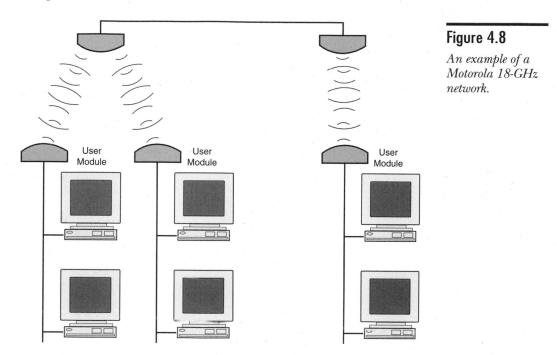

Figure 4.8

An example of a Motorola 18-GHz network.

18 GHz is a licensed frequency. To simplify licensing, Motorola has obtained licenses in all major metropolitan areas. Motorola handles all the licensing requirements for the customer.

Notice that the Motorola technology is not completely wireless. Computers communicate with hubs through user modules, which are connected by cables. Also, most hub-to-hub connections are cabled.

Note This discussion might have you wondering about the possibility of networking through the cellular telephone network. Using modems, this is possible to some degree when devices aren't moving. When a device crosses a cellular boundary, however, the process of handing off the signal from one cell to the next almost always interrupts data flow.

Observations on Wireless LANs

Vendors of wireless LANs are fond of quoting high estimates for the costs of moving PCs within an organization. Estimated costs of $500 to $1,000 per move are not uncommon. The claim is that the added cost of a wireless LAN is recovered quickly by money saved in moving computers.

It is difficult to see how these high costs can be justified in real life. With a modern structured cabling system (described later in this chapter), it is common to install cable in every place a computer is likely to be needed. Moving a computer is a simple matter of unplugging it from one location, moving the hardware, and plugging it into a new LAN outlet. Most of the labor is in moving the PC. Recabling the system takes only a few minutes.

As you saw in figure 4.8, many wireless LANs are not really wireless. Cables are needed to interconnect hubs or to enable devices to share LAN interface modules. Reorganizing the cabling of a "wireless" LAN could be a significant undertaking.

18-GHz radio and optical LANs cannot penetrate walls. Once again, you are faced with the need to use cables to interconnect different sections of the LAN. Few wireless LANs truly are wireless.

Wireless LANs are significantly outperformed by even low-end cabled LANs. Ethernet delivers a bandwidth of 10 Mbps. Wireless LANs seldom approach even half that level, and 1–2 Mbps of bandwidth are common. If your organization is moving into network-intensive applications, such as graphics or multimedia, it is unlikely that you will find a wireless LAN technology that fills your needs. LAN technologies such as 100-Mbps Ethernet or the emerging 455-Mbps ATM are unlikely to be supported by wireless media.

You probably should consider wireless LANs only when cabling is not an option. Some buildings do not structurally permit you to run cables, and some organizations require that workers be mobile with their PCs. Other than these two requirements, it is difficult to imagine applications where wireless LANs would be the technology of choice.

Topologies

Devices can communicate on networks in two ways, and all network configurations are variations on these two methods:

◆ The bus

◆ The point-to-point link

Bus Networks

Ethernet, the earliest LAN technology, was based on a bus configuration. An example of a bus is shown in figure 4.9. Notice that all the devices are connected to the same wire. Computer B is transmitting, and its signal travels down the wire in both directions. Every device on the network "hears" the signal. That is the distinguishing characteristic of a bus: If every device on the network can intercept every signal, the network is functioning as a bus.

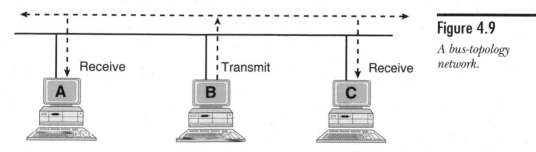

Figure 4.9

A bus-topology network.

A bus operates much like human conversation in a room—everyone can hear everything that is said by everyone else. Just like computers on a bus, humans in a room are sharing the same communication channel.

Point-to-Point Connections

The majority of networks are based on point-to-point (P-P) connections. Basic P-P links are illustrated in figure 4.10. A one-way link is established by connecting the transmitter of one device to the receiver of another. Two-way communication can be accomplished in a variety of ways.

Figure 4.10

*Types of point-
to-point
connections.*

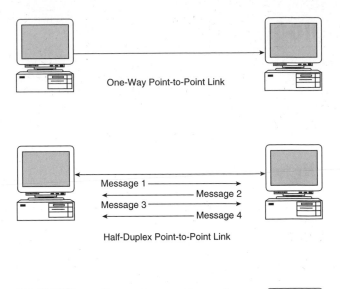

One-Way Point-to-Point Link

Half-Duplex Point-to-Point Link

Full-Duplex Point-to-Point Link

Two-way communication often is referred to as *duplex mode*. If only one communication channel exists, the devices must take turns transmitting; this is called *half-duplex mode*. In half-duplex mode, the devices take turns using a single wire. When one device is finished transmitting, it must "turn over" the communication channel so that the other device knows that it is permitted to transmit.

If both devices can transmit at the same time, the operation is called *full-duplex mode*. Full-duplex operation requires two communication channels. On LANs, full-duplex channels usually are created by adding a second pair of wires.

Building Complex Networks

Bus networks grow simply by extending the bus and adding devices. At some point, the bus will not be able to accommodate additional devices. At that point, additional buses can be connected together—usually with devices called *bridges*. A two-bus network is shown in figure 4.11. Ethernet is the most common network design based on a bus. The rules for extending Ethernet LANs are examined later in this chapter.

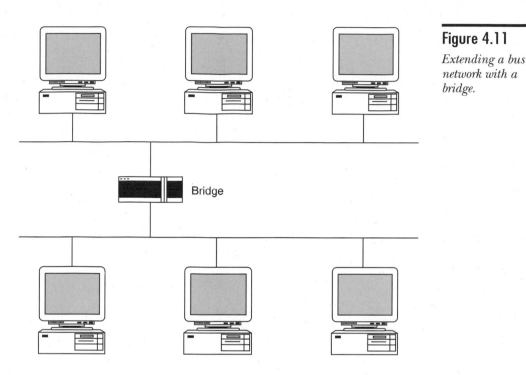

Figure 4.11

Extending a bus network with a bridge.

When P-P links are used, devices can be added simply by adding more P-P connections. Several multidevice networks are shown in figure 4.12. When each device is connected to every other device, the network design is called a *mesh*. You will notice that the number of P-P links in a mesh network rises rapidly as the number of devices increases. A three-device network requires three P-P links, but a four-device network requires six links. Obviously, this is not a practical way to network large numbers of devices.

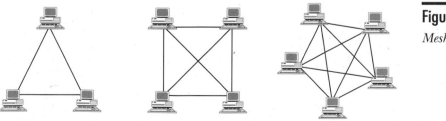

Figure 4.12

Mesh networks.

Mesh networks have several significant advantages. Each device has a dedicated communication link with every other device and has access to the full bandwidth available for that link. Devices on buses must share the bandwidth available on the bus medium. Another advantage of a mesh is that multiple paths exist between devices. If a direct path between devices goes down, messages can be routed through other devices.

Many large networks are constructed using a variation on the mesh design. The *hybrid mesh* approach shown in figure 4.13 uses extra links to establish redundant paths, but does not build in enough links to create a complete mesh. When the network links stretch for long distances, as in a countrywide or worldwide network, the redundancy of a hybrid mesh network can provide an important improvement in reliability.

Figure 4.13

A hybrid mesh network.

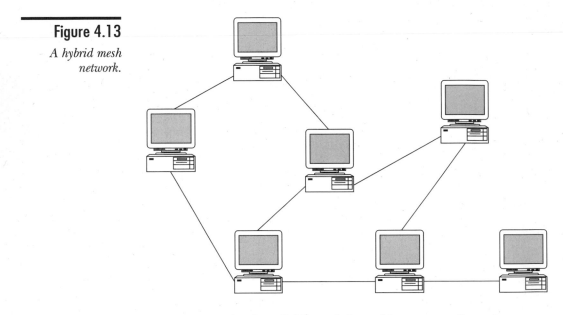

LANs generally are presumed to be reliable, and they seldom are configured as meshes. Meshes seldom are used to build LANs. The approaches most commonly used to build LANs with P-P links are rings and stars.

Figure 4.14 shows a *ring* network design. In this approach, the transmitter of one device is connected to the receiver of the next device in the ring. In this way, messages are forwarded around the ring until they are examined by each device on the network.

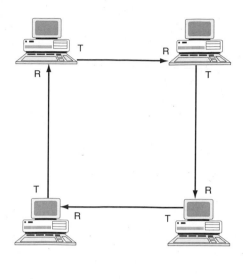

Figure 4.14

A ring network.

T = TRANSMIT
R = RECEIVE

Another common approach is the *star*, shown in figure 4.15. Star networks concentrate all network connections in wiring hubs. Each device connects to the network through a P-P link with the wiring hub.

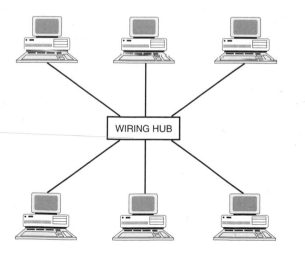

Figure 4.15

A star network.

Physical and Logical Topologies

The *topology* of a LAN is a description of the network's shape. The topologies you have seen up to this point are called *physical topologies* because they describe how the cabling of the network is physically laid out.

In addition to having a physical topology, every network design has a *logical topology*, which describes how the network looks from the perspective of the signals traveling through it. A given network design can have different physical and logical topologies. In other words, the way a network is cabled does not necessarily reflect the way in which signals flow through it.

> **Note** Here is another way to distinguish physical topology from logical topology:
>
> ◆ If you can see and touch it, it is physical.
>
> ◆ If you cannot see or touch it, it is logical.

Figure 4.16 is an example of a physical star network that functions logically as a ring. Each computer is connected to a central network hub with a cable that includes separate wires for receiving and transmitting signals. If you trace the cables through the figure, you will discover that the signal path is logically the same as that shown in figure 4.13. The network is wired in a star, but it functions as a ring as far as the network signals are concerned.

Figure 4.16

A network that is wired as a star but functions logically as a ring.

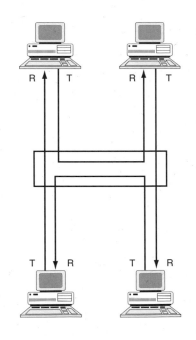

T = TRANSMIT

R = RECEIVE

Figure 4.17 shows a star-wired network that functions as a logical bus. In this case, the hub mixes the signals from all the attached devices. All messages are retransmitted to all devices attached to the hub. Recall that this is a defining characteristic of a bus: all devices hear all signals on the network. The network is a physical star because each device connects to the hub through an individual cable, but the network functions as a bus.

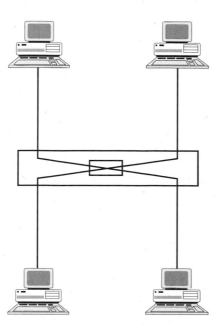

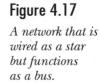

Figure 4.17

A network that is wired as a star but functions as a bus.

Most new LAN standards are based on star physical topologies. Star networks have several advantages. If each device is connected with its own cable, it is easy to move computers and reconfigure the network. This is, in fact, the basic principle behind structured wiring, a concept that is explained later in this chapter.

Star wiring also makes it easy to isolate malfunctioning devices. If a computer goes bad and starts corrupting data, it's easy to disconnect the faulty device by disconnecting its cable or by turning off its connection electronically at the hub.

When all devices connect to hubs, the hubs become central points from which to manage the network. It is increasingly common to build diagnostic capabilities into hubs, enabling them to detect problems and to notify network managers.

Hubs

Star-wired networks are based on hubs, and you should know something about the types of hubs that are available. Broadly speaking, there are two hub varieties: passive and active.

Passive hubs do not incorporate any powered electronic components. As a result, the only function of passive hubs is to provide a central point for connecting cables. Passive hubs cannot provide network management or improve the quality of network signals. You encounter only one type of passive hub in this chapter: the IBM model 8228, a relay-based hub that was developed for IBM's Token-Ring network.

The majority of hubs are *active,* meaning that they include electronic components that can process signals. Active hubs can include several interesting capabilities:

◆ Amplification of weakened signals

◆ Reshaping and retiming of distorted waveforms

◆ Detection of network problems

◆ Sending performance and error reports to management

◆ Remote management, enabling network administrators to control hubs that are located a considerable distance away

An interesting and fairly new category of active hub is the *switching hub* (see fig. 4.18). A switching hub can quickly switch signals between any two attached devices. Each device attached to the hub enjoys a private connection and has access to the full bandwidth capabilities available from its connection. Switching hubs improve network performance by freeing devices from the need to share the bandwidth of a common cable segment.

Figure 4.18

An example of a switching hub.

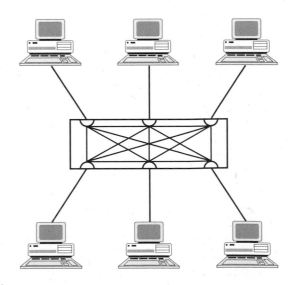

LAN Cabling Standards

The vast majority of local area networks are based on two standards: Ethernet and token ring. Both of these network types have been standardized by the International Electrical and Electronics Engineers (IEEE) organization, the largest professional organization in the world. The IEEE has a well-established standardization process that is open to a broad range of input. As a result, standards developed by the IEEE generally receive universal industry support.

IEEE LAN standards are grouped under the heading 802. A wide variety of 802 standards have been or are in the process of being defined. Some of those standards follow:

- **802.2.** Defines a network layer called the logical link control (LLC) layer.
- **802.3.** Defines the IEEE version of Ethernet.
- **802.5.** Defines the IEEE version of token ring.

Figure 4.19 illustrates the relationship of these standards to the OSI model. Notice that the 802.2 standard describes the upper half of the data link layer. Both the 802.3 and the 802.5 standards describe the physical layer, along with the lower half of the data link layer. All the lower-level 802.x standards are designed to work with the same LLC layer as defined by standard 802.2.

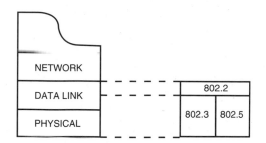

Figure 4.19

The relationship of several IEEE standards to the OSI reference model.

The 802.3 and 802.5 standards cover the OSI physical layer. They also cover the lower half of the data link layer—a sublayer called the medium access control (MAC) sublayer. The *MAC sublayer* defines the way that devices on the network share the network medium.

By defining a common LLC protocol for all LAN standards, the IEEE approach makes it unnecessary for the upper-layer protocols to be aware of the type of network on which they are operating. In fact, a network device can be moved from one network cabling system to another simply by changing the physical layer protocols.

You do not need to know a great deal about the 802.2 layer. You should, however, be at least somewhat familiar with the characteristics of the physical layer that is used on your LAN. The Ethernet (802.3) and token-ring (802.5) standards are discussed in the following sections.

The Fiber Distributed Data Interface (FDDI) is another network that Windows NT Server supports out of the box. FDDI is a standard for a fiber-based network that was developed by the X3T9.5 committee of the American National Standards Institute (ANSI). The ISO has adopted FDDI as standard 9314. FDDI was developed for wide area networks (WANs), but has been used in MANs and LANs as well. FDDI is designed around fiber-optic media and has a data bandwidth of 100 Mbps, but it has been adapted to copper media as well. FDDI is discussed later in this chapter.

Ethernet

Ethernet is the oldest LAN cabling system in current use—it dates back to the early 1970s. It developed originally out of research at the Xerox Palo Alto Research Center (Xerox PARC), and was refined through the joint efforts of Xerox, Intel, and Digital Equipment. Ethernet was submitted to the IEEE for standardization and, with some modification, became the IEEE 802.3 standard.

The original Digital/Intel/Xerox (DIX) Ethernet differs from the 802.3 standard. The most recent version of DIX Ethernet commonly is referred to as Ethernet II or Ethernet version 2. Ethernet II remains in common use on TCP/IP networks and on Digital's DECnet networks. The IEEE 802.3 standard is the dominant Ethernet version on most other network types.

Xerox has surrendered the Ethernet trademark to the public domain, and there is considerable controversy whether the DIX or the IEEE standard has the strongest claim to be called Ethernet. For what it's worth, the opinion of Robert Metcalf, credited as the inventor of Ethernet, is that the Ethernet label should be assigned to the latest standard, which is IEEE 802.3.

This book is not the place to settle the argument. The Ethernet variants are quite similar and are based on a medium access control method called CSMA/CD. Consequently, the term *Ethernet* is used in this book to describe features of both CSMA/CD networks. When it is important to make a distinction, the terms *Ethernet II* and *Ethernet 802.3* will be used.

How CSMA/CD Works

Ethernet is based on a bus, and you have learned that all devices on a bus share the same network medium. Because multiple frames on the same cable would interfere with each other, only one frame can be permitted on the network at a given time. CSMA/CD is the mechanism that enables devices to share the medium without excessively interfering with each other. This behavior sometimes is described as *listen before talking.*

CSMA/CD is an abbreviation for *Carrier Sense Multiple Access with Collision Detection.* That's a mouthful, but it's easy to understand if you take the name apart.

Carrier sensing describes the behavior of a device that wants to transmit on the network. When a device needs to access the network, it first listens to determine whether the network is busy. If the network is busy, the device waits for a bit and tries again. If the network is quiet, the device begins to transmit its frame. This behavior is quite similar to your behavior when you want to speak at a meeting. To avoid interrupting anyone, you listen for a lull in the conversation before you talk.

Multiple access means that many devices can share the network medium.

Collision detection describes the behavior of devices when they determine that two computers have sent frames at the same time. As a device is transmitting, it continues to listen to the network. If another frame appears on the network, it collides with the frame that the device is transmitting. Devices know collisions have occurred because they cause a higher than normal voltage to appear on the network.

When it detects a collision, a device stops sending its data and transmits a *jamming signal* that notifies all devices on the network of the collision. After the jamming signal is transmitted, each device waits for a random amount of time before attempting to retransmit. The random delay is important. If each device waited the same amount of time before retransmitting, another collision would occur. If devices wait for different lengths of time, collisions become less likely.

Collisions are a fact of life on CSMA/CD networks. This is because signals do not travel instantly down the entire length of the cable. Signals on cables travel somewhat slower than the speed of light. As figure 4.20 shows, when a device transmits, other devices will still sense a quiet network for a small period of time. A second device might, therefore, choose to transmit even though a signal from the first device was already on its way. Somewhere in the middle, the two signals will collide.

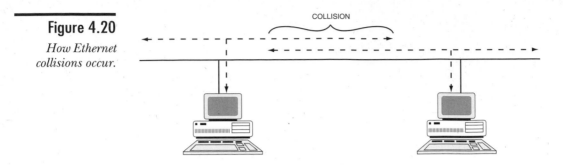

Figure 4.20

How Ethernet collisions occur.

You might correctly conclude that collisions are undesirable and that they detract from network performance. Unless an Ethernet is overloaded with traffic, however, collisions remain at a reasonable level and performance is excellent. An Ethernet frame can consist of no more that 1,518 bytes, and an Ethernet has a bandwidth of 10 million bits per second (1.25 million bytes). Unless the network is loaded heavily, collisions should occur with only a small percentage of frames transmitted.

At low LAN traffic levels, CSMA/CD is actually an extremely effective protocol. Little housekeeping is required to keep the network running, so the majority of the network's bandwidth is devoted to useful traffic.

When a CSMA/CD network is loaded too heavily, however, it is possible for collisions to become so frequent that little useful traffic can find its way onto the network. Under such circumstances, a device might find it impossible to transmit.

Ethernets tend to function very smoothly until some critical threshold is exceeded. At some point, traffic increases result in much more frequent collisions and network performance degrades, often catastrophically. You should make it a habit to monitor your LAN to determine whether usage levels are increasing to a potentially troublesome level. A good rule of thumb is that Ethernets work fine with constant traffic loads of 30 percent of capacity, and traffic bursts of about 60 percent of capacity. If your LAN is exceeding these levels, you should take steps to divide your Ethernet into additional segments to reduce the number of stations that are sharing a given segment's bandwidth.

CSMA/CD is a *probabilistic* access control method, meaning that a given device probably will have a chance to transmit at roughly the time it needs to, but that the opportunity to transmit is not guaranteed. On most LANs, probabilistic access control works fine. In some applications, however, it might be necessary to be more certain that devices can transmit. Suppose that the network is controlling a manufacturing process, and that things must happen at precise times. The possibility that a device might not gain access to the network at a critical time is unacceptable. This state of affairs is one reason why IBM invented the Token-Ring network.

Ethernet Cabling

Until recently, all Ethernets were cabled with thick or thin coaxial cable. Customers demanded a UTP configuration, however, and the IEEE responded with the 10BASE-T standard. This section reviews the three most common Ethernet cabling standards.

Thick Ethernet (10BASE5)

The original Ethernet cabling used a thick, half-inch diameter coaxial cable and is referred to as thick Ethernet or thicknet. As with most varieties of Ethernet, thick Ethernet operates in baseband mode with a bandwidth of 10 Mbps. The maximum cable length of a segment is 500 meters. The IEEE label 10BASE5 summarizes these characteristics: 10-Mbps bandwidth, baseband operation, and 500 meter segments.

Figure 4.21 illustrates the components of a thick Ethernet. Workstations do not connect directly to the thick coaxial cable. Instead, they attach by way of multistation access units (MAUs). An MAU can be installed on the cable by cutting the cable and installing N-type connectors. The more common practice is to use MAUs that clamp onto the cable. Pins in the clamp-on MAU penetrate the cable to make contact with the shield and center conductor. MAUs that attach in this way are called *vampire taps*. For best performance, MAUs should be attached to the thick coaxial cable at intervals that are even multiples of 2.5 meters.

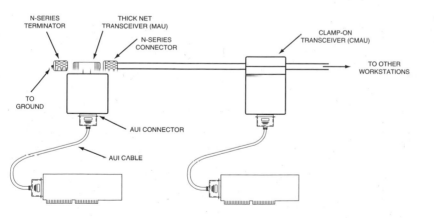

Figure 4.21

Components of a thick Ethernet.

Both MAUs and device network interfaces are equipped with a special 15-pin connector called an attachment unit interface (AUI) connector. A multi-conductor AUI cable of up to 50 meters can be used to connect the device to the MAU.

Figure 4.21 shows a common feature of networks based on coaxial cable. The ends of an Ethernet bus must be equipped with *terminators*—connectors that incorporate a 50-ohm resistor that matches the impedance characteristics of the cable. The terminators absorb any signals that reach them and prevent the signals from being reflected back into the cable as noise. One of the terminators must be connected to an electrical ground. Without the grounded connection, the cable's shield might not do an effective job of protecting against EMI. Only one terminator should be grounded. Grounding both connectors can produce electrical problems in the cable. A common source of an electrical ground is the screw in the center of an electrical wallplate. You should have your outlets tested to ensure that a good ground is present.

Two sets of terminology are used with thick Ethernet. The IEEE 802.3 standard refers to the connectors as *attachment unit interface connectors.* Practitioners of the older Ethernet II standard, however, refer to these connectors as *DIX (Digital-Intel-Xerox) connectors.* Also, although the IEEE 802.3 standard refers to the cable interface as a *medium attachment unit,* it more commonly is called a *transceiver* when used in an Ethernet II environment. You often will find these terms used interchangeably.

Apart from naming conventions, cabling is identical for Ethernet II and IEEE Ethernet 802.3. In fact, messages from both standards can coexist on the same cable segment.

An Ethernet *segment* consists of the coaxial cable between two terminators. The maximum length of a thick Ethernet segment is 500 meters, and each segment can support a maximum of 100 connections. When it is necessary to construct larger networks, segments can be connected by using repeaters, as shown in figure 4.22. Repeaters serve several purposes: they electrically isolate the coaxial segments, they amplify signals that pass between segments, and they reshape waveforms to correct distortions that arise as signals travel through cables.

Figure 4.22

Extending a thick Ethernet with a link segment.

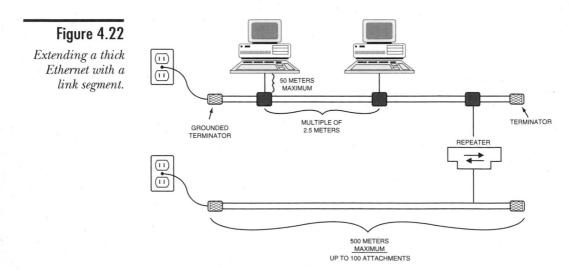

A repeater segment is called a *link segment.* At most, an Ethernet can include three coaxial cable segments and two link segments. Repeaters connect to coax segments using AUI cables, which are limited to 50 meters. The maximum length of a link segment, therefore, is 100 meters. If longer link segments are required, fiber-optic cable can be used to create a fiber-optic repeater link (FIORL) segment. FIORL segments can be up to 1 kilometer.

Thickwire Ethernet is seldom used in new LAN installations. The cable is expensive and bulky. Network components are also expensive, and are difficult to install.

Thin Ethernet (10BASE2)

The IEEE 10BASE2 specification describes a CSMA/CD network with these features: 10-Mbps bandwidth, baseband operation, and segment lengths of approximately 200 meters (the precise limit is 185 meters). The coaxial cable used with 10BASE2 is considerably thinner than thicknet coax. Consequently, this Ethernet cabling system often is called thin Ethernet, thinnet, or just Cheapernet.

You can examine the connectors used in thin Ethernet in figure 4.23. The connector used is a bayonet connector (BNC), which attaches and locks by twisting into place. NICs attach to the network by means of T connectors, which attach directly to the NIC. Although it is possible to use MAUs and AUI cables with thinnet, this seldom is done due to the high cost of components.

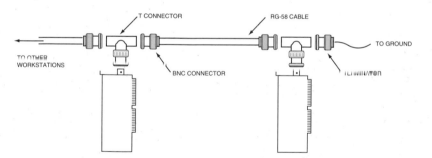

Figure 4.23

Components of a thin Ethernet.

As shown in figure 4.23, thinnet coaxial cable segments must have a terminator at each end. One of the terminators should be grounded (not both terminators).

A thin Ethernet segment should not exceed 185 meters or include more than 30 attached devices. For best performance, devices should be spaced along the cable at even multiples of one-half meter.

BNC connectors are easy to install with a few simple tools, or you can buy premade cables. Manufactured cables have two advantages: the connectors are securely installed, and cable lengths conform in length to the rule of one-half meter multiples. Thin Ethernet is easy to install in most situations.

Like thick Ethernet, thinnet networks can be extended using repeater links. A thin
Ethernet that includes two coax segments is shown in figure 4.24.

Figure 4.24

*A thin Ethernet
that includes a
repeater link
segment.*

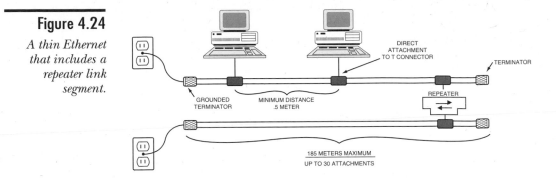

Each workstation connection involves three separate BNC connectors; these are the
cause of most problems with thin Ethernets. It is quite common for users to accidentally dislodge connectors or to pull the cable out of a connector—perhaps when
moving the PC. Any break in the coaxial segment can disrupt network communication for the entire segment.

Although thinnet gradually is being replaced by a preference for UTP networks, it
remains an excellent choice—especially for small networks. The cost of a connection
for thin Ethernet is the lowest of any network cabling system—easily less than $100
per device. No hubs are required, which can raise the cost of a network connection by
$20 to more than $100 per device. Thinnet cannot be surpassed as an inexpensive
medium for networking small organizations in a fairly restricted area.

One problem with thin Ethernet networks is that they can be difficult to reconfigure.
Adding a device requires you to add a T connector to the coax, which cannot be done
without cutting the cable. As a result, you can add users only when the network is shut
down.

For large networks or networks that must be reconfigured frequently, it's a good idea
to choose a star-wired network that includes intelligent hubs. These networks are easy
to reconfigure and manage. The next section describes the IEEE 10BASE-T standard,
which describes a hub-based version of Ethernet that uses UTP cable.

The features of 10BASE5 and 10BASE2 networks are summarized in table 4.2.

TABLE 4.2
Features of 10BASE5 and 10BASE2 Networks

Feature	10BASE5	10BASE2
Bandwidth	10 Mbps	10 Mbps
Maximum segment length	500 meters	185 meters
Maximum number of devices	100	30
Maximum link segments	2	2
Optimum device spacing	2.5 meters	.5 meter

Twisted-Pair Ethernet (10BASE-T)

The IEEE has developed an Ethernet standard called 10BASE-T, which describes 10-Mbps Ethernet that uses unshielded twisted-pair cable. Unlike coax Ethernet, 10BASE-T uses a star-wiring topology based on hubs. The length of the cable that connects a device to the hub is limited to 100 meters. A simple 10BASE-T network is shown in figure 4.25.

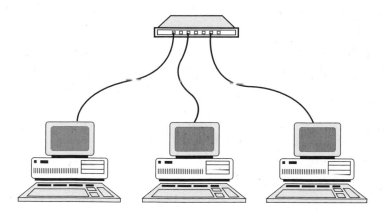

Figure 4.25

Connecting workstations to a 10BASE-T hub.

The cables used with 10BASE-T include two twisted pairs. These cables must be configured so that the transmitter of the device at one cable end connects to the receiver of the device at the other end. Figure 4.26 shows that this configuration can be accomplished in two ways:

◆ By crossing over the pairs of wires in the cable itself.

◆ By reversing the connections at one of the devices. The device in which connections are reversed is marked with an X by the manufacturer. This is a common approach with 10BASE-T hubs.

Figure 4.26

Methods of crossing pairs in 10BASE-T connections.

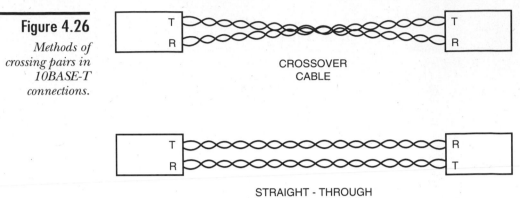

CROSSOVER CABLE

STRAIGHT - THROUGH CABLE

10BASE-T networks require at least Category 3 UTP cable connected with RJ-45 connectors. Never be tempted to use installed telephone wiring without determining whether it meets Category 3 specifications, and never use telephone-grade patch cables for connecting devices to hubs. Pairs of wires are not twisted in the flat satin cables that normally are used to attach telephones to the wall. Also, flat-satin cables are designed for voice-grade service, and they cannot support LAN data rates.

It is important for you to understand that the star physical topology of a 10BASE-T network does not alter the logical topology of Ethernet. A 10BASE-T network remains a logical bus. All devices on the network share the 10-Mbps bandwidth of the network, and only one device is permitted to access the network at a given time.

Your primary reason for choosing 10BASE-T should not be the goal of saving money with UTP cable. Instead, you should focus on the advantages a star network offers in terms of reconfiguration and management.

How 802.3 Ethernet Compares to Ethernet II

Although IEEE 802.3 Ethernet and Ethernet II networks can operate with the same cabling components, one significant difference exists between the two standards. This difference is illustrated by figure 4.27, which compares the frame formats defined for the two standards.

As shown in figure 4.27, data frames are organized into fields. In most cases, the fields used in 802.3 Ethernet and Ethernet II have the same formats, although the names often are different. Incidentally, the term for an 8-bit unit in an Ethernet frame is *octet*. This list summarizes the similarities and differences between the two frame formats:

◆ An Ethernet II frame starts with an 8-octet Preamble, which has the same format as the Preamble and the Start Frame Delimiter of the IEEE 802.3 frame.

◆ Ethernet II uses 6-octet source and destination address fields. 802.3 Ethernet can operate with 2- or 6-octet addresses, although 6 octets are used most commonly. Manufacturers are granted blocks of addresses by an Ethernet address registry, and a unique 6-octet address is burned into each Ethernet NIC during manufacture. This hardware address typically is used in the address fields.

◆ Ethernet II uses a Type field, using values that are defined by the IEEE. The 802.3 specification replaces the Type field with a Length field that describes the length in bytes of the LLC Data field. Because the LLC Data field has a maximum length of 1,500 octets, it is easy to distinguish an 802.3 frame from an Ethernet II frame by examining the value of the Type/Length field. If the value is 1501 or greater, the frame is an Ethernet II frame.

◆ The data fields have different names but otherwise are identical. The 802.3 standard calls the field the LLC Data field because it contains data that is passed down from the Logical Length Control sublayer. Data fields have a minimum length of 46 octets and are padded with extra data if they fall short of the minimum. The maximum length of an Ethernet data field is 1,500 octets.

◆ The Frame Check Sequence field contains a value that is used to detect transmission errors. Before it transmits a frame, a device calculates a mathematical value called a cyclic redundancy check (CRC) that summarizes all the data in the frame. The receiving device recalculates the CRC. If the calculated CRC matches the value in the Frame Check Sequence field, it can be assumed that the frame was transmitted without error.

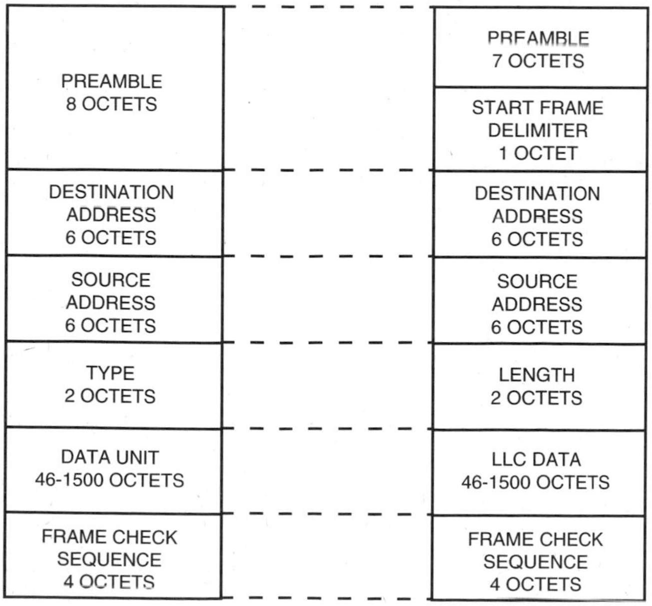

Figure 4.27

Frame formats for 802.3 Ethernet and Ethernet II.

Ethernet Frame Types

Several types of Ethernet frames are in common use. If you network only with Microsoft products, you are likely to encounter only two types of frames: IEEE 802.3 Ethernet and Ethernet II. When you configure Windows NT Server, the correct frame formats are selected for you. Windows NT Server is engineered to work smoothly with Novell networking products, however, and you frequently will see another frame type mentioned.

Novell began networking with Ethernet before the IEEE 802 standards were fully defined. The original Ethernet frame format used by NetWare did not include information associated with the IEEE 802.2 LLC standard. This frame format, which Novell now calls Ethernet_802.3, is incompatible with non-NetWare network implementations. It is supported by Windows NT Server when it is required for interfacing with a NetWare LAN, however.

Novell has begun to use the full IEEE 802.3 frame format. Because the format includes IEEE 802.2 data, Novell calls the frame format Ethernet_802.2. This is now the standard NetWare Ethernet frame format, and it also is supported by Windows NT Server.

In most cases, Windows NT Server can detect the frame format that is being used on a NetWare network, and no special configuration effort is required.

Ethernet Switches

The life of 10-Mbps Ethernet has been extended considerably by the use of switching hubs. These versatile devices enable you to configure an Ethernet in several interesting ways. Several options are shown in figure 4.28.

Each port on an Ethernet switch supports a full 10-Mbps bandwidth. Within the switch, frames are routed at high speeds, and the switch is capable of switching all the traffic that can be generated by the attached networks without causing performance bottlenecks.

Switching enables you to allocate bandwidth as required for various devices. The servers at the right end of figure 4.28 are each assigned an individual 10-Mbps segment. By eliminating the need to share a segment, each server experiences a significant increase in network performance.

Figure 4.28 also shows an interesting approach that can be taken with some switching hubs. In the middle, two hubs are connected using three ports each. This enables the switches to route traffic through any of the three network segments and results in an effective bandwidth between the switches of 30 Mbps.

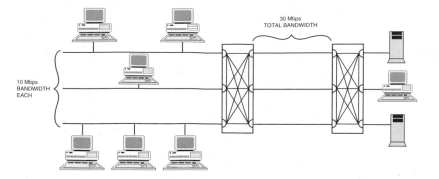

Figure 4.28

An Ethernet network using switching hubs.

10 Mbps is really quite a bit of bandwidth, capable of supporting many data-intensive applications. Switching is an expensive technology, but it does represent a practical way of extending the life of existing Ethernet networks.

Note | Switching hubs have become quite popular for Ethernet and now are being introduced for token ring as well.

Vendors have been introducing support for full-duplex communication along with switching hubs. Normally, when a device is connected to a switch, both the device and the switch send messages on the same cable. Full-duplex capability introduces two data paths between the device and the switch. The device has a dedicated Ethernet cable that it uses to send data to the switch, and the switch uses a separate cable to send data back to the device.

Full-duplex connections eliminate Ethernet collisions entirely and give each device a monopoly on the entire bandwidth available on the cable. Understandably, full-duplex communication is more expensive because additional cables are required, and hardware must be more elaborate. If you follow the advice in this chapter on installing new cable, however, you will be installing extra cables in your buildings anyway, so the extra cabling requirements might not be a problem. Full-duplex operation is yet another technology for extending the life of proven technologies, such as Ethernet and token ring.

High-Speed Ethernets

A significant marketplace change has taken place since the first edition of this book was published. Fast Ethernet has taken off like mad, driven by dozens of vendors and hundreds of products. Fast Ethernet offers 100-Mbps speeds, using technologies similar to 10BASE-T. A year ago, the technology was experimental and expensive, but now 100-Mbps Ethernet is available at attractive prices. Fast Ethernet hubs are available for less than $200 per port.

Often organizations will establish a mix of 10-Mbps and 100-Mbps Ethernet. Slower Ethernet is used for workstations with conventional needs. Fast Ethernet is used for workstations that need greater LAN bandwidth, and also for establishing high-speed backbones that interconnect servers. Two technologies are competing for your attention in the 100-Mbps Ethernet arena: 100BASE-T, the IEEE standard derived from 802.3 Ethernet; and 100VG-AnyLAN, which uses different technologies altogether.

Do you need a 100-Mbps LAN? First, you need large numbers of high-performance workstations equipped with PCI network cards. An ISA bus connection can't use the bandwidth available in 10-Mbps Ethernet, and a 100-Mbps connection would be a wasted expense. Second, you need applications that can't be resolved using a well-designed 10-Mbps network that uses switches strategically to manage traffic. Video conferencing is a good example of an application that needs lots of bandwidth.

100BASE-T

100BASE-T is standardized by the IEEE 802.3 committee and is part of the established IEEE Ethernet standards. Three variations of 100BASE-T are defined:

◆ 100BASE-TX uses two pairs of Category 5 UTP cable.

◆ 100BASE-T4 uses four pairs of Category 3, 4, or 5 UTP.

◆ 100BASE-FX uses multimode optical fiber.

The *collision domain*—the scope of a network that can be built without switches, bridges, or routers—of a 10BASE-T network can extend to 2,500 meters. 100BASE-T uses the same CSMA/CD media access method as 10-Mbps Ethernet, but operates at 10 times the speed. As the result, the collision domain of a 100BASE-T collision domain is limited to 250 meters. Switches, bridges, and routers can be used to extend the range of a 100BASE-T network.

10- and 100-Mbps Ethernet can coexist on the same network. Switches are available that support ports with both speeds. These 10/100- Mbps switches can be used to organize the network into different speed segments or as tools for migrating the network to 100-Mbps speeds.

100VG-AnyLAN

Although 100VG-AnyLAN is not an Ethernet technology, it is aimed squarely at 100BASE-T's market. The technology for 100VG-AnyLAN was developed and promoted by Hewlett-Packard and is standardized by IEEE 802.12. At this writing, Hewlett-Packard is the only major hub manufacturer supplying 100VG-AnyLAN products. The technology is supported by several smaller vendors.

The access method used is called *Demand Based Priority Access,* which eliminates collisions. This enables 100VG-AnyLAN networks to exceed the size limits imposed on 100BASE-T, and greatly reduces the need for repeaters.

Although 100VG-AnyLAN operates on completely different principles than Ethernet, it supports Ethernet frames and can be integrated with standard Ethernet networks. 100VG-AnyLAN also supports token-ring frames, and can be used as a high-speed LAN that integrates Ethernet and token-ring network segments. 100VG-AnyLAN may, therefore, be a better choice than 100BASE-T in environments that include both Ethernet and token-ring LANs.

Token Ring

Token-Ring is the major competitor to Ethernet in the LAN arena. Ethernet has been so successful that even IBM, the originator of Token-Ring technology, now markets Ethernet hardware. Although Ethernet has increasingly dominated the LAN market, Token-Ring has some unique advantages that make it preferable in many situations.

IBM originally developed the Token-Ring network technology, which was submitted to the IEEE to be considered as a standard. The IEEE 802.5 token ring is derived from IBM's Token-Ring network design.

Ethernet has been winning the LAN war for several reasons:

◆ The cost per device for Ethernet is considerably lower than the cost for token ring. Token-ring NICs cost from $300 to $600, compared to less than $100 for some Ethernet cards.

◆ Even though token ring is an IEEE standard, it is viewed by many as an IBM proprietary technology. Many customers and vendors have shied away from token ring for this reason.

◆ Token ring is more complex, and management of it requires more technical knowledge. Much of the added complexity, however, comes from the management tools that make it easier to diagnose and correct faults in a token-ring network than in an Ethernet.

You might want to choose token ring instead of Ethernet for the following reasons:

◆ Close integration with IBM technologies is required.

◆ The random nature of Ethernet medium access is unacceptable. In many applications, each device must be guaranteed an opportunity to transmit at regular intervals. Ethernet cannot guarantee this, but token ring can.

Token Access Control

All networks must provide a medium access control method that controls how devices can use the shared network medium. The method used by token ring is called *token access*. You can examine how token access control works in figure 4.29.

Figure 4.29

The token access control method.

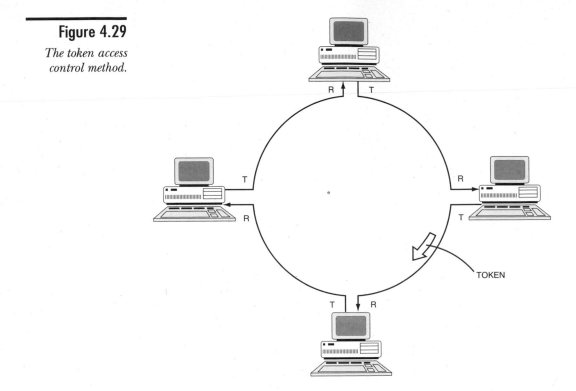

Token ring operates as a logical ring. The transmitter of each device is connected to the receiver of the next device in the ring. This enables the devices to pass messages around the ring.

A *token* is a special type of data frame that circulates around the ring. A device can transmit only when it is in possession of the token, and it must wait until the token arrives to transmit data. After a data frame is transmitted, the device releases the token to the network so that other devices can transmit.

The apparent simplicity of the token-passing method hides some complexities that had to be accounted for by the network designers, as these examples show:

◆ Like any network data, tokens can be lost. How is a lost token to be detected and how is a new token to be created?

◆ What steps should a station take if it stops receiving data?

◆ What if a station that was to receive a frame goes off the network? How is the network to identify frames that have circulated the network too many times?

To handle these and other potential problems, one device on a token ring is designated as a ring error monitor (REM). The REM can regenerate lost tokens and remove bad frames from the network. Additionally, each device is capable of signaling certain network problems by transmitting a beacon signal that notifies network management of the problem. The error-detection and diagnostic tools available on a token ring are quite extensive. By contrast, no such tools are built into Ethernet networks.

For these and other reasons, the development of token ring was a complex process. The mechanisms that control a token-ring network are much more involved than the mechanisms required for Ethernet. That is one reason that token-ring hardware costs more than Ethernet.

Token ring is preferred over Ethernet when a *deterministic* access method is required. Ethernet is probabilistic, and does not guarantee devices opportunities to transmit. On a token ring, however, every device is guaranteed a chance to transmit each time the token circulates the ring.

The IBM Cabling System

Unlike the IEEE 802.3 standard, the 802.5 token-ring standard does not specify a cabling technology. Therefore, it is common practice for vendors to base their equipment designs on the IBM cabling system.

IBM has specified a wide variety of cables for its Token-Ring network. The most common cable types follow:

◆ **Type 1.** Includes two data-grade, twisted pairs consisting of solid copper conductors. Both pairs are enclosed by a single shield.

◆ **Type 2.** Includes two solid-conductor, data-grade, twisted pairs enclosed by the same shield. In addition, the cable incorporates two voice-grade cables, enabling the same cable to be used for voice and data.

◆ **Type 3.** An unshielded twisted-pair cable similar to Category 3 UTP. IBM specifications originally limited use of Type 3 cable to 4-Mbps token ring.

◆ **Type 6.** Includes two data-grade twisted pairs constructed with stranded wires. The stranded wires make Type 6 cables more flexible and, therefore, better suited for cables that frequently are moved. Stranded cables, however, cannot carry signals as far as cables with solid conductors.

Cable Types 1, 2, and 6 are fairly thick and use a special IBM data connector (see fig. 4.30). The connector is fairly bulky but has several interesting features. When disconnected, it shorts pairs of conductors together, enabling you to disconnect devices from the network without introducing a break into the ring wiring.

Figure 4.30

An IBM data connector.

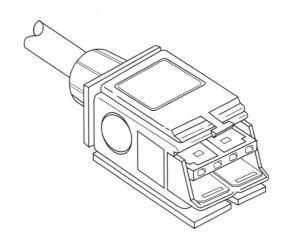

IBM's Token-Ring cabling uses a type of hub called a Multistation Access Unit (MSAU). The original IBM MSAU was called the 8228. It was a passive hub that used relays (electro-mechanical switches) to control network signal flow.

Although the 8228 still is available, more recent MSAU designs invariably use active designs with electronic switches replacing the relays. Active hubs are desirable because they enable hubs to correct signal distortion, to detect errors, and to be managed from a network-management console.

Figure 4.31 shows how MSAUs are used to build a network. The 8228 has eight ports, but modern MSAUs often have 16 or more ports to which devices can be connected. Each MSAU has two special ports called Ring In (RI) and Ring Out (RO). A ring network is created by connecting the Ring Out port of each MSAU to the Ring In port of the next MSAU in the ring.

Figure 4.31

How devices and MSAUs are connected to build a token-ring network.

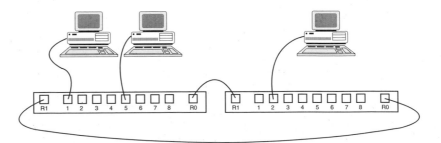

Token-ring networks have a ring logical topology, but they are wired as physical stars. For this reason, the token-ring topology frequently is described as a star-wired ring.

Each device on the network is connected to an MSAU by an individual cable. Figure 4.32 shows how the relays in an MSAU operate to configure the network as a logical ring. Relays in the MSAU normally are closed, permitting signals to flow around the ring. When a device connects to the network, the relay for that station opens, forcing signals to flow out to the device. The device returns the signal to the MSAU, and the signal continues around the logical ring.

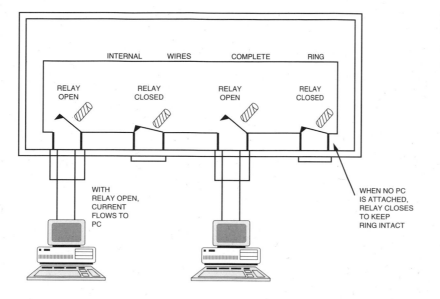

Figure 4.32

Operation of an 8228 MSAU.

STP Token Ring

Originally, IBM sanctioned two speeds for Token-Ring operation. IBM specified 4-Mbps data rates for use with STP and UTP cable. STP cable was required for 16-Mbps data rates. Type 1 and Type 2 cables commonly are used for running cables to workstations. These cables are called *lobe cables* in IBM token-speak. In general, lobe cables are limited to 100 meters.

Up to 260 devices and up to 33 8228 MSAUs can be attached to a ring. Repeaters can be used to extend the physical size of a ring, and they count as ring devices.

The actual number of devices a ring can accommodate depends on the ring size, the number of MSAUs, and the length of the longest lobe cable. Figuring out the capacities of a token ring is a fairly involved process. One IBM Token-Ring network planning guide devotes 22 pages to the subject of ring capacities and dimensions.

Most networks now are cabled with active MSAUs. IBM's active Token-Ring hubs are called controlled access units (CAUs). Active hubs and heavy use of UTP cable have rendered many of the old guidelines obsolete. The manufacturer's specifications of your network's token-ring components will be a better guide to the capacities you can expect on your network.

Originally, IBM blessed UTP cable only for 4-Mbps data rates. In the 1980s, numerous IBM engineers expressed the opinion that 16-Mbps data rates over UTP cable would never be practical.

UTP Token Ring

Other vendors, however, did not listen to that theory and did not wait for IBM to develop a 16-Mbps UTP specification. Vendors such as Proteon delivered MSAUs that could support 16-Mbps token-ring networks with UTP a couple of years before IBM announced comparable products. In fact, IBM, the inventor of Token-Ring, was among the last manufacturers to develop a 16-Mbps Token-Ring network that satisfied customer demands for UTP. UTP now has wide support for use at both 4-Mbps and 16-Mbps data rates. RJ-45 connectors are used with UTP cable.

In order to control noise on the network, token-ring devices must be connected to the UTP cable by a media filter. On older token-ring NICs, the media filter was often an extra item. Most currently manufactured NICs include the media filter on the network board and provide an RJ-45 connector for a network connection.

Because most token-ring NICs and MSAUs now support both 4-Mbps and 16-Mbps data rates, there is no cost advantage to opting for 4-Mbps operation. 16-Mbps token ring has been widely available for about five years and now can be regarded as a mature technology.

FDDI

Drivers for FDDI, the Fiber Distributed Data Interface, are included with Windows NT Server, and a brief discussion of the capabilities of FDDI are in order.

FDDI is a 100-Mbps network that functions much like token ring. FDDI networks are based on a ring topology and use token access control. Figure 4.33 illustrates several features of an FDDI network.

One feature to note is the manner in which FDDI networks can incorporate two rings that are configured to route signals in opposite directions. Devices that attach to both rings are called *dual-attached stations*. Devices that attach to only one ring are *single-attached stations*.

Because of the way in which FDDI rings are configured, the network can recover from a cable break between any two dual-attached stations. The right side of figure 4.33 shows what happens when a link is broken. The two stations next to the break rework their connections so the two counter-rotating rings are reconfigured into a single ring.

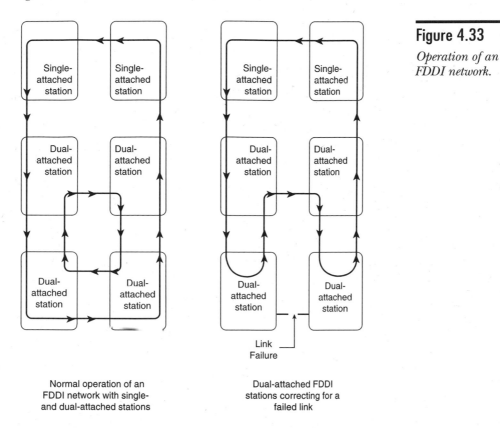

Figure 4.33

Operation of an FDDI network.

Normal operation of an
FDDI network with single-
and dual-attached stations

Dual-attached FDDI
stations correcting for a
failed link

FDDI is not well-suited to workstations because it does not expect devices to be turned on and off. Also, only the fastest PCs can keep pace with FDDI networks due to the limitations of most PC I/O bus designs.

FDDI does make an excellent high-speed backbone. Also, because dual-attached FDDI rings can extend to 100 kilometers in diameter, they can be adapted for use as a campus or metropolitan area network.

Acceptance of FDDI has been slow, however, due to the high cost of network hardware. Costs have been reduced somewhat by the introduction of standards for running FDDI protocols over copper cable, the so-called Copper Data Distributed Interface (CDDI).

High-speed Ethernet designs have more momentum than FDDI due to the lower cost of hardware based on Ethernet technologies. Nevertheless, FDDI is superior to Fast Ethernet in much the same way that token ring is superior to standard Ethernet. If your organization needs a deterministic, high-speed network that is fault-tolerant and highly manageable, FDDI is worth considering.

Network Components Hubs, Concentrators, and Structured Cabling Systems

Proper planning of your LAN's cabling system can pay big dividends. A well-designed LAN can be more reliable and easier to troubleshoot when problems occur. The LAN also can be easier and less costly to reconfigure. If you ever hear estimates indicating that it costs several hundred dollars to relocate a networked PC, you can bet that the cabling system is to blame. The key is to use a structured cabling system, along with a judicious selection of modern hubs and concentrators.

Structured Cabling Systems

If you are involved in planning a new LAN or upgrading an existing one, you should examine the merits of structured cabling systems. Although the equipment and installation of a structured cabling system represents a high up-front cost, network-maintenance costs are reduced considerably.

Structured cabling systems rely heavily on star wiring. Cabling from all devices converges in centralized wiring closets. Centralizing the distribution of all network cables is the key to making the system easy to configure.

Typically, network designers identify all the places where networked devices could be located and prewire those locations. Each location is equipped with a jack panel consisting of one or more RJ-45 jacks. A typical four-jack panel is shown in figure 4.34. These four jacks can be used for telephone or data purposes.

Each of the connectors in the jack panel corresponds to a matching connector in a patch panel in the wiring closet. Figure 4.35 shows a greatly simplified example of an equipment rack that includes a network concentrator and a patch panel. The patch panel enables network managers to connect any jack at the desktop to any resource on the patch panel quickly and inexpensively. Most network hubs already are equipped with RJ-45 connectors and are designed for convenient use with a patch panel.

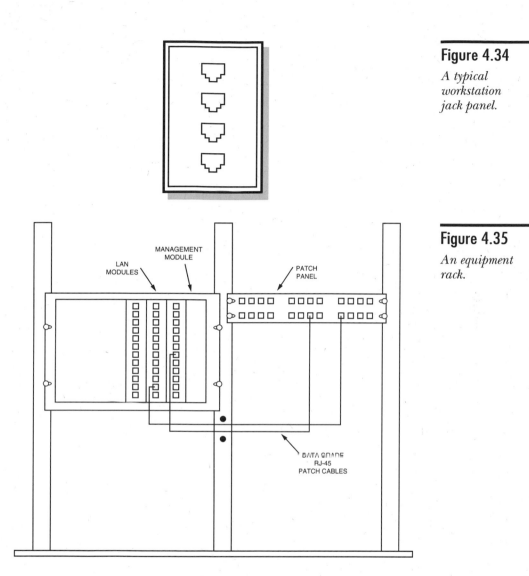

Figure 4.34

A typical workstation jack panel.

Figure 4.35

An equipment rack.

Most types of equipment are available in configurations that can be rack mounted. Although they represent an additional up-front cost, racks are a great way to exercise control over the cabling room, which quickly becomes an incredible mess unless the system is designed carefully.

In summary, the characteristics of a structured cabling system are as follows:

◆ A design based on star wiring that converges on centralized wiring closets

◆ Use of patch panels to make reconfiguration easier

◆ Prewiring anticipated locations with some extra cable thrown in for unanticipated needs

◆ Selection of hubs and concentrators that contribute to the goal of easy reconfiguration

A structured cabling system is a long-term investment in a network that is easy to manage and reconfigure. A properly installed cabling system, although costly, can be an ongoing asset. The workstations might change, your LAN servers might be upgraded, or you might completely change your network's physical layer (upgrading from standard to Fast Ethernet, for example); a structured cabling system can roll with the punches.

Hubs and Concentrators

This chapter has emphasized the tendency of the network industry to move toward network designs that are based on star wiring and centralized network hubs. These hubs can be basic, such as the IBM 8228, or they can be part of elaborate systems.

Basic passive and active hubs do not incorporate any management capabilities. If your LAN is of any size at all, you should pay serious attention to hubs that incorporate management features.

A few years ago, when manufacturers such as Synoptics and Cabletron were beginning to build components for structured networks, the cost of management capability was quite high, and designers attempted to spread that cost over as many devices as possible. This lead to the design of wiring concentrators, similar to the one shown in figure 4.36.

Figure 4.36

A typical wiring concentrator.

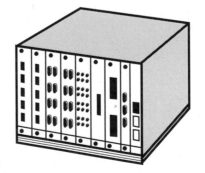

A *concentrator* is an enclosure with slots that accept slide-in modules. The concentrator supplies power to the modules and provides a means for the modules to communicate with one another. Network implementors can mix or match the modules to suit the requirements of their network. It is possible, for example, to install 10BASE2, 10BASE-T, and token-ring modules at the same time in some concentrator designs. Most concentrators can be equipped with a management module that adds management capabilities for all the options in the concentrator.

Wiring concentrators represent the high end of network cabling systems. These concentrators can include advanced features, such as redundant power supplies or other fault-tolerant options. Other concentrators enable you to configure several separate networks within the same concentrator, enabling you to move devices from one network to another, and so on, to balance network loading. Some concentrators even enable you to install server modules that can provide network services without the need for a separate PC.

Aside from high cost, the big disadvantage of concentrators is that they must be expanded in fairly large increments. If your concentrator accommodates 192 10BASE-T devices and you need to add device number 193, you will incur the cost of a new concentrator in addition to the 10BASE-T module that is required to support the new device.

For this reason, many LAN designers prefer the modularity of stand-alone hubs. Most hubs supports about 12 to 24 stations, and stack easily on shelves or in racks. If you need to add one more station, a single hub is less costly than a complete new concentrator.

New hub designs, known as *stackable hubs,* are designed for easy, incremental expansion. The hubs include connectors that enable you to easily add another hub to the stack. Some simply snap together.

The great thing about many modern hubs is that they include network-management capabilities. Now it is no longer necessary to invest in a concentrator-based system to have hubs that can be managed. With some stackable hub systems, the cost for managed Ethernet has dipped to less than $100 per port. If you don't need the more advanced features available in concentrators, stackable hubs can be an effective approach for your LAN.

Installing Network Cabling Systems

Installation of a structured cabling system is a job for experts. They will be adept at planning the network and installing the network components. They also will be able to muster the technicians required to install the network. Make no mistake about it: Installing a structured cabling system is a great deal of work.

The best time to install a new cabling system is when a building is under construction. Cables can be run in finished buildings, and most modern buildings are designed with the installation of cables in mind, but the process is more difficult.

You need to check building codes before you begin to install cable. If you will be pulling cables in the crawl spaces above suspended ceilings (the *plenum*), you need to select fire-resistant cables. Plenum-rated cables are coated with Teflon instead of plastic so that they will have a reduced tendency to burn and produce toxic gases.

Getting the right installer is especially important because many LAN problems can be traced to failures in the cable system. This is true particularly if your network will be based on Category 5 UTP. Many installers are not trained to respect the more stringent requirements of Cat 5.

Small networks, however, easily can be installed by do-it-yourselfers. You can simplify things by using premade cables that even eliminate the need for special tools. The easiest networks to install yourself use thin coax or Category 3 or 4 UTP.

If your network uses coaxial cable, the best connectors after factory installed are crimp-on connectors. Screw-on connectors are available but were not designed for LAN data rates. Be sure to obtain the right connectors and tools for the cable you will be using. A poorly installed crimped connector will pull right out of the cable. Expect to spend about $200 for the right tools, which include a cable stripper and a good crimper.

Don't look for bargains on coax connectors. The key to a reliable Ethernet is quality connectors that are installed properly. A good crimp-on BNC connector costs about $3.

If you are using UTP, don't buy your RJ-45 connectors from a telephone supply counter. Be sure that you are obtaining data-grade connectors that match or exceed the specifications of the cable you are installing. Expect to pay about $1 per connector. A good crimping tool costs from $40 to $150.

Ideally, you should invest in a cable tester for your type of cable. Unfortunately, prices for data cable test devices start at $2,000.

Small organizations always should hire an installer for fiber-optic cable. The tools are too expensive to be cost-effective unless they will be used extensively. In fact, few organizations will find do-it-yourself fiber installation cost-effective. After your long cable runs are in place, your primary need will be for patch cords, which can be purchased preassembled. Organizations determined to bring fiber-optic cabling capability in-house will not find the cost prohibitive, however. The primary difficulty of fiber-optic cable installation is the installation of connectors. Although termination of cables was once a complex task that required a variety of specialized tools such as a curing oven, new approaches have simplified the procedure. A kit for field-terminating fiber-optic cable costs about $1,000. Unfortunately, equipment to test fiber-optic cable is extremely expensive and seldom can be justified unless it will be used frequently.

Installing cable in existing construction often calls for ingenuity and patience. You might need to obtain specialized items to "fish" cables through walls. Fish tapes and long drill bits are available from electrical supply outlets.

If you cannot run cables through walls, you might want to install cable raceways. These consist of snap-together components that are attached to walls. After cables are installed, they can be covered, protecting the cables and making the installation more attractive.

You might have difficulty finding quality cable, tools, and connectors where you live, so here are a few sources:

The Black Box catalog is an excellent source of nearly any LAN components, and a copy should be on your bookshelf. In addition, Black Box offers excellent telephone technical support. For a catalog, contact Black Box at the following address:

> Attention: Vice President of Direct Marketing
> Black Box Corporation
> P.O. Box 12800
> Pittsburgh, PA 15241
> 800-552-6816

Another source of LAN components is South Hills Datacomm:

> South Hills Datacomm
> 760 Beechnut Drive
> Pittsburgh, PA 15205
> 800-245-6215

Finally, if you need tools, there is no better source than Specialized Products Company. Its catalog includes more than 300 pages of every imaginable tool, all of the highest quality. The address is as follows:

> Specialized Products Company
> 3131 Premier Drive
> Irving, TX 75063
> 800-866-5353

Testing Your Knowledge

1. The noise produced in cables by magnetic fields is called _____.

2. The measurement of data rates supported within a medium is called _____.

3. What are the four broad categories of cable?

    A. Coaxial, Jacketed, Non-jacketed, Fiber-optic

    B. Dielectric, Braided, Conductive, Insulated

    C. Coaxial, STP, UTP, Dielectric

    D. Coaxial, STP, UTP, Fiber-optic

4. What makes up the components of a coaxial cable?

    A. Center conductor, Jacketed layer, Shield, Sheath, Cladding

    B. Core, Dielectric, Sheath, Shield, Jacket

    C. Core, Insulation layer, Shield, Jacket

    D. Center conductor, Insulation layer, Shield Jacket

5. Which category of UTP can support 100 Mbps?

    A. Category 1

    B. Category 2

    C. Category 3

    D. Category 4

    E. Category 5

6. What makes up the components of a fiber-optic cable?

    A. Core, Cladding, Sheath

    B. Center conductor, Insulation layer, Shield, Jacket

    C. Center conductor, Cladding, Sheath, Shield

    D. Core, Insulation layer, Shield, Jacket

7. What are the two technology types of wireless media?

    A. Optical and Spread spectrum

    B. Optical and Radio frequency

    C. Radio frequency and Spread spectrum

    D. Spread spectrum and Point-to-point

8. Which IEEE standard defines the IEEE version of Ethernet?

   A. Logical link control

   B. 802.2

   C. 802.3

   D. 802.5

9. What does the abbreviation CSMA/CD stand for?

10. What is the maximum segment length in a 10BASE2 network?

    A. 185 meters

    B. 2.5 meters

    C. 500 meters

    D. 100 meters

11. What does the abbreviation FDDI stand for?

Review Answers

1. electro-magnetic interference

2. bandwidth

3. D

4. D

5. E

6. A

7. B

8. C

9. Carrier Sense Multiple Access with Collision Detection

10. A

11. Fiber Distributed Data Interface

CHAPTER 5

Selecting Hardware for Windows NT

From the beginning, one of the design goals for Windows NT was to make it easily portable to different hardware platforms. Windows NT version 4 supports systems based on four distinct hardware architectures:

- ◆ Intel x86
- ◆ MIPS RISC
- ◆ Digital Alpha AXP RISC
- ◆ PowerPC RISC

Because Windows NT is easily portable, you can expect it to show up on other hardware platforms as well.

Of course, Windows NT Server supports client workstation OSes that are based on other processors. Macintoshes traditionally have used microprocessors from the Motorola 68000 series, but a new line of Power Macintoshes is using the Power PC processor jointly developed by IBM, Apple, and Motorola. Additionally, a wide variety of system architectures is available on Unix workstations.

There are too many system types to discuss in one chapter or even in a book, so this chapter focuses on one narrow area of the workstation/server hardware market.

Given the popularity of Intel-based PCs, it seems likely that the majority of servers and workstations on your network will be based on Intel processors. Current systems trace their basic architecture back to the IBM Advanced Technology (AT) computer introduced in 1985. Although new features abound, the basic design of Intel-based PCs continues to reflect design decisions made 10 years ago.

You will not learn everything there is to know about Intel-based PCs in this chapter. Several more extensive PC hardware books are available if you would like additional information. These books often do not address the issues related to server performance. This chapter focuses on hardware and performance issues in the NT environment.

Note Some of the information in this chapter is based on data published in a white paper by IBM. It makes interesting reading. You should be able to get a copy by requesting the IBM Server Systems Performance white paper at the following address:

IBM LAN Systems Performance
IBM Boca Raton Laboratory
1000 N.W. 51st Street
Internal Zip 1214
Boca Raton, FL 33467

Performance curves similar to the one shown in figure 5.1 make it easy to illustrate the impacts of certain system changes on the performance of a server. Be sure to note the following features in figure 5.1:

◆ Under light loads, throughput increases smoothly to accommodate demand.

◆ At some point, throughput peaks. This is the greatest throughput that the server hardware configuration can support.

◆ The peak reflects the server's capability to service requests from memory. At some point, demand outstrips available memory and throughput begins to diminish as increasing numbers of requests must be fulfilled from disk.

◆ Throughput levels off at a point that is determined by the performance of the hard disks. At this point, most data requests are being serviced from disk rather than from memory cache.

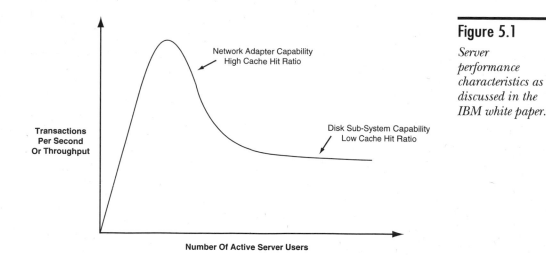

Figure 5.1

Server performance characteristics as discussed in the IBM white paper.

Features of Intel Microprocessors

The central component of a microcomputer is, of course, the microprocessor. This section takes an opinionated look at the Intel microprocessor family to point out the best choices for servers and workstations. Originally, Intel processors had names like 8086, 80286, and so on. Consequently, the family of compatible processors that has grown from that heritage is typically referred to as the x86 family. Beginning with the Pentium processor, Intel has abandoned the numeric processor designations, but the family resemblance remains. For current information about the Intel processor line, consult their web page at http://www.intel.com/.

The classes of Intel processors are summarized in table 5.1. Frankly, everything older than the 80486 is pretty much a dinosaur, and you would be hard-pressed to buy new hardware based on 80386 or earlier chips. As the first 32-bit x86 processor, the 80386 laid the groundwork for all Intel processors to follow, however, so this discussion begins with that model.

Here are brief definitions of the features discussed in table 5.1:

◆ **Register size.** The number of bits the microprocessor can process at one time.

◆ **Data bus size.** The number of bits the microprocessor can input and output in a single operation.

◆ **Address size.** The maximum number of bits in memory addresses determines how many bytes of memory the processor can manage.

◆ **Maximum memory.** Determined by the address size. The larger the memory address, the greater the amount of memory the processor can utilize.

◆ **Virtual memory.** Some models can use hard drives to simulate memory. Performance suffers, but the system does not run out of memory so readily. Intel processors starting with the 80286 have this feature.

◆ **Speed.** A clock determines how rapidly the processor performs operations. Until recently, microprocessors that operated faster than 33 MHz were forced to interface with outside components at 33-MHz speeds.

◆ **Math coprocessor.** Performs complex mathematical operations, such as floating-point arithmetic, more efficiently than a program running in a standard microprocessor. Originally purchased as an add-on item, coprocessors are included in newer Intel models. This feature is more important to workstations than to servers.

◆ **Real mode.** Enables the processor to simulate an original 8086 processor. Some programs, such as DOS, still require compatibility with the 8086. Real mode is limited to working with 1 MB of memory.

◆ **Protected mode.** Enables processors to directly utilize memory above 1 MB. Required for Windows NT and for all non-DOS operating systems.

◆ **Virtual real mode.** Enables processors to simulate multiple, real-mode processors. This feature was important to early versions of Microsoft Windows, but now seldom is used.

TABLE 5.1
Characteristics of Intel Microprocessors

	8086	80286	80386DX	80486DX	Pentium	Pentium Pro
Register size	16-bit	16-bit	32-bit	32-bit	32-bit	32-bit
Data bus size	16-bit	16-bit	32-bit	32-bit	64-bit	64-bit
Address size	20-bit	24-bit	32-bit	32-bit	32-bit	36-bit
Max. memory	1 MB	16 MB	4 GB	4 GB	4 GB	64 GB
Virtual memory	No	1 GB	32 TB	32 TB	32 TB	64 TB
Speed in MHz	4.77–10	6–20	16–33	25–33	60–166	150–200
On-chip L1 cache	No	No	No	8 KB or 16 KB unified	8 KB instruction 8 KB data	8 KB instruction 8 KB data
On-chip L2 cache	No	No	No	No	No	256 KB or 512 KB

	8086	80286	80386DX	80486DX	Pentium	Pentium Pro
Max. x86 instructions per clock cycle	1	1	1	1	2	3
Math coprocessor	Extra	Extra	Extra	Built-in	Built-in	Built-in
Real mode	Yes	Yes	Yes	Yes	Yes	Yes
Protected mode	No	Yes	Yes	Yes	Yes	Yes
Virtual real mode	No	No	Yes	Yes	Yes	Yes

Virtually all operating systems except DOS require at least an 80386 processor. The following discussion examines the 80386, 80486, and Pentium processors, including the most recent implementation, the Pentium Pro.

The 80386 Processor

The 80386 processor laid the groundwork for all later Intel processors. The 80386 introduced several features to the Intel line:

◆ 32-bit registers and data bus, making this the first Intel 32-bit processor.

◆ 32-bit address bus, enabling the 80386 to address 4 GB of memory.

◆ 32 TB (Terabyte=1,000 MB) of virtual memory. Virtual memory is an important performance enhancement because running out of RAM is a serious bottleneck to computer performance.

Earlier Intel processors were obsolete almost from the time they were introduced. Their limited capabilities were accepted due to the high cost of memory and 32-bit components. The 80386 architecture, however, left considerable room for growth.

No 32-bit bus architectures were available to match the 32-bit bus of the 80386 when it was introduced. The prevailing buses in the IBM PC world were the 8-bit and 16-bit versions of the ISA design (discussed later in this chapter). The first versions of the IBM Micro Channel Architecture (MCA) bus were limited to 16 bits.

Because the 32-bit capability of the 80386 often was not supported by external hardware, Intel introduced the 80386SX. Inside the 80386SX was a 32-bit 80386 processor. The standard version was redubbed the 80386DX. Outside, the 80386SX had a 16-bit bus, matching it to the most popular hardware of the period.

The 80386 processors could operate in *real* mode, enabling them to run software that expected to run on "real" 8086 or 8088 processors. Real mode is severely limited.

Most significantly, it is limited by its compatibility with the 20-bit addressing used by DOS, preventing real-mode programs from accessing memory above the 1-MB line.

Also available in the 80386 was *virtual real mode*, which enabled the processor to simulate multiple 8086 processors. Virtual real mode seldom was taken advantage of and was really only important for running DOS programs. Microsoft Windows 3.x was probably the most significant program to make use of virtual real mode.

Of greater significance was *protected mode*, which enabled the 80386 to work with memory above 1 MB as if it were a continuous memory range. Protected mode was introduced with the 80286, but seldom was exploited. The 80386 could work with 4 GB of protected mode memory—a capability that is taken advantage of by Windows NT and other 32-bit operating systems.

The 80486 Processor

The 80486 processor combines three sets of features:

◆ The architecture of the 80386

◆ A built-in math coprocessor

◆ A high-speed memory controller that significantly improves performance

The 80486 did not introduce any new external features and functions as a compatible upgrade of the 80386. Thanks to several internal improvements, performance was enhanced considerably, however.

The most important enhancement is a *cache controller*, which improves the speed with which the processor can access memory by building an 8-KB cache buffer into the microprocessor chip. Prior to the Pentium, x86 system designers were forced to implement caching with separate components. The cache controller stores recently read data and reads data in anticipation of future needs. Performance is improved because the processor can access memory in the cache controller more rapidly than memory on the motherboard. The 80486 has a single cache that is shared by code and data.

A math coprocessor can perform advanced mathematical operations by operating directly on decimal (*floating point*) numbers without the need to convert them into their decimal equivalents. Many applications take advantage of math coprocessors, which were extra-cost items prior to the 80486. Examples include CAD, graphics, spreadsheets, and financial and engineering software.

Many users do not run applications that require a coprocessor, however, so Intel introduced an 80486SX version that was identical to the 80486 except that the math coprocessor had been disabled. The version with a coprocessor now is called an

80486DX. You will notice that the SX and DX labels have different meanings for the 80386 and 80486 processor lines.

Intel persistently pushed up the clock speeds of the 80486 processors. First they introduced a clock-doubled series called the DX2 series that operated at 50 MHz and 66 MHz. Then they introduced the clock-tripled DX4 series, operating at 75 MHz and 100 MHz. In many cases, owners of 25-MHz and 33-MHz versions can purchase an Overdrive module that doubles the clock speed of the original processor.

Program data and code are stored in dynamic RAM (DRAM), which typically has an access time of 60–80 nanoseconds (ns). A 133-MHz processor, on the other hand, cycles at 7 ns. As a result, DRAM cannot be efficiently interfaced to the CPU. A high-speed cache provides a buffer between slow DRAM and the CPU, improving the speed with which the CPU can read and write data. Also, the cache can be used to retain recently or frequently used code or data in memory that can be rapidly accessed.

> **Note**   Although 80486 and Pentium processors have cache built-in, system performance can be improved by a well-designed secondary cache. You will encounter references to two types of CPU-related cache memory:
>
> ◆ Level 1 or L1 cache is cache built into the microprocessor.
>
> ◆ Level 2 or L2 cache is cache that is external to the microprocessor.
>
> L2 cache contains a subset of the contents of main memory, and L1 cache contains a subset of the contents of the L2 cache.
>
> The design of the memory and L2 cache is a significant way designers differentiate their systems. High-end Pentium systems may use 256–512 KB of pipelined, synchronous-burst L2 cache memory together with Extended Data Out Dynamic RAM (EDO DRAM). Mainstream systems may use less expensive memory alternatives, such as asynchronous static RAM (SRAM) with fast-page mode DRAM. Entry-level systems may dispense with L2 cache altogether.
>
> Because a 256-KB or 512-KB L2 cache is built into the Pentium Pro, L2 cache design will be a less significant differentiating factor in Pentium Pro systems.

The Pentium Processor

Intel found out that it could not copyright a numbered name for a processor, so it named the successor to the 80486 the Pentium.

The Pentium adheres to the 80386 external architecture with one exception: It incorporates a 64-bit data bus. The Pentium, therefore, can move data twice as rapidly as the 80486.

Pentiums also incorporate two 8-bit caches (the 80486 had one)—one for code and one for data—improving the processor's capability to move data to and from memory.

Pentium processors have been introduced with clock speeds up to 166 MHz. The earlier 60-MHz and 66-MHz versions were based on a 5-volt design. System designers had considerable trouble with the heat produced by the 5-volt Pentiums, so Intel changed to a 3.5-volt design for the 90-MHz and later versions. Both heat and power consumption are reduced greatly in the 3.5-volt chips.

Some of the features of the Pentium were new to the Intel processor line. One is *superscalar* technology that enables the processor to operate on two instructions during a single-clock cycle. The microprocessor is equipped with two *pipelines* in which instructions are executed. The Pentium uses a five-stage pipeline design: prefetch, decode 1, decode 2, execute, and writeback. This permits several instructions to be in different stages of execution, improving efficiency, and enables the CPU to execute many instructions in a single-clock cycle, whereas multiple-clock cycles might have been required in previous x86 processors.

Windows NT can utilize the Pentium superscalar capability, but many operating systems cannot. Programs and operating systems written for earlier x86 processors must be recompiled to take advantage of this superscalar capability.

> **Note** Two trends should be noted in Intel microprocessor design. One is the use of sub-micron technology. At microprocessor speeds, even the speed of electrical signals becomes a limiting factor. Reducing the size of the chip is a way to enable signals to arrive at their destinations more rapidly. Smaller fabrication methods also enable designers to pack more transistors on a chip. The size of a microprocessor component is measured in microns (μ).
>
> The other trend is to use lower voltages, significantly reducing the power consumption of the CPU and reducing the heat that is produced. The trend now is toward 2.9-volt designs that enable the chips to be used in desktop or laptop computers.
>
> Here is how these trends are manifested in various x86 microprocessors:
>
> ◆ 80486. 1.0μ technology operating at 5 volts.
>
> ◆ 60 and 66 MHz Pentiums. 0.8μ technology, operating at 5 volts.
>
> ◆ 120–166 MHz Pentiums. 0.35μ technology, operating at 3.3 volts.
>
> ◆ 150 MHz Pentium Pro. 0.6μ technology, operating at 3.1 volts.
>
> ◆ 166–200 MHz Pentium Pro. 0.35μ technology, operating at 3.3 volts.

As manufacturing processes improve, more and more transistors can be fitted on a chip. The 80486 includes a mere 1.6 million transistors, a number doubled by the Pentium processor, which incorporates 3.3 million transistors. The Pentium Pro has a staggering 5.5 million transistors.

Pentium Pro

The most recent member of the x86 processor family is the Pentium Pro. The design of the Pentium Pro was optimized for 32-bit operating systems, such as Windows NT and OS/2, and for 32-bit programs. The Pentium Pro uses a variety of tricks to enhance performance.

To begin with, the Pentium Pro superscalar design incorporates three pipelines and, in some circumstances, can execute three instructions in a clock cycle.

Another new feature is *superpipelining*. The Pentium Pro pipeline design has 14 stages, compared to 5 stages in the P5 pipelines. As a result, the Pentium Pro can operate at higher clock speeds. For a given fabrication process, the Pentium Pro can operate at a clock speed that is one third faster than the Pentium.

Dynamic execution enables the Pentium Pro to improve efficiency by manipulating data as processing takes place; it enables *out-of-order execution* whereby the Pentium Pro executes instructions in the most efficient possible order, rather than the order the instructions occupy in the program code. It has three components:

◆ **Multiple branch prediction.** The Pentium Pro can anticipate jumps in the instruction flow, enabling it to predict where instructions will be located in memory with great accuracy.

◆ **Data flow analysis.** The Pentium Pro can identify interdependencies among instructions in order to determine the best processing sequence.

◆ **Speculative execution.** Based on predicted branches, the Pentium Pro can look ahead for useful work to perform and store the results on a speculative basis.

Prior to the Pentium Pro, considerable engineering was required to construct a multiprocessor system. Up to four Pentium Pro processors, however, can be directly connected without additional logic. These processors share a transaction bus that enables overlapping access to I/O and main memory.

The Pentium Pro package incorporates either 256 KB or 512 KB of L2 cache. By tightly coupling the CPU with the L2 cache, cache performance is improved. The CPU can retrieve data from the built-in cache after a single wait state, whereas at least two wait states are required to retrieve data from the L2 cache of a Pentium system.

Superpipelining and out-of-order execution work together to improve processing of 32-bit code. Unfortunately, however, the Pentium Pro exacts a penalty for using 16-bit code because much 16-bit code cannot be executed out-of-order. 16-bit programs may actually execute more slowly on a Pentium Pro than on a similarly clocked Pentium. Therefore, the added cost of the Pentium Pro can be justified if you are using a 32-bit operating system, such as Windows NT, and the majority of programs to be used are available in 32-bit versions. The Pentium remains the better choice for Windows 95, which retains many 16-bit code components.

Selecting Intel Processors for Windows NT Servers

Windows NT loves powerful CPUs and will benefit from all the processing power you throw at it. If you are purchasing a new server, your choice almost certainly should be a Pentium or Pentium Pro system. Avoid systems based on 60-MHz and 66-MHz Pentium CPUs. These versions use more power and produce considerably more heat than the 90-MHz and faster versions.

You probably cannot buy an 80486 system, and you will give up a great deal of perform-ance if you make do with an older system. One thing you give up is multiple pipelines in the CPU, a feature supported by Windows NT. If you have a 66-MHz or better 80486 server, however, it could give you good service as a server on a small LAN.

Later in this chapter, you will read about buses and discover that the current favorite for server buses is the Intel PCI bus. PCI was designed for the Pentium and is available only on Pentium systems—another reason for choosing a Pentium server.

Windows NT has the capability to perform *asymmetrical multiprocessing*, meaning that it will take advantage of a second processor if one is available. This is an important capability that enables servers to be scaled up in processing power. If budget permits, you should consider a multiprocessor server for your LAN. The design of a multipro-cessor Pentium system is a tricky thing, however, and you should research your choices with caution.

The Pentium Pro is an excellent choice for a computer running Windows NT Server. All of the network utilities included with Windows NT Server are 32-bit programs. The superscalar design will improve the server's capability to satisfy service requests on a busy network. Because it adapts easily to multiprocessor configurations, the design of multi-CPU computers should be greatly simplified.

Otherwise, avoid frills on server computers. You shouldn't be running heavy-duty applications on a server, so you won't need a fancy video system. A simple 640×480 color VGA display will do just fine. Don't be tempted to use a fancy high-performance, high-resolution display adapter. These adapters achieve their high performance at the cost of performance in other areas. A high-performance video adapter can generate a lot of interrupts that distract the server from its primary duty of providing network services, for example.

Selecting Intel Processors for Workstations

About the only users who will be happy with an 80386 are those who still are using DOS. If you have moved to a graphics environment, working on an 80386 is sheer torture. For Windows, Windows NT, and other graphics 32-bit operating systems, a clock-doubled 80486 should be considered entry level.

When I first moved from a 50-MHz 80486 to a 90-MHz Pentium, I became convinced that even for mundane tasks such as word processing, it is difficult to have too much processing power. Tasks that used to inspire me to take coffee breaks now are performed almost instantaneously. Now, if I could just afford to upgrade to a dual 200-MHz Pentium Pro, or (sigh) a Digital AlphaStation.

Because time is money, processing power is a good investment. Has anyone ever estimated how many person-hours are wasted waiting for slow PCs to save files, print, perform spell checks, and so on? The estimate probably would surprise most managers who insist on economizing by buying the cheapest hardware available.

If you have an older PC, processor upgrades probably are not the way to go. The technologies built into 80386 PCs are hopelessly out of date. Most 80386s use older hard drive controller technologies, and all rely on video technologies that just cannot keep up with modern graphics-intensive environments. Upgrading your processor cannot improve the performance of your other systems.

For any modern operating system, such as Windows 3.1 or Windows NT, it's a good idea to have the following features:

- ◆ At least an 80486 66-MHz processor, preferably a Pentium
- ◆ A VESA local bus video for an 80486, or a PCI bus with a PCI video controller for a Pentium (buses are discussed in the next section)
- ◆ An IDE or SCSI hard drive controller with at least 1 GB capacity and 11 ms or better access time

If your system lacks the last two features, upgrading the processor will not buy you much.

When do you need a Pentium Pro workstation? The majority of your applications should be available in 32-bit versions, or you will suffer a performance penalty. You should need the added processing power, such as the improved floating point operation of the Pentium Pro's math coprocessor.

Features of RISC Processors

I've emphasized Intel processors in this chapter because the majority of Windows NT systems will likely be implemented on x86 computers. Please don't get the impression that Intel has a corner on running Windows NT, or even that Intel micro-processors are your best choice for a Windows NT computer. Many computers based on RISC processors are available, the best of which blow the doors off the fastest x86 systems. Depending on your requirements and budget, a RISC computer may better fit your needs.

RISC versus CISC

A major philosophical debate has pervaded the history of microprocessor design, with engineers arguing between two diametrically opposed viewpoints:

◆ Complex Instruction Set Computer (CISC) microprocessors incorporate a very large number of instructions. In some cases, a very complex task can be performed by a single instruction in the program code.

◆ Reduced Instruction Set Computer (RISC) microprocessors are based on a small set of instructions that perform discrete operations. The emphasis is on "lean and mean" efficiency.

Intel x86 processors started out with a CISC approach that Intel has been forced to maintain to ensure backward-compatibility with existing applications. Internally, however, the design of x86 processors has become increasingly RISC-like. The pipelines in a Pentium Pro are responsible for translating native x86 instructions into RISC-like *micro-ops,* which are the instructions actually executed by the CPU. As a result, many of the 5.5 million transistors in a Pentium Pro are devoted to interfacing the outside CISC environment to the RISC-like environment at the CPU.

The author is not qualified to argue the technical merits of the RISC versus CISC argument, but if you will examine some performance comparisons, you will always see that RISC systems have an edge over the best systems available using Intel x86 processors.

Part of this performance stems from higher cost. RISC system designs always emphasize performance and cost more—even considerably more—than the best x86 systems. This is particularly the case in I/O intensive applications, where RISC systems typically outshine x86 hardware. Entry-level RISC systems, however, are now available at costs that are comparable to better Pentium systems, and the RISC systems appear to have the edge on performance.

Other RISC Features

Many features that were added to the Intel Pentium processors are widely available on RISC processors, including on-CPU L1 cache, dynamic execution, and superscalar architectures.

Because it deals with a less complex instruction set, RISC processor architecture is often cleaner. The three processor pipelines on a Pentium Pro have different capabilities to match different levels of instruction complexity, resulting in an asymmetrical design. A RISC CPU, on the other hand, may have four pipelines that are fully symmetrical, enabling any instruction to execute in any pipeline.

For high-end users, RISC computers are the preferred platform for Windows NT. The best systems are, of course, quite costly, but entry-level RISC systems are approaching the costs of better Pentium systems. You have many choices of RISC computers that are configured for use with Windows NT Server and Windows NT Workstation. If you are focused on Windows NT and don't ever need to run MS-DOS, Windows 95, or OS/2, a RISC computer may be a good choice.

As it ships, Windows NT supports three RISC processor families: MIPS, Digital Alpha, and PowerPC. There are too many models of CPUs and systems, changing far too rapidly, to make a detailed discussion practical in this book. Here are the web pages where you can get more information about each processor:

- ◆ **MIPS.** http://www.mips.com/
- ◆ **Alpha.** http://www.alphastation.digital.com/
- ◆ **PowerPC.** http://www.motorola.com/SPS/PowerPC/

Note If you have made the transition to 32-bit applications, a RISC computer may be a good choice for you. Windows NT on a RISC computer can run 32-bit Windows applications. Sixteen-bit Windows and DOS applications, however, are not directly supported, but, rather, emulated.

Microcomputer Buses

The expansion bus is the primary means of adding hardware to a PC. It is made available in the form of expansion slots, which usually are mounted on the motherboard (systemboard) of the computer. In some cases, expansion slots are mounted on daughterboards that plug in to special slots on the motherboard.

Several bus designs have been used on Intel PCs. The connectors for these buses are shown in figure 5.2. Each connector is discussed in this section. The features of each bus are summarized in table 5.2.

Figure 5.2

Buses used in Intel-architecture PCs.

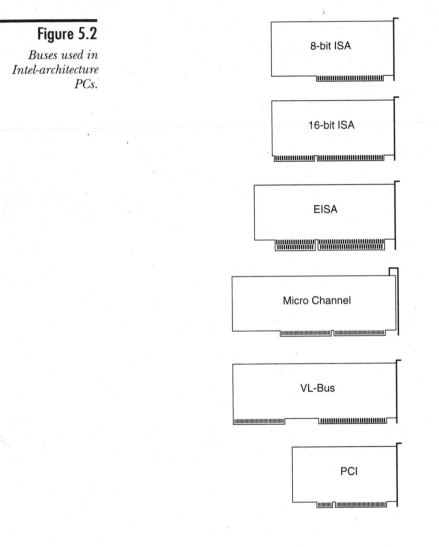

TABLE 5.2
Characteristics of Expansion Buses

	ISA	EISA	Micro Channel	VLB	PCI
Data bus (bits)	8/16	16/31	8/16/32	32	32/64
Data rates MB/Second	10	32	10–160	132	132–264
Available Connectors	8	12	8	2	3
DMA channels	7	7	15	N/A	System dependent
Data/Address Parity	No	No	Yes	No	Yes
Card ID	No	Yes	Yes	No	Yes
Auto Configuration	No	Yes	Yes	No	Yes

To take advantage of the many expansion options available for x86 PCs, vendors are incorporating ISA and PCI buses into increasing numbers of RISC computers.

Before examining the buses in detail, look at some of the characteristics that distinguish the bus designs:

◆ **Data bus.** The data bus of a bus serves the same function as the data bus of a microprocessor: moving data in and out of expansion devices. The wider the data bus, the more data can be moved in a given operation.

◆ **Data rate.** The amount of data a bus can move in a second is a function of both its data bus width and its clock rate measured in megahertz (MHz). A 16-bit bus can move 16 bits per operation and would move twice the data at the same clock rate as an 8-bit bus.

◆ **Maximum connectors.** Each bus design supports a maximum number of expansion slots.

◆ **DMA channels.** Direct memory access (DMA) enables expansion devices to directly manipulate memory without tying up the CPU. Some systems need additional DMA channels.

◆ **Data/address parity.** Parity is a basic means of checking for I/O errors.

◆ **Card ID.** If a bus supports a card ID, system-configuration software can determine the hardware that is in the bus, and it can configure the system accordingly.

◆ **Automatic configuration.** This option configures hardware options, such as interrupts and memory, by running a software-configuration program rather than setting jumpers. EISA and Micro Channel require you to run a special program to set up the system. PCI supports Plug and Play, which enables some operating systems to automatically identify and configure option cards.

The ISA Bus

The expansion bus IBM developed for the original PC was based on an 8-bit I/O bus that matched the capabilities of the 8088 microprocessor. When the Advanced Technology PC was introduced, a 16-bit version of the bus was introduced to support the 16-bit data bus of the 80286. This bus design has been adopted widely in almost all PCs based on the IBM/Intel architecture and has come to be called the Industry Standard Architecture (ISA) bus.

Performance of the ISA bus begins to run out of steam with VGA 640×480 video. The ISA bus is limited to a clock rate of 8 MHz, which is quite inadequate for 80386 and later microprocessors. ISA remains viable for options such as printer and com ports and mouse controllers, but is far too slow to support modern hard drives or video adapters.

Micro Channel Architecture

When IBM introduced the Micro Channel Architecture bus in 1987, it did so with the limitations of the ISA bus in mind. Micro Channel could be implemented with 16-bit and 32-bit data buses and, theoretically, could operate at clock rates of 100 MHz, although that speed has not been made available in an Intel-based IBM PC. Micro Channel supported a feature called *bus mastering*, which enabled controllers on expansion cards to take control of the bus. Bus mastering permitted bus operations to take place without requiring the CPU to control the process. Bus mastering is an important feature on a server that performs large amounts of I/O with the outside world.

IBM made several tactical errors with the Micro Channel Architecture. Most significantly, IBM treated it as a proprietary technology and expected vendors to license it. Because the ISA bus was free, almost no vendor chose to pay the license fees. Also, systems equipped with Micro Channel buses did not support older ISA cards, forcing customers to discard their investments in expansion cards. For some functions, ISA cards offered adequate performance, and many organizations were reluctant to make the hardware investment required to change over to Micro Channel Architecture.

Micro Channel Architecture now languishes in increasing obscurity. To my knowledge, only IBM continues to include Micro Channel in some of their systems.

The EISA Bus

Industry wanted the features of the Micro Channel; it just didn't want to pay for it. So a consortium of nine vendors developed the Extended Industry Standard Architecture (EISA) bus. EISA could do almost everything Micro Channel could do. It offered 32-bit I/O and bus mastering, for example. This was accomplished without sacrificing support for 8-bit and 16-bit ISA cards by designing a unique two-level connector. The top row of the connector was identical to the 16-bit ISA bus. The bottom row supported the new EISA features. ISA cards still could be used because they would contact only the top row of contacts. EISA cards would insert fully into the connector and use both rows.

The main problem EISA could not solve was the 8-MHz clock-rate limit, which is inherent in the design of the ISA connector. That was the main reason that IBM chose to abandon the ISA connector for the newer Micro Channel design. EISA has achieved some popularity in servers, but could not support the high speeds needed for advanced video. Like Micro Channel, EISA appears to have been eclipsed by PCI.

The VESA Local Bus

A superior video bus was required, and one was developed by the Video Electronics Standards Association (VESA). The VESA design uses a *local bus* technology that connects the expansion bus directly to the microprocessor. By eliminating intervening components and limiting the number of connectors the VESA bus would support, significant speed improvements became possible. The VESA Local Bus (VLB) can perform 32-bit data transfers at rates of 132 MB per second.

VLB connectors are installed in-line with ISA slots on the motherboard, as shown in figure 5.3. Only two VLB expansion slots are permitted.

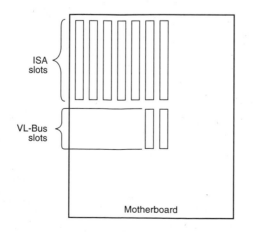

ISA slots

VL-Bus slots

Motherboard

Figure 5.3

Location of VESA Local Bus slots on the motherboard.

The VESA Local Bus was the first nonproprietary bus to significantly surpass the limits of the ISA design. Consequently, many vendors attempted to design nonvideo cards for the bus. Network interface cards and disk controllers have been introduced in VLB versions. VESA Local Bus, however, was designed for video; other technologies are a forced fit.

VLB has some significant constraints. First, it is limited to two expansion slots, making VLB less than ideal for servers that often must support more than two high-performance expansion options. The local bus approach is temperamental because the design must closely match a specific microprocessor. This drawback made it difficult to adapt VLB to the newer Pentium processor.

VESA began to run out of steam when the Pentium processor became popular. Pentiums require a 64-bit I/O bus. Although a 64-bit VESA II bus has been introduced, it arrived after PCI was well established and has received little support.

The PCI Bus

PCI is a high-performance bus that avoids many of the problems of a local bus by using a mezzanine approach, where an interface layer is sandwiched between the microprocessor and the bus, much like a mezzanine floor may be found between the first and second floors of a building. Special circuitry buffers the microprocessor from the PCI bus itself. Unlike previous nonlocal buses, the design used with PCI exacts a very small performance toll while greatly simplifying design.

Pentiums require a 64-bit bus, and PCI was the first design to deliver. PCI supports bus mastering and operates at clock rates of 33 MHz and 66 MHz, enabling it to support data-transfer rates of 132 MB to 264 MB per second.

PCI connectors generally replace ISA connectors on the motherboard, as shown in figure 5.4. A common implementation includes three PCI slots and five ISA slots. One PCI slot often is paired with an ISA slot; one slot can be used, but not both.

Early PCI designs were limited to three PCI slots. This might be acceptable for workstations, but servers generally need more high-speed slots. In the last year, Intel has introduced the *PCI-bridge* technology that enables it to support multiple three-slot PCI buses on a system. Expect to see more than three PCI slots on high-end systems.

Almost any type of expansion option now is available for PCI. Interestingly, the PCI design enables designers to work with reduced numbers of chips. Consequently, PCI expansion cards often have comparable costs to ISA cards.

One last feature of PCI is that it offers a new Plug and Play capability that is supported by operating systems such as Windows 95. Plug and Play enables operating systems to detect installed hardware and to set parameters such as interrupts, DMA channels, and address automatically, without the need for manual configuration.

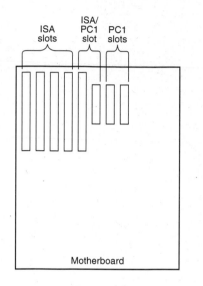

Figure 5.4

Location of PCI slots on the motherboard.

Selecting Buses for Servers

The Intel-designed Peripheral Component Interconnect (PCI) bus has become the dominant bus in high-performance Intel-architecture PCs and on many RISC computers as well. PCI has eclipsed EISA as the most common bus for network servers. Don't rush out to replace your old server for one with a PCI bus, however, unless you have some pretty demanding requirements.

Disk and network I/O are the most intensive tasks that a server bus must perform. Memory performance suffers too much when memory is installed on standard buses, although some manufacturers have designed proprietary buses to support memory expansion.

Unless you are supporting a 100-Mbps network, EISA or Micro Channel buses should be able to keep up with your network. An EISA bus can handle data rates as high as 33 Mbps, which should adequately handle three or four Ethernet segments.

Your hard drive subsystem might be another question, however. If you are using multiple, high-performance Redundant Arrays of Inexpensive Disks (RAID) hard drive systems, you might need to move to a faster bus.

One of the most significant improvements you can make in your hard drive subsystem is to use a 32-bit bus-mastering network interface card. A bus-mastering controller can improve server performance by raising the peak transactions-per-second level, as shown in figure 5.5.

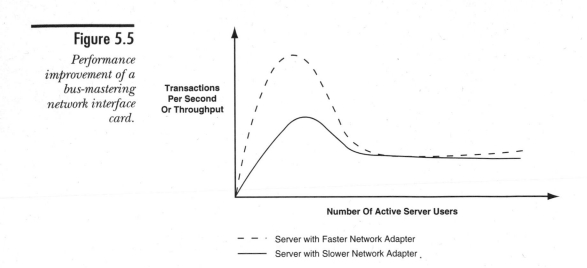

Figure 5.5

Performance improvement of a bus-mastering network interface card.

Selecting Buses for Workstations

Most I/O on workstations is related to video and hard drives, although that will change as LANs become vehicles for delivering graphics, video, and voice data to the desktop. In organizations that are examining these technologies, the days of the ISA bus are numbered. Don't even consider putting a PC on a 100-Mbps network if it has a 16-bit ISA bus.

In many cases, however, 16-bit buses provide adequate support for LAN I/O. Unless a PC is attached to a dedicated, full-duplex Ethernet channel, you are unlikely to exceed the performance of a 16-bit ISA. An 8-bit ISA is another story, however, and you should avoid using 8-bit ISA cards or PCs equipped with 8-bit buses. Your LAN is expensive. When a PC is transmitting, it is using all the LAN's capacity, and you don't want slow NICs tying up your network.

At present, the choice of bus is fairly simple. 80486 systems generally are equipped with a combination of VESA and ISA slots. Pentium systems nearly always include PCI and ISA slots, although a few include EISA slots instead of ISA.

Memory

PCs have become increasingly memory-hungry in recent years, and the minimum desirable memory seems to go up year by year. Now, 8 MB of memory is no longer a large amount; it is the minimum required in most situations. In this section, you examine the types of memory that are available.

Types of Memory

You probably know the types of memory well, but a review of them follows:

◆ **ROM (read-only memory).** Permanent memory that cannot be reprogrammed easily (or cannot be reprogrammed at all), and that retains its contents when the system is turned off. The basic input/output system software (BIOS) for a PC is installed in ROM.

◆ **DRAM (dynamic random-access memory).** Used for the main system memory in a PC. RAM is memory that can be modified easily by the computer. Each memory location in DRAM functions like a little battery that is charged and discharged to store data. The charges in DRAM fade with time, and a memory-refresh operation is required to maintain data in memory. DRAM is not as fast as SRAM, but it is considerably less expensive and generally is used for system memory for that reason.

◆ **SRAM (static random-access memory).** A type of RAM that does not require a refresh operation. Memory locations in SRAM work like switches that retain their settings as long as power is applied. SRAM is faster than DRAM but is used sparingly because SRAM costs considerably more. High-performance systems often use SRAM caches to buffer I/O to slower DRAM memory. Much of the performance of a high-speed system relates to the way in which the designers have used SRAM.

When you add memory, it is important to obtain memory that matches the speed requirements of your system. All memory types have a speed rating that is specified in nanoseconds (ns). Speeds range from 40 ns (fastest and most expensive) to about 100 ns (much too slow for most new PCs). Most memory you encounter will have a speed rating in the range of 70 ns. Your system will not run faster if you buy memory that is faster than it requires. You might want to purchase memory, however, that is slightly faster than the minimum. Memory performance varies, and some manufacturers hold tighter tolerances than others. Buying faster memory ensures that the memory you buy will meet or exceed your system's requirements.

Starting with the 80386, most CPUs have the capability of outrunning most DRAM, and system designers have used a number of techniques to slow down memory access. An early approach was to use *wait states*—"do-nothing" operations that slowed down processing to a speed that the memory could cope with. Wait states are a serious drag on system performance; you should avoid systems that require them. The need for wait states was eliminated largely by the incorporation of cache memory into the system design.

Memory Expansion

The discussion about buses makes the point that most expansion buses operate at much slower speeds than faster CPUs can support. A Pentium processor can perform burst-data transfers at rates as high as 528 Mbps and is capable of outrunning even a PCI bus, which is limited to 60–66 MHz operation. For that reason, it is not practical to install memory on expansion cards with most bus types.

With the exception of some proprietary memory-expansion designs, it has become common to install all memory directly on the motherboard, where it can be more directly serviced by the microprocessor. A special memory bus on the motherboard operates at CPU speeds.

Most memory sold today is packaged in single in-line memory modules (SIMMs), which consist of memory chips that are preinstalled on small circuit boards. When you obtain SIMMs, you need to be aware of several characteristics:

◆ SIMM modules have a width of either 1 or 4 bytes. One-byte wide SIMMs use a 30-pin package, and 4-byte wide SIMMs use a 72-pin package, as shown in figure 5.6.

◆ SIMM memory capacities typically range from 256 KB bits to 8 MB bits.

◆ SIMMs can be used individually. In many cases, however, SIMMs are used in banks of two or four SIMMs. You must review your system specifications to see what you need. On Pentium systems, SIMMs must be installed in matched pairs.

Figure 5.6

30-pin and 72-pin SIMM modules.

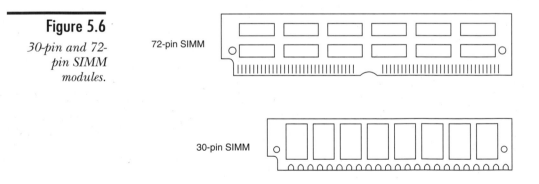

All SIMMs have a bit width. Traditionally, x86 PCs have used parity memory requiring nine bits of memory for each byte of storage. IBM designed PCs to use the ninth bit for parity checking of each byte of data. *Parity checking* is an elementary method for detecting memory errors. As a result, bit widths have typically been expressed in multiples of nine for Intel PCs.

Figure 5.7 shows how memory was arranged when individual chips were used. A byte of data is represented by one bit in each of eight chips. A ninth bit is used for parity.

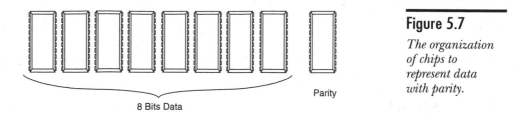

Figure 5.7

The organization of chips to represent data with parity.

8 Bits Data

Parity

Prior to the Pentium, many x86 systems used memory packaged on 9-bit SIMM modules. These modules incorporated memory that was one byte wide, usually with 9 bits per byte to implement memory parity. A SIMM with a 1-MB capacity would be configured as a 1×9 SIMM, meaning that its size is 1 MB bits by 9 bits.

Some 80486 and all Pentium systems use 32- or 36-bit SIMMs in a 72-pin package. A 1×36 SIMM contains 4 MB of memory because it has a width of 4 bytes.

Macintoshes have always used non-parity memory, a trick that has been recently adopted as a cost-saving measure by many manufacturers of x86 PCs. By discarding the parity chip, manufacturers can make use of less expensive 32-bit SIMMs. A 1×32 SIMM carries 4 MB of non-parity memory.

> **Note**
>
> Parity is a primitive error checking technique that can determine when most errors occur but cannot correct errors. With the philosophy that no data is better than bad data, IBM designed the original PC to lock up when a parity error was detected. Parity errors are now relatively rare, and nearly all vendors have abandoned use of parity memory.
>
> Better than parity is error correcting (ECC) memory. ECC is a technique that not only detects errors but can correct errors that affect a single bit. ECC is a feature of a few elite superservers. The Pentium Pro has features that enable it to support ECC memory.

Remember that it is very important to match SIMMs to your system's specifications. Also, if your system uses multiple SIMMs in banks, try not to mix brands or even different production runs in a bank. SIMMs can be arranged in banks so that a performance technique known as *paging* can be used. Paging distributes data for a byte across several chips, which might be in different SIMMs in the bank. Unless the SIMMs closely match each other's characteristics, bit-read errors or parity errors might occur.

Memory and Windows NT Server

Windows NT Server, like most servers, is designed to take full advantage of any memory that is available. So that it is not dependent on the performance limits of hard disks—often the slowest things on a server—a network operating system makes heavy use of memory in order to cache data. This is one of the most important techniques for improving server OS performance.

Although Windows NT Server will run with 16 Mbps of RAM, you almost certainly want to add more. Windows NT attempts to keep the programs and data it is using in memory. When memory is exhausted, Windows NT uses disk-based *virtual memory* as adjunct storage. Although virtual memory enables Windows NT to keep more tasks in operation, the necessity of swapping code and data between memory and disk slows down processing considerably. Windows NT will perform much better if the programs and data it needs fit entirely into RAM. Figure 5.8 shows how adding memory can extend the peak of the performance curve, extending the time data can be serviced out of cache rather than disk.

Figure 5.8

The effect of increasing memory in a server.

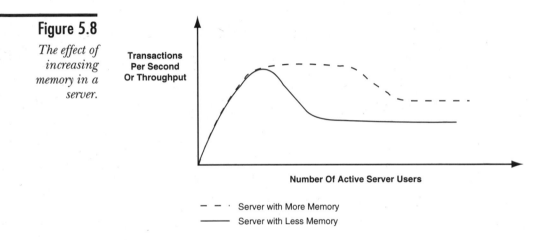

Workstation Memory Requirements

The memory required for a workstation depends on the operating system. Software vendors will state minimum requirements for marketing purposes, but you usually will be rewarded by adding memory. As with servers, extra RAM enables workstations to reduce reliance on hard drives to store data during processing.

Here are some suggestions for memory with various operating systems:

◆ **Microsoft Windows 3.1.** Although it will run with 4 MB of RAM, Windows will spend an exorbitant amount of time swapping data to disk unless you have a minimum of 8 MB.

◆ **Windows NT Workstation.** The specifications say 12 MB, but more will improve performance. Besides, it's easier to configure most systems with 16 MB of memory, so go for the extra 4 MB. Power users should have 24 MB or more for best performance.

◆ **IBM OS/2.** Again, ignore the stated minimum of 4 MB and install at least 8 MB.

◆ **Unix.** Install 16 MB or more.

DOS cannot directly access more than 1 MB of memory, but it can use expanded memory to increase the memory available to applications. *Expanded memory* consists of extra memory, installed outside the DOS range, that is swapped into DOS memory in 4-KB to 16-KB chunks by a memory manager. An application can access one memory chunk and then request another. That method is not as good as directly accessing several megabytes of memory, but it's better than being stuck with a 1-MB limit.

PCs equipped with 80386 and later processors can simulate expanded memory without the need for special expanded memory hardware. This is accomplished by using an extended memory manager to make memory above 1 MB available to an expanded memory manager, which then performs the memory swaps.

Hard Drives

Two major classes of hard drives are used on IBM-compatible PCs:

◆ Drives that owe their heritage to the original ISA-based drives used by IBM in the IBM XT. This family includes the currently popular IDE drives.

◆ Drives based on the Small Computer Systems Interface (SCSI).

Each of these classes meets a specific set of hard drive performance and cost needs. One class is ideal for workstations, and the other serves the more demanding needs of network servers admirably.

ISA, ESDI, and IDE Hard Drives

IBM designed the disk systems for the IBM XT computer around the ST506/412 interface developed by Shugart. This interface requires two cables to support a hard drive:

◆ **A control cable.** This cable supports two drives. The cable is daisy chained from one drive to the next and easily is distinguished by a twist in some of the wires in the otherwise flat cable.

◆ **A data cable.** Each drive was serviced by an individual data cable.

The IBM XT design could support two controller cards, each of which could support two hard drives for a total of four drives in a system. By today's standards, the

ST506/412 interface was outrageously slow, but with average seek times of 80 milliseconds, hard drives weren't very fast themselves. Data was transferred serially at a 5-MHz rate.

Data first were encoded on these drives using a method called modified frequency modulation (MFM), but MFM gradually was replaced by run length limited (RLL) encoding, which increased drive capacity by 50 percent. RLL required better performing controllers and more precisely manufactured drives, but it was an inexpensive way to increase hard drive capacity.

IBM introduced the Enhanced Small Device Interface (ESDI) with the PC AT. ESDI was essentially a better performing version of ST506/412. ESDI used the same cables as the older system, but it was not interchangeable with older devices. ESDI was too little, too late and quickly fell behind the performance needs of PCs. Both ST506/412 and ESDI hardware are difficult to locate these days.

In 1986, Compaq started work to integrate Western Digital controller technology with Control Data Corporation hard drives. The eventual result was the Integrated Drive Electronics (IDE) design, which had several advantages. Besides a power cable, only a single cable was required. More important, however, close integration of controller and hard drive has resulted in dramatic performance improvements, even while drive costs have been plummeting. IDE drives now offer outstanding performance at costs of less than 40 cents per megabyte.

IDE drives do not require an elaborate controller on the motherboard. A simple, inexpensive interface is all that is required. Virtually all motherboards now have built-in IDE controllers, but inexpensive IDE expansion boards also are available.

As with the older ISA technologies, a PC can support two IDE controllers, each of which can support two drives. A PC, therefore, can support four IDE drives.

When operating in pairs, one IDE drive is configured as master and the other as slave. The master drive controller manages all operations on both drives. One problem with this approach is that a failure of the master drive deactivates both drives.

IDE drives are excellent for workstations, but are poor choices for servers. The four-drive limit is an important disadvantage where servers are concerned. More important is the fact that only one drive in a master/slave set can be active at one time. This behavior is not well-suited to servers that must freely access all drives in the system. This characteristic also makes IDE drives poor candidates for *disk mirroring*—an important fault-tolerance capability that is built into Windows NT Server.

Today, hard disks are an unbelievable bargain, so don't skimp. Windows NT Workstation should be equipped with at least 1 GB of hard disk.

Note | Standard IDE drives allow for only 512 MB of disk space to be accessed without special drivers. This is due to a 1,024 cylinder limit in the original IDE specification. EIDE allows newer systems to access sizes above 512 MB on one drive, up to 2 GB.

Many new drives advertised as being greater than 512 MB are of the EIDE type. Make sure your system board and controller can support these types of drives and their entire capacity.

SCSI Subsystems

Objective B.7

Most high-performance disk subsystems are based on the Small Computer Systems Interface (SCSI). A SCSI host bus adapter (HBA) can support up to seven peripherals—including hard drives, CD-ROMs, tape drives, scanners, and other types of devices. (Newer *wide SCSI* controllers can accommodate 15 devices.)

Hard drive access on IBM PCs always has been managed by the BIOS, which directly controls hard drives in terms of tracks, sectors, and heads. SCSI, however, is a block-level interface. The application simply requests a block of data, and it is up to the SCSI subsystem to perform the disk-hardware operations that will retrieve the data. The physical structure of a SCSI hard drive is invisible to applications running on the computer. In order to adapt SCSI to PCs, hardware designers had to develop procedures that translated BIOS operations into SCSI terms so that the PC would view the SCSI subsystem as a conventional hard drive organized in tracks and sectors. Surprisingly, this approach works quite well, and SCSI has become a viable option on IBM-compatible PCs.

SCSI-1

SCSI, standardized by ANSI, has been enhanced several times. The original SCSI-1 standard had the following features:

- ◆ An 8-bit data bus
- ◆ Data transfers at 5 MB per second
- ◆ Seven devices per host bus adapter
- ◆ One command at a time per device

SCSI-2

The newer SCSI-2 standard is backward-compatible with the SCSI-1 command set, but adds several features:

- ◆ A *common command set* (CCS) that is supported by all SCSI-2 devices, enhancing compatibility among SCSI-2 hardware.

◆ Parity checking identifies errors and requests retransmission.

◆ A bus disconnect feature enables a disk to service a request while it is disconnected from the host bus adapter. This frees the HBA to service another device.
Bus disconnect makes SCSI-2 a multitasking interface that is ideally suited to the
needs of a server. Not all SCSI-2 adapters implement SCSI bus disconnect.

For servers, you should look for SCSI adapters that include the following extensions
to SCSI-2:

◆ Fast SCSI, which doubles the bus clock speed to 10 MB per second.

◆ Wide SCSI, which doubles the bus width from 8 bits to 16 bits. (A 32-bit wide
version is also defined, but is never encountered on PC equipment because two
68-conductor cables are required.)

A combination of Fast/Wide SCSI-2 can accomplish data transfers at rates up to 20
MB per second.

Another feature to look for on better SCSI-2 adapters is *Tag Command Queueing*
(TCQ). This feature enables the bus to queue up several commands for a given
device.

SCSI-1 and SCSI-2 use the same cables, which come in two variations. Standard 8-bit
SCSI devices require a 50-pin cable. Wide 16-bit devices require a 68-pin cable. It is
important to shop for the correct connectors when acquiring SCSI devices. External
cables make use of two connectors. Older devices used a 50-pin connector that
resembles a Centronics printer connector. Newer devices use a 50-pin, high-density,
miniature connector that uses a squeeze-to-release latch. You can mix connector types
in a SCSI daisy-chain, and adapter cables can be purchased to mate devices with
different connectors.

Internally, 8-bit devices use a 50-wire ribbon cable with a 50-pin unshielded pin
header. Wide SCSI devices use a high-density 68-pin ribbon cable with a hooded high-
density connector.

Because the Wide SCSI data bus doubles in width, you must purchase wide SCSI
components—principally hard drives—to mate with a Wide SCSI adapter. Many Wide
SCSI controllers include a standard SCSI-2 connector to support non-wide devices.
This enables the same controller to support Fast/Wide hard drives and standard
devices such as CD-ROMs.

SCSI-3

A new SCSI generation, SCSI-3, is navigating the standards process. Although the
standard is not complete, a number of products are being sold based on the draft
standard. Don't be too disturbed. Large numbers of SCSI-2 products hit the market
while SCSI-2 was but a draft standard.

One SCSI-3 development that is available is Fast-20 mode, also called Ultra SCSI, which quadruples the original 5 Mbps SCSI transfer rate. On a standard 8-bit bus, Fast-20 mode enables data transfers at 20 MB per second. On a Wide 16-bit bus, data transfers of 40 MB per second are possible. SCSI-3 also offers support for up to 32 devices.

A clear trend in SCSI evolution is that every advance has been accompanied by the need for additional wires in the cables. 32-bit Wide SCSI, for example, requires two 68-wire cables, probably the reason you are unlikely to encounter 32-bit Wide SCSI. To alleviate cable bloat, developers of SCSI-3 are working on a *serial SCSI* approach that offers high performance with only six wires. Even with the reduced wire count, serial SCSI will be capable of faster data transfers than 32-bit Fast/Wide SCSI. You won't see serial SCSI products on the market in the immediate future, but it is a technology to keep your eyes on.

Summary of SCSI Features

SCSI is practically required to implement RAID technologies, which are designed to improve the performance and fault-tolerance of hard drive subsystems. Windows NT Server provides excellent support for RAID, as you learned about in Chapter 17, "Managing Disk Storage."

Table 5.3 summarizes the features of various SCSI standards.

TABLE 5.3
Features of SCSI Standards

	SCSI-1 & SCSI-2	Fast SCSI-2	Wide SCSI-2	Fast/Wide SCSI-2	Fast 20 SCSI-3
Bandwidth	8 bits	8 bits	16 bits	16 bits	16 bits
Data transfer rate (MB/sec)	5	10	10	20	40
Cable type	50-pin	50-pin	68-pin	68-pin	68-pin

Here are some web pages where you can obtain information about SCSI adapters that are tested for Windows NT:

◆ **Adaptec and Future Domain:** http://www.adaptec.com

◆ **BusLogic:** http://www.buslogic.com

◆ **DPT:** http://www.dpt.com

Selecting Disk Subsystems for Servers

Figure 5.9 shows how server performance is improved by enhancements in the hard drive subsystem. A faster disk system raises and extends the peak of the maximum transactions curve and improves the cache hit rate because data can be written from cache to the hard drives more expediently. Finally, faster hard drives raise the plateau at the high-demand end of the curve.

Figure 5.9

Effects on server performance of an improved hard drive subsystem.

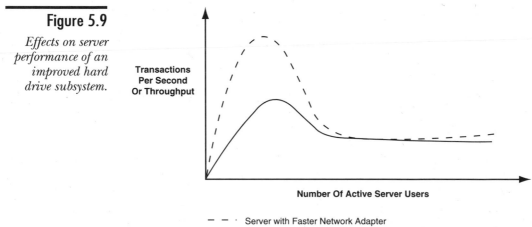

IDE drives are not well suited to the requirements of servers. Only one drive in a pair can be active at a given time. Consequently, a single IDE drive might perform as well as a single SCSI drive, but multiple SCSI drives always will outperform multiple IDE drives.

Although Windows NT Server will put IDE drives into RAID configurations, the fact that drives cannot function simultaneously prevents the RAID system from performing well.

SCSI is nearly ideal for use on servers. The many performance enhancements that are available for SCSI-2 make SCSI the only choice for top performance. Consider a Fast/ Wide PCI SCSI adapter coupled with suitable Wide SCSI-2 disk drives for optimal performance.

Selecting Disk Subsystems for Workstations

Workstations, on the other hand, can prosper with IDE drives. IDE is supported by nearly all operating systems, and single IDE drives perform comparably to SCSI drives at about half the cost. Currently, 1-GB IDE drives are available for less than $250.

If your organization has PCs that still are using older ST506/412 or ESDI hard drives, a drive upgrade is a great way to improve performance at a low cost. An IDE expansion board costs about $30, and drives are available for less than $200.

At present, IDE hard drives are limited to about 1 GB in capacity. If you require larger hard drives, SCSI is the way to go. Costs of SCSI drives have been coming down as well; SCSI-2 and IDE drives now have a comparable cost-per-megabyte. ISA SCSI adapters can be had for under $100, even from prestigious companies such as Adaptec. A Fast/Wide PCI-bus SCSI adapter from Adaptec retails for less than $300.

Many components are available in IDE and SCSI versions, including CD-ROM drives, tape backup units, and removable storage devices such as the Iomega Zip drive. Assuming that your PC is already equipped with IDE connectors, how do you decide when you should make the move to SCSI?

There are two driving factors: the number of devices to be supported, and the performance you require when multitasking several peripherals. IDE will support, at most, four devices per PC, including hard drives. IDE drives operate in pairs, and at any given time only one device in the pair can be active. On the other hand, SCSI can support up to 15 peripherals with a suitable adapter. SCSI bus disconnect and Tag Command Queueing enable a SCSI adapter to efficiently drive several devices. Together with the fact that many peripherals are available with SCSI interfaces but not with IDE, the flexibility and performance advantages of SCSI clearly provide an edge over IDE in demanding environments.

Testing Your Knowledge

1. The capability of NT to run on different hardware platforms is called
   _____.

2. The capability of a microprocessor to emulate an original 8086 processor limited to only 1 MB of memory is called _____.

3. Which Intel CPU introduced virtual real mode, enabling it to emulate multiple 8086 processors?

   A. 80186

   B. 8008

   C. 80386

   D. Pentium Pro

4. Which type of microprocessor technology utilizes a small set of instructions that perform discreet operations for high efficiency?

    A. RISC

    B. CISC

    C. MIPS

    D. Multi processors

5. Which expansion bus was introduced with the original IBM PC?

    A. Micro Channel

    B. PCI

    C. EISA

    D. ISA

6. Which of the following expansion buses allow for automatic resource configuration?

    A. ISA

    B. EISA

    C. Micro Channel

    D. VLB

    E. PCI

7. Which bus type provides 64 bits required by Intel Pentium processors?

    A. PCI

    B. VLB

    C. EISA

    D. PCMCIA

8. The elimination of performance degrading wait states was achieved by incorporating _____ memory into system designs.

9. What is the minimum amount of memory required on Microsoft Windows 3.1 workstations?

    A. 16 MB

    B. 12 MB

    C. 6 MB

    D. 4 MB

10. If you want to use a EIDE hard disk with a capacity greater than 512 MB, what do you need to verify before installing it?

    A. That the system BIOS or EIDE controller card supports these types of drives.

    B. That the drive has more than 1,024 cylinders.

    C. That it is set up as the primary or master drive.

    D. That it is not too expensive.

11. When considering using an adapter in a server platform, what SCSI-2 extensions should you verify a new adapter has?

    A. Common command set and parity checking

    B. Bus disconnect and parity checking

    C. Fast SCSI exclusively

    D. A combination of Fast SCSI and Wide SCSI

Review Answers

1. portability
2. real mode
3. C
4. A
5. D
6. B,C,E
7. A
8. cache
9. D
10. A
11. D

CHAPTER 6

Installing Windows NT Hardware

E very LAN administrator needs to know something about the hardware on his LAN. Emergencies always happen when your contract support people are unavailable. Some hardware vendors may attempt to sell you more hardware than you need, or they will push their favorite products rather than the products you really need. Ignorance is not bliss as far as network hardware is concerned.

You need to arm yourself with two things: basic knowledge and patience. Most installation and troubleshooting procedures are not outrageously difficult, but they can take a great deal of time. Keep your confidence and your cool. You can take care of most of the hardware problems on your LAN.

Note Unfortunately, Windows NT 4 does not support the Plug and Play features of many components that have been introduced for Windows 95. With some components, you will need to turn the Plug and Play feature off to have it configure properly for Windows NT.

Using the Proper Tools

A basic PC tool kit doesn't need to be expensive. You can buy one at just about any PC dealer for about $30. If you want to get unusual tools or tools of exceptional quality, a good source is Specialized Products Company. Its address is included at the end of Chapter 4, "Planning and Installing Network Media."

Your basic took kit will include the following:

- ◆ Large and small slotted screwdrivers.

- ◆ Large and small Phillips screwdrivers.

- ◆ Size 10 and 12 Torx drivers. You will probably get one driver with a reversible tip. A Torx driver is required for Compaq computers and used by some others. The Torx driver is the one with the funny tip that looks like a flower.

- ◆ 1/4-inch and 3/16-inch hex drivers.

- ◆ A chip puller and a chip-insertion tool. These tools were more useful in the days when chips were installed in sockets. Now that most chips are surface mounted and soldered, you seldom will need these tools.

- ◆ A pickup tool for retrieving the parts you will be dropping into the guts of your PC.

- ◆ A parts container so that you will only lose half of your loose parts.

Other useful tools include the following:

- ◆ A wire cutter/stripper.

- ◆ A wrist grounding strap. Use this to ground yourself when you are installing static-sensitive components, which include almost anything you can put into a PC.

- ◆ An anti-static work surface if you're particularly concerned about static damage to components.

- ◆ Some good needle-nosed pliers.

- ◆ An inexpensive volt/ohm meter.

- ◆ A variety of plastic wire ties. Have several sizes on hand. These little wonders have a hundred uses, from tidying up cable to attaching equipment labels and securing connectors so that they can't slip loose.

◆ A portable case that includes all the disks you need for troubleshooting the PCs in your office. As you use a new utility, add it to a disk in your tool kit. Start out with at least the following:

Disks for installing the standard version of DOS used in your office.

A bootable DOS disk with utilities such as FDISK and FORMAT.

Configuration software for any expansion cards used in your office.

Any configuration programs required for PCs in your office. Most PCs build the configuration program into the BIOS, but older PCs and PCs based on EISA and Micro Channel buses require configuration disks.

At least one diagnostic program.

Several good diagnostic programs are available. Microsoft Windows includes a basic program named MSD. Good commercial programs include CheckIt and QA Plus.

A popular diagnostic tool is Micro-Scope from Micro 2000. A unique feature of this product is that it boots up under its own operating system, enabling it to test even the memory areas that normally are occupied by DOS. Programs that run under DOS cannot test some memory areas. Micro-Scope includes several other unique features as well. Contact Micro 2000 for information:

Micro 2000, Inc.
1100 E. Broadway 3rd Floor
Glendale, CA 91205
818-547-0125

Binary and Hexadecimal Numbers

Computers don't work directly with the decimal numbers with which you are familiar. The heart of a computer consists of memory locations that are either on or off. These on and off states are used to represent 1s and 0s, from which all other numbers in computers are derived. Numbers in 1s and 0s are referred to as *binary* numbers. Another numbering system called *hexadecimal* makes large binary numbers easier to manage.

A single 1 or 0 in the computer numbering system is a *bit*. Numbers that can have only two values are called *binary*, and *bit* is an abbreviation for the phrase *binary digit*.

Patterns of bits can represent data, much like the dots and dashes of Morse code represent letters. Bits are strung together to build larger codes. The most common code is ASCII, which uses strings of 8 bits to represent characters. The capital letter A, for example, is represented by the binary pattern 01000001.

Unfortunately, to humans, 01000001 looks a lot like 01000010, so most people like to convert long binary numbers into forms with which they are more familiar. To convert binary numbers to decimal, you need to have an understanding of how decimal and binary numbering systems work.

Decimal numbers are based on powers of 10. The digits in the decimal number 5,432 have the following meanings:

5 represents 5×10^3, which is $5 \times 10 \times 10 \times 10$ or 5,000

4 represents 4×10^2, which is $4 \times 10 \times 10$ or 400

3 represents 3×10^1, which is 3×10 or 30

2 represents 2×10^0, which is 2×1 or 2

The same principle applies to binary numbers. Consider the binary number 1010, for example. The digits have the following meanings:

1 represents 1×2^3, which is $1 \times 2 \times 2 \times 2$ or 1×8

0 represents 0×2^2, which is $0 \times 2 \times 2$ or 0

1 represents 1×2^1, which is 1×2 or 2

0 represents 0×2^0, which is 0×1 or 0

As you can see, 1010 is the binary equivalent of the decimal number 10.

Here is a summary of the powers of 2:

$2^0 = 1$

$2^1 = 2$

$2^2 = 4$

$2^3 = 8$

$2^4 = 16$

$2^5 = 32$

$2^6 = 64$

$2^7 = 128$

$2^8 = 256$

A byte consists of 8 characters. The highest possible value of a byte is 11111111. If you convert this to decimal form by adding the values 2^0 through 2^7, you will see that a byte can represent values of 0 through 255.

When large binary numbers are encountered, it is common to convert them to *hexadecimal* (hex), which is a numbering system based on powers of 16. The easiest way to convert binary numbers is to organize them in blocks of four bits, which easily convert to hex equivalents. Table 6.1 lists hexadecimal, binary, and decimal equivalents for the numbers 0 through 15.

TABLE 6.1
Hexadecimal, Binary, and Decimal Equivalents

Binary	Decimal	Hexadecimal
0000	0	0
0001	1	1
0010	2	2
0011	3	3
0100	4	4
0101	5	5
0110	6	6
0111	7	7
1000	8	8
1001	9	9
1010	10	A
1011	11	B
1100	12	C
1101	13	D
1110	14	E
1111	15	F

Hexadecimal uses the letters A through F to represent digits ranging from 10 through 15 decimal. Hexadecimal numbers often are distinguished from decimal by adding an h to the number—for example, 3135h is a hex number. You also will encounter the C programming convention of attaching 0x to the beginning of a number, such as 0x5A29.

To convert a binary number to hexadecimal, just substitute the corresponding hexadecimal digit for each four-bit chunk:

0100	1010	0111	1110
4	A	7	E

You often run into some odd decimal numbers in association with computer characteristics. These apparently random choices make more sense when you remember that the numbers are based on binary equivalents. Here are some common values you will encounter:

Value	Decimal	Binary	Hexadecimal
1 KB	1024	0100 0000 0000	400h
640 KB	655360	1010 0000 0000 0000 0000	A0000h
1 MB	1048576	0001 0000 0000 0000 0000 0000	100000h

Note   The Calculator utility that is included with Windows can perform number base conversions. Just choose **V**iew, **S**cientific to put the calculator into scientific mode.

Objective B.5 Parameters Used to Configure Microcomputers

As you add devices to microcomputers, you need to ensure that they don't step on each others' toes. Each device needs to obtain access to certain system resources to get attention or exchange data. To enable devices to cooperate without conflicting, you need to attend to four system settings:

◆ Interrupts

◆ I/O addresses

◆ Shared memory addresses

◆ DMA channels

Interrupts

Computers are multitasking machines. When they are busy printing, saving files, or performing other operations, they need to be alert for key presses, messages from networks, or other systems that need attention. A couple of methods are available for meeting this requirement.

The CPU periodically can check each resource to see whether it needs attention; this process is called *polling*. Most of the time, though, this is a waste of the CPU's energy.

The CPU can recognize a mechanism by which systems can signal for attention on their own. That mechanism is based on *interrupts* (or IRQ for *Interrupt ReQuest*). Each device that might need attention is assigned an interrupt. When it wants to signal the CPU, the device *asserts* the interrupt. This interrupt signals the CPU to stop what it is doing and come to the aid of the device.

If two devices are configured with the same interrupt, considerable confusion can arise. An important step in system configuration is ensuring that each device in the system has a unique interrupt. Unfortunately, that can be more difficult than you might think.

All Intel PCs now being made inherit their basic interrupt mechanisms from the 16-bit ISA bus of the 1985 IBM AT. Table 6.2 lists the interrupts as defined by the AT architecture (interrupts 0 and 1 are not listed because they are reserved for the system).

TABLE 6.2
Interrupts Used in IBM PC Compatibles

IRQ	Use
2	Cascade to IRQ 9
3	COM2 and COM4
4	COM1 and COM3
5	LPT2
6	Floppy disk controller
7	LPT1
8	Real-time clock
9	Cascade from IRQ2
10	Available
11	Available
12	PS/2 and Inport mice (if present)
13	Math coprocessor

continues

TABLE 6.2, CONTINED
Interrupts Used in IBM PC Compatibles

IRQ	Use
14	Hard disk controller
15	Available

Lower numbered interrupts have higher priorities. That's why interrupts 0 and 1 were reserved for the system clock and keyboard. You can free up some of the low interrupts by disabling I/O ports. If your system doesn't support a directly attached printer, disable the LPT ports. Some ports are deactivated by removing jumpers on I/O cards. Newer systems usually enable you to disable ports from the BIOS setup program.

Interrupts 2 and 9 are special interrupts. To understand why, you need to understand how IBM implemented interrupts on the IBM AT. The 8259 interrupt controller chip used by IBM supports eight interrupts. When IBM designed the model AT, it elected to add eight new interrupts to the eight that had been supported by the IBM PC design. To do this, it added a second 8259 chip.

IBM chose to control the new 8259 by connecting IRQ 2 of the first 8259 controller to IRQ 9 of the new controller. IRQ 2 is called a *cascade interrupt* because it enables interrupts 8 through 15 to cascade down through IRQ 2 to get system attention.

When interrupts 8 through 15 fire, IRQ 9 is asserted, which cascades to IRQ 2. When the system is interrupted by IRQ 2, it knows that the real interrupt comes from the second 8259. It then checks to determine which of interrupts 8 through 15 actually was asserted.

Because of this cascade mechanism, some operating systems, such as MS-DOS, have trouble with interrupts 2 and 9. In most cases, Windows NT can handle devices using IRQ 9, but if you can avoid it, don't configure option cards for these interrupts. They might work, but you might get a flaky system if you try.

Because IRQ 2 has a high system priority, interrupts 8 through 15 inherit that priority. If possible, put your most critical option cards, such as NICs, in these interrupts. SCSI adapters generally use IRQs 10 or 11.

Note   COM ports can be scarce resources on a Windows NT Server. You will need one COM port for the interface cable to your uninterruptible power supply. If you need to configure remote access, you will need a COM port for a modem. Also, most mice interface with COM ports.

Even though PCs officially can support four COM ports, notice that interrupts are shared by COM1 and COM3 and by COM2 and COM4. It can be chancy to use two devices on the same interrupt at the same time, so you should avoid COM3 and COM4 on a server.

The solution to the dilemma is to use a PS/2-style mouse, possibly with a Microsoft Inport adapter. This option uses IRQ 12 and will not conflict with other uses for COM1 and COM2. Many computers are now equipped to use PS/2-style mice rather than serial mice.

I/O Addresses

After an expansion card has the CPU's attention, it needs to be able to communicate data. This is done by assigning memory blocks that can be used to exchange data. Two types of memory assignments can be made:

◆ I/O addresses or ports—small addresses that are located in lower system memory.

◆ Shared memory addresses that enable expansion cards to use larger amounts of system RAM.

I/O addresses (also called *ports*) are found in the memory range 100h through 3FFh. Typically, a port will be 8 bytes to 32 bytes. Unfortunately, the documentation for many option cards doesn't tell you how big a port the card requires. In general, assume that an 8-bit card requires 8 bits and that a 16-bit card requires 16 bits. If two cards overlap I/O address ranges, some very strange things can happen, so always suspect I/O address conflicts when two cards have neighboring addresses.

Table 6.3 lists some common I/O ports.

TABLE 6.3
Common I/O Port Assignments

Base Address	Device	Typical Address Range
200	Game port (joystick)	200–20F
260	LPT2	260–27F
2E8	COM4	2E8–2EF
2F8	COM2	2F8–2FF
300	Common factory setting for many network cards	300–31F

continues

TABLE 6.3, CONTINUED
Common I/O Port Assignments

Base Address	Device	Typical Address Range
330	Adaptec and other SCSI adapters	330–33F
360	LPT1	360–37F
3CD	EGA video display	3C0–3CF
3D0	CGA video display	3D0–3DF
3E8	COM3	3E8–3EF
3F8	COM1	3F8–3FF

Shared memory addresses are found in memory above the DOS 640 KB line. Actually, not much memory is available in that range, as shown in figure 6.1. A0000–BFFFFh are used by video systems, and F0000–FFFFFh are used by the system's ROM BIOS.

Consequently, shared memory addresses generally need to fit in the range of C0000h through EFFFFh. As with I/O ports, it is essential that shared memory addresses don't overlap. Table 6.4 lists some common shared memory addresses.

Figure 6.1

DOS memory usage.

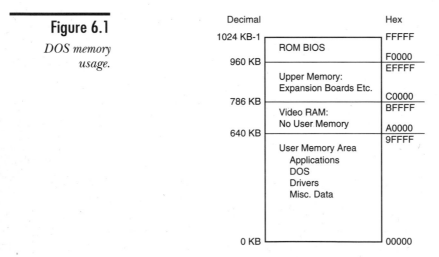

TABLE 6.4
Common Shared Memory Addresses

Device	Memory Range
Mono Video	B0000–B1000
CGA	B8000–C0000
EGA	A0000–C0
VGA	A0000–C4000
BIOS	F0000–FFFFF

DOS PCs that use expanded memory also require that an area above 640 KB be set aside as a page frame for swapping memory in and out of expanded memory. The location of this memory is declared as a parameter of the EMM386.EXE memory manager. Be sure that this page frame does not conflict with memory used by your expansion cards.

Windows NT provides automatic emulation of expanded memory as required by applications.

Note   You also should exclude expansion card shared memory from the extended memory used by your system. This is achieved by including the X= parameter when EMM386.EXE is run in CONFIG.SYS. Consult a DOS manual for more complete instructions.

DMA Channels

DMA channels enable peripherals to communicate with memory directly without bothering the CPU. Eight DMA channels are available, numbered 0 through 7. Lower numbered channels have the highest priorities.

The DMA address 0 is reserved for DRAM memory refresh.

Installing Expansion Cards

Objective B.5

Modern PCs generally include many options that were rare not too long ago. The majority of PCs purchased today have CD-ROM drives and sound cards, for example. As a result, interrupts and memory addresses represent some pretty precious real estate in many PCs. When buying an expansion option, it makes sense to obtain cards that support as many interrupt and address options as possible.

Cards that are designed to the limitations of 8-bit ISA are a definite liability. At one time, I was trying to add a Novell/Eagle NE2000 card to a system. Although it is a 16-bit card, it supports only 8-bit interrupts and is limited to IRQ settings of 2, 3, 4, and 5. The PC in question had no interrupts available in that range, and I couldn't find any way to reconfigure the existing options to free up an interrupt. Consequently, I had to dig up another, more versatile, card.

Things to look for when buying an expansion card include support for IRQ 8 through 15 (whenever possible) and easy setup procedures.

> **Note**
>
> Most of the components you can install in a PC are extremely sensitive to static electricity and can be damaged even by static charges you would not notice. For this reason, it is important that you ground yourself before installing most hardware.
>
> You probably will be advised to unplug the PC. Doing so, however, removes the ground connection from the PC—a great invitation for static electricity. Instead, leave the PC plugged in but make sure that it is turned off.
>
> Use a grounding strap to ensure that you don't build up a static charge. A grounding strap is a bracelet that you wear on your wrist. The bracelet connects to a wire that is attached to a ground, such as the metal chassis of your PC. Only after you are grounded properly should you remove a component from its anti-static bag.
>
> It's also a good idea to work on an anti-static mat—a surface that also is grounded. Grounding straps and portable anti-static mats can be obtained from Specialized Products Company. A field service kit with both components costs about $50. See the end of Chapter 4 for this company's address.

Configuring Cards with Jumpers and Switches

Many cards still configure with jumpers and switches. Figure 6.2 illustrates both options. Setting jumpers and switches is usually the pits. Many vendors don't provide clear instructions, and the pins and switches usually are not labeled in any sensible way. You might be told to add a jumper to pins 14 and 15 to set a memory address of 360h. (Now who could possibly forget that?) So, unless you work with a particular card every day, you need to consult the manual each time you set one up. Don't lose the manual or you're sunk.

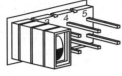 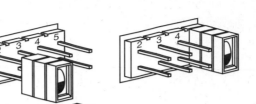

Figure 6.2

Examples of jumpers and switches for setting expansion options.

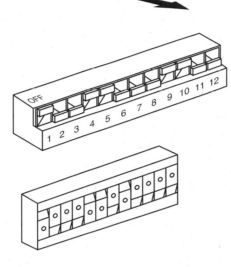

When you need to disable a jumper setting, don't completely remove the jumper. You might need it later when you reconfigure the card. Instead, place the jumper over one pin of the pair to keep the jumper with the card. Never throw a jumper away! Put it in your junk drawer. You will need it some day. There are at least two sizes of jumpers, so be alert to the difference and save some of both sizes.

Switches are easier to set and cannot be lost. They are called DIP switches because they are packaged in *dual-inline pin* assemblies, not because the guy who designed them was a dip.

Before you start reconfiguring a card, write down its settings so that you can restore them easily if things don't work. There is a lot of trial and error involved in configuring a PC, and proper documentation can save you a great deal of hassle.

Software Configurable Cards

Most cards are available in configurations that have replaced switches and jumpers with nonvolatile memory that is configured with a setup program. Many setup programs have the capability of examining systems to determine a configuration that will not conflict with existing options.

Configuring ROM BIOS

Some options are configured from the ROM BIOS. Most new motherboards include many features that once were located on expansion cards, including COM and LPT ports and disk controllers. In most cases, the ROM BIOS routine has an option for disabling or reconfiguring the settings for some or all of these features.

Configuring EISA and Micro Channel PCs

Option cards for EISA and Micro Channel buses do not have jumpers or switches. They incorporate a manufacturer's ID, which enables a setup program to determine which cards are installed in the expansion bus. When you run the configuration program, it generally does a pretty good job of configuring cards with nonconflicting settings.

The catch with EISA is that most EISA systems include non-EISA cards, which cannot be configured or read by the setup program. You will have to keep these settings in mind as you run the EISA setup. Micro Channel PCs don't accept non-Micro Channel cards and cannot have this problem.

Some EISA PCs don't enable you to set all system options from the EISA setup program. You still have to run a CMOS setup program to configure settings such as the system clock, hard drive configurations, and so on.

The setup programs for EISA and Micro Channel run from a disk that must be booted on the system. When you add a hardware option to the PC, you need to copy some configuration files to the setup program. These setup disks are among your most precious possessions. Store several copies that include all the setup files required by the systems in your organization.

| Note | After you configure the options in a system, be sure to record the settings you used. There is nothing more frustrating than having to remove every card and determine its settings before you can add a new board.

You should record settings in one of the following ways:

◆ **On a page in a configuration log.** The problem with this approach is that you are at the user's PC and the log is back at your desk.

◆ **On a tag that you attach to the PC.** One good choice is a cable tag, which is a self-adhesive label intended for use on cabling systems. They are durable and do not come off easily. Add one to the PC's monitor cable and record the settings. Get them from Black Box Corporation, whose address is at the end of Chapter 4.

◆ **Record the settings in a text file that you store in the PC's DOS directory.** Flag the file as System files, making them read-only and hidden, so that users cannot easily erase them.

Configuring PCI Devices

Actually, you can't do much, if anything, to configure a PCI device. PCI was designed as a "plug-and-play" bus, and it is supposed to be self-configuring. In most computers, you take the settings you get when you put a card in a PCI slot.

In most cases, that means you don't know the hardware configuration for a PCI card until it is installed and running. Then you can look at it to determine its settings. Windows NT Diagnostics, described in Chapter 19, "Managing the Server," can be used to determine the hardware settings.

After you know the resources being used by your PCI cards, you can use the remaining available settings to configure your ISA adapters.

Installing Memory

Some guidelines for selecting memory were covered in Chapter 5, "Selecting Hardware for Windows NT." There are, however, a few more considerations.

Take care when installing SIMMs in their sockets. There is no guaranteed way to repair a broken SIMM socket other than replacing the motherboard. Even with great patience, removing the old socket and soldering in a new one probably will not work.

Many cheap SIMM sockets secure the SIMM with plastic fingers that break off easily. When you buy a new PC, always look for metal fingers in the SIMM sockets. With rare exceptions, plastic fingers are a good tip-off that your vendor likes to use cheap components.

SIMMs will have cutouts and alignment holes that prevent the SIMM from being installed in the wrong position. If you have to force the SIMM, it isn't oriented in the right direction.

Memory size is set by the PC's CMOS configuration program. Always reconfigure CMOS after you change memory.

Some EISA systems automatically recognize changes in memory, but some do not and require you to run the setup program to register changes in memory. Micro Channel systems always require you to run the setup program to register changes in memory.

Installing Hard Drives

Only IDE and SCSI drives will be considered here. If you have older drives, you probably cannot buy replacement controllers or drives. Besides, the performance improvements of IDE and SCSI more than justify the cost of upgrading.

Installation Considerations

This section gives you some general guidelines that will be of interest when you are installing any type of hard drive.

Drive Bays

Desktop PCs are including fewer and fewer drive bays these days. If you will be adding many options to a desktop system, look for a minitower case.

Servers always should have full-tower cases with as many drive bays as possible. Be sure, however, that the case design provides proper ventilation. Large hard drives put out considerable heat, and you want to ensure that they will have good air circulation. It is often best to mount hard drives in individual, external drive cabinets. Then each drive has its own power supply and ventilation fan.

Some cases require drive rails in order to mount drives, but the best approach is to select a tower case that does not require drive rails. Then you will have more options for where you can install equipment. Drive rails don't really simplify much. You still have to screw something to the drive to hold it in place.

Be sure that your server cabinet provides plenty of ventilation. A second fan is a useful precaution. Also, with Pentium processors, it is a good idea to mount a cooling fan on the processor itself. Such a fan generally is included on better Pentium systems.

Power and Power Connectors

A server generally should be equipped with a power supply that has at least a 300-watt capacity. The power supply should be fitted with a large number of power connectors.

PCs use two power connectors (both are shown in figure 6.3). The larger connector is more common, but you will encounter the smaller connector on devices that are designed with a 3 1/2-inch form factor.

IDE Drives

IDE drives couldn't be much easier to install. Most new PC motherboards are equipped with an IDE connector.

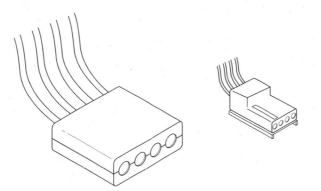

Figure 6.3

Power connectors used in PCs.

If your system includes only one IDE controller, the addresses are preset and standard. The I/O address for the first controller is always 1FE hex, and the interrupt is always 14.

If you need more than two IDE drives, you can include a second IDE controller if one is not present on your motherboard. IDE controllers are available for ISA, VESA, and PCI slots. The address for the second controller is usually 170 hex. You will need to determine an available interrupt.

Each IDE drive must be configured as a master or a slave, usually by setting jumpers. The first drive always is configured as a master and is seen by your system as drive C. If you add a second drive, set its jumpers to the slave setting.

A single ribbon cable with two drive connectors supports both the master and slave drive. Drives can be connected to the cable in any order. Be sure that line 1 of the ribbon cable attaches to pin 1 of the drive connector. Line 1 usually is identified by a stripe along one edge of the cable.

SCSI Adapters and Drives

You have to work a bit harder to install a SCSI subsystem. Each SCSI subsystem consists of a SCSI adapter (also called a *SCSI host bus adapter*), one or more SCSI devices, and a series of cables that connect the adapter and devices in a daisy chain configuration. There are a fair number of rules, but they are pretty easy to follow:

◆ SCSI is configured as a bus, and each device on the bus must be assigned a unique address in the range of 0 through 7. (Wide SCSI buses can support addresses ranging from 0 through 15. Consult the documentation for your SCSI adapter.)

◆ The SCSI adapter will always be assigned address 7, which is the factory default.

◆ Most SCSI adapters expect device 0 to be the hard drive that boots the system. Adapters also might expect drive 1 to be a hard drive. If that is the case, don't assign address 0 or 1 to other types of devices.

◆ Lower numbered SCSI addresses have higher priorities. If your server has hard drives and a CD-ROM, assign lower addresses to the hard drives.

◆ A system can support up to four SCSI adapters. You must, of course, ensure that each adapter is assigned unique settings for interrupts, memory, and so on.

◆ Most SCSI adapters are equipped with floppy drive connectors. If your floppy drives are attached to other controllers, be sure to disable floppy drive support on the SCSI adapter.

◆ Devices are added to the SCSI bus by daisy chaining cables from device to device.

◆ The first and last devices in the SCSI daisy chain must be terminated.

◆ Devices in the middle of the daisy chain must not be terminated.

◆ External SCSI devices must be separated by at least .3 meters of cable.

◆ The total length of the SCSI cable daisy chain cannot exceed 6 meters.

◆ At least one device must supply power to the SCSI bus. In most cases, this will be the SCSI adapter. All devices are protected by diodes, and it doesn't matter if more than one device is supplying power to the bus.

SCSI Addressing

SCSI is an attractive technology because one controller can manage seven devices (or more with Wide SCSI). Each device is identified on the SCSI bus by a unique SCSI address. Several precautions were mentioned in the preceding list.

A PC can support four SCSI buses, and devices on separate buses can share the same address.

The addresses on internal devices usually are set with jumpers. Many external devices are equipped with switches that make it easy to set the addresses.

Note A few new SCSI devices are being equipped with a SCSI Plug and Play feature that enables them to be configured with a SCSI address automatically. Plug and Play devices can coexist on the same bus with standard SCSI devices.

Connecting SCSI Devices

Internal SCSI devices connect to a 50-pin or 68-pin ribbon cable. The cable simply is daisy chained from one device to the next. Be sure that line 1 of the ribbon cable attaches to pin 1 of the SCSI connector. Line 1 usually is identified by a stripe along one edge of the cable. If you're lucky, when you reverse a cable, the attached device will only complain. If you're unlucky, it will die.

track is located the operating system boot loader, which begins the process of starting the OS. Once the boot loader has been located and executed, the operating system takes control of the PC.

On a SCSI disk, the operating system does not directly access tracks and sectors. Instead, data is stored in blocks and is retrieved simply by requesting a given block. This presents a problem on an IBM compatible because the BIOS can access data on disks via tracks and sectors. Somehow, the SCSI adapter must translate between the SCSI block-oriented storage and the track-sector storage favored by the PC BIOS.

This could be accomplished by installing a software driver that interfaces the OS with the SCSI adapter, but the driver program must be read from a hard disk. Also, the PC BIOS can't read the driver from a SCSI disk until the driver is loaded. Clearly a catch exists, and the SCSI adapter must perform a trick or two to enable the PC to access the SCSI disk and boot the operating system.

This slight of hand is performed by a SCSI BIOS that is loaded after the system test and prior to attempting to start the operating system. After the system test, you will typically see a message indicating that the SCSI BIOS is installed and identifying the devices that are attached. The SCSI BIOS enables the ROM BIOS to locate the boot track and start the operating system.

The SCSI BIOS is required only to enable the computer to boot from a SCSI disk. If the PC is booting from an IDE or ESCI hard disk, the operating system can load appropriate SCSI drivers that enable it to access non-bootable SCSI devices, such as additional hard drives and CD-ROMs. If the PC is not booting from a SCSI hard drive, you can disable the SCSI BIOS. You will save a bit of memory. More importantly, you will speed up the boot process because it is unnecessary for the SCSI adapter to initialize and scan the bus to identify devices. With ISA SCSI adapters, the SCSI BIOS is enabled using a jumper or a switch.

On many recent adapters, when the SCSI BIOS initializes, you are given the option of pressing a key to enter a SCSI setup program. Some of the settings you may see in the setup program are discussed in the following section. *The ROM-based setup program is available only when the SCSI BIOS is enabled.* To configure the adapter, you must enable the SCSI BIOS, run the configuration program, and then disable the SCSI BIOS.

Note | RISC computers are "SCSI-aware" and a SCSI BIOS is not required. See your system documentation for SCSI configuration procedures.

SCSI Adapter Hardware Settings

Many SCSI adapters are equipped with floppy-disk controllers, enabling them to replace the floppy/hard drive controller that was common in early PCs. Now, however, the majority of PCs are equipped with floppy disk controllers on the motherboard. If your SCSI adapter has a floppy drive port, you must disable floppy support on either the motherboard or the SCSI adapter. Floppy support is usually configured via a switch or jumper on the adapter card.

SCSI adapters require sole access to an interrupt and a range of memory addresses that functions as an I/O port. Many also require a DMA address. If your system has a single SCSI adapter, chances are the factory settings will work without alteration, although you should double check the IRQ. If you need to install multiple SCSI adapters—up to four can be supported—ensure that each adapter is set up with a unique set of communication parameters.

When the SCSI BIOS is enabled, you must specify the starting address for a memory range where the BIOS will be loaded. If multiple SCSI adapters are being installed, the BIOS must usually be enabled only on the adapter that supports the boot disk. The BIOS on other adapters needs to be enabled only when those adapters are being configured or when some features requiring the SCSI BIOS are enabled.

Termination must be considered, and you must determine whether termination should be enabled or disabled. On many recent adapters, an automatic termination mode is available that enables the adapter to configure itself depending on its position in the SCSI daisy chain.

Some new SCSI adapters are equipped with a plug-and-play feature that enables them to be configured automatically by some operating systems. Plug and Play is supported by Windows 95, but is not yet supported by Windows NT. You should disable Plug and Play if the adapter will be running under Windows NT.

Adding SCSI Adapters Device Drivers

Windows NT includes drivers on its resource CD-ROM for most standard SCSI controller cards, which are automatically detected during the Windows NT setup procedure. Adding SCSI adapters to a Windows NT Server manually is done through the Control Panel. Before adding SCSI adapter drivers, however, you must first install the card and configure its resources: IRQ, DMA, and I/O addresses according to the manufacturers instructions. Follow along with the next exercise to install a SCSI adapter device driver.

1. Click on the Start button and choose Settings and Control Panel.

2. Double-click on the SCSI Adapters icon.

3. Display the Drivers panel by clicking on the Drivers tab.

4. Click on the Add button.

5. Choose the SCSI Adapter manufacturer and model from the list box. If the adapter you are installing is not on the list, choose the Have Disk option to install the driver from the manufacturers installation diskette.

6. You may be prompted to insert the Windows NT Server CD-ROM or other media.

7. After the device driver has been added, you are prompted to restart the machine. Click on the Yes button to reboot.

Configuring SCSI Drive Startup

Hard drives consume the most power when they are spinning up to their operating speed. When a computer is equipped with several hard drives, it may exceed the capacity of the power supply to spin all drives up when the system is turned on. In these cases, it is possible to spin the drives up individually, under control of the SCSI adapter. Two configuration changes are required:

◆ You must configure the *remote start* capability of the hard drive by changing the appropriate jumper. Most hard drives are configured at the factory to start when power is applied.

◆ You must configure the SCSI adapter to send a *start unit command* to the drive. The SCSI BIOS must be enabled to send this command, even though this may not be the first SCSI adapter.

These procedures are required only for hard drives, and then only when several drives are present. In most cases, the boot drive will be configured to start automatically, and other hard drives will be started remotely. Other types of SCSI devices, such as CD-ROMs and tape drives, do not require configuration of remote startup.

Note Caution is required when configuring older SCSI-1 devices to operate on some Fast SCSI adapters. The SCSI-1 devices can function only at a 5 MBps transfer rate. A Fast SCSI controller, however, will attempt to negotiate 10 MBps transfers. Consult the documentation for your SCSI adapter if you are installing SCSI-1 devices.

Testing Your Knowledge

1. What is the decimal value of Hexadecimal value "D"?

    A. 8

    B. 1101

    C. 13

    D. 1000

2. Various configurable hardware settings permit devices to cooperate in a computer system without interfering with one another. Which of the following is not such as system setting?

    A. Interrupts

    B. Buses

    C. DMA channels

    D. I/O addresses

3. On a typical IBM-compatible PC, which IRQ is associated with the floppy disk controller?

    A. None

    B. 6

    C. 8

    D. 13

4. What I/O port base address assignment is typically associated with COM1?

    A. 2E8

    B. 360

    C. 3E8

    D. 3F8

5. What permits peripherals to communicate with memory directly without interrupting the CPU?

    A. DMU

    B. Cascading

    C. Thunking

    D. Shared memory address

6. Which bus type was designed to support plug-and-play technology?

    A. None

    B. All

    C. EISA

    D. PCI

    E. VL

7. Which device listed should be given the lowest SCSI address?

    A. CD-ROM

    B. Scanner

    C. Tape drive

    D. Hard drive

8. How many SCSI buses can a PC support?

    A. 1

    B. 2

    C. 4

    D. 7

9. Which methods are commonly used to configure SCSI adapters?

    A. Using switches or jumpers

    B. Through a configuration program on the adapters ROM

    C. Through EISA or MicroChannel setup

    D. Using the plug-and-play features within the PCI bus

10. Some new SCSI adapters are equipped with plug-and-play feature that enables them to be configured automatically by some operating systems. Which Microsoft operating system currently supports this feature?

    A. None

    B. Windows 95

    C. Windows NT 3.5x

    D. Windows NT 4

Review Answers

1. C

2. B

3. B

4. D

5. A

6. D

7. D

8. C

9. A, B, C, D

10. B

PART II

The Basics

CHAPTER 7

Installing Windows NT Server

Microsoft has put considerable thought into the installation procedures for Windows NT. The Setup program is highly automated and works with incredibly few flaws. It is sophisticated in its capability to identify computer hardware and select the proper drivers and driver settings. Most of what you as a user have to contribute during installation involves entering personal information such as your name, the license number, and so on.

This chapter walks you through the complete installation procedure. I'm assuming that your hardware has been installed and configured.

This chapter first covers planning, and then the actual installation. It follows with a look at some miscellaneous procedures related to installation, reconfiguration, and starting and stopping the server.

If you are familiar with the procedures for installing Windows NT version 3.5x, you will find that most changes for version 4 have to do with the program interface. Experienced users may, therefore, find it unnecessary to review this chapter.

Planning for Installation

Before charging into installation, you need to do some planning and preparation. This section discusses the plans you need to make.

Objective
B.8

Planning Disk Partitions

During system setup, you are required to designate a primary partition for Windows NT to use as a boot partition, the partition from which Windows NT boots. Chapter 17, "Managing Disk Storage," covers partitions in detail. When NT is installed on the active partition of a computer, it is referred to as the boot/system partition. If NT is installed on another partition, the active partition is the system partition, and the partition containing the Winnt folder is the boot partition.

In general, designate the entire first drive as the system partition. This partition becomes drive C after it is formatted. This configuration is done for you if you elect to perform an express setup.

The following exercise is a list of some guidelines for setting up partitions:

Setting Up the Partition

1. The boot partition must have a capacity of at least 90 MB for Intel x86 systems. Of course, 90 MB is a bare minimum; you should allow some room to grow. A suggested minimum is 500 MB.

2. The boot partition for a RISC computer must be configured with the FAT file system. The boot partition must have a capacity of at least 115 MB for x86 systems and 147 MB for RISC systems. Alternatively, a 2 MB FAT partition can be used to boot the RISC computer (as a system partition), after which all software can be run from an NTFS boot partition.

3. The system or boot partition cannot be configured as a volume set or a stripe set (see Chapter 17).

4. Partitions on a RISC computer are configured following procedures described in the system documentation. Windows NT Setup cannot configure partitions on RISC computers.

5. Windows NT cannot be installed in an existing partition if the partition is compressed.

6. If you want to configure the computer to dual-boot under both MS-DOS and Windows NT, the boot partition must use the FAT file system.

Note The Windows NT directory on the boot partition can always be referenced by the Windows NT system variable %SystemRoot%. Although the boot partition is virtually always drive C, the %SystemRoot% variable enables Windows NT (and you) to identify the boot partition without knowing which drive letter was assigned.

The default Windows NT directory for version 4 is C:\WINNT. The default directory for version 3.5 was C:\WINNT35.

Selecting File Systems

Windows NT supports the following file systems:

◆ **FAT (file allocation tables).** The file system used by DOS.

◆ **NTFS (NT file system).** A file system developed for Windows NT.

NTFS has the following advantages (which are particularly significant for network servers):

◆ Complete support for Windows NT security. NTFS is the file system of choice for Windows NT Server because it is the only one that provides file level security at the server computer. Unauthorized users cannot bypass security on an NTFS volume by booting the server from a floppy.

◆ Long file names—up to 256 characters—with support for mixed-case letters. OS/2 users can access long file names; MS-DOS users see shortened versions of the long file names.

◆ Disk activities can be logged to enable activities to be rolled back in the event of a system failure. Corrupt files due to hardware or power failures are much less common with NTFS.

Although only Windows NT computers can directly use NTFS files, network users can access files on Windows NT servers quite normally whether they are using MS-DOS, Unix, or Macintosh computers. Windows NT presents the files to non-NT computers in a form that the computers can accept.

**Objective
A.1**

With Intel x86 servers, the only reason not to use NTFS is that you need to dual-boot the computer using DOS or OS/2. Frankly, for servers, that's not an advantage. You want servers to be locked up tightly, and you most certainly don't want users to be able to boot the computer under DOS and attack your files.

With Advanced RISC computers, the system partition must be formatted with the FAT file system to enable the computer to boot. All other partitions can be formatted with NTFS.

In summary, all Windows NT computers should use NTFS whenever possible (with the sole exception of the system partition on a RISC-based server).

> **Note** With Windows NT version 4, Microsoft has dropped support for the High Performance File System (HPFS) developed for and still used by OS/2. You must convert HPFS volumes to NTFS if they are to be supported under Windows NT.

Objective A.2

Choosing Network Protocols

Network protocols—as covered in Chapter 1, "Understanding Networks"—are the languages that enable computers to carry on conversations on the network. Windows NT supports the following three transport protocols:

◆ **NetBEUI.** The protocol used in all earlier Microsoft network environments. NetBEUI is well-suited for small networks. Its primary disadvantage is that it cannot be forwarded through routers and is, therefore, unsuitable for large networks. NetBEUI is required if you need to communicate with other computers that are configured to use only NetBEUI.

◆ **NWLink.** A Microsoft-developed protocol that is compatible with Novell's IPX/SPX protocols. The Novell protocols are particularly notable for their plug-and-play nature—very little configuration is required. IPX/SPX is routable and can be used on large networks, providing solid performance. Network routing, long a weak spot with IPX/SPX, has improved greatly with a new routing protocol named NLSP, which is now available on most third-party network routers. Unfortunately, relatively few systems outside of the Novell network arena support IPX/SPX. If you don't need TCP/IP, NWLink is the best general-purpose protocol supported by Windows NT.

◆ **TCP/IP.** The most widely used network protocols in the computer industry. Virtually every combination of computer and operating system can be configured to support TCP/IP. TCP/IP provides outstanding reliability and performance. The primary disadvantage to TCP/IP is that it requires considerable configuration and management, and a fair amount of knowledge concerning how the TCP/IP protocols function.

As described in Chapter 4, "Planning and Installing Network Media," NDIS enables a Windows NT computer to load all three protocol stacks at the same time if required.

NWLink requires little or no configuration or maintenance and is a good choice for many networks. Installation of NWLink will be covered in this chapter. Because TCP/IP configuration is fairly involved, installation is treated in a separate chapter. Chapter 16, "Using TCP/IP," however, does examine TCP/IP concepts and installation.

Planning the Computer's Security Role

Objective
B.2

Windows NT Server computers and their clients are organized in *domains*, groups of computers that share a common administrative database. User accounts in a domain are all managed together, even though the domain may have many computers. Administration is considerably simpler than maintaining separate user accounts on each server. Domains and their relationships to servers are discussed in Chapter 9, "Understanding User Accounts, Groups, Domains, and Trust Relationships."

Windows NT Server computers can perform three security roles in a domain:

◆ **Primary Domain Controller (PDC).** The Windows NT Server computer that maintains the primary copy of the domain account database. The PDC's role is to maintain the account database, validate users, and synchronize change between the PDC and the BDCs.

◆ **Backup Domain Controller (BDC).** Additional Windows NT Server computers that keep backup copies of the domain account database. BDC will maintain a copy of the account database and validate users.

◆ **Server.** Windows NT Server computers that do not store copies of the domain database and does not validate domain users on the network.

A computer can only be configured as a domain controller during installation. Creating a PDC automatically creates its associated domain since the domain essentially consists of the domain database that is created on the primary domain controller. The first Windows NT Server computer in the domain must be a primary domain controller. Additional Windows NT Server computers can be BDCs or stand-alone member servers.

When you add a backup domain controller or a server to a domain, you must designate the domain to which the computer will be added. If a PDC has not been created for that domain, the domain doesn't exist, and you cannot add a computer to the domain.

When you add a BDC or a server to a domain, you must have a user name and password that has administrative access to the domain. Administrative privileges are required to add the new BDC to the domain database. (There is a way to add the BDC or server to the domain before it is installed. See Chapter 10, "Managing Domains and Trust Relationships," for the technique.)

To create a primary domain controller, the only real requisite is a working network. Setup examines the network to ensure that you are not duplicating an existing domain.

To set up a backup domain controller, you must have the following:

◆ A working network that enables the BDC to communicate with its intended PDC.

◆ A working domain with an operating PDC. You can't create a BDC without accessing a domain that is run by an active primary domain controller.

◆ An administrative user name and password for the domain.

Objective
B.1

Starting Installation

With Windows NT 4, Microsoft has dropped the option of installing from floppy disks; only CD-ROM installations are supported. At the time of this writing, a SCSI CD-ROM drive can now be purchased for less than $200, so it is inexpensive to add a CD-ROM to your server. If the CD-ROM drive is installed on the server, there is the added benefit that it can be easily shared with the network. You can, therefore, install Windows NT on other networked computers using a shared network CD-ROM drive.

Installation from a shared network drive makes a lot of sense if you need to install large numbers of servers on an established network or if some networked servers are not equipped with CD-ROM drives. You can use the same procedure to install from a non-SCSI CD-ROM.

Preparing for Installation

You will need to know the make and model of each network adapter card that is installed in the server. You must also know the resources used by each card, including interrupts, I/O ports, and DMAs. The Windows NT setup program can detect and properly identify most network adapter cards, but can't verify the settings. If you specify the wrong settings, a network connection cannot be established and you will be unable to complete the installation.

If the computer to which you are installing is equipped with an uninterruptible power supply, disconnect any serial cable that is used to enable Windows NT to monitor the UPS. During installation, Windows NT will examine the serial ports to identify attached devices, a procedure that may cause problems with the UPS.

Did you install the Shell Technology Preview on Windows NT 3.5x so that you could try out the Windows 95 interface? If so, it must be removed before upgrading to version 4. Execute the command `shupdate.cmd /u` from the directory on the installation CD-ROM that supports the microprocessor of the computer. For an Intel x86 computer, the command is:

```
\newshell\I386\shupdate.cmd /u
```

Before installing Windows NT on an ARC-compliant RISC computer, consult the documentation to determine how to configure partitions and how to run programs from CD-ROMs. The way you start the SETUP program depends on the configuration of your system.

Preparing to Upgrade

You can upgrade MS-DOS, Windows 3.x, Windows for Workgroups, Windows 95 (dual boot only), or Windows NT 3.x to Windows NT 4. When upgrading, you have the option of replacing the original operating system or of creating a dual-boot configuration. When a dual-boot configuration is established, a menu is presented when the system is booted, enabling you to select the operating system to be started.

To create a dual-boot configuration, two conditions must be met:

◆ The boot partition must be configured with the FAT file system (except dual boot with NT 3.x).

◆ You must install Windows NT 4 in a directory that is separate from the directory containing the earlier operating system.

It is difficult to justify installing Windows NT Server in a dual-boot configuration. A server should be configured with as much security as possible, and a FAT boot partition cannot be secured. Because servers are shared by many users, they must be available nearly 100 percent of the time. When, therefore, would you be booting a server to another operating system? Dual-booting may make sense for a workstation, but is seldom justifiable for a server.

Note The default installation directory for Windows NT 3.5x was C:\WINNT35. For Windows NT 4, the default installation directory has changed to C:\WINNT. When you install version 4, you have the following choices:

◆ You can install version 4 in C:\WINNT35 to upgrade to version 4, while retaining the obsolete directory name.

◆ You can install version 4 in C:\WINNT, resulting in a dual-boot configuration. This is not an upgrade, and NT version 4 won't inherit any of the settings from the earlier version.

Starting Installation from a Supported CD-ROM

Objective
B.3

When a supported CD-ROM is directly attached to a computer, the easiest way to install Windows NT is to boot the system using the installation floppy disks. With this method, the installation program will identify and install any disk drivers that are required. You will need the following to install Windows NT Server:

◆ Three setup floppy disks matched to your A drive. These should be copies of the setup floppies, not the originals!

◆ One high-density floppy disk, matching your A drive, that can be overwritten to prepare an emergency repair disk. Label this disk "Emergency Repair Disk."

◆ The Windows NT Server CD-ROM, installed in a properly connected CD-ROM drive. Don't worry about setting up drivers. Setup will select and install SCSI and CD-ROM drivers for you if you are using supported hardware.

To begin a CD-ROM installation, do the following:

CD-ROM Installation

1. Insert the Setup Boot Disk in Drive A: and turn on or reboot the computer.

2. Insert Setup Disk 2 when prompted. Setup Disk 2 begins to load a large number of drivers.

3. When you see the message Welcome to Setup, proceed to the section "Installing Windows NT Server." You will be prompted for disk 3 later on in the installation process.

Tip   If you are installing on a computer that is already configured with Windows NT 4 or with Windows 95, you have another option for starting installation. Simply insert the Windows NT installation CD-ROM in the drive. The disk will autostart and display the Windows NT CD-ROM startup screen. Simply double-click on the Windows NT Setup icon to begin installation. No floppy disks are required.

Starting Installation from a Shared Drive or an Unsupported CD-ROM

Objective
B.3

You can install directly from a CD-ROM or from files copied to a hard drive from the installation CD-ROM without having to boot from the setup floppies. This approach is valuable in two situations:

◆ When installing from a local CD-ROM drive that is unsupported

◆ When installing from a CD-ROM drive or a hard drive that is shared on a network

In both cases, you have two options for installation. You can create the bootable floppy disks during installation or install without the floppies. Installing without floppies requires a bit more free space on the destination hard drive.

| **Caution** | This method requires Setup to copy all required files to the destination partition before they can be installed. Consequently, you must have at least 108 MB of free space in addition to the free space required for Windows NT. The installation files will be temporarily stored during setup and will be removed when setup is complete. |

Preparing to Install from a Master Server

Objective B.3

To install from a master server, you must have already built a working network. This is probably not the first setup method you will try. Network installation requires the most knowledge about Windows NT Server networks.

Copying Master Files to a Server

Before installing from a network server, you must copy master files from the CD-ROM to the source server. The files are stored in the \I386, \Mips, \Alpha, and \Ppc directories on the master CD-ROM. You need only copy the files that are required for your network servers.

The master server must have access to a CD-ROM drive, which can be directly attached to the server or a shared drive that is connected through the network. To copy the master files, do the following:

Copying Master Files

1. Create a master file directory. This procedure assumes the directory will be named \NTMASTER.

2. Use the XCOPY command or File Manager to copy the appropriate subdirectory (or subdirectories if you have more than one type of server) from the CD-ROM to the \NTMASTER directory.

3. Share the master directory (see Chapter 14, "Using Windows and DOS Clients"). Only the Administrator group needs Read permissions to this share.

Starting Installation of Windows NT from a Network Server to a DOS Computer

Objective B.3

The following procedure is performed from DOS:

Over-the-Network Installation, Network Server to a DOS Computer

1. Use FDISK to create a FAT partition in which Windows NT will be installed.

2. Format the partition with the /S option to make it bootable.

3. Using procedures described in Chapter 14, install and activate DOS client software. Refer to Chapter 20, "Creating a Network Installation Startup Disk" for instruction on using Network Client Administration tool to create a network installation startup diskette.

4. Log on to the master server using an account that can access the shared master installation directory.

5. Connect a network drive to the shared master directory.

6. Change to the installation directory; for example, enter the command `CD \NTMASTER\I386`.

7. Type `WINNT` at the command prompt to create the three setup boot disks during the installation process. To install without creating the setup boot floppy disks, enter the command `WINNT /B`.

8. When prompted, enter the logical drive letter and directory path where the master files are located. Usually this is the same directory that WINNT was started from.

9. Supply disks as requested.

10. Follow the instructions to complete Setup. After the three setup disks are created, the procedures will closely follow the Setup walkthrough earlier in this chapter. Read the following section, "Installing Windows NT Server."

Starting Installation of Windows NT from a Network Server to a Windows NT Computer

To install to a computer that is running Windows NT, do the following:

Over-the-Network Installation, Network Server to an NT Computer

1. Log on to the server that contains the Master files.

2. In File Manager, connect a drive to the shared master directory.

3. Change to the directory that contains the master files for your hardware version (I386, Mips, Alpha, or Ppc).

4. Execute the command **WINNT32** to create the three setup boot disks during the installation process. To install without creating the setup boot floppy disks, enter the command **WINNT32 /B**.

Note   You can install from a shared drive under MS-DOS or Windows NT. The example procedure uses the command **WINNT32** to start the 32-bit (Windows NT) version of the setup program. You can also enter the command **WINNT** to start the MS-DOS version.

5. When prompted, enter the logical drive letter and directory path where the master files are locatcd.

6. Supply disks as requested.

7. Follow the instructions to complete Setup. After the three setup disks are created, the procedures will closely follow the Setup walkthrough in this chapter. Read the following section, "Installing Windows NT Server."

Starting Installation of Windows NT from a Non-SCSI CD-ROM to an MS-DOS Computer

The following procedure is performed from DOS:

1. Use FDISK to create a FAT partition in which Windows NT will be installed.

2. Format the partition with the /S option to make it bootable.

3. Install the appropriate drivers for your CD-ROM drive.

4. Reboot the computer to activate the CD-ROM drivcrs.

5. Insert the Windows NT CD-ROM in the CD-ROM drive.

6. Change the default drive to the CD-ROM.

7. Change to the directory that contains the desired software version; for example, enter the command **CD \I386**.

8. Execute the command **WINNT** to create the three setup boot disks during the installation process. To install without creating the setup boot floppy disks, enter the command **WINNT /B**.

9. When prompted, enter the logical drive letter and directory path where the master files are located.

10. Follow the instructions to complete Setup. After the three setup disks are created, the procedures will closely follow the Setup walkthrough in this chapter. Read the following section, "Installing Windows NT Server."

Installing Windows NT Server

A remarkable amount of Windows NT Server setup is automatic, and your actions will, in most places, be limited to a few key decisions. You might not even need to read this blow-by-blow description, but here it is just in case.

1. Choosing Installation or Repair

The Welcome to Setup screen branches in two directions:

◆ Press Enter to continue. This is what you'll do in this section.

◆ Press R to repair the server. Later in the setup procedures, you will create an Emergency Repair Disk, which enables you to use this repair option if crucial server files are damaged and the server cannot be started. Repair procedures are described later in this chapter.

> **Note** In most steps, press Enter to take Microsoft's preferred path through the setup procedure.
>
> Throughout Setup, you have these options:
>
> ◆ Press F1 for help tailored to the step you are executing.
>
> ◆ Press F3 to exit the Setup procedure.

Objective B.3

> **Note** Prior to Windows NT Server version 4, you had the option to select between an Express or a Custom setup process. NT Server 4 now automatically selects all the required networking options and prompts you to choose optional components.

2. Selecting Disk Controller Drivers

Next, Setup must select a disk controller driver. You can do the following:

◆ Press Enter to have Setup examine your hardware to detect mass storage devices and identify required drivers. I recommend having Setup scan for devices unless you have unsupported hardware.

◆ Press S to skip detection and select a driver from a list.

If your disk controller is on the supported hardware list, it is easy to permit Setup to detect your hardware and select the driver for you. The only disadvantage is that detection takes a few minutes because Setup loads every available driver and tries it to see if your hardware responds. All of the available drivers are tried even after a match is found because you might have two or more disk controllers of different brands or models.

Choose to skip detection if either of the following is true:

◆ You know which driver(s) you need, and it would be faster to choose the driver(s) from a list.

◆ You are using unsupported hardware and need to supply drivers on a disk.

2a. Detecting Mass Storage Devices

While Setup is scanning for mass storage devices, you are prompted to insert Setup Disk 3.

Setup can detect a wide variety of SCSI adapters. If Setup identifies one or more mass storage systems, you will be presented with a list that you can accept or reject. Devices such as IDE and ESDI hard drives don't appear in the list; these drivers are installed in a later step. You have a choice of the following:

◆ Pressing Enter to accept the list and continue.

◆ Pressing S to specify additional devices. If you choose this option, you will go through the manual driver selection procedure.

2b. Selecting Drivers Manually

If you press S to specify additional devices, Setup presents a scrolling list containing a wide variety of drivers for SCSI host bus adapters. To load a driver, use the following steps:

1. Scroll through the list by pressing the up and down arrow keys.

2. If the required driver is in the list, highlight it by pressing Enter.

3. If the required driver is not in the list and you have the driver on disk, select the bottom choice, Other (Requires disk provided by a hardware manufacturer).

   You are prompted, `Please insert the disk labeled Manufacturer-supplied hardware support disk into drive A:`. Do so and press Enter to load the driver.

4. The driver you selected will be added to the mass storage devices list. You may add other drivers by pressing S.

5. When all required drivers appear in the list, press Enter to continue installation.

3. Loading More Device Drivers

Setup now test loads every driver under the sun, including IDE, ESDI, and CD-ROM. By the end of this process, Setup will know almost everything about all of your mass storage devices unless you have something really unusual.

4. Choosing Upgrade or New Installation

If Setup detects an existing copy of Windows NT on the computer, you will be given the option to upgrade. Make one of the following choices:

◆ Press Enter to upgrade to Windows NT version 4. Most old configuration options will be retained. You cannot upgrade from NT Workstation to a Domain Controller; the installation procedure will continue as a stand-alone member server.

◆ Press N to replace the existing copy of Windows NT with a new installation of version 4. The old configuration will be lost. Pressing N will also enable you to set up a dual boot by choosing a different folder for the boot files.

The following discussion assumes a new installation.

**Objective
B.7**

5. Identifying Computer Hardware

Next, Setup examines your system to determine its basic hardware configuration. The following characteristics are typical for Intel x86 servers:

```
          Computer:  Standard PC
           Display:  VGA or Compatible
          Keyboard:  XT, AT, or Enhanced Keyboard (83-102 keys)
   Keyboard Layout:  US
   Pointing Device:  Microsoft Serial Mouse
```

Setup will probably be right about all this information, but you can change any item by using the up and down arrow keys to select an item and pressing Enter. A list of options will be presented.

If you are not located in the United States, for example, you might want to select a different international standard for the keyboard layout. A considerable number of nationalized keyboard layouts can be selected from a list.

When this list is correct, select The above list matches my computer and press Enter.

6. Partitioning the Hard Drive

Next Setup shows a list of the hard drives on your server, along with the partitions on each drive. The first partition on the first drive (Drive 0) is highlighted. This is the default partition for installing Windows NT. NT's system partition will always be the active partition. You must select or create a partition to hold the boot files for NT. This partition can be primary or extended and can reside on any hard drive.

6a. Deleting Existing Partitions

You might want to delete an existing partition by highlighting the partition entry and typing D. This enables you to create new partitions if required. You will be asked to confirm your request to delete the partition.

6b. Creating a Partition

**Objective
B.8**

To create a partition, use the following steps:

1. Select any area labeled `Unpartitioned space`. When you do so, a new option, `C=Create Partition`, appears at the bottom of the screen.

2. Enter C to create a partition.

3. A new screen is presented that declares the minimum size for the new partition (1 MB) and the maximum size (the full capacity of the unpartitioned space).

   In the box labeled `Create partition of size (in MB)`, enter a size for the partition that is in the minimum-to-maximum range.

4. Press Enter.

When you return to the partition list after creating a partition, you will see an entry similar to the following:

```
C:  New (Unformatted)              1016 MB
```

6c. Selecting a System Partition

You can select either of the following as a Windows NT Server system partition:

◆ A New (Unformatted) partition.

◆ An existing partition. Windows NT can be installed over existing software in a FAT or NTFS partition provided the partition is of sufficient size. (RISC-based servers must start from a FAT partition.)

Select a partition from the partition list and press Enter.

7. Formatting the System Partition

The options you see next depend on whether you have designated a New (Unformatted) partition or a partition that was previously formatted.

Objective
B.8

7a. Formatting a New (Unformatted) Partition

If you selected a New (Unformatted) partition, you have two choices on the next screen:

◆ Format the partition using the FAT file system

◆ Format the partition using the NTFS file system

Select one of these options and press Enter.

Note   NTFS partitions are first formatted with the FAT file system. The first time the server starts after setup has been completed, the FAT partition will be converted to NTFS.

FAT partitions can also be converted to NTFS at a later time. See Chapter 17 for the procedure.

7b. Formatting an Existing Partition

If an existing, formatted partition was selected in step 7, you will see the following four options:

◆ Format the partition using the FAT file system

◆ Format the partition using the NTFS file system

◆ Convert the partition to NTFS (visible for FAT partitions only)

◆ Leave the current file system intact (no changes)

Choose the last option if files exist on the partition that you want to retain. This is, of course, the option to use if you are upgrading, re-installing Windows NT Server, or setting up a dual boot.

8. Selecting a Directory for Windows NT

After the partition is selected and formatted, files can be installed. You will be asked to specify a directory for Windows NT. The default directory is \WINNT. Files will be installed on the boot partition that you designated in step 7.

If an existing Windows NT installation is found on the boot partition, you have the option of installing in the same directory or designating a separate directory for installation.

Note If you retain the existing Windows NT installation and install in a new directory, both versions will be entered into the boot menu, enabling you to boot the old OS as well as Windows NT.

9. Examining the Hard Disks

Next, Setup gives you the option of performing an exhaustive secondary examination of your hard disks. For first-time installations in particular, this test should always be performed, even though it can take quite a while on systems equipped with large hard drives.

- ◆ Press Enter to have Setup examine your hard disks.
- ◆ Press Esc to skip disk examination.

10. Copying Files

After the hard disks have been examined, Setup copies files to the system partition.

If you are installing from floppy disks, you will be prompted to change disks as needed.

11. Restarting the Computer

When files have been copied, the computer must be restarted. Remove any floppy disk from Drive A and press Enter.

12. Accepting the Software License Agreement

After the computer restarts, you will be shown the first window using the new user interface. If you are familiar with Windows 95, you will recognize the screen format.

The first window to appear is titled Software License Agreement. Read the license agreement and press F8 to continue installation. If you press Esc, installation will be halted.

Files are now copied to the installation drive.

Note Starting from this point, you can move both forward and backward through the installation procedure. In most cases, you can choose **B**ack to return to an earlier step and make changes.

13. Continuing Installation

As the next screen explains, the rest of the installation takes place in three stages:

- ◆ Gathering information about your computer
- ◆ Installing Windows NT Networking
- ◆ Finishing Setup

Choose **N**ext to begin the first stage, gathering information about the computer.

14. Entering Identification Information

After the system restarts, a Windows dialog box appears requesting the following information:

- ◆ Na**m**e (required)
- ◆ **O**rganization (optional)

Complete these free-form text entries and choose **N**ext to continue.

15. Selecting Server Licensing

The next window determines the server licensing mode, which is covered in greater detail later in this chapter. You have two options:

- ◆ Choose Per Ser**v**er if you want to license based on concurrent connections to this server. If, for example, you want to support up to 100 concurrent connections to this server, you must purchase 100 client access licenses.
- ◆ Choose Per **S**eat if you want to license based on the number of client computers on the network.

You may want to take the time to determine the relative costs of these two methods for your network. In general, per server licensing may be the most cost-effective if you have a single server. With per server licensing, however, a client that connects to two or more servers must be equipped with a client access license for each server being accessed concurrently.

If you have two or more servers, per seat licensing may work out better. A client can use a single license to access any number of servers that are configured for per seat licensing.

After selecting a licensing mode, choose **N**ext to continue.

> **Note** You must use the Network Administration program to specify the number of licenses that have been purchased for your server or network.

16. Specifying a Computer Name

Each computer on a Windows network must be assigned a unique name. This can be the name of the primary user of the computer, a designation of the computer's function, or some other meaningful name. Computer names can be as long as 15 characters. The name can include letters, numbers, and these characters: ! # $ % ^ & ( ) _ ' { } ~ , but should not include spaces.

Enter a name in the Na**m**e box and choose Continue. Choose Continue to confirm.

17. Selecting a Server Type

Windows NT Server can be installed with one of three configurations. Specify one of the following types in the next dialog box:

- ◆ **P**rimary Domain Controller
- ◆ Bac**k**up Domain Controller
- ◆ Member Server

Choose **N**ext to continue. (The rest of this example assumes that **P**rimary Domain Controller was chosen.)

18. Specifying an Administrator Account Password

If you are installing a PDC, you must specify a password for the Administrator account, which will be given full administrative permissions for the domain that is being created. Passwords are case sensitive and can contain up to 14 alpha-numeric characters. In the next window, complete the following fields with the password to be assigned to the Administrator user account:

- ◆ **P**assword
- ◆ **C**onfirm Password

These entries must match.

The password is optional; you can get away without entering one, which is fine while you are experimenting with Windows NT Server. (Because Setup regards no password as a questionable choice, you will be asked to confirm your decision.) You should be sure to enter a password for any in-service server, however, because the Administrator account has full control over all resources on the server.

Because domains have a global account database, installing a backup domain controller does not require you to create an Administrator account. The Administrator account for the domain is used. When installing a BDC in a domain, if the BDC's computer name has not been added to the domain, you must enter the user name and password for a user account that has administrative privileges in the domain.

If you are creating a stand-alone member server (the computer is not joining a domain), you are asked to specify both a member user name and a password for the server's administrator account.

Choose **N**ext to continue.

19. Creating the Emergency Repair Disk

An Emergency Repair Disk contains information about the hardware configuration of your server and can be used to recover the server from corruption in system files that prevents the server from starting up.

When Setup asks you if you want to create an Emergency Repair Disk, you should select **Y**es, Create an Emergency Repair Disk (Recommended) and follow the prompts.

Choose N**o**, Do Not Create an Emergency Repair Disk to skip this step. An emergency repair disk can be created at a later time using the RDISK utility.

20. Selecting Components

The next window enables you to specify which optional components will be installed. Options are organized in five categories:

◆ **Accessibility Options.** Options that enable you to configure the cursor, keyboard, sound, display, and mouse. Some of these options are decorative, but some enable you to make the computer easier to use for handicapped users. You can, for example, use sticky keys to enable users who cannot hold down two keys simultaneously to type shifted characters.

◆ **Accessories.** Here are 14 optional accessories such as the Calculator and Character Map utilities familiar from Windows 3.x. Also included are new utilities such as the Internet Jumpstart Kit, which provides a World Wide Web browser. All are briefly described in the Description box.

◆ **Communications.** Here you select from the following utilities: Chat, Hyper Terminal (a modem communication program), and Phone Dialer.

◆ **Games.** Four games are available: Freecell, Minesweeper, Pinball, and Solitaire. By default, none are selected.

◆ **Windows Messaging.** Components are Internet Mail, Windows Messaging (an integrated mail and messaging application), and Microsoft Mail (a mail client).

◆ **Multimedia.** A variety of applications for playing multimedia sound and video clips. None of these should be required for a dedicated server.

It is recommended that you install Windows NT Server on a computer that will be dedicated to providing network services. Users should not be playing games, sound, or video on a dedicated server computer. Therefore, the options you will require from this window are very limited. Pick and choose very carefully.

Choose **N**ext when components have been selected.

21. Beginning Network Installation

Next, you will be shown an installation status screen. The next task, which will be highlighted, is 2) Installing Windows NT Networking. Choose **N**ext to continue.

22. Specifying the Network Connection

In the next window, you specify how the computer will connect to the network. The following choices are given:

◆ **Wired to the network.** The computer can connect to the network through a network adapter card (such as Ethernet or token ring) or via an ISDN connection.

◆ **Remote access to the network.** The computer connects to the network through a modem. If you choose this option, you will be required to install Remote Access Service (RAS). See Chapter 21, "Using the Remote Access Server," for information about RAS configuration and usage.

You can check either or both of these options. Choose **N**ext to continue.

23. Installing the Internet Information Server

The Internet Information Server (IIS) includes a variety of components that enable a Windows NT Server to provide services on TCP/IP networks. A World Wide Web, FTP, and Gopher server are included.

In the next window, select Install Microsoft Internet Information Server if you want to set up an Internet server. Choose **N**ext to continue. This chapter assumes that the IIS is not installed. See Chapter 28, "Internet Information Server," for information about IIS.

> **Caution** The Internet Information Server requires the TCP/IP protocols. If you choose to install IIS, be prepared to configure TCP/IP as described in Chapter 16. This requires some planning, so don't install the IIS without doing the necessary up front work.

24. Setting Up Network Cards

Objective B.5

A primary or backup domain controller must have a network card because it must attach to the network before its domain security role can be established. Servers do not require network cards during setup, but you will need to install one later to enable network communication.

Setup has a sophisticated capability to scan your computer, identify network cards, and determine their settings. You can take advantage of this capability in the next dialog box.

It is recommended that you choose S**t**art Search to use automatic card detection, which is described in step 24a.

Choose **S**elect from list to skip card detection and go to step 24b, or to skip card selection altogether.

> **Caution** If the network card is conflicting with another device, it may lock up the system during this phase of the installation process. If this happens you will have to change the network card's resources, reboot the server, and restart the installation process.

24a. Using Automatic Card Detection

Objective F.1

> **Caution** If the network card is conflicting with another device, it may lock up the system during this phase of the installation process. If this happens, you will have to change the network card's resources, reboot the server, and restart the installation process.

If Setup is able to identify your adapter card, the name of the adapter will be added to the Network **A**dapters box.

◆ Choose **N**ext to accept the entry and continue with the next installation step.

◆ Remove the check mark to ignore the entry.

◆ Choose **F**ind Next to find another card if more than one is installed. (If your cards all use the same drivers, you do not need to do **F**ind Next.) You can, however, activate only one card at this stage in Setup. In step 24, additional cards can be installed.

◆ Choose **S**elect from List to select another card manually.

24b. Selecting Network Adapters Manually

If you choose **S**elect from List in step 24, you can use the Select Network Adapter box to select a driver from the **N**etwork Adapter list. In addition to drivers for supported hardware, you can choose **H**ave Disk if you have a floppy disk that includes drivers for your adapter. You will be prompted to specify the drive letter and path where the driver files can be found.

After you select a network adapter, choose OK. Choose Cancel to skip manual adapter selection. Either option returns you to the network adapter setup screen where you choose **N**ext to continue.

25. Selecting Protocols

Objective B.4

Next, Setup presents a dialog box with check boxes for three protocols:

◆ **TCP/IP Protocol.** This option is checked by default. If you choose it, you must be prepared to configure the adapter as described in Chapter 16. TCP/IP is required if you elected to install the Internet Information Server.

◆ **NWLink IPX/SPX Compatible Transport.** This option is checked by default.

◆ **NetBEUI Protocol.** This option is not checked by default and is not required. Enable it only if you require NetBEUI compatibility with existing systems.

You can choose **S**elect from list to obtain additional choices:

◆ **DLC Protocol.** This option supports printing to HP printers that are connected directly to the network.

◆ **Point-to-Point Tunneling Protocol.** This option is explained later.

◆ **Streams Environment.** This option supports applications written to the AT&T application programming interface. Check this option if you are running applications requiring Streams.

◆ **Have Disk.** Choose this button if you wish to install another protocol from a disk.

Check the desired protocols and choose **N**ext to continue installation.

26. Adding Network Components

The next window lists the network components that will be installed. You cannot remove components at this time, but you can add them by choosing **S**elect from list.

27. Installing Network Components

In the next window, choose **N**ext to install the network components you have selected.

Objective B.5

28. Configuring the Network Adapter

Next, you will be shown the network adapter Network Card Setup dialog box. Here you must specify the hardware settings for your adapter card, such as the IRQ and I/O port address.

Be careful when making these settings. Incorrect settings prevent the computer from communicating with the network and can cause installation to fail. Setup is unable to verify that the settings you enter are correct.

Choose OK when the settings are correct. The driver will be installed for the network adapter.

Caution You cannot back up once the driver is installed because Setup cannot unload the driver.

29. Copying Files

All required files are now copied to the computer.

Note If TCP/IP protocols are being installed, you have the option of having the IP address and other settings established by a DHCP server. If your network already includes a DHCP server and you want to obtain settings from DHCP, respond **Y**es to the TCP/IP Setup prompt. If you answer No, you must be prepared to provide an IP address and a subnet mask.

If you selected **R**emote access to the network in step 22, RAS must be installed and configured at this time. See Chapter 21 for RAS installation procedures.

30. Review Bindings

You can now review the bindings that have been established. A *binding* is a chain of drivers that are linked to a given service. A binding can be disabled by selecting the binding and choosing **D**isable.

Choose **N**ext to continue.

31. Start the Network

Next you have two choices:

◆ Choose **N**ext to start the network and continue setup.

◆ Choose **B**ack to stop the network if it is running.

You must choose **N**ext to continue setup.

32. Configuring the Computer Name

The contents of the next window depend on the server type:

◆ If you are configuring a primary domain controller, you will see two fields: Computer Name and Domain. You must enter values in the **D**omain field. If the domain you specify does not exist, it will be created and this computer will be established as the PDC. If the domain already exists, you must specify another domain name.

◆ If you are configuring a backup domain controller, you will see four fields: **C**omputer Name, **D**omain, **A**dministrator Name, and Ad**m**inistrator Password. The administrator name and password you specify will be used to add this computer to the domain you specify, where it will be configured as a BDC. If the user name and password you enter do not have administrator privileges in the domain, the computer cannot be added.

◆ If you are configuring a stand-alone server that will be joining the domain, you will see four fields: **C**omputer Name, **D**omain, **A**dministrator Name, and Ad**m**inistrator Password. The administrator name and password you specify will be used to add this computer to the domain you specify, where it will be configured as a stand-alone server. If the user name and password you enter do not have administrator privileges in the domain, the computer cannot be added.

Choose **N**ext to continue.

33. Finishing Setup

The next window informs you that you are at step 3, Finishing Setup. Choose Finish to continue. The computer will be configured to run Windows NT.

34. Entering Date and Time Properties

The next window is titled Date/Time Properties.

Select the **D**ate & Time tab to configure the system clock.

Select the Time Zone tab to select a time zone. Choose a time zone from the list provided. Be sure to check the box **A**utomatically adjust for daylight saving changes appropriately for your locale. This check box will be deactivated for some time zone choices, such as Indiana (East).

Choose Close to accept the settings and continue.

Objective B.7

35. Configuring the Display

Setup won't permit you to configure a video display setting that is nonfunctional with your equipment. Setup attempts to detect your video card, and the Detected Display information box shows you the hardware it identifies. Choose OK to continue.

The next dialog box, Display Properties, enables you to select settings that are appropriate to your display type. To set the video display mode, use the following steps:

Configuring Display Driver

1. Confirm that the adapter Setup has identified is correct. If not, choose Display **T**ype and select a different video adapter.

2. Select the video display modes you want by setting appropriate values in the **C**olor Palette, **D**esktop Area, **F**ont Size, and **R**efresh Frequency fields. Be sure that the settings you choose are supported by your monitor. Incorrect settings can damage your monitor circuitry.

3. Choose T**e**st. Setup displays a grid that tests the display mode you have selected. After a few seconds, the grid is cleared.

4. After the test, you will be shown the prompt Did you see the test bit map properly? If the display appeared to be correct, choose Yes to confirm that it functioned properly. Then choose OK. This mode can then be selected for the display adapter.

5. Some trial and error might be required to identify the best settings for your monitor. Keep going until you find a mode that passes the test. You cannot select a mode that you have not identified as OK.

6. After selecting a video display mode, choose OK in the Display Properties dialog box.

Setup now saves the configuration for the server and proceeds through several configuration procedures.

36. Creating the Emergency Repair Disk

If you chose **Y**es to create an emergency repair disk (recommended) in step 19, you will be prompted to insert a floppy disk labeled Emergency Repair Disk. All information on this disk will be overwritten.

Insert a floppy disk in the A drive and choose OK. The Emergency Repair Disk will be created.

37. Restarting the Computer

Next, you will need to restart the computer. Remove all floppy disks and choose **R**estart Computer to continue.

The first time a new server restarts, the process may be lengthy. For one thing, if you specified that the system domain should use NTFS files, the FAT partition that was created during Setup must be converted to NTFS.

Installation is now complete.

Logging On and Off, Restarting, and Shutting Down the Server

After the server restarts, the Begin Logon box invites you to Press Ctrl+Alt+Del to log on. Give the computer a three-finger salute to bring up a Logon Information dialog box.

To log on, supply the following information:

◆ **User name.** If this is the first time a primary domain controller has been started, only the Administrator account will exist.

◆ **Password.** For new PDCs, this password was declared during Setup in step 17.

◆ **Domain.** This is the domain you want to log on to. By default, this will be the domain you declared in step 17.

The first time you log on, you will see the Welcome to Windows NT dialog box. If you don't want to see it again, remove the check mark from the box **S**how the Welcome Screen next time you start Windows NT.

To log off, press Ctrl+Alt+Del any time when you are logged on. Unlike DOS, the Ctrl+Alt+Del key sequence does not immediately reboot the system. Instead, it produces a dialog box with the following options:

◆ **Lock Workstation.** Choose this option to lock the station when logged on. You will stay logged on, but will be required to enter your user password to regain access to your session. Only the account that locked the workstation or an administrator can unlock it.

◆ **Change Password.** Choose this option to change your password.

◆ **Logoff.** Logs out of the current session and displays the Welcome banner.

◆ **Task Manager.** Displays a list of running tasks and enables you to switch to a task or end the task. This option is especially useful to cancel a task that has hung or malfunctioned.

◆ **Shut Down.** Only administrators and server operators can shut down a server. This option gives you two further options:

    ◆ **Shutdown.** After Windows NT performs a controlled shutdown, the server does not restart. Use this option if you need to turn the server off.

    ◆ **Shutdown and Restart.** Use this option if you have made changes that require a server restart to be activated.

You can also initiate a shutdown from the Start menu:

1. Choose Start.

2. Choose Sh**u**t Down to open the Shut Down Windows dialog box.

3. Select one of the following shut down options:

   ◆ **S**hut down the computer?

   ◆ **R**estart the computer?

   ◆ **C**lose all programs and log on as a different user?

4. Choose **Y**es to execute the select action. Choose **N**o to return to Windows.

Reinstalling Windows NT

You might need to reinstall Windows NT for several reasons, for example:

◆ To change a computer security role. You can't upgrade a server to a domain controller without reinstalling Windows NT, for example.

◆ To repair corrupt files.

◆ To upgrade the operating system.

◆ To move this computer to a new domain.

To reinstall and change settings, follow the original installation procedures and choose New Version installation.

To upgrade the operating system or reinstall damaged files without changing any configuration settings, choose Upgrade installation.

There are some differences from first-time setup when you are upgrading. When Setup detects an existing Windows version after step 4, press Enter to upgrade. Do not press N to begin a new installation or the existing software will be overwritten.

If you upgrade, your existing partitions are used, along with all configuration information from the preceding version.

Caution Reinstalling a primary domain controller is a particularly tricky business. See Chapter 10 before you are tempted to try it.

continues

Actually, reinstalling any Windows NT computer can cause problems. You might think that no problems will arise provided you don't change the computer's name. Unfortunately, a computer is known by more than it's name. It also has a security ID (SID) that is created when you install Windows NT. When you reinstall and replace the old installation, a new SID is created. Even though the computer name might be the same, no other computers on the network will recognize the newly installed computer because they continue to use the old SID.

Repairing Windows NT

To repair Windows NT, it is best to have an Emergency Repair Disk (see step 32) that is up to date for your system. See Chapter 17 for information on updating the Emergency Repair Disk. You may be able to repair your problem without the Emergency Repair Disk, however.

Caution Repairing Windows NT restores the system configuration to the state it was in when the Emergency Repair Disk was last updated. If you repair the Registry using an old Emergency Repair Disk, you will lose recent changes to the Registry database. It is vitally important, therefore, that you keep the Emergency Repair disk current.

To repair Windows NT:

1. Boot the server with the Setup Boot Disk.

2. Select R to Repair the system.

3. Check the areas you want Setup to examine. You have four choices:

   ◆ Inspect Registry files

   ◆ Inspect startup environment

   ◆ Verify Windows NT system files

   ◆ Inspect boot sector

4. After checking areas you want, select Continue and press Enter.

5. You are now at step 3 in the Setup sequence. Work with Setup to identify the mass storage system drivers for your server.

6. Proceed with steps 3 through 5 of the standard Setup sequence.

7. When you are asked to supply an Emergency Repair Disk, you have two choices:

    ◆ Press Enter if you have an Emergency Repair Disk.

    ◆ Press Esc if you don't have an Emergency Repair Disk. Setup will make its best effort to repair Windows NT by looking for Windows NT on your hard drives.

8. When prompted, insert the Emergency Repair Disk. Follow subsequent prompts.

9. Setup will examine your system in the areas you checked in Repair step 3.

10. You can choose to restore Registry files. When prompted, select the files to be recovered from the following:

    ◆ SYSTEM (System Configuration)

    ◆ SOFTWARE (Software Information)

    ◆ DEFAULT (Default User Profile)

    ◆ SECURITY (Security Policy) and SAM (User Accounts Database)

    Choose Continue and press Enter to restore Registry files.

Caution   Restoring the Registry from this procedure will discard any changes that were made to the system since the Emergency Repair Disk was last updated.

11. If Setup identifies a version problem with a file, you can choose:

    ◆ Press Esc to not repair the file. Use this option if you have manually installed drivers or other files since the system was set up. Otherwise, your manual changes will be backed out.

    ◆ Press Enter to repair the file. It will be restored to the version that existed when the Emergency Repair Disk was created.

    ◆ To repair all files, type A.

12. When repairs are completed, you will be prompted to remove the disk from drive A and restart the computer.

Managing Licenses

Before users can log on from the network, you must add client licenses. As you learned during installation, Windows NT Server supports two licensing modes: per-server licensing and per-seat licensing. You must purchase a client license for each computer, regardless of the operating system installed on the client. Even Microsoft's own client operating systems, such as Windows NT Workstation and Windows 95, do not include a network client license.

It is necessary to monitor client licensing to ensure that your organization is in compliance with the software license agreement. To simplify license monitoring, you can arrange to maintain a central database of all license transactions. This is accomplished by replicating license information from individual Windows NT Server computers to a computer that serves as a central repository.

> **Note**   Other server products, such as Microsoft SQL Server, require their own client licenses. Registration of licenses for other products is similar to the procedure shown here.

License Replication

Figure 7.1 illustrates how license replication works. KEYSTONE1 is designated as the central license repository, an *enterprise server* in Microsoft licensing jargon. In each domain, licensing information is replicated from Windows NT Server computers in the domain to the PDC. The license information on the domain PDCs WIDGETS1 and DOODADS1 is replicated to KEYSTONE1.

It is not essential to replicate licenses, and you can elect to replicate licenses to multiple servers rather than a single enterprise server. The enterprise license database, however, is a valuable tool to ensure that your organization is in compliance.

Configuring Per Server Licensing

Under the per-server licensing approach, you must purchase a license for each user who connects to a specific server. If a maximum of 50 users will log on to server A, then 50 client licenses must be allocated to that server. If 25 users will log on to server B, 25 licenses must be allocated to B for a total of 75 licenses.

Per-server licensing tends to be the more economical approach if each user connects to a single server, particularly if they connect infrequently.

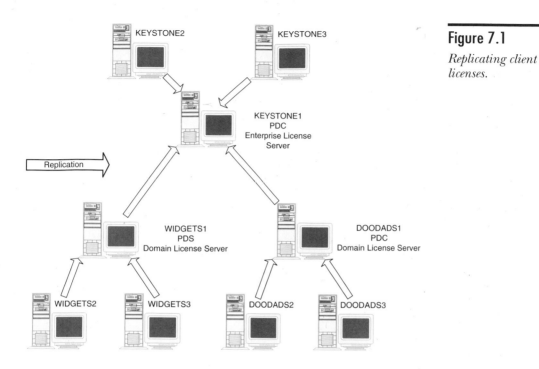

Figure 7.1

Replicating client licenses.

Note If you are uncertain which licensing approach to select, begin by selecting per-server licensing. You can make a one-time switch from per-server licensing to per-seat licensing if circumstances make per-seat licensing more desirable.

When licenses are on a per-server basis, licenses are installed "from the bottom up." You install licenses on individual servers and license replication passes the information to the central license server. You must configure per-server licensing on each Windows NT Server computer as follows:

1. Open the Licensing utility in the Control Panel. The utility is shown in figure 7.2.

Figure 7.2

The licensing utility.

2. If multiple products are listed in the **P**roduct field, select Windows NT Server.

3. Select the Per Ser**v**er radio button.

4. Choose **A**dd Licenses to open the New Client Access License dialog box (see fig. 7.3).

    4a. Enter the total number of licenses that have been purchased in the **Q**uantity field and choose OK.

    4b. Agree to the licensing agreement that is displayed by checking the box and choosing OK.

Figure 7.3

Adding client licenses.

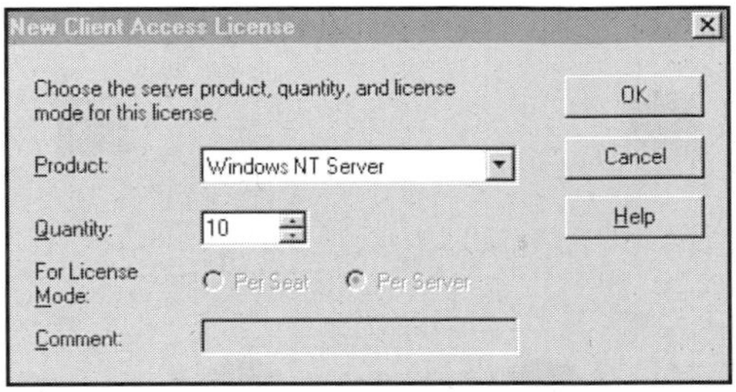

5. If per server licensing is in effect, you can remove licenses. To remove licenses, choose Re**m**ove Licenses to open the Select Certificate to Remove Licenses dialog box (see fig. 7.4).

    5a. Select a product in the Installed Certificates list.

    5b. Enter the total number of licenses that have been purchased in the Quantity field and choose OK.

    5c. Adjust the Number of Licenses to remove value to reflect the number of licenses you wish to remove from this product. (That is, if you have 15 licenses, specify 5 licenses to be removed to have 10 licenses remain.)

    5d. Choose Remove. You will be asked to verify your choice to remove the licenses.

    5e. Close the dialog box.

6. Choose **R**eplication to open the Replication Configuration dialog box (see fig. 7.5).

    6a. If this computer is an enterprise license server, select **D**omain Controller. Also select **D**omain Controller if this computer is a PDC that does not replicate license data any further.

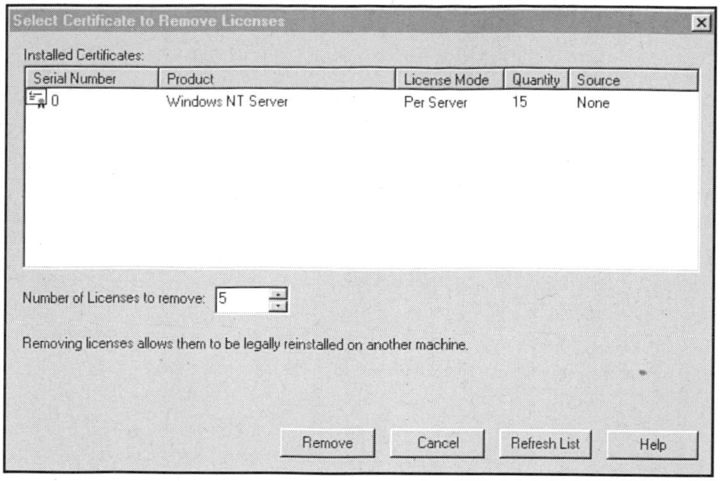

Figure 7.4

Removing client licenses.

6b. If this computer is a BDC, select **D**omain Controller to replicate license data to the PDC for the domain.

6c. If this computer is a PDC that replicates its data to an enterprise license server, select **E**nterprise Server and enter the name of the enterprise license server.

6d. It is best to manually specify when licenses will be replicated. By scheduling replication for slack hours, you can avoid adding traffic when the network is at high utilization levels. Alternatively, you can specify a replication frequency.

Specify a replication frequency in the Replication Frequency field of the dialog box.

6e. To specify when replication will start, select **S**tart At and enter a time.

6f. To specify a replication frequency, select St**a**rt Every and specify an interval. The default interval is 24 hours.

6g. Choose OK to return to the Choose License Mode dialog box.

7. Exit the License utility.

Configuring Per Seat Licensing

Under the per-seat licensing approach, you must purchase a license for each computer on the network. If you have purchased 100 licenses allocated on a per-seat basis, 100 users can access an unlimited number of servers.

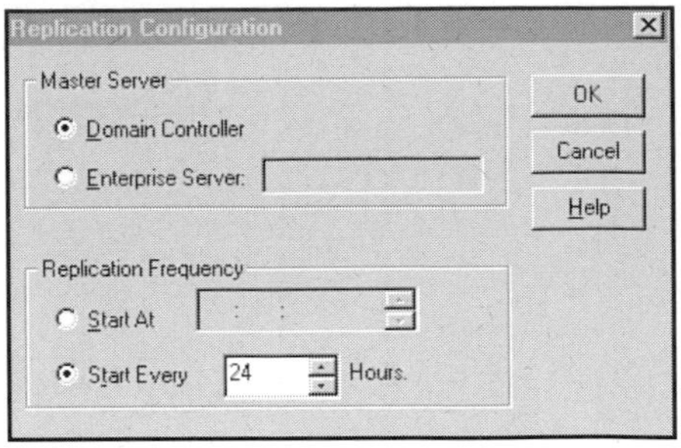

Figure 7.5

*Configuring
license
replication.*

Per-seat licensing tends to be the more economical approach if users routinely access multiple servers.

When licensing on a per-seat basis, licenses are installed "from the top down." You use License Manager to install licenses on a license server. You then configure servers to be licensed on a per-seat basis. Utilization data is replicated up to the license server where it is compared to registered licenses to monitor compliance. You must configure per-seat licensing on each Windows NT Server computer as follows:

1. Use the License Manager to add licenses to the license server that collects replicated license information for the domain or enterprise as appropriate.

2. Open the Licensing utility in the Control Panel.

3. If multiple products are listed in the **P**roduct field, select Windows NT Server.

4. In the Choose Licensing Mode dialog box, select Per **S**eat (refer to fig. 7.2). You must ensure that the number of computers on your network does not exceed the total number of licenses you have added.

5. Configure replication as described in steps 6 through 8 in the previous section.

6. Exit the License utility.

Monitoring Licensing

Licenses are monitored using the License Manager, which is installed in the Administrative Tools group of the Start menu. This utility has four tabs that enable you to monitor and manage licensing.

Purchase History

This tab displays a history of the licenses that have been purchased in your organization (see fig. 7.6).

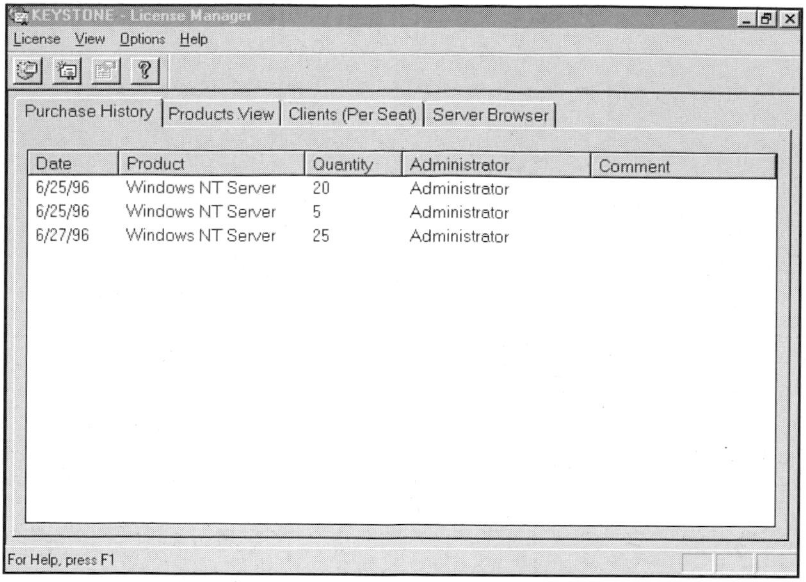

Figure 7.6

License purchase history.

Products View

This tab lists totals of licenses purchased and allocated (see fig. 7.7). This information enables you to determine whether you have purchased sufficient licenses for per-seat licensing, or whether you are running out of licenses allocated on a per-server basis.

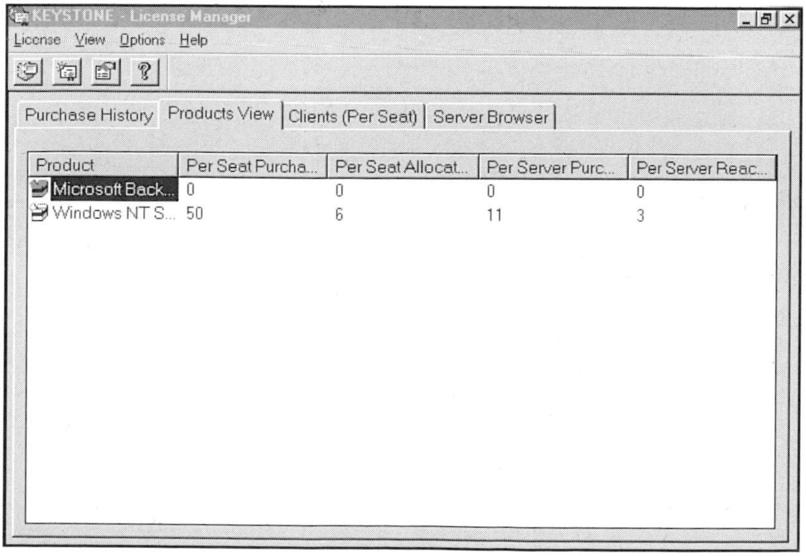

Figure 7.7

Licenses by product.

Clients (Per Seat)

This tab shows the users who are accessing servers licensed on a per-seat basis and informs you when unlicensed usage takes place (see fig. 7.8).

Server Browser

This versatile tab enables you to oversee the licenses on all Windows NT Server computers in the enterprise. As shown in figure 7.9, the tab displays a list of computers by domain. You can double-click on any server to display the licensing status for that server.

Adding Licenses

To add per-seat licenses, do the following:

1. Choose the New **L**icense command in the **L**icense menu.

2. In the New Client Access License dialog box (see fig. 7.10), select the product to be licensed in the **P**roduct field.

3. Specify a number of licenses to be added in the **Q**uantity field.

4. Agree to the licensing agreement by checking the OK box.

5. Add a comment if desired.

6. Choose OK.

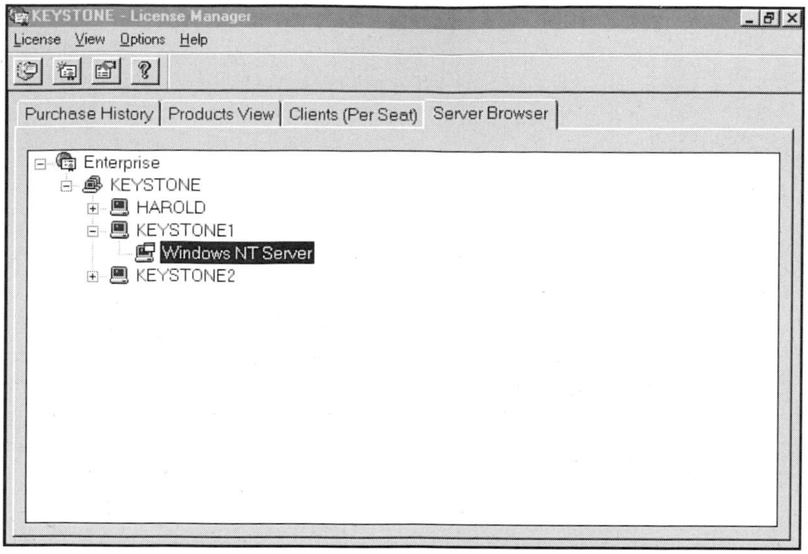

Figure 7.9

Browsing licensed servers.

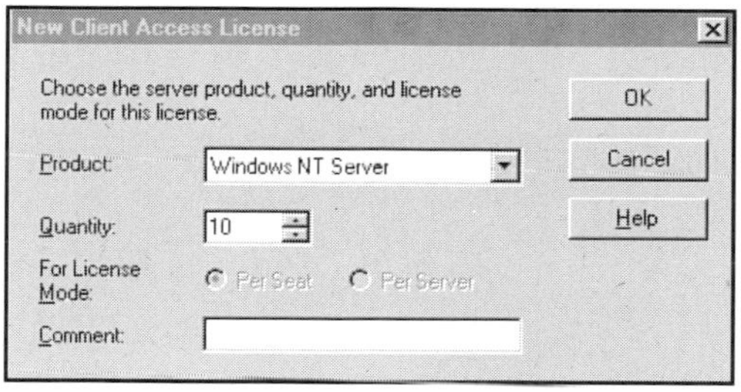

Figure 7.10

Adding licenses in License Manager.

Setting Up License Groups

When several users share computers, you should create a licensing group to ensure that license usage is properly reported. Otherwise, each user occupies one per-seat license.

To create a new license group:

1. Open the **O**ptions menu and choose **A**dvanced, **N**ew License Group. The New License Group dialog box is shown in figure 7.11.

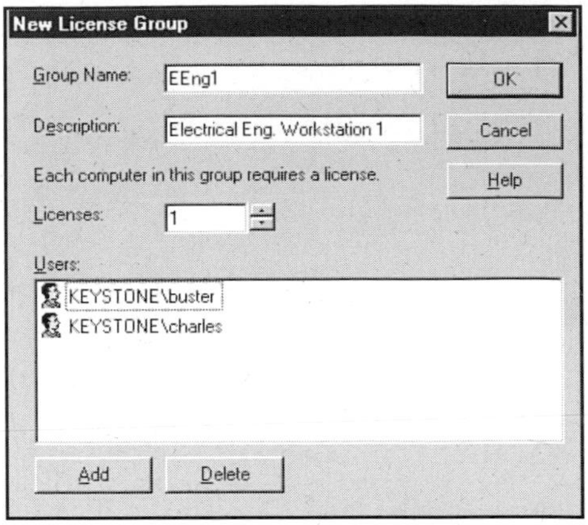

Figure 7.11

Creating a new license group in License Manager.

2. Enter a name for the license group in the **G**roup Name field.

3. Enter a description in the D**e**scription field.

4. In the **L**icenses field, specify the number of licenses to be dedicated to this group.

5. Choose **A**dd to add users to the **U**sers box.

6. An Add Users dialog box appears in which you can select from the users who have been registered on the license server (see fig. 7.12).

   6a. Select users to be added in the **U**sers list and choose **A**dd to add them to the Add **U**sers list.

   6b. Select users to be removed in the Add Us**e**rs list and choose **D**elete to remove them from the **U**sers list.

7. Choose OK to add users in the Add Us**e**rs list to the license group.

8. Choose OK to save the license group.

You can edit existing license groups by opening the **O**ptions menu and choosing **A**dvanced. In the Advanced submenu, choose **E**dit License Group.

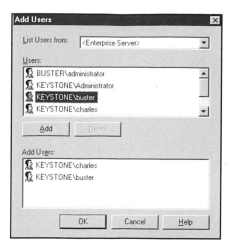

Figure 7.12

*Adding users to a
license group.*

Understanding the Windows NT Startup Process

The process of starting Windows NT has three distinct phases:

- ◆ The preboot sequence
- ◆ The boot sequence
- ◆ The Windows NT load phase

This section will examine these processes for Intel x86 and RISC computers.

The Startup Sequence on an Intel x86 Computer

Figure 7.13 illustrates the startup sequence for an Intel x86 computer. The steps in each sequence are described in this section. As you examine the sequence, take careful note of the files that are involved in each step.

Figure 7.13

Starting Windows NT on an Intel x86 Computer.

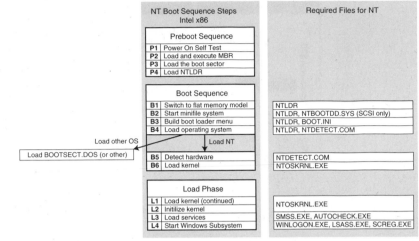

The Preboot Sequence

All events in the preboot sequence are controlled by the system firmware that is stored in the computer's ROM. The preboot sequence consists of the following four events:

P1. **Power On Self Test.** The system firmware conducts the initial hardware test.

P2. **Load and execute the Master Boot Record.** The Master Boot Record (MBR) is located in a system area of the boot hard disk. The MBR contains a program that continues the boot process.

P3. **Load the boot sector.** The MBR program examines the Partition Boot Record (PBR) to identify the active partition and loads the boot sector for the active partition.

P4. **Loading NTLDR.** NTLDR is executed from the boot sector. NTLDR is a hidden, read-only file that can start Windows NT and other operating systems. NTLDR is installed in the boot sector of the active partition when Windows NT is installed.

The Boot Sequence

The boot sequence begins when NTLDR begins to load the Windows NT operating system. Six events take place during the boot sequence:

B1. **Switching to a flat memory model.** NTLDR switches the microprocessor from 16-bit to 32-bit operation using a flat memory model. This switch enables Windows NT to access 4 GB of memory.

B2. **Starting the minifile system.** NTLDR loads the appropriate minifile system that enables it to load files from the file system (FAT or NTFS) in the boot partition. If the computer uses a SCSI disk subsystem with the BIOS disabled, NTLDR loads NTBOOTDD.SYS to enable it to access the hard disks.

B3. **Build the boot loader menu.** Even if Windows NT is the only operating system, NTLDR presents a menu that offers a choice between starting Windows NT in custom or VGA mode. (Starting in VGA mode enables you to start the operating system in a base video mode to correct display problems.) The menu is defined by entries in the BOOT.INI file. If other operating systems are available in a multi-boot configuration, the alternatives are defined in BOOT.INI. NTLDR uses the information in BOOT.INI to construct a boot loader menu.

B4. **Loading the operating system.** After the user selects an operating system from the boot loader menu, NTLDR loads the operating system.

If Windows NT was selected, NTLDR starts NTDETECT.COM and the boot process continues.

If another operating system was selected, NTLDR passes control to the appropriate startup files and the Windows NT boot process terminates. If the operating system is MS-DOS or Windows 95, NTLDR runs BOOTSECT.DOS.

B5. **Detecting hardware.** NTDETECT.COM examines the computer and determines its hardware configuration. This information is returned to NTDLDR.

B6. **Loading the kernel.** NTLDR runs NTOSKRNL.EXE, the operating system kernel, and passes it the hardware information received from NTDETECT.COM. (The *kernel* is the innermost component of Windows NT that directly manages the processors.) NTOSKRNL.EXE proceeds to supervise the load phase.

Note The hardware configuration information retrieved by NTDETECT.COM is stored in the Registry in the HKEY_LOCAL_MACHINE_HARDWARE hive. See Chapter 19, "Managing the Server," for information about the Registry.

The Load Phase

The preboot and boot phases are hardware dependent and differ between Intel x86 and RISC platforms. After control is passed to NTOSKRNL.EXE, however, the load process is identical on both platforms. The load phase has four steps:

L1. **Loading the kernel.** The kernel load phase begins when NTOSKRNL.EXE is loaded. Two distinct events occur in this phase:

◆ The Hardware Abstraction Layer (HAL) is loaded.

◆ The Registry System hive (a portion of the Registry described in Chapter 19) is scanned to identify drivers and services to be started.

This step of the load phase takes place after the screen clears and a series of (....) at the top of the screen indicates the process of loading the kernel.

Note The order in which drivers and services are loaded is determined by the LIST value entry under the following Registry subkey:

HKEY_LOCAL_MACHINE\SYSTEM\CurrentControlSet\Control\ServiceGroupOrder

See Chapter 19 for a description of the Registry.

L2. **Initializing the kernel.** The kernel initialization phase initializes the kernel and drivers after they have been loaded. The System hive is examined to identify high-level drivers that should be loaded after the kernel is initialized.

After drivers are initialized, the Registry's CurrentControlSet is saved, and a Clone control set is created. Information obtained from NTDETECT.COM (or OSLOADER on RISC computers) is used to update the hardware list in the Registry.

During kernel initialization, four different ErrorControl levels may be detected. Here are the ErrorControl levels and the actions taken:

◆ **0x0.** This code reports an Ignore error, which the boot sequence ignores. No error message is displayed.

◆ **0x1.** This code reports a Normal error, which the boot sequence ignores. The error generates an error message, however.

◆ **0x2.** This code reports a Severe error. If the system is not being booted with the LastKnownGood configuration, the LastKnownGood configuration is used. If the system is being booted with the LastKnownGood configuration, the error is ignored.

◆ **0x3.** This code reports a Critical error. The boot sequence aborts and restarts with the LastKnownGood configuration. If the LastKnownGood configuration is being used when the error is generated, the boot sequence fails and an error message is generated.

L3. **Loading the services.** During the service load phase, services are loaded by SMSS.EXE, the Session Manager. Events in this phase occur in the following sequence:

◆ The Session Manager runs programs listed in the Registry under the BootExecute value entry on the following Registry path:

> HKEY_LOCAL_MACHINE\SYSTEM\CurrentControlSet\Control\ SessionManager

The default value for the BootExecute value entry is `autocheck autochk *`, which executes AUTOCHK.EXE. During the boot sequence, AUTOCHK.EXE performs the same functions as CHKDSK on all volumes and reports information about each volume to the screen.

If the value for the BootExecute value entry is changed to `autocheck autochk /p *`, AUTOCHK.EXE performs the same operations as CHKDSK /F, which detects and corrects errors.

Additional programs can be added to the BootExecute value. Place each command on a separate line in the Multi-String Editor window of the Registry Editor.

◆ Session Manager configures the pagefiles defined under this Registry subkey:

> HKEY_LOCAL_MACHINE\SYSTEM\CurrentControlSet\Control\ SessionManager\MemoryManagement

◆ The CurrentControlSet and the Clone control set are written to the Registry.

◆ Session Manager loads the required subsystems that are defined in the Registry value entry under the following Registry path:

> HKEY_LOCAL_MACHINE\SYSTEM\CurrentControlSet\Control\ SessionManager\SubSystems

By default, only Win32 is defined as a required subsystem.

L4. **Starting the Windows subsystem.** Two events take place during this phase:

◆ The Win32 subsystem opens WINLOGON.EXE, which in turn opens LSASS.EXE, the Local Security Authority. LSASS.EXE displays the logon dialog box.

◆ SCREG.EXE, the Service Controller, is executed. SCREG.EXE examines the Registry to identify services that are configured to be loaded automatically. These services are loaded in order of their dependencies, as defined in the DependOnGroup and DependOnService value entries in the service subkeys. The subkey for the Workstation service, for example, is as follows:

HKEY_LOCAL_MACHINE\SYSTEM\CurrentControlSet\Services\
LanmanWorkstation

> **Note**   The boot sequence is not considered good until a user has successfully logged on to the system. Following a successful logon, the Clone control set is copied to the LastKnownGood control set.

The Boot Sequence on a RISC Computer

Figure 7.14 illustrates the startup sequence for a RISC computer. The steps in each sequence are described in this section.

Figure 7.14

Starting Windows NT on a RISC Computer.

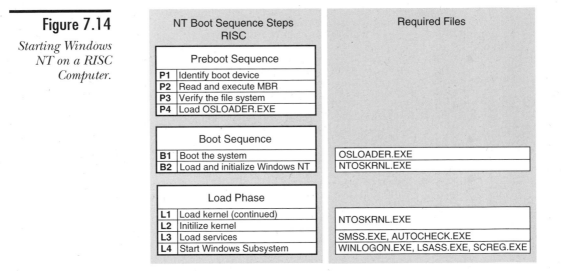

NT Boot Sequence Steps RISC		Required Files
Preboot Sequence		
P1	Identify boot device	
P2	Read and execute MBR	
P3	Verify the file system	
P4	Load OSLOADER.EXE	
Boot Sequence		
B1	Boot the system	OSLOADER.EXE
B2	Load and initialize Windows NT	NTOSKRNL.EXE
Load Phase		
L1	Load kernel (continued)	NTOSKRNL.EXE
L2	Initilize kernel	
L3	Load services	SMSS.EXE, AUTOCHECK.EXE
L4	Start Windows Subsystem	WINLOGON.EXE, LSASS.EXE, SCREG.EXE

The Preboot Sequence

The preboot sequence consists of the following four events:

P1. **Identifying the boot device.** The computer's firmware tests the system hardware and identifies the boot device.

P2. **Read the Master Boot Record (MBR).** The MBR on the boot device is loaded into memory and executed to determine whether a bootable partition is available.

P3. **Verify the file system.** The firmware reads the first sector of the bootable partition into memory. The BIOS Parameter Block (BPB) is examined to identify the file system and determine if it is supported.

P4. **Loading OSLOADER.EXE.** If the file system is supported, system firmware seeks the file OSLOADER.EXE, which is executed to continue the boot process.

The Boot Sequence

The boot sequence begins when OSLOADER.EXE begins to load the Windows NT operating system. Two events take place during the boot sequence:

B1. **Booting the system.** OSLOADER.EXE supervises the boot sequence and executes NTOSKRNL.EXE.

B2. **Loading and initializing Windows NT.** NTOSKRNL.EXE initiates the Load Phase.

The Load Phase

NTOSKRNL.EXE supervises the Load Phase on Intel x86 and RISC platforms. The steps for the Load Phase are identical on all Windows platforms.

Customizing the Boot Process

The Windows NT boot process is controlled by entries in the following places:

◆ The BOOT.INI file, used on Intel x86 platforms

◆ The Registry, used on all Windows NT platforms

This section will show you how to modify these resources to customize the boot sequence.

The BOOT.INI File

BOOT.INI is a text file that is stored in the root directory of drive C. BOOT.INI is created by the Setup program and is assigned the Read Only and System attributes.

To modify the BOOT.INI file, remove the Read Only and System attributes. The file can then be modified with any text editor, such as Notepad.

Here is a typical BOOT.INI file:

```
[boot loader]
timeout=30
default=multi(0)disk(0)rdisk(0)partition(2)\WINNT
```

```
[operating systems]
multi(0)disk(0)rdisk(0)partition(2)\WINNT="Windows NT Server Version 4.0"
multi(0)disk(0)rdisk(0)partition(2)\WINNT="Windows NT Server Version 4.0
➡[VGA mode]" /basevideo /sos
```

Before the BOOT.INI file can be examined in detail, you need to examine the ARC names that are used to identify partitions on hard drives in the BOOT.INI file and how the ARC names are used to identify the startup directories for operating systems.

ARC Naming Conventions

Partitions on Intel x86 Windows NT computers are identified in the BOOT.INI file by Advanced RISC Computer (ARC) naming conventions, which define the hard disk and partition on which the operating system resides. An example of an ARC name is `multi(0)disk(0)rdisk(0)partition(2)`. Before examining the details of the BOOT.INI file, you need to take a look at how devices are identified using ARC names.

ARC Name Syntax

When the BIOS is not enabled for a SCSI adapter, devices attached to the SCSI bus are identified by ARC names with the following format:

```
scsi (a) disk (b) rdisk (c) partition (d)
```

All other devices, including devices attached to SCSI adapters whose BIOS is enabled, are defined by the following format:

```
multi (a) disk (b) rdisk (c) partition (d)
```

> **Note**
>
> On an Intel x86 system, a SCSI BIOS translates the SCSI disk storage so that it looks like the conventional hard disk storage (ESDI, IDE, and so on) that is supported by the computer's own BIOS. In most cases, the SCSI BIOS is enabled on Intel x86 computers. Because RISC computers are more comfortable with SCSI devices, a SCSI BIOS is not required.
>
> When the MBIOS is disabled for a SCSI adapter, the scsi keyword is used in the ARC names for devices serviced by the adapter. NTLDR cannot use the SCSI adapter's BIOS to access attached devices; NTLDR loads NTBOOTDD.SYS to access the devices.
>
> Because the BIOS is enabled for most SCSI adapters, most ARC names in BOOT.INI files will use the multi keyword. For multi entries, rather than loading a device driver, NTLDR uses the BIOS on the SCSI adapter to access the hard disks supported by the adapter. If no scsi entries appear in the BOOT.INI file, NTBOOTDD.SYS is not required and is not loaded.

The keywords and parameters in an ARC name are as follows:

◆ `scsi/multi` (*a*) identifies the hardware adapter, where *a* is the ordinal number of the adapter. The first adapter is assigned the ordinal number 0, the second adapter is assigned the ordinal number 1, and so on.

◆ `disk` (*b*) identifies the device's address on the SCSI bus. When the `multi` keyword is used, *b* will always be 0.

◆ `rdisk` (*c*) identifies the ordinal number of the disk when the `multi` keyword is used. For the first disk, *c* will be 0. When the `scsi` keyword is used, *c* will always be 0.

◆ `partition` (*d*) identifies the partition on the drive that is specified by the foregoing parameters. The value of *d* will be 1 for the first partition on the hard disk, 2 for the second partition, and so on.

ARC Name Examples

Consider the first SCSI hard disk (the one with the lowest SCSI address, typically address 0), attached to the first SCSI adapter on a system, whose BIOS is enabled. If this disk has three partitions, the partitions would have the following ARC names:

```
multi(0)disk(0)rdisk(0)partition(1)
multi(0)disk(0)rdisk(0)partition(2)
multi(0)disk(0)rdisk(0)partition(3)
```

Next, consider a hard disk with SCSI address 2, attached to the second SCSI adapter on a system, whose BIOS is disabled. If this disk has three partitions, the partitions would have the following ARC names:

```
scsi(1)disk(2)rdisk(0)partition(1)
scsi(1)disk(2)rdisk(0)partition(2)
scsi(1)disk(2)rdisk(0)partition(3)
```

Finally, consider a Slave IDE drive (the second drive on an IDE controller) that is attached to the first IDE controller in a computer. If this drive is configured with three partitions, the partitions would have the following ARC names:

```
multi(0)disk(0)rdisk(1)partition(1)
multi(0)disk(0)rdisk(1)partition(2)
multi(0)disk(0)rdisk(1)partition(3)
```

Specifying Operating System Startup Directories in BOOT.INI

ARC names are used with directory paths to specify system startup directories. The directory \WINNT on the first partition of the first (Master) IDE drive on the first IDE controller would be identified as follows:

```
multi(0)disk(0)rdisk(0)partition(1)\WINNT35
```

In the case of MS-DOS, the startup partition is identified using a conventional drive letter. Within the BOOT.INI file, the DOS boot directory is identified by the path C:\.

Structure of the BOOT.INI File

The BOOT.INI file consists of two sections: [boot loader] and [operating systems]. This section examines how these sections are organized.

The [boot loader] Section

This section establishes the default operating system and determines whether the default operating system will be loaded if the user does not select an operating system after a timeout interval. The [boot loader] section accepts two optional parameters:

◆ **timeout=*n*** This parameter establishes a timeout interval of *n* seconds. If the user does not select an operating system within the timeout interval, the operating system specified by the default parameter will be loaded. If the timeout parameter is omitted, the system will wait indefinitely for the user to select an operating system. If the parameter is entered as timeout=0, the default operating system will be selected immediately without user action.

◆ **default=*partition**directory*** This parameter specifies the *partition* and *directory* of the default operating system that will be loaded when the timeout interval expires. If the default parameter is omitted, the first entry in the [operating systems] section will be taken as the default.

> **Note** The [boot loader] parameters can also be modified using the Startup/Shutdown tab of the System utility in the Control Panel as described in Chapter 19. Entries in the [operating systems] section may be modified only by directly editing the BOOT.INI file.

The [operating systems] Section

Each entry in the [operating systems] section specifies a directory from which an operating system can be started. Entries in the [operating systems] section accept the following optional switches:

◆ **/basevideo** This switch compels the system to be configured to use standard VGA video with 640×480 resolution. Setup always adds an option to the BOOT.INI file that includes the /basevideo switch. This option can be used to boot the system if video has been misconfigured for the adapter.

◆ **/sos** This option causes the boot loader to display the names of drivers being loaded as the system boots. If this option is omitted, NTLDR.EXE displays progress dots (....) as the boot process progresses but does not display file names.

◆ **/noserialmice=[COM*n*¦COM*x*,*y*,*z*]** This switch disables checking for pointing devices on the specified serial ports. /noserialmice=COM1 disables checking on COM1. /noserialmice=COM2,3,4 disables checking on COM2, COM3, and COM4. If the COM parameter is omitted, mouse checking is disabled on all ports.

Use this switch if NTDETECT tends to incorrectly identify a serial device as a mouse. Unless the port is excluded, the mouse driver will be bound to the wrong port and the device on the serial port will be unusable.

◆ **/crashdebug** Include this switch to enable the Automatic Recovery and Restart capability.

◆ **/nodebug** Include this switch to suppress monitoring of debugging information. Debugging information is useful to developers but slows system performance under normal circumstances.

◆ **maxmem:*n*** Use this switch to specify a maximum amount of RAM (*n* KB) to be used by Windows NT. This switch can be used to reduce the memory allocation for some hardware platforms and is useful if bad memory chips are suspected to be causing problems.

◆ **scsiordinal:*n*** If a system is equipped with two identical SCSI adapters, use this switch to distinguish the adapters. For the second adapter, the parameter *n* should be 1.

The Registry's Role in the Boot Process

Many entries in the Registry are used to configure Windows NT when the operating system is loaded. Reference was made to several Registry keys in the section "The Load Phase." First, you will take a look at some specific Registry keys. After that, you will examine use of the LastKnownGood Configuration.

Registry Keys Related to Loading Windows NT

Figure 7.15 shows the Registry Editor, focusing on the HKEY_LOCAL_MACHINE subtree. Several of the subkeys deserve special mention with regard to the Windows NT loading process.

◆ **HKEY_LOCAL_MACHINE\SYSTEM\CLONE.** This subkey is the temporary repository for Registry values that are collected while Windows NT is loading. Following initialization and a successful logon, values in the CLONE subkey are copied to a control subset, such as ControlSet001. This control subset is identified as the LastKnownGood configuration by the Select subkey. (Values in this subkey are mirrored in the HKEY_LOCAL_MACHINE\CLONE\CLONE subkey, a precaution that enhances Registry fault-tolerance.)

◆ **HKEY_LOCAL_MACHINE\SYSTEM\ControlSet00x.** These subkeys define control set configurations. Value entries in the Select subkey define the function of each of the control sets. As many as four control sets may be defined by the system, but it is most common to see two control sets in the Registry.

◆ **HKEY_LOCAL_MACHINE\SYSTEM\CurrentControlSet.** This subkey stores the Registry entries that define the current (running) system configuration. After system startup, the CurrentControlSet is identical to the LastKnownGood configuration. System configuration changes are reflected in the CurrentControlSet, but the LastKnownGood configuration retains the settings last used to successfully start the system.

◆ **HKEY_LOCAL_MACHINE\SYSTEM\Select.** This subkey stores value entries that define the functions of the various control sets. Consult figure 7.15 for examples of the value entries for this subkey. Each value entry includes a hex value that points to a control set. The value 0x1, for example, maps to ControlSet001. Four values appear in the Select subkey.

   ◆ **Current.** Points to the control set that was actually used to start the system.

   ◆ **Default.** Points to the control set that will be used to start the system the next time the computer is booted.

   ◆ **LastKnownGood.** Points to the control set that is a clean copy of the last control set that was successfully used to start the system.

   ◆ **Failed.** Identifies the control set that was replaced when the LastKnownGood control set was used. This key can be used to identify a bad control set so that it can be corrected.

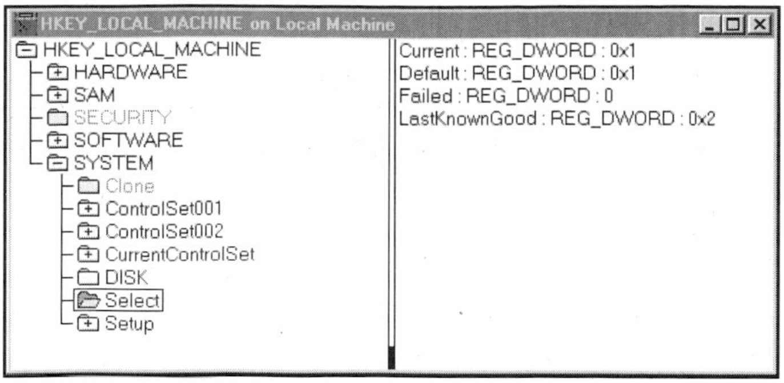

Figure 7.15

The Registry Editor focusing on the HKEY_ LOCAL_ MACHINE subtree.

Using the LastKnownGood Configuration

When Windows NT is booted, the user always has the option of invoking the LastKnownGood configuration, a copy of the control set that was used when Windows NT was last started successfully. (A successful boot is not achieved until a user logs on to the system. At that time, the LastKnownGood configuration is created.)

Objective F.1

The system will attempt to load the LastKnownGood configuration under two circumstances:

Objective F.2

◆ If the system must recover from a severe or critical error encountered when loading a device driver.

◆ If the user requests that the LastKnownGood configuration be used during startup. During system startup, NTLDR presents the option Press spacebar NOW to invoke the Hardware Profile/Last Known Good menu. If the user does not invoke the LastKnownGood configuration, the system uses the Default control set.

Objective F.3

Use the LastKnownGood configuration to recover from severe system startup problems. For example:

◆ You have installed a new driver and restarted the system to load the driver, but the system will not successfully boot. The LastKnownGood configuration will not invoke the new driver and can start successfully.

◆ You have introduced errors when editing the Registry. Use the LastKnownGood configuration to back out the changes. Of course, the LastKnownGood configuration can correct only those entries that were made to the CurrentControlSet and cannot recover from errors made in other areas of the Registry.

◆ You want to back out ALL configuration changes made during the previous session.

Testing Your Knowledge

1. What type of file system must be used in conjunction with a RISC computer's boot partition?

    A. HPFS

    B. NTFS

    C. HPFA386

    D. FAT

2. What type of file system must be used to support the dual boot feature included with Windows NT?

    A. NTFS

    B. FAT

    C. HPFS

    D. HPFS386

3. Which protocol suite included with Windows NT is typically best suited for small, simple LAN environments?

    A. NetBEUI

    B. TCP/IP

    C. NWLink

    D. DLC

4. To set up a backup domain controller, you must have which of the following?

    A. A working network that enables the BDC to communicate with its intended PDC.

    B. A working domain with an operating PDC. You can't create a BDC without accessing a domain that is run by an active primary domain controller.

    C. An established one-way trust relationship with the PDC's domain.

    D. An administrative user name and password for the domain.

5. Which methods listed can be utilized to install Windows NT Server 4?

    A. Floppy diskette installation

    B. Supported CD-ROM

    C. Over-the-network

    D. Unsupported CD-ROM

6. What is the default installation directory for Windows NT Server 4?

    A. \WINDOWS

    B. \WINNT35

    C. \WINNT

    D. \WINNT4.0

7. When may it be a better choice to choose the Per Seat licensing option?

    A. If you have two or more NT servers.

    B. If you have a single server.

    C. If you have a heterogeneous network environment.

    D. Strictly for cost effectiveness.

8. If you choose not to create an Emergency Repair Disk, what tool can be used after the installation process to create one?

    A. ERD

    B. Disk Administration tool

    C. FDISK

    D. RDISK

9. Which protocol suites are selected by default during the Windows NT server 4 installation process?

    A. TCP/IP

    B. NWLink IPX/SPX

    C. DLC

    D. NetBEUI

10. What does the Lock Workstation option provide you from the Ctrl+Alt+Del logon dialog box?

    A. Locks out all attached Windows NT Workstations attached to the NT Server you are administrating.

    B. Locks the station you are logged onto.

    C. Locks out all attached Windows NT Workstations attached to the PDC and BDCs.

    D. Locks out all attached workstations attached to the NT Server you are administrating.

11. When may it be necessary to reinstall Windows NT Server?

    A. To change a computer security role.

    B. To repair corrupt files.

    C. To upgrade the operating system.

    D. To move the computer to a new domain.

12. When running Windows NT setup, choose the option to perform a repair.

    A. R

    B. Verify

    C. Hot Fix

    D. ERD

13. The areas available to check during a repair session are:

    A. Verify option components.

    B. Inspect Registry files.

    C. Inspect startup environment.

    D. Verify Windows NT System files.

    E. Inspect boot sector.

14. The Windows NT Server tool used to monitor licenses is the _____?

15. When several users share computers, you should create a _____ to ensure that license usage is properly reported. Otherwise, each user occupies one per seat license.

16. During the preboot sequence, which hidden, read-only NT-specific file launches the boot sequence?

    A. BOOT.INI

    B. NTDETECT

    C. NTOSKRNL

    D. NTLDR

17. On an Intel x86 platform, which file can be modified to customize the boot process such as timeout, system startup directories, and crashdebug?

    A. BOOT.INI

    B. NTDETECT

    C. NTOSKRNL

    D. NTLDR

18. Which Registry subkey specifies a control set which was used to start the currently running system?

    A. HKEY_LOCAL_MACHINE\SYSTEM\Select

    B. HKEY_LOCAL_MACHINE\SYSTEM\ControlSet 00x

    C. HKEY_LOCAL_MACHINE\SYSTEM\CurrentControlSet

    D. HKEY_LOCAL_MACHINE\SYSTEM\CLONE

Review Answers

1. D
2. B
3. A
4. A, B, D
5. B, C, D
6. C
7. A
8. D
9. A, B
10. B
11. A, B, C, D
12. A
13. B, C, D, E
14. License Manager
15. licensing group
16. D
17. A
18. C

CHAPTER 8

Managing the Network Configuration

In Chapter 2, "Introducing Windows NT Server," you learned that Windows NT supports four sets of protocols—NetBEUI, NWLink, TCP/IP, and DLC—and will support them simultaneously if required. Figure 2.1 illustrates the Windows NT protocol model, so please take a moment to review that figure.

The figure shows you how the pieces fit together, but it can give the wrong impression. Simply because you can run four sets of protocols on a Windows NT computer doesn't mean that you should. There are two good reasons why you should load the least possible number of protocols.

The first reason is that anything you load on the computer uses memory. If you load a protocol stack you don't need, you are wasting computer resources; however, memory is getting pretty cheap. Is there another reason?

The other reason is that multiple protocol stacks mean that incoming messages are subjected to additional processing. All network communications include a timeout mechanism that calls off attempts to contact another computer if too much time elapses. If the destination computer is simultaneously processing packets through NetBEUI, NWLink, and TCP/IP, the likelihood increases that packets will not be responded to before they time out.

This chapter has two goals:

◆ To assist you in deciding which protocol stack or stacks you will run on your network.

◆ To show you how to install and configure protocols.

Because NetBEUI and NWLink are very easy to configure, they will be covered in this chapter. TCP/IP configuration is more involved, however, and gets its own chapter; see Chapter 16, "Using TCP/IP," for the details.

Objective A.2 | Guidelines for Selecting Protocols

Your goal, if possible, is to select a single protocol for your network. Let's reexamine the choices to see when each is most appropriate.

NetBEUI is the protocol of choice in one situation: when the network is small and does not include routers. NetBEUI is an efficient protocol that works quite well under those limited circumstances. Practically no management is required beyond installing the protocol on the computer. NetBEUI does not do anything that cannot be accomplished with NWLink or TCP/IP, and there appears to be no reason why you would need to load NWLink if one of the other protocol stacks is configured. In summary, NetBEUI is the protocol of choice if:

◆ Your network is small (and will remain so) and routing is not required.

◆ You don't require connectivity to NetWare servers.

◆ You don't require connectivity to the Internet or support of Internet services.

NWLink (IPX/SPX) is also extremely easy to configure. Although it is somewhat more complex than NetBEUI, that complexity gives it the capability of supporting routed networks. Even on larger networks, NWLink is easy to manage and requires little configuration. NWLink is required only in one situation: if you are supporting connectivity to NetWare servers using the NetWare Gateway the NetWare client. Otherwise, if you are running TCP/IP, you can dispense with NWLink. Choose NWlink when:

◆ Your network is large, or will grow to be large, and routing is required.

◆ You require connectivity to NetWare servers.

◆ You do not need to support Internet services.

◆ You don't want to undertake the planning and management required for TCP/IP.

TCP/IP is probably the preferred protocol on Microsoft networks, and it is clear that Microsoft is intent on improving TCP/IP support with each new release of Windows NT. TCP/IP supports networks of any size and has excellent routing support. More important, TCP/IP is required if you want to support the many tools that are emerging for the Internet and for intranets. Everything on the Internet is TCP/IP, from the World Wide Web to FTP. If you want your network to support Internet technologies, you must have TCP/IP. Your protocol of choice is TCP/IP when:

◆ Your network is large or will grow to be large, and routing is required.

◆ You require connectivity to the Internet or support for TCP/IP services.

◆ Your staff has the time and expertise to manage TCP/IP.

About the only network that requires two protocols is one that includes connectivity to NetWare as well as support for TCP/IP services.

 Tip   If in doubt when selecting protocols, choose TCP/IP. Some extra work is involved, but TCP/IP does everything well.

Characteristics of IPX/SPX Networks

NWLink consists of two protocols:

◆ **Internetwork Packet Exchange (IPX).** The protocol in the NetWare protocol suite that occupies the OSI network layer, and the workhorse protocol of the IPX/SPX suite.

◆ **Sequenced Packet Exchange (SPX).** An optional protocol that is used when robust communications are required, occupying the OSI transport layer.

When setting up an IPX network, there are only a few configuration considerations. To see what they are, examine the internetwork in figure 8.1. This internetwork consists of two network segments. As explained in Chapter 1, "Understanding

Networks," one issue on internetworks is how frames are to be routed to the correct destination network. Most of the configuration required for IPX has to do with network routing.

Figure 8.1

Example of an IPX internetwork.

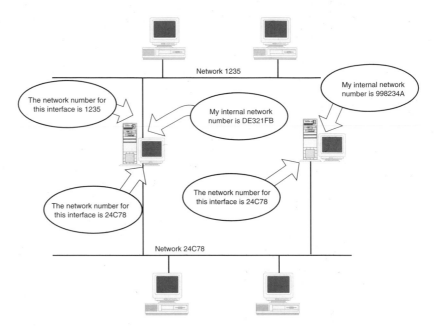

When a network interface card on a server is configured to connect to an IPX network, the configuration for the interface must declare a *network number* that is associated with the network segment. This network number can consist of up to eight hexadecimal digits. The network number that is declared for the interface becomes the network number for that network segment. Clients connected to that network learn the network number and include it in the destination fields of frames they transmit.

Two things should be noted about the network numbers in figure 8.1:

◆ Each network segment must be assigned its own network number, which must be unique throughout the IPX internetwork.

◆ All computers attached to the same network must agree to use the same network number; otherwise errors are generated.

> **Note** Actually, things are a bit more complicated because a given network can support more than one *frame type*. Clients on a given network might use IEEE 802.3 Ethernet frames for normal communication with the NetWare server. When they need to communicate with a TCP/IP computer, however, they must use Ethernet II frames.
>
> When two or more frame types are operating on a given network segment, a different network number is declared for each frame type. The network number is used to deliver frames not only to the correct network, but to the correct protocol stack on the destination computer.

Besides the network number assigned to its interface, each NetWare server is also configured with an *internal network number*. Also an eight-digit hex number, the internal network number is used to deliver data to the correct process within the NetWare server. The internal network number must also be unique, and cannot conflict with any other network numbers or internal network numbers on the internetwork.

Declaration of network numbers is the only essential task when setting up an IPX network. With Windows NT, you have the choice of specifying the network numbers to be used. In most cases, however, you can configure Windows NT to discover the network numbers that are active on the attached networks and configure itself appropriately.

Using the Network Utility

Figure 8.2 shows the Network utility, which is used to configure network adapters, protocols, and network characteristics in Windows NT. It can also be accessed using the Network utility in the Control Panel.

To start the Network utility:

1. Double-click the My Computer icon on the desktop.
2. Double-click the Control Panel icon in the My Computer window.
3. Double-click the Network icon in the Control Panel window.

The Network utility has five tabs, which access different network configuration functions.

Figure 8.2

The Identification tab in the Network utility.

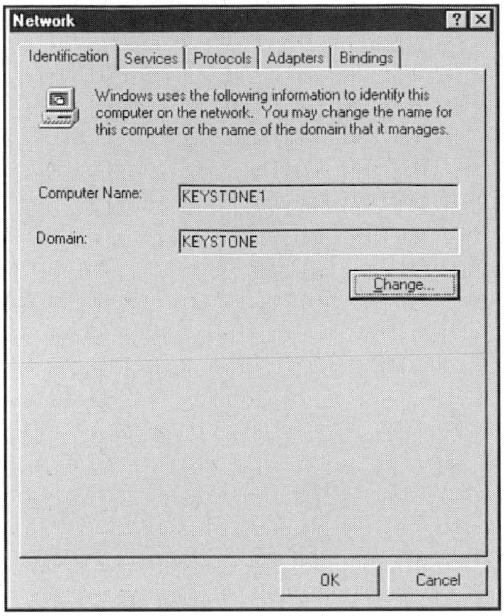

Changing the Computer Name and Domain Name

The Identification tab shows the computer's current name and domain. It does not show the computer's role in the domain. If you choose **C**hange, the dialog box shown in figure 8.3 appears. In this box, you can change the computer's name and domain.

Figure 8.3

Changing a computer's name and domain.

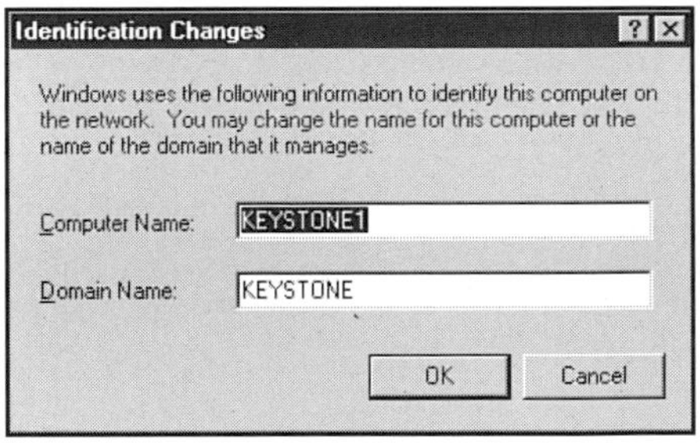

These options look simple, but are loaded with potential traps. Changing a computer name is risky business because on an established network, many computers may reference a particular computer by name, when, for example, they are accessing shared files. If you change the name of this computer, all those references will be made invalid. Chapter 9, "Understanding User Accounts, Groups, Domains, and Trust Relationships," and Chapter 10, "Managing Domains and Trust Relationships," describe how domain names are maintained and what you can and cannot do when renaming domains.

Managing Services and Protocols

Many services and protocols can be added to the Windows NT Server configuration. Although this section won't describe all of the items you can add, many features are described in other chapters.

Adding Services and Protocols

To add a service or a protocol:

Adding a Service or Protocol

1. Select the Services or Protocols tab. The Protocols tab is shown in figure 8.4.

2. Choose **A**dd to generate a list of items that can be added, such as the protocols list shown in figure 8.5.

3. Select an item from the list. (You can add an unlisted item if you have the required files. Choose Have Disk and follow the prompts.)

4. Choose OK. In most cases, files must be copied. Supply the drive path to the files, which will typically be found on the Windows NT Server installation CD-ROM.

5. Choose the Close button in the Network utility. In some cases, a dialog box will appear in which the software you installed must be configured.

6. Restart the computer to activate the new software.

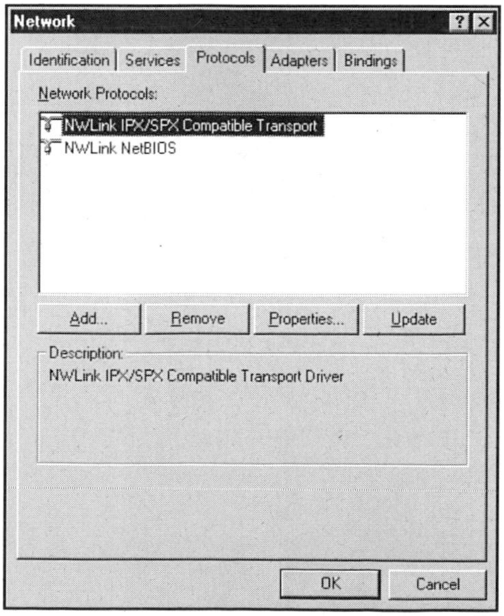

Figure 8.4

The Network Protocols tab.

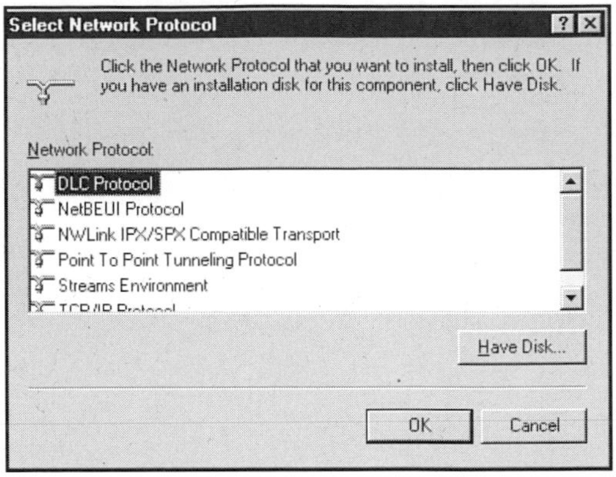

Figure 8.5

Adding a network protocol.

Select Network Protocol

Click the Network Protocol that you want to install, then click OK. If you have an installation disk for this component, click Have Disk.

Network Protocol:

DLC Protocol
NetBEUI Protocol
NWLink IPX/SPX Compatible Transport
Point To Point Tunneling Protocol
Streams Environment
TCP/IP Protocol

Have Disk...

OK   Cancel

Objective

B.4

Configuring NWLink Protocol Properties

Beginning with Windows NT 4, the configuration parameters of services and protocols are called properties. You can see how properties are configured by looking at the properties for NWLink.

To edit the properties for NWLink, follow the steps in the following exercise:

Editing NWLink Properties

1. Open the Network utility.

2. Select the Protocols tab.

3. Select NWLink IPX/SPX Compatible Transport in the Network Protocols box and choose Properties to open the NWLink IPX/SPX Properties box (see fig. 8.6).

4. NetWare servers also support an internal network number that supports interprocess communication among servers. An internal network number must be configured if this server will be an IPX router or will be running File and Print Services for NetWare. The default internal network number is 00000000, which instructs Windows NT to examine the network number and select one that does not conflict with numbers already in use. If you change the default number of 00000000, be sure that the number you enter does not conflict with other internal NetWare network numbers on the network.

5. If this computer is configured with two or more network adapter cards, select the adapter to be configured in the Adapter field.

6a. Select Auto Frame Type Detection if Windows NT should examine the network to identify the frame type in use. Unless your IPX network is using multiple frame types, this setting will typically enable the server to communicate with the network. With automatic frame type detection, only one frame type will be used.

In step 6b, you will observe that a network number must be specified when a manual frame type is added to the configuration. When you select A**u**to Frame Type Detection, Windows NT will detect the network number that is associated with the frame type that is selected; it is unnecessary to specify a frame type.

6b. Select **M**anual Frame Type Detection if you want to specify the frame type(s) that IPX will use. Manual frame type selection is necessary to prevent confusion in networks with multiple frame types, or to bind multiple frame types to an adapter. If you select **M**anual Frame Type Detection, you must add at least one frame type to the configuration. To add a frame type:

   a. Choose A**d**d to open the Manual Frame Detection dialog box.

   b. In the Frame Type field, select one of the frame types that is offered. You will only be shown frame types that are compatible with the network adapter card being configured.

   c. In the Network Number field, specify the network number that is used for this frame type on the attached network segment. All computers that use the same frame type on a given network segment must be configured with the same network number. If you add two or more frame types, each frame type must be associated with a unique network number.

7. Choose OK when configuration is completed.

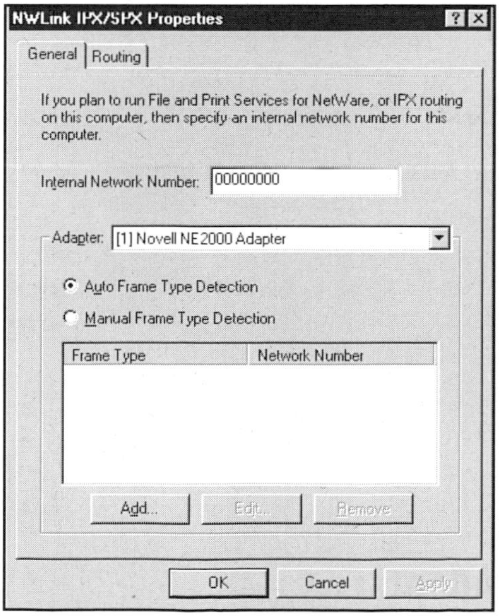

Figure 8.6

Configuring NWLink.

Note NWLink is the standard network protocol for Windows NT. NWLink was developed by Microsoft as a transport that is compatible with Novell's IPX/SPX protocols. The IPX/SPX protocols perform well and require little configuration.

One configuration item that you might need to attend to is the frame type for Ethernet or token-ring networks. A frame type is a variation on the basic frame format for a network. Novell NetWare supports four frame types for Ethernet and two for token ring. The primary reason for changing the frame type is to enable the Windows NT network to be compatible with another network.

Current Novell networks run the following default frame types:

◆ **Ethernet_802.2 for Ethernet networks.** This frame type fully conforms to the IEEE 802 standards and is the default frame type for current NetWare versions.

◆ **Token_Ring for token-ring networks.** This frame type conforms to IBM Token-Ring and to IEEE 802.5 standards and is the default token-ring frame type on NetWare networks.

The following frame types are also supported:

◆ **Ethernet_802.3.** An older Ethernet frame type Novell developed before the IEEE 802.2 standard was set. This frame type continues to be supported on Novell networks but is not preferred.

◆ **Ethernet_II.** The frame type that predated the IEEE 802.3 standard. This frame type is used on TCP/IP networks.

◆ **Ethernet_SNAP.** A variation used to support Macintosh EtherTalk networks.

◆ **Token_Ring_SNAP.** A token-ring variant that supports Macintosh TokenTalk networks.

Because Novell networks can bind multiple protocols, the best course of action is to have all networks bind to the Ethernet_802.2 or Token_Ring frame types. If your NetWare administrator is unable or unwilling to do that, you can add frame types to NWLink in the Protocol Configuration dialog box.

When you set NWLink to the recommended setting of Auto Frame Type Detection, NWLink examines the network and selects an active frame type. If Ethernet_802.2 frames are detected or no frames are detected, the Ethernet_802.2 frame type is selected. Otherwise, NWLink selects the frame type that is observed on the network.

Objective B.5

Adding Network Adapters

Figure 8.7 shows a single installed network adapter. You can have several if required. Before you install additional adapters, be sure that they are configured for non-conflicting settings. The following exercise performs the steps necessary to install network adapters.

To add an adapter:

Adding Network Adapters

1. Select the Adapters tab and choose **A**dd to display the Select Network Adapter dialog box (see fig. 8.8).

2. Select an item from the **N**etwork Adapter list. If a driver for your card is not listed, choose **H**ave Disk. You are required to supply the drivers on a floppy disk in the next step.

3. If a card of the selected type is already installed in the computer, you will see the question `A network card of this type is already installed in the system.` `Do you want to continue?` Choose OK to confirm your selection.

4. Next, a Network Card Setup dialog box appears in which you must specify the hardware settings for the card you are installing.

5. You might be asked to confirm adapter settings for installed protocols such as NWLink and TCP/IP. Protocol Configuration dialog boxes will be displayed. Make any desired changes. (NWLink configuration is discussed in the earlier section, "Configuring NWLink Protocol Properties." TCP/IP configuration is discussed in Chapter 16.)

6. Restart the computer to activate the new adapter.

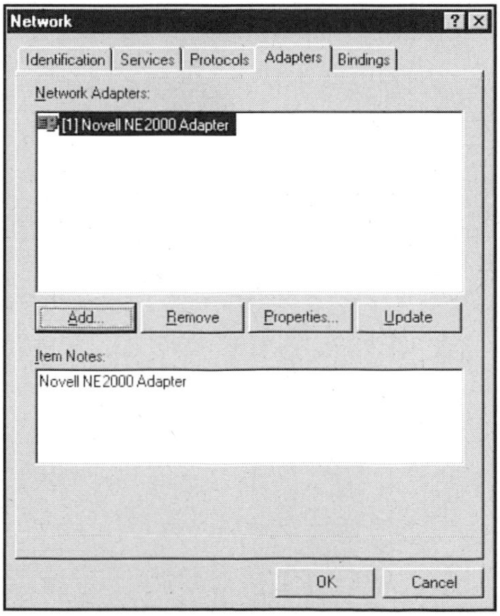

Figure 8.7

Installed network adapter.

Figure 8.8

*Installing a
network adapter.*

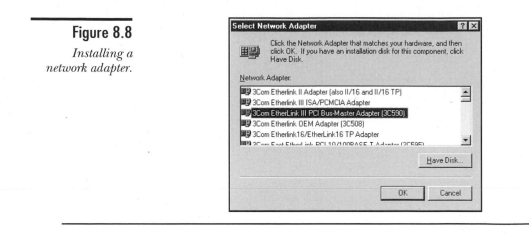

The adapter you specified will be added to the **N**etwork Adapter list. If you have installed two cards with the same driver, they will be identified as [1], [2], and so forth.

If more than one adapter is installed on a computer, you may want to enable routing support so that messages can be transferred between the attached network segments. To configure IPX routing, see the section, "Configuring IPX Routing," later in this chapter. Chapter 16 covers routing in the TCP/IP environment.

**Objective
B.5**

Configuring Network Adapters

After you add a network adapter, and whenever you change an adapter's hardware settings, you must change the network adapter configuration in the Network Settings.

To change the configuration of a network adapter:

1. Select the Adapters tab in the Network utility.

2. Select the adapter to be configured in the **N**etwork Adapter list.

3. Choose Properties to display a Network Card Setup dialog box similar to the one shown in figure 8.9.

4. Enter the hardware settings for your adapter.

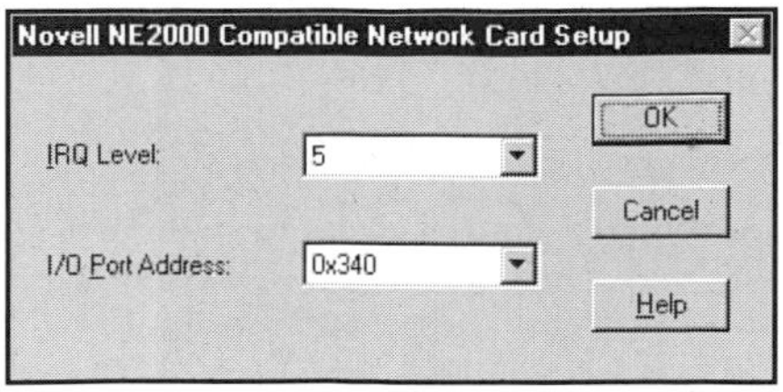

Figure 8.9 — Novell NE2000 Compatible Network Card Setup dialog box showing IRQ Level: 5, I/O Port Address: 0x340, with OK, Cancel, and Help buttons.

Figure 8.9

Configuring a network adapter.

Updating a Network Adapter

If you receive an updated version of a network adapter driver file, use the Update option to install the new file.

Removing a Network Adapter

To remove a network adapter:

1. Select the adapter in the Network Adapter list.

2. Choose Remove.

Caution   Removing software or an adapter, or entering improper configuration settings, can disrupt network functionality. Be careful what you modify, and make changes when you have time to pick up the pieces if something gets broken.

Managing Bindings

When network drivers and hardware are associated with one another, they are bound to one another. To display the bindings that are active on your computer, select the Bindings tab. The Bindings tab is shown in figure 8.10. The bindings panel can provide clues when troubleshooting network connectivity issues.

Each line in the binding list shows a series of software and hardware items that are bound together. Entries that are identified with a + can be expanded. In the figure, the NetBIOS Interface has been expanded two levels to show the bindings with the NWLink and TCP/IP transports. Notice that the lowest level cannot be expanded further, as indicated by the lack of a + sign to the left of the entry.

Objective B.4

Objective F.6

Figure 8.10

Network bindings.

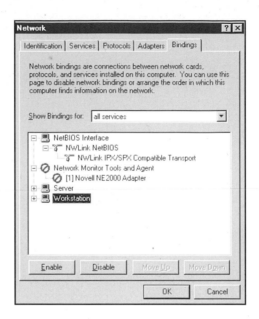

Bindings that are active are identified by a network icon. In some circumstances, you may want to deactivate a binding without removing the items from the computer configuration. This is done by selecting an item and choosing Disable.

To activate a deactivated binding, select the binding and choose Enable.

The order of bindings determines the order in which the computer will search for information via the bindings that are specified. You can raise and lower the priority associated with a binding by selecting the binding and choosing Move Up or Move Down. If, for example, you want the computer to use NWLink at a higher priority than TCP/IP, move the NWLink NetBIOS entry to the top of the NetBIOS Interface bindings.

Configuring IPX Routing

If you are configuring more than one network adapter card on a Windows NT computer, you probably want to enable Windows NT to forward network traffic between the network adapters. Figure 8.11 shows such a network, consisting of two network segments. Server B is attached to both network segments. Unless routing is enabled on server B, the user on computer A will be unable to communicate with server C.

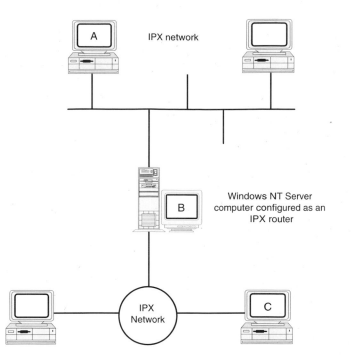

Figure 8.11

An IPX network that requires routing.

Windows NT 4 includes a router that supports the Routing Information Protocol that is the most common routing protocol on IPX networks. It is extremely easy to enable Windows NT to perform routing for the NWLink IPX/SPX transport protocol as described in the following exercise.

Configuring Windows NT as an IPX Router

To configure a Windows NT computer as an IPX router:

1. Install and configure two or more network adapter cards of either the same or different types.

2. In the Network utility, select the Services tab.

3. Choose Add to open the Select Network Service dialog box.

4. In the Network Service list, select the entry RIP for NWLink IPX/SPX Compatible Transport and choose OK.

5. When prompted for the source file location, specify the path of the directory where the installation files can be found. Typically, this path points to the installation CD-ROM.

6. When you see the prompt, `Netbios Broadcast Propagation (broadcast type 20 packets) is currently disabled. Do you want to enable it?` Choose Yes.

> **Note** When computers communicate using the NWLink protocol, browsing and name resolution are supported by NetBIOS over IPX, which is dependent on Type 20 packets. Type 20 broadcasts are broadcast on the network so that all computers receive the NetBIOS naming information. If NetBIOS Broadcast Propagation is disabled, type 20 broadcasts will not be forwarded by routers, and users will be prevented from browsing or resolving names for computers that are not attached to the local cable segment.
>
> When NetBIOS broadcast propagation is enabled, type 20 packets only propagate for eight hops from the computers that originate the packets. A hop occurs each time a packet crosses a cable segment. When NWLink is the only protocol on the network, clients cannot communicate with servers that are more than eight hops away. As a result, no more than seven routers can separate computers on a network that is running only NWLink. (Networks up to 15 hops can be implemented using TCP/IP.)

7. Close the Network utility and restart the computer.

8. Open the Network utility and select the Protocols tab.

9. Select NWLink IPX/SPX Compatible Transport and choose Properties.

10. RIP for NWLink is a network service installed separately of the NWLink protocol.

11. If the **E**nable RIP Routing check box is not selected, select it and choose OK. Restart the computer to activate routing.

Testing Your Knowledge

1. What are two reasons to load the least possible number of protocols?
   A. Too many protocols use up additional memory resources.
   B. The fewer the protocols, the more available processing resources.
   C. Few protocols guarantee a connection to a desired resource.
   D. Too many protocols use up additional processing resources.

2. Which Protocol does not provide connectivity to NetWare servers?
   A. NWLink IPX/SPX
   B. NetBEUI
   C. TCP/IP

3. What is a practical protocol candidate for a large network that requires routing but does not need to support Internet services?

    A. NetBEUI

    B. DLC

    C. TCP/IP

    D. NWLink IPX/SPX

4. Which protocol is the most difficult to manage but provides the most versatility, such as Internet services, routing, and support for large networks?

    A. NetBEUI

    B. NWLink IPX/SPX

    C. TCP/IP

    D. DLC

5. If you are installing a second network card into the server what needs to be considered?

    A. That they are configured with non-conflicting resource settings.

    B. That they are of the same type or model.

    C. That they use the exact same protocols and bindings as the first card.

    D. The second adapter must be configured as a router.

6. When network drivers and hardware are associated with one another, they are _____ together.

7. Windows NT 4 includes a router that supports _____, which is the most common routing protocol on IP networks.

Review Answers

1. A, D

2. B

3. D

4. C

5. A

6. bound

7. Routing Information Protocol (RIP)

CHAPTER 9

Understanding User Accounts, Groups, Domains, and Trust Relationships

I f networks were always simple, if they never had more than a single server or a few users, they would be easy to administer and to use. All resources would be in one place, and all users would be local. There would be no confusion regarding where a resource was located or how to gain access.

Today, however, increasing numbers of networks are not simple. They incorporate multiple servers (file, print, fax, mail, and so on) and often span multiple locations. More often than not, servers will be storing many gigabytes of files. Clearly, expecting users to simply know where things are under those circumstances is not very realistic.

Network designers, therefore, have sought ways to simplify the location of network resources. This chapter introduces you to the technique chosen by the designers of Windows NT Server, which is based on domains and trust relationships. These building blocks enable you to build enterprise networks that are easy for you to manage and easy for your users to use.

Organizing LAN Resources

In Chapter 1, "Understanding Networks," you learned that LANs provide services in two ways: through peer-to-peer resource sharing or through central servers. Which-ever method your network uses, the problem remains of enabling users to locate the resources that are available for use. This section surveys some of the following techniques that have been used for organizing network resources:

◆ Stand-alone services

◆ Directory services

◆ Workgroups

◆ Domains

Stand-Alone Services

The vast majority of early LANs incorporated only one server, so users had little difficulty locating files, printers, and other resources to be shared. NetWare 2.x and 3.x have long been the dominant network operating systems on small LANs, and statistics indicate that the average Novell 2.x and 3.x networks include a single server and 30 or fewer workstations.

With such an arrangement, there is little need for a sophisticated resource manage-ment service. Files can be found using DOS DIR commands, and printers can be selected easily from a list. In most cases, users' LAN environments are entirely pre-configured for them by the LAN administrator. Users are given access to specific printers, file access is preset, and users do not need a great deal of knowledge about the LAN to use it effectively.

Adding a second server can significantly complicate things, however. The problem arises because each stand-alone server maintains its own lists of users and resources. Figure 9.1 illustrates the problem. Server A is the host for applications such as WordPerfect and Lotus 1-2-3. Server B is the host for the company's e-mail, account-ing applications, and sales database. Users who need to access the sales database and use the applications must be given accounts on both servers. Each of these user accounts must be created and maintained separately. Notice that some users have accounts on only one server. It is easy for servers to get out of synchronization when they must be updated manually.

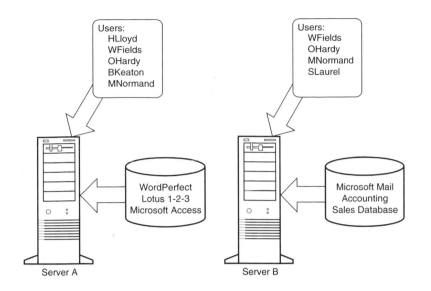

Figure 9.1

Administering two stand-alone servers.

The situation also complicates matters from the user's standpoint. The user must log on to and maintain a password on each server separately. This process can be automated, but it is a bit error-prone. Administrators of networks with several stand-alone servers are used to getting calls to re-synchronize user passwords among servers.

Two servers are about the most you would want to administer in this way, but even two servers can be too much. Assuming all users need to access all server resources, each user must be given an account on each server. It is easy to see how errors could occur in busy office environments where staff changes are frequent.

Users also have a problem with multiple stand-alone servers. To use a printer, the user must know which server hosts the printer. To access a file or program, the user must be aware of the server that maintains the file. Unless the user is given friendly tools for locating services, many of the network's capabilities will be difficult to access. The situation is much like trying to locate a plumber by using only the telephone directory's White Pages. Unless you already know the name of the plumber you want, finding one in your area of the city would be extremely difficult.

Given these limitations, LAN vendors have made considerable investments in making large LANs more manageable and usable. Two tools have come into use: directories and browseable services.

Directory Services

A network directory works much like a telephone directory's Yellow Pages. Resources can be grouped logically to make them easier to locate. Users can search the directory for the information they want, or they can browse the directory in a sensible fashion.

Directory services can be used to organize the resources on extremely large LANs. Several approaches are available:

◆ Banyan has long offered the StreetTalk directory service as part of its VINES network operating system. Banyan is now marketing StreetTalk as a directory service that can be used to integrate various network platforms.

◆ X.500 is an international standard for a directory service. It is not implemented currently in any LAN products.

◆ NetWare Directory Services (NDS) is incorporated into Novell's NetWare 4.x product line. NDS is based on X.500, but is not entirely compliant with the standard. At present, NDS can be used only with NetWare 4.x networks.

The concept of a directory service is attractive. Instead of logging on to several servers, a user now logs on to a network and is granted access to network resources by the directory service, regardless of which server is providing the service. The user sees a network directory with no indication of which server supports the user's account.

A directory service is an extremely formal way to organize network resources. Setting up such a service calls for careful planning that involves all departments in the organization. And directory services work best when one organization (such as a central MIS department) is responsible for maintaining the directory. Some directory services enable departments to have responsibility for portions of the directory, but one department must take primary responsibility. In organizations that do not have a central MIS department, it might be difficult to identify a primary directory manager.

In many organizations, LANs happened in departments long before they were discovered by the central MIS department. The departments that pioneered LANs often are reluctant to give up control and prefer to retain responsibility for managing their LAN resources. In Chapter 2, "Introducing Windows NT Server," you were cautioned that managing a LAN has political overtones. Setting up a directory service in a company that has well-established departmental networks can appear to threaten department autonomy and can run smack into those company politics. In most cases, users who are logged on to one directory structure cannot access resources that are controlled by another directory structure, making interdepartmental cooperation essential.

Directory services often add new complications as they solve old problems, and administrators of a directory need to be more skilled than administrators of stand-alone servers.

Almost any technology has up and down sides, and directory services are no exception. Although they can be very effective at organizing the resources of the largest LANs, directory services require skill and planning to administer correctly. They represent a formal approach to managing a network, and some organizations will take to directories more readily than others.

Workgroups

Workgroups are the conceptual opposites of directory services. Directories are formal and centrally administered; workgroups are informal and are operated by the users who are pooling their computing resources.

With a peer-to-peer approach to networking, users share the resources on their computers with other users. They might enable other users to print through their printers, access their files, or share a modem or CD-ROM. Individual users manage the sharing of resources on their PCs by determining what will be shared and who will be allowed access.

Peer-to-peer networking runs into two problems in large organizations:

◆ So many resources are available that users might have trouble locating them.

◆ Users who want to share resources often need an easy method of sharing resources with only a limited group of coworkers.

Microsoft introduced the metaphor of workgroup computing with the Windows for Workgroups (WfW) product. WfW enables users to share their workstation resources in a peer-to-peer mode, and workgroups make it easy to establish groups of related workers who easily can view and share each other's resources.

After someone joins a workgroup, he or she has access to all resources that are shared in that workgroup. You can share your hard drive with your coworkers simply by giving their workgroup rights to your printer. Figure 9.2 shows the Windows for Workgroups form that is used to share a printer.

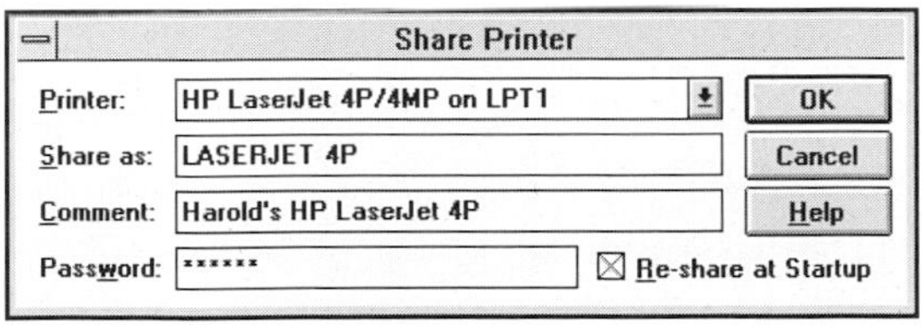

	Share Printer	
Printer:	HP LaserJet 4P/4MP on LPT1 ▼	OK
Share as:	LASERJET 4P	Cancel
Comment:	Harold's HP LaserJet 4P	Help
Password:	******	☒ Re-share at Startup

Figure 9.2

Sharing a printer with a workgroup.

Notice that the window in figure 9.2 enables the printer owner to assign a password that can be used to restrict access to specific individuals. Without a password, any member of the workgroup can use the printer. This is the only security provided by Windows for Workgroups.

To locate resources on a network, Microsoft uses a browsing service. Under Windows NT 4 or Windows 95, the Network Neighborhood or the Windows Explorer can be used to browse the network and identify resources to connect to. In figure 9.3, a user is browsing in the Network Neighborhood for sharable directories. Three such directories have been established on the workstation named Harold. Also shown is the Printers window which advertises a printer that is being shared by Harold.

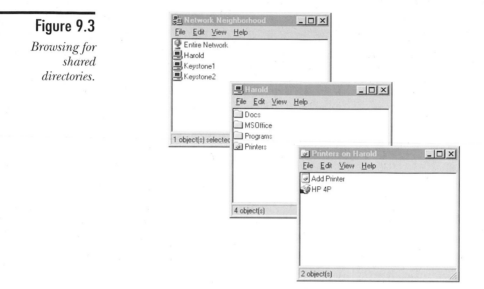

Figure 9.3

Browsing for shared directories.

Workgroups are more a convenience than anything else. They make resource sharing more efficient, but they do not organize services into a directory. They also do not make it easy to manage the shared resources in an efficient manner. Passwords can be used to restrict access to resources, but with one password for each resource, passwords proliferate rapidly. To change a password, everyone who uses the resource must be notified. If each resource has a different password, things get really complicated. It is difficult to maintain much security under those circumstances.

Figure 9.4 illustrates some of the problems with passwords in workgroups. When separate passwords are assigned by individual users, the number of passwords a user must remember can multiply rapidly. To make things easier, users tend to select passwords that are easy to remember, but such passwords also tend to be ones that are easy to guess.

To make matters worse, imagine that the network has dial-up capability, and that an employee has just left to work for your biggest competitor. You want to change all the passwords so that the employee cannot call in and get to your data. Obviously, changing all those passwords and informing everyone of the changes is going to be a big hassle.

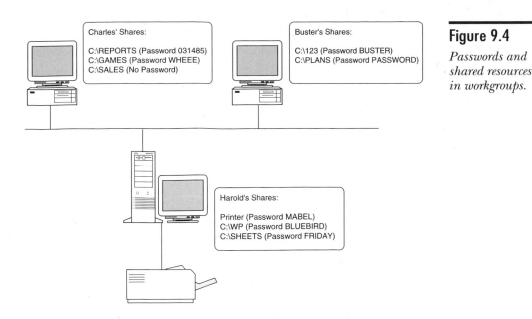

Charles' Shares:

C:\REPORTS (Password 031485)
C:\GAMES (Password WHEEE)
C:\SALES (No Password)

Buster's Shares:

C:\123 (Password BUSTER)
C:\PLANS (Password PASSWORD)

Figure 9.4

Passwords and shared resources in workgroups.

Harold's Shares:

Printer (Password MABEL)
C:\WP (Password BLUEBIRD)
C:\SHEETS (Password FRIDAY)

The following Microsoft products can share their resources in workgroups:

◆ Windows for Workgroups

◆ Windows 95

◆ Windows NT Workstation

◆ Windows NT Server

◆ MS-DOS with the Workgroup add-on feature

These Microsoft products enable workstations to access workgroup resources:

◆ Windows 3.x with the Workgroup Connection

◆ MS-DOS with the Workgroup Connection feature

◆ LAN Manager for MS-DOS Enhanced and Basic Clients (not covered in this book)

◆ LAN Manager for MS OS/2 Client (Since this client has not been updated for the most recent versions of OS/2, it is not covered in this book.)

Organizations that are large or that want more control over their networks need something more than workgroups. Therefore, Microsoft has incorporated the domain concept into Windows NT Server.

Domains

Domains borrow concepts from workgroups and from directory services. Like workgroups, domains can be fairly informal and can be administered using a mix of central and local controls. Domains can evolve fairly easily and can be set up with less planning than typically is required for a directory.

Like a directory, a domain organizes the resources of several servers into one administrative structure. Users are given logon privileges to a domain rather than to each individual server. Because a domain controls the resources of several servers, it is easier to administer than a network with many stand-alone servers.

Servers within the domain advertise their services to users. Users who log on to a domain gain access to all resources in the domain for which they have been granted access. They can browse the resources in a domain much as they would browse the resources in a workgroup; however, domains are hosted by Windows NT Servers and can be made more secure than workgroups.

When networks become large enough to require several domains, administrators can establish trust relationships among domains. Trust relationships simplify administration because a user is required to have an account in only one domain. Other domains that trust the user's logon domain can rely on the logon domain to authenticate the user's logon.

> **Note**   Windows NT Server domains are not the same as domains found on TCP/IP networks. TCP/IP domains are discussed in Chapter 16, "Using TCP/IP."

Domains and Trust Relationships

Domains are essentially improved workgroups. Access to domain resources is controlled by a domain controller. The user is assigned a single domain account and a password that is used to control access to all domain resources. Windows NT Server domains also support the use of groups that enable administrators to assign and change permissions for large numbers of users more efficiently. You will learn about managing users and groups in Chapter 11, "Managing Users and Groups."

Domains and Domain Servers

Objective B.2

A server in a domain has one of three roles:

- ◆ **Primary domain controller.** One Windows NT Server stores the master copy of the domain's user and group database. The PDC is responsible for synchronizing the account database with all BDCs.

◆ **Backup domain controller.** Other Windows NT Servers can store backup copies of the domain's user and group database.

◆ **Member or stand-alone server.** Servers can participate in a domain without being designated as primary or backup domain controllers.

Each of these roles is described more fully in the following sections.

The Primary Domain Controller

The first Windows NT Server in the domain is configured as a primary domain controller (PDC). The User Manager for Domains utility is used to maintain user and group information for the domain. This information is stored in a domain security database on the primary domain controller.

Backup Domain Controllers

Other Windows NT Servers in the domain can serve as backup domain controllers (BDC). Each backup domain controller stores a replica of the database on the primary domain controller, which is replicated periodically to distribute changes made to the main database on the PDC. Replication of the database has several advantages.

Objective B.2

If the primary domain controller experiences a hardware failure, one of the backup domain controllers can be promoted to the primary role. Having one or more backup domain controllers builds a degree of fault tolerance into your network. Each domain should have at least one BDC.

Backup domain controllers also can participate in the logon process. When a user logs on to a domain, the logon request can be handled by any primary or backup domain controller. This spreads the logon processing load across the available servers and improves logon performance. This can be an important benefit in domains with large numbers of users.

> **Note**
>
> Changes cannot be made to the domain database unless the PDC is functioning. If the PDC fails or is shut down for maintenance, you can promote a BDC to function as the PDC.
>
> Although the PDC is required to make changes to the domain database, other domain operations are not dependent on the PDC. Users can log on to the domain using a BDC if the PDC is unavailable.

Servers

Computers running Windows NT Server can also function as independent or *stand-alone* servers, which may or may not participate in domains. The term servers represents member server or stand-alone server. These servers do not function as primary or backup domain controllers. They can take advantage of the user and group databases, however, that are maintained for a domain, and you can assign user and group permissions for the server using the User Manager for Domains.

The server also can maintain its own database of users, and users can log on to the server independently of the domain. When this is done, the server cannot utilize the user and group database of a domain, and the server handles accounts much like computers running Windows NT Workstation.

You might choose to configure a stand-alone Windows NT Member Server for several reasons:

◆ The server can be administered by different staff members. Many Windows NT Servers are used for application servers, such as SQL databases. If you configure a database server as an independent server, you can assign a member of your database staff as the server administrator.

◆ Attending to logon requests can use a significant part of a server's processing capability. If you configure the server as an independent server, it can concentrate on servicing a single function, such as providing application services.

◆ When a server is functioning as a primary or backup domain controller, it is difficult to move the server to a new domain. If there is a chance the server will move to a different domain, configure it as an independent server.

Synchronizing the Domain Directory Database

All changes to the domain directory database are first made on the PDC, after which they are distributed to the BDCs in a process called *synchronization*. Changes made to the PDC database—consisting of password changes, new and modified user and group accounts, and changes in rights assignments—are recorded in a *change log* on the PDC. When a BDC requests a database update, the changes that took place since the last update are copied to the BDC's database. An update that consists only of recent changes is a *partial synchronization*.

The PDC change database has a limited capacity. It operates as a *circular buffer*, meaning that older changes will be purged to make room for new changes. Consequently, a BDC that is off-line for a lengthy period of time may have missed changes that have been purged from the change database. Under these circumstances, it is necessary to perform a *full synchronization* in which the BDC receives a complete copy of the domain directory database from the PDC.

The NetLogon service is tasked with synchronizing the domain database. By default, the NetLogon service synchronizes BDCs at five minute intervals, which is usually adequate given the default capacity of the change database to store approximately 2,000 changes. If changes are being lost, it becomes necessary to increase the frequency of synchronization events or the size of the change log, both of which are determined by settings in the Registry.

When BDCs are separated from the PDC by a slow WAN link, full synchronization is undesirable. In such situations, you may want to increase the size of the change log and reduce the synchronization frequency to reduce WAN traffic, even to the point of scheduling partial synchronization to take place at night.

Chapter 10, "Managing Domains and Trust Relationships," describes several Registry parameters that control operation of the directory synchronization process. See the section, "Configuring Domain Synchronization," in that chapter.

Trust Relationships

Many organizations own several LAN servers—this is fine because domains make multiple servers easy to administer. There are several reasons an organization might need to establish two or more domains; for example:

◆ If too many servers are put in a domain, performance can suffer.

◆ For best performance, the domain database should be restricted in size to 40 MB, limiting the numbers of workstations, users, and groups that can be defined in a given domain.

◆ Some departments prefer to manage their own resources, which is easiest if they have their own domains.

So your organization decides to have several domains. If a user needs to access resources in several domains, is it necessary to create an account for that user in each domain? That could be just as bad as administering several stand-alone servers.

Fortunately, Windows NT Server enables you to establish trust relationships between domains. Figure 9.5 illustrates a simple, two-domain trust relationship. Domain B is configured to trust Domain A. As a result, if a user is successful at logging on to Domain A, Domain B assumes that the user has been authenticated properly. Therefore, Domain B accepts the user without forcing the user to explicitly log on to Domain B.

Figure 9.5

A simple trust relationship.

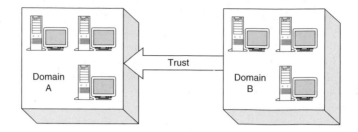

Trusts can flow both ways. In figure 9.6, Domains C and D are configured to trust each other. You will see several examples of network designs that use two-way trust relationships.

Figure 9.6

Domains configured to trust each other.

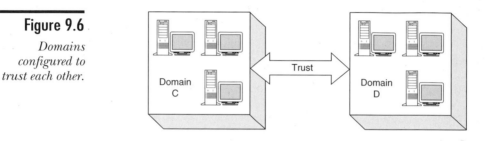

One more thing you should know about trust relationships is that trust does not flow through a domain. (Microsoft's term is that trusts are not *transitive*.) The top portion of figure 9.7 shows three domains that have established two-way trust relationships. Domains E and F trust one another, as do domains F and G. Domains E and G, however, do not trust each other because trusts do not pass through Domain F.

If all domains are to trust each other, it is necessary to establish trust relationships between each pair of domains. The bottom half of figure 9.7 shows how three domains can be made to trust each other.

Note Trust relationships do not automatically grant users access to resources in a trusting domain. A domain that trusts another domain relies on the trusted domain to authenticate users when they log on. The trusting domain still must grant those users access to resources.

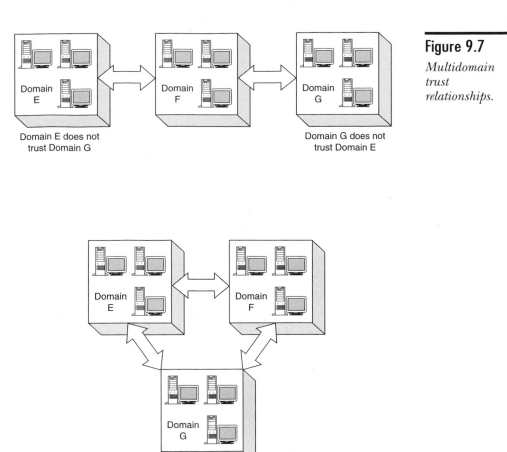

Figure 9.7

Multidomain trust relationships.

Domain Models

Proper use of trust relationships enables organizations to build enterprise networks that still require only a single logon procedure for resource access. Microsoft has defined four models for domain trust relationships. If you are configuring a multi-domain network, you will want to consider the merits and disadvantages of each model.

There are two reasons for adding domains:

◆ For organizational reasons

◆ To improve network performance

Regarding network performance, you will find that Microsoft's descriptions are a bit vague. You can use a single domain model, for example, "if your network doesn't have too many users..." That doesn't give you much help during the planning stages. Unfortunately, there are many variables, and it is difficult to come up with a simple prescription for adding domains. Windows NT Server can, after all, run on everything from an Intel 80486 PC to a multiprocessor RISC system. Such a broad range of hardware makes performance generalizations difficult. Fortunately, Windows NT Server domains make it easy to reorganize the LAN as it grows.

The four domain models defined by Microsoft follow:

◆ Single domain

◆ Master domain

◆ Multiple-master domains

◆ Complete trust

Each domain is discussed in the following sections.

The Single Domain Model

Figure 9.8 illustrates the *single domain model*—the preferred model for small organizations. (Remember, size descriptions are very vague. More powerful servers enable a single domain to grow in size.) When all servers are located in a single domain, administration is simplified greatly. Also, there is no need to administer trust relationships—an activity that can get quite involved.

Figure 9.8

A single domain network.

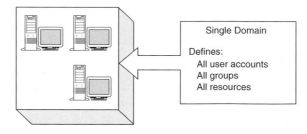

Large amounts of logon or browsing activity might degrade the performance of the domain. When a domain has a large number of servers, browsing can be inefficient, and you might find it advantageous to move some of the servers to another domain. Be alert to performance issues so that you can anticipate when you need to move to a different domain model.

A single domain network has several advantages:

◆ It is easier to manage because resources are centralized.

◆ No trust relationships are required.

◆ Group definitions are simpler.

You need to consider a multi-domain model in the following situations:

◆ If browsing is slow

◆ If too many users are degrading performance

◆ If your organization wants to assign domains to departments

◆ If you want to have some resources in their own domains

The Master Domain Model

The *master domain model* designates one domain to manage all user accounts. The master domain also supports global groups. *Global groups* can export group information to other domains. By defining global groups in the master domain, other domains can import the group information easily.

Figure 9.9 illustrates a network based on a master domain model. The master domain is named Keystone, and is managed centrally by the MIS staff. All users are defined in Keystone, as well as some groups that will make administration easier. Only the primary and backup domain controllers in the Keystone domain are used to store user and group account information. Because users cannot log on to the network without a working domain account database, a master domain always should include at least one backup domain controller in addition to the primary domain controller.

When users log on to the network, they always log on to the Keystone master domain. After they have logged on, they can access resources in other domains that trust Keystone.

In this example, the other domains are organized according to departments. After a user logs on through the master domain, most of the user's network activity relates to one of the department domains. Therefore, user network activity is distributed across several domains, removing much of the processing responsibility from the Keystone domain.

Figure 9.9

A network with a single master domain.

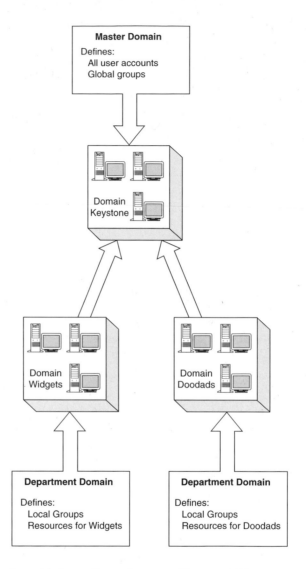

Each of the department domains is configured to trust Keystone. The assumption is that Keystone security will be sufficiently tight, and that other domains do not need to take special precautions of their own.

The department domains could be administered by MIS or by the individual departments. The master domain model makes it possible to delegate some management tasks while keeping the critical security function under the control of a central network authority. So that department domains are comfortable with the network security, administrators of the master domain should be well trained and security policies carefully defined.

A master domain network has several advantages:

◆ Security management is centralized.

◆ Non-master domains can be used to organize resources logically.

◆ Browsing activity is distributed through the department domains.

◆ Global groups in the master domain enable departments to easily establish local permissions.

◆ Departments that want to can manage the resources in their own domains.

The chief liability of the master domain model is that all logon activity takes place in a single domain. When performance begins to suffer in the master domain, you need to be prepared to move to a multiple master domain model.

> **Note** Groups are essential ingredients of effective Windows NT Server management. Groups enable you to manage the privileges of large numbers of users more efficiently than would be possible if privileges were assigned to users individually.
>
> Windows NT Server uses two types of groups: local and global. It can be difficult to grasp the differences between these group types and the appropriate uses of each. Consequently, this section does not dwell on that topic. Later in this chapter, the sections "Global Groups" and "Local Groups" investigate Windows NT Server groups thoroughly.

Because all accounts are concentrated in the master domain, a network designed with a single master domain is limited in scope by the size of the master domain's database. Typically, a master domain network will be limited to about 26,000 users and computers.

Although the master domain approach does not permit the network to support more users, it should result in performance improvements. After users have logged onto the network, their activities will be distributed across the department domains. There is less contention for network and server resources, and users should experience a performance improvement.

The Multiple Master Domain Model

The master domain model can be extended by introducing additional master domains. This is the primary technique used to scale Windows NT Server networks for larger enterprises. Figure 9.10 shows networks with two master domains and three department domains.

Figure 9.10

Networks with multiple master domains.

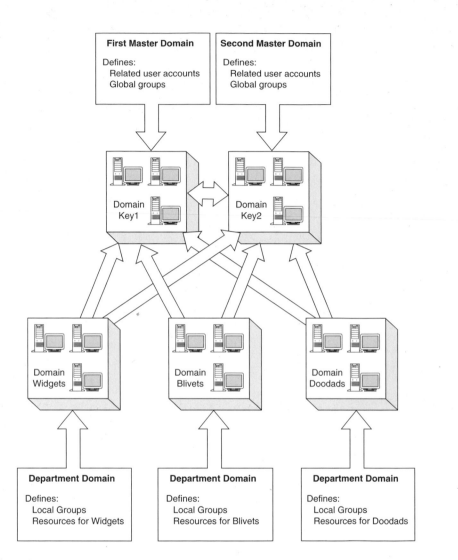

Each master domain supports about half the user accounts. This spreads the processing of logons over several domains. Each domain supports some of the groups that are accessed by the department domains.

Under this model, each master domain trusts every other master domain. This is a convenience for administrators, but is necessary for users only if they actually will be using resources on one of the master domains, which is not ordinarily the case. To reduce the likelihood of security holes, only administrators should be given permissions to access resources in the master domains. Users should be given permissions only in the department domains.

Each department domain trusts each master domain. It is not necessary for department domains to trust each other.

Because users are granted most privileges based on their memberships in master domain groups, it is a good idea to group related users into the same master domains. All your users in Accounting should log on to the same master domain, for example. Otherwise, you are forced to establish similar groups in each master domain. With more groups, it becomes far more difficult to establish privileges in the department domains.

The required number of trust relationships increases rapidly as you add domains. Figure 9.11 illustrates a network with three master domains and four department domains. The network in figure 9.10 required eight trust relationships. (Two trust relationships are required to enable the two master domains to trust one another.) The slightly larger network in figure 9.11 requires 18 relationships! Obviously, you do not want to expand the number of domains in your network unnecessarily.

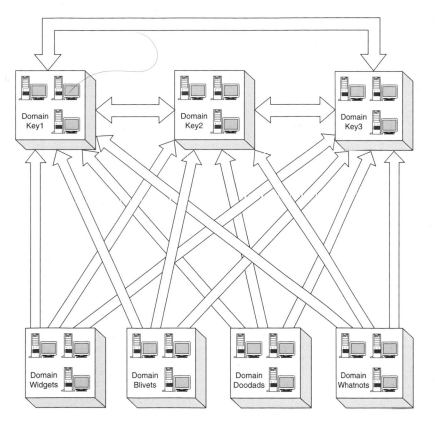

Figure 9.11

A larger network with multiple master domains.

The multiple master domain model has many desirable features:

◆ It is scalable to any organizational size.

◆ Security is managed centrally.

◆ Departments can manage their local domains, if desired.

◆ Related users, groups, and resources can be grouped logically into domains.

Disadvantages of the multiple master domain model include the following characteristics:

◆ The number of groups and trust relationships multiply rapidly as the number of domains increases.

◆ User accounts and groups are not located in a single location, complicating network documentation.

Theoretically, a multiple master domain network can grow to any size. Each master domain can support up to about 26,000 users and computers, and many master domains can be added. Because administration grows more complicated with each added master domain, however, it eventually becomes impractical to add more master domains to a network. It is probable, however, that few organizations will be faced with the limits. It is certainly practical to manage a network with three master domains, which can theoretically support 78,000 users. Is your network that large?

The Complete Trust Model

The master domain models assume that a central department exists that can take responsibility for managing user and group security for the complete organization. If no such department exists, or if departments want to retain full responsibility for managing their own domains, you might choose to implement a *complete trust model*. An example of a complete trust network is shown in figure 9.12.

In the complete trust model, every domain is configured to trust every other domain. Users log in to their department domains and then access resources in other departments by means of trust relationships.

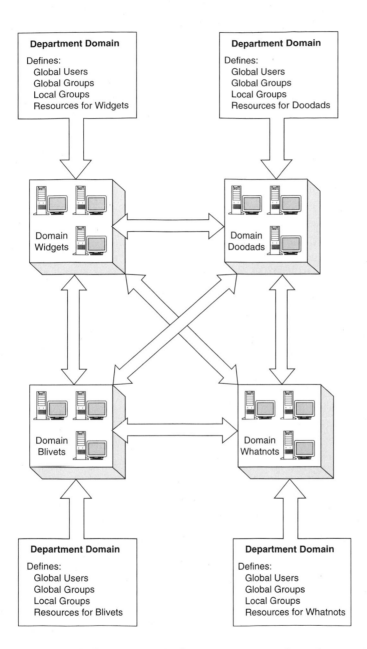

Figure 9.12

A network using a complete trust model.

As with the multiple master domain model, the number of trust relationships required increases rapidly as domains increase. Three domains require six trust relationships (two between each pair of domains), whereas five domains require 20 trust relationships. If *n* is the number of domains, then the network requires $n \times (n-1)$ trust relationships.

Caution   As a believer in tight network security, I find the implications of the complete trust model extremely disturbing. The administrators of each domain must have complete faith that the administrators of every other domain will maintain a high level of security. For me, that is carrying trust a little too far.

In fact, Microsoft itself has backed off from an endorsement of the complete trust model, and recommends a multiple master domain model for large installations. Although the complete trust model was featured prominently in the documentation for earlier versions of Windows NT Server, coverage is omitted from the Concepts and Planning manual for Windows NT Server 4.

If your organization does not have a central MIS department, networking is a great reason for establishing one. Besides the need to maintain tight security, several other functions are best when centralized. Here are some examples:

◆ File backup

◆ Communications services

◆ E-mail maintenance

◆ Management of the network infrastructure (media, hubs, and so on)

Few departments have personnel who possess the expertise to do these jobs well. Also, network management in a large organization calls for personnel who are devoted completely to the task.

Therefore, I don't put much credibility into the advantages that Microsoft attributes to the complete trust model, but here they are nevertheless:

◆ No central MIS department is required.

◆ The model scales to any organizational size.

◆ Departments retain control of their users and resources. (But, it can be argued, they surrender that control by trusting everybody.)

◆ Users and resources are grouped logically by departments.

A few of the disadvantages of the complete trust model follow:

◆ Central security control is lacking.

◆ Large numbers of trust relationships are required.

◆ Departments are dependent on the management practices of other departments.

Estimating Domain Capacity

The big question when planning a domain-based network is, "What is the recommended maximum size for a domain?" This turns out to be a fairly complex question that is affected by the numbers of user, computer, and group accounts. It is also affected by the processing horsepower of the computers that are assigned as domain controllers. All the issues come down to the size of the file that is used to store the Security Accounts Manager (SAM) domain database.

The size of the SAM database file matters because the entire database is made resident in a domain controller's RAM. Large SAM databases have two effects: they hog a lot of the domain controller's RAM, and they take a long time to load, prolonging the process of booting the computer.

Three types of objects are stored in the SAM domain database:

◆ User accounts use 1,024 bytes (1 KB) each.

◆ Computer accounts use 512 bytes (0.5 KB) each (only Windows NT computers require computer accounts).

◆ Global group accounts use 512 bytes plus 12 bytes per users.

◆ Local group accounts use 512 bytes plus 36 bytes per user.

Assume that you have 1,000 users and 500 NT computers that require accounts. To organize the domain, you require 10 global groups with an average membership of 200 users. You also require 10 local groups with an average membership of 20. How large a SAM database would that generate?

1,000 users × 1,024 bytes=1,024,000 bytes

512 computer accounts × 512 bytes=262,144 bytes

10 global groups × 512 bytes=5,120 bytes

2,000 global group members × 12 bytes=24,000 bytes

10 local groups × 512 bytes=5,120 bytes

200 local group members × 36 bytes=7,200 bytes

Total SAM database size=1,324,589 bytes

The total size of the SAM database would be approximately 1.5 MB. That's not particularly large as SAM databases go, and you can easily support this network in a single domain.

Depending on its processing power and on the services it provides, a domain controller can support between 2,000 and 5,000 users. A domain with 26,000 users, therefore, might require from 6 to 13 domain controllers to ensure adequate performance.

These two factors (the maximum size of the domain database and the number of users a given domain controller can support) suggest some situations that might make it desirable to design a multi-domain network.

Microsoft recommends that a SAM domain database file not exceed a size of 40 MB. Above this limit, performance is likely to be unacceptable. Of course, performance depends on the power of the computers that are functioning as domain controllers, and less powerful servers will probably require you to further limit the size of the domain database. Regardless of the server platform, however, it is unlikely that you will want the database size to exceed 40 MB.

How large is a 40 MB SAM database? It will accommodate approximately 26,000 users, 26,000 workstations, and 250 group accounts.

A 40 MB SAM database is practical only on high-performance hardware. Table 9.1 offers some suggestions on the hardware required to support SAM files of varying sizes.

TABLE 9.1
Selecting Domain Controller Hardware

Users	SAM Size	Minimum CPU	Minimum RAM
7,500	<10 MB	486DX/66	32 MB
10,000	<15 MB	Pentium or RISC	48 MB
15,000	<20 MB	Pentium or RISC	64 MB
30,000	<30 MB	Pentium or RISC	128 MB
15,000	<20 MB	Pentium or RISC	166 MB

If the SAM database for your planned domain exceeds the recommended capacity for your hardware, you should partition your network into two or more domains.

Domains and Workgroups

Microsoft has designed its network products so that users and network administrators can use a mix of peer-to-peer and centralized services. Users can participate in a workgroup at the same time they are logged on to a Windows NT Server domain. This capability enables you to mix formal and informal network services to meet the needs of your users. It also enables you to manage some resources centrally, while other resources are shared under user control.

Mixing workgroup and domain models can complicate your life as a LAN administrator, however. When a user reports a problem, it might be unclear whether the problem is related to the Windows NT Server network or to the user's workgroup. My recommendation is that you use a centralized approach whenever possible.

Files can always be shared simply by placing them on a network server. Although Windows for Workgroups users cannot share their printers with a Windows NT Server network (except through peer-to-peer resource sharing in a workgroup environment), users of Windows NT Workstation can configure their workstations as network print servers, enabling them to share their printers as domain resources. Thus, most of the resource sharing that is made possible by workgroups also is possible under domain management. Windows NT Server domains are, however, much easier to manage and troubleshoot.

> **Tip** If the data is important enough to share, it is important enough to protect. The best place to protect your data is on a Windows NT Server computer where it can be properly secured and backed up. In my opinion, workgroup computing has no place where important data is being exchanged.

Users and Groups

Windows NT Server security is based on the following four types of entities:

◆ **Global user accounts.** User accounts that originate in the Windows NT environment.

◆ **Local user accounts.** User accounts that originate in server environments other than Windows NT.

◆ **Global groups.** Used to manage groups in a domain. Also can be used to export groups of users to other domains.

◆ **Local groups.** Used to manage users and to import global groups from other domains.

These entities are discussed in detail in the following sections.

Note User and group account information is stored in the domain database, which is maintained by the PDC. Each user and group account is identified by a security identifier (SID). The SID is a number that is generated by Windows NT when the account is created. The following is an example of a SID:

S-1-5-21-2087915065-398913830-1877560073-500

The SID is the actual identifier of the user or group, not the name that is designated by the administrator. When a user is given permission to access an object such as a printer or a file, the user's SID is recorded in an *access control list* (ACL) associated with the object.

Consequently, it is not possible to recreate a user or group account once it has been deleted. Even though the recreated account can be given the same name, it will be assigned a different SID which will not be recognized by any references to the old account in the domain database.

When a user logs on to a domain, the WinLogon service generates an *access token* that determines which resources the user is permitted to access. The access token includes the following information:

◆ The user's SID

◆ Group IDs of groups to which the user belongs

◆ Privileges assigned to the user account

When a user attempts to access a network object, Windows NT compares the SID in the user's access token with the ACL for the object. If the SID appears in the ACL, the user is given permissions to the object as described in the ACL.

Global User Accounts

In Windows NT Server terminology, a *global entity* can be used by domains other than the domain in which the entity was created.

User accounts that are created on Windows NT Servers have a *global scope*—they can be used in any domain that trusts the domain in which the user account was created.

User accounts can be granted network privileges individually. It is more common, however, to include user accounts in groups and to grant privileges to the groups. This method makes it easier to alter the privileges of large numbers of users.

Because multi-domain Windows NT Server networks rely heavily on trust relationships, it is easy to see why global user accounts are desirable. A domain that trusts another domain can make use of any global user accounts that have been created in the trusted domain. This fact makes it unnecessary to give a user an account in more than one domain on the network.

Because global user accounts are the most common account types in Windows NT Networks, they simply are called *user accounts* in most situations.

Local User Accounts

When a user account originates on a network not running Windows NT, the account is a *local account*. Local entities cannot be used outside the domains in which they are created. Local user accounts can be placed in both global and local groups, however.

Local user accounts enable users from LAN Manager, IBM LAN Server, or NetWare environments to participate in Windows NT Server domains. Because they can be used only in the domains in which they are created, however, local user accounts are somewhat more difficult to administer than global user accounts.

Global Groups

Global groups are lists of user accounts from within a single domain. A global group can include user accounts only from the domain in which the global group was created. Global groups cannot contain other groups.

A global group created within one domain can be granted permissions in another domain. Figure 9.13 illustrates a two-domain network. The domain Keystone is used by all users to log on to the network. In Keystone, the administrator has created a global group named Domain Users. Users SLaurel, HLloyd, MNormand, and CChaplin have been established as members of Domain Users.

Figure 9.13

Global groups created in one domain can be granted privileges in domains that trust the host domain.

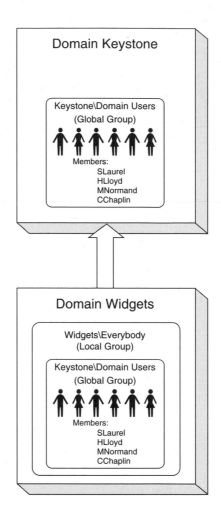

When Windows NT Server utilities reference the names of global groups, they frequently include the name of the domain in which the group was created. In the figure, the full name of the Domain Users group would be Keystone\Domain Users because the group is created in the Keystone domain. This notation is commonly used to describe a group in a domain other than the current domain.

The domain named Widgets trusts Keystone. This enables the Widgets administrator to assign permissions in the Widgets domain to the Keystone\Domain Users group. In figure 9.13, the administrator of Widgets has added the Keystone\Domain Users group as a member of the Widgets\Everybody local group. Any permissions that are assigned to the Widgets\Everybody group will be inherited by the members of Keystone\Domain Users.

Because it is important to understand this mechanism, let me express the idea a second way. When Widgets trusts Keystone, the Widgets administrator says, "I will accept the logon procedures in Keystone. Users who are authenticated by Keystone are also welcome in Widgets." Then the Widgets administrator proceeds to include global groups in Keystone as members of local groups in Widgets. By giving members of Keystone memberships in the Widgets local groups, those members are given permissions as though their accounts had been created directly in the Widgets domain.

The characteristics of global groups that you should remember follow:

◆ Global groups can contain users from the domain in which the group was created.

◆ Global groups cannot contain users from other domains.

◆ Global groups cannot contain other groups.

◆ Global groups can be assigned privileges in the domain in which the group was created.

◆ Global groups also can be assigned privileges in domains that trust the domain in which the group was created.

The word *global* indicates that global groups can be assigned privileges anywhere in the network (globally).

Local Groups

Local groups can be assigned privileges only in the account database in which they were created. The PDC and BDCs share an account database. Local groups can contain both users and global groups. This capability enables you to use a local group to collect entities from several domains and to manage them as a group in a local domain. When you assign privileges to a local group, all users and global groups in the local group inherit those privileges.

Figure 9.14 illustrates a three-domain network with the following features:

◆ The domain Blivets includes global users CChaplin, HLloyd, SLaurel, and MNormand.

◆ The domain Blivets includes a global group named SomeUsers. Users SLaurel, HLloyd, and MNormand are members of SomeUsers.

◆ Global users in the domain Doodads are BKeaton, FArbuckle, and OHardy.

◆ The domain Doodads includes a global group named MoreUsers. Only user OHardy is a member of MoreUsers.

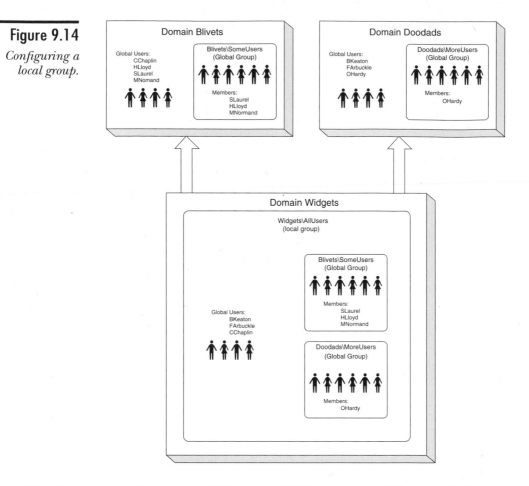

Figure 9.14

Configuring a local group.

The administrator of the domain Widgets would like to assign privileges to all the users in the Blivets and Doodads domains. One way to do that is to create a local group. In the figure, the local group is named Widgets\AllUsers. All the following entities can be added to AllUsers:

- **Blivets\SomeUsers.** A global group.

- **CChaplin.** A global user in the Blivets domain, who must be explicitly included since he is not a member of Blivets\SomeUsers.

- **Doodads\MoreUsers.** Another global group.

- **BKeaton and FArbuckle.** Global users in the domain Doodads, who must be explicitly included because they are not members of Blivets\SomeUsers.

A preferable approach would be to add all the users to the global groups Blivets\SomeUsers and Doodads\MoreUsers. This, however, would require the cooperation of the other domains. Fortunately, local groups enable you to include users when the global groups are not configured as you want.

The characteristics of local groups that you should remember follow:

◆ Local groups can contain users from the domain in which the local group was created.

◆ Local groups can contain global users from other domains that are trusted by the group's domain.

◆ Local groups can contain global groups from domains that are trusted by the local group's domain.

◆ Local groups can be assigned privileges in the group's local domain.

◆ Local groups cannot be assigned privileges in other domains.

Built-In Groups and Users

When you install Windows NT Workstation or Windows NT Server, several users and groups are created. These users and groups define various levels of access to workstations and servers and are the building blocks you use to secure your network.

The default users and groups can be modified by users with sufficient privileges. These groups cannot be deleted, however.

Built-In User Accounts

Every Windows NT Server or Windows NT Workstation has two default user accounts.

The *Administrator user account* enables you to manage the server when it first is installed. So that you cannot be locked out of the server, this account cannot be deleted or disabled, although it can be renamed. After you create other administrators, you can choose to give the Administrator account an especially secure password, store the password in a safe place, and put the Administrator account into semi-retirement.

The *Guest user account* cannot be deleted, but it can be disabled and renamed. Guest is disabled by default, but can be enabled if you want to permit guest users to have limited access to your domain or server.

Built-In Groups

You grant a user a set of capabilities on a domain, workstation, or server by adding the user to the correct group. The built-in groups are available in both global and local varieties to make management of the network more versatile.

Users can be assigned to multiple groups if required. To enable a user to manage printers and back up the system, add the user to the Print Operators and Backup Operators groups. These groups make it easy to configure layers of security on your network so that you can distribute responsibilities to various personnel.

Table 9.2 summarizes the built-in groups and whether they are installed on domain controllers, workstations, or servers. Each of the groups is discussed in the following sections.

TABLE 9.2
Windows NT Built-In Groups

Group	Local/ Managed by Global	Windows NT Server Domains	Workstations and Servers	Automatic Contents
Administrators	Local Administrators	Yes	Yes	Domain Administrator (user)
Domain Admins	Global Administrators	Yes	No	Administrator
Backup Operators	Local Administrators	Yes	Yes	None
Server Operators	Local Administrators	Yes	No	None
Account Operators	Local Administrators	Yes	No	None
Print Operators	Local Administrators	Yes	No	None
Power Users	Local Administrators	No	Yes	Setup user
Power Users	Local Administrators	Yes	Yes	Domain users

Group	Local/ Managed by Global	Windows NT Server Domains	Workstations and Servers	Automatic Contents
	Account Operators			Administrator (user)
Domain Users	Global Administrators	Yes	No	Administrators
	Account Operators			New users
Guests	Local Administrators	Yes	Yes	Domain Guest (user)
	Account Operators			
Domain Guests	Global Administrators	Yes	No	Guest
	Account Operators			
Replicator	Local Administrators	Yes	Yes	None

Administrators

◆ Local

◆ Domain Controllers, Workstations, and Servers

Members of Administrators local groups have nearly complete authority over the domain controllers, workstation, or server on which the group resides. Adding a user account to the Administrators group is all that is necessary to make the user an administrator. Administrators are limited in one respect: They cannot automatically access files on NTFS file systems. Each NTFS file has an owner who, by default, is the person who created the file. Unless the owner grants access permissions, even an administrator cannot access the file. Administrators can, however, take ownership of any file, as described in Chapter 12, "Sharing Drives, Directories, and Files."

Domain Admins

◆ Global

◆ Domain Controllers

Each domain also includes a built-in global group named Domain Admins. This group is added automatically to the Administrators local group, making all members of Domain Admins domain administrators.

You therefore have two ways to make a user a domain administrator: by adding the user directly to the Administrators local group, or by adding the user to the Domain Admins global group. The advantage of adding the user to the Domain Admins group is that this group can be included in the Administrators local group of other domains that trust this domain. This enables you to easily give administrators the permissions required to manage several domains.

When a Windows NT Workstation or a stand-alone Windows NT Server is brought into a domain, the Domain Admins group is added automatically to the workstation or server's Administrators group. If you want to prevent members of Domain Admins from managing the workstation or server, you must manually remove that entry from the Administrators group.

Backup Operators

◆ Local

◆ Domain Controllers, Workstations, and Servers

This group solves an old problem in LAN administration. Tape backups frequently are performed by operators who really should not have administrator privileges. Members of the Backup Operators group can back up and restore files, log on to the system locally, and shut down the system, but they are not granted the capability to manipulate security or perform other administrative functions.

Server Operators

◆ Local

◆ Domain Controllers

Each primary or backup domain controller has a Server Operators local group. Users in this group can perform many administrative functions but cannot manage security. They can share and stop sharing resources, format server disks, back up and restore files, log in locally to servers, and shut down servers.

Account Operators

- ◆ Local
- ◆ Domain Controllers

Account operators can manage user accounts and groups in the domain. They can create, delete, and modify most users, local groups, and global groups but cannot assign user rights. Account Operators cannot manage the accounts of administrators or modify the local groups' Administrators, Server Operators, Account Operators, Backup Operators, or Print Operators.

Print Operators

- ◆ Local
- ◆ Domain Controllers

Members of Print Operators can share, stop sharing, and manage printers running in a Windows NT Server domain. They can also log on to servers locally and shut them down.

Users

- ◆ Local
- ◆ Domain Controllers, Workstations, and Servers

Most users on workstations and servers will be members of the Users local group. On a PDC and BDCs, most users are members of Domain Users and Domain Users is a member of the Users local group. Members of Users are not permitted to log on locally to primary or backup domain controllers. They can access resources in the domain only through clients on the network. Users also can maintain a profile on a Windows NT Workstation (see Chapter 15, "Using Windows NT Clients"). Users can log on to domain controllers, workstations, and servers, however.

Power Users

- ◆ Local
- ◆ NT Workstations and Stand-alone Servers

Members of Power Users can perform user functions on workstations and servers. They can also create user accounts and modify the accounts they have created. Power Users can add user accounts to the built-in groups Users, Guests, and Power Users. They also can start and stop sharing of printers and files on the workstation or server.

If a Windows NT Workstation is operating in a Windows NT Server domain, a recommended strategy is to put the user's domain account into the Power Users group at the workstation. In that way, a single account enables the user to be a user in the domain and to administer the workstation.

Domain Users

- ◆ Global
- ◆ Domain Controllers

All user accounts in a domain are included in the Domain Users global group automatically. The Domain Users global group is in turn included in the local Users group, establishing all members of the Domain Users group as users of the domain.

In multi-domain networks, you can include the Domain Users group in the local Users groups of other domains that trust the logon domain. This is an easy way of granting users privileges on multiple domains.

Guests

- ◆ Local
- ◆ Domain Controllers, Workstations, and Servers

In domains, members of Guests are similar to members of Users. They can utilize domain resources, but may only do so by logging on through the network. Local server logons are not permitted.

Members of the Guests group on workstations and servers have limited rights. They can maintain a profile on a Windows NT Workstation, but they cannot manage local groups or lock the workstation.

Domain Guests

- ◆ Global
- ◆ Domains

The Guest user normally is included in the Domain Guests global group, which is included in the local Guests group. Other user accounts also can be added to the Domain Guests group. Members of the Domain Guests or Guest group have guest privileges in the domain.

In multi-domain networks, you can include the Domain Guests group in the local Guests groups of other domains that trust the logon domain. This is an easy way of granting users guest privileges on multiple domains.

Replicator

◆ Local

◆ Domain Controllers, Workstations, and Servers

Members of the Replicator group can manage the replication of files on the domain, workstation, or server.

What Happens When a Computer Joins a Domain

Windows NT computers cannot simply log on to a domain and start computing. Before they are permitted access to the domain, they must be added to the domain, a formal process by which the computer added to the Security Accounts Manager (SAM) database for the domain, in the process of which a SID is created for the computer. The effect this has depends on the computer's role in the domain.

Domain controllers (PDC and BDCs) fully participate in the domain security. This is most clearly seen in the case of administrators. Any user who is a member of the domain Administrators group (either directly or through membership in Domain Admins) is also an administrator of the domain controller computer. In other words, the Administrators group for the domain is also the Administrators group for the domain controller.

Stand alone servers and Windows NT Workstation computers, however, behave quite differently. Each server and workstation retains its own security database that regulates access to resources on that computer alone. And each computer has its own set of local groups, including Administrators, Backup Operators, Power Users, Replicator, and Users. Servers and workstations have only local groups and cannot create global groups. Membership in a domain group does not guarantee membership in the corresponding local group on a server or a workstation. A member of the domain Controller Backup Operators group, for example, is not a member of the workstation Backup Operators group.

Once a Windows NT server or workstation is added to a domain, however, administrators can administer the computer and users can use it. How is this accomplished?

When the server or workstation is added to the domain, two group membership assignments are established:

◆ The domain Domain Admins account is added to the local Administrators account on the server or workstation.

◆ The domain Domain Users account is added to the local Users account on the server or workstation.

In this way, the server or computer indirectly participates in the core security established by the domain. If you need to extend on the basic security provided by the Administrators and Users groups, you can assign any of the following permissions to file and printer resources shared by the server or workstation:

◆ Individual users from the domain to which the computer belongs

◆ Individual users from domains trusted by the domain to which the computer belongs

◆ Global groups from the domain to which the computer belongs

◆ Global groups from domains trusted by the domain to which the computer belongs

Because all groups on servers and workstations are local groups—and local groups cannot contain other local groups—you cannot assign permissions to domain controller local groups.

This close relationship between Windows NT servers and workstations is a key reason why Windows NT computers make the best clients on a Windows NT Server network. MS-DOS, Windows for Workgroups, and Windows 95 clients don't have the ability to use the domain database to secure the resources they share. That's another good argument for placing critical resources on Windows NT computers, where they can be properly secured.

Testing Your Knowledge

1. Which one of the following Microsoft products cannot share its resources in workgroups?

   A. Windows 3.x

   B. Windows NT Workstation

   C. Windows NT Server

   D. Windows 95

   E. Windows for Workgroups

   F. MS-DOS with the Workgroup add-on feature

2. Which of the following server roles are consistent with a Windows NT Server that is connected to a domain and contains a user and group database?

   A. Backup domain controller (BDC)

   B. Server

C. Workstation

D. Primary domain controller (PDC)

3. If a domain model is not desired, you may set up a Windows NT Server with the _____ role.

4. All changes to the domain directory database are first made on the PDC, after which they are distributed to the BDCs in a process called _____.

5. Why may it be necessary to establish two or more domains?

A. If too many servers are put in a domain, performance can suffer.

B. You may need to connect an additional NT Server to the network.

C. For best performance, the domain database should be restricted to 40 MB.

D. Some departments prefer to manage their own resources.

6. Which type of trust relationship permits both trusting domains users to access each other's domains resources?

A. One-way trust relationship

B. Two-way trust relationship

C. Two-domain trust relationship

D. Simple trust relationship

7. Which type of domain model is the most simple and is commonly used for small organizations?

A. Single domain model

B. Master domain model

C. Multiple master domain model

D. Complete trust model

8. What type of domain model uses one domain to manage all user accounts?

A. Single domain model

B. Master domain model

C. Multiple master domain model

D. Complete trust model

9. Which type of domain model is best suited for large enterprise situations?

A. Single domain model

B. Master domain model

C. Multiple master domain model

D. Complete trust model

10. Which type of domain model is practical if each domain within an organization wants to retain full responsibility for managing its own domain?

    A. Single domain model

    B. Master domain model

    C. Multiple master domain model

    D. Complete trust model

11. At what size of a SAM domain database file does Microsoft recommend you go to a multiple domain model type?

    A. 40 MB

    B. 166 MB

    C. 1,432,589 bytes

    D. 32 MB

12. When a user account originates on a network not running Windows NT, the account is a(n) _____.

13. A(n) _____ group is a list of user accounts from within a single domain. It can include user accounts only from the domain in which it was created and cannot contain other groups.

14. A(n) _____ group can be assigned privileges only in the domain in which it was created. It can contain both users and global groups.

15. Which of the following is not a built-in group?

    A. Administrators

    B. Domain Administrators

    C. Operators

    D. Guests

    E. Power Users

    F. Replicator

Review Answers

1. A

2. A, D

3. server

4. synchronization

5. A, C, D

6. B

7. A

8. A, B

9. C

10. D

11. A

12. local account

13. global

14. local

15. C

Managing Domains and Trust Relationships

As you probably have gathered from reading Chapter 9, "Understanding User Accounts, Groups, Domains, and Trust Relationships," proper management of domains and trust relationships is extremely important and can have critical implications for network security and performance. Chapter 9 focused on giving you background information about domains and trust relationships. In this chapter, you will learn to apply that understanding to real network-management operations.

Several terms are used frequently in this chapter, and it's worth reviewing their definitions:

- **Primary Domain Controller (PDC).** A computer running Windows NT Server, on which the primary domain user database is stored.

- **Backup Domain Controller (BDC).** A computer running Windows NT Server, on which replicas of the domain user database are stored.

- ◆ **Server.** A computer running Windows NT Server that is participating in a domain but is not serving as a domain controller.

- ◆ **Workstation.** A computer running Windows NT Workstation that is permitted access to a domain. Sometimes Microsoft also calls a Windows NT Workstation or Server a *computer*. For consistency and clarity, the terms *workstation* and *server* are used here.

Microsoft does not have a unique term for computers that are clients on a Windows NT Server network but are not running Windows NT software. Procedures for managing non-NT clients are somewhat different from procedures for Windows NT computers.

Creating Domain Controllers

Primary and backup domain controllers can be created only by the Setup process, which you examined in Chapter 7, "Installing Windows NT Server."

Selecting a Server Role

During Windows NT Setup, you are prompted to define the Windows NT Server Security Role. The following choices are available:

- ◆ Primary Domain Controller
- ◆ Backup Domain Controller
- ◆ Server

If you specify that the server is to be a domain controller, Setup takes you through the steps required to connect the server to the network. These steps are described in Chapter 7. Network communication is required so that Setup can determine which domains already are present. Each domain on the network must be named uniquely. A PDC cannot be added to an existing domain, and a BDC can be added to a domain only when the PDC for the domain is available.

Objective
B.2

Creating a Primary Domain Controller (PDC)

If you select Primary Domain Controller, you also must specify a domain name. Domain names cannot contain spaces.

Setup searches the network to ensure that a domain with the name you specify does not already exist. You are permitted to proceed only if the domain name specifies a new domain.

Setup creates an Administrator user for each new domain. The default Administrator user account has complete administrative authority for the domain. After the domain name you specified is approved, Setup prompts you for a password for the Administrator user. Blank passwords are permitted, but Setup warns you that `no password has been entered`. You need to choose OK to confirm your decision to leave the password blank.

You are required to enter the password twice as confirmation. Record this password in a safe place. If the Administrator password is lost before other Administrator accounts are created, the only way to change the password is to reinstall Windows NT Server.

After installation is completed and Windows NT Server is restarted, this server is the primary domain controller for the domain.

How Domain Security IDs Work

When you create the Primary Domain Controller for a domain, Windows NT Server assigns the PDC a Security ID (SID) that is used to identify everything in the domain. In fact, each time you add a backup domain controller or a computer to the domain, the domain SID is added as a prefix to the computer's own SID. It is the SID, not the domain name, that actually defines the identity of the domain. This has several potentially troublesome consequences.

Never perform a New Version installation of Windows NT Server on an existing primary domain controller. Even though you specify the same domain name, Setup will create a new SID for the PDC. Computers that have already been added to the domain were configured with the old SID and will be unable to find the new PDC. As a result, computers that could once attach to the domain will mysteriously be unable to do so.

Never install a domain controller when the PDC is down. Because Setup cannot find a PDC, the new computer may be installed as a PDC, creating a second SID for the same domain name. (Should this condition be called SIDling rivalry?) The new PDC will never be able to participate in the same domain as the old PDC. If you want to install a new computer to act as a PDC in a domain, install it as a BDC while the current PDC is running. Then promote the new computer to a PDC when both domain controllers are running.

Creating a Backup Domain Controller (BDC)

A BDC can be added to a domain in two ways:

◆ By first adding a computer account to the domain using the Server Manager utility, a procedure described later in this chapter. You then can install the BDC to that computer account.

◆ By creating the computer account during Setup, in which case, you must enter a user name and a password that has administrative privileges in the domain. This is the more common approach and the one that will be described in this section.

If, during installation, you select Backup Domain Controller, you also must specify the name of the domain that the backup domain controller will be joining.

If this computer already has been added to the domain (the procedure for doing so follows), you can choose OK. If the computer is being added to the domain during installation, you must specify the following:

◆ A **U**ser Name that has administrator privileges in the domain to be joined

◆ The **P**assword for the user name you have entered

You can use an Administrator account that originates in a domain that is trusted by the current domain. If Max is an Administrator in the trusted domain Keystone, for example, you would enter the name as **Keystone\Max**.

> **Note**   If you are moving existing Backup domain controllers to new domains, you will be required to reinstall Windows NT Server. During installation, Setup will determine that Windows NT is already installed on the hard drive and will ask you to choose between the following actions:
>
> ◆ To upgrade Windows NT in the directory shown, press Enter.
>
> ◆ To cancel the upgrade and install a fresh copy of Windows NT, press N.
>
> Be sure to request a New Version installation. Upgrading the current software retains the current system configuration and does not permit you to redefine the server's security role.
>
> Selecting New Version reinstalls Windows NT Server over the previous installation, and you lose your previous user account database. (You retain any applications and other files that have been installed on the computer's hard drives, however.)
>
> The only way to retain a user account database while changing a server's security role is to move a primary domain controller to a new domain. This isn't really

something you should count on, however, because it is probable that most of the permissions no longer will make sense because they pertain to the old domain name.

If you are reinstalling a backup domain controller to a new domain, it receives a copy of the domain account database from the PDC after it joins the domain.

Creating New Domains

New domains can be created in two ways:

◆ By installing a new primary domain controller into a new domain using the procedure described earlier in the section "Creating a Primary Domain Controller (PDC)."

◆ By using the Network utility in the Control Panel on a primary domain controller to create a new domain and set the server as the primary domain controller of the new domain. This procedure is described in the following section.

Creating a New Domain by Moving a Primary Domain Controller

On the primary domain controller, follow these steps:

1. In the Control Panel, choose the Network utility and select the Identification tab, shown in figure 10.1 or right-click on Network Neighborhood, and choose Properties.

2. Choose **C**hange to bring up the Identification Changes dialog box, shown in figure 10.2.

3. In the Domain Name box, enter a domain name that does not already exist on your network.

   A Warning box appears to warn you of possible consequences of this action (see fig. 10.3).

4. Choose **Y**es to complete the change. After a pause, you are greeted with a message welcoming you to the new domain.

5. Restart the server to make the change effective.

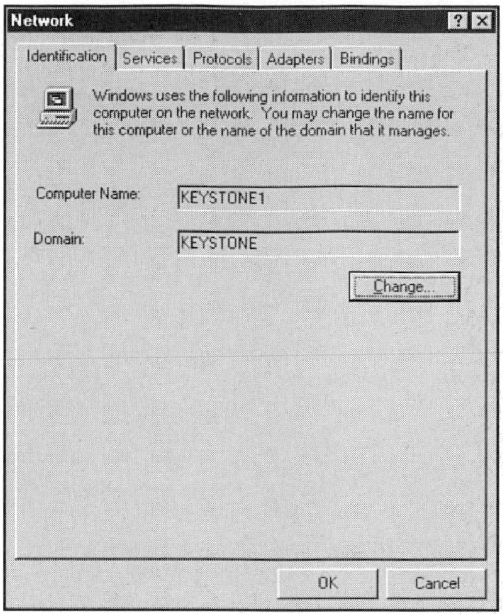

Figure 10.1

The Network dialog box.

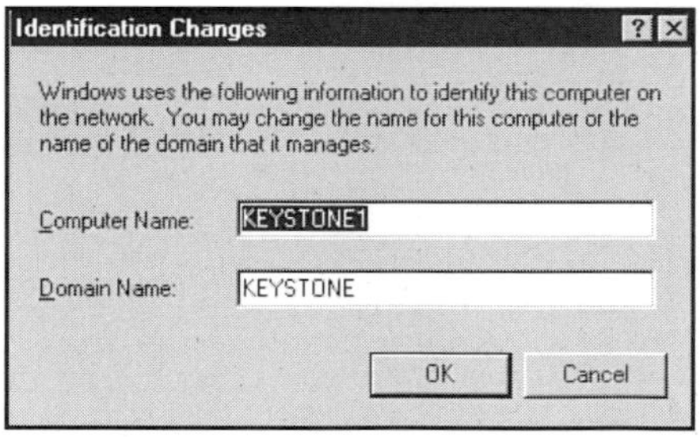

Figure 10.2

Renaming a domain.

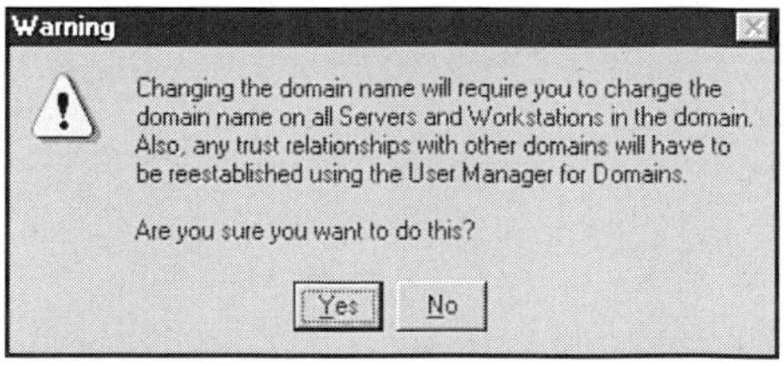

Figure 10.3

The Network Settings warning message.

> **Caution** | Moving primary domain controllers is not for the faint of heart. After you move the PDC, you might have a great deal of cleanup to do. You need to change the domains for any BDCs that you want to move to the new domain. You also need to update all the workstation logon configurations so that they will log on to the new domain.
>
> If you are moving the PDC to create a new domain, don't leave the old domain without a PDC. Be sure to promote one of the BDCs in the old domain to PDC.

Moving a Domain Controller to a New Domain

A primary domain controller can be moved to a new domain by using the procedures described in the previous section, "Creating New Domains." You can use the Control Panel to move a PDC, and you can move a PDC only if it is being moved to a domain that does not already exist.

A BDC cannot be moved to a new domain, but its domain can be renamed if the PDC's domain is renamed first. In that case, the SID for the domain remains the same and continuity is maintained when the domain name is changed. Chapter 7 reviewed a scenario whereby changing domain names can result in the establishment of two domains where one existed previously.

A domain controller can be moved to another domain by reinstalling Windows NT Server. You can reinstall a primary domain controller to a domain only if the domain does not exist. If the domain exists, a PDC already is established in the domain. You have to install the computer as a BDC and promote it to a PDC after setup.

To move a backup domain controller to another domain, you must reinstall Windows NT Server. During the Setup procedure, you can use the procedures described in the earlier section, "Selecting a Server Role," to specify the new domain for the server.

Although you can use the Identification tab in the Network utility to rename a domain, the procedure is by no means simple. To rename a domain, you must change the domain name in the Network utility for each computer in the domain. Change the PDC first, followed by each BDC. Finally, change the domains for the stand-alone servers and other workstations in the domain. When the domain has been renamed on each domain controller, you must reestablish trust relationships with other domains, as described in this chapter in the section "Setting Trust Relationships." This procedure should be performed when no users are accessing the domain, because services to connected users will be disrupted.

Suppose that the domain PRIMA includes three domain controllers: A is the PDC while B and C are BDCs. The following steps would successfully change the domain name to SECUNDA:

1. A's domain is changed to SECUNDA and A is restarted. This establishes the domain SECUNDA.

2. B's domain is changed to SECUNDA and B is restarted. B is established as a BDC in SECUNDA.

3. C's domain is changed to SECUNDA and C is restarted. C also is established as a BDC in SECUNDA.

Throughout the preceding procedure, continuity was maintained. A was the only PDC, and a single SID was associated with the domain, even when the domain was referred to by two different names. Until steps 2 and 3 were completed, however, the domain was not fully functional, and B and C could not participate in the domain as BDCs.

If the procedure is not carefully followed, it is possible for BDCs to lose their domains. While you are changing a domain name, there is a brief period when the PDC and BDCs belong to different domains, and confusion can result while the change is being made. Let's examine a scenario for a domain named ALPHA, which contains three domain controllers: A is the PDC, while B, C, and D are BDCs. Here is the chain of events:

1. A's domain is changed to domain BETA. After restarting, A is the PDC of domain BETA. For the time being, domain ALPHA does not have a PDC.

2. B's domain is changed to domain BETA. B is now a BDC in BETA.

3. C is promoted to become the PDC of ALPHA, a procedure that is described in the following section "Promoting Domain Controllers."

4. An attempt is made to change the domain of D to domain BETA. The attempt fails because ALPHA is managed by a PDC. When C became a PDC, ALPHA and BETA became two distinct domains.

A domain cannot have two PDCs. When C was promoted in step 3, it became necessary to distinguish between domains ALPHA and BETA, and each was assigned a unique SID. D remained associated with the SID for domain ALPHA and could no longer move to domain BETA, which was controlled by A using a different domain SID.

When you want to move a BDC from one domain to another, you must reinstall Windows NT Server on that computer when you make the change. Only reinstalling enables the BDC to acquire the SID for the new domain.

No problems are involved in moving workstations or stand-alone servers to a different domain. The computer must simply be added to the new domain by a user logged in with administrator permissions.

Note You must restart the computer to activate a change in the computer's name or domain.

Renaming a Domain

The preceding section demonstrated how it is possible to rename a domain under Windows NT Server 4. This procedure was not possible under earlier versions of Windows NT Server. Prior to version 4, it was necessary to reinstall BDCs to change their domain names.

Promoting Domain Controllers

You might need to promote a backup domain controller to the primary role for several reasons:

◆ If the server functioning as a primary domain controller will be shut down for maintenance, you should promote a backup domain controller so that the domain remains in full operation. You cannot make changes to the domain account database unless a PDC is active.

If a backup domain controller is promoted while the primary domain controller is available, the netlogon shares of the current PDC and BDC are stopped and their services are restarted under the new roles. The only difference between the PDC and BDC is responsibility for directory synchronization. Also, the old primary domain controller is demoted to the role of backup domain controller.

◆ If the primary domain controller is unavailable, the user account database on the backup domain controller will be established as the account database for the domain. Any changes that have not been replicated from the original PDC are lost. After the old PDC comes back online, you need to demote the old PDC to a backup role.

Note | If the PDC for a Windows NT Server domain is not available, changes cannot be made to the domain database. Although users can continue to log on to the domain and access secure resources, the following activities cannot take place:

◆ Changing, modifying, or deleting user accounts, including changes to user names, logon hours, and so forth

◆ Changes to user or group rights

◆ Creating, modifying, or deleting global groups

◆ Creating, modifying, or deleting local groups that belong to the domain controlled by the PDC

If the PDC will not be returned to the network in a reasonable time, it is necessary to promote a BDC (if the previous functions must be performed).

To promote a server to a primary domain controller, follow these steps:

1. Start the Server Manager utility (in the Administrative Tools folder).

2. Choose **S**ervers from the **V**iew menu. You then see a display similar to figure 10.4 that clearly indicates the domain controller function of each server. Notice the different icons that are used for primary and backup DCs.

3. Select the BDC to be promoted from the list.

4. Choose Promote to Primary Domain **C**ontroller from the **C**omputer menu.

   The warning shown in figure 10.5 appears.

5. Clearly, you should not promote a server when users are active in the domain. Choose **Y**es to proceed or **N**o to cancel.

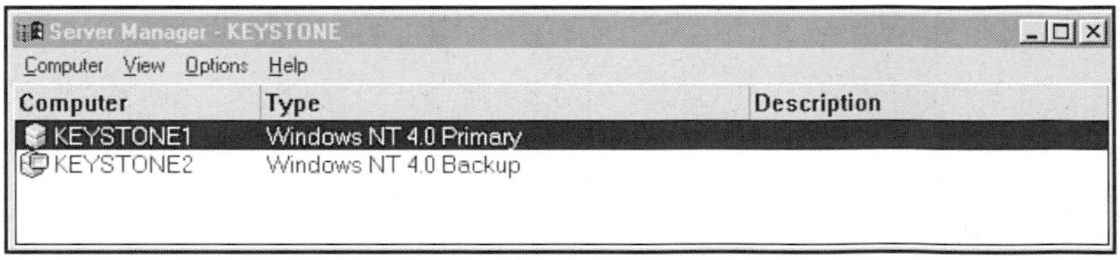

Figure 10.4

The servers list in Server Manager.

Server Manager - KEYSTONE		
Computer View Options Help		
Computer	**Type**	**Description**
KEYSTONE1	Windows NT 4.0 Primary	
KEYSTONE2	Windows NT 4.0 Backup	

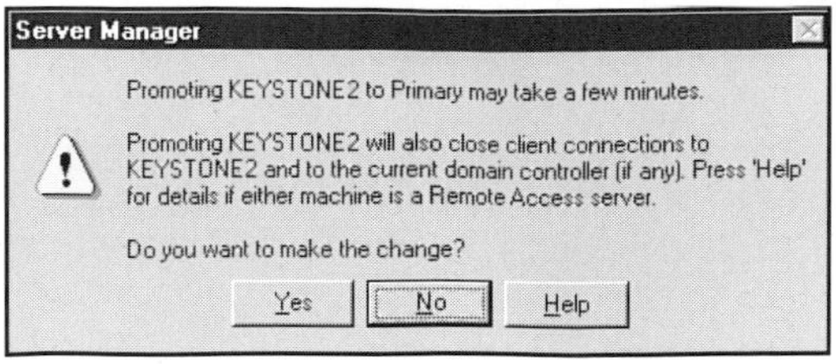

Figure 10.5

The warning you see when promoting a server.

Demoting a Primary Domain Controller

If a BDC is promoted while the PDC is off-line, you should be aware of the following differences from the procedure described in the last section:

◆ You are warned that the PDC is unavailable and that promoting the BDC might result in errors when the PDC returns to service.

◆ The status of the old PDC when it comes back online is uncertain. While experimenting with this scenario, I encountered two results:

The old PDC came online as a workstation.

The old PDC came online as an inactive PDC.

When a PDC attempts to reenter the domain after another server has been promoted to PDC status, Windows NT Server displays the message At least one service or driver failed during system startup. You are prompted to examine the Events log. Using the Events Viewer is covered in Chapter 19, "Managing the Server."

One event in the log has the source of NETLOGON. The Detail Description displays the message A Primary domain controller is already running in this domain.

If you examine the Servers list in System Manager on the new PDC and discover that two servers are shown as primary, the old PDC is not functioning (its icon appears as an outline) and must be demoted.

If you select a server that needs to be demoted, a new menu choice appears on the **C**omputer menu. This new choice is Demote to **B**ackup Domain Controller. This option is unavailable unless the selected computer is a duplicate PDC.

Choose the Demote to **B**ackup Domain Controller option to demote the old server.

Synchronizing Domain Computers

Under normal circumstances, Windows NT Server keeps all BDCs synchronized with the PDC in a domain. It seldom is necessary for you to force a domain to synchronize. Because it is possible for BDCs to lose sync with the domain, however, Windows NT Server provides a manual synchronization procedure as described in the following exercise.

Synchronizing Servers and Domains

To synchronize a BDC with the PDC, follow these steps:

1. Choose **S**ervers in the **V**iew menu of the Server Manager utility.

2. Select the backup domain controller to be synchronized.

3. Choose S**y**nchronize with Primary Domain Controller from the **C**omputer menu.

To synchronize an entire domain with the PDC, follow these steps:

1. Choose **S**ervers in the **V**iew menu of the Server Manager utility.

2. Select the primary domain controller.

3. Choose S**y**nchronize Entire Domain from the **C**omputer menu.

Adding Workstations and Servers to the Domain

Clients that are not running Windows NT enter a domain simply by running the correct protocols and logging on to a valid user account.

Because they participate more intimately in the domain, Windows NT Workstations and Servers must be explicitly added (create a computer account) to a domain before they are permitted to access domain services. They simply cannot connect up and log on.

Servers and workstations can join a domain in three ways:

◆ By adding the server or workstation computer to the domain first using the Server Manager utility

◆ By adding the server or workstation to the domain during installation

◆ By adding the server or workstation to the domain from the Control Panel

Adding Workstations and Servers to a Domain with Server Manager

You can prepare the way for a server or workstation to join a domain by adding it to the domain configuration with the Server Manager.

To add a workstation named Harold, for example, follow these steps:

Adding a Workstation with the Server Manager

1. Log on to the domain as an administrator.

2. Run the Server Manager utility in the Administrative Tools folder. The Server Manager box displayed by the utility is shown in figure 10.6. At present, this box lists only the primary domain controller computer KEYSTONE1.

3. Choose **A**dd to Domain from the **C**omputer menu. The Add Computer To Domain dialog box appears.

4. Figure 10.7 shows the Add Computer To Domain dialog box being used to add a server or workstation named HAROLD. You also can use this dialog box to add a backup domain controller to the domain prior to installing software on the BDC computer.

5. Choose **A**dd to add the computer you have specified.

6. After you add all required computers, choose Cancel.

7. The computer(s) you add appear in the Server Manager list (see fig. 10.8).

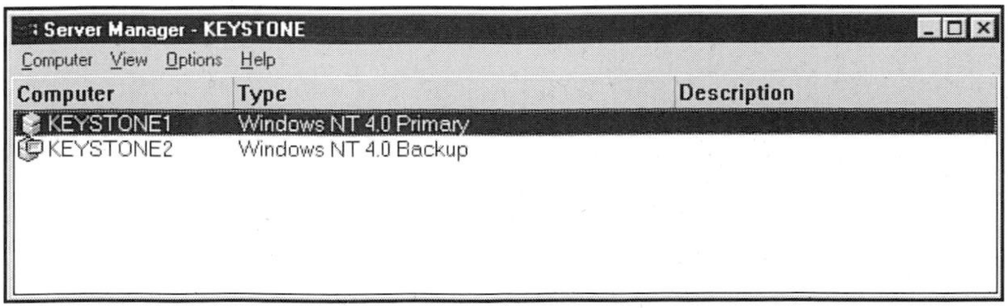

Figure 10.6

Server Manager with two domain controllers installed.

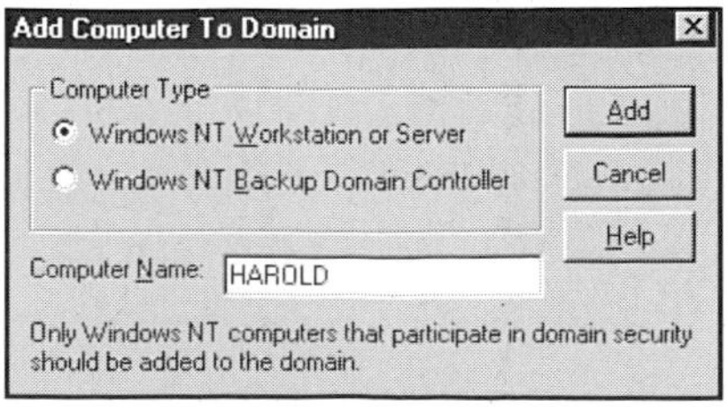

Figure 10.7

Adding a computer to a domain.

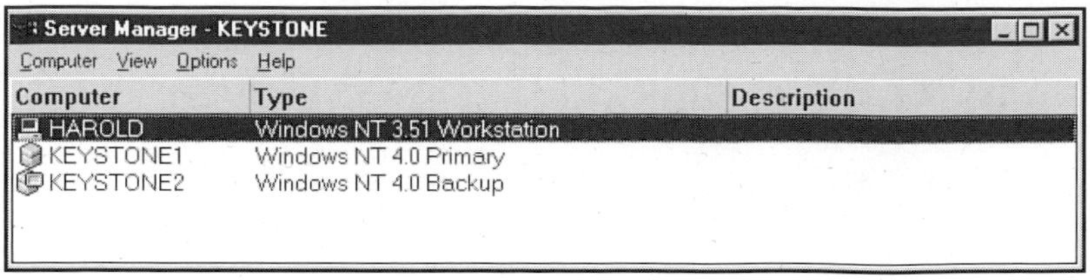

Figure 10.8

Server Manager after a new computer has been added.

Once a computer account has been created, you can then join the domain from the Workstation or Server.

To join a domain from a Windows NT Workstation, follow these steps:

Joining an NT Domain from a Workstation

1. Choose the Network utility from the Control Panel and select the Identification tab.

2. Check the Computer **N**ame entry to ensure that it matches the name that was specified in the Server Manager. If it does not match, choose the **C**hange button. An Identification Changes dialog box enables you to enter a new computer name. You need to restart the computer to put the new computer name into effect before you resume this procedure from step 1.

3. Choose **C**hange to open the Identification Changes dialog box.

4. Enter the domain to which the computer will be added in the **D**omain field. The Identification Changes dialog box shown in figure 10.9 is being used to add the computer Harold to the domain KEYSTONE.

   Because the computer already has been created, you do not need to check the **C**reate Computer Account in the Domain check box or use the other fields of the dialog box. If the computer successfully enters the domain, you will see a message "Welcome to the...domain."

5. When you exit the Network utility, you will be prompted to restart the computer to activate the network changes.

6. After restarting the computer, press Ctrl+Alt+Del to log on again.

7. In the Begin Logon dialog box, change the **D**omain entry to the name of the domain to which you want to log on. Be sure that the **U**ser Name and **P**assword entries match a valid user account in the domain.

8. Choose OK to log on.

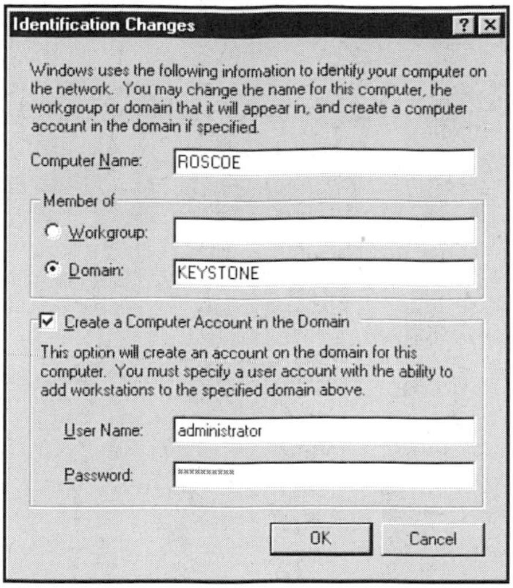

Figure 10.9

The Identification Changes dialog box on a Windows NT Workstation.

Note You might want to look at the computer list in Server Manager before and after a new computer has logged on for the first time. Prior to the logon, the computer's icon is presented as an outline. Following a successful logon, the icon is filled in.

Adding Workstations or Servers to a Domain During Installation

Windows NT Workstations and Servers also can join a domain during installation. In this case, installation must be performed by a domain administrator because an administrator logon is required to access the domain database and add the new workstation or server.

During Windows NT Server installation, you are prompted to define the Windows NT Server Security Role. Three choices are available:

◆ Primary Domain Controller

◆ Backup Domain Controller

◆ Server

When you are installing Windows NT Workstation or Windows NT Server in Server mode, after Setup connects to the network, you are prompted to enter information that will add the computer to a domain. This is discussed in step 32 of the Windows

NT Server installation procedure in Chapter 7. The information you enter depends on the role of the computer that is being installed and whether the computer has already been added to the domain using Server Manager.

Adding Workstations or Servers to a Domain from the Control Panel

Windows NT Workstations and Servers also can join a domain after setup is completed. This procedure must be performed by a domain administrator, because an administrator logon is required to access the domain database and add the new workstation or server.

To add the computer to the domain, follow these steps:

Adding a Computer to a Domain from the Control Panel

1. Choose the Network utility from the Control Panel and select the Identification tab.

2. Check the Computer **N**ame entry to ensure that it matches the name that was specified in the Server Manager. If it does not match, choose the **C**hange button. An Identification Changes dialog box enables you to enter a new computer name. You need to restart the computer to put the new computer name into effect before you resume this procedure from step 1.

3. Enter the domain to which the computer will be added in the **D**omain field. The Identification Changes dialog box (see fig. 10.9) is being used to add the computer ROSCOE to the domain KEYSTONE.

4. Check the **C**reate Computer Account in the Domain check box. In the **U**ser Name and **P**assword fields, enter the user name and password for a user account that has administrator privileges in the domain specified in the **D**omain field.

5. Choose OK and exit the Network utility. You will be prompted to restart the computer to activate the network changes.

6. After restarting the computer, press Ctrl+Alt+Del to log on again.

7. In the Begin Logon dialog box, change the **D**omain entry to the name of the domain you want to log on to. Be sure that the **U**ser Name and **P**assword entries match a valid user account in the domain.

8. Choose OK to log on.

| Note | Just as installing a primary domain controller defines a security ID (SID) for the domain, each computer that is added to the domain is assigned an SID that uniquely identifies it in the domain. |

It is the computer SID that permits the computer to participate in the domain. The computer's name is included as a convenience for users. This approach makes it difficult for another computer to masquerade as a computer that already has been added to a domain. Suppose that a computer named Harold has been added to a domain. Another Windows NT computer cannot log on to the domain simply by changing its name to Harold. It also is required to duplicate the SID that was created for the first Harold.

Unfortunately, only Windows NT computers are secured on the network using SIDs. Non-NT clients, such as Windows 95 and Windows 3.x, are not assigned computer accounts or SIDs and cannot communicate with the same level of security as is possible with Windows NT.

Removing Computers from Domains

Computer accounts are not deleted when a computer stops using a domain. When you move a domain controller to a new domain, for example, the old domain retains a computer account. If a user's workstation begins to access the network from a new domain, its computer account remains in the old domain.

There will be times, therefore, when you need to remove a computer from a domain. This is performed from the Server Manager using the following procedure:

Removing Computers from Domains

1. Log on to the domain as an administrator.

2. Run the Server Manager utility in the Administrative Tools folder.

3. Select the computer to be removed from the domain.

4. Choose **R**emove from Domain from the **C**omputer menu. You are asked to confirm your decision.

The computer might not be removed from the Server Manager computer list immediately. It might be several minutes before periodic server housekeeping updates the computer list.

Setting Trust Relationships

The operations required to add and remove trust relationships can be illustrated in a simple two-domain network. The example network has two domains:

◆ Keystone, which will be trusted by Widgets

◆ Widgets, which will trust Keystone

Each trust relationship is the result of two actions:

◆ The trusted domain must be configured to allow another domain to trust it.

◆ The trusting domain then must be configured to trust the trusted domain.

The following example demonstrates the steps required to enable the Widgets domain to trust the Keystone domain.

Permitting Widgets to Trust Keystone

First, an administrator of Keystone must add Widgets to the list of domains that are permitted to trust Keystone. The steps to accomplish this follow:

Establishing a One-Way Trust

1. Start the User Manager utility in the Administrative Tools folder.

2. Choose **T**rust Relationships in the **P**olicies menu. The Trust Relationships dialog box shown in figure 10.10 appears.

   Choose the A**d**d button beside the Tr**u**sting Domains list. This brings up the Add Trusting Domain dialog box. The example shown in figure 10.11 is adding Widgets to the list of domains that trust the keystone domain.

3. An optional password can be specified. The password must be used to enable the trusting domain to complete the establishment of the trust relationship. If a password is specified, it must be entered in Initial **P**assword and **C**onfirm Password fields.

4. Choose OK. When you return to the Trust Relationships dialog box, the domain you specified is added to the Tr**u**sting Domains list.

5. The Cancel button changes to Close after a domain has been added or removed. Choose Close to exit the dialog box.

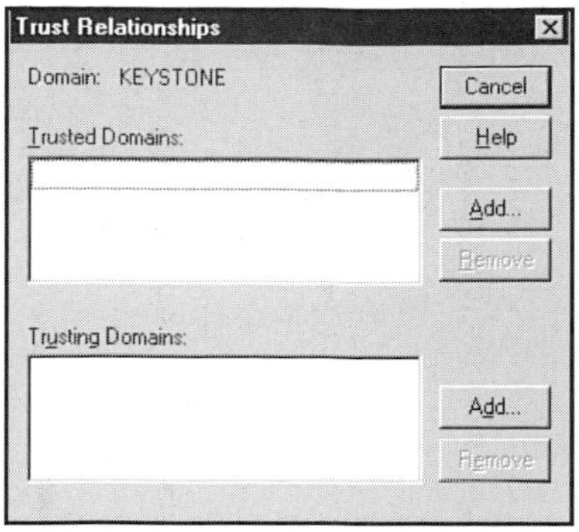

Figure 10.10

The Trust Relationships dialog box.

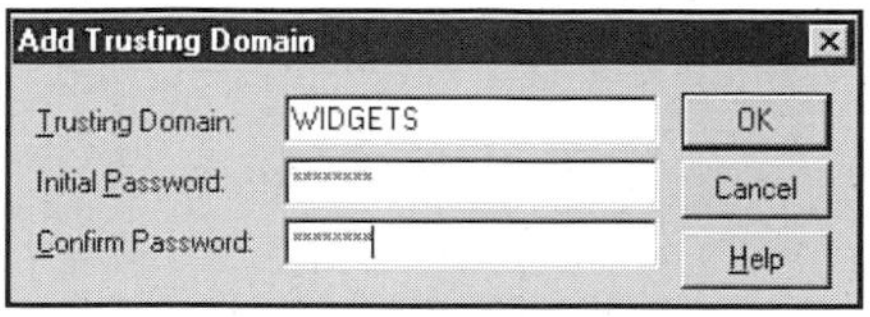

Figure 10.11

Adding a trusting domain.

Trusting Keystone

Next, an administrator must add Keystone to the list of trusted domains for the Widgets domain. After logging on to Widgets, an administrator should perform the following actions in the following exercise:

Confirming that Trust Is Established

1. Start the User Manager for Domains utility in the Administrative Tools folder.

2. Choose **T**rust Relationships from the **P**olicies menu to display the Trust Relationships dialog box.

3. Choose the **A**dd button next to **T**rusted Domains. The Add Trusted Domain dialog box shown in figure 10.12 appears.

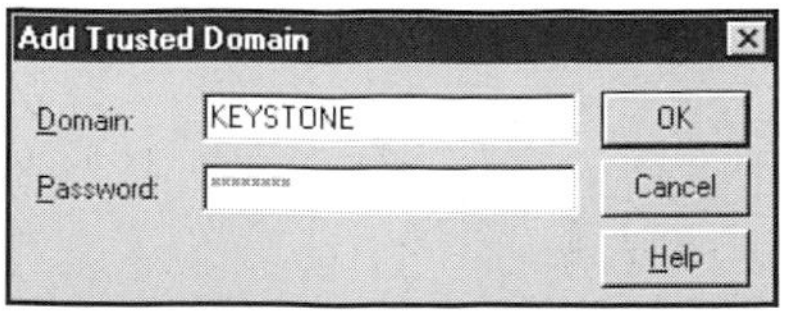

Figure 10.12

The Add Trusted Domain dialog box.

4. Enter the name of the domain to be trusted in the **D**omain field. If a password is specified by the trusted domain, enter the password in the **P**assword field. Figure 10.12 shows a completed dialog box that adds Keystone to the domains that are trusted by Widgets.

5. Choose OK to return to the Trust Relationships dialog box.

6. If all goes well, a message is displayed stating `Trust Relationship with KEYSTONE successfully established.`

    An error message results if the domains are unable to establish contact to confirm the trust relationship. An error also results if you have specified a domain name that does not exist or a password that does not match the password specified by the trusted domain.

7. Confirm that the domain has been added to the domains listed in the **T**rusted Domains box.

8. Choose Close to close the Trust Relationships dialog box.

Note   Trusting another domain does not immediately give users in the trusted domain access to resources in the trusting domain except if the group "everyone" is used. The group everyone now contains all users in the first domain and the trusted domains. You also must grant permissions that enable users who log on through the trusted domain to access resources in the trusting domain. The procedures for assigning permissions are described in Chapter 11, "Managing Users and Groups."

Removing Trust Relationships

Two steps are required to remove a trust relationship. The trusting domain must stop trusting the trusted domain, and the trusted domain must cancel its permission to be trusted.

How to Remove the Keystone/Widgets Trust

Removing a domain from the **T**rusted Domains list is accomplished by following these steps:

Trust Relationship Removal

1. Log on as a domain administrator for the trusting domain widgets and start the User Manager for Domains utility in the Administrative Tools folder.

2. From the **S**elect Domain option in the **U**ser menu, select the trusting domain widgets whose trust relationship is to be removed.

3. Choose **T**rust Relationships from the **P**olicies menu to display the Trust Relationships dialog box.

4. In the **T**rusted Domains list, select the domain to be removed. Then choose **R**emove (located beside the **T**rusted Domains list).

Because canceling a trust relationship can have far-reaching effects, User Manager for Domains displays the warning shown in figure 10.13.

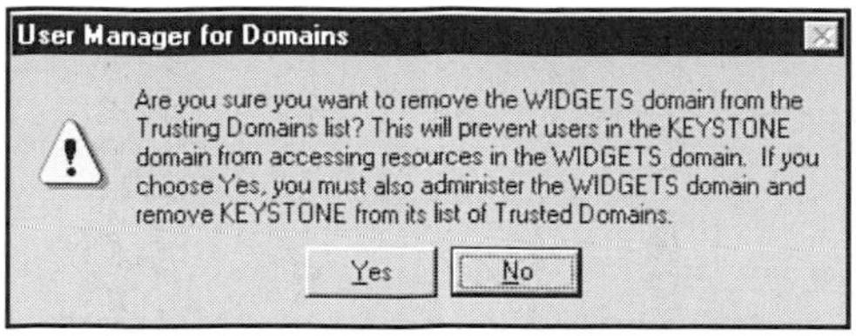

Are you sure you want to remove the WIDGETS domain from the Trusting Domains list? This will prevent users in the KEYSTONE domain from accessing resources in the WIDGETS domain. If you choose Yes, you must also administer the WIDGETS domain and remove KEYSTONE from its list of Trusted Domains.

Figure 10.13

The warning displayed when removing a trust relationship.

5. Choose **Y**es to complete the action. You are returned to the Trust Relationships dialog box, and the domain you removed is no longer listed.

6. Choose Close to exit the Trust Relationships dialog box.

Canceling Permission to Trust a Domain

Next, an administrator on the trusted domain must cancel permission to trust the domain. Canceling a trust permission is accomplished with this procedure:

1. Log on to the trusted domain as a domain administrator and start the User Manager for Domains utility in the Administrative Tools folder.

2. Choose **T**rust Relationships from the **P**olicies menu to display the Trust Relationships dialog box.

3. In the Tr**u**sting Domains list, select the domain to be removed. Then choose R**e**move (located beside the Tr**u**sting Domains list).

Because this action also can create havoc on the LAN, User Manager for Domains displays a warning message.

4. Choose **Y**es to complete the action. You are returned to the Trust Relationships dialog box, and the domain you removed no longer is listed.

5. Choose Close to exit the Trust Relationships dialog box.

After the trust relationship has been removed on both the trusting and the trusted server, the complete trust relationship has been removed.

Planning Domains on WANs

When a domain spans a WAN link, special care must be taken to support the domain properly. In particular, you should take steps to minimize the amount of WAN traffic that is devoted to overhead, such as browsing and domain synchronization.

Figure 10.14 illustrates a domain that supports three sites. The PDC and one BDC are located at the corporate headquarters. Two remote sites are connected to the corporate site via WAN links. Notice that each remote site is equipped with a BDC. This enables users to browse the domain using the local BDC without the need to browse using a domain controller on the other end of the WAN link. WAN traffic will be generated to synchronize the BDC with the PDC, but synchronization traffic can be configured, as described in the next section, and in any case will be less than browsing traffic.

Figure 10.14

Domain controllers on a WAN.

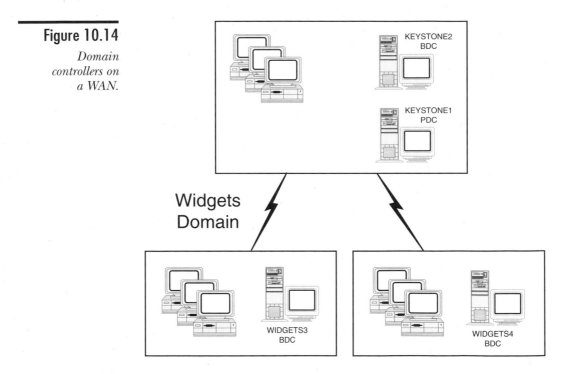

A larger organization might choose to use a master domain model to organize the network. The logon domain would be located at a central site, and each site would be equipped with its own domain to support local users. Because users must be able to browse the logon domain and the local domain, the arrangement of domain controllers is a bit more complicated.

Figure 10.15 illustrates such a network, consisting of four domains. Keystone is the master logon domain. Three department domains are included: New York, Chicago, and Los Angeles.

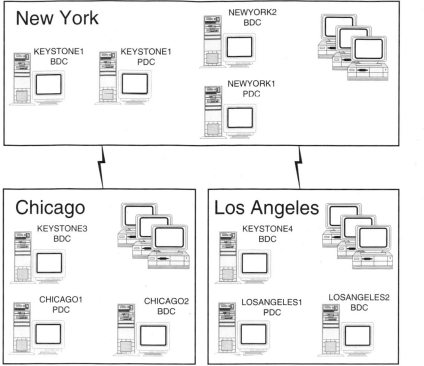

Figure 10.15

Domain controllers in a master domain model.

The PDC for the Keystone domain is located in New York, along with a BDC for fault tolerance. BDCs for the Keystone domain are also located in Chicago and Los Angeles to support user logons.

The Chicago and Los Angeles domains are each supported by a PDC and a BDC.

Because a Windows NT Server cannot be a domain controller for two domains, three or more domain controllers are required for each site:

◆ New York has the PDC and BDC for the Keystone domain. New York also has the PDC and BDC for the New York domain.

◆ Chicago has a BDC for the Keystone domain, and also has a PDC and a BDC for the Chicago domain.

◆ Los Angeles has a BDC for the Keystone domain, and also has a PDC and a BDC for the Los Angeles domain.

That makes for a total of ten (10!) domain controllers to do the job right. Each additional site under this scheme would need three domain controllers of its own.

What happens if the network grows and needs two master domains? The number of domain controllers may increase further. Suppose New York had two master domains. Each remote site would need a BDC for each master domain, meaning that Chicago would need at least four domain controllers, and that the total of domain controllers would now be 14! To minimize the number of remote BDCs, plan your master domains so that all users at a remote site log onto the same master domain. This will enable you to support the remote site with a single master domain BDC.

Configuring Domain Synchronization

As changes are made to the domain security database on the PDC, they are recorded in a *change log*. From time to time, it is necessary for a PDC to synchronize its database with all BDCs in the domain. Synchronization can be full or partial.

◆ A *full synchronization* is performed when the PDC sends a complete copy of the domain account database to a BDC.

◆ A *partial synchronization* is performed when the PDC sends the BDC only the changes that have been made to the domain account database since the last time the PDC and BDC were synchronized. The PDC tracks the synchronization status of each BDC in the domain and forces synchronization only when a BDC's data is out of date.

When a PDC determines that one or more BDCs must be synchronized, the PDC notifies the BDCs in a message called a *pulse*. BDCs must respond to the pulse to initiate synchronization. The PDC staggers pulses to prevent all BDCs from attempting to synchronize at the same time.

Domain Synchronization Registry Parameters

The domain synchronization process is one of the functions of the NetLogon service, which is also responsible for validating logons and for pass-through authentication. Many characteristics of the accounts database synchronization process can be configured in the Registry. (See Chapter 19 for a description of the Registry.) The Registry value entries are found in the following Registry key:

    HKEY_LOCAL_MACHINE\SYSTEM\CurrentControlSet\Services\Netlogon\
    Parameters

You can add the following value entries to the Registry to control domain synchronization. All are of type REG_DWORD.

◆ **ChangeLogSize.** This value entry determines the size in bytes of the change log, which is stored in memory and on disk in %SystemRoot%\netlogon.chg. Partial synchronizations are performed using entries in the change log. If they are performed at infrequent intervals, increase the change log size to ensure that changes will remain in the change log. If changes have been scrolled out of the change log, a full synchronization will be necessary. A typical change log entry consists of 32 bytes, enabling a 65,536 byte change log to store approximately 2,000 entries. Default value: 65536 (64 KB); range: 65536 to 4194304 (64–4,096 KB).

◆ **Pulse.** This value entry determines the pulse frequency in seconds. At the expiration of the pulse interval, the PDC sends a pulse to BDCs that need the changes accumulated since the last pulse. Default value: 300 (5 minutes); range: 60–3600 (1 minute to 1 hour).

◆ **PulseConcurrency.** This value entry determines the maximum number of BDCs that will be pulsed at any one time. In large networks or WANs it may be desirable to pulse a limited number of BDCs at any one time to minimize network traffic and load on the PDC. Increasing PulseConcurrency increases LAN traffic and load on the PDC while synchronizing BDCs more rapidly. Decreasing PulseConcurrency reduces load on the PDC but prolongs synchronization. Default value: 20; range: 1–500.

◆ **PulseMaximum.** This value entry determines the maximum interval at which BDCs will be pulsed, whether or not changes have been made to the domain database. Default value: 7200 (2 hours); range 60–86400 (1 minute to 1 day).

◆ **PulseTimeout1.** This value entry determines how many seconds a PDC will wait for a BDC to respond to a pulse before declaring the BDC to be non-responsive. Non-responsive BDCs do not count against the PulseConcurrency count. This mechanism enables the PDC to stop attempting to update non-responsive BDCs and accelerate updates of the remaining BDCs. If a domain has a large number of non-responsive BDCs, a large value for this parameter may result in slow partial synchronization of the domain. A small value may cause the PDC to mistakenly classify BDCs as non-responsive. Default: 5 (5 seconds); range 1–120 (1 second to 2 minutes).

◆ **PulseTimeout2.** This value entry determines how many seconds a PDC will permit for a BDC to complete a partial synchronization. When this timeout is exceeded, the synchronization process is presumed to be stalled and the BDC will be declared to be non-responsive. The BDC is given PulseTimeout2 seconds to complete each partial synchronization attempt. If this value is too large, a slow BDC may consume an excessive portion of a PulseConcurrency slot. If this value is too small, the number of BDCs that fail to complete a partial synchronization may rise, increasing demand on the PDC. Default: 300 (5 minutes); range: 60–3600 (1 minute to 1 hour).

◆ **Randomize.** This value entry specifies the time a BDC will wait before responding to a pulse. Each BDC will wait a random number of seconds in the range of zero through Randomize before calling the PDC. Randomize should always be smaller than PulseTimeout1. Default: 1 (1 second); range: 0–120 (0 to 2 minutes).

The time to synchronize all changes to BDCs in a domain will be greater than:

((Randomize/2)×NumberOfBDCs)/PulseConcurrency

To activate changes in these Registry parameters, you must use the Service tool in the Control Panel to stop and start the NetLogon service.

Synchronizing a Domain over a Slow WAN Link

When BDCs are separated from the PDC by a slow WAN link, you may want to configure the Registry ReplicationGovernor parameter to improve performance of the WAN link. This parameter can be configured if the PDC and BDC are both configured with Windows NT Server version 3.5x or higher.

The ReplicationGovernor parameter determines two things:

◆ The size of data transferred for each call from the BDC to the PDC

◆ The frequency of calls from the BDC to the PDC

The ReplicationGovernor value entry must be added to the following Registry key:

HKEY_LOCAL_MACHINE\SYSTEM\CurrentControlSet\Services\
Netlogon\Parameters

Create a parameter with the following characteristics:

◆ Name: ReplicationGovernor

◆ Type: REG_DWORD

◆ Value: 0–100

The value assigned to ReplicationGovernor determines two factors. First is the size of the data buffer that will be used. A value of 100 establishes the maximum size data buffer of 128 KB. Smaller values specify a percentage of 128 KB; for example, a value of 50 specifies a data buffer of 64 KB.

The second factor is the percent of time the BDC will have an outstanding synchronization call on the network. If the value of ReplicationGovernor is 66, the BDC will have an outstanding synchronization call on the network no more than 66 percent of the time.

The effect of reducing the value of the ReplicationGovernor parameter is to reduce the WAN traffic related to domain synchronization. The value must be configured individually for each BDC. If the value is too low, the BDC may remain out of synchronization for unacceptably long periods of time. If the value is zero, synchronization will not take place.

Testing Your Knowledge

1. A Primary Domain Controller (PDC) can be added to an existing domain.

   A. True

   B. False

2. If you are moving existing Backup Domain Controllers (BDCs) to new domains, you will be required to reinstall Windows NT Server.

   A. True

   B. False

3. In what two manners can a new domain be created?

   A. By installing a new PDC using NT setup.

   B. Simply by renaming the domain name of any PDC server in the NT Registry.

   C. By using the Network utility on an existing PDC to create a new domain, and then setting the server as the PDC of the new domain.

   D. By promoting a BDC to a PDC and assigning it a new domain name.

4. It is not necessary to restart the computer to activate a change in the computer's name or domain assignment.

   A. True

   B. False

5. If a BDC is promoted to a PDC and the original PDC is unavailable, the user account database on the BDC will be used as the account database for the domain.

   A. True

   B. False

6. Because Windows NT Server automatically synchronizes all BDCs with the PDC, NT does not supply any method to manually synchronize the domain computers.

   A. True

   B. False

7. NT Servers and NT Workstations can join a domain in which three ways?

   A. By utilizing a roaming profile.

   B. By adding the computer to the domain first using the Server Manager utility.

   C. By adding the computer to the domain during installation.

   D. By adding the computer to the domain from the Control Panel's Network utility.

8. Domain trust relationships are established with which utility?

   A. Server Manager

   B. User Manager for Domains

   C. Control Panel–Network utility

   D. Command prompt

9. Trust relationships must be established on both affected domains.

   A. True

   B. False

10. Once a domain trust is established, all users can immediately take advantage of resources on the trusting domain.

   A. True

   B. False

11. A(n) _____ synchronization is performed when the PDC sends the BDC only the changes that have been made to the domain account database since the last time the PDC and BDC were synchronized.

Review Answers

1. B
2. A
3. A, C
4. B
5. A
6. B
7. B, C, D
8. B
9. A
10. B
11. partial

CHAPTER 11

Managing Users and Groups

LAN administration would be considerably more pleasurable if there were no LAN users. You can set up your network perfectly, install your software, and test everything for days until every last problem is ironed out, but it will do you no good. The moment you add the first user is the moment your problems really begin. Applications that once worked perfectly will begin to have bugs. Files that are critical to your organization will disappear mysteriously. Your phone will ring off the hook, and every problem the users experience will be the fault of "the LAN." Users! You might begin to wish that you had chosen a more secluded way to make a living.

Without users, however, your LAN can't pay its keep, so you have no choice but to let them in. The key is to let users into the LAN the right way. There are several key ingredients to configuring the user environment:

♦ Establishing solid user security

♦ Creating productive environments for users

♦ Training users on anything you can't make self-evident

Part III of this book delves into the details of setting up user environments for Windows and DOS clients. The groundwork for your users' working environments begins in this chapter, however.

User accounts enable users to log on to the network and access network resources. Setting up user accounts involves two almost contradictory goals:

◆ Helping users access the resources they need

◆ Keeping users away from everything else

To meet these goals, you will grant users permissions to use network resources. Doing so involves assigning privileges to users themselves and to groups to which the users belong.

The tool you will use for managing users and groups is User Manager for Domains; most of its features are covered in this chapter.

> **Note**   Windows NT Workstation includes a similar tool called User Manager to manage user accounts and groups on the workstation. Because User Manager is designed to manage the resources of a single workstation, there are many differences, but experienced users of Windows NT Workstation should have no difficulty making the transition to User Manager for Domains.

Who Can Manage Users and Groups?

Rights to administer user accounts and groups are conferred on members of three Windows NT groups:

◆ **Administrators.** Members of this local group can perform all user and group management functions.

◆ **Domain Admins.** In most domains, the Domain Admins global group is a member of the Administrators local group. All users who are members of Domain Admins, therefore, are granted Administrator privileges for the domain.

> **Note**   To enable Administrators to manage users and groups in other domains, first trust the Administrators' logon domains. Then add the Domain Admins global group from the logon domain to the Administrators local group of the domain you want the Administrators to manage.

◆ **Account Operators.** Users in the Account Operators group can create user accounts and groups, delete most users and groups, and manage many characteristics of user accounts and groups.

Members of the Account Operators group cannot manage the administration groups set up by Windows NT Server: Administrators, Domain Admins, Account Operators, Server Operators, Print Operators, or Backup Operators. Also, members of the Account Operators group cannot manage the accounts of domain Administrators or establish domain security policies.

Getting Started with User Manager for Domains

User Manager for Domains can be used to manage any domains for which you have been given administrative access.

In most cases, you will run User Manager for Domains by choosing User Manager for Domains in the Administrative Tools folder. The User Manager for Domains window, shown in figure 11.1, is displayed when you start the utility. When started from the Start menu, User Manager for Domains displays the domain where your user account is defined.

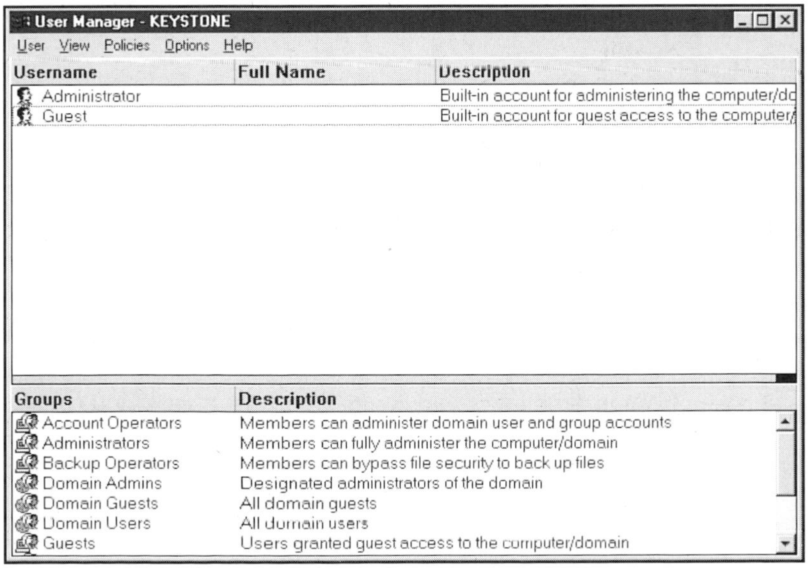

Figure 11.1

The opening window for User Manager for Domains.

Sorting User Accounts

By default, user accounts are listed in alphabetical order. You can control the order in which user accounts are listed by choosing a sort order from the **V**iew menu. Two commands are available:

◆ Sort by **F**ull Name

◆ Sort by **U**sername

These options are unavailable when **L**ow Speed Connection is specified.

Managing User Accounts

A user account enables users to access resources on domains and Windows NT computers. When you manage a user account, you configure a wide variety of security features that restrict how, where, and when the user can access the network. You also grant privileges that permit the user to access resources.

This user information is stored in a user account database, and it is that database on a primary domain controller that you are actually managing as you use User Manager for Domains. The database is replicated to any backup domain controllers that are included in the domain.

Managing Built-In User Accounts

Two user accounts, Administrator and Guest, are created when Windows NT is installed. These accounts cannot be removed, but can be managed in specified ways.

> **Note**   If you install the Internet Information Server, an Internet user account is added to the domain. This user account is used to provide anonymous access to Internet services. It is not a special account, however, like the Administrator and Guest accounts, and can be deleted if desired. The Internet user account is discussed in Chapter 16, "Using TCP/IP."

The Administrator User Account

The Administrator user account is created to enable you to manage Windows NT after the software is installed. You can rename the Administrator user account, but you cannot remove it from the domain.

Administrator is a member of the following built-in groups, from which it cannot be removed:

◆ Administrators (local group)

◆ Domain Admins (global group)

◆ Domain Users (global group)

To create other user accounts that are equivalent to Administrator, you must include them as members of these three groups.

By default, the Domain Admins global group is added to the Administrators group for every Windows NT computer in the domain. A user logged on as Administrator can manage the domain and all Windows NT computers in the domain.

Note Administrator users (members of the Administrators group) are extremely powerful and operate with very few restrictions. When logged on as an Administrator, take care not to perform actions that could damage network operations. It can be very easy, for example, to accidentally delete files that are crucial to network operation by selecting the wrong file or directory in File Manager.

An Administrator has unrestricted access to most files in the domain and can easily disseminate viruses throughout the network. Make frequent use of virus-detection software to ensure that viruses are not present on an Administrator's computer.

You also should assign Administrators two user accounts: one with Administrator privileges to be used when administering the network, and another with user privileges to be used at other times. When logged on under the user account, the risk of infecting the network with a virus is reduced considerably. Administrators will find it extremely useful to use Windows NT Workstation on their personal computers because the process of logging on and off is simplified greatly.

The Guest User Account

The Guest user account is a member of the Domain Guests built-in group and initially is disabled on a domain controller. You can enable the account by using the Disable Account option described in the section "Modifying User Account Properties," later in this chapter. The Guest user account can be renamed, but it cannot be removed.

The initial account password for Guest is blank. Unless a password is added to the account, users can use Guest to access the domain even from untrusted domains.

Activate the Guest user account if your network supports resources that should be accessible to individuals who do not have formal user accounts.

Before enabling Guest user accounts, it is important to remember that adding a user account requires little effort and is repaid in substantially improved security. Few of the programs or data that you will put on the LAN are so unimportant that security ceases to be a concern.

> **Caution** | The really risky thing about enabling the Guest account is that it provides a back door that enables unauthenticated users to gain access to network shares. It turns out that any Microsoft network client can browse any domain, whether that client is logged on to the domain or not. Any Microsoft network client can access the shares in the domain that are accessible to the Guest account.
>
> Here's a scenario. A user CCHAPLIN logs on locally to a Windows NT Workstation computer named CHARLES. Then the user browses the network to see what's available. Lo and behold, the domain KEYSTONE is there clear as day. The user never logged on to KEYSTONE, but there it is. Worse, any share Guest can use CCHAPLIN without being authenticated to the domain. MS-DOS, Windows for Workgroups, and Windows 95 can accomplish the same because these operating systems permit users to log on without being authenticated to the network.
>
> What makes this particularly nasty is that Guest is a member of the special group Everyone, and Everyone typically has Full Control access to newly created directories, and to lots of other things besides. Guest provides a means for unauthenticated users to access nearly any directory you create and share on the network.
>
> Unless you intend to be very careful, disable the Guest account.

Adding a User Account

You need to create a user account for each user who requires access to the network. User accounts are created and managed from the New Users window, which is accessed by choosing the New **U**ser command from the **U**ser menu of User Manager for Domains. The New User window is shown in figure 11.5. The figure illustrates an example of a completed New User form.

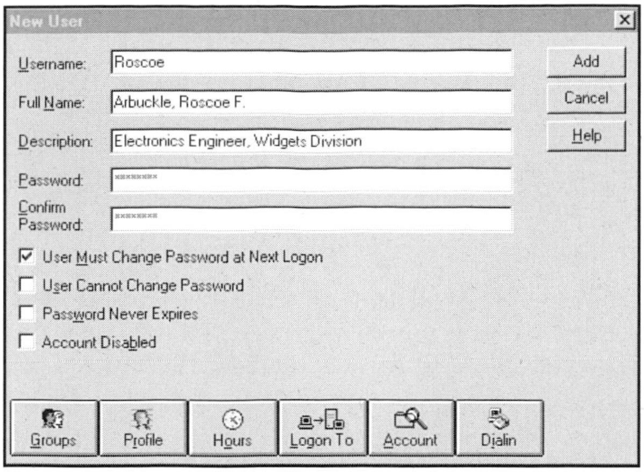

Figure 11.5

The New User window.

After the fields in the New User window have been completed, click on Add to create the user account. Each of the fields in the window is discussed in the following sections.

Username

Each user in a domain or computer must have a unique user name. A user name can include up to 20 characters, including upper- and lowercase letters, numbers, and punctuation. The following characters cannot appear in a user name:

= + [ ] / \ < > ; : ' " * ?

You should establish a network policy for user names. Consistent naming conventions make it easier to remember user names and to find them in lists. First names are used for user names in the examples in this book, but that approach works only for very small LANs. You might work in a 15-person department that includes three Roberts, for example.

If your network includes users of DOS and Windows 3.1, it makes some sense to restrict user names to eight characters. Then user names also can be used as the names of users' home directories.

Some alternative naming standards follow:

◆ First name plus a number, such as Jim338. User names of this type can be difficult to remember and recognize.

◆ First name plus last initial, such as JimA. Numbers can be added in case of duplicates. You might create accounts for JimA1 and JimA2, for example.

◆ First initial plus last name. An example is JAnderson (or JAnderso if you want to restrict the user name to eight characters). In case of duplication, include a digit, as in JAnders1 and JAnders2.

The third option is probably the best because it results in fewer name duplications. The number of first names in common use is surprisingly limited, and user names based on first names quickly produce duplications in organizations of any size.

Note If your network includes users of MS-DOS or Windows 3.x, you will find it convenient to restrict user names to eight characters. This will enable you to use the user name to create user directories that are compatible with the MS-DOS 8.3 file name format. If you permit longer user names, you must create the directories manually to ensure that the user directory names can be easily read by MS-DOS users.

Full Name

This optional field enables you to specify a more complete name for the user. The full name appears in several lists of user names that are presented by network utilities. Use of the Full **N**ame field is especially important when the convention you select for the user name does not produce names that are easily recognizable.

As with user names, you should establish a convention for full names. These names can be used by programs on the network, and might provide the user name folder for your network's e-mail program, for example. In such cases, it probably is preferable to enter the last name first (Lloyd, Harold H.), rather than the first name first (Harold H. Lloyd).

Description

The **D**escription field is optional. You might, for example, want to use it to identify the user's job title and department.

Password and Confirm Password

If you choose to specify an initial password, enter it in both fields. Passwords are never displayed in open text when they are entered, and the **C**onfirm Password field verifies that you have correctly typed the password.

Passwords are case-sensitive and can consist of up to 14 characters. Administrators can set policies that establish the types of passwords that are permitted. For more information, see the section "Managing the Account Policy," later in this chapter.

User Must Change Password at Next Logon

If the User **M**ust Change Password at Next Logon box is checked (the default value), the user is forced to change the password the first time he or she logs on.

Windows NT Server security is so versatile that even Administrators can be restricted from openly accessing some user resources. By forcing users to select a password that is unknown to the Administrator, you can enforce this capability.

You always should check this field if you are entering blank passwords for newly created user accounts.

User Cannot Change Password

There are at least two reasons for activating the U**s**er Cannot Change Password option:

◆ Several users share an account.

◆ Passwords are entered manually by the network administrator, and users are not permitted to enter passwords.

Users have a tendency to enter passwords that are easy for them to type and remember. Unfortunately, these passwords tend to be easy to guess—such as children's names, birthdates, and so on.

Some organizations that require especially high levels of security assign passwords centrally so that they cannot be guessed easily. Because Administrators cannot examine user-entered passwords to determine whether they meet security guidelines, it is necessary for such passwords to be administered by a central security staff.

Password Never Expires

Your account policy probably will specify the number of days that a password is valid before a user is forced to specify a new password. In rare instances, you might want to override automatic password expiration for some accounts.

If you check the Pass**w**ord Never Expires option, the value of the User **M**ust Change Password at Next Logon field is overridden.

> **Note** Passwords are key ingredients to network security. Unfortunately, it is extremely difficult to obtain the cooperation of users where passwords are concerned. Users want passwords that are easy to remember; security demands passwords that are difficult to guess. You would be amazed at how many passwords are cracked simply because they are obvious: users' names, family names, and obvious associations with the organization are common.

continues

A common technique for cracking passwords is to use a dictionary consisting of common words that are systematically entered. Encourage your users to select non-obvious passwords. An effective technique is to combine two unrelated words to form a password. A password such as BLUEFACE is easy to remember but difficult to guess.

In the most extreme cases, passwords should be determined by the network security administrator. This can be a lot of work because passwords must be changed periodically, and users must learn the new passwords in a secure fashion. It is the only way, however, for the administrator to enforce a password policy. Avoid being too draconian, though. If you create passwords such as X12Z!@FQP, you are openly inviting users to remember their passwords on a Post-It note attached to their monitors.

Establishing a strong user rights policy (as described later in this chapter) helps security considerably. If an account locks up after several bad logon attempts have been made, the likelihood is reduced that an intruder can guess users' passwords.

Account Disabled

Check this box to prevent users from accessing a user account. Here are several reasons for using the Account Disabled option:

◆ To disable an account while a user is on extended leave

◆ To disable an account that is used by a person filling a particular role when the position is vacant

◆ To create a template account that is used only to create other accounts

Additional Account Properties

At the bottom of the New User window are six buttons: **G**roups, P**r**ofile, H**o**urs, **L**ogon To, **A**ccount, and D**i**alin. Each button produces a window that enables you to specify additional properties for user accounts. Each of these sets of properties is discussed later in this chapter.

Copying a User Account

If an existing user account is substantially similar to a new user account you want to create, you can copy the existing account and modify it as required for the new user.

To copy a user account, perform the steps outlined in the following exercise:

Copying User Accounts

1. Select the account to be copied in the User Manager for Domains window.

2. Choose **C**opy from the **U**ser menu. This produces a window labeled `Copy of username`, where *username* is the name of the account you are copying.

3. In the **U**sername field, enter the user name and other user-specific information.

4. Make any modifications you want to other user properties.

5. Choose **A**dd to create the user account.

Note You will find it useful to configure a template account that is used to create other accounts. After you have configured the properties of the template, check the Account Disa**b**led box in the New User window so that the account cannot be used. Create new users by copying the template account.

Modifying User Account Properties

You can modify user accounts one at a time or in groups. The following sections explain the ways in which to do this.

Modifying Individual User Accounts

You can select a single user account for modification in three ways:

◆ Locate the user account entry in the User Manager for Domains window and double-click on the entry.

◆ Select the user account entry in the User Manager for Domains window and press Enter.

◆ Select an entry in the User Manager for Domains window and choose the **P**roperties command from the U**s**er menu.

Either way, the user account properties are presented in the User Properties window, which is nearly identical to the New User window that was used to create the account. The User Properties dialog box is shown in figure 11.6.

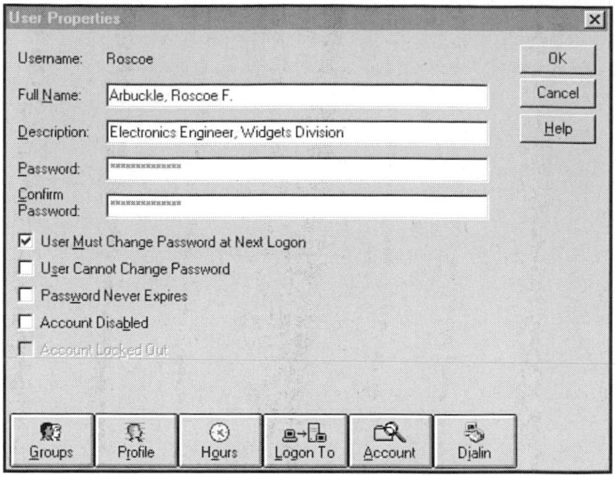

Figure 11.6

*The User
Properties
dialog box.*

Make any required changes in the properties in this window. Notice that you cannot change the Username field. You can access any of the additional property windows by clicking on the appropriate button at the bottom of the window.

Note   When a user logs on and is authenticated to a domain, Windows NT Server constructs an *access token* consisting of the user's security ID (SID), group IDs, and assigned privileges. Subsequently, when the user attempts to access a network resource, Windows NT checks this access token to determine whether the user has the required access rights.

Because the access token is constructed when the user logs on, any security changes that affect the user do not become active until the next time the user logs on.

Disabling User Accounts

You might want to disable a user account without removing it from the domain. To disable a user account, check the Account Disabled check box.

Unlocking User Accounts

The Account Locked Out field usually is inactive (shown in gray). Under certain circumstances, a user account can be locked out by Windows NT Server. If that is the case, the Account Locked Out field will be active. You can unlock the account by checking this field.

Modifying Two or More User Accounts

If you need to perform the same action on several user accounts, you can do so by selecting the accounts in the User Manager for Domains accounts list.

You can select accounts in several ways:

◆ Select individual accounts by holding down the Ctrl key as you click on each account. If you select accounts by pressing Ctrl and clicking, previously selected accounts remain selected.

◆ Select a range of accounts by selecting an account at one end of the range. Then locate the account at the other end of the range and hold down the Shift key as you click on the account. A range of accounts is selected, starting with the account you first selected and extending to the account that you Shift+clicked.

◆ Use the Select Users command in the User menu to display a Select Users list of groups, as shown in figure 11.7.

If you highlight a group and choose Select, users in that group are added to the selected users in the main window.

If you highlight a group and choose Deselect, users in that group are deselected in the main window.

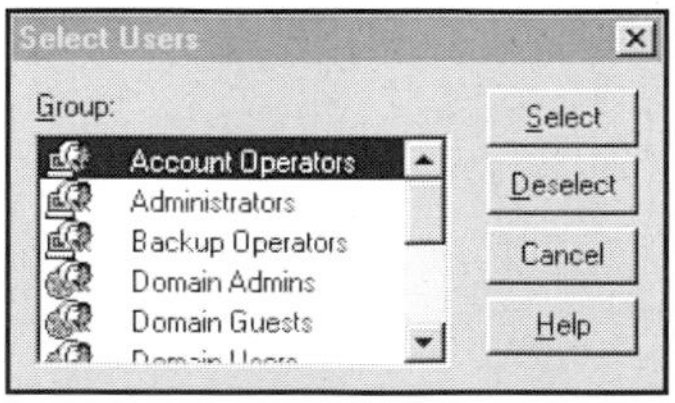

Figure 11.7

The Select Users list.

After you select the user accounts to be modified, choose the Properties command from the User menu to reveal the User Properties window. The User Properties window in figure 11.8 is being used to modify properties for four users.

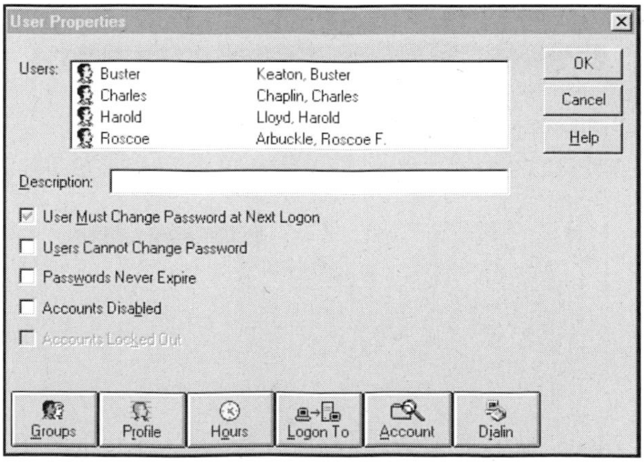

Figure 11.8

Managing properties for multiple users.

When you are modifying two or more users, some options in User Manager will be unavailable:

◆ The User Properties window does not permit you to modify these fields:

Full **N**ame

Description

Password and **C**onfirm Password

Pass**w**ords Never Expire

◆ The Group Memberships window permits you to manage only group memberships that are common to all the users you have selected.

◆ The User Environment Profile window can be used to assign common or custom profile assignments.

◆ The Logon Hours window can be used only to set the same logon hours for all selected users.

◆ The Logon Workstations window can be used only to set the same logon workstations for all selected users.

◆ The Account Information window can set uniform properties for all selected users.

Assigning Group Memberships

The **G**roups button in the New User, Copy of, and User Properties windows enable you to assign group memberships. Clicking on **G**roups reveals the Group Memberships window shown in figure 11.9. The options in this window are described in the following sections.

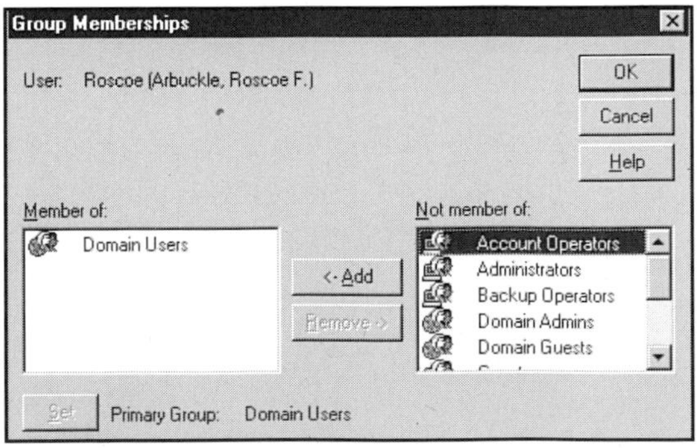

Figure 11.9

The Group Memberships window.

Adding a Group Membership to a User Account

The **N**ot member of list box lists groups to which this user account does not belong. To add a group membership to the user's account, select the group name and click the **A**dd button. The group name is removed from the **N**ot member of box and added to the **M**ember of box.

You are permitted to select multiple groups in the **M**ember of box prior to removing them from the user account.

You are not permitted to remove the group that is designated as the user's primary group. If you want to remove that group, you first must designate a different group as the user's primary group, as described in the following section.

Removing a Group Membership from a User Account

The **M**ember of list box lists the groups to which this user account does not belong. To remove a group membership from the user account, select the group name in the **M**ember of box and click **R**emove. The group name is removed from the **M**ember of box and added to the **N**ot member of box.

You are permitted to select multiple groups in the **N**ot member of box prior to adding them to the user account.

Setting the Primary Group for a User Account

The primary group is used only by users who are accessing Windows NT Server through Services for Macintosh. When a Macintosh user creates a folder, the user's primary group is associated with the folder.

Whether or not they are using a Macintosh, each user account must designate one group as its primary group. To set the primary group, select a group in the **M**ember of list box and click on **S**et. See Chapter 24, "Windows NT Server for Macintosh," for more about how the primary group is used.

Managing Group Memberships of Two or More Users

When you select two or more users in the User Manager for Domains window, the Group Memberships window resembles figure 11.10.

This window has the following features:

◆ The Users box lists the names of the users you have selected.

◆ The All Are **M**embers Of box lists only the groups that are assigned to all the users in the Users box. In figure 11.10, no groups are listed because Administrator is not a member of any groups to which the other users belong.

◆ The **N**ot All Are Members Of box lists all groups that are not already assigned to all users in the Users box.

◆ The **S**et button for the Primary Group selection is inactive.

When you add or remove a group, it is added or removed from all groups in the Users list box.

To ensure that none of the selected users is a member of a group, follow these steps:

1. Select the group in the **N**ot All Are Members Of box and click **A**dd to add the group membership to all listed users.

2. Choose OK to save the change and return to the User Properties window.

3. Click on **G**roups in the User Properties window.

4. Select the group in the All Are **M**embers Of box that is to be removed from all user accounts and choose **R**emove.

5. Choose OK to save the changes.

Managing User Profiles

The P**r**ofile button in the New User, Copy of, and User Properties windows enables you to assign user profile information. Choosing P**r**ofile reveals the User

Environment Profile dialog box shown in figure 11.11. This dialog box has fields for several items that are explained in the following sections.

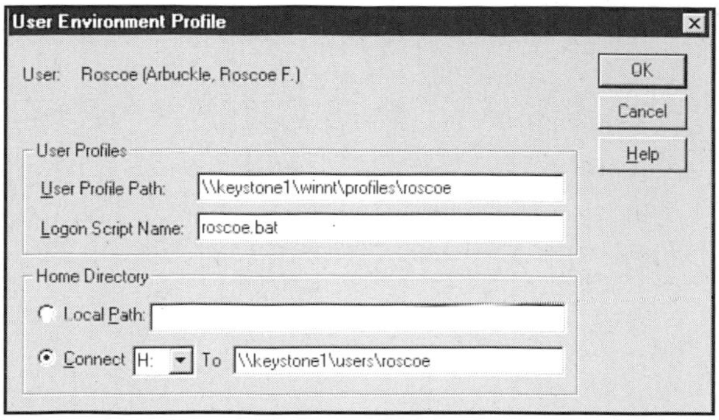

Figure 11.11

*The User
Environment
Profile dialog box.*

User Profile Path

Windows NT users can take advantage of *user profiles*—the most powerful means provided by Windows NT Server to configure users' network environments. A user profile can specify most of the startup features of a Windows NT session, including program groups and available applications. Profiles can be managed by users, or Administrators can take over profiles for users when it is necessary to exercise greater control over actions users can perform on the network. You will learn the details of user profiles in Chapter 15, "Using Windows NT Clients."

When working on a Windows NT computer, each user maintains a user profile that is associated with the user's name on the computer. This profile is stored on the workstation computer, and users who access several computers must maintain a profile on each computer. A profile that is maintained on a workstation is called a *local profile* because it can be accessed only while working on the computer on which the profile was created.

Users who log on to a Windows NT Server network have the option of maintaining their profiles on the network server. This capability enables them to access the same profile regardless of the Windows NT Workstation from which they are logging on. A profile that is maintained on the network is called a *roaming profile* because users can access their profiles from any computer on the network.

Windows NT Server supports two types of roaming user profiles:

◆ **Personal user profiles.** An individual profile is assigned to each user. Users can modify their personal profiles and changes will be preserved from logon to logon.

◆ **Mandatory user profiles.** Administrators also can assign mandatory profiles that users are not permitted to permanently modify. Although they can make changes, the changes are not stored in the profile and are lost at the end of a logon session. Mandatory user profiles ensure that users work in a common environment and prevent problems that can result from users' modifications to profiles.

By default, user profiles are stored in subdirectories of C:\Winnt\Profiles. The location of a user's profile file is specified in the **U**ser Profile Path field of the User Environment Profile window. To specify a user profile, follow these steps:

1. Enter the path to a shared profile directory in the **U**ser Profile Path field. For the share PROFILES on server KEYSTONE1, you would enter the profile path for Roscoe as follows:

   \\KEYSTONE1\PROFILES\ROSCOE

2. Optionally, create the ROSCOE profile following the procedure described in Chapter 15. If you do not create a user profile, the user will access the local profile on the workstation when next logging on to the network. This local profile, along with changes the user makes, is saved to the user's roaming profile path you specified in step 1.

> **Note**   Administrators familiar with Windows NT Server 3.5x profiles are accustomed to specifying the name of a profile file; for example, C:\WINNT\PROFILES\ROSCOE.USR. Starting with Windows NT 4, profiles are stored in a directory structure, not in an individual file. The **U**ser Profile Path field, therefore, now specifies a directory path rather than a path and file name.
>
> With Windows NT 4, user profile data are stored in a file named Ntuser.dat. To change a personal profile to a mandatory profile, rename Ntuser.dat to Ntuser.man.

You do not need to create the profile directory structure unless you want to assign an initial profile to establish a starting environment for the user. If you do not create the profile directory structure, it will be created when the user next logs on. Because Administrators are not required to create personal user profiles, it is easy to create large numbers of user accounts.

> **Note**   In the next section, you will learn that logon script files generally are replicated to each domain controller in the domain. This is possible because all logon script files can be maintained in a single place and replicated to other specific places. It does not matter which copy of the logon script actually is used during the logon process.
>
> Replication is a one-way street. Administrators specify export and import directories on Windows NT computers, and files are copied from the export directories to the import directories by the Replicator service. Replication is not sophisticated enough

to identify which of several copies of a file is most current and replicate that copy to all other servers.

For this reason, user profiles cannot be replicated in the same manner as logon scripts. Suppose that the Replication service was configured to replicate a profile file from Keystone1 to Keystone2. If users on Keystone2 made modifications to the replicas of their user profiles, those changes would not be replicated back to the master copies of the profiles on Keystone1.

Because a user's profile can be stored on one server only, you should avoid shutting down servers on which user profiles are stored while users are logged on to those servers.

Logon Script Name

Logon scripts are batch files that are executed when users log on from Windows NT, DOS, Windows for Workgroups, and OS/2. Logon scripts are less versatile than profiles, and you probably will want to use profiles for users of Windows NT computers.

Logon scripts have the extension BAT for DOS, Windows for Workgroups, and Windows NT Workstations. The CMD extension is used when users log on from OS/2 workstations. Because logon script files are tailored for specific client operating systems, users who log on from both Windows and OS/2 operating systems might require more than one user account.

By default, logon scripts are stored in the directory C:\WINNT\SYSTEM32\REPL\ IMPORT\SCRIPTS. The directory can be modified by changing a logon script path specification using the Server Manager. This feature is part of the Windows NT Server directory Replicator service and is discussed in Chapter 22, "Managing Directory Replication."

In most cases, a master copy of each logon script is kept on one domain controller—usually the PDC. The directory Replicator service then is configured to replicate the logon script files to other domain controllers. In this way, the logon scripts are available to users regardless of the DC that is used to authenticate their connection to the domain.

The **L**ogon Script Name may be expressed as a relative path specification in the following situations:

◆ If you specify only a file name such as **HAROLD.BAT**, Windows NT Server will look for the file in the default logon script directory.

◆ If you specify a relative path name (one that does not begin with a drive letter or a backslash), Windows NT Server looks for the logon script file in a subdirectory of the logon script default directory. If you enter

WIDGETS\ALLUSERS.BAT, Windows NT Server looks for a file named ALLUSERS.BAT in the WIDGETS subdirectory of the logon script directory. For the default logon script directory, the complete directory path would be as follows:

C:\WINNT\SYSTEM32\REPL\IMPORT\SCRIPTS\WIDGETS\ALLUSERS.BAT

You can assign individual logon script file names for each user or the same file for a group of users. By sharing the same logon script with groups of users, you can ensure that they are working in a consistent network environment.

Specific information about logon scripts is presented in the following chapters:

- Chapter 14, "Using Windows and DOS Clients"
- Chapter 15, "Using Windows NT Clients"

Home Directory

In most cases, each user should be assigned a home directory on the network. This directory can be used by the user to store personal files. It also can be designated by the system Administrator as a location for certain user-specific files.

The home directory can be located on the user's local hard drive. In this case, the user will be able to access only the home directory from a single workstation. To specify a local logon script path, follow these steps:

1. Select the Local **P**ath option in the User Environment Profile dialog box.

2. Enter a local path in the Local **P**ath field, such as **C:\HOME**.

You will want to locate home directories on the network. Users can access a network home directory when they log on to any client on the network. To specify a network home directory, follow these steps:

1. Create a share that points to the directory that contains the users' home directories; for example, create a share named USERS that points to C:\USERS on Keystone1.

2. Select the **C**onnect option in the User Environment Profile window.

3. Specify a drive letter that will identify the home directory. Click on the arrow button to choose an available drive letter from a list.

4. Enter a complete path to the home directory. You should use UNC notation and specify the server so that the user can log on from any domain controller. To place Roscoe's home directory on the KEYSTONE1 computer in the USERS share, for example, you enter **KEYSTONE1\USERS\ROSCOE** as the home directory path.

Windows NT Server will create a user home directory following the home directory path name you have entered. Privileges for user home directories are configured so that only the specified user has access to the directory contents.

> **Note** When the user logs on, the drive letter you indicate will be connected to the common users directory. The user will need to open the network drive and change to his personal directory to access personal files unless a distinct share has been created for each user.

Managing User Profiles for Two or More Users

You probably will configure your users with nearly identical user profiles, and you often will want to configure all their profiles in a single operation.

When you select two or more users in the User Manager for Domains window, the User Environment Profile window resembles figure 11.12. The window in the figure has been preconfigured to illustrate techniques for defining group user profiles.

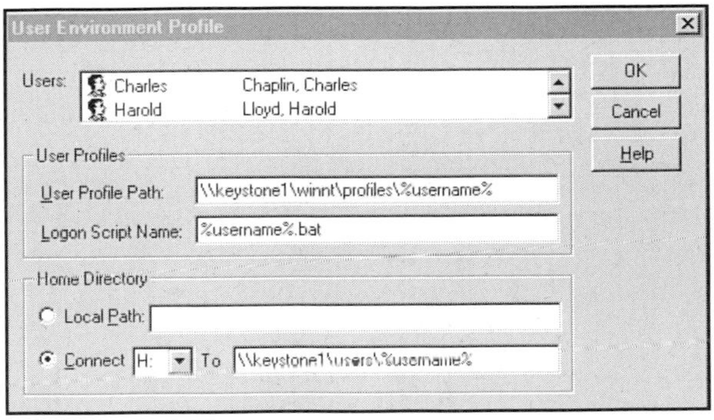

Figure 11.12

Specifying user profiles for two or more users.

The trick is to use one of the variables available on Windows NT Server computers. The variable %username% stores the user name of the current user. This variable is used in two fields in the figure.

Specifying User Profiles for Two or More Users

The **U**ser Profile Path field in figure 11.12 establishes a personal user profile for each user. For the user named Buster, the user profile path will be \\KEYSTONE1\ PROFILES\BUSTER. The profiles name should be the share name.

If you will be using a mandatory profile, it is probable that you will be assigning the same profile to several, or even all, of your users. In that case, you might specify a user profile path, such as \\KEYSTONE_PROFILES\ALLUSERS. (Be sure to create the ALLUSERS mandatory profile, or users will be unable to log on.)

Specifying Logon Scripts for Two or More Users

If you want to create personal logon scripts for users, you can specify the file names in the **L**ogon Script Name path by entering **%USERNAME%.BAT** (or **%USERNAME%.CMD**, as appropriate). Remember that DOS and Windows users can easily access only files that conform to the 8.3 format. If you use this technique, be sure that the user names you have selected do not exceed eight characters.

Creating Home Directories for Two or More Users

Figure 11.12 also shows the use of the %username% variable to create personal home directories. A user named Roscoe will be assigned a home directory on the KEYSTONE1 server in the directory \USERS\ROSCOE. When users log on, Windows NT Server assigns the specified drive letter—in this case H—to each user's home directory.

> **Note**
>
> The concept of a home directory applies only to users who log on from a Windows NT computer. Users who log on from MS-DOS, Windows for Workgroups, or Windows 95 are unaffected by the home directory specification. Windows 95 clients can be configured to use the Home directory as their network-based profiles.
>
> If your server is configured with FAT volumes, you cannot create directory names that do not conform to the 8.3 format. If any of the user names you have selected are longer than eight characters, do not use the %username% variable to create user profiles or home directories on FAT volumes.

> **Caution**
>
> Officially, this technique for creating home directories should work, but in my experience, it is not always reliable. Check things out with File Manager to determine that directories were created and properly secured. You might need to do part or all of the job manually.

Managing Logon Hours

The H**o**urs button in the New User, Copy of, and User Properties windows enables you to restrict the hours during which a user can log on to the network. Choosing H**o**urs reveals the Logon Hours window shown in figure 11.13.

The Logon Hours window shows a weekly schedule of hours during which the user is permitted to log on to the network. Hours that are marked with a dark bar are hours when the user is permitted to log on. Hours that are cleared are hours when the user is not permitted to log on.

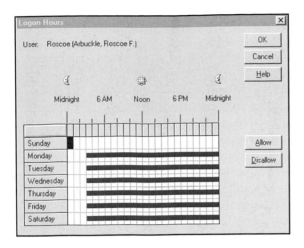

Figure 11.13

The Logon Hours window.

The example in figure 11.13 gives the user the following log restrictions:

◆ The user is permitted to log on daily from 3 a.m. through midnight.

◆ The user is not permitted to log on between midnight and 3 a.m. because this is the time during which daily backups are performed.

◆ The user is not permitted to log on on Sunday because that day is reserved for comprehensive network backups and system maintenance.

To permit logon during a time period, select the hours and click on **A**llow. The hours you selected are marked after clicking OK; hours that are allowed are shown in white with a blue bar through them, indicating that these hours will be allowed after you click on OK.

To prevent logon during a time period, select the hours and click on **D**isallow. The hours you selected are marked in after clicking OK; hours that are disallowed are shown as plain white, indicating that these hours will be disallowed after you choose OK.

You can select hours in several ways:

◆ Choose a specific hour.

◆ Choose a day label to select that entire day.

◆ Click at the top of an hour column to select that hour for all days.

◆ Choose the square above Sunday to select the entire week.

After you make your changes, choose OK to save the changes.

Managing Logon Hours for Two or More Users

When you select two or more users in the User Manager for Domains window, and those users are configured with different logon hours, clicking on H**o**urs in the User Properties window produces an information box warning you that The selected users have different Logon Hours settings. If you choose to continue, the logon hours for all selected users are reset. You then can configure new logon hours for all users with the procedure described in the preceding section.

Note Users of Windows NT computers are fully affected by the logon hours you specify for their accounts. Users are permitted to log on only during hours allowed in their account properties. If they are logged on when their hours expire, the effect is determined by settings made by the Domain Administrator in the Account Policy window (described later in the section "Managing the Account Policy").

Normally, users are allowed to remain logged on, but they cannot make new connections.

If the Administrator has selected **F**orcibly disconnect remote users from server when logon hours expire in the Account Policy window, users will receive a warning to log off. Users who have failed to log off when the time expires are disconnected.

This disconnection is considerably less draconian than it sounds. Users of non-NT computers are not booted off the network when the logon time interval expires, and they can continue to use the network without restriction. They are not permitted to log on to the domain during a restricted time interval, however.

Managing Permitted Logon Workstations

The **L**ogon To button in the New User, Copy of, and User Properties windows enables you to restrict the computers from which users can log on to the domain. Choosing **L**ogon To reveals the Logon Workstations window shown in figure 11.14.

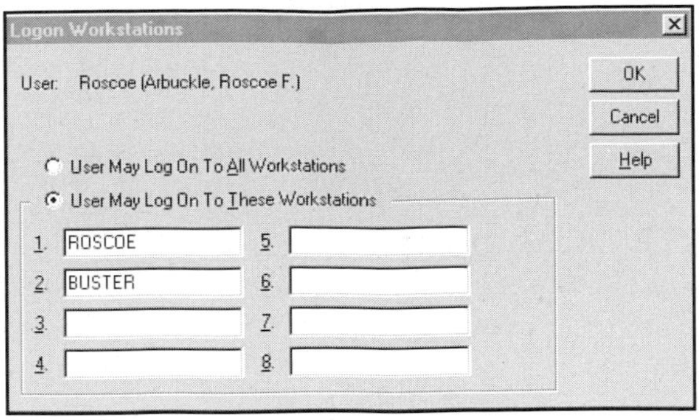

Figure 11.14

The Logon Workstations window.

By default, the User May Log On To **A**ll Workstations option is selected, and no workstation restrictions are in effect.

If you select the User May Log On To **T**hese Workstations button, you may enter up to eight workstation names from which the user is permitted to log on.

Note

For many reasons, Windows NT computers are the preferred workstations on Windows NT Server networks. Non-NT computers are not formally added to the domain and are not assigned SIDs that make it possible to establish secure communication. A user of a non-NT computer needs only a valid user name and password to log on to the domain.

You can prevent users from logging on from unapproved workstations by using workstation logon restrictions. For each user, configure the Logon Workstations window to permit the user to log on using only known Windows NT computers. When that is done, someone who steals or guesses a user's name and password cannot log on without gaining physical access to a computer the user account can use.

Managing Permitted Logon Workstations for Two or More Users

When you select two or more users in the User Manager for Domains window, choosing **L**ogon To in the User Properties window produces a Logon Workstations window that displays only information that is true of all workstations.

If you select one of the buttons, that option will be selected for all the users you have selected.

The workstations you enter replace the workstation lists that were established previously for the selected users.

Note   Users of non-NT workstations are not restricted by any logon workstation properties you assign to their accounts.

Managing Account Information

The **A**ccount button in the New User, Copy of, and User Properties windows enables you to assign user account information. Choosing **A**ccount reveals the Account Information window shown in figure 11.15. You use this window to configure two properties of user accounts.

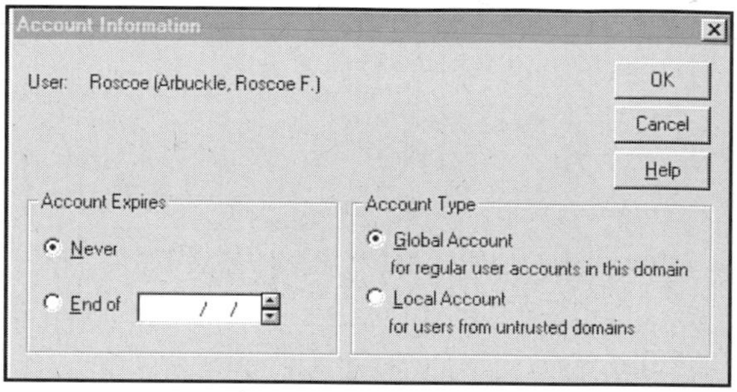

Figure 11.15

The Account Information window.

By default, user accounts never expire. You can configure an account to expire by choosing **E**nd of and specifying a date. Automatic account expiration is useful in several situations; two follow:

◆ You receive notice that an employee will terminate on a certain day, and you want to ensure that the account will become inactive at that time.

◆ A temporary employee requires access for a specific period of time. This might be a good use of the Guest account. You also could set up a user account named Temp to reuse in similar situations.

The Account Information window also enables you to specify whether the user account will be a local or global account:

◆ Select **G**lobal Account if you want the account to be recognized by other domains that trust the user's logon domain.

◆ Select **L**ocal Account if this user will be logging on to the domain from an untrusted domain, such as LAN Manager 2.x.

Managing Account Information for Two or More Users

When you select two or more users in the User Manager for Domains window, clicking on **A**ccount in the User Properties window produces an Account window that displays only information that is true of all workstations. When workstations do not share a common configuration for a given set of buttons, neither button is selected.

Any changes you make in the window replace the previous settings for all the accounts you have specified.

Managing the Account Policy

The account policy determines password and lockout policies that affect all users in the domain. You can access the Account Policy window, shown in figure 11.16, by choosing the **A**ccount command from the User Manager for Domains **P**olicies menu. Figure 11.16 does not show default settings. Instead, it presents minimum settings that I recommend you establish on your network.

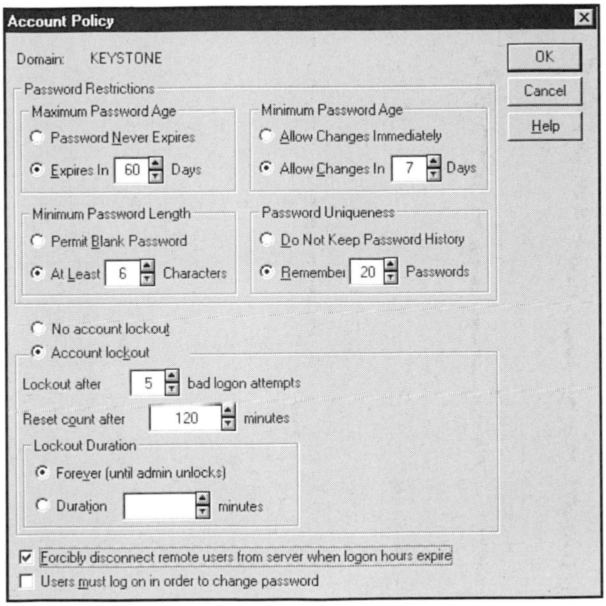

Objective

C.1

Figure 11.16

The Account Policy window.

Setting Password Restrictions

The account policy can define four password restrictions:

◆ **Maximum Password Age.** This setting determines how long passwords can be in effect before they expire. If you select the **E**xpires In button, users are forced to change their passwords after the specified number of days. The default for this setting is Password **N**ever Expires. I recommend that you allow a maximum of 60 days before users are forced to change their passwords.

◆ **Minimum Password Age.** In most cases, you want Windows NT Server to remember users' recent passwords so that they don't simply enter the same old password when their passwords expire. Unless you establish a minimum password age, some users simply will enter some dummy passwords until they can reuse their favorite old password. The default for this setting is **A**llow Changes Immediately. A minimum setting of seven days is recommended.

◆ **Minimum Password Length.** Short passwords are easier to guess or determine by trial and error. The default setting is Permit **B**lank Password. To ensure security, you should require a minimum password length of at least six characters.

◆ **Password Uniqueness.** If you choose the **R**emember option, Windows NT Server remembers the users' most recent passwords. To avoid having users reuse the same easily remembered passwords, select **R**emember and set the number of remembered passwords to 10 or more.

Setting Policy for Changing Expired Passwords

At the bottom of the Account Policy window, you see a box labeled Users **m**ust log on in order to change password. If you check this box, a user whose password has expired will not be permitted to log on and must obtain assistance from an Administrator.

Setting Account Lockout Actions

Many passwords can be guessed if you give an intruder enough opportunities. To prevent someone from attempting to determine passwords by trial and error, establish account lockout properties. If you select Account loc**k**out, the following options are active:

◆ **Lockout after *n* bad logon attempts.** If a user cannot log on after five attempts, it is due to a forgotten password.

◆ **Reset c**o**unt after *n* minutes.** This field determines the interval (from 1 to 99999 minutes) in which the minimum number of bad logon attempts will lock out the account. Setting a high value ensures that a user will contact an administrator when the account is locked out. In that way, you learn if a user is having problems, and you may be tipped off to attempts to breach security.

◆ **Lockout Duration.** If a user cannot successfully log on after five attempts, it is a good bet that the user has forgotten the password or is an intruder. If an intruder locks up a user's workstation, and you have set the reset count to a low value, the lockout condition will have cleared when the legitimate user attempts to access the network. Both of you will be unaware of the intrusion attempt. It is recommended, therefore, that you set the value to Fore**v**er (until admin unlocks), forcing users to contact an administrator when they have been locked out.

Restrictive account lockout policies are particularly important if your network can be accessed from outside your organization through a wide area network or a dial-up connection. There is a myth that all computer intruders are exceptionally clever computer geeks who know how to crack their way into the most secure systems. In fact, most intruders are successful because system administrators have been careless in setting security policies.

Setting Disconnection Policy

At the bottom of the Account Policy window is the **F**orcibly disconnect remote users from server when logon hours expire option. If time restrictions have been established for a user account, checking this option instructs Windows NT Server to disconnect users whose time has expired.

Users of non-NT computers are unaffected by this option.

> **Note** In Windows NT terminology, a *local user* is a user who is working with files that reside on the local computer. A *remote user* is a user who is accessing files through the network via shares. Only remote users are affected by the account disconnection policy.

Managing Groups

Objective C.1

The bottom portion of the User Manager for Domains window lists groups that have been defined in the domain. A number of groups are created for you when Windows NT is installed. These groups were described in Chapter 9, "Understanding User Accounts, Groups, Domains, and Trust Relationships."

Take a moment to examine the group listing shown in figure 11.17. You will notice that global groups are identified by an icon that includes a world globe in the background. Local groups are identified by an icon that includes a workstation in the background.

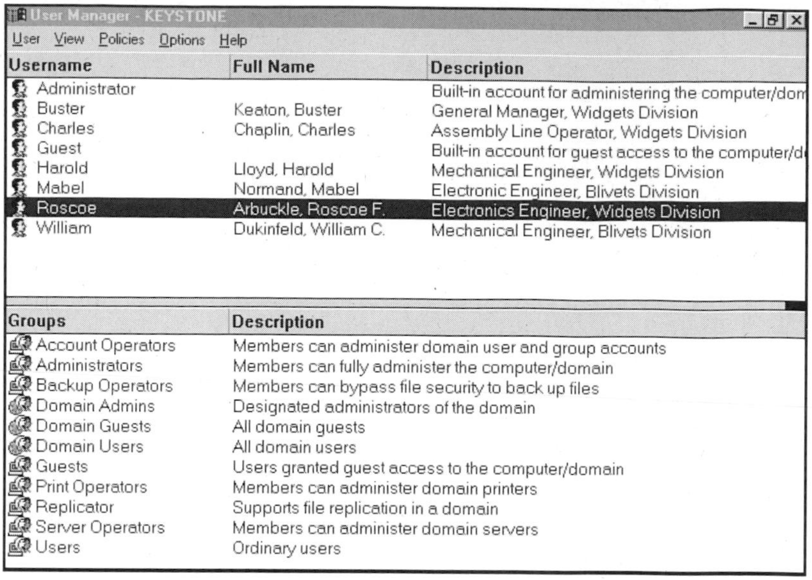

Figure 11.17

Groups listed in User Manager for Domains.

User Manager for Domains can be used to create and delete groups and to add and remove user accounts from groups. Later, you will examine how to determine the rights that a group can exercise.

Adding a Global Group

To create a new global group, follow these steps:

1. Choose the New **G**lobal Group command from the **U**ser menu. The New Global Group dialog box appears, as shown in figure 11.18. Figure 11.18 illustrates an example global group.

2. The group name is required. Enter a group name of up to 20 characters in the **G**roup Name field.

3. The description is optional. In long listings of groups, descriptions can be extremely useful, and it is recommended that you make an entry.

4. Only user accounts can be members of global groups. To add users to the group, select the user or users in the **N**ot Members list. Then click on **A**dd.

5. To remove users from the group, select the user or users in the **M**embers list. Then click on **R**emove.

6. Click on OK to add the group.

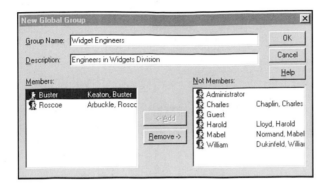

Figure 11.18

Adding a new global group.

Adding a Local Group

To add a local group, follow the steps covered in the following exercise:

Adding a Local Group

1. Choose the New **L**ocal Group command from the **U**ser menu. The New Local Group window is shown in figure 11.19. This figure illustrates a local group. Group members include two global groups and two user accounts.

2. The group name is required. In the **G**roup Name field, enter a group name of up to 20 characters.

3. The description is optional. In long listings of groups, descriptions can be extremely useful, and making an entry is recommended.

4. To add names to the group, choose **A**dd. The Add Users and Groups window shown in figure 11.20 appears. Members of local groups can include users and global groups from the local group's own domain as well as global users and global groups from other domains that this domain trusts. You have several options in this window:

   ◆ **List Names From.** Local groups can include users and groups from other domains that this domain trusts. To select names from a trusted domain, click on the arrow for this option and choose a domain from the list that is provided.

   ◆ **Add.** To add a user account or a group to the members of the group, select the entry in the **N**ames list and choose **A**dd. The name is added to the Ad**d** Names box.

   ◆ **Members.** To view the members of a global group, select the group in the **N**ames list and choose **M**embers. You can choose members of the global group to add to the group you are creating.   .

◆ **Search.** Because the list of domain names may be quite long, you might want to choose **Search** to find a particular entry. After you find a user or group, you can add it to the members of the group you are creating.

5. After you choose the names you want to add, choose OK.

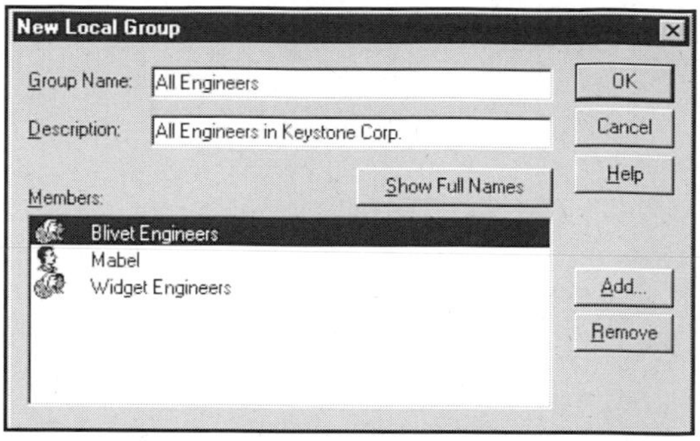

Figure 11.19

Adding a new local group.

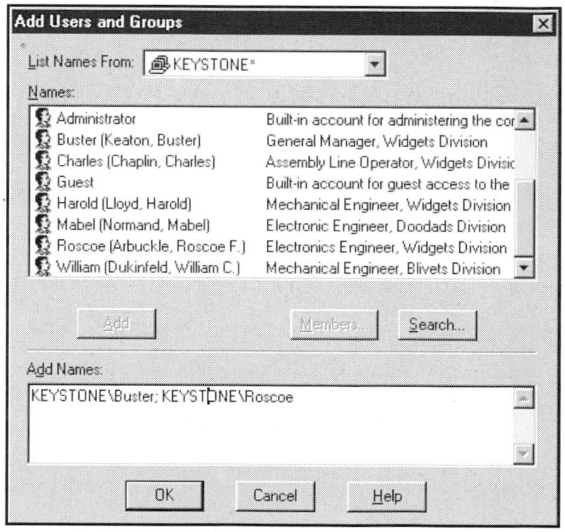

Figure 11.20

Adding users and groups to a local group.

6. To remove names from the group, select the name or names and choose **R**emove.

7. Choose OK when you have defined the group's members as you want.

Note   Examine figures 11.18 and 11.20. Notice that the chief difference between global and local groups is the **L**ist Names From field that is available for local groups. This field enables you to include users and global groups from other domains as members of a local group.

You can only trust users and global groups from other domains if the local group's domain trusts the domain in which the user and global group accounts are created. See Chapter 10, "Managing Domains and Trust Relationships," if you need to refresh your memory on the procedures for setting up trust relationships.

Managing Group Properties

To manage the properties of a global or local group, double-click on the group entry in the Groups list; or, select a group name from the list and choose **P**roperties from the **U**ser menu. The Global Group Properties window and the Local Group Properties window enable you to manage group properties.

Copying a Group

To create a copy of a group, select a group in the User Manager for Domains window. Then choose **C**opy from the **U**ser menu. A New Group window enables you to configure a new group with the same list of members. You will, of course, need to specify a unique name for the new group.

Deleting a Group

Groups that have been created by domain administrators can be deleted, but built-in groups cannot.

Deleted groups cannot be recovered. Like other entities in Windows NT Server networks, groups are identified by a security ID (SID). If you delete a group and then re-create it, the SID for the new group is different from the original SID. The newly created group does not have the rights and privileges of the old group, and it is not recognized by other groups that once recognized the SID of the old group.

To delete a group, follow the steps covered in the following exercise:

Deleting a Group

1. Select the group in the User Manager for Domains window.

2. Choose **D**elete from the **U**ser menu (or press the Delete key). The warning in figure 11.21 appears.

3. Choose OK to delete the group or Cancel to cancel the action.

4. A second box asks you to confirm your decision. Choose Yes to delete the group.

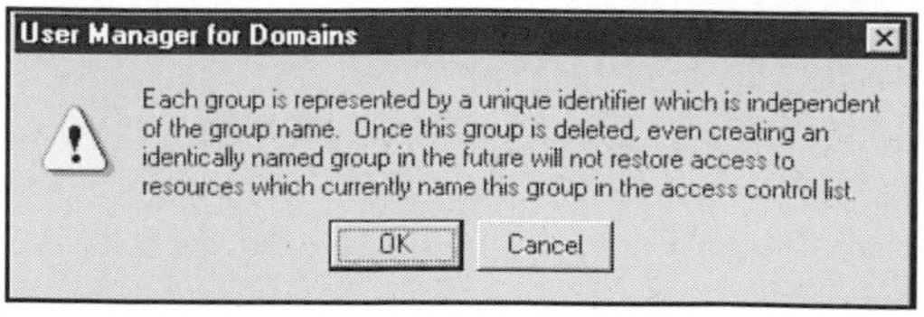

Figure 11.21

The warning you see when deleting a group.

> **User Manager for Domains** ☒
>
> ⚠ Each group is represented by a unique identifier which is independent of the group name. Once this group is deleted, even creating an identically named group in the future will not restore access to resources which currently name this group in the access control list.
>
> [OK]   [Cancel]

Enabling Users in Trusted Domains to Access Resources in Trusting Domains

In Chapter 10, you were shown how to enable a domain to trust another domain. If the domain Widgets trusts the domain Keystone, users who log on to the network through Keystone can be given permissions to access resources in Widgets. Without trust, users would be required to log on to Widgets directly.

Setting up a trust relationship does not permit users in Keystone to access resources in Widgets, however, until an Administrator in Widgets has given Keystone users permissions in Widgets. Also, if the group "everyone" is used and the guest account is active, keystone users will have access.

This is most commonly done by adding global groups from the trusted domain to local groups in the trusting domain. Here are some memberships you might set up:

◆ Add Keystone\Domain Users to Widgets\Users

◆ Add Keystone\Domain Admins to Widgets\Administrators

◆ Add Keystone\Domain Guests to Widgets\Guests

You can create other global groups in trusted domains. This is the easiest way to give users in trusted domains access to trusting domains.

Suppose that you want to have one set of backup operators back up multiple domains. Windows NT Server does not have preconfigured groups for doing this, but you easily could make the arrangements by doing the following:

◆ Make sure that each domain to be backed up trusts the backup operator's logon domain.

◆ In every domain to be backed up, create a global group named Backup.

◆ Add the Backup Operators global group from the logon domain to the Backup local group in each domain to be backed up. This will only allow the backup of domain controllers. If you want to backup member series or workstations you must also add the global group backup to the local group operator.

This approach can be used for any user group that you want to have access to a trusting domain. It seldom should be necessary to assign individual user accounts permissions in trusting domains.

The User Rights Policy

Objective
C.1

The actions that users and groups can perform depend on the rights and privileges they have been assigned. Rights and privileges are distinct sets of capabilities:

◆ *Rights* apply to the system as a whole. Because rights are assigned with User Manager for Domains, they are covered in this chapter.

◆ *Permissions* apply to specific objects such as files, directories, and printers. You will learn about permissions in other chapters, including Chapter 12, "Sharing Drives, Directories, and Files."

Rights have fundamental effects on the tasks that a user can perform on the network. In fact, rights can exceed the privileges that the user has been assigned.

Consider the Backup Operators group. Users in this group must be able to back up all files on the network—even files that they are not explicitly permitted to read. This capability is given to the Backup Operators group by assigning the Backup files and directories right.

The various built-in groups you have learned about are distinguished by the default rights that have been assigned to them by Windows NT Server.

What Are the Windows NT Server Rights?

Two categories of rights are defined: basic and advanced. The basic rights are listed here. After basic rights are discussed, the advanced rights will be examined.

Because the capabilities of the built-in groups are in part the result of the rights that initially are assigned to the groups when they are created, each right is identified with the groups to which it is assigned by Setup.

◆ **Access this computer from network.** Permits users to log on to the computer through the network.

Administrators

Power Users (Windows NT Workstation)

Everyone

◆ **Add workstations to domain.** Enables users to create computer accounts in a domain. This right can be granted to users who are not members of the groups that have the Add workstation to domain built-in capability.

◆ **Back up files and directories.** Allows users to back up all files on the computer.

Administrators

Backup Operators

Server Operators

◆ **Change the system time.** Permits users to set the time on the computer's clock.

Administrators

Power Users (Windows NT Workstation)

Server Operators

◆ **Force shutdown from a remote system.** This right is not implemented in current versions of Windows NT.

Administrators

Power Users (Windows NT Workstation)

Server Operators

◆ **Load and unload device drivers.** This right may show as an advanced right if the server was upgraded from a Windows NT Server prior to version 3.5.

Administrators

◆ **Log on locally.** Enables users to log on to a Windows NT computer. Without this right, a user cannot log on to a computer that is running Windows NT Server. Notice that ordinary users are not given the Log on locally right for Windows NT Server computers.

Account Operators

Administrators

Backup Operators

Power Users (Windows NT Workstation)

Print Operators

Server Operators

◆ **Manage auditing and security log.** Permits users to specify resources to be audited and to manage the security logs. This right does not enable users to set up system auditing—an ability that is held by Administrators.

Administrators

◆ **Restore files and directories.** Allows backup operators to restore all files and directories, regardless of any permission restrictions.

Administrators

Backup Operators

Server Operators

◆ **Shut down the system.**

Account Operators

Administrators

Backup Operators

Power Users (Windows NT Workstation)

Print Operators

Server Operators

◆ **Take ownership of files or other objects.**

Administrators

Additionally, there are several advanced rights. Most of these rights are of interest only to programmers and will not be discussed. If you cannot control your curiosity, you can read about these rights in the *Windows NT Server System Guide*.

The following advanced user rights may be useful when operating a Windows NT network:

◆ **Bypass traverse checking.** Permits a user to traverse a directory tree, even if permissions to access the directory have not been assigned.

Everyone

◆ **Load and unload device drivers.** This right appears as an advanced right if the server was upgraded to Windows NT Server 3.5 from an earlier version.

Administrators

◆ **Log on as a service.** Enables users to log on as a service. The Replicator service uses this right.

(None)

Managing the User Rights Policy

You seldom will need to redefine the default rights assignment. Microsoft has done a thoughtful job of setting up the built-in groups. At the very least, do not try to outguess Microsoft until you have gained some experience with Windows NT Server.

| Note | One change you might need to make is to permit users to log on to the server computer directly rather than through the network. To enable a user to log on at the server, assign the Log on locally right. In the next chapter, you will learn there is a risk to granting users this capability because share restrictions do not apply to local logons. |

To manage the user rights policy, follow the steps in the following exercise:

Managing User Rights

1. Choose the **U**ser Rights command from the **P**olicy menu of User Manager for Domains. This action displays the User Rights Policy dialog box, which is shown in figure 11.22.

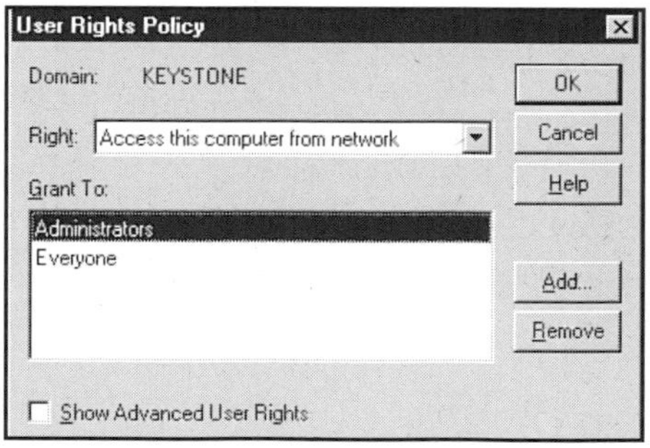

Figure 11.22

Managing the user rights policy.

2. To include advanced rights in the Rights list, check the **S**how Advanced User Rights box. This seldom will be necessary.

3. Click on the arrow beside the Righ**t** box to display a list of rights.

4. Select the right you want to examine. As you select rights, the **G**rant To box shows you the groups and users who have been assigned that right.

5. To add a group or user to the **G**rant To list, choose **A**dd and choose users and groups from the Add Users and Groups list. This list permits you to specify users and groups in the current domain or in trusted domains.

6. To remove a group or user, select it in the **G**rant To list. Then choose **R**emove.

7. To confirm your changes, choose OK. To cancel changes, choose Cancel.

The Capabilities of Built-In Accounts

The special characteristics of built-in accounts are determined by two sets of capabilities:

◆ *Rights*, which can be administered as you learned in the previous section

◆ *Built-in capabilities*, which are assigned by Windows NT Server to each built-in account and cannot be altered or assigned to new accounts

Now that you have examined rights, you should take a moment to examine the following list of built-in capabilities, along with the local groups that possess those capabilities:

◆ **Add workstation to domain**

Administrators

Account Operators

◆ **Assign user rights**

Administrators

◆ **Create and manage global groups**

Administrators

Account Operators (limited)

◆ **Create and manage local groups**

Administrators

Account Operators (limited)

Power Users (Windows NT Workstation)

Users (can modify only local groups they create)

◆ **Create and manage user accounts**

Administrators

Account Operators (limited)

Power Users (Windows NT Workstation)

◆ **Create common groups**

Administrators

Power Users (Windows NT Workstation)

Server Operators

◆ **Format server's (Windows NT Workstation: computer's) hard disk**

Administrators

◆ **Keep local profile**

Administrators

Power Users (Windows NT Workstation)

Everyone

◆ **Lock the server (Windows NT Workstation: computer)**

Administrators

Everyone

Power Users (Windows NT Workstation)

Server Operators

◆ **Manage auditing of system events**

Administrators

◆ **Override the lock of the server (Windows NT Workstation: computer)**

Administrators

Server Operators

◆ **Share and stop sharing directories**

Administrators

Power Users (Windows NT Workstation)

Server Operators

◆ **Share and stop sharing printers**

Administrators

Power Users (Windows NT Workstation)

Print Operators

Server Operators

In many cases, the built-in capabilities of non-administrators are limited. Although a member of Account Operators possesses the Create and manage local groups capability, he cannot modify the Domain Admins global group or the Administrators, Servers, Account Operators, Print Operators, or Backup Operators local groups. Nor can he modify global groups that are members of these groups.

Understanding the Windows NT Security Model

You have seen Windows NT security in action in the form of user and group permissions. The time has come to go behind the scenes and see how Windows NT security works.

Under MS-DOS, Windows 95, and other popular operating systems, it is routine for applications to bypass the operating system and directly poke around on the hard disk, in video memory, or in system memory. Programmers like to do this because accessing the system through the operating system slows things down. Game programmers especially like to program "down to the bare metal" so that they cke out every last bit of performance.

One concept of an operating system adhered to by Windows NT is that applications and users should be subject to control by the OS, which serves as a gatekeeper to every aspect of the system hardware and software. A well-designed operating system will prevent applications from conflicting or performing illegal operations. It also will offer other benefits as well, such as preemptive multitasking.

Multitasking can be performed over MS-DOS, but the multitasking applications must be on their best behavior and must cooperate wholeheartedly. This style of "cooperative multitasking" often goes awry. When applications can bypass the operating system they are free, through malice or error, to trash memory and files without restraint. Because Windows NT controls the machine with an iron fist, applications cannot interfere with one another and cannot hurt the operating system.

The Windows NT security model is based on a straightforward premise: All users must be granted permission to access any resource. To make this simple premise work, several things are required:

◆ Only Windows NT can directly access computer resources. Users must access resources through NT. Users and applications cannot bypass the operating system, as is commonly the case with MS-DOS.

◆ Each user accessing the computer must be identified to the system. On Windows NT, that means that each user is required to log on prior to doing any work, a feature called *mandatory logon*.

◆ Each resource on the computer is associated with a list of the users (called an *access control list*) who can access the object and the operations each user can perform.

Each of these areas requires some expansion so that you can understand the complete picture of Windows NT security.

Components of Windows NT Security

The primary components of the Windows NT Security subsystem are:

◆ The Local Security Authority (LSA)

◆ The Security Account Manager (SAM)

◆ The Security Reference Monitor (SRM)

The following sections examine the purpose and function of each of these subsystems.

The Local Security Authority

The LSA has the following responsibilities:

◆ Authenticates users during the logon process

◆ Generates access tokens during the logon process

◆ Manages the Security policy

◆ Manages the Audit policy

◆ Logs audit messages to the event log

The Security Account Manager

The SAM maintains the *security account database,* commonly referred to as the SAM database, which contains information about all user and group accounts. SAM is used by the LSA to authenticate users during the logon process by comparing the user name and password entered by the user to the user's record in the SAM database.

SAM also generates the security identifiers (SIDS) that uniquely identify each user and group account. A SID is a very long number, such as the following:

S-1-5-21-2087915065-388913830-1877560073-500

The user or group is identified to the system by the SID, not by the name, which is provided as a convenience for users. When a user or group account is deleted, the SID is retired. It is, therefore, impossible to recreate the same user or group account. A new account might have the old name but would be assigned a new SID.

Note | SIDs are the reason you need to be very careful when you delete a user or group account because you cannot get the same account back again.

Incidentally, each Windows NT computer has a SID as well. If you reinstall Windows NT (as opposed to performing an upgrade), following the installation the computer may have the same name, but it will have a new SID. It is essentially a new computer on the network. Network security databases will retain entries for the old SID but will not recognize the new computer configuration due to the change in the SID.

The Security Reference Monitor

The SRM enforces access validation and the audit policy that is established by the LSA. All attempts to access resources must go through the SRM, which validates access to objects (files, directories, and so forth), tests user accounts for permissions, and generates audit messages as required.

The SRM has the only copy of the account validation code on the system, ensuring uniform object protection throughout Windows NT. When an application attempts to reference an object, the SRM examines the object's *access control list* (ACL) and checks the *access control entries* (ACEs) in the list to determine whether the user has the required permissions to perform the requested operation. SRM will either grant or deny access based on information in the ACL.

The Logon Process

Mandatory logons are a key component of the Windows NT security model. The Windows NT logon process is shown in figure 11.23, and follows these steps:

Figure 11.23

*The Windows NT
logon process.*

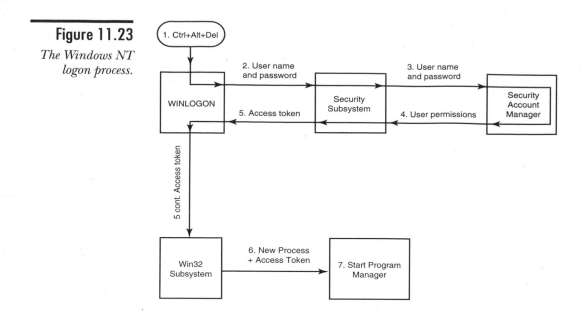

1. All logons are initiated by the Ctrl+Alt+Del key sequence, the familiar key
   combination that has reset IBM PCs from their inception. Under Windows NT,
   Ctrl+Alt+Del always vectors to the WinLogon process and serves as a strong
   defense against Trojan horses—programs that masquerade as system logon
   programs in an attempt to intercept user names and passwords.

   The WinLogon, a component of the LSA, displays the Welcome dialog box
   which accepts a user name, domain, and password. If either the user name or
   password is incorrect, the system replies with a "User Authentication Failure"
   message. The system does not explain whether the user name or password was
   invalid.

2. If the user name and password are valid, LSA passes the user's input to the
   security subsystem.

3. The security subsystem passes the user input to the SAM.

4. SAM consults the security accounts database to determine whether the user
   name and password match an account in the database. This information is
   returned to the security subsystem, together with information about the user's
   permissions, home directory location, and profile. If the user has a script file,
   the file is retrieved for execution.

5. If a match was found for the user name and password, and if the user account
   has permissions on the system, the security subsystem generates an *access token*
   that represents the user and serves as a key containing the user's credentials on
   the system. The access token is passed to the Win32 subsystem.

6. The Win32 subsystem generates a new process that is associated with the access token.

7. The process created by Win32 is used to initiate the Win32 NT Desktop, and the NT Desktop screen is displayed.

Note Two types of logons take place in the Windows NT Server domain environment:

◆ **Interactive logons.** These are logons that take place in response to a logon request in the logon dialog box. The user logs on to a domain or to the local computer, depending on whether a the **D**omain field specifies a domain or the name of the local computer.

◆ **Remote logons.** When a user is already logged on to a user account and attempts to establish a network connection to another computer, a *remote logon* takes place. An example of a remote logon is an attempt to map a network drive or to access a shared printer.

By supporting remote logons, Windows NT Server enables users to access resources on other computers and in other domains.

The NetLogon Service

The logon process is controlled by the *NetLogon service*, which is dependent on the Workstation service. The NetLogon service has three responsibilities with regard to the logon process:

◆ **Discovery.** When a Windows NT computer starts up, the NetLogon service attempts to locate a domain controller (either a PDC or a BDC) for the domain that is specified in the **D**omain field of the Logon dialog box. When a domain controller is identified, it is used to authenticate the user logon.

◆ **Establishing a secure communications channel.** Windows NT computers that communicate issue challenges and responses to establish the existence of valid user accounts. After verification, a communication session is established between the computers, and user identification data are exchanged.

◆ **Pass-through authentication.** When a user attempts to access a network resource and the access request cannot be authenticated by a domain controller of the user's logon domain, the request is passed to a domain controller in the destination domain for authentication.

Pass-through authentication makes the structure of the network considerably more transparent to the user who is attempting to access shared resources. The user is explicitly authenticated when logging on to one domain. Attempts to access resources in other domains are handled through pass-through authentication, eliminating the need to explicitly log on to additional domains. The domains that a user can access through pass-through authentication are determined by trust relationships that are established between the domains, as described in Chapter 10.

The NetLogon service is also responsible for replicating changes in the SAM database on the PDC to the BDCs in the domain. The process of reconciling the various copies of the SAM database is called *synchronization*.

Objects and Access Tokens

Subsequent to the logon process, the access token is used to control access to all secured objects. An access token includes the following information:

◆ The user's SID

◆ IDs of groups to which the user belongs

◆ Rights assigned to the user

The access token is generated during the logon process and is not updated. Therefore, changes that are made to a user's permissions will not take effect until the next time the user logs on to the system.

Access tokens are used to validate users' access to objects in the Windows NT system. The following are examples of objects in Windows NT:

Directories	Printers
Devices	Processes
Files	Symbolic links
Network shares	Threads
Ports	Windows

Each object has the following characteristics:

◆ **Type.** For example, file or printer.

◆ **Attributes.** The data stored in the object; for example, the contents of a file.

◆ **Functions.** The operations that can be performed on the object; for example, open a file. All operations that can be performed are part of the object.

If security is explicitly defined for an object, the object will have an *Access Control List* (ACL) consisting of *Access Control Entries* (ACEs) that identify a user or group that is assigned permissions for the object and the permissions that are assigned. The absence of an ACL indicates that all users are permitted access to the object.

The ACEs in an ACL are organized starting with ACEs that deny access, followed by ACEs that permit access. This sequence holds unless a custom application generates ACLs that are organized differently.

ACLs for objects are managed by various utilities. From an administrator's viewpoint, the most important tools are File Manager for files and directories and Print Manager for printers.

Evaluating Permissions

Following a successful logon, the security subsystem evaluates all attempts to access objects. The user's access token, created during the logon process, is compared to the ACL of the object to be accessed. The evaluation sequence is as follows:

1. Starting with the beginning of the ACL, the security subsystem looks for ACEs that deny access to the object for the user or for any group to which the user belongs. Because ACEs that deny access are organized at the beginning of the ACL, all denials will be encountered first.

2. The request is denied if any ACE is encountered that denies access.

3. If access is not denied, the security subsystem looks for ACEs that explicitly grant the requested access to the user's account or to groups to which the user belongs. ACEs are evaluated until sufficient permissions are accumulated to grant the user's access request.

4. The access request is denied if the security subsystem is unable to identify sufficient permissions to satisfy the request.

5. The access request is approved if sufficient permissions are found to satisfy the request.

Note To emphasize the point, in standard ACLs, ACEs that deny access always come first and take precedence over ACEs that grant access. The ultimate denial is the No Access permission, which overrides all other permissions.

The process of granting access to an object is shown in figure 11.24. The events shown in the figure are as follows:

1. The user requests access to an object.

2. The user is validated to the object's ACL.

3. If the user has the required access permissions, a *handle* is generated. A handle is an identifier used internally by Windows NT to identify a particular access to a resource. With the handle, the system generates a *list of granted access rights*, which

describes the user's permissions for the object. This list is stored in the user's process table.

4. After the object is opened, subsequent actions are checked against the list of granted access rights in the user's process table.

Figure 11.24

Granting a user access to an object.

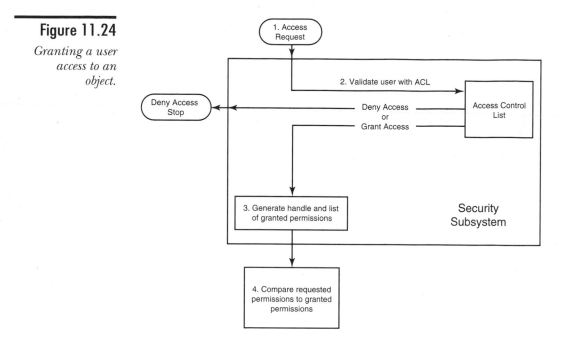

The ACL is consulted for permissions only when the user first accesses the object. As a result, permissions remain in effect as long as the handle that is created remains open. Changes to the ACL take effect only when the user closes the current handle and opens a new one. If, for example, the administrator changes the attribute of a file to Read Only while a user has it open, the user can continue to write to the file until the current handle is closed.

Customizing Windows NT Logons

The Windows NT Logon sequence can be customized in a variety of ways. This section describes several options. All Registry values discussed in this section are located in this Registry key:

    HKEY_LOCAL_MACHINE\SOFTWARE\Microsoft\Windows NT\
    CurrentVersion\Winlogon

Omitting the Default Logon Username

By default, the WinLogon Welcome dialog box displays the last user name that was used to log on to the system. This is a convenience but reduces security because it announces a valid user name. The value entry to add is:

DontDisplayLastUserName:REG_SZ:1

With a value of 1, this value entry prevents display of the last logon name. With a value of 0, the last logon name is displayed.

Displaying a Custom Logon Message

Some organizations have a policy to display a message to all users before they log on to a computer system. This message often describes organization security policies and warns of the penalties for misuse of the system. Such a message can be displayed after Ctrl+Alt+Del is pressed and before the Welcome dialog box is displayed.

To create a message, perform the steps outlined in the following exercise:

Displaying a Custom Logon Message

1. Enter the caption as a string in the data field of the following value entry:

   LegalNoticeCaption:REG_SZ:*caption of the message box*

2. Enter the message as a string in the data field of the following value entry:

   LegalNoticeText:REG_SZ:*text displayed in the message box*

The legal notice box will be displayed unless both Registry value entries are blank.

Changing the Shutdown Computer Options

The default Windows NT Workstation Welcome dialog box includes a Shutdown button that can be used to shut down the computer without logging on. To disable the Shutdown button, edit the following Registry entry, giving it the data value shown:

   ShutdownWithoutLogon:REG_SZ:0

By default, the value of this value entry is 1 and the Shutdown button is active.

If the computer hardware is equipped with a BIOS that enables the computer to be powered off under software control, you can add a button to the Shutdown Computer dialog box: Shutdown and **P**ower Off. To add this option, edit the following value entry as shown:

   PowerdownAfterShutdown RE6SZ-1

By default, the value of this value entry is 0, and the Shutdown and <u>P</u>ower Off option does not appear in the Shutdown Computer dialog box.

Configuring Automatic Logon

By default, you are prompted to enter a user name and password when logging on to Windows NT. If logon security is not required, you can configure a user name, domain, and password that will be automatically used to log on to the system.

Store the automatic logon entries in the following Registry values:

> DefaultUserName:REG_SZ:*username*

> DefaultDomainName:REG_SZ:*domainname*

You will need to create the following value entries:

> DefaultPassword:REG_SZ:*password*

> AutoAdminLogon:REG_SZ:1

To disable automatic logon, change the value of the AutoAdminLogon value entry to 0.

Testing Your Knowledge

1. Rights to administer accounts and groups are conferred on members of three Windows NT groups: Administrators, Domain Admins, and _____.

2. On Windows NT Server, what is the name of the tool used to manage user accounts and groups?

3. User Manager for Domains can be used to mange any domains for which you have been given administrative access.

    A. True

    B. False

4. Under Windows NT Server, you may only have one active session of the User Manager for Domains running at a given time.

    A. True

    B. False

5. If you are using the Low Speed Connection option with the User Manager for Domains, it restricts the tool in which of the following three ways?

 A. The View menu commands are inactive.

 B. User accounts no longer will be listed in the main window, and the Select Users option on the User menu is inactive.

 C. Access to trusted domains is not available.

 D. Groups no longer will be listed in the main window. Local groups can be created and managed using options from the User menu. Global groups cannot be created or managed.

6. Two user accounts, Administrator and _____, are created when Windows NT is installed.

7. A user name can include up to 20 characters, including upper- and lowercase letters, numbers, and punctuation. There are some illegal characters, however. Name at least four characters that are illegal to use for user names.

8. Passwords are case-sensitive and can consist of up to how many characters?

 A. 12

 B. 14

 C. 16

 D. 20

9. For increased security, it is not permitted to copy accounts.

 A. True

 B. False

10. Under the User Manager for Domains tool, it is possible to modify two or more user accounts simultaneously.

 A. True

 B. False

11. The Primary group is used only by users who are accessing Windows NT Server through Services for Macintosh.

 A. True

 B. False

12. Under the user environment profile, the Home Directory option must be assigned to the user's local hard drive.

 A. True

 B. False

13. When managing the account policy, several password settings are available to the administrator to manage, including: minimum and maximum password age, minimum password length, and password uniqueness. What purpose does the password uniqueness provide?

   A. To retain a historical record of a specified number of past passwords used by the user, and restrict that user from using them again.

   B. To restrict the user from utilizing characters that the administrator specifies in the password selection.

   C. To prevent users from using passwords that other users have already selected.

   D. To force a set of mandatory restrictions imposed by the administrator, such as a combination of alpha and numeric characters and upper- and lowercase characters.

14. The User Manager tool can be used to create and delete groups and to add and remove user accounts for groups. NT Server uses Global groups exclusively, and NT Workstation uses Local groups exclusively.

   A. True

   B. False

15. Setting up a trust relationship does not permit users from domain A to access resources in domain B until the administrator gives domain A users permissions in domain B.

   A. True

   B. False

16. Rights are predetermined by Microsoft and assigned to the built-in groups and accounts, and cannot be altered.

   A. True

   B. False

17. What NT Security component does the abbreviation SRM stand for?

18. Each user, group, and NT computer has a unique security identifier (SID). If you delete a user, group, or NT computer, you can reestablish the SID by recreating the deleted object.

   A. True

   B. False

Review Answers

1. Account Operators
2. User Manager for Domains
3. A
4. B
5. A, B, D
6. Guest
7. = + [ ] / \ < > ; : ' " * ?
8. B
9. B
10. A
11. A
12. B
13. A
14. B
15. A
16. B
17. Security Reference Monitor
18. B

CHAPTER 12

Sharing Drives, Directories, and Files

Unless users can access network resources, they have no reason to access the network at all. In previous chapters, you learned how to set up computers so they could communicate, and you learned how to set up user accounts so users could log on. Before users can benefit from the network, however, you need to share the network's resources with its users.

Sharing is the basic technique used by all Microsoft networking products to make directories and files on servers available to clients. The capability to share files in a workgroup setting is available in Windows for Workgroups, Windows 95, and Windows NT Workstation. Workgroup file sharing is informal and is not always suitable for large numbers of users or for sharing critical files. It is difficult to maintain a high level of security and to back up files in a workgroup environment, for example.

Windows NT Server contributes the capability to share files in a robust, centrally controlled environment. An extremely high level of security is possible, and files are located on central servers where they can be accessed by many users.

Merely sharing files with Microsoft networking products is easy. Any user can learn to share files on Windows for Workgroups in a few minutes. Taking advantage of the advanced security offered by Windows NT Server is a more involved topic, and it is the focus of this chapter.

Windows NT Server security is based on four sets of capabilities that can be given to users:

- ◆ **Abilities.** Users gain these by being assigned to built-in groups.

- ◆ **Rights.** Initially are assigned to built-in groups but can be assigned to groups or users by an Administrator.

- ◆ **Shares.** Pools of files that are shared on the network and can be assigned share-level security. Partition can be formatted as FAT or NTFS.

- ◆ **NTFS Permissions.** File system capabilities that can be assigned to groups or directly to users. Only partitions with NTFS can implement NTFS local permissions.

Administrators seldom get deeply involved in rights and have no direct control over abilities. Your involvement with rights and abilities probably will be limited to granting users membership in built-in groups.

You will be heavily involved in sharing files and setting NTFS permissions, however, and the activities related to sharing and permissions are the focus of this chapter.

Understanding File Sharing

Until at least one directory has been shared, users are unable to access files on the server by logging on through the network. This section shows you a very basic example of setting up and using a directory share.

Figure 12.1 illustrates a directory tree on a Windows NT Server, as shown in the Windows NT Explorer. Before users can access any of the directories through the network, the directories must be shared. Two directories are shared. The icon for the \WINNT directory shows a hand, indicating that it is shared. This directory is shared only for Administrators, and the share was established when Windows NT Server was installed. The Root directory of the C drive is also shared, again for use by administrators. When the figure was captured, no shares were configured for access by non-administrators.

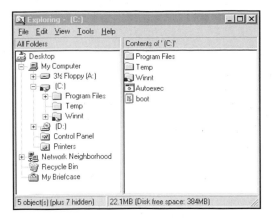

Figure 12.1

*Windows NT
Explorer showing
shared directories.*

Note   One other directory is created when Windows NT Server is installed on a PDC or a BDC. A share named NETLOGON enables users to access their logon scripts. Do not remove this share, which is assigned to C:\Winnt\system32\Repl\Import\ Scripts.

To share a directory in Windows NT Explorer, follow these steps:

**Objective
C.4**

1. Right-click on the directory to be shared.

2. Choose Sharing from the options menu to open the Winnt Properties window with the Sharing tab selected, as shown in figure 12.2.

Figure 12.2

*Editing share
properties.*

3. Choose S**h**ared As to activate sharing for the directory.

4. In the **S**hare Name field, enter a name that will be used to advertise the share. Other information that can be added to the share definition is discussed later in the chapter.

   If the share will be used by MS-DOS or Windows 3.x clients, the share name must conform to the 8.3 naming rule. Windows NT and Windows 95 clients can use long share names.

5. In the **C**omment field, you have the option of entering a description for this share. The description will identify the share in users' browse lists.

6. If you do not want to limit the number of users who can simultaneously connect to the share, select **M**aximum Allowed.

   If you want to limit the number of users who can access a share, select Allo**w** and specify a number in the Users field. You might want to limit users to conform to software licensing requirements or to reduce activity on busy servers. Remember, though, that users must explicitly stop sharing a directory to free a share count for other users. Users tend to forget such housekeeping details.

7. Choose OK to save the share information. Check the Windows NT Explorer display to see the new icon assignment for the shared directory.

Tip   You can also manage shares in My Computer. Simply right-click the drive or directory to be shared, choose S**h**aring, and complete the Sharing tab in the Properties window.

Now that a directory has been shared on the server, users can log on to the server and access the shared directory. By default, the group Everyone is given Full Control of a share. If that is what you want, you don't need to change the permissions assigned to the share.

Users access shares differently from different types of clients:

◆ On a Windows NT 4 client, shares can be accessed through Windows NT Explorer or through the Network Neighborhood. The NET USE command can also be used from batch files and the command line.

◆ Windows 3.x and Windows NT 3.x clients can access shares through File Manager or the NET USE command.

◆ MS-DOS and OS/2 users must access shared files by using the command line.

To use a shared directory, a user must connect the share to a free drive letter. On most PCs, drive letters E through Z are available for use as network drives. After a shared directory is connected to a drive letter, the user can access the shared directory as if it were an extra hard drive on the local computer.

To connect a network drive using the Network Neighborhood, perform the following steps:

1. Double-click on Network Neighborhood to open the network browser, as shown in figure 12.3.

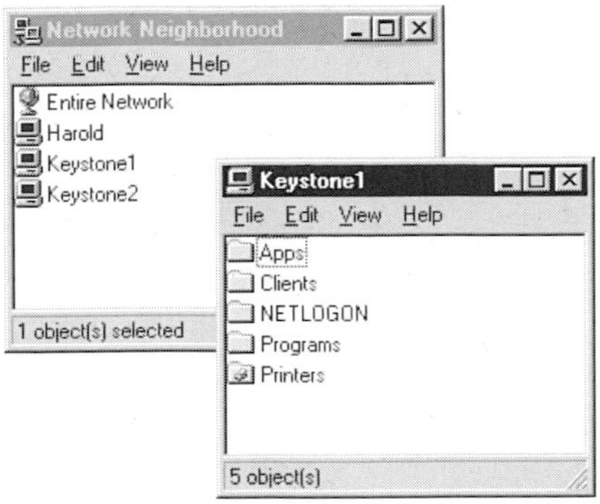

Figure 12.3

Browsing the Network Neighborhood.

2. Browse the Network Neighborhood to locate the share you want to connect to. In figure 12.3, the user has isolated the shares available on Keystone1.

3. Right-click on the desired share and choose **M**ap Network Drive from the Options menu to open the dialog box shown in figure 12.4.

4. In the **D**rive field of the Map Network Drive dialog box, specify a drive letter that will be used to connect to the share.

5. If necessary, choose **P**ath and edit the UNC name to correct the path to the share. This is available only when working in the Network Neighborhood.

6. If you do not have permission to access the share but of a user account that does have access, enter the user name in the **C**onnect As field.

7. If this drive connection should be reestablished whenever you log on to the network, check **R**econnect at Logon.

8. Choose OK.

Figure 12.4

*Connecting a
drive letter to
a share.*

In figure 12.4, a user mapped drive G to the Apps share on Keystone1, a share that connects to the Applications folder. After the mapping is accomplished, the user can access the Applications Folder in My Computer or in Windows NT Explorer by selecting drive G, as shown in figure 12.5. Notice that the subdirectory Program Files displays as though it were the root of drive G.

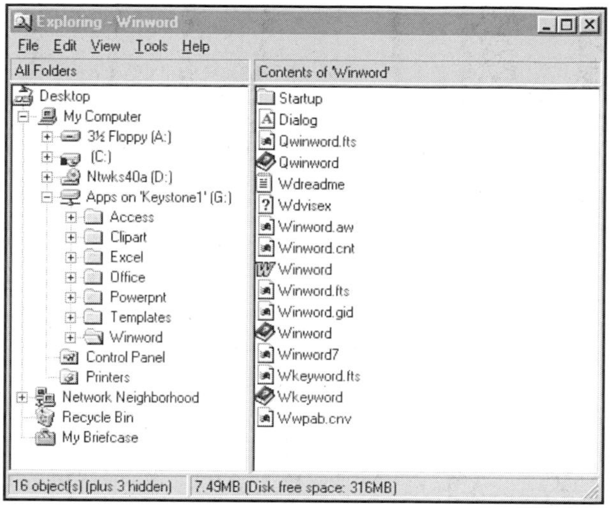

Figure 12.5

*Accessing a
connected network
directory.*

As you can see, sharing directories is extremely easy from the user's viewpoint. Additionally, users access shared directories using the same technique, whether the files are on a Windows NT Server or a workgroup computer running Windows NT Workstation or Windows for Workgroups. The network appears to the user as a large pool of shared resources, and the user doesn't need to know much about how the resources actually are being provided.

Note   Microsoft uses *universal naming convention* (UNC) names to identify computers and shares on the network. UNCs are occasionally entered in graphic utilities. More commonly, you will use them in conjunction with command-line utilities such as the NET command. A UNC name has the following format:

`\\`*computername*`\`*share*

The *computername* is the NetBIOS name assigned to the computer that is offering the share. The *share* is an existing share on the computer. The following example employs the NET USE command to establish a connection between drive j: and a share. The UNC identifies the share USERS on the computer KEYSTONE1:

```
net use j: \\keystone1\users
```

It is a good idea to leave spaces out of your host and share names. If you include spaces, users must remember to enclose the UNC in quotation marks like this:

```
net use m: "\\my computer\public"
```

Using Windows NT Explorer

If you have been using Windows 95, you are probably familiar with Windows 95 Explorer, which is quite similar to the Windows NT Explorer. The Explorer is such an important tool, however, that I want to make sure you are familiar with its features before getting into the details of sharing files and setting file-system permissions. Even if you have some experience with Explorer, please scan the topics in this section to see if anything is new to you.

Note All of the results described in this section can be obtained using the My Computer tool as well. I'm most comfortable, however, with the tree-oriented approach of Windows NT Explorer as opposed to the many windows that must often be navigated in My Computer. Try working with both tools and choose the one that fits your style.

Browsing the Desktop

Figure 12.6 shows the Explorer. In the left-hand All Folders pane of Explorer, the Desktop is displayed as a large tree that contains both local and network resources. Thus the Explorer provides one-stop-shopping for all available resources. Windows NT uses a "folders" metaphor for directories, and directories in the file system are typically referred to as folders when they are displayed graphically.

The right-hand Contents pane shows the contents of the folder that is selected in the All Folders pane.

Items displayed in the Explorer are identified by icons. Some of the icons you will encounter are described in the following list and are labeled in figure 12.6. Many resources can contain other resources. A hard drive can contain folders, for example. By default, the contents of many resources are not expanded in All Folders. A resource that is not expanded is tagged with a +. A resource that has been expanded is tagged with a –. Click a resource to expand it and display its contents.

Here are some of the icons you will encounter in Explorer:

◆ **Hard Drives.** Each hard drive is identified with a drive icon and a drive letter. The hard drive icon indicates a fixed storage device, one that cannot be removed during normal computer operation.

◆ **CD-ROM.** A CD-ROM is a read-only device and is assigned a distinctive icon.

◆ **Floppy Drive.** Floppy disk drive and other removable storage devices share the same icon. The media can be ejected from a removable storage device.

◆ **System Folders.** Some folders have special uses and are identified by distinctive icons. The Control Panel, for example, is indicated by a special folder, as is the Printers folder.

◆ **Closed Folders.** When a folder is closed, its contents are not expanded in the directory tree. If a closed folder has contents that can be displayed, it is labeled with a +. Click on a closed folder to open it.

◆ **Open Folders.** When a folder is opened, its contents are displayed. Opened folders and subfolders will be displayed in the All Folders pane.

◆ **Shares.** A drive or a folder that is tagged with a hand icon is being shared. Not all shares are available to the end users. Some shares are administrative shares, available only to members of the Administrators group.

◆ **Network Drives.** When a connection has been mapped to network share, the connected drive is shown with a network drive icon.

◆ **Network Neighborhood.** Open this icon to browse the network.

◆ **Recycle Bin.** This folder stores files and directories that have been deleted. Deleted resources can be recovered until the Recycle Bin has been emptied.

◆ **My Briefcase.** This folder is used to maintain copies of files that must be synchronized between computers. Don't confuse this with the directory replication service discussed in Chapter 22, "Managing Directory Replication." My Briefcase is a manual synchronization tool primarily designed to support end users.

◆ **Data Files.** Data files that have been associated with an application are identified by an icon related to the application. By default, Windows NT does not display the file name extensions of files that are associated with an application.

◆ **Applications.** Each application can be identified by an icon. By default, application and system file name extensions (such as EXE, COM, and SYS) are not displayed.

In the right-hand pane, Explorer displays the contents of the resource that is selected in the directory tree.

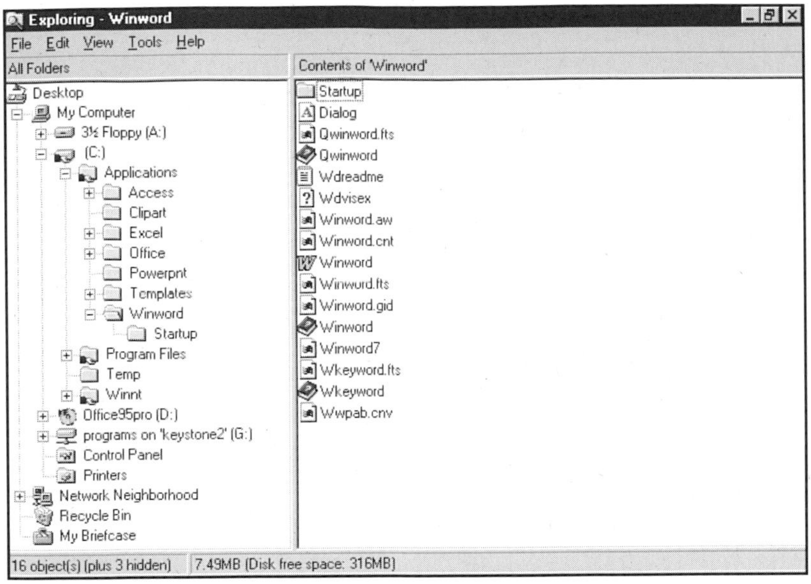

Figure 12.6

Windows NT Explorer.

Tips on Selecting Files

Selecting individual files and directories.

◆ With the mouse, click on the item.

◆ With the keyboard, press the Tab key to select the desired pane, then highlight the desired item with the arrow keys.

Selecting a range. Several techniques can be used to select a range:

◆ Clicking with the mouse: Select one end of the range by clicking on the item. Then hold down Shift and click on the other end of the range. The entire range is selected.

◆ Dragging with the mouse: An alternate technique with the mouse is to drag a selection box around the items. Point to a spot in the window that is outside the area to be selected. Press and hold the mouse, then drag the mouse to the other end of the range. A selection box will follow the mouse. Adjust the selection box to cover the desired items. When you release the mouse, the items within the selection box will be selected.

continues

◆   With the keyboard: Select the first item. Then hold down Shift and use the arrow keys to extend the selection range.

Extending a selection. If items already are selected, you can select additional files with the mouse, hold down Ctrl and click on the other selections.

Creating Folders

To create a folder, follow these steps:

1. In the All Folders pane, select the parent directory that will contain the new directory.

2. Right-click in the Contents pane and select New in the Options menu. Then choose Folder in the submenu that is opened. A new folder will be added to the Contents pane. It will be named New Folder, and the name will be selected for editing.

3. Edit the name of the folder and press Enter.

Naming NTFS Directories Files

The NTFS file system supports long file names, which can consist of up to 255 characters. The following characters may not be used:

? * / \ < > | :

Although NTFS supports upper- and lowercase letters, case is not significant. These file names are functionally identical: barney, Barney, BaRNey, and BARNEY.

Remember that your DOS and Windows 3.1x users cannot display long file names. When a DOS or Windows user displays a long NTFS file name, it is shortened and converted according to the following rules:

◆   All spaces are removed.

◆   Characters not allowed in DOS are converted to underscore characters (_).

◆   The name is shortened to the first six characters, unless a period appears in the first six characters, in which case only the characters that precede the period are retained.

◆   A tilde (~) and a digit are added to the characters that are retained. The digit is incremented if files are encountered that duplicate the first six characters.

> ◆ If a period is found in the long name, the first three characters following the period are used as a file-name extension (the file name `Sales report for 10/94 by Sam R,` for example). Green is converted to `SALESR~1.GRE`.
>
> Because the resulting file names can be illogical or confusing, you might want to conform to DOS file-naming conventions on a network that includes DOS or Windows clients.

Deleting Directories and Files

To delete directories or files, select the items then:

◆ Press the Delete key.

   or

◆ Choose **D**elete in the **F**ile directory.

Note | When you delete items from the Network Neighborhood or the Windows NT Explorer, they are not deleted but are moved to the Recycle Bin, which has an icon on the desktop. You can recover items from the Recycle Bin until it has been emptied.

To empty the Recycle Bin:

1. Right-click the Recycle Bin icon on the desktop.

2. Choose Empty Recycle **B**in from the Option menu.

3. Confirm deletions as requested.

Copying Directories and Files

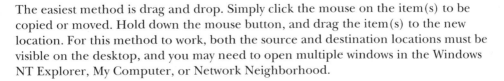

Objective C.4

After you select one or more directories or files, you can copy them to a new location by using menu commands or mouse actions.

The easiest method is drag and drop. Simply click the mouse on the item(s) to be copied or moved. Hold down the mouse button, and drag the item(s) to the new location. For this method to work, both the source and destination locations must be visible on the desktop, and you may need to open multiple windows in the Windows NT Explorer, My Computer, or Network Neighborhood.

When you drag items with the mouse, be aware of the following:

◆ Dragging a directory or files to a different disk drive makes a copy of the items on the new drive. If you want to move an item(s) to a new drive, removing the item(s) from the original drive, hold the Shift key while dragging and dropping.

◆ Dragging a directory or files to a location on the same drive moves them. The directories and files are removed from the old location and stored in the new location.

◆ To copy files to a new location the same drive, you must hold down the Ctrl key as you drag the files.

When you drag an executable file (EXE or COM) three results are possible:

◆ Normally, the executable file remains in the original location and a shortcut icon is created in the destination.

◆ If you hold down the Ctrl key while dragging, a copy of the file is placed in the destination and the original file remains in the source location.

◆ If you hold down the Shift key while dragging, the file is moved to the new location.

You can also use cut and paste techniques:

◆ To cut an item or items, select the items and choose Cut in the Edit menu. Cutting removes the original items, placing a copy in the Clipboard.

◆ To copy an item or items, select the items and choose Copy in the Edit menu. Cutting places a copy in the Clipboard, leaving the original items intact.

◆ To paste the contents of the clipboard, select the destination folder and choose Paste in the Edit menu. The contents of the clipboard will be placed in the selected folder.

Opening Additional File Management Windows

You will often find it handy to have two or more folders open. If you are doing a drag and drop, for example, the source and destination folders must be visible on the desktop. You can open any combination of the following:

◆ Multiple copies of Explorer

◆ Windows opened in My Computer

◆ Windows opened in Network Neighborhood

Simply drag and drop between any two visible locations.

Customizing the View

You might want to customize the manner in which Explorer displays directories and files. The **V**iew menu supplies a number of options that enable you to tailor your display.

Check the **T**oolbar option to display an icon bar at the top of the Explorer window. By default the toolbar is disabled, but it was enabled when figure 12.6 was prepared.

Check the Status **B**ar option to display a status bar at the bottom of the display. The status bar describes the current action when you are accessing a menu. At other times, it displays information about the objects that are selected in the All Folders pane. By default, the status bar is enabled.

Three commands specify whether File Manager should display icons or a list in the Contents pane. **L**ist, the default option, displays a vertical listing. If you prefer another format, choose Lar**g**e Icons or S**m**all Icons. If you have specified an icon display, the Lin**e** up Icons command is active and can be used to clean up the arrangement of the icons in the Contents pane.

By default, only folder and file names are listed in the Contents pane. If you want to see more information, check **D**etails in the **V**iew menu. Figure 12.7 illustrates a detailed display. You can change the widths of the columns in the Contents pane by dragging the dividers between the column headers. In the figure, the divider between the All Folders and the Utilities panes was dragged to permit more space for the detailed display.

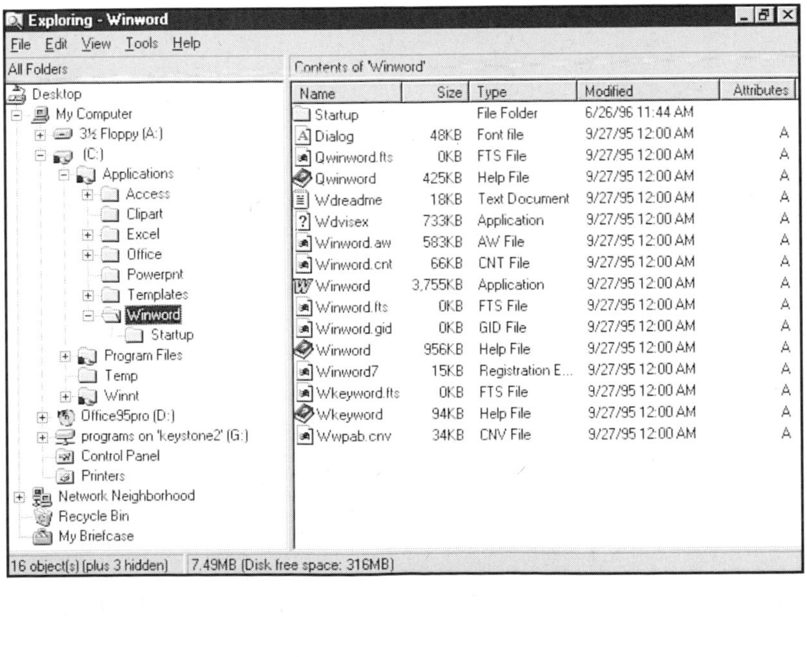

Figure 12.7

Windows NT Explorer with details enabled.

The Arrange Icons option opens a submenu where five commands are available for controlling the order in which listed files are sorted:

- ◆ by **N**ame
- ◆ by **T**ype
- ◆ by Si**z**e
- ◆ by **D**ate
- ◆ **A**uto Arrange

The **A**uto Arrange option is available only when large or small icons are displayed. Choose this option if you want Explorer to clean up the icons arrangement as changes are made.

Windows NT Explorer will update its display to reflect changes made locally, but it does not check the network to determine whether changes have been made elsewhere. If you want to bring the contents of the Explorer displays up to date, choose **R**efresh.

The final command in the **V**iew menu is **O**ptions, which is important enough to deserve a section of its own.

Selecting Explorer Options

The **O**ptions command in the **V**iew menu produces the Options utility shown in figure 12.8. The Options utility has two functions: determining which files will be excluded from the Explorer lists, and registering file types to associate them with applications.

The following options are available in the View tab, which is shown in figure 12.8:

- ◆ **Show all files.** Select this option if all files should be listed in Explorer, including system files.

- ◆ **Hide files of these types.** Select this option to exclude system files from the Explorer display. The types of files that are excluded are listed in the scroll box. This is the default value.

- ◆ **Display the full path in the title bar.** Check this option to display the full path of the selected resource in the Explorer title bar. By default, this option is not checked.

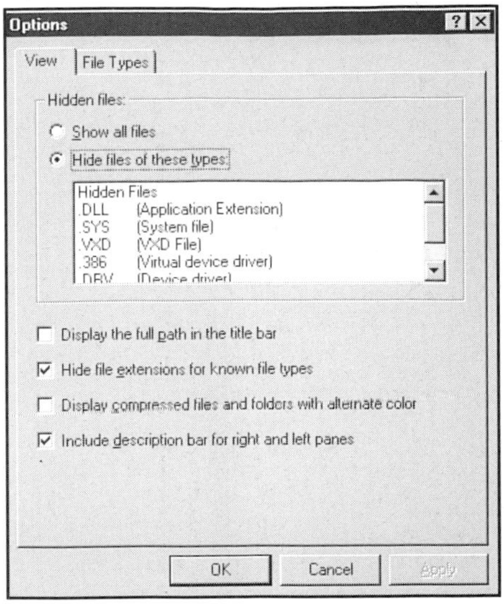

Figure 12.8

Configuring the file view in the Options utility.

◆ **Hide file extensions for known file types.** If you have added an extension to the list of known file types, check this option to prevent Explorer from displaying the extension in listings. This option is a matter of choice. Many administrators will prefer to display the extensions and will want to remove the check from this option.

◆ **Display compressed files and folders with alternate color.** In Chapter 17, "Managing Disk Storage," you will learn how to compress folders and files. If you want to display compressed folders and files in a distinctive color, check this option.

◆ **Include description bar for right and left panes.** This option determines whether the panes will be labeled with the All Folders and Contents legends. Remove the check mark to permit a bit more room for data display.

The File Types tab is shown in figure 12.9. Using this tab, you can associate file-name extensions with particular applications. Doing so informs Windows NT to run the associated application whenever you open the data file. If files with the extension DOC are associated with Microsoft Word for Windows, for example, the Word application is launched whenever you open a file with a DOC extension.

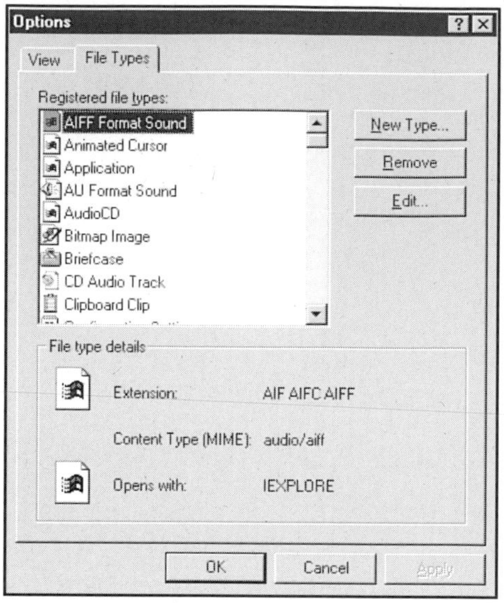

Figure 12.9

Examining a file type registration.

Figure 12.9 shows an association between the DOC file-name extension and the Microsoft Word for Windows application. From this display, you can examine associations in the Registered file types list. You can also remove an association by selecting it and choosing **R**emove.

Although it is possible to add your own file type registrations, the details are beyond the scope of this book, often requiring a knowledge of DDE. Typically, when Windows applications are installed the related file type registrations are established for you.

Managing Directory and File Properties and Attributes

Directories and files have several properties that are managed by Windows NT.

Files and directories also can be assigned several attributes that determine actions that can be performed with them. The attributes follow:

- ◆ **Archive.** Assigned by the operating system to indicate that a file has been modified since it was backed up. Backup software usually clears the archive attribute. The archive attribute makes it possible to identify modified files when performing incremental backups.

- ◆ **Compress.** Identifies folders and files that have been or should be compressed. This option is available only on NTFS partitions.

◆ **Hidden.** Files and directories do not usually appear in directory lists. You can direct File Manager to display hidden files by choosing the **O**ptions command in the **V**iew menu and checking the **S**how all files box.

◆ **Read Only.** Files and directories cannot be erased or modified.

◆ **System.** Files usually are given this attribute by the operating system or by the OS Setup program. This attribute rarely is modified by Administrators or users. System files and directories behave as if they have both the Read Only and Hidden attributes. You can display the attributes in File Manager listings using the technique described for hidden files.

Note | Assign the Compress attribute to directories or files that you want Windows NT to compress. Compression takes place in the background and can dramatically reduce the space required to store files. There is some performance penalty because compressed files must be decompressed before use, but the cost is reasonable in most cases, considering the storage savings that result. Do not, however, compress files that are used frequently, such as large data files that many users share. Compression/decompression will reduce file access performance, and, because the file will spend most of the time in a decompressed state, nothing of real benefit is gained.

Managing Properties and Attributes for Directories

You can configure Windows NT Explorer to display file attributes by choosing the **D**etails command in the **V**iew menu.

To display the properties for a folder or a file:

1. Right-click on the folder or file and choose the **P**roperties command from the Options menu.

2. Select the General tab. The General tab for a folder is shown in figure 12.10.

3. Check the attributes you want to assign to the folder or file.

4. Choose OK.

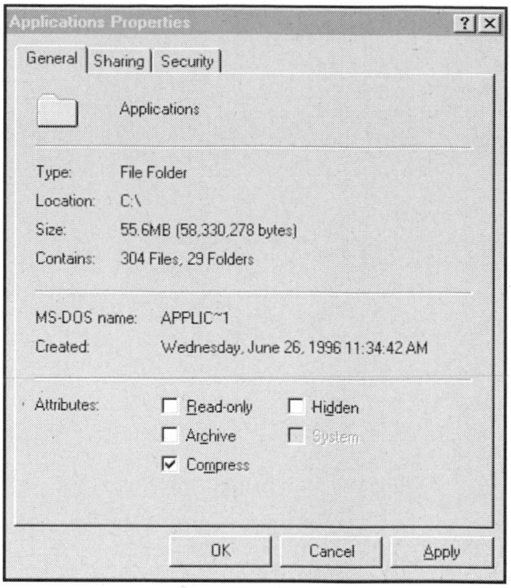

Figure 12.10

Attributes for a folder.

Formatting and Copying Floppy Disks

You can format and copy disks from Explorer. To format or copy a disk:

1. If necessary, Insert the disk to be formatted.

2. Right-click the disk icon in the All Folders pane.

3. To format a disk, choose the For**m**at command in the Options menu and follow the prompts.

4. To copy a disk, choose the Cop**y** Disk command in the Options menu and follow the prompts.

Note   You cannot format the system partitions (usually C:) from Explorer.

Searching for Files

Servers typically have many files in large directories on very large drives. If you had to remember where every file was located, you would be in trouble. Fortunately, Windows NT Explorer provides a search option. To search for a file, follow the steps outlined in the following exercise:

File Searching

1. Right-click on the object in the All Folders pane where you would like to begin the search. The search will proceed down the tree from this point.

2. Choose the **F**ind command in the Options menu to open the Find: All Files window shown in figure 12.11.

3. Select the Name & Location tab, shown in figure 12.11.

4. In the **N**amed field enter a file name, which can include the ? and * wildcards. You can pull down a list of typical file name search targets.

5. You can change the starting point for the search by pulling down the **L**ook in field to select another disk object. If desired, choose **B**rowse to browse for a particular directory.

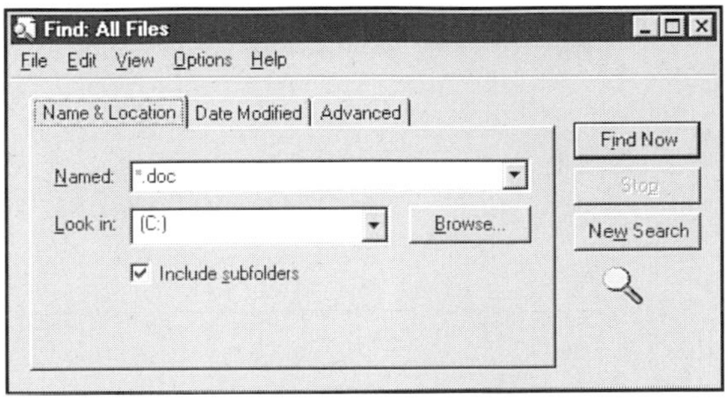

Figure 12.11

Specifying parameters for a file search.

6. Select the Date Modified tab, shown in figure 12.12.

7. Select **A**ll files to search all files, regardless of their date stamps.

8. Select Find all files created or **m**odified to search for files with specific date stamps. Select one of the available date criteria and enter the required parameters.

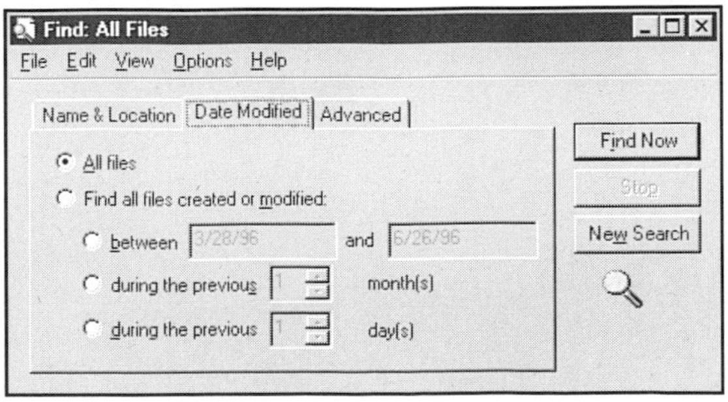

Figure 12.12

Specifying date parameters for a file search.

9. Select the Advanced tab, shown in figure 12.13, if it is necessary to further narrow the search.

10. To narrow the search to a particular file type, pull down the Of type field and select a file type from the list. These file types reflect the file type registrations that have been established on this computer.

11. To search for a specific text string in the file contents, enter the text in the **C**ontaining text field.

12. To search for files in a particular size range, select At least or At most in the **S**ize is field. Then specify a file size in the KB field.

13. Choose F**i**nd Now to initiate the search.

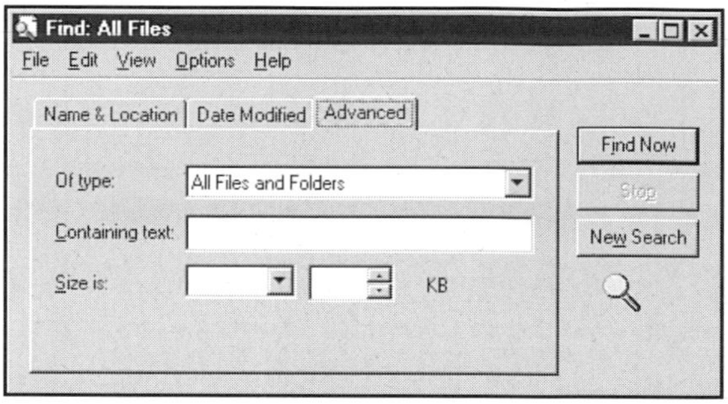

Figure 12.13

Specifying advanced parameters for a file search.

When the search is complete, File Manager displays a list of files that met your specifications. You can perform any operation on files in this list that you could perform in the Contents pane of Windows NT Explorer.

Running Applications from Windows NT Explorer

You can start applications directly from Explorer. An application file is any file with an extension of EXE, COM, BAT, or PIF. (PIF files are Program Information Files that can be used to configure the operating environment for an EXE or COM file. Running a PIF file automatically executes the program file specified in the PIF file.) Several techniques can be used to run an application from File Manager:

◆ Double-click on the icon for the application file.

◆ Right-click on the icon and choose **O**pen from the Options menu.

◆ Drag a data file icon to the icon for the appropriate application file. This approach works only if both icons are visible and is difficult to perform in Windows NT Explorer when the file and application are in different directories. You may need to open a second copy of Explorer to have both file icons visible.

◆ Double-click on a data file that has been registered for a particular application, as described earlier in this chapter.

Managing Directory Shares

Unless a directory is shared, it is unavailable to users who access the server through the network. Even Administrators, who have free access to all directories and files when logged on to the server, cannot access unshared resources through the network. Early in this chapter you saw a brief demonstration of the way in which shares are created and used. This section covers the details.

Sharing works with both FAT and NTFS file systems. You will find that the security you can implement with sharing is pretty limited, however. To enhance share security, you need to be able to assign directory and file permissions, which are available only with the NTFS file system. Directory and file permissions are discussed in the section "Directory and File Permissions."

Keep in mind some of the significant limitations of shares:

◆ Shares control user access only with remote logins. Shares have no effect on users who are permitted to log on locally to the server.

◆ Because shares have no effect on security for users who log on locally to the server, security on FAT and HPFS volumes is practically nonexistent for users who have physical access to the server.

◆ When you share a directory, you share all its files and subdirectories. If you need to restrict access to part of a directory tree, you must use file and directory permissions and the NTFS file system.

Sharing a Directory

To share directories, you must be logged on as a member of the Administrators or Server Operators group.

All file sharing procedures are performed in Windows NT Explorer. To share a directory, use the steps outlined in the following exercise:

Directory Sharing

1. Right-click on a directory.

2. Choose the **Sh**aring command from the Options menu to display properties for that directory. The Sharing tab will be selected as shown in figure 12.14.

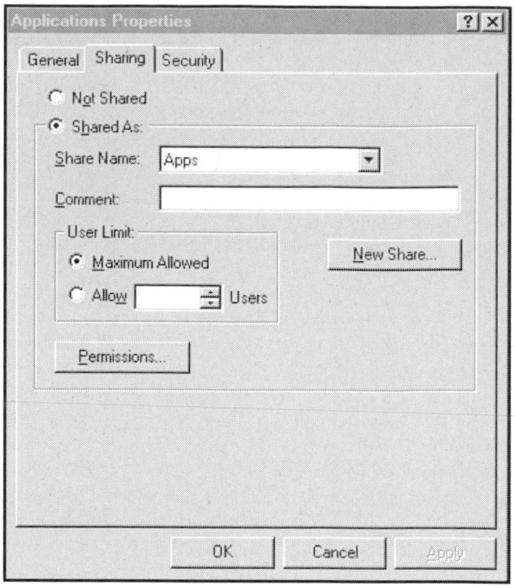

Figure 12.14

*Sharing a
directory.*

3. If this directory is already shared and you want to establish a new share for the same directory, choose **N**ew Share.

4. Select S**h**ared As.

5. Enter a share name in the **S**hare Name field. The name of the directory you selected is displayed as a default, but you can change the share name if desired. The share name can consist of up to 12 characters.

Caution   MS-DOS and Windows 3.x users cannot see share names that exceed the restrictions of the 8.3 file name format. Although Windows NT converts long file names to a format that can be viewed by MS-DOS users, it does not convert share names.

6. Enter a comment in the **C**omment field. This comment can describe the share to your users in greater detail than the short share name.

7. Set a user limit. By default, **M**aximum Allowed is selected and an unlimited number of users can access a share. You can set a fixed limit by selecting Allo**w** Users and entering a number.

8. By default, everyone in the network has full control of the directory you share. If you want to restrict access, click on the **P**ermissions button. Setting share permissions is described in the next section.

9. Choose OK.

The icon for the directory you shared now includes a hand to indicate that it is shared.

Creating a New Share for a Shared Directory

You might want to share the same directory more than once. To add a new share to a shared directory, follow the steps covered in the following exercise:

Establishing Multiple Shares

1. Right-click the shared directory in the directory tree.

2. Choose the **Sh**aring command from the Options menu to display properties for that directory.

3. Choose **N**ew Share to create a new share.

Each share must have a unique name. If you are creating two or more shares for the same directory, be sure your share names and comments explain what each share is for and who can use it.

Understanding Special Identities

You have been introduced to most of the entities that can be assigned permissions on Windows NT Server: local and global users, as well as local and global groups.

Permissions also can be assigned to five entities that Microsoft calls *special identities* or *special groups*:

- ◆ **Everyone.** Includes all users and can be used to assign permissions that all users in a domain hold in common, including guests and users from other domains.

- ◆ **SYSTEM.** Represents the operating system. Setup assigns initial permissions to SYSTEM that you should not modify. In fact, you should seldom, if ever, need to directly manipulate the permissions for SYSTEM.

- ◆ **NETWORK.** Includes all users who access a file or directory through the network. Rights assigned to NETWORK are active only when a user logs on remotely.

- ◆ **INTERACTIVE.** Includes users who log on locally to the server. Rights assigned to INTERACTIVE are in force only when a user logs on to the server computer itself.

- ◆ **CREATOR OWNER.** Represents the user who creates a directory or file.

continues

> Permissions given to CREATOR OWNER for a directory are assigned to any files or subdirectories that are created in the directory. As a result, users are given the rights assigned to CREATOR OWNER for any subdirectories or files they create.
>
> Of these five special identities, only Everyone and CREATOR OWNER apply to shares. Because share permissions affect only users who log on through the network, SYSTEM, NETWORK, and INTERACTIVE have no genuine role with regard to share security even though you can choose to assign share rights to those groups.
>
> All special identities can be used with directory and file permissions, which are discussed later in this chapter.

Objective C.4

Setting Share Permissions

Share permissions establish the maximum set of permissions that are available within a shared directory tree. Other permission assignments can further restrict access, but cannot add to the permissions established by the share permissions.

Four types of permissions can be assigned to shared directories. From most restrictive to least restrictive, the permissions follow:

◆ **No Access.** No permissions are granted for the share.

◆ **Read.** Users have the following capabilities:

Displaying subdirectory names and file names

Opening subdirectories

Displaying file data and file attributes

Running program files

◆ **Change.** Users have Read permissions plus the following capabilities:

Creating subdirectories and files

Modifying files

Changing subdirectory and file attributes

Deleting subdirectories and files

To set share permissions, choose the **P**ermissions button in the Sharing tab of the Properties window. The Access Through Share Permissions window shown in figure 12.15 appears.

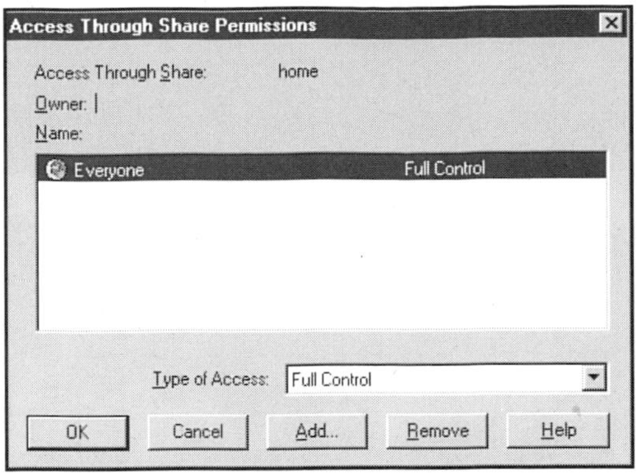

Figure 12.15

Setting share permissions.

When you create a new share, the default permissions give Everyone Full Control over the share. This default assumes that you will be assigning directory and file permissions when it is necessary to restrict users' access to other directories. If your server uses NTFS and you will be setting file and directory permissions, you do not need to restrict share permissions.

If you are using FAT volumes, share permissions are all you have to work with. Here are some suggestions:

◆ Users often need only Read permissions in application directories because they do not need to modify files.

◆ Users generally need Change permissions in any directory that contains shared data files.

◆ Often, the only place you will permit users to have Full Control privileges is in their personal directories.

The permissions a user can exercise are cumulative. Take the case of a user who belongs to a group named Widgets. If Everyone is given Read permission to a directory and Widgets is given Change permission, the user can exercise Change authority in the directory.

As a general rule, create shares and grant permissions on a group basis. You will quickly become overwhelmed if you attempt to manage permissions for individuals.

Modifying Permissions

You can modify permissions easily from the Access Through Share Permissions window. To change share permissions for a group or user, follow the steps described in the following exercise:

Modifying Group and User Permissions

1. Right-click the shared directory in Windows NT Explorer.

2. Choose the **S**haring command from the Options menu.

3. Choose **P**ermissions to display the Access Through Share Permissions window shown in figure 12.15.

4. Select the entry in the **N**ame box.

5. Pull down the **T**ype of Access list and select the access privilege you want to assign.

6. Choose OK.

Removing a User or Group from Share Permissions

To cancel permissions for a user or group, you can change the permissions to No Access, or you can remove the group. Use the steps in the following exercise:

Removing a Group or User from Share Permissions

1. Right-click the shared directory in Windows NT Explorer.

2. Choose the **S**haring command from the Options menu.

3. Choose **P**ermissions to display the Access Through Share Permissions window.

4. Select the entry in the **N**ame box.

5. Choose **R**emove.

6. Choose OK.

Adding User or Group Permissions to a Share

You can add a user to the **N**ame list. Of course, it only makes sense to do this if you have changed the privileges of Everyone from Full Access.

To add privileges for a group or user, follow the steps in the following exercise:

Adding Group or User Permissions to a Share

1. Right-click the shared directory in Windows NT Explorer.

2. Choose the **S**haring command from the Options menu.

3. Choose **P**ermissions to display the Access Through Share Permissions window.

4. Choose **A**dd in the Access Through Share Permissions window. This displays the Add Users and Groups window shown in figure 12.16.

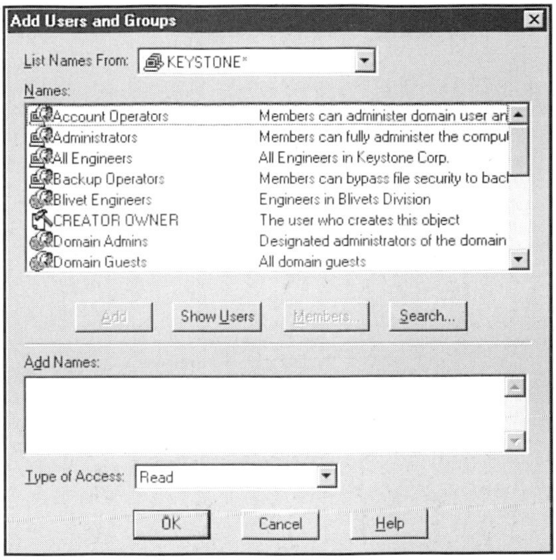

Figure 12.16

Adding a group to a share permissions list.

5. Pull down the **L**ist Names From list if you need to select a domain. You can specify share privileges for the following:

   ◆ Local users in this server's domain

   ◆ Global users in domains this server's domain trusts

   ◆ Local groups on this server

   ◆ Global groups in domains this server's domain trusts

   ◆ Special identities in this server's domain or in trusted domains

6. Choose Show **U**sers to display user accounts in the selected domain. (Remember that it is not a good idea to assign permissions to individual users.)

7. Select a name to which permissions are to be assigned and choose **A**dd. The name is added to the A**d**d Names list.

8. Pull down the **T**ype of Access list and select the access to be granted to the names you have selected.

9. Choose OK. The names are added to the **N**ame list for the share.

Stopping Directory Sharing

To stop sharing a directory, follow the steps outlined in the following exercise:

Stopping Directory Sharing

1. Right-click the shared directory in Windows NT Explorer.

2. Choose the **S**haring command from the Options menu.

3. Select N**o**t Shared in the Properties sharing tab.

> **Caution**   Obviously, you need to be careful. Explorer does not ask you to confirm your action when stopping a share, and stopping a share can seriously disrupt a network.
>
> Do not delete a shared directory before you stop sharing it. If you fail to stop sharing the directory, Windows NT will attempt to reestablish the share the next time the computer is started. This will result in an error that will be recorded in the Event Log, reporting that a directory to be shared does not exist.

Using Administrative Shares

Windows NT Server creates several administrative shares to assist Administrators who need to access server drives through the network:

◆ **ADMIN$.** An ADMIN$ share on each server is associated with the directory that stores the Windows NT Server operating system files—usually C:\WINNT.

◆ ***driveletter$.*** An administrative share is created for each partition drive on the server. C$, for example, is an administrative share that is associated with the root of drive C.

◆ **IPC$.** This resource is used by the named pipes mechanism that enables communication between programs. IPC$ supports remote administration of a computer.

◆ **PRINT$.** This share supports sharing printers.

◆ **REPL$.** When a replication server is configured, this share is created. It is required to perform export replication.

Administrative share names end with a $. Any share whose name ends with a $ will not be advertised in network browse lists.

Note Windows NT Server also maintains a share named NETLOGON, which is used by the Net Logon service to process logon requests. Although NETLOGON is not, strictly speaking, an administrative share, it should not be removed or modified.

To connect to an administrative share in Windows NT Explorer, follow the steps described in the following exercise:

Connecting to Administrative Shares

1. Choose the **M**ap Network Drive command in the **T**ools menu to open the Map Network Drive dialog box shown in figure 12.17.

2. In the **D**rive field select a free drive letter to be mapped.

3. In the **P**ath field enter the UNC identifier for the desired share. Because you cannot browse for administrative shares, you must be aware of the share name. In figure 12.17, the user has specified the C$ share on computer KEYSTONE1.

4. Choose OK.

Figure 12.17

Connecting to an administrative share.

Administrators can use administrative shares to manage remote servers. After connecting to an administrative share, you can even add and manage shares on the drive.

You might need to create shares that are not publicly known. Any share whose name ends with a $ will not appear in the Connect Network Drive window. To use the shares, users must be aware that the share exists and enter the share path manually.

Note Do not worry that users will discover administrative shares and get into the roots of your server drives. To access the root of a server's drive from a remote location, you must be logged on as a member of the Administrators, Server Operators, or Backup Operators group.

Connecting Network Drives

Users can connect a network drive to any share for which they have access permissions. A connection to a shared directory appears to a user to be a local hard drive.

Figure 12.18 shows how a shared directory appears on a user's local computer, viewed in a window under My Computer. The share shown is for the Applications folder on Keystone1, which is not the root directory of the server. When the user connects to the share as drive G, however, Applications is treated as the root directory of G. No matter how deeply nested the shared directory is in the server directory structure, the same effect applies. As a result, users are shown a simplified view of what might be a very complex directory structure.

Figure 12.18

How connections to shared directories work.

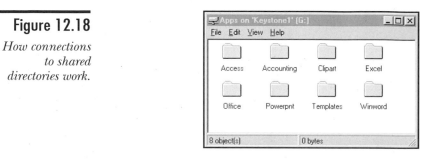

Connecting a Network Drive

The technique for connecting to a share differs depending on the client operating system. DOS and Window are considered in Chapter 14, "Using Windows and DOS Clients." Windows for Workgroups is used here as an example.

To connect a network drive, a user performs the following actions as detailed in the following exercise:

Connecting to a Network Drive with Windows for Workgroups

1. Choose the Connect **N**etwork Drive from the **D**isk menu to display the Connect Network Drive window shown in figure 12.19.

2. If desired, pull down the **D**rive list and select an available drive letter.

3. To select the **P**ath entry, use one of these techniques:

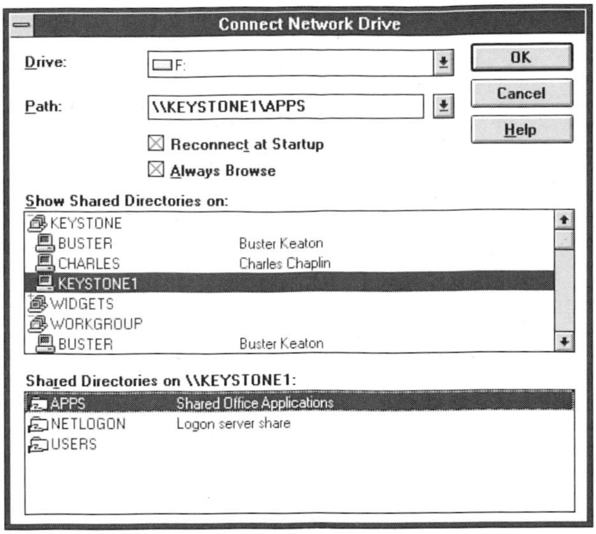

Figure 12.19

Connecting a network drive with Windows for Workgroups.

◆ Browse the network tree in the Sha**r**ed Directories box to locate available shares. When you identify the share you want, double-click on it to copy it to the **P**ath field.

◆ Type the computer and share name in the field. For example, type **\\keystone1\apps**.

4. If you want this connection to be established each time you log on to the network, check the Reconnec**t** at Startup check box. If this box is cleared, the connection will be for this logon session only.

5. Choose OK.

The drive letter specified in step 2 is added as an icon to the drive bar. This drive can be used as a local resource, subject to any permissions that might apply.

Disconnecting a Network Drive

To disconnect a network drive, follow the steps outlined in the following exercise:

Disconnecting a Network Drive under Windows for Workstations

1. Choose **D**isconnect Network Drive in the **D**isk menu.

2. Choose a network drive from the Disconnect Network Drive window and choose OK.

NTFS Security Features

Under NT, any partition formatted as NTFS has several additional features—local folder and file level permissions, ownership, and auditing. The rest of this chapter will discuss ownership and file and folder permission. For Audition information, see Chapter 19, "Managing the Server."

All directories and files in Windows NT have an owner who has a special status. Although a user usually must be an Administrator to manage permissions, a user can grant permissions for directories and files the user owns.

When you read about directory and file permissions in the next section, you will learn that a user can restrict directories and files he or she owns to prevent even Administrators from accessing them. This enables users to configure their personal directories for complete privacy.

Users cannot give away ownership of directories and files that they own. They can give another user permission to take ownership, however. This approach prevents users from creating files and then making them appear to belong to another user.

Administrators can take ownership of any file or directory on the network. This is necessary because Administrators must be able to access files of users who leave the company or change departments. Because Administrators cannot return ownership to the original owner, however, they cannot casually access private files without leaving some evidence behind.

Directory and File Permissions

Directory and file permissions enable Administrators and owners to fine-tune security on directories and files down to the individual file level. Directory and file permissions are available only on partitions that use the NTFS file system.

How File and Directory Permissions Work

Six individual permissions can be assigned to directories and files. Each permission has an abbreviation, which is included in parentheses in the following list. Permissions can be assigned to directories and files. The list describes the effect of each permission on a user's capabilities with directories and files.

◆ Read (R)

    Directory: Permits viewing the names of files and subdirectories

    File: Permits reading the file's data

◆ Write (W)

>   Directory: Permits adding files and subdirectories

>   File: Permits changing the file's data

◆ Execute (X)

>   Directory: Permits changing to subdirectories in the directory

>   File: Permits running of the file if it is a program file

◆ Delete (D)

>   Directory: Permits deleting the directory

>   File: Permits deleting the file

◆ Change Permissions (P)

>   Directory: Permits changing the directory's permissions

>   File: Permits changing the file's permissions

◆ Take Ownership (O)

>   Directory: Permits taking ownership of the directory

>   File: Permits taking ownership of the file

Assigning Standard Permissions

To simplify the task of assigning permissions, Microsoft has defined a series of standard permissions that can be used to assign useful sets of permissions in a single operation. Table 12.1 summarizes the standard permissions for directories.

TABLE 12.1
Standard Permissions for NTFS Directories

Standard Permission Name	Individual Permissions for Directory	Individual Permissions for Files	Explanation
No Access	None	None	No access to directory or to files
List	RX	Not Specified	List directory contents Change to subdirectories No access to files unless otherwise given

continues

TABLE 12.1, CONTINUED
Standard Permissions for NTFS Directories

Standard Permission Name	Individual Permissions for Directory	Individual Permissions for Files	Explanation
Read	RX	RX	List directory contents Change to subdirectories Read data from files Execute programs
Add	WX	Not Specified	Create subdirectories Create files No access to existing files unless otherwise given
Add & Read	RWX	RX	List directory contents Create subdirectories Change to subdirectories Read file data Execute programs
Change	RWXD	RWXD	List directory contents Create subdirectories Change to subdirectories Delete subdirectories Read file data Create and modify files Execute programs Delete files
Full Control	All	All	All directory permissions All file permissions Change directory and file permissions Take ownership

Each of the standard permissions defines two sets of privileges:

◆ Permissions that will be assigned to the directory, which are shown in the second column of table 12.1.

◆ Permissions that will be assigned to files that are created in the directory. These are the permissions shown in the third column of table 12.1. When you assign permissions, you have the option of assigning these file permissions to the existing files as well.

When the third column states that permissions are "Not Specified," it means that users are not granted any file-access permissions by the standard permissions. If you want users to have access to files in the directory, you can specify file permissions separately. Under that scenario, however, users will not have access to files that are subsequently created in the directory, because permissions for those files will be Not Specified.

Windows NT Server also offers standard permissions for files:

◆ No Access

◆ Read (RX)

◆ Change (RWXD)

◆ Full Control (All)

How Working Permissions Are Determined

The operations a user can apply to a directory or file are the sum of the permissions the user acquires through the following sources:

◆ Membership in a special identity (special group)

◆ All group memberships

◆ Permissions directly assigned to the user

Here is an example. The Widgets division maintains a directory of engineering specification documents named \SPECS. Several groups have privileges in \SPECS:

◆ **Engineers.** Members have read privileges (R)(R)

◆ **Sr_Eng.** Members can add and update documents (W)(W)

◆ **Eng_Mgt.** Members can delete documents (D)(Not Specified)

Mabel is a member of all three groups. In addition, her user account has been given the privilege (X)(D) so that she can administer the directory. Consequently, her privileges in the \SPECS directory are the sum of all the following:

```
(R    )(R     ) from the group Engineers
( W   )( W   ) from the group Sr_Eng
(    D)(      ) from the group Eng_Mgt
(   X )(    D) from assignment to Mabel's user account
```

Mabel's working privileges to files in the directory are (RWXD)(RWD).

Any permissions a user has for a file augment permissions the user has from directories.

There is one big exception to all of this: the No Access standard permission. If a user is assigned No Access permissions in any group, all permissions for the directory are revoked, even if the user is an Administrator. Try it. Log on as an Administrator and assign the No Access permission to Everyone for the USERS directory. Even as an Administrator, you will be unable to access the directory.

If the No Access permission has been used to lock users out of a directory, only the owner can remove the No Access permission. An Administrator can take ownership of the directory and remove the No Access permission if necessary.

Assigning Standard Directory Permissions

To assign standard permissions for a directory, use the following steps covered in the following exercise:

Assigning Standard Directory Permissions

1. Right-click the directory and choose **P**roperties from the Options menu.

2. Select the Security tab in the Properties box. The Security tab is shown in figure 12.20.

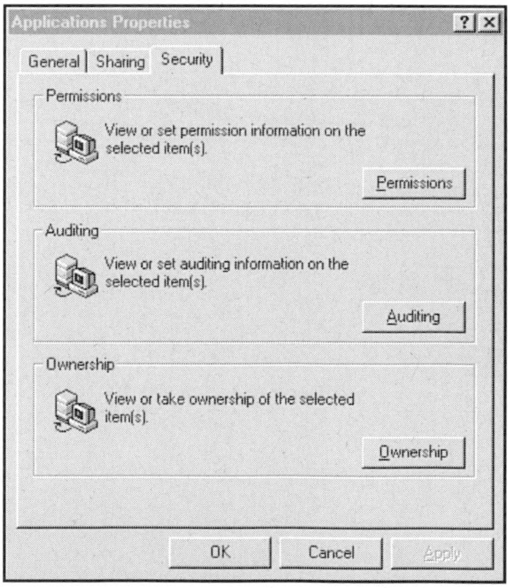

Figure 12.20

The Security tab in the Properties box.

3. Choose **P**ermissions in the Security tab to open the Directory Permissions box shown in figure 12.21.

The example in figure 12.22 shows a newly created directory named Applications. New directories inherit the permissions of the directory in which they were created. APPS was created in the root directory, which is configured with default permissions.

4. To change permissions for a group or user that is already in the **N**ame box, follow these steps:

◆ Select the group or user.

◆ Pull down the **T**ype of Access list and select one of the standard permissions. This list is shown in figure 12.22.

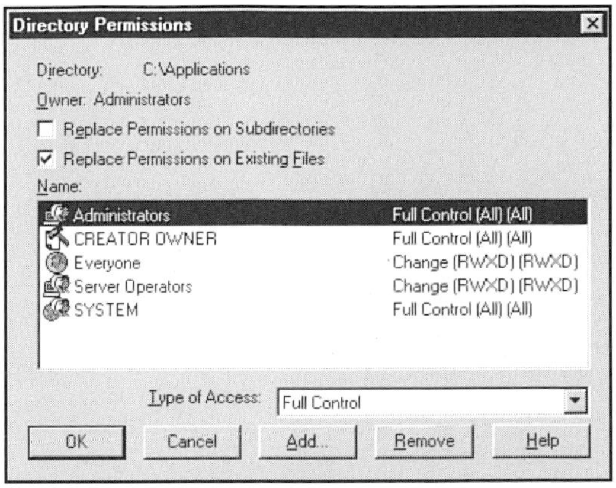

Figure 12.21

Managing directory permissions.

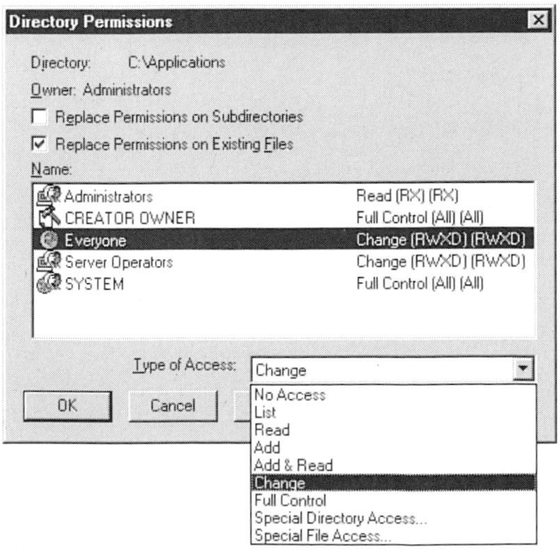

Figure 12.22

Selecting a type of access.

5. To add a group or user, follow these steps:

◆ Choose **A**dd to display the Add Users and Groups window shown in figure 12.23.

◆ To display names from another domain, pull down the **L**ist Names From list and choose a domain.

◆ To show users in the **N**ames list, choose the Show **U**sers button.

◆ Double-click on the groups or users to be added from the **N**ames list. Each group or user you select is added to the A**d**d Names list.

◆ Select standard permissions from the **T**ype of Access list. All names in the A**d**d Names list will receive the same standard privileges.

◆ Choose OK to add the names and return to the Directory Permissions window.

6. If you want existing files in the current subdirectory to be assigned the file permissions you have specified, check the Replace Permissions on Existing **F**iles box in the Directory Permissions window. (If you do not choose this option, files retain the permission assignments they already have.)

7. If you want to assign the rights you have selected to all subdirectories of this directory, check the Replace Permissions on Subdirectories box. (If you do not choose this option, subdirectories retain the permission assignments they already have.)

8. Choose OK to save the directory permissions.

Assigning Special Access Permissions

When the Directory Permissions window is displayed, you can assign special directory and file access permissions to any name in the **N**ame list.

To assign directory access permissions, use the steps outlined in the following exercise:

Assigning Special Access Permissions to Directories

1. Pull down the **T**ype of Access list and choose Special Directory Access to display the Special Directory Access window shown in figure 12.24. The currently assigned privileges are checked.

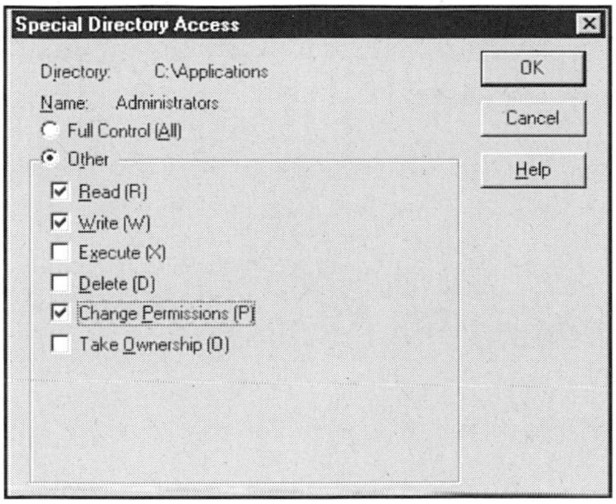

Figure 12.24

Assigning special directory access permissions.

2. Check the boxes of the privileges you want to assign.

3. Choose OK to assign the checked privileges.

To assign file access permissions, follow the steps outlined in the following exercise:

Assigning Special Access Permissions to Files

1. Pull down the **T**ype of Access list and choose Special File Access to display the Special File Access window shown in figure 12.25. The currently assigned privileges are checked.

2. Check the boxes of the privileges you want to assign.

3. Choose OK to assign the checked privileges.

Figure 12.25

*Assigning special
file-access
permissions.*

Figure 12.25

*Assigning special
file-access
permissions.*

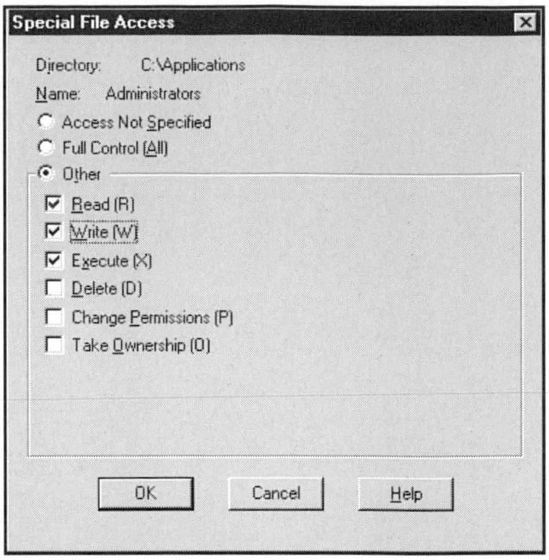

Managing File Permissions

File permissions are managed in much the same way as directories. Follow the steps detailed in the following exercise:

Managing File Permissions

1. Select the file or files you want to manage. Unlike directories, you can assign privileges to multiple files at one time.

2. Right-click one of the selected files and choose **P**roperties from the **O**ptions menu.

3. Select the Security tab in the Properties box.

4. Choose **P**ermissions in the Security tab to open the File Permissions dialog box shown in figure 12.26.

Figure 12.26

*Assigning special
file-access
permissions.*

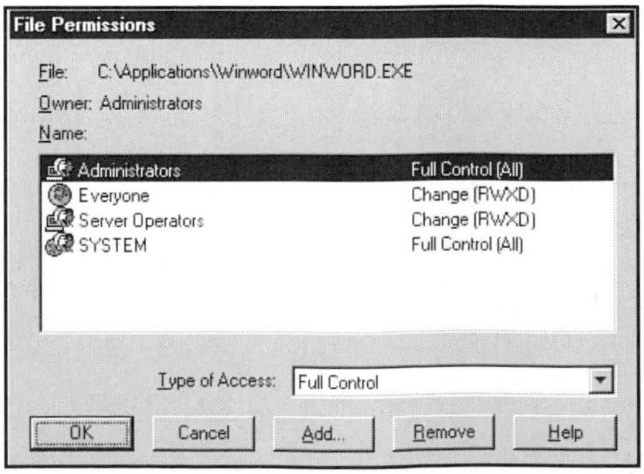

5. Manage names and permission assignments as described for directories. The Special File Access choice in the **T**ype of Access list enables you to specify custom file privileges. If you have selected two or more files, permissions that are not held in common by all selected files are shown with gray Xs.

Changing Ownership of Directories and Files

Directory and file owners cannot give away ownership, but can grant permission to other users to take ownership. In emergencies, Administrators can take ownership of directories and files owned by users.

If you see that a user or group has All privileges for a file or a directory, remember that All includes the Take Ownership privilege.

Giving Users the Right to Take Ownership

Use the procedures described for assigning special directory or file access permissions. Assign the Take Ownership right to the group or user you want to have that privilege.

Taking Ownership

To take ownership, follow the steps covered in the following exercise:

Taking Ownership

1. Right-click the directory or file you want to own.

2. Choose **P**roperties from the **O**ptions menu.

3. Select the Security tab in the Properties box.

4. Choose **O**wnership in the Security tab. The dialog box you see depends on whether you have permissions to view the directory.

5. If you selected a directory for which you have the Take Ownership permission, the dialog box will resemble figure 12.27. Choose **T**ake Ownership to take ownership of the directory and its contents.

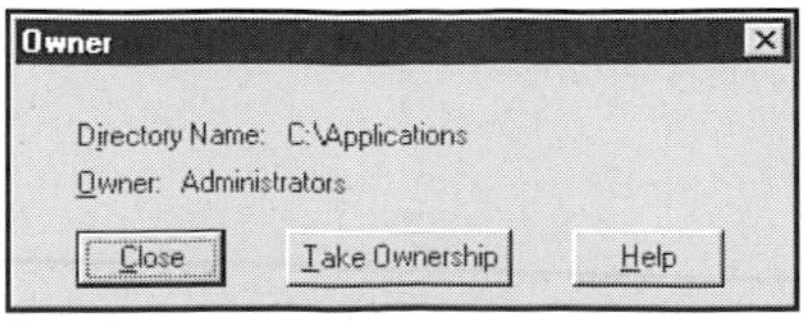

Figure 12.27

Ownership information for a directory.

6. When taking ownership of a directory, you will see the warning shown in figure 12.28. Choose **Y**es to complete the ownership change.

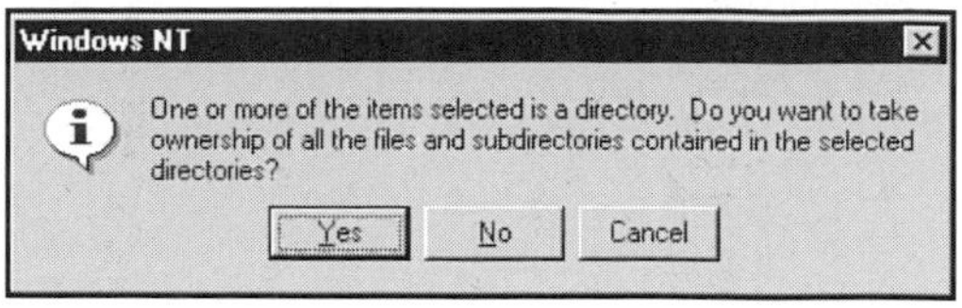

Figure 12.28

Warning when taking ownership of a directory.

7. If you do not have the permissions required to view the owner, you will see the message in figure 12.29. If you have the Take Ownership permission for the directory, choose **Y**es to overwrite the existing permissions and take ownership.

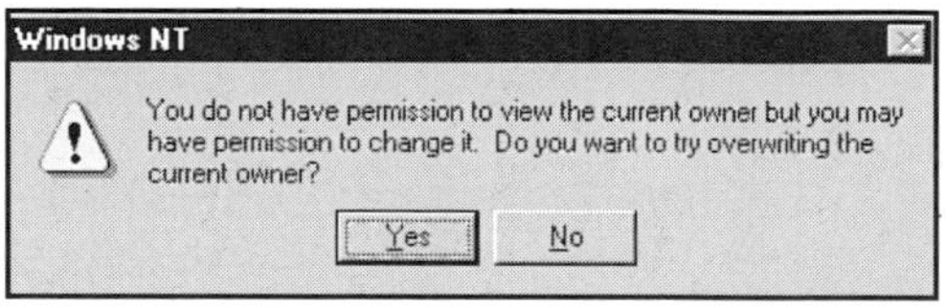

Figure 12.29

Overriding current permissions to take ownership.

Using the No Access Permission

Remember, if you assign No Access permissions to a directory or file for any group a user belongs to, the user loses all privileges for the directory. No Access overrides permissions from other groups and permissions made directly to the user's own user account. Even Administrators lose access to directories if a No Access permission has been assigned. Obviously, No Access should be used with caution. It often is preferable to revoke permissions instead of using No Access because revoking permissions from one group does not affect permissions for another group.

Use No Access when you want to be absolutely certain that users do not have access, but be aware of potential side effects.

Default Directory Permissions

When Windows NT Server is installed, default permissions are assigned to all directories on the server. You seldom will need to change these permissions. Because newly created directories inherit privileges from the directory in which they were created, it is useful for you to be aware of the default permissions created during system setup. Here is a summary:

◆ \(Root directory of an NTFS volume)

Administrators	Full Control
Server Operators	Change
Everyone	Change
CREATOR OWNER	Full Control
SYSTEM	Full Control

◆ \SYSTEM32

Administrators	Full Control
Server Operators	Change
Everyone	Change
CREATOR OWNER	Full Control
SYSTEM	Full Control

◆ \SYSTEM32\CONFIG

Administrators	Full Control
Everyone	List
CREATOR OWNER	Full Control
SYSTEM	Full Control

◆ \SYSTEM32\DRIVERS

Administrators	Full Control
Server Operators	Full Control
Everyone	Read
CREATOR OWNER	Full Control
SYSTEM	Full Control

◆ \SYSTEM32\SPOOL

Administrators	Full Control
Server Operators	Full Control
Print Operators	Full Control
Everyone	Read
CREATOR OWNER	Full Control
SYSTEM	Full Control

◆ \SYSTEM32\REPL

Administrators	Full Control
Server Operators	Full Control
Everyone	Read
CREATOR OWNER	Full Control
SYSTEM	Full Control

◆ \SYSTEM32\REPL\IMPORT

Administrators	Full Control
Server Operators	Change
Everyone	Read
CREATOR OWNER	Full Control
Replicator	Change
NETWORK	No Access
SYSTEM	Full Control

◆ \SYSTEM32\REPL\EXPORT

Administrators	Full Control
Server Operators	Change
CREATOR OWNER	Full Control
Replicator	Read
SYSTEM	Full Control

You probably are surprised that groups such as CREATOR OWNER and Everyone have privileges dispersed throughout these directories. Remember that these privileges can be exercised by network users only if they access a directory through a share. If you do not share a directory where Everyone has permissions, they cannot exercise their permissions in the directory.

This restriction does not apply to users who can log on to the server directly, however. If you will be permitting non-Administrators to log on to the server computer, you should consider adjusting permissions, especially to Everyone.

Examples of Directory and File Permissions

Figure 12.30 shows a simplified directory tree that illustrates how shares and permissions can be set up. Because permissions can be assigned only to NTFS volumes, these examples apply only to servers that are using the NTFS file system.

This directory tree has several directories that will be shared on the network:

◆ **\Applications.** The location for all shared application files. All these applications are capable of being shared on a network. Users will need to be permitted to read files from these directories, but personalized files will be kept in their home directories or on their C drives. Therefore, only Read and Execute permissions are required and the standard List permission can be assigned.

◆ **\Applications\Accounting.** Contains the company's accounting application. Of course, only members of the accounting department should have access, so an Accounting group will be created and given appropriate permissions. Permissions are revoked for all other users.

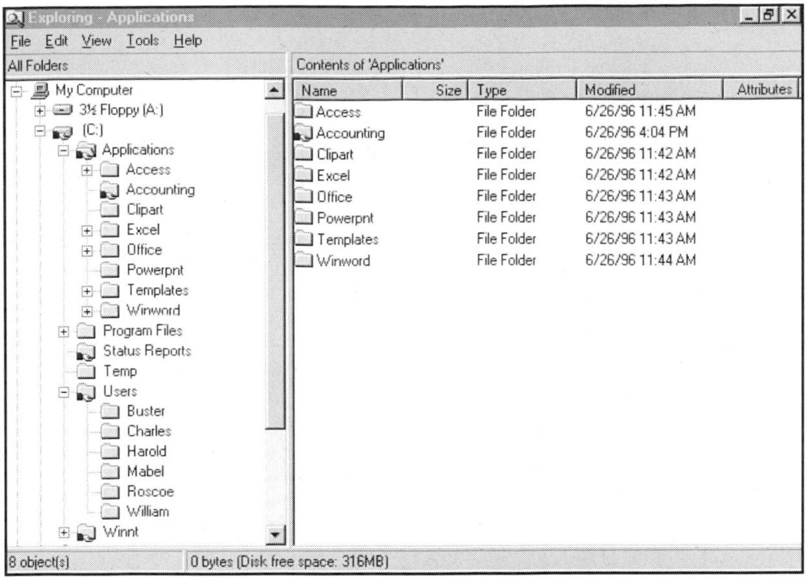

Figure 12.30

Example of a directory tree.

◆ **\Users.** Contains a personal directory for each user. Personal directories are secured so that only the directory owner has access to the files.

◆ **\Status Reports.** A directory in which all employees maintain their weekly status reports. Each user must have the capability to modify his or her own files. Only engineering managers should be permitted to read the reports.

The first step in securing the directory tree is to create the following groups:

◆ **Accounting.** Membership is restricted to the accounting staff.

◆ **Eng Managers.** Includes all managers who should have access to status reports.

Users of the \Applications directory require only List permissions. They will read and execute files, but they will not create or modify files. Figure 12.31 shows the permissions assigned for \Applications. Notice that the check boxes are selected so that files and subdirectories inherit the appropriate permissions.

The \Applications\Accounting directory must have different permissions. In figure 12.32, notice that the Accounting group has been added with Change permissions given to the \Accounting subdirectory, but that no other users, including Administrators, have access.

Figure 12.31

Setting permissions for the \Applications directory.

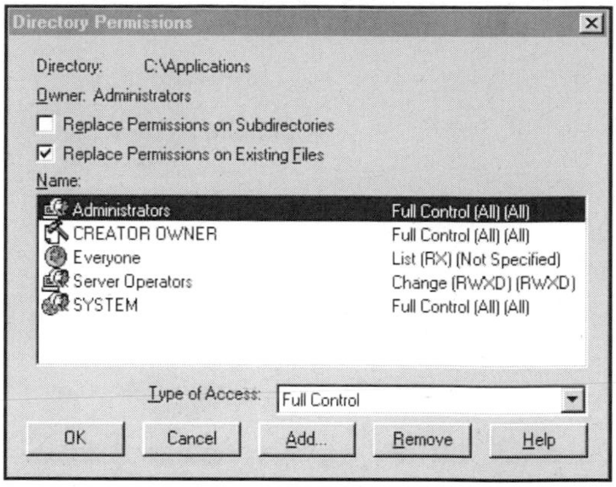

Figure 12.32

Setting permissions for the\Applications\ Accounting directory.

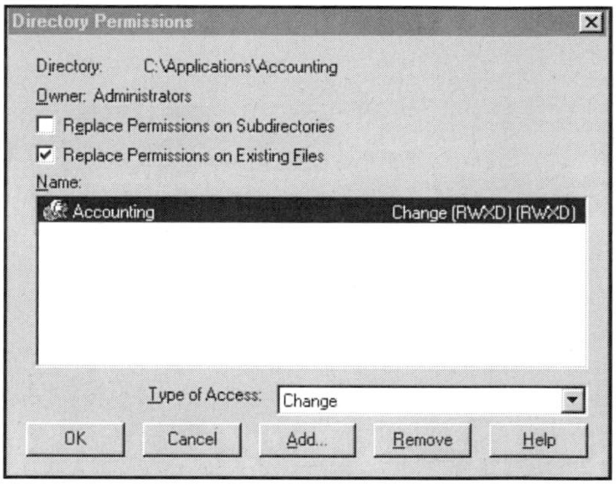

To configure the \Status Reports directory, use the special identity CREATOR OWNER. By assigning Change permissions to CREATOR OWNER, users are given the capability of modifying the status reports they create. The group Everyone is given Add privileges in the directory to enable users to create the files in the first place. The group Eng Managers is given Change permissions. Permissions for \Status Reports are shown in figure 12.33.

No action should be needed to secure the home directories. The user directories were created using the technique described in Chapter 11, "Managing Users and Groups," in the section "Creating Home Directories for Two or More Users." When home directories are specified in the User Profile window of User Manager for Domains, the directories are created, the user is established as the owner, and default permissions are assigned. The default permissions for a home directory permit Full Control for the directory's owner. No other users, including Administrators, have access. (The structures of home directories are discussed in greater detail later in this chapter. See the following section, "More about Home Directories.")

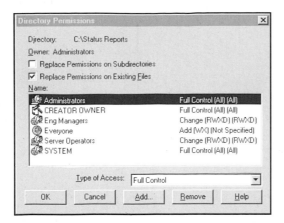

Figure 12.33

Setting permissions for the \Status Reports directory.

Now that the required permissions have been assigned, the only remaining step is to assign shares so that networked users can access the directories. One approach is to create the following shares:

◆ USERS for the \USERS directory

◆ APPS for the \APPS directory

◆ STATUS for the \Status Reports directory

Note   Even though Status Reports has a long directory name, it will have no effect on DOS and Windows users because they will not see the directory name when they connect to the share. Remember, however, that shares must have 8.3 format names to be used by DOS and Windows users. You might, therefore, use StatRep as the share name.

More about Home Directories

In the majority of cases, you will want to provide each user with a personal directory on the network. To manage personal directories effectively, you need to understand the proper manner for establishing the directory structure and the default characteristics Windows NT Server assigns to user directories.

Prior to NT Server version 4, a directory entitled Users was automatically created during the setup process. The Users directory was ideal for establishing home directories. Under version 4, you will need to create a home directory structure from scratch. Assuming that personal directories are stored within Users, figure 12.34 illustrates the structures of the personal directories.

Figure 12.34

Structure of an example Users directory.

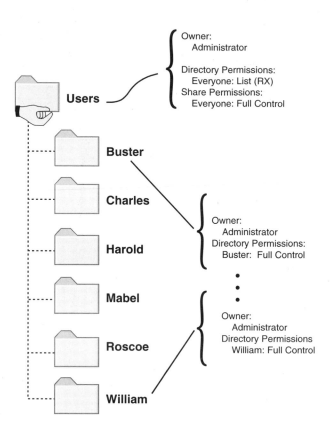

Owner:
  Administrator

Directory Permissions:
  Everyone: List (RX)
Share Permissions:
  Everyone: Full Control

Users

Buster

Charles

Owner:
  Administrator
Directory Permissions:
  Buster: Full Control

Harold

Mabel

Owner:
  Administrator
Directory Permissions
  William: Full Control

Roscoe

William

Figure 12.35 shows the default permissions that are assigned to the Users directory. By default, the group Everyone has List (RX) permissions to the Users directory.

Consequently, any user who accesses the Users directory can list the directories it contains.

Figure 12.35

Default permissions for the Users directory.

Directory Permissions

Directory: C:\Users
Owner: Administrators
☐ Replace Permissions on Subdirectories
☑ Replace Permissions on Existing Files
Name:

Administrators	Full Control (All) (All)
CREATOR OWNER	Full Control (All) (All)
Everyone	Change (RWXD) (RWXD)
Server Operators	Change (RWXD) (RWXD)
SYSTEM	Full Control (All) (All)

Type of Access: Full Control

OK   Cancel   Add...   Remove   Help

Of course, to enable users to access the Users directory through the network, the directory must be shared. Simply create a share that gives Change share permissions to the group Everyone or Users.

Within the Users directory, each user is assigned a personal directory. In Chapter 11, you saw how User Manager for Domains can be used to create home directories. For review, examine the User Environment Profile tab shown in figure 12.36. The home directory for Charles is established by connecting drive letter Z: to \\keystone1\ users\Charles where

◆ **keystone1** is the server on which the directory resides.

◆ **users** is a share name offered by the server.

◆ **Charles** is the user's personal directory within the directory being shared.

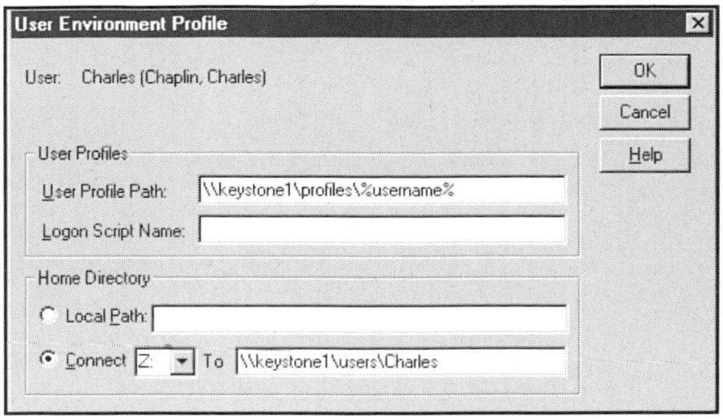

Figure 12.36

Setting up a user's home directory.

When a home directory is created using the User Environment Profiles tab, the user associated with the directory is given Full Control permissions for the directory. No other users have access to the directory.

There is a sneaky exception to the last statement. Because an administrator created the home directory, an administrator is the owner of the directory. As you have learned, the owner of a directory can do just about anything to the directory, including placing his or her name in the directory permissions. The administrator who created a user's home directory, therefore, can gain access to the directory fairly easily.

Note Users who don't want administrators to access their home directories need to take ownership of the directories. In a large organization, there is a surprising amount of material that is handled on a "need-to-know" basis. Personal records are an excellent example. If you are a supervisor, you don't want administrators snooping around your personal directory to read employee performance reviews. If you restrict ownership of your home directory, any administrator who takes ownership will leave a record in the security logs. Also, since the administrator cannot give ownership back, you can establish who has been snooping in your files.

Access Control Lists

A user can be given permissions to a file, directory, or other secured object in several ways, including permissions assigned to their user accounts and to groups to which they belong. At times, due to the various possible sources, it can be rather difficult to determine what the user's effective permissions are. To understand how Windows NT grants access to secured objects, you need to understand how access tokens and access control lists work.

When a user is authenticated during the logon process, an *access token* is generated for the user. Subsequent to the logon process, the access token is used to control access to all secured objects. An access token includes the following information:

◆ The user's SID

◆ IDs of groups to which the user belongs

◆ Rights assigned to the user

The access token is generated during the logon process and is not updated. Changes that are made to a user's permissions, therefore, will not take effect until the next time the user logs on to the system.

Access tokens are used to validate users' access to objects in the Windows NT system. The following are examples of objects in Windows NT:

Directories	Printers
Devices	Processes
Files	Symbolic links
Network shares	Threads
Ports	Windows

Each object has the following characteristics:

◆ **Type.** For example, file or printer.

◆ **Attributes.** The data stored in the object. For example, the contents of a file.

◆ **Functions.** The operations that can be performed on the object. For example, open a file. All operations that can be performed are part of the object.

If security is explicitly defined for an object, the object will have an Access Control List (ACL) consisting of Access Control Entries (ACEs) that identify a user or group that is assigned permissions for the object and the permissions that are assigned. The absence of an ACL indicates that all users are permitted access to the object.

The ACEs in an ACL are organized starting with ACEs that deny access, followed by ACEs that permit access. This sequence holds unless a custom application generates ACLs that are organized differently.

ACLs for objects are managed by various utilities. From an adminstrator's viewpoint, the most important tools are Explorer for files and directories and Printer objects for printing objects.

Evaluating Permissions

Following a successful logon, the security subsystem evaluates all attempts to access objects. The user's access token, created during the logon process, is compared to the ACL of the object to be accessed. The evaluation sequence is as follows:

1. Starting with the beginning of the ACL, the security subsystem looks for ACEs that deny access to the object for the user or for any group to which the user belongs. Because ACEs that deny access are organized at the beginning of the ACL, all denials will be encountered first.

2. The request is denied if any ACE is encountered that denies access.

3. If access is not denied, the security subsystem looks for ACEs that explicitly grant the requested access to the user's account or to groups to which the user belongs. ACEs are evaluated until sufficient permissions are accumulated to grant the user's access request.

4. The access request is denied if the security subsystem is unable to identify sufficient permissions to satisfy the request.

5. The access request is approved if sufficient permissions are found to satisfy the request.

> **Note** To emphasize the point, in standard ACLs, ACEs that deny access always come first and take precedence over ACEs that grant access. The ultimate denial is the No Access permission, which overrides all other permissions.

The process of granting access to an object is shown in figure 12.37. The events shown in the figure are as follows:

1. The user requests access to an object.

2. The user is validated to the object's ACL.

3. If the user has the required access permissions, a *handle* is generated. A handle is an identifier used internally by Windows NT to identify a particular access to a

resource. With the handle, the system generates a *list of granted access rights* describing the user's permissions for the object. This list is stored in the user's process table.

4. After the object is opened, subsequent actions are checked against the list of granted access rights in the user's process table.

Figure 12.37

Granting a user access to an object.

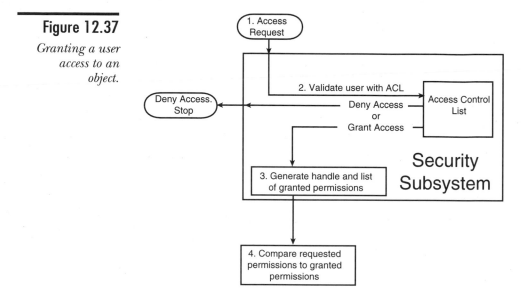

The ACL is consulted for permissions only when the user first accesses the object. As a result, permissions remain in effect as long as the handle that is created remains open. Changes to the ACL take effect only when the user closes the current handle and opens a new one. If, for example, the administrator changes the attribute of a file to Read Only while a user has it open, the user can continue to write to the file until the current handle is closed.

Guarding Against Viruses and Trojan Horses

Windows NT is much more resistant to viruses and trojan horses than MS-DOS and Windows 95. Nevertheless, it pays to be careful. A virus outbreak on a LAN can take considerable effort to cure, and the cost in downtime can be horrendous.

A *virus* is a program that attempts to replicate itself to new computers, and networks are fertile breeding grounds for viruses. Some viruses are simply annoying, but some can be quite destructive, resulting in lost data or, in some cases, damage to hardware.

A *trojan horse* is a program that pretends to be another program. A common trojan horse masquerades as a logon screen in order to capture a user's name and password. Windows NT is highly resistant to logon trojan horses. Logons are always initiated by a Ctrl+Alt+Delete key sequence that vectors to the logon routine in Windows NT, making it impossible for another program to be the target of a logon request.

Of course, "impossible" is often another word for "it hasn't been done yet." So do not be too relaxed about viruses and trojan horses. Some wise precautions are:

◆ Own two or more virus detection programs and use them regularly.

◆ Educate your users and make virus detection software available to them so that they can scan disks and programs that they obtain off-site or download from a service.

◆ Be careful when setting file permissions to protect executable files from being modified while users are running programs. Any component of a program can become a host for a virus.

◆ Be fanatical about backups and be sure you have a sufficiently long retention time of old backup tapes. Some viruses attack after a time delay. A backup tape may be the easiest way to recover a version of a file as it was before it was corrupted.

◆ Test new programs on an isolated computer before installing them on the network. After installing, scan the computer for viruses.

Troubleshooting Network Access and Permission Issues

Objective
F.7

In the event that one or more of your users has difficulty accessing a resource on the NT Server, use the following troubleshooting list to aide you in alleviating the problem:

◆ Verify that the physical network connection is good. Keep in mind that if other workstations can access resources on the server, the cable and network adapter on the server is good. This can be a clue to check cable connections and adapter at the workstation. You should also check the hub and network adapter for proper link status and proper termination. Manufactures of hubs and adapter card usually include a diagnostic routine you may want to utilize.

◆ Check the affected computer for hardware resource conflicts. Often a user will add an additional hardware option to the computer without realizing that there is a conflict. Also verify that the network card is using the proper device drivers, as often end users inadvertently corrupt or change them.

◆ Verify that the affected computer is using the correct protocols, domain name, and frame type settings. End-users often get themselves in trouble here as well by tinkering around where they should not be.

◆ For the ultimate test, log on to the affected workstation as an Administrator and see if you can connect. If you can then you are probably looking at resource permissions, bad or locked user account or logon profile restriction issues.

Testing Your Knowledge

1. By default, which three shares are established when a PDC is created with NT Server 4?

    A. C:\WINNT

    B. C:\

    C. C:\WINNT\SYSTEM32\REPL\EXPORT\SCRIPTS

    D. C:\WINNT\SYSTEM32\REPL\IMPORT\SCRIPTS

2. When creating a share that will be used by MS-DOS or Windows 3.x clients, the share name must conform to the _____ naming rule?

3. Windows NT Server provides the ability to limit the number of users who can simultaneously connect to a share.

    A. True

    B. False

4. Which of the Microsoft operating systems support connecting to shares by using the command line?

    A. Windows NT Server and Workstation

    B. Windows for Workgroups

    C. MS-DOS

    D. Windows 95

5. When connecting to a network drive with the Explorer, which you want to reestablish whenever you log on to the network, check the _____ option.

6. What does the abbreviation UNC stand for?

7. Which UNC wording is correct if you want to connect to a share entitled APPS on an NT Server called Keystone1 with a drive assignment of J?

    A. net connect j: "\\keystone1\APPS"

    B. net use j: \\keystone1\apps

    C. net connect j: \\keystone1\apps

    D. net use j: \\"keystone1"\"apps"

8. Unique to Windows 95 and NT 4 is a folder used to maintain copies of files that must be synchronized between computers. What is the folder called?

9. NTFS file system supports file names, which can consist of up to _____ maximum characters.

    A. 254

    B. 255

    C. 256

    D. 128

10. Which characters listed are illegal in NTFS file names?

    A. ? * / \ < > | :

    B. ? * ~ \ < > | ; :

    C. ? * ~ \ < > | :

    D. ? * @ \ < > | ; :

11. Under NT 4, deleted files are moved to the _____, which has an icon on the desktop?

    A. Recycle bin

    B. Trash can

    C. Recycler

    D. task bar

12. Which key must be held down while dragging a file to a new location that you want to have copied?

    A. Spacebar

    B. Alt

    C. Shift

    D. Ctrl

13. The menu option that brings the contents of the Explorer up to date reflecting any changes made on the network is called _____ .

14. The search tool brought up with the Find option in the Explorer permits you to search for files based on a files size in KB under the Advanced tab.

    A. True

    B. False

15. In order to share a directory under Windows NT Server, the directory must be located on a partition that has been formatted with NTFS.

    A. True

    B. False

16. What groups are given the right to share directories by default?

    A. Administrators

    B. Server Operators

    C. Power Users

    D. Backup Operators

17. If a directory is already established as a share, it cannot be setup as a new share.

    A. True

    B. False

18. MS-DOS and Windows 3.x users cannot see share names that exceed the restrictions of the 8.3 file name format.

    A. True

    B. False

19. Share permissions establish the maximum set of permissions that are available within a shared directory tree. Other permission assignments can further restrict access, but cannot add to the permissions established by the share permissions.

    A. True

    B. False

20. Which of the following is not a permission type that can be assigned to a shared directory?

    A. No Access

    B. Read

    C. Change

    D. Write

    E. Full Control

21. If you are using FAT volumes, share permissions are all you have to work with.

    A. True

    B. False

22. Which of the following is not a legitimate administrative share?

    A. ADMIN$

    B. *driveletter*$

    C. IPC$

    D. PRINT$

    E. NET$

    F. REPL$

23. If you are logged on as an Administrator, you can connect to and use an administrative share using the proper UNC and administrative share designator.

    A. True

    B. False

24. Users can give away ownership of directories and files that they own.

    A. True

    B. False

25. Under NTFS, six individual permissions can be assigned to directories and files. What are these six permissions and their correct abbreviation?

    A. Read (R), Write (W), Execute (X), Delete (D), Change Permission (C), Take Ownership (O)

    B. Read (R), Write (W), Execute (X), Delete (D), Change Permission (C), Take Ownership (T)

    C. Read (R), Write (W), Execute (X), Delete (D), Change Permission (P), Take Ownership (O)

    D. Read (R), Write (W), Execute (X), Erase (E), Change Permission (P), Take Ownership (T)

26. Directory and file owners cannot give away ownership, but can grant permission to other users to take ownership.

    A. True

    B. False

27. If a directory or file is assigned the No Access permission, only Administrators can access it.

   A. True

   B. False

28. An access token contains the following information:

   A. The user's SID

   B. IDs of groups to which the user belongs

   C. Rights assigned to the user

   D. The user's logon password

29. What does the abbreviation ACL stand for?

30. If a user is unable to access a share what can you do as a quick check to see if it is a share permission issue and not a hardware problem?

Review Answers

1. A, B, D

2. Eight dot three (8.3—filename.doc)

3. A

4. A, B, C, D

5. Reconnect at Logon

6. universal naming convention

7. B

8. My Briefcase

9. B

10. A

11. A

12. D

13. Refresh

14. A

15. B

16. A, B

17. B

18. B

19. A

20. D

21. A

22. E

23. A

24. B

25. C

26. A

27. B

28. A, B, C

29. Access Control List

30. Log on from the users workstation as an Administrator to see if you can establish a connection to the share.

CHAPTER 13

Managing Printing Services

E ven though printer prices have fallen dramatically in recent years, it continues to make good sense to share printers on a network. If there are any personal printers in your office, keep an eye on them. What percentage of the time are they actually busy printing? At most times, most printers are idle. An idle personal printer might be a nice status symbol, but many organizations feel that idle printers make little economic sense. There are also specialty devices, such as high-quality color printers, costing many thousands of dollars. Very seldom does it make sense to dedicate such a valuable device to a single user, and sharing it on the network is an ideal situation.

Today, a high-capacity printer, capable of printing 16 pages per minute, can be purchased for less than $2,000. Such a printer easily can fill the needs of 20 or more typical users if it is configured properly for sharing. Windows NT is quite capable of sharing such printers effectively.

This chapter will examine printing in a Windows NT Server environment.

Selecting Network Printers

Practically any printer can work in a network environment, but some printers are a better fit than others.

An important consideration for shared printers is the duty cycle. Just because a printer can print 10 pages per minute doesn't mean that it can work at that rate constantly, eight or more hours a day. The *duty cycle* of a printer is a statement of the maximum number of pages a printer should be expected to produce in a given period of time, often a month. Forcing a printer to exceed its recommended duty cycle significantly shortens its life and probably makes it less reliable.

A wide variety of printers are designed with networks in mind. One of the special characteristics of network-ready printers is that they are designed for high duty cycles. Often, the difference in cost between printers does not show up in speed or print quality, but appears in different duty cycles. Unfortunately, the duty cycle is a specification that tends to be left off most product data sheets. You might have to call the manufacturer to get this information.

Virtually all network-ready printers provide the option of directly connecting to an Ethernet network. Most also have the option to be connected to a Token Ring. Of these printers, the vast majority are capable of participating in a Windows NT network. Depending on the exact hardware and the level of network activity, direct network attachment might not make a big difference in performance because documents still must be managed by a print server, and data must be transmitted over the network. The chief advantage of network attachment is that printers can be placed anywhere on the network. They do not need to be within 100 feet of a print server, as do printers that must connect through a serial port.

Hewlett-Packard produces a wide variety of printers that can attach to networks using HP's JetDirect network interfaces. Windows NT directly supports network-attached HP printers.

Other printer brands might provide support for Windows NT, but you will be dependent on the manufacturers to provide the necessary software to make the connections.

A feature that might be more important than speed is paper capacity. When many users are printing, paper supplies are exhausted rapidly. If you are selecting a printer for a busy office, be sure that it has the paper capacity required to handle the printing volume.

If your office needs a special-purpose printer, such as a high-quality color printer or a 1,200 dpi black-and-white laser, a network is an excellent way to connect users to the printer. Such printers are far too expensive to be dedicated to the use of one individual, and because color printers are expensive to use, you do not want them used to print the office football pools. Network security enables you to restrict the users who can access the printer and to audit the activity.

Expensive printers are not the only ones you should consider sharing. If your office has a Windows NT Server network, you have everything in place to share any printer you want. By all means, share the personal laser printers in your office. Just be sure they are suited to the job you are asking them to perform.

Windows NT enables you to place printers anywhere on your network. Any Windows NT computer can function as a print server. You can dedicate the Windows NT computer for use as a print server or permit it to be used as a workstation. Of course, if a workstation is supporting a great deal of printing, its performance as a workstation could suffer.

Planning Network Printing

Network printing must cope with a few problems:

◆ Many users send jobs to a few printers. Orderly procedures must be established so that all users' printing needs are served.

◆ Access to some printers should be restricted, or should be restricted to certain times of day.

◆ Some users' jobs require special treatment. Some jobs must be printed immediately, while others can wait for overnight printing.

These problems are solved through a mechanism called *spooling*. Figure 13.1 illustrates the process:

1. When a user prints a job, it is not sent directly to a printer. Instead, it is stored in a file on a print server. The print server software is capable of accepting print jobs from many users at one time. All jobs are stored in the spooler files.

2. When a printer becomes available, the print server retrieves jobs one by one from the spooler files and directs them to the printer. Print servers can despool jobs to several printers at once.

Figure 13.1

Spooled printing.

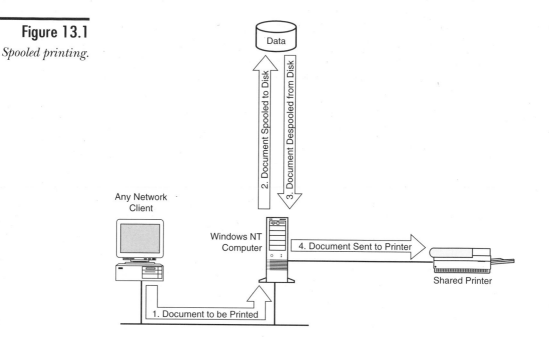

The print spooler serves as a gigantic buffer that can store many megabytes of printer data until printers become available. Print servers can be configured in a wide variety of ways to meet different printing requirements.

Because the entire shared printing process is controlled centrally, a wide variety of special printing needs can arise, such as the following:

◆ Delayed printing of low-priority jobs—even delaying for overnight printing

◆ Restriction of users' access to printers

◆ Printing of identification pages (banners) to identify jobs

◆ Printing of spooled jobs on the first available printer in a printer pool

The need for some of these functions becomes clearer when more than one printer is on the network. In that case, there is a wide variety of ways that the printers can be shared.

Users print to the print spooler by printing to logical printers. A *logical printer* consists of software that is running on a Windows NT computer. Users use a logical printer just as they would a printer that was attached to their computer, but the data that is printed to a logical printer is directed through the network to a shared network printer.

A Windows NT computer that supports logical printers is called a *print server*. Both Windows NT Workstation and Windows NT Server can function as print servers.

The print server associates logical printers with physical printers (actual printer hardware), and it is the job of the print server to ensure that jobs a user sends to a logical printer are directed to the correct physical printer.

> **Note**
>
> Microsoft's terminology is a bit muddy. They generally use the term *printer* to refer to a logical printer, but a printer is sometimes a hardware device. When Microsoft talks about "creating a printer," they are discussing the creation of a logical printer. Typically, they refer to a physical printer as a *printing device*. There are times, however, when you need to look at the context for the word printer to determine whether the manuals are describing a logical or a physical printer.
>
> To avoid confusion, the term *logical printer* is used in this book to refer to a Windows NT printer that is created in the Print Manager and functions as a print spooler. The term *physical printer* is used to describe the hardware printing device.

Figure 13.2 illustrates the three ways in which logical printers and physical printers can be related:

◆ One logical printer can be associated with a single physical printer. All jobs that are directed to the logical printer eventually wind up being printed by the same physical printer.

◆ One logical printer can be associated with two or more physical printers. The print spooler sends each job to the first physical printer that becomes available. There is no way to predict which printer actually will service a given job. This approach is called a *printer pool*.

Objective B.9

◆ Two or more logical printers can be associated with a single printer. The advantage to this approach is that the logical printers can be configured differently. One might be configured for normal printing, while another might accept jobs that will be printed overnight, for example. Logical printers also could be serviced at different priority levels.

Figure 13.2

Possible relationships between logical and physical printers.

One Logical Printer Associated With One Physical Printer

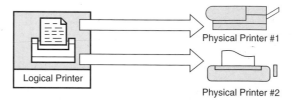

One Logical Printer Associated With Two Physical Printers

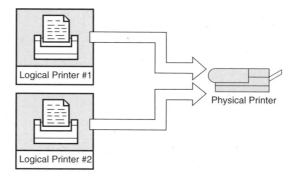

Two Logical Printers Associated With One Physical Printer

The three printer relationships can be mixed up a bit. Figure 13.3 shows one possibility for combining two approaches. The high-priority logical printer is serviced by only one of the printers in the pool.

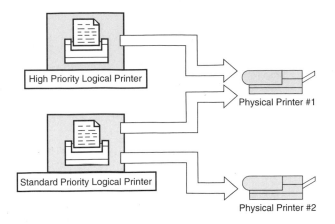

Figure 13.3

A more complex logical and physical printer arrangement.

Installing Printer Hardware

Printers can be attached to print servers through parallel or serial interfaces. Windows NT supports up to 256 COM ports, named COM1 through COM256. Computers based on the Intel/IBM architecture are limited in the numbers of ports they can support. RISC computers are far less limited.

Parallel interfaces are considerably easier to set up than serial interfaces. Most Intel PCs are equipped to support two parallel ports:

◆ LPT1, which uses IRQ7

◆ LPT2, which uses IRQ5

A third parallel port can be added. You will need to obtain a parallel port adapter that supports LPT3. Be sure that the adapter can be set for an interrupt that is not in use on the print server. For reliable operation, parallel printer cables should not exceed 20 feet in length.

Serial ports are considerably more difficult to configure. The most common serial interface standard, RS-232, was not designed with printers in mind. Consequently, manufacturers differ in the way they design printers to work with serial interfaces. You will need to obtain a cable that is wired according to the specifications for your printer. Cables for serial ports can be up to 100 feet.

Serial ports typically use the following interrupts:

◆ COM1 uses IRQ4

◆ COM2 uses IRQ3

With most serial port hardware, COM3 and COM4 reuse interrupts IRQ4 and IRQ3, respectively. Because COM ports share interrupt real estate, some device combinations work well and others do not. If you want to use both COM1 and COM3 (or COM2 and COM4) simultaneously, your serial port hardware must enable you to configure the interrupts for COM3 and COM4 so that they do not conflict with COM1 and COM2.

With standard hardware, serial ports can be in short supply on Intel/IBM AT computers. You certainly do not want to manage Windows NT without a mouse, and most mice use a serial port. If the computer also has a modem, it has used up standard IRQs for COM ports. Consider getting a mouse that uses an InPort interface card, which does not use up a COM port IRQ. InPort mice take a little effort to locate, but it's worth the trouble.

Several vendors provide expansion cards that support 4, 8, or 16 serial ports on a PC. Special drivers are required to enable the operating system to support the expansion card. Because Windows NT is relatively new on the market, not all multiport serial cards provide drivers for Windows NT. Be sure to check with the card's manufacturer to be sure Windows NT is supported by its hardware.

RISC computers do not have these interrupt problems or arbitrary limitations on the number of ports you can add. You can add parallel and serial ports up to the expansion limits of your computer hardware.

Configuring Serial Ports

Serial ports are configured using the Ports utility of the Control Panel. If you run the Ports utility, you see the Ports window shown in figure 13.4. This window shows the ports that Windows NT knows about. In this example, COM1 is dedicated to the computer's mouse and is not available for configuration. COM2 was present when Windows NT was installed.

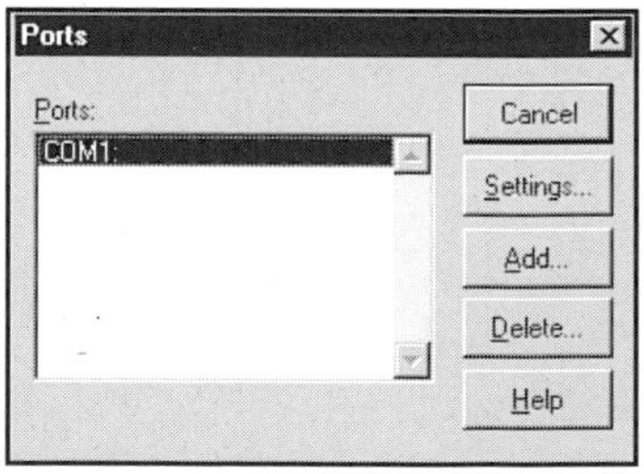

Figure 13.4

The Ports window in the Control Panel.

The Ports window only displays information for COM1 and COM2. If you have added COM port hardware, you need to choose **A**dd and specify the advanced port settings as described in the following sections.

Configuring Serial Port Settings

If you select a port and choose **S**ettings in the Ports window, you access the Settings dialog box shown in figure 13.5. This box enables you to configure serial communication parameters for the port you selected.

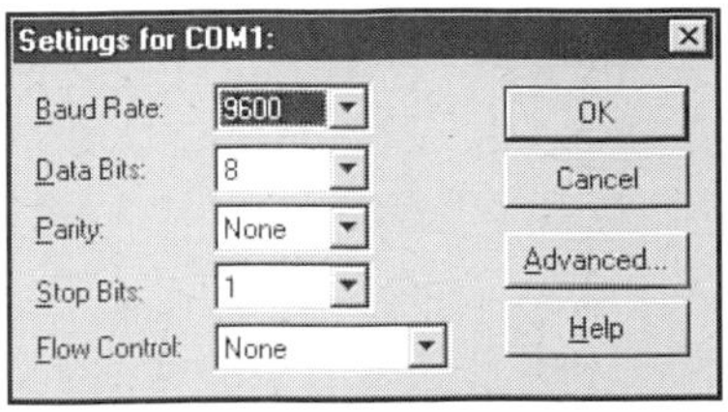

Figure 13.5

Serial port settings.

Serial ports must be configured with a variety of parameters. Both the computer port and the printer port must be configured with the same settings. These settings follow:

◆ **Baud Rate.** A measure of the bits-per-second rate at which the port will operate. The most common setting for printers is 9600.

◆ **Data Bits.** Serial communication takes place one character at a time. Each character contains four to eight bits of data. In almost all cases, you will want to work with eight data bits, which support advanced character sets and graphics.

◆ **Parity.** A rudimentary form of error detection that seldom is employed for computer-printer communication. In general, you can configure both devices for None. Other options are Even, Odd, Mark, and Space.

◆ **Stop Bits.** One or more stop bits signal the end of a serial character. It is not important how many are used, as long as the computer and printer agree. (Extra stop bits do waste a bit of the communication bandwidth, however, and one stop bit will do fine.)

◆ **Flow Control.** This parameter determines how the computer and printer inform each other when data is ready to transmit and when the printer's input buffer is full. Options for this setting follow:

Hardware. The computer and printer communicate through extra wires in the serial cable. This is the most commonly implemented handshaking method.

XON/XOFF. Software handshaking transmits control characters called XON and XOFF to start and stop transmission.

None. Risky if the volume of data potentially could overflow the printer's input buffer, which is often the case.

Choose OK to save settings. Click **A**dvanced to configure hardware settings for the port.

Configuring Advanced Serial Port Settings

Click on the **A**dvanced button in the Settings for COM*x* window to configure additional settings for a serial port. The Advanced Settings for COM*x* dialog box, shown in figure 13.6, can be used to configure Windows NT if your serial ports use non-standard hardware settings or exceed the COM1 and COM2 port configurations that Windows NT knows by default.

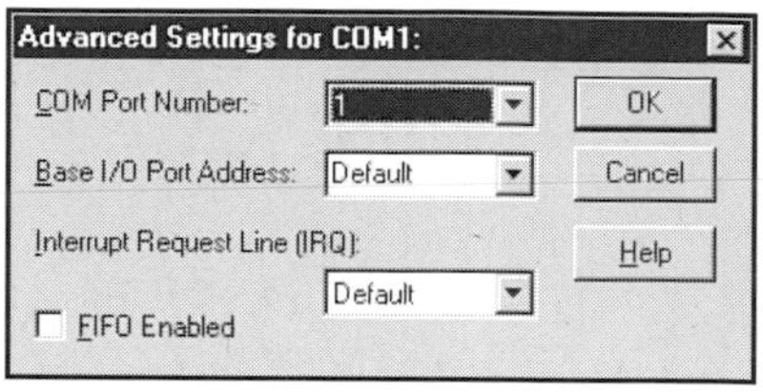

Figure 13.6

Advanced settings for a COM port.

The settings in the Advanced Settings window follow:

◆ **COM Port Number.** This field enables you to specify the COM port that you want to configure. If you add a new port, it should be numbered COM3 or above.

◆ **Base I/O Port Address.** COM ports must be configured with an address in the memory range 2E0h through 3ffh. This address supports communication between the OS and the port. Avoid changing the default settings for COM1 through COM4, which have standard and nonconflicting port addresses.

◆ **Interrupt Request Line (IRQ).** If your serial port hardware permits you to configure custom interrupts, you can configure NT for those interrupts here. To use COM1 and COM3 at the same time (or COM2 and COM4), you need to configure custom, nonconflicting interrupts. Interrupts must be in the range of 2 through 15, although most of the interrupts in this range are unavailable.

◆ **FIFO Enabled.** Enables Windows NT to take advantage of the capability of some advanced serial chips (called UARTs) to buffer incoming signals. Check your serial port documentation before you enable this feature.

Choose OK to save the settings.

Configuring Network-Attached Printers

To support network-attached printers, you must be sure that the proper protocol support has been installed in Windows NT. To support network-attached Hewlett-Packard printers, the Data Link Control (DLC) protocol is required.

To install DLC, follow these steps:

Configuring Network-Attached Printers

1. Start the Network utility from the Control Panel.

2. In the Network utility, select the Protocols tab.

3. In the Protocol tab, choose **A**dd.

4. In the Select Network Protocol box, choose DLC Protocol from the list under **N**etwork Protocol.

5. Choose OK.

6. Provide any disks and path information that are requested.

Creating Printers

Objective B.9

Microsoft calls the process of setting up a logical printer *creating a printer*. Remember, when you create a printer, your actions do not set up the printer hardware itself. Creating a printer is the process of setting up a logical printer that enables users to print on the network.

Logical printers are created and managed using Print Manager. The icon for Printers is found in the Control Panel or through start settings. This section covers the basics of creating a printer. Later, in the section "Configuring Printer Properties," you will be shown some more advanced features of printers.

Any Windows NT computer can be configured as a print server. You must be a member of one of the following groups to create printers:

◆ Administrators (NT Workstation and Server)

◆ Server Operators (NT Server)

◆ Print Operators (NT Server)

◆ Power Users (NT Workstation)

When you create a printer, the procedure you follow depends on how you will be connecting to the printer. You can create a printer to use a printing device that is attached to a part on your computer, or you can connect to a printing device to access a printer that is shared on the network. The procedures are sufficiently different that they will be covered separately.

Creating a Printer on a Print Server

After a printing device has been attached to a port on your computer, follow these steps to create a new logical printer:

Creating a Printer on a Print Server

1. Open the Printers icon in the Control Panel or in start settings. Doing so opens a Printers window containing an icon for each printer, as shown in figure 13.7. One of the icons is named Add Printer.

2. Double-click on Add Printer to open the Add Printer Wizard, shown in figure 13.8.

Figure 13.7

The Printers window.

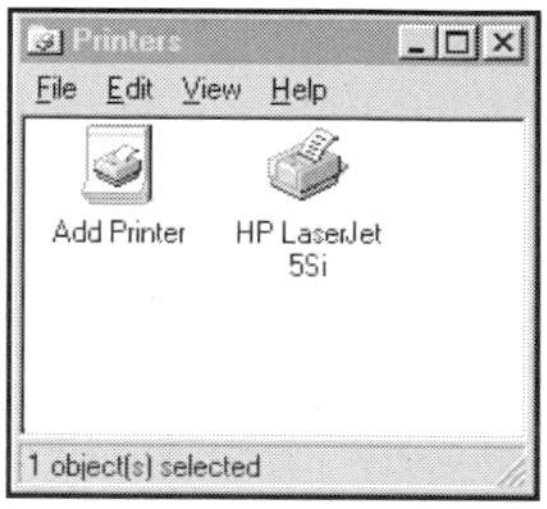

Figure 13.8

The Add Printer Wizard.

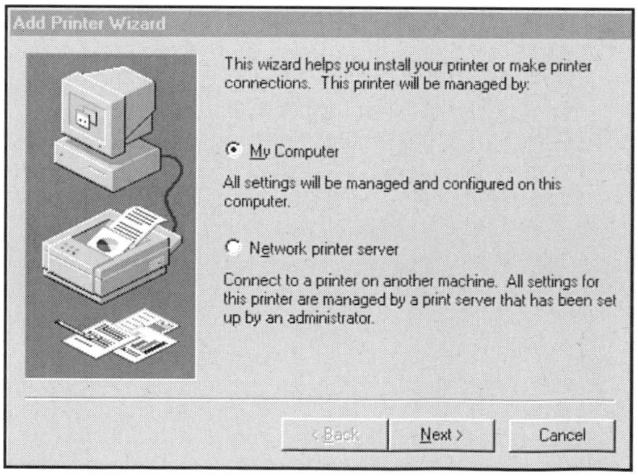

3. First specify the type of printer to be created. You have two choices:

    ◆ **My Computer.** Select this option to create a printer that is physically attached to this computer.

    ◆ **Network printer server.** Select this option to establish a connection with a printer that is shared on the network.

    The remainder of this procedure assumes that **M**y Computer is chosen.

4. Next, the dialog box in figure 13.9 is used to specify the port to which the printer is attached. You can select an LPT port or a COM port. You can also elect to print to FILE:. When printing is directed to FILE:, the printer-ready output is stored in a file.

5. If you want to add one of the following additional ports, choose Add Po**r**t and select one of the following:

   ◆ **Appletalk Printing Devices.** Available when AppleTalk protocol support is installed, this choice enables users to print to AppleTalk printers.

   ◆ **Digital Network Port.** Available when TCP/IP or DECNet protocols are installed, this choice enables users to print to DEC print devices.

   ◆ **Hewlett-Packard Network Port.** Available when the DLC network protocol is installed, this choice enables users to print to printers attached to the network through an HP JetDirect adapter.

   ◆ **LPR Port.** Available when Microsoft TCP/IP Printing service is installed, this choice enables applications using the LPR protocol to print to a printer supported by Windows NT.

To configure a port, select the port and choose **C**onfigure Port. The parameters that are presented depend on the port type. Configuration of a serial port is described earlier in this chapter in the section, "Configuring Serial Ports."

Check one of the ports in the **A**vailable ports dialog box and choose Next.

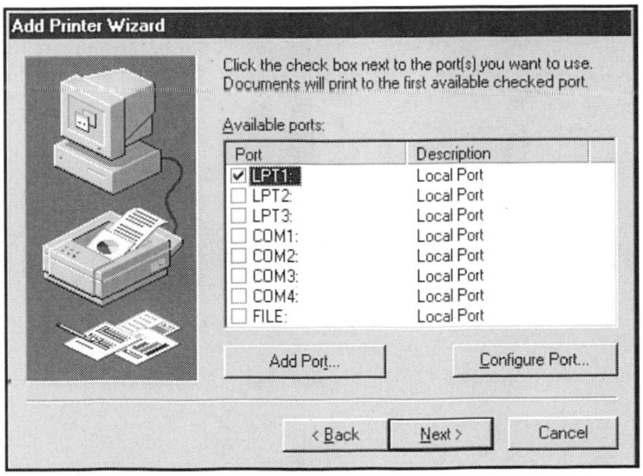

Figure 13.9

Specifying a printer port.

6. The next step is to choose a printer driver, which is performed in the dialog box shown in figure 13.10. (If you are installing printer drivers from a diskette, choose **H**ave Disk and follow the prompts.)

First choose an option in the **M**anufacturers list.

Then choose a printer in the **P**rinters list.

Choose **N**ext.

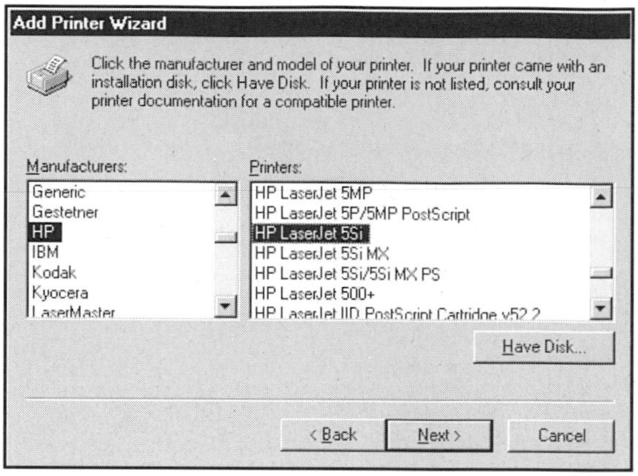

Figure 13.10

*Specifying a
printer.*

Note   Few printer manufacturers actually design proprietary printer control languages. Virtually all laser printers can emulate a Hewlett-Packard LaserJet by supporting some level of HP's Printer Control Language (PCL). Three versions of PCL have been used in laser printers. Here they are, along with basic drivers that should work with compatible printers:

- ◆ PCL3—HP LaserJet Plus
- ◆ PCL4—HP LaserJet II
- ◆ PCL5—HP LaserJet III

The problem with using HP drivers is that they might not support special features in your printer, such as multiple paper sources.

If your printer uses PostScript, try using the Apple LaserWriter Plus driver.

The majority of dot-matrix printers will emulate at least one model in the Epson or IBM Proprinter lines. Here are some possibilities to try:

- ◆ IBM compatible—IBM Proprinter (9-pin), IBM Proprinter X24 (24-pin)
- ◆ Epson compatible—Epson FX-80 (9-pin) standard carriage, Epson FX-100 (9-pin wide carriage), or Epson LQ-1500 (24-pin)

Windows NT computers do not require their own copies of driver files to print with a Windows NT print server. The required driver files are read from the print server when a connection is made to a printer.

Different drivers are required for Intel and RISC-based Windows NT computers. If your network includes both hardware platforms, you must install drivers for both Intel and RISC computers on the print server.

7. In the next dialog box, specify a name for the printer. This is the name that will identify the printer to users on the network.

8. The next dialog box, shown in figure 13.11, prepares the printer to be shared on the network.

9. Select **S**hared if the printer will be shared. Select N**o**t Shared if the printer will be used only by users logged on locally to this computer.

   If you selected **S**hared, a share name will be suggested. MS-DOS and Windows 3.x users cannot access printer share names that do not conform to 8.3 format. Edit the Share Name field if desired.

   If you selected **S**hared, select the operating systems that are used on your network. The Add Printer Wizard will copy drivers for each supported operating system so that they are available for users. Drivers for Windows NT 4 x86 computers are installed by default.

Note | The Windows NT Server 4 installation CD-ROM includes drivers for Windows NT version 4 only, including I386, MIPS, Alpha, and PPC drivers. Drivers for prior versions of Windows NT, or for Windows 95, must be copied from the installation disks for those operating systems. Be sure that you have the disks available and that you know the paths to the installation files before you attempt to install these drivers.

Choose **N**ext.

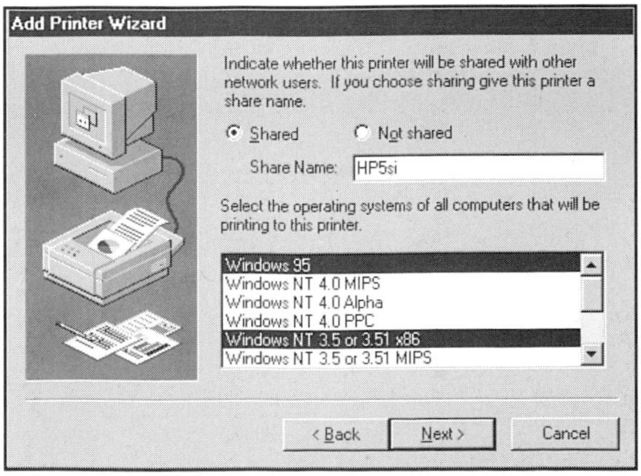

Figure 13.11

Configuring printer sharing.

10. Next you are asked, `Would you like to print a test page?` To test the printer configuration, select **Y**es. To skip the test, select **N**o.

11. Choose Finish to complete the installation.

12. When prompted, specify the path where the installation files are located.

Connecting to a Network Printer

After a printer has been created, any user with at least print privilege can connect to the printer. This section shows you how to connect a printer in Windows NT. Specific procedures for other operating systems are covered in the chapters devoted to those environments.

Windows NT computers can print to the network immediately. They can access the printer driver that was installed on the print server computer and do not need to have a driver installed locally.

To connect to a logical printer on a Windows NT computer, follow these steps:

Connecting to a Network Printer

1. Open the Printers icon in the Control Panel. Doing so opens a Printers window containing an icon for each printer, as shown in figure 13.7. One of the icons is named Add Printer.

2. Double-click on Add Printer to open the Add Printer Wizard, shown in figure 13.8.

3. Choose Network printer server. Then choose Next.

4. A Connect to Printer dialog box opens a browse list (see fig. 13.12). Browse the network and select a shared printer. Then choose Next.

5. Choose Finish to complete the installation.

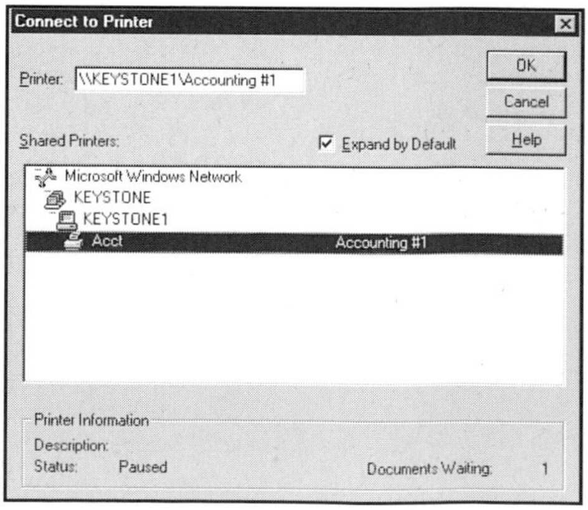

Figure 13.12

Connecting to a shared printer.

If you are familiar with printing in Windows for Workgroups, you probably are surprised that the network printer was not connected to a port. In Windows NT, a port assignment is not necessary when printing to a shared network printer.

Note   Many DOS applications require you to specify a port assignment, which is done with the NET USE command. To assign the printer LASER1 on the server Widgets to your parallel port LPT3, enter this command:

```
NET USE LPT3: \\WIDGETS\LASER1
```

The logical printer now appears as an icon in the Printers window and can be selected for printing in applications. Figure 13.13 shows the Print Setup window in Windows NT Winpad.

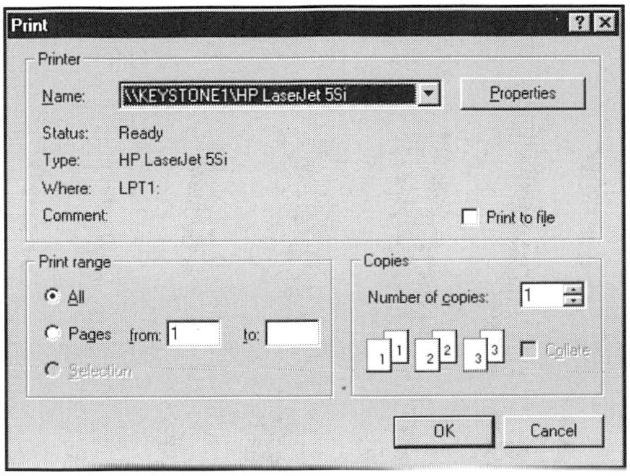

Figure 13.13

Selecting a network printer in Windows NT Winpad.

Selecting the Default Printer

At any given time, a user can have several printer connections in effect. One of these connections is the default printer, which is used for printing unless the user specifies otherwise.

To select the default printer in Windows NT, right-click on the desired icon in the Printers window. Then choose the command Set As Default in the Options menu.

Configuring Printer Properties

In this section, you will be shown how to configure properties of logical printers. To manage the properties for a printer, right-click on the desired icon in the Printers window. Then choose the **P**roperties command from the Options menu. A printer Properties box is shown in figure 13.14. Each of the tabs will be examined in the following sections.

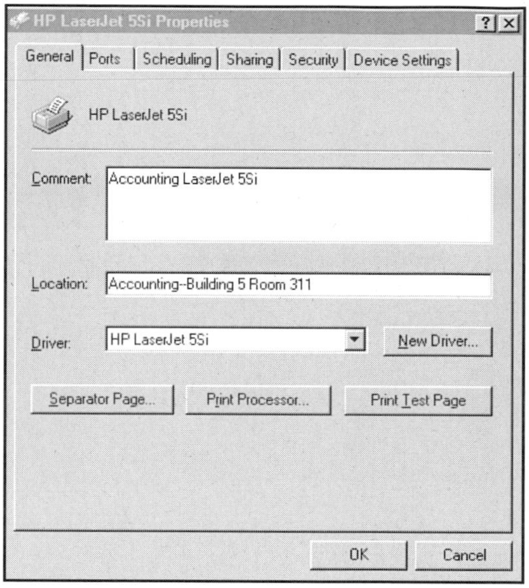

Figure 13.14

Printer General properties.

Configuring General Properties

This tab supports a potpourri of general configuration functions.

Configuring Printer Comment and Location Information

The first property in the General tab, shown in figure 13.14, is **C**omment. This field accepts a freeform comment. Perhaps the best use is to provide contact information identifying the person who is responsible for maintaining the printer hardware. If the printer has special features, such as a letterhead paper bin or an envelope feeder, those features might be worth mentioning as well.

The **L**ocation field accepts freeform text that describes the printer's location.

Changing the Printer Driver

The **D**river field describes the driver that is currently assigned to the printer. If other drivers are installed, you can pull this field down to change the driver. Or you can choose **N**ew Driver to install a new driver.

Specifying a Separator Page

A *separator page* is a file that contains text and commands to be placed on a page that is printed prior to the print job. If a separator page is to precede each job, choose **S**eparator Page and enter the path to the separator page file in the **S**eparator Page field of the dialog box that is provided. Three standard print separator files are included with Windows NT:

◆ **PCL.SEP.** For use with Hewlett-Packard printers and other printers that use the HP Printer Control Language (PCL). In dual-protocol printers, PCL.SEP switches the printer into PCL mode.

◆ **PSCRIPT.SEP.** For use with HP printers equipped with PostScript. In dual-protocol printers, PSCRIPT.SEP switches the printer into PostScript mode.

◆ **SYSPRINT.SEP.** Prints a separator page on PostScript printers.

Each of these files can be edited, and you can create custom separator pages easily. Later in this chapter, the section "Creating Separator Files" describes the procedure.

To cancel use of a separator file, select the text in the **S**eparator Page box and delete it.

Configuring the Print Processor

The Print Processor button opens the dialog box shown in figure 13.15. This dialog box specifies the driver that is responsible for processing print jobs for this printer. Windows NT includes only one print processor named WINPRINT. You need to change the entry in the Print Processor box only if you install software that provides its own print processor. Consult the software documentation for details.

In rare instances, you might need to change the Default Datatype entry. Choices for this field include the following:

◆ **RAW.** Data are passed to the printer as raw bit streams. Required for printing graphics jobs, for PostScript, and for printing with Windows TrueType fonts. In fact, this setting is required for most printing and works for most other types of printing. You seldom will need to use other options.

◆ **RAW [FF appended].** Use in the rare instances when an application does not force a form feed at the end of a print job.

◆ **RAW [FF auto].** Data are passed to the printer as raw bit streams. A form feed will be sent if WINPRINT determines that one is not sent to terminate the job.

◆ **NT EMF 1.002.** A special Windows NT format to be used if your applications require it.

◆ **TEXT.** Use this choice for printing with applications that print only ASCII text. A form feed is forced at the end of the print job. Some text-mode DOS applications print more effectively with this setting.

Printing a Test Page

After you configure changes on a printer, you should test them by printing a test page. Choose Print **T**est Page to do so.

Configuring Ports Properties

Objective B.9

This tab configures several port-related configuration characteristics and is shown in figure 13.15.

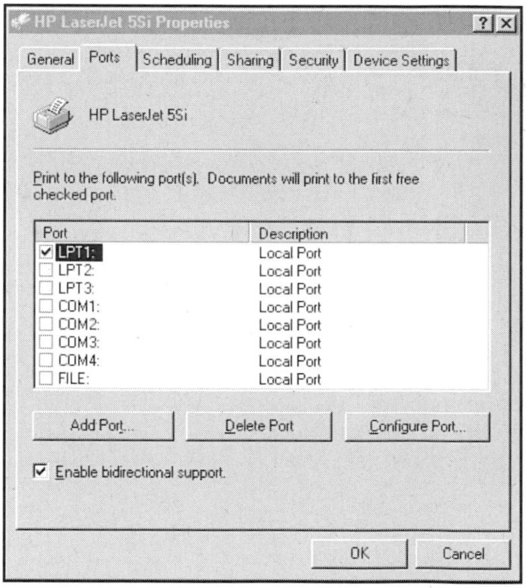

Figure 13.15

Printer Port properties.

A logical printer can send jobs to several printers. This arrangement is called a *printer pool*, and was described earlier in the chapter. Two conditions apply:

◆ The printer devices must be connected directly to the same print server, although you can mix different types of ports.

◆ The printer devices must be identical. Otherwise, the configuration information entered in Print Manager will not apply to all printers. If printers differ, configure the logical printer so that it matches the specifications of the most limited printer hardware.

To create a printer pool or to add a physical printer to an existing pool, enable printer pooling and select the ports by clicking the entry in the Ports tab.

To deselect a port, remove the check mark.

To delete a port from the list, select the port and click the **D**elete Port button. You might want to remove a port if it is not available in the print server's hardware configuration.

To add a port to the list, choose Add Po**rt** to open the Printer Ports dialog box, which is shown in figure 13.9. Consult the description for that figure for the procedures and options when adding ports.

To configure a port, select the port and choose **C**onfigure Port. A dialog box will be displayed with configuration options for the type of port that has been selected.

Many new printers are capable of engaging in a two-way dialog with the driver software. They can, for example, tell the driver when they are low on toner. If your printer supports bidirectional communication, check **E**nable bidirectional support.

Configuring Scheduling Properties

Actually, not all the options on this tab have to do with scheduling, but that is the first topic to be considered. The Scheduling tab is shown in figure 13.16.

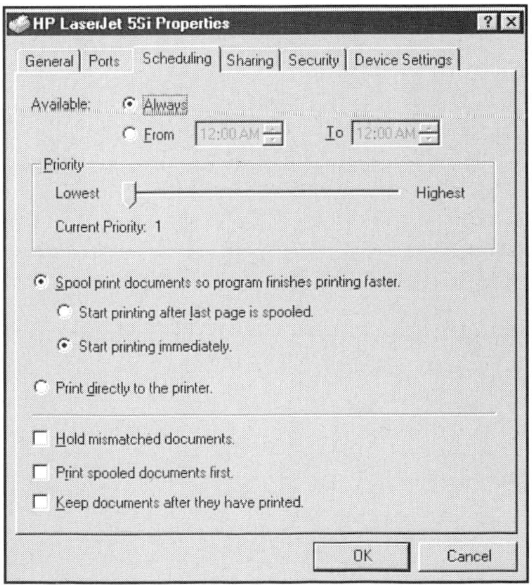

Figure 13.16

Printer Scheduling properties.

Scheduling Printer Availability

It can be extremely useful to delay print jobs for later printing. This is most commonly done so that large or low-priority jobs can print overnight when printers ordinarily are idle.

You can establish several logical printers, associating them with the same printer. Each logical printer can be configured with different scheduling properties, enabling you to have distinct restrictions for different users, priorities, or types of jobs.

If the logical printer is to be available at all times, select Al**w**ays.

To restrict the availability for the logical printer, select **F**rom and specify a time interval in the **F**rom and **T**o boxes.

<table>
<tr><td>

Objective

B.9

</td></tr>
</table>

Setting Printer Priority

The **P**riority field determines the printing priority associated with this logical printer. If several logical printers are serviced by the same physical printer, the logical printer having the highest priority will be given preference in the order of printing jobs.

Configuring Spooler Operation

You can tune operation of the spooler using several options on the Scheduling tab, shown in figure 13.16.

By default, spooling is enabled by selecting **S**pool print documents so the program finishes printing faster. When spooling is enabled, you have a choice of two modes of operation:

- ◆ **Start printing after last page is spooled.** This option ensures that the entire print job is available in the spooler, but printing cannot begin until the entire job has been spooled.

- ◆ **Start printing immediately.** By default, jobs start printing as soon as the first page of the job has been spooled. Printing can begin earlier in the print cycle, and print jobs are completed more quickly.

To disable spooling, select Print **d**irectly to the printer. The following choices are available only when spooling is active:

- ◆ **Hold mismatched documents.** When this option is checked, the spooler will hold jobs that do not match the form that is currently mounted on the printer. When this option is not checked, jobs of the same priority are printed in the order submitted, and form changes must be performed as required. Although this is not checked by default, check it to minimize the frequency of form changes.

◆ **Print spooled documents first.** When this option is checked (the default), a job that has completed spooling will be printed before a job in the process of spooling, even when the spooling job has a higher priority. The default is typically the better choice.

◆ **Keep documents after they have printed.** If you are printing documents that cannot be easily recreated, check this option. The document will remain in the spooler after printing is completed. If a printing problem occurs, you can reprint the spooled jobs. Because jobs must be manually deleted when this option is enabled, you should use this option only in special instances.

Configuring Printer Sharing

The Sharing tab (see fig. 13.17) is used to determine printer sharing characteristics. If a printer is not to be shared, select N**o**t Shared.

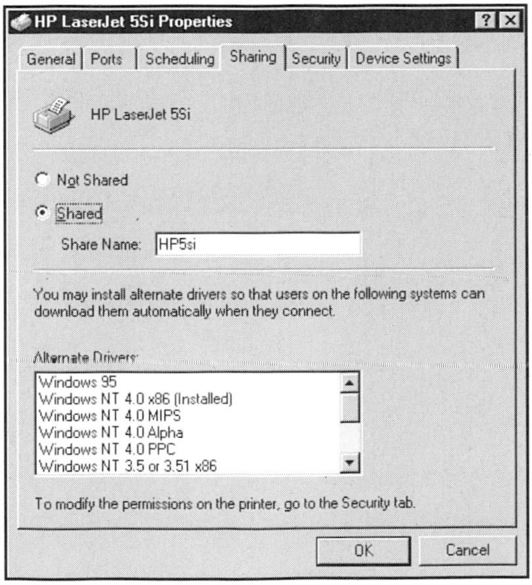

Figure 13.17

Printer Sharing properties.

To share a printer, select **S**hared and specify a shared name. Windows NT and Windows 95 users can operate with long share names, but you must restrict the name to 8.3 format if the printer is to be shared by MS-DOS and Windows 3.x users.

Tip Just as you can create file shares that do not appear when users browse the network, you can conceal printer shares by adding a dollar sign ($) to the end of the share name. Users who want to access the printer must enter the share name manually when connecting to the printer.

Drivers for Windows 4 x86 computers are installed by default. If other Windows NT platforms must be supported, select the platforms in the Alternate Drivers list so that drivers will be copied for those computers.

> **Note**   The Windows NT Server 4 installation CD-ROM includes drivers for Windows NT version 4 only, including I386, MIPS, Alpha, and PPC drivers. Drivers for prior versions of Windows NT, or for Windows 95, must be copied from the installation disks for those operating systems. Be sure that you have the disks available, and that you know the paths to the installation files before to attempt to install these drivers.

Configuring Printer Security

The Security tab has three buttons addressing different areas of security:

- ◆ **P**ermissions
- ◆ **A**uditing
- ◆ **O**wnership

Auditing is addressed in Chapter 19, "Managing the Server." Permissions and ownership are discussed in the following sections.

Taking Printer Ownership

The user who creates a printer is the printer's owner and can administer all characteristics of the logical printer. The owner can enable other users to administer the printer by giving the users Manage Documents or Full Control permissions.

Any user who has Full Control permissions can take ownership of the printer by selecting the **O**wnership option on the Security tab. This opens the Owner box, which includes a **T**ake Ownership button. Click the button to assume ownership of the printer.

Managing Printer Permissions

Printer permissions can be managed by the owner of the printer or by users who have Full Control permissions. Four permissions can be assigned to printers:

- ◆ No Access
- ◆ Print
- ◆ Manage Documents
- ◆ Full Control

Users with the Manage Documents permissions can perform the following actions:

- ◆ Controlling document settings
- ◆ Pausing, resuming, restarting, and deleting documents

Users with Full Control permissions can perform the actions permitted by Manage Document permissions. In addition, they can perform these actions:

- ◆ Changing document printing order
- ◆ Pausing, resuming, and purging logical printers
- ◆ Changing logical printer properties
- ◆ Deleting logical printers
- ◆ Changing logical printer permissions

> **Note** The user who creates a document is established as the document's owner. All users can perform Manage Document operations on documents they own.

The procedure for setting printer permissions is nearly identical to the procedure for setting file permissions. Use the following steps:

Setting Printer Permissions

1. Select Security tab to open the Printer Permissions box shown in figure 13.18.

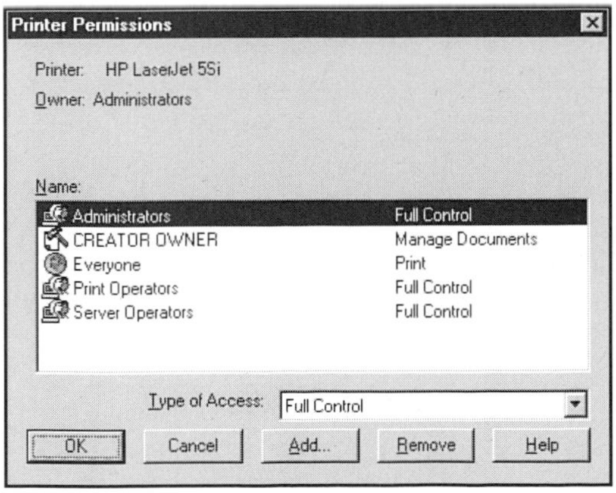

Figure 13.18

Setting printer permissions.

2. To change permissions for a user or group:
   - ◆ Select a name in the **N**ame box.
   - ◆ Pull down the **T**ype of Access list and select the desired access.

3. To add a user or group to the permissions list:

   ◆ Click Add in the Printer Permissions box. The Add Users and Groups dialog box appears, as shown in figure 13.19.

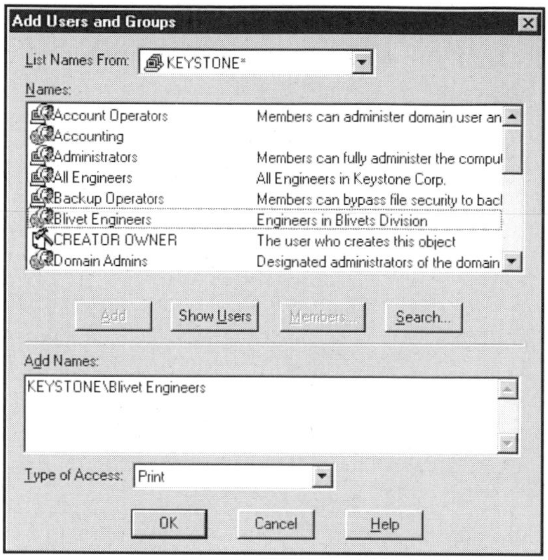

Figure 13.19

Adding users and groups to printer permissions.

◆ If required, select a different domain from the **L**ist Names From drop-down list.

◆ To display user names in the **N**ames box, click on Show **U**sers.

◆ Add names to the A**d**d Names box by double-clicking entries in the **N**ames box or by selecting entries in the **N**ames box and choosing **A**dd.

◆ In the **T**ype of Access box, select the permissions to be assigned to the names you have selected. All selected users and groups receive the same permissions.

◆ Choose OK to add the users or groups to the permissions list for the printer and return to the Printer Permissions box.

4. To remove a name, select the entry in the **N**ames box of the Printer Permissions dialog box, and choose **R**emove.

5. Choose OK to save the permissions.

Configuring Printer Device Settings

Figure 13.20 shows the Device Settings tab. This tab presents a hierarchical list of the printer's hardware features. The details you see will depend on the printer driver that is being used for this printer. To view or change a setting, select the property in the list. In some cases, options will appear on the Settings tab for changing settings. In other cases, a button will be displayed that opens a secondary dialog box.

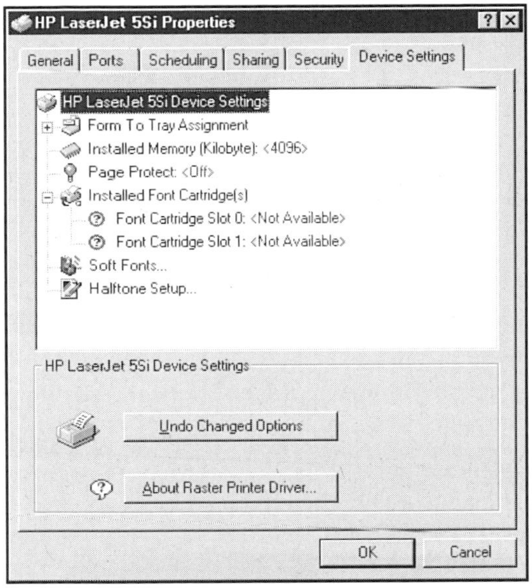

Figure 13.20

The Device Settings tab.

Identifying Available Forms for a Printer

You can assign a different type of form to each paper tray on the printer. If a print job requests an available form type, the appropriate paper tray will be accessed. If a print job requests a form that is unavailable, a printer operator can load the form in a paper tray and modify the printer properties to show that the form type is available.

In figure 13.21, the Form To Tray Assignment category has been opened to reveal the trays available on this printer. To assign a form, select one of the paper trays that is listed to open the **C**hange...Setting list. Scroll through this list and select the form type that is to be associated with the paper tray you have selected.

Specifying Printer Memory

It is particularly important for Windows NT to know how much memory is installed in a laser printer. When graphics are printed to a laser printer, the entire page must be imaged in memory before the page is printed. This cannot be achieved if the memory installed in the printer is insufficient for the graphics being printed.

15. Windows NT permits you to specify when a logical printer is available to be used.

    A. True

    B. False

16. If several logical printers are serviced by the same physical printer, the logical printer having the lowest priority setting will be given preference in the order of printing jobs.

    A. True

    B. False

17. By default, jobs start printing after the last page is spooled.

    A. True

    B. False

18. As with directory shares, printer shares must be restricted to the 8.3 standard if it is to be available to MS-DOS clients.

    A. True

    B. False

19. What is not a legitimate permission that can be assigned to printers?

    A. Take Ownership

    B. No Access

    C. Print

    D. Manage Documents

    E. Full Control

20. The page protection option instructs the printer to image the entire page in memory before printing.

    A. True

    B. False

21. What are the three types of fonts a printing device can use?

    A. Software fonts

    B. Hardware fonts

    C. Screen fonts

    D. Soft fonts

    E. Vector fonts

22. Under Windows NT, you can configure default document settings that will be used when settings are not specified by the application printing the document. What are two instances where printing defaults are valuable?

    A. Printing from a Windows NT 3.1 machine

    B. Printing utilizing a printer pool

    C. Printing from a non-Windows application

    D. Printing from the command line, using the PRINT command or copying a document to the PRN: device

23. When an administrator pauses a logical printer, users cannot spool documents to it.

    A. True

    B. False

24. The priority setting has a range of 1 to _____, where 1 is the lowest priority.

    A. 100

    B. 99

    C. 256

    D. 10

25. When using seperator files, what escape code prints the name of the user who submitted the print job?

    A. \U

    B. \N

    C. \W

    D. None

Review Answers

1. duty cycle
2. C
3. printer pool
4. A
5. C
6. D
7. D
8. PCL (Printer Control Language)
9. B
10. D
11. B
12. A
13. C
14. A
15. A
16. B
17. B
18. A
19. A
20. A
21. B, C, D
22. C, D
23. B
24. B
25. B

PART III

Installing and Using Clients

CHAPTER 14

Using Windows and DOS Clients

The overwhelming popularity of Microsoft MS-DOS and Windows practically ensures that your network will include DOS and Windows clients. Microsoft produces two distinct families of Windows products:

◆ Windows versions that run over MS-DOS:

Windows 3.1. A Windows product that is intended primarily for stand-alone computing but is capable of being networked.

Windows for Workgroups 3.11 (WfW). An extended version of Windows 3.1 that has many built-in networking features.

Windows 95. Microsoft's next-generation Windows product that replaces the 16-bit Windows 3.x architecture with a 32-bit architecture. Much of the underlying technology of Windows 95 can be traced back to MS-DOS.

◆ Windows NT (new technology):

Windows NT Workstation. Version 3.5 has a user interface that looks much like Windows 3.1, but Windows NT was designed from the ground up as an advanced 32-bit operating system, completely free from any dependence on DOS technology.

Windows NT Server. Version 3.5 is an extended version of Windows NT Workstation that provides a full range of network server features.

Because Windows NT is so dramatically different from DOS-based Windows products, the two product groups will be considered in separate chapters. Look for coverage of Windows NT clients in the next chapter.

Windows for Workgroups (WfW) is ready to network out of the box and is considered first.

To network MS-DOS with Windows 3.1, you must install and configure a network add-on called the Workgroup Connection. Procedures are similar for both environments, and they will be considered together.

Finally, the chapter looks at networking with Microsoft's Windows 95.

Windows for Workgroups 3.11

Windows for Workgroups can be used by itself to build peer-to-peer networks that support file and printer sharing. The utilities included with WfW are network-ready. Print manager can share local printers and connect to shared printers elsewhere on the network. File Manager can share files and connect to shared files. Although you can network Windows 3.1, the utilities in Windows 3.1 cannot participate in the network with the same facility as the utilities in WfW.

Everything you need to configure a WfW 3.11 client is included with the product. In this section, you will learn how to install networking software, connect to a domain, and access domain resources.

Installing WfW Network Software

When WfW is installed on a networked computer, SETUP will normally install the network software and configure WfW to participate in a workgroup. If the WfW computer is already participating in a workgroup, the network software is already installed, and you can skip this section and go to the section "Connecting to a Domain."

The following exercise covers step-by-step procedures for adding network software to an installed copy of Windows for Workgroups:

Installing WfW Network Software

1. Run the Windows Setup utility. The icon for Windows Setup is normally stored in the Main program group. In the Windows Setup dialog box, the Network field will indicate `No Network Installed`.

2. Choose the Change **N**etwork Settings command in the Options menu. The Network Setup dialog box will be displayed as shown in figure 14.1. This box is the focus for most WfW network configuration procedures. In figure 14.1, no networking features are enabled.

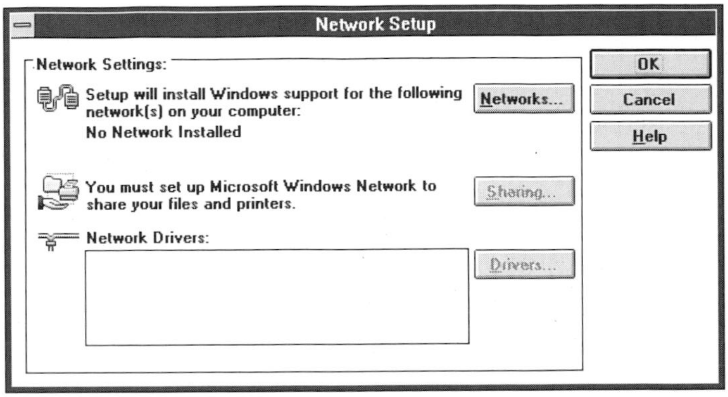

Figure 14.1

The Network Setup dialog box.

3. To install network support, choose **N**etworks to display the Networks dialog box shown in figure 14.2.

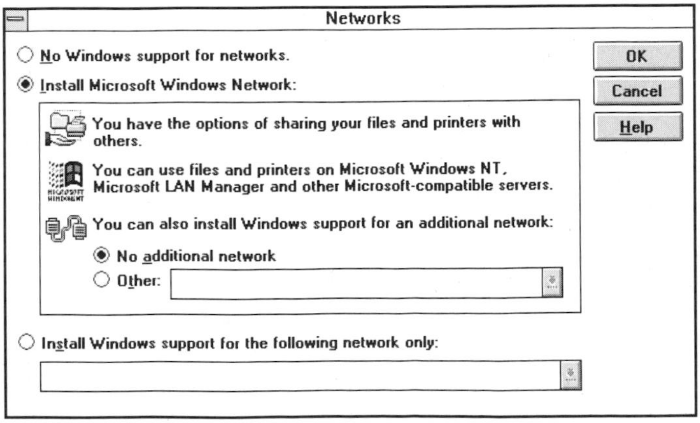

Figure 14.2

Selecting Network support options.

Although WfW can be configured with protocol stacks provided by other vendors, such as the Open Datalink Interface (ODI) stack from Novell, you will probably want to use the NDIS stack that is provided by Microsoft. NDIS supports multiple, simultaneous protocols including NetBEUI, NWLink (a transport that is compatible with Novell's IPX/SPX), and TCP/IP.

4. To install the protocols, select the **I**nstall Microsoft Windows Network radio button and choose OK. (If your network includes NetWare or other supported networks, you will also need to select O**t**her and follow the required procedures for the other network type.)

   You will be returned to the Network Setup dialog box, which now indicates that Setup will install the Microsoft Windows Network (version 3.11). Choose OK to continue.

5. Setup attempts to discover any network cards in the PC and will probably be successful.

   Some cards will fool the detection programs. If the card Setup detects is incorrect, you must choose **N**o to enter the Add Network Adapter dialog box.

Note   In my case, the computer had a card that was compatible with the Novell/Eagle NE2000. Setup thought it was an NE1000, and displayed the message shown in figure 14.3. I had to choose **N**o and select the card manually.

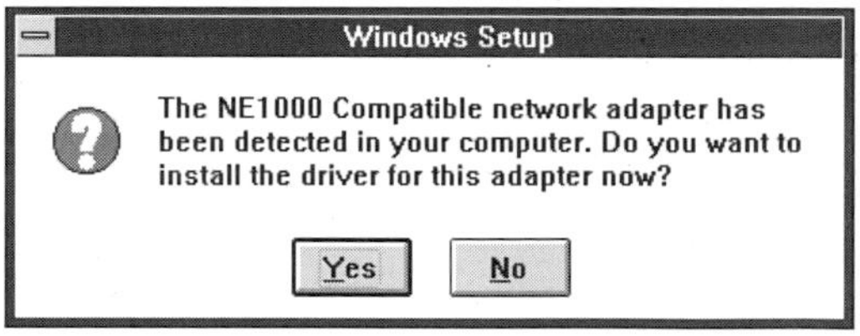

Figure 14.3

Setup requesting confirmation of a discovered network card.

6. If you must manually select a network card driver, you will do so from the list in the Add Network Adapter dialog box, shown in figure 14.4. In the figure, an NE2000 has been chosen.

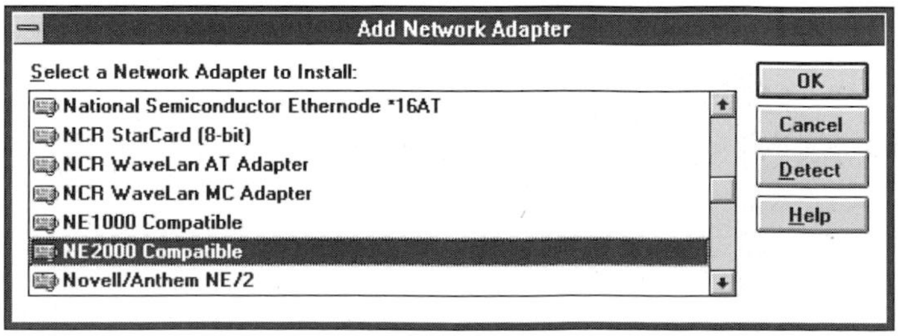

Figure 14.4

Choosing a network adapter.

7. Next, a series of boxes enables you to specify settings for your network card. In the case of the NE2000, the interrupt and the I/O port had to be confirmed.

If you select an interrupt that is normally dedicated to another resource, Setup warns you. Figure 14.5 shows the warning shown when Interrupt 3 was selected.

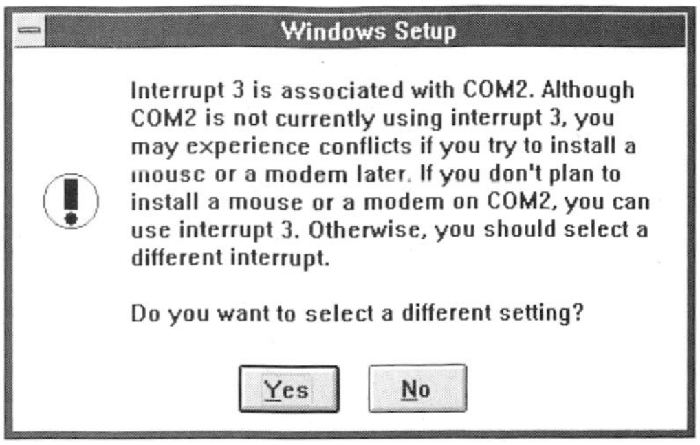

Figure 14.5

Setup warning of a potential resource conflict.

8. After specifying card settings, Setup presents the Microsoft Windows Network Names dialog box shown in figure 14.6. Here you must specify the following:

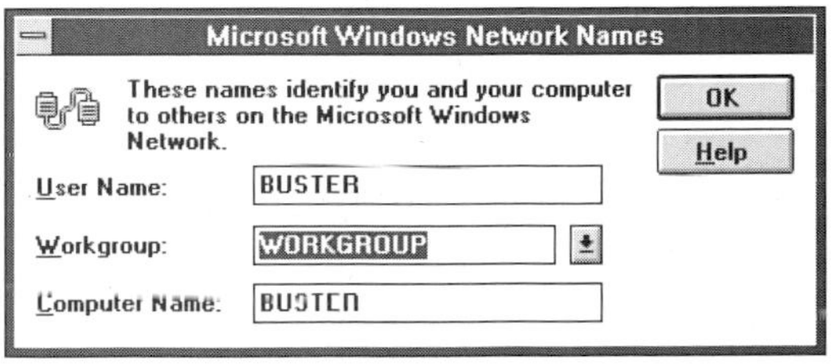

Figure 14.6

Specifying network names.

◆ **User Name.** Should match a user name that is recognized by the domain this user will access.

◆ **Workgroup.** Can be a WfW workgroup (the default is WORKGROUP) or a domain. It is suggested that you leave this setting at WORKGROUP and connect to the NT domain as described in the next section.

◆ **Computer Name.** Should uniquely identify this computer on the network.

Workgroup and computer names can consist of up to 15 characters and may include the following characters:

! # $ % ( ) - _ . @ ^ ' ~

Spaces are not permitted.

> **Note** The entry specified in Workgroup determines which computers a WfW computer can share resources with. If the entry is the name of a workgroup, the WfW computer can share resources with other computers in the Workgroup but not with Windows NT computers or with computers that are connected only to a domain.
>
> If the entry in Workgroup is the name of a domain, the WfW computer can share resources with Windows NT computers, WfW computers, and DOS computers that are running Microsoft Network software. The computer, however, will not enable the WfW computer to share resources with computers that are not logged on to the domain.
>
> A WfW computer can share resources with a workgroup and log on to a domain by specifying a workgroup in the Workgroup entry and entering a domain, as described in the later section, "Connecting to a Domain."

9. Choose OK when network names have been specified. Setup will begin to install files. Insert disks and specify file locations when prompted.

   You are notified that Setup will modify the files AUTOEXEC.BAT, SYSTEM.INI, and PROTOCOL.INI. The changes made to these files will be discussed later in the chapter.

10. After files are installed, the computer must be rebooted to activate the network software. You are given the option Restart your computer now?. Choose **R**estart Computer to activate the network.

11. When you restart Windows, you will see a Welcome to Windows for Workgroups dialog box. This dialog box has the following two fields:

    ◆ **Logon Name.** Matches the name you specified in step 8.

    ◆ **Password.** You should enter the password this user will enter to access the workgroup network.

> **Note** WfW is capable of logging users on to a variety of resources while it is starting up. For this to work smoothly, a user should have the same user name on each network. It is also useful to enter the same password on each network. There is no way to discover a password once it has been created, and one password is easier to remember than three or four.

12. Next you will see the message There is no password list file for the user name. Do you want to create one now?. Respond by choosing **Y**es.

13. A Confirm User Password dialog box requests that you enter the password a second time. Type the password again in the **C**onfirm New Password dialog box and click on OK.

    WfW will encrypt the password you entered and store it in a file named *username*.PWL in the Windows directory (where *username* matches the user's logon name). The next time this user logs on to WfW, a password will be requested and checked against the password in the PWL file. If a blank password was entered, no password is requested when WfW starts.

The computer is now set up to participate on a network, but cannot yet log on to a domain. The next section covers the steps to connect the computer to a Windows NT domain.

Note After installing networking on Windows for Workgroups, you should obtain two update files from the Windows NT Server 4 CD-ROM. Copy the files in \Clients\Update.wfw of the CD-ROM to the \Windows\System directory for Windows for Workgroups.

Connecting to a Domain

After a WfW computer has been configured to connect to a network you can enable it to log on to a domain. Start the Network utility in the Control Panel. The Microsoft Windows Network dialog box that is shown can be used to reconfigure many WfW network settings (see fig. 14.7).

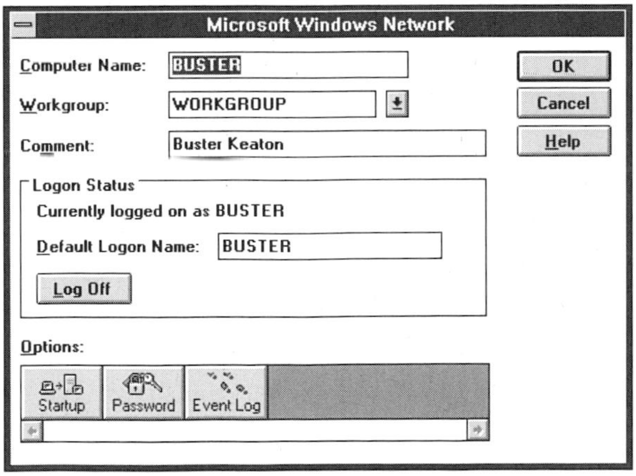

Figure 14.7

Windows for Workgroups network settings.

To configure WfW to log on to a domain when starting, follow the steps covered in the following exercise:

Configuring WfW to Log on to a Domain

1. Choose the Startup button to display the Startup Settings dialog box shown in figure 14.8.

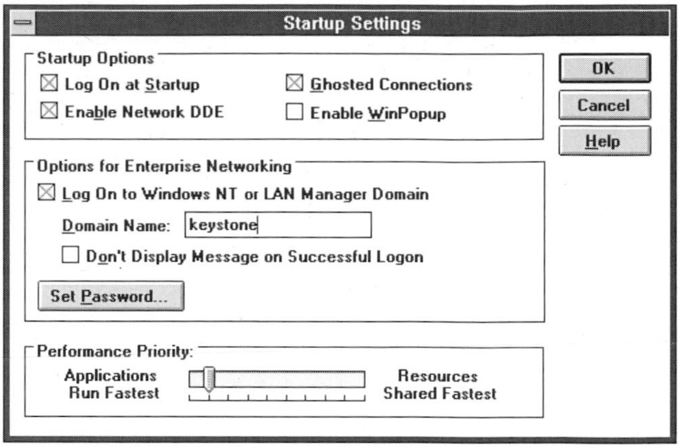

Figure 14.8

Specifying WfW network startup settings.

Several check boxes are included:

◆ **Log On at Startup.** Check this box to have WfW log you on automatically when it starts.

◆ **Enable Network DDE.** If you will be using network DDE with your applications, check this box. Check the box only if network DDE is required because enabling this option uses about 50 KB of memory.

◆ **Ghosted Connections.** Selecting this option saves time at startup by not establishing connections to resources until they are actually placed in use. Drive letters are reserved for persistent connections, but connections are not established.

◆ **Enable WinPopup.** WinPopup is a message display utility that displays network messages in Windows. If you will be broadcasting messages to users, enable this option. WinPopup also receives confirmation messages from domain print servers.

2. Check the box labeled **L**og On to Windows NT or LAN Manager Domain to enable Windows NT Server logon when WfW starts up.

3. Enter the log on domain name in the **D**omain Name box.

4. Choose Set **P**assword to enter the logon password at this time.

5. If you do not want to receive a message confirming a successful logon, check the box D**o**n't Display Message on Successful Logon.

6. Click OK. You will be prompted to restart the computer.

7. When WfW restarts, you will be presented with the Domain Logon dialog box shown in figure 14.9. Enter the password for the domain that was selected. If desired, you can change the domain or choose **B**rowse to browse for one.

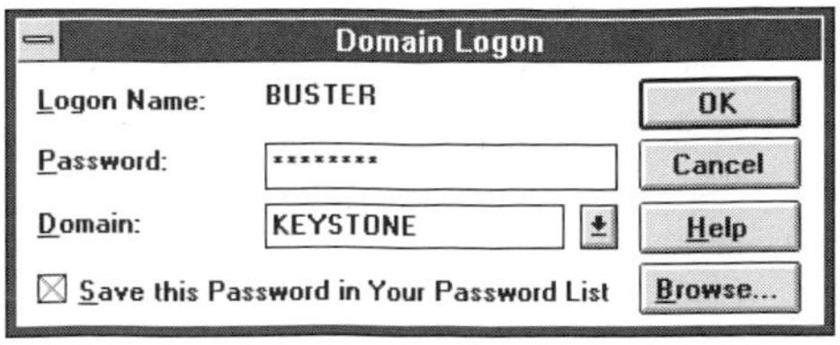

Figure 14.9

Logging on to a domain.

8. If you check the box **S**ave this Password in Your Password List, WfW will encrypt the domain password and store it in this user's PWL file.

9. Following a successful domain logon, WfW displays a confirmation message similar to the one shown in figure 14.10. (This box will not display if D**o**n't Display Message on Successful Logon was checked in step 5.)

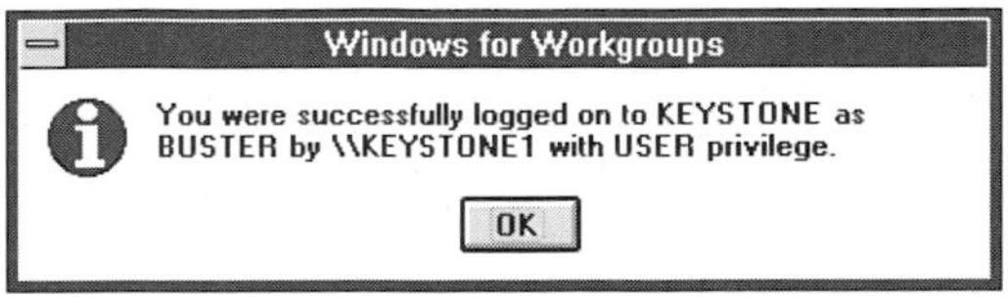

Figure 14.10

Confirmation of a successful domain logon.

After workgroup and domain passwords have been stored in a password file, WfW will not request them when starting unless they are refused by the workgroup or the domain.

If a password has changed or if you want to change your password, do the following:

◆ Change your domain password by choosing the Set **P**assword button in the Startup Settings window (refer to fig. 14.8).

◆ Change your workgroup password by choosing the Password button in the Microsoft Windows Network window (refer to fig. 14.7).

If you have not logged on to a domain and attempted to browse domain resources, you will be shown the logon message displayed in figure 14.11, which gives you the option of logging on to the domain.

Figure 14.11

Logging on to the domain in mid-session.

Connecting to Shared Directories

WfW computers can connect to shared directories on Windows NT computers, using
File Manager, as detailed in the following exercise:

Connecting WfW to Shared NT Directories

1. Run File Manager.

2. Choose the Connect **N**etwork Drive command in the **D**isk menu.

3. Specify a drive letter and browse the network for a shared directory.

4. Specify whether the disk should be reconnected at startup.

5. Choose OK.

The disk connection can be used as a virtual hard drive.

Connecting to Shared Printers

Unlike Windows NT, WfW computers cannot read print drivers from a print server.
Before a WfW computer can use a printer that is shared by a Windows NT print
server, the proper print drivers must be installed on the WfW computer.

To install a printer driver in Windows for Workgroups, follow the steps in the following exercise:

Installing Printer Drivers Under WfW

1. Start the Print Manager.

2. Choose the **P**rinter Setup command from the **O**ptions menu.

3. In the Printers box, choose **A**dd to display the **L**ist of Printers box, shown in
   figure 14.12. Browse the list to determine if a driver is available to support your
   printer. If so, select the driver and choose **I**nstall. You will be prompted to insert
   disks from the WfW installation set.

   Unfortunately, the drivers that are included with Windows for Workgroups
   haven't been updated since the product was introduced two years ago, and many
   newer printer models are not directly supported. You might need to supply
   drivers on a floppy disk. To do so, choose Install Unlisted or Updated Printer
   from the **L**ist of Printers box and then choose **I**nstall. You will be prompted to
   enter a path where WfW can locate the print drivers, usually on drive A.

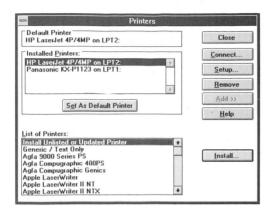

Figure 14.12

Installing a printer in Windows for Workgroups.

4. The new printer will be automatically installed on LPT1:, even if another printer already occupies that port. If you are sharing a workgroup printer on LPT1:, you must assign the network printer to a new port. To do so, do the following:

◆ Choose **C**onnect in the Printers window. The Connect dialog box appears (see fig. 14.13).

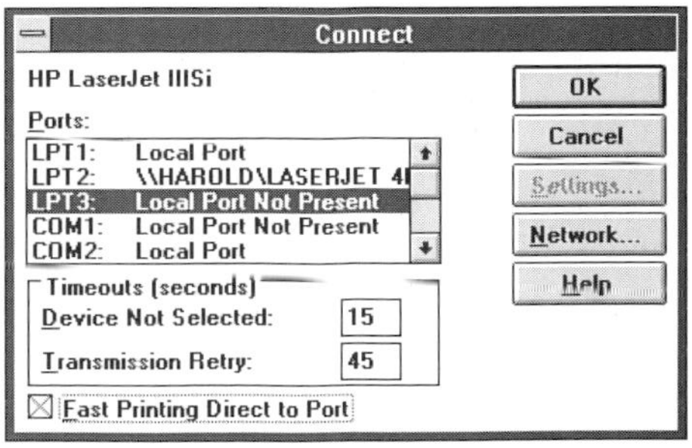

Figure 14.13

Connecting a printer to a port in Windows for Workgroups.

◆ Select an unoccupied port in the **P**orts box.

◆ Choose OK. You will be returned to the Printers dialog box. The printer will now be installed on the port you have selected.

Note   Windows uses background printing through the print manager to enable applications to print without waiting for a printer to become available. The approach works much like spooled printing on a network. Since printing on a network is already being spooled, you can improve network printing performance by enabling WfW to print directly to a port. To make the change, check the box **F**ast Printing Direct to Port in the Connect dialog box.

To enable an installed printer to print to the network, you must connect it to a shared printer. This is also done in Print Manager, as covered in the following exercise:

Connecting to a Shared Printer with WfW

1. Start the Print Manager.

2. Select a printer that is labeled (not shared).

3. Choose **C**onnect Network Printer from the **P**rinter menu. This will display the Connect Network Printer dialog box in which you can browse for a network printer (see fig. 14.14).

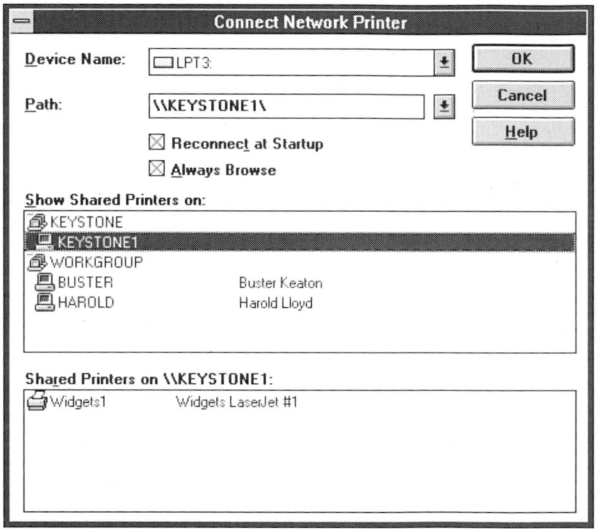

Figure 14.14

Browsing for printers in Windows for Workgroups.

4. Browse for a shareable printer and select it to store the path in the **P**ath box, or enter the path manually.

5. Indicate whether the printer should Reconnec**t** at Startup by checking the box.

6. Choose OK to return to the Connect dialog box. The **P**orts box will now show that the port you specified is connected to the shared network printer.

7. Choose OK to return to the Printer Manager. The printer list will now indicate the resource path to which the printer is connected.

Print Manager need not be running to print to the network unless you are sharing a local printer with a workgroup. WfW will open Print Manager if it is required.

MS-DOS

Objective

B.10

Windows NT Server includes software that enables MS-DOS and Windows 3.1 computers to function as clients on a Windows NT Server network. The client software is called Microsoft Network Client 3.0 for MS-DOS.

Note	Do not use software called Workgroup Connection, which is available from several sources, including CompuServe and the Microsoft TechNet CD-ROMs. Workgroup Connection uses very old technology from the first version of Windows for Workgroups, version 3.1. Workgroup Connection will enable workstations to log on to the network, but does not enable them to take advantage of many Windows NT Server features, such as logon scripts.

Creating an Installation Disk

Objective

B.3

You will need to create installation disks before the client software can be installed on the workstation. Disks are created using the Network Client Administrator utility. To start Network Client Administrator, open the Start menu and choose Programs, Administrative Tools, Network Client Administrator.

When you start the Network Client Administrator, you will see the Network Client Administrator dialog box with several options, shown in figure 14.15.

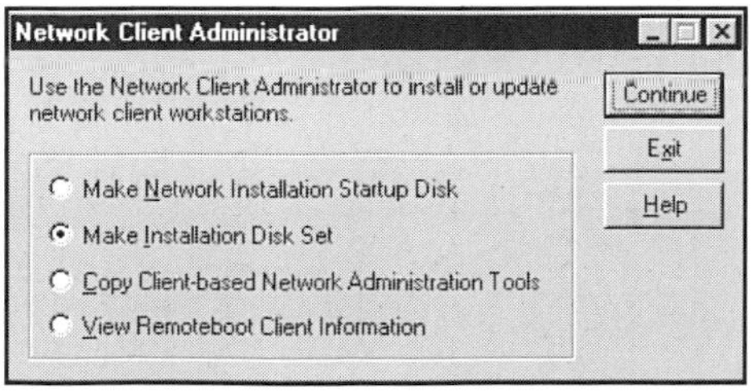

Figure 14.15

The Network Client Administrator options.

The DOS client can be installed in the following two ways:

◆ Using a network installation startup disk that you boot on the workstation. This disk has enough information to connect to the network and download client software from a directory on the server.

◆ Using client installation disks that enable you to manually install the software on the workstation.

Using a network installation startup disk has a number of catches:

◆ The disk must be formatted as a system disk using the same DOS version as the computer on which it will be installed. This can be problematic unless all your PCs have exactly the same DOS version.

◆ The disk must include a driver for the network card that will be on the workstation. Unless all your computers use the same network card, you will need several disks.

◆ It doesn't always work, and you might have to resort to manual installation in any case.

The procedure described here, therefore, involves use of a conventional client installation disk set.

To create the disk set, select the option Make **I**nstallation Disk Set and choose Continue. This will take you to the Share Network Client Installation Files dialog box, shown in figure 14.16.

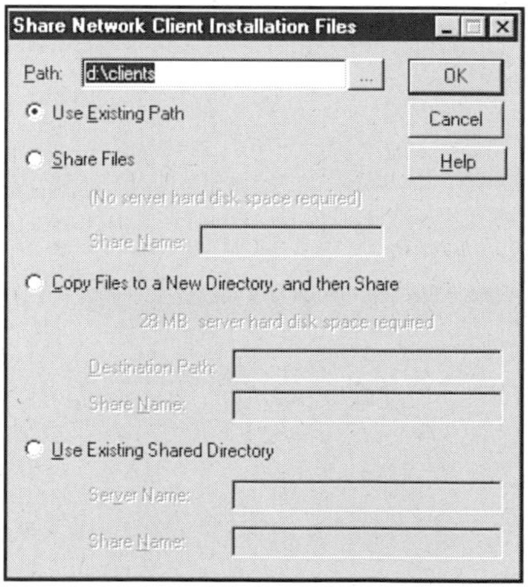

Figure 14.16

Network client installation options.

Network Client Administrator can copy the drivers for various network clients to the server, where they can be available to support client installation using network installation startup disks. Because the method described here uses the client installation disk set, it is not necessary to copy files to the server. They can be copied directly from the Windows NT Server installation media (in my case, a CD-ROM) to the floppies.

To create the installation disk set, follow the steps covered in the following exercise:

Creating Installation Disk Sets

1. Locate two high-density disks. All files on these disks will be erased. Label these disks Network Client v3.0 Disks 1 and 2.

2. Start Network Client Administrator, select the Make Installation Disk Set option, and choose Continue.

3. In the Share Network Client Installation Files dialog box, select Use Existing Path. Be sure that the drive letter in the Path box is correct for your CD-ROM.

4. Choose OK to display the Make Installation Disk Set dialog box shown in figure 14.17.

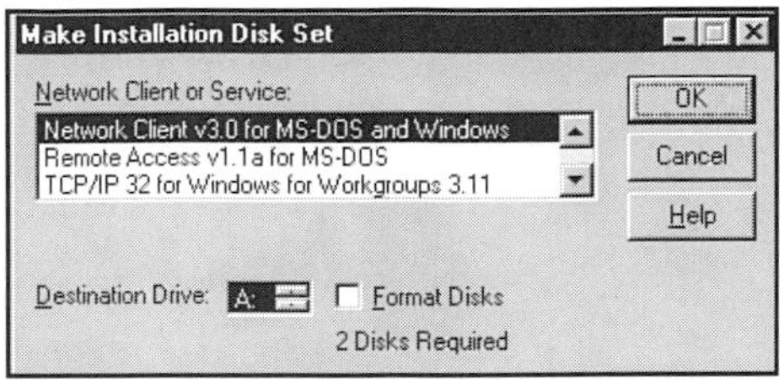

Figure 14.17

Preparing to create client installation disks.

5. In the Network Client or Service box, select Network Client v3.0 for MS-DOS and Windows.

6. Select the Destination Drive you will be using.

7. Check the Format Disks box. It is always a good idea to format. A quick format will be performed if possible to save time.

8. Choose OK and follow the prompts to create the disks.

Installing Network Client for MS-DOS

Objective B.3

Network Client requires MS-DOS version 3.3 or later. To install the Network Client on a DOS PC, follow the steps in the following exercise:

Installing Network Client for MS-DOS

1. Insert Disk 1 and, depending on the drive that holds the disks, type **A:SETUP** or **B:SETUP** from the C: prompt.

2. Press Enter once to reach a screen where you can enter a directory in which files will be installed. The default is C:\NET. Change this path if desired and press Enter.

3. SETUP will examine your PC hardware. You might see the message shown in figure 14.18. Network Client requires a substantial amount of DOS memory. Unless you will be using a memory manager to move programs to upper memory, you will need to do everything you can to conserve memory.

Figure 14.18

The Set Network Buffers message.

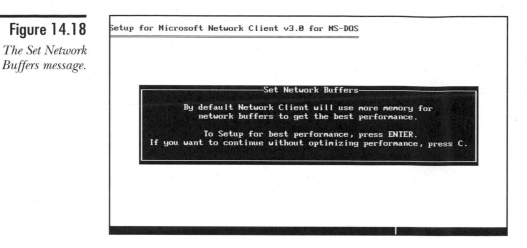

```
Setup for Microsoft Network Client v3.0 for MS-DOS




                      ┌──────────Set Network Buffers──────────┐
                      │  By default Network Client will use more memory for  │
                      │     network buffers to get the best performance.     │
                      │                                                      │
                      │     To Setup for best performance, press ENTER.      │
                      │ If you want to continue without optimizing performance, press C. │
                      └──────────────────────────────────────┘
```

Press Enter if SETUP should maximize performance at the expense of higher memory overhead.

Press C to conserve memory at the cost of reducing performance.

4. Enter a computer name of up to 15 characters. The name can include letters, numbers, and these characters: ! # $ % ^ & ( ) _ ' { } ~, but not spaces.

After you enter a computer name, you will see the screen shown in figure 14.19. This screen accesses three other screens that configure the Network Client. Use the arrow keys to highlight an option, and press Enter to select the option.

Figure 14.19

The main menu in Setup for Network Client v3.0.

```
Setup for Microsoft Network Client v3.0 for MS-DOS

        Names:
             Your User Name is harold

        Setup Options:
             Use the Full Redirector.
             Run Network Client.

        Network Configuration:
             Modify your adapter and protocols with this option.

        ┌──────────────────────────────────────────────┐
        │ Change Names                                   │
        │ Change Setup Options                           │
        │ Change Network Configuration                   │
        │ ██The listed options are correct.████████████  │
        └──────────────────────────────────────────────┘

ENTER=Continue   F1=Help   F3=Exit
```

5. Select the Change Names option to display the screen shown in figure 14.20. The computer name you entered in step 4 will appear in the Change User Name and Change Computer Name fields.

```
Setup for Microsoft Network Client v3.0 for MS-DOS

        This screen allows you to change your user name, computer name,
        workgroup name, and domain name.

        ┌──────────────────────────────────────────────────────────┐
        │ Change User Name      : harold                           │
        │ Change Computer Name  : harold                           │
        │ Change Workgroup Name : WORKGROUP                        │
        │ Change Domain Name    : keystone                         │
        │ The listed names are correct.                            │
        └──────────────────────────────────────────────────────────┘




F1=Help  F3=Exit  ESC=Previous Screen
```

Figure 14.20

Changing Network Client names.

The other fields will show the default entry of WORKGROUP. In the figure, the domain name has been edited.

To change a field, highlight it with the arrow keys and press Enter. Modify the entry in the Change Domain Name field to match the domain this computer will log on to.

6. Select The listed names are correct, and press Enter to save the changes and return to the Setup menu.

7. Select Change Setup Options. This will bring up the screen shown in figure 14.21. This screen has four options that you may choose to modify:

```
Setup for Microsoft Network Client v3.0 for MS-DOS

        This screen enables you to change your redirector,
        startup, logon, and net pop-up options.

        ┌──────────────────────────────────────────────────────────┐
        │ Change Redir Options    : Use the Full Redirector.       │
        │ Change Startup Options  : Run Network Client.            │
        │ Change Logon Validation : Logon to Domain.               │
        │ Change Net Pop Hot Key  : N                              │
        │ The listed options are correct.                          │
        └──────────────────────────────────────────────────────────┘





F1=Help  F3=Exit  ESC=Previous Screen
```

Figure 14.21

Entering setup options.

◆ **Change Redir Options.** You can choose to use the Full Redirector or the Basic Redirector. The Basic Redirector works for many users and saves memory (only 10 K). The Full Director is required to support Microsoft Windows, Remote Access Service, and other advanced functions (110 K).

◆ **Change Startup Options.** You can choose from these options:

Run Network Client. The client runs when the computer is booted.

Run Network Client and Load Pop-Up. The pop-up is a utility that enables you to connect to network resources from a menu interface. It can be easily loaded later if needed.

Do Not Run Network Client. The client software must be started manually.

◆ **Change Logon Validation.** You can choose the following depending on your network model:

Do Not Logon to Domain.

Logon to Domain.

◆ **Change Net Pop Hot Key.** When the NET pop-up utility is loaded, it can be displayed with a hot key, normally Alt+N. You can change the letter for the hot key if it is used by another utility.

When you have configured these options, choose The listed options are correct.

8. Select Change Network Configuration to display the screen shown in figure 14.22, which is used to configure network adapters and protocols.

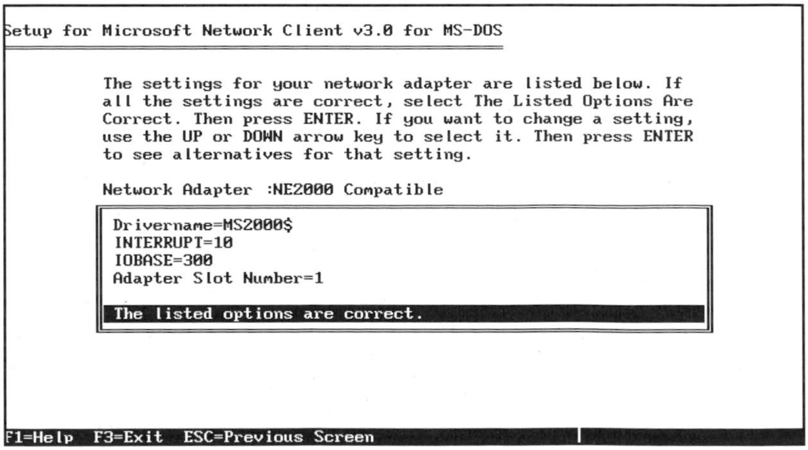

Figure 14.22

Configuring network adapter settings.

```
Setup for Microsoft Network Client v3.0 for MS-DOS

        The settings for your network adapter are listed below. If
        all the settings are correct, select The Listed Options Are
        Correct. Then press ENTER. If you want to change a setting,
        use the UP or DOWN arrow key to select it. Then press ENTER
        to see alternatives for that setting.

        Network Adapter :NE2000 Compatible

        Drivername=MS2000$
        INTERRUPT=10
        IOBASE=300
        Adapter Slot Number=1

        The listed options are correct.



F1=Help  F3=Exit  ESC=Previous Screen
```

9. Examine the network adapter in the Installed Network Adapter(s) box.

   This screen has two boxes: Installed Network Adapters and Protocols and Options. To change the active box, press Tab.

10. If the listed adapter is incorrect, select Remove in the Options box. You will be asked immediately to add a network adapter. Select an adapter from the list provided.

11. To add an adapter, choose Add Adapter and select an adapter from the list provided. To supply a driver for a card that is not listed, choose Network Adapter not Shown on the List Below.

12. Choose Change Settings and review the settings for your adapter. Figure 14.22 shows the settings screen. Change any setting by selecting it and choosing new values from a list.

    The default protocol NWLink is probably the only protocol you will require. If you want to install other protocols, choose Add Protocol.

    ◆ **Microsoft NetBEUI.** Add this protocol if you want to access shared resources on workgroup computers that are not running NWLink.

    ◆ **Microsoft TCP/IP.** Add to support the TCP/IP protocol suite. See Chapter 16, "Using TCP/IP," for more information.

13. Choose Network Configuration Is Correct to return to the Setup menu.

14. After all settings are correct, continue installation by choosing The listed options are correct in the Setup menu.

15. You will be prompted to reboot the computer to activate the network software.

Tip You may rerun the SETUP utility in the network directory to reconfigure options. This is much more efficient than attempting to edit configuration files manually. Do not reconfigure by running SETUP from the client installation disks.

Note Network Client v3.0 uses a significant amount of DOS memory. Unless you optimize memory, you might find that some applications will not run. You might also find that NET commands in logon scripts cannot be run due to memory limitations. Full redirector uses 110 K, while basic redirector uses only 10 K. The basic redirector does not allow for domain logons.

It is strongly recommended that you run a memory manager on all DOS clients. If possible, configure your system without expanded memory because EMS page frames occupy high DOS memory that could be used to relocate DOS TSRs and drivers.

Logging On with Network Client

After the system boots, you can log on to the network.

1. The logon procedure depends on the option you chose for the Startup Option field in Setup.

   ◆ If you chose Run Network Client and Logon to Domain, you will receive the prompt Type your user name. The user name you entered during setup will be presented as a default. Enter a user name or press Enter to accept the default.

   ◆ If you chose Do Not Logon to Domain, you must type the command NET LOGON at the DOS prompt when you want to connect to the network.

2. After you log on, you will be prompted for a workgroup password. Workgroup passwords might be stored in a file. You will be asked if you want to create a password file for this user. The password file has nothing to do with domain security. If you create one, you will need to enter two passwords when logging onto the network, one for the workgroup and another for the domain. It's a whole lot easier to simply respond N so that a local password file is not created.

3. If the DOS client is logging on to a Windows NT Server domain, you will be prompted to enter a domain password.

4. If the full redirector has been loaded, after logging on, any commands in the user's logon script will be executed.

Connecting Drives and Printers with the Workstation Connection NET Pop-Up

Network functions are accessed with the NET utility, which has both a command-line and a pop-up interface. The default hot key for the pop-up utility is Ctrl+Alt+N.

To connect a drive, follow the steps covered in the following exercise:

Connecting Drives with the Workstation Connection Net Pop-Up

1. Activate the NET pop-up by typing **NET**. If it is already loaded, press the hot key to display the Disk Connections dialog box, shown in figure 14.23. Select fields in Disk Connections by pressing the Tab key.

2. If desired, change the drive letter in the Drive field.

3. Connect to a shared directory by entering a path in the Path field and choosing Connect.

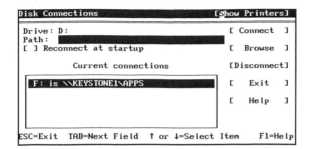

Figure 14.23

Connecting drives with the NET pop-up utility.

4. Choose Reconnect at startup if you want this connection to be reestablished when the Network Client starts up.

5. Press Esc when done.

To connect a printer, follow the steps detailed in the following exercise:

Connecting Drives with the Workstation Connection NET Pop-Up

1. Start the NET utility by typing **NET** or by pressing the hot key if NET is already loaded.

2. Select **S**how Printers to display the Printer Connections box shown in figure 14.24.

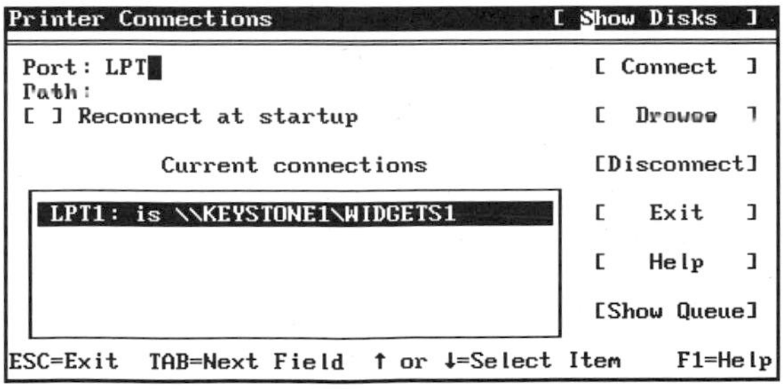

Figure 14.24

Printer Connections in the Network Client pop-up.

3. Select a Port. No default value is provided.

4. Enter a printer path in the Path field and choose Connect to make a connection.

5. Check Reconnect at startup to have this printer connect when the Network Client is started.

6. Press Esc to leave the pop-up utility.

Format of Autogenerated Names

When MS-DOS and Windows 3.x users view files on a Windows NT computer, long file names must be translated to a form that is compatible with the MS-DOS 8.3 file name format. The process of generating 8.3 file name aliases is automated; you have no control over the names that are created. Because the names can be a bit difficult to fathom, this section looks at the rules Windows NT obeys when producing the aliases.

Table 14.1 shows some long file names and their aliases. The first four aliases are easy to understand. Windows NT simply did the following:

◆ Removed spaces.

◆ Retained the first six characters of the file name.

◆ Added a ~ character, followed by a digit from 1–4.

◆ Restored the file name extension.

TABLE 14.1
Converting LFNs to Aliases

LFN	Alias
Annual Report 1990.doc	ANNUAL~1.DOC
Annual Report 1991.doc	ANNUAL~2.DOC
Annual Report 1992.doc	ANNUAL~3.DOC
Annual Report 1993.doc	ANNUAL~4.DOC
Annual Report 1994.doc	ANE9A3~1.DOC
Annual Report 1995.doc	ANF9A7~1.DOC

The first four names aren't difficult to understand, although an important bit of information is lost because the aliases no longer relate to the year associated with the file. You can probably discern how the aliases came about, however.

How in the world did Windows NT get to a name like ANE9A3~1.DOC? After encountering four file names having the same first six characters and extension, Windows NT uses a process called *hashing* to generate characters three through five of the file name. Here are the steps Windows NT used to generate the next two names:

1. Removed spaces.

2. Retained the first two characters of the file name.

3. Hashed characters three through six to obtain the next four characters of the alias.

4. Added a ~ character followed by the digit 1.

5. Restored the file name extension.

Notice that the ANE9A3~1.DOC and ANF9A7~1.DOC both include the characters ~5. Windows will use ~1 in all additional files until hashing the middle characters fails to produce a unique name, and will then use ~2. You might, for example, see files with the names ANE8B4~2.DOC and ANE8B4~6.DOC.

| Note | Programmers are very fond of processes called *hashing* or *hash algorithms* that run data through digital meat grinders. Hashing serves a legitimate purpose, but it isn't something non-programmers need concern themselves with. Just take the hashing part of generating alias names for granted and with a sense of humor. |

Using Network Client Commands

The NET command accepts several command arguments that control functions such as logon, logoff, and resource connections. These commands can be used interactively, but are probably most valuable when included in logon scripts. Examples of logon scripts will be provided in the "Logon Scripts" section, later in this chapter.

Because the NET commands can be used with a variety of network clients, some of the most useful are briefly discussed here.

NET HELP

NET HELP displays a summary of the NET command options. You can display details about any command by including a command as an option. To see a help listing on the LOGON command, for example, type:

```
NET HELP LOGON
```

NET LOGON

NET LOGON initiates a logon dialog. Entered alone, NET LOGON prompts you for a user name and a password. You can also enter the name and password as parameters; for example, buster would log on the default domain or workgroup with the password general like this:

```
NET LOGON BUSTER GENERAL
```

A different domain can be specified with the /domain:*domainname* option. For example:

```
NET LOGON HAROLD CLOCK /DOMAIN:WIDGETS
```

NET LOGOFF

NET LOGOFF breaks your logon connection with the network. If you include the /YES option, you will not be asked to confirm your logoff request.

NET USE

Disks and printers are both connected and disconnected with the NET USE command. To connect drive C to the APPS share on KEYSTONE1, use this command:

```
NET USE C: \\KEYSTONE1\APPS
```

The following command connects LPT1: to printer WIDGETS1 on server KEYSTONE1:

```
NET USE LPT1: \\KEYSTONE1\WIDGETS1
```

Add the option /PERSISTENT:YES to specify connections that should be made when the Workstation Connection starts up.

To see a list of your connected resources, enter the NET USE command without options.

NET VIEW

Use the NET VIEW command to list computers and shared resources. Enter NET VIEW without options to list computers that are sharing resources in your domain.

Include a computer name to list shared resources on the computer. NET VIEW \\KEYSTONE1 lists shared resources on KEYSTONE1.

NET TIME

NET TIME provides a convenient means of synchronizing a computer's clock with the clock on another computer. It is generally preferable to synchronize clocks in a share environment so that users can be assured that time and data stamps are meaningful.

To synchronize a client clock with the computer \\KEYSTONE1, you would use this command:

```
NET TIME \\KEYSTONE1 /SET /YES
```

The /YES parameter carries out the NET TIME command without prompting you for confirmation.

NET START

The NET START command loads services. To unload the pop-up, enter the command:

```
NET START POPUP
```

NET STOP

The NET STOP command unloads services. To unload the pop-up, enter the command:

```
NET STOP POPUP
```

You can stop the default redirector, which disconnects you from the network, by entering the command:

```
NET STOP WORKSTATION
```

NET PASSWORD

Change your password with the NET PASSWORD command. Remember that users can have passwords in several places, including the password list file on the client and the user name database on a domain or workstation.

Entered without parameter, the command prompts you for old and new passwords. You can also include old and new passwords as parameters. To change the password in the client password list file, the command syntax would be:

```
NET PASSWORD oldpassword newpassword
```

To change a password on a specific computer, include the computer name as a parameter. A user name is also required:

```
NET PASSWORD \\WIDGETS1 MABEL oldpassword newpassword
```

To specify a domain, use the /DOMAIN option:

```
NET PASSWORD /DOMAIN:KEYSTONE MABEL oldpassword newpassword
```

> **Note**
>
> When working in MS-DOS, there are actually two passwords to be concerned with. One password is used to access Microsoft workgroup networking and is maintained in a local, encrypted file. Another is your domain password, which is stored in the domain security database.
>
> If you enter the NET PASSWORD command without specifying a computer name, you are updating your local workgroup password.
>
> You must specify a domain name to update your domain password.
>
> Because it is possible to crack the password in the local password file, you should not use the same password for workgroup and domain computing. Better yet, don't create a local workgroup password file. Then you won't be asked for a workgroup password.

Windows 3.1

The Network Client can be used to enable Windows 3.1 computers to access Windows networks. Although Windows 3.1 workstations lack the workgroup features of Windows for Workgroups, they can become clients of Windows NT Server domains and of Windows workgroups.

Installing Networking for Windows 3.1

Network Client should be installed as described in the section "Installing Network Client for MS-DOS," earlier in this chapter. This is a standard DOS installation, and no differences are required when Windows will be supported.

You might be tempted to install the Network Client files in the same directory as Windows, but this will not be permitted. The primary reason is probably that both Windows and Network Client rely on files named SYSTEM.INI, and Setup is not permitted to overwrite the Windows SYSTEM.INI file. (Windows for Workgroups is more fully integrated for networking, and one SYSTEM.INI file serves both WfW and the network drivers.)

After Network Client is installed, reboot the computer. Then start Windows and configure networking as follows:

1. Start the Windows Setup utility in the Main program group.

2. Choose **C**hange System Settings in the Windows Setup **O**ptions menu. This will display the Change System Settings dialog box.

3. Pull down the **N**etwork box in Change System Settings to display a list of network options. From this list, choose the entry Microsoft Network (or 100% Compatible).

4. Choose OK to save the settings. Then close Windows Setup.

5. When you exit Windows setup, you will be told that You need to exit Windows so that the changes you made will take effect. Choose **R**estart Windows to activate networking.

6. You should check two settings in the Control Panel. Start the Network utility in the Control panel.

   ◆ If you want to have connections established in Windows reestablished when Windows starts, check the box **R**estore all Connections at Startup.

   ◆ Normally, you will receive warning messages if network services are not running. To eliminate these messages, check the box **D**isable Warning When Network not Running.

   Choose OK when network settings have been made.

You are now ready to connect to network resources.

Connecting to Network Resources

You can connect to network resources in the following ways:

◆ By entering NET USE commands before starting Windows or from an MS-DOS prompt in Windows. These connections will be reestablished if you include the /PERSISTENT:YES option.

◆ By connecting to files with File Manager and printers with Print Manager. These connections will be reestablished when Windows restarts if you checked the box **R**estore all Connections at Startup in the Network utility of the Control Panel.

Connecting Drives with File Manager

To connect a drive with File Manager, follow the steps in the following exercise:

Connecting Drives with File Manager

1. Choose Network Clients in the **D**isk menu. The Network Connections dialog box is some- what different from the same box in Windows for Workgroups (see fig. 14.25).

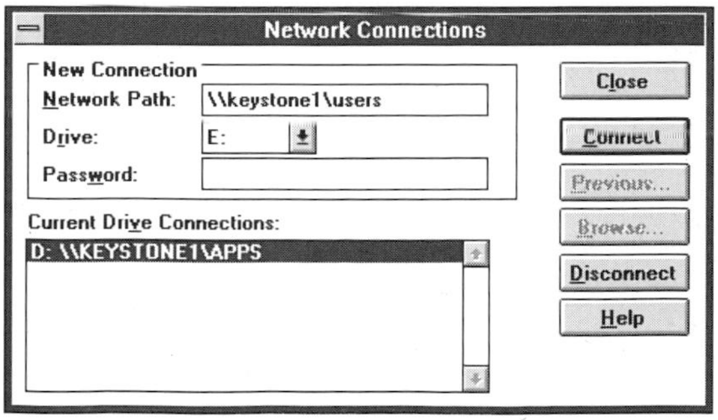

Figure 14.25

Connecting a drive in Windows 3.1.

2. Select an available drive letter in the D**r**ive box.

3. Enter the path in the **N**etwork Path box. The Windows Networking driver does not enable you to browse for network resources.

4. If a password is required for this share, enter it in the Pass**w**ord box.

5. Choose **C**onnect.

6. Choose C**l**ose when all required connections are established.

The drives you have connected can now be used by any Windows program.

Connecting Printers with Print Manager

To connect a printer with Print Manager, follow the steps covered in the following exercise:

Connecting Printers with Print Manager

1. Choose Network Clients in the **O**ptions menu. The Printers - Network Connections dialog box, shown in figure 14.26, will be displayed.

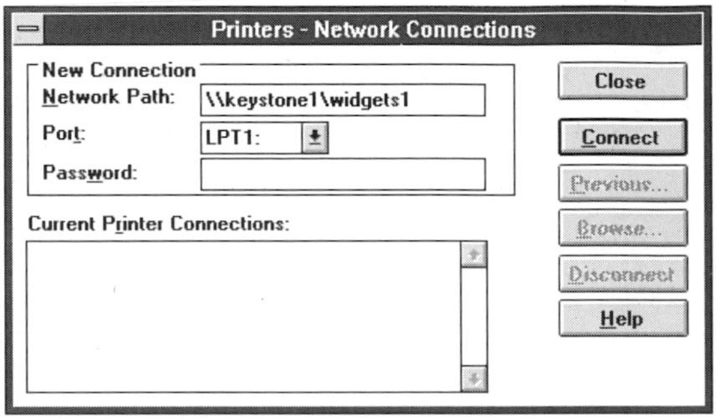

Figure 14.26

Connecting printers with Print Manager.

2. Enter a path in the **N**etwork Path box. As with File Manager, you will be unable to browse for resources.

3. If a password is required for this share, enter it in the Pass**w**ord box.

4. Choose **C**onnect. The printer connection will appear in the Current P**r**inter Connections box.

5. Add other printer connections if desired by selecting other ports and entering the desired paths. Choose **C**onnect to complete each connection.

6. Choose Close to return to the Print Manager.

The printers you have connected can now be used for printing with any Windows program.

Files Used with DOS and Windows Clients

When Microsoft network software is installed on a computer, several files are modified or added. Some of these modifications define parameters that you might need to modify, so it is a good idea to take the time to familiarize yourself with the files discussed in the following sections.

CONFIG.SYS

Windows for Workgroups 3.11 and Network Connection 3.0 require two new lines in the CONFIG.SYS file:

```
LASTDRIVE=Z
DEVICE=C:\NET\IFSHLP.SYS
```

`LASTDRIVE=Z` configures DOS to support drive letters up to Z. (By default, DOS supports drives A through E.)

AUTOEXEC.BAT

If you have configured the computer to start the network automatically when booting, the NET START command will be added to the AUTOEXEC.BAT file, along with an appropriate path to locate the NET.EXE file. For example

```
C:\WINDOWS\NET START
```

Windows for Workgroups performs most network functions within Windows. The Workgroup Connection must perform all network configuration functions from DOS. Workgroup Connection 3.0, therefore, adds some other lines to AUTOEXEC.BAT.

With Network Connection, when protocols other than NetBEUI are loaded, the following command is added to the beginning of AUTOEXEC.BAT to load protocols and drivers without binding them to the Protocol Manager:

```
C:\NET\NET INTTIAI T7F
```

If you are using NWLink with Network Connection 3.0, you will see this line in the AUTOEXEC.BAT file, which loads the NWLink protocol:

```
C:\NET\NWLINK
```

Finally, Network Connection adds a NET START command. With Network Connection, NET START can be configured to log the user on to the network. Windows for Workgroups logs the user on after WfW starts.

PROTOCOL.INI

The PROTOCOL.INI file defines the configuration for the NDIS drivers. If several network card drivers or protocols are being loaded, PROTOCOL.INI can get quite elaborate, so this section will examine only a simple example that loads an NE2000 adapter and the NETBEUI protocol. In general, you will find it much easier to let

Microsoft setup programs build the PROTOCOL.INI file for the hardware you want to support. You will be required to make only small manual modifications to PROTOCOL.INI, if any are needed at all. The file can be modified by any text editor, including the Windows Notepad.

Windows for Workgroups places the PROTOCOL.INI file in the Windows installation directory (usually C:\WINDOWS). Network Client setup places PROTOCOL.INI in the Network Client installation directory.

Here is a listing of a PROTOCOL.INI that was created by Network Client. I have added numbers to the lines to simplify discussion. This section won't go through the file line-by-line, but it will point out some significant features.

```
[network.setup]
version=0x3110
netcard=ms$ne2clone,1,MS$NE2CLONE,1
transport=ms$nwlink,MS$NWLINK
transport=ms$ndishlp,MS$NDISHLP
lana0=ms$ne2clone,1,ms$nwlink
lana1=ms$ne2clone,1,ms$ndishlp

[MS$NWLINK]
FRAME=ETHERNET_802.2
DriverName=nwlink$
BINDINGS=MS$NE2CLONE
[MS$NE2CLONE]
IOBASE=0x300
INTERRUPT=10
DriverName=MS2000$
[MS$AE2]
IOBASE=0x300
INTERRUPT=3
[MS$NE1CLONE]
IOBASE=0x300
INTERRUPT=3

[protman]
DriverName=PROTMAN$
PRIORITY=MS$NDISHLP

[MS$NDISHLP]
DriverName=ndishlp$
BINDINGS=MS$NE2CLONE
```

This file is divided into several sections, each beginning with a label in square brackets; for example, [MS$NDISHLP]. These labels enable network components to locate the lines that are relevant to them.

The [network.setup] section defines the basic characteristics of the network by cross-referencing other sections. The line beginning with netcard, for example, states that the driver to be used is MS$NECLONE, and that parameters for the card can be found in the section [MS$NE2CLONE].

The [protman] section defines parameters for the protocol manager. If additional protocols are added to the NDIS protocol stack, this section tells the protocol manager which protocols have priority.

The [MS$NDISHLP] section supports configuration of the NDIS protocol stack and binds the NE2CLONE driver to the stack. You should not need to edit this section.

Each network board will have a section dedicated to it (in this example, [MS$NECLONE]). This is the only section that is likely to require manual attention if a card is recon- figured or if the setup program will not permit you to enter a setting that your hardware supports.

SYSTEM.INI

A file named SYSTEM.INI is used by Windows and by Network Client. For Windows, this file is located in the Windows installation directory, which is C:\WINDOWS by default.

Network Client Setup will not permit you to install Network Client in the same directory as Windows, so you will have SYSTEM.INI files for both Windows and for Network Client.

SYSTEM.INI in Network Client

For Network Client, SYSTEM.INI has the following structure:

```
[network]
sizworkbuf=1498
filesharing=no
printsharing=no
autologon=yes
computername=HAROLD
lanroot=C:\NET
username=HAROLD
workgroup=WORKGROUP
reconnect=yes
```

```
dospophotkey=N
lmlogon=1
logondomain=KEYSTONE
preferredredir=full
autostart=full
maxconnections=8

[network drivers]
netcard=ne2000.dos
transport=ndishlp.sys,*netbeui
devdir=C:\NET
LoadRMDrivers=yes

[Password Lists]
*Shares=C:\NET\Shares.PWL
HAROLD=C:\NET\HAROLD.PWL
```

You will recognize in this file many of the parameters that you entered when you set up the software. In fact, you can reconfigure most of the startup features of Network Client by editing this file. It is generally more prudent, however, to make changes with the SETUP utility.

Each user who establishes a password list file (PWL extension) on the client will be given an entry in the [Password Lists] section.

SYSTEM.INI in Windows for Workgroups

Windows has a SYSTEM.INI file that contains settings both for Windows and for the network. The changes made to SYSTEM.INI are different for Windows for Workgroups 3.11 and network-enabled Windows 3.1. You will find it useful to scan SYSTEM.INI using either the Windows NOTEPAD or SYSEDIT utilities to identify features that are modified or added when networking is configured.

In WfW, you will find [network] and [Password Lists] sections that serve similar purposes to the sections defined for Network Client, but which might be more elaborate. WfW can share resources in addition to connecting to shares, and extra settings are required in the WfW SETUP.INI file.

Most of the network-related features of SYSTEM.INI can be reconfigured in Windows using the Control Panel or Windows Setup utilities. If you will be editing this file (or any configuration file for that matter), save a backup copy in case you introduce an error.

Windows 95

Objective

B.10

Windows 95 integrates effortlessly into most networks. The details of installation won't be discussed here, but some of the most important features of using Windows 95 in a Windows NT Server network will be covered.

Despite being a 32-bit operating system and a significant enhancement over Windows 3.x, Windows 95 retains many of the underlying technologies that are found in Windows for Workgroups and DOS. If you browse the WINDOWS directory, you will find a PROTOCOL.INI file, for example. All features of Windows 95 networking, however, can be set up from the Control Panel, and manual editing should seldom, if ever, be required.

Installing Windows 95 Networking

The installation program for Windows 95 uses Microsoft's Wizard technology to take you through the procedure step-by-step. Network installation and configuration is highly automated; you will need to do little more than answer a few questions.

During installation, you are asked if you want to identify network adapters in your computer. If you check the Network Adapter box, the Setup Wizard will scan your system for an adapter and will probably succeed in identifying not only the adapter but its settings as well.

> **Note**   If you are using a compatible card, automatic card identification may fail. My card can be configured in two modes, including NE2000 compatible. Windows 95 identified the card by its default mode, and manual configuration was required. It is difficult for automatic configuration to cope with hardware that has multiple personalities. By and large, however, with the most hardware, Windows 95 should set up without a hitch.

After Windows 95 is set up, you can add or reconfigure network adapters using the Network utility, which you start by opening the My Computer icon on the desktop and then choosing Control Panel. Figure 14.27 shows the Network utility after a network adapter has been added and configured. (If you haven't seen Windows 95, take note of the new tabs, which make it easy to flip through various configuration boxes. Just click the tab to select a different set of configuration options.) The following procedures demonstrate how to get to this point.

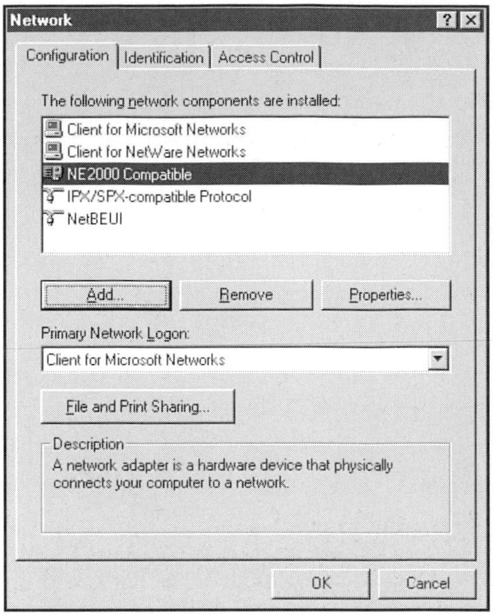

Figure 14.27

*The Network
window with an
installed and
configured
network adapter.*

To add a network adapter under Windows 95, conduct the steps in the following
exercise:

Adding a Network Adapter Under Windows 95

1. Choose **A**dd in the Configuration tab to display the Select Network Component
   Type dialog box (see fig. 14.28).

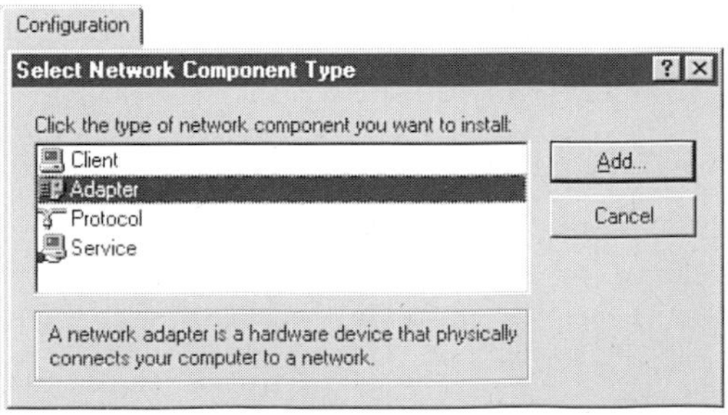

Figure 14.28

*Selecting a
network
component to
install.*

2. In most cases, you will select an adapter and permit Windows 95 to select
   protocols. To select an adapter, click Adapter and choose **A**dd to display the
   Select Network adapters window (see fig. 14.29).

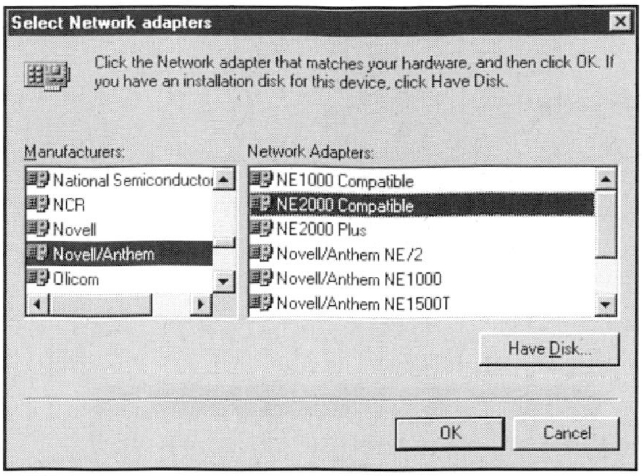

Figure 14.29

Selecting a network adapter.

3. Select Network adapters has two lists of options. First select an entry in the **M**anufacturers list. Then select a specific card in the Network Adapters list. If your card is not supported by drivers shipped by Windows 95, you can supply drivers on a disk by choosing the Have **D**isk button. After specifying an adapter, you will be returned to the Network window, which will be completed, as shown in figure 14.27.

   Notice that support is automatically installed for both Microsoft and NetWare networks. Also, both the NWLink (IPX/SPX compatible) and the NetBEUI protocols are installed. In its default configuration, Windows 95 will integrate smoothly into Windows NT Server, Microsoft workgroup, and NetWare networks.

4. By default, the Primary Network **L**ogon field will be set to Client for Microsoft Networks. You can pull down this list to change the default logon to Client for NetWare Networks or to Windows Logon. Choose Windows Logon if you do not want Windows 95 to access the network each time it is started.

5. To enable sharing, click the **F**ile and Print Sharing button. You can check the following options:

   ◆ I Want to Be Able to Give Others Access to My **F**iles.

   ◆ I Want to Be Able to Allow Others to **P**rint to My Printer(s).

   After you enable these options, the network components list will include File and printer sharing for Microsoft Networks.

6. Select the Identification tab to enter the following information:

   ◆ **Computer Name.** If you will be logging in to a Windows NT Server network, enter your computer name (up to 15 characters).

◆ **Workgroup.** Enter a workgroup name or the name of an Windows NT Server domain.

◆ **Computer Description.** Enter a more extensive identification of the computer, such as your full name.

7. To configure adapter settings, select the adapter in the network components window and choose <u>P</u>roperties. Figure 14.30 shows an example of a Properties dialog box. The options you will have in Properties will depend on your network adapter. The NE2000 Compatible Properties dialog box has three tabs:

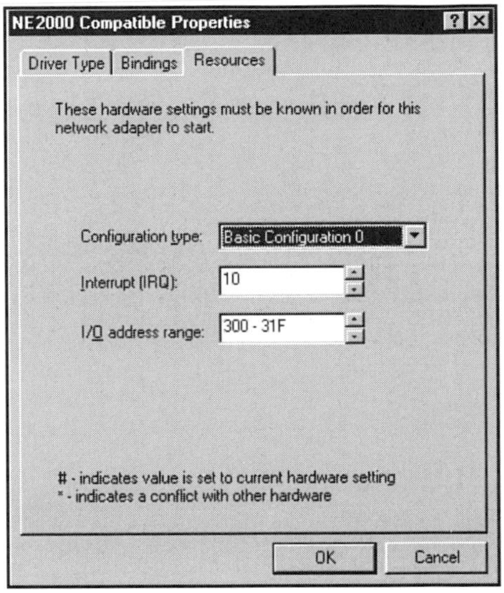

Figure 14.30

Configuring resources for an NE2000 compatible.

◆ Driver Type (16- or 32-bit)

◆ Bindings (protocols)

◆ Resources (network adapter settings)

8. After you have configured network settings, choose OK in the Network window. Respond to the prompts if disk changes are required. Then restart the computer when prompted to activate network support.

Logging On to the Network

When Windows 95 restarts, it should connect to the network. Assuming that you entered a domain name in the workstation identification dialog box, you will be asked to `Type your password to enter the Microsoft Network`.

Windows 95 does not remember your Microsoft Network password; it must be re-entered each time you log on to the network.

Accessing Shared Directories with Windows 95

Windows 95 includes the Network Neighborhood browsing tool, which is installed as a desktop icon. Figure 14.31 shows a series of windows that were opened starting with the Network Neighborhood icon. Eventually, a window for the Keystone1 server was encountered that shows all resources that the server is sharing. Connections to shared directories and printers can be established starting from this window. (Notice that I could have gotten directly to Keystone1 in the Network Neighborhood window, but I wanted to give you a more extensive tour.)

If you prefer, you can also browse the network using the Windows Explorer. The Windows NT and Windows 95 browsing tools are very similar.

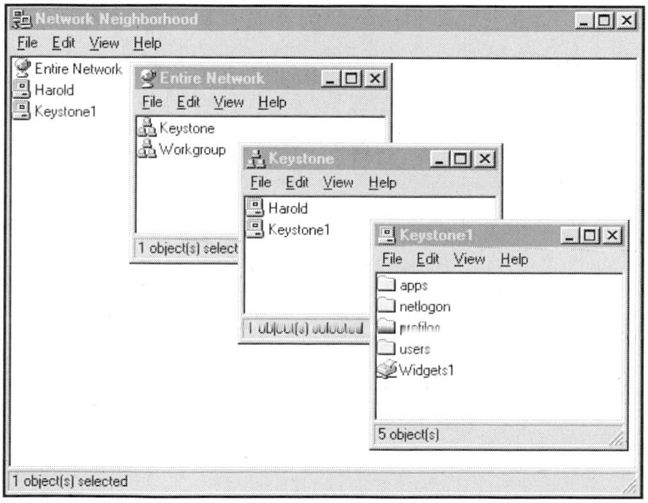

Figure 14.31

Browsing for resources in Windows 95.

Connecting to a Shared Directory

To connect to a shared directory in Windows 95, follow the steps in the following exercise:

Connecting to a Shared Directory Under Windows 95

1. Browse the Network Neighborhood to find the icon for the directory.

2. Point to a shared directory and click the right mouse button (That's right. Finally a version of Windows has put that right mouse button to good use.) to open a command menu that includes the option **M**ap Network Drive.

3. Choose **M**ap Network Drive to display the Map Network Drive dialog box shown in figure 14.32.

4. Choose a different drive letter in the **D**rive box if desired.

5. Check Reconnec**t** at logon to have this connection reestablished when Windows 95 logs you on to the network.

6. Choose OK when settings are complete. A new drive window will be created on your desktop. It will also be added to the My Computer window.

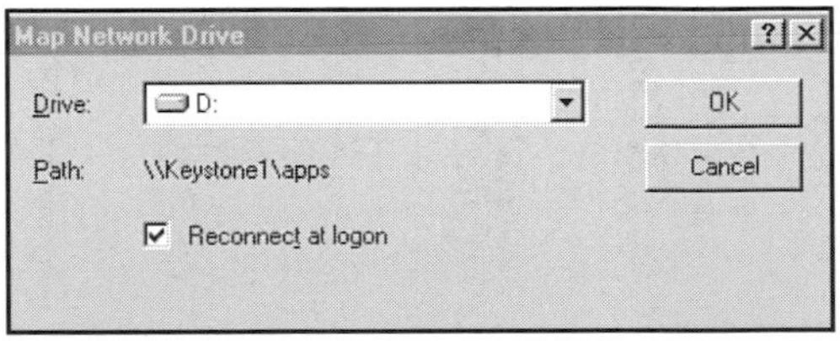

Figure 14.32

Connecting to a shared directory with Windows 95.

Connecting to a Shared Printer

Before you can connect to a shared printer, you must first install printer drivers on Windows 95. Adding printers is controlled by a wizard. To start the wizard, choose the Add Printer icon in the Printers folder of the My Desktop window.

The Add Printer Wizard asks you if you are creating a local or network printer. If you create a network printer, the wizard gives you the option of selecting a shared printer. Windows 95 can identify the printer driver that is required for the shared printer, but cannot load the driver from the server as Windows NT can do. After identifying printer type, the wizard will copy appropriate drivers from your installation disks.

To connect to a shared printer after a printer has been installed, follow the steps in the following exercise:

Connecting to a Shared Printer Under Windows 95

1. Browse the Network Neighborhood to find the icon for the printer.

2. Point to a shared printer and click the right mouse button to open a command menu that includes the option **C**apture Printer Port.

3. Choose **C**apture Printer Port to open the Capture Printer Port dialog box (see fig. 14.33).

4. Change the port in the **D**evice box if desired.

5. Check Reconnect at logon to have this connection reestablished when Windows 95 logs you on to the network.

6. Choose OK when settings are complete.

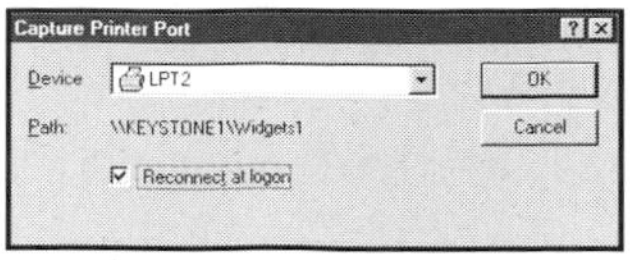

Figure 14.33

Capturing a printer port in Windows 95.

Using Windows NT Server Tools for Windows 95

Objective
C.3

Several of the Windows NT Server management tools are available in versions that can be run under Windows 95. The following tools are supported under Win32s: User Manager for Domains, Server Manager, Event Viewer, Print Manager for Windows NT Server, and File Manager.

To install Server Tools for Windows 95, conduct the steps in the following exercise:

Installing Windows 95 Server Tools

1. Open the Control Panel.

2. Open the Add/Remove Programs utility.

3. Select the Windows Setup tab.

4. Choose **H**ave Disk and specify a path to locate the \Clients\Srvtools\Win95 directory on the Windows NT Server 4 installation CD-ROM. This CD-ROM can be directly attached to the PC or can be accessed through a network share.

5. Choose OK.

6. Check the box next to Windows NT Server Tools and choose **I**nstall. Files are copied to the \srvtools directory.

7. Choose OK after files are copied.

8. Edit the PATH statement in the computer's AUTOEXEC.BAT file to include a path to the C:\SRVTOOLS directory. Add the text ;c:\srvtools to the end of the PATH statement, for example.

9. Restart the computer.

The installation program creates a Windows NT Server Tools program group in the Start/Programs menu. It also extends the capabilities of Windows Explorer to enable you to manage the security settings of an NTFS drive or a printer on a Windows NT computer.

> **Note** When you use the Server Tools for Windows 95, you will, from time-to-time, be asked to log on and enter your password. This procedure is required when you are logging on to a new server and is necessary to ensure that you have administrative privileges on the server.

> **Caution** You can use the Windows 95 version of User Manager for Domains to establish trust relationships, but you cannot verify that the links are established. Be especially careful that you enter correct user names and passwords when configuring a trust relationship.

Objective B.10 Logon Scripts

Logon scripts are an effective way to configure Windows NT Server clients when they are logging on to the network. Logon scripts are particularly effective for configuring a group of users so that they log on with the same set of drive and printer connections.

A logon script is usually a batch file, and has a BAT file name extension for DOS and for Windows clients. Program files with the EXE extension can also be executed as logon scripts.

The name of a user's logon script is specified in the user's account profile. The procedure for specifying logon script names was described in Chapter 11, "Managing Users and Groups."

By default, logon scripts are stored in the directory C:\WINNT\SYSTEM32\REPL\ IMPORT\SCRIPTS. In most cases, you won't want to change this location, particularly if you are operating a domain with more than one domain controller because you will want to use directory replication to copy logon scripts to all domain controllers in the domain.

When users log on to a domain, their logons can be authenticated by any active domain controller. If a logon script is specified for the user, the domain controller will look for the script on the local directory that matches the logon script directory location defined for the domain. In other words, each domain controller looks for logon scripts on its local C drive.

You can use the Windows NT Server Replicator service to replicate copies of logon scripts from one domain controller to all other DCs in the domain. The procedure for replicating files is described in Chapter 22, "Managing Directory Replication."

Logon Script Example

Logon scripts don't need to be elaborate. The following is an example of a logon script that defines resources by department. It might be set up for Widgets Engineering:

```
@echo off
net time \\keystone1\set /yes
net use g: \\keystone1\apps /yes
net use s: \\widgets1\status /yes
net use lpt1: \\widgets1\laser1 /yes
```

This script uses NET TIME to synchronize each client workstation to the clock of KEYSTONE1. By synchronizing all clients to the same clock, you know that you can rely on the time and date stamps on files.

The /YES option is included with each command and has two effects. First, /YES eliminates the need for users to respond to any prompts. Second, /YES ensures that these settings will replace any persistent settings that users have established.

> **Tip**
>
> Because Windows for Workgroups users generally log on to the network after WfW has started, logon scripts execute in a virtual DOS session.
>
> Logon scripts are simply batch files, and they can contain any batch file commands that are valid in the user's operating system environment. If you want to know more about DOS batch files, I recommend New Riders Publishing's outstanding and extensive *Inside MS-DOS 6.22*.

Testing Your Knowledge

1. Windows for Workgroups and Windows 95 are both _____-to-_____ networkable.

2. Windows for Workgroups can be setup to connect to either a LAN Manager or NT domain.

    A. True

    B. False

3. Why should you use the Enable Network DDE startup settings option only if necessary?

   A. DDE is an outdated technology.

   B. It uses an additional 50 KB of memory.

   C. It may require additional protocols to be loaded.

4. If you are logging onto a domain with Windows for Workgroups, you cannot utilize the Save password option.

   A. True

   B. False

5. Just as with Windows NT, WfW computers can read print drivers from a print server.

   A. True

   B. False

6. You can improve network printing performance from a WfW workstation by letting the network spool the print job instead of using background printing. This option is selected by choosing the Connect option in the Printers window, and checking which option?

   A. Enable Network spooling

   B. Fast Printing Direct to Port

   C. Disable background printing

7. Windows NT Server includes software that enables MS-DOS and Windows 3.1 computers to function as clients on a Windows NT Server network. The client software is called _____.

8. What NT tool is used to create client installation disks?

   A. Client Administrator

   B. Network Client Administrator

   C. Client Network tool

   D. Client Installation Administrator

9. Network Client requires MS-DOS version 3.0 or later.

   A. True

   B. False

10. When entering a name for a Microsoft client computer, what characters and length is permitted?

   A. ! # $ % ^ @ ( ) _ ' { } ~ and 12 characters

   B. ! # $ % ^ @ ( ) _ ' [ ] ~ and 24 characters

    C. ! # $ % ^ & ( ) _ ' [ ] ~ and 32 characters

    D. ! # $ % ^ & ( ) _ ' { } ~ and 15 characters

11. What is the default protocol used on a Microsoft client computer?

    A. NetBEUI

    B. NWLink IPX/SPX

    C. TCP/IP

    D. DLC

12. What is the default hot key for the Net pop-up utility?

    A. Ctrl+Alt+P

    B. Ctrl+Alt+N

    C. Ctrl+Shift+P

    D. Ctrl+Shift+N

13. MS-DOS and Windows 3.1 client can not see NT files that are not 8.3 compliant.

    A. True

    B. False

14. What is the command line to list coputers and share resources?

    A. NET USE

    B. NET LIST

    C. NET VIEW

    D. NET BROWSE

15. Network clients are installed in the same fashion for Windoes 3.1 clients as are MS-DOS clients.

    A. True

    B. False

16. Which of the following files is not used with both DOS and Windows clients?

    A. CONFIG.SYS

    B. AUTOEXEC.BAT

    C. PROTOCOL

    D. WIN.INI

    E. SYSTEM.INI

17. Windows 95 does away with the PRotocol.INI file.

    A. True

    B. False

18. Installing NT client support for Windows 95 is done locally at the Windows 95 workstation with a setup wizard.

    A. True

    B. False

19. Windows 95 can auto-detect installed network adapter cards with its plug-and-play funtionality.

    A. True

    B. False

20. Windows 95 does not remember your Microsoft Network password; it must be reentered each time you log on to the network.

    A. True

    B. False

21. To connect to a shared directory with Windows 95, simply browse the Network Neighborhood to locate the desired directory and then right-click on it and choose the _____ option.

22. When connecting a Windows 95 client to a shared printer, it can load the printers driver from the server just as Windows NT does if the NT Server has the 95 drivers available.

    A. True

    B. False

23. Windows 95 can not be enabled to administer an NT Server.

    A. True

    B. False

24. By default, which NT Server directory stores logon scripts?

    A. C:\WINNT\SYSTEM32\REPL\IMPORT\SCRIPTS

    B. C:\WINNT\SYSTEM\REPL\IMPORT\SCRIPTS

    C. C:\WINNT\SYSTEM32\REPL\SCRIPTS

    D. C:\WINNT\SYSTEM32\IMPORT\REPEL\SCRIPTS

Review Answers

1. peer-to-peer
2. A
3. B
4. B
5. B
6. B
7. Microsoft Network Client 3.0 for MS-DOS
8. B
9. B
10. D
11. B
12. B
13. B
14. C
15. A
16. D
17. B
18. A
19. A
20. A
21. Map Network Drive
22. A
23. B
24. A

CHAPTER 15

Using Windows NT Clients

B ecause Windows NT computers are the most capable clients of a Windows NT Server network, I have used Windows NT to demonstrate most of the functions discussed in this book.

In Chapter 12, "Sharing Drives, Directories, and Files," you saw how Windows NT computers could connect to shared directories. And in Chapter 13, "Managing Printing Services," you saw how easy it is to access a shared printer from a Windows NT computer.

Even though Windows NT clients are discussed in other chapters, I will summarize them briefly in this chapter.

Windows NT Workstation Clients

A Windows NT Workstation client consists of three general components:

◆ Network protocol

◆ Network client redirector

◆ Resource configuration

This section demonstrates installation and configuration of these components. When you have completed this chapter, you will be able to do the following:

◆ Install and configure network protocols

◆ Install and configure client redirector

◆ Log on and log off a Windows NT Workstation as a local or domain user

◆ Connect to and disconnect from shared network drives

◆ Share and stop sharing local drives

◆ Connect to and disconnect from shared network printers

◆ Share and stop sharing local printers

◆ Identify troubleshooting tools available on Windows NT Workstation

The following sections assume that Windows NT has been installed and that a network adapter is installed in the workstation and is connected to the network. The Windows NT Workstation CD-ROM is also required.

The network protocol installation process demonstrated here is the same as the network protocol installation process for a new workstation installation.

Installing a Windows NT Client

Windows NT Workstation ships with four network protocols:

◆ NetBEUI

◆ NWLink (IPX/SPX Compatible Transport Protocol)

◆ TCP/IP

◆ DLC (Data Link Control protocol)

The next section steps you through installing the TCP/IP protocol. This is actually the most complex of the three protocols to configure. Having accomplished the TCP/IP installation, NetBEUI and IPX/SPX are child's play.

Installing the TCP/IP Protocol

1. Start the Windows NT Workstation and log on.

2. Double-click the Network applet in Control Panel. Because no network is installed, you are prompted to install Windows NT Networking.

3. Click the Yes button. Windows NT Setup starts. You are prompted for the path to the Windows NT distribution files. Enter the path to the install directory for the Windows NT workstation (usually D:\I386, where D is your CD-ROM device) and click the Continue button.

4. Setup takes a few moments to prepare network adapter driver choices. The Network Adapter Card Detection dialog box prompts for autodetection of the network adapter. Click the Continue button to let Setup attempt to detect the make and model of the installed network adapter.

Note | Sometimes, Setup cannot detect a network adapter if the network adapter is a Plug and Play device and the Plug and Play feature is enabled. You may need to disable Plug and Play per the manufacturer's instructions.

5. If autodetection succeeds, Setup prompts for confirmation. If the card listed in the dialog box is correct, click the Continue button and skip to step 9 in this exercise.

6. If autodetection fails, you are prompted either to install Remote Access Services or to select a network adapter, which you may need to do manually (see fig. 15.1). Click the Continue button to select a network adapter manually.

> **Note** If autodetection fails, Setup assumes that either it did not find a network adapter or there is no network adapter installed. If there is no network adapter installed on the workstation, Setup thinks that you want to install the Windows NT Remote Access Service (dial-up networking), hence the **R**emote button on the dialog box shown in figure 15.1.

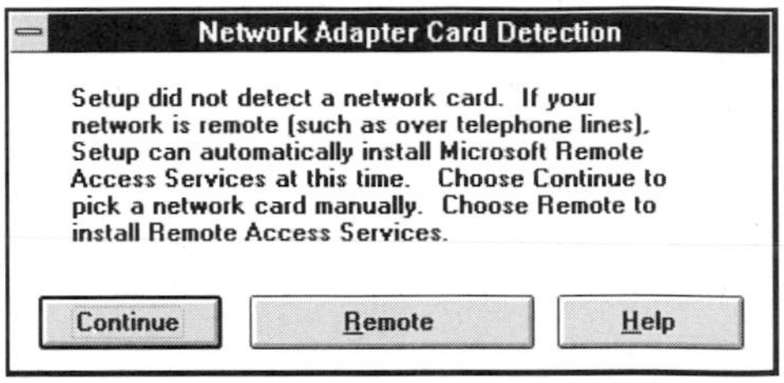

Figure 15.1

If Setup cannot detect the network adapter, you will need to perform a manual installation.

Network Adapter Card Detection

Setup did not detect a network card. If your network is remote (such as over telephone lines), Setup can automatically install Microsoft Remote Access Services at this time. Choose Continue to pick a network card manually. Choose Remote to install Remote Access Services.

[Continue] [Remote] [Help]

7. The Add Network Adapter dialog box appears. Select the appropriate make and model for your network adapter from the Network Adapter Card drop-down list and click the Continue button.

8. A network adapter card setup dialog box appears. Setup does not always detect network adapter settings correctly. Confirm that the settings listed are correct and modify as necessary. Click the Continue button.

   The Adapter Card Setup dialog box varies with network adapter manufacturer and model. Many network adapters require no configuration and step 8 is skipped.

9. After network adapter identification, Setup offers a choice of three network protocols to install (NetBEUI, TCP/IP, IPX/SPX). Select the TCP/IP check box and click the Continue button.

10. Windows NT Workstation offers quite a few TCP/IP options, as shown in figure 15.2. Complete the Windows NT TCP/IP Installation Options dialog box as follows:

    ◆ **TCP/IP Internetworking.** The minimum TCP/IP implementation. This component is required.

    ◆ **Connectivity Utilities.** Utility toolbox that includes the command-line tools such as Finger, FTP, and Telnet. Install these—they'll be very useful.

    ◆ **SNMP Service.** Simple Network Management Protocol. Select this option if you use SNMP network management tools on your network. Your network administrator can tell you whether this should be selected.

    ◆ **TCP/IP Network Printing Support.** Select this option if your network uses Unix print services and you want to print to Unix print devices from the Windows NT workstation.

◆ **FTP Server Services.** Select this option to provide file transfer services to FTP clients.

◆ **Simple TCP/IP Services.** Services include the TCP/IP character generator, echo, and quote of the day. These services come from the Unix TCP/IP world and may be used on your network if you have Unix devices connected.

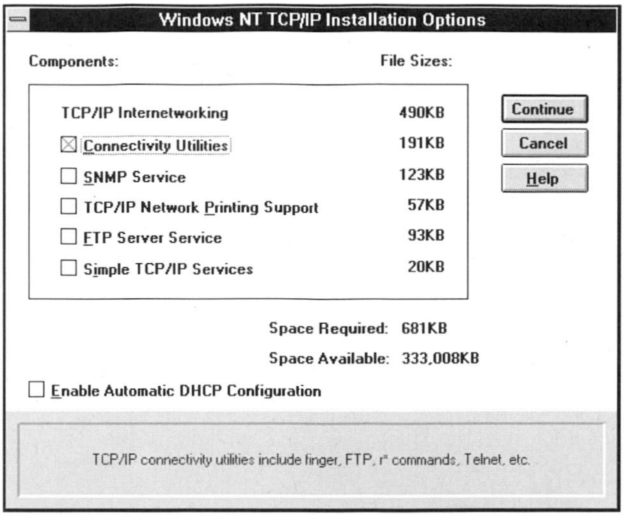

Figure 15.2

A good collection of TCP/IP add-ons.

11. After selecting desired TCP/IP options and clicking the OK button, the next dialog box presented is Network Settings (see fig. 15.3). Although you may be tempted to begin configuring the protocols and network adapter here, resist the urge. Click the OK button.

12. After Setup copies the necessary files and configures the preliminary installation, the TCP/IP Configuration dialog box appears, as shown in figure 15.4. Complete this dialog box as follows:

◆ **Adapter.** Confirm that this is the correct network adapter make and model.

◆ **Enable Automatic DHCP Configuration.** Select this check box if DHCP is being employed.

If DHCP is not being used, complete the following fields:

◆ **IP Address.** Enter a unique IP address for this client.

◆ **Subnet Mask.** Enter the subnet mask for the client IP address.

◆ **Default Gateway.** If the client is on a routed network, enter the IP address of the default router port.

◆ **Primary WINS Server.** If you are using Windows Internet Naming Service server, enter the address of the primary server.

◆ **Secondary WINS Server.** IP address of a secondary WINS server, if applicable.

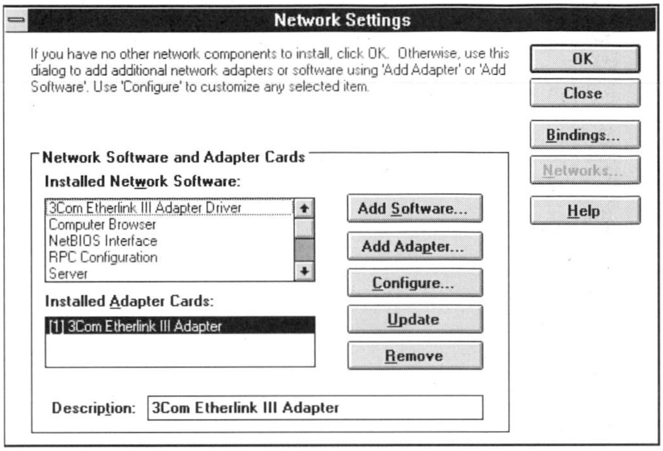

Figure 15.3

The Windows NT Network Settings dialog box is the heart of network configuration.

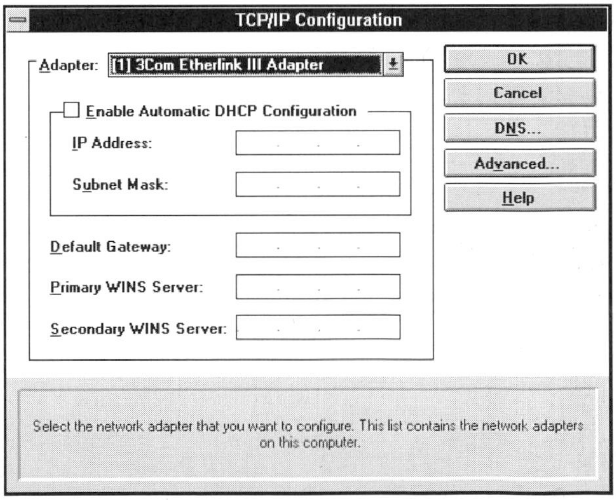

Figure 15.4

The Windows NT TCP/IP Configuration dialog box. Look familiar?

13. Click on the DNS button. The DNS Configuration dialog box appears, as shown in figure 15.5. Complete the DNS Configuration dialog box as follows:

◆ **Host Name.** Should be the same name as the Microsoft Network name for the client.

◆ **Domain Name.** Name of your network's TCP/IP domain. This domain name is not the Windows NT domain name. It is a TCP/IP domain name that is used by DNS to manage host names. Your network administrator should know the correct TCP/IP domain name.

◆ **Domain Name Service (DNS) Search Order.** Enter the IP addresses of DNS servers on your network and set the order in which you want the client to search when attempting to resolve names.

◆ **Domain Suffix Search Order.** Enter up to six domain suffixes that are appended to the name to be resolved.

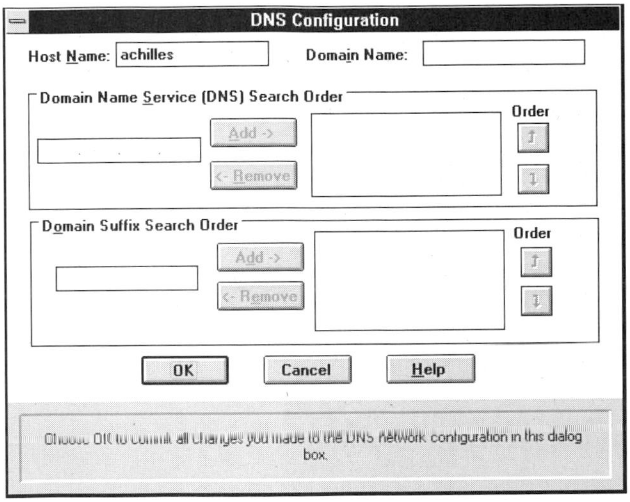

Figure 15.5

The DNS Configuration dialog box.

14. Click the OK button to return to the main TCP/IP Configuration dialog box.

15. Click the Advanced button to get to the Advanced Microsoft TCP/IP Configuration dialog box (see fig. 15.6). Complete this box as follows:

◆ **IP Address and SubnetMask.** These options are used if the client workstation has two network adapters installed or if more than one IP address is assigned to a single network adapter.

◆ **Default Gateway.** If the client is installed on a routed network segment with more than one router connected, specify the IP addresses of the other routers and set the order in which they are sent out-of-segment packets.

◆ **Enable DNS for Windows Name Resolution.** Domain Name Service provides host name resolution on IP-based networks. Select this option if you employ a DNS server on your network. The client workstation must know the address of the DNS server; DNS must therefore be configured if this option is selected (see step 13).

◆ **Enable LMHOSTS Lookup.** The LMHOSTS file is a text database of NetBIOS computer names and their respective IP addresses. This enables a client to reference other clients without WINS name resolution. The LMHOSTS file is usually stored locally on each client workstation. This is a useful option for small, stable, routed networks. It is not required on non-routed networks.

◆ **Scope ID.** WINS resolution may be restricted by assigning scope IDs in the WINS server configurations. This field associates the client with one of the defined WINS scopes. When Scope ID is defined on the WINS servers, a member of a given scope can only "see" other members of that scope. Use this feature with care.

◆ **Enable IP Routing.** If the client has more than one network adapter installed and configured with TCP/IP, this option allows routing between the two cards.

◆ **Enable WINS Proxy Agent.** Selecting this option makes the client emulate a WINS server for remote clients. A WINS server must be implemented on the network in order to use this option.

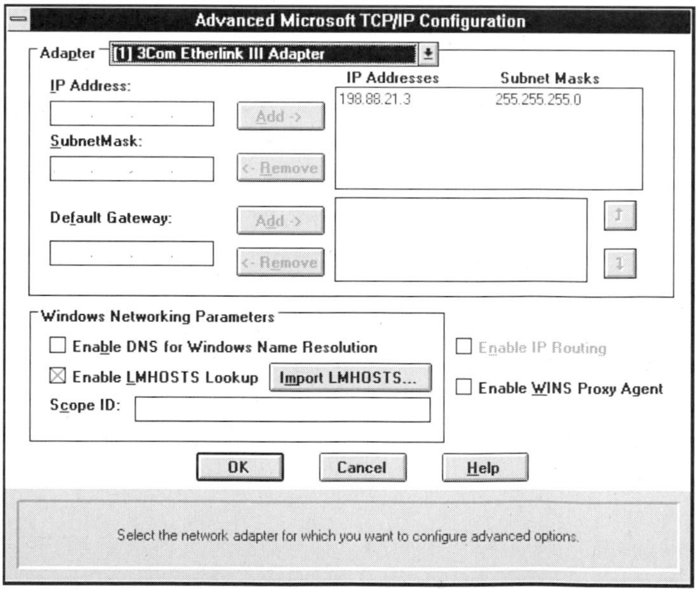

Figure 15.6

The Windows NT Advanced Microsoft TCP/IP Configuration dialog box.

16. Click the OK button.

17. You are returned to the main TCP/IP Configuration dialog box. Click the OK button to save your work. Setup opens a domain configuration dialog box.

18. Windows NT Workstation now wants you to select a domain or workgroup. Enter either a workgroup name or a domain name, depending on your network design. If this workstation is to belong to a domain, then a computer account must be added to the domain. Workgroups cannot be added to a domain and do not need a computer account. Complete the dialog box (shown in figure 15.7) as follows:

   ◆ **Member of.** Select the workgroup or authenticating domain for this workstation.

   ◆ **Create Computer Account in Domain.** This option is active only when a domain is selected. Enter the user name and password for an account that already exists on the target domain. The user account entered must have the right to add workstations to the domain (Administrator is the best choice and is most commonly used).

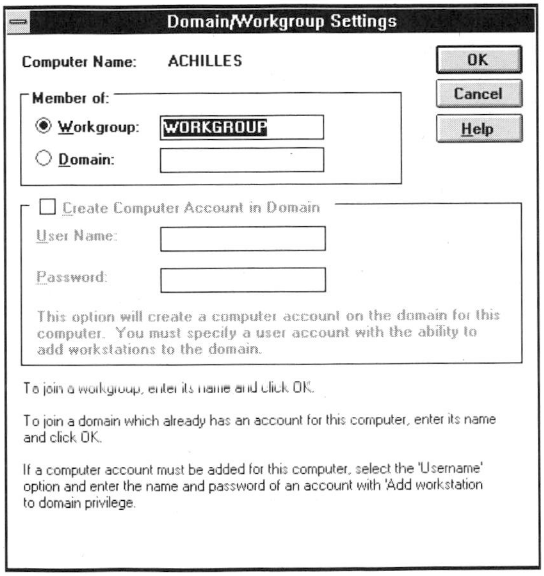

Figure 15.7

Domain/ Workgroup selection can be tricky stuff.

Note The settings in the **C**reate Computer Account in Domain section of the Domain/ Workgroup Settings dialog box are probably as clear as mud to most people. What is not conveyed to the user is the fact that a Windows NT Workstation must join the domain if you want to use domain resources. When a Windows NT Workstation joins a domain, it has an account on that domain the same as any user. Although a computer and user account are similar in name, their purposes are much different. Note that the check box label in figure 15.7 says Create *Computer* Account in Domain.

continues

In order for a user to log on to a domain from a Windows NT Workstation, a valid user name, password, and workstation account are required.

In order for a workstation to join a domain, it requires the assistance of a user with explicit rights to add workstations to the domain; this user is generally the administrator.

19. When the Windows NT Workstation has successfully joined the target domain, a success dialog box appears.

Logging On from a Windows NT Client

The mechanics of logging on to a Windows NT Workstation are simple. The more important aspect of logging on is the type of logon performed (local or domain) and the difference between the two. At the end of this section, you will understand:

◆ Logon and logoff procedures

◆ Local logons

◆ Domain logons

Logon and Logoff Procedures for Windows NT Workstation

There are three ways to get to a Windows NT logon dialog box:

◆ Restart the workstation and press Ctrl+Alt+Del after Windows NT starts.

◆ If a user is already logged on to the Windows NT Workstation, press Ctrl+Alt+Del while running Windows NT. A Security Manager dialog box appears. One of the options in the Security Manager dialog box is Logon.

◆ If a user is already logged on to the Windows NT Workstation, choose the Logon option from either the File menu or the System menu in Program Manager.

In any case, you are prompted for a user name, a password, and the user account database to which you want to authenticate. The logon dialog box also has a drop-down list labeled From. The From drop-down list contains any domains known to the Windows NT workstation and the computer name for the local workstation. The From field defaults to the domain or name used at last logon.

Selecting the computer name in the From field facilitates a local logon using the user accounts database. Using a domain name logs on to the selected network domain and its domain user accounts database.

Local Logons

When you logon using the computer name in the From field, you are logged on locally. In order to log on locally, you must have a valid user name defined on the Windows NT workstation local accounts database. The local logon to this user name gives you all of the permissions defined for that user account. These permissions are limited to the local workstation.

A local logon may have external permissions if the workstation belongs to a workgroup rather than a domain. If a given user has a local user account on another Windows NT workstation, for example, he may connect to permitted resources on the remote machine. If the remote Windows NT workstation password is the same as the local password, then such a connection is completed without a password prompt.

A user logged on to a Windows NT workstation that is a member of a workgroup can connect to and share resources with other members of that workgroup.

Domain Logons

When you log on using a domain name in the From field, you are logging on to a domain's user account database. Two things must be true to achieve a successful domain logon:

◆ The logon user account must be valid and known to the authenticating domain.

◆ The Windows NT workstation must be a member of that domain.

> **Note**   Joining a domain is unique to Windows NT Workstation. None of the other workstation platforms that have been addressed in this chapter have a domain membership attribute.
>
> Domain membership for a Windows NT workstation is mutually exclusive; that is, a given Windows NT workstation may belong to only one domain at a time. If you want to log on to a second domain, the Windows NT workstation must relinquish membership in the first domain.
>
> Windows NT workstation may access resources in other domains if the appropriate trust relationship(s) exists between the domains.

As stated at the beginning of this section, the mechanics of logging on and off a Windows NT Workstation are not nearly as important as understanding the differences between local and domain logons.

User Profiles

User profiles are exceptionally rich tools for configuring users' network environments. Unfortunately, profiles can only be used with Windows NT and Windows 95 clients, but that's simply because profiles take advantage of capabilities that aren't supported by other operating systems.

In Chapter 11, "Managing Users and Groups," you learned to assign a profile path to a user's account properties. In this chapter, you will learn the details about setting up and managing user profiles.

To this point, you haven't seen how versatile and powerful profiles are. Profiles can do everything that logon scripts can do, but they also are capable of almost fully describing the user's Windows NT computing environment.

<table>
<tr><td>Objective
C.2</td></tr>
</table>

Planning User Profiles

When users work on a stand-alone Windows NT Workstation, each user account maintains a local personal profile that is stored on the workstation. Local user profiles maintain users' personal settings from session to session. These local profiles are created automatically when the user account is created. Guests are the only users who do not maintain local user profiles.

Things change when a user of a Windows NT computer logs on to a Windows NT Server network. If a user account is assigned a network profile, the network profile will replace the local profile when the user logs on to a domain. A user can access his or her network profile while logging on from any Windows NT computer on the network. For this reason, network-based profiles are called *roaming profiles*.

This approach has the following two benefits:

◆ Profiles can be centrally administered.

◆ Users can obtain the same profile when logging on to different Windows NT computers.

User profiles can be deployed in several ways:

◆ Individual users can be given personal profiles that maintain their settings on an individual basis.

◆ Individual profiles can be configured to restrict the modifications users can make. This ensures that the user always logs on to a standard environment.

◆ Groups of users can be given the same profile, which they can modify for a specific session only.

◆ Users and groups of users can be given a common profile that they are restricted from modifying.

Two types of profiles can be defined: personal and mandatory. In addition, there is a default profile that users access if they have not been assigned a profile. Each profile type has useful features.

Note Users on a Windows NT computer also have a locally cached profile that is used when the network profile is unavailable: for example, when the user logs on to a workstation local account rather than a domain account. The locally cached profile also is used when the user account has not been assigned a network profile.

Locally cached profiles exist only on individual computers. If a user logs on to another Windows NT computer, a different locally cached profile will be used.

User Profile Folders

Each user who has an account in a Windows NT 4 domain can be assigned a profile folder in which the user's personal settings can be stored from session to session. As shown for the user Buster in figure 15.8, this directory supports a directory structure used to store session configuration data in several areas. The folders and their purposes are:

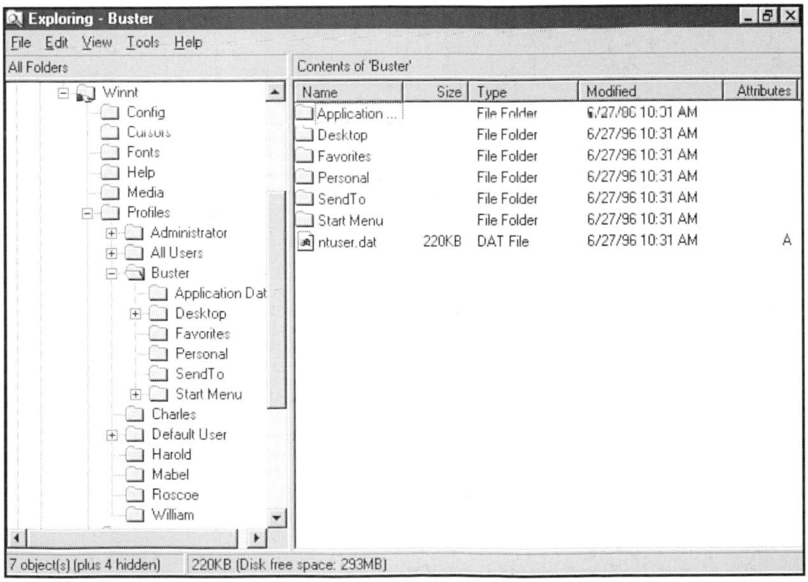

Figure 15.8

Structure of a user's profile folder.

◆ **Application Data.** Stores application-specific data for some Windows applications, such as personal settings for Word for Windows.

◆ **Desktop.** Icons that appear on the user's desktop, including files and shortcuts.

◆ **Favorites.** Shortcuts to favorite programs and locations.

◆ **NetHood.** Shortcuts to items in the Network Neighborhood.

◆ **Personal.** Shortcuts to personal program items.

◆ **PrintHood.** Shortcuts to items in the printer folder.

◆ **Recent.** Shortcuts to items that have been used recently.

◆ **SendTo.** Shortcuts to documents.

◆ **Start Menu**. Shortcuts appearing in the user's Start menu.

◆ **Templates.** Shortcuts to application templates.

> **Note** The NetHood, PrintHood, Recent, and Templates folders are hidden and are not normally shown in Windows NT Explorer.

Table 15.1 summarizes the parameters that are stored in the user's profile.

TABLE 15.1
Parameters Stored in User Profiles

Source	Parameters Stored
Accessories	User-specific parameters for all applications that configure the user's working environment, including Calculator, Clock, Notepad, and Paint.
Control Panel	All settings defined by the user in the Control Panel.
Online Help	Bookmarks the user places in the online help system.
Printer Connections	The user's network printer connections.
Taskbar	User-specific settings for program groups, program items, and Taskbar configurations.

Source	Parameters Stored
Windows Applications	Parameters established by the user in applications that are Windows NT compatible.
Windows NT Explorer	Settings that configure the user environment in Windows NT Explorer.

For the most part, users need not be concerned with the structure of their profile directories. As an administrator, however, you will need to be aware of the structure and locations of user's profile directories to manage their configurations.

Besides the personal profile menus, there are two special-purpose profile directories: Default User and All Users.

The Default User Profile Folder

Every Windows NT computer has a Default User profile that is used when both of the following are true:

◆ The user has not logged on to this computer before, and

◆ A profile has not been assigned to a user account.

You can copy another profile to replace the Default User profile if desired.

The All User Profile Folder

The All Users profile contains entries that are included in the profiles of all users on this computer. These entries are not part of the domain profile and apply specifically to resources available on the local computer. Typically, the All Users profile includes desktop icons that are common to all users, as well as items that appear in all users' Start menus.

Windows NT 3.x administrators are experienced with creating two types of program groups. The type, personal or common, is declared when the program group is created. The window title for a personal group is not given any special designation, but common program groups are labeled with (Common) in the window title bar.

Windows NT 4 does not support common and personal program groups in the same manner as Windows NT 3.x. For Windows NT 4, program groups placed in the user's personal profile folder are personal and are shown only to that user. Program groups placed in the All Users profile folder are common, and are visible to all users of the computer.

An example of a Windows NT 4 common program group is Administrative Tools (Common). This program group is created in the All Users folder and is, therefore, a common program group. The (Common) designation is actually part of the name of the folder. Figure 15.9 shows a Start menu that includes two common program groups: Administrative Tools and Startup.

Figure 15.9

Personal and common program groups.

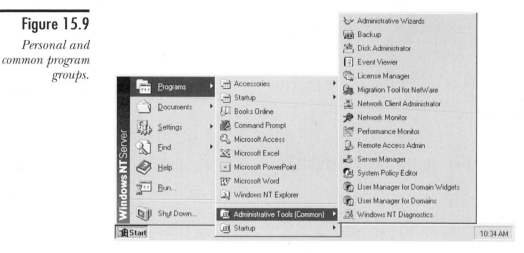

Note   The method of changing profiles has changed radically with Windows NT version 4. Prior to Windows NT 4, user profiles were stored in a single file, and all user profile files could be stored in the same designated profile directory. If the profile file had a USR extension (for example, BUSTER.USR), the user could make changes to the profile that would be saved from session to session. If the profile file had a MAN extension (for example, CHARLES.MAN), it was a mandatory profile that could not be altered by the user.

Objective C.2

Personal Profiles

A portion of each user's profile is stored in the Registry. The Registry data is stored in a file named NTuser.dat, which is stored in the root directory of each user's profile folder. When the user logs on, the user's profile data is copied to the HKEY_CURRENT_USER Registry key. As the user makes changes to the working environment, the user's NTuser.dat file is updated. The user's profile directory also contains a file named ntuser.dat.LOG, which serves as a transaction log, providing fault tolerance as updates are made to the Registry database.

Figure 15.10 shows the structure of the HKEY_CURRENT_USER Registry key. See Chapter 19, "Managing the Server," for more information about the Registry.

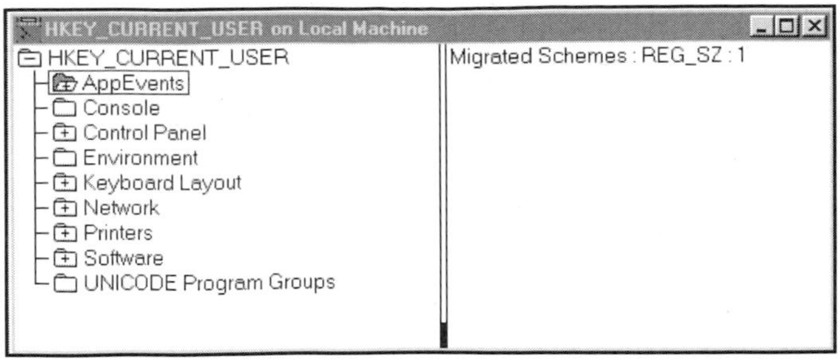

Figure 15.10

The HKEY_CURRENT_USER Registry key.

| Caution | Personal profiles should never be shared by multiple users because a user's changes will affect the environment of other users who share the profile. |

Mandatory Profiles

Objective C.2

Mandatory profiles have the same structure as personal profiles. Registry data for a mandatory profile, however, is stored in a file named NTuser.man. Although users with mandatory profiles may be permitted to modify their desktops, changes are not saved to the profile. As a result, the user always logs on with the same environment settings.

Mandatory profiles are especially useful when they are assigned to groups of users. In many cases, users perform a well-defined and restricted set of tasks, such as entering orders or bank transactions. It is essential to prevent users in restricted environments from introducing changes that could impair performance of a critical function. Mandatory profiles can be locked up tight.

Mandatory profiles also provide a great way to manage applications locally. If you need to deploy a new application to the users of a mandatory profile, you need only to install the application in one place and update the mandatory profile. All users of the mandatory profile will automatically receive the application on their desktops.

| Note | Users can share mandatory profiles. When users make changes to a mandatory profile, the changes are not saved to the network profile. Instead, they are saved to the locally cached profile on the user's Windows NT computer. |

| Tip | If you want to give users the benefits of personal profiles while retaining some ability to set up environments locally, consider using a combination of profiles and logon scripts. You can, for example, include NET USE commands in logon scripts to create a consistent environment of network connections. Printer connections can be established in the logon script, and users can be prevented from creating new printer connections from the desktop. |

Planning Profiles for Different Workstation Hardware

Some of the settings that are stored in user profiles are hardware-dependent, particularly video display cards and monitors. Ideally, therefore, all users of a shared profile should have the same video hardware.

Virtually all graphics adapters and monitors are capable of functioning in standard 640×480 VGA mode, and you can use this mode as a common configuration for shared profiles regardless of computer hardware variations. When users must use more advanced graphics modes, you might need to create several mandatory profiles for each hardware configuration.

When you create a profile, you should create the profile on a computer that has a hardware configuration that matches the machine on which the profile will be used. Characteristics to consider are:

◆ Video resolution and color settings

◆ Locations of application and data files on the local hard drives

◆ Drive letter assignments for hard drives and CD-ROMs

Planning Profiles for Applications

All users who share a profile share a common application setup. The properties for each application icon determine where the application files can be found. The information in the shared icons must be valid for all users of the profile. You can ensure that program items are valid for all users in two ways:

◆ By installing applications on local workstations in exactly the same directories

◆ By installing applications on the network file server

The network approach makes a great deal of sense because you can more easily maintain and upgrade one copy of an application on the server than many copies on individual workstations. Further, users can move applications on their personal computers, but can be restricted from moving application files on the file server.

If users have home directories on the server, you can specify individual home directories by using variables in program property paths. The variable string %HOMEDRIVE%%HOMEPATH%, for example, will always point to each individual user's home directory. You can use each user's home directory as a working directory by specifying %HOMEDRIVE%%HOMEPATH% in the Working Directory box for the properties of an application icon.

Planning Profile Directories

In general, I recommend that you store user profiles in the standard directory, which by default is C:\WINNT\Profiles. Personal profiles, however, can be stored in other directories, including the users' home directories, if desired. User directories are normally shared, so it's unnecessary to establish a new share, and users have full permissions to manage files in their personal directories. The downside to this approach is that administrators normally cannot access files in home directories; you will be unable to manage users' personal profiles unless they give you access.

Before setting up profiles on a server, establish a share to the profiles directory. This share will be used to specify the path to the users' profiles in their user account properties. In the examples, this share is named PROFILES.

Creating User Profiles

To create a user profile, follow the steps in the following exercise:

Creating User Profiles

1. Create a user account that will be used to create user profiles. In the examples, this account has the user name Profile Admin.

2. Log on with the Profile Admin account and configure the desktop environment as desired, thereby creating the Profile Admin profile.

3. Copy the Profile Admin profile to user accounts that will use the profile.

4. If desired, convert the profile to a mandatory profile.

The following sections discuss the details of the previous procedure.

Creating a Profile Administration Account

You probably don't want to create user profiles using your personal user account because you might be making extensive changes to the environment. You should create a special user account that has similar group memberships and permissions to the users who will use the profile. Be sure to assign a Profile Path property to the user account. I call my user Profile Admin.

Configuring the Desktop Environment

The first step in creating a profile is to log in with the profile administrator user account and to configure the desktop as desired. Table 15.1 can serve to remind you of all the features you can customize in a profile.

Don't forget to remove program items and groups that are assigned to administrative applications.

If you want applications to start automatically when the user logs on, place an appropriate alias into the Startup folder.

Copy the User Profile

After you have configured the desktop as desired, log out from the profile administrator account and log on using an account with Adminstrator permissions. Copy the profile as outlined in the following exercise:

Copying the User Profile

1. Open the System utility in the Control Panel.

2. Select the User Profiles tab to display user profiles on this computer (see fig. 15.11).

Figure 15.11

Managing user profiles.

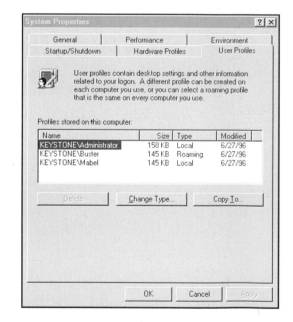

3. Select the profile entry for the Profile Admin user and choose Copy **T**o, thereby opening the Copy To dialog box (see fig. 15.12).

4. First, specify the location to which the profile will be copied. You can copy the profile to another computer on the network if desired. Choose **B**rowse if you want to browse for the location. In figure 15.12, the destination has already been set.

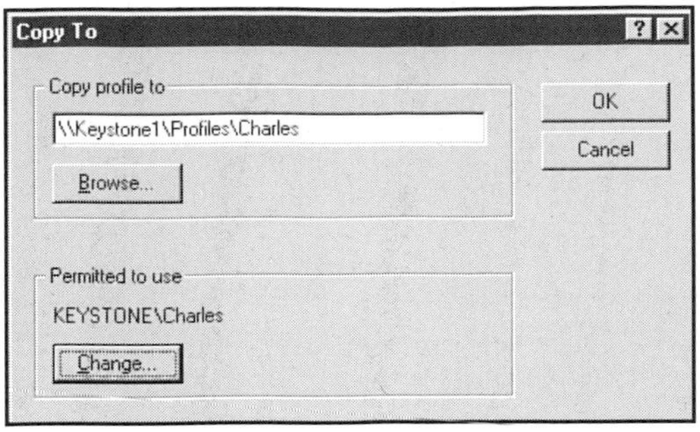

Figure 15.12

Copying a user profile.

5. Only one user or group can use a profile at a given time. After the profile has been copied, the Profile Admin user remains the only user who can modify the profile. If you want the new owner of the profile to be able to modify the profile, you must change the Permitted to Use entry.

   Choose **C**hange to open a dialog box in which you can select a user or a group. In figure 15.12, the user has been changed to KEYSTONE\Charles.

6. Choose OK to copy the profile.

Creating a Mandatory Profile

If the profile you have copied will be a mandatory profile, locate the NTuser.dat file in the user's profile directory and change the name to NTuser.man.

Setting the User Account Profile Path Property

To review the procedure for specifying the profile path that was covered in Chapter 11, figure 15.13 shows the User Environment Profile dialog box for the user Buster. The **U**ser Profile Path field contains the path that locates Buster's profile directory on the network.

The elements of the user profile path are as follows:

◆ **Server name.** In the example, the server is \\keystone1. The server can be any Windows NT Server computer, and does not have to be the PDC.

◆ **Share name.** The second element is the share name that is associated with the profiles directory. In the example, the share name is profiles.

◆ **User name.** The final element is the user name. If you are entering user profile paths for two or more users simultaneously, use the variable %username% to create a profile named appropriately for each user.

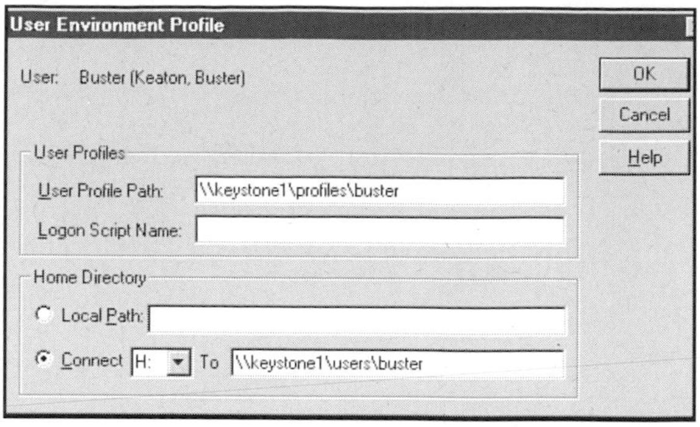

Figure 15.13

Configuring a user's profile path property.

> **Note** Before placing the user profile path in a user's account properties, create the profile directory and assign a share to the directory. Assign Full Control permissions to Everyone.

Creating Profiles as a User

If you assign a personal profile to a user but do not copy a profile to that user's profile directory, Windows NT attempts to create the profile automatically the first time the user logs on.

When a user has been assigned a profile and the profile is unavailable when the user logs on, the message `Unable to load your central profile` is displayed. This message displays whenever the user cannot access the profile, which might be the case if the directory is missing or the user does not have sufficient permissions to access the file.

If a user has been assigned a profile path and the profile cannot be accessed when the user logs on, Windows NT retrieves the user's locally cached profile if one exists. The locally cached profile (the user's local profile on the Windows NT computer) will be used to create the user's personal profile on the network.

If the user has been assigned a profile path but the profile has not been created and the user has never logged on from the existing Windows NT computer, the default user profile on the workstation is used to create the user's personal profile on the network.

Network and Local Profiles

When you work on a Windows NT computer with a network roaming profile, you actually have two profiles: the profile that is stored on the network, and a *locally cached* profile, which is a copy of your network profile. The locally cached profile enables you to retain your profile settings even though you are not connected to the network.

Suppose that you are working on your laptop computer, connected to the network. Changes made to your profile are stored in both your network and your local profile.

Later, when you are detached from the network, Windows NT will configure your computer using the locally cached profile. Any changes you make will be stored in your local profile.

You return to the office and connect up to the network. When you log on to the network, your local profile is more up-to-date than your network profile. Which takes precedence? When you log on under these circumstances, you are shown this message: Your locally stored profile is newer than your roaming profile. Would you like to use the locally stored profile? If you answer No, you will use your local profile, which will be copied to your roaming profile. If you answer Yes, you will use your network roaming profile, and changes made to your local profile will be lost.

Working with Profiles on Slow Network Connections

When users log on to the network through slow connections such as a RAS modem connection, the process of accessing and updating the roaming profile can consume considerable bandwidth on the connection. In such situations, it is generally preferable to work with a local profile. In such cases, users can switch the type of profile with which they are working.

Switching Between a Remote and a Local Profile

1. Log on to the remote computer.

2. Open the System utility in the Control Panel and select the User Profiles tab.

3. Select **C**hange Type to open the Change Type dialog box (see fig. 15.14).

4. Select **L**ocal profile or Use **c**ached profile on slow connections option.

5. Choose OK.

If desired, select **R**oaming profile at the end of the session to update the server-based roaming profile.

Figure 15.14

Configuring the type of a user's profile.

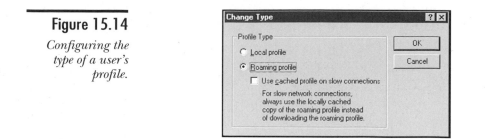

Upgrading Windows NT 3.5x Profiles to Windows NT 4

Considerable conversion is required to adapt Windows NT 3.5x profiles to Windows NT 4. When upgrading to Windows NT 4, profile upgrades are handled as follows:

◆ The Windows NT 3.5x profile file is retained.

◆ The data in the Windows NT 3.5x profile file is used to create a Windows NT 4 profile folder for the user.

◆ Users can access profiles from Windows NT 3.5x and 4 workstations, but the profiles are updated separately, and users cannot access changes that were made under the other environment.

◆ On Windows NT computers that are upgraded to Windows NT 4, the local profile is converted to a profile folder format. The local profile file is not retained.

When a Windows NT 3.5x profile is upgraded to Windows NT 4, a personal profile originally stored in *username*.usr is converted to a profile folder named *username*.pds. A mandatory profile stored in a file named *username*.man is converted to a profile folder named *username*.pdm.

When a user logs on from a Windows NT 3.5x computer, the profile path *server**share**username*.usr is used to retrieve the profile file *username*.usr.

When a user logs on from a Windows NT 4 computer and the profile path is *server**share**username*.usr, the profile folder *username*.pds is used. It is, therefore, not necessary to edit the Profile Path property of the user account to indicate which profile is to be used.

Caution When upgrading to Windows NT 4, mandatory profiles are not automatically upgraded. To create a mandatory profile that can be accessed from Windows NT 3.5x and 4 computers, you must do the following:

1. Use a Windows NT computer to create the profile with the desired settings.

2. Log on using a user account with Administrator permissions.

3. Use the System utility in the Control Panel to copy the profile to the user's profile folder.

4. In the destination profile folder, rename the NTuser.dat file to NTuser.man.

When a user logs on to a computer running Windows NT, the mandatory profile will be downloaded to the local computer.

Supporting Windows 95 Profiles

Both Windows NT and Windows 95 support user profiles, but the mechanisms used are somewhat different. Here is how Windows 95 and Windows NT profiles compare:

◆ Local profiles operate in the same manner.

◆ Windows 95 clients running the Client for Microsoft Networks can access roaming user profiles on a Windows NT Server network if their primary logon is Microsoft Network.

◆ Windows 95 clients running the Client for NetWare Networks can also access roaming user profiles on a Novell server if the primary logon is Client for Novell. The profile is stored in the user's mail directory on the Novell server.

◆ Mandatory user profiles are supported but cannot be shared. A separate mandatory user profile must be created for each user.

◆ Windows 95 profiles do not support common groups.

◆ Windows 95 profiles are less comprehensive, and include only shortcut (.lnk) files and program information (.pif) files.

◆ Windows 95 clients can obtain their roaming profiles only from their home directories. The User Profile Path property of the user account is not used.

Differences in Profile Files

Windows NT and Windows 95 maintain profiles using different files, which have slightly different purposes. Comparable files are listed in Table 15.2.

TABLE 15.2
Comparison of Windows NT and Windows 95 Profile Files

Windows NT Server	Windows 95
NTuser.dat	user.dat
ntuser.dat.LOG	user.da0
NTuser.man	user.man

Windows 95 profiles are less robust than Windows NT profiles. On Windows NT, the ntuser.dat.LOG file functions as a transaction log that enables Windows NT to recover the profile if it is corrupted during an update. On Windows 95, user.da0 is simply a copy of user.dat, which is updated when the user logs off.

Creating Windows 95 Profiles

Because Windows 95 profiles have their own file structure, you cannot create a Windows 95 profile using Windows NT. Create the profile on a Windows 95 work-station and copy the profile folder to the user's home directory on the network server.

Managing the System Policy

The *system policy* provides a means of tightening administrative control over user environments and actions. The system policy can be enforced for all Windows NT Workstation and Windows NT Server computers on the network.

The system policy is enforced by overwriting settings in two areas of the Registry:

◆ *System policy for users* overwrites settings in the current user areas of the Registry (HKEY_CURRENT_USER). These policy settings determine the user's profile on the computer.

◆ *System policy for computers* overwrites settings in the local machine areas of the Registry (HKEY_LOCAL_MACHINE). These policy settings determine logon and network access settings.

The system policy is managed using the System Policy Editor to create a file named NTConfig.pol, which is placed in the \NetLogon share of the PDC and all BDCs. The NetLogon share is found on the boot partition under Winnt\system32\repl\import\ scripts. When a user logs on to the domain, Windows NT looks for a NTConfig.pol file in the NetLogon share. If found, NTConfig.pol is used to overwrite the user and local machine areas of the local Registry.

If desired, you can specify custom system policies for users, groups, or computers, enabling you to closely tailor the policy to users' needs and to department policies.

| Caution | If the system policy is implemented, it should be implemented in all domains to which users log on. Consider the following sequence of events:

1. Buster logs on to domain Keystone, which enforces a security policy. The policy settings are downloaded to Buster's computer and update his Registry.

2. Buster logs on to the domain Fubar, which does not enforce a security policy. His Registry retains the policy settings that were established when he logged on to Keystone.

This problem is avoided if a security policy is established for the Fubar domain as well.

Creating the System Policy

Objective

C.2

The system policy is created and managed using the System Policy Editor, which is installed in the Administrative Tools (Common) program group.

To begin creating the system policy, open the System Policy Editor and choose the **N**ew Policy command in the **F**ile menu. When a system policy has been opened, two icons will be displayed in the System Policy Editor, as shown in figure 15.15.

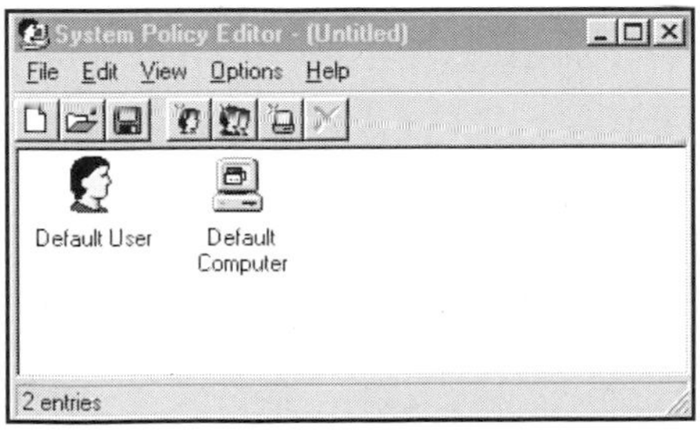

Figure 15.15

Editing a system policy in the System Policy Editor.

Adding Users, Groups, and Computers to the System Policy

You can create custom system policies for three groups of entities:

◆ Specific users

◆ Groups of users

◆ Specific computers

All users not covered by a custom policy in one of the previous categories are covered by the default users and/or default computer system policy.

To add a custom system policy, do one of the following:

◆ To add a system policy for a specific user, choose Add **U**ser in the **E**dit menu and supply the name of the user to add. A user icon will be placed in the System Policy Editor window.

◆ To add a system policy for a specific group, choose Add **G**roup in the **E**dit menu and supply the name of the group to add. A group icon will be placed in the System Policy Editor window.

◆ To add a system policy for a specific computer, choose Add C**o**mputer in the **E**dit menu and supply the name of the computer to add. A computer icon will be placed in the System Policy Editor window.

In all of these cases, a Browse button is provided, enabling you to browse for the desired resource. Figure 15.16 shows the System Policy Editor window after a user, group, and computer have been added.

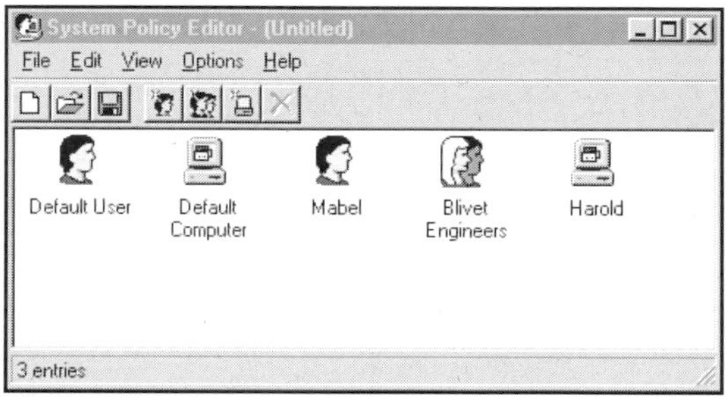

Figure 15.16

User, group, and computer icons in the System Policy Editor.

If the default user or default computer settings are filled in before you create a new user or computer, the system will copy all the settings to your new items.

Editing the User System Policy

To edit the System Policy Editor for a user, double-click the user icon to open the User Properties window (see fig. 15.17). The properties in this window are arranged in a hierarchical list. In the figure, the Desktop heading was opened to reveal two settings:

◆ **Wallpaper.** The check box for Wallpaper is gray, indicating that no setting has been established.

◆ **Color scheme.** Here the administrator has clicked the check box to activate the setting. Doing so opened the **S**ettings for Color scheme box in which the administrator has selected the color scheme Rose 256.

All other properties are configured in much the same way. Check the property heading to open a window in which settings are entered.

Note If a check box is gray in the System Policy Editor, no policy has been specified for that property.

A selected check box indicates that the policy is in effect.

A deselected check box indicates that the policy is not in effect.

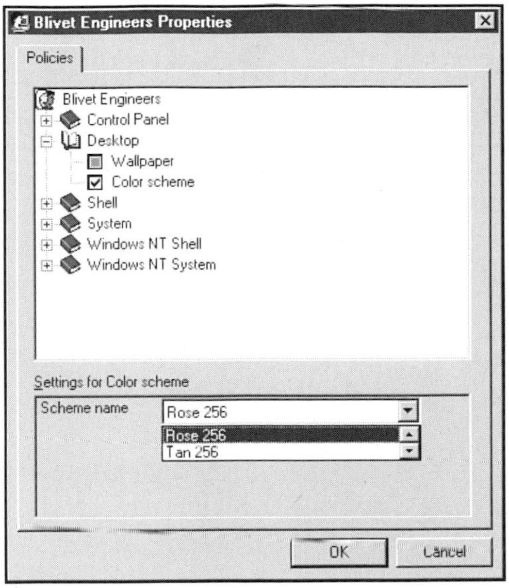

Figure 15.17

Example of changing a desktop property.

Users can waste a lot of time fiddling around with their desktops, playing with screen savers, and so forth. If you would like to put an end to that sort of thing, examine figure 15.18. Under the Control Panel heading you will find options that enable you to restrict the changes users can make to their displays. If you check Restrict display, five check boxes appear that enable you to block users from making changes to their displays. You can deny access to the Display icon entirely, or you can hide specific tabs in the Display utility.

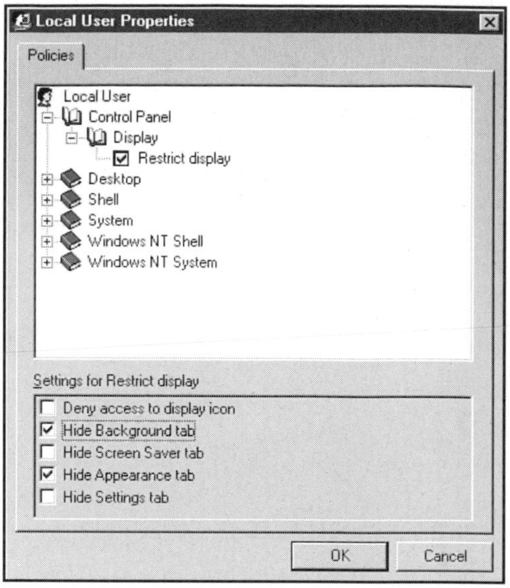

Figure 15.18

Restricting access to Display properties.

From the system administrator's point of view, much more interesting properties can be found under other headings. In figure 15.19, the Shell heading has been opened to reveal a variety of powerful properties. Here are just a few properties that can prove valuable:

◆ **Remove Run command from Start menu.** Use this property to prevent users from running programs that are not defined as icons in the Start menu.

◆ **Remove Taskbar from Settings on Start menu.** This property can be used to prevent users from modifying the structure of the Start menu.

◆ **Hide drives in My Computer.** You can prevent users from running programs from icons in My Computer with this property. You can also prevent them from using My Computer to examine the contents of drives and from moving files and folders.

◆ **Don't save settings at exit.** Use this property to prevent users from making permanent changes to their environment.

As you can see, you can lock up a user's options pretty tightly using properties under the Shell heading.

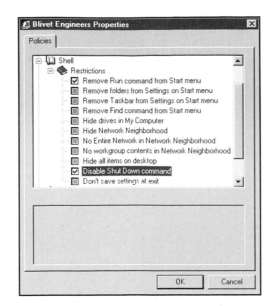

Figure 15.19

Shell properties.

As shown in figure 15.20, two properties under the System heading enable you to prevent users from modifying the Registry or from running any but allowed Windows application.

Figure 15.20

System properties.

Caution The System Policy Editor is a Registry editor, and you would expect it to be affected by the Disable Registry editing tools restriction. Unfortunately, it isn't, and the System Policy Editor can be used to override the effects of policies on a local

continues

Registry. If you're serious, therefore, about restricting Registry access, keep the System Policy Editor out of the hands of your users.

The Windows NT Shell heading has two subheadings:

◆ **Custom folders** contains properties that restrict users' ability to create and customize a variety of folders.

◆ **Restrictions** contains properties that restrict users from using custom shell extensions and from removing common program groups from the Start menu.

Because there are so many settings in the User Properties list, I'm going to leave it to you to take the time to scan the descriptions. You will find that most are self-explanatory. Use your imagination and ingenuity to establish the correct restrictions for your users.

Caution Policies can get pretty restrictive. In fact, they can get downright nasty. They can even lock things up so that you can't repair the damage. Try the effects of a policy change on a test user account before you turn the policy loose on the entire network. After a policy has been implemented on the network, its contents are merged into the computer's registry and are not removed when the NTConfig.pol file is deleted.

Editing the Computer Policy

When you double-click a computer icon in System Policy Editor, you open the Computer Properties window shown in figure 15.21. This window also presents a hierarchy of property categories. To illustrate, the Windows NT Network heading has been opened.

Once again, there are far too many properties to discuss here. The majority of properties are self-explanatory, so it's up to you to review the options.

Saving the System Policy

After you have edited the system policy as required, save a new policy as follows:

1. Choose the Save **A**s command in the **F**ile menu.

2. Save the policy as C:\Winnt\system32\Repl\Import\Scripts\ntconfig.pol on all domain controllers. (Change the path if the root volume has been assigned a different drive letter.)

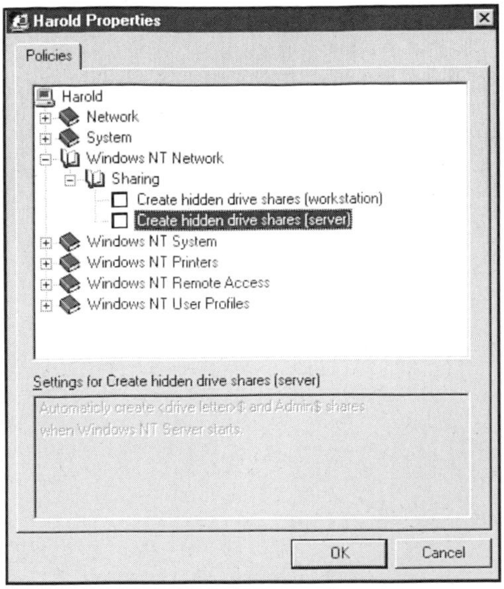

Figure 15.21

*Computer
properties.*

Using System Policy Editor to Edit the Registry

Choose the Open **R**egistry command in the **F**ile menu to immediately write system
policy changes to the Registry on the local computer. The changes are saved to the
Registry when you choose **S**ave in the **F**ile menu.

To connect with a Registry on another computer, choose the Connec**t** command on
the **F**ile menu. This option enables you to maintain users' Registries remotely.

Logon Scripts

Chapter 11 explained how to define the logon script name for a user account. To
refresh your memory, figure 15.22 shows a User Environment Profile dialog box in
which a logon script name has been specified. By default, logon scripts are stored in
C:\Winnt\system32\Repl\Import\Scripts. You will need to reconfigure directory
replication, as described in Chapter 22, "Managing Directory Replication," if scripts
are stored in a different directory.

Logon scripts are batch files (.BAT extension) that contain executable commands.
You will find the NET commands extremely valuable when creating logon scripts.
The NET commands for Windows NT are more extensive than they are for DOS.

Logon scripts for Windows NT clients can make use of several logon variables, which
are listed in table 15.3.

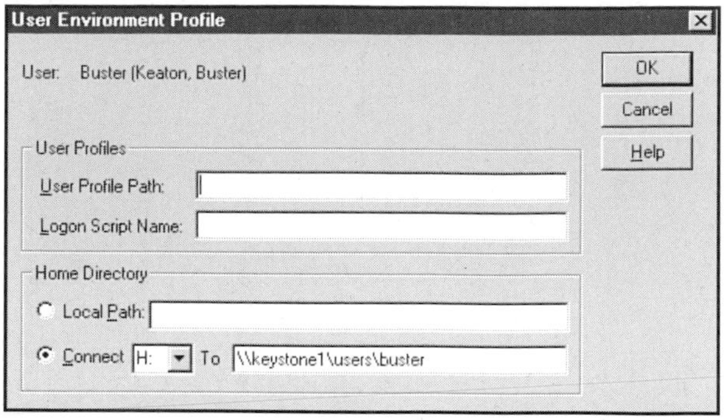

Figure 15.22

Figure 15.22

Specifying a logon script name for a user profile.

TABLE 15.3
Windows NT Logon Script Variables

Variable	Description
%HOMEDRIVE%	The drive letter that connects to the user's home directory
%HOMEPATH%	The complete path name of the user's home directory
%HOMESHARE%	The name of the share that contains the user's home directory
%OS%	The operating system running on the user's workstation
%PROCESSOR%	The processor type installed in the user's workstation
%USERDOMAIN%	The domain name in which the user's account is defined
%USERNAME%	The user name of the user

The %USERNAME% variable was encountered in Chapter 11, when it was used to specify logon script and profile names. Other variables can be used to enable logon scripts to adjust to changes in the user's environment when moving from computer to computer.

Variables also can be used to enable a single logon script file to service users in different departments. You could use the %USERDOMAIN% printer to enable the logon script to connect different printers, depending on the user's home domain, as in the following examples:

```
IF %USERDOMAIN% == WIDGETS NET USE LPT1: \\WIDGETS1\LASER1 /YES

IF %USERDOMAIN% == ACCT NET USE LPT1: \\ACCT\ACCTLASR /YES
```

Another useful thing to do in a logon script is to synchronize client clocks with a given server, ensuring that all computers on the network will be set to approximately the same time. To synchronize client clocks with the server KEYSTONE1, you would add the following command to the logon script:

```
NET TIME \\KEYSTONE1 /SET /YES
```

Tip If you are synchronizing clocks on the network, it would be nice if the master computer had the right time. The best way to set the master clock is to synchronize it with a standard time service, such as the US Naval Observatory or the National Institute of Standards and Technology. Such a program is included with the *Windows NT Resource Kit*. Read the "Time Service for NT" documentation file for more information.

Using Windows NT Server Tools on Windows NT Workstation

Objective C.3

You can easily install a set of Windows NT Server management tools on a Windows NT Workstation client. To install the tools, connect to the Windows NT Server installation CD-ROM and execute the SETUP.BAT file from the \Clients\Srvtools\Winnt directory. The following programs will be installed on the workstation:

◆ DHCP Manager

◆ Event Viewer

◆ RAS Administrator

◆ Remoteboot Manager

◆ Server Manager

◆ User Manager for Domains

◆ User Profile Editor

◆ WINS Manager

A program group and icons are not created by SETUP; these will need to be created manually.

Testing Your Knowledge

1. What kind of profile is stored for each user of a stand-alone NT Workstation?

    A. Locally cached profile

    B. Local user profile

    C. Roaming profile

    D. Stand-alone user profile

2. What kind of profile can be accessed by a user from any NT workstations on an NT network?

    A. Locally cached profile

    B. Local user profile

    C. Roaming profile

    D. Stand-alone user profile

3. Users on a Windows NT computer have a _____ profile that is used when the network profile is unavailable.

4. Every Windows NT computer has a Default User profile that is used when following conditions are true:

    A. A profile has not been assigned to a user account.

    B. Only the locally cached profile is available.

    C. The users roaming profile is the only profile available.

    D. The user has not logged on to this computer before.

5. Common groups are identical in nature between Windows NT 3.5x and NT 4.

    A. True

    B. False

6. Personal profiles should never be shared by multiple users because user's changes will affect the environment of other users who share the profile.

    A. True

    B. False

7. Which type of profile will force the users to log on with the same environment settings even if they change their desktops?

    A. Mandatory profile

    B. Local user profile

    C. Roaming profile

    D. User profile

8. What extension does a mandatory file have?

9. If a user logs on to the network through a slow connection such as a RAS modem, the process of accessing and updating the roaming profile can consume considerable bandwidth on the connection. In such situations, the user may want to use a local profile.

   A. True

   B. False

10. Windows NT 3.5x profiles require little or no modification to work with NT 4.

   A. True

   B. False

11. Similar to Windows NT, mandatory user profiles are supported under Windows 95 but can not be shared. A separate mandatory user profile must be created for each user.

   A. True

   B. False

12. The system policy is created and managed using the _____.

13. Which property can be set within the system policy?

   A. Wallpaper

   B. Remove Run command from the Start menu

   C. Color scheme

   D. Don't save settings at exit

14. Which of the following logon scripts will attach the logical printer LASER1 which is shared on the server named WIDGETS1 to a user who is defined in the domain called WIDGETS?

   A. `IF %USERNAME% == WIDGETS NET USE LPT1: \\WIDGETS1\LASER1 /YES`

   B. `IF %USERDOMAIN% == WIDGETS NET USE LPT1: \\WIDGETS1\LASER1 /YES`

   C. `IF %USERDOMAIN% == WIDGETS1 NET USE LPT1: \\WIDGETS\LASER1 /YES`

   D. `IF %DOMAIN% == WIDGETS NET USE LPT1: \\WIDGETS1\LASER1 /YES`

15. You can easily install a set of Windows NT Server management tools on a Windows NT Workstation client. These tools are installed from the NT Server installation CD-ROM.

   A. True

   B. False

Review Answers

1. B
2. C
3. locally cached
4. A, D
5. B
6. A
7. A
8. MAN
9. A
10. B
11. A
12. System Policy Editor
13. A, B, C, D
14. B
15. A

CHAPTER 16

Using TCP/IP

TCP/IP is without question the most widely used family of network protocols. Several factors contribute to the popularity of TCP/IP:

◆ **Maturity.** Definition of the TCP/IP protocols began in the 1970s to satisfy a requirement of the Department of Defense for a robust wide-area-networking protocol. TCP/IP gained wide distribution when it was written into Berkeley Standard Distribution (BSD) Unix, and has been a standard feature of Unix implementations for a long time. As a result, TCP/IP received thorough field trials when other protocols were in their early developmental stages.

◆ **Openness.** TCP/IP is the only protocol suite with an open standards definition process. Discussion takes place in the form of Requests for Comments (RFCs) that are posted and debated publicly on the Internet. Proposals and debates are open, not restricted to members of a standards committee.

◆ **Non-proprietary ownership.** In a real sense, TCP/IP is owned by the user community. Other protocols, almost without exception, are proprietary protocols, which are owned by vendors. Users have little or no input into these proprietary protocols, and manufacturers must often pay licensing fees to build them into their products.

◆ **Richness.** TCP/IP is actually a suite of protocols that provides a vast set of capabilities. Just about anything a network should be able to do can be done using TCP/IP.

◆ **Compatibility.** TCP/IP is the only protocol suite that runs on almost anything; name the hardware, and you will probably find at least one TCP/IP implementation for it. Computer system manufacturers now regard TCP/IP as a requirement.

Unfortunately, a single chapter can only skim the surface of TCP/IP, a subject that would require many volumes in order to be covered thoroughly. The goal in this chapter is to cover the topics that you need to know about to get TCP/IP running in a Windows NT network, along with a few of the configuration techniques you must be aware of. If you want more details, please check out *Networking with Microsoft TCP/IP*, also published by New Riders Publishing.

Before you can appreciate TCP/IP and understand how to set it up, you need to know something more about how small and large networks work.

Networks and Internetworks

On simple networks, such as the one in figure 16.1, delivering messages between devices is quite simple. Each device is assigned a device address (a numeric name). When device A wants to send a message to device C, device A simply adds C's device address to the message and puts the message on the network. C, like every device on the network, is looking at all of the messages that zip by. If C sees a message that bears its device address, it can retrieve the message. Other devices, such as B (see fig. 16.1), will ordinarily ignore messages not addressed to them.

Message delivery on a simple network is just like finding your luggage on the conveyor belt at the airport. The baggage handlers aren't aware of where you're standing or even if you're present at all. They just throw your bags on the conveyor, and it's up to you to spot the pieces that have your name on them.

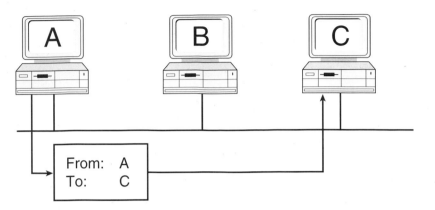

Figure 16.1

Message delivery on a simple network.

Large networks and real luggage delivery, however, are a lot more complicated than simply getting suitcases from the airplane to the owner. Consider what really happens on a long flight with several stops and some plane changes. When you arrive at your departure airport, your bags are marked by a tag that identifies the destination airport. When you change planes, your bags are supposed to change planes with you, and baggage handlers at the intermediate airport must sort through the incoming bags and route them. Each bag is tagged with a destination. Some bags stay at this airport, some go to another airport, and some, whose destination can't be reached directly from this location, need to be routed through another intermediate airport as the next hop toward their destination. If the destination on a luggage tag matches the current airport, the bag needs to go onto the conveyor belt for local delivery. If an item is sent to the wrong airport, a mechanism must be in place to identify the error, discover how to get the item to its correct destination, and start it on its way.

Airport baggage handling is a concrete example of the problems large networks face thousands of times during every second that they operate. Here is a summary of the problems that must be solved to deliver messages through a complex network:

◆ Each device must have a unique identification on its local network. Imagine there were two Bill Roberts with the same street address trying to pick up the same luggage with an LAX (Los Angeles International) airport tag.

◆ Each intermediate and final destination must have an identification. No two networks or airports can use the same identification symbol.

◆ Procedures must be in place for routing messages between the source and the final destination. Airports use baggage handlers. Networks use routers and routing protocols.

◆ If an intermediate destination is of a different type from the source and/or destination, all must agree on procedures so that confusion does not arise.

Imagine what it would be like flying from New York to Saudi Arabia if every country along the way required you to route your baggage with a completely different procedure.

◆ When problems occur, as they surely will, mechanisms must be in place to attempt to correct the error.

Figure 16.2 shows a fairly involved wide area network. With this network, a message from A that was addressed to B could hypothetically take several routes to reach its destination. Devices called *routers* are placed in every place that networks interconnect. Routers serve the same function as baggage handlers in an airport; they route packages toward their destinations, hopefully along the fastest route.

Figure 16.2

A complex network.

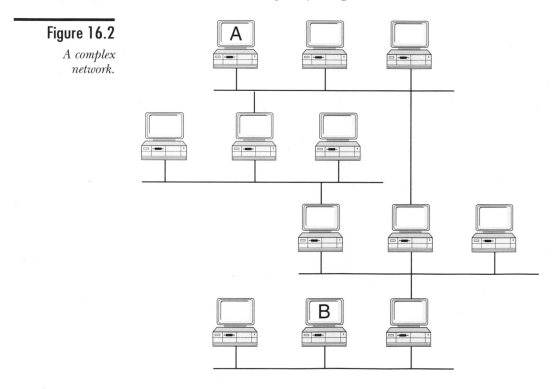

The network in figure 16.2 consists of several networks that are interconnected. A "network of networks" is commonly called an *internetwork* or *internet*. The network of networks, a vast, international network that originated from the original Defense Department networks of the late 1970s, is called the *Internet*.

Following are the elements of an internetwork, expressed in somewhat more technical terms:

◆ **Each device on a network is identified by a unique address, often called a device or node address.** These addresses are often permanently coded into the network hardware. Each Ethernet and token-ring card possesses a 48-bit address number that is guaranteed to be unique throughout the world.

◆ **A local delivery mechanism enables devices to place messages on the medium and retrieve messages that are addressed to them.** Using the OSI reference model discussed in Chapter 1, "Understanding Networks," local delivery is performed by the physical and data link layers.

◆ **A mechanism for delivering messages that must travel through the internetwork.** In the TCP/IP protocol suite, internetwork delivery is the responsibility of the Internet Protocol (IP).

◆ **A way to determine good ways of routing messages.** With TCP/IP, routing in complex networks is performed by IP, usually with support of a routing protocol, such as Routing Information Protocol (RIP) or Open Shortest Path First (OSPF).

◆ **A way to detect and recover from errors.** The Transmission Control Protocol (TCP) is responsible for error detection and recovery on TCP/IP networks.

TCP/IP isn't the only way of solving these problems, but it is an excellent approach, and the approach with the widest acceptance. If your Windows NT network is participating in an internetwork, there is a good chance that it will need to run TCP/IP.

Protocols and Windows NT

Objective
A.2

Windows NT ships with support for three transport protocols:

◆ **NetBEUI.** The traditional protocol on Microsoft networking products. Its primary limitation is that it can be used only on simple networks because it cannot be routed.

◆ **NWLink.** A Microsoft-developed transport that is compatible with Novell's IPX/SPX protocols. A significant advantage of these protocols is that they require virtually no configuration. NWLink is routable and can be used to build small to medium internetworks.

◆ **TCP/IP.** It is the most commonly implemented network protocol, particularly on internetworks, and has excellent networking capabilities. Unlike NWLink, TCP/IP requires considerable configuration.

All of these protocols can coexist on Windows NT, thanks to two technologies:

◆ **NDIS.** The Network Driver Interface Specification, which enables multiple protocol stacks to share network adapters.

◆ **TDI.** The Transport Driver Interface, which enables various upper-layer Windows NT services to interface freely with the installed protocols.

Figure 16.3 shows how the protocols fit together.

Figure 16.3

NDIS supporting multiple protocols.

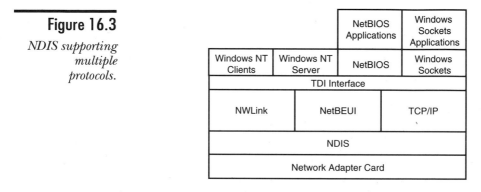

Although the TCP/IP protocol stack was developed before the OSI network model was implemented, a fairly close relationship can be drawn between IP and the network layer. Also, TCP is closely related to the OSI transport layer. Purists will argue against trying to forcefit TCP/IP into the OSI model, but for the sake of simplicity, we will regard these protocols and layers as a match.

> **Note** The TCP/IP layer that corresponds to the OSI transport layer is called the *host-to-host layer.* The TCP/IP layer most similar to the OSI Network layer is called the *Internet layer.*

TCP/IP and Internetworks

Now that you can see the layered structure of TCP/IP, you can look at how the layers solve the internetwork problems that were introduced earlier.

Local Network Addresses

TCP/IP can use a wide variety of lower layer protocols, including X.25 packet switching, Ethernet, and token ring. In fact, TCP/IP was explicitly designed without data link and physical layer specifications because the goal was to make the protocol suite adaptable to most types of media.

TCP/IP relies on physical addresses to deliver messages on the local network. On LANs, physical addresses are functions of the medium access control (MAC) sublayer of the OSI data link layer. Most LAN standards make provisions for assigning physical (hardware) addresses to cards. Each Ethernet and token-ring card has a 48-bit address that is burned into the card's hardware when it is manufactured. A central address registry assigns address ranges to each manufacturer so that each card will have a unique address.

> **Note**   Computers on TCP/IP networks are called *hosts*. When TCP/IP was being developed, there were no personal computers or workstations. All computers were multi-user computers that were, and still are, called hosts. Today, even a single user computer on a TCP/IP network is called a host.

Local Message Delivery

TCP/IP refers to each local network as a *subnet*. You see how each subnet is defined later in the chapter. Whenever IP sends a message that is directed to a device on the local subnet, it tags the message with the physical address of the message recipient and sends the message down the protocol stack. The physical layer places the message on the network, where it circulates past all devices on the subnet (local broadcast). The device that matches the physical address retrieves the message.

Routing Messages Through Internetworks

When a message is not destined for a device on the local subnet, it must be routed. Each subnet is assigned a subnet address. Each computer is configured with a default router to which it sends messages that must be sent to a remote subnet.

The responsibility of determining how messages should be addressed is one of the tasks of IP, the Internetwork Protocol. IP identifies whether each message is destined for a computer on the local network or whether it should be sent to the default router. The physical address for either the local host or the default router is added to each message that is sent.

IP makes use of addresses called *IP addresses* to logically identify subnets and devices, which are called *hosts* in TCP/IP terminology. IP addresses are explained later in this chapter, in the section "IP Addresses."

IP receives frames from higher-level protocols. One of IP's responsibilities is to attach to each frame a header containing address information. Once the IP header has been attached to the frame, the combination is generally referred to as a *packet*.

Determining routing paths between routers is usually the responsibility of one of two protocols: Routing Information Protocol (RIP), an older and less efficient protocol that remains in widespread use, and Open Shortest Path First (OSPF), a newer and more efficient protocol. Thorough discussion of RIP and OSPF is beyond the scope of this book. IP makes use of routing tables built by RIP or OSPF to determine the next router to which a packet should be sent.

Detecting and Recovering from Errors

IP provides what is known as *unreliable network service*, meaning that IP assumes that packets will be delivered correctly and does nothing to verify delivery. Generally speaking, this is insufficient, and a mechanism is required to detect and recover from errors.

Error recovery is the responsibility of the Transmission Control Protocol (TCP), the second protocol that identifies the TCP/IP protocol suite. Among the responsibilities of TCP are:

◆ Fragmentation of large messages from upper-layer protocols into *frames* that fit within the limitations of the network. (No network can transmit a 100-megabyte file in a single chunk because that would monopolize the network for too long a time. The file must be broken into smaller units.)

◆ Reassembly of received frames into messages that are passed to upper-layer protocols.

◆ Error detection and recovery.

When TCP sends a frame, it expects an acknowledgment when the frame is received. When no acknowledgment is forthcoming, TCP assumes that the frame was lost, and retransmits. TCP is an extremely robust protocol, enabling TCP/IP to function reliably on surprisingly flaky networks. After all, the protocol was developed with the goal of running critical defense networks when networks weren't all that reliable under normal use, let alone during wartime conditions.

The reliable features of TCP come at the cost of reduced performance. When "best effort" delivery is sufficient, an alternative protocol can be utilized. User Datagram Protocol (UDP) provides unreliable transport service for less critical functions. One use of UDP is to transmit network management information for the Simple Network Management Protocol (SNMP).

IP Addresses

Network addresses, unlike physical addresses, are not burned into any hardware anywhere. Network addresses are assigned by network administrators and are logically configured into network devices.

In addition to logical addresses for subnets, TCP/IP assigns a logical address to each host on the network. Although they complicate network setup, logical IP addresses have some advantages:

◆ They are independent of the specific physical layer implementation. Upper-layer processes can use logical addresses without concerning themselves with the address format of the underlying physical layer.

◆ A device can retain the same logical IP address even though its physical layer may change. Converting a network from token ring to Ethernet doesn't affect the IP addresses.

IP Address Format

IP addresses are 32-bit numbers that contain both a subnet address and a host address. The method used for encoding addresses in an IP address is a bit confusing for newcomers and is the primary stumbling block for TCP/IP newbies.

Following is an example of an IP address. Please commit it to memory.

11000001000010100001111000000010

It's not that easy to scan, is it? It's really hard to quickly identify differences between two numbers. Assuming that the two numbers were not nearby on the same page, how quickly could you spot the difference between the previous number and this one:

11000010000010100001111000000010

That little change makes a big difference in the way the address functions. To make IP addresses easier to work with, the 32-bit addresses are typically divided into four *octets* (8-bit sections):

```
11000001 00001010 00011110 00000010
```

Still not easy, but the next step considerably simplifies things. Each of the octets can be translated into a decimal number in the range of 0 through 255. This leads us to the more conventional method of representing the example IP address:

```
193.10.30.2
```

This format is commonly called *dotted-decimal notation*.

> **Note**   Although IP addresses are most commonly represented in dotted-decimal notation, it is important to keep in touch with the underlying binary numbers. IP functionality is defined by the bit patterns, not by the decimal numbers we commonly use. The vast majority of IP addressing problems result because the network administrator failed to closely examine the bit patterns for the IP addresses that were selected.

> **Tip**   If you are among the 99.44 percent of the population who doesn't think it's fun to convert binary to decimal in your head, make use of the Windows Calculator application. Switch it into Scientific mode by checking the **S**cientific option in the **V**iew menu. Then you can use the Binary and Decimal mode buttons to convert numbers from one representation to another.

IP Address Classes

Each IP address consists of two fields:

◆ A *netid* field, which is the logical network address of the subnet to which the computer is attached

◆ A *hostid* field, which is the logical device address that uniquely identifies each host on a subnet

Together, the netid and the hostid provide each host on an internetwork with a unique IP address.

When the TCP/IP protocols were originally developed, it was thought that computer networks would fall into one of three categories:

◆ A small number of networks that had large numbers of hosts

◆ Some networks with an intermediate number of hosts

◆ A large number of networks that would have a small number of hosts

For that reason, IP addresses were organized into *classes*. You can identify the class of an IP address by examining the first octet:

◆ If the first octet has a value of 0 through 127, it is a *class A* address. Because 0 and 127 in this octet have special uses, 126 class A addresses are available, each of which can support 16,777,214 hosts.

◆ If the first octet has a value of 128 through 191, it is a *class B* address. 16,384 class B addresses are possible, each of which can support up to 65,534 hosts.

◆ If the first octet has a value of 192 through 223, it is a *class C* address. 2,097,152 class C addresses are available, each of which can support up to 254 hosts.

The number of hosts that a class address can support depends upon the way the class allocates octets to netids and hostids. Figure 16.4 shows how octets are organized for each class.

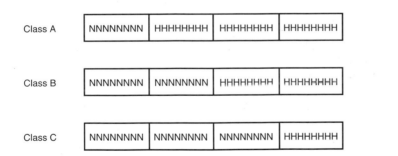

Class A | NNNNNNNN | HHHHHHHH | HHHHHHHH | HHHHHHHH |

Class B | NNNNNNNN | NNNNNNNN | HHHHHHHH | HHHHHHHH |

Class C | NNNNNNNN | NNNNNNNN | NNNNNNNN | HHHHHHHH |

Figure 16.4

Organization of octets in classes of IP addresses.

As you can see, a class A address uses only the first octet for network IDs. The remaining three octets are available for use as host IDs.

Class B addresses use the first two octets to designate the netid. The third and fourth octets are used for host IDs.

Class C addresses use the first three octets for network IDs. Only the fourth octet is used for host IDs.

> **Note** | Technically, the class of an address is defined by the leftmost bits in the first octet:
>
> ◆ If the first bit is a 0, the address is class A.
>
> ◆ If the first two bits are 10, the address is class B.
>
> ◆ If the first three bits are 110, the address is class C.
>
> ◆ If the first four bits are 1110, the address is class D.
>
> ◆ If the first four bits are 1111, the address is class E.
>
> Class D and E are not available for standard network addressing and aren't discussed much in this book. Class D is mentioned later in this chapter under routing tables.

Special IP Addresses

You might have noticed that the numbers don't add up to the subnets and hosts that a particular address class can support. That is because several addresses are reserved for special purposes. If you set up a TCP/IP network, you are assigning IP addresses and should keep the following restrictions in mind:

◆ Any address with a first octet value of 127 is a loopback address, which is used in diagnostics and testing. A message sent to an IP address with a first octet of 127 is returned to the sender. 127 cannot be used as a netid, therefore, even though it is technically a class A address.

◆ 255 in an octet designates a broadcast or a multicast. A message sent to 255.255.255.255 is broadcast to every host on the local network. A message sent to 165.10.255.255 is multicast to every host on network 165.10.

◆ The first octet cannot have a value above 223. Those addresses are reserved for multicast and experimental purposes.

◆ The last octet of a hostid cannot be 0 or 255.

Network IDs and Subnets

The rule for configuring TCP/IP subnets is quite simple: every host on the network must be configured with the same subnet ID. Figure 16.5 shows an internetwork with three subnets:

◆ A class A subnet with the subnet address 65

◆ A class B subnet with the subnet address 140.200

◆ A class C subnet with the subnet address 201.150.65

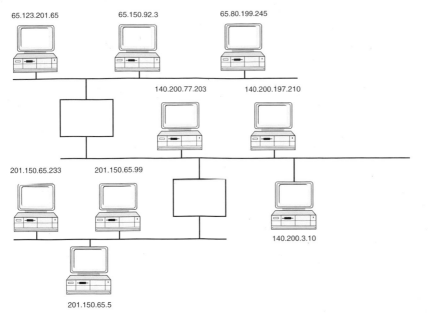

Figure 16.5

An internetwork based on three IP network IDs.

Each host on each subnet is shown with its internet ID. These subnets function in the same fashion. The only difference is that the class A subnet can support many more hosts. The subnets are internetworked with routers. Routing is described later in this chapter.

> **Note** Actually, you can configure devices on the same cable segment with different netids, and nothing will blow up. The devices behave as though they are on different subnets, however, and cannot communicate without a router. As you can see, the netid, not the cable segment to which the hosts are attached, is the crucial identifier of a subnet.

Subnet Masks

A *subnet mask* is a bit pattern that defines which portion of the IP address represents a subnet address. Because the octet organization of each IP address class is clearly defined, the purpose of subnet masks is not obvious at first, but subnet masks have good reasons for existing.

Here is a basic example. Consider the class B address 170.203.93.5. The binary equivalent for this address is:

```
10101010 11001011 1011101 00000101
```

The default subnet mask for a class B address is:

```
11111111 11111111 00000000 00000000
```

As you can see, the subnet mask has a 1 in each bit position that corresponds to a bit in the netid component of the address. When a 1 appears in the subnet mask, the corresponding bit in the IP address is part of the netid of the subnet. The netid of this subnet, therefore, is:

```
10101010 11001011
```

A 0 (zero) in a subnet mask indicates that the corresponding bit in the IP address is part of the host ID.

Like IP addresses, subnet masks are usually represented in dotted decimal notation. The preceding subnet address is 255.255.0.0.

Note | The RFCs do not allow a hostid that is all 1s or all 0s. Similarly, the RFCs do not permit the subnet portion of the netid in an IP address to be all 1s or all 0s.

Many implementations of TCP/IP, however, permit the use of subnetids that are all 0s, and it appears that Windows NT is among them. To my knowledge, however, Microsoft hasn't made an explicit statement that 0 subnetids are permitted.

Even though NT appears to support 0 subnetids, you need to look further before configuring the 0 subnet on your network. Be sure that all of the routers and clients are compatible with the 0 subnet. Not all devices are, particularly devices that are written in exact conformity with the standards.

Because the 0 subnet is problematic, I have chosen not to use it in the examples in this book.

Subnet masks make it easier and faster for IP to identify the netid portion of the IP address. Subnet masks have another benefit, as well; they permit you to suballocate network addresses.

This capability is particularly important when your network is attached to the Internet. This is because you will be assigned your IP addresses, and you probably won't get all the addresses you would like to have. Internet addresses are getting scarce, and you might not be able to secure enough addresses to assign an address to each subnet. Suppose that you have been assigned one class C address, but you need to organize your network with three subnets? That's where subnet masks really come in handy.

Consider the class C network address 205.101.55. The default subnet mask would be 255.255.255.0. It is possible, however, to extend the subnet mask into the fourth octet. Consider this binary subnet mask, which would be expressed as 255.255.255.224 in dotted-decimal notation:

11111111 11111111 11111111 11100000

This mask designates the first three bits of the fourth octet of the IP address as belonging to the subnet ID. To see how this works, apply the subnet mask to an IP address on this network. The IP address 205.101.55.91 would have this binary address:

11001101 01100101 00110111 01011011

After applying the subnet mask, the network ID for the subnet is:

11001101 01100101 00110111 01000000

The host ID consists of the five bits that correspond to zeros in the subnet mask. The host ID is binary 11011, which is decimal 27.

The first three bits of the fourth octet of the IP address can have values ranging from 001 through 110. Because 000 and 111 are not valid subnet IDs, a total of six subnets are made available by a subnet mask of 11100000.

The subnet mask designates that hostids in the fourth octet will fall in the range 00001 through 11110, with decimal values ranging from 1 through 30. (Again, 00000 and 11111 are invalid, and decimal addresses 0 and 31 may not be used.) This range of host IDs can be reused with each of the available subnet IDs.

The six subnets designated by a subnet mask of 255.255.255.224 would be associated with the following ranges of values in the fourth octet of the IP addresses:

00100001 through 00111110 (33 through 62)

01000001 through 01011110 (65 through 94)

01100001 through 01111110 (97 through 126)

10000001 through 10011110 (129 through 158)

10100001 through 10111110 (161 through 190)

11000001 through 11011110 (193 through 222)

> **Note** If you choose to use the 0 subnet, you can also use the range of 00000001 through 00011110 (1 through 30).

As you can see, the use of the subnet mask has made a considerable number of possible values unavailable. The benefit of creating multiple subnets with a single class C address must be weighed against the cost in terms of unavailable addresses.

Figure 16.6 shows an internetwork that requires a single class C network ID to implement three network segments. This would not be possible without using subnet masks.

Figure 16.6

An internetwork based on one class C address.

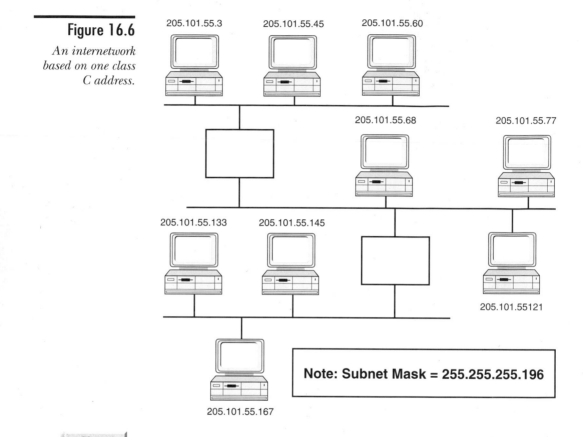

205.101.55.3   205.101.55.45   205.101.55.60

205.101.55.68   205.101.55.77

205.101.55.133   205.101.55.145

205.101.55121

Note: Subnet Mask = 255.255.255.196

205.101.55.167

Note When expressed in decimal form, subnet masks can appear to be somewhat of a mystery. For subnet masks to make sense, you must see them in terms of their binary patterns. Fortunately, subnet masks almost always use adjacent, high-order bits, so there are only eight common subnet mask octets:

Binary	Decimal
00000000	0
10000000	128
11000000	192
11100000	224

11110000	240
11111000	248
11111100	252
11111110	254
11111111	255

Delivering Packets on the Local Subnet

One of IP's responsibilities is to determine whether a packet can be delivered on the local subnet or must be routed to another subnet for final delivery. Subnet IDs make it much easier for IP to make this determination.

Before examining how routing takes place, take a look at the steps IP uses to deliver a packet to another host on the local subnet:

1. IP receives a frame from TCP, the next highest layer in the protocol stack. This frame is addressed to a particular IP address.

2. IP compares the subnet ID of the frame's IP address to the subnet ID of the local subnet. If the two subnet IDs match, the frame can be delivered locally.

3. Before sending the frame on the subnet, IP must determine the hardware address of the device that corresponds to the destination IP address. To get this information, IP utilizes the Address Resolution Protocol (ARP). Given an IP address of a host, ARP can determine the associated physical address for the host.

4. IP adds the following information to the frame, which is now referred to as a packet:

   ◆ The source IP address

   ◆ The source hardware address

   ◆ The destination IP address

   ◆ The destination hardware address

5. IP passes the packet with the address information down the protocol stack to the protocols that actually place the packet on the network.

Since the packet is tagged with the hardware address of a host on the local subnet, the destination host is able to spot the packet and retrieve it.

Routing Packets to Remote Subnets

What happens if IP determines that the source and destination subnet addresses don't match? That's a clear indication that the packet must be routed through the internetwork. IP in the local host doesn't perform the routing, but does send the packet to a device where it can be routed.

When hosts are connected to an internetwork, each host is configured with the IP address of a *default gateway* or *router*. (*Gateway* is an older term for *router;* it is also the term Microsoft NT uses.) When IP determines that the destination of a packet is not on the local subnet, IP addresses the packet to the default router (or an alternative router if the default router is unavailable).

Figure 16.7 illustrates the routing process. For the first time, the devices that connect the subnets have been labeled as routers. A router is essentially a computer running a TCP/IP protocol stack that is equipped with network adapters on all of the attached subnets. The adapter on each subnet is assigned an IP address that is appropriate for that subnet. Thus, a router is assigned two or more IP addresses and has a presence on two or more subnets.

Figure 16.7

Simple IP routing.

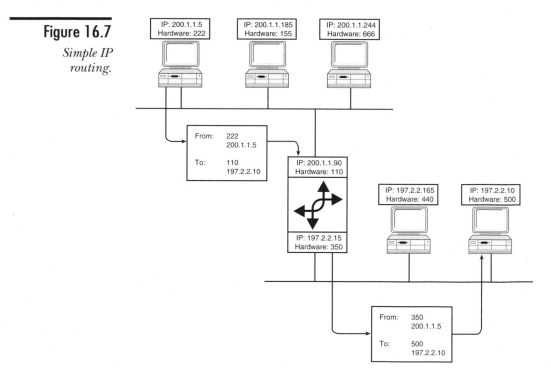

Routing algorithms can be very simple or very complex. To illustrate the simple approach, assume that the default class C subnet mask (255.255.255.0) is configured on all hosts. Suppose that host 200.1.1.5 is sending a packet addressed to host 197.2.2.10. The simple approach works like this (refer to figure 16.7 for illustration):

1. IP on host 200.1.1.5 determines that the destination host is not on the local subnet because the subnet addresses of source and destination don't match.

2. Because the packet must be routed, IP addresses the packet with the following information:

   ◆ Source Hardware Address: 222

   ◆ Source IP Address: 200.1.1.5

   ◆ Destination Hardware Address: 110

   ◆ Destination IP Address: 197.2.2.10

   Notice that the destination hardware address identifies the default router. The destination IP address matches the ultimate destination of the packet.

3. IP on the router receives the packet from subnet 200.1.1 and determines from the IP address that the packet is addressed to a host on subnet 197.2.2.

4. A local network adapter on the router has been configured with an IP address on subnet 197.2.2. IP, therefore, will use that adapter to forward the packet.

5. If the hardware address of the destination host is not already known, IP on the router uses ARP to determine it.

6. IP addresses the packet with this information and sends it on subnet 197.2.2:

   ◆ Source Hardware Address: 600

   ◆ Source IP Address: 200.1.1.5

   ◆ Destination Hardware Address: 500

   ◆ Destination IP Address: 197.2.2.10

7. When host 197.2.2.10 examines the packet, it determines that the addressee of the packet is itself and retrieves the packet from the network.

Notice two things in the routing process:

◆ The source and destination IP addresses don't change as the frame is routed. They always represent the original source and the ultimate destination of the packet.

◆ The hardware addresses change to indicate the host that last sent the packet
and the host that should receive it.

Complex IP Routing

IP determines where to route packets by consulting routing tables. The simple
routing in the previous discussion is an example of the routing capabilities of
Windows NT. Any Windows NT computer can be configured as a basic router by
adding a second network adapter card and configuring TCP/IP to enable routing.

By default, Windows NT routing tables only contain information about subnets to
which the computer is directly attached. A default configuration, therefore, would be
unable to route a packet from subnet 65 to subnet 90 in figure 16.8. Router A is
simply unaware that subnet 90 exists and cannot forward the frame.

Figure 16.8

*More complex
routing.*

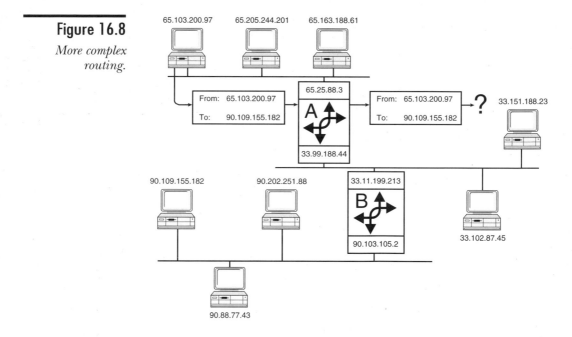

To route packets through more complex internetworks, it is necessary to enhance the
richness of the routing table information that is available to IP. There are two
approaches to building routing tables: *static* and *dynamic* routing.

Static Routing

A router can be configured with a *static routing table* that contains routing information
that is manually defined by a network administrator. The term *static* is used because

the table is not automatically updated when the network changes. When you reconfigure TCP/IP, a routing table is maintained on the computer.

Windows NT provides the route command-line utility, which can be used to print and directly modify the routing table on a host. The command to display a routing table is route print. Figure 16.9 shows the Windows NT routing table that is associated with the router that is set up later in this chapter. A full description of this table and of configuring static routing is beyond the scope of this book. Some essential features are:

◆ The *Network Address* column defines destination IP addresses.

◆ The *Netmask* indicates the portion of the network address that must match if this route is to be used. A binary 1 in the netmask indicates that a bit in the IP address must match the corresponding bit in the network address. Thus, a netmask of 255.255.255.255 is used for a host entry because a host is uniquely identified by its complete IP address. Netmasks for network addresses have 1 bits indicating the bits reserved for the netid and subnetid, and 0 bits indicating bits reserved for hostids.

◆ The *Gateway Address* column defines the gateway (router) that should be used next when sending a frame to the address shown in the Network Address column. Network addresses can consist of subnet IDs or complete host IP addresses.

◆ The *Interface* column states the interface associated with this table entry.

◆ The *Metric* column indicates the cost of reaching the destination address. Cost is measured in hops: a hop count of 1 indicates that the destination is on the local subnet. An additional *hop* is incurred whenever a frame crosses a router.

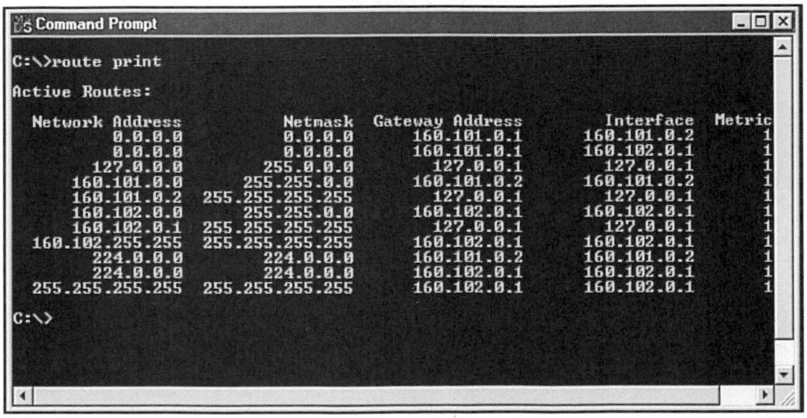

Figure 16.9

Example of a Windows NT routing table.

Let's take a closer look at some of the entries in this table:

◆ Entries with the network address 0.0.0.0 are *default routes*. When the router table does not have an explicit entry for a destination, the gateway address in the default route entry will be used. Most hosts are configured with default routes to be used in events when a destination is not covered by an explicit route.

◆ The entry for the network address 127.0.0.0 defines routes to loopback network. All messages directed to addresses 127.0.0.1 through 127.0.0.255 should be directed back to the interface from which they originate. This is accomplished by using a *netmask* of 255.0.0.0, which indicates that all destination addresses that match the first 8 bits of 127.0.0.0 (that is, all addresses with 127 at the start of the address) should be routed to address 127.0.0.1.

◆ The entry for network address 160.101.0.0 is an example of a network destination. The netmask 255.255.0.0 indicates that all addresses matching the first 16 bits of 160.101.0.0 should be routed to the specified gateway. As a result, any data directed to any host on the 160.101.0.0 network will be routed to interface 160.101.0.2.

◆ The entry for network address 160.101.0.2 defines a table entry for a specific destination IP address. The netmask 255.255.255.255 indicates that the destination address of a message must match all 32 bits of the network address before the message will be routed to the specified gateway.

◆ The entries for 224.0.0.0 are *multicast* entries. Network 224.0.0.0 is a class D network, and class D addresses are reserved for use with multicasts. A multicast is a message that is directed to a specified group of hosts. Multicasts are often used by TCP/IP protocols for communication among hosts.

◆ The entry for 255.255.255.255 specifies that all messages sent to the broadcast address should be directed to 160.102.0.1.

Each time the network configuration changes, static routing requires a network administrator to use the route command to update the routing table. You can readily see that this could become a time-consuming and error-prone task.

Dynamic Routing

Because maintaining static routing tables is a pain, most networks rely on routers that can use routing algorithms to dynamically maintain routing tables. Windows NT does not have this capability, and you must turn to commercial routers to get it.

Routing algorithms is quite complex, and the details far exceed the scope of this chapter. Only a brief description of two algorithms commonly employed on TCP/IP internetworks is included.

Routing Information Protocol

The Routing Information Protocol (RIP) is known as a *distance vector* routing algorithm. If a router knows several routes to a destination, it assigns a cost to the route in terms of the *hops* the route involves. The hop count is incremented each time a packet crosses a router. Each router broadcasts its routing table every 30 seconds. In this way, routers in the internetwork share their routing tables, and routing information gradually propagates through the internetwork.

Distance vector algorithms have a number of practical problems. One, called the *count-to-infinity* problem, has to do with routes that loop back on themselves, causing packets to circulate the network indefinitely. Count-to-infinity is controlled by setting a maximum hop count of 16. Any packet that registers 16 hops is discarded. This limits the maximum number of hops a packet can take to 15 and limits the scope of networks that RIP can manage.

Another problem is that it can take considerable time for a change to propagate through the network. This is called the *convergence* problem.

Finally, because all routers broadcast routing information every 30 seconds, considerable traffic is generated. RIP traffic can really bog down a network, particularly when slower WAN links are involved.

RIP is available in two versions: RIP I and RIP II. RIP II supports the use of subnet masks. Some routers can support both RIP versions simultaneously.

Open Shortest Path First

The Open Shortest Path First (OSPF) algorithm is based on a different approach called *link state*. Each router broadcasts periodic *link state packets* that describe its connections to its neighbors. Using this information, routers build a link state database that is used to identify routes. OSPF enables networks to use costs as high as 65535, enabling designers to build internetworks without the 16 hop limitation.

Link state algorithms do not suffer from the count-to-infinity problem. They also generate much less broadcast traffic than RIP. Link state packets are retransmitted only when the network changes or at infrequent intervals.

As such, OSPF is a significant improvement over RIP and can be expected to become the TCP/IP routing protocol of choice.

Host Names and Naming Services

It would be a real nuisance to have to refer to each host by its IP address. Let's face it, humans don't remember numbers very well. A system was developed, therefore, that enabled users to refer to hosts by name.

Originally, the system involved a file named "hosts," a text file that was stored on each host that mapped IP addresses to host names. A hosts file might contain entries like this:

```
201.150.63.98   widgets.keystone.com
```

Conventionally, the hosts file is stored with other TCP/IP configuration files on Unix computers in a directory named "etc." By default, Windows NT stores the hosts file in C:\WINNT\SYSTEM32\DRIVERS\ETC.

The hosts file must be manually maintained by the network administrator. One of the big hassles of maintaining a TCP/IP network is updating this file and ensuring that the updates make it onto each computer on the network.

Maintenance of host files should qualify for mental hazard pay, and would be even worse on really large networks. To get around the problem, you need a naming service.

Windows NT offers the Windows Internet Naming Service (WINS), which is discussed later in this chapter in the section "Installing and Managing WINS."

Domain Name Services (DNS) protocol was developed to serve as a central repository of names on the Internet. DNS is discussed later in the examination of issues involved in connecting Windows NT to the Internet. DNS names are discussed in the section "Internet Domain Names."

Note Two categories of names are involved in a Windows NT TCP/IP environment:

◆ NetBIOS names are the native names used for Windows networking. These are the computer names you enter when you install Windows NT or when you configure Microsoft networking on Windows for Workgroups. NetBIOS names are used when Microsoft network clients are browsing the network.

◆ DNS names are supported by a TCP/IP Directory Name Service. DNS names identify TCP/IP hosts by name and are recognized by TCP/IP applications.

The Windows Internet Naming System (WINS) permits NetBIOS names to be used in a TCP/IP environment by maintaining a NetBIOS name database.

WINS is a Microsoft-only standard, and names that are maintained by WINS are not usable by non-Windows hosts on an internetwork. If you want your network to have a naming service that is usable by Windows and non-Windows hosts, you need to implement DNS.

Connecting to the Internet

More and more private networks are being connected to the Internet, a giant TCP/IP internetwork descended from the ARPAnet, a network built by the Defense Advanced Research Projects Agency (DARPA) to connect the Department of Defense (DoD) with educational institutions and defense contractors. The Internet has recently been made public and now interconnects millions of hosts throughout the world.

When you connect your TCP/IP network to the Internet, you enter a larger world with restrictions, risks, and responsibilities. One of your responsibilities is to obtain an IP address for your organization that does not conflict with addresses of other organizations on the Internet.

After you obtain an IP address, you need to obtain a connection to the Internet, usually through a commercial Internet provider.

Obtaining an Internet Address

If you are running a TCP/IP network in isolation, you can use any addresses you choose. On the Internet, however, you need to use an address that is assigned by the Internet Network Information Center (InterNIC).

Until fairly recently, individual organizations contacted the InterNIC directly to register Internet addresses. As the Internet accelerated, however, the InterNIC chose to allocate blocks of addresses to Internet access providers (IAPs), who in turn assign addresses to their clients. Unless you are one of the rare organizations that has a direct connection to the Internet, you will be working with an IAP who will supply you with the addresses you need.

If you need to register with the InterNIC, you can obtain the required documents by using FTP to connect to is.internic.net. Log on as anonymous and transfer the documents you require.

If you don't have Internet access, contact InterNIC at:

> Network Solutions
> InterNIC Registration Service
> 505 Huntmar Park Drive
> Herndon, VA 22070

Applications and questions can be e-mailed to hostmaster@internic.net.

Incidentally, don't expect to obtain a class A or B address at this late date. Class A and B addresses were used up long ago by the early occupants of the Internet. All that's really left are class C addresses, and even those are in short supply. In fact, the Internet will run out of class C addresses in a year or two. Consequently, a new approach has been taken when assigning IP addresses to smaller organizations. If your organization has 50 hosts, it would be wasteful for you to be given a class C address that would waste 204 addresses. Instead, you will be assigned a block of addresses called a Classless Internetwork Domain Routing (CIDR) block. Your assignment includes an IP address, and a subnet mask that grants you use of a subset of the addresses in the complete IP address. If you need 50 addresses, for example, you would likely be assigned a class C address with a subnet mask of 255.255.255.192. This combination gives you use of 64 addresses. CIDR (pronounced "cider") blocks are identified by the number of 1 bits in the subnet mask. A CIDR block with a subnet mask of 255.255.255.192 has 26 1 bits and is a "slash 64" CIDR block.

> **Note**
>
> You may chafe at the thought of receiving less than a full class C address, but inefficient address usage is at the heart of the IP address crisis. If every possible address were available for host assignment, 32-bit IP addresses could support several billion hosts. Few organizations who register a class A, B, or C address, however, use their allocations to 100% capacity. How many organizations have the 16,777,216 hosts required to fully utilize a class A address?
>
> It is necessary, therefore, to get away from the concept of "owning" a block of IP addresses. Organizations must learn to be satisfied with addresses that meet their operational needs with reasonable room for growth. They should not expect to stake a claim on a substantial part of the IP address territory when they do not have the resources to fully exploit that claim.

To fix the IP address problem, a new generation of TCP/IP protocols (IP next generation, or IPng) is being developed. Because much current TCP/IP equipment does not support IPng, however, it will take considerable time for the entire Internet to migrate to the new standards.

> **Note**
>
> It's a good idea to obtain addresses from InterNIC, even if your network is not currently attached to the Internet. If you do connect to the Internet in the future, you won't have the headache of reassigning all the IP addresses on your network.

Internet Domain Names

Domain Name Services was mentioned earlier as the solution used on the Internet to assign names to IP addresses. DNS was developed as a means of organizing the nearly 20 million host names that are using the Internet.

DNS names are organized in a hierarchy. Before looking closely at how DNS manages its name space, you should review the characteristics of a naming hierarchy by examining a familiar example, the Windows NT file system directory structure.

File System Hierarchies

You are already familiar with a common form of hierarchical organization: the hierarchical directory structure used by virtually all operating systems, including Unix, DOS, and Windows. Figure 16.10 illustrates a Windows NT directory hierarchy, more commonly called a *directory tree*. (Even though real trees and family trees—perhaps the oldest hierarchical databases—frequently place their roots at the bottom, database trees are always upended as shown. The upside-down trees commonly used to depict computer data structures are called *inverted trees*.)

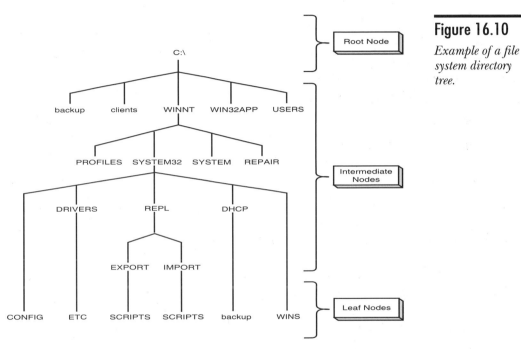

Figure 16.10

Example of a file system directory tree.

Data in a tree are represented by the intersections or end-points of the lines that describe the tree structure. These points are called *nodes*, of which there are three kinds:

◆ **Root.** Every tree has exactly one root node. On a file system, this is called the root directory, represented by a \ (DOS and Windows) or a / (Unix).

◆ **Intermediate nodes.** An indefinite number of nodes can be made subordinate to the root node. Intermediate nodes may themselves have subordinate nodes. On file systems, intermediate nodes are called subdirectories and are assigned logical identifiers, such as WINNT.

◆ **Leaf nodes.** A leaf node is the end of a branch in the tree.

Nodes are frequently referred to as *parent* and *child* nodes. Leaf nodes are always children. Intermediate nodes are parents of their child (subordinate) nodes and children of their parent nodes. The root node is a parent to all first-level intermediate nodes. Nodes that are children of the same parent are *siblings*.

Any given node on the tree may be fully described by listing the nodes between itself and the root. Figure 16.10 shows an example identifying the node (in this case a subdirectory) \WINNT\SYSTEM32\REPL\EXPORT. Names that list all nodes between a node and the root are called *fully qualified* names. Note that fully qualified names for file systems begin with the root and proceed down the tree to the node in question.

A fully qualified name can uniquely identify any node in the tree. The names \WINNT\REPAIR and \WINNT\SYSTEM describe separate nodes (subdirectories) in the directory tree.

Figure 16.11 illustrates an important rule of hierarchies: siblings may not have identical node names. Thus, the \WINNT directory cannot have two subdirectories named MSAPPS. It is perfectly all right, however, to have two nodes named MSAPPS when their fully qualified names are different. It is permissible, for example, to have directories named \APPS\MSAPPS and \WINNT\MSAPPS on the same file system.

Figure 16.11

Each node in a hierarchy must have a unique fully qualified name.

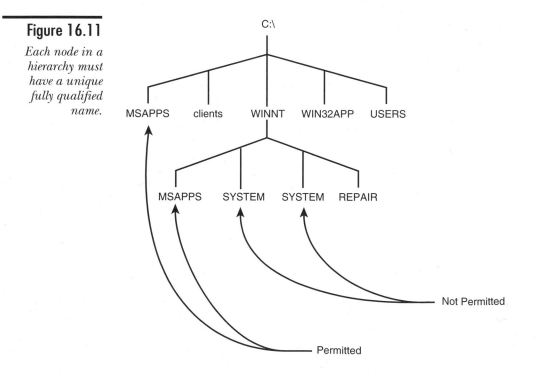

The Domain Name Space

The DNS hierarchical database is called the *domain name space*. Each host in the domain name space has a unique fully qualified name. Figure 16.12 shows a simple DNS hierarchy that might be employed in an organization. The root node of a DNS tree is called either "root" or the "root domain." The root domain is often designated with empty quotation marks (" "). Each node in the tree has a name, which can contain up to 63 characters.

The fully qualified name for a DNS node is called the *fully qualified domain name* (FQDN). Unlike fully qualified path names in file systems, which start from the root, the FQDN convention in DNS starts with the node being described and proceeds to the root. Figure 16.12 illustrates charles.sw.keystone as an example of a FQDN. The convention with DNS names is to separate node names with a period (referred to as "dot"). The root node may be represented by a trailing dot (as in charles.sw.keystone.), but the trailing dot is ordinarily omitted.

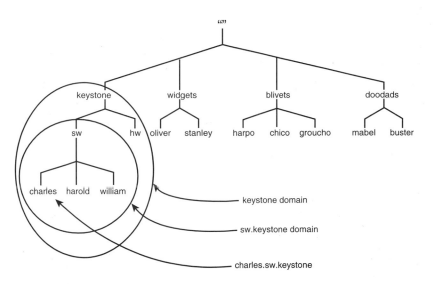

Figure 16.12

DNS tree for an organization.

DNS trees can be viewed in terms of domains, which are simply subtrees of the entire database. Figure 16.13 illustrates how subdomains can be defined within domains. The eng domain has two subdomains: sw.eng and hw.eng. The name of a subdomain is simply the FQDN of the topmost node in the domain. Subdomains always consist of complete subtrees of the tree, a node and all of its child nodes. A subdomain cannot be designated to include both eng and mkt, which are located at the same level of the tree.

Subdomains are DNS management structures. It is possible to delegate management of any subdomain to distribute management responsibility for the complete name space.

As shown in figure 16.13, DNS trees obey the same naming rules as directory trees: siblings must have unique node names. Nodes that are children of different parents may have the same node names.

Note Domain names can be assigned *aliases*, pointers from one domain name to another. The domain pointed to by the alias is called the *canonical* (the "real") domain name.

Domain and subdomain are relative terms and are used somewhat interchangeably. Every domain except the root domain is, in a real sense, a subdomain. When discussion focuses on a particular node, however, that node is generally referred to as a domain. Use of the terms domain and subdomain is primarily a function of perspective. DNS domains are typically referred to in terms of levels:

◆ A *first-level domain* is a child of root. The more commonly used name for first-level domain is *top-level domain*.

◆ A *second-level domain* is a child of a first-level domain.

◆ A *third-level domain* is a child of a second-level domain, and so forth.

Notice that eng.keystone has two functions. It is a name of a host in the DNS hierarchy, and it points to a particular IP address. eng.keystone, however, is also a structure in the DNS database that is used to organize its children in the database hierarchy.

Figure 16.13

Naming rules for DNS nodes.

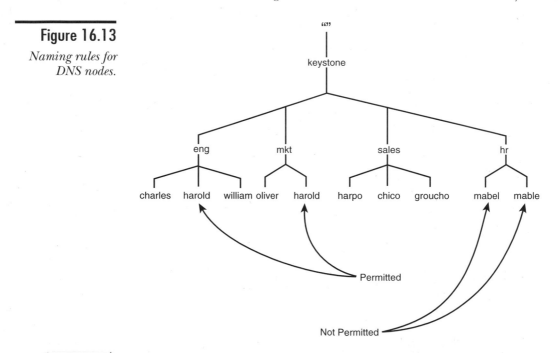

Note Note that the term *domains* used with regard to DNS has no relationship to Windows NT Server domains. Windows NT Server domains provide a means of organizing Windows NT computers into manageable groups that share a common security database. DNS domains are related only to the Internet naming service. It is quite possible for a Windows NT computer to participate in a Windows NT domain under one name and in a DNS domain under another name.

> **Note** Beginning with Windows NT 4, UNC names can include TCP/IP host names. If your network is fully converted to TCP/IP, the following UNC identifies the share APPS on the computer charles.keystone.com:
>
> ```
> \\charles.keystone.com\apps
> ```
>
> Of course, charles.keystone.com must be a Windows NT computer. You cannot use this UNC to connect to a Unix computer because Unix servers don't offer Windows-compatible shares.

Reverse-Lookup Domains

You most often use DNS to resolve a name to its associated IP address. Some processes, however, find it necessary to resolve an IP address to a domain name. The standard DNS hierarchy provides no easy way to do this. A given IP address can appear anywhere in the name space. DNS uses reverse-lookup domains to provide address-to-name resolution.

Figure 16.14 shows the portion of the Internet reverse-naming tree that describes mcp.com (Macmillan Computer Publishing's Internet domain), which has the IP address 198.70.148.1. Suppose a host needs to resolve that IP address to determine the domain name. It starts at the root of the reverse-naming tree, as follows:

◆ It identifies the root naming tree, in which the first-layer name is arpa.

◆ It walks down the tree through the domain in-addr. All reverse-name data are stored beneath this node.

◆ It looks for the first part of the IP address (198) under in-addr.

◆ It looks for the second part of the IP address (70) under 198.

◆ It looks for the third part of the IP address (148) under 70.

◆ Finally, it comes to the hostid (1) under 148. Beneath the last part of the IP address is found a pointer to the domain name mcp.com.

When you set up your DNS server, you need to establish reverse-lookup domains in addition to the forward-lookup domains.

Domain Administration

DNS was designed to handle the Internet, which is too vast to be centrally administered as a single name space. It was essential, therefore, to be able to delegate administration of subdomains.

Name servers are programs that store data about the domain name space and provide that information in response to DNS queries. The complete name space can be organized into *zones*, which are simply subsets of the DNS tree. A given name server has authority for one or more zones. Figure 16.15 shows a sample tree as it might be organized into three zones. Notice that zones do not require regular boundaries. In the example, eng is maintained in a separate zone on its own name server. Notice that zones, unlike domains, need not be simple slices of the NDS tree, but can incorporate different levels of different branches.

Figure 16.14

The in-addr.arpa reverse-lookup domain.

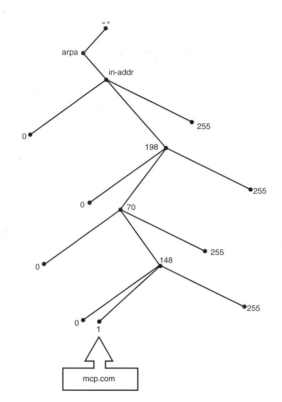

Administration for zones can be delegated to name servers, as required. When administration for a domain is delegated to a name server, that name server is responsible for the domain's subdomains as well, unless administration for those subdomains is delegated away.

Each zone must be serviced by a *primary master name server*, which obtains the data for the zone from files on its host. Secondary master domain servers obtain zone data by performing *zone transfers* from the primary master name server for the zone. Secondary masters will periodically update their databases from the primary to keep the various name servers for the zone synchronized.

DNS is very flexible in the way name servers and zones can be related. Recall that name servers may be authoritative for more than one zone. Beyond that, it is possible for a name server to be a primary on some zone(s) and a secondary for other zone(s).

The provision for multiple name servers provides a level of redundancy that enables the network DNS to continue to function with secondaries despite a failure of the primary master name server.

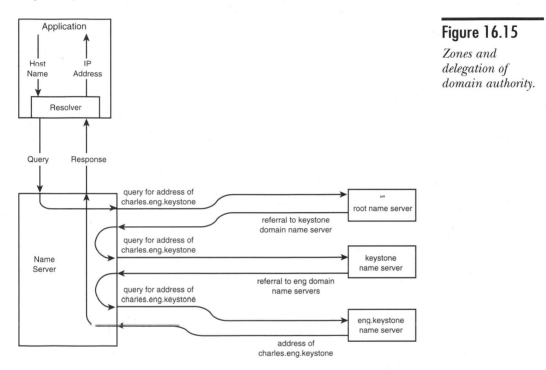

Figure 16.15

Zones and delegation of domain authority.

Resolving DNS Queries

When an application requires DNS data, it uses a *resolver* to query a DNS server. A resolver is simply the client side of the DNS client/server relationship. The resolver generates a DNS query and sends it to a name server, processes the response from the name server, and forwards the information to the program that requested the data.

Resolver queries are fulfilled by DNS servers. The process is shown in figure 16.16. The resolver in a host is configured with the IP address of at least one DNS server. When the resolver requires an IP address, it contacts a known DNS server, which is responsible for processing the request.

Resolution is a matter of querying other DNS servers, starting with one that is authoritative for the root domain. The root name server provides the address of a first-level domain in the queried name. If required, the first-level domain supplies the address of a second-level domain server, and so on, until a domain server is reached that can satisfy the query.

Note The most popular implementation of DNS is Berkeley Internet Name Domain (BIND), originally written for 4.3BSD Unix and now at version 4.8.3. BIND has been ported to most versions of Unix, and a Windows NT version is included with the *Windows NT Resource Kit*. BIND supports tree depths of 127 levels, sufficient to enable BIND to be used on the root name servers for the Internet.

BIND makes use of so-called *stub resolvers*. A stub resolver has no DNS search capability. It simply knows how to send a query to a DNS server. Actual resolution of the query is performed by the name server.

To diminish the effort required to resolve DNS queries, DNS servers will cache the results of recent queries. Data in the cache may enable the server to satisfy a DNS query locally or to shorten the search by starting at a DNS server that is authoritative for a lower-level domain. In the event that cached information cannot be used to initiate a search, the process begins with the root domain. Entries in a DNS cache table are assigned a *time to live* (TTL), which is configured by the domain administrator. Entries that exceed the TTL will be discarded, and the next time a resolver places a request for that domain the name server must retrieve the data from the network.

Figure 16.16

Resolution of a DNS query.

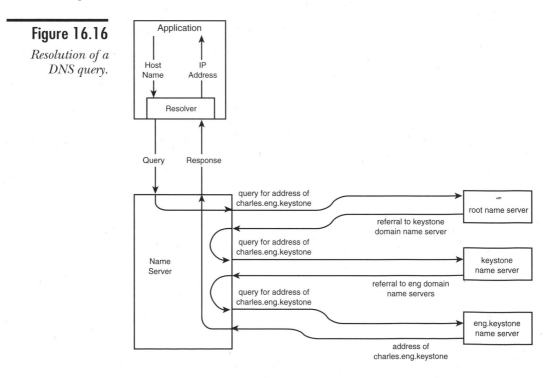

Resolvers are actually components of applications and processes running on a host. When compiling programs, developers will include library routines for the name service to be supported. Thus, programs like ftp and telnet are compiled with the capability to construct DNS queries and to process the response. The DNS server is responsible for searching the database, however.

Clearly, the capability of supporting secondary DNS servers in domains is crucial to providing a reliable name service. If no DNS server is available for the root domain, for example, all name resolution will eventually fail, as entries in the cache tables in lower-level DNS servers expire and must be renewed.

The Internet DNS Name Space

If you are connecting your private TCP/IP to the Internet, you need to fit your DNS name space into the Internet name space. Your organization will not be established as a first-level domain, and perhaps not as a second-level domain. Instead, you will occupy the Internet name space as a child of an existing domain.

DNS names are organized in a hierarchical fashion, as shown in figure 16.17.

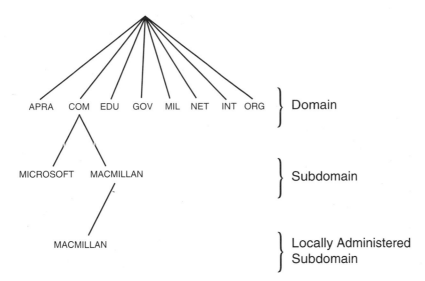

Figure 16.17

The DNS name hierarchy.

The first layer of the hierarchy consists of *domain names* that are assigned by the Network Information Center (NIC). Table 16.1 summarizes the top-level domain names. Each domain is given its own administration authority.

TABLE 16.1
Top-Level Domain Names

Domain Name	Description
ARPA	Advanced Research Projects Agency network (ARPAnet)
COM	Commercial organizations
EDU	Educational institutions
GOV	Government agencies
MIL	Military agencies
NET	Network support centers, such as Internet service providers
INT	International organizations
ORG	Non-profit organizations
country code	Two-letter X.500 country codes

Second-level domain names, called *subdomain names,* must be registered with the NIC. The application can be found in the file DOMAIN-TEMPLATE.TXT, which can be retrieved by anonymous ftp from hostmaster@internic.net. If you are running a DNS service on your local LAN, register the name even if you are not currently connected to the Internet. When you do connect, you can be sure that the name you want is available.

Third-level domain names usually name a particular host in the subdomain. (You can have as many levels as you want, provided the entire name does not exceed 255 characters.) The NIC only registers domain and subdomain names. Additional levels of the name hierarchy are maintained locally.

Windows NT 4 includes a DNS name server that is compatible with BIND, the most popular name server on the Internet. The Windows NT 4 DNS server has the unique capability to connect with WINS, which enables you to advertise the names of WINS-registered hosts in the DNS name space. Configuration and management of the Windows NT 4 DNS server is covered later, in the section "Managing DNS."

Getting Access

Unless you are well-connected with an organization that is already connected to the Internet, you will probably gain access through a commercial provider.

Access can be through a dial-up connection if you don't need your site to be consistently accessible from the outside. You can set up a dial-up connection using the Remote Access Server (RAS), which is the subject of Chapter 21, "Using the Remote Access Server." RAS supports dial-up connections through conventional modems using the SLIP and PPP protocols. RAS also enables you to use the high-speed dial-up capabilities of ISDN.

A permanent connection usually means that you will be leasing a dedicated phone line from a local communication provider. This line will connect you with your local Internet access provider. In most cases, you will install a router between your network and the dedicated line to route traffic to the Internet.

When you connect to the Internet, you open your network to the world. There is considerable risk in doing so, because a TCP/IP connection gives outside users significant access capabilities to your network. The Internet is filled with people who know how to infiltrate your system through an Internet connection.

To protect yourself, you should consider installing a *firewall* at your Internet access point. Just as firewalls in buildings slow the spread of fires, a network firewall impedes the ability of outsiders to gain access to your network. New Riders Publishing offers an excellent book on firewalls, titled *Internet Firewalls and Network Security*.

Installing and Managing TCP/IP Services

Objective
B.4

This section covers installation of TCP/IP, along with two services that greatly simplify administration of Windows NT TCP/IP networks.

Installing TCP/IP is easy, but proper configuration takes time, planning, and probably some troubleshooting. Much of the time involves planning IP addresses and configuring each host with the correct address information. Because you need to know how to plan and configure hosts with fixed IP addresses, the manual procedures are covered first. You first learn how to set up a network with a single subnet. Then you learn how to configure a Windows NT computer to serve as an IP router between two subnets.

After you know how to assign addresses manually, you are introduced to an easier way to assign host addresses. Windows NT provides a protocol that considerably simplifies host addressing. The Dynamic Host Configuration Protocol can assign host names dynamically.

Finally, this section examines the Windows Internet Naming Service (WINS), which provides a naming service for users of Windows network products that are connected to a TCP/IP network.

Setting Up a TCP/IP Subnet with Fixed IP Addresses

Before you start addressing any network, it is essential that you plan your address scheme. If you are using an Internet IP address that was assigned by InterNIC, you need to make the most of the address you have, which means planning any subnetting that will be required.

Start with a basic network with a single subnet. With the basics out of the way, it will be easier for you to understand how to set up multiple subnets and routers.

Figure 16.18 illustrates the subnet that will be configured first. It is based on the class B address 160.100. The figure shows only two hosts, but once the basic subnet is configured, adding more hosts is not complicated.

Figure 16.18

A network with one subnet.

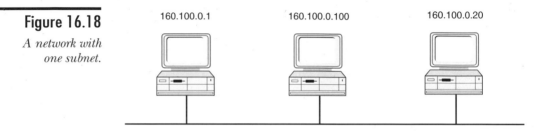

The first computer you install is given the IP address 160.100.0.1. To install TCP/IP on the computer, follow the steps in the following exercise:

Installing TCP/IP

1. Start the Network utility in the Windows NT Control Panel and select the **P**rotocols tab.

2. Choose **A**dd to display the Select Network Protocol dialog box.

3. Select the entry TCP/IP Protocol. Then choose OK.

4. You are shown the prompt, `Do you wish to use DHCP?` In this example, IP addresses are installed manually, and DHCP is not to be installed. Select **N**o.

5. When prompted, supply the path where files can be found on the installation CD-ROM. Files are copied and TCP/IP is installed. You are returned to the Network utility window.

6. Choose Close.

7. After bindings for other protocols are reviewed, the Microsoft TCP/IP Properties window is displayed, as shown in figure 16.19.

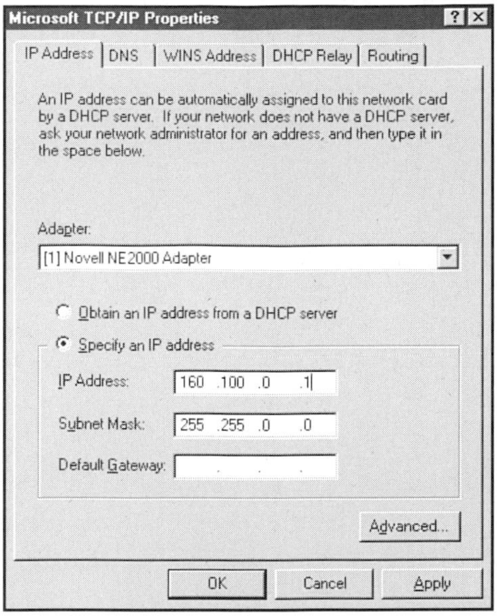

Figure 16.19

Configuring TCP/IP properties.

8. The only settings required in this example are:

    ◆ Check **S**pecify an IP Address.

    ◆ Enter the desired IP address in the **IP** Address field.

    ◆ Enter a subnet mask in the Su**b**net Mask field. The dialog box will propose the default mask for the address class you entered in the **IP** Address box.

    No default gateway is specified because a single subnet does not require any routing.

9. Choose OK to save the settings.

10. When prompted, restart the computer to activate the protocol.

The second computer on the subnet will have the IP address 160.100.0.100. This computer is configured using the same procedures; only the **IP** Address entry differs. After TCP/IP is installed on the second computer and both computers have been restarted, they should be able to communicate through TCP/IP.

Testing the TCP/IP Installation

The basic tool for testing TCP/IP networks is the ping command. ping accepts an IP address or a name that is recognized by the active naming service. ping sends a message to another host that requests a reply. Figure 16.20 shows the result of a successful ping request. When the other host does not respond, the result resembles figure 16.21.

Figure 16.20

Result of a successful ping.

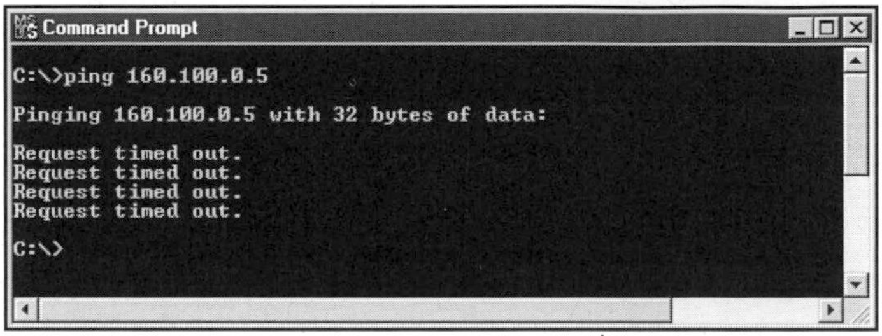

Figure 16.21

Result of an unsuccessful ping.

Use the Unix ping command to test your network as it is built. Work through the network gradually to ensure that hosts are reachable, particularly when routing is involved.

You can also use ping to test the basic configuration of an individual host. Earlier it was mentioned that IP addresses with a first octet value of 127 were used as loopback addresses. If you ping a loopback address, the attempt loops back without being sent to another host. If ping works with a loopback address, TCP/IP has been properly installed.

The following exercise performs a suggested sequence for testing a newly installed host using ping:

Testing a Newly Installed Host with Ping

1. Ping the loopback address with the command:

   ping 127.0.0.1.

2. Ping the host's own IP address.

3. Ping another host on the segment. If the host's default gateway has been installed, it is a good ping target. Successfully pinging the default gateway is the first step in determining whether the host can reach other segments on an internetwork.

4. Ping a host on another segment that should be attached through a router.

5. If a name service such as WINS or DNS is configured on the network, try pinging host names as well as addresses.

Failure in steps 1 or 2 indicates improper TCP/IP installation.

Failure in step 3 could mean several things:

◆ You are pinging the wrong address.

◆ The host you are pinging is improperly configured.

◆ One of the hosts has a bad network adapter.

◆ The network media has failed.

Failure in step 4 could indicate the same sorts of failures. First perform tests on the individual segments to ensure that hosts on each segment can ping one another. If the individual segments are functioning, the problem probably lies with the configuration of the router. Setting up Windows NT as an IP router is the subject of the next section.

Setting Up a Two-Segment Network with Routing

Figure 16.22 shows a network with two segments connected by a Windows NT computer that is configured as a router. The router must meet the following requirements:

◆ A separate network adapter must be installed to connect the computer to both segments.

◆ Each adapter must be configured with an IP address that matches the network segment to which it is connected.

◆ Routing must be enabled on the routing computer.

Figure 16.22

A two-segment network with a router.

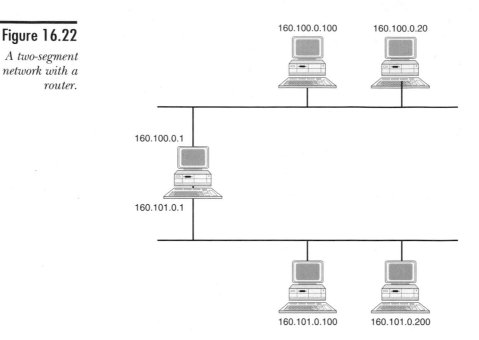

A router essentially has two network personalities. It functions as a host on each of the networks to which it is attached and is assigned an IP address for each network. Internally, a routing function routes packets as required between the two networks.

The following exercise details the procedures for implementing an NT router.

Configuring a Windows NT Router

The first step in configuring a Windows NT router is to install a second network adapter in the computer. Then some reconfiguration of TCP/IP is required:

1. Install a network adapter card. Be sure it does not conflict with any hardware settings for existing components.

2. Open the Networks utility in the Control Panel and select the Adapters tab.

3. Choose **A**dd to open the Select Network Adapter window.

4. Select an adapter from the **N**etwork Adapter list and choose OK.

5. In the Adapter Card Setup dialog box, specify the hardware settings for the adapter you have selected.

6. If your computer has more than one bus (for example ISA and PCI), specify the bus supporting the adapter in the Adapter Bus Location dialog box.

7. Choose OK when shown the prompt `The current netcard parameters are not verifiably correct and may result in usage problems or system failure. Use them anyway?`

8. When prompted, supply the path where files can be found on the installation CD-ROM. Files will be copied and the adapter software will be installed. You will be returned to the Network utility window.

9. Choose Close in the Network dialog box. While bindings are configured, you will be shown the TCP/IP Properties window.

10. Select the adapter to be configured in the Ada**p**ter field.

11. Select **S**pecify an IP address.

12. Complete the **IP** Address and **S**ubnet Mask fields.

13. Repeat steps 12–14 for any additional network adapter cards.

14. Select the Routing tab and check **E**nable IP Forwarding.

> **Note** In the network of figure 16.22, it is not necessary to configure a default gateway for the router computer. It is directly attached to both network segments and does not require a default gateway address to route data.
>
> You must, however, configure default gateway addresses on the workstations attached to each network segment. If a default gateway is not specified, the computers will not be able to route data to computers on the other subnet unless the route command is used to add appropriate routing information to the computers' routing tables.

15. Choose OK to save the settings.

16. When prompted, restart the computer to activate the protocol.

After the other hosts have been configured, ping can be used to test out the gateway's routing capabilities. It should be possible to ping 160.100.0.100 from either subnet, for example. If that doesn't work, it is necessary to double-check addressing on the adapters in the router and to ensure that IP routing has been enabled.

> **Note** Another example would be to ping 160.100.0.100 from machine 160.101.0.100, which would show that the NT box is routing IP packets.

Setting Up Additional Segments

Windows NT computers can function as routers. Windows NT can include a protocol such as RIP or OSPF, routing tables can be manually configured whenever segments are separated by more than one hop, or the use of RIP can dynamically adjust the routing table.

Figure 16.23 illustrates such a network. Two routers are used to internetwork three network segments. As installed, the routers can handle the following routing:

◆ Router A can route frames between segment 160.100 and 160.101.

◆ Router B can route frames between segment 160.101 and 160.102.

Figure 16.23

A three-segment network.

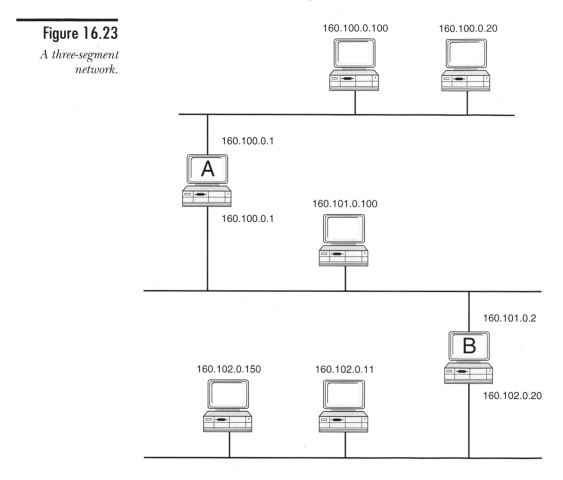

If a host on segment 160.100 attempts to send a frame to 160.102.0.100, however, router A is unaware of the existence of subnet 160.102 and is unable to route the frame. It is, therefore, necessary to give A a more sophisticated routing capability. Windows NT Server 4 offers enhanced routing in two forms:

◆ Dynamic routing using the Routing Information Protocol (RIP)

◆ Static routing using the `route` command

Both approaches are discussed in the next two sections.

Dynamic Routing with RIP

Windows NT Server 4 includes a Multiprotocol Router that supports the RIP protocol, enabling Windows NT Server computers to provide a dynamic routing capability. RIP for IP is extremely easy to install and configure, as outlined in the following exercise.

To install RIP for IP, follow these steps:

Installing RIP for IP

1. Open the Network utility in the Control Panel and select the Services tab.

2. Choose **A**dd and select RIP for Internet Protocol in the **N**etwork Service box.

3. Choose OK.

4. When prompted, supply the path where files can be found on the installation CD-ROM. Files will be copied and the adapter software will be installed. You will be returned to the Network utility window.

5. RIP is installed as a service. Restart the computer to activate the protocol.

After RIP for IP has been installed and the computer has been restarted, the RIP service is started and routing is enabled on the computer. To enable and disable routing, do the following:

1. Open the Network utility in the Control Panel and select the Routing tab.

2. Check **E**nable IP Forwarding.

3. Choose OK.

Note The IP RIP router included with Windows NT Server does not support routing through dial-up WAN links.

When RIP is installed on a computer that is equipped with a single network adapter card, RIP operates in *Silent Mode*. RIP will collect RIP route advertisements from the network and use them to update the computer's routing table, but RIP will not broadcast route advertisements.

If you add a network adapter to a Windows NT computer running RIP in Silent Mode, you must disable Silent Mode by editing the following Registry value:

HKEY_LOCAL_MACHINE\CurrentControlSet\Services\IpRip\
Parameters\SilentRip

Silent Mode is enabled when the SilentRip value entry has a value of 1. Disable Silent Mode by editing the SilentRip value entry, changing the value to 0.

Using Static Routing

The route command, which was previously mentioned, is used to manually maintain routing tables and can add the routes that are required on this network.

> **Note**   Static routing is deactivated when RIP for Internet Protocol is installed. To enable static routing, you must remove RIP.

Routes are added to the static routing table with the route add command, which has the following syntax:

```
route [-f] [-p]
      [command ip_address] [MASK netmask] [gateway] [METRIC metric]
```

The parameters are as follows:

- **-f.** When present, this option clears the routing table of all entries. If a command is included, the routing table is cleared before running the command.

- **-p.** When used with an ADD command, -p makes the entry permanent. Permanent entries will remain in the routing table when the computer is restarted. If the -p option is omitted, the routing table entry will be removed when the computer is restarted.

- ***command.*** Specifies the action to be taken where:

    - ADD adds a new entry to the routing table

    - CHANGE modifies an existing table entry

    - PRINT displays the current routing table

    - DELETE removes a table entry

- ***destination.*** Specifies a destination, either a destination network or host IP address.

- **MASK.** If this keyword is present, the next parameter must be an IP subnet mask. The *netmask* parameter indicates the portion of the *destination* IP address that is to be examined when performing routing.

- ***gateway.*** This parameter specifies the IP address of the gateway (router) that is the next hop to *destination*.

- **METRIC.** If this keyword is present, the next parameter must be an integer indicating the cost metric for the route being specified.

To enable router A to route to network 160.102.0.0, the following command would be entered:

```
route -p add 160.102.0.0 netmask 255.255.0.0 160.101.0.2 metric 2
```

The command states, "If this router receives a frame addressed to network 160.102.0.0, the frame will be routed to 160.101.0.2 at a cost of two hops." The -p parameter establishes a *persistent* route that is retained in the router's configuration.

The metric parameter indicates that two networks must be crossed to reach the destination.

Similarly, this command would be entered on router B:

```
route -p add 160.100.0.0 netmask 255.255.0.0 160.101.0.1 metric 2
```

If more than three segments are used, the route command must be used at each router to ensure that frames are forwarded from router-to-router and segment-to-segment. If you configure such a network, be sure to ping it out thoroughly to ensure that all of the routing tables have been configured properly.

When do you need to add more than the default route to a host's routing table? It depends on whether the host is functioning as a router.

The general rule is that multihomed computers that are configured as routers should be configured with routing tables that contain routes to every network. Only a few of the computers on your network will be configured as routers, so the effort required to beef up their router tables isn't too much of an inconvenience.

In most cases, however, single homed hosts will be configured with a default gateway only. Your network will probably include large numbers of hosts, and you don't want to visit each one to reconfigure its routing table when the network configuration changes. Simply configure your singly homed hosts with default gateway addresses that enable the hosts to forward data to a router.

When to Use Static and Dynamic Routing

Dynamic routing sounds like the hands-down choice as a routing method. Why would you want to administer routing manually when you can simply install RIP and forget it?

Unfortunately, RIP exacts two costs from the network:

◆ Increased traffic is generated when RIP routers exchange their routing tables at 30 second intervals. This traffic can become quite significant on networks with multiple routers.

◆ Running the RIP protocol uses some of the available processing power of the router, which may require you to use more expensive hardware for Windows NT Server computers that are working as routers. The alternative is to install separate routers, but those are even more costly.

You should choose static routing when your network routing configuration changes infrequently. Static routing is not difficult to set up and requires no maintenance unless the network routing configuration changes. While "there ain't no such thing as a free lunch," static routing is as close to free as routing gets.

Static routing cannot adapt to changes in the network, however. If your network has redundant paths, it is advantageous to have routers that can use alternate routes when a router fails. That calls for dynamic routing. A network that is frequently reconfig-ured is also a candidate for RIP. Be aware of the traffic RIP is generating, however, and be prepared to adopt a different routing strategy if network performance is suffering due to excess routing traffic.

Adding Default Gateways

Windows NT computers can specify additional gateways to be used when the default gateway is not available or when the default gateway does not have routing informa-tion for a segment. Figure 16.24 shows the three-segment network with an additional router. If desired, hosts on the various network segments can be configured with alternative gateways.

Figure 16.24

A three-segment network with three routers.

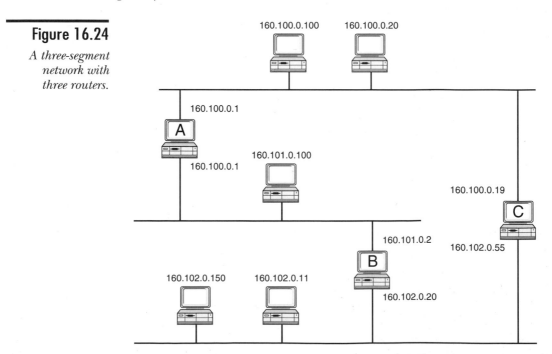

A network that is configured in this way with extra routers is more reliable because any one router can fail without disrupting the network.

To add a default gateway to a computer, follow the steps in the following exercise:

Adding a Default Gateway

1. Open the Network utility in the Control Panel and select the Protocols tab.

2. Select TCP/IP Protocol in the **N**etwork Protocols box.

3. Choose A**d**vanced in the TCP/IP Properties window to open the Advanced IP Addressing window shown in figure 16.25.

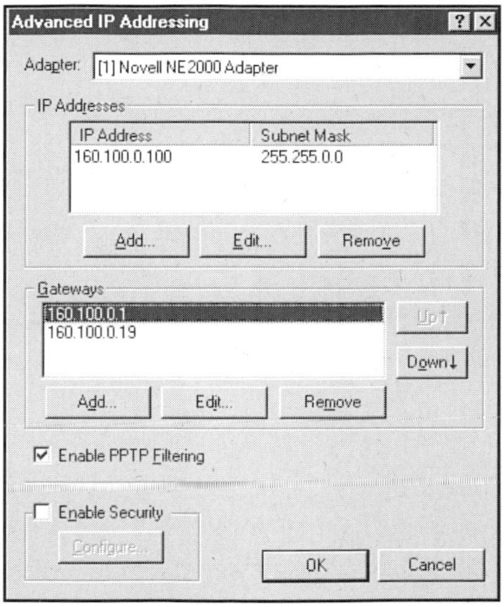

Figure 16.25

Adding multiple default gateways to a computer.

4. Under the **G**ateways box, choose A**d**d.

5. Enter the gateway address in the TCP/IP Gateway Address dialog box.

6. Choose **A**dd. The gateway address will be added to the host's address configuration.

Note	The order in which the default gateway addresses appear in the **G**ateways list determines their precedence. The first address in the list will be used unless its host is unavailable. Only then will the second address be used.
	You can adjust the order of the addresses in the list, perhaps to compensate for changes in the network.

continues

◆ To move an address to the top of the list, select the address and choose **U**p.

◆ To move an address to the bottom of the list, select the address and choose **D**own.

Installing TCP/IP Client Software on Windows for Workgroups 3.11

Windows NT includes TCP/IP client software for Windows for Workgroups 3.11, Windows 3.1, and MS-DOS.

TCP/IP software for Windows for Workgroups 3.11 is included in "TCP/IP 32 for Windows for Workgroups 3.11." This client software is available in the Windows NT Server Workgroup Administrator, which is described in Chapter 20, "Monitoring and Managing the Network."

To install TCP/IP on Windows for Workgroups 3.11, follow the steps described in the following exercise:

Installing TCP/IP on WFW

1. Prepare the client installation disk using Workgroup Administrator.

2. Run the Windows Setup utility in the Main program group.

3. Choose Change **N**etwork Settings in the **O**ptions menu.

4. Choose **D**rivers in the Network Setup box.

5. Choose Add **P**rotocol in the Network Drivers dialog box.

6. Select Unlisted or Updated Protocol in the Add Network Protocol list and choose OK.

7. Insert the TCP/IP client diskette and specify a path to the correct diskette drive.

8. When Microsoft TCP/IP-32 v3.311 is added to the Network Drivers list, select the entry and choose **S**etup.

9. Enter TCP/IP addresses and other parameters as described previously for Windows NT.

10. Choose OK and close Setup.

11. Restart the computer.

Installing TCP/IP Client Software on MS-DOS and Windows 3.1

TCP/IP software for MS-DOS and Windows 3.1 is included in "Network Client v3.0 for MS-DOS and Windows." This client software is available in the Windows NT Server Workgroup Administrator, which is described in Chapter 20.

Procedures for installing the Network Client v3.0 are described in Chapter 14, "Using Windows and DOS Clients." When you install the client kits, select the TCP/IP protocols for installation. Configure the protocols using the same settings as described in the previous sections about configuring TCP/IP on Windows NT.

Using the Dynamic Host Configuration Protocol

The procedures required to manually configure IP addresses on just a few computers have probably made you wonder what it would take to configure large numbers of hosts on a changing network. It doesn't take much thought to realize that managing IP addresses can send you screaming into the night.

With Dynamic Host Configuration Protocol (DHCP), you need to hard code only one IP address. All other addresses may be allocated from a pool when a computer demands TCP/IP access to the network. Network administrators are relieved of the necessity of maintaining logs that record every IP address in the organization and to whom it is assigned.

Simplifying the assignment of IP addresses is just one reason the DHCP was developed. Another reason is that DHCP enables a network support more TCP/IP users than it has TCP/IP addresses. Suppose that you have a class C address on the Internet, which gives you the potential for 253 connections (your router takes one). Unfortunately, your company has 500 employees. Fortunately, only 50 of those employees stay connected for a significant portion of the day. Others are on the Net only occasionally. After you dedicate an IP address to each one of your "regulars," you have about 200 addresses that can be shared. Those 450 occasional users can share the 200 address pool thanks to DHCP.

How DHCP Works

Figure 16.26 illustrates a network that is supporting DHCP. A single DHCP server can support the network, although multiple DHCP servers may be installed if desired. Notice in the figure that a single DHCP server can support addressing on multiple subnets.

A DHCP client is a computer that requests IP addresses from a DHCP server. When a DHCP client initiates access to the TCP/IP network, the following events take place:

1. The client broadcasts a discover message that is forwarded to DHCP servers on the network.

2. DHCP servers respond by offering IP addresses.

3. The client selects one of the IP addresses and sends a request to use that address to the DHCP server.

Figure 16.26

A network offering DHCP support.

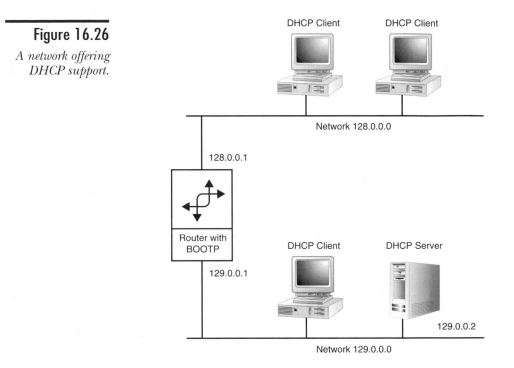

4. The DHCP server acknowledges the request and grants the client a lease to use the address.

5. The client uses the address to bind itself to the network.

DHCP addresses are leased for a specific duration. When the lease is halfway through, an active client negotiates to renew the lease. If the current address cannot be reassigned, a new address is assigned to the client. Addresses that are not renewed are returned to the address pool. If a client computer and DHCP server are on-line, the leased address will always be renewed and thus never be released.

> **Note**   BOOTP was the first protocol that was used to automate address assignments on TCP/IP networks and is still an integral supporting part of DHCP. BOOTP enables a TCP/IP host on one subnetwork to request an IP address from another subnetwork.

In figure 16.26, BOOTP is enabled on the router, which has interfaces on both networks and must of course be configured as a TCP/IP router. When a DHCP client on network 128.0.0.0 requests an IP address from the DHCP server, the BOOTP router appends the network number 128.0.0.0 to the request. The DHCP server will respond to the request only if it can offer an address on the appropriate network.

Installing a DHCP Server

To support DHCP on a network, at least one Windows NT computer must be configured as a DHCP server. After the DHCP server software is installed, DHCP manager is used to configure and manage the service. After at least one DHCP server has been configured, computers can be configured as DHCP clients.

Because a computer cannot function simultaneously as a DHCP client and a DHCP server, Windows NT computers functioning as DHCP servers must be configured with fixed IP addresses. Before you begin the following procedure, use the techniques described earlier ("IP Addresses") to configure adapters and IP addresses on the computer you plan to use as a DHCP server.

To install a DHCP server, follow the steps in the following exercise:

Installing a DHCP Server

1. Open the Network utility in the Control Panel and select the Services tab.

2. Choose **A**dd.

3. In the **N**etwork Service box, select Microsoft DHCP Server and choose OK.

4. When prompted, supply the path where files can be found on the installation CD-ROM. Files will be copied and the adapter software will be installed.

5. Next, you will be shown a message box that states `If any adapters are using DHCP to obtain IP addresses, they are not required to use a static IP address`. Choose OK.

6. Choose Close in the Network utility.

7. When the Microsoft TCP/IP Properties window is displayed, review the configurations of the network adapters on the computer to ensure that each is configured with a static IP address.

8. Choose OK.

The Microsoft DHCP service will be added to the computer, and the DHCP Manager will be added to the Administrative Tools group in the Start menu.

Enabling BOOTP Forwarding

You must enable BOOTP forwarding on any routers that must pass on DHCP discover messages. This is done in Network utility in the Control Panel. To enable BOOT forwarding, follow the procedures in the following exercise:

Enabling BOOTP Forwarding

1. Open the Network utility and select the Protocols tab.

2. In the **N**etwork Protocols box, select TCP/IP Protocol and choose **P**roperties.

3. Select the Routing tab and ensure that the Enable IP Forwarding check box is checked.

4. Select the DHCP Relay tab, shown in figure 16.27.

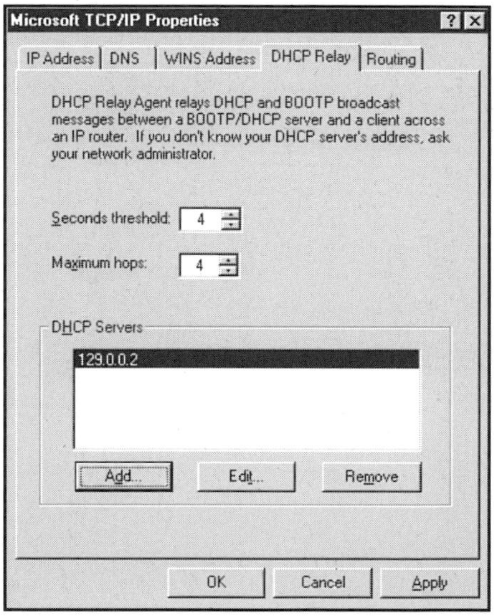

Figure 16.27

Configuring DHCP forwarding.

5. The value of the **S**econds threshold field determines how long DHCP broadcast messages will be permitted to remain on the network.

6. The value of the Ma**x**imum hops field specifies the maximum number of networks that can exist between this router and the DHCP server. DHCP discover messages that exceed this hop count will not be delivered. This value limits the degree to which DHCP broadcast messages will be dispersed through the network.

7. The D**H**CP Servers list must contain the IP address of at least one DHCP server. Choose A**d**d to add an address to the list.

8. Quit the Network utility when configuration is completed and restart the computer.

Managing DHCP Scopes

Before clients can obtain addresses from DHCP, you must create one or more scopes on each DHCP server. A *scope* is a range of IP addresses that can be leased by clients. DHCP Manager, the utility used to manage DHCP scopes, is installed in the Network Administration program group when DHCP is installed on the computer.

Figure 16.28 shows the main window for DHCP Manager. The left pane lists scopes that have been defined on this server, while the right pane defines options that have been configured.

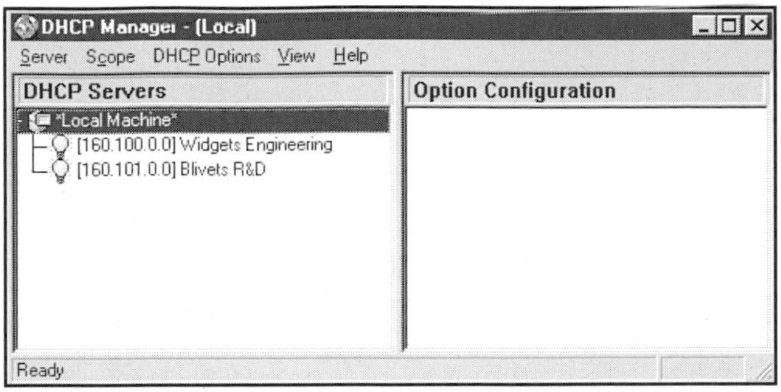

Figure 16.28

The DHCP Manager main window.

Creating and Modifying a Scope

To create a scope, follow the steps in the following exercise:

Creating a Scope

1. Open DHCP Manager, which is the Administrative Tools program group in the Start menu.

2. At least one computer should be displayed in the left DHCP Servers pane. The computer on which DHCP Manager is running will be listed as Local Machine.

   Double-click the server on which the scope will be created. Then choose **C**reate in the S**c**ope menu to display the Create Scope dialog box shown in figure 16.29.

3. The address range of a scope is defined by a **S**tart Address and an **E**nd Address field. Enter a valid IP address range in these two fields. The IP addresses in the scope include the values you enter.

4. Specify a subnet mask in the Subnet Mas**k** box. Unless you are using address subranges, this entry will be the default mask for the address class you entered in the **S**tart Address and **E**nd Address boxes.

5. If you do not want to have some of the addresses in the scope range assigned to DHCP clients, you can exclude ranges of addresses from the scope.

To exclude a range, under Exclusion Range, enter a Start Address and an End Address. Then choose Add.

To exclude a single address, enter the address in the Start Address box and choose Add.

To remove an excluded address or range, select it in the Excluded Addresses list and choose Remove.

Figure 16.29

Creating a scope.

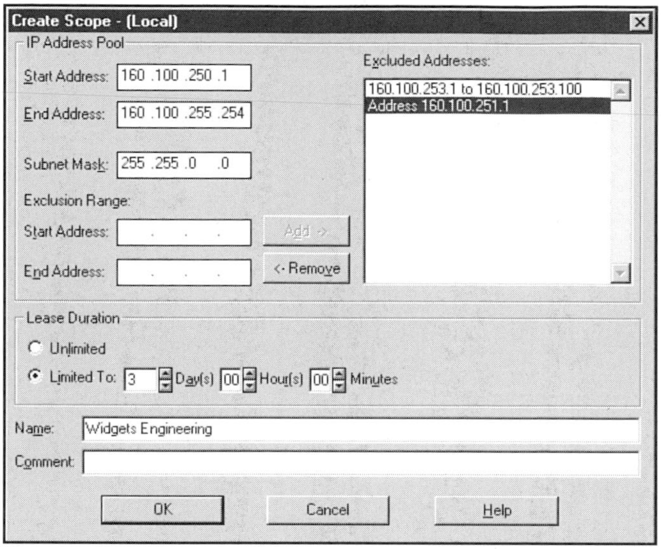

6. Specify the lease duration for this scope.

   If leases should not expire, select Unlimited.

   If leases should expire, select Limited To and specify a lease duration in days, hours, and minutes.

7. Optionally, you can complete the Name and Comment fields for this scope. The name you enter will help identify the scope in the DHCP Manager window.

8. When the scope has been defined, choose OK. DHCP Manager will notify you: `The scope has been successfully created, but has not yet been activated. Activate the new scope now?` Choose Yes to activate the scope.

9. When the DHCP Manager window is displayed, the new scope will appear. The light bulb icon will be lit (yellow) indicating that the scope is active.

To modify an existing scope, follow the steps in the following exercise:

Modifying a Scope

1. Select the scope in the DHCP Manager window.

2. Choose **P**roperties in the S**c**ope menu.

3. Make the required changes in the Scope Properties dialog box, which is identical in content to the Create Scope dialog box shown in figure 16.29.

4. Choose OK to save the changes to the scope.

> **Note**   Now that DHCP scopes are active, you can activate DHCP clients. When you configure TCP/IP on the clients, check the **O**btain an IP address from a DHCP server box in the Microsoft TCP/IP Properties window (see fig. 16.12). It is not necessary to specify an IP address or subnet mask.
>
> Restart the client, and it should connect to the DHCP server and lease an address.

Activating, Deactivating, and Deleting Scopes

To activate a deactivated scope, follow these steps:

1. Select the scope in the DHCP Manager window.

2. Choose **A**ctivate in the S**c**ope menu.

To deactivate an active scope, follow these steps:

1. Select the scope in the DHCP Manager window.

2. Choose De**a**ctivate in the S**c**ope menu.

> **Note**   Deactivating a scope will not disconnect active leases, but will cause DHCP to stop leasing addresses from that scope.

To delete an active scope, use the following steps:

1. Deactivate the scope.

2. Verify that active leases have been released. You can wait for leases to expire or have users disconnect from the DHCP server.

3. Select the scope in the DHCP Manager window.

4. Choose **D**elete in the S**c**ope menu.

Viewing and Managing Active Leases

To view or manage the leases that are active for a scope, do the following:

1. Select the scope in the DHCP Manager window.

2. Choose Active **L**eases in the S**c**ope menu to display the Active Leases dialog box shown in figure 16.30.

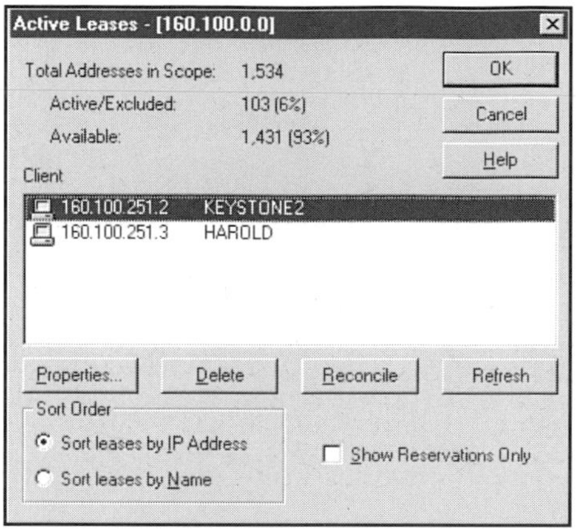

Figure 16.30

Active leases in a DHCP scope.

Information at the top of the dialog box lets you determine how many of the available addresses in the scope are available.

3. To delete a client and terminate the lease, select the lease and choose **D**elete. DHCP Manager knows that this can cause problems and asks you to confirm.

   Delete only entries that are no longer in use. If you delete an active client, deleted addresses can be reassigned to new clients and duplicate IP addresses can be created on the network.

4. To edit the properties for the lease, select the lease and choose **P**roperties. The Client Properties dialog box is shown in figure 16.31.

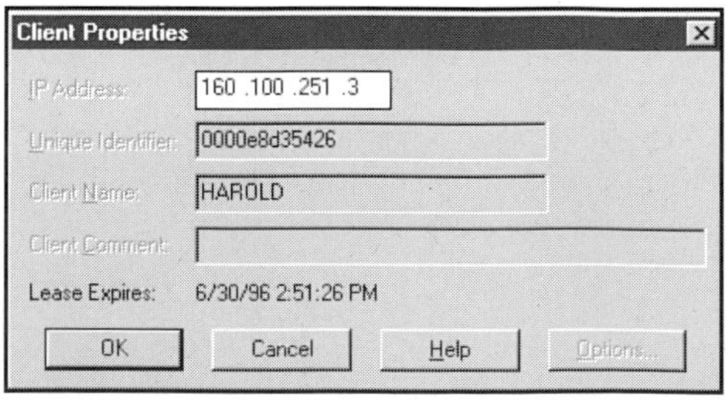

Figure 16.31

Client properties for an active DHCP client.

You can edit the following items:

- **Client Name.** This does not necessarily match the user's computer name, and changing the client name will not affect the computer name.

- **Unique Identifier.** This is the hardware MAC address for the client and is determined automatically when the lease is established.

- **Client Comment.** Any comment text you want to add.

Tip

You can determine the IP address assigned to a DHCP client by entering the command `ipconfig` at a command prompt on the client. The ipconfig utility is installed when you install TCP/IP on a computer.

You can also cut and paste the address within DHCP Manager. First view a client that does not have a reservation in the Client Properties box. Although you cannot edit the **U**nique Identifier field, you can select it and copy the contents (press Ctrl+C). Then you can paste the value to the **U**nique Identifier field of the Add Reserved Clients dialog box when creating the reservation.

Note

You can install more than one DHCP server on a network. This improves DHCP responsiveness and also enables DHCP clients to continue to access the network when one DHCP server is down.

The catch is that DHCP servers don't communicate with each other. If two or more DHCP servers are operating with the same address pool, it is possible that more than one client might obtain a lease to the same address from different DHCP servers.

Consequently, when setting up multiple DHCP servers, you should ensure that unique address ranges are assigned to the scopes on each DHCP server on the network.

Reserving DHCP Addresses

It is significantly more convenient to allocate addresses from DHCP than by hard coding them into individual computers. Nevertheless, there will be times when you want to configure a DHCP client to always have the same IP address. You can accomplish this while retaining many of the advantages of DHCP by reserving addresses within DHCP for specific clients.

To reserve an address for a client, follow these steps:

1. Start DHCP Manager.

2. Select a scope and choose Add **R**eservations in the S**c**ope menu. This will display the Add Reserved Clients dialog box shown in figure 16.32.

Figure 16.32

Adding a reserved client.

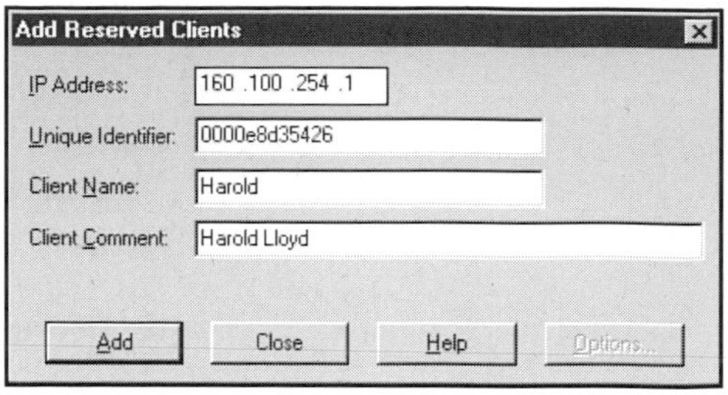

3. In the **I**P Address field, enter an IP address that falls within the range of addresses reserved for this scope.

4. In the **U**nique Identifier box, enter the hardware address for the client that will use this IP address. You can determine this address by typing the command **net config wksta** at a command prompt at the client. For Ethernet or token ring, this will be a 12-digit hexadecimal number. The unique identifier, not the client name, is the crucial bit of information that enables a client to access the reserved address. Other information is informational only.

5. Enter a client name in the Client **N**ame box. This doesn't have to match the user's account name and is entered here for informational purposes only.

6. If desired, add a comment in the Client **C**omment box.

7. Choose **A**dd.

If you select this scope and choose Active **L**eases, you will see the reservation listed in the Active Leases box, as shown in figure 16.33. A reservation that is actively being used is labeled as `Reservation in use`.

Figure 16.33

An address reservation in the Active Leases list.

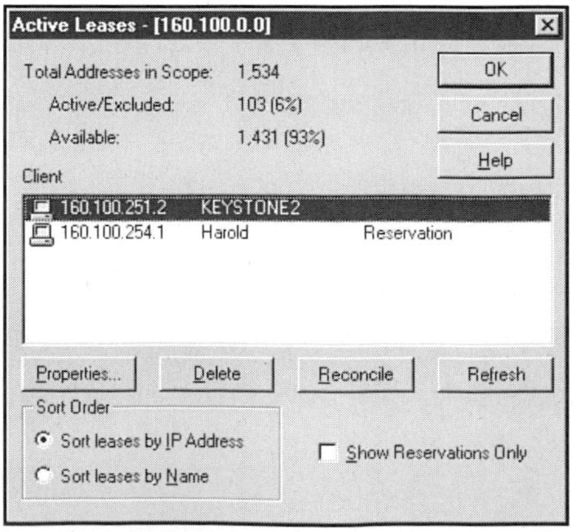

> **Note** Once a reservation has been created, its properties are managed from the Active Leases dialog box. Select the reservation and choose **P**roperties to display information about the reservation.

Configuring Multiple Scopes for a Network

It's always a good idea to have two of anything that is important on a network. Two domain controllers are a good idea (for example, a PDC and at least one BDC). Can you configure multiple DHCP servers so that a failure won't disrupt the network? Yes, but there is a catch.

Suppose that you configure two DHCP servers to support the network (200.100.3.0, for example). You create scopes on both servers that include the address range 200.100.3.10 through 200.100.3.254. How do things work out?

Quite badly, as a matter of fact. There is no mechanism to enable one DHCP server to determine that an IP address has been assigned by another DHCP server. Both servers, therefore, could assign the IP address 200.100.3.25 to different two hosts. Now, two hosts with the same IP address are a recipe for disaster, and communications get hopelessly mixed up.

The only way around the problem is to allocate different ranges of IP addresses to each DHCP server. For the above network, one DHCP server could be permitted to assign addresses in the range 200.100.3.10 through 200.100.3.125. The second DHCP server would control addresses 200.100.3.126 through 200.100.3.254.

This method looks like a recipe for wasting addresses, but it really isn't. Both servers will respond to DHCP discovery messages and will offer addresses for this network. All the addresses on the network, therefore, remain available for assignment. Only when one of the DHCP servers is shut down does part of the address range become unavailable.

Configuring DHCP Options

When DHCP is used to assign IP addresses, the TCP/IP environment of the DHCP client is defined by the options that are assigned to the scope from which the address is obtained. DHCP has about 60 predefined options, only some of which will ever concern you. Among their many functions, you can use options to specify the addresses of default gateways and DNS servers, domain names, and support for WINS.

Options can be assigned at three levels:

◆ **Defaults.** Options that apply to all scopes unless they are overridden by options assigned globally or to a specific scope.

◆ **Global.** Options that apply to all scopes and override default options.

◆ **Scope.** Options that apply only to a specific scope and override global and default options.

The following procedure illustrates how options are added to a scope and configured. The example defines default router addresses for a scope. Since default routers are specific to each network segment, this option would logically be assigned to a specific scope.

To add an option to a specific scope, follow these steps:

1. Select the scope in the DHCP Manager main window.

2. Choose the **S**cope command in the DHC**P** Options menu. The DHCP Options dialog box is shown in figure 16.34.

Figure 16.34

Adding a DHCP option to a scope.

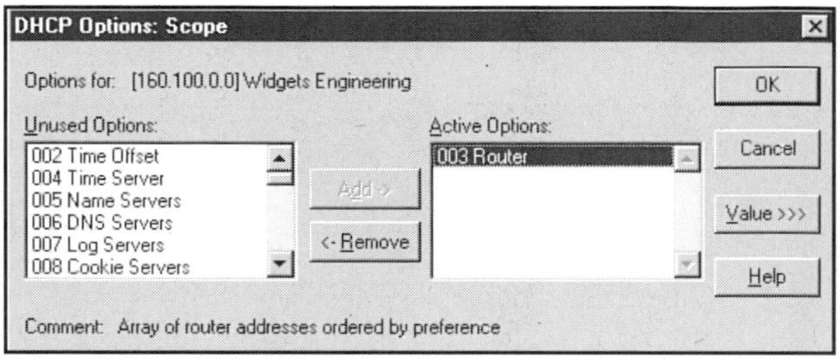

3. Select an option in the **U**nused Options list and choose A**d**d. The option will be moved to the **A**ctive Options list. In figure 16.34, the 003 Router option has been added.

4. For options that must be configured, select the option in the **A**ctive Options list and choose **V**alue. An Options dialog box will be added to the DHCP Options window, as shown in figure 16.34. At first, the IP Address box contains the legend <None>, indicating that no entries have been made. Figure 16.35 shows the list after one address has been added.

Figure 16.35

Values for a DHCP option.

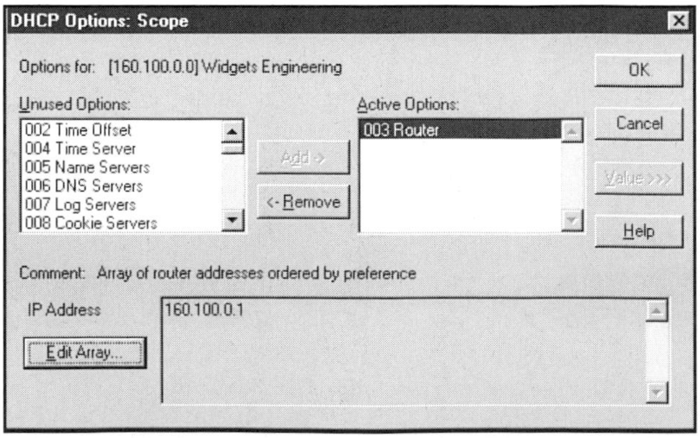

5. Some options can be edited directly in this box. Options that accept multiple values require you to display another dialog box by choosing **E**dit Array. Figure 16.36 shows the IP Address Array Editor.

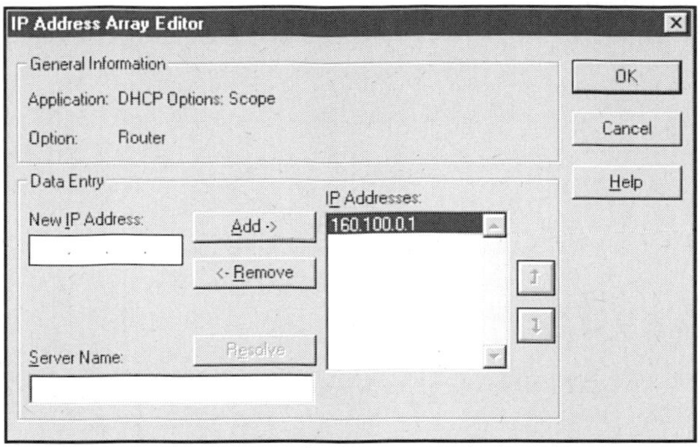

Figure 16.36

Editing an array of values for a DHCP option.

To configure a default router, follow these steps:

◆ Remove the initial value of 0.0.0.0 by selecting the entry in the **IP** Addresses list and by choosing **R**emove.

◆ Add a value by entering the default router address in the New **IP** Address box and choosing **A**dd.

Figure 16.36 shows the dialog box after an address of 160.100.0.1 has been added.

6. Choose OK twice to save the option and return to the DHCP Manager main menu.

Besides the default router option, you may require these options:

◆ **006 DNS Servers.** Specifies an address list of available DNS servers.

◆ **015 Domain Name.** Specifies the DNS domain name the client should use for DNS host name resolution.

Two other options you can use to relate to WINS are discussed in the following section, "Installing and Managing WINS." Although many other options appear in the options list, they do not apply to Microsoft DHCP clients. These options are offered to enable the Windows NT DHCP server to be a general DHCP server for non-Windows clients.

To manage options for a DHCP reservation, follow these steps:

1. Select the scope that supports the reservation in the DHCP Manager main window.

2. Choose Active **L**eases in the S**c**ope menu.

3. Select the reservation in the Active Leases box.

4. Choose **P**roperties.

5. Choose **O**ptions to display the DHCP Options: Reservation dialog box. This dialog box enables you to manage options for a reservation using the procedures to manage options for a scope.

Configuring Clients for DHCP

You must configure TCP/IP clients to take advantage of TCP/IP. Use the Network utility in the Control Panel to configure the TCP/IP protocol. On the IP Address tab (shown in figure 16.19), check **O**btain an IP address from a DHCP server. You need not specify the address of a DHCP server because DHCP discovery messages are broadcast.

When changes are made to the configuration of a DHCP scope, clients are not affected until their leases expire and must be renewed. If leases have a duration of three days (the default), some clients may not learn of a change until three days after the change occurs.

It is impossible to push changes out to clients. DHCP configuration information must be pulled from the client when a lease is accepted or renewed. This can complicate things when a change must be made in the DHCP configuration.

If you are planning to make a change, such as the address of a WINS server or a change in IP addresses, you should arrange things so that all client leases expire soon after the change is made. You can do that by adjusting the lease durations for the affected scopes. Starting on the third day from the change, gradually reduce the lease durations a day at a time. Finally, on the last day, lease durations should be set to one day. In that way, all leases will expire the next day after the change has gone into effect.

Backing Up the DHCP Database

Once scopes are in effect and leases are taken, the DHCP database begins to become a valuable commodity. Consequently, the DHCP database is automatically backed up at regular intervals, when the DHCP server is stopped, or when the server is shut down. The master database files are stored in C:\WINNT\SYSTEM32\DHCP, and the backup files are stored in the directory C:\WINNT\SYSTEM32\DHCP\BACKUP.

If the DHCP database becomes corrupted, you may be able to restore the database from the backup files using the steps in the following exercise:

Restoring the DHCP Database

1. Stop the Microsoft DHCP Server service using the Services utility in the Control Panel.

2. Back up the C:\WINNT\SYSTEM32\DHCP\BACKUP directory.

3. Use the Registry Editor (described in Chapter 19, "Managing the Server") to edit the HKEY_LOCAL_MACHINE\SYSTEM\CurrentControlSet\Services\ DHCPServer\Configuration\Parameters key. Change the value of the RestoreFlag value entry to 1.

4. Start the Microsoft DHCP Server service.

If a server crash forces you to reinstall Windows NT Server, you will need to reinstall the DHCP server as well, which is established with a newly initialized database. Unfortunately, some of your clients probably own leases that were granted prior to the server crash, which means that the DHCP database is out of sync with the leases that are in active use. When clients attempt to renew their licenses, the DHCP server is unaware the licenses exist, and errors will occur.

Assuming that you are backing up the server nightly, you should be able to restore the DHCP database from the last backup taken prior to the crash. Stop the Microsoft DHCP Server service using the Services utility in the Control Panel, restore the files, and restart the DHCP Server service.

| Tip | If you aren't satisfied with nightly backups of the DHCP database, consider replicating the database to another computer using the Windows NT Replicator service. The replica of the database will be updated every few minutes, enabling it to be more current than a daily backup tape. See Chapter 22, "Managing Directory Replication," to learn about directory replication. |

NetBIOS over TCP/IP

NetBIOS Over TCP/IP (NBT) is a capability that is enabled automatically when TCP/IP is installed on a Microsoft networking client. NBT enables applications written to the NetBIOS API to run over a TCP/IP protocol stack.

Consequently, Microsoft TCP/IP supports two application APIs:

◆ **NetBIOS via NBT.** This enables Microsoft TCP/IP clients to run NetBIOS applications such as the NET commands.

◆ **Windows Sockets (WinSock).** This enables Microsoft TCP/IP clients to run a wide variety of applications that are targeted explicitly for TCP/IP.

Because two APIs are supported, Microsoft TCP/IP clients have two identities. In the NetBIOS environment, they are known by their NetBIOS names, such as KEY-STONE1. Assuming that the network is properly configured, all Microsoft networking clients will recognize these NetBIOS names. A client on a TCP/IP network segment can exchange NetBIOS names with a client on a NWLink network segment, provided the two segments are properly connected by a Windows NT Server computer.

Microsoft TCP/IP clients need some help to learn NetBIOS names. The names can be learned from WINS servers or from static LMHOSTS files.

WinSock applications, however, do not work with NetBIOS names. Instead, they rely on TCP/IP host names. These names can be learned from DNS servers or from static HOSTS files.

The following sections show you how to manage naming in a TCP/IP environment using WINS, LMHOSTS files, HOSTS files, and DNS.

Installing and Managing WINS

This chapter has been peppered with references to naming services, such as Domain Name Service (DNS). Naming services are crucial tools for humanizing access to a network. That's why DNS was invented for the TCP/IP community. Names have another advantage, however—they insulate us from changes in network and host IDs.

Suppose that you're used to referring to a host as 203.95.160.3. One day, the department housing that computer moves to another building on another segment of the network. All of a sudden, the computer has a new address of 199.180.65.43. Lots of other computers probably moved with it, and you have considerable work to do forgetting old numbers and learning new numbers. If you've ever worked for a company that has moved to new quarters, think about the hassle it was getting used to the new phone numbers.

If you think about it, users on a DHCP-managed network face that problem every day. DHCP allocates addresses dynamically, and a given user's TCP/IP address changes from time to time.

The solution to this problem is to get a name service. Although IP addresses may change, a name service will keep itself up-to-date. Users continue to use familiar network names, regardless of alterations in the network structure.

Naming is one of the problems the Windows Internet Naming Service (WINS) solves by enabling users to use the familiar NetBIOS computer names in a TCP/IP environment. (NetBIOS names are the names that are assigned to a computer when Windows NT or another network client is configured to access the Microsoft network.)

As users connect to the network and as IP addresses change, they register with WINS, which maintains a database of NetBIOS names and their respective IP addresses. This database is available for reference by Windows and TCP/IP programs on the Microsoft network.

> **Note** Unfortunately, WINS is a Microsoft-only protocol. Only WINS clients on the Microsoft network can use names in the WINS database. Users who are entering your network from the outside cannot use WINS names to identify hosts. For that, you need DNS.

WINS Support for NetBIOS over TCP/IP

NetBIOS was not developed with large networks in mind. Microsoft enables NetBIOS to operate on the TCP/IP protocol stack (NetBIOS over TCP/IP is referred to as NBT), but that facet isn't enough to enable NetBIOS applications to fully access a TCP/IP network. Without help, NetBIOS cannot operate in a network that incorporates routers, as all large networks must.

The problem is that NetBIOS relies heavily on broadcast messages, messages that are addressed to all other computers on the network. When a Windows computer starts up on the network, it announces itself by broadcasting a message with its name to see if any other computer on the network is already using that name. When the computer shares resources, broadcast messages are also used to announce the resources that the computer is sharing with the network.

Unfortunately, broadcast messages are not passed over routers, which means that NetBEUI network services are limited to the local subnet. Unless, that is, WINS is enabled on the network.

WINS enables NetBEUI network clients to access name databases using point-to-point communication modes that are routable. Each WINS client is configured with the IP addresses of one or more WINS servers. These IP addresses enable the client to access the WINS server even if client and server are separated by a router.

A WINS server should be assigned a fixed address. Each client must be configured to use a specific address in order to use the WINS services.

Figure 16.37 illustrates a routed network that incorporates WINS servers and clients. Three types of computers are shown:

◆ **WINS servers.** Several WINS servers can be present on a network. They can replicate each other's databases and improve WINS performance.

◆ **WINS-enabled clients.** Windows NT and Windows for Workgroups 3.11 can interact directly with WINS servers.

◆ **Non-WINS clients.** Clients that support a feature called *b-node* can interact with WINS clients on their local network segments. The WINS clients can be configured as a proxy to obtain name information from WINS servers on the local or remote segments and provide this information to non-WINS clients. Not all WINS-enabled clients function as WINS *proxies* for non-WINS computers. A segment can only support one WINS-proxy to service non-WINS clients.

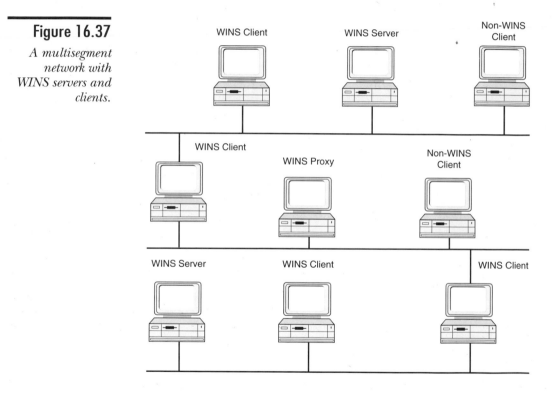

Figure 16.37

A multisegment network with WINS servers and clients.

As mentioned at the beginning of this section, two or more WINS servers can be configured on a network. Since these WINS servers can be configured to replicate their databases, multiple WINS servers improve the fault tolerance of WINS services on the network.

Name Resolution Modes

Four modes of name resolution are used on Windows networks. These modes are referred to as b-node, p-node, m-node, and h-node.

B-node relies exclusively on broadcast messages and is the oldest name resolution mode. A host needing to resolve a name request sends a message to every host within earshot, requesting the address associated with a host name. B-node has two short-comings: broadcast traffic is undesirable and becomes a significant user of network bandwidths, and TCP/IP routers don't forward broadcast messages, which restricts b-node operation to a single network segment.

P-node relies on WINS servers. Clients register themselves with a WINS server and contact the WINS server with name resolution requests. WINS servers communicate using directed messages, which can cross routers, so p-node can operate on large networks. Unfortunately, if the WINS server is unavailable, or if a node is not config-ured to contact a WINS server, p-node name resolution fails.

M-node is a hybrid mode that first attempts to resolve names using b-node. If that fails, an attempt is made to use p-node name resolution. M-node was historically the first hybrid mode put into operation, but it has the disadvantage of favoring b-node operation, which is associated with high levels of broadcast traffic.

H-node is also a hybrid mode, which favors WINS. First, an attempt is made to use p-node to resolve a name via WINS. Only if WINS resolution fails does the host resort to b-node to resolve the name via broadcasts. Because it typically results in the best network utilization, h-node is the default mode of operation for Microsoft TCP/IP clients configured to use WINS for name resolution.

Note Although networks can be configured using mixtures of b-node and p-node computers, Microsoft recommends against it. P-node hosts ignore b-node broad-cast messages, and b-node hosts ignore p-node directed messages. Two hosts, therefore, conceivably could be established using the same NetBIOS names.

Installing WINS Servers

To install a WINS server, follow the steps in the following exercise:

Installing WINS Server

1. Open the Network utility in the Control Panel and select the Services tab.

2. Choose **A**dd.

3. In the **N**etwork Service box, select Windows Internet Name Service and choose OK.

4. When prompted, supply the path where files can be found on the installation CD-ROM. Files will be copied and the adapter software will be installed.

5. Review the configuration in the Microsoft TCP/IP Properties window, and choose OK.

6. Restart the computer when prompted.

WINS is installed as a Windows NT service. It is configured to start automatically when Windows NT starts.

Note | A multihomed computer—a computer with more than one network adapter attached to more than one network—cannot be used as a WINS server because a WINS server cannot register its name on more than one network.

Managing WINS Servers

When WINS services are installed, the WINS Manager is added as a program item in the Network Administration program group. The main window for the WINS Manager is shown in figure 16.38. This window lists several statistics that enable you to track the operation of WINS. Since many of these statistics have to do with WINS database replication, you'll return to this screen after replication is discussed.

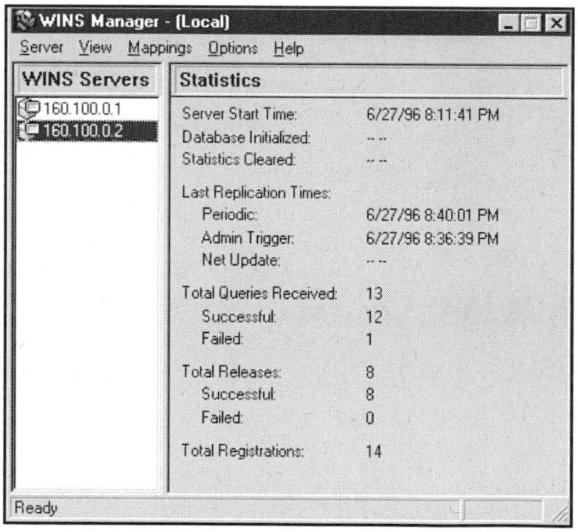

Figure 16.38

Statistics in the WINS Manager main window.

Several parameters on a WINS server can be adjusted. To configure a WINS server, follow the steps in the following exercise:

Configuring a WINS Server

1. Select a server in the WINS Servers pane of the WINS Manager main window.

2. Choose the Configuration command in the **S**erver menu to display the WINS Server Configuration dialog box shown in figure 16.39.

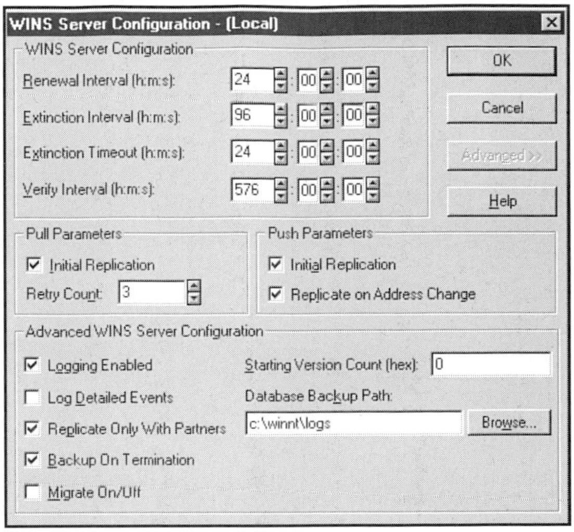

Figure 16.39

Configuring properties of a WINS server.

The fields in this dialog box are as follows:

◆ **Renewal Interval.** Specifies the intervals at which a WINS client must reregister its name. A name that is not reregistered is marked as *released* in the WINS database. The maximum value is four days (96 hours). If clients are forced to renew very frequently, network traffic is increased. Try reregistering at one to two day intervals.

◆ **Extinction Interval.** Specifies the interval between the time a name is marked *released* and when it is marked *extinct*. Extinct records are eligible to be purged. Try setting this value to four times the renewal interval.

◆ **Extinction Timeout.** Specifies the interval between the time a name is marked extinct and when the name is actually purged from the database. The minimum value is one day.

◆ **Verify Interval.** Specifies the interval after which a WINS server must verify that names it does not own are still active. The maximum value is 24 days (576 hours).

3. Pull Parameters and Push Parameters are discussed in the section about WINS database replication.

4. To access **A**dvanced WINS Server Configuration parameters, choose Advan**c**ed.

5. Check L**o**gging Enabled if logging to JET.LOG should be turned on.

6. Check Log **D**etailed Events to turn on detailed logging. Because verbose logging can consume considerable resources, it should be turned on only during performance tuning.

7. Check Re**p**licate Only With Partners if replication should take place only with push and pull partners specifically configured for this server. If this option is not checked, an administrator can force push or pull replication with this server.

8. Check **B**ackup On Termination if the database should be backed up automatically when WINS Manager is stopped (except when the server is shutting down).

9. Database Bac**k**up Path accepts a path to a file that is used to back up the database. Backup can be initiated automatically, as discussed in step 8, or manually, by using the **B**ackup Database command in the **M**appings menu. Choose Bro**w**se to browse for a path if desired.

10. Check **M**igrate On/Off if you are upgrading non-Windows NT systems to Windows NT. This option enables static records to be treated as dynamic and reassigned to eliminate conflicts.

11. Choose OK to save the configuration settings.

Configuring WINS Database Replication

Although a single WINS server can service the entire network, ideally you should activate at least two WINS servers to provide a level of fault tolerance. WINS servers can be configured to replicate their databases with one another so that each remains up-to-date with changes on the network. WINS servers can perform two database replication operations, *pushing* and *pulling*.

Because each segment of a network should include either a WINS server or a WINS proxy, the best approach on a multisegment network is to have WINS servers on different network segments. Remember, however, that a multihomed server can't be a WINS server, so you can't add WINS support to two segments with a single computer.

A replication *push partner* is a WINS server that notifies other WINS servers of changes, and then sends database replicas upon receiving a request from a pull partner.

A replication *pull partner* is a WINS server that requests replication data from a push partner and then accepts replicas of new database entries.

Figure 16.40 illustrates one manner in which WINS servers might be configured for database replication. A combination of one- and two-way relationships is shown, although I suspect two-way replication by far will be the more common configuration.

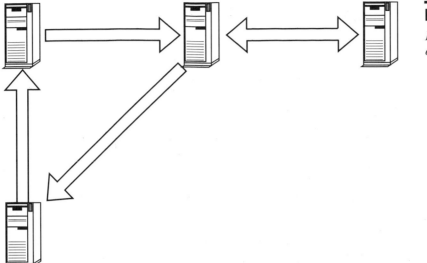

Figure 16.40

Replicating WINS databases.

To configure replication on a WINS server, follow the steps in the following exercise:

Configuring Replication on a WINS Server

1. Select a WINS server in the WINS Manager main window.

2. Choose the **R**eplication Partners command in the **S**erver menu. The Replication Partners dialog box appears, as shown in figure 16.41.

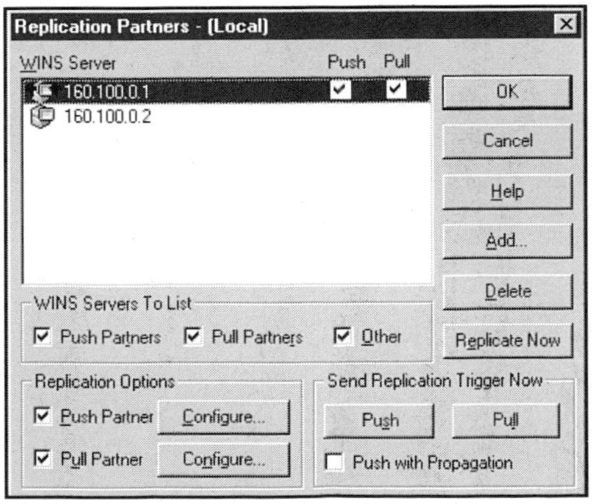

Figure 16.41

Configuring replication partners.

3. Select another WINS server in the Replications Partners dialog box.

4. If the server is to be a push partner

◆ Check the **P**ush Partner box under Replication Options.

◆ Choose **C**onfigure to display the Push Partner Properties dialog box shown in figure 16.42. This dialog box has one item, **U**pdate Count, where you specify the number of updates that must take place to the local database before partners will be notified. (Entries pulled from other partners do not count in this context. Only local updates are taken into consideration.)

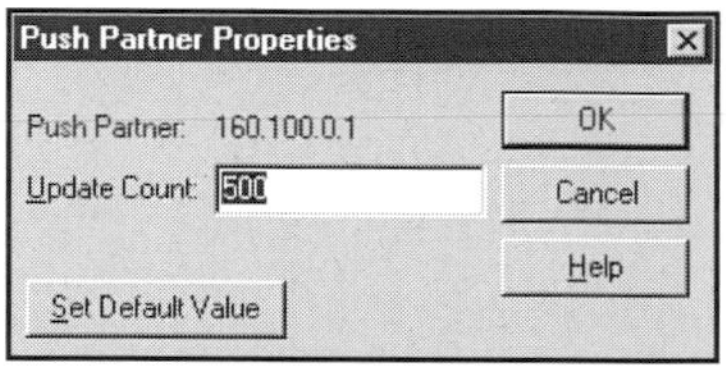

Figure 16.42

Configuring a push partner.

Forcing updates to occur too frequently will generate excess network traffic. The minimum value is 5. You can set a default push partner update count in the Preferences window, as described in the next section.

5. If the server is to be a pull partner

◆ Check the **Pu**ll Partner box under Replication Options.

◆ Choose Co**n**figure to display the Pull Partner Properties dialog box shown in figure 16.43. In this box, you can specify an hour in the day when replication should begin and the intervals at which scheduled replications should occur.

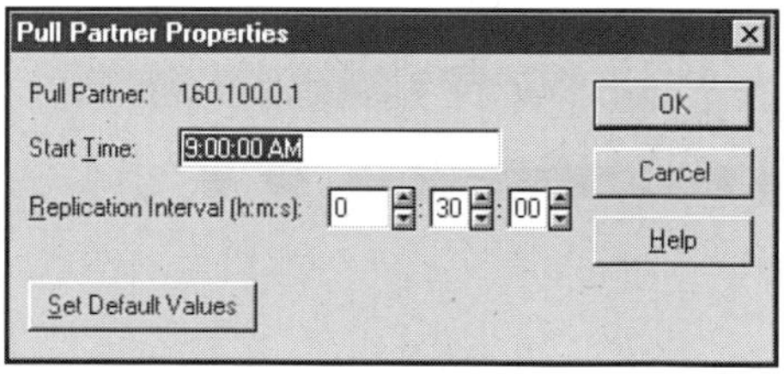

Figure 16.43

Configuring a pull partner.

6. Choose OK to save the replication configuration.

Note   You must configure both sides of a push-pull pair.

◆ If you have specified server A as a pull partner of server B, be sure to use WINS Manager to make server B a push partner of server A.

◆ If you have specified server C as a push partner of server D, be sure to use WINS Manager to make server D a pull partner of server C.

You are walking a tightrope when setting push and pull configurations. Changes can only propagate through the network as rapidly as you specify, and the ideal case would be to propagate all changes immediately. Doing so, however, could slow down the network, so you need to make a compromise.

Forcing Database Replication

There are times when you might want to force database replication to occur. You can initiate replication by sending replication triggers, or you can force an immediate replication.

To send a push replication trigger to a pull partner, follow these steps:

1. Select a pull replication partner in the Replication Partners dialog box.

2. Check the Push with Propagation box if the selected server should send a push trigger to its pull partners after it has pulled replicas from the source server.

   Leave the box unchecked if the selected pull partner should not send.

3. Choose Push in the Send Replication Trigger Now box to send a replication trigger to the server's pull partners. This trigger takes effect only for other servers that have been configured as pull partners.

To send a pull replication trigger:

1. Select a replication partner in the Replication Partners dialog box.

2. Choose Pull in the Send Replication Trigger Now box to send a replication trigger to the server's push partners. This trigger takes effect only for other servers that have been configured as push partners.

To start immediate replication, choose Replicate Now.

Setting WINS Preferences

You can configure several WINS preferences by choosing the **P**references command in the WINS Manager **O**ptions menu. The Preferences dialog box is shown in figure 16.44. The figure shows how the window appears after the Pa**r**tners box has been checked to display options for configuring new pull and push partners. Following are the options:

◆ Options in the Address Display box specify whether the address should be displayed in the main window by IP address, computer name, or both.

◆ Check Auto Re**f**resh to specify that statistics should be updated automatically at the interval specified.

Figure 16.44

Configuring WINS Manager preferences.

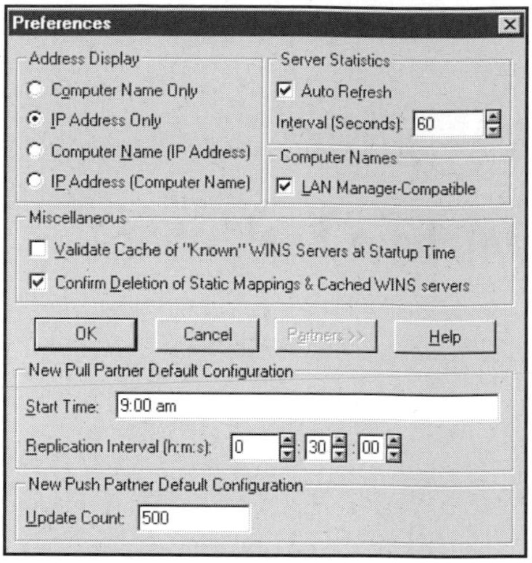

◆ Under Computer Names, the **L**AN Manager-Compatible box should always be checked unless your network will be receiving NetBIOS names from sources other than Microsoft networks. (All Microsoft network clients use LAN Manager compatible names.)

◆ Check **V**alidate Cache of "Known" WINS Servers at Startup Time if this server should query its list of known WINS servers each time Windows NT Server starts up. Ordinarily, this option is not required.

◆ Check Confirm **D**eletion of Static Mappings & Cached WINS servers if warnings should be displayed when you delete a static mapping or the cached name of a WINS server. This option is recommended.

◆ Specify default options for pull partners in the New Pull Partner Default Configuration box.

◆ Specify default options for push partners in the New Push Partner Default Configuration box.

Managing Static Mappings

When WINS maps a name to an IP address, the mapping is dynamic. It must be periodically renewed, or it is subject to removal. In most cases, dynamic mapping is in keeping with the nature of a name service, which should adapt to changes in the network without the need for frequent intervention by network administrators.

A *static mapping* is a permanent mapping of a computer name to an IP address. Static mappings cannot be challenged and are removed only when they are explicitly deleted by the network administrator.

If DHCP is run on the network with WINS, reserved IP addresses assigned in DHCP will override static mappings assigned in WINS.

Static WINS mappings permit you to post names and addresses in the WINS database computers that are not WINS-enabled. Static WINS mappings should not be assigned to WINS-enabled computers.

Adding Static Mappings

To add a static mapping, follow these steps:

1. Choose **S**tatic Mappings in the **M**appings menu. The Static Mappings dialog box is shown in figure 16.45.

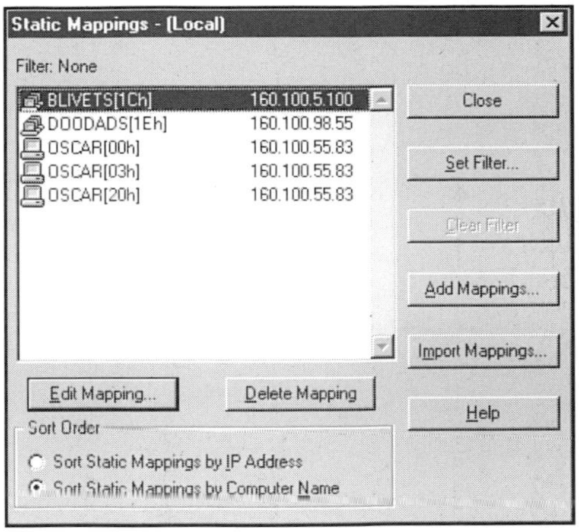

Figure 16.45

Static mappings.

2. Choose **A**dd Mappings to display the Add Static Mappings dialog box shown in figure 16.46.

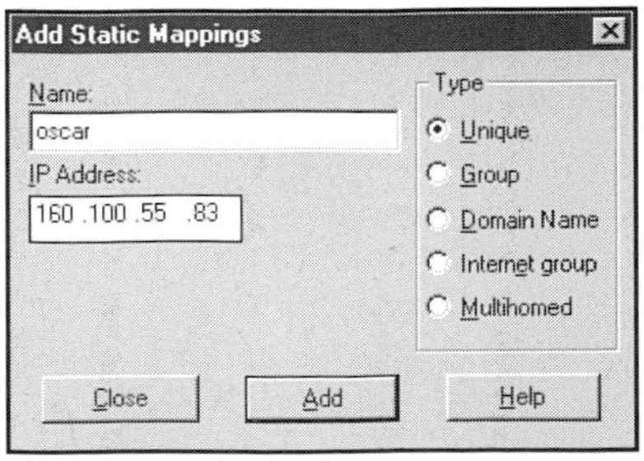

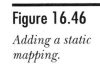

Figure 16.46

Adding a static mapping.

3. Type the computer name in the **N**ame box. (WINS Manager will add the leading \\s if you forget them.)

4. Type the address for the computer in the **IP** Address box.

5. Choose an option in the Type box. Here are the choices:

   - ◆ **Unique.** A unique name in the database with a single address per name.

   - ◆ **Group.** No address is associated with a group, and addresses of individuals are not stored. The client broadcasts name packets to normal groups.

   - ◆ **Domain Name.** Enables you to create a Domain Name type entry for a Remote Domain Name.

   - ◆ **Internet group.** A group on an internet that stores up to 25 addresses for members.

   - ◆ **Multihomed.** A name that maps from 1 to 25 addresses. This corresponds to adding multiple IP addresses in the Advanced dialog box for TCP/IP settings.

6. Choose **A**dd.

Static mappings are added to the database immediately when you choose **A**dd. Modification of added static mappings is limited, and you will need to delete the static mapping if you want to cancel it.

Editing a Static Mapping

The IP address of a static mapping can be modified as follows:

1. Choose **S**tatic Mappings in the **M**appings menu.

2. Select the mapping to be modified in the Static Mappings dialog box.

3. In the Edit Static Mapping dialog box, enter a new IP address in the **I**P Address box.

4. Choose OK. The change is saved to the WINS database immediately.

Managing the WINS Database

Several operations should be performed periodically to maintain the WINS database. The database consists of four files, which are stored by default in the C:\WINNT35\ SYSTEM32\WINS directory:

- ◆ **JET.LOG.** The database transaction log, used to recover the database in the event of error.

- ◆ **SYSTEM.MDB.** Stores information about the structure of the WINS database.

- ◆ **WINS.MDB.** The actual WINS database file.

- ◆ **WINSTMP.MDB.** A temporary file created while WINS is operating.

These files should not be deleted or modified. They should be backed up when the WINS server is backed up, and they should be managed only by utilities in the WINS manager. I suggest that you set up a schedule for performing these duties on a weekly basis.

Scavenging the WINS Database

Extinct and old entries in the database should be removed periodically by choosing the I**n**itiate Scavenging command in the **M**appings menu.

Owned active names for which the renewal interval has expired are marked *released*. Owned released names for which the extinct interval has expired are marked *extinct*. Owned extinct names for which the extinct timeout has expired are deleted, as are replicas of extinct and deleted names.

Compacting the WINS Database

After entries have been scavenged, holes in the database will reduce WINS performance. The database, therefore, should be compacted. This must be performed when users will not be accessing WINS.

To compact the WINS database, follow the steps in the following exercise:

Compacting the WINS Database

1. Use the Services utility in the Control Panel to stop the WINS Internet Name Service service.

    Alternatively, you can stop the service from the command line by typing the command **net stop wins** at the command prompt.

2. Run JETPACK.EXE (which is installed by default in \WINNT\SYSTEM32).

3. Restart WINS with the Services utility or by entering the command **net start wins**.

Tip	Because WINS must be shut down to compact the database, consider putting these commands in your nightly backup batch file prior to running the backup jobs. Presumably, this batch file runs at a time when users have been logged out of the network. See Chapter 18, "Backing Up Files," for more information about scheduling batch files for overnight execution.

Viewing the WINS Database

The Show **D**atabase command in the **M**appings menu displays the Show Database window, which can be used to examine the contents of the WINS database. An example is shown in figure 16.47.

Figure 16.47

Contents of a WINS database.

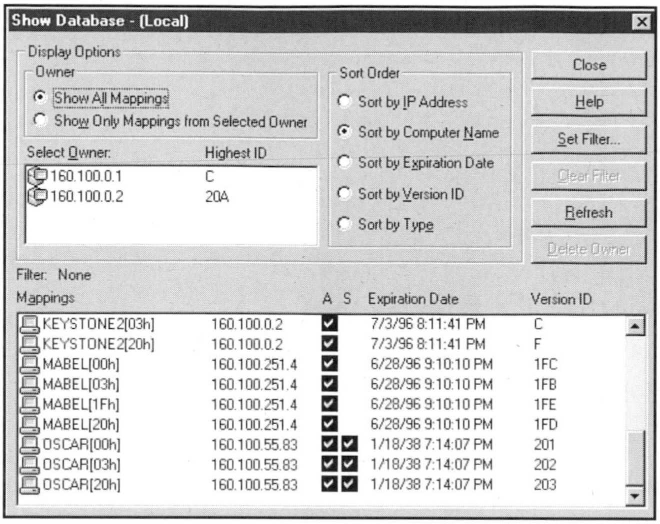

With WINS, the owner of a mapping is the WINS server that originated the mapping, not a particular user account. To view mappings owned by a particular server, do the following:

1. Select Sho**w** Only Mappings from Selected Owner in the Owner box.

2. Select a WINS server in the Select **O**wner list.

If you want to view all mappings in the database, select Show A**l**l Mappings.

If you want to view only mappings for a particular computer, follow these steps:

1. Choose **S**et Filter.

2. In the Set Filter dialog box, specify a value in the Computer **N**ame or **IP** Address field.

3. Choose OK.

To delete all mappings owned by a particular WINS server, follow these steps:

1. Select a WINS server in the Select **O**wner list.

2. Choose **D**elete Owner.

Note In figure 16.47, notice that most hosts appear more than once in the mappings table. In fact, a given NetBIOS computer can be identified by as many as 16 names, which consist of two parts:

◆ A text name up to 15 characters—the name you specify when you configure the computer name when setting up networking

◆ A 16-bit hexadecimal number suffix that describes the program with which the name is associated

WINS is one of the few places where you will observe NetBIOS names complete with their numeric suffixes. In figure 16.44, the computer MABEL is linked to four NetBIOS names:

◆ MABEL[00h] is the name associated with the Workstation service. Every Microsoft network client will be associated with at least a Workstation service name.

◆ MABEL[03h] is the name associated with the Messenger service, the name used to send messages to this computer. This name is observed if the Messenger service is active.

◆ MABEL[1Fh] is the name associated with the NetDDE service, and is observed if a NetDDE application is running on the computer.

◆ MABEL[20h] is associated with the Server service, and is seen on any Microsoft computer that is configured to share resources with the network.

You can observe the NetBIOS names associated with a computer by entering the command **nbtstat -n** from a command prompt.

Backing Up and Restoring the WINS Database

In the earlier section, "Managing WINS Servers," you were introduced to options that specify the WINS backup path and whether the WINS database should be backed up when exiting WINS Manager. You can also force a backup of the WINS database.

To back up the WINS database, follow the steps in the following exercise:

Backing up the WINS Database

1. Choose the **B**ackup Database command in the **M**appings menu.

2. In the Select Backup Directory dialog box, browse for a backup directory. You must back up to a local hard drive because the WINS database cannot be restored from a network drive.

3. Check Perform **I**ncremental Backup if you want to back up only records that have been created since the most recent backup.

4. Choose OK.

To restore a WINS database, follow the steps in the following exercise:

Restoring the WINS Database

1. Choose the **R**estore Local Database command in the **M**appings menu.

2. Browse for the directory to be restored from.

3. Choose OK.

Configuring WINS Clients

From the client side, WINS configuration could hardly be easier. All that is necessary is to specify WINS server addresses in the TCP/IP Configuration dialog box. Figure 16.48 shows an example taken from Windows for Workgroups 3.11.

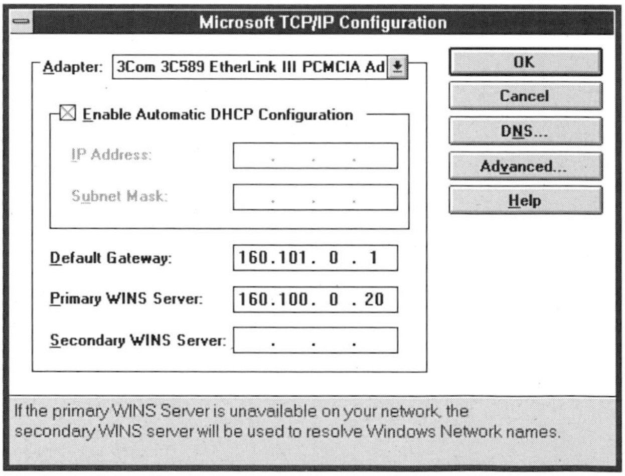

Figure 16.48

Configuring a client for WINS.

If the WINS client is also using DHCP, you need to configure the client using DHCP options. If all clients use the same WINS servers, these can be global options. Otherwise, they should be added as scope options.

The required options are:

◆ **044 WINS/NBNS Servers.** As values for this option, specify the IP address(es) of WINS servers to be used by the client.

◆ **046 WINS/NBT Node Type.** Enter a value of 0×8 for this option, which configures the client for h-node mode. See the following note for a brief explanation of client modes.

| Note | Clients can be configured to perform registration in four modes:

◆ **b-node.** The client uses broadcasts, which are restricted to the local subnet. This mode is supported by older Microsoft network clients.

◆ **p-node.** Clients neither create nor respond to broadcasts. Computers register with a WINS server using point-to-point communication. If a WINS server is unavailable, the client is unable to register with the network.

◆ **m-node.** The client first attempts to register with b-node mode. If successful, it attempts to switch to p-node. The initial registration in b-node generates high levels of broadcast traffic and does not achieve the goal of connecting to a WINS server.

◆ **h-node.** This is the most recently developed mode, supported by Windows NT 3.5 and Windows for Workgroups 3.11. The client first attempts to register with a WINS server using p-node. If registration fails, the client attempts to register on the local subnet with b-node.

Configuring WINS Proxies

If some network clients support only b-node operation, you should make sure that at least one computer on each network segment is either a WINS server or a WINS proxy. Any Windows NT 3.5x or Windows for Workgroups 3.11 client can be configured as a WINS proxy. To configure a WINS proxy, follow the steps in the following exercise:

Configuring a WINS Proxy

1. Display the TCP/IP Configuration dialog box for the client.

2. Choose Ad**v**anced to display the Advanced Microsoft TCP/IP Configuration dialog box.

3. Check Enable **W**INS Proxy Agent.

4. Choose OK.

Managing LMHOSTS Files

Before there was WINS, Microsoft TCP/IP clients used files named LMHOSTS to resolve NetBIOS names to IP addresses. An LMHOSTS file has a very simple structure, as with the following:

```
160.100.0.1      KEYSTONE1
160.100.0.100    CHARLES
160.100.0.20     BUSTER
160.101.0.100    MABEL
```

Each entry in LMHOSTS appears on a separate line and consists of two fields: an IP address and a name. The fields must be separated with at least one space or tab character. You will find a sample LMHOSTS file in the directory C:\Winnt\ system32\drivers\etc. The sample file is LMHOSTS.SAM and will not be queried by NT. Only a file named LMHOSTS can be used.

LMHOSTS Files Keywords

Several keywords can appear in LMHOSTS files. Here is an example of a file with keywords:

```
160.100.0.1      KEYSTONE1     #PRE    #DOM:KEYSTONE
160.101.0.2      KEYSTONE2     #PRE

#BEGIN_ALTERNATE
#INCLUDE \\KEYSTONE1\PUBLIC\LMHOSTS
#INCLUDE \\KEYSTONE2\PUBLIC\LMHOSTS
#END_ALTERNATE
```

The #PRE keyword specifies that the entry should be preloaded into the name cache. Ordinarily, LMHOSTS is consulted for name resolution only after WINS and b-node broadcasts have failed. Preloading the entry ensures that the mapping will be available at the start of the name resolution process.

The #DOM: keyword associates an entry with a domain. This may be useful in determining how browsers and logon services behave on a routed TCP/IP network. #DOM entries may be preloaded in cache by including the #PRE keyword.

The #INCLUDE keyword makes it possible to load mappings from a remote file. One use for #INCLUDE is to support a master LMHOSTS file that is stored on logon servers and is accessed by TCP/IP clients when they start up. Entries in the remote LMHOSTS file are examined only when TCP/IP is started. Entries in the remote LMHOSTS file, therefore, must be tagged with the #PRE keyword to force them to be loaded into cache.

If several copies of the included LMHOSTS file are available on different servers, you can force the computer to search several locations until a file is successfully loaded. This is accomplished by bracketing #INCLUDE keywords between the keywords #BEGIN_ALTERNATE and #END_ALTERNATE, as was done in the preceding example file. Any successful #INCLUDE causes the group to succeed.

> **Note**   In the example listing, note that the hosts KEYSTONE1 and KEYSTONE2 were explicitly defined so that the names could be used in the parameters of the #INCLUDE keywords. If a name resolution fails in the first INCLUDE server NT will not access the other server. Only when the first server is not responding will NT continue its search.

Enabling Clients to Use LMHOSTS Files

LMHOSTS files are unnecessary on networks that have a properly functioning WINS name service. If an internetwork will not be using WINS, LMHOSTS lookups should be enabled and LMHOSTS files should be configured to enable computers to find critical hosts.

Any TCP/IP client can be enabled to use LMHOSTS files by checking the Enable **L**MHOSTS Lookup check box in the WINS tab of the Microsoft TCP/IP Properties dialog box.

Guidelines for Establishing LMHOSTS Name Resolution

B-node computers that are not configured to use WINS name resolution can use LMHOSTS to resolve names on remote networks. If the majority of name queries are on the local network, it is not generally necessary to preload mappings in the LMHOSTS file. Frequently accessed hosts on remote networks may be preloaded with the #PRE keyword.

#DOM keywords should be used to enable non-WINS clients to locate domain controllers on remote networks. The LMHOSTS file for every computer in the domain should include #DOM entries for all domain controllers that do not reside on the local network. This ensures that domain activities, such as logon authentication, continue to function.

To browse a domain other than the logon domain, LMHOSTS must include the name and IP address of the primary domain controller of the domain to be browsed. Include backup domain controllers in case the primary fails or in case a backup domain controller is promoted to primary.

LMHOSTS files on backup domain controllers should include mappings to the primary domain controller name and IP address, as well as mappings to all other backup domain controllers.

All domain controllers in trusted domains should be included in the local LMHOSTS file.

Managing HOSTS Files

Both WINS and LMHOSTS files have serious shortcomings. They do not enable non-Microsoft TCP/IP computers to learn host names from the Microsoft TCP/IP environment, nor can they be used as a basis for a naming system that enables Microsoft TCP/IP clients to use host names for non-Microsoft computers.

When non-Microsoft hosts are involved, to establish a comprehensive naming system, you need to include one of the following in your network:

◆ A Domain Name Services (DNS) naming server

◆ Static HOSTS naming files

Although Windows NT Server 4 includes a DNS server, the concepts involved in managing a DNS naming service are beyond the scope of this book. DNS is covered in greater detail by the following resources:

◆ *Networking with Microsoft TCP/IP* by Drew Heywood, New Riders Publishing. *Networking with Microsoft TCP/IP, Certified Administrator's Resource Edition* is due in September 1997.

◆ *Unlocking Internet Information Server*, New Riders Publishing.

◆ *DNS and BIND*, by Paul Albitz & Cricket Liu, O'Reilly & Associates, Inc.

In the next section, you learn how to use HOSTS files to support TCP/IP naming. HOSTS files function much like LMHOSTS files, and are static files listing IP addresses and corresponding host names. But HOSTS files work on Windows NT, Unix, and other TCP/IP clients.

Structure of HOSTS Files

A HOSTS file is simply a text file that you can create with any text editor, such as Notepad. If your network does not incorporate a DNS server, you might elect to use a simple, non-hierarchical naming system for your TCP/IP hosts. Here is a sample HOSTS file that uses non-hierarchical names:

```
127.0.0.1         localhost
160.100.0.1       KEYSTONE1
160.100.0.100     CHARLES
160.100.0.20      BUSTER
160.101.0.100     MABEL
```

Note | The entry for the name `loopback` creates a name that is associated with the local loopback adapter. This entry makes it possible to test the local interface with the command `ping loopback` as alternative to the command `ping 127.0.0.1`.

If, on the other hand, your network incorporates a DNS server that supports a hierarchical name space, you might include entries that add the domain structure to the host names; for example:

```
127.0.0.1        localhost
160.100.0.1      KEYSTONE1
160.100.0.1      KEYSTONE1.keystone.com
160.100.0.1      CHARLES
160.100.0.100    CHARLES.keystone.com
160.100.0.20     BUSTER
160.100.0.20     BUSTER.keystone.com
160.101.0.100    MABEL
160.101.0.100    MABEL.keystone.com
```

With this HOSTS file, users can use CHARLES or CHARLES.keystone.com to refer to host 160.100.0.100. (Incidentally, the names are not case sensitive; CHARLES is the same name as charles.)

HOSTS File Locations

To enable your hosts to use these names, it is only necessary to create the HOSTS file and place it in the appropriate directory of each TCP/IP computer on the network. The location is determined by the operating system:

◆ Windows NT expects the file to be in the directory *%systemroot%*\system32\ Drivers\ etc. By default, this directory is C:\Winnt\system32\Drivers\etc.

◆ By convention, Unix hosts expect the HOSTS file to be stored in the directory \etc.

Apart from creating HOSTS files and copying them to the appropriate directories, no further steps are required to enable Windows TCP/IP clients to use HOSTS files for name resolution. A host will use the HOSTS file unless it has been configured to use DNS for name resolution.

Tip | If you decide to use HOSTS files, consider using a logon script to copy the file to your Windows NT clients. This will ensure that users receive any changes each time they log on. Unfortunately, non-NT hosts must obtain the file manually.

Managing DNS

HOSTS files can be made to provide all the naming support a network needs, but they can be very inconvenient to manage. Every host on the network must be equipped with a HOSTS file. Updating the HOSTS file on each host can be a major administrative headache.

HOSTS files cannot be used to advertise your internal host names to outside users. If your organization has a presence on the Internet, you probably want to advertise at least some of your host names, such as your FTP and WWW servers, to Internet users. Unless the users have a copy of your HOSTS file, however, they remain blissfully ignorant of your internal host names.

In the Windows NT environment, HOSTS files have yet another disadvantage. Microsoft network clients are identified by their NetBIOS names. These NetBIOS names can be made available to Windows TCP/IP clients through WINS, but what about to the rest of the world? If you want non-Windows TCP/IP computers to share your Windows client names, you need a link between the WINS database and DNS. That's what the Windows NT 4 DNS server provides: a means of bringing together your NetBIOS names and DNS. When you make the WINS-DNS connection, you retain the chief advantage of the NetBIOS naming system, that the host name database adapts automatically when hosts change their configurations or move to different networks.

Deciding Whether to Implement DNS

If your Windows TCP/IP network is not connected to non-Microsoft TCP/IP networks, you do not require DNS. WINS can provide all of the naming services required on a Microsoft Windows network. Because WINS configures name-address mappings dynamically, WINS requires little or no maintenance to cope with network equipment changes. A user can move a portable computer from one network on the private internet to another network with no requirement for changes in WINS. WINS will recognize the new location of the host and adjust its database accordingly.

You need DNS if you wish to connect your TCP/IP hosts to the Internet or to a Unix-based TCP/IP network, but only if you wish to enable users outside the Windows network to access your TCP/IP hosts by name. If outside users will not be using services hosted on your computers, or if it is acceptable to identify your computers by IP address, it is not necessary to identify your network hosts in DNS.

In other words, if your network is attached to the Internet, you do not need to include your hosts in the Internet DNS tree to enable your users to connect to outside resources. DNS name-support is needed only if outsiders will be connecting to resources on your network.

If it is decided that hosts on your network must be identified in DNS, ask the following questions:

◆ Must all hosts be added to DNS, or only a select few?

◆ How often with host name-address information change?

◆ Should the names of local hosts be provided by WINS?

◆ Will you be obtaining a domain name on the Internet?

The right answers to these questions may mean that you can hire an Internet access provider to manage your portion of the DNS tree. As you learned earlier in the chapter, a single DNS server can manage multiple zones in the DNS tree. Many commercial Internet providers will manage your zone for a fee often considerably less than the labor cost of maintaining two private DNS servers. (At least two are generally preferred to ensure fault tolerance.)

Consider contracting management of your portion of the DNS tree if:

◆ You obtain your Internet access through an Internet provider who offers DNS management as a service.

◆ You do not wish to have local names of Windows TCP/IP hosts provided by WINS. The majority of Internet access providers will be running DNS on Unix computers, which will not support links to WINS.

◆ Your network is too small to justify training two DNS administrators, allocating a portion of their work time, and maintaining two computers with capacity to provide DNS services.

◆ Your network is fairly stable and you do not require immediate posting of changes.

Consider managing your own DNS server if:

◆ You wish to use WINS to provide host names of your Windows computers.

◆ You want local control of your organization's part of the DNS tree.

◆ Your network changes frequently.

◆ Your organization can justify the expense of administrative labor and DNS server hardware.

Local networks that include Unix hosts cannot use WINS for name resolution. Although DNS might seem the best solution for providing a local database, HOSTS files remain an option under some circumstances. Naming through HOSTS files generates no network traffic for name resolution, and HOSTS files can be easily maintained if the network is fairly stable. If the network changes frequently, it is easier to maintain DNS than it is to frequently distribute HOSTS files to all computers on the network.

An Example Network

Figure 16.49 illustrates an internetwork that will be used as an example of configuring DNS. The internetwork consists of two networks, connected by a multihomed host serving as an IP router. The internetwork will connect to the Internet via a Cisco router. The primary DNS server will be keystone1. (The configuration for keystone1 will assume a secondary name server will be set up on keystone2. The details of configuring the secondary name server are discussed later in the chapter.)

Figure 16.49

The example network.

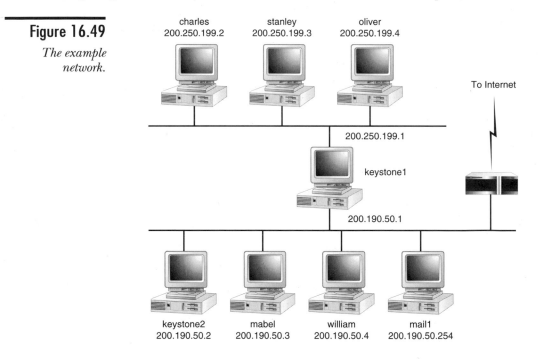

Only three computers require fixed IP addresses:

◆ **keystone1.** The primary DNS server; has two interfaces that will be named under DNS.

◆ **keystone2.** A secondary DNS server; also will be the WINS server.

◆ **oliver.** Will be hosting an FTP server.

◆ **mail1.** The mail server.

The Microsoft DNS server can be set up either graphically or by importing data from BIND database files. Frankly, the graphic approach is considerably simpler than the process of creating BIND database files and is far less error-prone. For that reason, I have chosen to focus on using the graphic DNS Manager in this chapter.

If you need to port data from an existing BIND server, you need to thoroughly understand the BIND data file format. I discuss BIND files at some length in *Inside Microsoft TCP/IP*, published by New Riders Publishing. *Inside Microsoft TCP/IP, Certified Administrator's Resource Edition* updated for Windows NT 4, will be available in September 1997.

For even more details about BIND, consult *DNS and Bind* by Paul Albitz and Cricket Liu (O'Reilly & Associates). This book is the standard reference for BIND, good enough that no one else has bothered to try to compete with it.

Installing the Microsoft DNS Server

The procedure for installing the Microsoft DNS Server is accomplished by following the steps in the following exercise:

Installing DNS Server

1. Install TCP/IP on the DHCP server computer. DNS servers must be configured with static IP addresses so that the addresses can be entered into host configurations.

2. Open the Microsoft TCP/IP Protocols properties dialog box and select the WINS Address tab. Be sure that E**n**able DNS for Windows Resolution has been checked.

3. Open the DNS tab (see fig. 16.50) in TCP/IP Properties and complete the following fields:

    ◆ **Host Name.** This field should contain the name of this host, which by default is the same as the host's NetBIOS name.

    ◆ **Domain.** In this field, enter the fully qualified name of the domain in which this host resides.

    ◆ **DNS Service Search Order.** In this box, add the IP addresses of this and any other DNS servers on the network. DNS servers will be queried in the order they appear in this box. Use the U**p** and Do**w**n buttons to adjust the order of multiple entries.

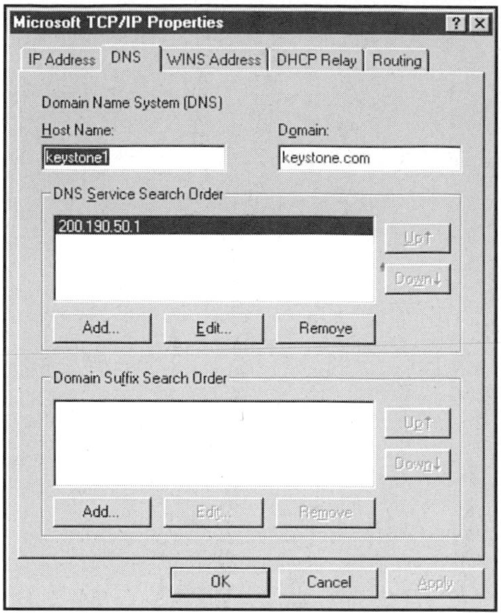

Figure 16.50

Configuring DNS client properties.

4. Choose OK to exit Microsoft TCP/IP Protocols.

5. Open the Network utility in the Control Panel.

6. Select the Services tab.

7. Choose **A**dd.

8. In the **N**etwork Service list, select Microsoft DNS Server, and choose OK.

9. Supply the path to the installation files when prompted.

10. Close the Network utility and restart the server.

About Resource Records

The DNS name space is organized into *zones*, and each zone is defined by a zone database. The information in the zone databases takes the form of *resource records*. There are many types of resource records, but only a few are commonly encountered. Before going too deeply into the details of setting up DNS, it is a good idea to briefly examine these record types.

◆ **The Start of Authority Record.** A Start of Authority (SOA) resource record is found at the beginning of each mapping database file. This block of information declares the host that is most authoritative for the domain, and also declares contact information and some DNS server parameters.

◆ **Name Server Records.** A name server (NS) record must declare each primary and secondary name server that is authoritative for the zone.

◆ **Address Records.** Each host name that DNS resolves must be specified using an address (A) resource record, unless the name will be resolved through WINS. Multihomed hosts require an address declaration for each network adapter, as with the host keystone1 in the example database file.

◆ **Alias Records.** Many networks employ aliases. In most cases, aliases are declared using CNAME ("canonical name") resource records. On the keystone.com network, host stanley will be configured as an FTP server. An alias will be established so that users can access the FTP server with the name ftp.keystone.com.

◆ **E-Mail Server Records.** The most popular electronic mail environment in the TCP/IP world is based on a program called sendmail. If your network incorporates an electronic mail system that uses sendmail, the MX (*mail exchanger*) records enable mail to be delivered to the correct mail server in your domain.

◆ **WINS Records.** The WINS resource record is unique to the Microsoft DNS Server, enabling it to resolve names by looking them up in WINS.

You encounter these resource records during the following discussion, and the details of each are examined.

Initializing the DNS Server

By default, database files for the Microsoft DNS Server are installed in *%systemroot%* system32\dns. When the DNS Server is installed, only a cache.dns file is installed in this directory.

When DNS Manager is run for the first time, it attempts to initialize using database files in the *%systemroot%*\system32\dns directory. Depending on the contents of this directory, one of two things can happen:

◆ If the dns directory contains only the cache.dns file, the DNS Server is initialized with an empty database. This section assumes that only the default files are present in the dns directory.

◆ If you have placed a set of BIND data files in this directory, DNS Manager will initialize the server database from those files. These files must be properly configured using syntax that the Microsoft DNS Server will accept, or errors will be generated and DNS server startup will fail. Discussion in this chapter assumes that BIND database files are not present.

The icon for the DNS Manager is installed in the Administrative Tools program group. At first, no DNS servers are listed, and the display is entirely uninteresting, so I haven't provided you with a picture. The first step is to add one to the DNS Manager configuration. Figure 16.51 shows DNS Manager after a DNS server has been added.

Figure 16.51

DNS Manager after a DNS server has been added.

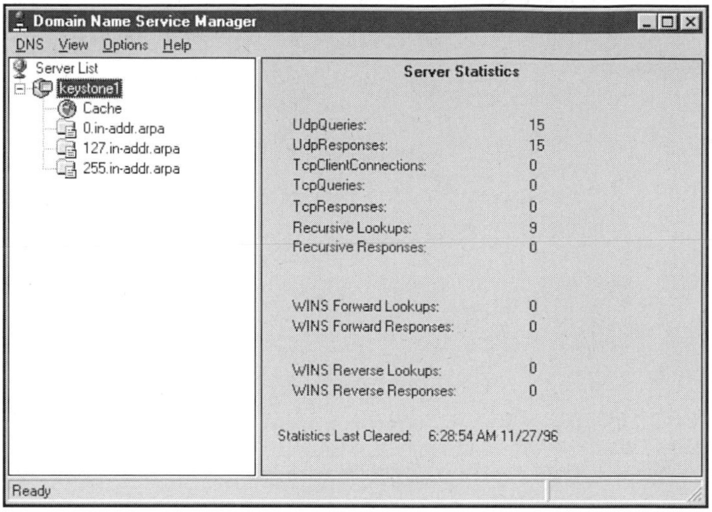

To create a DNS server:

1. Right-click on the Server List icon and select the **N**ew Server command from the menu that is displayed.

2. Enter the host name or IP address of the DNS server in the Add New Server dialog box, shown in figure 16.52. If you enter a host name, Microsoft DNS Server must be installed on the host. Additionally, this host must be able to resolve the host name to an IP address using WINS or some other means.

Note　If the server icon is marked with a red X, the DNS Server service is not running on the server you specified. It may be that the service has not been installed, or it may be that an error occurred when an attempt was made to start the service. Check the Event Viewer to determine the nature of the error.

If an existing set of BIND files is stored in the %*systemroot*%\system32\dns directory, it may be that an error exists in one or more of the files. Troubleshooting those files is not covered in this book. Refer to one of the resources mentioned earlier in this chapter, or simply remove all files except Cache.dns from the dns directory and start from scratch.

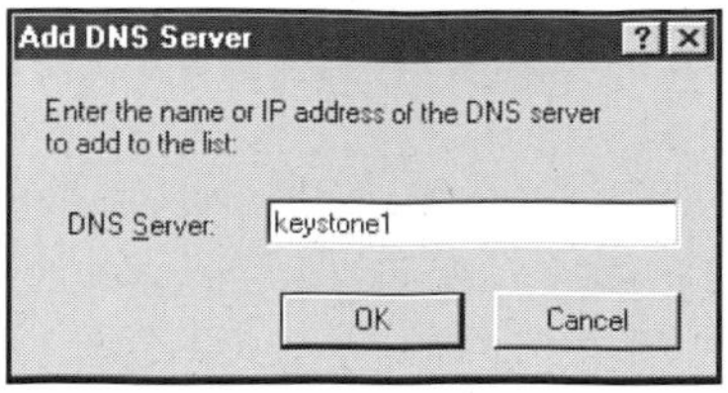

Add DNS Server [?][X]

Enter the name or IP address of the DNS server
to add to the list:

DNS Server: keystone1

[OK] [Cancel]

Figure 16.52

*Adding a new
DNS name server
to DNS Manager.*

Adding the server creates an icon for the DNS server object, which is assigned a
default set of properties. In addition, the following zones are automatically created:

◆ **Cache.** This zone is filled with records defining the root name servers for the
Internet.

◆ **0.in-addr.arpa.** This zone prevents reverse-lookup queries for the address
0.0.0.0 from being passed to the root name server.

◆ **167.in-addr.arpa.** This zone supports revers-lookup queries for the
loopback address.

◆ **255.in-addr.arpa.** This zone prevents broadcast name queries from being
passed to the root name server.

> **Note**
>
> With the exception of the Cache zone, the automatically created zones are
> concealed by default. To enable display of these zones, as was done to create
> figure 16.2, choose the **P**references command in the **O**ptions menu. Then check the
> **S**how Automatically Created Zones check box. Finally, press F5 to refresh the
> display and display the zone icons.
>
> Because these zones require no maintenance on your part, you can safely leave
> them hidden, as was done in the other figures.

The Cache Zone

The Cache zone, shown in figure 16.53, may require some maintenance on your part.
This zone lists the name servers that are authoritative for the root domain, information that is vital if your network is to be connected to the Internet, because hosts must
resolve names starting at the root and working down through the DNS name space.
The entries in this file change infrequently, and you can probably use the Cache zone
as it is created by DNS Manager. If you wish to obtain the latest list of Internet root
name servers, try one of the following sources:

◆ **FTP.** FTP the file /domain/named.root from FTP.RS.INTERNIC.NET.

◆ **Gopher.** Obtain the file named.root from RS.INTERNIC.NET under menu
InterNIC Registration Services (NSI), submenu InterNIC Registration Archives.

◆ **E-mail.** Send e-mail to service@nic.ddn.mil, using the subject "netinfo root-servers.txt."

Each entry in the Cache zone takes the form of an NS (*name server*) record. (Records in DNS databases are called *resource records*). The period in the Name column designates the root domain. NS is the record type, and the entry in the Data column is the name of a root domain name server. You will see how to create and modify NS records later in this chapter.

Figure 16.53

*Contents of the
Cache zone.*

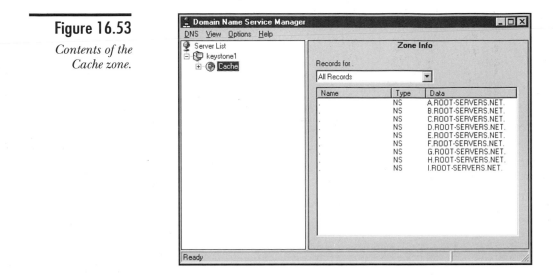

Adding Reverse-Lookup Zones

Before you create a zone for the domain that is to be managed, you should create the zones that support reverse-lookups, the in-addr.arpa zones. These zones contain PTR (*pointer*) records that associate IP addresses with host names.

If you create the reverse-lookup zones first, you can populate them with PTR records automatically, as you add A records to the primary domain zone.

To create a primary reverse-lookup zone, follow the steps in the following exercise:

Creating a Primary Reverse-Lookup Zone

1. Right-click on the icon of the primary DNS server.

2. Select the New **Z**one command from the object menu to open the Create new zone wizard shown in figure 16.54.

3. Click the **P**rimary radio button and choose **N**ext to open the Zone Info dialog
   box shown in figure 16.55.

4. In the **Z**one Name field, enter the name of the reverse-lookup zone. Because this
   is a reverse-lookup zone, adhere to the naming convention (*reverse-netid*.in-addr.
   arpa). DNS server will realize this is a reverse-naming zone and will configure it
   accordingly. To create the reverse-lookup zone for network 200.250.199.0, you
   would enter `199.250.200.in-addr.arpa` in the **Z**one Name field.

   Do not move to the next field except by pressing the Tab key.

5. Press Tab to automatically generate a file name in the Zone **F**ile field. The file
   name can be anything you want, but the default adheres to the conventions
   established for the Microsoft DNS Server.

6. Choose **N**ext. You will be rewarded with the message, `All of the information for the new zone has been entered.`

7. Press **F**inish to create the zone, or press **B**ack to change any information you have entered.

Figure 16.56 shows DNS Manager after entry of the reverse-lookup zones required for the example network. Notice that the NS and SOA resource records have been entered for you. You can probably leave the default values for both records. Later, you will learn how to edit these records.

> **Note** | Two networks are included in the example internetwork. A reverse-lookup zone must be created for each zone. The second zone will appear in later figures.

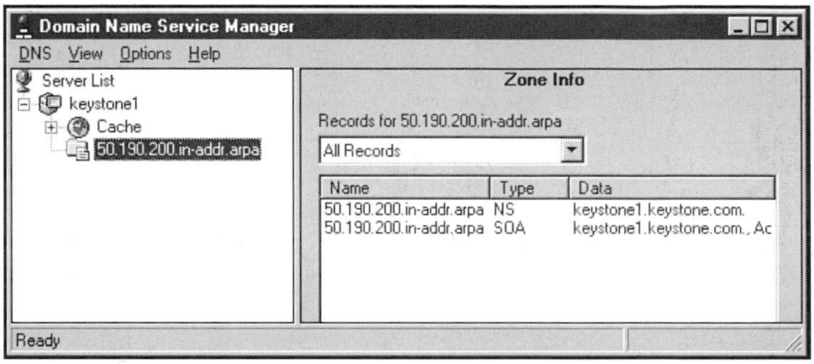

Figure 16.56

A newly created reverse-naming zone.

Adding a Primary Zone

After the reverse-lookup zones have been created, you can begin to create the name-lookup zones. The procedure is quite similar to that shown in the preceding section:

1. Right-click on the icon of the primary DNS server.

2. Select the New **Z**one command from the object menu to open the Create new zone wizard.

3. Click the **P**rimary radio button and choose **N**ext.

4. Enter the zone name in the **Z**one Name field and press Tab to generate the file name. Then press **N**ext.

5. Press **F**inish to create the zone, or press **B**ack to change any information you have entered.

Figure 16.57 shows the keystone.com zone after it has been created. Notice that the NS and SOA resource records have been created for you. Check to ensure that an A record has been entered for the DNS server host. If not you will need to add one. If the host is multihomed, you must add an A record for each interface. The second interface for keystone1 will be added later.

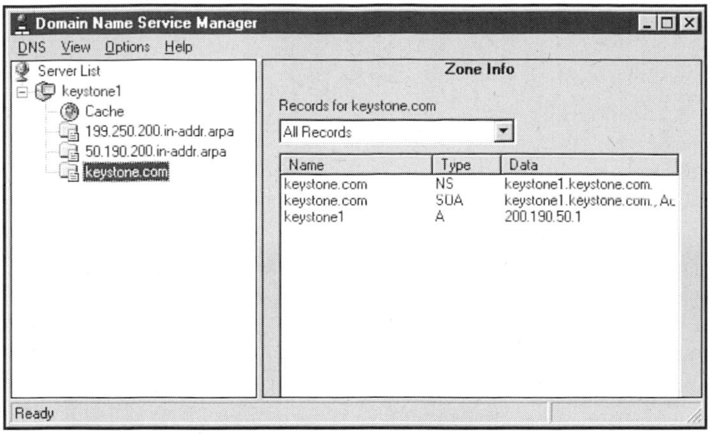

Figure 16.57

DNS Manager after the keystone.com name-lookup zone has been created.

Adding Pointer Records

You must add a PTR to the reverse lookup domain or domains that define networks to which this host is attached. Without these pointer records, DNS clients are unable to contact the DNS server.

To create a pointer record for the DNS server:

1. Right-click on the reverse-lookup zone that is to contain the record. In the New Resource Record dialog box for a reverse-look zone, only three record types can be created, as shown in figure 16.58.

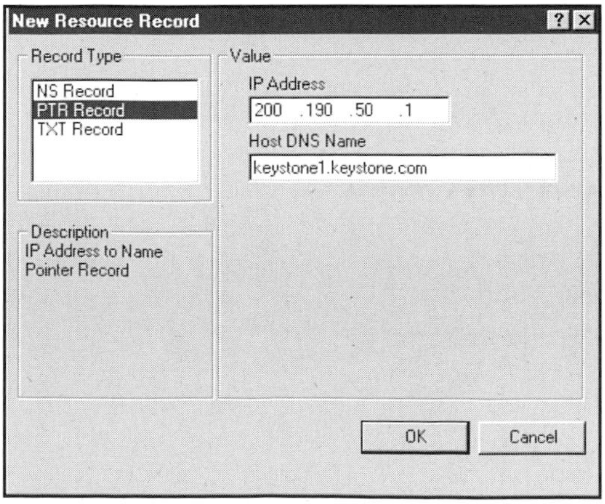

Figure 16.58

Creating a PTR resource record for a reverse-lookup zone.

2. Select PTR Record in the Record Type list.

3. In the IP Address field, enter the IP address of the DNS server. Enter the address fields in their conventional order. Do not enter the fields in their reverse order.

4. In the Host DNS Name field, enter the fully qualified host name of the DNS server. Do not enter the host name alone. The reverse-lookup domains are not tied to a particular name domain.

5. Choose OK to create the record.

Figure 16.59 shows the PTR record for a DNS server host in the reverse-lookup zone.

Figure 16.59

The PTR record for the DNS server in a reverse-lookup zone.

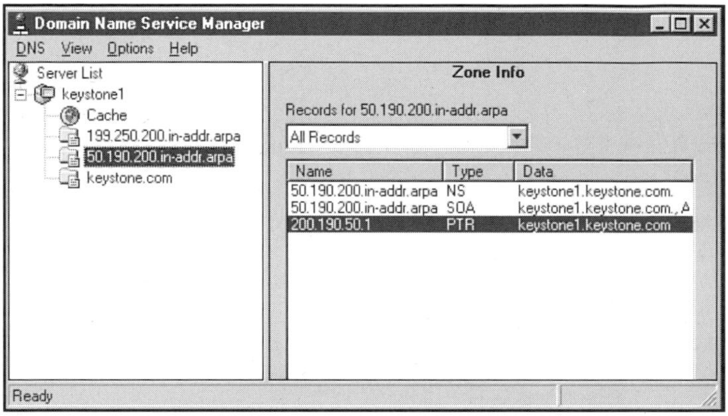

Editing the Start of Authority Record

Every zone database includes a Start of Authority or SOA record. Although you can probably operate with the default SOA record that is created when the zone is established, you may wish to make a few changes. Figure 16.60 shows the SOA record for keystone.com. To open the editor for any resource record, double-click the record in the Zone Info pane.

The fields in an SOA record are as follows:

◆ **Primary Name Server DNS Name.** This field contains the FQDN of the primary name server for the domain that is being defined. Notice that the FQDN must be terminated with a period. This is a result of the way BIND defines records.

All names are interpreted in the context of the zone that is being defined; in this case, keystone.com. If the entry read oliver.keystone.com, then keystone.com would be appended, resulting in the name oliver.keystone.com.keystone.com. The trailing period indicates that the name is a FQDN starting from the root domain, and that the domain context is not appended.

◆ **Responsible Person Mailbox DNS Name.** This is an e-mail name. Because @ is a special character in BIND databases, it cannot appear here. Administrator.keystone.com. appears instead, indicating an e-mail name of Administrator@keystone.com. Notice that a trailing period is required, as in the Primary Name Server DNS Name field. The default value for this field is Administrator@*domain*. Edit this field to specify the designated DNS contact person for this domain.

◆ **Serial Number.** A serial number that indicates the revision level of the file. The DNS administrator increments this value each time the file is modified. (DNS Manager increments this value automatically when changes are made.)

◆ **Refresh Interval.** The interval in seconds at which a secondary name server checks in to download a copy of the zone data in the primary name server. The default value for DNS Server is a refresh interval of 60 minutes.

◆ **Retry Interval.** The time in seconds a secondary name server waits after a failed download before it tries to download the zone database again. The default value for DNS Server is a retry interval of 10 minutes.

◆ **Expire Time.** The period of time in seconds that a secondary name server continues to try to download a zone database. After this time expires, the secondary name server discards data for the zone. The default value for DNS Server is 24 hours

◆ **Minimum Default TTL.** The minimum time of life in seconds for a resource record. This parameter determines how long a DNS server retains an address mapping in cache. After the TTL expires for a record, the record is discarded. Short TTL values enable DNS to adjust to network changes more adroitly, but increase network traffic and loading on the DNS server. A short TTL might be appropriate in the early days, while a network evolves, but you might want to extend the TTL as the network stabilizes. The default value for DNS Server is a TTL of one hour.

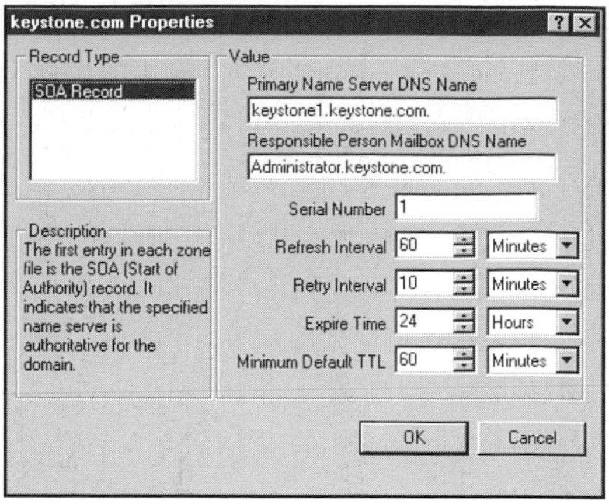

Figure 16.60

Contents of the SOA record.

Adding Resource Records

Figure 16.61 shows DNS Manager after a variety of records have been added to the keystone.com domain. This section and the following ones examine the creation of address, CNAME, MX, and WINS resource records.

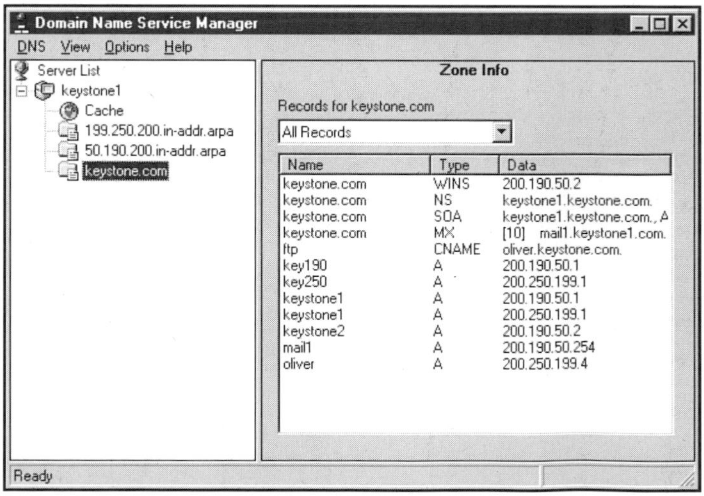

Figure 16.61

Various resource records in the keystone.com domain.

Adding Address Records

Next you must add essential address (A) records to the name-lookup zone. You must add address records only for hosts that are associated with fixed IP addresses or are not registered with WINS. Hosts that are registered with WINS can be entered into the zone database through WINS lookups.

You should add an A record for any host that must have a fixed address-to-name mapping or that cannot be resolved using WINS. Oliver, which will be the FTP server, and mail1 are good examples of hosts that require fixed mappings. As shown in figure 16.61, the database for keystone.com contains a number of address records. Of particular interest are the following:

```
key250          A    200.250.199.1
key190          A    200.190.50.1
```

These records are for the convenience of the network administrator, assigning, as they do, individual names to each interface of the multihomed keystone1 host. These names enable the administrator to, for example, ping each interface by name without having to enter the entire IP address.

When a multihomed host is entered in the database, each interface should be defined. Notice that two entries have been made for keystone1:

```
keystone1       A    200.190.50.1
keystone1       A    200.250.199.1
```

To add an address resource record:

1. Right-click on the name-lookup zone icon (in this example, keystone.com) and choose **N**ew Host from the object menu.

   or

   Right-click in the database area of the Zone Info pane and choose **N**ew Host from the menu.

2. In the New Host dialog box, shown in figure 16.62, enter the host name in the Host **N**ame field.

Note   In most cases, when you are entering a host name, DNS Manager expects only the host name portion of the FQDN. When necessary, the host name will be combined with the domain name to create the FQDN.

3. Enter the host's IP address in the Host IP Address field.

4. If you wish to create a record in the appropriate reverse-lookup database, check Create Associated PTR Record. The reverse-lookup zone has to have been previously created.

> **Note** In my experience, automatic pointer record creation can fail, in which case you will need to enter the records manually, as described later in this chapter.

5. Choose **A**dd Host to create the database records.

6. Repeat steps 2 through 5 as required to enter additional address records.

7. Choose **D**one when you are finished.

When do you create a PTR record? In most cases, you want to add host addresses to the reverse-lookup zones, but there are some exceptions. In the examples created in this chapter, pointer records were created for all A records except for key250 and key190. Because those records were added for administrative convenience and not for public consumption, and because a PTR record for keystone1 already exists, entries were not added to the reverse-lookup directories. To have done so would have been to create conflicting mappings, where an IP address mapped to two host names.

Figure 16.62

Creating an address record.

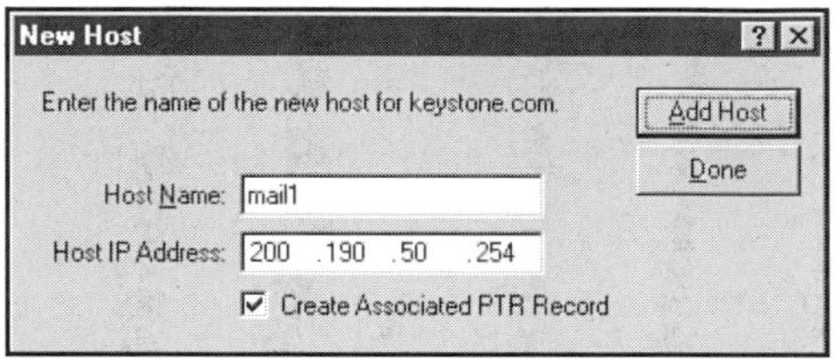

Adding Other Resource Records

Besides address records, all other types of resource records are entered from the New Resource Record dialog box, shown in figure 16.63. The fields you see in the Value box depend on the record type that has been selected. In this section, we will examine the procedures for creating CNAME, MX, and PTR resource records.

Figure 16.63

Adding a CNAME resource record.

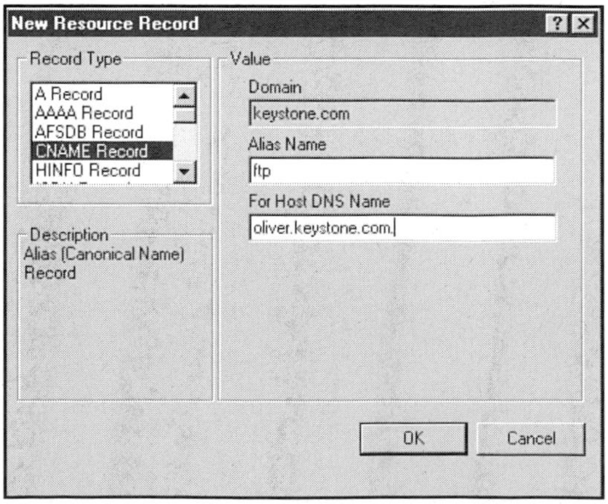

Adding CNAME Records

An alias is established by adding a CNAME record. In the example network, the alias ftp.keystone.com will be created for oliver.keystone.com. To add a CNAME resource record, follow these steps:

1. Right-click on the zone that is to contain the record.

2. Choose New Record from the object menu to open the New Resource Record dialog box shown in figure 16.60.

3. Select CNAME Record in the Record Type list.

4. Enter an alias in the Alias Name field.

5. Enter the fully qualified domain name for the host in the For Host DNS Name field.

6. Choose OK to add the record. The completed records for the example network can be observed in figure 16.61.

Adding MX Records

Each mail exchanger should be specified in an MX record. To add an MX resource record, follow these steps:

1. Right-click on the zone that is to contain the record.

2. Choose New Record from the object menu to open the New Resource Record dialog box shown in figure 16.64.

3. Leave the Host Name field blank to establish a mail exchanger for the domain specified in the Domain field.

4. Enter the host name of the mail exchange server in the Mail Exchange Server DNS Name field.

5. Enter a preference number in the Preference Number field.

6. Choose OK to add the record. The complete record can be seen in figure 16.61.

The preference number comes into play when several mail exchangers are servicing a zone. When mail is to be delivered, outside mail exchangers will look for the mail exchanger that has the lowest preference number. The mail exchanger with the lowest preference number will be the first to receive mail. If that mail exchanger is unavailable, the mail exchanger with the next lowest preference number will receive mail.

The mail exchanger host must be defined by an A and an NS record.

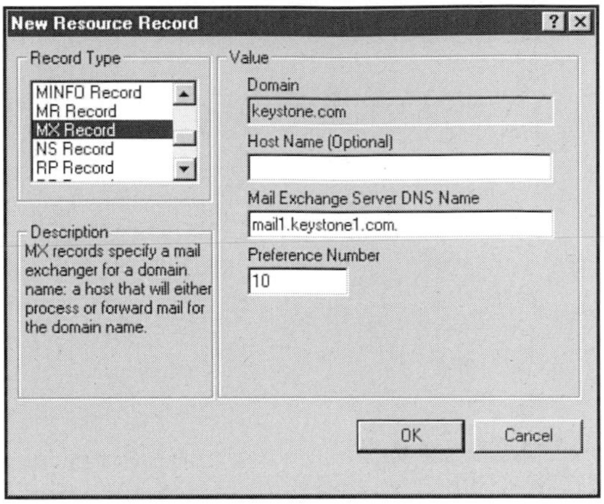

Figure 16.64

Creating an MX resource record.

Adding PTR Records

If you create the pointer records when you add an address record to the zone database, you may seldom need to add PTR records manually. To add a PTR resource record to a reverse-lookup zone, follow these steps:

1. Right-click on the reverse-lookup zone that is to contain the record. In the New Resource Record dialog box for a reverse-look zone, only three record types can be created, as shown in figure 16.65.

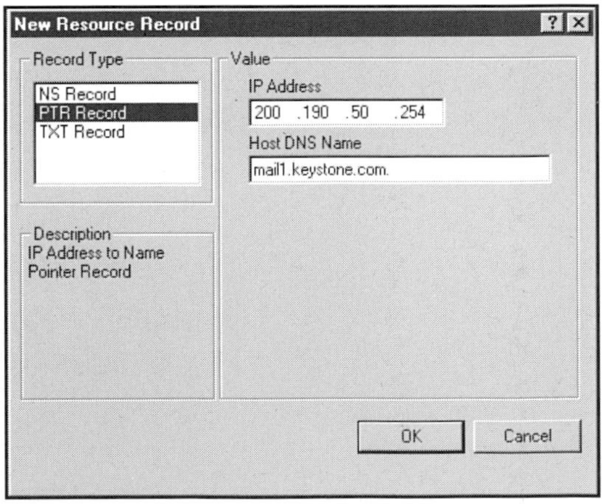

Figure 16.65

Creating a PTR resource record for a reverse-lookup zone.

2. Select PTR Record in the Record Type list.

3. In the IP Address field, enter the IP address of the host. Enter the address fields in their conventional order. Do not enter the fields in their reverse order.

4. In the Host DNS Name field, enter the fully qualified host name of the host. Do not enter the host name alone. The reverse-lookup domains are not tied to a particular name domain.

5. Choose OK to create the record.

Figure 16.66 shows the records for a reverse-lookup zone after PTR records have been created.

| Caution | Don't rely on DNS Manager to create all the required PTR records for you. In particular, review the appropriate reverse-lookup zones to ensure that pointer records are entered for each name server. Clients cannot contact the DNS server unless the reverse-lookup records are available. |

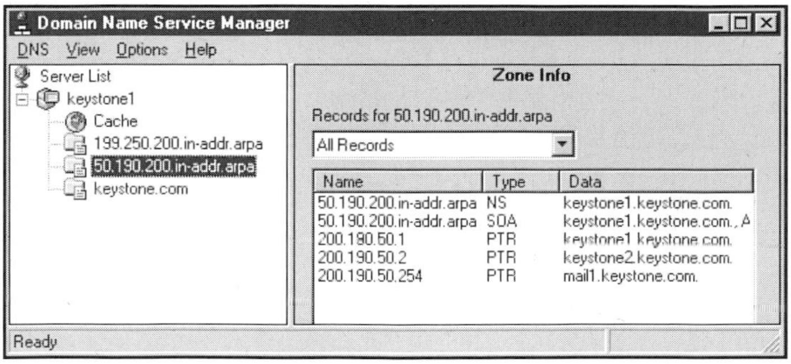

Figure 16.66

PTR records in a reverse-lookup zone.

Modifying Resource Records

You can open a dialog box to modify any resource record by double-clicking the resource record in the Zone Info box.

Modifying Zone Properties

When a zone is created, it is assigned a default set of properties, and a Start of Authority record is established. You should review the zone properties and the SOA record to ensure that the properties are correct for your network.

To review the zone properties, right-click on the zone icon and choose **P**roperties from the object menu. The Zone Properties dialog box is shown in figure 16.67. Four tabs are included in the dialog box, and are examined in the following sections.

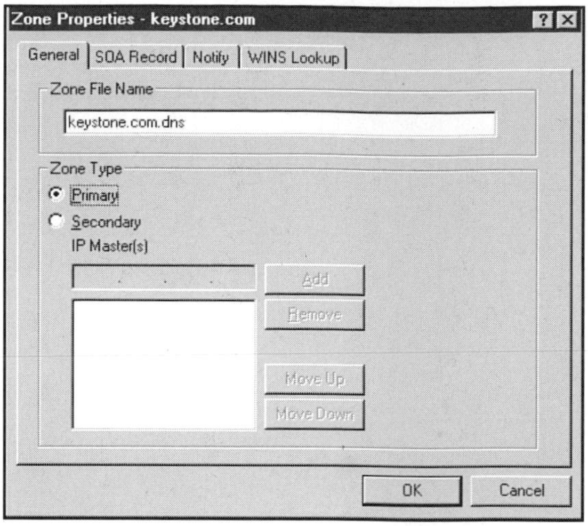

Figure 16.67

The General tab of the Zone Properties dialog box.

Zone General Properties

The General properties tab, shown in figure 16.67, has the following fields:

◆ **Zone File Name.** This file name specifies the file name that is used to create a server data file for the zone. You can change this file name at any time.

◆ **Primary.** When the **P**rimary radio button is selected, this server is a primary DNS server for the zone. Primary DNS servers maintain a database for the zone locally on the computer on which they are running.

◆ **Secondary.** When the **S**econdary radio button is selected, this server is a secondary DNS server for the zone. Secondary DNS servers obtain zone data from another DNS server and do not maintain a local database for the zone.

◆ **IP Master(s).** If the **S**econdary radio button is selected, this list is active. You must specify the IP addresses of one or more master DNS servers, servers from which zone transfers will be performed to populate the database of the secondary DNS server.

SOA Record Properties

The SOA Record tab (see fig. 16.68) establishes properties for the SOA record in the zone database. The SOA record was discussed in considerable detail earlier in the chapter, in the section "Editing the Start of Authority Record."

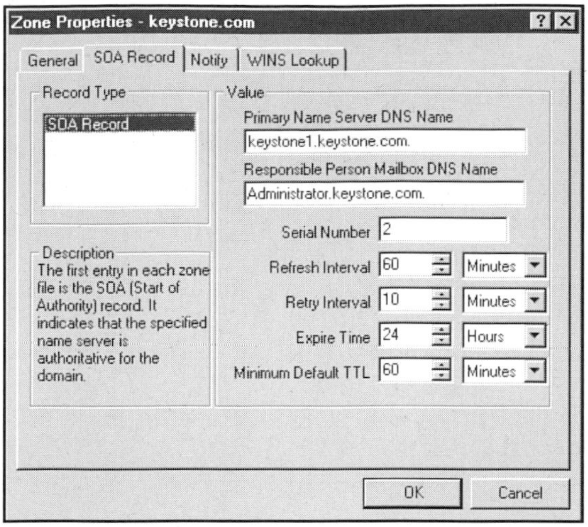

Figure 16.68

The SOA Record properties tab.

Notify Properties

The Notify tab, shown in figure 16.69, lists the IP addresses of secondary DNS servers that obtain zone data from this server. A DNS server will notify servers appearing in the **N**otify List field when changes are made to the zone database.

Zone transfers can be driven by secondary DNS servers, and it is not essential for notification to take place. If, however, you wish to restrict the secondary DNS servers that can transfer records from this server, check **O**nly Allow Access From Secondaries Included on Notify List.

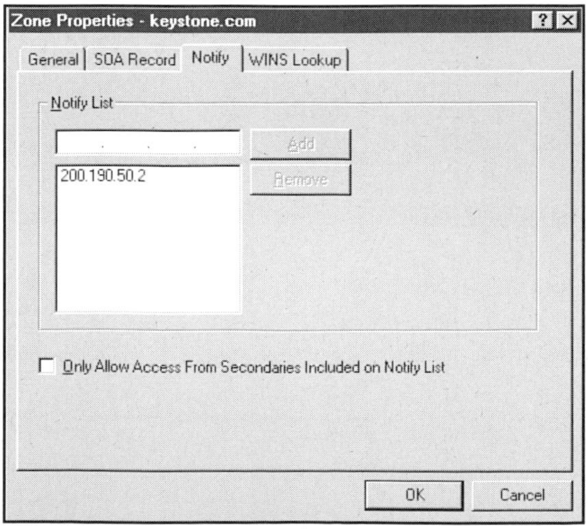

Figure 16.69

Specifying secondary DNS servers in the Notify List.

WINS Lookup Properties

This tab (see fig. 16.70) is used to enable DNS Server to use WINS to resolve names that do not appear in the zone database. On the sample network, a WINS server is running on 200.190.50.2. This tab has three fields:

◆ **Use WINS Resolution.** When this box is checked, WINS lookup is enabled. A WINS resource record will be added to the zone database, as shown in figure 16.61.

◆ **Settings only affect local server.** When WINS resolution is enabled, this field determines how records are handled on secondary DNS servers. Ordinarily, when a record learned from WINS is sent to a secondary DNS server in a zone transfer, the record is flagged as read-only. Such records cannot be modified on the secondary server. When this box is checked, the read-only protection is removed, enabling records to be modified at the secondary DNS server, and preventing modified records from being overwritten in a zone transfer.

◆ **WINS Servers.** When WINS resolution is enabled, this list must include the IP addresses of one or more WINS servers that will be used to resolve names.

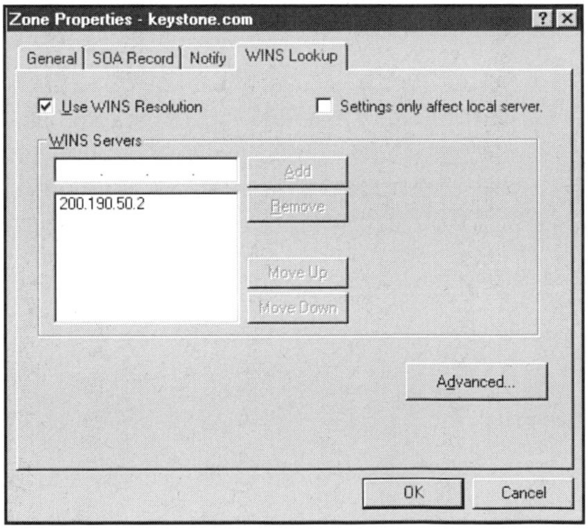

Figure 16.70

Establishing WINS lookup properties.

Several advanced WINS properties can be configured by clicking the A**d**vanced button to open the Advanced Zone Properties dialog box shown in figure 16.71. The dialog box has the following fields:

◆ **Submit DNS Domain as NetBIOS Scope.** NetBIOS scopes permit administrators to specify a character string (a scope ID) that is appended to NetBIOS and is used for all NetBT (NetBIOS over TCP/IP) names. The effect is that only computers having the same NetBIOS scope can communicate with each other. In the words of the *Windows NT Resource Kit,* "Use of NetBIOS Scope is strongly discouraged if you are not already using it, or if you use Domain Name System (DNS) on your network." Who am I to question Microsoft? Given the many problems that can ensue if NetBIOS scopes are used, I don't recommend them. Unless they are used, there is no reason to check this box.

◆ **Cache Timeout Value.** The DNS Server maintains a cache of addresses that have been recently resolved via WINS. These records are retained for a limited time, determined by the settings in these fields. Long timeouts can reduce the number of calls to WINS, but can increase memory demand by the DNS Server. By default, this value is 10 minutes.

◆ **Lookup Timeout Value.** This value determines how long DNS Server will wait for a response from WINS before giving up and returning an error to the sender. By default, this value is 1 second.

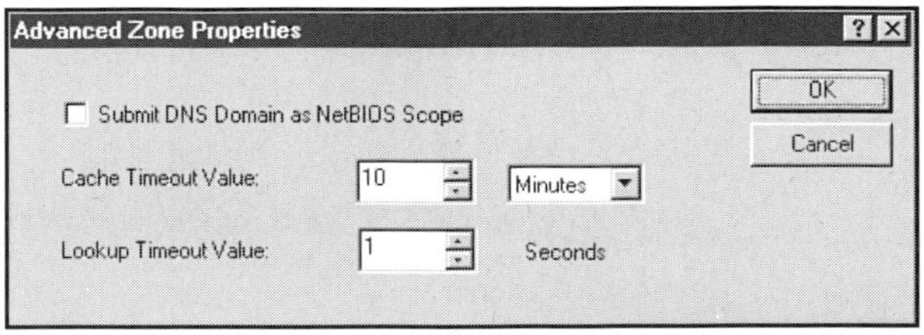

Figure 16.71

Configuring WINS lookup advanced properties.

Resolving Names with WINS

Very little is required to link Microsoft DNS Server with WINS:

◆ At least one WINS server must be operating to register hosts in the zone.

◆ WINS lookup must be enabled in the zone database.

The previous section, "WINS Lookup Properties," showed how to enable WINS lookup. Figure 16.72 shows an example of a database record that has been retrieved from WINS.

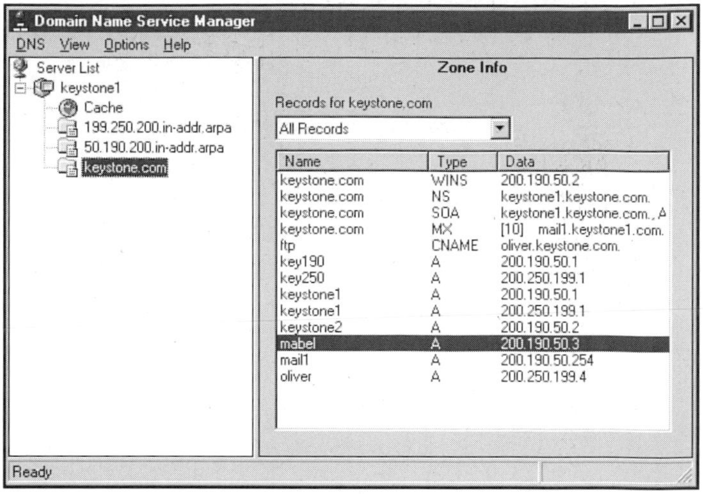

Figure 16.72

The resource record for mabel was obtained through a WINS lookup.

Managing Multiple DNS Servers

DNS Manager can manage many DNS servers. Besides consolidating DNS management on a single console, this capability simplifies certain operations by enabling you to use drag-and-drop to copy data. You will see how in the following section, "Creating a Secondary DNS Server."

Figure 16.73 shows DNS manager with two DNS servers appearing in the Server list (no zones have been created for the second server). To add a remote DNS server to the list:

1. Install Microsoft DNS Services on the remote server.

2. Right-click on the Server List icon.

3. Choose **N**ew Server in the object menu.

4. Enter the host name or the IP address of the remote DNS server in the DNS **S**erver field of the Add DNS Server dialog box.

5. Choose OK.

> **Note**   DNS Managers communicate with remote DNS Servers using RPCs (Remote Procedure Calls). To communicate with DNS Manager, the DNS Service must be running on the computer that is being managed. If DNS Manager cannot communicate with a DNS Service, the icon will be marked with a red X. You will also see an error message in the Server Statistics box stating that `The RPC service is unavailable`.

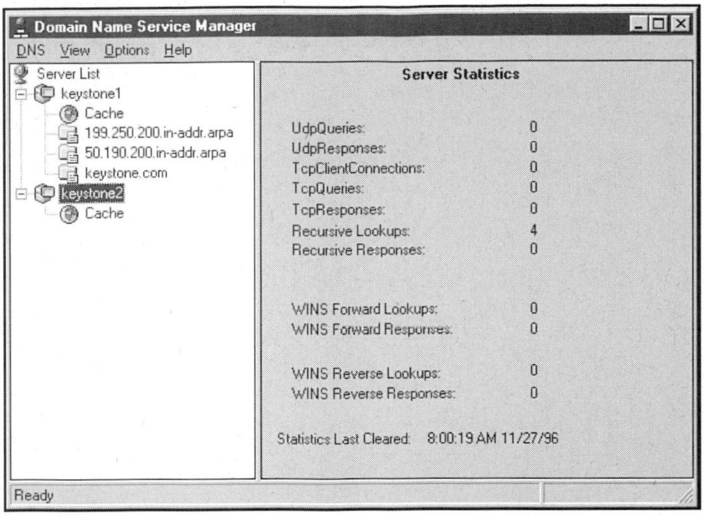

Figure 16.73

DNS Manager with two managed servers.

Creating a Secondary DNS Server

On the sample network, keystone2 will be set up as a secondary DNS server for the keystone.com domain. I'll show you two ways to set up a secondary domain, one hard, one easy.

Creating a Secondary Server the Hard Way

The hard way is as follows:

1. Right-click on the server icon and select **N**ew Zone from the object menu.

2. Click the **S**econdary radio button in the Creating new zone dialog box, shown in figure 16.74.

3. Enter the zone name in the Zon**e** field.

4. In the Serve**r** field, enter the name of the server from which zone transfers will be made.

5. Choose **N**ext.

6. The **Z**one Name field will already be completed with the name of the zone that was specified in step 3. Press the Tab key in this field to generate the name for the database file in the Zone **F**ile field.

7. Press **N**ext.

8. In the IP Masters list (see fig. 16.75), specify the IP address list of at least one DNS server that will be a master server for this secondary.

9. Choose **N**ext. Then choose **F**inish to create the zone.

Figure 16.74

Creating a zone on a secondary DNS server.

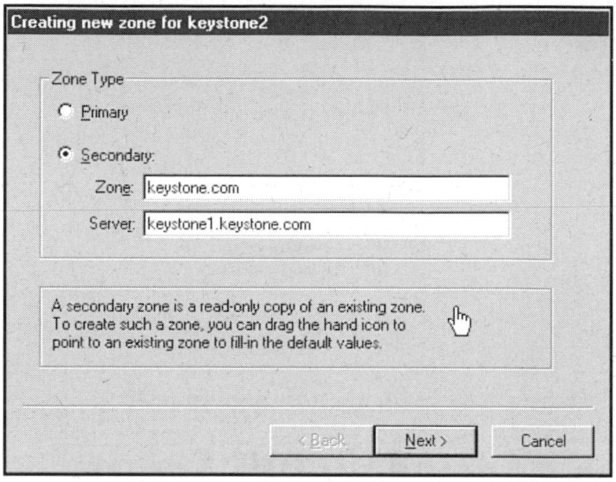

Figure 16.75

Specifying the address for an IP master.

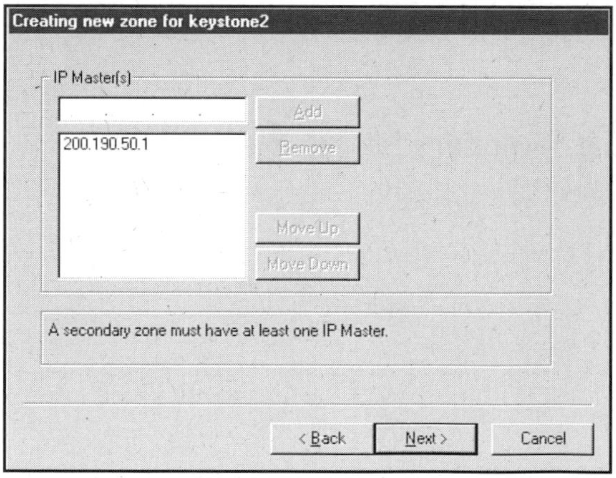

> **Note** Because the Cache zone is the same on every DNS server, there is no sense in transferring zone data between servers. Every DNS server, therefore, is a primary server for the Cache zone. The same holds true for the automatically created zones. Only the zones you create must be duplicated through zone transfers.

And Now, the Easy Way

Now let's use the easy method to add the secondary zones for the two reverse-lookup zones. For this to work, the primary zone must be displayed in DNS Manager. If necessary, add the server supporting the primary zone and open the server icon to display the icon for the primary zone. After that, here's the procedure:

1. Right-click on the server icon and select **N**ew Zone from the object menu.

2. Click the **S**econdary check box in the Creating new zone dialog box.

3. If you examine figure 16.74, you will notice a hand icon that was ignored in the previous procedure. Use the mouse to drag the hand icon and drop it on the appropriate primary zone. All of the fields in the Create new zone dialog box will be completed as required.

4. Use the **N**ext button to review the fields in the Create new zone dialog box.

5. Choose **F**inish to complete creation of the secondary zone.

If every network management task was that easy, we network administrators would be out of jobs.

Adding Subdomains

As you have learned, the DNS name space is a hierarchy, and you can extend the name space hierarchy by adding domains below existing domains. Although the sample network has only a single domain, it is worth looking at the techniques for adding lower-level domains.

Suppose, for example, that you want to add the domains, such as widgets.keystone .com, and blivets.keystone.com, to provide subdomains for various departments. Let's examine the procedure.

To create a widgets.keystone.com subdomain, follow these steps:

1. Right-click on the icon for the keystone.com zone.

2. Choose New **D**omain in the object menu.

3. In the New Domain dialog box, enter the domain name in the **D**omain Name field.

4. Choose OK.

Subsequently, you would add address records to the subdomain just as you add them to the primary domain. The subdomain uses the same name server and SOA parameters as the primary domain does.

Figure 16.76

Two subdomains have been added to keystone.com.

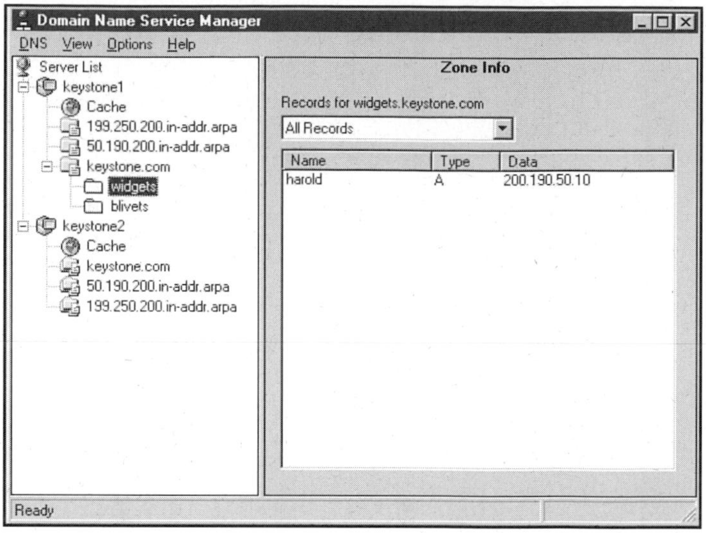

Subdomains have no effect on the reverse-lookup files. The reverse-lookup database is flat and includes all hosts with the same netid, whether or not they are in the same name domain. Figure 16.77 shows how harold.widgets.keystone.com is entered into the reverse-lookup database.

Figure 16.77

The reverse-lookup record for a host in a subdomain.

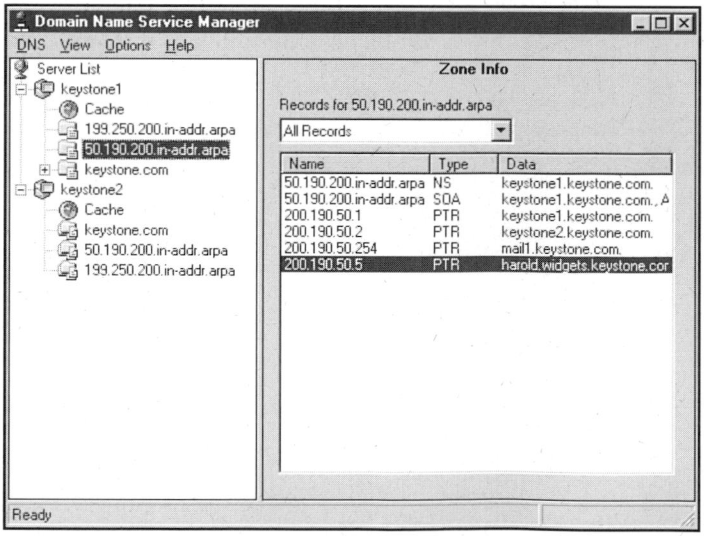

Updating the Database Files

DNS Manager maintains a standard set of BIND data files, which can be used to back up the server database or to export the configuration to a BIND name server. To back up the database, choose the **U**pdate Server Data Files command in the **D**NS menu.

Setting DNS Manager Preferences

Several preferences determine the behavior of DNS Manager. To open the preferences dialog box, shown in figure 16.78, choose the **P**references command in the **O**ptions menu. The options in this dialog box are as follows:

◆ **Auto Refresh Statistics.** Ordinarily, DNS Manager updates server statistics only when you click on a server icon. If you check this check box, statistics will be updated at the interval specified in the **I**nterval field.

◆ **Show Automatically Created Zones.** Check this box to display the zones that are automatically created when a new DNS server is created.

◆ **Expose TTL.** Each resource record is assigned a Time to Live. Ordinarily, you don't see the value of the TTL parameter, but you can see and adjust TTL if you check this option. When **E**xpose TTL is checked and you open the properties for a record (by double-clicking the record), a TTL field is added to the properties dialog box, as shown in figure 16.79. You can change the TTL value if desired.

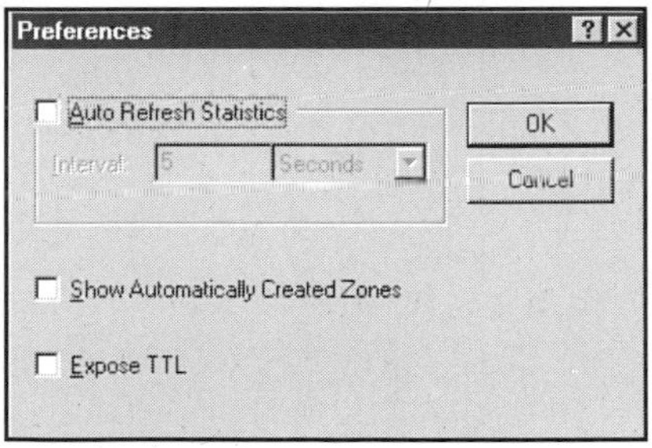

Figure 16.78

Setting DNS Manager preferences.

DNS Server Statistics

DNS Manager maintains several statistics that describe the operation of the DNS Server. Figure 16.80 shows statistics for the keystone1 DNS Server. These statistics give you an idea of the activity and health of the DNS server.

Ordinarily, DNS Manager does not dynamically update these statistics. You can update them manually by selecting a server icon and pressing F5, or you can configure DNS Manager preferences so that the statistics are updated at periodic intervals. See the previous section, "Setting DNS Manager Preferences," for the technique.

1. In the Properties tab, open the Microsoft TCP/IP Protocols properties dialog box.

2. Select the WINS Address tab. Be sure that **E**nable DNS for Windows Resolution has been checked.

3. Open the DNS tab (see fig. 16.50) in TCP/IP Properties and complete the following fields:

   ◆ **Host Name.** This field should contain the name of this host, which by default is the same as the host's NetBIOS name.

   ◆ **Domain.** In this field, enter the fully qualified name of the domain in which this host resides.

   ◆ **DNS Service Search Order.** In this box, add the IP addresses of this and any other DNS servers on the network. DNS servers will be queried in the order they appear in this box.

   ◆ **Domain Suffix Search Order.** If you want to search for host names under DNS domains other than the one specified in the D**o**main field, enter the domain names in this list. Domains will be searched in the order they appear in the list. Use the **U**p and Do**w**n buttons to adjust the order of multiple entries. These entries are not required to search for fully qualified domain names, only to search for a host name without a domain name (for example, to search for buster in widgets.keystone.com without specifying FQDN buster.widgets.keystone.com).

4. Choose OK to exit Microsoft TCP/IP Protocols.

5. Open the Network utility in the Control Panel.

6. Select the Services tab.

7. Choose **A**dd.

8. In the **N**etwork Service list, select Microsoft DNS Server and choose OK.

9. Supply the path to the installation files when prompted.

10. Close the Network utility and restart the computer.

Other TCP/IP Options

Two auxiliary TCP/IP services can be installed via the Services tab in the Control Panel Network utility. Here are some brief descriptions.

Simple TCP/IP Services

The Simple TCP/IP Services option includes a variety of useful utilities, including the following:

◆ **ftp.** File transfer protocol is an interactive, command-line utility used to transfer files between ftp-enabled hosts. The Windows NT Help files include descriptions of the commands available under ftp.

◆ **finger.** Finger is a command-line utility that can be used to display information about a host that is running the finger service.

◆ **telnet.** Telnet supports terminal-emulation access with remote hosts running a telnet service. Telnet is a graphic utility that is added as a program item to the Accessories program group.

◆ **tftp.** Tftp is similar to ftp but does not provide user authentication.

Experienced Unix users will be comfortable with the command-line interfaces of ftp, finger, and tftp, and will probably not balk at the large command set for ftp. They are, however, a bit out of place in a graphic environment such as Windows NT. Shareware versions are readily available from Internet providers, information services, and ftp servers, but Windows versions of ftp and finger are recommended.

SNMP Service

The SNMP Service includes support for the Simple Network Management Protocol, the standard network management protocol in the TCP/IP environment. SNMP enables the computer to be managed by network management consoles such as Sun NetManager or Hewlett-Packard Open View. SNMP services are also required to enable the Windows NT Performance Monitor utility to receive statistics from the computer.

Testing Your Knowledge

1. Manufacturers must pay licensing fees to use the TCP/IP protocol in their products.

    A. True

    B. False

2. The Network Driver Interface Specification (NDIS), enables multiple protocol stacks to share network adapters.

    A. True

    B. False

3. TCP/IP refers to each local network as a _____.

4. Error recovery is the responsibility of the Transmission Control Protocol (TCP), the second protocol that identifies the TCP/IP protocol suite. Among the responsibilities of TCP are:

    A. Fragmentation of large messages from upper-layer protocols into frames that fit within the limitations of a network

    B. Error detection and recovery

    C. Reassembly of frames from upper-layer protocols

    D. Reassembly of received frames into messages that are passed to upper-layer protocols

5. What IP address class starts with the first octet value having a value of 132.

    A. A

    B. B

    C. C

6. Any IP address with a first octet value of _____ is a loopback address, which is used in diagnostics and testing.

    A. 255

    B. 0

    C. 223

    D. 127

7. A _____ is a bit pattern that defines which portion of the IP address represents a subnet address.

8. What does the abbreviation ARP stand for?

9. A routing table which is manually defined by a network administrator is called a _____.

    A. static routing table

    B. complex routing table

    C. dynamic routing table

    D. mask

10. What does the abbreviation RIP stand for?

   A. Routing Independent Protocol

   B. Routing Information Packet

   C. Routing Information Protocol

   D. Routing Internet Protocol

11. The Domain Name Services (DNS) protocol was developed to serve as a central repository of names on the Internet.

   A. True

   B. False

12. If you are running a TCP/IP network in isolation, you must obtain an address from the Internet Information Center (InterNIC).

   A. True

   B. False

13. What command is used to test IP addresses.

   A. pong

   B. ping

   C. pang

   D. poke

14. To setup a two-segment network, a separate network adapter must be installed to connect the computer to both segments.

   A. True

   B. False

15. The IP RIP router included with Windows NT Server supports routing through dial-up WAN links.

   A. True

   B. False

16. Windows NT includes TCP/IP client software for which three of the following four Microsoft operating systems?

   A. MS-DOS

   B. Windows 3.1

   C. Windows for Workgroups 3.11

   D. MS OS/2 1.3

17. With Dynamic Host Configuration Protocol (DHCP), you need to hard code all IP addresses utilized in the subnet.

    A. True

    B. False

18. What does the abbreviation WINS stand for?

19. What does the abbreviation SNMP stand for?

Review Answers

1. B

2. A

3. subnet

4. A, B, D

5. C

6. D

7. subnet mask

8. Address Resolution Protocol

9. A

10. C

11. A

12. True

13. B

14. A

15. B

16. A, B, C

17. B

18. Windows Internet Naming Service

19. Simple Network Management Protocol

PART IV

Management

CHAPTER 17

Managing Disk Storage

When you get right down to it, file storage is the heart and soul of a network server. Users need to store their data (often in large quantities), share it, and know that it still will be intact tomorrow.

The typical server has a considerably more sophisticated hard drive system than the typical workstation. At the very least, server drives are likely to be considerably larger. Server drives also tend to be faster, and a premium tends to be placed on reliability.

In this chapter, you will encounter the capabilities Windows NT Server brings to hard drive management. A wide variety of hard drive configurations is available to meet different sets of cost, performance, and reliability needs. In particular, Windows NT Server has the capability to create groups of disks called redundant arrays of inexpensive disks (RAID) using only Windows NT Server software, standard SCSI adapters, and off-the-shelf hard drives. Making RAID technology available to budget-conscious LAN users is one of Microsoft's most significant achievements with Windows NT Server.

How Hard Drives Are Organized

As you read through this chapter, you will notice that the hard drives you hold in your hand often have no direct relation to the drive letters that you actually use to manipulate file systems. You might have two hard drives but only one drive letter. You also might have one hard drive but four or more drive letters. Before you learn how to configure hard drives, you need to know something about how hard drives and software drive letters are associated.

Physical Hard Drives

The basic storage unit is the physical hard drive, commonly available with capacities of about 200 megabytes up to almost 10 gigabytes. The individual hard drive has the advantage of simplicity, and it's the most common way to organize hard drive storage. You will see, however, that it is worthwhile to evaluate the alternative of using *arrays*—two or more hard drives that work in association.

Physical hard drives must be low-level formatted, a task that generally is performed by the manufacturer. SCSI hard drives can be low-level formatted in the field using utilities that accompany the SCSI adapter card. IDE and ESDI hard drives cannot be low-level formatted by the user.

SCSI hard drive subsystems are by far the most appropriate for LAN file storage. Their performance is high, and they are the only systems that can be productively organized into arrays. Windows NT Server enables you to configure arrays of other drives such as IDE, but you will not gain the fault-tolerance advantage that is possible with an array of SCSI drives.

Each hard drive in a system is assigned a logical number. Drives on the primary drive controller are numbered starting with 0. Logical numbers are assigned differently for SCSI, IDE, and ESDI drives.

◆ For SCSI, hard drives on the primary controller are numbered from 0 to as high as 6 (one of the eight possible addresses on a SCSI bus, almost always address 7, is reserved for the bus adapter). Drives on the secondary bus adapter start numbering where the first adapter leaves off. As many as four host bus adapters and 28 drives theoretically can be accommodated.

◆ For IDE and ESDI, hard drives on the primary controller are numbered 0 and 1 (if a second drive is present). A second hard drive controller can support drives numbered starting where the first controller leaves off—usually 2 and 3.

Partitions

Before data can be stored on a hard drive, the hard drive must be partitioned. A *partition* is a designated portion of a hard drive that functions as a separate unit. Partitions can be formatted to create storage volumes. Each hard drive can be configured with as many as four partitions in one of two configurations:

◆ One to four primary partitions

◆ One to three primary partitions and one extended partition

A primary partition can be configured to enable an operating system to boot in the partition.

An extended partition is not directly usable for file storage. Extended partitions must be configured with one or more logical drives that are used to store files. Extended partitions are used when it is necessary to have more than four logical drives on a hard drive.

> **Note** MS-DOS is capable of recognizing only a single primary partition—the partition from which it is booted. If there is a chance that you will want to boot your Windows NT computer under MS-DOS, you should restrict each hard drive to a single primary partition and create additional logical drives in extended partitions.

Logical Drives

Before files actually can be stored, partitions must be formatted to establish drive letters. You are familiar with drives such as the C, D, E, and other lettered drives that you use to organize the file system on a DOS or Windows NT computer. Drive letters are assigned differently to primary and extended partitions:

◆ A primary partition may be formatted with a single drive. Each primary partition, therefore, will be represented by a single drive letter.

◆ Extended partitions may be formatted with one or more logical drives.

Figure 17.1 illustrates primary and extended partitions, as shown by the Windows NT Disk Administrator.

Disk 0 has one primary partition, which has been formatted as drive C. This partition has been formatted with the NTFS file system. Disk 0 also has one extended partition, which has been formatted into three logical drives: E, L, and O.

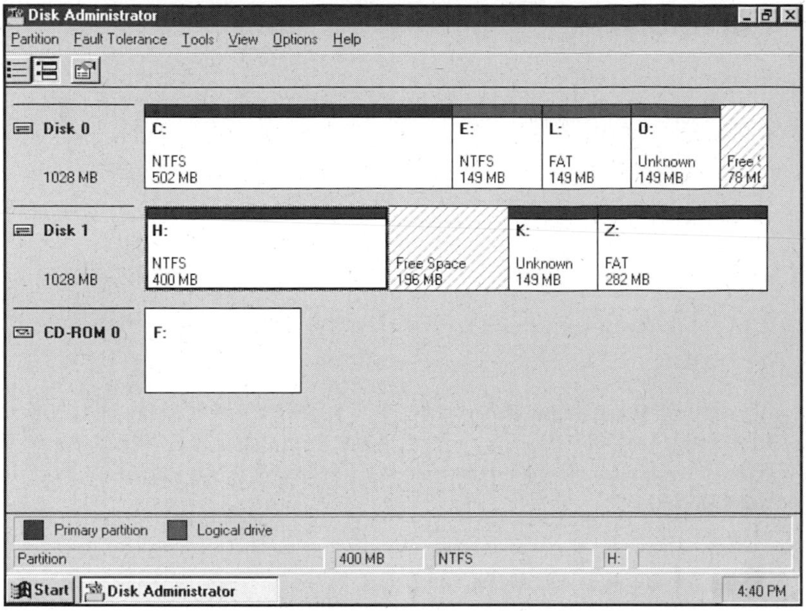

Figure 17.1

Examples of partitions and drives.

Disk 1 has three primary partitions, which are formatted as drives H, K, and Z. Although K has not been formatted, it has been assigned a drive letter.

Each disk has a partition labeled Unknown, an indication that the partition has not been formatted.

Each disk also has one area in which a partition has not yet been created. This area is crosshatched and is designated as Free Space. This space is unusable until it has been used to create a partition.

Several features should be noted in this figure. If you are familiar with DOS, you might have been surprised that drive lettering did not follow DOS conventions. DOS assigns letters automatically, and letters hard drives continuously starting with drive C. This approach often causes havoc when partitions are deleted or added and drive letters change.

Windows NT enables you to specify the drive letter for each drive. You can always use letters C through Z. The letter B might be available if the system does not have a second floppy drive. A drive letter must be set aside for each CD-ROM drive on the computer.

If the server has more than 25 hard drives, you can create partitions that do not have drive letters.

Some of the partitions in the figure have been formatted with the FAT or NTFS file systems. Others have not been formatted and are labeled Unformatted.

> **Note** Each type of drive is designated by a color in the Disk Administrator display. A color key appears at the bottom of the Disk Administrator window. I'm not telling you what the colors are since they are user-definable. To change the colors, choose **C**olors and Patterns from the **O**ptions menu.

Drive Sets

**Objective
B.8**

In many cases, volumes will be configured to occupy more than one partition on more than one hard drive. This might be done to create volumes larger than the capacity of a single hard drive or to enhance the fault tolerance of the volume. Windows NT supports the following types of drive sets:

◆ **Volume sets.** A volume is extended by using two or more partitions, which can be on multiple hard drives.

◆ **Stripe sets.** A volume is extended by using two or more partitions, each on a separate drive. A special technique called *striping* is used to write data on all the volume segments.

◆ **Stripe sets with parity.** Similar to a stripe set, a stripe set with parity uses parity error checking to create a fault-tolerant drive array. Any one drive in the set can fail without causing a loss of data.

◆ **Mirror sets.** Two partitions on two drives are configured so that each will contain the exact same data. If one drive fails, the mirror contains a replica of the data so that no data is lost and processing can continue.

Now that you have learned the characteristics of partitions, drives, and drive sets, the remainder of this chapter shows you how to create and delete them.

> **Note** In addition to RAID, Windows NT uses another trick to improve the reliability of disk storage. *Disk sparing* is a technique that enables Windows NT to compensate for bad sectors on a hard disk. When Windows NT detects a bad sector, the data in the sector is moved to a good sector and notifies the disk device driver of the new location of the data. Then Windows NT maps out the bad sector so that it will no longer be used.
>
> Disk sparing is available only on SCSI disk subsystems, and is not supported for IDE or ESDI disks.

Creating and Deleting Partitions and Drives

All operations required to create, manage, and delete hard drives can be performed with the Disk Administrator utility. In this section, you learn the basics of creating and managing partitions and standard logical drives.

Creating Primary Partitions

A primary partition can be as small as 1 MB or as large as the free space on the hard drive. Up to four primary partitions can be created on a given hard drive.

To create a primary partition in Disk Administrator, follow these steps:

Creating a Primary Partition in Disk Administrator

1. Select an area marked Free Space. The area you select is marked with a wider, black border.

2. Choose **C**reate from the **P**artition menu. The Create Primary Partition dialog box shown in figure 17.2 appears. This box indicates the maximum and minimum sizes allowed for the partition.

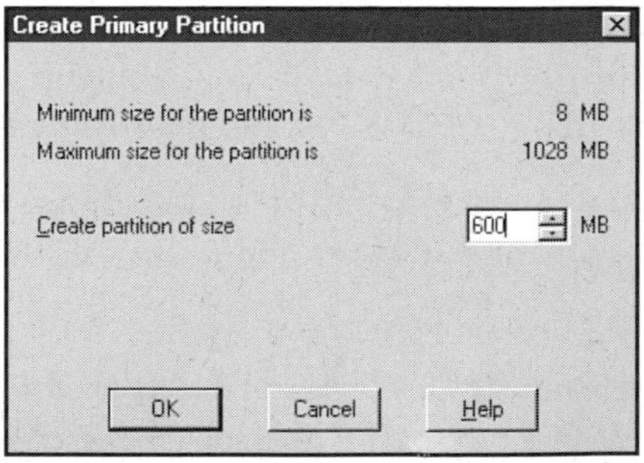

Figure 17.2

Designating the size of a primary partition.

```
Create Primary Partition                          [x]

  Minimum size for the partition is           8  MB
  Maximum size for the partition is        1028  MB

  Create partition of size              [600] ÷  MB


          OK          Cancel          Help
```

3. Enter the desired size in the **C**reate partition of size field.

4. Choose OK. Figure 17.3 shows the new, unformatted partition that appears, with the label Unformatted.

5. To create the partition, choose C**o**mmit Changes Now from the **P**artition menu. After the partition is committed, it is marked as Unformatted.

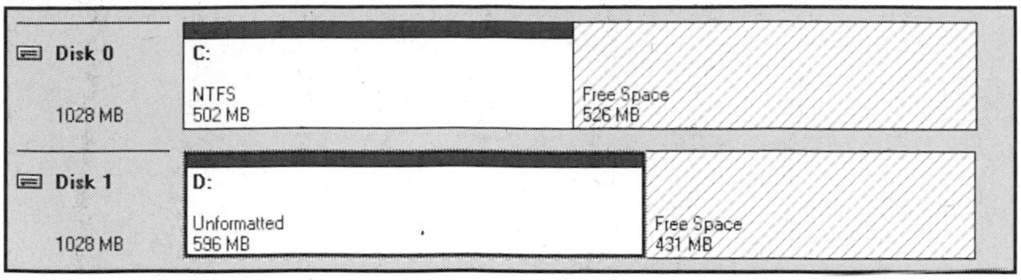

Figure 17.3

An unformatted primary partition.

> **Note**
>
> Many changes made in Disk Administrator do not take effect until they are committed. This feature enables you to quit Disk Administrator and discard any changes you made since changes were committed last. It's a lot like having to save a file after you have edited it in the word processor. You can get the old version back simply by not saving your changes.

Before you can work with a partition, changes must be committed. You cannot format a New Unformatted partition because the partition is not really created until changes are committed.

When you quit Disk Administrator, you might see the following message: `Changes have been made to your disk configuration. Do you want to save the changes?` Choose **Y**es to save the changes or **N**o to cancel.

You can also commit changes without leaving Disk Administrator by choosing the C**o**mmit Changes Now command from the **P**artition menu.

MS-DOS can access only one primary partition on a hard drive. Ordinarily, this is not a concern because you seldom will be booting a Windows NT Server under DOS.

If you begin to create more than one primary partition on a hard drive, the warning shown in figure 17.4 appears.

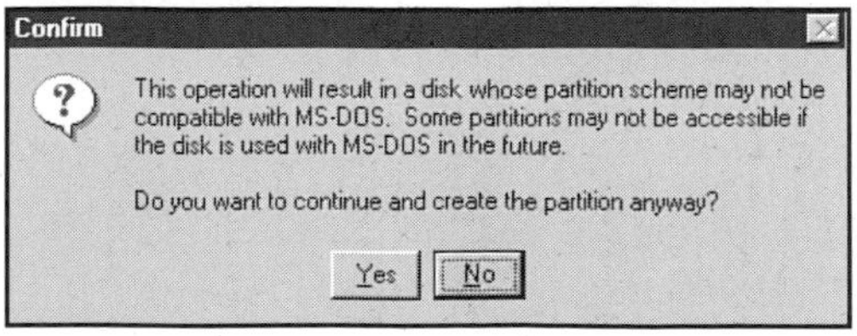

Figure 17.4

The warning you see when creating additional primary partitions on a hard drive.

Designating the Active Partition

Windows NT designates two special partitions, which may or may not be the same physical partition:

- ◆ **System partition.** Contains hardware-specific files (NTLDR, BOOT.INI, and NTDETECT.COM or OSLOADER.EXE) that are used to load Windows NT. On Intel x86 computers, the system partition must be a primary partition that has been marked as active. On RISC computers, the system partition is configured by setup software provided by the manufacturer.

  On RISC computers, the system partition must be formatted with the FAT file system. On Intel x86 computers, the system partition may be formatted for FAT or NTFS files.

- ◆ **Boot partition.** Contains the Windows NT operating system. It may be formatted for the FAT or NTFS file system. The boot partition is generally the same as the system partition. The operating system files are installed in a directory identified by the %systemroot% variable, which by default refers to C:\WINNT.

The hard drive that boots the system must have one partition designated as the active partition. On an Intel x86 system, an active partition is created when Windows NT is installed. You might need to change the active partition, however, if you have created other primary partitions to support other operating systems. You change the active partition to a Unix partition, for example, if you will be rebooting the computer and want it to start up with the Unix operating system.

Operating systems can boot only from an active primary partition on Disk 0. You cannot designate a partition on another drive as the active partition. The active partition on drive 0 is marked by an asterisk (*) in the colored bar above the partition box.

To mark the active partition on an Intel x86 computer, follow these steps:

1. Select the primary partition on Disk 0 that contains the start-up files for the desired operating system. The selected partition is outlined with a bold, black border.

2. Choose the Mark **A**ctive command from the **P**artition menu.

3. Choose OK in the Disk Administrator information box.

Creating Extended Partitions and Logical Drives

You can create a single extended partition on a hard drive, which can range in size from 1 MB to the size of the free space available on the drive. If you create an extended partition, the maximum number of primary partitions on the drive is reduced to three.

To create an extended partition, follow these steps:

Creating an Extended Partition

1. Select an area marked `Free Space`. The area you select is marked with a wider, black border.

2. Choose Create **E**xtended from the **P**artition menu. The Create Extended Partition dialog box shown in figure 17.5 appears. This box indicates the maximum and minimum sizes allowed for the partition.

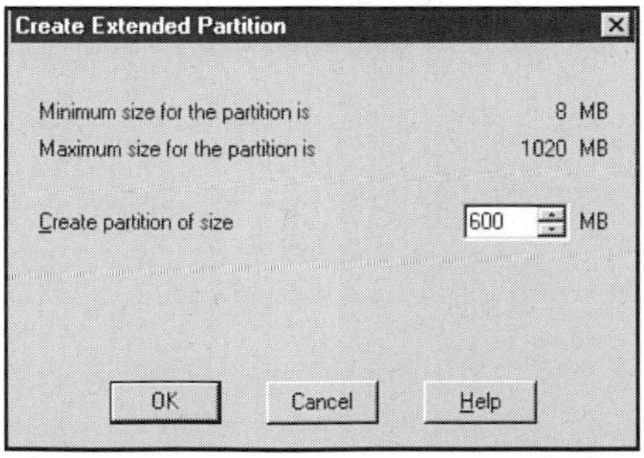

Figure 17.5

Designating the size of an extended partition.

3. Enter the desired size in the **C**reate partition of size box.

4. Choose OK. Figure 17.6 shows the new extended partition that appears. No drives have been created. The area simply is designated as `Free Space`, with crosshatching in a different direction. In figure 17.6, the Free Space with 596 MB is the newly created extended partition.

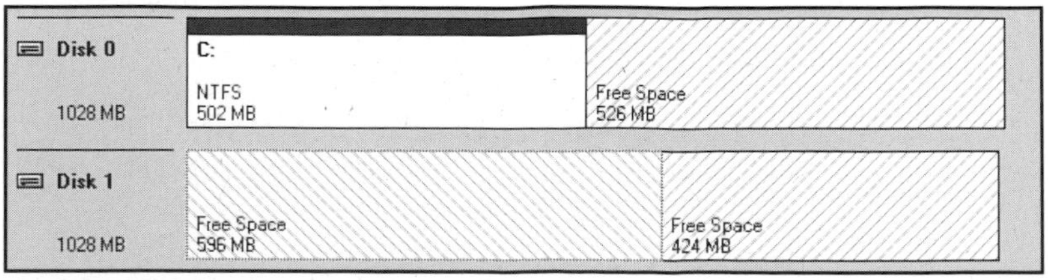

Figure 17.6

A new extended partition.

To create a logical drive in an extended partition, follow these steps:

Creating a Logical Drive in an Extended Partition

1. Select an area marked `Free Space` that is crosshatched to indicate that it is an extended partition. The area you select is marked with a wider, black border.

2. Choose **C**reate from the **P**artition menu. The Create Logical Drive dialog box appears. This box indicates the maximum and minimum sizes allowed for the partition.

3. Enter the desired size in the Create logical drive of size box.

4. Choose OK. Figure 17.7 shows the new, unformatted logical drive that appears.

Figure 17.7

A new, unformatted logical drive.

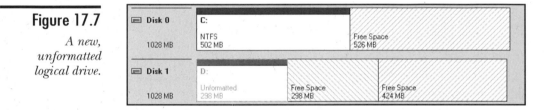

5. To create the partition, choose C**o**mmit Changes Now from the **P**artition menu. After committing changes, the logical drive is labeled as `Unformatted`.

Committing Changes

Partitions and drives are not actually created by the procedures described up to this point. Changes must be committed before they are written to disk. Until you commit changes, you can cancel any changes you have made since the last time changes were committed.

To have the changes you make written to the disks, choose the C**o**mmit Changes Now option in the **P**artitions menu. To cancel changes made since the last commit, quit Disk Administrator and respond **N**o to the prompt `Changes have been made to your disk configuration. Do you want to save the changes?`.

Objective B.8

Formatting Partitions and Logical Drives

To format a partition, follow these steps:

Formatting Partitions

1. If the partition is marked `New Unformatted`, it has not been physically created. Choose **C**ommit Changes Now from the **P**artition menu. After changes are committed, the drive is designated as `Unformatted`.

2. Select the partition. You can click on the partition's box in the Disk Administrator window or press the Tab key until the desired partition is selected. The selected partition is outlined with a bold line.

3. Choose **F**ormat from the **T**ools menu. The Format Drive dialog box appears, as shown in figure 17.8.

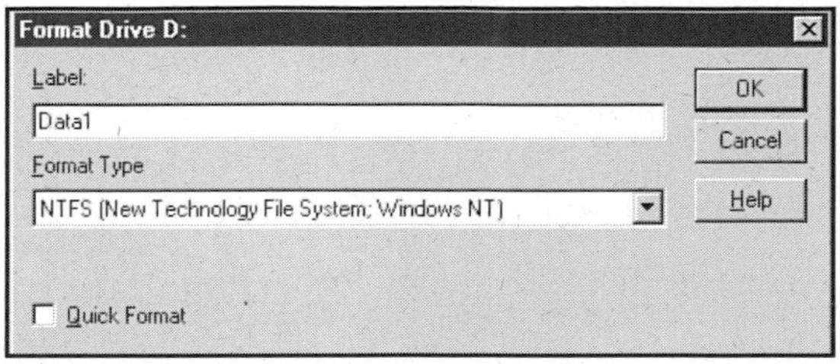

Figure 17.8

Specifying format parameters.

4. Select the file system type (NTFS or FAT are available) in the **F**ormat Type box.

5. In the **L**abel box, enter a volume label if desired

6. Select the **Q**uick Format check box if you want the partition formatted without checking for errors. (Quick Format is not available with mirror sets or stripe sets with parity.)

7. When asked to confirm that you want data in the partition overwritten, choose **Y**es. As the partition is formatted, progress is displayed on a bar graph.

   Normal formatting might be slower than you would like because Disk Administrator is ordinarily very thorough about identifying and locking out bad spots on the disk.

8. When the `Format Complete` message is displayed, choose OK. Figure 17.9 shows a logical drive after it has been formatted.

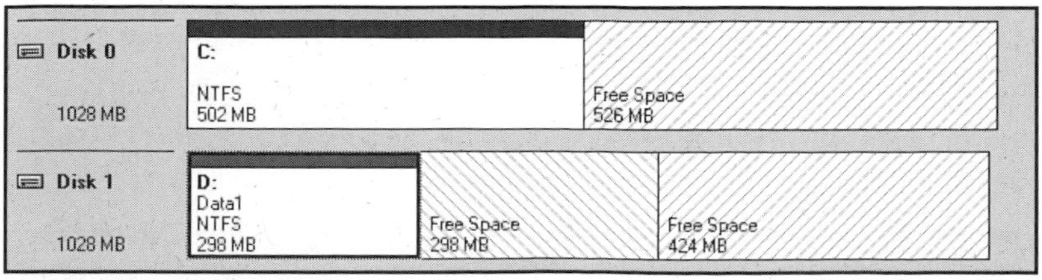

Figure 17.9

A formatted logical drive.

Reformatting a Volume

When you reformat a volume that contains data, all data stored on that volume is lost. Be sure that you back up any files you want to save.

You cannot make any changes to the Windows NT system partition using Windows NT. To modify this partition, back up all data you want to retain. Then reinstall Windows NT, using a Custom installation. You can request that Setup deletes, re-creates, or reformats the partition.

Changing and Deleting a Volume Label

A label can be assigned to any volume. This label may describe the function or the contents of the volume and is reproduced in a variety of situations when the volume contents are displayed. To change or delete a volume label, follow these steps:

1. Select the formatted volume.

2. Choose **L**abel from the **T**ools menu. The Label dialog box appears.

3. Enter the new volume name or delete the name that is shown.

4. Choose OK.

Converting a Volume to NTFS

You can convert a FAT volume to NTFS with the CONVERT.EXE utility. To convert a volume, follow these steps:

Using the Convert Utility

1. Open a command prompt by double-clicking the Command Prompt icon in the Main program group.

2. To convert drive D to NTFS, enter the following command:

```
CONVERT D: /FS:NTFS
```

Note   The boot partition cannot be converted while Windows NT is running. If you specify that CONVERT should process the active partition, you will see this message:

```
Convert cannot gain exclusive access to the C: drive, so it cannot
convert it now. Would you schedule it to be converted the next time
the system restarts?
```

If you respond **Y**es, you can then shut down Windows NT and restart it. The partition is converted when the system starts backup. The system must boot several times in order to complete the conversion. Be patient. Everything will work fine in the end.

Assigning Drive Letters

Unlike DOS, Windows NT enables you to assign specific drive letters to volumes. This is called *static assignment* of drive letters.

Prior to assigning static drive letters with Disk Administrator, drive letters are assigned automatically using DOS rules. Adding drives or changing partitions can change drive letters for other volumes.

To assign a drive letter to a volume, follow these steps:

Assigning a Drive Letter to a Volume

1. Select a drive.

2. Choose Dri**v**e Letter from the **T**ools menu. The Assign Drive Letter dialog box appears, as shown in figure 17.10.

3. To assign a drive letter, choose **A**ssign drive letter and select an available letter in the box.

4. To create a drive without a drive letter, choose Do **n**ot assign a drive letter.

5. Choose OK.

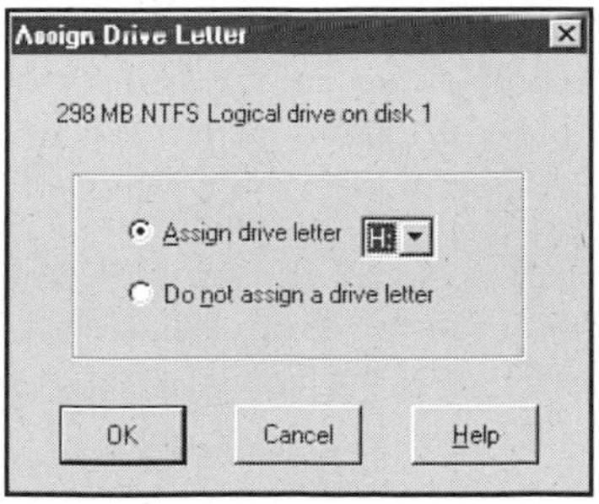

Figure 17.10

Assigning a drive letter.

Note The **C**D-ROM Drive Letters option on the **T**ools menu enables you to specify the drive letters for your CD-ROM drives.

Deleting Partitions and Drives

From time to time, you need to reorganize your disks and to delete partitions and drives. To delete a partition or drive, follow these steps:

Deleting Partitions

1. Select the partition or drive.

2. Choose **D**elete from the **P**artition menu.

3. In the confirmation box that is displayed, confirm that the partition should be deleted by choosing **Y**es.

4. Commit the change by choosing C**o**mmit Changes Now from the **P**artition menu or by quitting Disk Administrator and choosing **Y**es.

Note To delete an extended partition, you first must delete each logical drive in the partition.

Fixing Sector Failures

When a volume is formatted, Windows NT performs an exhaustive check to identify bad sectors. Windows NT Server has the fault-tolerant capability that can recover bad sectors.

When an error is detected in a sector, Windows NT attempts to spare the bad sector by removing it from use. On SCSI systems, the fault-tolerant subsystem asks the disk driver to spare the sector from use. When a sector cannot be spared, as is the case on ESDI and IDE disk subsystems, Windows NT receives a status message identifying the I/O error. The operating system attempts to isolate the bad sector and remove it from the file system sector map. An error is logged, which can be examined in the Event Viewer.

You can manually check for errors in Disk Administrator by selecting a volume and choosing the **C**heck for Errors command in the **T**ools menu.

Running Chkdsk

Chkdsk is a command-line utility that verifies the integrity of FAT and NTFS file systems. To test drive D, enter the command **chkdsk d:**. To repair errors that are identified, include the /f switch as follows: **chkdsk d: /f**.

The Chkdsk utility can be run from Disk Administrator. First select a volume and then choose the **C**heck for Errors command in the **T**ools menu. The Check for Errors dialog box offers three choices:

◆ **D**o not fix errors

◆ **F**ix file system errors

◆ **S**can for bad sectors

You can also check for errors in Windows NT Explorer. Select a volume and choose **P**roperties in the **F**ile menu. Select the Tools tab, and then choose **C**heck now to check the disk. In the Check Disk dialog box, you have the following options:

◆ **A**utomatically fix file system errors

◆ **S**can for and attempt recovery of bad sectors

Defragmenting Disks

Although the problem is less acute on NTFS than on FAT volumes, both file systems can develop a syndrome called *fragmentation*. When files are erased from a disk, the space they occupied leaves a group of blank sectors. If a large file must be stored, Windows NT will attempt to locate a contiguous area that can receive the entire file. When no single space is large enough, Windows NT must store the file in multiple small spaces, resulting in file fragmentation.

Windows NT does not include a tool for correcting file fragmentation, but you would be wise to obtain one. Microsoft has made room for a defragmentation tool on the Tools tab of the Drive properties window. I assume that Microsoft or third-party vendors will be marketing defragmentation utilities that can be installed and accessed from the Tools tab.

Volume Sets

A *volume set* is a volume that is made up of several free space segments from as many as 32 disk drives. Later, you will be introduced to striped sets, which might seem similar to volume sets. Volume sets and striped sets are significantly different, however.

Figure 17.11 shows two disk drives. Three areas on the two drives are designated as Free Space. These Free Space areas can be combined into a volume set. Figure 17.12 shows volume D—a volume set that occupies three of those areas.

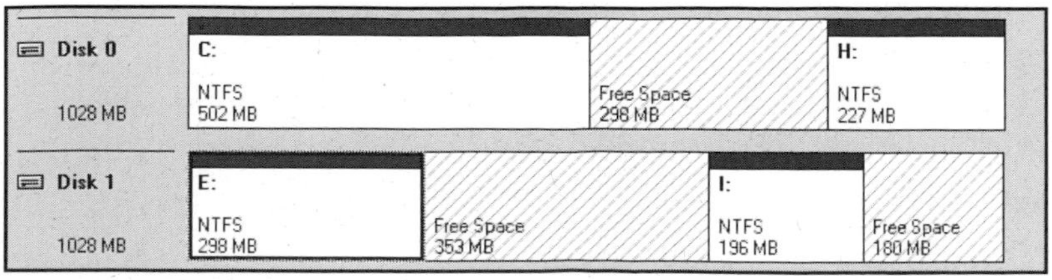

| 🖳 Disk 0 | C: | | Free Space | H: |
| 1028 MB | NTFS 502 MB | | 298 MB | NTFS 227 MB |

| 🖳 Disk 1 | E: | Free Space | I: | Free Space |
| 1028 MB | NTFS 298 MB | 353 MB | NTFS 196 MB | 180 MB |

Figure 17.11

Drives prior to creation of a volume set.

Figure 17.12

Drives after the creation of a volume set.

Disk 0	C:	D:	H:
1028 MB	NTFS 502 MB	NTFS 298 MB	NTFS 227 MB

Disk 1	E:	D:	I:	D:
1028 MB	NTFS 298 MB	NTFS 353 MB	NTFS 196 MB	NTFS 180 MB

Even though they are constructed from bits and pieces, volume sets function much like standard hard drives. Figure 17.13 illustrates the hard drives in a volume set. As files are stored in the volume set, they are stored first at the beginning of the first segment in the volume set. After the first segment is filled, the second segment is used, then the third, and finally the fourth.

Figure 17.13

How volume sets store files.

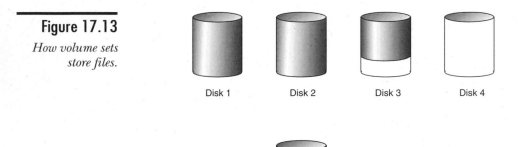

Disk 1   Disk 2   Disk 3   Disk 4

= Disk Space in Use

Creating a Volume Set

To create a volume set, follow these steps:

Creating a Volume Set

1. Select the first area of free space.

2. Select additional areas while holding down the Ctrl key.

3. Choose Create **V**olume Set from the **P**artition menu.

4. The Create Volume Set dialog box appears, as shown in figure 17.14. You use this box to specify the size the volume set will be. The maximum size is the total of the sizes of all free space partitions that were selected.

5. Choose OK to create the volume set.

6. Choose C**o**mmit Changes Now from the **P**artition menu to create the volume set.

7. Restart the system so that the changes will take effect.

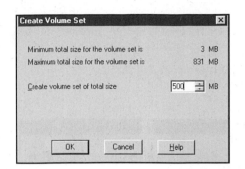

Figure 17.14

Designating the size of a volume set.

If, in step 4, you select a size that is smaller than the maximum allowed, as was done in figure 17.14, space is deallocated from each of the free space areas. This can create many small, free space gaps in the hard drives, as shown in figure 17.15.

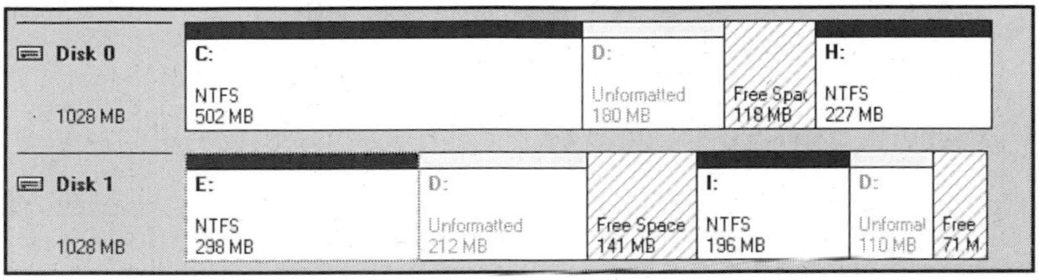

Figure 17.15

Unused free space after a volume set was created with less than the maximum size.

Formatting a Volume Set

To format the volume set, select any segment of the volume set. Notice that all the segments are selected. Then format it as you would a standard partition. After the volume set is formatted, all the segments are identified with the same drive letter, as was shown in figure 17.12, where the volume set is drive D.

Extending a Volume Set

Individual volumes and volume sets can be extended by adding free space. Extending an individual volume turns it into a volume set. Only NTFS Partitions can be extended.

Note   Stripe sets and mirror sets cannot be extended.

To extend a volume or a volume set, follow these steps:

Extending a Volume or Volume Set

1. Select the volume or volume set.
2. While holding down the Ctrl key, select a free space area to be added to the volume set.

3. Choose Ex_t_end Volume Set from the _P_artition menu. The Extend Volume Set dialog box appears, as shown in figure 17.16. Minimum total size for the volume set is reflects the size of the existing volume or volume set.

4. Specify the new size for the volume set.

5. Choose OK.

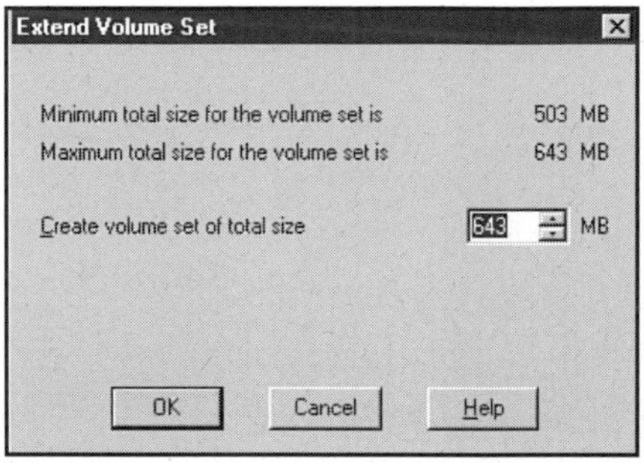

Figure 17.16

Extending a volume set.

There is no need to commit the changes or to format the new segment of the volume set.

Note After free space is used to extend a volume set, the free space cannot be removed. To reduce the space of a volume set, back up the data, delete the volume set, create a new volume set of the desired size, and restore the data.

Considering the Pros and Cons of Volume Sets

Volume sets have two significant advantages:

◆ They enable you to use small, free space segments in volumes of useful size. The segments used can be of virtually any size.

◆ They enable you to create volumes that are larger than your largest hard drive. Because a volume set can incorporate free space from up to 32 hard drives, truly huge volumes are possible.

Nothing is free, however; a cost is associated with volume segments. The cost is an increased risk that a drive failure will result in loss of data on the volume. If any hard drive in the volume set fails, all data in the volume set is lost.

Note The reliability of hardware is rated in a statistic called mean time between failure (MTBF)—the average number of hours the equipment is expected to operate without failure. When volume sets are created with two or more hard drives, the MTBF for the volume set is significantly less than the MTBF for the individual drives. The formula Microsoft provides follows:

$$MTBF_{set} = MTBF_{disk}/N$$

Where:
$MTBF_{set}$ is the MTBF for the volume set.
$MTBF_{disk}$ is the average MTBF for an individual disk.
N is the number of disks in the set.
As you can see, a four-drive set has one-quarter the MTBF of an individual drive.

Using Stripe Sets

Objective B.8

Like volume sets, *stripe sets* enable you to build hard volumes with multiple hard drives. Stripe sets store data in a significantly different way, however, using a technique called *striping*. Figure 17.17 shows how striping works.

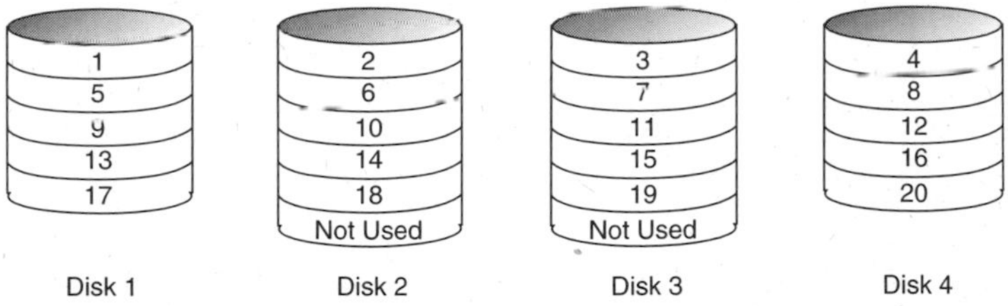

Disk 1	Disk 2	Disk 3	Disk 4
1	2	3	4
5	6	7	8
9	10	11	12
13	14	15	16
17	18	19	20
	Not Used	Not Used	

Figure 17.17

Storing data on a stripe set.

When files are written to stripe sets, the written data is broken into stripes, which are written sequentially to all drives in the stripe set. As a result, a file is actually spread out across all the drives in the stripe set.

"Why," you might ask, "would anyone want to split files up in that way? I can build large volumes with volume sets, so what does striping buy me?" The answer is *performance*. Hard drives spend a great deal of time just moving their heads around to seek out the right track. When these head-seeks are spread across multiple drives, the time required to retrieve a file is reduced nearly by a factor of the number of drives. The performance improvement is particularly apparent with applications that frequently read data from the disk.

Because data is striped across disks, the disk segments on the various disks must be roughly the same size. Figure 17.17 shows what happens when some segments are larger than others: portions of some segments are not used. Because space would be wasted otherwise, Disk Administrator always ensures that the segments that are added to a stripe set are the same size.

Disk striping has the same disadvantage as volume sets—the reliability of a stripe set is less than the reliability of an individual drive. Also, if a single drive fails, all data on the stripe set is lost. Stripe sets can be created over two to 32 disks. The system and boot partitions cannot be included in a stripe set or stripe set with parity.

Using Stripe Sets with Parity

A technique called *parity* can make a stripe set considerably more reliable. Figure 17.18 shows how data is recorded on a stripe set with parity. With each set of stripes, a parity record is created on one of the drives in the set. This parity record is created by performing a set of calculations on all the stripes in that "row." If a drive fails, the information on that drive can be reverse engineered by combining all the stripes in that row with the parity record. A stripe set with parity, therefore, can continue to function with one drive failure.

Figure 17.18

How data is stored on a stripe set with parity.

Disk 1	Disk 2	Disk 3	Disk 4
1A	1B	1C	Parity 1
2A	2B	Parity 2	2C
3A	Parity 3	3B	3C
Parity 4	4A	4B	4C
5A	5B	5C	Parity 5

Disk striping with parity produces a fault-tolerant disk array with less drive overhead than mirroring (see the section, "Using Mirror Sets," later in this chapter). A pair of mirrored drives loses 50 percent of total drive capacity to achieve fault tolerance. A disk stripe with parity set consisting of four drives loses just 25 percent of total capacity to create the parity records. A set with five drives loses just 20 percent of total capacity to produce a fault-tolerant configuration. Stripe sets can be constructed from free space on a minimum of three disks to as many as 32 disks.

Disk striping with parity generally has better read performance than mirroring when all drives in the set are functioning. When one drive fails, performance suffers due to the need to recover stripe contents using the parity information. Microsoft recommends disk striping with parity for all read-intensive systems.

Tip

The need to create the parity records reduces write performance and requires additional memory. Microsoft recommends 25 percent additional memory to support disk striping with parity. Windows NT Server can perform most tasks with 16 MB of memory, but 20 MB is recommended when using disk striping with parity.

Note

Redundant arrays of inexpensive disks (RAID) describes several methods of using multiple disks to improve performance, enhance reliability, or both. Several types of RAID configurations, called *levels*, have been developed, of which only three are of interest to microcomputer LAN users:

Objective A.1

- ◆ **RAID 0.** Microsoft calls RAID 0 stripe sets.
- ◆ **RAID 1.** Mirror sets.
- ◆ **RAID 5.** Stripe sets with parity.

It is important to realize that RAID is not a hierarchy. RAID 5 is not inherently better than RAID 1. Both meet different needs and have different advantages and disadvantages. You need to choose the RAID technology that is right for your network.

Windows NT makes it possible to implement RAID systems using only standard microcomputer hardware. When you don't use special RAID hardware, you give up several advantages:

- ◆ More robust hardware, possibly with fault-tolerant power supplies
- ◆ The capability to replace failed hard drives without shutting down the server (hot swapping)

Microsoft also admits that a hardware-based RAID system should yield greater performance than the Windows NT Server software-based approach.

If RAID 5 meets your needs, you might want to consider a commercial RAID subsystem to obtain some extra fault tolerance and reduce the likelihood of down time.

Creating a Stripe Set (RAID 0)

To create a stripe set, follow these steps:

Creating a Stripe Set (RAID 0)

1. Select an area of free space.

2. Hold down the Ctrl key and select additional areas—up to one each on a total of up to 32 hard drives.

3. Choose Create **S**tripe Set from the **P**artition menu.

4. In the Create Stripe Set dialog box, the size Disk Administrator displays takes all of the selected free space areas into account (see fig. 17.19). If you reduce the size, space is removed from each of the drives on which you have selected free space. This size is selected based on the creation of equal-sized segments on all disks.

Figure 17.19

Specifying the size of a stripe set.

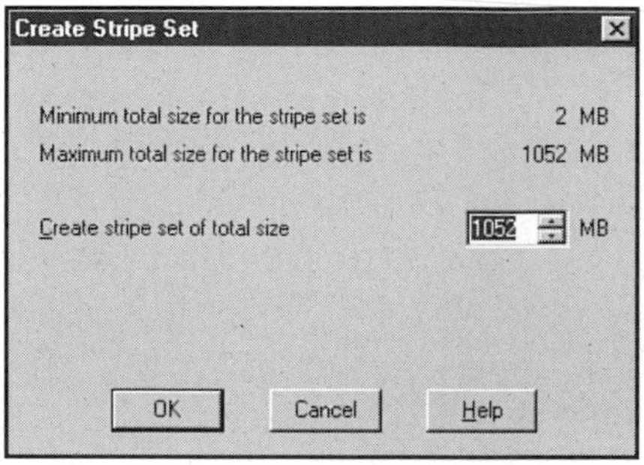

Create Stripe Set

Minimum total size for the stripe set is — 2 MB
Maximum total size for the stripe set is — 1052 MB

Create stripe set of total size — 1052 MB

OK   Cancel   Help

5. Choose OK. Disk Administrator creates a disk stripe with parity logical volume and assigns a single drive letter to the set.

6. Choose C**o**mmit Changes Now from the **P**artition menu.

7. Select the partition.

8. Choose the **F**ormat command from the **T**ools menu to format the partition.

As you can see in figure 17.20, Disk Administrator creates equal-sized unformatted partitions on each of the drives in the stripe set. If you choose a stripe set capacity that cannot be distributed evenly on the disks, Disk Administrator rounds up to the next acceptable value.

Figure 17.20

A stripe set on two disks.

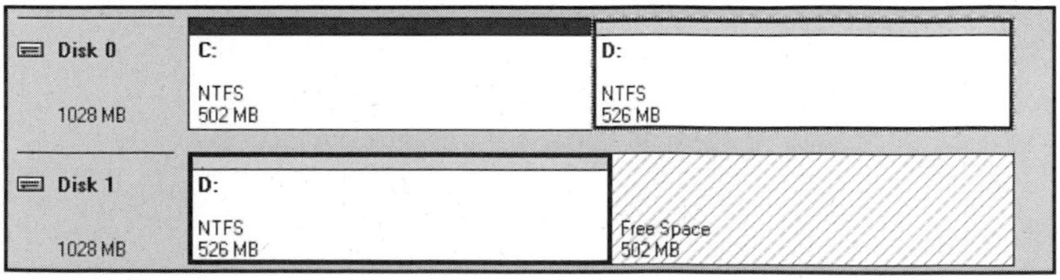

Disk 0 — 1028 MB — C: NTFS 502 MB — D: NTFS 526 MB

Disk 1 — 1028 MB — D: NTFS 526 MB — Free Space 502 MB

Creating a Stripe Set with Parity

At least three hard drives are required to create a stripe set with parity: two to store data and one for the parity stripe. To create a stripe set with parity, follow these steps:

Creating a Stripe Set with Parity

1. Select an area of free space on one hard drive.

2. Hold down the Ctrl key and select two or more additional areas—one each on a total of up to 32 hard drives.

3. Choose Create Stripe Set with **P**arity from the **F**ault Tolerance menu.

4. In the Create Stripe Set with Parity dialog box that appears, the size that Disk Administrator displays takes all of the selected free space areas into account. If you reduce the size, space is removed from each of the drives on which you have selected free space.

5. Choose OK.

6. Format the partition.

Disk Administrator creates equally sized, unformatted partitions on each of the drives in the stripe set. If you choose a stripe set capacity that cannot be distributed evenly on the disks, Disk Administrator rounds up to the next acceptable value.

Deleting a Stripe Set

In the event of a drive failure, a stripe set is invalidated and must be deleted.

A stripe set with parity can be recovered from a single drive failure and should not be deleted unless you are through using it.

To delete a stripe set, select any of the segments of the stripe set and choose the **D**elete command from the **P**artition menu.

Using Mirror Sets

Mirror sets consist of two drives that are maintained as mirror images. All data on the two drives is identical. Two different hardware configurations are possible:

◆ Both drives are connected to the same disk controller. In this case, failure of the disk controller halts both drives, and the mirrored set is unavailable.

◆ Each drive is connected to a separate disk controller. If one disk controller fails, the disk drive on the other controller continues to function, and the mirror set remains functional. This configuration frequently is called *disk duplexing*.

Mirror sets and disk stripe with parity sets are equally fault tolerant. Mirror sets tend to perform better when writing data because the parity stripe does not have to be created. Disk stripe with parity sets tend to perform better when reading data because drive seeks are spread out over a greater number of drives.

> **Note** Mirror sets are the only form of fault tolerance that can be used with the system or boot partitions of a server. Stripe sets cannot be booted.

Creating a Mirror Set

Creating a mirror set consists of creating a new partition that duplicates an existing partition on another drive. The same drive letter will be assigned to both disks.

To create a mirror set, follow these steps:

Creating a Mirror Set

1. Create and format a standard volume.

2. Select the volume.

3. While holding down the Ctrl key, select an area of free space on another disk that is at least as large as the volume created in step 1.

4. Choose Establish **M**irror from the **F**ault Tolerance menu.

5. Choose C**o**mmit Changes Now from the **P**artition menu to create the mirror set.

The new mirrored partition is displayed with the status of Unformatted. That status remains until the two partitions are synchronized. Figure 17.21 shows hard drives with a mirror set for drive C.

| **Note** | If the partitions in a mirrored set ever get out of synchronization, Windows NT automatically resynchronizes them. If you look at Disk Administrator while resynchronization is occurring, the drive that is catching up is displayed with its description in red text. |

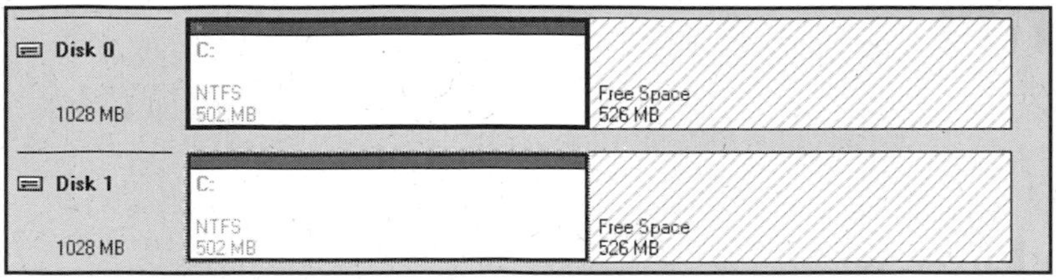

Figure 17.21

A mirrored set for drive C.

Breaking a Mirror Set

To break a mirror set, follow these steps:

Breaking a Mirror Set

1. Select the mirror set.

2. Choose **B**reak Mirror from the **F**ault Tolerance menu.

3. Disk Administrator presents the message:

   This will end mirroring and create two independent partitions. Are you sure you want to break the selected mirror?

   Choose **Y**es to confirm.

4. Choose **Y**es after you see the message:

   Do you wish to continue with this operation?

5. Choose C**o**mmit Changes Now from the **P**artition menu to break the mirror set.

6. Choose OK after you see the message:

   Changes have been made which require you to restart your computer.

After the computer restarts, Disk Administrator displays two independent partitions where the mirror set formerly was. You can delete the unmirrored portion if desired.

> **Note** | After you break a mirror set for the system partition, you must reboot the system.

Fixing Mirror Sets and Stripe Sets with Parity

When a drive fails in a mirror set or a stripe set with parity, the failed drive is known as an *orphan*. The action you must take to repair the set depends on the set type.

Objective F.8

Repairing a Mirror Set

When a drive of a mirror set fails, you must break the mirror set. This exposes the working drive of the mirror set so that it can resume working as a standard volume. The working member of the mirror set retains the drive letter that was assigned to the set. You then can establish a new mirror set relationship with a replacement hard drive or with another hard drive on the system.

> **Note** | Keep in mind that if you're repairing a mirrored set that is used in a duplexed situation, the affected hard disk's controller may actually be what has gone bad rather than the disk itself.

Objective F.8

Creating a Fault-Tolerance Boot Disk

If the system partition is protected by a mirror set and the primary drive fails, you can use an emergency boot disk to start the server by using the mirror copy. First, you need to create a boot disk with the proper files. Then, you may need to edit the BOOT.INI file so that it boots from another disk.

To create the boot disk for an x86 computer, copy the following files from the root of the system partition to a floppy disk that you have formatted with Windows NT:

- ◆ NTLDR
- ◆ NTDETECT.COM
- ◆ NTBOOTDD.SYS (if present on your system)
- ◆ BOOT.INI

Editing BOOT.INI

Edit the content of the BOOT.INI file on the floppy disk. Remove the System and Read Only properties from the file so that it can be edited.

Your BOOT.INI file will resemble this one:

```
[boot loader]
timeout=30
default=multi(0)disk(0)rdisk(0)partition(1)\WINNT
[operating systems]
multi(0)disk(0)rdisk(0)partition(1)\WINNT="Windows NT Server Version 4"
multi(0)disk(0)rdisk(0)partition(1)\WINNT="Windows NT Server Version 4
➥[VGA mode]" /basevideo
```

The BOOT.INI file contains information that helps NTLDR find the boot partition. The information is found in entries like this:

```
multi(0)disk(0)rdisk(0)partition(1)
```

This is called an *ARC name*—a format that is borrowed from Advanced RISC Computers. Each field in the ARC name defines a characteristic of the boot partition:

◆ **multi(*n*).** This field is multi(*n*) for non-SCSI systems and for SCSI systems using a SCSI BIOS. This field is scsi(*n*) for SCSI systems that do not use a SCSI BIOS. If the server has only one hard drive controller, then *n* will be 0. Additional hard drive controllers will be numbered 1 through 3. Edit this field if the mirror partition is attached to a different disk controller.

◆ **disk(*o*).** For scsi, *o* is the SCSI bus number for multiple-bus SCSI adapters. Edit *o* to reflect the SCSI address of the drive with the mirror partition. For multi, *o* is always 0.

◆ **rdisk(*p*).** For scsi, *p* is always 0. For multi, *p* is the ordinal number of the disk on the adapter. Because IDE and ESDI adapters support only two drives, *p* will be 0 or 1.

◆ **partition(*q*).** Edit *q* to indicate the partition number on the drive that contains the mirror of the system partition. Partitions are numbered 0 through 3. Extended partitions are always numbered after all primary partitions. Unused partitions are not numbered.

Note When I was testing, the address for the mirror on disk 1 was as follows:

```
multi(0)disk(0)rdisk(1)partition(1)
```

After you edit the BOOT.INI file on the emergency boot floppy disk, use it to boot the system. It should fail, fill the screen with numbers, and include the following message:

```
***STOP 0x000006B (0xC00000D,0X0000002,0X00000000,0X00000000)
PROCESS1_INITIALIZATION_FAILED
```

If this message fails to appear, your floppy disk is not properly configured to boot your system.

> **Note** I know that an error message is a roundabout way to tell you things are working as they should, but trust me, this error shows that everything is working fine. I tried it by replacing my disk 0 with an unformatted drive. The mirror of the boot partition on disk 1 started up without a hitch.

Recovering a Failed System Partition Mirror Set

If the primary drive of the mirror set fails, replace the failed hard disk. Then follow these steps to recover the system:

Recovering a Failed System Partition Mirror Set

1. Boot the system with the Fault Tolerance boot floppy disk.

2. Use Disk Administrator to break the mirror. Because you are breaking the mirror of the system partition, you must reboot the server.

3. Reestablish the mirror between disk 0 and the mirror partition and exit Disk Administrator.

4. Boot again using the boot floppy disk. The disk 0 mirror partition is rebuilt from the working mirror partition.

5. Use Disk Administrator again to break the mirror.

6. Change the drive letters of the partitions that were part of the mirror set so that the partition on disk 0 is drive C, and the other partition from the mirror set is a different drive letter.

7. Exit Disk Administrator.

8. Remove the boot floppy disk and reboot the system.

Note | The BOOT.INI file on the emergency boot floppy disk must be updated each time changes in partitions affect the ARC path of the partition that is mirroring the system partition.

Microsoft notes that this procedure works best when the drives in the mirror set have the same disk geometry: the same heads, cylinders, and sectors per track.

If you add a new hard drive to the system, you might see a message similar to the one shown in figure 17.22. Choose **Y**es to have the drive signature written.

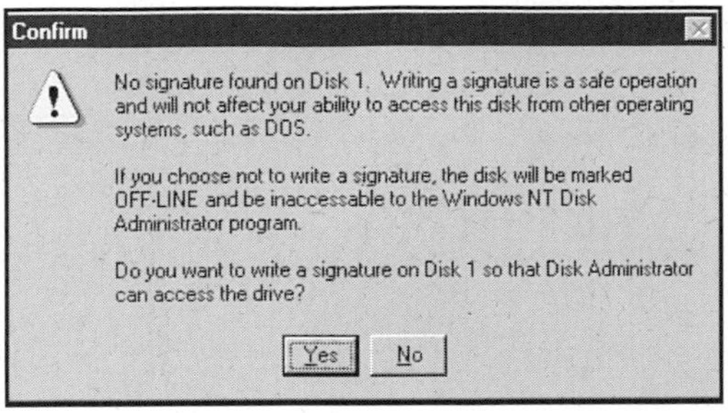

Confirm ☒

⚠ No signature found on Disk 1. Writing a signature is a safe operation and will not affect your ability to access this disk from other operating systems, such as DOS.

If you choose not to write a signature, the disk will be marked OFF-LINE and be inaccessible to the Windows NT Disk Administrator program.

Do you want to write a signature on Disk 1 so that Disk Administrator can access the drive?

[Yes]   No

Figure 17.22

Warning that a new disk requires a signature.

Repairing a Stripe Set with Parity

**Objective
F.8**

If a member of a parity stripe set fails, you see the message: A disk that is part of a fault-tolerant volume can no longer be accessed.

After you identify the failed hardware item and replace it, run Disk Administrator and conduct the following steps:

Repairing a Stripe Set with Parity

1. Select the stripe set with parity that experienced the drive failure.

2. Hold down the Ctrl key and select an area of free space at least as large as the partitions that are members of the stripe set.

3. Choose **R**egenerate from the **F**ault Tolerance menu.

4. Restart the server. The stripe set with parity regenerates the image for the new partition.

Using the Volumes View

The Volumes view, shown in figure 17.23, is a quick source of statistics about the volumes on a Windows NT computer. You can access this view in two ways:

- Select the **V**olumes command in the **V**iew menu.
- Click the Volumes View button.

Figure 17.23
Viewing volume statistics.

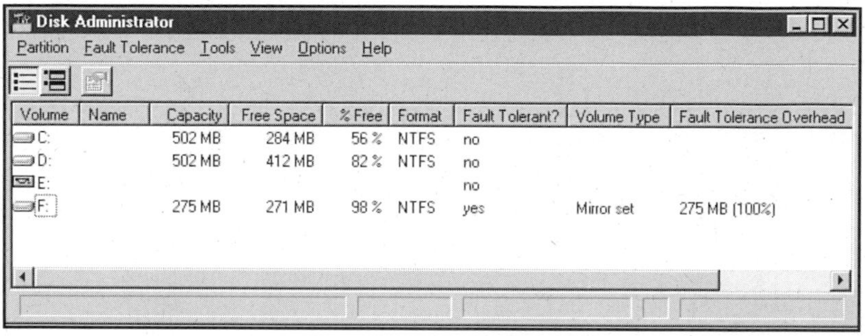
Disk Administrator
Partition Fault Tolerance Tools View Options Help
Volume | Name | Capacity | Free Space | % Free | Format | Fault Tolerant? | Volume Type | Fault Tolerance Overhead
C: 502 MB 284 MB 56 % NTFS no
D: 502 MB 412 MB 82 % NTFS no
E: no
F: 275 MB 271 MB 98 % NTFS yes Mirror set 275 MB (100%)

Viewing Properties of Disks and Volumes

If you select a volume in the Volumes view or the Disks view and click the Examine Properties button, you will see a Volume Properties window similar to figure 17.24. This window displays statistics about the volume and has other options as well.

Change the value of the **L**abel field to add a volume name or change an existing name.

Choose **F**ormat to format the volume.

Choose **C**heck Now to open a Check for Error box in which you can run a disk integrity check, similar to the check performed by the Chkdsk command-line utility (see fig. 17.24). You have three options:

- **D**o not fix errors
- **F**ix file system errors
- **S**can for bad sectors

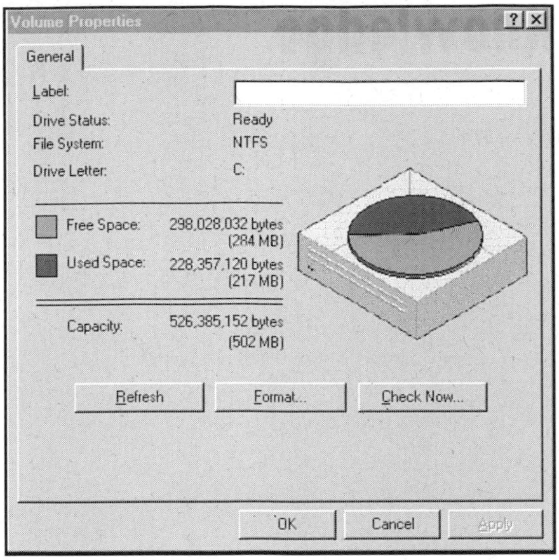

Figure 17.24

Properties for a volume.

Updating the Emergency Repair Disk

When you change the partitions on a Windows NT server, you see a message advising you to update the Emergency Repair disk that you created when the system was installed.

The Emergency Repair disk is updated with the RDISK.EXE utility. You can access RDISK by using the **R**un command from the **S**tart menu. The command window for RDISK is shown in figure 17.25. Just select an option and follow the prompts to create or update an Emergency Repair disk.

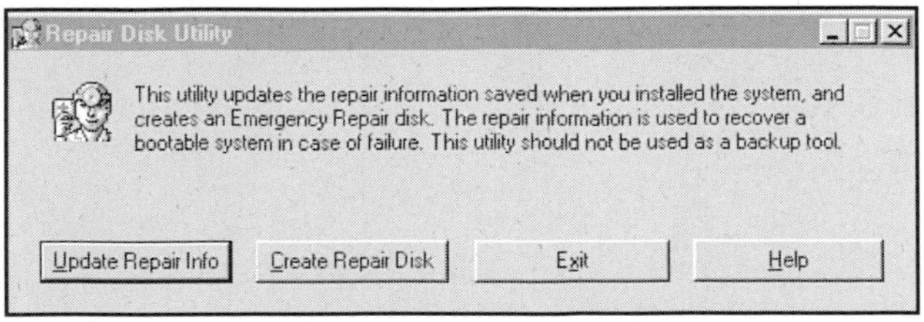

Figure 17.25

The command window for RDISK.

If you will be frequently changing the partitions on your system, you probably will want to add an RDISK program item to the Administrative tools group of your Start menu.

Testing Your Knowledge

1. What does the abbreviation RAID stand for?

2. SCSI, IDE, and ESDI hard drives can be low-level formatted by the user.

   A. True

   B. False

3. A(n) _____ is a designated portion of a hard drive that functions as a separate unit.

4. How many partitons can a hard drive be configured with?

   A. 1

   B. 64

   C. 4

   D. 256

5. Extended partitons may be formatted with one or more logical drives.

   A. True

   B. False

6. Windows NT supports which of the following types of drive sets?

   A. Mirror sets

   B. Stripe sets

   C. Volume sets

   D. Stripe sets with parity

7. Disk sparing is available only on SCSI disk subsystems.

   A. True

   B. False

8. How many primary partitions on a disk drive can MS-DOS access?

   A. 1

   B. 2

   C. 4

   D. 256

9. On a RISC computer, the system partition must be formatted with the NTFS file system.

   A. True

   B. False

10. After choosing the Format option from the Tools menu under Windows NT version 4, which type of file system types are available to choose from?

    A. FAT

    B. HPFS

    C. HPFS386

    D. NTFS

11. What utility is used to convert a FAT volume to NTFS?

12. To delete an extended partition, you must first delete each logical drive in the partition.

    A. True

    B. False

13. To repair errors that are identified with the CHKDSK command, use the _____ switch.

14. Microsoft Windows NT 4 does not include a disk defragmentation utility.

    A. True

    B. False

15. A volume set is made up of several free space segments from as many as _____ disk drives.

    A. 16

    B. 32

    C. 64

    D. 256

16. What does the abbreviation MTBF stand for?

17. What is the key advantage of using stripe sets?

    A. Performance

    B. Reliability

    C. Cost

    D. Capacity

18. Which RAID level is stripe sets with parity considered?

    A. RAID 0

    B. RAID 1

    C. RAID 5

    D. RAID 3

19. What is the minimum number of drives that can be used to create a stripe set with parity?

    A. 1

    B. 2

    C. 3

    D. 4

20. What is the term for a mirrored set that uses separate controller cards?

21. When a drive fails in a mirror set or a stripe set with parity, the failed drive is known as a(n) _____.

22. What is the name of the utility that is used to create and update emergency repair disks?

Review Answers

1. Redundant Array of Inexpensive Disks

2. B

3. partition

4. C

5. A

6. A, B, C, D

7. A

8. A

9. B

10. A, D

11. CONVERT.EXE

12. A

13. /f

14. A

15. B

16. mean time before failure

17. A

18. C

19. C

20. disk duplexing

21. orphan

22. RDISK.EXE

CHAPTER 18

Backing Up Files

Backing up the files on your LAN is among your most important responsibilities as a LAN administrator. File backups are your front-line defense against everything from users losing files to total disasters. Unfortunately, having good, reliable backups is something most organizations fail to think about until disaster already has struck.

Today's computer hardware is pretty reliable. Few users experience hard drive failures, and many PCs run for years without problems. Also, few users take the time to back up their personal hard drives, and this thinking often spills over into LAN administration. Here are some reasons to take the situation seriously:

◆ Most LANs store many more times the files than individual users store on their PCs.

◆ Most LANs have more mission-critical data than is found on personal PCs. Ask your users what the impact would be of totally losing the data that is stored on the LAN.

◆ Multiple hard drives are common on LAN servers, and the chances of a piece of equipment failing are multiplied.

Planning for Disasters

Think the worst. An earthquake has just struck and the building that houses your LAN is now rubble. How soon could you restore basic LAN services and have critical data available for your company?

Just order up backup tapes from the off-site storage, go buy a new server, and restore the data. Sounds simple, right? But have you actually tried it? Where are the master software disks for your server? You need to restore Windows NT Server before you can restore any data, and you can't restore Windows NT Server if your installation disks are under a ton of rubble.

> **Note** I had a situation that was nearly as bad as an earthquake. A pipe in the ceiling of my LAN room burst. When I arrived at work, water was pouring down right on my server, soaking my manuals, and threatening to flood the drawer that held my on-site backup tapes. Luckily, the pipe had broken only a few minutes before I arrived. A few more minutes and I probably would have found a dysfunctional server and ruined tapes.

If you think about the situation of a real disaster in terms of doing business for a few days without your LAN and re-creating all your data from scratch, it will become clear why managers of corporate mainframe computers take disaster recovery very seriously. The biggest corporations actually maintain duplicate mainframes at a *hot site* that can take over in short order if the main data processing site is down. Smaller companies often have agreements with other companies to serve as hot sites for each other in the event of a disaster.

It is not unreasonable, therefore, for your company to maintain a basic backup LAN at another site—a LAN hot site. The hot site should be supplied with everything needed to quickly take over your essential computing needs and should, as much as possible, use the same hardware and software as the main site.

Identical hardware and software are especially important with tape backups, which seem to be a bit finicky about being restored on the same type of system on which they were created. There are relatively few standards that ensure portability of data tapes between different hardware systems. The only way to be sure that you can restore the tapes you create is to eliminate software and hardware differences between the source and target systems.

So, don't store only your backup tapes off site. Be sure that your off-site archives include copies of the same rglease of Windows NT Server as your server is running, along with any patches you might have obtained and copies of any drivers you are using that didn't come on the Windows NT Server distribution disks.

The only way you can be sure that your backup and recovery plan works is to test it, not just once, but periodically. Before you know things work, you're going to have to blow away your server files and try to restore the server. There is no other way. Ideally, such a test should be performed before your server goes into service.

Storing Data Long Term

There is a tendency to forget about data after it is backed up and in the vault. Magnetic tapes are living things, however, and they are deteriorating from the moment they are recorded. The data on a magnetic tape can be trusted only for three to five years.

How far back do you need to be able to recover any given file on your LAN? You would be surprised how many managers would answer that question, "Forever!" The need for reliable, long-term data archives increases as more and more company documentation is stored in electronic form. Many companies are rapidly eliminating paper forms.

As a result, a need exists for reliable ways of storing large amounts of data affordably but reliably. Magnetic tape can meet these needs, provided that you periodically retrieve tapes from storage and copy them. Three years should be the most you should rely on a tape without refreshing it with a new copy.

You might want to consider various types of write-once optical media. *Write-once optical media* record data by using a laser to burn pits in the plastic surface of the disk. Data recorded in this way should be reliable for about 20 years. Optical media are fairly delicate, however, and you should make at least two copies of any vital files.

Backup Hardware

As the need for volume and speed have increased, backup technologies have evolved. Interfaces have become faster, and new tape formats have evolved as engineers have tried different approaches to solving the data-storage problem. This section helps you select hardware to meet your needs.

Data Backup Formats

You will encounter four major standards for tape media. They differ significantly in terms of cost, capacity, and performance, and you should choose carefully because it is very difficult to convert a tape archive to another format. Consequently, it makes sense to overbuy, obtaining tape equipment that will meet your needs for a number of years.

I strongly feel it should be your goal to back up your entire LAN every night. Doing so requires you to obtain equipment that has not only the capacity to hold your data, but the speed to back up that data in the time you can allot. As more and more LANs are called on to function 24 hours a day, 7 days a week, the time available for backing up files increasingly is scarce.

The following sections discuss the most common tape formats used on LANs.

The DC-6000 Tape Format

DC-6000 is the latest in a long evolution of tape formats based on technology originated by 3M in 1971. *Quarter-inch cartridge* technology was developed specifically for recording data. With the DC-6000 format, 600 feet of quarter-inch wide magnetic tapes are housed in a fairly large shell—4×6×0.665 inches—that is reinforced by a thick metal bottom plate. The cartridges were designed to be extremely gentle to the tape. An elastic drive belt moves the tape, and is designed to avoid stretching the tape medium. The cartridge is designed so that nothing touches the delicate magnetic surface of the tape.

Data is stored on quarter-inch cartridges using a system called *serpentine recording*, which is illustrated in figure 18.1. The tape is divided into parallel tracks, and the tape head moves up and down to select a particular track. The tape is streamed in one direction and then reverses direction to record the next track.

Figure 18.1

Serpentine recording.

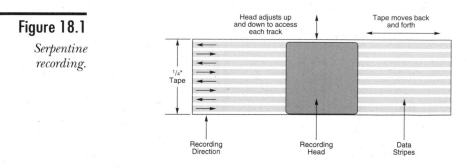

The capacity of quarter-inch cartridges can be increased by extending three parameters: the length of the tape, the bits recorded per inch of tape, and the number of tracks. The practical limit for tape that can fit in the cartridge and yet be stable enough to be reliable is about 600 feet. The remaining tools for increasing capacity, therefore, are to increase data density and to add tracks. The largest technologies, with capacities of up to about 2.1 GB, use 30 tracks and a density of 68 kilobits per inch. Standards have been proposed that could record up to 35 GB per data cartridge if engineers can solve the problem of recording 216 tracks on a quarter-inch tape.

Standards for quarter-inch cartridges are established by a consortium of equipment manufacturers generally called the QIC Committee. Standards developed for DC-6000 cartridges are named after the capacities they support. QIC-525 supports capacities of 525 MB per cartridge, for example.

> **Note** In my experience, the quarter-inch cartridge is reliable but slow. Data throughput is slower than other formats—about 5 MB per minute seems typical. Another problem is that locating files involves a sequential search to the entire serpentine track path, resulting in long file searches. Another disadvantage is that the cartridges are mechanically complex and tend to be somewhat more expensive than cartridges for other formats.

The DC-2000 Tape Format

The minicartridge was designed to lower the cost of tape backup using quarter-inch cartridges. This format has become popular for backing up personal computers. Also invented by 3M, DC-2000 uses a smaller shell (2.4×3.2×0.57 inches) to house 205 feet of quarter-inch magnetic tape.

Until fairly recently, capacities have been fairly limited for this format, but manufacturers have recently introduced systems that can store 850 MB of data in compressed form.

To reduce hardware costs, the tape format was designed to enable the drives to be managed by a floppy-disk controller. However, high-density floppy disk controllers are capable of supporting data-transfer rates of only about 500 kilobits per second.

Two significant problems limit the usefulness of DC-2000 media on LANs:

◆ Media must be formatted. This is a time-consuming process that can take about one hour for 40 MB. Formatting has the advantage of identifying and locking out bad spots on the tape. Preformatted tapes are available.

◆ Data-transfer rates are far too low to back up large hard drives in short time intervals. Performance can be improved by using a dedicated tape controller interface instead of a floppy-disk controller, although manufacturers' claims of data throughput rates are notoriously optimistic.

A significant advantage of DC-2000 is that tapes are fairly portable between drives from different manufacturers. The most important formats follow:

◆ **QIC-40.** Uses 20 tracks and supports up to 40 MB of uncompressed data on a single DC-2000 data cartridge.

◆ **QIC-80.** Uses 32 tracks to record up to 80 MB of uncompressed data on a DC-2120 data cartridge. Recently introduced extended-length cartridges can record up to 120 MB of uncompressed data. Data-compression techniques frequently are employed to double this capacity to about 250 MB.

◆ **QIC-3010.** A new format that records 340 MB of uncompressed data (700 MB compressed).

◆ **QIC-Wide.** Another recently introduced format that records 420 MB of uncompressed data (850 MB compressed).

Note   I feel that minicartridges are most appropriate for workstations, although they might be sufficient for small LANs. Because tapes are usable on many brands of equipment, minicartridges can be an effective means of exchanging large amounts of data with other systems.

8mm Cartridges

This format was developed by Exabyte, which is still the only manufacturer of OEM drive hardware. The format is based on the 8mm tape format developed by Sony for its Betamax video recorders and cameras. The 8mm format became popular when it was the only format that could back up more than 1 GB of data to a cartridge. Most units back up 2.2 GB of uncompressed data, with larger capacities available.

The 8mm and 4mm data cartridges use a technique called *helical-scan recording*, borrowed from the videotape industry, to increase data density on tapes. Figure 18.2 illustrates the way in which helical-scan recording works. The tape moves at a relatively slow speed past a drum that contains the recording head and revolves at high speed. The drum is tilted, and the recording head records data in diagonal stripes on the tape.

Figure 18.2

Helical-scan recording.

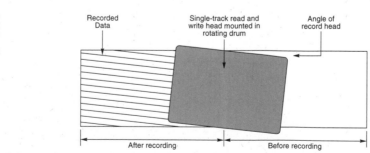

Serpentine recording methods increase the amount of data that can be recorded on a track by moving tape more rapidly past the recording head. Eventually, a limit is reached at which increasing speed would place too much stress on the fragile magnetic tape.

Helical-scan recording increases data density by revolving the recording head more rapidly. Tape speeds are low and tape stress is minimized. The tape-drive mechanics are significantly more complicated than DC-6000 drives, however, and costs of helical-scan tape drives have been reduced only recently to the level of less than $1,000.

Although 8mm drives use the same cartridge shells as 8mm video tapes, the magnetic media must be of much higher quality. A lost flake of metal oxide might cause only a white streak in a video picture, but it can invalidate an entire file on a data cartridge.

You can get 8mm data-recording equipment with capacities of 2.2 GB and 5 GB per tape, with data-compression enabling capacities of 10 GB per data cartridge. The 8mm option is an excellent format for backing up LAN data, but it is less popular than other formats, and the basic hardware is manufactured by only one company, Exabyte. Many LAN administrators prefer to select equipment standards that have a broader manufacturer base.

4mm Cartridges

The 4mm data-cartridge format is derived from the Digital Audio Tape (DAT) format developed by Sony. The 4mm format uses helical-scan recording to store 1.3 GB of uncompressed data on a 60-meter tape. Compression techniques have raised capacity per tape to the neighborhood of 9 GB.

Data-recording densities are extremely high, and tape speeds are only about 3 seconds per inch. The tape drum rotates at 2,000 revolutions per minute and records 1,869 tracks per inch of tape. Data-transfer rates are extremely high, and I have observed rates up to 30 MB per second with low-end 4mm hardware.

One consequence of these slow tape speeds is that 4mm tapes can be searched extremely rapidly. Typically, the tape can be positioned to any file on its length in 15 seconds or less.

Note | The 4mm format is the hot tape format these days, and manufacturers are competing to raise capacities and lower costs. I just purchased a 2 GB capacity unit for under $800. Units with capacities of up to 16 MB are available at costs of just over $2,000. Because many manufacturers are competing in this format, you have a wide range of options for cost and features.

Because 4mm is a digital format, an innovative approach to increasing data through-put is to operate two tape drives in tandem, writing data to both simultaneously. Now, two data cartridges are required to store data, but throughput is effectively doubled. On LANs that have limited backup windows, this might be the most effective way to back up large amounts of data in a short time.

The 4mm format gets my vote as the best format for backing up most LANs. Costs are low and getting lower, capacities are high and getting higher, and data-transfer rates are as high as they get for tape media.

Optical Disks

Three types of optical media generally are available:

◆ Compact disc read-only media (CD-ROM)

◆ Write once read many (WORM)

◆ Magnetic optical (MO) read/write

CD-ROM is primarily a read-only medium, although recordable CD-ROM (CD-R) technology is becoming more readily available. CD-R is intended primarily for mastering CD-ROM discs, however, not for backing up LANs.

WORM systems are available with large capacities, and are intended primarily for archiving large amounts of data. WORM systems record data by using a laser to burn pits in a plastic medium, as shown in figure 18.3. Recorded media are insensitive to magnetic fields and have a storage life of about 20 years, making WORM an effective archive medium. High costs and the inability to reuse recorded media, however, make WORM unsuitable for daily backups.

Figure 18.3

WORM data recording.

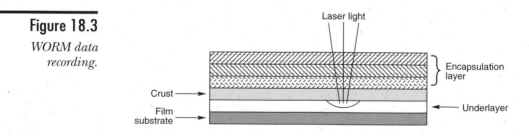

Magnetic optical drives use a combination of lasers and sophisticated magnetic recording technology to store high data densities on a read/write medium. A laser is used to heat small areas of a magnetic medium so that a magnetic field can change the polarization of the area. Figure 18.4 shows how the process works.

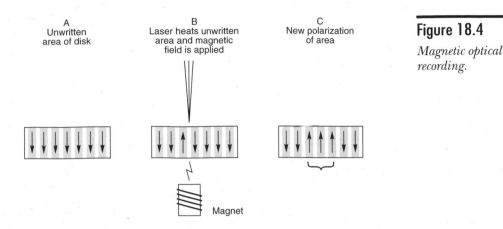

Figure 18.4

Magnetic optical recording.

Shrinking costs of high-capacity, read/write optical disks have made this medium a contender as a backup medium in certain critical situations. Data throughput generally is higher than tape, and file random access is much higher, making optical disks an excellent place to store seldom-used files that must remain available on short notice.

Some vendors are promoting optical storage as an alternative to tape. Unfortunately, standards are lacking and optical cartridges from one manufacturer seldom are usable on another vendor's equipment. If you are seeking to avoid proprietary technologies in your backup equipment, this can be an important concern.

A recent trend has been toward reduced costs of hardware for writing data to CD-ROM media. Costs for recordable CD-ROM drives are approaching the price points of better standard CD-ROM drives. The capacity of a CD-ROM disc is limited to 650 MB, however, which is insufficient to back up the typical modern server. The emphasis of the inexpensive recording CD-ROM drive is to master CD-ROMs, not on speed. The typical, low-cost RECORDABLE CD-ROM drives offer only slight advantage over tape where speed is concerned.

Costs of optical storage remain significantly higher than tape, in part due to the relative newness of optical technology compared to tape. If your network is running 24 hours a day, 7 days a week, however, optical storage might be the best way to make the most of limited backup intervals.

Selecting Backup Hardware

File backup is complicated by the fact that open files cannot be backed up reliably or, in most cases, at all. Getting good backups, therefore, means forcing all users to log out. You can do this by using User Manager for Domains to limit the logon hours for user accounts and disconnect them after hours, although this works only for users of Windows NT computers.

In some organizations, the staff leaves at 5:00 p.m. and doesn't return until 8:00 the next morning. This backup situation is easy, and even slow equipment can cope. In most offices, however, there's always someone who *must* use the LAN at any time of the day or night. The best you might be able to ask for is about a two-hour window starting at 3:00 a.m. If you have a couple of hours, you probably can get the job done if you are permitted to obtain the right backup hardware.

Unfortunately, as LANs mature, the available backup window shrinks even as the volume of data to be backed up grows. If you are hard pressed to back up your data, there are four strategies you can examine:

◆ **Back up data by copying it to other hard drives, then back up the auxiliary hard drives at your leisure.** Hard drives on a fast SCSI sub-system are among the fastest backup systems you can obtain—expensive, but often the only way.

◆ **Use faster tape drives.** Speeds as high as 60 MB per minute are possible with some DAT systems.

◆ **Make use of faster file access.** Fast-wide SCSI on a PCI bus can deliver extremely fast data transfers. Remember, however, that bus speed only affects backup of data on the local server. If you are backing up data on other servers, you are limited by the speed of the medium that connects the servers. You need to install a tape drive on each server or install a high-speed link between your servers, such as FDDI or dedicated 100 Mbps Ethernet links.

◆ **Use more tape drives.** The fastest way of backing up multiple servers might be to simply add a tape drive to each server. Yes, you need to manage more tapes, but all the drives can operate simultaneously.

> **Note** | I strongly recommend that you back up your entire LAN every night if possible. Otherwise, two or more tapes are required to restore the LAN in the event of a catastrophic data loss. Although most backup software spans tapes (continues backup jobs on two or more tapes), someone generally must be available to switch tapes after one tape fills up.

You should either purchase a drive that has the capacity for your entire LAN, purchase multiple drives, or get a tape auto-changer that switches tapes automatically.

Incidentally, the only way to copy a data tape is to copy it to another identical tape drive. It's a good idea to purchase two identical drives if possible. You can use the drives to speed backup operations and have them available when a critical tape must be duplicated. Remember that archive tapes should be copied about every three years to refresh the magnetic image.

Note Databases present a special problem where backups are concerned. Files on a database server generally are held open as long as the database engine is running. This prevents you from backing up the files at the same time you back up other files on the LAN. In general, databases must be backed up using software that is included with the database engine.

Issues in Tape Backup

You should consider several issues when planning your LAN backup procedures. These issues are examined in the following sections.

Security Issues

The designers of Windows NT Server showed considerable foresight by creating the Backup Operators group, which enables users to back up all files on the server without having full administrative access to the server.

When a backup is being performed with a Backup Operators account, it is logged on with a level of security that exceeds normal user security. For that reason, computers that will be performing backups should be placed in a secure location. If the system is not under lock and key, install a screen saver that is password protected so that the computer will be locked with a password when it is unattended.

A backup tape can be a complete snapshot of your LAN data. If your data is sensitive, you don't want one of your tapes to get into the wrong hands. Windows Backup enables you to lock tapes so that they can be read only by the tape owner or by members of the Administrators or Backup Operators groups.

Backups of Open Files

Open files are one of the big headaches where backups are concerned. Most backup software does not even attempt to back up open files because they are moving targets that might be modified in the middle of the backup operation. Windows NT Backup simply tries for a specified period of time and reports an error if the file is not closed.

Some software that runs continuously keeps files open around the clock. Many mail systems fall into this category. You should periodically stop this software to close the files so that they can be backed up.

Backups that Span Multiple Tapes

Almost any tape backup software continues jobs on additional tapes as data cartridges fill up; this procedure is called *spanning*. Unfortunately, spanning usually involves manually changing tapes, which requires an operator's intervention. If your organization does not maintain an overnight operations staff, a spanning feature is of little value to you.

Workstation Backup Capability

Any computer that can share its resources with the domain (it is configured with a domain name as its workgroup setting) can be connected to for backup. Windows NT Backup recognizes connections established through File Manager and can back up connected volumes.

Automation Features

The degree of automation available on tape backup software varies significantly. Windows NT Backup is somewhat in the middle of the spectrum of automation capabilities. You can automate tasks, but it is a bit of a nuisance, and the automation isn't tremendously well integrated with the backup software. If your backup needs are more complicated, you might want to investigate third-party software for backing up your LAN.

Backup Activity Reporting

The best backup software does more than merely log messages in files. It ensures that backup operators are notified of problems by e-mail, fax, or pager. Ideally, backup operators should receive a report of each night's backup activity.

This is another area where Windows NT Backup is limited. Operators must remember to check the logs to ensure that errors are detected. Backups usually run fine and, unfortunately, most operators eventually stop checking the details of the log. For that reason, some form of automatic notification of errors is extremely valuable.

Record Keeping and Storage Rotation

Some of your tapes should be rotated into off-site storage—preferably the vault of a commercial data-storage service. Unfortunately, doing so is a hassle that requires considerable manual bookkeeping. Windows NT Backup does not have the capability of tracking vault rotations for you, so you have no choice but to set up clear procedures and tracking forms.

If you are tempted to store your off-site tapes anywhere but the vault of a media storage service, be sure that you obtain a fire safe that is rated for computer media. Ordinary fire safes are designed only to keep paper from combusting. Plastic storage media have a much narrower comfort range than paper.

Scheduling Backups

How you schedule backups depends on a number of factors:

◆ The capacity of the backup system

◆ The speed of the backup system

◆ The frequency with which files are being modified

◆ The importance of the data

Ultimately, all your decisions hinge on the last factor. If the data is critical enough to your business, you can justify almost any level of expense to obtain reliable backups.

I am strongly in favor of a full backup every day with tapes retained for various lengths of time. In the following sections, various types of backup schedules are discussed.

Types of File Backups

Windows NT Backup can perform five types of backups. To understand how the backup types differ, you need to understand the file *archive bit* (also called the *archive attribute*). The archive bit is a marker on a file that can be turned on and off to indicate whether the file has been backed up since it was last modified.

Whenever a file is modified in Windows NT (or DOS), the archive bit is set. Some backup operations look only for files for which the archive bit has been set.

Backup operations do one of two things to the archive bit when the file has been backed up: they leave the bit in its current state, or they clear the bit to indicate that the file has been backed up.

The five types of backups are discussed in the following sections.

Normal Backups

A *normal* backup does two things:

◆ Backs up all files that have been selected, regardless of the setting of the archive bit

◆ Clears the archive bit to indicate that the files have been backed up

Obviously, a normal backup performs a thorough backup of the selected files. By clearing the archive bit, a normal backup indicates that all files have been backed up. A normal backup is sometimes referred to as a full backup.

Copy Backups

A *copy* backup does the following:

◆ Backs up all files that have been selected, regardless of the setting of the archive bit

◆ Leaves the archive bit in its prebackup state

In other words, a copy backup does not alter the files that are backed up in any way, including changing the archive bit.

Differential Backups

Differential backups are so named because they record all the differences that have taken place since the last normal backup. A differential backup does the following:

◆ Backs up only files that have the archive bit set to show that the file has been modified

◆ Leaves the archive bit in its prebackup state

Differential backups often are used in combination with normal backups. A normal backup of all files is performed each weekend to archive all files on the LAN, for example. Then a differential backup is performed each night of the week to back up all files that have been modified since the weekend. Figure 18.5 shows how this schedule would work.

To restore all files on the LAN, you would need to restore two sets of tapes:

◆ The normal backup for the previous weekend

◆ The differential backup for the previous night

Differential backups commonly are used to reduce the amount of time in which backup jobs must run during the week. If you can schedule a normal (full) backup for the weekend but have limited time during the week, a differential backup still might fit into the weekday backup window.

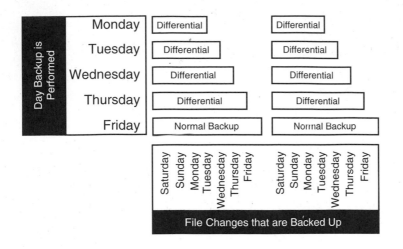

Figure 18.5

Differential backups.

Incremental Backups

Incremental backups record is similar to a differential backup. Incremental backups are usually smaller than differential and thus can take less time to backup, but will require more work to restore. An incremental backup does the following:

◆ Backs up only files that have the archive bit set to show that the file has been modified

◆ Clears the archive bit to indicate that the file has been backed up

Figure 18.6 shows how a combination of normal and incremental backups would work. The figure assumes that a normal backup is performed during the weekend, while an incremental backup takes place each week night. Notice that each incremental backup only records files that have been modified since the previous backup took place.

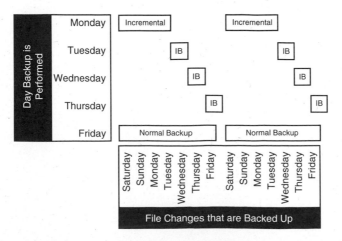

Figure 18.6

Incremental backups.

Incremental backups are used to further reduce the time interval required to back up networks. If your LAN includes critical data, you might want to run incremental backups more than once a day so that an entire day's worth of work cannot be lost.

The disadvantage of incremental backups is that several tapes can be required to restore the network. If the LAN fails on Thursday, you must restore the last normal backup plus the incremental backups for Monday, Tuesday, and Wednesday.

Daily Backups

Daily backups identify files to be backed up by examining the date stamp. If a file has been modified on the same day the backup is being made, the file will be backed up.

Both incremental and daily backups can be used to make checkpoint backups during the working day to capture changes at intervals shorter than 24 hours.

| **Note** | Notice that none of these backup types protects you against loss of data in files that have been modified since the most recent backup. What if you cannot afford to lose a single change that is made to any file, regardless of when the last backup was made? If you are running computers for a bank, how do you ensure that not a single transaction is lost? |

There is no such thing as continuous backup, and open files can't be backed up. If your data is so critical that nothing may be lost, you need to be looking into one or more of the following options:

- ◆ **RAID disk storage.** So that a single hard drive failure will not lose data.

- ◆ **Fault-tolerant hardware.** Has redundant power supplies, error-correcting memory, and other goodies that keep you from losing data.

- ◆ **Fault-tolerant software.** Can rebuild damaged files. A good database system keeps a log file that can reconstruct all transactions that take place. As long as the hard drives that contain the log file survive a disaster, you can restore last night's backup and roll the log forward to reconstruct the database to the point of failure.

Tape-Rotation Schedules

Your goal in rotating tapes is to have as much of your data as possible both on-site and safely off-site in storage. Ideally, your on-site tapes would be sufficient to rebuild the LAN, and you would need files from the off-site archive only in an emergency. The following sections explain several rotation schemes, each of which has advantages and disadvantages.

Two-Set Rotation

A basic scheme simply uses 10 tapes divided into 2 sets of 5. One set is used one week, and the other set is used the next week. Figure 18.7 illustrates the process.

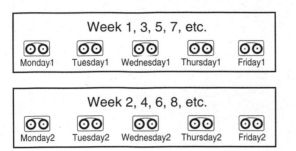

Figure 18.7

Two-set rotation.

This method does not provide for long-term archives and does not enable you to reach back very far in time. Suppose that you find that an unknown virus infected your LAN a month ago. Wouldn't it be nice to be able to restore all your program files (the only ones the virus could infect) from a tape that was made before the virus infection began?

You also may need greater scope in your archive if you have data that must be stored for long periods of time.

Grandfather-Father-Son Rotation

The *grandfather-father-son* (GFS) method is simple to manage and is adequate for most small- to medium-sized LANs. Several GFS tape rotations could be developed, but here is one that works well without being unduly complicated. You need the following tapes:

◆ Four tapes for each weekday: Monday, Tuesday, Wednesday, and Thursday

◆ Five Friday tapes, one for each Friday of the month, labeled Friday1 through Friday5 (the fifth tape is for months with five Fridays)

◆ Twelve monthly tapes

The GFS rotation scheme is shown in figure 18.8.

Monday through Thursday, a backup is performed using the appropriate tape. These tapes are reused weekly. Normal, differential, or incremental backups may be performed, depending on your requirements.

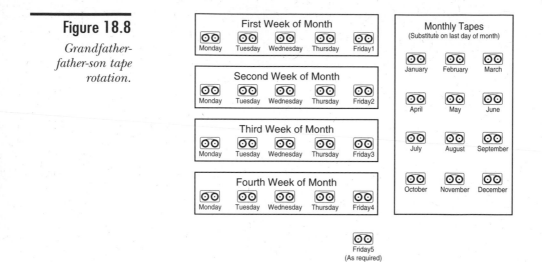

Figure 18.8

Grandfather-father-son tape rotation.

Friday1 through Friday4 are used on the first through fourth Friday of the month. These tapes are stored off-site and are retrieved after two weeks. In this way, the two most recent Friday tapes are stored off-site.

On the last day of each month, the appropriate monthly tape is used. These tapes are stored off-site for at least one year. If your organization needs a longer archive period, monthly tapes could be stored off-site indefinitely.

If you own two tape drives, you could make an on-site copy of each tape before it is sent to off-site storage. This ensures that you can locate any file in your archive without the delay of retrieving files from the vault.

Note   Of course, if all your files will not fit on a single tape, you will be working with spanned tape volumes. Work out an appropriate labeling scheme to keep related tapes together, such as MONDAYA, MONDAYB, and so on.

Ten-Tape Rotation

The GFS method has many desirable qualities, and is probably the most commonly used approach; however, GFS rotation uses some tapes much more heavily than others. The daily tapes are used 52 times a year, while the monthly tapes are used only one time. A ten-tape rotation spreads the wear on all tapes.

This method uses a series of four-week cycles. During each cycle, the same tapes are used on each Monday, Tuesday, Wednesday, and Thursday. A new tape is rotated in on Friday. Figure 18.9 shows how the process works. As you can see, the rotation begins to repeat after 40 weeks.

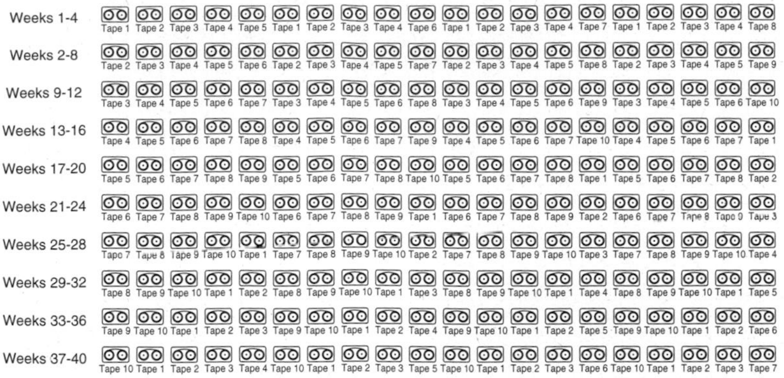

Weeks 1-4																			
Tape 1	Tape 2	Tape 3	Tape 4	Tape 5	Tape 1	Tape 2	Tape 3	Tape 4	Tape 6	Tape 1	Tape 2	Tape 3	Tape 4	Tape 7	Tape 1	Tape 2	Tape 3	Tape 4	Tape 8

Weeks 2-8 Tape 2 Tape 3 Tape 4 Tape 5 Tape 6 Tape 2 Tape 3 Tape 4 Tape 5 Tape 7 Tape 2 Tape 3 Tape 4 Tape 5 Tape 8 Tape 2 Tape 3 Tape 4 Tape 5 Tape 9

Weeks 9-12 Tape 3 Tape 4 Tape 5 Tape 6 Tape 7 Tape 3 Tape 4 Tape 5 Tape 6 Tape 8 Tape 3 Tape 4 Tape 5 Tape 6 Tape 9 Tape 3 Tape 4 Tape 5 Tape 6 Tape 10

Weeks 13-16 Tape 4 Tape 5 Tape 6 Tape 7 Tape 8 Tape 4 Tape 5 Tape 6 Tape 7 Tape 9 Tape 4 Tape 5 Tape 6 Tape 7 Tape 10 Tape 4 Tape 5 Tape 6 Tape 7 Tape 1

Weeks 17-20 Tape 5 Tape 6 Tape 7 Tape 8 Tape 9 Tape 5 Tape 6 Tape 7 Tape 8 Tape 10 Tape 5 Tape 6 Tape 7 Tape 8 Tape 1 Tape 5 Tape 6 Tape 7 Tape 8 Tape 2

Weeks 21-24 Tape 6 Tape 7 Tape 8 Tape 9 Tape 10 Tape 6 Tape 7 Tape 8 Tape 9 Tape 1 Tape 6 Tape 7 Tape 8 Tape 9 Tape 2 Tape 6 Tape 7 Tape 8 Tape 9 Tape 3

Weeks 25-28 Tape 7 Tape 8 Tape 9 Tape 10 Tape 1 Tape 7 Tape 8 Tape 9 Tape 10 Tape 2 Tape 7 Tape 8 Tape 9 Tape 10 Tape 3 Tape 7 Tape 8 Tape 9 Tape 10 Tape 4

Weeks 29-32 Tape 8 Tape 9 Tape 10 Tape 1 Tape 2 Tape 8 Tape 9 Tape 10 Tape 1 Tape 3 Tape 8 Tape 9 Tape 10 Tape 1 Tape 4 Tape 8 Tape 9 Tape 10 Tape 1 Tape 5

Weeks 33-36 Tape 9 Tape 10 Tape 1 Tape 2 Tape 3 Tape 9 Tape 10 Tape 1 Tape 2 Tape 4 Tape 9 Tape 10 Tape 1 Tape 2 Tape 5 Tape 9 Tape 10 Tape 1 Tape 2 Tape 6

Weeks 37-40 Tape 10 Tape 1 Tape 2 Tape 3 Tape 4 Tape 10 Tape 1 Tape 2 Tape 3 Tape 5 Tape 10 Tape 1 Tape 2 Tape 3 Tape 6 Tape 10 Tape 1 Tape 2 Tape 3 Tape 7

Figure 18.9

Ten-tape rotation.

The biggest problem with ten-tape rotation is that it is easy to get the schedule confused. Unfortunately, automated scheduling of a ten-tape rotation is beyond the scope of most tape backup software systems, and scheduling becomes a manual affair.

Using Windows NT Backup

Windows NT Backup is a reasonably capable backup system. Its main deficiency is its lack of a versatile macro language. Scheduling jobs is a bit complicated, due to an involved process of editing batch files and scheduling them with a separate utility. Still, before you invest in third-party backup software, live with Backup for a while. It may be all you need. At the very least, it will help you learn the features you want most in backup software.

Before you can back up files, you need to install tape-device support on the server. First, you learn how to install these devices, and then you look in detail at using Windows NT Backup to save and restore files.

Note   Before you buy a tape device for use with Windows NT, be sure it is on the list of supported hardware. Most SCSI devices should work fine. I have worked with several SCSI tape subsystems and had good results. Even though several models are supported, I have not tried to work with any QIC-40/QIC-80 tape drives, so I can't be sure what configuration issues you might encounter.

Installing Tape Drives

If you have never installed a tape device on your server, you need to install drivers using the following procedure:

Objective B.7

Installing Tape Drive Device Drivers

1. Open the Tape Devices utility in the Control Panel.

2. Windows NT will attempt to detect any attached tape devices. If successful, you will see a message similar to the one in figure 18.10.

Figure 18.10

A detected tape device.

New SCSI Tape Device Found

HP HP35470A
Required Driver:
4 millimeter DAT drive
Click OK to install the driver now.

OK   Cancel

3. Choose OK to install the driver for the detected device.

4. When prompted, verify the path to the installation files.

5. After the driver is installed, the Tape Devices window appears as shown in figure 18.11. It is not necessary to restart the computer to activate the tape device.

Figure 18.11

An installed tape device.

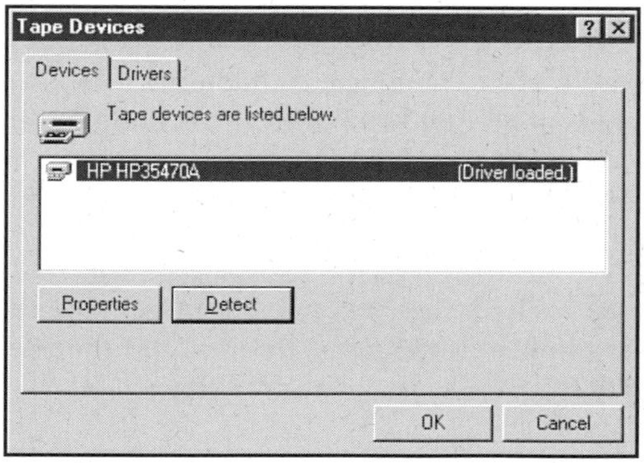

Tape Devices

Devices | Drivers

Tape devices are listed below.

HP HP35470A   [Driver loaded.]

Properties   Detect

OK   Cancel

Backing Up Files

The Backup utility is installed in the Administrative Tools program group. Figure 18.12 shows the Backup utility window and identifies several features. The Drives window normally will be open when you start Backup to display drive letters that currently are connected to the computer. Any drives that have been connected locally or through the network are displayed in the Drives window. Devices in the figure include:

◆ **D:** a high-capacity, removable media drive

◆ **E:** a CD-ROM drive

◆ **F:** a network connection to \\keystone1\accounting

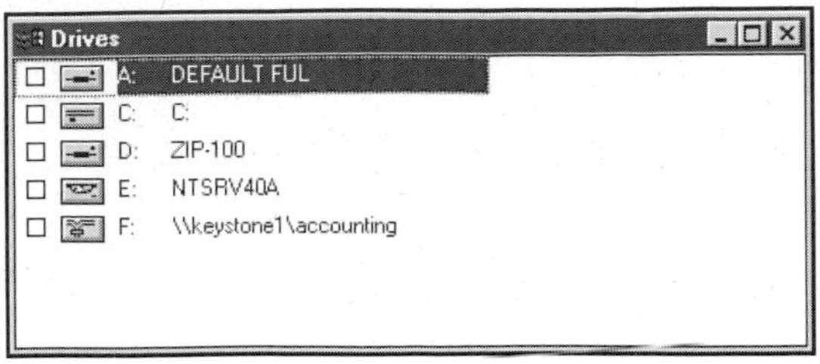

Figure 18.12

The main window in Backup.

Backing up files is a five-step process as outlined in the following exercise:

Backing Up Files

1. Prepare the tape media.

2. Select the files to be backed up.

3. Specify the backup options.

4. Run the backup.

5. Verify the backup.

Note To make backups or restore files, you must be a member of the Administrators or Backup Operators group.

Preparing the Tape Media

In most cases, new tapes require little or no preparation. If tapes have existing data from another backup system, they might need to be erased or formatted. Several tape options are found on the **O**perations menu.

◆ **Erase Tape.** Choose this operation to erase records of previous backups. You have two choices:

Quick Erase. Simply erases the tape label and makes the tape usable with Windows NT Backup. Existing data remains on the tape and can be accessed.

Secure Erase. Physically erases all data from the tape so that it cannot be accessed.

◆ **Retension Tape.** DC-6000 and DC-2000 data cartridges should be retensioned prior to first use and every 20 backup operations. *Retensioning* fast forwards and rewinds the tape to equalize tension on the tape medium. The 4mm and 8mm tapes do not require retensioning.

◆ **Eject Tape.** Ejects a tape if a tape device supports software tape ejection.

Note You should erase any tapes that will be used during unattended operation, because no one will be present to correct errors if Backup is unable to read the tape.

If Backup produces an error message such as `Tape Drive Error Detected` or `Bad Tape`, you might not be able to erase the tape with Backup in normal mode. To erase a tape that causes these errors, start Backup by choosing **R**un from the **F**ile menu and add the /nopoll switch. (The command would be `NTBACKUP /NOPOLL`.)

After you format tapes with the /NOPOLL switch, stop Backup and restart it normally. Do not attempt to execute normal operations with the /NOPOLL switch.

Selecting Files for Backup

To select entire volumes, simply enable the check boxes of the desired volumes in the Backup window.

Tip You also can check and uncheck items by using the Check and Uncheck icons on the toolbar or by choosing the **C**heck and **U**ncheck commands from the **S**elect menu.

To select directories or files, follow these steps:

Selecting Directories or Files

1. Double-click a drive name to open a drive tree window similar to that shown in figure 18.13.

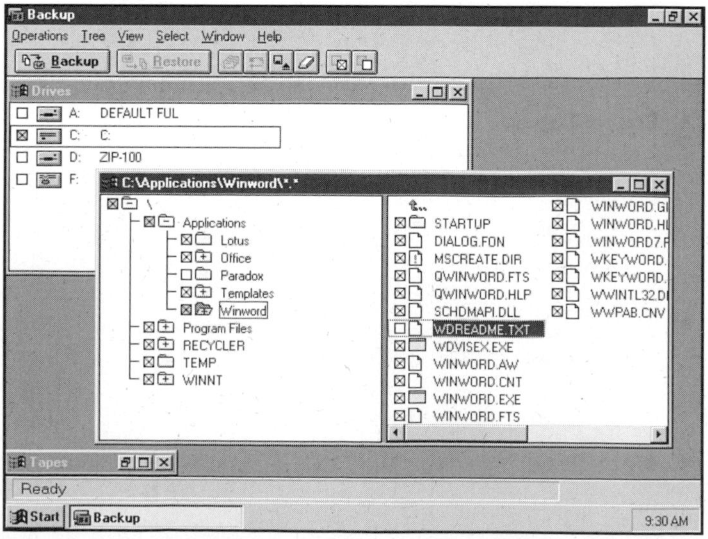

Figure 18.13

Selecting files and directories for backup.

2. This drive tree window works much like trees in utilities such as Windows NT Explorer. You double-click a directory to open a directory, for example.

3. Choose the files or directories to be backed up by checking the associated box. Checking a directory selects all subdirectories of that directory. If you want, you can open the subdirectories and remove the check marks.

Notice that a directory check box is filled with gray if any files or subdirectories under that directory are unchecked.

Tip

As the cost of removable storage hardware has decreased, it has become more common for computers to be equipped with high-capacity removable storage devices, such as Bernoulli, SyQuest, and writable CD-ROM drives. Unfortunately, the Windows NT Backup program does not permit you to select removable volumes for backup.

The trick is to share the drive that you want to back up; then connect a drive letter to the shared drive. You can then back up the storage device by selecting the drive letter that is connected to the removable drive.

Specifying Backup Options

After you have selected the items to be backed up, begin the backup by choosing the **B**ackup command from the **O**perations menu, or click the Backup button in the toolbar. This displays the Backup Information dialog box shown in figure 18.14.

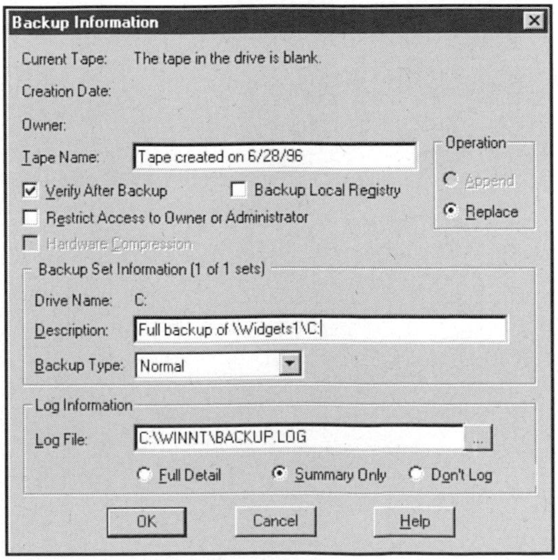

Figure 18.14

Specifying backup job information.

The options in this box follow:

◆ **Current Tape.** The name of the currently mounted tape, unless the tape is blank or has an unrecognized format.

◆ **Creation Date.** The date the first backup set on the tape was created.

◆ **Owner.** The user who placed the first backup set on the tape.

◆ **Tape Name.** You can specify a tape name or permit Backup to use the default name "Tape created on *date*." This box is available only when you choose the **R**eplace option.

◆ **Append.** Select this button to add the new backup set to the end of the tape.

◆ **Replace.** Select this button to overwrite existing backup sets on the tape with the current backup.

◆ **Verify After Backup.** Check this item to have Backup compare the tape contents to the original files to ensure that file data was written to tape without error.

◆ **Backup Local Registry.** The Registry is the heart and soul of Windows NT, and contains all the system's vital operational data. You should include the Registry in every backup of drive C to ensure that you have a valid, recent copy in case the Registry files are damaged.

◆ **Restrict Access to Owner or Administrator.** Check this option to make the tape more secure. Data from the tape can be retrieved only by the tape owner, or by a member of the Administrators or Backup Operators group. This box is available only when you choose the **R**eplace option.

◆ **Hardware Compression.** This option is active only if your tape device supports hardware data compression. Check this box to activate the feature. Be aware, however, that using hardware compression can prevent you from restoring the tape from another brand of drive or from a drive that does not support data compression.

◆ **Drive Name.** This field displays the name of a drive that you checked in the Backup window. If you checked more than one drive letter, you see a scroll bar that can be used to display each of the drives. For each drive, you can enter a description and select a backup type.

◆ **Description.** Enter a brief description of the job.

◆ **Backup Type.** Choose the backup type from the options: Normal, Copy, Differential, Incremental, and Daily. Each type was discussed earlier in the chapter.

◆ **Log File.** Enter a path describing a file where log messages will be recorded.

Full Detail. Logs all operations, including the files and directories that are backed up.

Summary Only. Logs only major operations, such as starting and completing the backup and backup errors.

Caution | Windows NT Backup does not back up Registries on remote computers.

If you want to back up your network from a central location, two utilities found in the *Windows NT Resource Kit* enable you to back up a Registry to files that can in turn be backed up through the network to tape. Use REGBACK.EXE to back up a Registry, and REGREST.EXE to restore it.

Running the Backup

When you have completed entries in the dialog box, choose OK to continue with the backup.

If the tape in the drive already contains data and you have specified **R**eplace as the backup operation, you will see an error message. Be sure that you don't mind whether the files on the tape will be destroyed before you choose **Y**es to continue.

Verifying the Backup

As the backup proceeds, the Backup Status box updates you on events (see fig. 18.15). Pay particular attention to two statistics:

◆ **Corrupt files.** High or increasing numbers of corrupt files might indicate hardware problems.

◆ **Skipped files.** These files were, of course, not backed up. If you see skipped files, check the log to ensure that missing these files is not a critical omission. You might need to force a user to log out to close the files.

It is always a good idea to check the backup log, which is a text file you can print or review with Notepad.

Restoring Files

To restore files, first review your logs to identify the appropriate tape. If you are restoring a complete volume from a combination of several backup sets, be sure to restore the backup sets in the order they were made so that newer copies of files overwrite older copies.

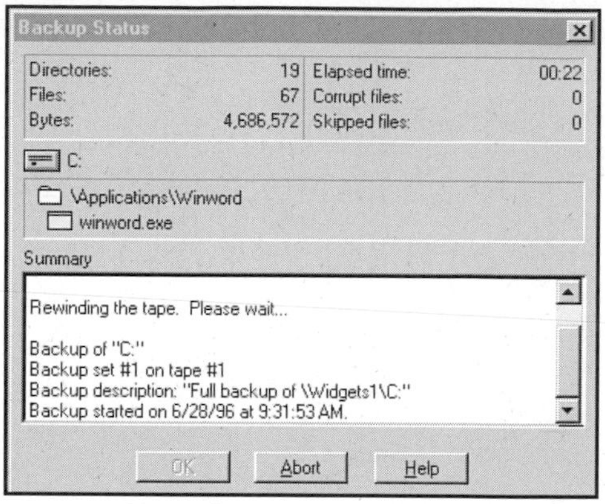

Figure 18.15

*The Backup
Status dialog box.*

| Note | Windows NT Backup does not restore the following files:

◆ Tape files that are older than the corresponding file on disk. You will be asked to confirm replacement of newer files.

◆ Files that are to be restored to a directory for which the user does not have the Write permission. Users are also prevented from overwriting files for which they do not have Write permissions.

Selecting Files to Restore

Prior to a restore, you must select the files to be restored. Backup enables you to restore entire tapes, specific backup sets, or individual files or directories. To select files to restore, follow these steps:

Selecting Files to Restore

1. Open the Tapes window by double-clicking the Tapes icon.

2. Insert the desired tape. After you insert a tape, Backup reads a catalog of items on the tape and creates an icon for the tape in the Tapes window. Figure 18.16 shows a Tapes window with two tape catalogs loaded.

    You can request loading of a tape catalog by selecting the tape icon and choosing **C**atalog from the **O**perations menu.

3. You can restore entire tapes, specific backup sets, or individual directories or files by selecting the items you want in the Tapes window. You can open folders to locate subdirectories and files on a drive. Check all items that are to be restored.

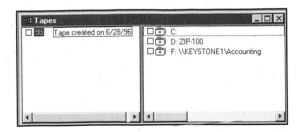

Figure 18.16

Selecting a tape to restore.

> **Note**   Creating catalogs is a time when you will really appreciate the fast seek times that are possible with 4mm data cartridges. The catalog is stored as the last item on the tape, and Backup must search the entire tape. This can take considerable time with QIC cartridges, but takes less than a minute with a 4mm drive.

Specifying Restore Options

After selecting items to be restored, choose the Restore icon in the toolbar or choose **R**estore from the **O**perations menu. The Restore Information dialog box appears, as shown in figure 18.17.

Figure 18.17

Specifying restore options.

If you have selected two or more tape sets to restore, a scroll bar will be included in the Restore Information dialog box. You can select each set by moving the scroll handle.

For each tape set being restored, the following information and options are displayed:

- ◆ **Tape Name.** The name of the tape from which files are being restored for this set.

- ◆ **Backup Set.** The name you assigned to the backup set.

- ◆ **Creation Date.** The date the backup set was created.

- ◆ **Owner.** The user who created the backup set.

- ◆ **Restore to Drive.** Specify a different destination drive by entering the drive path here. This path can include local hard drives or drives that are created by network connections.

- ◆ **Alternate Path.** If files will not be restored to their original directories, specify the base directory to which the directory tree should be restored.

- ◆ **Verify After Restore.** Check this option to have restored files compared to the image on tape to ensure that errors have not occurred.

- ◆ **Restore File Permissions.** Check this box if you want to retain file permissions that originally were assigned to the directories and files. This option is available only if you are restoring to an NTFS volume.

- ◆ **Restore Local Registry.** Check this box to restore the server Registry. This option is active only if the Registry was backed up to the tape set and if it would be restored to the same volume on which it originally was located.

- ◆ **Log File.** Enables you to specify where messages should be logged. Options are the same as the options available in the Backup Information dialog box.

Restoring Files

After you have completed the Restore Information dialog box, begin the restore operation by choosing OK. A Restore Status box similar to figure 18.18 displays the progress of the file restoration.

Restoring from Spanned Tape Sets

If the tape set you are restoring spans more than one physical tape, the catalog will be on the last tape on the set. Backup asks you to mount the appropriate tape so that it can read the catalog.

If a tape from the spanned set is missing or damaged, you might need to force Backup to rebuild a catalog by scanning each tape. To do this, start Backup by choosing **R**un from the Start menu and typing the command `NTBACKUP /MISSINGTAPE`. Backup then scans each tape to build a catalog—a lengthy process, but one that is preferable to losing your data.

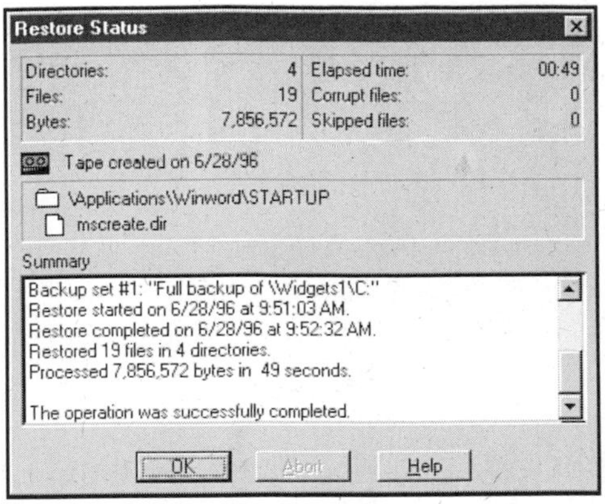

Figure 18.18

The Restore Status dialog box.

Restoring a Registry

You can restore only the Registry files to the volume from which they were archived, if you prefer. With the Windows Backup utility, you must select at least one file to activate the **R**estore button. Then you can check the Restore Local Registry box in the Restore Information dialog box.

To restore from the command line, specify the following directory:

`\WINNT\SYSTEM32\CONFIG`

You cannot restore this directory to any disk other than the disk from which it was backed up.

Note   If you need to restore files to a newly installed server, be sure that the software on the new server is identical to the software on the old server. If any patches or upgraded drivers were installed on the old server, be sure that they go on the new server before you try to restore the files. Otherwise, the backup software might not be able to read your tapes.

Backing Up from the Command Line

A command-line interface is available for Backup. The primary use for the command-line interface is to build batch files that can be executed manually or using the Windows NT command scheduler.

The syntax for the NTBACKUP command follows:

```
NTBACKUP operation path [/A][/B][/D "text"][/E][/HC:[ON¦OFF]]
     [/L "filename"][/R][/T option][/TAPE:n][/V]
```

The command recognizes several options (square brackets indicate that a parameter is not required in Microsoft syntax diagrams). The parameters and options for NTBACKUP follow:

operation	Always specify BACKUP.
path	Enter one or more path specifications of directories to be backed up.
/A	Include this option to have Backup append this job to tape. Omitting this option instructs Backup to replace the tape contents with the current job.
/B	Include this option to back up the local Registry.
/D "text"	Use this option to specify a description of the backup set. Place the description in quotation marks.
/E	If this option is used, the backup log includes exceptions only. Without this option, a full backup log is created.
/HC:[ON¦OFF]	Use this option to force a backup device to operate with hardware compression on or off. Specify the option as /hc:on or /hc:off. This option is effective only when the /A option is omitted, because the compression mode of the tape is determined by the mode used for the first set on the tape.
/L "filename"	This option specifies the name of the backup log. Include the file name and path in quotation marks.
/R	Secures the backup set by restricting access to the tape owner and to members of the Administrators or Backup Operators group. This option is effective only when the /A option is omitted.
/T option	Specify the backup type. Replace option with normal, copy, incremental, differential, or daily.
/TAPE:n	If the server has more than one tape drive, specify the drive to be used with a number n from 0 through 9 to reference the drive's number as listed in the Registry.
/V	Include this option to have Backup verify the tape.

Now look at some examples. Following is a command that backs up the APPS directory of drive C:

```
ntbackup backup c:\apps /a/e/v /l "c:\winnt\backup.log"
/t differential
```

Notice that the order of the options does not matter. This command accomplishes the following:

◆ Backs up all files and subdirectories of C:\APPS

◆ Appends the tape set to the current tape

◆ Restricts tape log entries to exceptions only

◆ Verifies the backup

◆ Places the log in the file C:\WINNT\BACKUP.LOG

◆ Performs a differential backup

Here is another example:

```
ntbackup backup c: d: h: /r/b /t normal /l:c:\tape.log
```

This example does the following:

◆ Backs up drives C, D, and H

◆ Backs up the Registry on local drives

◆ Replaces contents of the tape (no /a option)

◆ Restricts access to the backup set

◆ Performs a normal backup

◆ Records a full detail log (no /e flag) in C:\TAPE.LOG

Because the interactive Backup utility is so quick and easy to use, you probably will use the command-line format primarily to create batch files. Because Backup does not support a macro language, however, the command-line approach is the only way to store backup procedures for repeated execution.

In the next section, you see how backup batch files can be scheduled for delayed or repeated execution. Here is a batch file that backs up drives on several servers:

```
net use g:\\widgets1\c$ /yes
net use h:\\widgets2\c$ /yes
net use i: \\acct\c$ /yes
ntbackup backup c: d: g: h: i: /e/v /l "c:\winnt\backup.log"
/t normal /d "Complete backup of KEYSTONE, WIDGETS, and ACCT domains"
```

Of course, a backup operator must be trusted on other domains before being permitted to back up his or her data in those other domains.

Note The administrative shares such as C$ and D$ are available only to members of the Administrators local group. If members of Backup Operators will be backing up remote servers, you need to create shares that can be accessed by them.

Scheduling Backup Jobs

Windows NT has a Schedule service that can be used to schedule execution of commands. The Schedule enables you to schedule jobs to execute overnight or over the weekend, and to execute repeatedly without the need for rescheduling. This section shows you how to set up and use the Schedule to make tape backups. You learn more about managing services in Chapter 19, "Managing the Server."

Starting the Schedule Service

The Schedule service can run in two modes:

◆ **As a system account.** In this mode, Schedule operates in the current logon session, using the permissions assigned to the logged-on user account. Schedule cannot operate when no user is logged on.

◆ **In its own logon session.** In this mode, it uses permissions assigned to its own user account. Schedule can operate whenever the server is active and can function in the background when users are logged on to the server.

The first choice is useful when you are scheduling tasks that will take place while you are logged on.

In many cases, however, you will want to use the second approach with tape backups. By assigning a user account to the Schedule, you make it possible for backups to take place even when no one is logged on to the backup server.

Starting the Schedule Service as a System Account

Services are managed using the Service utility in the Control Panel. Open the Service utility to see a list of services, as shown in figure 18.19. Notice that the Schedule service status is not started and its Startup mode is Manual. Services that are configured with an Automatic Startup mode are started when Windows NT Server is booted.

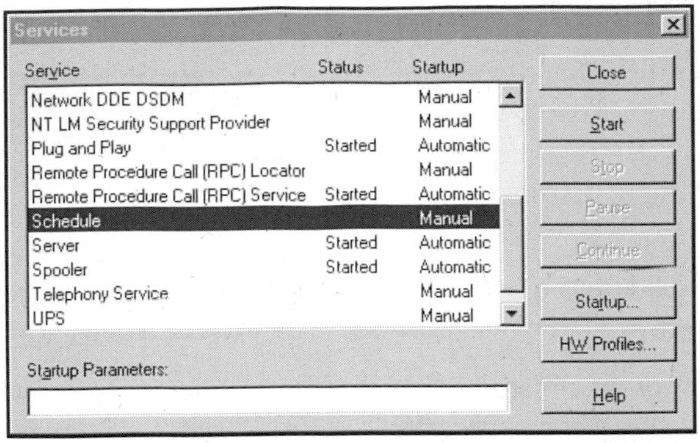

Figure 18.19

*Services in the
Services utility.*

To set up the Schedule service as a system account, follow these steps:

Setting Up the Schedule Service as a System Account

1. Open the Service utility in the Control Panel.

2. Select the Schedule service in the Services box.

3. Choose Startup to display the Service dialog box shown in figure 18.20.

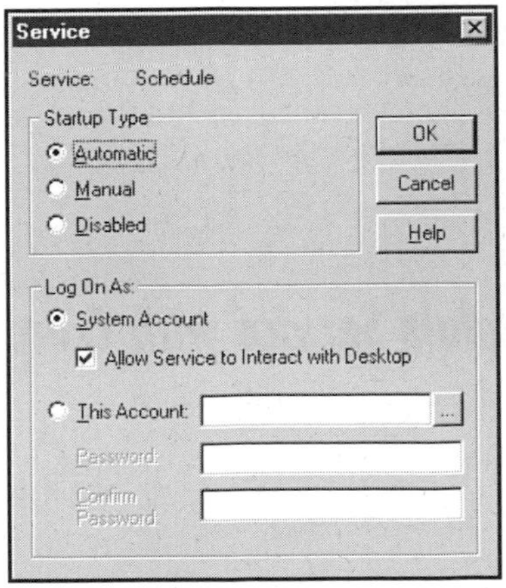

Figure 18.20

*Setting Service
options.*

4. Select **A**utomatic so that Schedule service will be started automatically.

5. Select **S**ystem Account.

6. Select A**l**low Service to Interact with Desktop if you want to monitor backup jobs as they run. (I recommend using this option when you are learning to schedule backups.)

7. Choose OK. You will be returned to the Services window.

8. Choose **S**tart to start the Schedule service. It restarts automatically each time the server is booted.

9. Exit the Service utility.

> **Note** When you are experimenting, set up the Schedule service as a System service. You will find it much easier to learn the ropes and to set up your regular backup jobs.
>
> Any time you change the settings for the Schedule service, you must stop and restart the service to have the changes take effect.

Starting the Schedule Service with Its Own User Account

Create a user account that will be used by the scheduler. The user ID also must be a member of the Backup Operators local group of any domain that it will be responsible for backing up. Of course, proper trust relationships must be set up between domains before cross-domain memberships can be assigned.

Because the Schedule service will be running backup jobs, the user account must be made a member of the Backup Operators local group. Other group memberships might be required as well.

Before you go further, log on with the user account you have created and be sure you can perform the required functions.

To set up the Schedule service to log on with the user account you have created, follow these steps:

Logging On to the Schedule Service with Created Account

1. Open the Service utility in the Control Panel.

2. Select the Schedule service in the Services box.

3. Choose **S**tartup to display the Service dialog box.

4. Select **A**utomatic so that Schedule service will be started automatically.

5. As shown in figure 18.21, select **T**his Account and enter the user account name you have created for backups. You can click the Browse (...) button to browse the network and select the user name.

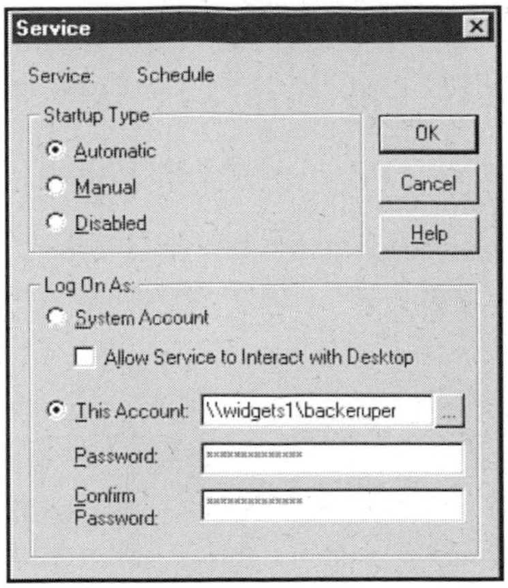

Figure 18.21

Configuring a service to log on with a user account.

6. Enter the password for the user account in the two password fields.

7. Choose OK. You will be returned to the Services dialog box.

8. Stop the service if it is running. Then choose **S**tart to activate the service with the changes you have made.

9. Exit the Service utility.

Note   You only need to set up the Schedule service to log on with a user account if you are planning to have it run jobs in the background or when a user is not logged on. If the backup computer is located in a secure, locked area, you can do just as well by configuring Schedule as a system service and leaving it logged on with appropriate privileges. If you are concerned about security, install a password-protected screen saver so that the computer will be locked with a password when it is unattended.

Scheduling Jobs with the AT Command

Now that the Schedule service is started, you can enter scheduled jobs with the AT command. AT commands are entered at a command prompt. The syntax of the AT command follows:

```
AT [\\computer] [[id][/DELETE] ¦ /DELETE [/YES]]
```

or

```
AT [\\computer] time [/INTERACTIVE][/EVERY:date[,...] "command"
```

or

```
AT [\\computer] time [/INTERACTIVE][/NEXT:date[,...] "command"
```

The AT command typed alone lists all currently scheduled jobs.

The command recognizes several options (square brackets indicate that a parameter is not required in Microsoft syntax diagrams). The parameters and options for AT follow:

`\\computer`	Specify the name of a Windows NT computer on which the command will execute. If this command is omitted, the current computer is assumed.
`id`	The identification number that is assigned to a scheduled command.
`/DELETE`	Include this option to cancel a schedule command. If an *id* is specified, only the jobs associated with that *id* are deleted. Otherwise, all scheduled commands are deleted.
`/YES`	When used to cancel all jobs, /YES eliminates the need to confirm the request.
`time`	Specifies the time in 24-hour format when the job should be scheduled.
`/INTERACTIVE`	Include this option to enable the current user to interact with the job. Without this flag, the job operates in the background.
`/EVERY:date`	Use this option to schedule repeating jobs. Specify one or more dates, where *date* is a day of the week (Monday, Tuesday, and so on) or a day of the month (1 through 31). If *date* is omitted, the current day of the month is assumed.
`/NEXT:date`	Use this option to schedule a job the next time *date* occurs. Specify one or more dates, where *date* is a day of the week (Monday, Tuesday, and so on) or a day of the month (1 through 31). If *date* is omitted, the current day of the month is assumed.
`"command"`	The command to be executed.

Assuming that BACKUP.BAT is a batch file, here are some examples of scheduling jobs with the AT command. This first example schedules the job once at 3:00 a.m. If it is later than 3:00 a.m., the job is scheduled for the morning of the next day.

```
AT 3:00 "backup"
```

To schedule a job to happen regularly on Wednesdays at midnight, use the /EVERY option:

```
AT 0:00 /every:Wednesday "backup"
```

If you want the job to happen every weekday, just add the extra days:

```
AT 0:00 /every:Monday,Tuesday,Wednesday,Thursday "backup"
```

Particularly when you are debugging backup procedures, you might want to have the job operate in interactive mode. Here is an example:

```
AT 15:00 "backup" /interactive
```

After each job is scheduled, you see this message where *n* is the job number:

```
Added a new job ID=n
```

To delete a job, use the job ID with the /DELETE command.

> **Caution** Do not use the /INTERACTIVE option with backup jobs that will run overnight without a user logged on to the desktop. Interactive jobs will attempt to connect with an active desktop and will fail.

Scheduling Jobs with Command Scheduler

The *Windows NT Resource Kit* includes a useful utility called Command Scheduler that enables you to schedule and manage jobs in an interactive windows-based environment. Figure 18.22 shows the main window of Command Scheduler with three jobs scheduled.

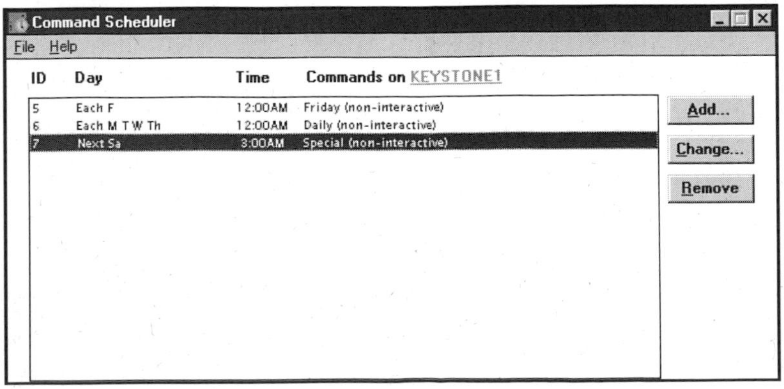

Figure 18.22

The main window of Command Scheduler.

If you start the Command Scheduler and the Schedule service is not started, Command Scheduler asks whether you want to start the service.

From the main window, choose **A**dd to add a new command using the dialog box shown in figure 18.23. The fields in the Change Command dialog box follow:

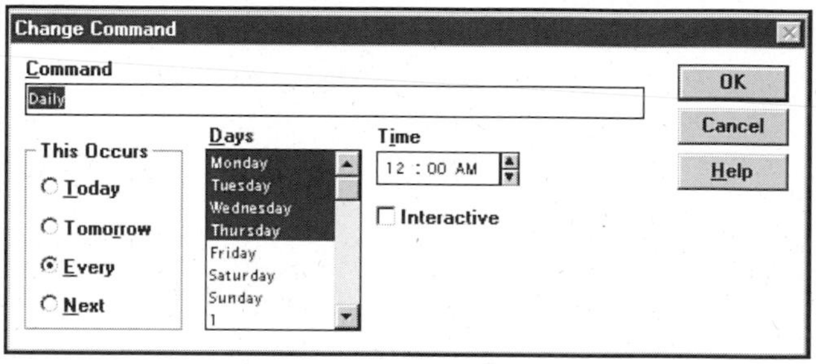

Figure 18.23

Adding a job in Command Scheduler.

◆ **Command.** Enter the command to be executed.

◆ **This Occurs.** Specify whether the job should occur:

Today

Tomo**rr**ow

Every—Day(s) specified in the **D**ays box

Next—Day(s) specified in the **D**ays box

◆ **Days.** If **E**very or **N**ext is selected, select one or more days in this box.

◆ **Time.** Enter the time. You can tab to each time field and enter a number, or select each field in turn and change the value with the arrow buttons.

◆ **Interactive.** Check this box if the job should be available on the desktop of the currently logged-on user. (See the earlier warning about interactive jobs.)

After you have completed the dialog box, choose OK to add the job and return to the Command Scheduler main window.

To change or remove a job, select the job and choose **C**hange or **R**emove in the Command Scheduler main window.

Note   The Command Scheduler is distributed with the *Windows NT Resource Kit* for Windows NT version 3.5. As I write this, I can't be sure it will be included in the *Windows NT Resource Kit* for version 4. If it is not included, it is worth doing some legwork to obtain a copy. The AT command leaves just a bit to be desired.

Recovering a Server

If you experience total failure of a server's boot hard drive, Microsoft recommends the following procedure for recovering the drive, as detailed in the following exercise.

Drive Recovery Procedure

1. After replacing the drive, reinstall Windows NT Server on the system partition. Use the Repair option and the server's Emergency Repair Disk to recover the BOOT.INI file and critical portions of the Registry.

2. Restart the server.

3. Use a tape drive attached to the server to restore the boot partition. Start with the last normal backup, and then restore any incremental or differential backups that are required.

4. Restart the server.

Tip   To shorten the time a boot drive failure puts a server out of service, I suggest that you create an emergency hard drive that is preconfigured with Windows NT Server. In the event of failure, disable the current boot drive, attach the emergency drive to the SCSI bus, and use it to boot the server. Finally, recover your backups to the emergency hard drive and restart the server. Your server will be up and running without the delay of reinstalling Windows NT Server. You can swap the hard drives and reinstall a new boot drive during a scheduled maintenance period.

Testing Your Knowledge

1. Data stored on quarter-inch cartridges uses a system called _____, which divides the tape into parallel tracks, and the head moves up and down to select a particular track.

2. QIC format tapes are more than adequate for an NT Server platform.
    A. True
    B. False

3. What manufacturer developed the 8mm cartridge?

4. Which tape drive types use the helical-scan recording method?
    A. DC-6000
    B. DC-2000

C. 8mm

D. 4mm

5. What three types of optical disk technology are available?

A. Compact disc read-only media (CD-ROM)

B. Write once read many (WORM)

C. Magnetic optical (MO) read-only

D. Magnetic optical (MO) read/write

6. WORM media is ideal for daily backups.

A. True

B. False

7. What factors can determine how you schedule backups?

A. The capacity of the backup system

B. The speed of the backup system

C. The frequency with which files are being modified

D. The importance of the data

8. What are the four types of file backups are normal, copy, _____, and _____.

9. A copy backup leaves the archive bit in its prebackup state.

A. True

B. False

10. What is a key difference between a differential and an incremental backup operation?

A. A differential backup only backs up files that have the archive bit set to show that the file has been modified

B. What is done with the files archive bit after being successfully backed up

C. An incremental backup only backs up files that have the archive bit set to show that the file has been modified

D. A differential backup only backs up files that have the archive bit set to show that the file has not been modified

11. Which tape rotation schedule puts the least amount of wear on the tapes?

A. Two-set rotation

B. Grandfather-father-son rotation

C. Ten-tape rotation

D. No rotation

12. Because Windows NT 4 does not support plug-and-play, it will not attempt to detect any attached tape devices. You must manually select the device from a list box.

    A. True

    B. False

13. What two NT Server groups are permitted to make backups or restore files?

    A. Account Operators

    B. Power Users

    C. Backup Operators

    D. Administrators

14. What are the two types of logs available when backing up?

    A. Full detail

    B. Error only

    C. User defined

    D. Summary only

15. Windows NT Backup does not back up Registries on remote computers. What utility is included in the NT resource kit that enables you to back up remote registries to files on the server that can then be backed up on tape?

    A. RDISK

    B. REGBACK

    C. REGREST

    D. REGEDIT

16. Windows NT Backup does not provide the means to restore files to an alternate path.

    A. True

    B. False

17. You can restore only the Registry files to the volume from which they were archived.

    A. True

    B. False

18. When backing up from the command line, which switch secures the backup set by restricting access to the tape owner and to members of the Administrators or Backup Operators group?

    A. /S

    B. /R

      C. /E

      D. /L

19. The NT scheduling service permits backups to run unattended.

      A. True

      B. False

20. To schedule a backup job to happen regularly on Wednesdays at midnight, what AT command would you enter?

      A. AT 12:00 Wednesday backup

      B. AT 12:00 /every:Wednesday backup

      C. AT 0:00 Wednesday "backup"

      D. AT 0:00 /every:Wednesday "backup"

Review Answers

1. serpentine recording

2. B

3. Exabyte

4. C, D

5. A, B, D

6. B

7. A, B, C, D

8. differential, incremental

9. A

10. B

11. C

12. B

13. C, D

14. A, D

15. B

16. B

17. A

18. B

19. A

20. D

CHAPTER 19

Managing the Server

This chapter explores the tools that are provided to manage Windows NT Server. You have encountered some of these tools in earlier chapters, but some features still require discussion. You will examine a few tools in this chapter for the first time.

The following utilities are covered in this chapter:

- ◆ **Control Panel.** Actually a collection of tools for managing Windows NT hardware and software.

- ◆ **Server Manager.** The primary tool for managing server resources. You examined this tool extensively when domains and workstations were discussed. This chapter examines the remainder of Server Manager's features.

- ◆ **Service Manager.** The utility for starting, stopping, and configuring services.

- ◆ **UPS.** A utility for monitoring the status of an uninterruptible power supply.

- **Network Client Administrator.** A tool for creating client installation disks and for installing client software through the network.

- **Registry Editor.** The tool that enables you to directly manipulate the contents of the Windows NT Server Registry database.

- **File Properties.** This chapter covers the use of file properties to audit network file activities.

- **Printer Properties.** This chapter covers the use of printer properties to audit network printing activities.

- **Administrative Wizards.** A wide variety of administrative tasks are encapsulated in wizards.

Using the Control Panel

Anyone who has used Windows will be familiar with the Control Panel. Because this book isn't a basic tutorial on Windows, not much attention is lavished on the Control Panel, but a few of the tools are discussed. (If you want to change your cursor to a walking dinosaur by using the Cursors utility, you'll just have to get curious and figure it out for yourself.) Figure 19.1 shows the Control Panel window. The exact tools you have vary a bit depending on the features that are installed.

Figure 19.1

The Control Panel.

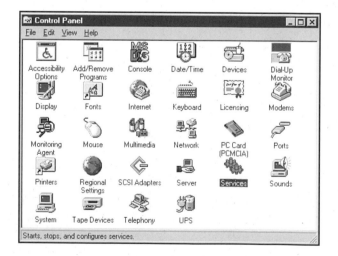

Only the tools that relate closely to server management are mentioned here:

- ◆ **Date/Time.** Computer clocks drift, and you occasionally should use this utility to keep your computers' clocks in reasonable agreement.

- ◆ **Devices.** This utility provides a means for examining and configuring most of the hardware on the computer. This utility is examined in this chapter.

- ◆ **Regional Settings.** A tool for defining language, time, date, currency, and other characteristics. You must select international characteristics during installation and seldom need to change them.

- ◆ **Licensing.** This utility is used to manage the client licenses on your network. It is discussed in this chapter.

- ◆ **Network.** Following installation, this is the tool used to add and remove network card drivers and protocols and network services.

- ◆ **Ports.** A tool for adding, configuring, and deleting communication ports. The Ports tool was discussed in detail in Chapter 13, "Managing Printing Services."

- ◆ **Printers.** This icon opens a window that contains the icons for the various printers defined on this computer. See Chapter 13 for further information.

- ◆ **Services.** The tool that configures, starts, pauses, and stops services. The Services tool is discussed in this chapter.

- ◆ **System.** A utility for configuring several characteristics of the Windows NT operating system environment. The System tool is discussed later in this chapter.

- ◆ **Tape Devices.** A utility for adding, removing, and configuring tape devices. See Chapter 18, "Backing Up Files."

- ◆ **UPS.** The utility that monitors an uninterruptible power supply and takes action during power failures. UPS is described later in this chapter.

Server Manager

Figure 19.2 shows the main window of Server Manager, which is used to manage Windows NT Servers and Workstations. Chapter 10, "Managing Domains and Trust Relationships," demonstrates how Server Manager is used to add and remove network servers and computers.

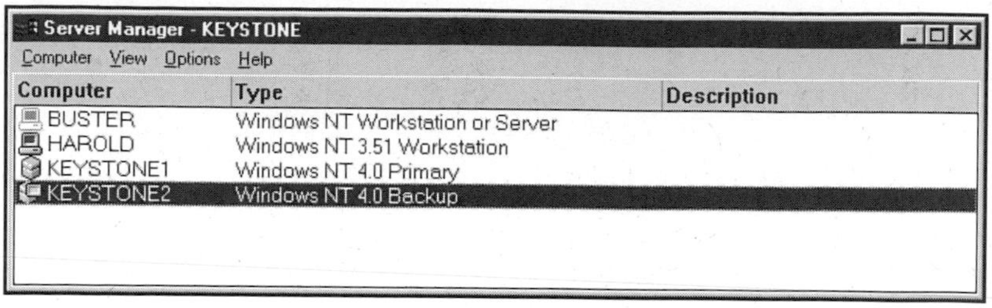

Figure 19.2

*The Server
Manager main
window.*

Server Manager has three command menus, each of which has features that still require further discussion. Each menu is described in the following sections.

The Computer Menu

The **C**omputer menu contains commands that enable you to manage Windows NT computers on the network. Some commands are discussed in more detail in other chapters but they are reviewed here for the sake of completeness. To manage a server with commands in the **C**omputer menu, first select the computer in the Server Manager window.

Managing Windows NT Computer Properties

The **P**roperties command displays the computer Properties dialog box shown in figure 19.3. This dialog box is used both to view and to manage properties of computers. The Properties dialog box has one input box that enables you to enter a description of the server. It also has five buttons you can use to manage specific categories of computer properties.

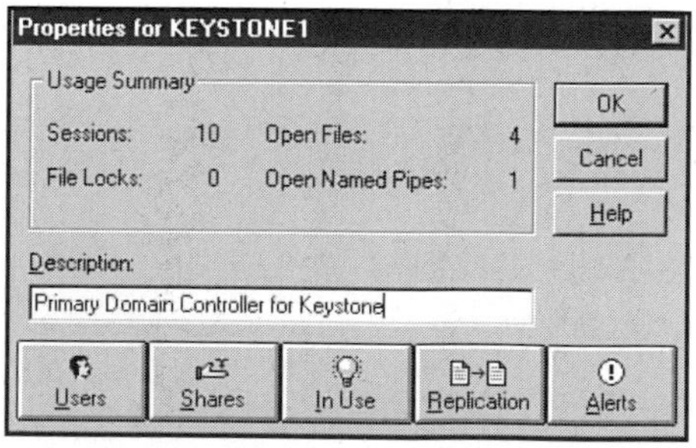

Figure 19.3

*The computer
Properties
dialog box.*

Viewing and Disconnecting Users Connected to a Server

The **U**sers button calls up the User Sessions dialog box shown in figure 19.4. Each user who is connected to the computer is listed in the **C**onnected Users scroll box. When you select a user, any shares that it has connected are listed in the Resource box.

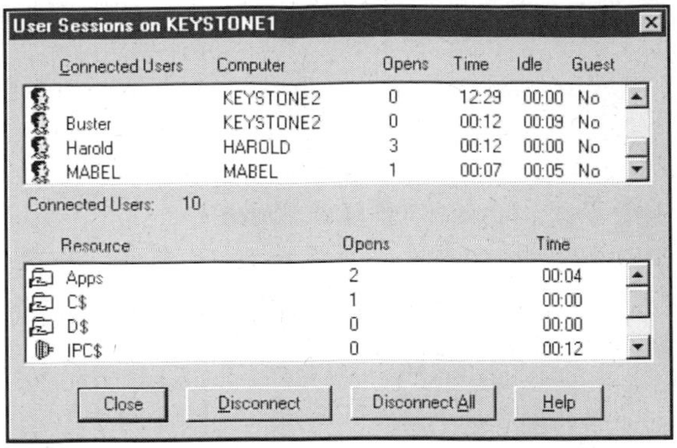

Figure 19.4

The User Sessions dialog box.

For each user, the following information is displayed:

◆ **Opens.** The number of files the user has open.

◆ **Time.** The time that has elapsed since the connection was established.

◆ **Idle.** The time that has elapsed since the user accessed this connection.

◆ **Guest.** Whether the user is logged on as Guest.

◆ **Resource.** Shares to which the user is connected.

Note It is important not to confuse being logged on to a domain with being connected to a computer. Simply being logged on to the domain does not guarantee that a user will appear in this list. The user must be actively connected to a share on this computer to be listed.

It is common for users to create persistent connections to a server. Persistent connections are easily reused each time the user logs on, but in most cases, persistent connections are reestablished in a disconnected state. Until the user actually uses a directory in the connected share (by displaying the directory in File Manager, for example), the connection does not go active and the user doesn't appear in the **C**onnected Users list.

Administrators and Server Managers can take the following actions with connected users displayed in this window:

◆ To disconnect a single user from this computer, select the user in the **C**onnected Users box and click the **D**isconnect button. You will need to confirm this action.

◆ To disconnect all users from this computer, click the Disconnect **A**ll button.

Disconnecting a user does not log the user out. Disconnecting simply closes any resources to which the user is connected. If the user uses the resource again, they are reconnected immediately. To prevent the user from reconnecting, change the access rights before disconnecting.

Viewing and Disconnecting Users Connected to a Share

The **S**hares button reveals the Shared Resources dialog box shown in figure 19.5. In many ways, the Shared Resources dialog box does the opposite duty of the User Sessions dialog box. Instead of displaying users first and then their shares after users are selected, the Shared Resources dialog box enables you to select a share and see who is connected to it. For each share, you see how many users are attached and the path to which the share is assigned.

Figure 19.5

The Shared Resources dialog box for a server.

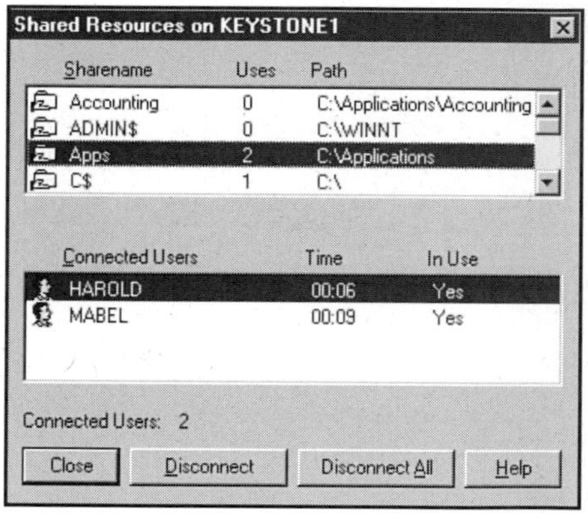

Administrators and Server Managers can take the following actions with connected users displayed in this window:

◆ To disconnect a single user from all connected resources, select the user in the **C**onnected Users box and click the **D**isconnect button. You will need to confirm this action.

◆ To disconnect all users from a share, select the share in the **S**harename box and click the Disconnect **A**ll button.

Disconnecting a user does not log out the user. Disconnecting simply closes any resources to which the user is connected.

Viewing and Closing Open Resources

After a user opens a shared resource, it is listed in the Open Resources dialog box (see fig. 19.6) that is displayed by choosing **I**n Use in the computer Properties dialog box.

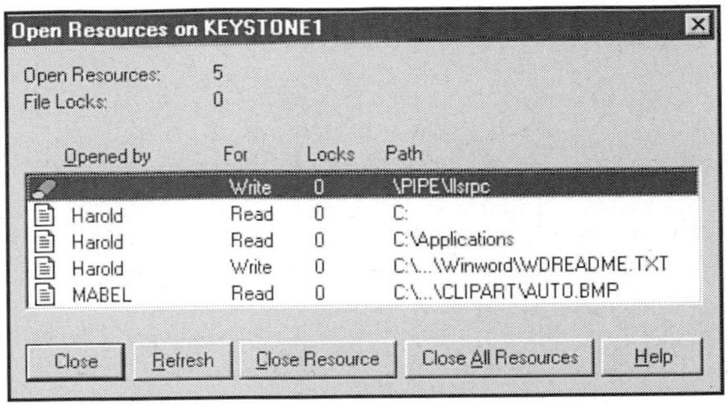

Figure 19.6

The Open Resources dialog box.

Unlike the User Sessions and Shared Resources dialog boxes, the Open Resources dialog box displays resources that are actually opened by users. This information is especially useful when you are attempting to manage an open resource because open resources cannot be copied, deleted, or modified. With the Open Resources dialog box, you can identify users who are holding a resource open so that you can ask them to release it.

If you must force users off a resource, you have two button choices:

◆ **Close Resource.** Closes a single, selected resource.

◆ **Close All Resources.** Forces all resources on the server to close.

Managing Directory Replication

The Directory-Replication feature accessed by the **R**eplication button in the computer Properties dialog box brings up the Directory Replication dialog box. This feature is thoroughly explained in Chapter 22, "Managing Directory Replication."

Configuring Computer Alerts

The **A**lerts button in the computer Properties dialog box reveals the Alerts dialog box shown in figure 19.7. In this box, you determine which users and computers receive administrative alerts that are generated by this computer.

Figure 19.7

*The Alerts
dialog box.*

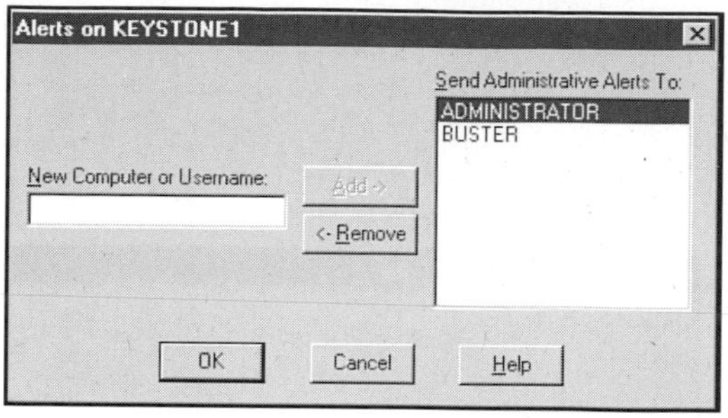

◆ To have a user or computer receive alerts from this computer, type the user or computer name in the **N**ew Computer or Username box and choose **A**dd.

◆ To disable alerts for a user or computer, select the user or computer in the **S**end Administrative Alerts To box and choose **R**emove.

> **Note** The Alerter service must be running for alerts to be sent. See the section "Service Manager" later in this chapter for instructions about starting and stopping services.

Managing Shared Directories

Shared directories can be managed with File Manager or with the Shared Directories dialog box which is accessed by choosing the Shared **D**irectories command from the **C**omputer menu of Server Manager. The Shared Directories dialog box is shown in figure 19.8.

Figure 19.8

*The Server
Manager Shared
Directories
dialog box.*

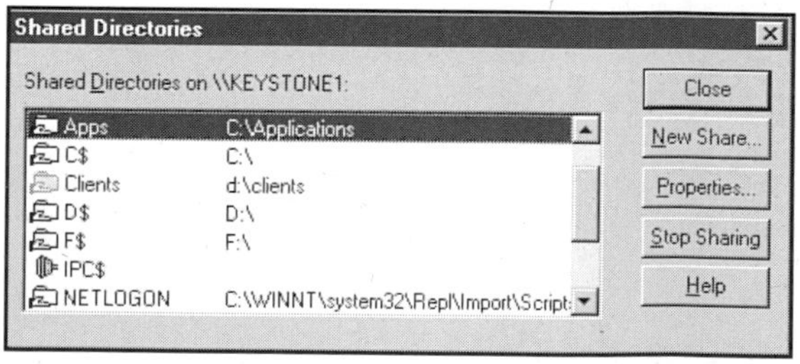

This is the place where you can see *all* the shares on a server. Each share type has a distinctive symbol, as you can see in figure 19.8. You can manage these shares by using techniques similar to those used with Windows NT Explorer and the printer management windows.

Managing Computer Services

You can start the Service Manager by choosing the Services command from the **C**omputer menu. The Service Manager is described later in this chapter in the "Service Manager" section.

Sending Messages to Users

You can choose the Send **M**essage command from the **C**omputer menu to communicate with users on the network. Simply enter the text of the message in the Send Message dialog box, as shown in figure 19.9, and click OK to send the message to all users who are connected to the server. Only connected users receive the message—not all users in the domain.

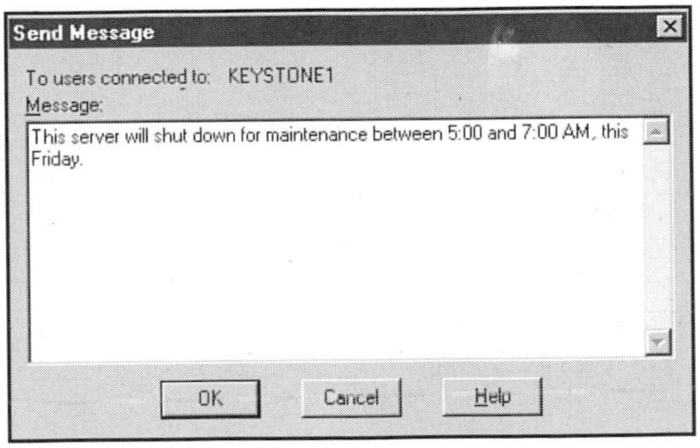

Figure 19.9

Sending a message to connected users.

Users of Windows 3.*x* must be running the Windows Popup program. See Chapter 14, "Using Windows and DOS Clients," for information on configuring this option.

Promoting a Domain Controller

The next option on the **C**omputers menu is Promote to Primary Domain **C**ontroller. Chapter 10 explains how and why this option is used to promote a backup domain controller, in order to enable it to be a primary domain controller.

Synchronizing the Domain Database

On rare occasions, the copies of the domain database on the various backup domain controllers can get out of synchronization with the database on the primary domain controller. Synchronization is performed automatically, but also can be initiated manually.

To synchronize the database of a single BDC, follow these steps:

◆ Select the computer name of the BDC in the Server Manager window.

◆ Choose **S**ynchronize with Primary Domain Controller from the **C**omputer menu.

The database on the BDC is synchronized with the database on the domain PDC.

To synchronize all BDCs in the domain, follow the steps covered in the following exercise:

Synchronizing All Domain BDCs

1. Select the computer name of the domain PDC in the Server Manager window.

2. Choose **S**ynchronize Entire Domain from the **C**omputer menu.

The database is copied from the PDC to all BDCs in the domain, which can be a time-consuming process.

Adding and Removing Domain Computers

Chapter 10 explains how the **A**dd to Domain and **R**emove from Domain commands on the **C**omputer menu are used.

Selecting a Domain to Manage

By default, Server Manager selects your logon domain to manage. You can change to another trusting domain by choosing the **S**elect Domain command from the **C**omputer menu.

The View Menu

Use options in the **V**iew menu to determine which computers are displayed in the Server Manager window. You have the following choices:

◆ **Servers.** Choose to display only Windows NT Servers.

◆ **Workstations.** Choose to display only Windows NT Workstations.

◆ **All.** Choose to display all Windows NT computers.

◆ **Show Domain Members Only.** Choose to limit displayed computers to computers that are members of the current domain.

The Options Menu

Commands in the **O**ptions menu enable you to configure the operation of Server Manager. Two of the commands on this menu follow:

◆ **Save Settings on Exit.** If you want Server Manager to retain your current setup each time you quit, check this option. If you want to have Server Manager restore default settings or savings you saved at an earlier time, remove the check.

◆ **Font.** Use this option to select a new font to be used in Server Manager. A larger or different style of font may make it easier to read the details.

Service Manager

The Service Manager can be started in two ways:

◆ Choosing the **S**ervices command from the Server Manager **C**omputers menu

◆ Double-clicking on the Services icon in the Control Panel

Starting Service Manager displays the Services dialog box, shown in figure 19.10.

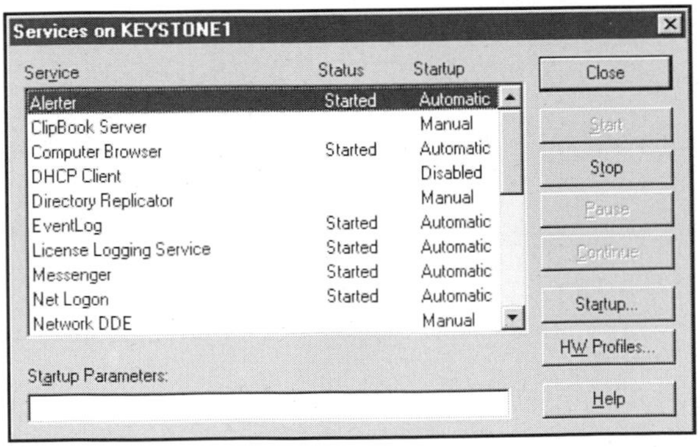

Figure 19.10

The Services dialog box in Server Manager.

Table 19.1 lists the default services for Windows NT Server.

TABLE 19.1
Service Manager Utilities

Service	Function
Alerter	Sends alert messages to designated recipients, as declared in the Alerts dialog box of Server Properties. Requires the Messenger service.
ClipBook Server	Supports ClipBook Viewer, and enables remote ClipBooks to see local pages.
Computer Browser	Maintains resource lists used by applications when browsing the network.
Directory Replicator	Supports directory replication between computers.
EventLog	Writes application, security, and system events in the Event log.
Messenger	Transmits and receives messages sent by the Alerter service or by Administrators.
Net Logon	Authenticates user logons. Synchronizes the domain database among domain controllers in a domain.
Network DDE	Transports and provides security for network DDE conversations.
Network DDE DSDM	The DDE share database manager (DDSM) supervises shared DDE conversations.
NT LM Security Support Provider	Provides security to RPC applications using transports other than named pipes.
Remote Procedure Call (RPC) Locator	Provides RPC name service to distributed applications. RPC servers register names with the RPC Locator Service. RPC clients query the RPC Locator Service for server applications.
Remote Procedure Call (RPC) Service	The RPC subsystem for Windows NT.
Schedule	Enables delayed jobs to be scheduled and supports their execution.
Server	Remote Procedure Call (RPC) support for file, print, and named pipes sharing.

Service	Function
Spooler	Supports print spooler.
UPS	Monitors uninterruptible power supply and responds to UPC conditions.
Workstation	Provides workstation network connectivity.

Starting, Stopping, and Pausing Services

Select a service and choose the **S**tart, S**t**op, or **P**ause button to change the status of the service.

To pass arguments to a service, type them in the St**a**rtup Parameters box before choosing **S**tart.

Note
The Server service supports all remote user connections. Stopping the Server service disconnects all users, including Administrators. Therefore, remote Administrators cannot stop and restart this service; it must be restarted locally.

Before stopping the Server service, use the Send Message command to alert users so that they have the opportunity to close any open files and can prepare to be disconnected.

When the Server service is paused, members of the Administrators and Server Operators groups can establish new connections with the server, but other users cannot.

Some services require a user name or service account to start. You can specify a service account under the startup options. Make sure this account has the Logon as Service privilege. These privileges can be set from the User Manager for Domains under the Policies, User Rights menu.

Configuring Services

Follow the steps in the following exercise to define the characteristics of a service:

Configuring Services

1. Select a service in the Services window.

2. Choose Sta**r**tup to display the Service startup dialog box shown in figure 19.11.

Figure 19.11

The Service startup dialog box.

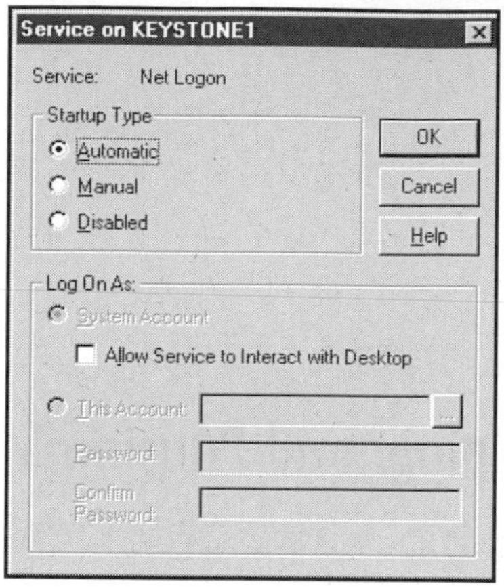

```
Service on KEYSTONE1                          [x]
  Service:     Net Logon
 ┌Startup Type──────────────┐
 │  ⊙ Automatic             │        ┌────────┐
 │  ○ Manual                │        │   OK   │
 │  ○ Disabled              │        └────────┘
 └──────────────────────────┘        ┌────────┐
                                      │ Cancel │
 ┌Log On As:────────────────────────┐└────────┘
 │  ⊙ System Account                 │┌────────┐
 │    □ Allow Service to Interact with Desktop
 │                                   ││  Help  │
 │  ○ This Account:  [          ] [..]└────────┘
 │     Password:     [            ]  │
 │     Confirm       [            ]  │
 │     Password:                     │
 └───────────────────────────────────┘
```

3. Choose the service startup type from the following:

   ◆ **Automatic.** The service starts when the server is booted.

   ◆ **Manual.** The service must be started manually from the Service dialog box.

   ◆ **Disabled.** The service cannot be started.

4. Choose **S**ystem Account if the service should log on using the system account. This setting is used for almost all services.

5. Choose **T**his Account to have the service log on with a user account. The Directory Replicator and Schedule services log on using other accounts as well as Back-Office services. See Chapter 18, "Backing Up Files," for information about setting up the Schedule service. See Chapter 22 for information about setting up the Directory Replicator service and Part V, "Exploring the BackOffice Suite," for more BackOffice information.

   If **T**his Account has been chosen, enter a user account and passwords in the appropriate boxes.

6. Click OK.

7. Start the service.

Service startup settings take effect only when the service is started. A running service must be stopped and restarted if startup settings change.

Chapter 18 shows an interesting use of the Schedule service, which illustrates some advanced configuration characteristics that apply to some services. In that chapter, you can see how the Schedule service can be made to log on with a user account, enabling it to perform tasks in the background.

The System Utility

Double-clicking on the System icon in the Control Panel reveals the System Properties dialog box shown in figure 19.12. This window has six tabs that are used to configure several Windows NT settings.

Environment

The Environment tab is shown in figure 19.12. Windows NT is much less dependent on environment variables than is Windows 3.x or DOS. Nevertheless, a few environment variables are maintained. In fact, two sets are available:

◆ **System variables.** Used by the system regardless of the user who is logged on.

◆ **User variables.** Can be customized for each user.

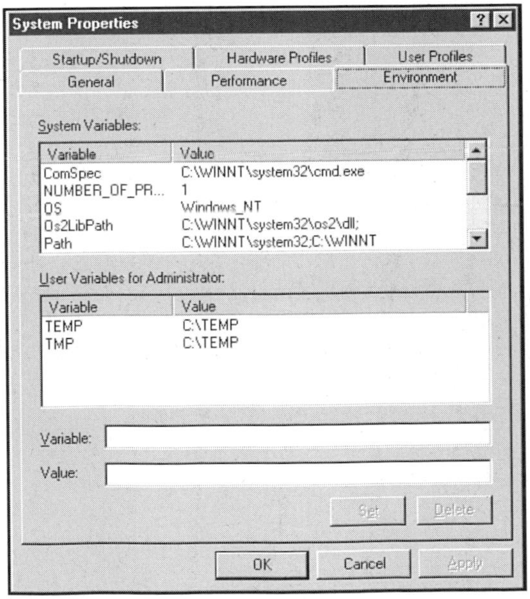

Figure 19.12

The Environment tab of the System utility.

To delete a variable, select the variable and click the **D**elete button.

To add an environment variable, follow the steps in the following exercise:

Adding an Environment Variable

1. Select an entry in the Ṣystem Variables or the Ụser Variables for Administrator box.

2. Enter the variable name in the Ṿariable box.

3. Enter a value for the variable in the Vaḷue box.

4. Click the Ṣet button.

To edit an environment variable, follow the steps in the following exercise:

Editing an Environment Variable

1. Select the variable.

2. Change the value in the Vaḷue box.

3. Click the Ṣet button.

Changes made to system environment variables take effect the next time the computer is started.

Changes made to user environment variables take effect the next time the user logs on to the computer.

If an Autoexec.bat file is present any variable set in the file will be read first. The order that variables are read indicates which value overrides the others.

1. Autoexec.bat

2. System variables

3. User variables

Note It is instructive to select a system environment variable and observe the value in the Vaḷue box. Notice that the values make extensive use of Windows NT variables such as %SystemRoot%.

Use extreme caution when changing system environment variables. Most are vital to the proper functioning of Windows NT.

Users can only change their user variable, not system variables.

General Properties

The General tab, shown in figure 19.13, is informational only, displaying information about the operating system, the registered owner, and the computer.

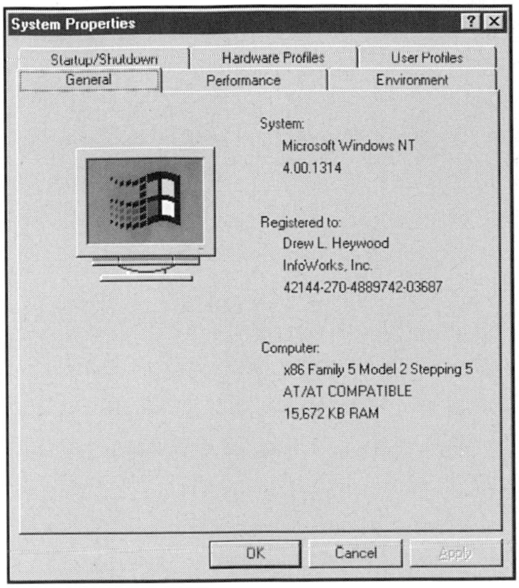

Figure 19.13

The General tab of the System utility.

Hardware Profiles

The Hardware Profiles tab supports the capability of Windows NT to define multiple hardware profiles, which may be selected when the system is booted. Hardware profiles enable a user to, for example, have one configuration for a laptop PC when it is docked at a desk and another configuration when the computer is undocked and mobile.

Hardware profiles are not very applicable to network servers and are not considered in this book.

User Profiles

The User Profiles tab is used to copy user profiles, as described in Chapter 15, "Using Windows NT Clients."

Performance

The Performance tab is shown in figure 19.14. This tab has one setting and enables you to access the window where virtual memory is configured.

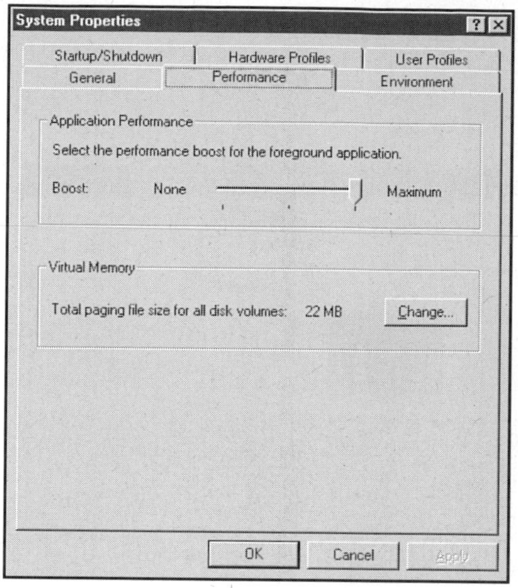

Figure 19.14

The Performance tab of the System utility.

The Application Performance setting determines the responsiveness of the foreground Windows application, that is, of the application whose window has the focus. Set the Boost to Maximum if the foreground application should be given the greatest share of available processing. Set the Boost to Minimum if you require background windows to receive improved service. If, for example, you are programming and want to compile programs in the background, you would lower the Boost setting to ensure that compilation receives reasonable access to the processor.

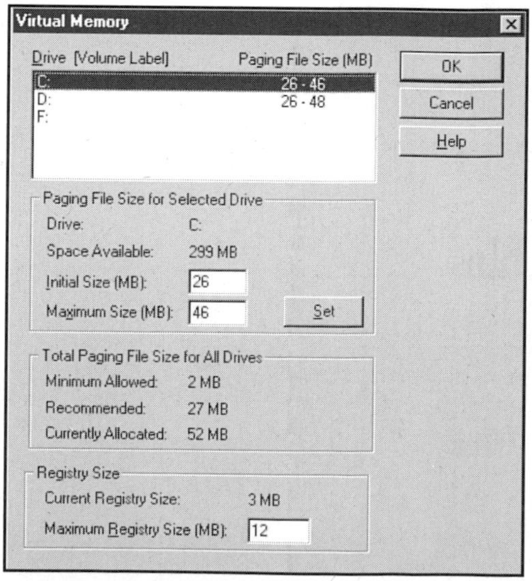

Figure 19.15

Configuring Windows NT virtual memory.

The **C**hange button in the Virtual Memory area opens the Virtual Memory dialog box shown in figure 19.15. Windows NT uses the virtual memory capability of Intel 386 and later processors to significantly increase the memory that is available to the operating system. Virtual memory uses disk storage to simulate RAM—a process called *paging*, which uses a *paging file* to create virtual memory. Although virtual memory is much slower than RAM, it is much better to have slow memory than to run out.

Microsoft recommends that you create a paging file for each volume. Depending on the capabilities of the computer hard drive controller, multiple paging files can enhance virtual memory performance.

A paging file is created automatically when the system disk is created. Paging files for other disks must be created manually. A minimum and maximum size is declared for each paging file.

Configuring Virtual Memory

To create or modify the paging file for a volume, follow the steps in the following exercise:

Creating and Modifying the Paging File

1. Select a volume in the **D**rive box.

2. Enter the paging file parameters in the Paging File Size for Selected Drive box. A recommended total value is displayed in the Total Paging File Size for All Drives box.

3. Click the **S**et button to save the changes.

4. Restart the system to have the changes go into effect.

Note　Virtual memory is stored in a file named pagefile.sys, which cannot be deleted under Windows NT. If the file is deleted under another operating system, it is re-created when Windows NT is restarted.

Limiting Registry Size

The Virtual Memory dialog box also includes the Maximum **R**egistry Size field that is used to set a limit to the growth of the Registry, and sets an upper bound both for the page pool (in RAM) and for the Registry disk space. This parameter does not allocate space, and space will be used only as required. Also, this parameter does not guarantee that the memory specified will be available.

Startup/Shutdown Properties

The Startup/Shutdown tab, shown in figure 19.16, contains two categories of settings: System Startup and Recovery.

Figure 19.16

*Configuring
startup and
shutdown
properties.*

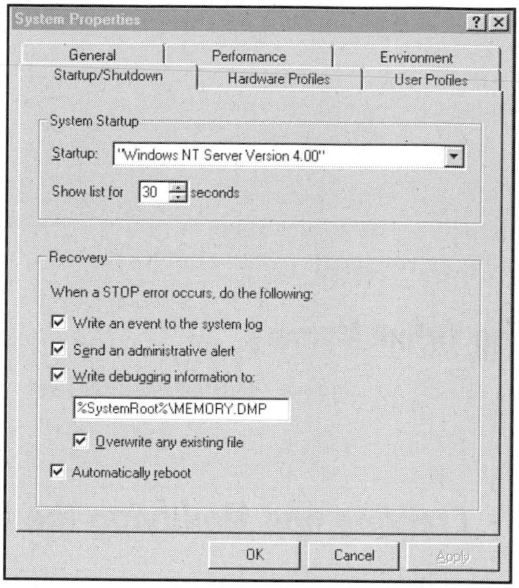

Specifying Startup Options

The properties in the System Startup area determine two options in the boot.ini file. The **S**tartup property determines which startup option in the boot.ini file will be the default. The structure of the boot.ini file was described in Chapter 7, "Installing Windows NT Server." Each option in the [operating systems] section of the boot.ini file appears as a choice in the **S**tartup field.

To specify the time that the startup configuration menu is displayed, edit the time in the Show list **f**or spin box. It is not recommended that you set this value to 0 because that will make it difficult to start the computer in default VGA mode.

Specifying Recovery Options

When Windows NT Server encounters a critical error, called a *STOP error* or a *fatal system error*, the system records an event in the System log, transmits an Administrator alert, and optionally reboots itself. Because Windows NT Server reboots itself without waiting for an Administrator to intervene, downtime is reduced.

The Recovery box includes several fields that determine what will happen when a STOP error occurs. The fields in this box are as follows:

◆ **Write an event to the system log.** The system log can be examined by using the Event Viewer, which is described later in this chapter.

◆ **Send an administrative alert.** Check this option if administrators should receive an alert message through the network.

◆ **Write debugging information to *file name.*** Debugging can assist Microsoft with the diagnosis of your problem. If you select this option, you must specify a file name. By default NT will use %SystcmRoot%\MEMORY.DMP.

◆ **Overwrite any existing file.** If this option is checked, an existing debugging file will be overwritten if a new STOP error occurs. If you have a lot of crashes you may not want this feature on. This way you can compare dump files. Make sure to delete or move the files manually or your hard drive will fill up very fast.

◆ **Automatically reboot.** Check this option if the server should attempt to reboot after STOP error actions have been executed.

Using Windows NT Diagnostics

The Windows NT Diagnostics (WINMSD) program enables you to observe configuration information for some features of the server hardware and software. It isn't a full-blown diagnostics program. In particular, Windows NT Diagnostics is not capable of testing hardware. For that, you should obtain a third party program. Third party programs generally are oriented around DOS, however, so you would need to bring the server down to perform any diagnostics. Windows NT Diagnostics is a Windows NT program that can be run while the server is operating and, of course, it is free.

The Windows NT Diagnostics icon is not installed in the Start menu, although you can do so if you want. Start the program by executing the command WINMSD at the Run prompt in the Start menu. When you run the utility, you will see the window shown in figure 19.17. This window has nine tabs that access different categories of data.

The following sections cover entries on the various tabs.

Version

The Version tab (refer to fig. 19.17) describes the processor, the Windows NT serial number, and the registered owner.

System

The System tab (see fig. 19.18) describes the BIOS version and describes the microprocessor in greater detail. In the figure, an x86 Family 5 CPU describes an Intcl Pentium processor.

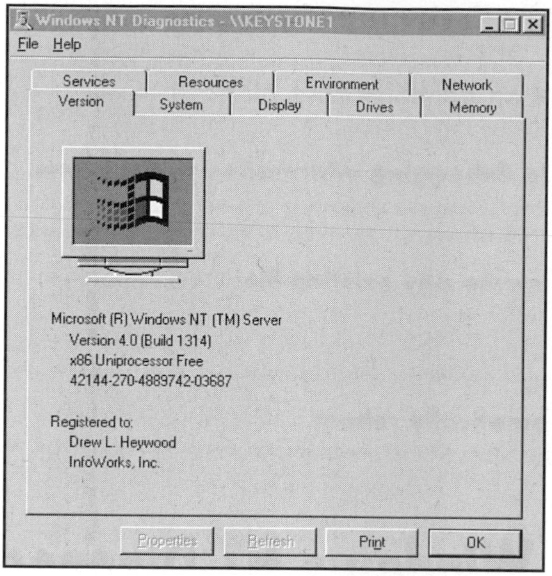

Figure 19.17

The main window of the Windows NT Diagnostics dialog box.

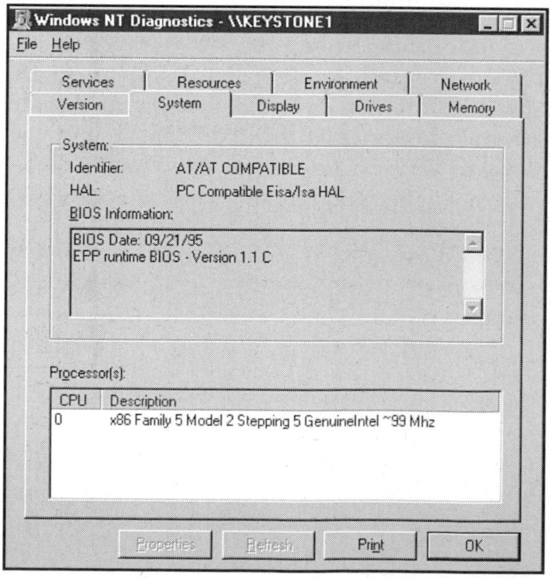

Figure 19.18

The System information tab.

The item labeled "HAL" refers to the *Hardware Abstraction Layer*, the component of Windows NT that interfaces the operating system to the computer hardware. Although the operating system code remains the same from platform to platform, a HAL must be designed for each type of computer hardware. In this case, the HAL is designed for a PC-compatible (x86).

Display

The Display tab describes the video adapter, current video settings, and the video driver that is installed.

Drives

The Drives tab displays a hierarchy consisting of all disk drives on the system. Figure 19.19 shows the basic display, opened to reveal the entries for the hard drives. Two buttons enable you to determine the order in which drives will be listed:

◆ Drives by type

◆ Drives by letter

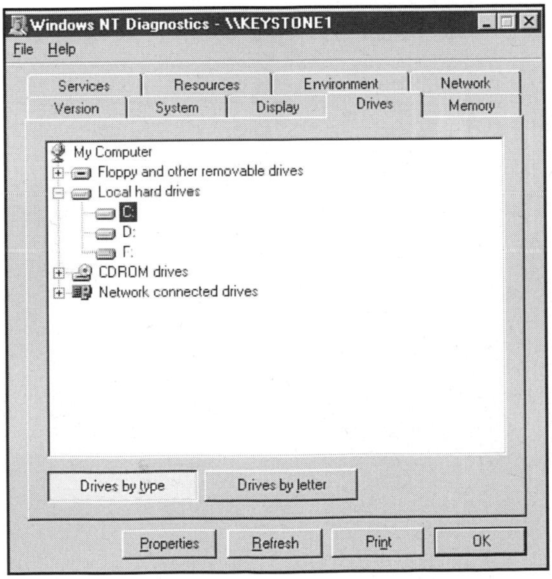

Figure 19.19

Drives listed in the Drives tab.

If you open a drive entry, you are shown the properties for that device. Figure 19.20 shows the details for the C drive. The General tab (see fig. 19.20) describes the storage utilization, while the File System tab (see fig. 19.21) describes the file system with which the drive is formatted.

NTFS is the only file system in which Unicode characters are allowed in file names. *Unicode* is a means of representing many different character sets so that applications can be written to support languages that could not be comprehended by ASCII.

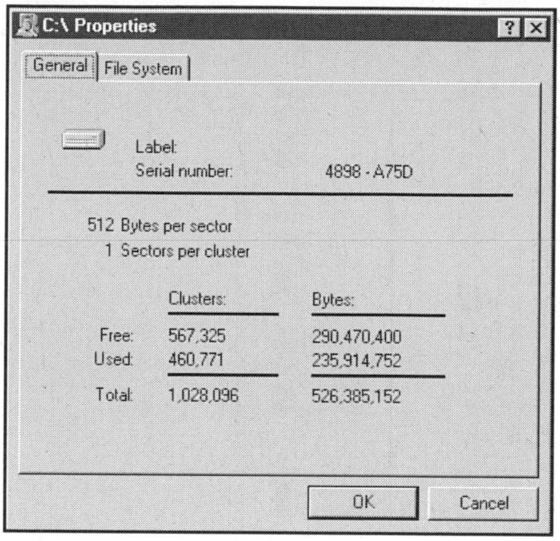

Figure 19.20

*Properties of a
hard disk.*

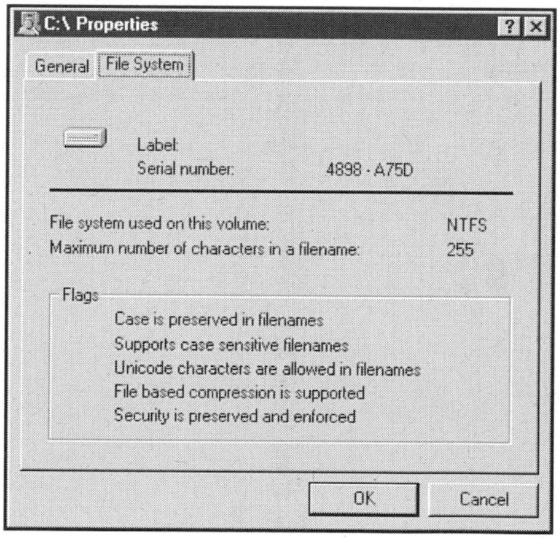

Figure 19.21

*File system
properties of
a hard disk.*

Memory

The Memory tab shows details of the system memory including available memory and memory in use by various resources. As figure 19.22 shows, the Memory tab is a good way to keep track of the use of physical and virtual memory to determine whether memory should be added or the pagefile size should be increased. You can also determine pagefile location and sizes.

Services

The Services tab displays listings of all services and devices that are installed on the computer. The display in figure 19.23 lists services. Click the **D**evices button to switch to a listing of devices.

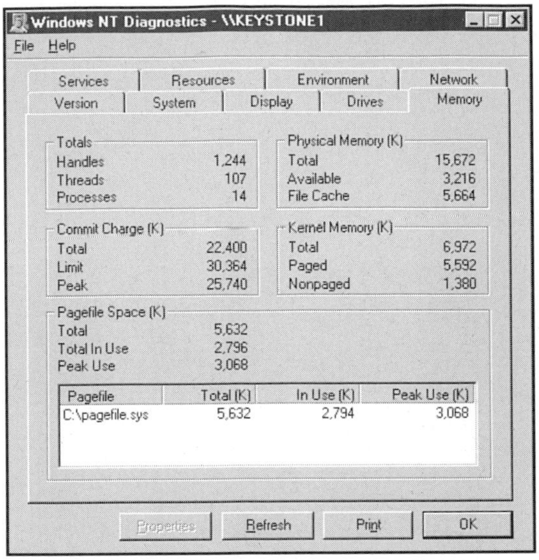

Figure 19.22

Memory diagnostic information.

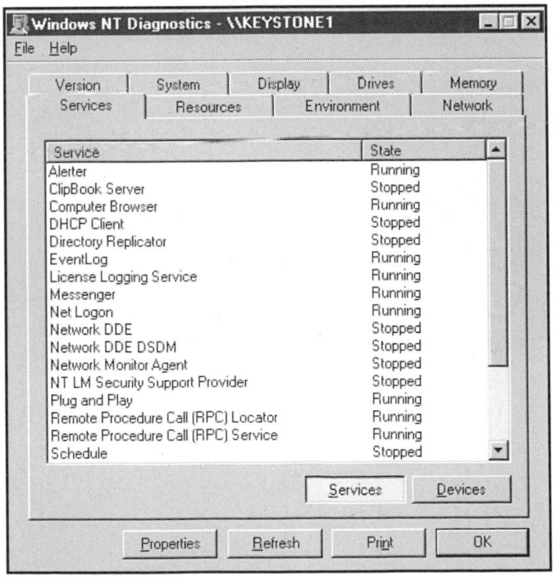

Figure 19.23

Services in the Services tab.

You can double-click any service or device to obtain more detail. Figure 19.24 shows properties for the Net Logon service. The Dependencies tab lists any other services that this service depends on for its operation.

Figure 19.24

*Properties of the
Net Logon service.*

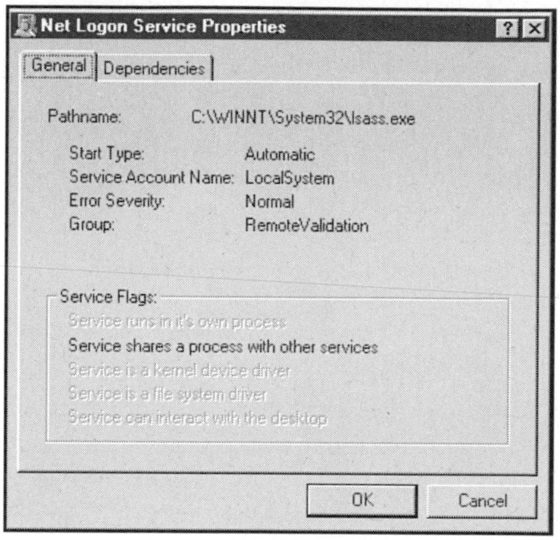

Resources

The Resources tab (see fig. 19.25) provides information about various characteristics of hardware that has been added to the Windows NT configuration. Unlike Windows 95, Windows NT does not automatically detect most devices. Devices are added to the configuration during installation and manually by using various Control Panel utilities. Therefore, hardware may be present in the system that is not reported in this list. A sound card that has not been added to the configuration, for example, will not be reported in this list.

Figure 19.25

*Interrupts
listed in the
Resources tab.*

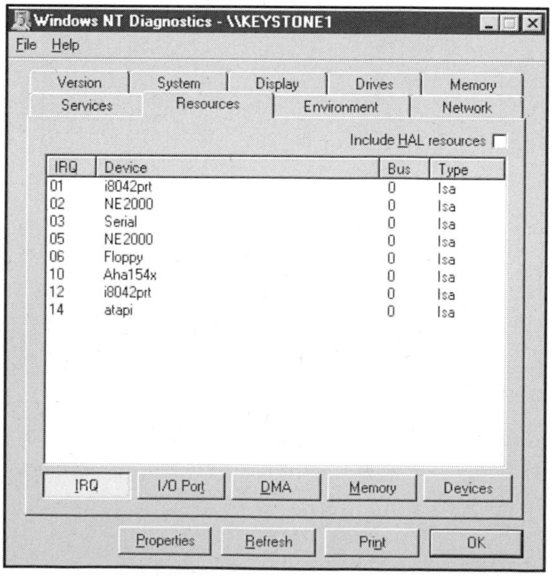

Five buttons display different categories of information. Use the information in these lists to identify available resources and to determine when resource conflicts exist:

◆ **IRQ.** Displays the IRQ, bus, and bus type for each installed device, as shown in figure 19.25.

◆ **I/O Port.** Displays the I/O port addresses associated with installed devices.

◆ **DMA.** Displays the DMA channel, port, bus, and bus type for any installed DMA-driven device.

◆ **Memory.** Displays any blocks of memory that have been dedicated to specific hardware devices.

◆ **Devices.** Lists the installed hardware devices.

You can display properties for all the entries in the five categories by selecting an entry and choosing **P**roperties. Figure 19.26 shows the properties for the Adaptek Aha154x SCSI adapter installed in this computer. First, the De**v**ices button was chosen to list installed hardware, and then **P**roperties was chosen to produce the window shown in the figure.

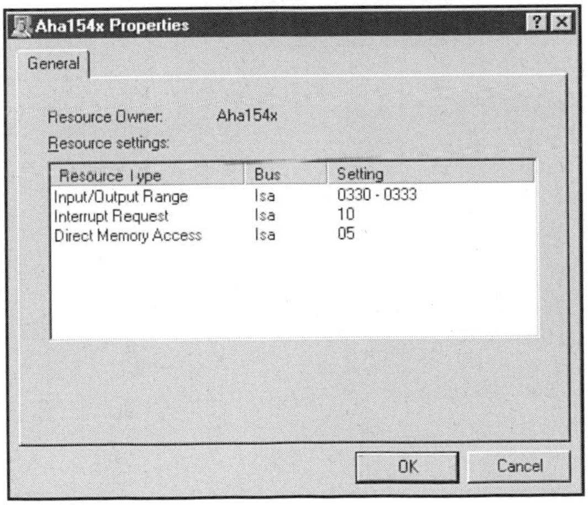

Figure 19.26

Properties for a device.

Environment

The Environment tab lists the environment variables that are in memory (see fig. 19.27). Click the **S**ystem button to display system variables, and click the **L**ocal User button to display variables for the currently logged-on user.

Network

The Network tab displays information that is not readily available elsewhere (see fig. 19.28). It is extremely useful for you to examine this screen as you configure and reconfigure your server. If you are running a service in the background with its own logon name, it appears as a logon count in the Network information box, for example.

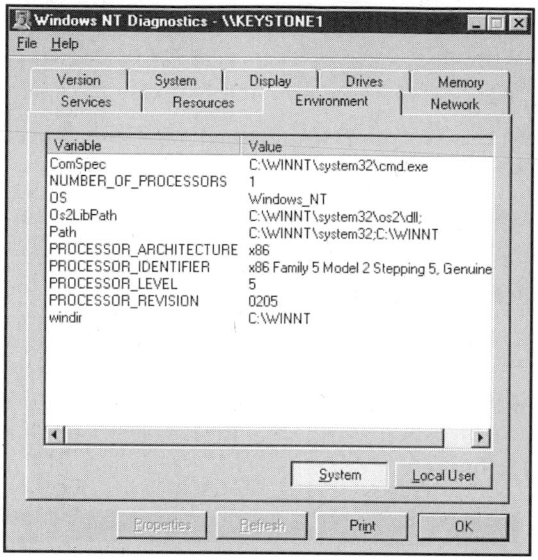

Figure 19.27

Environment variables.

Figure 19.28

Network information.

Four buttons access different categories of information:

◆ **General.** This button lists information about the computer's network configuration and currently logged-on users.

◆ **Transports.** This gives descriptions about the transport protocol layers that are installed along with configuration information.

◆ **Settings.** Shows the current values of numerous Windows NT Server settings.

◆ **Statistics.** WINMSD keeps a running total of dozens of events that occur as the server operates. Of particular interest are various reports of errors. If you see that the Network Errors statistic is climbing, for example, you might suspect a problem in your network hardware or cabling.

Auditing Files and Printers

Auditing is a useful function in any large LAN. Auditing is a way of gathering statistics about how resources are being used. More important, auditing is a way to determine who is responsible if resources are being misused. As LANs take on increasingly critical tasks, it becomes more desirable to implement auditing.

Windows NT Server enables you to audit the use of domains, files, directories, and printers.

> **Note**   You must be logged on as a member of the Administrators group to audit files and directories.

Auditing Domains

Domain auditing is configured by using User Manager for Domains. In some ways, domain auditing is the most important auditing category, particularly if your network is part of a wide area network. WANs—particularly when they participate in the Internet—are more vulnerable to intruders than networks that are confined to a company's own buildings. Domain auditing can tell you whether large numbers of attempted security breeches are taking place, which might indicate that someone is trying to break into your system.

To define the audit policy for a domain, follow the steps in the following exercise:

Defining the Audit Policy

1. Open User Manager for Domains.

2. Choose the **S**elect Domain command from the **U**ser menu to select the domain to be audited.

3. Choose the Au**d**it command from the **P**olicies menu to display the Audit Policy dialog box shown in figure 19.29.

Figure 19.29

Setting the domain audit policy.

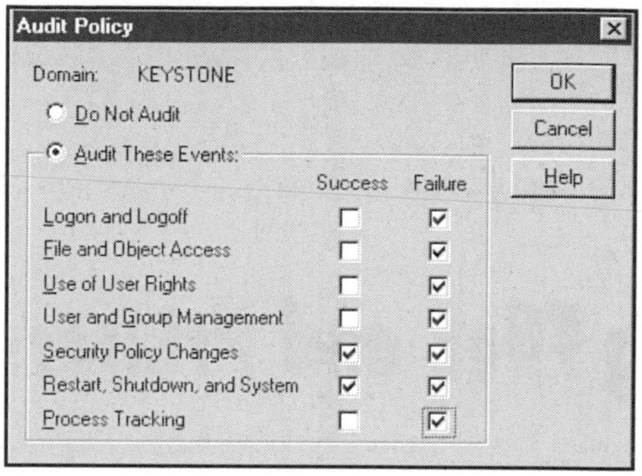

4. Choose **A**udit These Events to activate auditing for the domain.

5. Check the events to be audited.

6. Click the OK to save the auditing policy.

The following domain events can be audited:

◆ **Logon and Logoff.** A user logs on, logs off, or makes a connection through the network.

◆ **File and Object Access.** A directory or file was accessed that had been configured for auditing in File Manager. A print job was sent to a printer that was configured for auditing in Print Manager. This option must be turned on if any file auditing is to take place.

◆ **Use of User Rights.** Use of a user right apart from rights related to logging on or off. A user right that can be audited is something like: Who changed the server's clock over the weekend?

◆ **User and Group Management.** The following activities are audited with respect to user accounts or groups: creation, changing, deleting, renaming, disabling or enabling, and password changes.

◆ **Security Policy Changes.** Any change to user rights, audit, or trust relationships policies.

◆ **Restart, Shutdown, and System.** Shutting down or restarting the server. Any action that affects system security or the security log.

◆ **Process Tracking.** Program activation, process exit, handle duplication, and indirect object access.

Objective C.1

> **Tip**
>
> When you are setting up auditing, audit the success and failure of everything you are tracking. This makes it easy to determine that you have set up your auditing to track the resources you want. When you are confident that you are tracking the correct resources, pare back the audited events to the events you really want to know about.

Auditing Directories and Files

The auditing of directories and files is managed through File Manager. Setting up auditing is a simple matter of declaring the groups or users whose use of a file or directory will be audited along with the events to be audited. Auditing is available only for NTFS volumes.

To view or change auditing for a directory or file, follow the steps in the following exercise:

Auditing a Directory or File

1. Right-click the directory or file to be audited in Windows NT Explorer.

2. Choose **P**roperties from the **O**ption menu and open the Security tab.

3. Choose **A**uditing from the Security tab to display the Directory Auditing dialog box shown in figure 19.30.

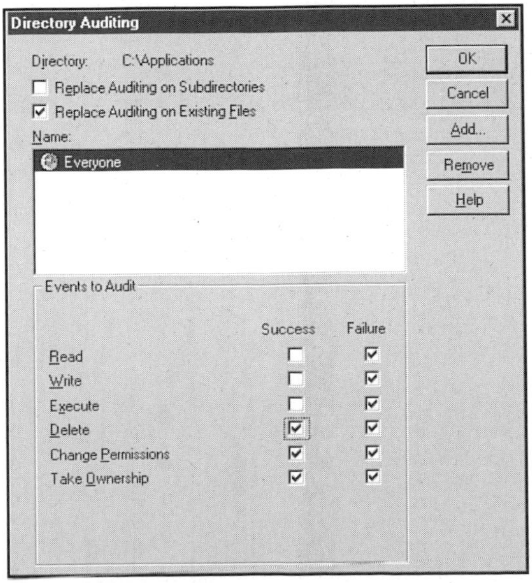

Figure 19.30

Auditing a directory.

4. Check **R**eplace Auditing on Subdirectories if all subdirectories of this directory are to be audited in the same fashion.

5. Check Replace Auditing on Existing **F**iles if existing files should be audited in the same fashion. If this box is not checked, auditing affects only the directory.

6. To add a user or group, choose the **A**dd button to display a Browse list. Select each name to be added in the Browse list and choose **A**dd. Click OK when all desired names have been added. When you return to the Auditing window, the names are listed in the **N**ame box.

7. To remove a user or group, select the entry in the **N**ame box and click the Re**m**ove button.

8. For each event that is to be audited, check the appropriate box in the Events to Audit box.

9. Click OK to save the auditing information.

Tables 19.2 and 19.3 summarize the actions that are audited by each event that can be checked in the Auditing dialog box.

Table 19.2

Actions audited by directory audit events.

	Read	Write	Execute	Delete	Change Permissions	Take Ownership
Display attributes	●	○	●	○	○	○
Display filenames	●	○	○	○	○	○
Change attributes	○	●	○	○	○	○
Create subdirectories and files	○	●	○	○	○	○
Go to a subdirectory	○	○	●	○	○	○
Display owner and permissions	●	●	●	○	○	○
Delete directory	○	○	○	●	○	○
Change directory permissions	○	○	○	○	●	○
Change directory ownership	○	○	○	○	○	●

Table 19.3

Actions audited by file audit events..

	Read	Write	Execute	Delete	Change Permissions	Take Ownership
Display file attributes	●	○	●	○	○	○
Read file data	●	○	○	○	○	○
Display owner and permissions	●	●	●	○	○	○
Change file attributes	○	●	○	○	○	○
Change file attributes	○	●	○	○	○	○
Change file data	○	○	●	○	○	○
Execute program file	○	○	○	●	○	○
Change file permissions	○	○	○	○	●	○
Change file ownership	○	○	○	○	○	●

Note Directory and file events are audited only if you have activated **F**ile and Object Access auditing in the Audit Policy for the domain. The procedure for setting the domain audit policy is described in the preceding section.

Auditing Printers

Printing is a service that often is abused. If you don't want users printing football pools on the $10,000 color printer, or if you want to know which user is going through all those reams of paper, printer auditing might give you the support you need.

Printer auditing is configured with Print Manager. To configure auditing for a printer, follow the steps in the following exercise:

Configuring Printer Auditing

1. Open the printer window for the printer to be audited.

2. Choose the P**r**operties command from the **P**rinter menu and select the Security tab.

3. Choose **A**uditing from the Security tab. The Printer Auditing dialog box appears, as shown in figure 19.31.

4. To add a user or group, click the **A**dd button to display a Browse list. Select each name to be added in the Browse list and click the Add button. Click OK when all desired names have been added. When you return to the Auditing window, the names are listed in the **N**ame box.

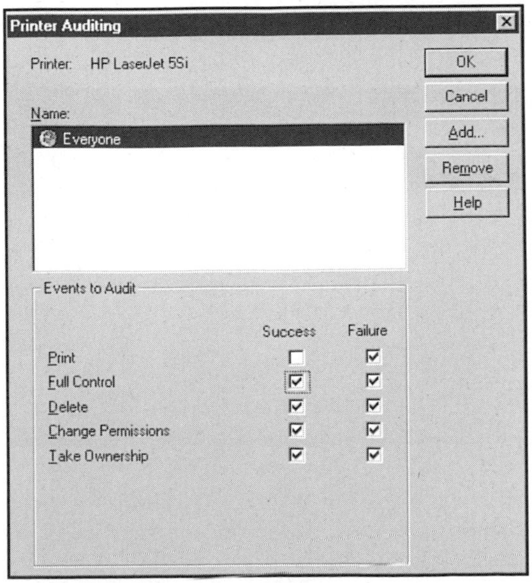

Figure 19.31

Configuring printer auditing.

5. To remove a user or group, select the entry in the Name box and click the Remove button.
6. For each event that is to be audited, check the appropriate box in the Events to Audit box.
7. Click OK to save the auditing information.

The printer events that can be audited are:

- **Print.** Printing documents.
- **Full Control.** Changing document job settings. Pausing, restarting, moving, and deleting documents.
- **Delete.** Deleting a printer.
- **Change Permissions.** Changing printer permissions.
- **Take Ownership.** Taking ownership of a printer.

Note Printer events are audited only if you have activated File and Object Access auditing in the Audit Policy for the domain. The procedure for setting the domain audit policy is described in the previous section "Auditing Domains."

Reviewing the Security Log

All the auditing facilities record their messages in the Security log, which is examined by using the Event Viewer. Figure 19.32 shows an example of Security log entries. Use of the Event Viewer is described in the following section.

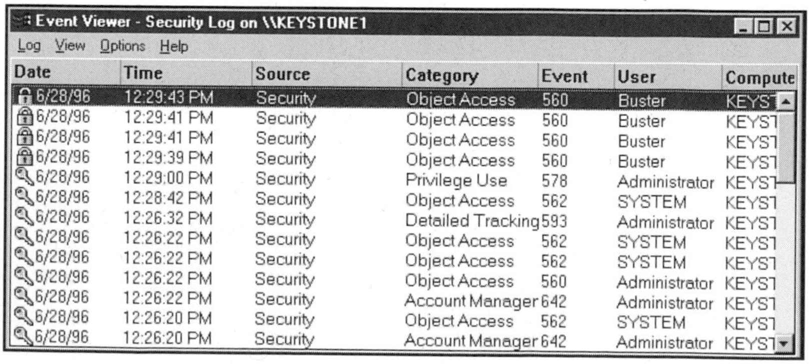
Event Viewer - Security Log on \\KEYSTONE1

Log View Options Help

Date	Time	Source	Category	Event	User	Compute
6/28/96	12:29:43 PM	Security	Object Access	560	Buster	KEYS1
6/28/96	12:29:41 PM	Security	Object Access	560	Buster	KEYS1
6/28/96	12:29:41 PM	Security	Object Access	560	Buster	KEYS1
6/28/96	12:29:39 PM	Security	Object Access	560	Buster	KEYS1
6/28/96	12:29:00 PM	Security	Privilege Use	578	Administrator	KEYS1
6/28/96	12:28:42 PM	Security	Object Access	562	SYSTEM	KEYS1
6/28/96	12:26:32 PM	Security	Detailed Tracking	593	Administrator	KEYS1
6/28/96	12:26:22 PM	Security	Object Access	562	SYSTEM	KEYS1
6/28/96	12:26:22 PM	Security	Object Access	562	SYSTEM	KEYS1
6/28/96	12:26:22 PM	Security	Object Access	560	Administrator	KEYS1
6/28/96	12:26:22 PM	Security	Account Manager	642	Administrator	KEYS1
6/28/96	12:26:20 PM	Security	Object Access	562	SYSTEM	KEYS1
6/28/96	12:26:20 PM	Security	Account Manager	642	Administrator	KEYS1

Figure 19.32 *Viewing the Security log on Event Viewer.*

Security log entries are identified with two icons. A key designates a successful action, and a lock designates an unsuccessful action. In the figure, the user BUSTER attempted an action for which he did not have the required permissions, resulting in several entries in the Security log.

Event Viewer

The Event Viewer is used to examine three Windows NT Server logs:

◆ **System log.** Records events logged by the Windows NT system.

◆ **Application log.** Records events logged by applications. A Windows NT Server-aware application, for example, might log a message when a file error is encountered.

◆ **Security log.** Records events that have been selected for auditing in User Manager for Domains, File Manager, or Print Manager.

Viewing Event Logs

To view a log, choose System, Security, or Application from the Log menu of the Event Viewer. Figure 19.33 shows an example of a System log.

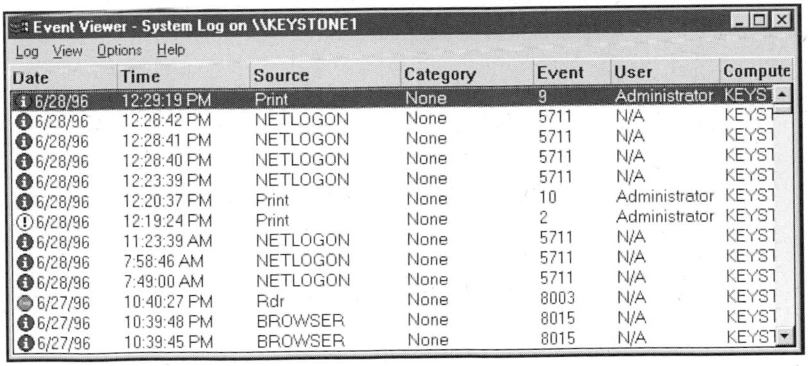

Figure 19.33

Events in the System log.

For each entry, you see the following information in addition to the date and time when the log entry was recorded:

◆ **Source.** The software that logged the event—either an application name or a component of Windows NT.

◆ **Category.** An event classification.

◆ **Event.** Each source is assigned a unique number, which appears in this column.

◆ **User.** The user name of the account that was logged in when the event was logged.

◆ **Computer.** The computer name where the event occurred.

To make it easy to scan events visually, each event is labeled with an icon. The icons in the event logs are: information, warning, critical error, success audit, and failure audit.

Here are more complete descriptions of the events:

◆ **Information.** Infrequent significant events that describe the successful operation of Windows NT Server services.

◆ **Warning.** Non-critical errors that may predict future problems.

◆ **Critical Error.** Data loss or failure of major functions.

◆ **Success Audit.** Audit events that are associated with the successful execution of an action.

◆ **Failure Audit.** Audit events that are associated with the unsuccessful execution of an action.

You can display a detailed view of each event by double-clicking the event entry. An example of a detailed display is shown in figure 19.34.

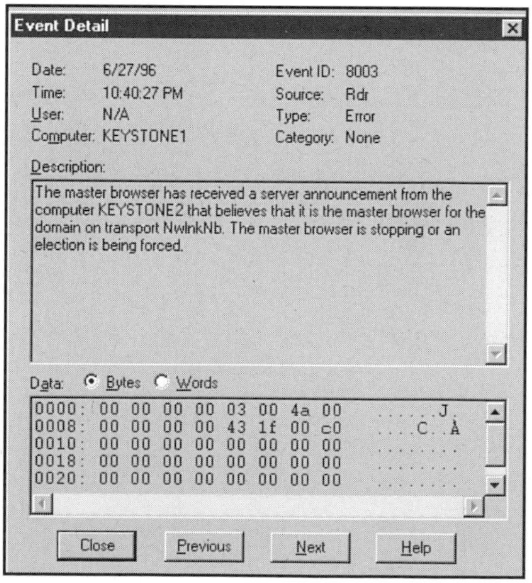

Figure 19.34

Detailed information about an event.

Configuring Event Log Options

The Event Log Settings dialog box enables you to determine how large log files will grow (see fig. 19.35). Unless they are properly controlled, log files can grow to a significant percentage of server file capacity.

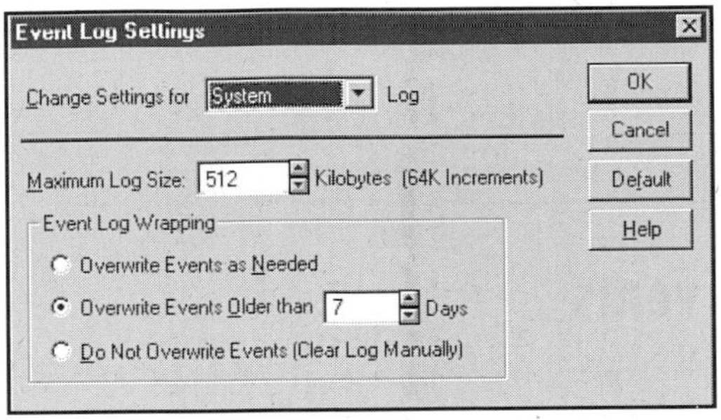

Figure 19.35

The Event Log Settings dialog box.

To configure event log settings, follow the steps in the following exercise:

Configuring Event Log Settings

1. Choose Log Settings from the **L**og menu to access the Event Log Settings dialog box.

2. Select a log in the **C**hange Settings for Log box.

3. Enter a maximum size in the **M**aximum Log Size box. If the log reaches this size and you have not specified a means of trimming old records, event logging ceases.

4. To have new events overwrite old events after the log is full, choose Overwrite Events as **N**eeded.

5. To limit the log by discarding old records, choose Overwrite Events **O**lder than… Days and specify a number in the box. If logs will be archived weekly, a good choice is 7 days.

6. To clear the log manually, choose **D**o Not Overwrite Events (Clear Log Manually). Avoid using this option unless there are events you cannot afford to miss. Security on a critical server might be an example of such information.

7. Click OK after the Event log settings are entered.

Clearing a Log

To clear an Event log, follow the steps in the following exercise:

Clearing an Event Log

1. Select the log to be cleared from the **L**og menu.

2. Choose C**l**ear All Events from the **L**og menu. You are asked to verify your decision to clear the log.

Viewing Specific Events

Event Viewer has several tools that enable you to more easily identify specific events. You can change the order for sorting events and add filters to determine which events are displayed.

Sorting Events

To change the sorting order for events, choose either **N**ewest First or **O**ldest First from the **V**iew menu.

Filtering Events

Event logs can grow to be quite large, and you might find yourself wanting to limit the events that are displayed, or limiting yourself to a specific type of event to enable you to focus on a problem. Event Viewer enables you to filter events in a wide variety of ways.

To filter events, follow the steps in the following exercise:

Filtering Events

1. Choose Fi**l**ter Events from the **V**iew menu to display the Filter dialog box shown in figure 19.36.

2. To restore default filters, choose **C**lear.

3. Specify the filters to be used. The various filters are discussed in the following list.

4. Click OK to activate the filters.

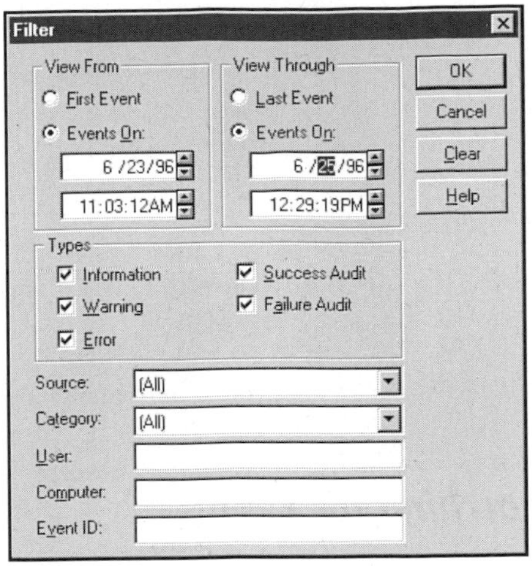

Figure 19.36

Filtering Event Viewer events.

The following event filters can be selected:

◆ **View From.** Specifies a date of the oldest records that should be displayed. Choose First Event to display events starting from the beginning of the log. Choose Events On to start displaying events occurring on the specified day.

◆ **View Through.** Specifies a date of the newest records that should be displayed. Choose Last Event to display events through the end of the log. Choose Events On to display events through the specified day.

◆ **Information.** Infrequent significant events that describe successful operation of Windows NT Server services.

◆ **Warning.** Non-critical errors that may predict future problems.

◆ **Error.** Critical errors. Data loss or failure of major functions.

◆ **Success Audit.** Audit events that are associated with the successful execution of an action.

◆ **Failure Audit.** Audit events that are associated with the unsuccessful execution of an action.

◆ **Source.** The application, computer, or driver that originated the log entry.

◆ **Category.** Event categories specific to the log source.

◆ **User.** User name of the account that was logged on when the log entry was generated (not case-sensitive).

◆ **Computer.** Computer from which the log message originated (not case-sensitive).

◆ **Event ID.** The number that corresponds to the specific type of event.

To disable event filtering, choose **A**ll Events from the **V**iew menu.

Searching for Events

You can search for specific events. This capability is useful when it is necessary to locate specific events in large log files.

To search for specific events, follow the steps in the following exercise:

Searching for Events

1. Choose **F**ind from the **V**iew menu to display the Find dialog box shown in figure 19.37.

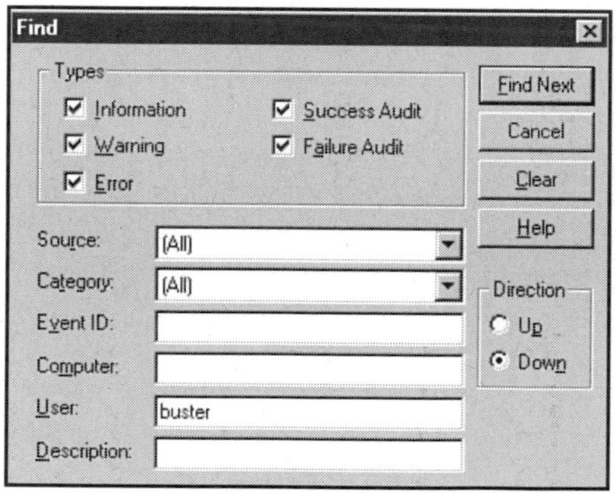

Figure 19.37

Finding events in Event Viewer.

2. Click the **C**lear button to restore default values to the dialog box.

3. Enter the criteria of the events to be found.

4. Select U**p** or Dow**n** to specify the search direction.

5. Click the **F**ind Next button to locate successive records that meet the criteria.

6. Click the Cancel button to exit the dialog box.

Archiving Event Logs

Logs can be archived in three forms:

◆ Event log format that you can review later in the Event log

◆ Text files, which may be read by any text editor

◆ Comma-delimited format that can be read by many other programs for analysis of the data

To archive a log, follow the steps in the following exercise:

Archiving Event Logs

1. Select the log in the **L**og menu.

2. Choose Save **A**s from the **L**og menu.

3. In the Save As dialog box, select a directory and a log file name (see fig. 19.38).

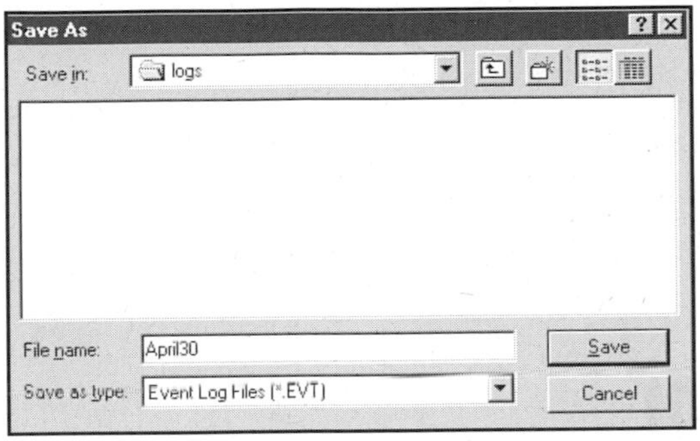

Figure 19.38

Specifying the file name and directory for an archive log file.

4. Select the file format in the Save as **t**ype box.

5. Click OK to save the file.

To view an archived log, follow the steps in the following exercise:

Viewing Archived Logs

1. Choose **O**pen from the **L**og menu.

2. Select the directory and file name in the File **n**ame list of the dialog box.

3. Click OK to retrieve the archive file.

4. In the Open File Type dialog box, specify the type of log you are retrieving: S**y**stem, Se**c**urity, or **A**pplication.

| Note | Logs that are archived in text file or comma-delimited format include data in the following fields: |

1. Date

2. Time

3. Source

4. Type

5. Category

6. Event

7. User

8. Computer

9. Description

Comma-delimited files can be imported by most spreadsheet and database applications.

Registry Editor

The *Registry* is the database that serves as the central repository for configuration data on a Windows NT computer. If you are familiar with Windows and DOS, you will find that the functions of many files are brought together in the Registry, including the following:

◆ config.sys

◆ autoexec.bat

◆ system.ini

◆ win.ini

◆ protocol.ini

Although Windows NT still supports INI files for the sake of compatibility with applications not written with Windows NT in mind, the Registry is a significantly improved means of storing configuration data.

The Registry is configured as a fault-tolerant database that is nearly impossible to crash. If a system failure occurs when entries are being written to the database, log files enable Windows NT to recover the database and fix any damage.

A considerable amount of data is stored in the Registry. Some data is of little concern to users or administrators, and much of the information is stored in a binary form that cannot be easily interpreted or modified. In the vast majority of cases, you will make modifications to the Registry by means of utilities, such as the Control Panel, policies, or Setup.

On rare occasions, however, you might be instructed to make a change directly to the Registry. Or you might find it useful to examine the Registry contents directly. At those times, it is handy for you to understand the structure of the Registry and the use of the Registry Editor.

Viewing the Registry

No icon is assigned to the Registry Editor when Windows NT is installed. You can run the Registry Editor by entering the command **REGEDT32** after choosing **R**un from the Start menu. Or, you can add an icon to the Start menu or desktop.

> **Tip**
>
> After you run the Registry Editor, convert the editor to read-only mode by choosing the **R**ead Only Mode command from the **O**ptions menu. When this option is checked, you can browse the Registry all you want without fear of damaging critical data.

When you start the Registry Editor, four windows are available, as shown in figure 19.39. The Registry is organized in a tree, and you navigate the Registry tree just as you navigate directory trees in File Manager. The windows in figure 19.39 have been arranged so that you can see the information in the topmost level of each tree.

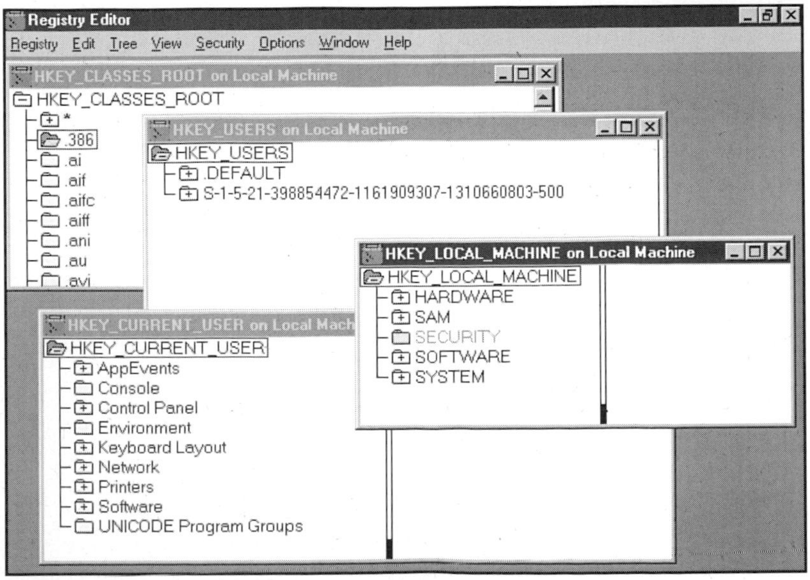

Figure 19.39

The Registry Editor window.

The organization of the Registry database is shown in figure 19.40. As you can see, the database has five subtrees. Close examination reveals that the name of each subtree corresponds to a window in the Registry Editor. Each entry in the tree is called a *key*, and each key can have *subkeys*.

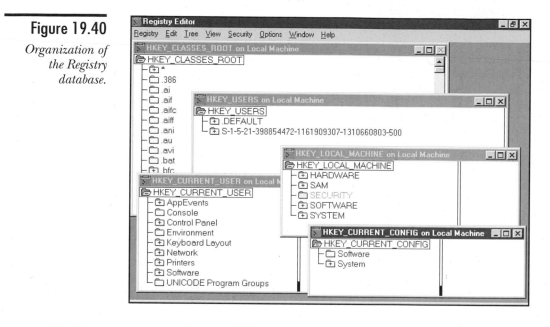

The five subtrees in the Registry follow:

- ◆ **HKEY_LOCAL_MACHINE.** Contains computer hardware information. Part of this subtree is reconstructed each time the computer is started to reflect the current hardware configuration.

- ◆ **HKEY_CURRENT_CONFIG.** Contains current hardware configuration, derived from the configuration used to boot Windows NT. This is the area of the Registry that is used and modified during the current session. When the system shuts down, the current configuration is copied back to HKEY_LOCAL_MACHINE under the appropriate area.

- ◆ **HKEY_CLASSES_ROOT.** Contains object linking and embedding (OLE) and file-class association data. Information in this subtree is duplicated in HKEY_LOCAL_MACHINE.

- ◆ **HKEY_CURRENT_USER.** Contains user-profile data for the currently logged-on user.

- ◆ **HKEY_USERS.** Contains all actively loaded user profiles, including the default profile and a duplicate of information in HKEY_CURRENT_USER. Profiles for remotely logged-on users are stored in the Registries of their local computers.

Much of the information that concerns you is stored in HKEY_LOCAL_MACHINE, which makes a good starting point for examining the structure of the Registry. The symbol for a key is a folder, and open keys are represented by open folders. To open subkeys in a window, double-click any folder that shows a plus sign (+). To close a subkey, double-click the open folder.

Looking at the Structure of Registry Values

Figure 19.41 shows the HKEY_LOCAL_MACHINE window after taking the following actions:

1. Double-clicking on the SYSTEM key to open the SYSTEM subtree.

2. Double-clicking on the CurrentControlSet key to open the subtree that describes the current state of the computer.

3. Double-clicking on the Control key.

4. Double-clicking on the ComputerName key.

5. Clicking on the ActiveComputerName key. Notice that this key is not flagged with a plus sign (+), indicating that it is the final key in the branch.

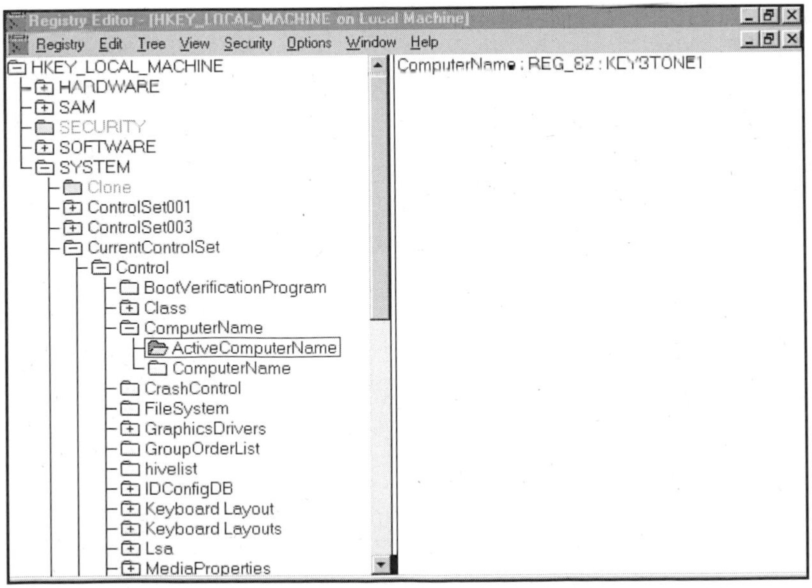

Figure 19.41

Opening keys in HKEY_LOCAL_ MACHINE.

> **Note** | To describe the complete path to a file, the same convention is used as for files in subdirectories; each level of the tree is represented by a backslash. The path that was opened in figure 19.41 is
>
> ```
> HKEY_LOCAL_MACHINE\SYSTEM\CurrentControlSet\Control\
> ComputerName\ActiveComputerName
> ```

Each key and subkey can be assigned one or more *values*, which are displayed in the right-hand pane of the window. These values have a specific structure. ActiveComputerName key has only one value, but you will see examples of keys that have many values. A value has three fields:

◆ **Name.** The name of the value.

◆ **Data type.** Programmers are familiar with the concept that data has a type that restricts the information that the data can display. Each data type is discussed in this section.

◆ **Value.** The actual data. The type of value stored depends on the data type.

Each value is classified by a data type that describes the types of values that can be stored. You encounter some other data types if you browse around, but these five types are the ones that most concern you:

◆ **REG_BINARY.** This data type describes raw binary data, the form used to store most hardware data, which can be viewed in more readable form in WINMSD. An example of such an entry follows:

```
Video:REG_BINARY:00 00 00 00
```

◆ **REG_DWORD.** Data represented by a number up to four bytes long. This data can be displayed in binary, hexadecimal, or decimal form. An example follows:

```
ErrorMode:REG_DWORD:0
```

◆ **REG_EXPAND_SZ.** Data represented in an expandable data string, which contains a system variable. The following example makes use of the %SystemRoot% variable:

```
SystemDirectory:REG_EXPAND_SZ:%SystemRoot%\system32
```

◆ **REG_MULTI_SZ.** Data represented in a multiple string consisting of lists or multiple values. Most human-readable text is of this type. Here is an example that has three values (autocheck, autochk, and *):

```
BootExecute:REG_MULTI_SZ:autocheck autochk *
```

◆ **REG_SZ.** Character data used to store human-readable text. For example:

```
DaylightName:REG_SZ:US Eastern Standard Time
```

Hives, Files, and Subtrees

The data in the four Registry subtrees is derived from six or more sets of files called hives. The term *hive* was coincd by a Microsoft systems programmer to reflect the way Registry data is stored in compartmentalized forms. Each hive consists of two files: a data file and a log file. The log file is responsible for the fault tolerance of the Registry and is described in greater detail later.

Each hive represents a group of keys, subkeys, and values that are rooted at the top of the Registry tree; it is easy to identify the keys in the Registry that are associated with each hive. Figure 19.42 shows a composite of two windows: the HKEY_LOCAL_MACHINE window from Registry Editor, and a File Manager window that shows the C:\WINNT\SYSTEM32\CONFIG subdirectory.

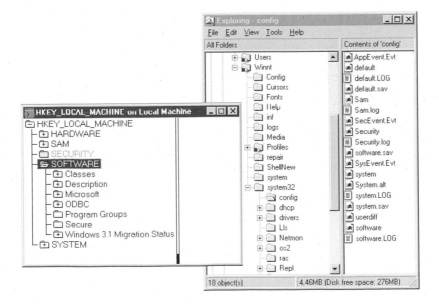

Figure 19.42

Relationship of Registry hives to files in the CONFIG subdirectory.

You easily can identify files in the directory that are related to keys in the Registry. The SOFTWARE key, for example, is associated with the files SOFTWARE and SOFTWARE.LOG.

The Registry hives and files are summarized in table 19.4.

TABLE 19.4
Registry Hives and Associated Files

Registry Hive	Associated Files
HKEY_LOCAL_MACHINE\SAM	SAM and SAM.LOG
HKEY_LOCAL_MACHINE\SECURITY	SECURITY and SECURITY.LOG
HKEY_LOCAL_MACHINE\SOFTWARE	SOFTWARE and SOFTWARE.LOG
HKEY_LOCAL_MACHINE\SYSTEM	SYSTEM, SYSTEM.LOG, and SYSTEM.ALT
HKEY_USERS\DEFAULT	DEFAULT and DEFAULT.LOG
HKEY_CURRENT_USER	Ntuser.dat and ntuser.dat.LOG

Beginning with Windows NT 4, the user part of the Registry, corresponding to HKEY_CURRENT_USER, is stored in the files Ntuser.dat and ntuser.dat.LOG in the user's profile directory. In prior versions of Windows NT, the user profile files were stored in the CONFIG subdirectory.

Notice that in figure 19.42 hives are associated with all the subtrees in HKEY_LOCAL_MACHINE except HARDWARE. The information in the HARDWARE subtree is regenerated each time the computer is booted and therefore is not stored permanently in hives. On Intel x86 computers, the information is gathered by the NTDETECT program. On Advanced RISC computers, the information is gathered by the ARC configuration database.

The hives are responsible for storing different categories of information:

◆ **HKEY_LOCAL_MACHINE\SAM.** Stores security information for user and group accounts. This information is used by the Windows NT Server Security Access Account Manager (SAM).

◆ **HKEY_LOCAL_MACHINE\SECURITY.** Security information regarding local account policy, used by the Windows NT security subsystem.

◆ **HKEY_LOCAL_MACHINE\SOFTWARE.** The configuration database for locally installed software. Serves the same purpose as application INI files for Windows NT applications.

◆ **HKEY_LOCAL_MACHINE\SYSTEM.** The system startup database. Data is configured during installation and when the computer is reconfigured. The computer cannot start without this information.

◆ **HKEY_USERS\DEFAULT.** The default user profile.

◆ **HKEY_CURRENT_USER.** The profile for the current user of the computer. This information is duplicated in the HKEY_LOCAL_MACHINE\SYSTEM hive. If entries in the hives disagree, HKEY_CURRENT_USER takes precedence.

Editing Values in the Registry

You will seldom—if ever—need to directly edit values in the Registry. There are a few features in Windows NT, however, that can be configured only in Registry Editor.

An example is the behavior of Windows NT computers that function as browsers on the network. A *browser* is a computer that maintains a network Browse list of all domains and servers that are available. It isn't my intention to explain the details of browsers. The point is that a computer functions as a browser depending on the value of its HKEY_LOCAL_MACHINE\SYSTEM\CurrentControlSet\Services\Browser\Parameters key. To change a computer's behavior as a browser, you must edit the value of this key, which can be No (never a browser), Yes (preferred browser), or Auto (potentially a browser).

Let's look at a harmless example of using the Registry Editor, editing the Registry value that describes the wallpaper file that is used on the computer desktop. (The example will work for you only if you installed wallpaper files on your computer.)

The current user's working environment is defined in the HKEY_CURRENT_USER subtree of the Registry. The window associated with this subtree is shown in figure 19.43.

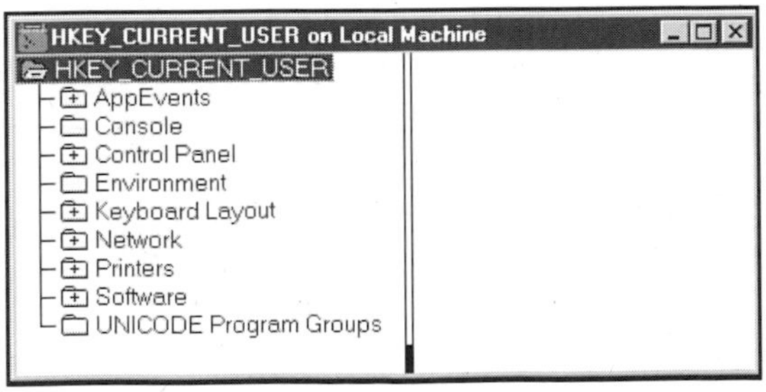

Figure 19.43

*The HKEY_
CURRENT_
USER subtree.*

Much of the information in this subtree will be quite familiar, and you might want to browse around to see what you can find. Then, you might want to try a little experiment to see what editing the Registry is like. Follow along in the following exercise:

Editing the Registry

1. Start the Registry Editor. If you have not created a program item, choose the **R**un command from the Start menu. Enter **REGEDT32** in the **O**pen field and choose OK.

2. After Registry Editor starts, check the **O**ptions menu. If the **R**ead Only Mode option is checked, remove the check mark. Otherwise, you will be unable to save changes.

3. If the HKEY_CURRENT_USER window is not open, open it by doing one of the following:

   ◆ Choosing HKEY_CURRENT_USER in the **W**indow menu

   ◆ Double-clicking on the HKEY_CURRENT_USER icon

4. Double-click the Control Panel key. After this key opens, you see the subkeys shown in figure 19.44. In the figure, the Desktop subkey has been selected, which contains the field you will be editing.

Figure 19.44

Subkeys for the Control Panel key.

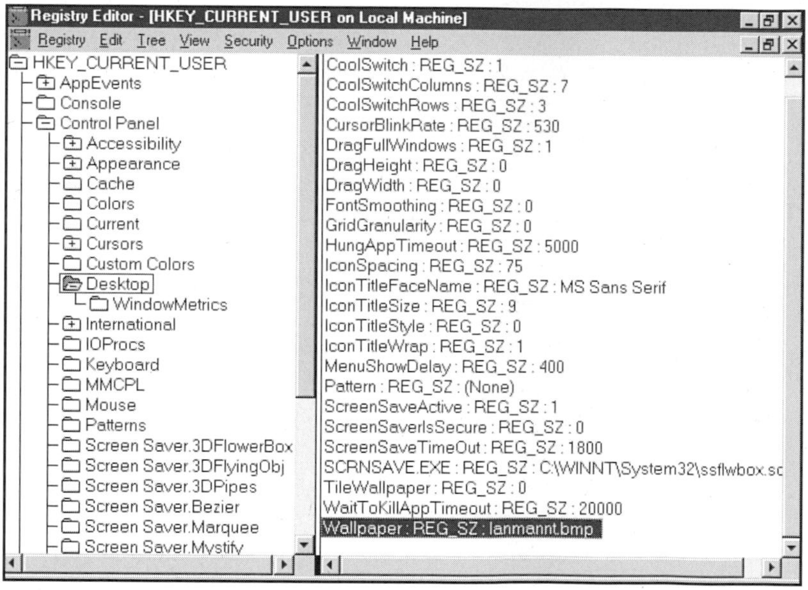

5. Double-click the Desktop key to display its values.

6. Double-click the entry named wallpaper. A dialog box opens that contains the value of the current wallpaper file. Edit this entry to read `lanmannt.bmp`, which will configure the wallpaper file to a file that should exist on your system. (The change has already been made in figure 19.44.)

7. Choose OK to save the entry.

8. Quit Registry Editor and restart Windows NT. When Windows NT restarts, the wallpaper will have changed.

| Note | If you have Administrative access, you can use the Registry Editor to edit hives on remote PCs. The **L**oad Hive command on the **R**egistry menu can be used to load a hive through a connected drive. After you are through with the hive, use the **U**nload Hive command to save the files back to the remote computer. |

Examining User Profiles in the Registry

User profile information is duplicated in two subtrees: HKEY_CURRENT_USER and HKEY_USERS. If information conflicts in these two subtrees, Windows NT uses the values in HKEY_CURRENT_USER.

If you open the HKEY_USERS subtree, you see two keys, as shown in figure 19.45. One key is named DEFAULT. The subtree under the DEFAULT key stores the default profile that is accessed by users who do not have an assigned profile. The other key is labeled with a number that begins with an S. This is a copy of the Registry profile for the current user of the computer.

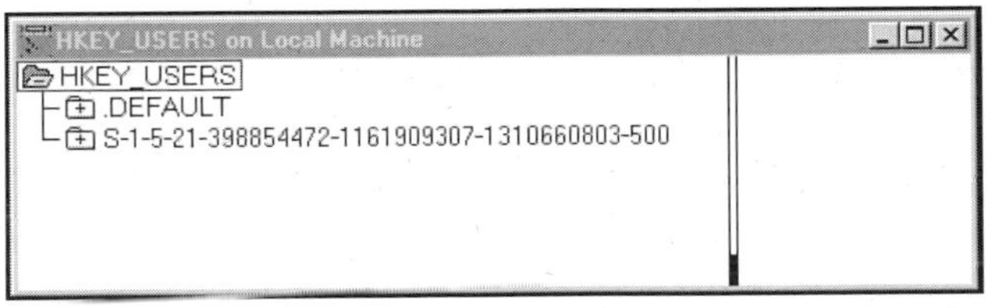

Figure 19.45

Subtrees in the HKEY_USERS window.

The number is the user security ID (SID) that was assigned to the user account when it was created. Different users result in different numbers in the name of this key.

User profiles are associated with hive files, which are located with other hive files in C:\WINNT\SYSTEM32\Config. If you look in that directory, you see a hive profile file for each user who has logged on the computer locally. The file is based on the first five characters of the user name plus the number 000. The file for the user Buster would be named BUSTE000, for example. The currently logged-on user also will have a file with a LOG extension—for example, BUSTE000.LOG.

You can examine the SIDs and profile file information for user accounts by opening HKEY_LOCAL_MACHINE\SOFTWARE\Microsoft\Windows NT\ProfileList. Although you could, don't be tempted to edit the SIDs. Doing so prevents the user from accessing any resources for which the user account has been given permissions.

Finding Registry Keys

The Registry is a big place, and you might be wondering how to locate specific keys. After you become familiar with the Registry structure, you can find a great deal by browsing, but Registry Editor does have a **F**ind Key command. The catch is that you need to know which subtree to look in. After that, it's pretty straightforward. The Find command will only look through keys, not values.

As an example, look for entries regarding installed printers. Because this is hardware, the keys appear in the HKEY_LOCAL_MACHINE subtree. To search for the information, follow the steps in the following exercise:

Searching for Registry Keys

1. Open the HKEY_LOCAL_MACHINE window.

2. Select the root key of the tree HKEY_LOCAL_MACHINE.

3. Choose the **F**ind Key command from the **V**iew menu.

4. Type **printer** in the Fi**n**d What box.

5. Do not check the Match **W**hole Word Only box because many of the names of keys are compound words, and *printer* might be only part of the key name.

6. Do not check Match **C**ase unless you are trying to find a specific entry for which the case of the letters is known.

7. Select **D**own if it is not already selected.

8. Choose **F**ind Next to initiate the search.

9. The search result is shown in figure 19.46. (I opened the Printers key after it was found that it held the information I wanted.) The specific printer information probably differs on your computer, but the key under which the information is located should be found without trouble.

Registry Fault Tolerance

The Registry is an extremely robust database that can survive even critical system failures in the middle of writing data. This capability to shrug off faults results from the use of a technique borrowed from databases. When a key value is saved to a hive in the Registry, the following events take place:

1. The change is written to the LOG file associated with the hive.

2. File buffers are flushed to force data to be physically written out to the LOG file. Normally, file writes are stored in buffers until Windows NT has some spare time to write data to files. Flushing the buffers ensures that the change is stored safely in the LOG file.

3. The information in the LOG file is used to update the hive file.

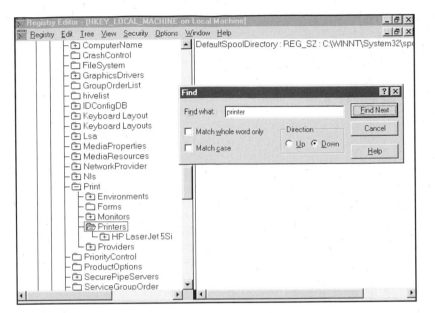

Figure 19.46

Results of finding a key in the Registry.

Suppose the server crashes while the change is half written to the hive file. A half-written change is a corrupt change, and the hive file would be unreliable. Fortunately, when the system restarts, information in the LOG file can be used to roll back the hive file to a stable state.

In one case, the Registry goes even further to ensure reliability and data integrity. The System hive is stored in two files: system and system.alt. If the server cannot boot with the primary copy, the alternate copy can be used.

Using the LastKnownGood Configuration

The control settings most recently used on the computer are stored in the Registry in the key HKEY_LOCAL_MACHINE\SYSTEM\CurrentControlSet. Information in this key is accessed when the computer is started.

The CurrentControlSet can be damaged in a number of ways that can prevent the system from being able to start. Installing bad drivers or options with conflicting settings might have this effect. Or, you accidentally might configure the video adapter so that you simply cannot see data on-screen.

Besides the current control set, Windows NT keeps a copy of the last control set that was used successfully to start the computer. If, for any reason, the computer does not start with the current control set, you can invoke the LastKnownGood control set by pressing the spacebar when you see the message `Press spacebar NOW to invoke the Hardware Profile/LastKnownGood menu`.

After you invoke the LastKnownGood menu, you lose any changes that were made to the system configuration since the last time the computer was started.

The UPS Utility

An uninterruptible power supply is essential equipment for any network server. You simply cannot have servers crashing with every power outage. Files get damaged and user productivity is interrupted. There are actually several electrical conditions from which you want to protect your server:

- **Power outages.** Complete losses of power.

- **Voltage variations.** You know how the lights in your house dim when you start the vacuum cleaner? Power-hungry systems can cause the voltage at an AC outlet to vary by a surprising degree. I've seen more than one server problem caused by these periodic "brownouts."

- **Voltage spikes and surges.** Equipment can be damaged by a voltage spike so short that you might not even notice it. Lightning is a prime cause of voltage spikes.

- **Noise.** Radio frequency noise on the AC line might get past the filtering in your computer power supply, which is really designed only to cope with the 50 Hz to 60 Hz frequency of line current. Noise also can cause computers to act erratically.

Equipment for Surges, Spikes, Noise, and Power Fluctuations

Depending on your equipment, you might need more than one device to deal with all these problems. Many UPS units don't provide spike protection or filtering, and most cannot protect against voltage variations in the AC line.

At a minimum, every computer should be plugged into a surge and spike protector, and you need to plug your UPS into one unless the UPS provides surge and spike protection. Don't even think about using a $10 special. Expect to spend at least $50 for a spike and surge suppressor—particularly one that also filters out high-frequency noise. This device is a must.

A surge and spike suppressor is designed to eliminate relatively short voltage changes. If your power line experiences periodic brownouts or overvoltages, the device you need is the *power-line conditioner*. These devices are capable of leveling off low and high voltages, maintaining a constant output voltage within a reasonable range of line fluctuations. Expect to spend about $300 for a power-line conditioner. If you have an electrician install a dedicated power line for your server, however, chances are you won't need a power conditioner.

Uninterruptible Power Supplies

All UPS devices work by charging a battery during normal operation. The power in the battery can be converted to AC current that can be used to power a computer. A UPS can be designed in two ways: to operate with the battery online or offline. Figure 19.47 shows how the two types of UPS devices work.

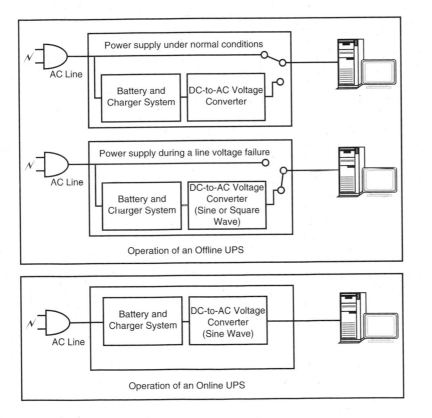

Figure 19.47

Offline and online UPS systems.

The majority of UPSs use the offline approach. Under normal conditions, the AC line is switched directly to the outlets that service the computer. AC power also is directed to the battery system, which is kept constantly charged. When power fails, an electronic switch connects the UPS outlets to the inverter circuits that convert DC power from the battery into AC power that can run the computer.

The most significant problem with an offline UPS is the period of time that is required to switch from direct AC power to the inverter. Most UPS devices now are designed to make the switch rapidly enough that few computers are bothered, but this was once a common problem.

The online UPS makes it unnecessary to switch power because the computer is always connected to the battery/inverter system. The outside AC power runs the charging circuits that keep the battery topped off, but it is never directly connected to the computer. Because there is no switch-over, a power outage is handled much more smoothly. Because the AC line voltages are never connected to the computer, an offline UPS inherently functions as a surge, spike, and power-line conditioner.

Every battery-powered UPS must be capable of converting battery direct current (DC) into the alternating current (AC) required by the protected computer. In the majority of UPS devices, the AC voltage produced is not a true sine wave, like the AC current you get from the wall. Most UPS devices produce a square wave that can cause problems with some computer equipment. Some manufacturers design their equipment to produce a simulated sine wave, which is a stepped-square wave. Simulated sine waves are acceptable to most equipment. Figure 19.48 illustrates the various waveforms.

Figure 19.48

Wave forms produced by UPS systems.

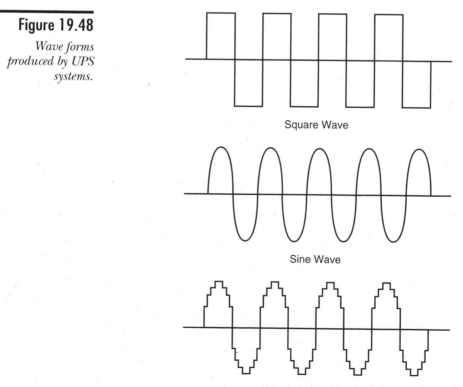

Square Wave

Sine Wave

Simulated Sine Wave

Because an online UPS is constantly supplying the computer with remanufactured AC, it must produce a true sine wave. Equipment operating too long on a square wave AC will be damaged.

Most offline UPS systems produce square-wave voltages, which can be used to operate the majority of computers for relatively short periods of time, such as the few minutes it takes to shut down the server properly in the event of a long power failure.

UPS systems can power a server only for a limited time before their batteries are depleted. Therefore, it is desirable to have a means of automatically monitoring the UPS and shutting down the server before the UPS can no longer sustain the required operating voltage. Windows NT includes a UPS service that can provide UPS monitoring with many UPS systems.

Connecting the UPS to the Server

To use the UPS service, your UPS must be equipped with a monitoring interface—usually a DB-9 connector that uses RS-232 serial interface signaling. A cable is used to connect the UPS to a serial port on the computer.

Unfortunately, there are no standards for how UPS monitoring should be done, and every manufacturer seems to have a different way of configuring the monitoring port. It is always best, therefore, to obtain a cable that is designed for Windows NT Server. Contact the manufacturer of the UPS to obtain cables or cable specifications.

You might, in a pinch, be able to reverse-engineer the hardware and build a cable yourself. Be aware, however, that this might not be straightforward or even possible. The cable for my UPS, for example, requires a CMOS integrated circuit to support Windows NT Server. In case you want to attempt it, table 19.5 shows the pin requirements for Windows NT Server.

TABLE 19.5
Pin Requirements for Windows NT Server

Signal	DB25	DB9	Purpose
CTS	5	8	The UPS can supply a positive or negative voltage at this pin to signal the UPS service that a power failure has occurred.
DCD	8	1	The UPS can supply a positive or negative voltage at this pin to signal the UPS service that a low-battery condition exists.

continues

TABLE 19.5, CONTINUED
Pin Requirements for Windows NT Server

Signal	DB25	DB9	Purpose
DTR	20	4	Windows NT can send a positive voltage at this pin to signal the UPS that it can shut itself off.
TXD	2	3	Windows NT maintains a negative voltage at this pin for use with contact-closure signaling from some UPSs.
RTS	4	7	Windows NT maintains a positive voltage at this pin for use with contact-closure signaling from some UPSs.

Before you can configure the UPS service, you must know whether your UPS will generate a positive or a negative signal at the CTS and DCD pins.

After you connect the UPS to your server with a suitable cable, you can configure the UPS service.

Objective B.7

Configuring the UPS Service

You access the UPS dialog box from the UPS icon in the Control Panel. The UPS dialog box is shown in figure 19.49.

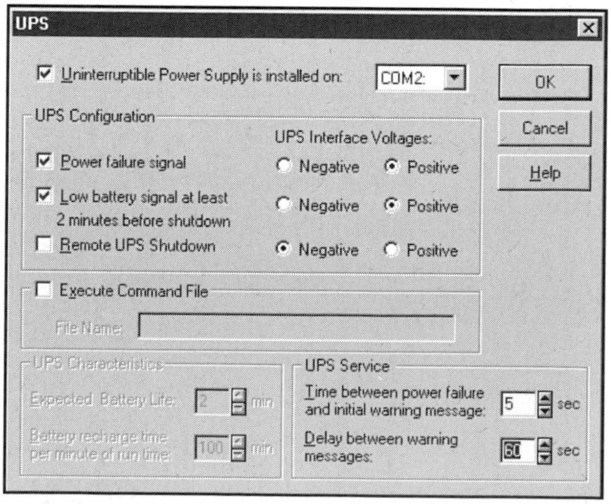

Figure 19.49

Configuring the UPS service.

Configure the UPS settings as described in the following exercise:

Configuring the UPS Service

1. Open the UPS utility in the Control Panel.

2. Check the **U**ninterruptible Power Supply is installed on box to activate the other options in the window.

3. Select a COM port. You might need to use the Ports utility in the Control Panel to activate the port you need.

4. If your UPS can send a signal indicating that a power failure has taken place, check the **P**ower failure signal box. Indicate whether the signal will consist of a Negative or a Positive voltage.

5. If your UPS can send a signal indicating that its battery is low, check the **L**ow battery signal at least 2 minutes before shutdown box. Indicate whether the signal will consist of a Negative or a Positive voltage.

6. If your UPS can accept a signal that orders it to shut itself off, check the **R**emote UPS Shutdown box. Indicate whether the signal will consist of a Negative or a Positive voltage.

7. If you did not check the **L**ow battery signal at least 2 minutes before shutdown box, options in the UPS Characteristics box will be active.

   ◆ Enter a conservative estimate of the time the UPS can power the server in the **E**xpected Battery Life box.

   ◆ Enter a conservative estimate of the time required to recharge the UPS battery in the **B**attery recharge time per minute of run time box.

   The manufacturer of your UPS is the best source of information for the values to put in these fields. Because the UPS cannot signal a low-battery condition, the UPS service uses these values to estimate when a low battery condition is likely.

8. Most UPSs send a power failure warning immediately, even for a very short loss of service. If the UPS service interpreted such a short loss as the start of a serious outage, it would often notify network users to log off when logging off was unnecessary.

   You can specify a delay between the signaling of a power failure by entering a value in seconds in the **T**ime between power failure and initial warning message box. If power is restored within this time period, no message is sent.

9. UPS sends periodic messages as long as the power outage continues. You can specify the delay between these messages by entering a value in seconds in the **D**elay between warning messages box.

10. You can instruct the UPS service to execute a command file when a low-battery condition exists. This command file could be a batch file that shuts down special applications, such as a database server. The UPS service will shut down most server functions normally, so a command file is required only in special instances.

    To activate the feature, follow these steps:

    ◆ Check the E**x**ecute Command File box

    ◆ Enter a command file name in the File Name box

11. When you have configured the service, click OK.

When you activate the UPS service, it automatically configures its own startup parameters so that it will start automatically. It also ensures that the Alerter, Messenger, and EventLog services are started.

When the UPS service starts up, it tests the interface to the UPS hardware by assuming that normal power conditions prevail. If you have specified a positive voltage at the CTS pin to signal a power failure, the UPS service assumes that a negative voltage will be found at the pin. Each pin you have activated in the UPS Control Panel will be tested. If the expected voltages are not found, the UPS service will not start.

Testing the UPS

Never assume that your UPS works. After you have configured the UPS service, plan a test. If the server is being used, schedule the test for after hours. You can use the Send Message command in Server Manager to notify users that a test will take place. Users must log out for the duration of the test.

Testing is simple. Pull the plug on your UPS and see what happens.

After the delay you specified (in the **T**ime between power failure and initial warning message box), a message is broadcast to the domain: `A power failure has occurred at server name. Please terminate all activity with this server.` This message repeats at the intervals you specified. During this period, new users cannot attach to the server.

At this time, the server can resume normal function if power is restored. When power comes back up and the UPS hardware clears the power failure signal to the UPS service, a message is sent to users: `Power has been restored at server name. Normal operations have resumed.` Users can reconnect to the server and resume their work.

The next step is initiated in one of two ways:

◆ If you configured the UPS service to expect a low-battery signal, the UPS initiates the next phase of the shutdown.

◆ If you configured the UPS service to use a timed shutdown (**E**xpected Battery Life), the next phase starts when the shutdown timer expires.

After a low-battery condition occurs, UPS executes any command you specified in the UPS command screen. This command must execute in 30 seconds or less if the server is to be shut down smoothly within two minutes.

After executing the command, the UPS service starts a controlled shutdown of the server. After it begins, the shutdown process cannot be aborted.

You should let your test continue until the UPS service shuts down the server.

Administrative Wizards

You have probably seen wizards in action. A wizard supervises the second half of the Windows NT installation process. Another wizard assists you when configuring a new printer. If you like the wizard approach, you will want to check out the Administrative Wizards, which are installed in the Administrative Tools group in the Start menu. Figure 19.50 shows the Administrative Wizards program window.

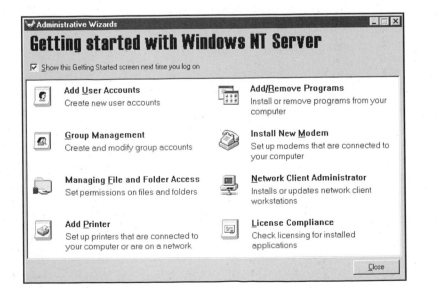

Figure 19.50

Administrative Wizards.

Testing Your Knowledge

1. The Licensing tool is located in the Control Panel.

   A. True

   B. False

2. The Server Manager tool has three command menus; these include:

   A. Computer menu

   B. View menu

   C. File menu

   D. Options menu

3. When viewing users connected to a server with the Server Manager tool, users only need to be connected to the domain to appear on the connected users list.

   A. True

   B. False

4. It is possible to disconnect all users connected to a specific share with the Server Manager tool.

   A. True

   B. False

5. The _____ service must be running for specific users or computers to be configured to receive alerts.

6. The domain database synchronization process is entirely automatic, therefore NT does not provide a method of manually synchronizing the domain database.

   A. True

   B. False

7. By default, Server Manager selects your logon domain to manage. What must exist between the logon domain and the domain you want to manage before you can select it by choosing the Select Domain command from the Computer menu?

8. What command must be selected from the Options menu if you want Server Manager to retain your current setup when quiting?

9. Name at least four of the default Services for Windows NT Server.

10. When the Server service is paused, members of the Administrators and Server Operators groups can reestablish connections with the server, but others cannot.

    A. True

    B. False

11. The three Service startup types are Automatic, Manual, and _____.

12. When using the System utility with the Environment panel activated, which types of environmental variables are used by the system regardless of the user who is logged on?

    A. System

    B. User

    C. Static

    D. ComSpec

13. Under Windows NT, virtual memory uses disk storage to simulate RAM. This process is referred to as _____.

14. What happens if NT's pagefile.sys file is deleted under another operating system in a dual boot environment?

    A. Windows NT must be fixed using setup with the "r" or recovery option.

    B. Windows NT will prompt the administrator that the pagefile.sys file has been corrupted and instruct him to recreate the file.

    C. Windows NT will recreate the file when NT is restarted.

15. The Windows NT Diagnostics (WINMSD) program enables you to observe configuration information for all software and hardware components.

    A. True

    B. False

16. The WINMSD's Network panel's Statistics button can be useful for tracking potential network hardware issues.

    A. True

    B. False

17. To audit files and directories you must be logged on as a member of which group?

    A. Administrators

    B. Power User

    C. Backup Operator

    D. Server Operator

18. Auditing Security Policy Changes tracks any changes to audits, user rights, or _____.

19. Printer auditing is configured with Print Manager.

    A. True

    B. False

20. What are the three NT Server logs used in conjunction with the Event Viewer?

    A. System

    B. Application

    C. Event

    D. Security

21. When archiving event logs, there are three formats available. These formats are:

    A. Event log

    B. Text Files

    C. Comma-delimited

    D. ASCII files

22. Which subtree of the NT Registry contains user-profile data for the currently logged on user?

    A. HKEY_LOCAL_MACHINE

    B. HKEY_CURRENT_CONFIG

    C. HKEY_CLASSES ROOT

    D. HKEY_CURRENT_USER

    E. HKEY_USERS

23. A surge and spike suppressor is designed to eliminate relatively short voltage changes. If your power line experiences periodic brownouts or overvoltages, the device you need is a _____.

24. To use the UPS service your UPS must be equipped with a monitoring interface.

    A. True

    B. False

Review Answers

1. A

2. A, B, D

3. B

4. A

5. Alerter

6. B

7. A trusting relationship

8. Save Settings on Exit

9. Alerter, ClipBook Server, Computer Browser, Directory Replicator, EventLog, Messenger, Net Logon, Network DDE, Network DDE DSDM, NT LM Security Support Provider, Remote Procedure Call (RPC) Locator, Remote Procedure Call (RPC) Service, Schedule, Server, Spooler, UPS, Workstation

10. A

11. Disabled

12. A

13. paging

14. C

15. B

16. A

17. A

18. trust relationships

19. A

20. A, B, D

21. A, B, C

22. E

23. power-line conditioner

24. A

CHAPTER 20

Monitoring and Managing the Network

A network is a dynamic, almost living thing. It has a heartbeat, a pulse, and measurable health. Another of your many jobs as a LAN administrator, in fact, is monitoring the network so you can anticipate when it is healthy and when its health is in decline. This chapter covers the following tools, which focus on monitoring and managing the network and network clients:

- ◆ Network Client Administrator
- ◆ Performance Monitor
- ◆ Network Monitor

You will also take a look at some tools in the *Windows NT Resource Kit* that solve particular network management problems.

Network Client Administrator

Network Client Administrator is a central resource for managing client installation.

You can make five different sets of client software installation disks. These disk sets contain all the files required to install client software on the following clients:

◆ Network Client 3.0 for MS-DOS and Windows (covered in Chapter 14, "Using Windows and DOS Clients")

◆ Remote Access v1.1a for MS-DOS (discussed in Chapter 21, "Using the Remote Access Server")

◆ TCP/IP 32 for Windows for Workgroups 3.11 (covered in Chapter 16, "Using TCP/IP")

◆ LAN Manager 2.2c for MS-DOS (not covered in this book)

◆ LAN Manager 2.2c for OS/2 (also not covered)

Network Client Administrator also can build network installation startup disks. Network installation startup disks contain only the files required to enable a client to access the network and connect to installation files on a server. The actual client files are then installed to the client from a shared network directory. Network installation is supported for two clients:

◆ Windows for Workgroups 3.11

◆ Network Client for MS-DOS and Windows

Creating Client Installation Disk Sets

A client installation disk set contains all the files required to install client software on a computer. In general, installing from a client installation set is the most successful method of installing client software. Clients can have varying hardware configurations without requiring you to rebuild the installation disks.

To create a client installation disk set, perform the steps in the following exercise:

Creating a Client Installation Disk Set

1. Start Network Client Administrator. The program icon is installed in the Administrator Tools program group in the Start menu. When the program starts, the Network Client Administrator window appears (see fig. 20.1).

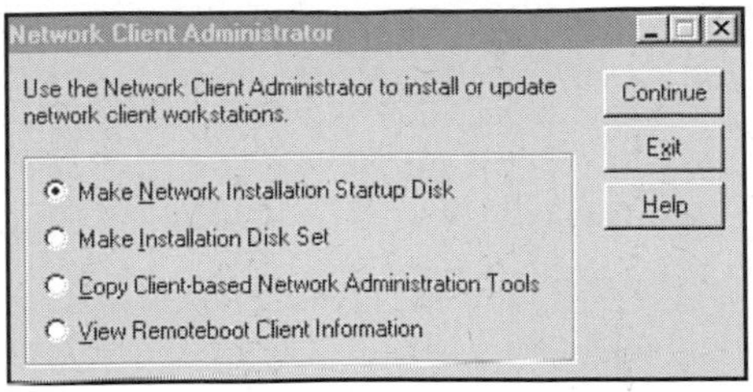

Figure 20.1

The Network Client Administrator main window.

2. Choose Make **I**nstallation Disk Set and choose Continue. The Share Network Client Installation Files dialog box appears (see fig. 20.2).

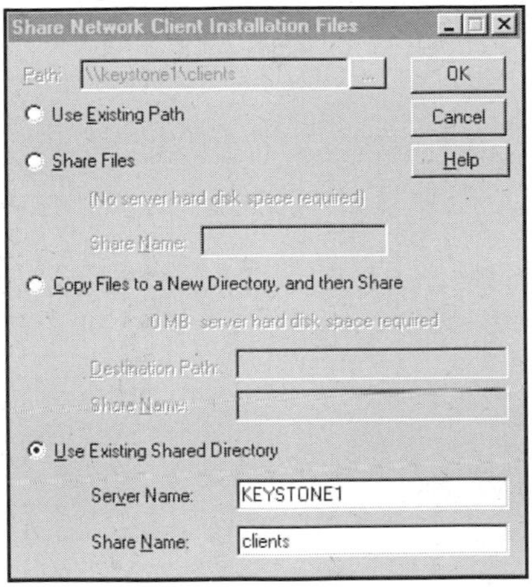

Figure 20.2

The Share Network Client Installation Files dialog box.

3. Specify the location of the installation disk files.

   ◆ If the installation files are on CD-ROM or in an unshared directory, choose Use **E**xisting Path and specify the path in the **P**ath box. If desired, click the Browse button and browse for the file path. The required files are in the \clients subdirectory of the CD-ROM.

   ◆ To share installation files on a CD-ROM, choose **S**hare Files, specify a path in the **P**ath box, and enter a share name in the Share **N**ame box. This option is more applicable to the network installation method.

   ◆ If you want to copy the files to a hard disk and share them, choose **C**opy Files to a New Directory, and then Share. Specify entries in the **D**estination Path and Share **N**ame fields. Although 49 MB of hard disk space are initially required, you can delete client software you don't require after the files are copied.

◆ If files are already copied and shared, choose **U**se Existing Shared Directory. Complete the Ser**v**er Name and the Share **N**ame entries.

4. Choose OK to continue.

   If you choose **C**opy Files to a New Directory, and then Share, files will be copied. This process is a rather lengthy one, so take a break afterward.

   When ready to proceed, Network Client Administrator displays the Make Installation Disk Set dialog box shown in figure 20.3.

5. In the **N**etwork Client or Service list, select the client you want to create. The dialog box tells you how many disks will be required.

6. If multiple floppy drives are available, select one in the **D**estination Drive field.

7. Check **F**ormat Disks if the disks are unformatted or already contain files.

8. Choose OK. Supply disks as requested. Be sure to label the disks as specified in the prompts.

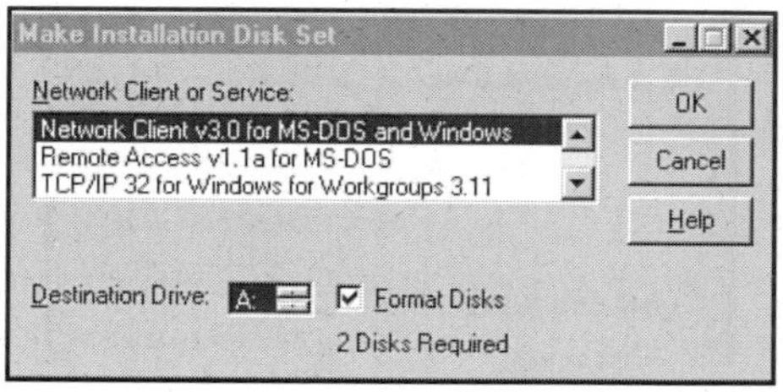

Figure 20.3

Specifying which client software disks to make.

The procedure for using the installation disks depends on the operating system being used. Chapter 14 covers the installation of client software for MS-DOS and Windows 3.1. Chapter 16 discusses installation of the TCP/IP client software for MS-DOS and Windows for Workgroups 3.11.

Objective B.3

Creating a Network Installation Startup Disk

To create a network installation startup disk, perform the steps in the following exercise:

Creating a Network Installation Startup Disk

1. Format a bootable disk for the target computer. Ideally, all computers on which you will be using network installation will be configured with the same version of MS-DOS.

2. Start Network Client Administrator. The program icon is installed in the Network Administration program group. When the program starts, the Network Client Administrator window appears (refer to fig. 20.1).

3. Choose Make **N**etwork Installation Startup Disk and choose Continue. The Share Network Client Installation Files dialog box appears (refer to fig. 20.2).

4. Network installation must be performed from a shared directory. In the Share Network Client Installation Files dialog box, you can use all options except Use **E**xisting Path.

   ◆ To share installation files on a CD-ROM, choose **S**hare Files, specify a path in the **P**ath box, and enter a share name in the Share **N**ame box. Sharing installation files in this way is particularly useful for network client installation because you can share the CD-ROM during installation and no hard drive space is required.

   ◆ If you want to copy the files to a hard disk and share them, choose **C**opy Files to a New Directory, and then Share. Complete the **D**estination Path and Share **N**ame fields.

   ◆ If files are already copied and shared, choose **U**se Existing Shared Directory. Supply appropriate entries in the Ser**v**er Name and the Share **N**ame fields.

5. Click OK to continue. Network Client Administrator displays the Target Workstation Configuration dialog box (see fig. 20.4).

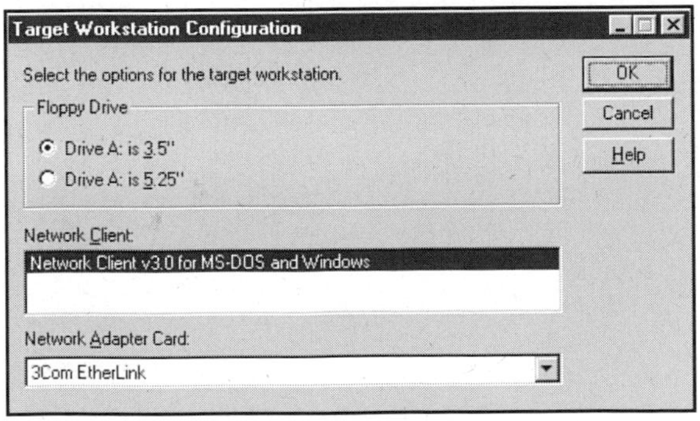

Figure 20.4

Building a network installation startup disk.

6. Select the desired software in the Network **C**lient list. Only one disk is required for each client.

7. Select the destination drive.

   Installation must be made to a disk in drive A. In the Floppy Drive box, choose whether you are using a 3 1/2-inch or a 5 1/4-inch disk.

8. Select a network adapter card in Network **A**dapter Card drop-down list. If your network uses more than one model of network adapter, you must create a network installation startup disk for each card model.

9. Choose OK. A license warning appears. Choose OK again.

10. The Network Startup Disk Configuration dialog box appears (see fig. 20.5). This box configures the client that is to be used when the startup disk connects to the server containing the installation files.

Figure 20.5

Configuring the network installation startup disk.

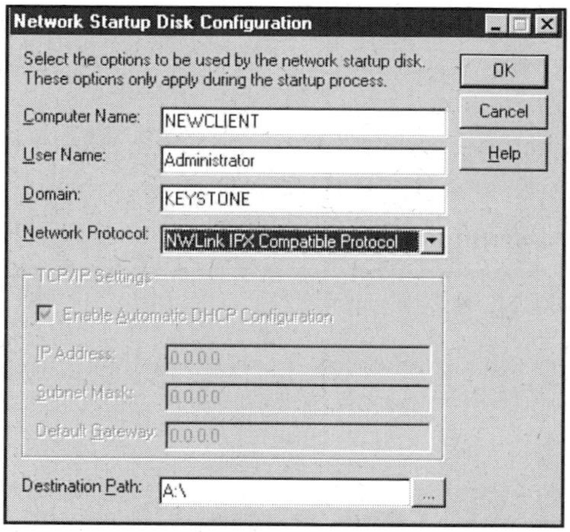

◆ In the **C**omputer Name field, enter a computer name that is to be used while the network installation is taking place. This computer name should not be in use by any other computer. Designate a computer name that is reserved for use during network client installation.

◆ In the **U**ser Name field, specify an account that can access the shared directory. An administrator account is often best here.

◆ In the **D**omain field, specify the domain in which the computer resides.

◆ Select a protocol in the **N**etwork Protocol box. NetBEUI is installed by default on all Windows NT Servers. NetBEUI can only be used if the client is attached to the same network segment as the server.

If TCP/IP is installed on the server, TCP/IP can be used to install clients through the internetwork. If TCP/IP is selected, enter the required TCP/IP settings. See Chapter 16 for guidance.

11. The Destination **P**ath is almost always the disk drive on which you are installing the startup files.

12. Insert the formatted system disk in drive A and choose OK after entering the required information. Files are copied to the disk

To use the network installation startup disk, perform the steps in the following exercise:

Using the Network Installation Startup Disk

1. Install the appropriate client operating system on the new client computer.

2. Make sure the source server is active and the share containing the files is available.

3. Boot the network client computer with the network startup disk.

4. Install the client software. Procedures are similar to those described in Chapter 14. Be sure to verify the settings for the network adapter card. The network setup disk is configured with default settings.

Monitoring Computer Performance

The Windows NT Performance Monitor is capable of monitoring quite a few performance characteristics of Windows NT computers. The resulting data can be displayed in the form of charts, can be used to generate alerts, or can be captured into data files for statistical analysis.

Performance Monitor is actually four related utilities, each having its own screen and command set. This section doesn't attempt to tell you everything there is to know about Performance Monitor. It does, however, show you some of its most useful features.

Charting Performance Statistics

Figure 20.6 shows an example of a chart produced by Performance Monitor. The chart displays a line graph, although bar charts (histograms) are available and more appropriate for some data types. This particular line graph example is tracking processor utilization on two computers. The two lines at the bottom of the window describe the collected statistics.

The statistics are summarized in the *value bar* below the chart:

- ◆ **Last.** Shows the most recent reading taken.
- ◆ **Average.** Shows the average of all readings since the chart was created.
- ◆ **Min and Max.** Show the lowest and highest readings recorded.
- ◆ **Graph Time.** Shows the time in seconds displayed on one screen of the graph.

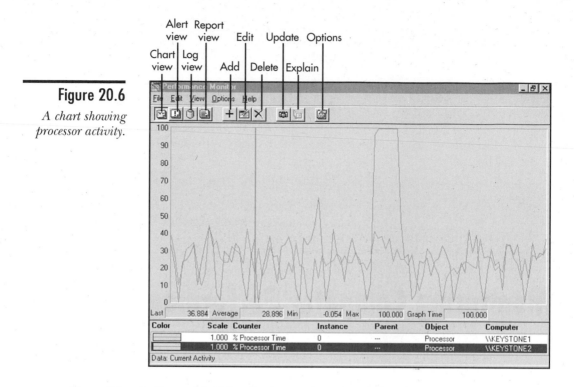

Figure 20.6

A chart showing processor activity.

The callouts in figure 20.6 identify the toolbar buttons. Performance Manager consists of four related tools (Chart, Alert, Log, and Report) with differing commands in their menus, but these four buttons are always available.

The easiest way to understand how a chart works is to create one. To create a performance chart, perform the steps in the following exercise:

Creating a Chart

1. Select chart view by choosing the **C**hart command in the **V**iew menu, or by clicking the Chart icon in the toolbar.

2. If you want to clear an existing chart, choose **N**ew Chart in the **F**ile menu.

3. To create a new chart line, choose **A**dd to Chart in the **E**dit menu, or click the Add button in the toolbar. The Add to Chart dialog box appears (see fig. 20.7).

4. Enter the computer to be monitored in the **C**omputer box. If you want to browse for a computer, click on the Browse button (...).

5. Pull down the **Ob**ject list and select an object to be monitored. Objects are processes running on the computer. Each object has a number of different counters that you can select. The objects displayed in the **Ob**ject list are different depending on the operating system, and on the services, protocols, and programs that are installed.

6. Select an **I**nstance if more than one is listed. If the example had been created on a multiprocessor server, there would have been more than one instance of a processor. You also would see multiple instances for disk drives in a multi-drive computer.

   If you choose **E**xplain, as was done in figure 20.7, each counter is described briefly in the Cou**n**ter Definition scroll box at the bottom of the window.

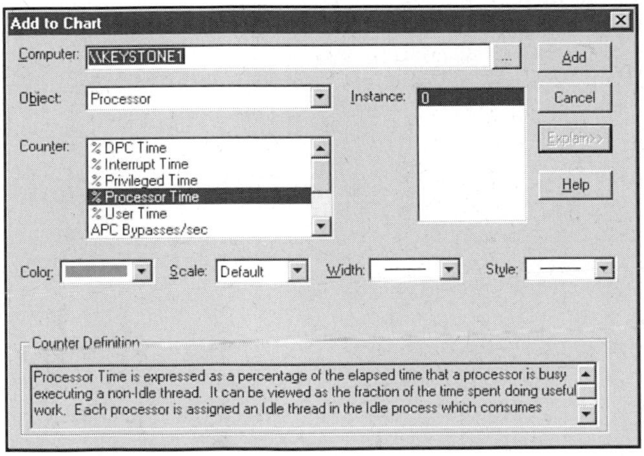

Figure 20.7

Adding an item to a chart.

7. Select a Coun**t**er to be monitored.

8. Select the Colo**r**, **S**cale, **W**idth, and St**y**le for the line associated with this object. Line width and style are probably more useful than color if you want to print these graphs on a monochrome printer.

   The **S**cale factor determines how the data is to be scaled on the chart. The default scale is generally 1.000, which is especially appropriate for percentages because the chart scale runs from 0 to 100. Change this factor to increase or reduce the height of the graph as required.

9. Choose **A**dd when you have defined the chart line to your satisfaction.

10. Define and add other chart lines if desired.

11. When all chart lines are defined, choose **D**one. You return to the Add to Chart screen, and the data is displayed.

| Tip | If you plan to run Performance Monitor for an extended period of time, I suggest you turn off any screen savers you have configured, or choose a screen saver that simply blanks the screen. Animated screen savers typically peg the processor at 100 percent and probably distort other readings as well. You are attempting to monitor the actual work the computer is performing, not the effort that goes into putting on a show. |

To edit the characteristics of any chart line, perform the steps in the following exercise:

Editing Chart Characteristics

1. Select the legend at the bottom for the chart line to be modified.

2. Choose the **E**dit Chart Line command in the **E**dit menu, or click the Edit icon in the toolbar. The Edit Chart Line window has the same dialog items as the Add to Chart dialog box. (You can also double-click on the legend to display the Edit Chart Line window.)

3. After making the desired changes, choose OK.

To delete a chart line, perform the steps in the following exercise:

Deleting a Chart Line

1. Select the legend at the bottom for the chart line to be deleted.

2. Choose **D**elete From Chart in the **E**dit menu or press the Delete key.

| Note | Disk performance counters are not ordinarily active, because they typically slow disk access time. Although any user can run Performance Monitor, only an administrator can turn on the disk performance counters.

To activate or deactivate disk performance counters, execute the command `diskperf` at a command prompt. Answer Y to turn counters on or N to turn counters off. (-Y and -N can also be included as command-line parameters, as can a computer name in the format `\\computername`.) The computer must be restarted to put the change into effect. |

Setting Chart Options

Several options are available for customizing the chart display. The Chart Options dialog box, shown in figure 20.8, controls these options.

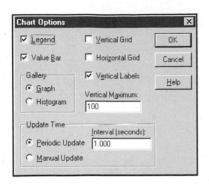

Figure 20.8

Configuring chart options.

◆ **Legend.** Check this box to display the chart legends at the bottom of the chart window. Remove the check to hide the legends.

◆ **Value Bar.** Check this box to display the value bar. Remove the check to hide it.

◆ **Gallery.** These choices determine whether the data is to be displayed as a Graph (line chart) or as a Histogram (bar chart). A *graph* displays each item as a line that is tracked by time. A *histogram* displays a single bar for each item, which is updated at each update time. Graphs are usually more useful.

◆ **Update Time.** Choose Periodic Update if you want the data to be updated at regular intervals; the interval in seconds is specified in the Interval box. Choose Manual Update if you want to trigger updates yourself.

◆ **Vertical Grid and Horizontal Grid.** Check these options to display grid lines. Remove the checks to suppress them.

◆ **Vertical Labels.** Check this option to display labels on the Y (vertical) axis. Remove the check if you do not want the vertical axis to be labeled.

◆ **Vertical Maximum.** This value specifies the maximum value on the Y (vertical) axis. For percentages, 100 is good, but Performance Monitor also tracks many characteristics that are not percentages. To track megabytes in use on a 512 MB drive, for example, you might set this value to 512.

Tip

Performance Monitor does not have a provision for printing data directly. Any screen can be copied to the clipboard, however, by pressing Alt+Print Screen. Then you can open Paintbrush, paste the image there, and print it.

Setting Alerts

Performance Monitor enables you to set alerts that can monitor any of its counters. Alerts log and can notify administrators when counters rise above or fall below specified values. You might, for example, set an alert on each disk drive so that you are notified when the percent in use rises above 90 percent. Figure 20.9 shows such an alert.

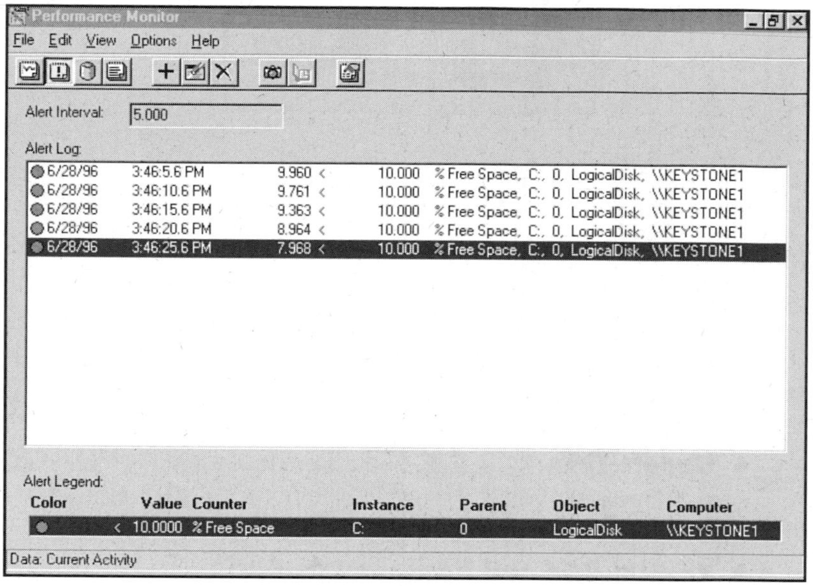

Figure 20.9

Alerts in Performance Manager.

You have the option to arrange to send network messages when alerts occur (see fig. 20.10).

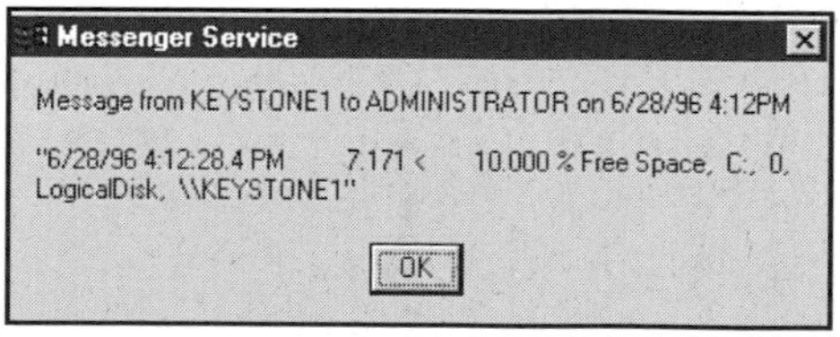

Figure 20.10

A Monitor alert message.

To add an alert, perform the steps as outlined in the following exercise:

Adding an Alert

1. Select alert view by choosing the **A**lert command in the **V**iew menu or by clicking the Alert icon in the toolbar.

2. Choose **A**dd to Alert in the **E**dit menu, or click the Add icon in the toolbar. The Add to Alert dialog box appears (see fig. 20.11). This screen shot was taken after the **E**xplain button had been chosen, so explanations of the options appear at the bottom of the window.

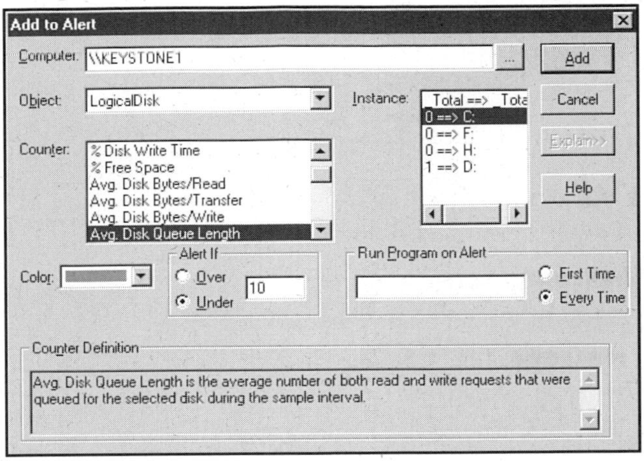

Figure 20.11

Adding an alert.

3. Enter the computer to be monitored in the **C**omputer box. If you want, click the ... button to browse for a computer.

4. Select an O**b**ject to be monitored.

5. Select an **I**nstance if more than one is listed.

6. Select a Coun**t**er to be monitored.

7. Select the Colo**r** to be associated with the alert.

8. In the Alert If box, choose **O**ver or **U**nder and specify a value that is to be used as the alert threshold.

9. If a program is to be run when an alert occurs, enter the program name in the Run **P**rogram on Alert box. Then choose whether the program should run the **F**irst Time the alert occurs or E**v**ery Time the alert occurs.

10. When the alert has been configured, choose **A**dd.

Setting Alert Options

You can configure options by choosing the **A**lert command in the **O**ptions menu when the alert view is displayed, or by clicking the Options icon in the toolbar when the alert view is displayed. Figure 20.12 shows the Alert Options dialog box. The available options are the following:

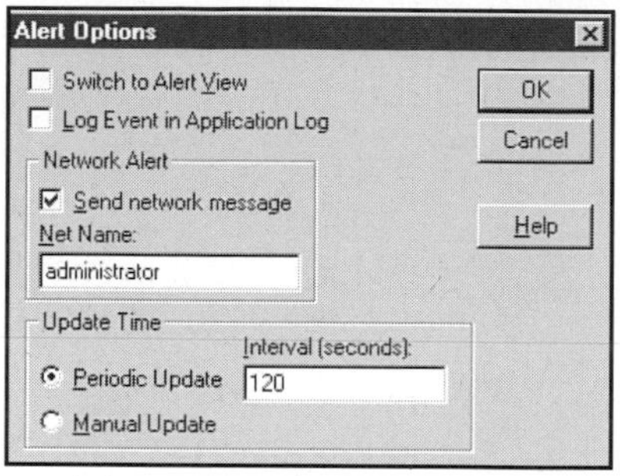

Figure 20.12

The Alert Options dialog box.

- ◆ **Switch to Alert View.** Check this option if you want Performance Monitor to switch to alert view when an alert condition is detected.

- ◆ **Log Event in Application Log.** Check this option if you want the event logged. Logged events can be viewed in the Event Viewer.

- ◆ **Send network message.** Check **S**end network message and enter the user name in the **N**et Name box if a network message should be sent to notify users of the alert.

- ◆ **Periodic Update.** Check this option if you want to display alerts at regular intervals. Specify the **I**nterval in seconds. (Don't specify an interval too short, or you'll find yourself doing nothing but clearing messages during a crisis.) Check **M**anual Update if you want to display alerts on demand.

> **Note**
>
> The messages generated by Performance Monitor are NetBIOS messages, and you need to make sure that the NetBIOS messenger service is running and has been alerted of your message recipients. To set up messaging, enter the following commands at a command prompt:
>
> ```
> net start messenger
> net name username add
> ```
>
> The *username* should match the name you entered in the **N**et Name box in the Alert Options dialog box.

Using Log Files

One task you should perform consistently with Performance Monitor is recording periodic logs of the status of the network. If you record logs when the network is functioning well, the data can help you spot what's wrong when the network starts to falter. You can, for example, record a log for the entire day every Monday, sampling the network at five-minute intervals, and then archive these logs for future review.

Recording a Log File

To record a log file, perform the following exercise steps:

Recording a Log File

1. Select the log view by choosing the **L**og command in the **V**iew menu or by clicking the Log icon in the toolbar.

2. Choose **N**ew Log Settings in the **F**ile menu to clear out existing log settings.

3. Choose **A**dd To Log in the **E**dit menu. The Add To Log dialog box appears (see fig. 20.13).

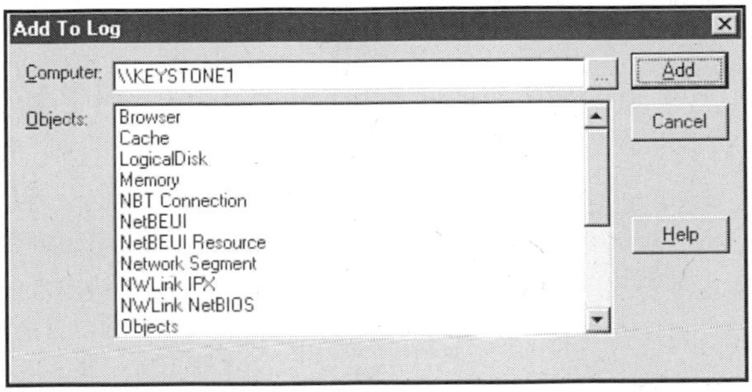

Figure 20.13

Adding to a log.

4. In the **C**omputer box, enter the computer to be monitored. If you want to browse for a computer, click the Browse button (...).

5. Select an object to be logged from the **O**bjects list. All the instances for the objects you select are logged.

6. Choose **A**dd to add the object to the log.

7. Repeat steps 5 and 6 for any other objects you want recorded in the log.

8. Choose **D**one when all objects have been added. You return to the log view, which specifies the objects to be monitored.

9. Next, specify a log file and turn on logging. Choose **L**og in the **O**ptions menu, or click the Options button in the toolbar. The Log Options dialog box appears (see fig. 20.14).

10. In the Directories box, browse for the directory in which log files are to be stored. Choose the Network if you want to browse for a shared network directory.

11. Specify a file name for the log file in the File **n**ame box. Performance Manager supplies the default LOG file name extension.

    Alternatively, select an existing log file.

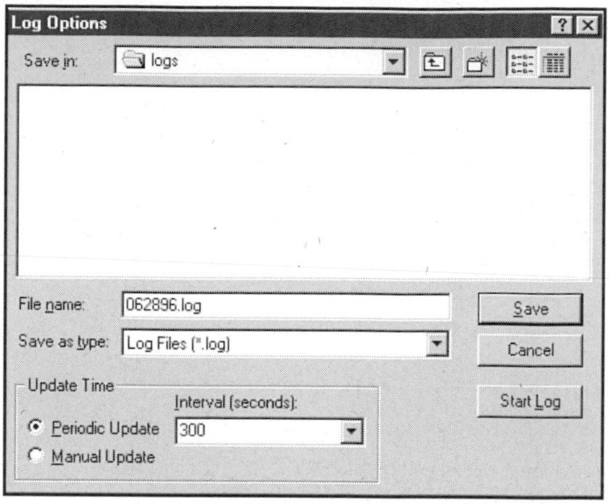

Figure 20.14

Specifying log options.

12. In the Update Time box, specify the log updates desired. Choose **P**eriodic Update and specify an update **I**nterval if updates should take place at automatic intervals. Choose **M**anual Update if you want to record updates only on demand.

13. Turn on logging by choosing Start **L**og. Then choose OK to return to the log view. The log view in figure 20.15 shows a log that has been configured and started.

14. When you want to stop logging, open the Log Options dialog box and choose **S**top Log.

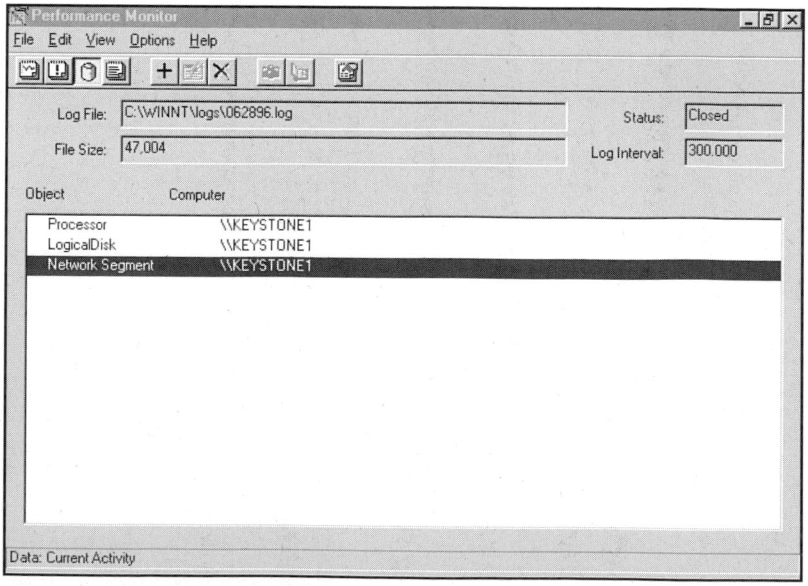

Figure 20.15

A log being recorded.

Using a Log File

After recording a log file, it can be opened for analysis. To open a log file, perform the steps in the following exericse:

Using a Log File

1. If the log file is still collecting data, it must be closed. Select the log view by choosing the **L**og command in the **V**iew menu or by clicking on the Log icon in the toolbar.

   Open the Log Options window and choose **S**top Log.

2. Up to this exercise, Performance Monitor has been using data from the current activity. To display data from a log file, do the following:

   ◆ Choose the Data **F**rom command in the **O**ptions menu. The Data From dialog box appears (see fig. 20.16).

   ◆ Select **L**og File.

   ◆ Specify the path and file name in the **L**og File box. Click on the Browse button (...) to browse for a directory and file.

   ◆ Choose OK.

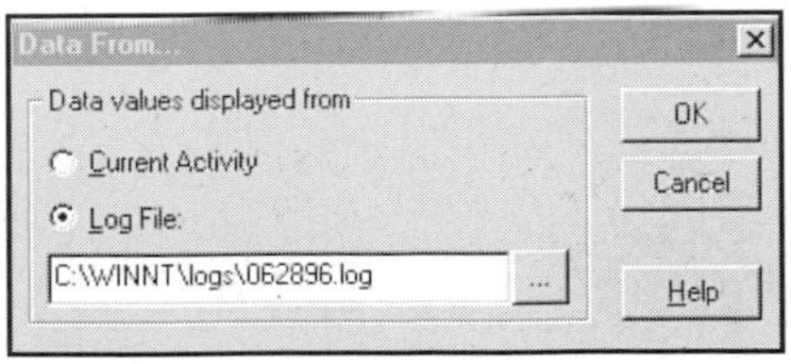

Figure 20.16

Selecting where data is to be taken from.

3. If you desire, you can specify a time window within the log file.

   Choose the **T**ime Window command in the **E**dit menu. This command is active only when data is coming from a log file. The Input Log File Timeframe appears, as shown in figure 20.17.

   The bar above the **B**ookmarks box graphically indicates the time line in the log file.

   The **B**ookmarks box lists events when data were logged.

   ◆ To select a start time for the data window, do the following:

   Select a bookmark in the **B**ookmarks box and choose Set As **S**tart.

   or

   Drag the start time handle of the timeline to the desired start time.

Figure 20.17

Specifying an input log file time frame.

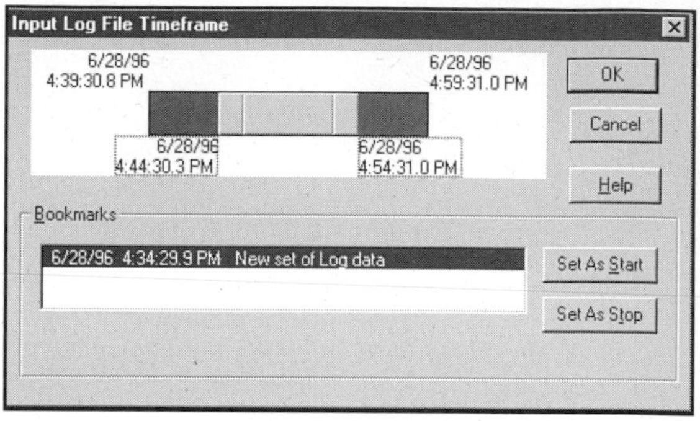

◆ To select a stop time for the data window, do the following:

Select a bookmark in the **B**ookmarks box and choose Set As S**t**op.

or

Drag the stop time handle of the timeline to the desired stop time.

4. Choose OK.

Now, you can enter the chart, alert, or report views and examine the data. You can chart old data, set alert parameters to see if any thresholds were exceeded, or generate reports, just as if data were being actively collected. The only restriction is that you can only include those objects you added to the log.

To resume real-time data analysis, be sure to reset the Data From command to Current Activity.

Creating Reports

Reports enable you to capture data in a tabular format. Reports represent a snapshot of the current activity data, and are most valuable when prepared using a log file, because you can scan through the log file to find the data on which you want to report. Reports are configured in a manner similar to charts and alerts. Perform the steps in the following exercise:

Creating Reports

1. Select the report view by choosing the **R**eport command in the **V**iew menu or by clicking on the Report icon in the toolbar.

2. If you want to clear a displayed report, choose **N**ew Report Settings in the **F**ile menu.

3. To create a new report item, choose **A**dd to Report in the **E**dit menu. The Add to Report dialog box appears, from which you can select the objects and counters to be reported.

4. When all desired objects and counters have been added to the report, choose **D**one. The report is displayed in the report view.

Exporting Reports

Reports can be exported in tab- or comma-delimited format, enabling report data to be transferred to spreadsheet and database programs for more detailed analysis.

To export a report, perform the steps in the following exercise:

Exporting Reports

1. Select the report view.

2. Define the report.

3. Choose **E**xport Report in the **F**ile menu.

4. In the Performance Monitor—Export As dialog box, specify the directory and file name for the export report file.

5. Select the file format in the List Files of **T**ype box.

   ◆ TSV files delimit data fields with tab characters.

   ◆ CSV files delimit data fields with commas.

6. Choose OK to export the file.

Filing Performance Monitor Settings

You may spend quite a while defining the settings for a view to meet your needs. You can save the settings you have created for any view and retrieve them for use at another time.

To save settings for a view, complete the steps in the following exercise:

Saving Settings for a View

1. Select the desired view.

2. Choose **S**ave ... Settings in the **F**ile menu. If you have not previously saved the settings, a Save As dialog box appears.

   Or choose Save ... Settings **A**s.

3. In the Save As dialog box, specify the Directory and File for the saved settings. The following default file name extensions are used:

   ◆ Chart: PMC

   ◆ Alerts: PMA

   ◆ Log: PML

   ◆ Reports: PMR

Save As saves only the view settings, not the data. To save data in a file, you must create a log.

To save all settings for all four windows, choose the Save **W**orkspace command in the **F**ile menu. You are prompted for a file name that is used to store the workspace data.

Tips on Using Performance Monitor

The number of objects and counters available in Performance Manager might overwhelm you. Fortunately, you probably won't need too many of them. (If you want a complete list, consult Appendix A in the *Optimizing Windows NT* volume of the *Windows NT Resource Kit.*)

Most problems are manifested in terms of system throughput, and you can focus on several areas when the system seems to be slowing down:

◆ The processor(s)

◆ Memory

◆ Hard drive performance

◆ Network hardware and software

Objective E.1

Processor Object

A good indicator of whether the processor is overloaded is %Processor Time, which indicates the percentage of time the processor is busy. If this value consistently exceeds 80 percent, and disk and network counter values are low, consider upgrading the processor to relieve performance bottlenecks.

Another good counter to watch is Interrupts/second. If you observe excessive interrupt activity, be on the lookout for misbehaving hardware (such as network adapters with faulty drivers) or applications. There's no easy to way to isolate the source of the excessive interrupts, but this counter gives you some tips on whether you are solving a potential problem.

Memory Object

A good way to check memory is to examine cache performance. If the cache is working smoothly, your system probably has enough memory. Monitor the Memory object for Cache Faults/sec and Page Faults/sec. Increasing numbers of errors in these areas indicates that the system is finding data less frequently in memory and must increase the frequency with which data is retrieved from disk. Eventually, a phenomenon called *thrashing* occurs, which means virtually all data accesses require data to be swapped between memory and the hard drive. Thrashing is death to system performance.

Paging File Object

Virtual memory makes use of a file named *pagefile.sys*. The Paging File object has counters that can help indicate whether pagefile.sys is large enough. If %Usage Peak approaches the maximum size you have specified for the paging file, reconfigure virtual memory so that the paging file has a larger maximum size.

Logical Disk Object

Check several statistics for the Logical Disk object. %Disk Time indicates the percentage of time the disk is active. If this value is high, check the Disk Queue Length counter, which indicates the number of pending I/O requests. Microsoft recommends that the Disk Queue Length value not exceed 1 1/2 to 2 times the number of physical drives that comprise the logical drive.

Avg. Disk sec/Transfer is a good indicator of how rapidly data can be transferred to and from the disk. An increasing value for this counter might indicate a pending hardware failure that is slowing disk throughput.

Physical Disk Object

Microsoft recommends that the Current Disk Queue Length value should not exceed the number of drives on the computer by more than 2.

Server Object

To determine whether network capacity is being exceeded, examine the Bytes Total/sec counter under the Server object. If the sum of Bytes Total/sec for all servers on a network segment is approaching the maximum bandwidth capacity of the segment, consider segmenting the network.

Network counters are organized by protocol. Select the protocols used most heavily on your network, and check a few counters. Monitor the Failures Adapter, which might predict impending failure of a network adapter. Also check Frame Bytes Re-Sent/sec because frame bytes are re-sent due to errors. Always expect to see some errors on a network, but be concerned if the number of errors begins to increase.

The absolute number of errors on a network is often less important than changes in the error rates. You should periodically log critical counters on your network and save the log files. Logging statistics when the network is performing well is called *baselining*. Your baseline measurements can serve as a basis for comparison when the network slows down. Differences in the statistics help isolate the system that is having problems.

You also can use Performance Monitor to compare statistics on several servers. If one server is working harder than another, move applications or other shared files to the less busy server.

Logons consume a considerable amount of a domain controller's processing capability. Consider monitoring Logons/second and Logons total under the Server Object to determine if logon activity is accelerating on your network. If it is, you should consider adding to the number of BDCs in the logon domain.

The Process Object

The Process object has an instance for every process running on the computer. It is time-consuming, but if you suspect that a particular process is dominating a computer, add a chart line for each process. Track the %Processing Time counter for each process to see if any of the processes is consuming an excessive amount of processor time. (Another option is to use the Process Viewer described at the end of this chapter.)

Network Monitor

Performance Monitor is limited to reporting statistics related to network performance. You cannot use Performance Monitor to examine the network traffic itself. Although you can, for example, gauge NWLink protocol performance by charting the numbers of frame bytes sent and received and the numbers of errors that are encountered, you cannot examine the frames to determine the nature of the traffic, the types of protocols, or the types of errors that are taking place. To diagnose your network in detail, you need a tool that can perform *protocol analysis*, enabling you to look inside the actual data circulating on your network.

Note   Unfortunately, protocol analysis can be very involved, requiring a detailed understanding of the protocols being analyzed. Thorough coverage of protocol analysis for the NetBEUI, IPX/SPX, and TCP/IP protocol suites would require another book nearly as large as this one. Therefore, all that can be done in this chapter is to introduce Network Monitor, and identify the components that can be used conveniently by the majority of LAN administrators.

Before you learn about Network Monitor, you may find it useful to review the following sections in this book:

◆ "A Formal Approach to Defining a Network" in Chapter 1, "Understanding Networks"

◆ "LAN Cabling Standards" in Chapter 4, "Planning and Installing Network Media"

◆ Chapter 8, "Managing the Network Configuration"

Network Monitor extends your capability to manage the network by enabling you to capture network data for detailed examination. You can look inside the frames to perform a detailed analysis of the network's operation.

Network Monitor is equipped with a wide variety of *protocol parsers*, which are modules that examine network frames to decode their contents. Among the 62 or so included protocol parsers are many you will recognize from discussion in this book, including Ethernet, token ring, IPX, IP, TCP, and PPP. A complete discussion of the protocol parsers, however, is far beyond the scope of this book. Although they are not books on protocol analysis, you can find more detailed descriptions of the network standards and protocols supported by Windows NT in the following resources:

◆ *Windows NT Server Professional Reference*, by Karanjit Siyan, published by New Riders Publishing

◆ *Networking with Microsoft TCP/IP*, by Drew Heywood, published by New Riders Publishing

As shipped with Windows NT 4, Network Monitor's one significant limitation is that it can capture only those frames that originate from or are delivered to the computer on which it is running, including broadcast and multicast frames that the computer receives or originates. You cannot use Network Monitor to monitor frames associated with other computers on the network.

Note   To monitor the entire network from a single computer, you need Microsoft's Systems Management Server (SMS), which includes a more powerful version of Network Monitor. SMS can monitor network traffic associated with any computer that is running a Network Monitor Agent. (*Agents* are proxy programs that collect data and forward them to another computer for analysis.) The Network Monitor Agent is included with Windows NT 4.

Ordinarily, computers on a network are selective and will only receive frames that are addressed to them. As shipped with Windows NT 4, Network Monitor is designed to work with standard network adapter cards, which in part accounts for the restriction of Network Monitor being only able to capture those frames that

continues

originate from or are delivered to the computer on which Network Monitor is running. Network Monitor works with NDIS 4, new with Windows NT 4, to capture network data with little or no degradation in computer performance.

The SMS Network Monitor captures network traffic in *promiscuous mode*, meaning that it can capture all network data regardless of the destination of the frames, thus enabling SMS to monitor any computer running a Network Monitor Agent. Capturing data in promiscuous mode is intense work, however, and performance will suffer on the computer running SMS. Therefore, monitoring the network with SMS Network Monitor is an activity best reserved for a dedicated network management computer. (On some network types, such as token ring, special network adapters are required to support promiscuous mode. Because the Network Monitor included with Windows NT 4 does not operate in promiscuous mode, special network adapters are not required.)

SMS has other capabilities as well, including hardware and software inventory, and remote administration and troubleshooting tools.

Installing Network Monitor

To install Network Monitor, open the Network utility in the Control Panel and open the Services tab. You can add two services related to the Network Monitor:

◆ **Network Monitor Agent.** Choose this option if this computer will be monitored by another computer running the SMS.

◆ **Network Monitor Tools and Agent.** Choose this option if this computer will be used to collect and analyze network data. This option also installs the Network Monitor Agent, enabling SMS to monitor this computer remotely.

Network Monitor is added to the Administrative Tools group of the Start menu. Network Monitoring Agent is added to the Control Panel as the Monitoring Agent utility. The computer must be restarted to activate Network Monitor.

Setting Up Network Monitor Security

The data captured by Network Monitor can include very sensitive information. Suppose, for example, that you are logging into a terminal session with a remote computer that does not use encrypted logins. Data frames sent to the remote computer would include your password in clear text, so the password could be discovered by any user with access to the Network Monitor. You should, therefore, prevent unauthorized users from using Network Monitor by assigning two types of passwords:

◆ A *capture password* is used to restrict the users who can use Network Monitor to capture and display statistics and data associated with this computer.

◆ A *display password* is used to determine which users can open previously saved capture files.

A capture password also restricts SMS access to the Network Monitor Agent. SMS can be used to capture data from a given agent only when the capture password is known.

To assign or change the Network Monitor passwords, complete the steps covered in the following exercise:

Assigning and Changing Network Monitor Passwords

1. Open the Monitoring Agent utility in the Control Panel to open the Configure Network Monitoring Agent dialog box shown in figure 20.18.

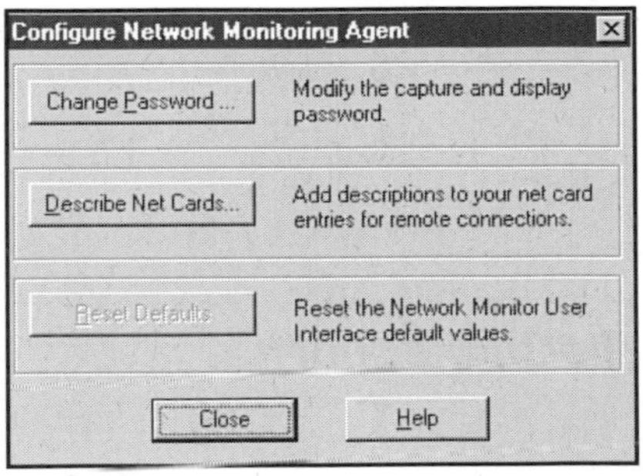

Figure 20.18

The Configure Network Monitoring Agent dialog box.

2. Choose Change **P**assword to open the Network Monitoring Password Change dialog box shown in figure 20.19.

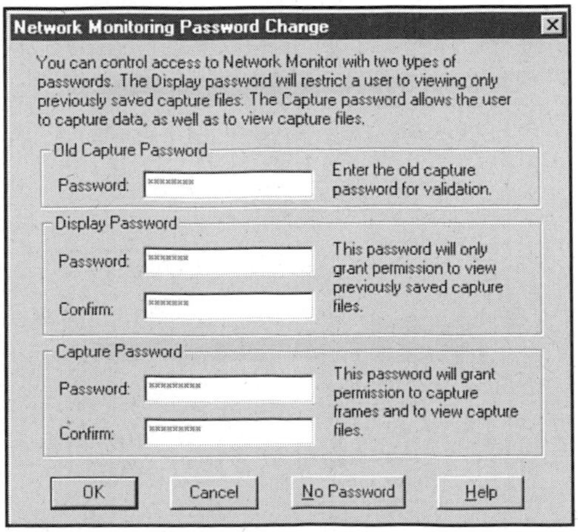

Figure 20.19

Configuring Network Monitor passwords.

3. To remove all passwords, choose **N**o Password, then OK.

4. To change the capture password, first enter the current password in the Old Capture Password box.

5. To specify a display or capture password, complete the appropriate Password field. Then enter the password again in the associated Confirm field to verify the entry.

6. Choose OK when passwords have been specified as desired. Then exit the Monitoring Agent utility.

Describing Your Network Cards

When one computer will be monitored by another, you should enter descriptions for each of the network adapters in the Network Monitor Agent. These descriptions enable the administrator who is monitoring the network to more easily identify the computer's network interfaces.

To describe network cards, follow these steps:

Exporting Reports

1. Open the Monitoring Agent utility in the Control Panel to open the Configure Network Monitoring Agent dialog box shown in figure 20.18. In figure 20.20, a description has been entered for the NE20001 adapter. The NE20002 adapter has not yet been described.

2. Choose **D**escribe Net Cards from the Configure Network Monitoring Agent dialog box to open the Describe Net Cards dialog box shown in figure 20.20.

Figure 20.20

Describing network cards.

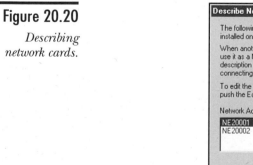

3. To change the description of a network adapter, select the entry and choose **E**dit Description to open a Change Net Card Description dialog box. Enter a new description and choose OK.

4. Repeat step 3 for each network card to be described.

Capturing Network Frames

The Network Monitor Capture window is shown in figure 20.21.

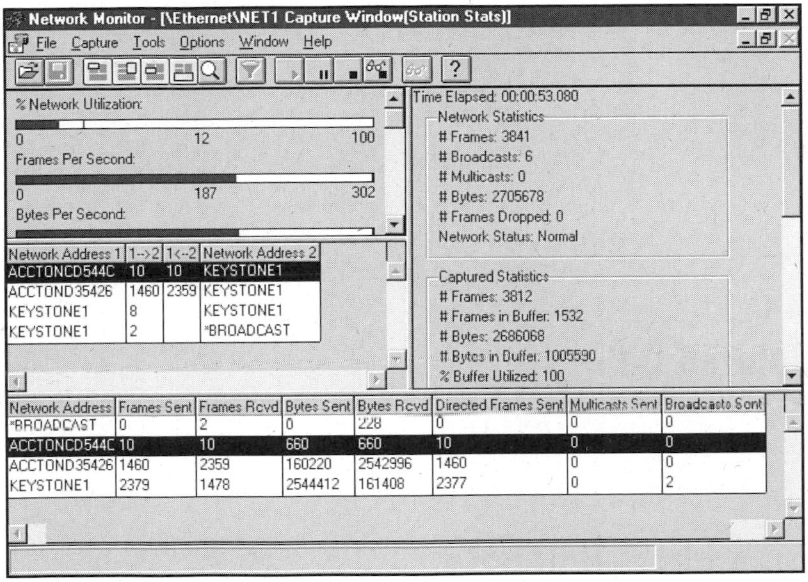

Figure 20.21

Elements of the Network Monitor window.

The window contains four panes:

◆ **Graph Pane.** This pane includes bar charts that dynamically display current activity. The five bars in this pane are % Network Utilization, Frames Per Second, Bytes Per Second, Broadcasts Per Second, and Multicasts Per Second. You can display or hide this pane by clicking the Toggle Graph Pane button. (A line in the % Network Utilization bar designates the highest utilization encountered during the current capture. The numbers at the right ends of the other bars describe the highest measurement encountered.)

◆ **Total Statistics.** This pane displays cumulative network statistics. These statistics summarize network traffic in five areas: Network Statistics, Captured Statistics, Per Second Statistics, Network Card (MAC) Statistics, and Network Card (MAC) Error Statistics. You can display or hide this pane by clicking the Toggle Total Statistics Pane button.

◆ **Session Statistics.** This pane displays statistics about sessions that are currently operating on the network. You can display or hide this pane by clicking the Toggle Total Session Statistics Pane button.

◆ **Station Statistics.** This pane displays statistics about sessions in which this computer is participating. You can display or hide this pane by clicking the Toggle Total Station Statistics Pane button.

When capturing is active, network frames are captured into a buffer that is limited in size. When the buffer fills up, older data are discarded to make room for new entries. Control capture status using the following options in the **C**apture menu: **S**tart, **S**top, Stop and **V**iew, **P**ause, and **C**ontinue. These functions can also be controlled using buttons in the toolbar, identified in figure 20.21.

Figure 20.21 was prepared while a capture was taking place. The information in the various panes is updated dynamically while capturing is active.

> **Tip**   If you want, you can focus on the activity in one of the panes. Simply select the pane and click the Zoom Pane button in the toolbar. The pane you selected will expand to fill the available space. To return to normal display, click the Zoom Pane button again.

Saving Captured Data

After you stop capturing data, choose **S**top in the **C**apture menu to stop the capture. The data in the capture buffer can now be analyzed as required, or it can be saved for future study.

Creating an Address Database

When you first capture data in Network Monitor, most devices will be identified by their physical network addresses (such as their Ethernet MAC addresses). Data captured in figure 20.21 identify most computers by their physical network addresses.

Because Microsoft network administrators generally prefer to identify computers by their NetBIOS names, Network Monitor includes a feature that identifies the NetBIOS names of computers from which data are captured.

To build the address database, start capturing data on the network and let Network Monitor continue to collect data for an extended period of time. As traffic is generated, computers will be added to the Session Statistics and Station Statistics panes, identified by their network addresses.

After capturing a large number of frames, stop capturing. Then select the Find All Na**m**es command in the **C**apture menu. The frames in the capture buffer will be scanned and the names will be added to the address database. During future capture operations, computers will be identified by name, as shown in figure 20.22.

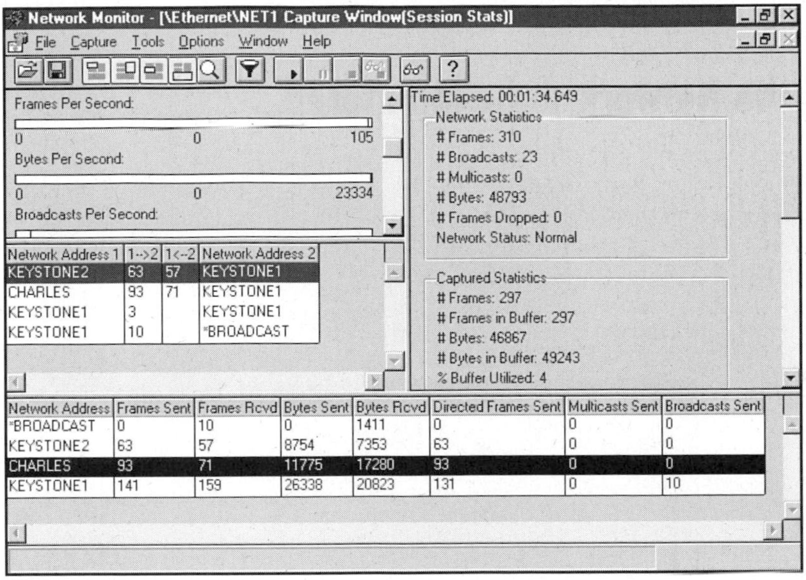

Figure 20.22

Computers identified by name in Network Monitor.

| **Note** | A bit of luck is required to capture frames that include computer names. Each time you capture data, collect names and add them to the database until the list is complete. |

You can view the address database, shown in figure 20.23, by choosing the **A**ddresses command in the **C**apture menu. Notice in the figure that a given computer may be represented by multiple entries, associated with different protocols and network types.

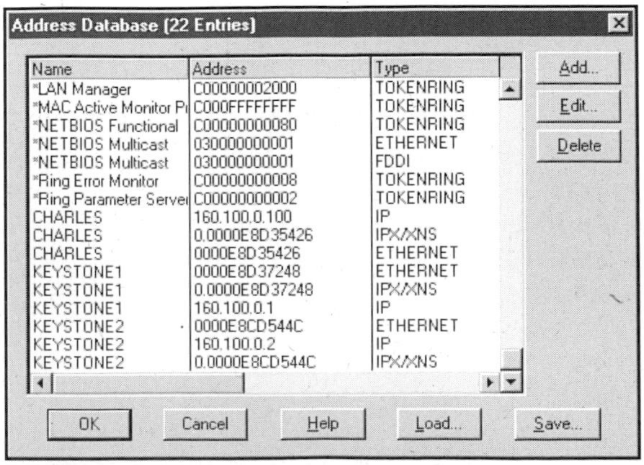

Figure 20.23

Viewing the address database.

In the Address Database dialog box, you can add, edit, and delete specific entries. You can save the database to a file with a .ADR extension, and load existing address files. The default address database, which is used unless you load another, is saved as DEFAULT.ADR.

Selecting the Network to be Monitored

When the Network Monitor computer is attached to two or more networks, it can monitor only one at a time. You can specify which network will be monitored by using the **N**etworks command in the **C**apture menu to open the Select Capture Network dialog box, shown in figure 20.24. The network that will be monitored is identified by the word CONNECTED in the Connect State column.

To change the connected network, select the network and choose **C**onnect.

Figure 20.24

Selecting the connected network.

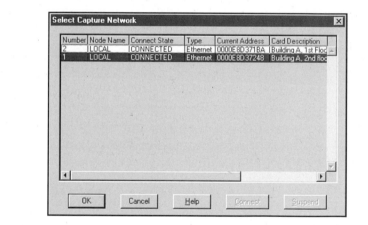

Managing the Capture Buffer

Data captured by Network Monitor are stored in system memory in a *capture buffer.* Due to lower performance of hard disks, disk storage cannot be used without the risk of losing frames during the capture process.

Ideally, the capture buffer should reside entirely in RAM. Virtual memory can be used, but frames may be lost. Therefore, setting the size of the capture buffer involves compromise. If the buffer is too small, it will not be large enough to capture a reasonable sample of network traffic. If the capture buffer is too large, part of it may be swapped into virtual memory and the efficiency of network data capture may be impaired.

To adjust the size of the capture buffer, choose the **B**uffer Settings command in the **C**apture menu to open the Capture Buffer Settings dialog box, shown in figure 20.25. In the **B**uffer Size (in MB) field, adjust the size of the capture buffer as desired. By default, the maximum size of the capture buffer is 8 MB less than the amount of RAM installed in the computer. To maximize the amount of RAM available for the capture buffer, stop as many applications as possible. Ideally, only Network Monitor should be running when you do this.

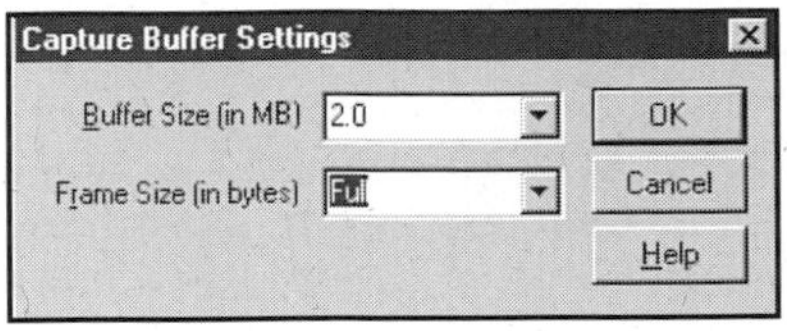

Figure 20.25

Configuring the capture buffer.

On a busy network, captured frames can quickly fill a capture buffer. In many cases, to ensure that the frames you need are captured, you will need to capture more frames than will fit in the capture buffer at one time. Fortunately, the most critical bytes are often found at the beginning of the frame. In many cases, you can use the capture buffer more efficiently by capturing only the frame header to obtain the information you need. In other cases, you need only capture the header and a limited portion of the data field.

The F**r**ame Size (in bytes) field in the Capture Buffer Settings dialog box specifies the number of bytes to be captured from the start of each frame that is captured. By default, the value of this field is Full, indicating that complete frames are to be captured. Suppose, however, that you are capturing data from an Ethernet network, and that you require only the bytes in the Ethernet frame headers, which make up the first 22 bytes of the frame. In that case, you can set the value of the F**r**ame Size (in bytes) field to 64 (the smallest setting). Other size increments are also available.

Avoiding Dropped Frames

When data are being captured, a significant part of the computer's processing capacity is required to dynamically update the Network Monitor display. When the CPU is busy, frames may be lost. You can reduce CPU loading by placing Network Monitor in dedicated capture mode.

Choose the Dedicated Capture Mode command in the Capture menu. When capturing is active, the Dedicated Mode dialog box will be displayed, as shown in figure 20.26. If capturing is currently stopped, the Dedicated Mode box will be displayed when capturing is started.

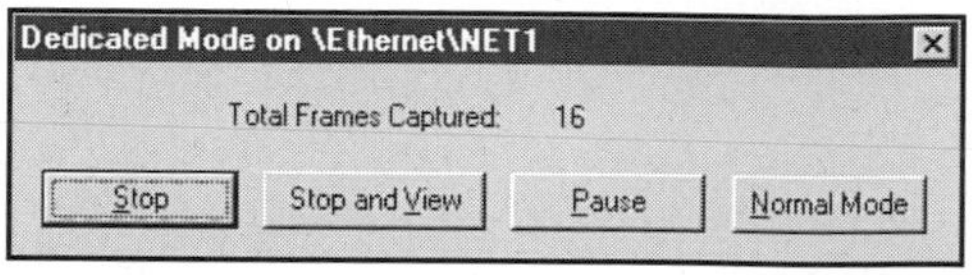

Figure 20.26

Capturing in dedicated mode.

Dedicated Mode on \Ethernet\NET1

Total Frames Captured: 16

| Stop | Stop and View | Pause | Normal Mode |

When capturing in dedicated mode, only the number of captured frames is updated in the display. You can stop and pause capturing in the Dedicated Mode dialog box. If you choose Normal Mode, capturing will continue while the full Network Monitor window is displayed. If you choose Stop and View, capturing will stop and the Capture window will be displayed. See the following section, "Examining Captured Data," for a discussion of the Capture window.

Using Capture Filters

On a large network, the volume of data can overwhelm you unless you have a way of focusing on specific types of data. *Capture filters* enable you to specify which types of frames will be captured, enabling you to capture data from a specific subset of computers or protocols.

> **Note**   Capture filters determine which frames will be stored in the capture buffer; however, all frames are reported in the performance statistics, regardless of any capture filter that may be in effect.

Structures of Capture Filters

Figure 20.27 shows the default capture filter, which is organized as a *decision tree*. Filters consist of three sets of criteria, connected by AND keywords. Frames will be captured only if they meet all three of the following criteria: SAP/ETYPE, address, and pattern match.

The capture filter criteria are described in the following sections.

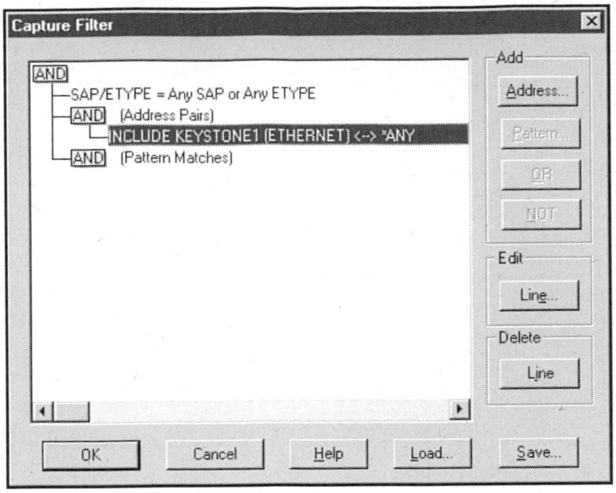

Figure 20.27

The default capture filter.

SAP/ETYPE Filters

The frames associated with specific protocols are identified by hexadecimal numbers referred to as SAPs or ETYPEs. By default, Network Monitor captures frames matching all supported protocols, but you can restrict capturing to specific protocols by selecting the SAPs and ETYPEs that will pass through the filter.

ETYPEs (*EtherTypes*) and SAPs (*service access points*) are used to specify the upper-layer protocols that are associated with a frame. An EtherType of 800 hex is associated with the IP protocol, for example. An EtherType of 8137 hex is associated with NetWare running on an EtherNet II LAN.

To establish capture filters for specific SAPs or ETYPES, select the SAP/ETYPE= line in the Capture Filter dialog box. Then choose Lin**e** in the Edit box to open the Capture Filter SAPs and ETYPEs dialog box, shown in figure 20.28. Network Monitor will capture frames matching protocols that are specified in the E**n**abled Protocols list; by default, all supported ETYPEs and SAPs are listed in this list.

To disable protocols, use the **D**isable and Disable A**l**l buttons to move protocols to the D**i**sabled Protocols list. In the representation in figure 20.28, several protocols have been disabled in this way.

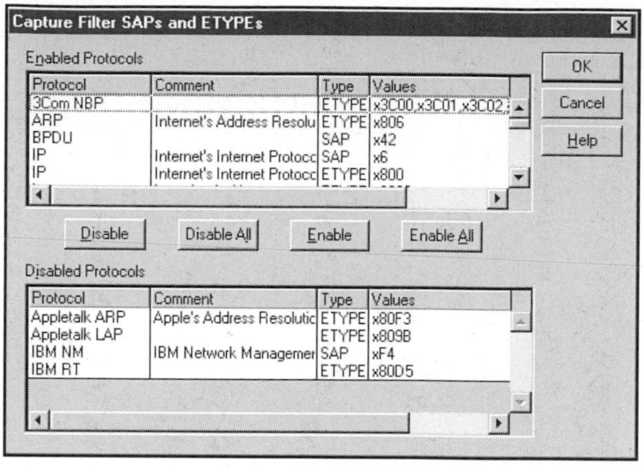

Figure 20.28

Filtering SAPs and ETYPEs.

To enable disabled protocols, use the **E**nable and Enable **A**ll buttons to move protocols to the E**n**abled Protocols list.

Address Filters

Every frame is associated with a source-destination address pair. By default, frames will be captured for all source-destination address pairs, but you can limit capturing to specific address pairs if you want to.

An address pair consists of the following components:

◆ A source address (or computer name)

◆ A destination address (or computer name)

◆ A direction arrow (- ->, <- -, or <- ->) specifying direction(s) in which traffic should be monitored

◆ The keyword INCLUDE or EXCLUDE specifying whether frames should or should not be captured for this address pair

Address pairs are established in the Address Expression dialog box, shown in figure 20.29. Open this dialog box as follows:

◆ To edit an existing address pair, select the entry in the entry under (Address Pairs) and choose Lin**e** in the Edit box, or double-click the entry.

◆ To create a new address pair, select any line in the (Address Pairs) section and choose **A**ddress in the Add box, or double-click the (Address Pairs) line.

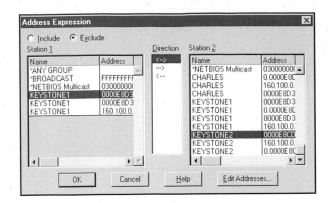

Figure 20.29

*Filtering on
address pairs.*

You can specify up to four address pairs. Suppose that you want to display all traffic between the KEYSTONE1 server and clients, but that you want to ignore traffic with the KEYSTONE2 server. The following address pairs establish a filter to accomplish that goal:

```
INCLUDE KEYSTONE1 <--> ANY
EXCLUDE KEYSTONE1 <--> KEYSTONE2
```

Tip   When multiple address pairs are specified, EXCLUDE statements have priority. If a frame matches an EXCLUDE statement, it will not be captured even though it may also match one or more INCLUDE statements.

Data Pattern Filtering

In some cases, you may want to filter frames by whether they include or do not include a specific pattern of bytes. In that case, you must specify one or more entries in the Pattern Matching section.

A pattern consists of two components:

◆ The pattern of bytes to be matched, which can be specified as a series of hexadecimal numbers or as a string of ASCII characters.

◆ An offset that specifies the position of the bytes in the frame. The offset can specify the position relative to the beginning of the frame or relative to the end of the topology header. (An offset of 0 specifies the first byte, which is 0 bytes from the beginning of the frame. Therefore, an offset of 19 specifies the 20th byte of the frame.) Specify the offset from the beginning of the topology header if the topology protocol permits variable length headers, such as Ethernet or token-ring MAC frames.

> **Tip**   You don't get much help when constructing capture filters based on data patterns. When you need to analyze frames based on data patterns, you may find it easier to construct data filters instead. As you will see in the following section "Display Filters," considerable expertise is built into the expression editor, which knows the structures of the headers for all the supported protocols.

Clearly, to set up filters, you must have a thorough understanding of the structures of the frames on your LAN. It is, unfortunately, beyond the scope of this book to consider the details of the message structures associated with the various protocols supported by Windows NT.

To add a filter, select the (Pattern Matches) line and chose **P**attern in the Add box, or double-click the (Pattern Matches) line. This will open the Pattern Match dialog box, shown in figure 20.30.

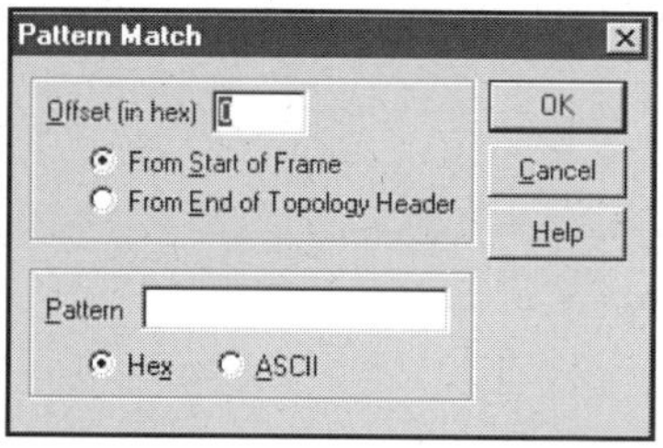

Figure 20.30

Entry form for a pattern match filter.

Using Logical Operators

When two or more patterns have been entered, you can set up complex filtering criteria using AND, OR, and NOT logical operations. Select the line to receive the logic operator, and choose **A**ND, **O**R, or **N**OT in the Add box. After you add a logical operator, you can drag the operators and expressions around to construct the logic tree that you require.

The logical operators function as follows:

◆ An AND branch of the tree will be true if all of the expressions under the AND are true. Otherwise, the AND branch will be false.

◆ An OR branch of the tree will be true if any of the expressions under the OR are true. The OR branch will be false if all of the expressions under the OR are false.

◆ A NOT will be true if the expression under the NOT is false. A NOT will be false if the expression under the NOT is true.

Note	Pattern matching is the one place in this book where we enter the esoteric realm of Boolean algebra. The programmers among you will be comfortable enough, but readers new to Boolean logic should be wary when setting up complex filters. It is quite easy to get the logic wrong and to establish filters that misbehave in mysterious ways. If you aren't capturing the frames you want, check the logic in your capture filter.

Using Capture Triggers

On occasion, you may want a particular action to occur when a particular network situation occurs. A *trigger* describes a set of network conditions and an action that takes place when the conditions are met.

To define a capture trigger, choose the **T**rigger command in the **C**apture menu to open the Capture Trigger dialog box shown in figure 20.31. The following trigger types can be selected:

◆ **Nothing.** No triggers are specified. This is the default setting.

◆ **Pattern match.** The trigger is initiated when a specified pattern is identified in a captured frame. Specify the pattern in the **P**attern box.

◆ **Buffer space.** The trigger is initiated when the free buffer space falls below the threshold specified in the Buffer Space box.

◆ **Pattern match then buffer space.** The trigger is initiated when the pattern specified in the **P**attern box is identified in a captured frame, followed by a free buffer space that falls below the threshold specified in the Buffer Space box.

◆ **Buffer space then pattern match.** The trigger is initiated when the free buffer space falls below the threshold specified in the Buffer Space box, followed by the detection of a frame that includes the pattern specified in the **P**attern box.

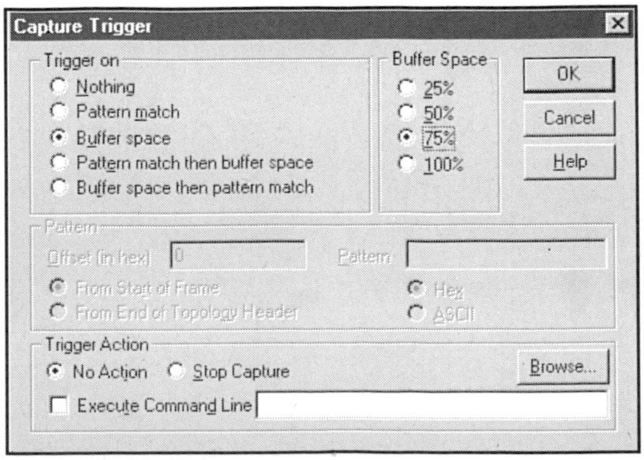

Figure 20.31

Establishing a capture trigger.

When the trigger occurs, one of three events can take place, as specified in the Trigger Action box:

◆ **No Action.** No action is taken when the trigger occurs.

◆ **Stop Capture.** Capturing will halt when the trigger occurs. This option ensures that the frame that initiated the trigger will remain in the capture buffer.

◆ **Execute Command Line.** The command specified will be executed when the trigger occurs. Include the path and command to be executed.

Saving Capture Data

After you have stopped capturing data, you can save the contents of the capture buffer for later analysis. Use the **S**ave command in the **F**ile menu to save the capture buffer in a file with a .CAP name extension. Load previously saved data with the **O**pen command in the **F**ile menu.

Examining Captured Data

After frames have been captured, you can examine them in considerable detail. To examine captured frames, do one of the following:

◆ When capturing is active, click the Stop and View Capture toolbar button, choose the Stop and **V**iew option in the **C**apture menu, or press Shift+F11.

◆ When capturing is stopped, click the Display Captured Data toolbar button, choose the **D**isplay Captured Data option in the **C**apture menu, or press F12.

These actions open the Capture dialog box, shown in figure 20.32. At first, this dialog box includes one pane, which lists all frames currently in the capture buffer.

To examine details for a frame, double-click on the entry for the frame. This will add two more panes to the dialog box, as shown in figure 20.33.

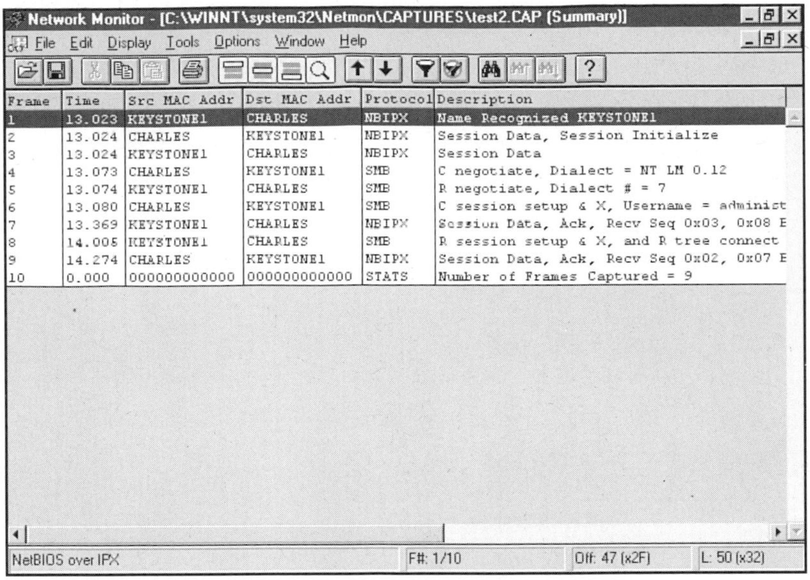

Figure 20.32

The Capture window showing captured frames.

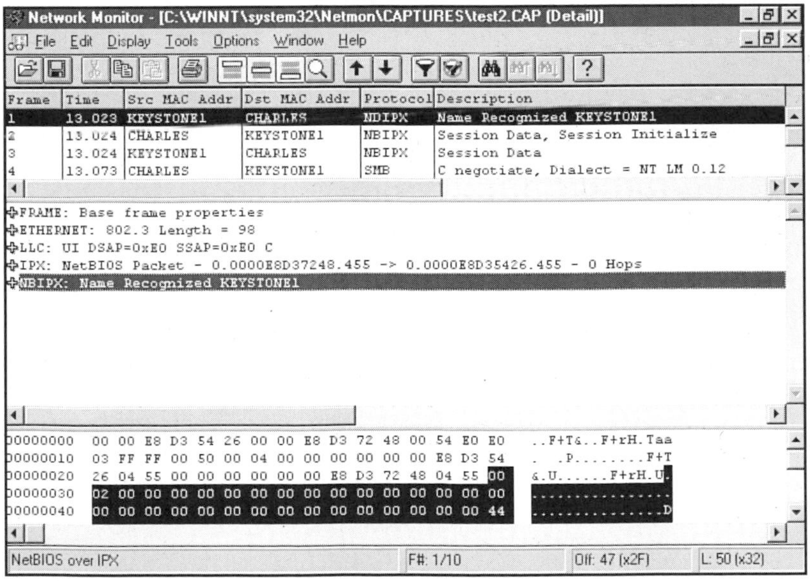

Figure 20.33

The Capture window showing all panes.

The panes are as follows:

- **Summary Pane.** This pane includes a one-line summary of each frame in the capture buffer.

- **Detail Pane.** This pane displays the contents of the frame, organized by protocol layer.

- **Hex Pane.** This pane displays the data in the pane in hexadecimal and in ASCII characters. The bytes that are highlighted are associated with the protocol section that is highlighted in the Detail Pane.

The following sections discuss the Summary and Detail Panes.

The Summary Pane

The Summary Pane briefly describes each frame that is held in the capture buffer. To open a frame for detailed analysis, select the entry in the Summary Pane. In figure 20.33, the frames were captured when a user logged on to the KEYSTONE domain from the workstation CHARLES. Filtering was used so that only frames sent between KEYSTONE1 and CHARLES would be captured.

The source and destination computers are identified by the Src MAC Addr and Dst MAC Addr fields. If a name database has been created, NetBIOS names will appear in place of hexadecimal physical addresses.

The frames shown in figure 20.33 are associated with two Windows NT protocols. In the Protocol column, NBIPX identifies frames associated with running NetBIOS over the IPX protocol. SMB identifies frames associated with the Server Message Block protocol. SMB is the protocol used to format messages on Windows NT networks. SMB messages fall into four categories:

- **Session Control.** Commands that establish or release connections with shared network resources.

- **File.** Commands that access shared remote file systems.

- **Printer.** Commands that access shared remote printers.

- **Message.** Commands used by applications and the operating system to send messages.

The entries in the Description column can be reasonably clear (for example, "Name Recognized KEYSTONE1") or downright obscure (such as "R negotiate, Dialect # = 7"). To decode the descriptions, you will need to learn the operational details of the protocols that are being analyzed.

The Detail Pane

Unless you are knowledgeable enough to undertake a byte-by-byte analysis of the data, the Detail Pane will probably be the pane that occupies most of your analytical effort. This pane translates the data in the various header layers into human-readable form. In figure 20.34, the Detail Pane was expanded by selecting it and clicking the Zoom Pane button.

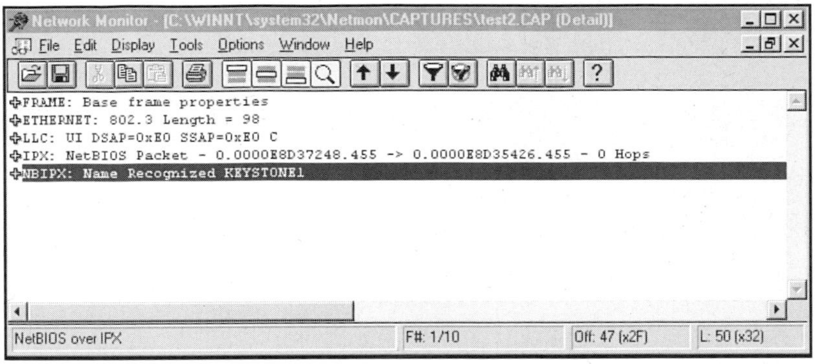

Figure 20.34

The Detail Pane.

The frame that is represented is identified by the description "Name Recognized KEYSTONE1." This frame is associated with NetBIOS over IPX. As shown in figure 20.34, Network Monitor has organized the frame contents in terms of the protocol layers that are embedded in the frame. This frame contains five layers of protocol data:

◆ **FRAME.** Basic physical properties of the frame, including when it was captured and its length in bytes.

◆ **ETHERNET.** Ethernet physical and MAC layer data. Here, for example, you learn that the frame type is IEEE Ethernet 802.3.

◆ **LLC.** IEEE LLC (logical link control) sublayer data.

◆ **IPX.** Novell IPX protocol network layer data.

◆ **NBIPX.** Microsoft NetBIOS over IPX data.

This organization enables you to examine the layers that are encapsulated within the frame with relative ease.

In figure 20.34, notice that each entry is tagged with a + to the left, indicating that the entry can be expanded to show greater detail. In figure 20.35, the ETHERNET entry has been expanded by clicking on the +. Within the entry you can see how Network Monitor has decoded entries such as the destination and source addresses, the frame length, and the length of the data field. While becoming familiar with Network

Monitor, take some time to compare the frame data by comparing the decoded frame data in the Detail Pane to corresponding "raw" data in the Hex pane. This will give you an appreciation for the way the Detail Pane translates data for easier analysis.

Figure 20.35

Details of the Ethernet frame.

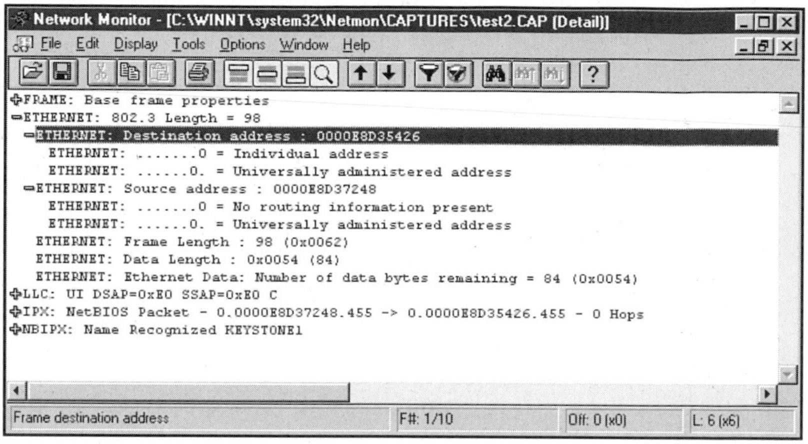

When you select a field in the Detail Pane, the legend at the bottom of the window provides some useful information about the field:

◆ First shown is a brief description of the field.

◆ `F#:`. This box designation specifies the frame's position in the capture buffer. For example, `F#: 4/10` designates that this is the fourth of ten frames captured.

◆ `Off:`. This box specifies the offset of the selected byte from the start of the frame. For example, `Off: 74(x4A)` specifies that the selected byte is offset 74 (decimal) bytes (4A hex) from the first byte of the frame. The first byte of the frame has an offset of 0. (This field is a valuable guide when setting up capture and display filters.)

◆ `L:`. This box specifies the length of the field in bytes.

Clearly, given the complexity of the data, there is nothing easy about protocol analysis, and I regret that I have to leave this discussion, without getting down to the details. In truth, however, few readers of this book will need to thoroughly comprehend the information in Network Monitor. Many organizations find it more comprehensive to hire a consultant who is an expert in protocol analysis, rather than maintaining an expert on staff. You will still find it useful, however, to learn how to perform network captures. At the very least, you can collect network traffic when problems are encountered, so that the data can be analyzed later by an expert.

Display Filters

Okay, you've collected a buffer full of frames and you want to focus your attention on just a few without scrolling through the thousands that are available? No problem, just design a display filter. Choose **F**ilter in the **D**isplay menu to open a dialog box in which you can design a display filter. Display filters are a bit different from capture filters, so let's take a brief look at the procedure.

Figure 20.36 shows the Display Filter dialog box. The default display filter, shown in figure 20.36, displays frames for all protocols and computer addresses.

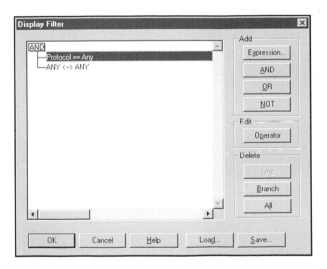

Figure 20.36

The default display filter.

Adding Expressions

To add an expression to the Display Filter, select the line that will precede the new expression, and choose E**x**pression in the Add box to open the Expression dialog box, shown in figure 20.37. This dialog box has three tabs, enabling you to enter expressions based on three types of properties: Address, Protocol, and Property. Figure 20.37 shows the Address tab.

Figure 20.37

Constructing an address expression for a display filter.

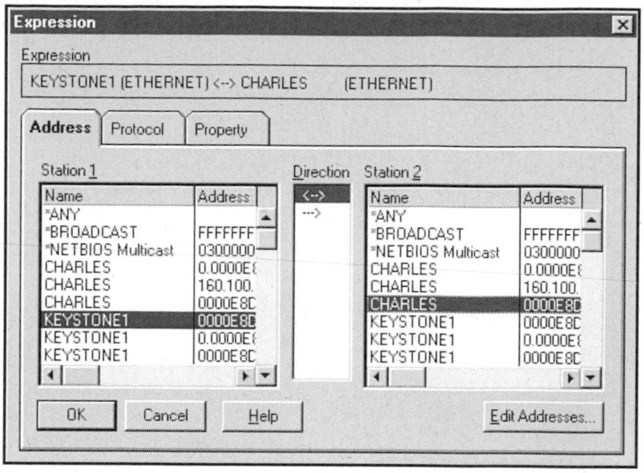

Address expressions specify the addresses of two computers whose frames are to be captured together with a direction specification. As you select entries for Station **1**, **D**irection, and Station **2**, the expression you are constructing is displayed in the Expression box.

The Protocol tab enables you to enable and disable filters for specific protocols (see fig. 20.38). If a protocol is listed in the D**i**sabled Properties list, frames for that protocol will not be displayed.

Figure 20.38

Constructing a protocol expression for a display filter.

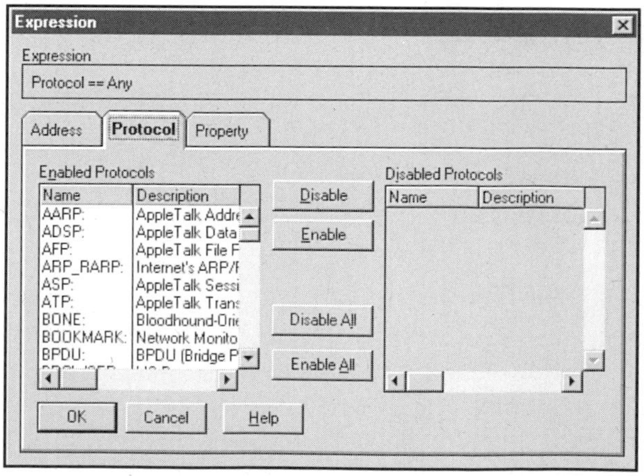

The Property tab is used to construct filters based on data patterns (see fig. 20.39). As you saw, you receive no help when establishing data patterns for capture filters; however, you can expect considerable help when constructing display filters.

Each of the protocols in the **P**rotocol Property list can be opened to list the data fields in the protocol header. In figure 20.39, the Ethernet protocol has been expanded to reveal the fields of an ETHERNET header. After selecting Ethernet Type (EtherType), a list of valid options is revealed in the **R**elation list. And, although I could have manually entered a hex number in the **V**alue field, I was able to select one of the predefined options. In this case, NetWare IPX has an Ethernet type of E0 hex.

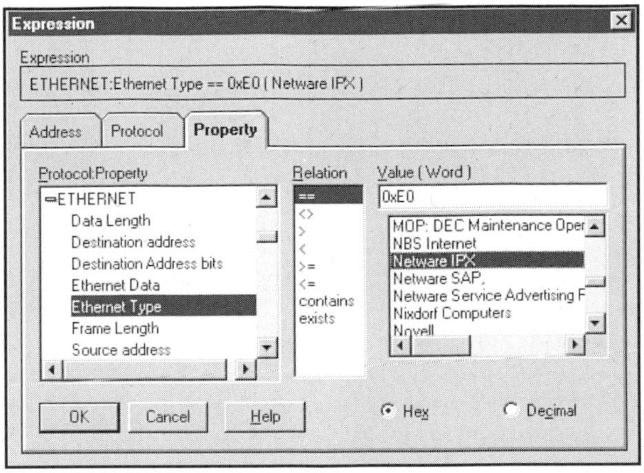

Figure 20.39

Constructing a protocol property expression for a display filter.

> **Tip**
> It is clearly easier to construct display filters rather than capture filters. You may want to filter in two stages. So that you don't have unwanted frames cluttering the capture buffer, construct capture filters to limit the general categories of frames that are captured, perhaps sorting by protocol (using SAP or ETYPE filters). Then use display filters to zoom on the details and isolate specific frames.

Using Logical Operators

You can use AND, OR, and NOT operators to modify the expressions in display filters. To add a logical operator to an expression, select the expression, and choose **A**ND, **O**R, or **N**OT. The easiest way to organize the structure of the logic tree is to drag expressions and operators around.

> **Tip**
> To change a logical operator in a display filter, click on the operator icon. The icon will change from AND to OR to NOT with each click.

Managing Browsers

You have seen many instances of using browsing to locate resources on the network. Browsing is yet another service that is supported on the network, and you should be aware of how browsing works, in case your users have trouble browsing.

How Browse Monitors Work

Each domain has a *master browser,* which is usually the primary domain controller. If a master browser announces that it is shutting down, other computers hold an election to determine which is best able to become the domain master browser. If a client cannot find a browser, it can force an election of a new master browser.

As additional computers are added to the network, they may become backup browsers. By default, Windows NT computers become backup browsers, although computers can be configured as standby browsers. The master browser can instruct standby browsers to become backup browsers, attempting to maintain about one backup browser per 30 computers, with a maximum of three per domain/segment. Backup browsers spread the work of browsing around. Backup browsers check in every 15 minutes with the master browser to update their databases.

Any Windows NT computer that is running the Server service will be advertised via the browser mechanism. When a server comes onto the network, it announces itself to the master browser. Periodically, the server checks in with the master browser, decreasing the frequency until it is checking in about every 12 minutes.

When a master browser fails, it might be 15 minutes before backup browsers detect the failure. The first backup browser to detect the failure forces an election to select a new master browser.

When clients browse the network, they use a browser API call to identify browsers on the network, to select a browser, and to browse the database in the browser.

A computer's browser behavior is determined by a key in the Registry: HKEY_LOCAL_MACHINE\SYSTEM\CurrentControlSet\Services\Browser\ Parameters. The MaintainServerList value entry for this key can have three values:

◆ **No.** Indicates that the computer will never be a browser.

◆ **Yes.** Indicates that the computer will be a browser. It will attempt to contact the master browser and become a backup browser. If no master browser is found, the computer forces an election for a master browser.

◆ **Auto.** Indicates that the computer is a standby browser and can become a backup browser if a master browser notifies it do so. Auto is the default value.

With a Windows for Workgroups computer, you can control the computer's browser behavior by adding a line to the [network] section of the system.ini file. To prevent the computer from functioning as a browser, add the following line:

```
MaintainServerList=No
```

Note The list of servers maintained by a master browser is limited to 64 KB of data. As a result, a domain or workgroup is limited to about 2,000–3,000 computers.

In rare instances, you may have a Windows NT computer that is configured as a server (it is running the Server service) but that you don't want to be advertised in browser lists. To prevent the server from appearing in browser lists, use the Registry editor to add a value to the key HKEY_LOCAL_MACHINE\System\CurrentControlSet\Services\ LanManServer\Parameters. Add a value entry with the name Hidden, the type REG_ DWORD. Set the value to 1 to remove the computer from browse lists. Set the value to 0 to enable the computer to appear in browse lists.

Monitoring Browser Status

The *Windows NT Resource Kit* includes a Browser Monitor that can be used to monitor the status of browsers on a network. The icon for this program is installed in the Resource Kit program group.

When you start the Browser Monitor utility, you must tell it which domain or domains to display. Choose the **A**dd Domain command in the **D**omain menu. Then select a domain from the Select Domain list. Workgroups count as well as Windows NT domains; you can add either or both. After you have added domains, you should have a list similar to the one in figure 20.40.

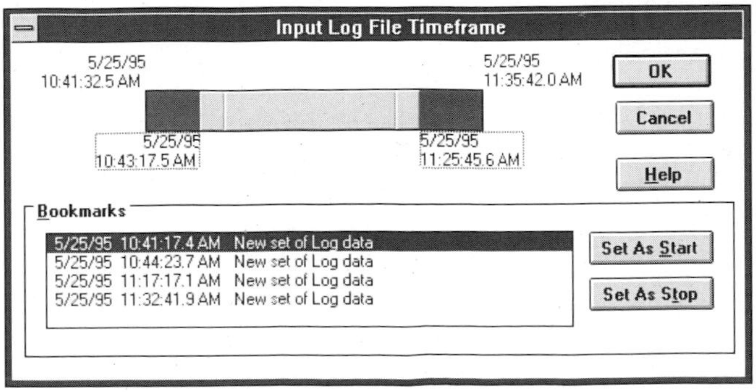

Figure 20.40

A master browser list.

Each protocol that supports browsing should show a master browser. This figure shows a master browser for the Keystone domain, for the *NWLinkNB* (NetBIOS over NWLink) protocol, and for *Nbf* (NetBIOS Frame Protocol, Microsoft's name for TDI-compliant NetBEUI).

You can determine from this window which computer is functioning as the master browser for each domain. KEYSTONE1 is the master browser for the KEYSTONE domain, which isn't surprising, since it is the primary domain controller. The Windows for Workgroups computer named BUSTER is the master browser for Workgroup.

Each of these entries can be used to access a separate browser status window, which you can examine by selecting an entry and choosing the **P**roperties command in the **D**omain menu. Figure 20.41 shows the browser status display for the KEYSTONE domain NBF protocol. From this window, you can determine that KEYSTONE1 and KEYSTONE2 servers are both functioning as browsers for the KEYSTONE domain. They are also backup browsers for WORKGROUP.

Figure 20.41

*Browser status
for a domain.*

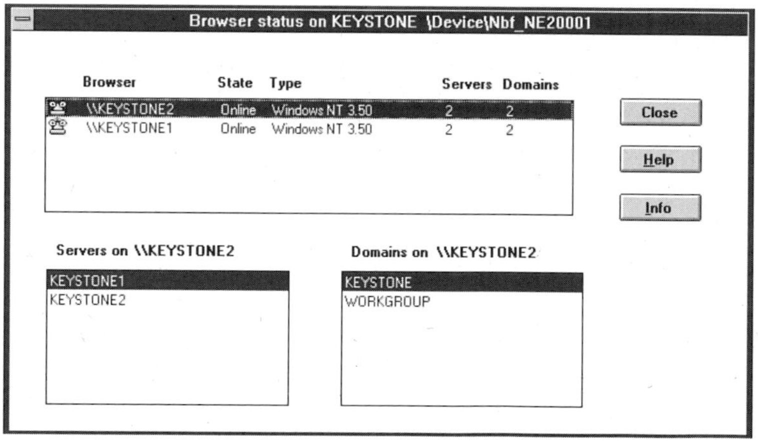

Remember that it takes some time for backup browsers and servers to register their presence with the master browser. If you are running Browser Manager immediately after starting computers on the network, it might take a while before the data catches up with your expectations.

If you want to see details about one of the browsers, double-click on its entry in the Browser list. You are rewarded with a list containing more statistics than you probably care to have. Figure 20.42 offers an example.

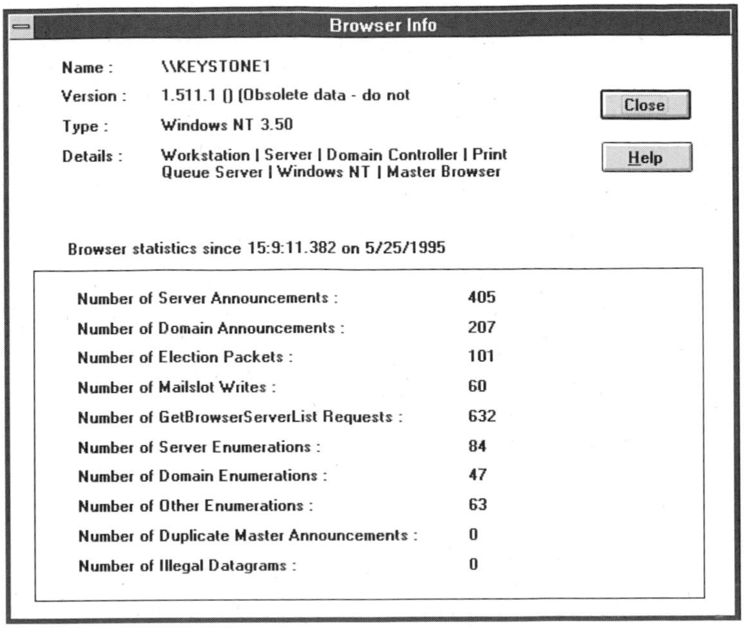

Figure 20.42

*Detailed infor-
mation about a
browser.*

Other Mini Network Utilities

The *Windows NT Resource Kit* includes some other simple utilities that you might find
useful for network monitoring.

Using Net Watcher

Net Watcher displays a browseable list of shares and users in the domain, an example
of which is shown in figure 20.43. You can double-click on any of these items for more
detail.

Process Viewer

This utility shows you detailed information about every process running on a computer. Figure 20.44 offers an example of a Process Viewer display. You need to dig in
to the *Windows NT Resource Kit* to find out what all the statistics are, but that is true of
Performance Monitor as well. The **M**emory Detail button in Performance Viewer
enables you to examine the detailed memory usage of a process.

> **Caution**   You can kill processes with the **K**ill Process button, so Process Viewer can make you
> very dangerous.

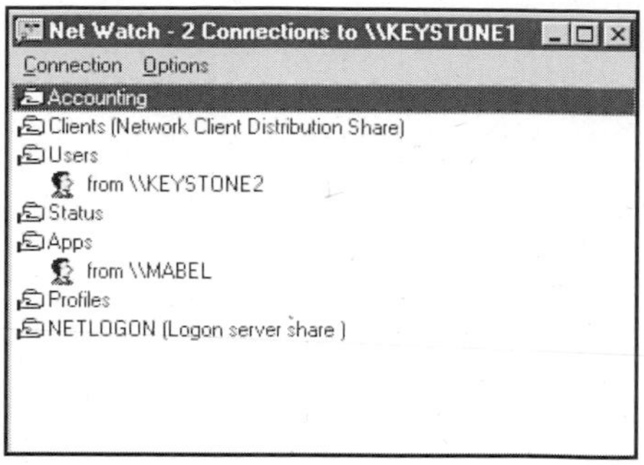

Figure 20.43

You can double-click on shares and users to see more information about them.

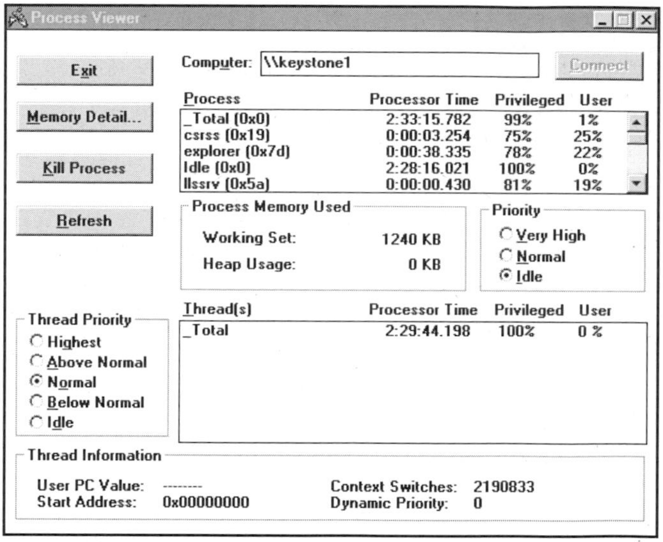

Figure 20.44

The Process Viewer dialog box.

Testing Your Knowledge

1. The Network Client Administrator can build network installation startup disks for which two types of clients?

    A. Windows for Workgroups 3.11

    B. Windows 95

    C. MS-DOS and Windows

    D. OS/2 1.X

2. Under Windows NT Server 4, the Network Client Administrator tool only allows for the creation of 3 1/2" disk sets.

   A. True

   B. False

3. If your network uses more than one model of network adapter, you must create a network installation startup disk for each card model.

   A. True

   B. False

4. What is the term for a process running on the computer as it relates to the Performance Monitor tool?

   A. Counter

   B. Instance

   C. Token

   D. Object

5. If more than one object is available for monitoring, such as a multiprocessor server, you need to select the desired _____ to monitor.

6. When choosing a specific object and counter to monitor with the Performance Monitor tools chart view, you can optionally select which of the following options for the line associated with it?

   A. Color

   B. Scale

   C. Width

   D. Style

7. When a server called Keystone1 is restarted, what is the proper command line that an administrator can use to turn on disk performance counters?

   A. diskperf on \\Keystone1

   B. diskperf \\Keystone1 on

   C. diskperf \\keystone1 -y

   D. diskperf -y \\Keystone1

8. What are the four types of views supported under the Performance tool?

   A. Chart

   B. Report

   C. Alert

   D. Archive

   E. Log

9. The Performance Monitor does not support printing data directly.

    A. True

    B. False

10. If you are setting up alert options and want to use the Send network message option, you must start the _____ service.

11. When using a log file, you can view chart, alert, and report views of the logged data. The only restriction is that you can only include those objects you added to the log.

    A. True

    B. False

12. Which Performance Monitor view type enables you to capture data in a tabular format?

13. The Performance Monitor does not allow you to save settings created for views.

    A. True

    B. False

14. Which object should be monitored to see if network capacity is being exceeded?

    A. Process

    B. Paging File

    C. Server

    D. Memory

15. What are the two services related to the Network Monitor that can be installed in the Network Utility in the Control Panel?

    A. Network Monitor Tools and Agent

    B. LAN Manager Master Browser Service

    C. Network Performance Monitor Agents

    D. Network Monitor Agent

16. Which type of password is used under the Network Monitor to determine which users can open previously saved capture files?

    A. display password

    B. capture password

    C. logon password

17. On large networks, the volume of data can overwhelm you unless you have a way of focusing on specific types of data. What enables you to specify which types of frames will be captured?

   A. Frame buffers

   B. Capture filters

   C. Capture buffers

   D. Frame filters

18. When a capture trigger occurs, three events can take place. They are:

   A. Send Alert

   B. Stop Capture

   C. Execute Command Line

   D. No Action

Review Answers

1. A, C

2. B

3. A

4. D

5. Instance

6. A, B, C, D

7. D

8. A, B, C, E

9. A

10. Messenger

11. A

12. report

13. B

14. C

15. A, D

16. A

17. B

18. B, C, D

CHAPTER 21

Using the Remote Access Server

Executives, sales, and marketing staffs are used to traveling, but increasingly other categories of staff members are finding themselves working away from the office. A few companies have even closed entire offices, given their employees a desk and a business telephone, and sent them home to work. When users travel, or when they work at home, they still expect to maintain contact with the central office. Increasingly, that means that users are demanding remote access to their company LANs.

Offices that can be anywhere have come to be called *virtual offices*, and you can expect to see a lot more virtual offices as portable computers become less expensive and telecommuting becomes easier. Consequently, it is extremely likely that users will be demanding remote access to your LAN to send e-mail, to access central databases, or to exchange files with their coworkers.

Remote LAN access has been possible for several years, thanks to programs such as PC Anywhere and Carbon Copy. But adding dial-up capability has generally meant buying additional products, integrating them, and training your users to use them and live with the quirks.

Microsoft has simplified remote LAN access considerably by building a Remote Access Server (RAS) into Windows NT and Windows for Workgroups. RAS integrates smoothly with Windows and doesn't require users to learn a new method of using LAN resources. The only difference between a remote user and a local user is the initial dial-in step. Once the dial-in is set up, everything works as though the computer were directly attached to the LAN cable.

RAS isn't a telecommunication program, and it can't be used for accessing, say, CompuServe or a BBS. But it is easy to integrate TCP/IP with RAS, and RAS can be used as a way to access the Internet.

This chapter will teach you how remote access works with an emphasis on RAS. You will learn how to add remote access capability to your LAN, how to connect to the LAN from a remote location, and how to use RAS to access the Internet.

Styles of Remote Access

Remote access wasn't a big problem when applications and terminals were based on text and when all controls were typed commands. But PCs eliminated that simplicity long ago by introducing graphic interfaces and non-keyboard input devices. Windows users want to be able to use their mice, they don't want to give up their graphic interfaces, and they certainly don't want to learn a complicated command language for transferring files or using central computer resources. Therefore, a successful remote access strategy must enable users to carry their desktop graphic environments with them.

There are two approaches to remote network access that meet the needs of a graphic environment: remote control and remote node. You need to comprehend the differences to understand when RAS is appropriate and when you should examine another approach.

Remote Access Using Remote Control

Remote control is the older and better-established of the two approaches. It was pioneered by programs such as Carbon Copy and PC Anywhere, and works as shown in figure 21.1. For every remote user, you need two computers: one remote and one with a local LAN attachment.

The local PC operates just like a normal PC. It connects to the LAN, runs applications, reads and writes network files, and prints as if it were a stand-alone PC. The trick with remote control is that special software enables a remote computer to clone the local computer's screen, keyboard, and mouse. When the remote user types a key, the keystroke is transferred to the local computer that treats the keystroke as its own.

When the screen on the local computer is updated, data describing the change is sent to the remote computer, which also updates its screen.

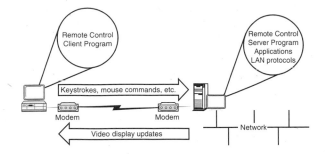

Figure 21.1

Remote computer access using remote control.

The only thing running in the remote computer is the remote control software. When the user runs Lotus 1-2-3, the program is loaded in the local computer. Files are opened and calculations take place all on the local computer. The only things that travel between the remote and the local computer are control codes: keystrokes, screen updates, and mouse commands.

The remote control approach was not developed for LANs but works fine in a LAN environment. A user might leave Carbon Copy running on his desktop PC when leaving for the night, enabling him to dial in from his home PC. Or a department might install a bank of PCs strictly for dial-in support, leaving PC Anywhere running on those computers full-time.

Remote control works well, but often not as well as we would like. Graphics screen data in particular can fill up a 14.4 Kbps modem line. You can buy a faster modem, but unless you have ISDN—and what hotel rooms do?—you are lucky to be able to push more than 1400–2800 characters through a phone line in a second. When the display is a 640×480 color VGA display, modem bandwidth gets bogged down in a hurry. Consequently, users often complain that remote control access is too painfully slow to work with.

Another problem with remote control is that users need to learn how to use the remote control software. If they want to copy a file from their remote computer to the LAN, they can't use File Manager. Instead, they must use the copy utility that is built into the remote control software. As a result, remote control is not as natural as using a local computer.

Remote Access with Remote Nodes

Remote node technology was developed with LANs in mind. The basic idea is that, instead of connecting to the LAN through a network adapter card, a remote computer connects through a modem and a network access server. Yes, the modem connection is slower than a LAN card, but many LAN operations don't transfer a lot of data and a modem can often keep up just fine.

Figure 21.2 shows how remote node operation works. A big difference is that applications are now running on the remote computer. All the local computer is doing is running a modem program that enables the user to dial in and access the LAN. Since the local computer doesn't have to run applications for the dial-in user, it can often support several users. Windows NT RAS can theoretically support up to 256 remote users.

Figure 21.2

Remote access using a remote node.

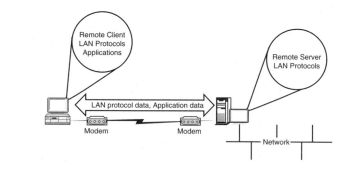

So what's passing through the modems? Data, of course. If a user copies a file, it is transferred through the phone line. Also going through the remote node is LAN protocol traffic. In fact, the remote computer is running almost exactly the same software it would be running if it were directly attached to the LAN. If the LAN runs on NetBEUI, the remote computer must load a NetBEUI protocol stack. The difference is that traffic to and from the protocol stack is routed through the phone line.

After a user achieves a dial-up connection, the remote computer is used as though it is locally attached. Users don't need to learn a new software package. File Manager copies files to the LAN just as it would if the user were directly attached.

The down side to remote node is that it doesn't work well in a lot of situations. Suppose a remote user needs to edit an Excel spreadsheet that is stored on the LAN. Excel spreadsheet files are big! If the user opens a 546 KB file, nothing happens until 546 KB of file data is transferred through the modem connection and into the users PC, which can take about ten minutes. When the file needs to be saved, the process is reversed. To make matters worse, what if the Excel program itself is being run from the LAN? Excel makes use of several megabytes of files, swapping file data in and out of memory almost constantly. A LAN can handle that much data transfer, but a modem can't.

Remote control works better with large files and applications being run from the LAN because the files and the applications are never transferred through the modem; they only need to get as far as the local PC that is functioning as a remote control host.

Only screen, keyboard, and mouse data goes through the modem, which constitutes a much smaller volume of data than an Excel spreadsheet.

Remote node access is the preferred approach when:

◆ All applications required by the user are loaded on the remote PC.

◆ Data transfer volumes when running applications are relatively low.

◆ Users don't want to learn a new procedure.

Remote control is the preferred approach when:

◆ Users must access applications that are only stored on the LAN. A custom database application is a good example.

◆ Users must interact with large files.

Eventually, ISDN will do away with the need to make this distinction. When users have access to over 100 Kbps of data bandwidth, remote node becomes a viable technology even when large data transfers are required. Until that time, however, planning a remote access installation requires some strategy and analysis of tradeoffs.

Introduction to Remote Access Service

RAS is both a dial-in and a dial-out utility. As a dial-in utility, RAS can be configured to support modems on as many as 256 serial ports, which can be configured into a modem pool.

Dial-out capability enables the user of the RAS computer to dial out to remote RAS hosts. Unfortunately, RAS does not support a dial-out modem pool that can be accessed by users on the local LAN.

Before looking at installation, management, and use of RAS, you need to examine Remote Access Service features so that you can plan your RAS installation.

Security

Objective D.2

Security is a significant concern for any LAN with dial-in capabilities. Unfortunately, the world is full of people who have made breaking into computers a hobby or a profession, and a modem tone on a phone line is a challenge to too many people.

RAS can support a very high level of security. Dial-in users are authenticated by Windows NT Server standard security, which can be enough for many organizations.

If added security is desired, RAS can be configured to operate in dial-back mode. When a user calls in dial-back mode, RAS hangs up and calls the user at a specific telephone number. That way, it isn't enough for an intruder to have a valid user name and password; the intruder must also be calling from a specific telephone to get in. Dial-back makes dial-in access extremely secure.

Dial-back operation has another benefit because the bulk of long-distance calling charges will be born by the organization's company lines, which probably have a better cost structure than telephone credit cards.

When the tightest dial-in control is desired, RAS can interface with a separate security access system. These systems typically require users to carry a calculator-like security card that incorporates a security algorithm. The dial-in security host issues a challenge to the user in the form of a numeric code. The user's security card is used to generate a secure response that the user enters into the terminal. Only if the response matches the anticipated result is the user granted access.

Communication security between RAS computers is maintained through support for data encryption using the RC4 algorithm licensed from RSA Data Security Incorporated.

Another security feature available with RAS is the ability to configure each user's dial-in restrictions to determine whether the user will be permitted to access the entire LAN or will be limited to accessing files on the RAS server itself.

RAS Communication Methods

RAS is equally versatile in terms of available communication methods. Users can connect through conventional analog modems, Integrated Services Digital Network (ISDN), or widely available X.25 networks. Null-modem connections are also supported for local access.

Analog Modems

RAS supports a wide variety of modems. Windows NT supports up to 256 modems, which can be configured in modem pools that support dial-in and dial-out traffic.

Objective D.2

RAS supports three modem protocols: PPP, SLIP, and a proprietary RAS protocol, enabling a variety of clients to dial in to and out of a RAS server. To support more than four modems on an Intel x86 PC, you will need to install multi-port serial adapters. Consult the Hardware Compatibility List for supported multi-port adapters.

| **Note** | Microsoft recommends using the same brand and model of modem on both ends of communication because mixing models can result in difficult-to-troubleshoot problems. Of course, unless you are starting from scratch, you will seldom have a single-model modem pool, so be prepared to experiment. |

The following list describes the modem protocols that RAS supports:

◆ **SLIP.** The Serial-Line Internet Protocol (SLIP) is an extremely basic protocol developed for the Unix environment. SLIP operates without error checking, flow control, or security. SLIP remains popular, however, because it operates with little overhead and provides good performance. RAS supports SLIP for dial-out operating, enabling RAS clients to access Unix computers and many Internet providers.

◆ **PPP.** The Point-to-Point (PPP) protocol is sometimes referred to as "SLIP done right." PPP performs error checking and recovery and can cope with noisier lines than SLIP. Although PPP has slightly higher overhead than SLIP, PPP is becoming the preferred protocol for remote access. RAS supports PPP for dial-in and dial-out operation.

◆ **RAS Protocol.** The RAS protocol is a Microsoft proprietary protocol that supports NetBIOS, and is supported by all versions of RAS. The RAS protocol is required to use the NetBEUI protocol.

RS-232C Null Modem

A *null modem* is a cable that crosses wires to enable two RS-232 ports to connect as though there were modems between. This setting can be used for local testing of the RAS server. It also enables a PC to attach through a serial connection to a local network when it is not equipped with a network adapter on that network. Wiring of null-modem cables is described in the last section of this chapter.

X.25

X.25 is an old and clunky but reliable and widely available wide area network service that is based on packet switching. In most cases, companies lease the use of a commercial X.25 network, gaining access through a dedicated phone line or a dial-up port. Several commercial X.25 networks are available, and a company could easily plan an affordable WAN strategy using X.25.

Figure 21.3 illustrates how X.25 might be used with RAS. X.25 networks are typically drawn as clouds, because the operation of the X.25 network is invisible to users. A customer simply sends a packet into a cloud at one point, and the packet emerges from the cloud at the destination. The route the packet took through the network is not the customer's concern.

Figure 21.3

*Features of an
X.25 network.*

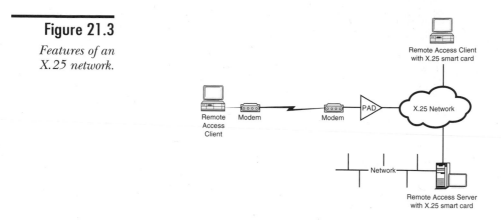

Computers can access an X.25 network in two ways:

◆ Through a direct connection, using a device such as an X.25 smart card.

◆ Through a modem, using a device called a packet assembler-disassembler (PAD), which performs the task of formatting user messages into packets that can travel through the network and reassembling messages from received packets.

For organizations with large volumes of remote access, X.25 might be preferable to relying on long-distance modem access. Performance is potentially better, and costs will be lower for high-volume users.

ISDN

Integrated Services Digital Network (ISDN) is the state-of-the-art for dial-up digital communications. Modems working with voice telephone lines must convert digital signals to analog, a process that limits bandwidth typically to 14,400 bps, although higher rates can be achieved using data compression. Unfortunately, much of the data that is transmitted between computers is already compressed, and compression of the data communication channel yields little improvement in bandwidth. Although speeds higher than 14,400 bps are practical, even the slightest degradation of line performance can cause modems to shift down to a lower speed.

ISDN is digital all the way. Several levels of service are available and multi-megabit speeds are possible. Service is offered in several channel configurations that are assigned an identifying letter. A basic rate ISDN line for a customer is configured with two B channels that operate at 64 kilobits per second (Kbps). A D channel is included to support 16 kilobits per second.

Ordinarily, the two B channels provide separate routes of communication. Some ISDN interface devices and drivers have the capability of aggregating the B channels to provide 128 Kbps of channel bandwidth.

ISDN requires use of ISDN cards in place of modems. Both ends of the communication must be equipped with ISDN, which can be a significant problem. Local telephone companies have been inconsistent in their eagerness to offer ISDN to their customers. While some providers have committed to offering ISDN to all their customers, others have dragged their feet. As a result, you might have ISDN service, but the place you are calling might not.

RAS Clients

RAS supports a variety of remote clients. Windows NT and Windows for Workgroups include RAS. RAS software is also available for MS-DOS. Additionally, clients that communicate with the PPP protocol (described later) can connect with RAS.

Windows NT and Windows 95 Clients

Windows NT Workstation and Server include RAS and introduce support for the PPP protocol, as does Windows 95. Windows NT and Windows 95 clients can dial in to and negotiate security with RAS servers using the RAS, PPP, or SLIP protocols. They can also access other remote services, such as Unix or the Internet, using PPP or SLIP.

Windows NT 3.1 is compatible with RAS with the exception that version 3.1 lacks support for the PPP protocol. Users of Windows NT 3.1 must use the proprietary RAS protocol to call a RAS server.

Windows for Workgroups Clients

WfW includes RAS. If you are not using WfW version 3.11, you might want to upgrade the network client software using the WfW client that is included with Windows NT Server. See Chapter 14, "Using Windows and DOS Clients," for information about the WfW client.

MS-DOS and Windows 3.1 Clients

The Microsoft Network Client version 3.0 for MS-DOS and Windows provides RAS support. You must install the full redirector and access RAS using the *rasphone* command.

RAS for MS-DOS supports only NetBEUI applications and does not support client applications that require TCP/IP or IPX.

PPP Clients

Terminal-mode PPP clients can access RAS. The RAS server will automatically initiate an authentication dialog. This mode enables Unix and other non-Microsoft clients to access files on the RAS server or the Windows NT Server network.

Installing and Configuring RAS

Objective D.2

RAS is configured as a network service. In many ways, installation and configuration procedures resemble the procedures used with a network adapter card, and much of the material in this chapter will be familiar to you from earlier chapters.

The RAS installation and configuration procedure has these major stages:

1. Hardware installation

2. Configuration of serial ports

3. Installation of the RAS software

4. Configuration of RAS LAN protocols

5. Configuration of RAS user accounts

Because hardware installation is highly varied, it won't be addressed here; it is beyond the scope of this book.

Serial port configuration is performed with the Ports utility in the Control Panel. This tool was described in Chapter 13, "Managing Printing Services." Only serial ports that have been configured with the Ports utility can be configured to support RAS.

X.25 PADs are installed as serial devices on RS-232C ports.

ISDN adapters should be installed according to the manufacturer's instructions. Installation of this hardware is beyond the scope of this book.

Adding Serial Ports

Before installing modems, you must add serial ports to the system configuration using the Port utility in the Control Panel. The procedure for adding a COM port is described in Chapter 13.

Install Modems

Objective
B.7

Before attempting to install RAS, you must install at least one communications device. Modems are installed using the Modem utility in the Control Panel. The procedure to install a modem is covered in the following exercise:

Installing a Modem

1. Open the Modem utility in the Control Panel.

2. If no modems have been installed, the Install New Modem Wizard will be invoked.

3. Windows NT is very adapt at detecting modem hardware. In the majority of cases, you should *not* check Don't detect my modem; I will select it from a list in the first window of the Installation Wizard.

4. Choose **N**ext. The Wizard will scan your COM ports and attempt to identify a modem. The modem may not be identified by brand. A standard Hayes-compatible modem is identified as a Standard Modem.

5. If you don't like the modem choice, choose **C**hange. You can then select a specific make and model.

6. Choose **N**ext when you are satisfied with the modem choice.

7. When you are informed Your modem has been set up successfully, choose **F**inish.

If at least one modem has been installed, the Modem utility looks like figure 21.4. You can use this window to add, remove, and change the properties of modems. Choosing **A**dd starts the Install New Modem Wizard.

Note   To enable RAS to communicate through a null-modem cable, the computers at both ends of the connection must be configured to use null-modem connections. To install null-modem support, select the modem manually. In the Install New Modem dialog box, specify (Standard Modem Types) in the **M**anufacturers list, and specify Dial-Up Networking Serial Cable between 2 PCs in the Mode**l**s list.

Advanced Modem Configuration

The modem utility is used to configure the configuration properties for modems (see fig. 21.4). To configure a modem follow the steps in the following exercise:

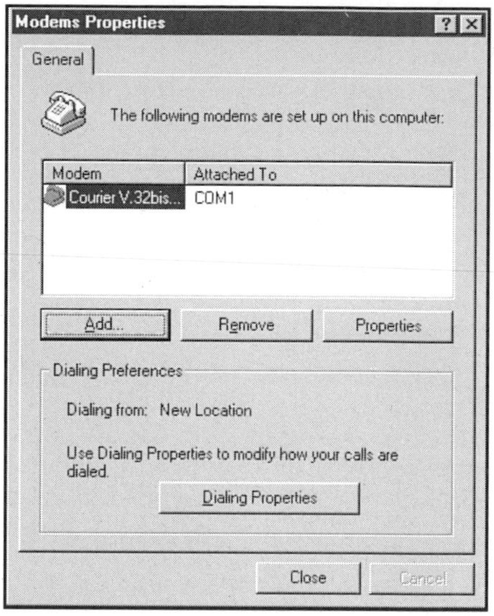

Figure 21.4

*The modem
utility.*

Configuring a Modem

1. Select a modem in the modem list of the Network utility and choose Properties to open the Modem Properties window shown in figure 21.5.

2. The General properties tab (refer to fig. 21.5) has three settings:

   ◆ **Port.** Describes the COM port to which the modem is connected.

   ◆ **Speaker volume.** Determines the loudness of the modem speaker.

   ◆ **Maximum speed.** Specifies the maximum speed at which software should attempt to operate the modem.

3. The Connection properties tab, shown in figure 21.6, defines a number of modem communications characteristics:

   ◆ **Data bits.** Specifies the size of the data character to be used, with 8 bits being the most common and the default setting.

   ◆ **Parity.** Specifies the type of parity checking to be used. The most common setting is None, which is specified by default.

   ◆ **Stop bits.** Specifies the stop bits to be sent after a data character is sent. 1 stop bit is the most common choice and is the default setting.

   ◆ **Wait for dial tone before dialing.** When checked (the default), the modem will not commence dialing until a dial tone is detected.

   ◆ **Cancel the call if not connected within ... secs.** Check this option if calls should time out if a specified number of seconds elapse before a connection is established.

◆ **Disconnect a call if idle for more than ... mins.** Check this option if connections should be terminated if no traffic is generated within a specified period of time.

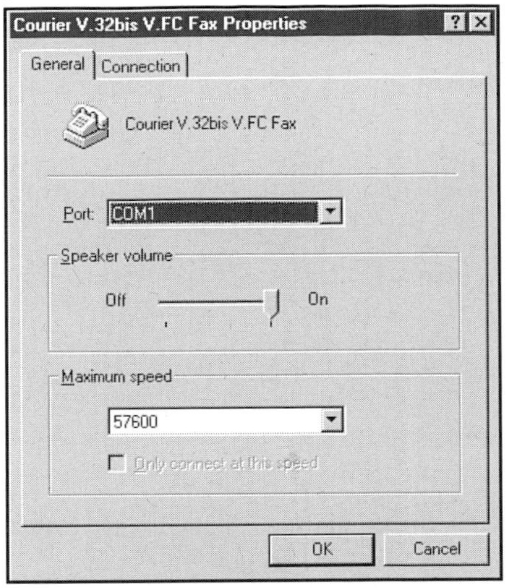

Figure 21.5

Configuring modem properties.

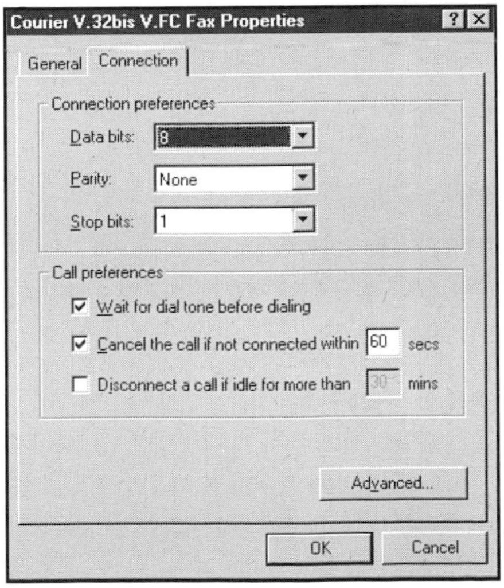

Figure 21.6

Configuring modem connection properties.

4. Choose Advanced on the Connection tab to open the Advanced Connection Settings dialog box (see fig. 21.7). This dialog box has a variety of options.

4a. Many modems have advanced features that may or may not be desirable to use. Four of the options in the Advanced Connection Settings dialog box have to do with error control:

   ◆ **Use error control.** Check this option if the modem's hardware error control should be used. Modems at both ends of the connection must be capable of performing the same type of error control. Typically, error control is provided by the RAS communication protocol.

   ◆ **Required to connect.** If hardware error control is enabled, check this option if error control is required to establish a connection. If this option is not checked, connections can be established without error control in effect.

   ◆ **Compress data.** If hardware error control is enabled, check this option if hardware data compression should be used. Modems at both ends of the connection must be capable of performing the same type of compression.

   ◆ **Use of cellular protocol.** If the modem is capable of communicating through a cellular telephone link, check this option to enable cellular communication.

4b. Flow control techniques smooth the process of communication between a serial interface and the modem, preventing either device from overwhelming the other with excess traffic. Flow control options are as follows:

   ◆ **Use flow control.** Check this option to enable flow control.

   ◆ **Hardware (RTS/CTS).** Hardware flow control uses two wires in the serial interface cable to signal when the modem is ready to receive data. This is more efficient than software error control because extra traffic is not generated.

   ◆ **Software (XON/XOFF).** Software flow control consists of sending special XON and XOFF characters to start and stop data transmission. Software flow control is generally used only when hardware flow control is not supported.

4c. The Modulation type field can be used to specify nonstandard modulating techniques if required in certain circumstances.

4d. The Extra settings accepts special product-specific settings.

4e. If you want to maintain a log file for events related to this modem, check Record a log file. A log file can be a valuable troubleshooting tool.

4f. Choose OK when advanced settings are completed.

5. Choose OK to exit the Modem utility.

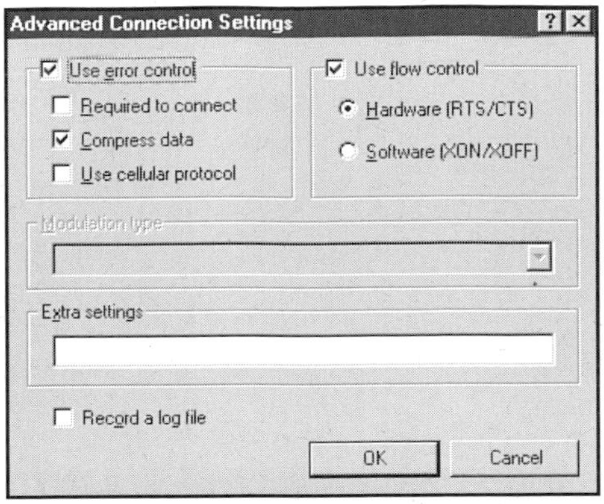

Figure 21.7

Configuring modem advanced properties.

Installing RAS Software

As with all network services, RAS is installed and its protocols are configured using the Network utility in the Control Panel. This tool has been encountered several times in this book, most notably in Chapter 7, "Installing Windows NT Server." This chapter will only dwell on procedures that are specific to RAS.

To install the RAS software, follow the steps in the following exercise:

Installing RAS Software

1. Open the Network utility in the Control Panel and select the Services tab.

2. Choose **A**dd and select Remote Access Service in the **N**etwork Service box.

3. Choose OK.

4. When prompted, supply the path where files can be found on the installation CD-ROM. Files will be copied and the adapter software will be installed. You will be returned to the Network utility window.

5. After files are copied, the Add RAS Device dialog box appears, as shown in figure 21.8. Review the current configuration by pulling down the RAS Capable **D**evices list.

5a. Choose Install **M**odem to add a modem to the configuration. This will start the Install New Modem Wizard.

5b. Choose Install X25 **P**ad to add an X.25 packet assembler-disassembler.

5c. Choose OK to accept the RAS device configuration.

Note To install modem-pooling equipment:

◆ Configure the equipment to function as one of the modem types supported by RAS. The equipment must interface via standard RS-232 signals.

◆ Connect a COM port to the equipment and configure RAS with the same modem type that was configured for the modem-pooling equipment.

Microsoft recommends configuring modem-pooling equipment as standard Hayes-compatible modem devices.

Note ISDN adapters are installed as network adapters using the Network utility in the Control Panel.

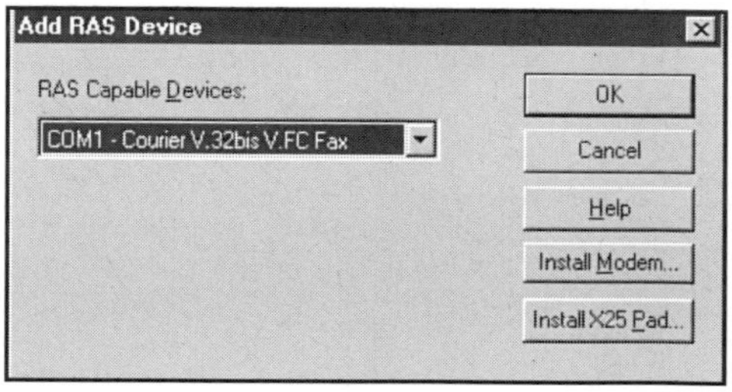

Figure 21.8

Adding a RAS port.

6. Next, the Remote Access Setup dialog box appears (see fig. 21.9). In this dialog box, you add ports and devices to the RAS configuration. At this point, you should configure any ports that are currently installed.

6a. Select a port and choose **C**onfigure to open the Configure Port Usage dialog box (see fig. 21.10). Each port can be configured with one of the following options:

◆ Dial **o**ut only

◆ **R**eceive calls only

◆ **D**ial out and Receive calls

Select a Port Usage option and choose OK.

6b. Review the configuration in the Remote Access Setup dialog box and choose Continue when satisfied.

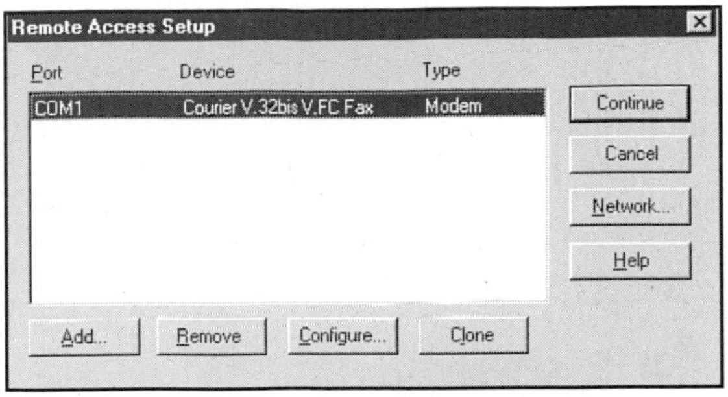

Figure 21.9

The Remote Access Setup dialog box.

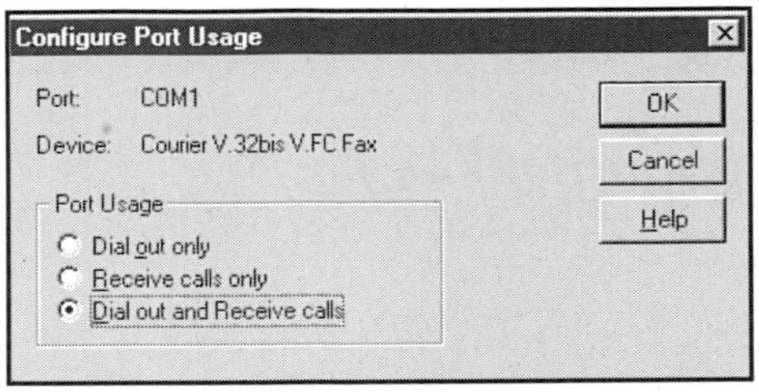

Figure 21.10

Configuring a Port Usage option.

7. If NetBEUI protocol support is installed on the computer, the RAS Server NetBEUI Configuration dialog box appears next. See the section "RAS Server Configuration for NetBEUI" later in this chapter for more information about this dialog box.

8. If TCP/IP protocol support is installed on the computer, the RAS Server TCP/IP Configuration dialog box appears next. See the section "RAS Server Configuration for TCP/IP" later in this chapter for more information about this dialog box.

9. If IPX protocol support is installed on the computer, the RAS Server IPX Configuration dialog box appears. See the section "RAS Server Configuration for IPX" later in this chapter for details about this dialog box.

10. If NWLink is installed on the computer, you will see the message shown in figure 21.11. Typically, NWLink is not configured to propagate NetBIOS broadcast packets (type 20 packets), that is, to forward NetBIOS broadcast packets over routers and throughout a network. If your network requires NetBIOS broadcasts, choose **Y**es. Typically, the default response of **N**o will be appropriate.

11. When you see the message Remote Access Service has been successfully installed, choose OK.

12. Close the Network utility and restart the server.

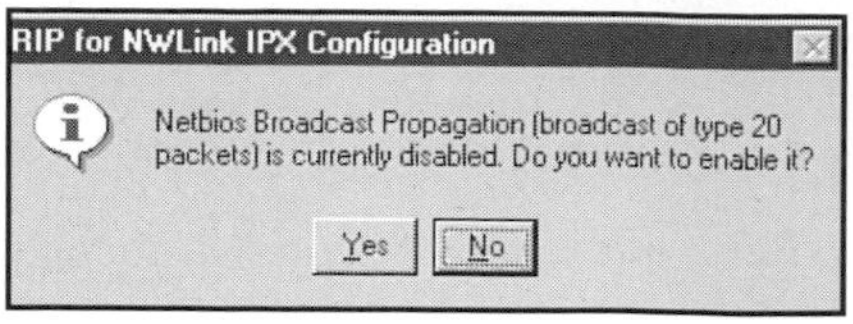

Figure 21.11

NWLink configuration for NetBIOS broadcast propagation.

Configuring RAS Ports

The Network utility in the Control Panel is used to reconfigure RAS ports. To reconfigure RAS ports follow the procedures in the following exercise:

Configuring RAS Ports

1. Open the Network utility in the Control Panel and select the Services tab.

2. Select Remote Access Service in the **N**etwork Services box and choose **P**roperties to open the Remote Access Setup dialog box (refer to fig. 21.9).

3. Use the Remote Access Setup dialog box to add, remove, and configure ports.

4. To configure port usage, select a port and choose **C**onfigure to open the Configure Port Usage dialog box (refer to fig. 21.10). After configuring ports, choose OK to close the dialog box.

5. The **N**etwork button in the Remote Access Setup dialog box is used to configure the protocols that RAS will support. Choose this button to display the dialog box shown in figure 21.12.

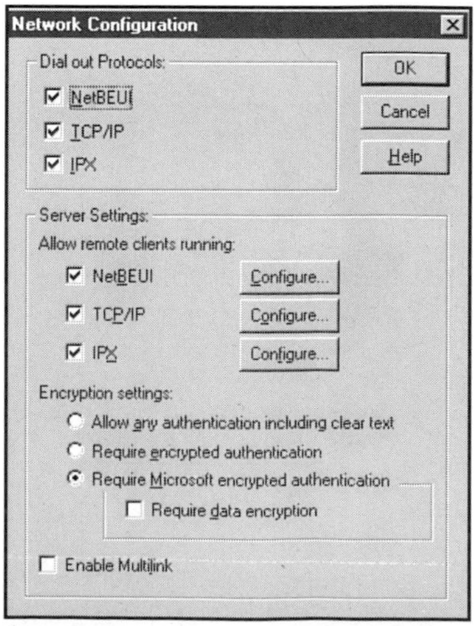

Figure 21.12

RAS Network Configuration dialog box.

5a. Check the protocols that will be supported for dial-in and dial-out operation.

Note Windows 3.x clients can use only NetBEUI with RAS.

Windows NT clients can use NetBEUI, NWLink, and TCP/IP with RAS.

Windows 95 will also support all protocols with RAS.

5b. In the Dial out Protocols box, check the protocols to be supported by RAS. Configuration of the protocols is discussed in the section "Configuring RAS LAN Protocols" later in this chapter.

5c. In the Server Settings box, select the encryption setting:

◆ **Allow <u>a</u>ny authentication including clear text.** This choice permits clear text authentication as well as encrypted authentication using MS-CHAP, MD5-CHAP, SPAP, and PAP. This setting is useful with clients that do not support data encryption.

◆ **Require <u>e</u>ncrypted authentication.** This option enables users to connect with MS-CHAP, MD5-CHAP, and SPAP.

◆ **Require <u>M</u>icrosoft encrypted authentication.** For clients that support Microsoft encryption (MS-CHAP), this is the preferred setting. If you check the box Require <u>d</u>ata encryption, all data transferred between the client and server are encrypted using the RSA Data Security Incorporated RC4 algorithm.

5d. Dial-up multilink capability enables RAS to aggregate multiple physical links into a logical bundle. Bundling is a common technique used with ISDN links. Check Enable Multi<u>l</u>ink to support the feature.

5e. Choose OK when the Network Configuration settings are complete.

6. Exit the Network utility when RAS ports have been configured.

Note CHAP, *challenge handshake authentication protocol*, adds considerable security to the RAS session. When a connection is being established, the CHAP server sends a random challenge to the client. The challenge is used to encrypt the user's password, which is returned to the server. This has two advantages: the password is encrypted in transit, and an eavesdropper cannot forge the authentication and play it back to the server at a later time because the challenge is different for each call.

continues

MS-CHAP is the most secure encryption protocol supported by RAS. MS-CHAP, also known as RSA Message Digest 4 (MD4), uses the RC4 algorithm to encrypt all user data during the RAS session.

PAP, the *Password Authentication Protocol*, is a clear-text authentication protocol that is associated with the PPP protocol. PAP authentication should be used only when dialing in to servers that do not support encrypted authentication, such as SLIP and PPP servers.

SPAP, the *Shiva Password Authentication Protocol*, is supported on the RAS server only and is an implementation of PAP on Shiva remote client software.

Objective D.2

Configuring RAS LAN Protocols

When you are installing RAS, you will need to configure the protocols that RAS will support. It is important to remember that RAS clients must be running a network protocol stack—NetBEUI, IPX, or TCP/IP—that is supported by RAS. If you accept the default values, little protocol configuration is required. RAS will make most address assignments.

If you need to reconfigure RAS LAN protocol support, return to the Network utility in the Control Panel and open the properties for the Remote Access Service. In the Remote Access Setup dialog box (refer to fig. 21.9), choose **N**etwork to open the Network Configuration dialog box (refer to fig. 21.12). Access the configuration dialog boxes of the RAS protocols by choosing the appropriate Configure button.

RAS Server Configuration for NetBEUI

Choose **C**onfigure in the Network Configuration dialog box to open the RAS Server NetBEUI Configuration dialog box (see fig. 21.13). In this dialog box, choose the network access that will be granted to RAS users. Your choices are:

◆ Entire **n**etwork

◆ This **c**omputer only

After you make your selection, choose OK.

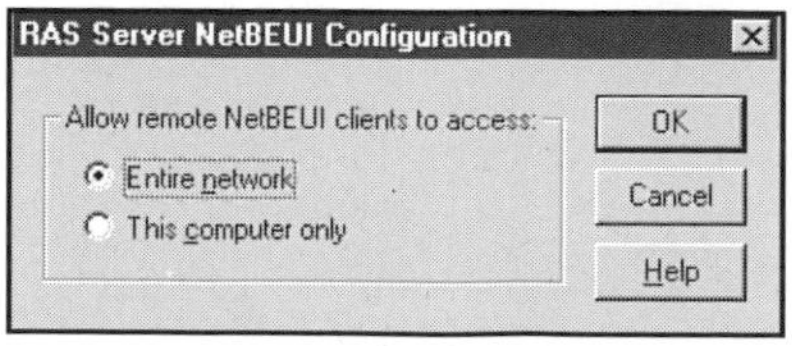

Figure 21.13

*RAS Server
NetBEUI
configuration.*

RAS Server Configuration for TCP/IP

Choose C**o**nfigure in the Network Configuration dialog box to open the RAS Server TCP/IP Configuration dialog box (see fig. 21.14). Issues such as TCP/IP addressing are discussed in detail in Chapter 16, "Using TCP/IP."

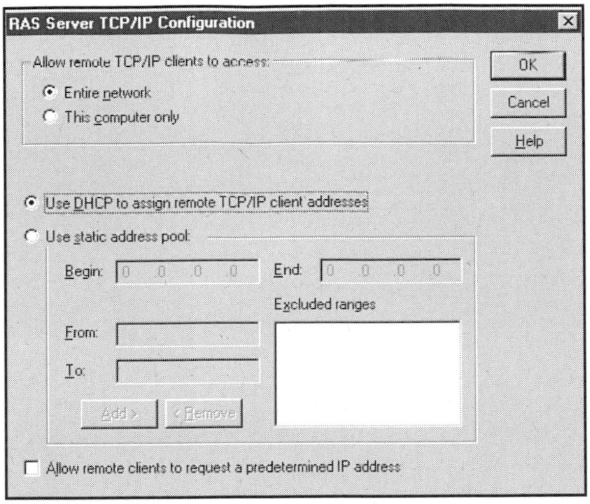

Figure 21.14

RAS server TCP/IP configuration.

As with NetBEUI, you can determine whether TCP/IP clients will be given access to the Entire **n**etwork or to This **c**omputer only.

Three approaches are available to determine IP addresses that will be assigned to dial-up users:

◆ **Use** **D**HCP **to assign remote TCP/IP client addresses.** If the Dynamic Host Configuration Protocol (DHCP) is running on your network, this is the most satisfactory approach because no further address configuration is required.

◆ **Use** **s**tatic **address pool.** You can select a range of addresses from which an address will be assigned to dial-in users. You will need to specify the address range in the **B**egin and **E**nd fields.

If you want, you can exempt some addresses from the address pool. Specify a range of addresses in the **F**rom and **T**o fields and choose **A**dd to exclude that address range from the address pool.

◆ **Allow remote clients to request a predetermined IP address.** Use this option only if users must have control over their IP address.

When TCP/IP has been configured, choose OK.

RAS Server Configuration for IPX

Choose Con**f**igure in the Network Configuration dialog box to open the RAS Server IPX Configuration dialog box (see fig. 21.15).

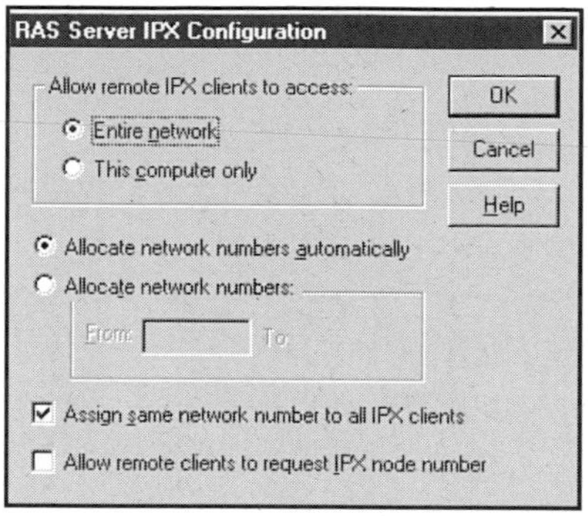

Figure 21.15

RAS Server IPX Configuration dialog box.

As with the other protocols, you determine the access that will be granted to IPX clients by selecting Entire **n**etwork or This **c**omputer only.

If you configure network and node number settings as shown in figure 21.15 (the default settings), no further IPX configuration is required.

Assigning IPX Network Numbers

IPX requires all clients to be associated with a network number for routing purposes. In most cases, a given network segment is assigned a single network ID for each protocol and frame type that the segment supports. An IPX network number is a hexadecimal number up to eight digits.

The IPX Routing Information Protocol (RIP, similar in principle to TCP/IP RIP) advertises network numbers by having routers announce them at one minute intervals. As the quantity of network numbers increases, RIP traffic increases rapidly. It is desirable to minimize the number of network numbers whenever possible.

Therefore, the default setting is to check Assign **s**ame network number to all IPX clients.

You can choose two methods of assigning network numbers:

◆ **Allocate network numbers automatically.** RAS will assign a network number that does not conflict with existing network numbers.

◆ **Allocate network numbers.** Use this option to specify a range of addresses from which network numbers will be assigned.

Assigning IPX Node Numbers

Each device on a network has a node number, a hexadecimal number up to 16 digits. For clients that are attached to the network, this number is usually derived from the hardware address of the Ethernet or token-ring card.

You can, if you want, enable users to specify their own IPX node address by checking Allow remote clients to request IPX node number. This is a risky option because it can permit users to impersonate other users by using their node numbers.

Configuration of RAS User Accounts

When RAS is installed, two new programs are installed:

◆ **Dial-Up Monitor.** This utility echoes status lights for several of the modems' most critical lines. It is especially useful with internal modems. The icon is installed in the Control Panel.

◆ **Remote Access Admin.** Use this utility to configure a RAS server. You can also use it to start a RAS server. It is located in the Administrative Tools submenu of the Start menu.

The Dial-Up Networking utility is installed in a standard Windows NT setup. This is the RAS dial-out program, which is installed in the Start menu. Look in the **P**rograms/Accessories submenu.

Before users can use a RAS server, you must use Remote Access Admin or User Manager for Domains to set up user permissions. The main window for Remote Access Admin is shown in figure 21.16. This window displays the status of each RAS communication channel and is used to access RAS administration functions.

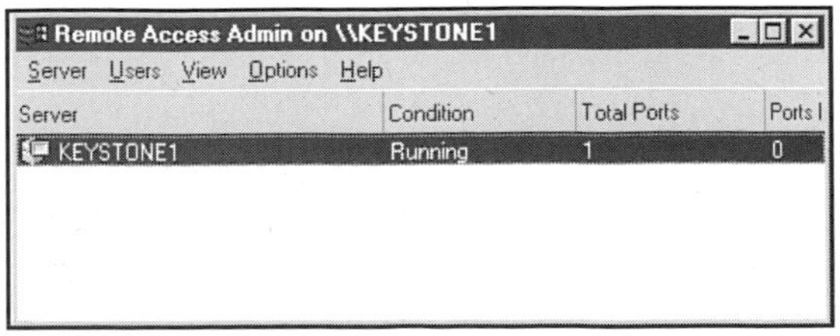

Figure 21.16

The main window for Remote Access Admin.

Objective D.2

To administer RAS user permissions, choose the **P**ermissions command in the **U**sers menu. The Remote Access Permissions dialog box appears (see fig. 21.17). In this dialog box, you can administer remote access permissions for individuals or for all network users.

Figure 21.17

Granting remote access permissions.

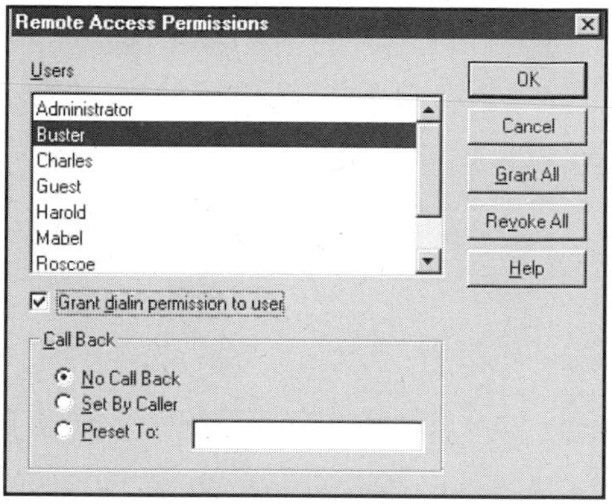

To revoke RAS permissions from all users, choose Re**v**oke All.

To grant the same permissions to all users, set the permissions and choose **G**rant All.

To grant permissions to an individual user, select the user account name in the **U**sers box. Then set the permissions to apply to that user.

Check the Grant **d**ialin permission to user box to grant RAS dial-in access.

Three options are available in the **C**all Back box:

◆ **No Call Back.** This option enables users to call in and connect with the network on the same call.

◆ **Set By Caller.** With this option, the caller will be asked to enter a telephone number. RAS will disconnect, call the user at the number specified, and connect the user to the network.

◆ **Preset To.** This option requires you to specify a number that RAS will call to connect the user. Using a specified number enhances security because a user must have physical access to a particular telephone to enter a remote session.

After making the required settings, choose OK.

| Tip | You can also manage user dial-in permissions in User Manager for Domains. Open the User Properties dialog box and choose Dialin to open the Dialin Information dialog box, which has the options shown in figure 21.17. |

| Caution | Because the Guest account does not ordinarily have a password, you should avoid giving this account dial-in permissions. If you intend to grant guests dial-in access, either strictly restrict permissions assigned to this account or assign a password. |

Managing the Remote Access Server

The Remote Access Admin utility can be left active to monitor RAS operation. The main window lists the status of active RAS servers in the current domain (refer to fig. 21.16). The status indicates the number of ports that are configured for each server, as well as the number of active connections.

| Note | Remote Access Admin can manage RAS servers in any domain on the network. Use the Select Domain or Server command in the Server menu to change domains.

If you are managing another domain through a modem or other slow connection, choose the Low Speed Connection option in the Options menu to reduce the amount of data that will be transmitted through the communication link. |

Starting and Stopping the Server

After RAS has been installed and the server has been restarted, the Remote Access Service should be started. The Server menu in Remote Access Admin has four options for starting, stopping, and pausing the RAS server:

◆ **Start Remote Access Service.** Starts the Remote Access Service.

◆ **Stop Remote Access Service.** Stops the Remote Access Service.

◆ **Pause Remote Access Service.** This action prevents users from accessing the service, but leaves it enabled for administrators and server operators.

◆ **Continue Remote Access Service.** Changes the status of the service from Paused to Started.

All of these actions can also be performed using the Services utility in the Control Panel, as described in Chapter 19, "Managing the Server." When the RAS software is installed, the Remote Access Service is configured to start automatically when Windows NT Server is restarted.

Managing Server Ports

To obtain details about server ports, double-click on the entry in the main window, or select the server and choose the **C**ommunication Ports command in the **S**erver menu. Figure 21.18 shows an example of a Communication Ports display. Four buttons can be used to access port management features:

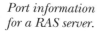

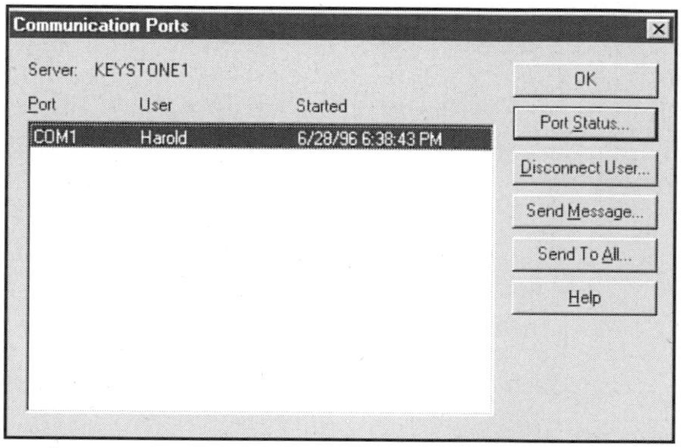

Figure 21.18

Port information for a RAS server.

◆ **Port Status.** This button displays a detailed status report for the selected port. An example is shown in figure 21.19. Click on the **R**eset button to zero out the statistics. This display is extremely useful for troubleshooting RAS connections. (Much of this information is also available in the Dial-Up Networking Monitor in the Control Panel.)

◆ **Disconnect User.** Select a user and click on this button to break a remote connection.

◆ **Send Message.** Use this option to send a message to the selected port.

◆ **Send To All.** Use this option to send a message to all users connected to this server.

A similar display is available for connected users. Choose the **A**ctive Users command in the **U**sers menu to display the Remote Access Users dialog box (see fig. 21.20). Options are similar to the detailed port status display with the exception of the **U**ser Account button, which displays information about the user's account.

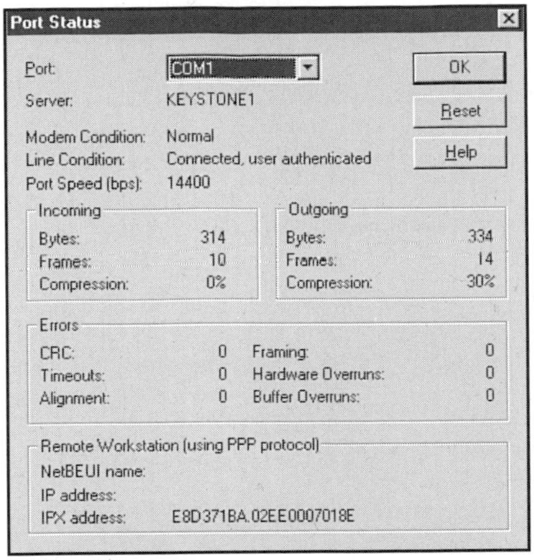

Port Status

Port:	COM1 ▼	OK
Server:	KEYSTONE1	Reset
Modem Condition:	Normal	Help
Line Condition:	Connected, user authenticated	
Port Speed (bps):	14400	

Incoming
Bytes:	314
Frames:	10
Compression:	0%

Outgoing
Bytes:	334
Frames:	14
Compression:	30%

Errors
CRC:	0	Framing:	0
Timeouts:	0	Hardware Overruns:	0
Alignment:	0	Buffer Overruns:	0

Remote Workstation (using PPP protocol)
NetBEUI name:	
IP address:	
IPX address:	E8D371BA.02EE0007018E

Figure 21.19

Detailed port status.

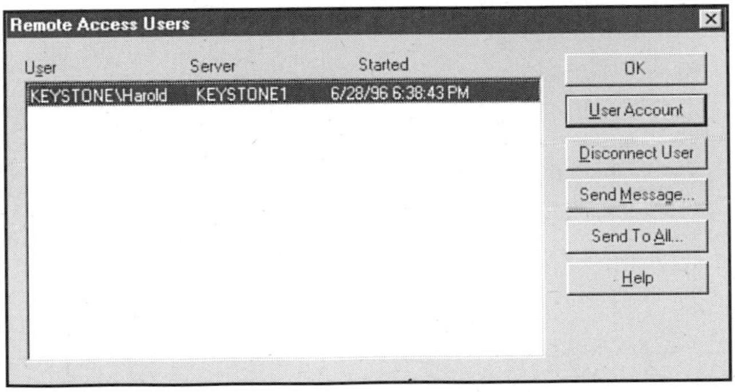

Remote Access Users

User	Server	Started	
KEYSTONE\Harold	KEYSTONE1	6/28/96 6:38:43 PM	OK
			User Account
			Disconnect User
			Send Message...
			Send To All...
			Help

Figure 21.20

The active RAS users list.

Installing the RAS Clients for Windows for Workgroups

Objective
D.2

RAS client software is included with Windows for Workgroups. As with Windows NT, RAS is considered a network service. To install RAS on WfW, use the steps in the following exercise:

Installing RAS on WfW

1. Start the Windows Setup utility.

2. Choose Change **N**etwork Settings in the **O**ptions menu.

3. In the Network Settings dialog box, choose **D**rivers.

4. In the Network Drivers dialog box, choose Add **A**dapter.

5. In the Add Network Adapter box, scroll the adapters in the **S**elect a Network Adapter to Install list until you find Remote Access Service. Select that option and choose OK.

6. When installation begins, supply the path name for files and change disks as requested.

7. In the Remote Access Configuration dialog box, select a COM port in the **P**ort box. Then pull down the **D**evice list and select a communication device. Then choose OK.

8. Choose Close in the Network Drivers box. Then choose OK to close Network Setup.

9. In the Microsoft Windows Network Names box, specify:

   ◆ **User Name.** The user name to be used to access the network.

   ◆ **Workgroup.** The workgroup or domain to be accessed.

   ◆ **Computer Name.** A name for this computer that is not in use on the network to be accessed.

   Choose OK when this information has been entered. Remote Access files will be copied to the computer.

10. Restart the computer when prompted.

The Remote Access program icon will be installed in the Network program group.

Dialing Out with RAS

If you're used to using RAS dial-out under Windows NT 3.x, you have a lot of relearning to do for version 4. Everything has changed. You will, however, be pretty comfortable if you are experienced with Windows 95.

Note When RAS is installed on a computer, a **L**ogon using Dial-Up Networking option is added to the Logon Information dialog box. This enables you to log on to a remote network during the standard logon procedure.

Configuring Telephony Services

Optionally, you may choose to configure Telephony Services, which establish contexts for dialing out from various locations. To manage your dialing locations, follow the steps in the following exercise:

Managing Dialing Locations

1. Open the Telephony utility in the Control Panel. The window is shown in figure 21.21.

2. In the I am **d**ialing from field, enter a name for a new location or choose an existing location to be modified.

3. In the The area **c**ode is field, enter the local area code. An area code will not be added to the phone numbers of calls placed in this area code.

4. In the **I** am in field, select the country for this location.

5. In the To access an **o**utside line, 1st dial:…x for local,…y for long dist. fields, enter any dialing prefixes that are required to obtain a local and a long distance outside line.

6. If your long-distance charges are to go on a calling card, check Dial **u**sing Calling Card to open the Change Calling Card dialog box. Select the service in the Calling Card to **u**se field and enter your PIN in the **C**alling Card number field. Choose OK to save the entry.

7. If your location has call waiting, disable the feature by selecting the This location has call **w**aiting. To disable it, dial check box and enter the code to disable call waiting in the field provided.

8. Specify the dialing mode by selecting **T**one dialing or **P**ulse dialing.

9. Choose **A**pply to save the entry, and choose OK to exit.

Using Dial-Up Networking

The Dial-Up Networking application is used to manage your dial-up configurations and to connect to remote locations. After you learn how to manage phonebook entries, you are ready to dial out to RAS and other servers.

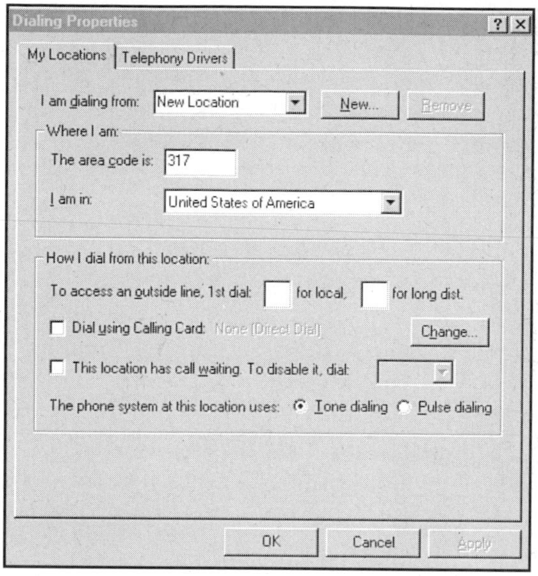

Figure 21.21

Adding a location to Telephony Services.

Installing Dial-Up Networking

The first time you start Dial-Up Networking, you see the message The phonebook is empty. Press OK to add an entry. When you choose OK, you are shown the New Phonebook Entry Wizard. You need to configure at least one phonebook entry to use Dial-Up Networking. The following information is required:

◆ A name for the new phonebook entry

◆ Whether you are calling the Internet

◆ Whether it is okay to send your password in plaintext if requested by the server

◆ If you are calling a non-Windows NT server, whether the server expects you to enter login information after connecting

◆ The phone number (and alternate phone numbers if available)

◆ Whether the phonebook entry will use telephony dialing properties

When the phonebook entry is completed, it will be shown in the Dial-Up Networking dialog box (see fig. 21.22).

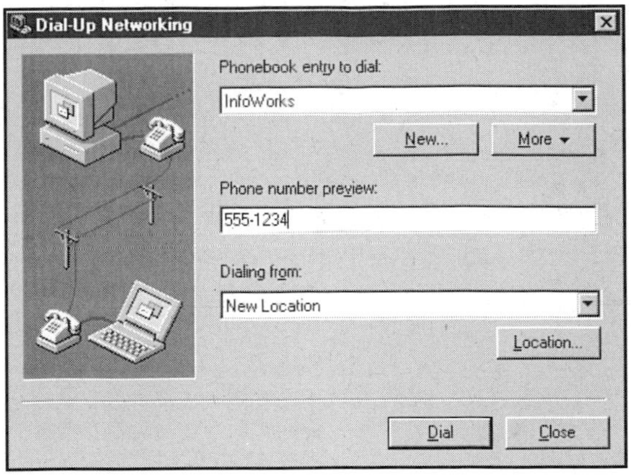

Figure 21.22

A phonebook entry in Dial-Up Networking.

To edit the phonebook entry, choose **M**ore. Select **E**dit entry and modem properties from the menu that is opened to open the Edit Phonebook Entry dialog box (see fig. 21.23). The Edit Phonebook Entry dialog box has five tabs. A thorough discussion of the tabs is beyond the scope of this book, but basic configuration is not at all difficult.

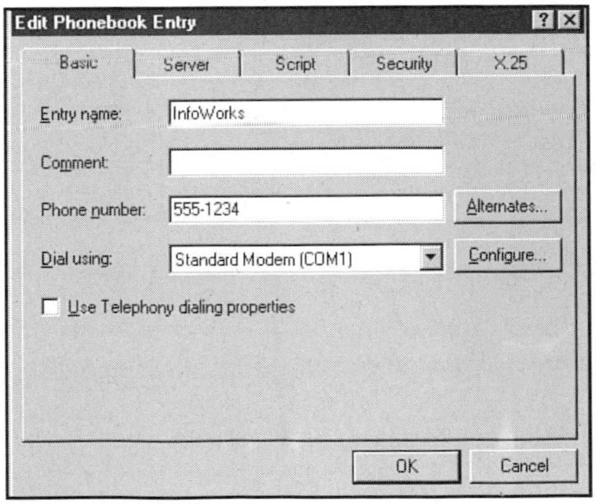

Figure 21.23

Basic properties of a phonebook entry.

Basic Dialing Properties

The Basic tab, shown in figure 21.23, defines the basic dial-out configuration. If you want to use settings established in your Telephony configuration, check **U**se Telephony dialing properties. The entries for this tab should require no explanation.

Choose <u>C</u>onfigure to open a dialog box in which you can configure the following modem properties:

◆ **<u>I</u>nitial speed (bps).**

◆ **Enable hardware <u>f</u>low control.** Hardware flow control is enabled by default.

◆ **Enable modem <u>e</u>rror control.** Modem error control is enabled by default.

◆ **Enable modem <u>c</u>ompression.** Modem compression is enabled by default.

◆ **Disable modem <u>s</u>peaker.** Speaker is enabled by default.

Note	Compressed data cannot be further compressed, and it is a waste of processing to enable both hardware and software data compression. Typically, on today's faster computers, because software data compression outperforms hardware data compression, hardware data compression should be disabled.

Server Protocol Properties

The Server tab defines the protocols that will be used to communicate with the server (see fig. 21.24).

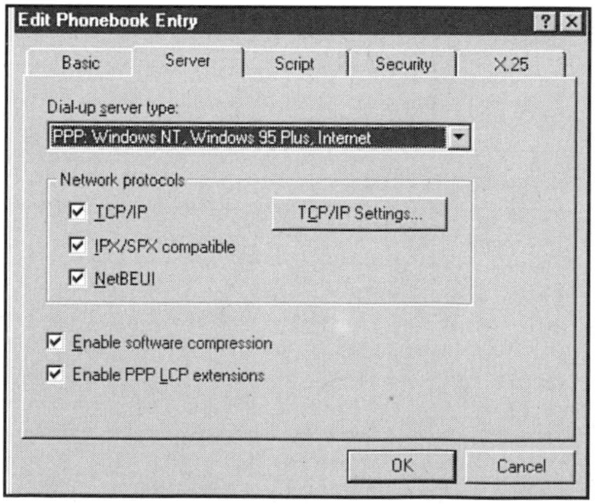

Figure 21.24

Configuring RAS server protocols.

You have the following options:

◆ **Dial-up <u>s</u>erver type.** In this field, you have three choices:

◆ **PPP: Windows NT, Windows 95 Plus, Internet.** The Point-to-Point Protocol (PPP) is the most commonly used protocol for TCP/IP dial-up services and is supported by all of the sources mentioned. This is the default, and the best all-around choice. When PPP is selected, you can select any or all of the available protocols.

◆ **SLIP: Internet.** The Serial-Line Internet Protocol (SLIP) is an older Internet protocol that remains quite popular. SLIP is less reliable and has fewer features than PPP, but is more efficient and provides somewhat better performance. When SLIP is selected, only TCP/IP is available as a protocol option.

◆ **Windows NT 3.1, Windows for Workgroups 3.11.** This option selects the older RAS protocol that was standard prior to Windows NT 3.5. It should be used only when backward-compatibility is required. When the RAS protocol is selected, only the NetBEUI protocol is available.

◆ **Network protocols.** In this box, check the protocols that are to be supported. Only PPP gives you a choice. TCP/IP is required for SLIP, and NetBEUI is required for the RAS protocol.

If **T**CP/IP is selected, the TCP/IP Settings dialog box can be accessed. The options you see depend on whether the PPP or SLIP protocol is selected. The PPP TCP/IP Settings dialog box is shown in figure 21.25. The options in this window are as follows:

◆ **S̲erver assigned IP address.** Select this option if the PPP dial-in server will assign an IP address for you; this is the most common situation.

◆ **Specify an I̲P address.** Select this option and specify an IP address in the IP a̲ddress field if the PPP server does not assign an IP address.

◆ **S̲erver assigned name server addresses.** Select this option if the PPP dial-in server adds the address of a DNS server to your configuration when you dial in. This is less commonly done than automatic IP address assignment.

◆ **Specify na̲me server addresses.** Select this option to manually specify the IP addresses of DNS and WINS name servers.

◆ **Use IP header c̲ompression.** Header compression—also known as Van Jacobson IP header compression, or VJ header compression—is almost always used to reduce the amount of traffic. Check with the manager of the dial-in server to determine if header compression is used.

◆ **Use default gateway on remote network.** This option applies to computers that are connected to local networks at the same time they are dialing remotely. When this option is checked, packets that cannot be routed to the local network are routed to the default gateway on the remote network.

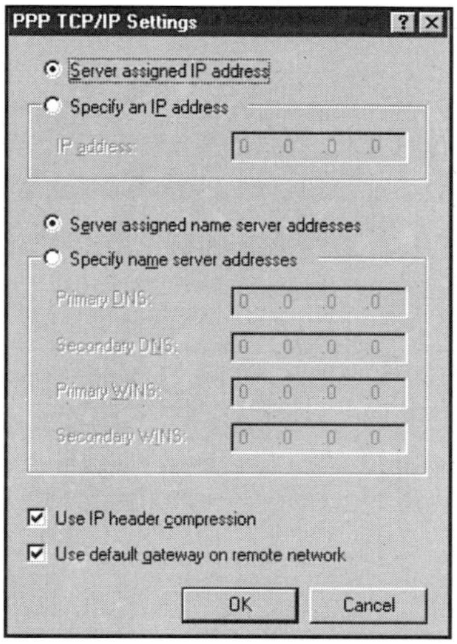

Figure 21.25

TCP/IP protocol configuration options for PPP.

Figure 21.26 shows the SLIP TCP/IP Settings dialog box. The options in this window are as follows:

◆ **IP address.** You must specify an IP address. SLIP servers cannot assign addresses.

◆ **Name server addresses.** You must specify IP addresses for the applicable DNS and WINS name servers.

◆ **Force IP header compression.** Check this option if the SLIP server uses header compression.

◆ **Use default gateway on remote network.** This option applies to computers that are connected to local networks at the same time they are dialing remotely. When this option is checked, packets that cannot be routed to the local network are routed to the default gateway on the remote network.

◆ **Frame size.** This value determines the size of frames that will be used. Adjust this value, if required, for the SLIP server. Frame sizes of 1006 and 1500 can be selected.

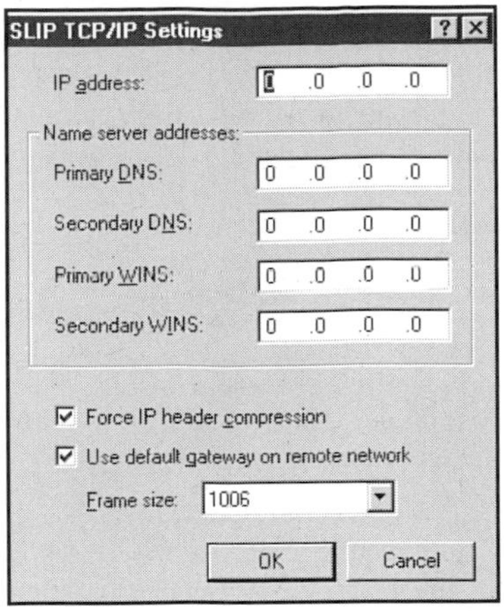

Figure 21.26

TCP/IP protocol configuration options for SLIP.

◆ **Enable software compression.** When this option is checked (the default), the communication software will compress and decompress communications data. It is unproductive and unnecessary to enable both hardware (modem) and software (protocol) compression. Typically, software compression is more efficient, particularly on higher-end computers. Software compression is not supported by the SLIP protocol.

◆ **Enable PPP LCP extensions.** LCP is a component of newer PPP implementations but is not supported by older PPP servers. Try deselecting this box if problems occur when using PPP.

Script Properties

Figure 21.27 shows the Script tab. Scripts are text files that contain commands that automate dial-in events such as logon. The details of scripts are beyond the scope of this book, and are discussed in the Windows NT Server documentation.

Scripts are typically unnecessary when dialing into PPP servers. PPP includes the Password Authentication Protocol (PAP), which automates the acceptance of user IDs and passwords. Because no automation is available for SLIP, however, scripts may be of benefit.

The Script tab provides options for scripts to be executed after dialing. The options are:

◆ **None.** No script will be executed. This is the default, and will work with most PPP servers.

◆ **Pop up a terminal window.** If this option is selected, a terminal window will be opened when a connection is established. The terminal will be used to accept the user's password and other required logon information.

◆ **Run this script.** If this option is selected, enter the path name for a script. You can choose **E**dit scripts to create and modify script files.

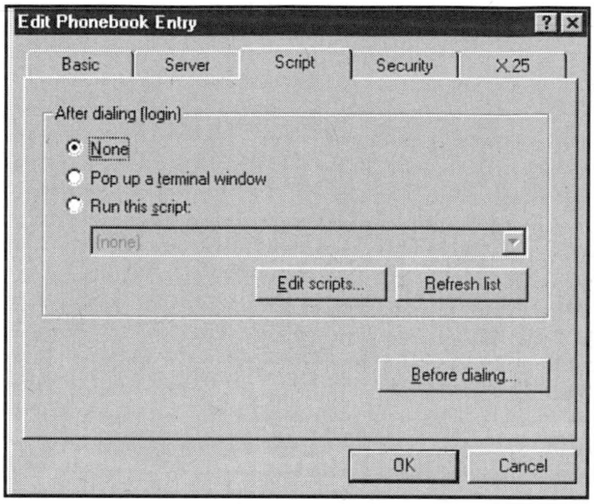

Figure 21.27

The Script tab's After dialing options.

You can also specify scripting to take place before dialing. Choose **B**efore dialing to open the Before Dialing Script dialog box, which is practically identical to the After dialing box shown in figure 21.27.

Security Properties

The Security tab, shown in figure 21.28, determines the types of encryption that will be used. The option chosen must match the requirements of the server. These choices were discussed in the section about RAS server configuration. See the discussion accompanying figure 21.12.

If you want to use your user name and password on the Windows NT network, check **U**se current username and password.

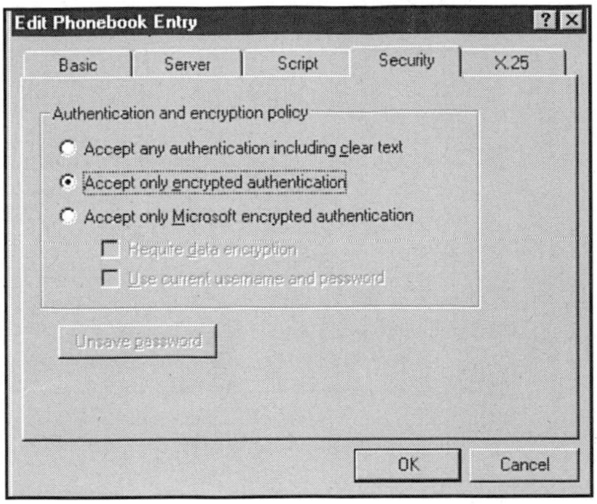

Figure 21.28

The Security tab.

X.25 Properties

If you are connecting to an X.25 network, select the X.25 tab, shown in figure 21.29. Entries on this tab are as follows:

◆ **Network.** Select the name of the X.25 network you are calling.

◆ **Address.** Specify the X.25 address supplied by the X.25 network provider.

◆ **User Data.** Enter additional connection data supplied by the X.25 network provider. This field may be left blank.

◆ **Facilities.** Enter parameters to request facilities from your X.25 provider. Consult the provider for appropriate parameters. This field is optional.

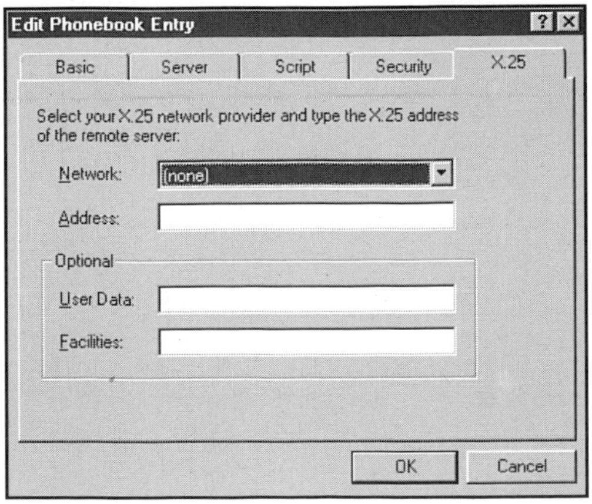

Figure 21.29

The X.25 tab.

Dialing with a Phonebook Entry

After you have entered a phonebook entry, choose OK in the New Phonebook Entry window to open the Dial-Up Networking window (refer to fig. 21.22). The actual events that take place depend on:

◆ Whether the host is a RAS server or a TCP/IP network

◆ Whether the host is configured for dial-back operation

The following exercise steps through the sequence of events when a RAS client calls a RAS server:

RAS Client to RAS Server Connection Sequence

1. Select a phonebook entry in the Phonebook entry to dial field.

2. Verify the entry in the Dialing from field. You can select another location by choosing **L**ocation. (New locations must be entered using the Telephony utility in the Control Panel.)

3. Verify the number in the Phone number preview field. If the number is not complete and correct, check the configuration for the location.

4. Choose **D**ial to open the Connect dialog box (see fig. 21.30).

Figure 21.30

Completing your dial-up account information.

5. Complete the fields in the Connect dialog box as follows:

◆ **User name.** Enter your user name on the destination network. This field and the **P**assword field will be completed with your Windows network user name if you checked **U**se current username and password in the Security tab when configuring this phonebook entry.

◆ **Password.** Enter your password on the destination network.

◆ **Domain.** If you are dialing to a RAS server, enter the domain you want to log on to. If you are dialing a non-RAS server, clear this field.

◆ **Save password.** Check this field if you want to have your password saved with the phonebook entry. This can be hazardous. Saving your password enables any user to dial your remote account without entering a password.

Choose OK when you have configured the Connect dialog box.

6. The client dials and enters a conversation with the RAS server.

7. The RAS server sends a challenge to the client.

8. The client sends an encrypted response.

9. The server checks the response against its database.

10. If the response is valid, the server checks for remote access permission.

11. If the user has been given remote access permission, the client is connected.

12. If callback is enabled, the server disconnects, calls the client, and completes steps 6 through 11 again.

13. If the server does not support all of the protocols that you enabled in the Protocols tab for the phonebook entry, you will see the message shown in figure 21.31. If you check Do **n**ot request the failed protocols next time, the protocols will be removed from the phonebook entry. Typically, because these protocols are unneeded, you can safely remove them.

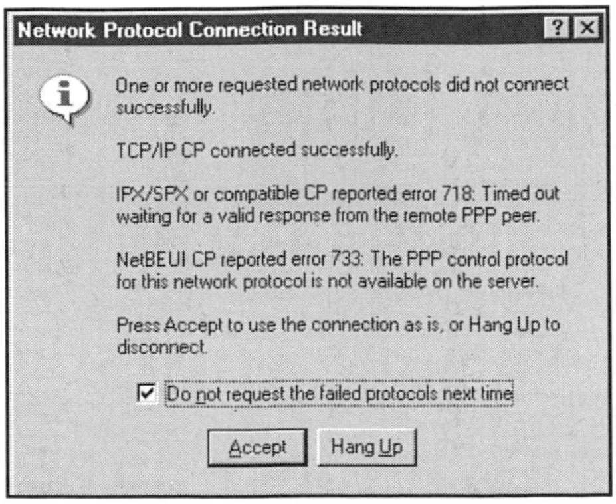

Network Protocol Connection Result

One or more requested network protocols did not connect successfully.

TCP/IP CP connected successfully.

IPX/SPX or compatible CP reported error 718: Timed out waiting for a valid response from the remote PPP peer.

NetBEUI CP reported error 733: The PPP control protocol for this network protocol is not available on the server.

Press Accept to use the connection as is, or Hang Up to disconnect.

☑ Do **n**ot request the failed protocols next time

Accept   Hang Up

Figure 21.31

Reporting unsupported protocols on the dial-up server.

14. Choose **A**ccept to continue the connection with the supported protocols. Choose Hang **U**p if a required protocol is not supported and you want to try another server.

15. Next, a message box informs you that the connection is complete. At this point, you can specify two actions that will take place when you make future connections:

   ◆ **Close on dial.** If this box is checked, the Dial-Up Network will be closed when a connection is established.

   ◆ **Do not display this message again.** If this box is checked, you will not see this message in the future when a connection is completed.

16. When the session is complete, choose the Hang Up button in the Dial-Up Networking application. You will need to reopen the application if you checked Close on dial in step 11.

You are now connected. The connection mimics a direct network connection, and you can use any applications that are appropriate to the environment. For example, you can use Windows NT applications to access files on a remote RAS server. Or you can use Winsock compatible TCP/IP to access remote TCP/IP services, such as those offered by the Internet.

When the session is finished, disconnect as covered in the following exercise:

Disconnecting a Session

1. Reopen the Dial-Up Networking application.

2. Choose Hang Up in the Dial-Up Networking dialog box.

Objective D.2

More Options in the Dial-Up Networking Application

Return to the Dial-Up Networking application. If you choose the More button, a menu opens with the following options:

◆ **Edit entry and modem properties.** Choose this option to use the phonebook editor to modify this phonebook entry.

◆ **Clone entry and modem properties.** Use this option as a shortcut for creating a new phonebook entry that has similar settings to an existing entry.

◆ **Delete entry.** Use this option to remove the entry shown in the Phonebook entry to dial field.

◆ **Create shortcut to entry.** This option opens a dialog box that enables you to create a shortcut. To put the shortcut on your desktop, place it in C:\Winnt\ Profiles*username*\Desktop. To put the shortcut in the Start menu, place it in C:\Winnt\Profiles*username*\Desktop\Start Menu\Programs*folder*, where *folder* is the submenu that should contain the shortcut.

◆ **Monitor status.** This option opens the Dial-Up Networking Monitor (see fig. 21.32). This utility, which can also be started from the Control Panel, displays a variety of information about the dial-up session and enables you to configure certain options for the dial-up session. In the Preferences tab, you can determine whether status lights will be displayed as a taskbar icon or as a window on the desktop. See the "Troubleshooting RAS" section for more information about the status lights.

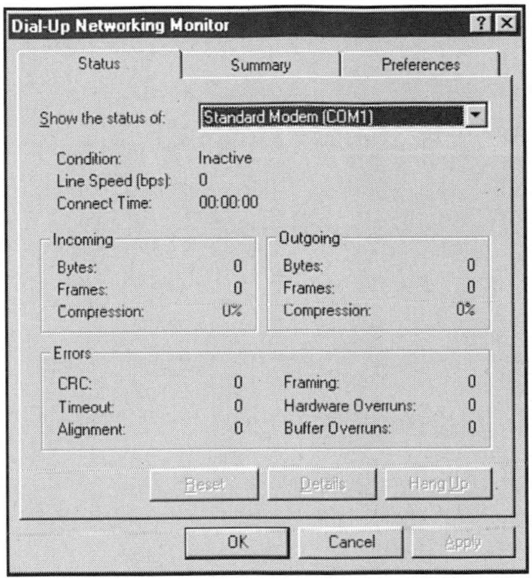

Figure 21.32

The Dial-Up Networking Monitor.

◆ **Operator assisted or manual dialing.** Use this option if the phone number must be entered manually or by an operator.

◆ **Logon preferences.** This option opens the Logon Preferences utility shown in figure 21.33. Use this utility to configure a variety of options that affect the dial-up process. Of particular interest is the Callback tab, shown in the figure. You must configure this tab to enable callback operation.

Using RAS Automatic Dialing

With Windows NT 4, an automatic dialing feature has been added to RAS. When a connection is established, automatic dialing associates a network address with a phonebook entry. RAS AutoDial also learns about every connection that is established over a RAS link.

If you are not connected to a dial-up network, whenever the address is referenced, RAS will automatically be invoked and will attempt to connect using the appropriate phonebook entry.

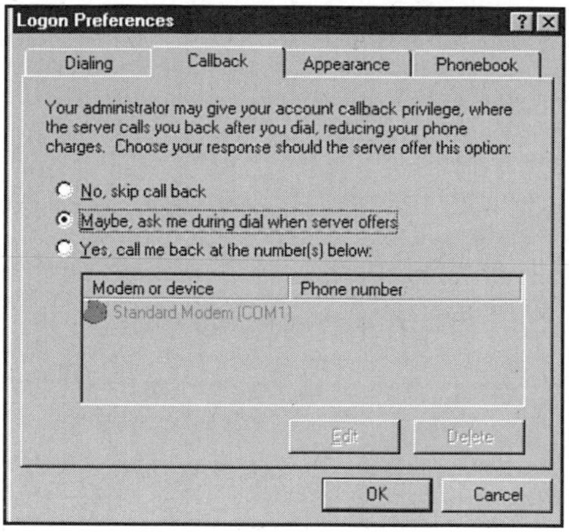

Figure 21.33

*The Logon
Preferences utility.*

Figure 21.33

The Logon Preferences utility.

Under certain circumstances, you may want to disable the AutoDial feature. To do so, follow the steps in the following exercise:

Disabling AutoDial

1. Choose **M**ore in the Dial-Up Networking dialog box and select the Logon Preferences option in the Options menu.

2. Select the Appearance tab.

3. Deselect the Always prompt **b**efore auto-dialing entry.

Using the Point-to-Point Tunneling Protocol

Using RAS, you can construct a dial-in server that enables clients to access your network from anyplace in the world. RAS works well and provides a high-level of security. What more could you want?

Lower cost, for one thing. If you have dozens of users calling in via RAS, you can run up a lot of long-distance charges. If your network is connected to the Internet, you might begin to wonder whether your users could connect to your network by dialing into the Internet. They would be making a local call to an IAP, and their traffic would be routed to your RAS server for free through the global Internet. Nice and cheap!

Unfortunately, the Internet is not a very secure place. The majority of traffic is unencrypted and is vulnerable to eavesdropping. Sensitive communications should always be secured when it passes through the public Internet, but until recently, RAS has not had that capability.

The Point-to-Point Tunneling Protocol (PPTP) is a new feature in Windows NT version 4. PPTP using *tunneling* to enable packets for one protocol to be carried over networks running another protocol. For example, NWLink packets can be encapsulated inside IP packets, enabling the IPX packets to be transported through the TCP/IP world of the Internet. PPTP has the added benefit of enhancing security, because it works hand-in-hand with the encryption capability of RAS.

Let's look at two scenarios for using PPTP. In figure 21.34, both the RAS client and the RAS server are directly connected to the Internet. A PPTP tunnel between the client and the server establishes a secure communication channel between them. The use of PPTP enables the client and server to connect via the Internet, without a need for the client to dial in to RAS through a switched connection. While communicating, RAS encrypts traffic between the client and server, providing a secure communications data stream.

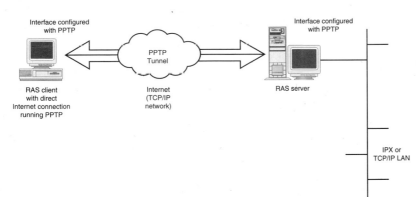

Figure 21.34

Client and server can communicate through the Internet using PPTP.

A slightly more elaborate example is shown in figure 21.35. The RAS server is connected to a LAN running NWLink. By establishing a PPTP tunnel through the Internet, the client can connect with the NWLink network even though it is communicating through the TCP/IP Internet. This is accomplished by loading the NWLink protocols on the client together with PPTP. The client dials in to the Internet and opens a PPTP tunnel with the RAS server. From that point, the NWLink packets are encapsulated in PPP packets for transfer through the Internet. The RAS server decapsulates the PPP packets to recover the NWLink messages, which are forwarded to the LAN.

Figure 21.35

*A dial-up client
can communicate
with an NWLink
or TCP/IP LAN
through the
Internet using
PPTP.*

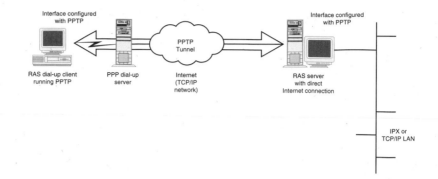

Microsoft refers to PPTP tunnels as *virtual private networks* (VPNs) because the
establish a logical private network that runs over the public network infrastructure.

PPTP configuration is not difficult. The following sections show how to configure
PPTP support on the RAS server and client.

Configuring PPTP

PPTP must be enabled for each RAS server or client that will use PPTP. To enable
PPTP, follow the steps in the following exercise:

Configuring PPTP

1. Using the Network applet in the Control Panel, install the Point-To-Point
   Tunneling Protocol in the Protocols tab.

2. After the protocol is copied from the installation disks, the PPTP Configuration
   dialog box is displayed (see fig. 21.36). The **N**umber of Virtual Private Networks
   specifies the number of PPTP connections that will be supported. In the example, two VPNs will be established.

Figure 21.36

*Specifying the
number of
connections
PPTP will
support.*

PPTP Configuration

Number of Virtual Private Networks: 2

OK

Cancel

3. Next, the RAS setup utility is started. Here, you will add the virtual ports that support the Virtual Private Networks you want to establish.

4. Choose **A**dd to open the Add RAS Device dialog box shown in figure 21.37. In the example, I have opened the RAS Capable **D**evices list to show you the two virtual ports that correspond to the two VPNs that were specified in step 2. Select an entry (for example VPN1-RASPPTPM) and choose OK.

5. In the Remote Access Setup dialog box, select each new entry and choose **C**onfigure to open the Configure Port Usage dialog box. Select one of the following options to define how the port will be used: Dial **o**ut only, **R**eceive calls only, or **D**ial out and Receive Calls.

   For a PPTP client, at least one VPN port must be configured to permit dial-out.

   For a PPTP server, at least one VPN port must be configured to permit receiving calls.

6. Repeat steps 4 and 5 for each VPN virtual device you want to add. Figure 21.38 shows Remote Access Setup after both VPNs have been added.

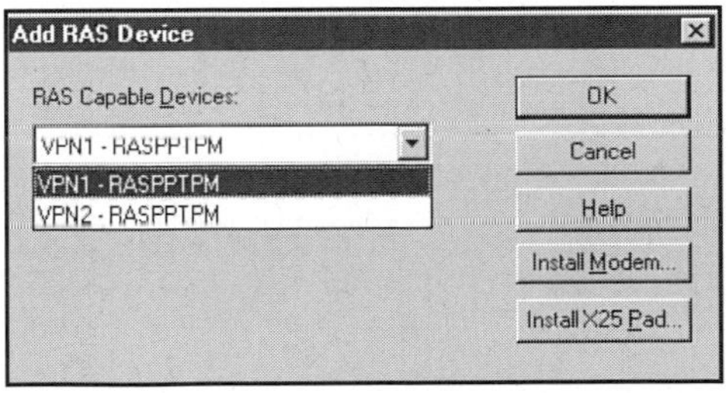

Figure 21.37

Adding VPN virtual devices.

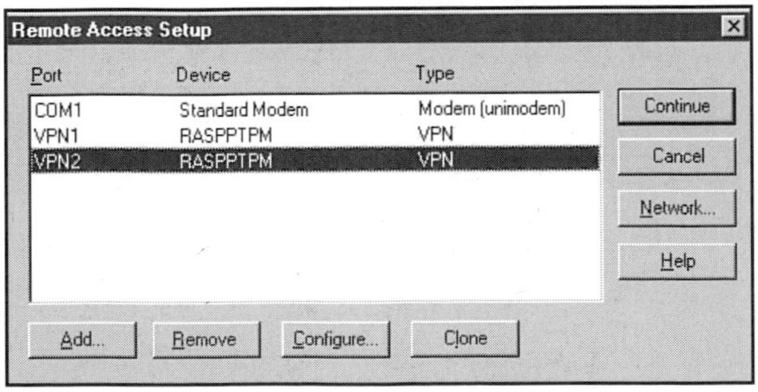

Figure 21.38

Remote Access Setup after VPN devices have been added.

7. When all virtual devices have been added, choose Continue.

8. When you are returned to the Protocols tab, choose Close.

9. Restart the computer.

Enabling PPTP Filtering

After PPTP is installed, the RAS server will support both PPTP and non-PPTP connections, a potential security hole. If you want, you can enable PPTP filtering, disabling support for any traffic except PPTP.

To enable PPTP filtering, follow the steps in the following exercise:

Enabling PPTP Filtering

1. Select the Protocols tab in the Network applet.

2. Select TCP/IP Protocol and choose **P**roperties.

3. Select the IP Address tab.

4. Select a network adapter for which PPTP filtering is to be enabled.

5. Click A**d**vanced.

6. Check Enable PPTP **F**iltering.

7. Repeat steps 4 through 6 for each interface that will support PPTP filtering.

8. Restart the computer to activate the changes.

Monitoring Server PPTP Support

You can monitor the PPTP ports in the RAS Server Admin utility by choosing the **C**ommunication Ports command in the **S**erver menu. As shown in figure 21.39, VPN ports are listed with modem ports and can be managed in the same way. Ports will only appear if they are configured to receive calls. Dial-out only ports will not be listed.

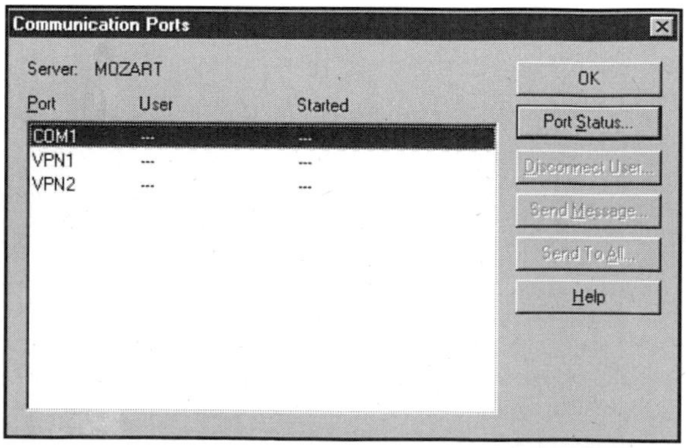

Figure 21.39

VPN ports being monitored in RAS Server Admin.

Enabling Client PPTP Support

When a client is dialing into the Internet, as in figure 21.35, establishing a PPTP tunnel to the RAS server has two steps:

◆ The client establishes a dial-up connection to the Internet through an Internet access provider.

◆ The client establishes a PPTP connection to the RAS server.

When a client is directly connected to the Internet, it is unnecessary to establish a dial-up connection. The procedure for starting a PPTP connection to the RAS server remains the same, however.

To establish a PPTP connection, you need to create a special entry in the Dial-Up Networking phonebook. This entry, and example of which appears in figure 21.40, has two distinguishing characteristics:

◆ The **D**ial using field is configured with one of the VPN virtual devices that was added to the RAS configuration when PPTP was installed. In figure 21.40, the field has been pulled down to show the available ports. VPNs will appear in this list only if they have been configured to support dial-out.

◆ The Phone number pre**v**iew field is completed with the DNS name or the IP address of the PPTP server.

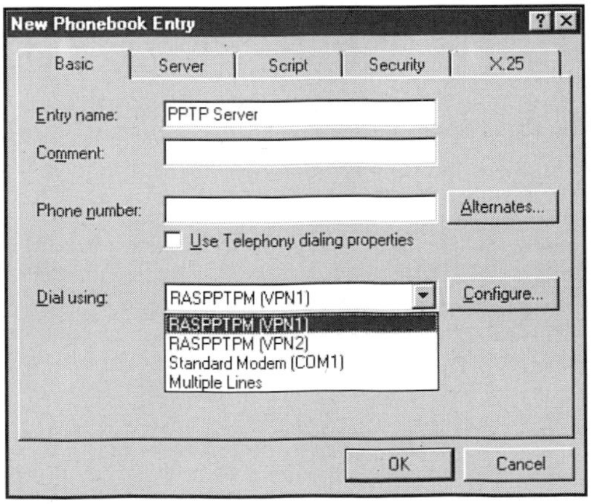

Figure 21.40

Configuring a PPTP client phonebook entry.

Creating a dial-up connection to PPTP has two steps:

◆ In Dial-Up Networking, run the phonebook entry that connects to your IAP using a telephone number and a modem.

◆ After the connection is established, run the phonebook entry that connects to the PPTP tunnel using a DNS hostname or IP address.

If the client is directly connected to the Internet, it is only necessary to run the phonebook entry that creates the PPTP tunnel.

RAS Serial Cable Requirements

Table 21.1 summarizes the pin connection requirements RAS expects in a cable that is used to connect a RAS computer to a modem. If you purchase a commercial cable, be sure it supports these wiring configurations.

TABLE 21.1
Pin Connection Requirements

Computer 25-pin connector	Computer 9-pin connector	Modem 25-pin connector	Modem 9-pin connector	Signal
1		1		Ground
2	3	2	3	Transmit Data
3	2	3	2	Receive Data
4	7	4	7	Request to Send
5	8	5	8	Clear to Send
6	6	6	6	Data Set Ready
7	5	7	5	Signal Ground
8	1	8	1	Carrier Detect
20	4	20	4	Data Terminal Ready

Table 21.2 lists the RAS cable requirements for a null-modem cable.

TABLE 21.2
Cable Requirements for a Null-Modem Cable

Server 25-pin connector	Server 9-pin connector	Client 25-pin connector	Client 9-pin connector	Signal
1		1		Ground
2	3	3	2	Transmit Data
3	2	2	3	Receive Data
4	7	5	8	Request to Send
5	8	4	7	Clear to Send
6, 8	6, 1	20	4	Data Set Ready, Carrier Detect
7	5	7	5	Signal Ground
20	4	6, 8	6, 1	Data Terminal Ready

Troubleshooting RAS

Objective F.5

By far the most common problems you will have, at least while you are learning RAS, will result from misconfiguration of the client or the server. Start with a basic setup, get everything working, and then add modem pools and other fancy features.

If possible, do your initial testing with two identical modems. If that works and other modems don't, you can be pretty sure the modems are incompatible with RAS.

The Dial-Up Networking Monitor (see fig. 21.41), an extremely useful tool for testing flaky connections, pops up when dialing commences. The Dial-Up Monitor displays modem status lights during a session, either in a window or as an icon on the taskbar. The window version is more informative, showing the status of the TX (transmit data), RX (receive data), and CD (carrier detect) lines and whether errors are detected.

Especially look for high error rates that might be causing lost connections.

Figure 21.41

*The Dial-Up
Networking
Monitor.*

Logging RAS Events

You can enable two RAS logs by changing Registry entries. The PPP log can be used to troubleshoot problems with PPP connections. To enable the PPP log, change the following Logging parameter to 0×1 in the key HKEY_LOCAL_MACHINE\ SYSTEM\ CurrentControlSet\Services\RasMan\PPP.

The device log records all communication from serial ports to connected devices when modem commands are being executed. To enable the device log, change the Logging parameter to 0—1 in the key HKEY_LOCAL_MACHINE\SYSTEM\ CurrentControlSet\Services\RasMan\Parameters. Log data is stored in the file DEVICE.LOG in the C:\WINNT\SYSTEM32\RAS directory.

> **Note** See Chapter 19 for information about changing values in the Registry.

By default, the logs are stored in the directory C:\WINNT\SYSTEM32\RAS. The PPP log file is named PPP.LOG and the device log is named DEVICE.LOG. You can view these files using Notepad.

Testing Your Knowledge

1. How many modems can Windows NT Server support in a modem pool?

    A. 256

    B. 64

    C. 32

    D. None

2. Which three protocols does the RAS service support with analog modems?

    A. PPP

    B. NetBIOS

    C. SLIP

    D. NWlink

    E. RAS Protocol

3. What does the abbreviation SLIP stand for?

    A. Single-Line Interconnect Protocol

    B. Serial-Line Interface Protocol

    C. Single-Line Internet Protocol

    D. Serial-Line Internet Protocol

4. A _____ is a cable that crosses wires to enable two RS-232 ports to connect as though there were modems between.

5. ISDN has two B channels that have the potential (with a compatible device and drivers) to support up to _____ Kbps of channel bandwidth.

    A. 36.6

    B. 14.4

    C. 64

    D. 128

6. Which Microsoft operating systems support the PPP protocol?

    A. MS-DOS

    B. Windows NT Server 3.5x and 4

    C. Windows 95

    D. Windows NT Advanced Server 3.1

    E. Windows NT Workstation 3.5x and 4

7. Installing the RAS service is done in the Control Panel by opening the Network utility and selecting which tab?

    A. Bindings

    B. Protocols

    C. Services

    D. Adapters

8. The RAS service requires that you have network interface adapters installed.

    A. True

    B. False

9. What is the name of the Microsoft encryption protocol (MS-CHAP)?

    A. Certified handshake authorization protocol

    B. Challenge handshake authentication protocol

    C. Certified handshake authentication protocol

    D. Challenge handshake authorization protocol

10. For optimal RAS security, you can set the _____ option, which disconnects the client and returns a call at a preset phone number.

11. PPTP is an abbreviation for _____, which is a new feature in Windows NT Server 4.

    A. Point-to-Point Tunneling Protocol

    B. Point-to-Point Telecommunications Protocol

    C. Peer-to-Peer Tunneling Protocol

Review Answers

1. A

2. A, C, E

3. D

4. null modem

5. D

6. B, C, E

7. C

8. B

9. B

10. call back

11. A

CHAPTER 22

Managing Directory Replication

Directory replication is one of the surprise bonus features of Windows NT Server. As a LAN administrator, I have often needed to duplicate data between servers. To accomplish this I have had to rely on indirect approaches involving job schedulers and copy procedures. Between the times I scheduled the copy jobs to run, the directories gradually went out of synchronization. So I appreciate the ease with which Windows NT Server directory replication works.

The most common use of directory replication is probably to copy logon scripts and policy files from one domain controller to other DCs, enabling users to log on through any DC and access a copy of their logon script and policies on the local domain controller. Because the logon script is local to the network, it need not be retrieved from another server (across a WAN link), and both network traffic and server demand are reduced.

Directory replication can be used with any data that is shared on multiple computers or domains. Suppose, for example, that your company maintains an employee directory or online newsletter. Rather than having everyone in the enterprise hit on the same server, you can replicate the files to as many computers as you like.

Directory replication does not merely perform "one time" copies. It is a dynamic service that continuously identifies changed files and new files and replicates them to other computers, all without the need for administrator intervention. Essentially, directory replication keeps directory trees on different computers synchronized. It does not merely copy files, but removes files and creates subdirectories (it does not delete subdirectories) to keep the two directories identical.

How Directory Replication Works

Directory replication copies files from computers called *export servers* to computers called *import servers/computers.* Although only Windows NT Server computers can be configured as an export server, both Windows NT Workstations and Servers can be import computers.

When you configure an export server, you designate two things:

◆ An export directory. All subdirectories and files created in the export directory are eligible for export.

◆ An "export to" list of computers and domains to which files will be exported. If an export server exports to a domain, every computer that is configured to import files will receive the import.

When you configure an import computer, you designate similar properties:

◆ An import directory to receive imported files.

◆ An "import from" list of computers and domains from which import files will be accepted.

Figure 22.1 illustrates directory trees on an export server and an import computer. The figure is based on the default export and import directories that are established when Windows NT is installed. The default export directory is \Winnt\system32\Repl\ Export, and the default import directory is \Winnt\system32\Repl\Import. The result of directory replication is that subdirectories and files in the Import subdirectory will mirror images of subdirectories and files in the Export directory.

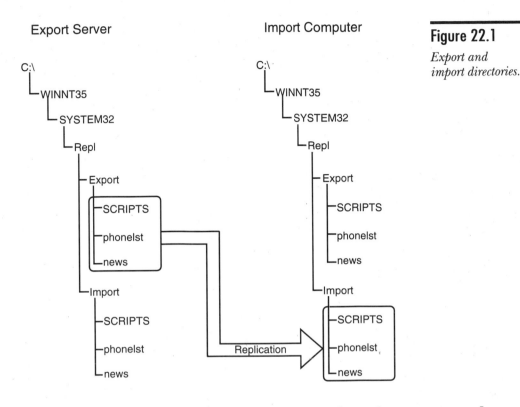

Figure 22.1

Export and import directories.

The same computer can function as an export server and as an import computer. In fact, an export server can replicate files to its own import directory. Figure 22.2 shows some of the possibilities.

Note   A given computer can export only one replication directory tree. In some cases, however, you might want to replicate two or more trees on a network. In addition to replicating the logon script directory tree, for example, you might want to replicate a company telephone directory database.

The best solution is to place the trees on separate export servers. Configure one server to export the logon script directory tree and configure another to export the database directory tree.

Directory replication under NT 4 does not function properly unless Service Pack 1 or later is installed.

Figure 22.2

Examples of export servers and import computers.

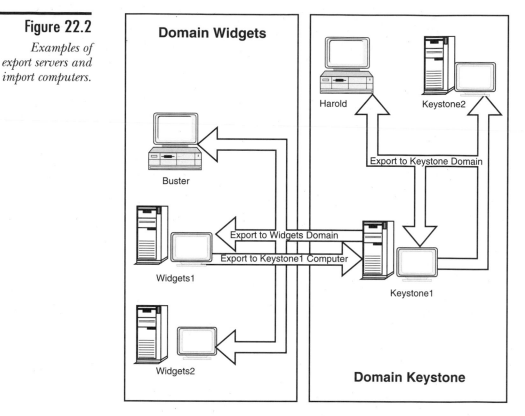

Using the Directory Replicator Service

Every export server and import computer must be running the Directory Replicator service. This service must be configured to log on with a user account that has the privileges needed to replicate files. First you need to create the user account, and then you must configure and start the Directory Replicator service.

Creating the Directory Replicator User Account

In each domain that will be importing or exporting files, create a user account with the following properties:

◆ Pass**w**ord Never Expires has been checked.

◆ The account Logon Hours enable it to log on 24 hours a day, 7 days a week.

◆ The account is a member of the Replicator local group.

You won't be able to name this user account Replicator because a built-in local group already exists with that name. I called my user "RepUser" in the examples.

Configuring the Directory Replicator Service

Objective

B.6

After you have created the user account, you can configure and start the Directory Replicator service. Services are managed with the Service Manager, which is accessible through the Control Panel Services utility or through the Server Manager. This section uses the Server Manager in the following exercise.

Configuring the Directory Replicator Service

1. Open the Services dialog box for the server using one of the following methods:

    ◆ Run the Server utility in the Control Panel.

    ◆ Select the server in Server Manager and choose Ser**v**ices from the **C**omputer menu. The Services dialog box is shown in figure 22.3.

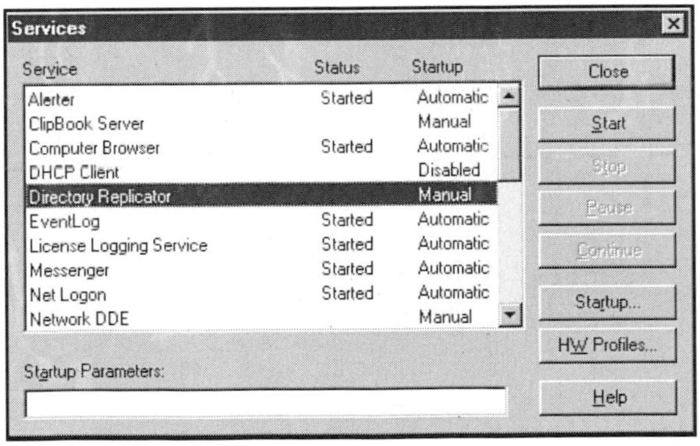

Figure 22.3

The Service scroll list in the Services dialog box.

If you have not replicated directories, the Directory Replicator service will not show an entry in the Status column and will be configured as Manual in the Startup column.

2. Select the Directory Replicator service and choose Sta**r**tup to configure the startup options for the service. Figure 22.4 shows how this box appears when the Directory Replicator service has been properly configured.

Figure 22.4

*Configuring
startup options
for the Directory
Replicator service.*

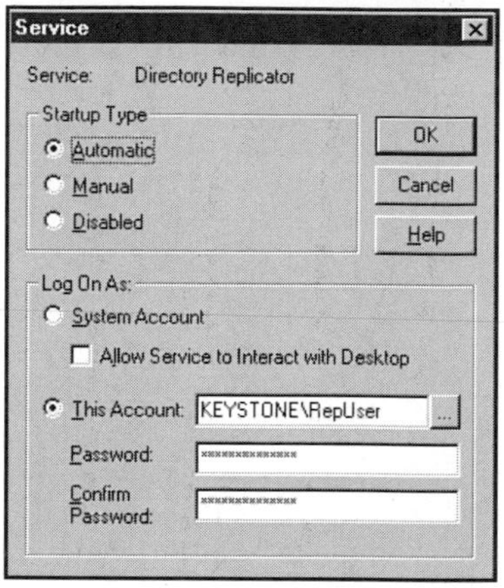

3. Choose the **A**utomatic option in the Startup Type box.

4. Select the **T**his Account radio button and enter the user name of the replicator account you created. You can click on the Browse (...) button next to the **T**his Account button to choose the account from a browse menu.

5. Enter the password in the **P**assword and **C**onfirm Password boxes.

6. Choose OK to return to the services list. You will see the message shown in figure 22.5. As you can see, the user account used by the Directory Replicator service is granted some special permissions.

Figure 22.5

*Message verifying
setup of the
Directory
Replicator user
account.*

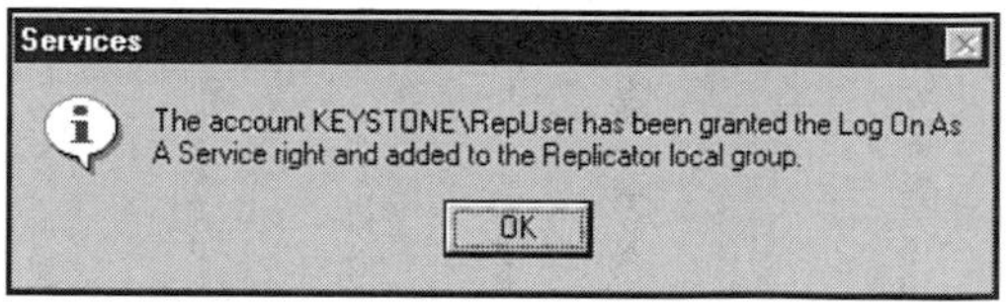

7. Select the Directory Replicator service and choose **S**tart. You will see this message: Attempting to Start the Directory Replicator service. If the service starts successfully, the confirmation message shown in figure 22.5 is presented.

   The Directory Replicator service should show as Started in the Status column and as Automatic in the Startup column.

8. Choose Close to return to Server Manager.

Repeat this procedure on each computer that will be an export server or an import computer.

Configuring Trust Relationships

Every domain that will be importing files from another domain must trust the export domain. The procedures for configuring trust relationships were described in Chapter 10, "Managing Domains and Trust Relationships."

Be sure that each exporting domain permits the importing domain to trust it. Then configure each importing domain to trust the exporting domain.

If directories will be replicated in both directions, two one-way trust relationships must be established.

If a trust is not established, the same user account and password must exist on each domain.

Configuring the Export Server

Any Windows NT Server can be configured as an export server. Recall that Setup configures the server with a default export directory. I don't recommend that you change the default export directory. If you want to do so, however, create the directory and assign Full Control permissions for the directory to the Replicator local group.

The permissions you give to other users and groups depend on how the directories and files are used. You can enable users to create files in the export directory tree if desired.

Follow the steps in the following exercise to configure the export server:

Configuring the Export Server

1. Open the Server properties dialog box for the server using one of the following methods (see fig. 22.6):

    ◆ Run the Servers utility in the Control Panel.

    ◆ Select the server in Server Manager and choose **P**roperties from the **C**omputer menu.

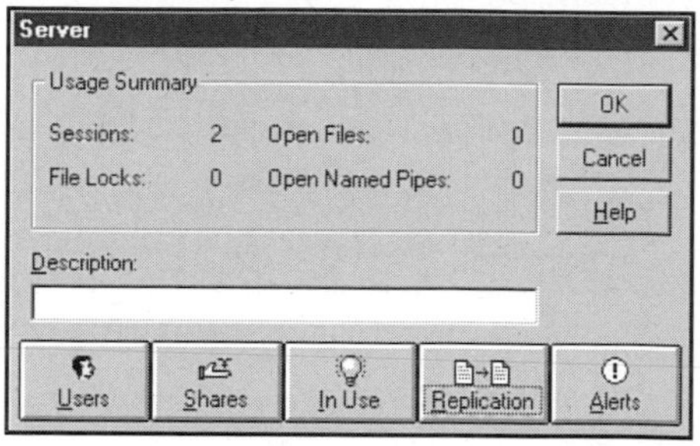

Figure 22.6

The Server properties dialog box.

2. In the Server properties box, choose **R**eplication to display the Directory Replication dialog box shown in figure 22.7. By default, the Do Not E**x**port and Do Not I**m**port options are selected. The example in the figure has already been set up as an export server that exports to the domains KEYSTONE (its own domain) and WIDGETS.

> **Note**   If you are viewing properties for a Windows NT Workstation computer, you will see only the options related to directory importing. A stand-alone server cannot be an export replication server.

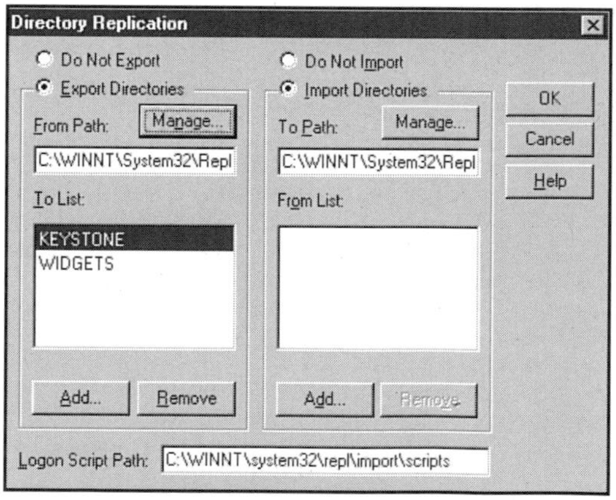

Figure 22.7

Directory replication configuration for an export server.

3. Select **E**xport Directories.

4. If you are not using the default export directory, edit the entry in the **F**rom Path box.

5. At least one import computer or import domain must be specified in the **T**o List box. To add an import destination, choose **A**dd to display the Select Domain dialog box shown in figure 22.8. Only the current domain and domains that trust this domain are shown in the **S**elect Domain box.

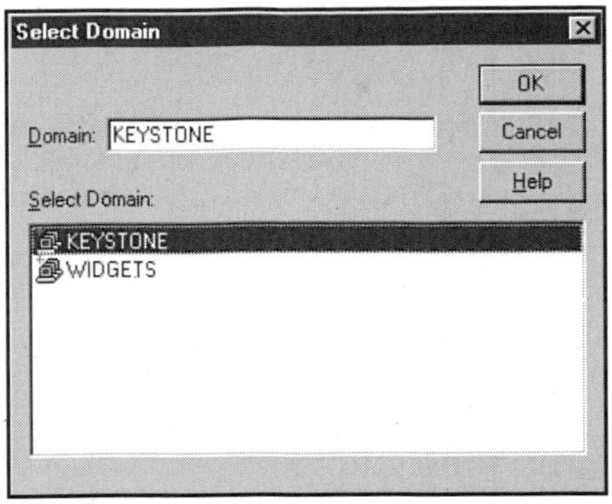

Figure 22.8

Selecting an import domain.

6. If the domain you want to add is shown, you may browse the **S**elect Domain box and select a domain or a computer. If the domain is not shown, type the domain or computer name in the **D**omain box.

> **Tip**
>
> The browse list contains only the domains that trust this domain. In most cases, you will be exporting from a master domain to a department domain, and master domains typically are not trusted by master domains. Therefore, you will usually have to explicitly enter the computer or domain name when you are setting up an import computer in a department domain.

7. Choose OK to save the entry and return to the Directory Replication dialog box.

8. Add any other desired destinations to the **T**o List box.

9. Choose OK to save the server properties.

> **Note**
>
> Directory replication to a domain may fail if the export and import domains are connected through a wide area network connection. With a WAN connection, you should export to individual computers in the import domain.

Configuring the Import Computer

Import computers can be Windows NT workstations or servers. They are also configured with the server Properties dialog box as shown in the following exercise:

Configuring the Import Server

1. Open the Properties dialog box for the server using one of the following methods:

◆ Run the Servers utility in the Control Panel.

◆ Select the server in Server Manager and choose **P**roperties from the **C**omputer menu.

2. In the Properties dialog box, choose **R**eplication to display the Directory Replication dialog box shown in figure 22.9. By default, the Do Not Export and Do Not Import options are selected. The example in the figure has already been set up as an import server.

Figure 22.9

The Directory Replication properties box for an import computer.

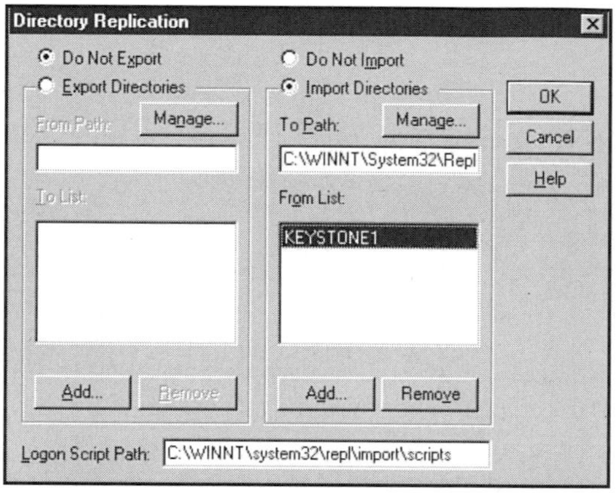

3. Select **I**mport Directories.

4. If you are not using the default import directory, edit the entry in the To **P**ath box.

5. At least one export computer or export domain must be specified in the Fr**o**m List box. To add an export source, choose A**d**d to display the Select Domain dialog box.

6. If the domain you want to add is shown, you may browse the Select Domain dialog box and select a domain or a computer. If the domain is not shown, type the domain or computer name in the **D**omain dialog box.

7. Choose OK to save the entry and return to the Directory Replication dialog box.

8. Add any other desired sources to the Fr**o**m List.

9. Choose OK to save the server properties.

Testing Directory Replication

Now that you have started the Directory Replication services and configured the export and import servers, directory replication should commence. Some delay is always present in the directory replication process, so don't expect things to happen immediately.

To verify that directory replication is working, follow these steps:

1. Open a window in File Manager to view the export directory.

2. Open another window in File Manager to view the import directory.

3. Create a file in the export directory. You can copy a file to the directory or use Notepad to create a text file.

4. Create a subdirecotry in the export directory.

5. Wait. Take a break and check the import directory in a few minutes. It should be a mirror image of the export directory.

Note Replication takes place after a stabilization period has been completed. The length of the stabilization period is determined by the value of the Stabilize option specified for the properties of the export computer. The Stabilize option is described in the section "Managing Export and Import Computers."

Troubleshooting Directory Replication

Directory replication errors are recorded in the applications log, which you may view with the Event Viewer utility, which is installed in the Administrative Tools program group. Choose **A**pplications from the **L**og menu to view any errors.

If directory replication is not working, check the following items:

◆ Examine the user account being used by the Directory Replicator service. Is the user account a member of the Replicator group?

◆ Has the Directory Replicator service been configured in each export and import computer with the following?

Startup Type: **A**utomatic.

This Account is selected and an account specified that has Backup Operators membership.

Proper passwords.

◆ Do all export domains permit themselves to be trusted by the appropriate import domains?

◆ Do all import domains trust the appropriate export domains?

◆ Is the Directory Replicator service started on each export and import computer?

◆ On NTFS volumes, does the directory replicator user account have Full Control permissions in the Export and Import directories, either through direct or group assignments?

◆ Are files that are not being replicated being held open by a user or an application? Files must be closed to be replicated.

◆ Are the system clocks on the export and import domains reasonably close in settings?

Tuning the Replication Process

Several Registry parameters can be used to tune the operation of the Replicator service. The value entries are located in the following Registry key:

`HKEY_LOCAL_MACHINE\SYSTEM\CurrentControlSet\Services\Replicator\Parameters`

These values cannot be set using the Services tool and must be modified using the Registry Editor. Consult Chapter 19, "Managing the Server," for a description of the Registry and instructions for using the Registry Editor to modify Registry contents. The following value entries must be added to the Parameters subkey. All are of type REG_DWORD.

◆ **Interval.** This value entry determines the interval in minutes at which the export server checks replicated directories for changes. Range: 1–60 (minutes); default: 5.

◆ **Pulse.** This value entry specifies the frequency with which the export server repeats sending the last update notice. To ensure that no import server misses the notice, the export server continues to send change notices even when no changes have occurred. The server waits Pulse×Interval minutes between notices. Range: 1–10; default: 3.

◆ **Guard Time.** This value entry determines the number of minutes the export directory must be stable before the import server can import its files. Range: 0–1/2 of Interval (minutes); default: 3.

Remember that these parameters take effect only when the Directory Replicator is restarted.

Managing Export and Import Computers

The Directory Replication properties dialog box (see fig. 22.7) enables you to manage several characteristics of export servers and import computers.

Choose the Ma**n**age button in the **E**xport Directories box to display the Manage Exported Directories dialog box, shown in figure 22.10. An entry is listed for each subdirectory that is in the export directory. The following information is displayed for each subdirectory:

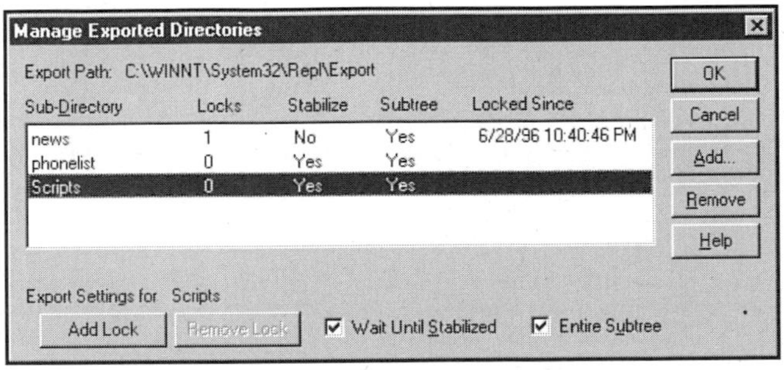

Figure 22.10

Managing exported directories.

◆ **Locks.** Unless the lock count is 0, this subdirectory will not be exported. Locks are added with the Add Lock button, discussed in the next list.

◆ **Stabilize.** Indicates whether the Wait Until **S**tabilized option has been selected. If this field is No, files are eligible to be exported as soon as they are modified. If this field is Yes, modified files will be allowed to stabilize for at least two minutes.

◆ **Subtree.** Indicates whether the Entire S**u**btree option has been selected. If this field is No, subdirectories of this directory will not be exported. If this field says Yes, subdirectories will be exported.

◆ **Locked Since.** For locked subdirectories, indicates the time and date when locks were applied.

To manage a subdirectory, select it and use the following controls:

◆ **Add Lock.** If a lock is added to a subdirectory, nothing will be exported from it or from its subdirectories. You can add more than one lock (several administrators may be working on the same export directories). Exporting will not resume until all locks are removed.

◆ **Remove Lock.** Choose this option to reduce the lock count by one. Exporting resumes when the lock count is 0.

◆ **Wait Until S̲tabilized.** Check this box to force Directory Replication to wait at least two minutes after a file is modified before exporting the file. Use this option to help eliminate partial replication. If this box is checked, the Stabilize column will indicate Yes for this subdirectory.

◆ **Entire S̲ubtree.** If this box is checked, subdirectories of this directory will be exported whenever this directory is exported. If the box is not checked, only this directory will be exported, without its subdirectories.

◆ **Add.** If a subdirectory in the export directory is not listed in the Manage Export Directories window, choose the A̲dd button to add it to the display. In most cases, subdirectories will be added and removed by the system.

◆ **Remove.** To remove a subdirectory from the window, select the subdirectory and choose R̲emove.

The Manage button in the Import Directories box displays a slightly different window, as shown in figure 22.11. The following information is displayed for each subdirectory:

◆ **Locks.** Unless the lock count is 0, this subdirectoy will not be imported. Locks are added with the Add Lock button, discussed in the next list.

◆ **Status.** This field can have the following values:

  ◆ *OK* indicates that the subdirectory is receiving regular imports.

  ◆ *No Master* indicates that imports are not being received. The export server may not be running or a configuration error may exist.

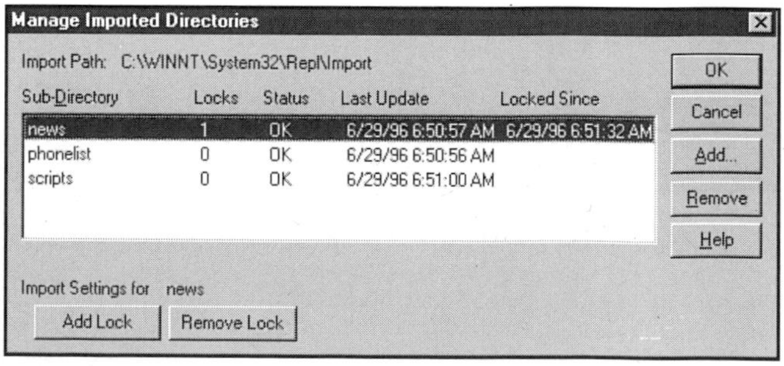

Figure 22.11

Managing imported directories.

- ◆ *No Sync* indicates that imports have taken place, but that data is not current. This condition can result from communication error or incorrect permissions at the export server.

  - ◆ If the field is blank, replication has not occurred in this subdirectory.

- ◆ **Last Update.** The date and time the subdirectory last received an import.

- ◆ **Locked Since.** For locked subdirectories, indicates the time and date when locks were applied.

The Manage Imported Directories window has only two controls:

- ◆ **Add Lock.** As with export directories, you can place locks on import subdirectories. Files will not be imported to a subdirectory if any locks are applied.

- ◆ **Remove Lock.** Select this button to remove a lock from the selected subdirectory.

- ◆ **Add.** If a subdirectory in the export directory is not listed in the Manage Export Directories window, choose the **A**dd button to add it to the display. In most cases, subdirectories will be added and removed by the system.

- ◆ **Remove.** To remove a subdirectory from the window, select the subdirectory and choose **R**emove.

Managing Logon Scripts

The Directory Replication dialog box is used to declare the location of logon scripts for the server (see fig. 22.7). Directory replication is commonly used to replicate master copies of logon scripts to all domain controllers in a domain or on the entire network.

The logon script path is a subdirectory of the default export directory. By default, the logon scripts path is C:\Winnt\system32\Repl\Import\Scripts (this is the NetLogon share used by logon scripts and policies). To replicate logon script files, the master copies should be placed in the same subdirectory of the export subdirectory. The default subdirectory for master logon scripts that are to be exported is C:\Winnt\ system32\Repl\Export\Scripts.

Users whose logons are replicated by the master export server must be able to access logon scripts in the Import\Scripts subdirectory. The easiest way to achieve this is to configure the master export server to export to its own domain. This configuration causes scripts to be replicated to the Import\Scripts directory on the master export server at the same time it is replicated to other import computers in the domain.

Testing Your Knowledge

1. Both Windows NT Servers and NT Workstations can be configured as import and export servers.

    A. True

    B. False

2. What is the default export directory that is created when Windows NT is installed?

    A. \WINNT\SYSTEM32\RPL\EXPORT

    B. \WINNT32\RPL\SCRIPTS\EXPORT

    C. \WINNT\SYSTEM32\REPL\SCRIPTS\EXPORT

    D. \WINNT\SYSTEM32\REPL\EXPORT

3. A given computer can be configured to export multiple directory trees.

    A. True

    B. False

4. It is only necessary for the export server, rather than the import server, to be running the Directory Replicator service.

    A. True

    B. False

5. When creating the Directory Replicator user account, which three of the listed properties need to be used?

    A. Password Never Expires

    B. No account lockout

    C. Log on hours of 24 hours a day, 7 days a week

    D. Membership in the Replicator group

6. The Directory Replicator Service is started with the Service Manager in the Control Panel.

    A. True

    B. False

7. Every domain that will be importing files from another domain should trust the export domain.

    A. True

    B. False

8. What is the default interval value, in minutes, which the export server checks replicated directories for changes?

    A. 2

    B. 10

    C. 1

    D. 5

9. Subdirectory locks can be added to both export and import servers, preventing them from replicating.

    A. True

    B. False

Review Answers

1. B

2. D

3. B

4. B

5. A, C, D

6. A

7. A

8. D

9. A

CHAPTER 23

Windows NT Server and NetWare

N ovell NetWare is found on approximately two-thirds of all network servers in the world. When Microsoft's staff developed Windows NT Server, they realized that it had to coexist in a NetWare world. Several technologies promote this coexistence:

◆ NDIS enables Windows computers to run protocol stacks for both Windows NT and NetWare, enabling users to access data on both server types.

◆ A NetWare Gateway enables users on a Windows NT Server network to access files and printers on the NetWare server without the necessity of running a dual protocol stack or dual clients.

◆ A NetWare migration tool enables Windows NT Server administrators to move NetWare user accounts and file structures to Windows NT Server if desired.

This chapter discusses issues and procedures for all of these technologies. Before starting the how-to, however, you are provided with some background information comparing the use of multiple protocol stacks to gateways.

Technologies for Accessing Different Servers

NetWare and Windows NT Server differ significantly in the protocols they use. As a result, computers that need to access both environments require special configuration.

NetWare servers rely on two key protocols:

- ◆ **IPX/SPX.** Provide network and transport layer network functionality.
- ◆ **NetWare Core Protocols (NCP).** These are the protocols that enable NetWare clients to request services from NetWare servers.

Windows NT Server, on the other hand, relies on the following protocols:

- ◆ **NetBIOS.** (Actually an API that is usually run over NBF, the NetBIOS Frame Protocol, an updated form of NetBEUI.) NetBIOS is also supported over NWLink, Microsoft's implementation of IPX/SPX.
- ◆ **Server Message Blocks (SMB).** Provide much the same service for Windows NT Server as NCP messages do for NetWare.

Windows NT supports the IPX/SPX protocols with NWLink, so that aspect doesn't present a problem. NCP and SMB, however, are wholly incompatible, and Microsoft had to do some extra work to give a client access to both network service protocols.

In fact, Microsoft has made two approaches available. You can configure clients to access Windows NT Server by installing both protocol stacks on the client, or you can use a NetWare Gateway. Both alternatives are examined.

Accessing Different Environments with Multiple Client Protocol Stacks

NDIS was designed with multi-protocol support in mind. You have seen throughout the book how NDIS enables Microsoft network clients to simultaneously support NetBEUI, NWLink, TCP/IP, and DLC protocols. In fact, you can access both Windows NT and NetWare using NWLink. All that remains is to support NCP in addition to SMB messaging.

Windows NT is capable of supporting two network software interfaces. Novell's ODI architecture enables you to support the Novell and Microsoft protocols in the MS-DOS environment by using the ODINSUP program to support NDIS drivers. When the appropriate software is installed and configured, client network communication resembles figure 23.1.

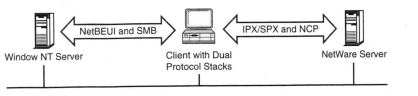

Figure 23.1

Client network access with multiple protocol stacks.

This approach has several advantages:

◆ Each server environment is accessed in its native environment. All services and security features are in force.

◆ No performance is lost because protocols do not require translation.

The following two disadvantages must be noted, however:

◆ Dual protocol stacks require increased client maintenance.

◆ Dual server environments require separate maintenance.

Two approaches are available for supporting Microsoft and NetWare protocols on DOS and Windows 3.1 computers:

◆ Microsoft NDIS technology

◆ Novell's Open Datalink Interface (ODI) technology

Windows for Workgroups 3.11 can support more than one server environment if you install the Novell ODI drivers and use the ODINSUP to support NDIS protocols.

Windows NT supports NetWare as a secondary protocol stack using the Client Services for NetWare, which are installed as part of the Gateway service.

Accessing Different Environments with a Gateway

A gateway is a heavy-duty translator. Although routers translate network protocols at the OSI network layer, a more powerful approach is required above that layer because the environments can differ in fundamental ways. The NetWare NCP command to open a file is nothing like the Microsoft SMB command to do the same thing.

Figure 23.2 shows a network that incorporates a Windows NT NetWare gateway. On the Windows side of the gateway, clients communicate using any supported protocol and server message blocks. The gateway translates client messages into IPX/SPX and NCP format and communicates with the NetWare server.

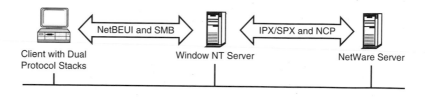

Figure 23.2

A network with a Windows NT Server NetWare gateway.

The interesting thing about the gateway approach is that the NetWare server appears to users as just another shared resource on the Windows NT gateway server. No changes to Windows network clients are required to enable them to access the NetWare server through the gateway.

As you can see, a gateway approach has several advantages:

◆ Clients do not require multiple protocol stacks, and client maintenance is simplified.

◆ Users access all resources in the same way.

◆ Very little additional maintenance is required on the NetWare side. A gateway is a great way for a NetWare-based department to share files with Windows NT Server users in another department without maintaining a NetWare user account for each user.

◆ Administration can be simplified because access to resources is controlled by the gateway.

A gateway may not be an ideal solution, however, for the following two reasons:

◆ The translations the gateway must perform are extensive, and performance is generally slower than a connection with the proper protocol stack.

◆ Some features on the NetWare host might not be available. In particular, the NetWare gateway cannot access NetWare 4.x NetWare Directory Services, and users must access NetWare 4.x servers in bindery mode.

Note   Opinions on gateways differ. I'll give you mine, but you'll need to study the pros and cons in light of your organization's needs.

I've operated Windows networks with multiple protocol stacks with no real trouble. It is extremely easy to add support for a second network with Windows NT,

Windows 95, or Windows for Workgroups clients. Performance doesn't take a hit with multiple protocols, and I haven't seen a user yet who wasn't performance-conscious. I also prefer native NetWare security to the share-level security that is available with the Windows NT Gateway. Yes, it means extra administration, but good security is worth the effort.

Consider using a gateway if your users require fairly casual access to NetWare, particularly if they need to access printers on the NetWare network. Thanks to print queues and spooling, printing performance isn't as critical to most users as application performance. A gateway also is an easy way to enable users to pass files between the two networks.

Setting Up a Gateway

Configuring a gateway has four major steps:

1. Preparing NetWare to support the gateway

2. Installing the gateway

3. Activating the gateway and sharing NetWare files with users

4. Sharing NetWare printers with users

Each step is covered. Throughout this discussion, it is assumed that you are familiar with NetWare administration so that I don't have to write a book within a book. If you need to know more about NetWare, please allow me to recommend my book *Inside NetWare 3.12, Fourth Edition*, also from New Riders Publishing.

Preparing the NetWare Server to Support a Gateway

Very little setup is required on the NetWare side. Essentially, all you need to do is add accounts that let the gateway into the NetWare LAN.

Gateway Services for NetWare consists of two components:

◆ A client service that enables the user of the gateway computer to log directly on to the NetWare server

◆ A gateway service that enables Microsoft network users to access shared NetWare resources

Each of these services can be configured to access the NetWare server through a separate NetWare user account. Users do not have the gateway privileges on the NetWare network. The share permissions will govern the access Microsoft clients have on the NetWare server.

To set up the NetWare server to support Gateway Services for NetWare, use SYSCON to create the following entities:

◆ A group named NTGATEWAY. Grant this group the rights that should be available to NT Gateway accounts that will access the NetWare server through the gateway.

◆ A user account with the same user name that is used to log on to the Windows NT network from the gateway computer. Give this user the appropriate rights. Because I'm logging in as the Windows NT Administrator user, I created a user account named ADMINISTRATOR on the NetWare server. Configure passwords so that they are the same on the Windows NT Server and the NetWare server.

◆ A user account that will be used by the gateway service. I named my user account GATEWAY. Make this user account a member of the NTGATEWAY group on the NetWare server. To create other gateways, create a user account for each gateway and add each account to the NTGATEWAY group. Only one user account is required per gateway computer.

Installing the Gateway Service

The Gateway Service is installed from the Network utility in the Windows NT Server Control Panel. To install the service, use the steps in the following exercise:

Installing the Gateway Service

1. Open the Network utility in the Control Panel and select the Services tab.

2. Choose **A**dd and select Gateway (and Client) Services for NetWare in the **N**etwork Service box.

3. Choose OK.

4. When prompted, supply the path where files can be found on the installation CD-ROM. Files are copied, and the adapter software is installed. You will be returned to the Network utility window.

5. Restart the computer to activate the changes.

Note | If NWLink was not previously installed on the computer, it is added when you install Gateway Service for NetWare. Unless your network has specific protocol requirements, no configuration should be needed. Consult Chapter 7, "Installing Windows NT Server," for information about configuring NWLink.

Activating the Gateway Server and Adding Shares

After the server reboots and you log on within the Welcome box, you are shown a new dialog box, Select Preferred Server for NetWare. In this window, you can specify the first NetWare server that the logon process attempts to connect you with. You can name a preferred server for a binder-mode NetWare server or a default tree for an NDS network. The server or tree you select will be the preference for your personal NetWare user ID.

The dialog box that appears at logon resembles the dialog box in Gateway Services for NetWare, and the specifics will be discussed in the next section. If you want, you can choose Cancel to skip the logon dialog box and use Gateway Services for NetWare to establish the NetWare connection configuration.

If you specify a preferred server or a default tree, Windows NT attempts to authenticate you on the NetWare server using your Windows NT account name and password. If the logon fails, you are asked to enter a user name and password for NetWare.

Configuring the User Account Information

When Gateway Service for NetWare is installed, a new GSNW icon is added to the Control Panel. This tool is used to configure NetWare services on the computer (see fig. 23.3).

Information in the Gateway Service for NetWare box pertains to the user whose name is shown after Username. This information is used to configure this user's personal NetWare environment.

You have the following options in this dialog box:

◆ Select Pr**e**ferred Server to make a bindery mode server the default server. Specify a server name in the **S**elect Preferred Server field. Use this option when connecting to NetWare 3.x or to NetWare 4.x in bindery mode.

◆ Select **D**efault Tree And Context to connect to a NetWare Directory Services tree in NDS mode. Specify the tree name in the **T**ree field and the user context in the **C**ontext field.

◆ Check **R**un Login Script if a NetWare login script is to be executed when logging into NetWare.

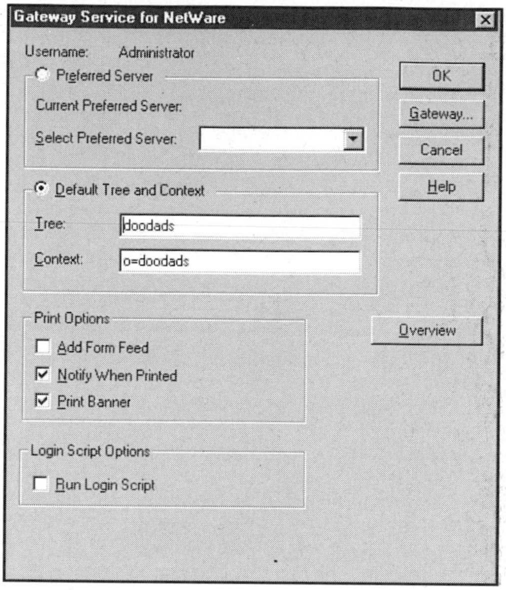

Figure 23.3

User account information for Gateway Service for NetWare.

Choose OK when you have completed the dialog box. (If you prefer, you can choose Cancel and enter the information later in Gateway Service for NetWare. Refer to figure 23.3.) Print options for printing to NetWare printers can be set as follows:

◆ **Add Form Feed.** Check this box if NetWare should force a form feed at the end of print jobs. Most software sends a form feed, and this option should not be checked.

◆ **Notify When Printed.** Check this box if you want to receive a message when a job has been sent to a printer.

◆ **Print Banner.** When this option is checked, NetWare prints a banner page before each job. Do not check this option if printing to a PostScript printer. Most organizations do not find it necessary to activate banners.

At this point, you have configured the computer so that locally logged on users can log on to NetWare. If you will not be configuring a gateway, choose OK to exit the utility.

Note When the NetWare account was set up for the locally logged on user, the password was probably not synchronized to the user's password on the Windows network. As a result, the user is asked to enter a password each time a connection is established with the NetWare server.

To change the password on the NetWare server, use the steps in the following exercise:

Changing the Password on the NetWare Server

1. Open a command prompt.

2. Use the net use command to connect a drive to the NetWare SYS volume. For example, enter the command:

   `net use s: \\nw4\sys`

3. Change to the connected drive.

4. CD to the \PUBLIC directory.

5. Enter the command **SETPASS**. Follow the prompts to change the NetWare password.

After passwords match in Windows NT and NetWare, you will need to enter your password only once when logging on to the network.

Configuring the NetWare Gateway and Sharing Directories

To configure the gateway, click on the **G**ateway button in the Gateway Service for NetWare dialog box to open the Configure Gateway dialog box (see fig. 23.4). At first, the **A**dd, **R**emove, and **P**ermissions options are not active because the gateway service has not been started.

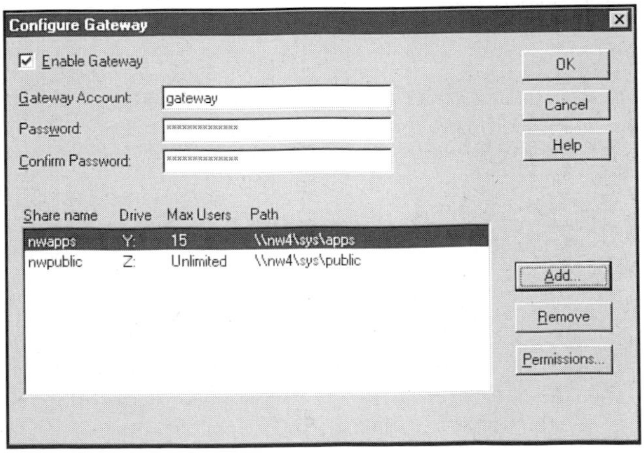

Objective

D.1

Figure 23.4

Configuring a gateway.

To configure a gateway, use the steps in the following exercise:

Configuring a Gateway

1. Check **E**nable Gateway. Checking this option instructs Windows NT Server to start the gateway service when the server starts. You can disable the gateway without removing the software by removing the check mark from this box.

> **Note** Do not stop the Gateway Service for NetWare service using the Service utility in the Control Panel. Several other vital services are stopped with it. Instead, disable the gateway in the GSNW utility.

2. Enter the NetWare user account name that you created for the gateway server in the **G**ateway Account box. When an account name has been entered, the **A**dd button is activated.

3. Enter the password for the NetWare user account in the Pass**w**ord and **C**onfirm Password boxes.

4. To make directories on the NetWare server available to gateway users, you must define them as shares. To add a share, click on **A**dd to display the New Share dialog box shown in figure 23.5. Complete the following information for the share you are adding:

    ◆ **Share Name.** Enter the name by which the share will be known to gateway users.

    ◆ **Network Path.** Enter the path to the NetWare directory that will be shared. The utility accepts uniform naming convention (UNC) names, which have the following format:

    `\\server\volume\directory\subdirectory...`

    Figure 23.5 shows the UNC name for the APPS directory on the SYS volume of the NW4 server.

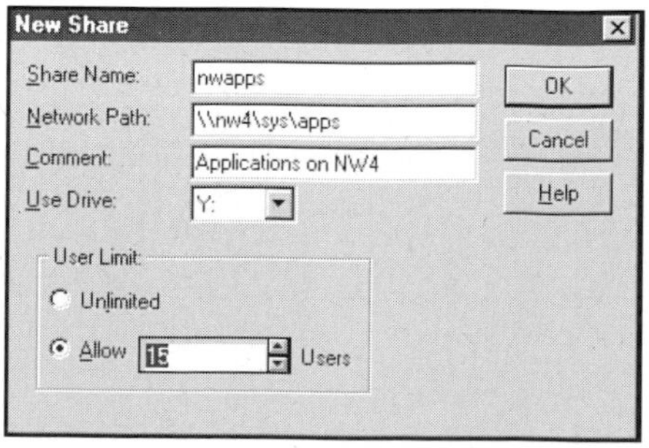

Figure 23.5

Adding a gateway share.

    ◆ **Comment.** You can add a comment to describe the share if desired. This comment will be shown when the share is listed in users' browse lists.

◆ **Use Drive.** Select an available drive letter from the list. Drive letters that correspond to physical drives on the computer are not available, and available drives are usually limited to the letters E through Z because a gateway can provide access to 22 or 23 directory shares at the most.

◆ **Unlimited.** Choose this option if you do not want to restrict the number of users who can access the share.

◆ **Allow.** Choose this option and specify a number to restrict the number of users who can access the share. Because performance will suffer if too many users connect to a given share, a limit is desirable.

Choose OK when you have configured the share. The Gateway service will attempt to locate the shared directory on the specified NetWare server. If the share can be validated, it will be added to the **S**hare name list in the Configure Gateway dialog box.

Note Unfortunately, you cannot modify a gateway share once it is added. To make changes, you must remove the existing share and add a new share with the desired settings.

5. By default, the group Everyone is given Full Control permissions to a newly created Gateway share. If you want to change the default permissions, select the entry in the **S**hare name box and choose **P**ermissions. The Access Through Share Permissions dialog box (see fig. 23.6) functions like the share permissions dialog boxes in File Manager. Consult Chapter 12, "Sharing Drives, Directories, and Files," for details about setting share permissions.

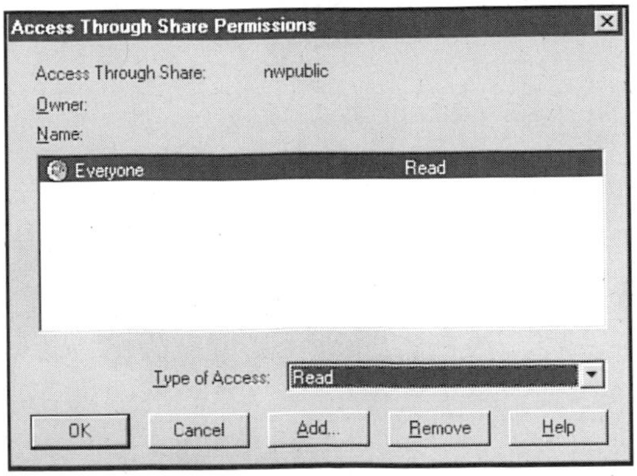

Figure 23.6

Managing permissions for a share.

6. After you have configured the desired gateway shares, choose OK to quit the Gateway Services For NetWare utility.

Note | Gateway Service shares must be created, and their permissions managed, in the Gateway Services For NetWare utility. Gateway file shares cannot be managed in File Manager. As a result, you cannot use File Manager to fine-tune directory and file permissions.

You can, however, assign detailed NetWare rights to the NTGATEWAY group. Directory and file rights will set maximum permissions for all gateway users, regardless of the share permissions that may be assigned by the Gateway Service.

As a result, NetWare directories that are accessed through the gateway should generally be regarded as group directories, not personal directories. You could add a share that would grant permissions to only one user, but because you are restricted to 22 gateway shares, assigning shared directories on the gateway is not very practical.

If any users require personal directories on the NetWare sever, you should assign them individual NetWare accounts and equip their computers with NetWare client software.

Sharing NetWare Printers

NetWare users do not print directly to printers. They print to print queue files, from which jobs are printed by a print server. Gateway Service for NetWare enables users on the Windows network to connect to NetWare print queues and print to NetWare-managed printers.

Although NetWare directory sharing is managed with the GSNW utility instead of File Manager, NetWare printers are shared using fairly standard procedures in the Print Manager.

To share a NetWare-based printer, use the steps in the following exercise:

Sharing a NetWare Printer

1. Log on to the NetWare network from the gateway computer. The account you use must have NetWare rights to use the desired print queue.

2. Open the Printers icon in the Control Panel.

3. Double-click on Add Printer to open the Add Printer Wizard.

4. Choose Network printer server. Then choose Next.

5. Next a Connect to Printer dialog box opens a browse list (see fig. 23.7). Browse the network and select a shared printer. Choose Next.

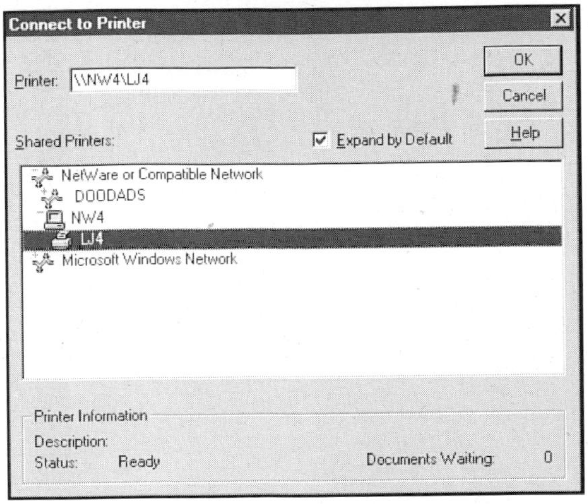

Figure 23.7

Connecting to a shared printer.

6. Windows NT ordinarily expects to find a suitable printer driver on the computer to which it is connecting. Because NetWare servers don't come equipped with Windows print drivers, you will see the warning in figure 23.8. Before you can print to the NetWare queue, a suitable printer driver must be added to the local computer. Choose OK in this message box and go through the steps of selecting and installing a print driver. See Chapter 13, "Managing Printing Services," if you want more information.

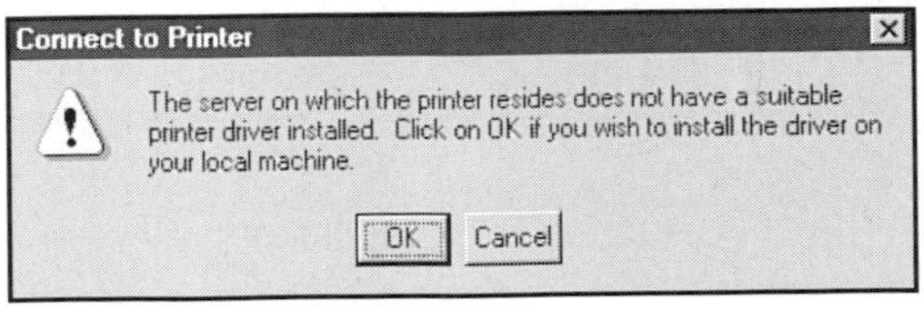

Figure 23.8

Warning to install printer drivers.

7. After the print driver has been installed, the printer is added to the local printer configuration and an icon is added to the Printers window. The locally connected user can now print to the printer. Before gateway users can use the printer, however, it must be shared.

8. To share the printer with the gateway, select the printer in the Printer window. Then choose the Properties command in the Printer menu. The Sharing tab of the Printer Properties dialog box is shown in figure 23.9.

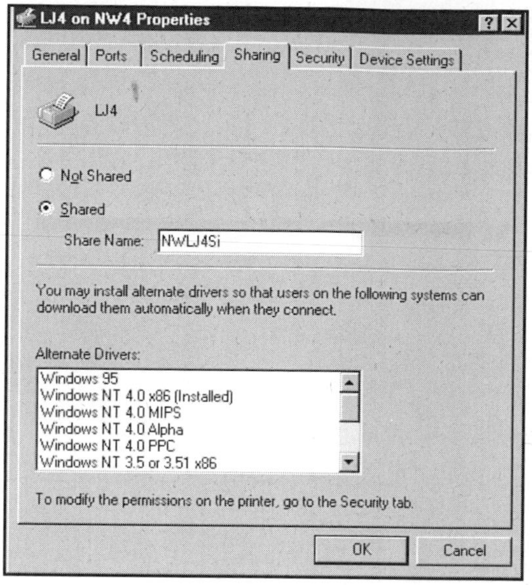

Figure 23.9

*Configuring
share properties
for a gateway
printer.*

9. To share the printer, select **S**hared. Enter a share name in the Share Name field. Select any additional drivers to be supported in the Alternate Drivers list.

   You can, if desired, configure the other properties for the share, such as security. Consult Chapter 12 for thorough coverage of these options.

10. Choose OK when the share properties are specified.

Windows users can now access this shared printer as though it were directly attached to the gateway computer.

Accessing NetWare Resources from the Gateway Server

A user who logs on to the Windows NT Server Gateway for NetWare is logged on to the NetWare server as a NetWare client. As a result, resources offered by the NetWare server are available using standard browsing tools.

Figure 23.10 shows the Network Neighborhood dialog box of a gateway computer. Notice that entries appear for the NetWare 4.1 server, a printer, and for the two volumes. When logged on to NetWare, your access is controlled by standard NetWare security, and you are unaffected by permissions assigned to the gateway shares.

Figure 23.10

Network Neighborhood for the logged in user.

After gateway shares are established, they appear in your My Computer window as shared volumes. Figure 23.11 shows some examples.

Figure 23.11

NetWare Gateway shares.

Client Access to Gateway Shares

Shared printers and directories are advertised in the browse list for the gateway computer, just as though they resided physically on that computer. As a result, most of the NetWare gateway mechanism is invisible to network users.

Using NetWare Applications through the Gateway

A wide variety of NetWare MS-DOS utilities can be run through the gateway:

chkvol	grant	pconsole	rights	slist
colorpal	help	psc	security	syscon

dspace	listdir	pstat	send	tlist
flag	map	rconsole	session	userlist
flagdir	ncopy	remove	setpass	volinfo
fconsole	ndir	revoke	settts	whoami
filer				

NetWare menu utilities, such as RCONSOLE, require access to files such as SYS$MSG.DAT, which is installed in the SYS:PUBLIC directory. To access these files, either make SYS:PUBLIC your default directory before running the utility, or add SYS:PUBLIC to your search path.

Not all NetWare-aware applications run in a Windows NT gateway environment. Consult your program documentation for information about supported environments. Some applications may require that the NWLink or IPX/SPX protocol stacks be loaded on the client.

Many NetWare-aware applications that are written for 16-bit Windows require DLL files that are provided by Novell. The NWIPXSPX.DLL file is included with the NetWare DOS client software. If the NetWare client software has ever been installed on the client, this file should have been installed. To make the file available to gateway clients, obtain NWIPXSPX.DLL and copy it to the directory C:\WINNT\SYSTEM32.

Some NetWare-aware applications directly send and receive NCP packets. These applications might require a copy of NETWARE.DRV, which is copied to the C:\WINNT\SYSTEM32 directory when the Gateway Service is installed. NETWARE.DRV is used in combination with either NWNETAPI.DLL or NWCALLS.DLL, depending on the version of NetWare being used. Consult the NetWare documentation for the correct file to use. Copy these files to the directory C:\WINNT\SYSTEM32.

For MIPS and ALPHA AXP clients, the file TBMI2.COM must be copied to the directory C:\WINNT\SYSTEM32. Also, add the following line to the AUTOEXEC.NT file and restart the computer:

```
lh winnt\system32\tbmi2.com
```

Applications do not generally perform as well through the gateway as they would with a direct logon connection. This is particularly true if large amounts of data must flow through the gateway. Gateway translation takes time.

Caution One particular area of incompatibility is tape backup. You might be tempted to use the backup program from Windows NT Server because it's already included with the product. When backing up NetWare, however, you must use a backup product that is aware of the existence of the NetWare bindery files. Windows NT Backup was written for Windows NT, not for NetWare.

Note | Gateway Service for NetWare must translate several file system characteristics when users access NetWare files. Among the features that require translation are file attributes. Following is a comparison of Windows NT file attributes and the way they are translated for NetWare files:

Windows NT Attribute *NetWare Attribute*

R (Read Only)   Ro, Di (Delete Inhibit), Ri (Rename Inhibit)

A (Archive)   A

S (System)   Sy

H (Hidden)   H

The NetWare Ci (Copy Inhibit), P (Purge), RW (Read Write), S (Shareable), T (Transactional), Ra (Read Audit), and Wa (Write Audit) attributes are not supported by the gateway, although they do restrict the operations that gateway users can perform on NetWare-based files.

Migrating Users from NetWare to Windows NT

Objective D.1

If you dislike the idea of maintaining two types of servers and have decided to move all of your servers over to Windows NT Server, you are faced with the big problem of moving user accounts from NetWare to Windows NT. If you have a large number of NetWare users, you might decide that the task of creating new accounts in the Windows NT Server environment is too daunting.

Microsoft includes the Migration Tool for NetWare with Windows NT Server that reduces the pain of moving users to Windows NT networks. The Migration Tool is not installed as an icon, and, because you will probably not be running it frequently, you will probably choose to run it from a Run command.

The server that is running the migration must meet the following conditions:

◆ Volumes to which NetWare files will be migrated must be formatted with the NTFS file system so that NetWare directory and security information can be migrated.

◆ The NWLink protocols must be installed.

◆ The Gateway Service for NetWare must be installed. The Gateway Service enables the Migration Tool to access the NetWare server from which you are migrating.

The icon for Migration Tool for NetWare is installed in the Administrative Tools program group when you install Gateway Services for NetWare. The first dialog box you see, Select Servers For Migration, is shown in figure 23.12. Specify the names of the NetWare and Windows NT Server computers and choose OK. If you need to log on to either server, you are prompted for a user name and a password. The NetWare user account should be secured as a Supervisor equivalent. The Windows NT user account should have administrator permissions on the target server.

Figure 23.12

Selecting file servers for migration.

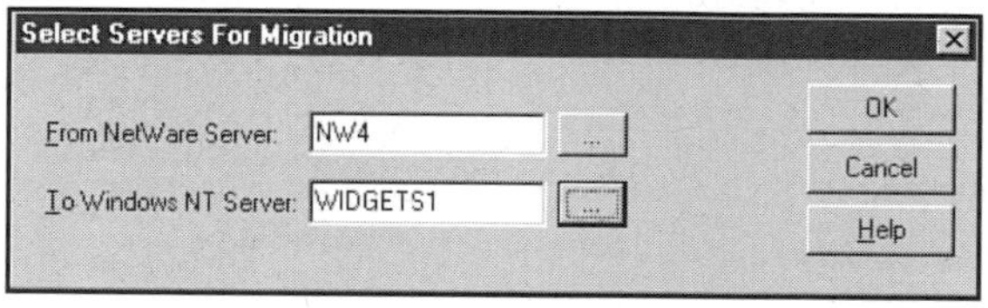

After logging on to the source and destination servers, the main Migration Tool dialog box is displayed (see fig. 23.13).

Figure 23.13

The main window for the Migration Tool.

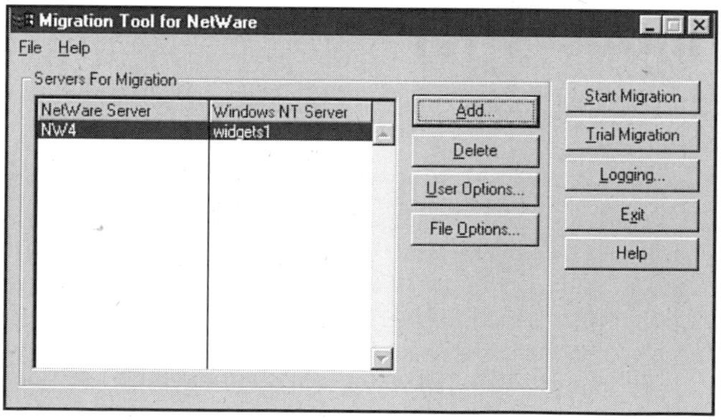

The **A**dd and **D**elete buttons are used to add and delete source and destination servers.

Setting Migration User Options

The **U**ser Options button in the Migration Tool is used to access the User and Group Options dialog box (see fig. 23.14), which has four subboxes that are accessed by clicking tabs: Passwords, Usernames, Group Names, and Defaults. Each of these boxes is covered in turn.

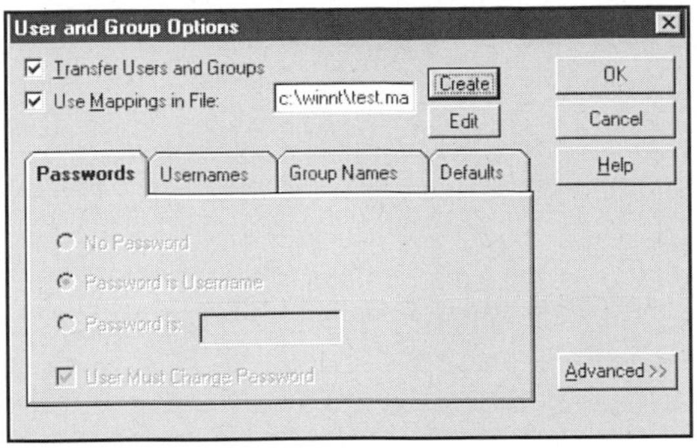

Figure 23.14

User and group options for the Migration Tool.

Selecting the Transfer Option

Check **T**ransfer Users and Groups if you want to migrate NetWare groups and users. If you want, you can turn this option off to transfer only files.

Using a Mappings File

If you want to control how names of users and groups are handled during the migration, use a mappings file. To use a migration mapping file, conduct the steps in the following exercise:

Using a Migration Mapping File

1. Check Use **M**appings in File.

2. Enter a file name in the box. The file the Migration Tool creates is a text file that will have a MAP extension.

3. After you choose OK in the User and Group Options window, you are shown this message: Mapping file created successfully. Do you want to edit it? If you choose **Y**es, Notepad is started, and the mapping file is loaded for editing. An example is shown in figure 23.15. The example was kept very simple. As you can see, you can map the user's NetWare account name to a new name on the Windows NT server. You can also change user group names and specify an initial user password.

Selecting Password Options

Not even a NetWare Supervisor can discover user passwords, so passwords cannot be migrated to Windows NT. The passwords box has three options for creating passwords:

◆ **No Password.** This option makes it unnecessary for you to distribute passwords to users.

◆ **Password is Username.** The password for the user account will be the same as the user name.

◆ **Password is.** The initial password will be the password you specify.

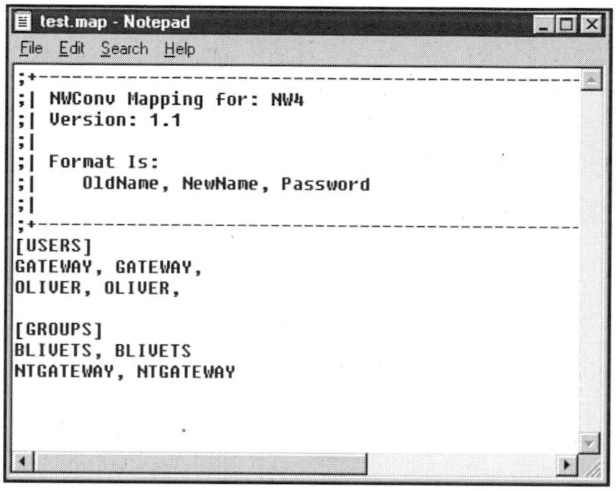

Figure 23.15

Editing a migration mappings file.

Figure 23.15

Editing a migration mappings file.

It is recommended that you check User Must Change Password if you use the No Password option so that users will be forced to change or create a password when they first log on.

Selecting Username Options

Select the Usernames tab in the User and Group Options box to display the Usernames options (see fig. 23.16). Options in this box specify the action that will be taken if a user name on the NetWare server is duplicated by an existing name on the Windows NT Server.

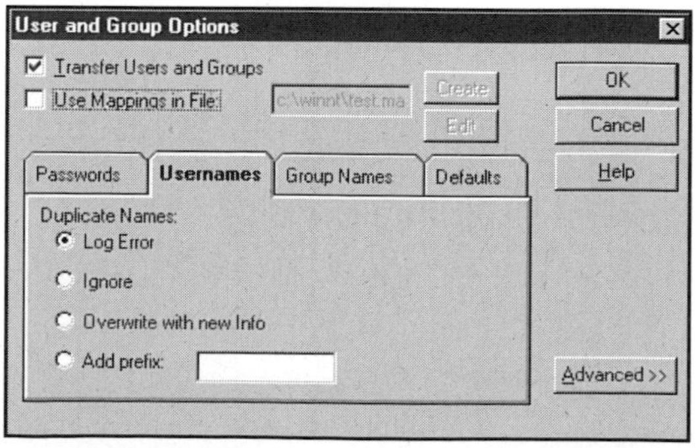

Figure 23.16

Specifying migration action when duplicate user names are encountered.

◆ **Log Error.** This option records conflicts in the ERROR.LOG file that is created during migration.

◆ **Ignore.** This option ignores accounts on the NetWare server that already exist on the Windows NT Server.

◆ **Overwrite with new Info.** This option replaces account information on the Windows NT Server with account information from NetWare.

◆ **Add prefix.** You can specify a prefix that is appended to the NetWare name if a conflict occurs.

Selecting Group Name Options

Click on the Group Names tab to display the box shown in figure 23.17. Because these options duplicate options on the Usernames tab, they require no discussion.

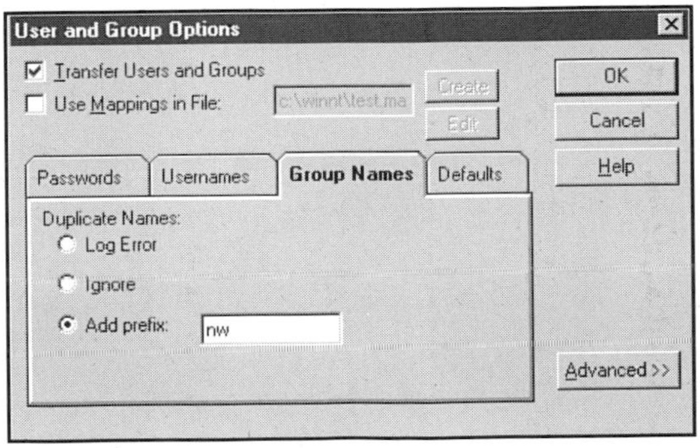

Figure 23.17

Specifying migration action when duplicate group names are encountered.

Selecting Supervisor Defaults

Click on the Defaults tab to determine how supervisor rights will be transferred to the Windows NT Server environment. Options are shown in figure 23.18.

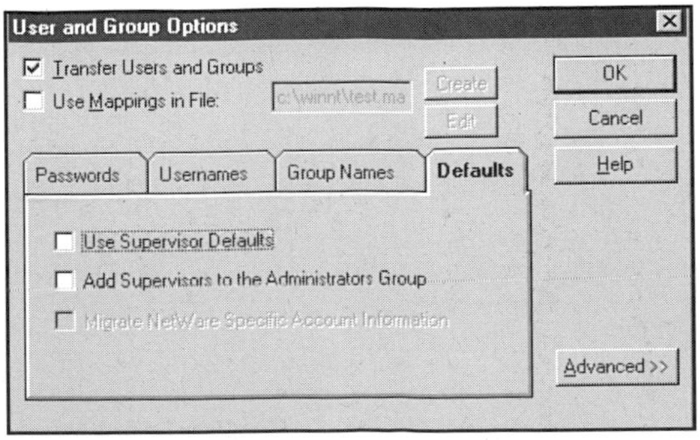

Figure 23.18

Specifying supervisor rights transfer.

◆ **Use Supervisor Defaults.** Check this box to transfer account restrictions from NetWare to Windows NT Server. Remove the check mark if Windows NT account policy settings should be used.

◆ **Add Supervisors to the Administrators Group.** Check this box if users who are user-equivalent to the NetWare Supervisor should be added to the Administrators group. Remove the check mark if supervisor equivalents should not be made administrators of the Windows NT Server.

Setting Migration File Options

The File **O**ptions button in the Migration Tool main window produces the File Options dialog box shown in figure 23.19. This box enables you to control where files will be placed on the Windows NT Server. The NetWare server used in this example has only one volume, named SYS. All of the volumes on the NetWare server should be listed, and the **A**dd button will only be activated if you delete a volume.

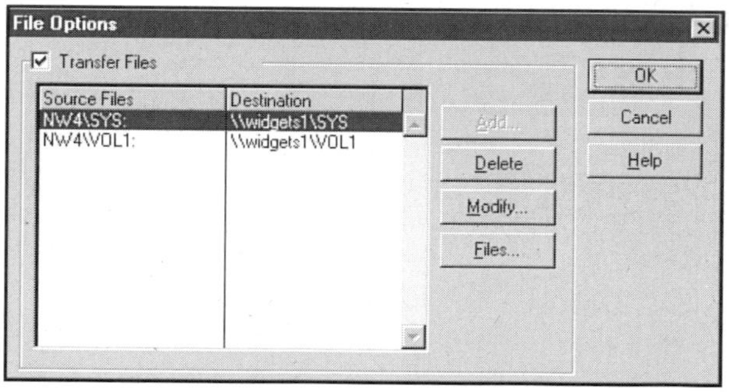

Figure 23.19

Setting file migration options.

The **M**odify button displays the Modify Destination dialog box shown in figure 23.20. By default, files in a NetWare volume are copied to a directory with the same name as the volume. The share name assigned to the directory will be the same as the original volume name.

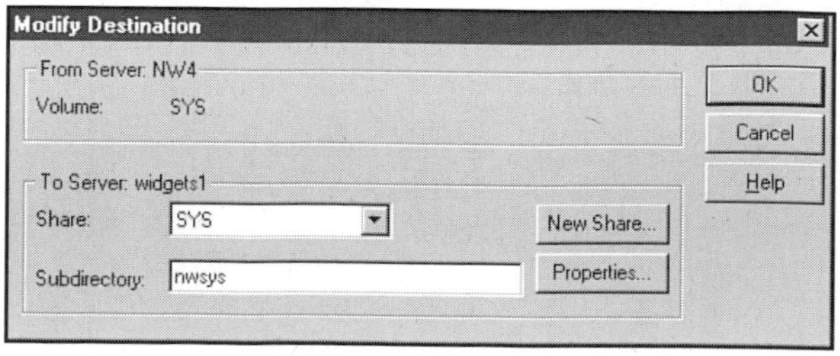

Figure 23.20

Specifying the file migration destination.

You can modify the destination directory and share name in this dialog box. Change the Share entry to specify the share name that is assigned to the directory to which these files are copied. You can also specify a different directory by clicking on Properties.

If you want to select specific files and directories to be transferred, choose the **F**iles button in the File Options dialog box to display the Files To Transfer dialog box shown in figure 23.21. Select directories and files much as you would in File Manager. Double-click a closed folder icon to examine the directory contents. Check the directories and files to be transferred and clear check marks for items that should not be migrated.

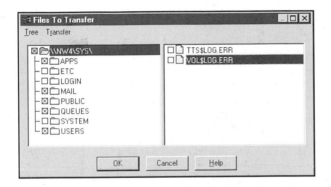

Figure 23.21

Selecting directories and files to migrate.

In figure 23.21, the SYS volume was opened to reveal the first-level directories. By default, several directories are not checked. It would make no sense to migrate the SYSTEM directory, for example, which contains the NetWare system files. You can go down to the file level if you want to exercise that much control over files that will migrate. You will probably want, for example, to exclude most if not all of the files in the PUBLIC directory.

The T**r**ansfer menu in the Files To Transfer dialog box contains two options, **H**idden Files and **S**ystem Files, that determine whether these files will be transferred.

Setting Migration Logging Options

You can determine the amount of logging that will take place during migration by choosing the **L**ogging button in the Migration Tool main window. Logging options are shown in figure 23.22.

The View Log Files button is only active if log files have been created.

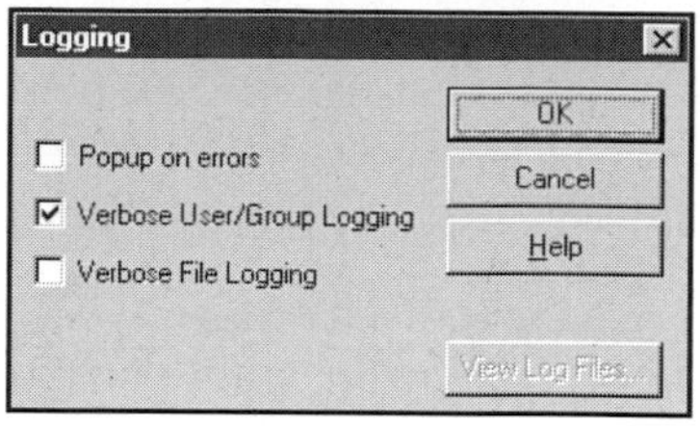

Figure 23.22

Options for logging during migration.

Running a Trial Migration

Before you perform an actual migration, run a trial by clicking on the **T**rial Migration button in the Migration Tool main window. Your migration settings will be tested without actually migrating anything.

After the trial migration is completed, a summary box reports the results (see fig. 23.23).

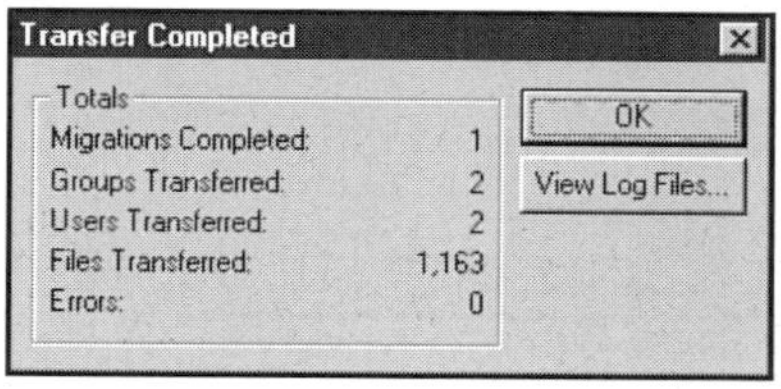

Figure 23.23

The Transfer Completed summary box.

A trial migration creates log files just as would be created by an actual migration. Three log files are created:

◆ *LOGFILE.LOG* contains information about users, groups, and files.

◆ *SUMMARY.LOG* contains an overview of the migration process.

◆ *ERROR.LOG* reports any migration errors that were encountered.

You can view these logs by clicking the View Log Files button in the Transfer Completed box. The LogView utility (see fig. 23.24) that is invoked includes windows for the three migration logs. You can select logs for review as required.

Be especially sure that the ERROR.LOG file does *not* report critical errors, such as the following:

◆ User and group names that did not transfer

◆ Network errors, such as a failure to access the source server

◆ System errors, such as insufficient space for transferred files on the destination drives

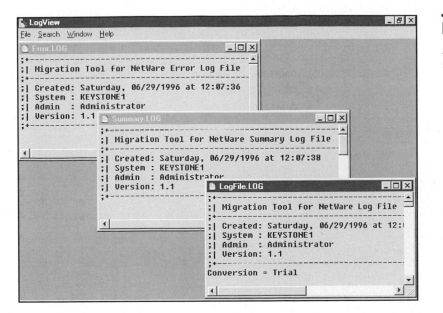

Figure 23.24

Reviewing the migration logs.

The following listing contains part of the LOGFILE.LOG file that is created. This file was created with the Verbose User/Group Logging option and contains a detailed record of the migration.

```
;+----------            ---------------------------------------------------------+
;¦ Migration Tool for NetWare Log File                                          ¦
;+------------------------------------------------------------------------------+
;¦ Created: Saturday, 06/28/1997 at 12:07:38                                    ¦
;¦ System : KEYSTONE1                                                           ¦
;¦ Admin  : Administrator                                                       ¦
;¦ Version: 1.1                                                                 ¦
;+------------------------------------------------------------------------------+
Conversion = Trial


Number of Migrations = 1


[Servers]
   From: NW4          To: widgets1


;+-----------------------------------------------------------------------------+
;¦ Server Information                                                          ¦
;+-----------------------------------------------------------------------------+


[widgets1]
   Windows NT(R) Server
   Version: 4.0
```

```
[Drives]
   C: [NTFS]
      Free Space: 1,584,993,792
   D: [NTFS]
      Free Space: 414,729,216
   E: [     ]
      Free Space: 0
   F: [     ]
      Free Space: 0


[Shares]
   NETLOGON
      Path: C:\WINNTSRV\system32\Repl\Import\Scripts

[NW4]
   NetWare(R) Server
   Version: 4.10

   [Shares]
      SYS
      VOL1


;+------------------------------------------------------------------------------+
;¦ Setting User Defaults from Supervisor Defaults                               ¦
;+------------------------------------------------------------------------------+
;+------------------------------------------------------------------------------+
;¦ From: NW4                                                                    ¦
;¦ To:   widgets1                                                               ¦
;+------------------------------------------------------------------------------+
;¦ Converted: Saturday, 06/28/1997 at 12:07:38                                  ¦
;+------------------------------------------------------------------------------+


[Transfer Options]
   Convert Users and Groups: Yes

   User Transfer Options:
      Use mapping file: No
      Passwords: 2 - Password is username
         User must change password: Yes
      Duplicate Names: Log Error

      Duplicate Groups: Pre-pend constant: nw

      Use supervisor defaults: No
      Add Supervisors to the Administrators Group: No
```

```
[File Options]
   Convert Files: Yes

[New Shares]
   SYS
      Path: C:\SYS
   VOL1
      Path: C:\VOL1

[Users]
   Number of Users = 2

   Users to Transfer
   +--------------------------------------------------+
    GATEWAY
    OLIVER

   [GATEWAY]                                      (Added)
   Original Account Info:
      Name:
      Account disabled: No
      Account expires: (Never)
      Password expires: (Never)
      Grace Logins: (Unlimited)
      Initial Grace Logins: (Unlimited)
      Minimum Password Length: 0
      # days to Password Expiration: (Never)
      Maximum Number of Connections: (Unlimited)
      Restrictions:
         Anyone who knows password can change it
         Unique passwords required: No
      Number of login failures: 0
      Max Disk Blocks: (Unlimited)

   Login Times:
   Midnight            AM             Noon            PM
      12 1  2  3  4  5  6  7  8  9 10 11 12 1  2  3  4  5  6  7  8  9 10 11
      +-----------------------------------------------------------------+
   Sun ** ** ** ** ** ** ** ** ** ** ** ** ** ** ** ** ** ** ** ** ** ** ** **
   Mon ** ** ** ** ** ** ** ** ** ** ** ** ** ** ** ** ** ** ** ** ** ** ** **
   Tue ** ** ** ** ** ** ** ** ** ** ** ** ** ** ** ** ** ** ** ** ** ** ** **
   Wed ** ** ** ** ** ** ** ** ** ** ** ** ** ** ** ** ** ** ** ** ** ** ** **
   Thu ** ** ** ** ** ** ** ** ** ** ** ** ** ** ** ** ** ** ** ** ** ** ** **
   Fri ** ** ** ** ** ** ** ** ** ** ** ** ** ** ** ** ** ** ** ** ** ** ** **
   Sat ** ** ** ** ** ** ** ** ** ** ** ** ** ** ** ** ** ** ** ** ** ** ** **
```

```
New Account Info:
   Name:
   Password: GATEWAY
   Privilege: User
   Home Dir:
   Comment:
   Flags:
      Execute login script: Yes
      Account disabled: No
      Deleting prohibited: No
      Home dir required: No
      Password required: Yes
      User can change password: Yes
   Script path:
   Full Name:
   Logon Server:

Logon Hours:
 Midnight               AM               Noon               PM
   12 1  2  3  4  5  6  7  8  9  10 11 12 1  2  3  4  5  6  7  8  9  10 11
   +-----------------------------------------------------------------------+
Sun ** ** ** ** ** ** ** ** ** ** ** ** ** ** ** ** ** ** ** ** ** ** ** **
Mon ** ** ** ** ** ** ** ** ** ** ** ** ** ** ** ** ** ** ** ** ** ** ** **
Tue ** ** ** ** ** ** ** ** ** ** ** ** ** ** ** ** ** ** ** ** ** ** ** **
Wed ** ** ** ** ** ** ** ** ** ** ** ** ** ** ** ** ** ** ** ** ** ** ** **
Thu ** ** ** ** ** ** ** ** ** ** ** ** ** ** ** ** ** ** ** ** ** ** ** **
Fri ** ** ** ** ** ** ** ** ** ** ** ** ** ** ** ** ** ** ** ** ** ** ** **
Sat ** ** ** ** ** ** ** ** ** ** ** ** ** ** ** ** ** ** ** ** ** ** ** **

[OLIVER]                                        (Added)
Original Account Info:
   Name:
   Account disabled: No
   Account expires: (Never)
   Password expires: (Never)
   Grace Logins: (Unlimited)
   Initial Grace Logins: (Unlimited)
   Minimum Password Length: 0
   # days to Password Expiration: (Never)
   Maximum Number of Connections: (Unlimited)
   Restrictions:
      Anyone who knows password can change it
      Unique passwords required: No
   Number of login failures: 0
   Max Disk Blocks: (Unlimited)
```

```
Login Times:
  Midnight                AM                    Noon                  PM
    12 1  2  3  4  5  6  7  8  9  10 11 12 1  2  3  4  5  6  7  8  9  10 11
    +------------------------------------------------------------------+
Sun ** ** ** ** ** ** ** ** ** ** ** ** ** ** ** ** ** ** ** ** ** ** ** **
Mon ** ** ** ** ** ** ** ** ** ** ** ** ** ** ** ** ** ** ** ** ** ** ** **
Tue ** ** ** ** ** ** ** ** ** ** ** ** ** ** ** ** ** ** ** ** ** ** ** **
Wed ** ** ** ** ** ** ** ** ** ** ** ** ** ** ** ** ** ** ** ** ** ** ** **
Thu ** ** ** ** ** ** ** ** ** ** ** ** ** ** ** ** ** ** ** ** ** ** ** **
Fri ** ** ** ** ** ** ** ** ** ** ** ** ** ** ** ** ** ** ** ** ** ** ** **
Sat ** ** ** ** ** ** ** ** ** ** ** ** ** ** ** ** ** ** ** ** ** ** ** **

New Account Info:
   Name:
   Password: OLIVER
   Privilege: User
   Home Dir:
   Comment:
   Flags:
      Execute login script: Yes
      Account disabled: No
      Deleting prohibited: No
      Home dir required: No
      Password required: Yes
      User can change password: Yes
   Script path:
   Full Name:
   Logon Server:

Logon Hours:
  Midnight                AM                    Noon                  PM
    12 1  2  3  4  5  6  7  8  9  10 11 12 1  2  3  4  5  6  7  8  9  10 11
    +------------------------------------------------------------------+
Sun ** ** ** ** ** ** ** ** ** ** ** ** ** ** ** ** ** ** ** ** ** ** ** **
Mon ** ** ** ** ** ** ** ** ** ** ** ** ** ** ** ** ** ** ** ** ** ** ** **
Tue ** ** ** ** ** ** ** ** ** ** ** ** ** ** ** ** ** ** ** ** ** ** ** **
Wed ** ** ** ** ** ** ** ** ** ** ** ** ** ** ** ** ** ** ** ** ** ** ** **
Thu ** ** ** ** ** ** ** ** ** ** ** ** ** ** ** ** ** ** ** ** ** ** ** **
Fri ** ** ** ** ** ** ** ** ** ** ** ** ** ** ** ** ** ** ** ** ** ** ** **
Sat ** ** ** ** ** ** ** ** ** ** ** ** ** ** ** ** ** ** ** ** ** ** ** **

[Groups]
  Number Groups = 2
  BLIVETS                                       (Added)
```

```
          NTGATEWAY                                    (Added)

            [BLIVETS]
               OLIVER

            [NTGATEWAY]
               GATEWAY

      [Security Equivalences]
            [GATEWAY]
               NTGATEWAY

            [OLIVER]
               BLIVETS


      [Print Operators]
               Domain Admins
      [Files]

          Copying Files From Volume: SYS
          To Share: SYS
             [Files]

          Copying Files From Volume: VOL1
          To Share: VOL1
             [Files]
```

After a trial migration has been performed, none of the accounts or files that were chosen to be transferred are on the NT Server. You can perform as many trial migrations as needed.

Completing the Migration

When the trial migration runs satisfactorily, use the **S**tart Migration button in the Migration Tool main window to start the actual migration.

Testing Your Knowledge

1. What Microsoft technology enables Windows computers to run multiple protocol stacks for both Windows NT and NetWare?

2. IPX/SPX is currently the default network protocol for Microsoft Windows products.

    A. True

    B. False

3. Which two approaches are available for supporting Microsoft and NetWare protocols on DOS and Windows 3.1 computers?

    A. Microsoft NDIS technology

    B. Microsoft NetBEUI

    C. Novell's Open Datalink Interface (ODI) technology

    D. Novell's Server Message Blocks

4. How does an NT NetWare gateway server translate client messages?

    A. The client uses any NWLink, which the gateway translates into IPX/SPX and NCP before passing the message along to the NetWare server.

    B. The client uses any supported protocol and NCP, which the gateway translates into IPX/SPX and SMB before passing the message along to the NetWare server.

    C. The client uses NWLink and SMB, which the gateway translates into IPX/SPX before passing the message along to the NetWare server.

    D. The client uses any supported protocol and SMB, which the gateway translates into IPX/SPX and NCP before passing the message along to the NetWare server.

5. Before installing the gateway service, you must create a user account on the NetWare server. Which NetWare tool is used to create this account?

    A. Account Manager

    B. SYSCON

    C. PCON

    D. User Manager

6. The gateway service is installed using the run command setup from the NT Server CD-ROM.

    A. True

    B. False

7. Which of the following is true regarding the installation of the Gateway Service for NetWare?

    A. You must install NWLink prior to installing the Gateway Service for NetWare, otherwise the installation process will prompt you to do so and exit.

B. You must install NWLink after the installation of the Gateway Service for NetWare to ensure proper bindings.

C. NWLink is not required to be used with the Gateway Service for NetWare.

D. If NWLink was not previously installed on the computer, it is added when you install Gateway Service for NetWare.

8. In addition to Preferred Server settings, Default Tree and context settings, and a Logon script option, the GSNW tool also provides NetWare printing options.

A. True

B. False

9. The preferred method of stopping the Gateway Service for NetWare is by using the Service utility.

A. True

B. False

10. When establishing shares on a NetWare Server available to gateway users, you must enter the path to the NetWare directory using the universal naming convention (UNC).

A. True

B. False

11. How many drive letters can theoretically be available for NetWare share assignments on a gateway for NetWare?

A. 26

B. Unlimited

C. 23

D. 25

12. What is the maximum number of users that can be permitted to access a share made available through a NetWare gateway?

A. 15

B. 255

C. Unlimited

D. 254

13. Unfortunately, you cannot modify a gateway share once it has been added. To make changes, you must remove the existing share and add a new share with the desired settings.

A. True

B. False

14. Gateway Service shares must be created, and their permissions managed, in the Gateway Services for NetWare utility. Gateway file shares cannot be managed in File Manager or Explorer.

     A. True

     B. False

15. Sharing NetWare printers is done with the Add Printer Wizard, but it requires you to load the drivers on your local machine because the NetWare Server does not come equipped with Windows print drivers.

     A. True

     B. False

16. No NetWare MS-DOS utilities can be run through the gateway.

     A. True

     B. False

17. Which one of the following file attributes are not translated correctly for NetWare?

     A. NT = R (Read Only)   NetWare = Ro, Di, Ri

     B. NT = A (Archive)   NetWare = Ar

     C. NT = S (System)   NetWare = Sy

     D. NT = H (Hidden)   NetWare = H

18. What three conditions must be met on the NT Server before running the NetWare migration tool?

     A. Volumes to which the NetWare files will be migrated must be formatted with the NTFS file system.

     B. NWLink protocols must be installed.

     C. All desired NetWare user accounts and groups must be manually created on the NT Server before the migration process.

     D. The Gateway Service must be installed.

19. Passwords cannot be migrated to Windows NT. The migration tool provides three options for password assignments including: No Password, Password is (specified by administrator), and _____.

20. Before actually performing the NetWare migration, you can test it by running _____.

Review Answers

1. NDIS
2. A
3. A, C
4. D
5. B
6. B
7. D
8. A
9. B
10. A
11. C
12. C
13. A
14. A
15. A
16. B
17. B
18. A, B, D
19. Password is Username
20. a trial migration

CHAPTER 24

Windows NT Server for Macintosh

Macintosh computers were the first PCs to have network interfaces as standard equipment. Every Mac ever made has been equipped with a connector for Apple's proprietary AppleTalk network. The Mac network philosophy goes so far as to build networking into Apple LaserWriter printers. A Mac that prints to a LaserWriter is doing so through an AppleTalk.

Apart from Apple's own efforts, however, the majority of LAN designs have taken a PC-centric approach, reflecting the numeric dominance of IBM-compatible PCs in the computer marketplace. Microsoft's various network operating systems have all been aimed at the PC. Prior to Windows NT, a barrier remained in place between Microsoft and AppleTalk networks that prevented PCs and Macs from being smoothly integrated.

The technical differences between PCs and Macs are quite significant, and it is no mean trick to build a network that enables them to be smoothly integrated. But the trick has been accomplished with Windows NT Services for Macintosh. Now, with very little effort, Mac users can be included in Windows NT networks, enabling them to seamlessly share files and printers with DOS and Windows NT users.

Before you can plan, implement, and manage Services for Macintosh, you need to know about the features of an AppleTalk network.

Characteristics of AppleTalk Networks

An AppleTalk network is different from anything else. Apple designed Macs to network, but wanted to make network setup as invisible as possible. Therefore, you don't need to concern yourself with installing network software on a Mac, or setting up physical node ids. Network software is installed by default, and physical node ids are negotiated invisibly among the Macs on a given network segment.

Nevertheless, there are several things you need to know about Mac networks. This chapter briefly examines the following characteristics:

- Network cabling systems
- Zones
- Network numbers
- Routing
- Applications and files
- Printing

Network Cabling Systems

Although Ethernet was available when the Mac was introduced, networks cost several hundred dollars per node, far too much to build into a mass-market personal computer. Because Apple had designed a new computer, they took it upon themselves to design a new network as well, one that would be affordable and very easy to configure. They came up with LocalTalk.

Everything about LocalTalk was new, from the cable to the connectors. LocalTalk was designed around shielded twisted-pair cables that attached using DIN connectors. Users simply daisy chained cables and connectors to build a network that could include up to 254 devices in a non-routed network. Apple visualized even printers as network devices, and LaserWriter printers were typically attached to the network rather than to serial or parallel ports. If there was a downside to LocalTalk, it was that speeds were abysmal, in the neighborhood of 150,000 kilobits per second.

Soon after the Mac was introduced, it became clear that the faster Ethernet and token-ring networks would come to dominate the LAN market. Apple redubbed the Mac network protocols, calling them AppleTalk. LocalTalk now referred only to the cabling system. This enabled Apple to adapt AppleTalk to other networks. To date, the following flavors of AppleTalk have emerged:

◆ **LocalTalk.** The original STP cabling system.

◆ **EtherTalk.** AppleTalk protocols running over Ethernet.

◆ **TokenTalk.** AppleTalk on a token-ring network.

◆ **FDDITalk.** AppleTalk adapted to FDDI.

All of these cabling systems can be supported by Windows NT. If economy is required, a LocalTalk network adapter can be added to a Windows NT Server computer. However, it is clearly preferable to choose a more speedy network system, and Ethernet is probably the most popular choice on modern Mac networks.

Appletalk has evolved in two phases:

◆ Phase 1 offered support for 254 connections on a network and did not support routing.

◆ Phase 2 supports up to 16 million nodes on a routed internetwork.

Zones

Devices on a Macintosh network are organized into *zones*, which serve much the same purpose as workgroups in a Microsoft network. Users who are connected to a zone can see only those computers and printers that are in the same zone. This reduces the amount of clutter that appears on a network; users see only the resources that they need to see.

LocalTalk networks are restricted to a single zone. EtherTalk, TokenTalk, and FDDITalk networks can have multiple zones.

Each Macintosh computer functions in one zone at any given time. On any given network, one zone will be identified as the *default zone*, which is the zone that clients will use unless a different zone is specified by the user.

Network Numbers

Each AppleTalk network segment has one or more network numbers, and each network number can support multiple devices.

A LocalTalk network has one network number and can support up to 254 devices, although the LocalTalk media capacity has a practical limit of 32 devices.

EtherTalk, TokenTalk, and FDDITalk networks can support up to 253 devices per network number. If more than 253 devices occupy a network segment, multiple network numbers can be assigned. An internetwork can support up to 16.5 million devices.

Routing

AppleTalk networks tend to be organized in internetworks consisting of several small networks. LocalTalk networks in particular are limited in scope; the cabling system can support only about 32 computers on a non-routed cable segment.

A variety of third-party devices are available to support AppleTalk routing. Figure 24.1 illustrates an example of a routed AppleTalk network that consists of four segments: two Ethernet, one token ring, and one LocalTalk.

Figure 24.1

An AppleTalk internetwork.

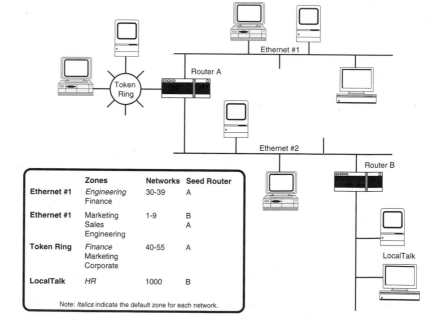

	Zones	Networks	Seed Router
Ethernet #1	*Engineering* Finance	30-39	A
Ethernet #1	Marketing Sales Engineering	1-9	B A
Token Ring	*Finance* Marketing Corporate	40-55	A
LocalTalk	*HR*	1000	B

Note: *Italics* indicate the default zone for each network.

Each network segment is labeled with the network numbers and zones that it supports. The LocalTalk segment is assigned one network number, which is the limit for a LocalTalk cable. The Ethernet and token-ring segments are each assigned a range of network numbers to allow room for growth. Although network numbers must be unique, zones can span multiple network segments. Zones are a means of keeping workgroups organized and are independent of the network topology.

Seed Devices

The network numbers and zones that apply to a given network segment are supplied by special devices called *seed devices* because they seed the network with routing information. Each network segment must be configured with at least one seed device, typically a router, which should be the first device that is started when the network is initialized. The configuration of a seed device specifies which, if any, of the attached networks the device will seed. If multiple seed devices are configured on a network, the first device to start will become the functioning seed device. The seed device will discard conflicting information from seed devices that enter the network at a later time.

Figure 24.1 illustrates how zones and network numbers are assigned to the network segments. It also specifies which router functions as the seed router for each network segment. Because Ethernet #2 is connected to two routers, both are configured as seed routers for that network.

Applications and Files

The Macintosh filing system differs significantly from either FAT or NTFS. Each Macintosh file is stored with two components, called *forks*:

◆ **Data fork.** The *data fork* consists of the data content of the file.

◆ **Resource fork.** The *resource fork* contains file type and creator information that identifies the application used to create the file. The resource fork also contains application-specific information, such as formatting and fonts.

Data files typically have relatively large data forks and small resource forks. Application files have relatively large resource forks and small data forks.

Macintosh users are used to being able to launch a data file in an application by double-clicking the icon for the data file. This is possible because the resource fork enables the Macintosh operating system to identify and start the application that created the file. This process has no parallel in MS-DOS or Windows NT; adaptation is required to enable Macintosh users to access applications on Windows NT servers in a natural way.

The Macintosh file system supports long file names that consist of up to 31 characters. Files can be stored in folders, and folders can be nested in other folders, similar to nested subdirectories in FAT and NTFS. When folder levels must be distinguished by name, a colon (:) character separates the folder names, serving the same purpose as the backslash (\) under FAT or NTFS.

> **Note** Because Macintosh files incorporate a data and a resource fork, Macintosh users can only share files that are stored on NTFS volumes on Windows NT Server.

Printing

The typical shared Macintosh printer is an Apple LaserJet laser printer (or compatible) that is attached to the network. Users print files through the network.

From the first days of the Macintosh, the standard printer has been a laser printer configured with the Adobe PostScript page description language. Because the license cost of PostScript was rather high in the 1980s, this requirement elevated the cost of printing for Macintosh users. PostScript is now significantly less expensive, but remains a rarity on printers used in the PC arena.

Ordinarily, files that are being printed are spooled on the local user's Mac before they are directed through the network. After spooling, the files are printed, a process that monopolizes the Mac until printing is completed.

When a network print server is available, such as an AppleShare server, print jobs can be spooled through the network to the print server from which they are printed. The Mac that originated the print job can resume printing as soon as the print spooler has received the print job.

Architecture of Services for Macintosh

You can integrate Macintoshes into a Windows NT network by running Services for Macintosh on a Windows NT Server computer. Services for Macintosh is a bit more than a simple extension of the Macintosh network. As you will see, Macintosh users gain a few advantages when working in the Windows NT environment. They lose a bit as well, and you need to understand Services for Macintosh thoroughly to enable Macintosh users to work as normally as possible.

> **Note** All of the features discussed in this chapter are available when Services for Macintosh is installed in a Windows NT Server computer.
>
> Services for Macintosh can also be installed on Windows NT Workstation computers. These computers can share files and printers, but can function as AppleTalk routers or as seed devices.

Security

One thing Macintosh users gain is a way to store files on Windows NT servers, providing C2 level security. An authenticated logon is required to access files on the Windows NT Server computer. Logon passwords are encrypted when transmitted through the network, preventing users with network analyzers from learning passwords by snooping through packets on the network. As a result, files shared from the Windows NT Server computer are more secure than files shared from the Macintoshes themselves.

To obtain authenticated logon security, Macintosh users must copy logon software to their computers. This software enables them to log on using a Windows NT user name and password. Macintosh users who log on without the Windows NT Macintosh client software are restricted to working with files that are accessible to the Guest user account.

Macintosh user accounts are standard Windows NT Server user accounts, managed using User Manager for Domains. Therefore, you don't need to learn any new skills to manage user accounts for Macintosh users.

File Sharing

NT Folders are shared with Macintosh users using a mechanism that is similar to that used to share files with Microsoft network users. Folders that are shared can be mounted as *volumes* on the Macintosh computers. Each mounted volume appears as a volume icon on the Macintosh user's desktop. NTFS volumes can be shared with Macintosh users.

The first volume that is shared is named MICROSOFT UAM VOLUME, where UAM stands for *User Accounts Manager*. This volume is available to all Macintosh users when logging in as Guest, and contains the MS UAM file that enables Macintosh users to gain access to the Microsoft network using encrypted logons. Guest can be given access to other shared volumes as well, but the usual practice is to require Macintosh users to gain access to additional volumes through a personal user account. This enables each user to be authenticated using a secure password.

When Windows NT files are viewed from a Mac, file name extensions are carried over to the Macintosh desktop. That is an inconvenient but necessary consequence of the need to share files between both environments.

Volume Security

Shared Macintosh volumes are secured similarly to Windows NT shares, applying the same level of security to the entire share. When it is necessary to fine-tune security, NTFS directory and file security permissions can be assigned. All administration is performed with File Manager.

Macintosh volume security is applied to three entities:

   ◆ **Owner.** Each volume has an owner, typically the user who created the volume. The owner normally has all permissions for the shared volume and need not be a member of any group that has access to the volume. This option permits you to establish private volumes that are accessible to a single individual.

   ◆ **Primary Group.** Each volume has one primary group to which you can assign specific permissions. This option permits you to establish group volumes that are accessible to a limited number of users.

   ◆ **Everyone.** Finally, you can assign permissions that are available to all Macintosh users who are not members of the primary group.

To each of these entities, you can assign the following permissions:

   ◆ **See Files.** Permits a user to see which files are in a folder and to read those files. This corresponds to the Windows NT Read permission for files.

   ◆ **See Folders.** Permits a user to see which folders are contained within a folder. This corresponds to the Windows NT Read permission for folders.

   ◆ **Make Changes.** Permits a user to modify the contents of folders, rename files, move files, create new files, and delete files. Corresponds to the Windows NT Write and Delete permissions.

A folder's owner can manage permissions for the folder from a Macintosh client. The owner of a folder is assigned the Windows NT Change Permission permission for the folder. The owner can also manage from Windows NT File Manager.

If desired, *volume passwords* can be established that require all users to enter a password when accessing a volume, regardless of the permissions the users have for the volume. By default, volume passwords are not created. Volumes that are protected by volume passwords cannot be automatically mounted at startup or by double-clicking an alias.

File Name Support

Files that are shared with Macintosh users must reside on NTFS volumes, which support the long file names expected by Macintoshes. When files are shared by MS-DOS, Macintosh, and Windows NT users, some file name conversion may take place when long file names are displayed.

Each operating system has different file name requirements:

◆ MS-DOS and Windows 3.x restrict file names to the 8.3 format. A three-character file name extension typically identifies the application that created the file.

◆ Macintosh computers accept file names up to 31 characters in length and do not typically use a file name extension because the resource fork identifies the application that created the file. The : character may not appear in a file name.

◆ Windows NT computers accept file names up to 256 characters in length and use file name extensions to identify the application that created the file.

Ideally, when files are shared by users with several types of computers, users should restrict file names to the lowest common denominator. If MS-DOS users will share files, for example, Mac and NT users should name the files according to the 8.3 file name rules. If Mac and NT users will share files, NT users should restrict names to 31 characters and avoid use of the : character in a file name.

If users fail to name files according to the requirements of other operating systems, users will see shortened versions of those file names that do not meet the requirements of their operating system. For example:

◆ Under MS-DOS, file names longer than the 8.3 requirement will be truncated according to the rules described in Chapter 14, "Using Windows and DOS Clients."

◆ Macintosh users can see long file names created by Windows NT users that are up to 31 characters in length, including the three-character extension and the period separator.

◆ When Macintosh users access files with names that exceed 31 characters in length, the file names will be truncated according to the rules for displaying long file names to MS-DOS users. Extensions will be preserved.

As you saw in Chapter 14, the 8.3 file names that Windows NT generates from long file names are often confusing. Therefore, it is always best for users to cooperate and name files so that all users can see the file name in its original form.

Associating Files with Applications

Macintosh files that are stored on Windows NT Server computers lose the type and creator information that is normally stored in the resource fork. Without this association, the Macintosh cannot associate an application icon with a data file that is displayed on the desktop. Nor can the Mac automatically start an application when the user double-clicks a data file icon.

To circumvent this problem, Macintosh users can include extensions in their file names, just as MS-DOS and Windows NT users are used to doing. Services for Macintosh provides a mechanism that associates file name extensions with applications, enabling the Mac to obtain the file type and creator codes. This mechanism works with the Macintosh client to identify icons that should be displayed on desktops and to identify applications that should be started when a data file is double-clicked.

Extensions are not an ideal solution to the problem from the Macintosh frame of reference, but they do provide a way for MS-DOS, Windows NT, and Macintosh users to share the same data files.

Printer Sharing

Services for Macintosh enables Macintosh users to access the following types of printers:

◆ Printers that are attached to the serial or parallel port of a Windows NT Server computer that is running Services for Macintosh.

◆ Printing devices, such as the Apple LaserWriter, that can be attached directly to a LocalTalk network.

◆ Printing devices that are connected to the network through Ethernet or token-ring attachments.

Macintosh users gain two benefits by printing through Windows NT Server. The first benefit is that the Windows NT Server print server functions as a print spooler. Once the Macintosh client has transferred the print job to the print server, the client can return to work as normal while the print server completes the print job.

The second benefit is that the Windows NT print server functions as a translator between PostScript and the native language of the destination printer. Macintosh users can print to any printer that is attached to the Windows NT Server print server, whether or not the printer is equipped with a PostScript interpreter.

Note On AppleTalk networks, LaserWriter printers are configured for printing by sending the printer a file called LaserPrep. When a Mac prints, it sends the LaserPrep file to the printer, which retains it for future use.

The next time the Mac prints, it checks the printer to see if the correct version of LaserPrep is resident, in which case the Mac does not need to send LaserPrep again.

If the Macs are equipped with different versions of Chooser Packs, they will be using different versions of LaserPrep. This can result in significant performance degradation because each Mac that prints must reset the printer, download its own version of LaserPrep, and print a startup page. This condition is known as *LaserPrep Wars*.

Windows NT Services for Macintosh avoids LaserPrep Wars by capturing the printer and handling all print jobs. NT sends its own LaserPrep file with each job. The printer saves time because it never needs to make the LaserPrep file or print a startup page.

AppleTalk Routing Support

Any Windows NT Server that is equipped with Services for Macintosh can function as an AppleTalk router. In figure 24.1, either router could be a Windows NT Server computer.

Seed Device Support

Any Windows NT Server that is equipped with Services for Macintosh can serve as an AppleTalk seed device. The computer can be configured as a router, in which case it can seed multiple networks, or it can be configured with a single interface and seed a single network only.

Installing Services for Macintosh

Before installing Services for Macintosh, plan your network. You will need to know the following about each network that connects to the computer running Services for Macintosh:

◆ Zones supported

◆ Network numbers supported

◆ Which, if any, networks this computer will seed

Services for Macintosh is installed like any other network software. The procedure is covered in the following exercise:

Installing Macintosh Services

1. Open the Network utility in the Control Panel.

2. Add **Services for Macintosh** in the Services tab.

3. During network software configuration, you will see the Microsoft AppleTalk Protocol Properties window (see fig. 24.2).

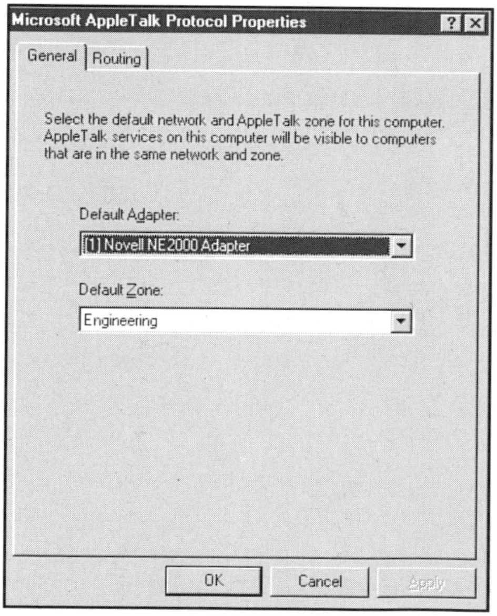

Figure 24.2

Configuring AppleTalk properties.

4. In the Default **Ad**apter field, select a network adapter that is attached to a network that will be configured with AppleTalk.

4a. In the Default **Z**one field, select the zone in which you want Services for Macintosh to appear on this network. You will be able to select a zone only if a seed device has established zones on this segment. If this computer will be the seed device, you will be unable to select a zone. Proceed with step 6 to establish zones that this router will seed and select a default zone.

5. To configure zones and routing, select the Routing tab (see fig. 24.3). Complete this tab as follows:

    5a. Select an adapter in the Ada**p**ter box.

    5b. If this computer is equipped with two or more interfaces, you can configure it as a router by checking Ena**b**le Routing. You should also enable routing if this computer will seed an attached network.

    5c. If routing is enabled, you can elect to have this server seed an attached AppleTalk network. To configure this computer as a seed router, check **U**se this router to seed the network.

    5d. If this server is a seed router, you must specify a network range and the names of zones that this router will seed:

        ◆ In the Network Range box, complete the Fr**o**m and **T**o boxes with the first and last network numbers that will be used on this network.

        ◆ To add a zone to the Default **Z**one list, choose A**d**d and enter the name of the zone in the Add Zone dialog box that is provided.

        ◆ To remove a zone, select the zone name in the Default **Z**one list and choose **R**emove.

        ◆ If other devices are seeding the network, you can obtain a list of active zones by choosing **G**et Zones. The zone list that is obtained will replace the entries in the Default **Z**one list.

        ◆ To specify a default zone, select the zone in the Default **Z**one list and choose Ma**k**e Default.

6. Repeat step 5 for other attached networks.

7. When the AppleTalk properties are complete, choose OK.

8. Restart the computer when prompted.

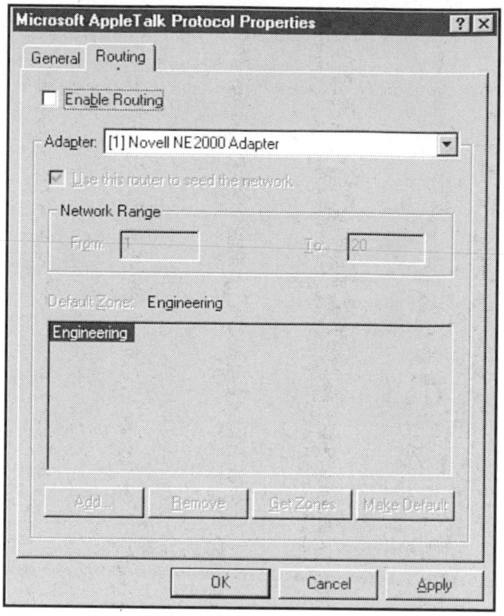

Figure 24.3

Configuring a router.

Microsoft AppleTalk Protocol Properties

General | Routing |

☐ Enable Routing

Adapter: [1] Novell NE2000 Adapter

☑ Use this router to seed the network.

Network Range
From: 1   To: 20

Default Zone: Engineering

Engineering

Add | Remove | Get Zones | Make Default

OK | Cancel | Apply

The following components of Services for Macintosh will be installed:

◆ File Server for Macintosh will be added as a service and configured to start automatically. You can start, stop, and configure this service using the Service utility in the Control Panel.

◆ Print Server for Macintosh will be added as a service and configured to start automatically. You can start, stop, and configure this service using the Service utility in the Control Panel. Additional configuration is required, as described in the later section, "Managing Printing."

◆ A MacFile utility is added to the Control Panel.

◆ Commands are added to the menus for File Manager and Print Manager.

◆ The Microsoft UAM Volume will be created and will be shared as a Macintosh volume.

Configuring Macintosh User Accounts

No special steps are required to configure user accounts for Macintosh users. You will probably wish to create groups for Macintosh users to be used when setting security on shared Macintosh volumes.

Macintosh users who are not assigned personal user accounts can log on using the Guest account. Initially, the directory Microsoft UAM Volume is the only volume accessible to Guest, but you can grant Guest access to other volumes if desired. In general, however, it is better to assign Macintosh users their own user accounts so that they can be individually authenticated using encrypted passwords.

Managing Shared Volumes and Files

Macintosh shared volumes are established much like Windows NT shares. When Services for Macintosh is installed, a MacFile menu is added to the menu bar of Server Manager.

To create a shared Macintosh volume, follow these steps:

Creating a Shared Macintosh Volume

1. Start Server Manager and select the server that stores the volume to be shared.

2. Choose the **V**olume command in the MacFile menu to open the volumes list shown in figure 24.4. At first, only the MICROSOFT UAM VOLUME will be listed.

Figure 24.4

The volumes list prior to creating a shared Macintosh volume.

3. To add a volume, choose **C**reate Volume to open the Create Macintosh-Accessible Volume dialog box (see fig. 24.5).

4. In the **V**olume Name box, specify the name by which Macintosh users will identify this volume.

5. In the **P**ath box, verify the path to the directory to be shared.

6. If you wish to require a password when accessing this volume, specify a password in the Pa**s**sword box. This field is optional.

7. In the Volume Security box, check **T**his volume is read-only if users should be prevented from modifying files or directories in this volume.

Figure 24.5

Creating a shared Macintosh volume.

8. In the Volume Security box, check **G**uests can use this volume if users should be permitted to access this volume using the Guest account, in which case access is not restricted by a user account password.

9. In the User Limit box, specify whether a limited number of users should have access to the shared volume.

10. Choose Pe**r**missions to open the Macintosh View of Directory Permissions dialog box (see fig. 24.6). The permissions that are available were described earlier in this chapter in the section "Volume Security." Complete this dialog box as follows:

   ◆ In the **O**wner field, specify the owner of the directory. Check the permissions to be available to the owner of the directory.

   ◆ In the **P**rimary Group field, select the primary group that will have access to this directory. Check the permissions to be available to this group.

   ◆ Specify the permissions to be available to the group Everyone.

   ◆ If the permissions specified should be applied to subdirectories of this directory, check **R**eplace permissions on subdirectories.

   ◆ If users should be prevented from modifying the directory or its subdirectories, check **C**annot move, rename, or delete.

   ◆ Choose OK to return to the Create Macintosh-Accessible Volume dialog box.

11. Choose OK to create the volume and return to File Manager.

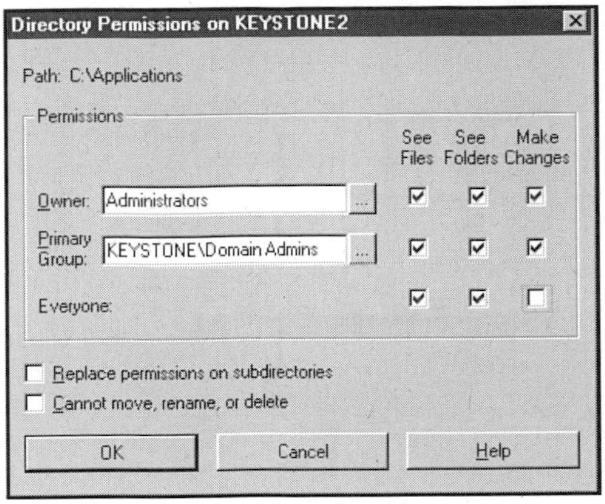

Figure 24.6

Setting permissions for a Macintosh-accessible volume.

Associating Application Extensions

Because Mac data files stored on NTFS volumes do not retain their resource forks, it's necessary to have another mechanism that enables the Mac to identify which application created the data file. This mechanism establishes associations between the following:

◆ The MS-DOS file name extension.

◆ The Macintosh *type* associated with the file, which classifies the file as, for example, a chart, spreadsheet, document, or template.

◆ The Macintosh *creator*, which identifies the Mac application that created the file.

Services for Macintosh comes preloaded with the type and creator codes for a variety of Macintosh applications. You can add your own associations, but must determine the type and creator codes for the application. This information is often available in the application documentation or can be obtained from the application's creator.

You must manually associate an MS-DOS file name extension with the type and creator codes.

To establish an association, follow these steps:

Establishing an Association

1. In File Manager, choose the **A**ssociate command in the MacF**i**le menu. This will open the Associate dialog box shown in figure 24.7.

2. In the **F**iles with MS-DOS Extension box, click the arrow to open a list of pre-entered extensions. If an association already exists for the extension you have selected, the application will be highlighted in the box below.

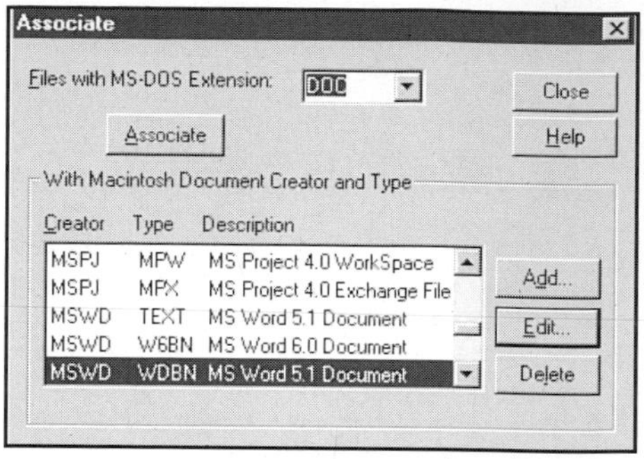

Figure 24.7

Associating an extension with an application.

If the extension you require does not exist, you can enter a new extension and establish an association from scratch.

3. To change an association or establish a new one, select one of the applications listed in the box labeled With Macintosh Document Creator and Type.

4. If your application is not listed, choose A**d**d. The Add Document Type dialog box appears in which you can add a new set of application codes.

5. Choose **E**dit to open the Edit Document Type dialog box in which you can modify the codes entered for an application.

6. Choose **A**ssociate to complete the association.

Connecting Macintosh Clients

After user accounts and shared volumes have been established, Macintosh users can connect to the Windows NT Server via AppleTalk. First, a user will connect as a Guest and copy the user authentication software from the server to the Macintosh. After that, the user can log on using a personal user account and password.

First-Time Connections

To set up a Macintosh client, follow these steps:

Setting Up a Macintosh Client

1. Ensure that the Mac has a network connection that can communicate with the Windows NT Server running Services for Macintosh. Also verify that the Mac is running version 6.0.7 or later of the Macintosh operating system.

2. Open the Chooser in the Apple menu.

3. In the Chooser, click AppleShare to display a list of available servers, as shown in figure 24.8.

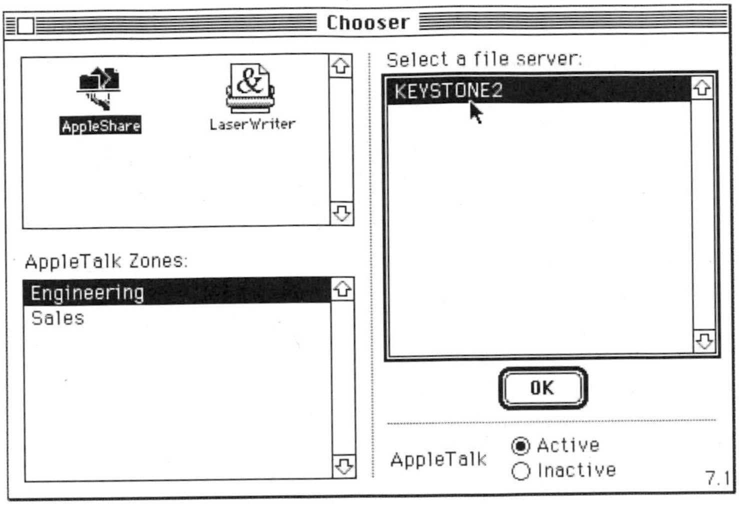

Figure 24.8

Selecting a file server in Chooser.

4. Select the Windows NT Server in the Select a File Server list and choose OK to open the connection window shown in figure 24.9.

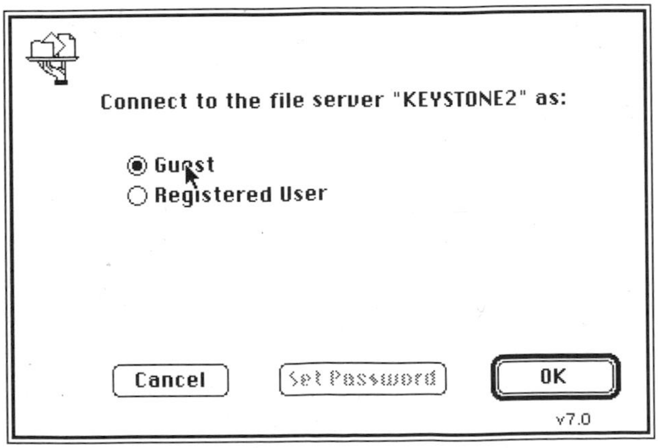

Figure 24.9

Connecting to the Windows NT Server as a guest.

5. Because the Windows NT client software has not been copied to the Mac yet, you can log on as a guest only. The Registered User option will be inactive. Select Guest and choose OK to open the volume selection window shown in figure 24.10.

Figure 24.10

Selecting a volume to be used.

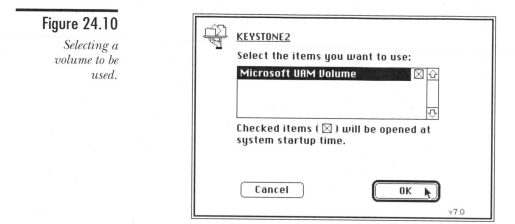

6. This window lists shared volumes that you can use. At present, you are logged in as Guest, and it is likely that only the Microsoft UAM Volume will be available. Unavailable volumes will be listed, but will be grayed-out. Select Microsoft UAM Volume and choose OK. The Microsoft UAM Volume will appear as an icon on your desktop (see fig. 24.11).

Figure 24.11

The Microsoft UAM Volume icon on the Mac desktop.

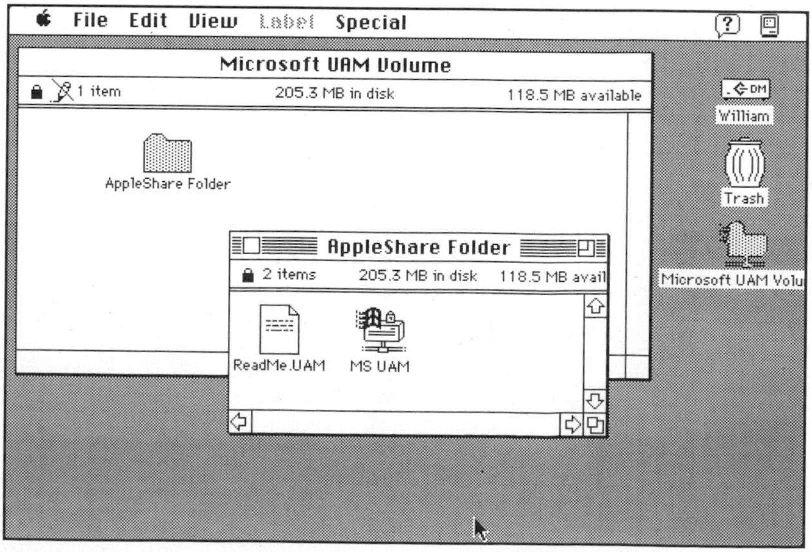

7. Close Chooser.

8. Open the Microsoft UAM Volume. In it you will find a folder named AppleShare Folder. Depending on the contents of your System folder, do one of the following:

   ◆ If your System folder does not already have an AppleShare Folder, drag the AppleShare Folder from the Microsoft UAM Volume to the System Folder.

   ◆ If your System folder already has an AppleShare folder, drag the contents of the AppleShare Folder of the Microsoft UAM Volume to the AppleShare Folder of the System folder. You will be dragging two items: ReadMe.UAM and MS UAM.

9. Restart the Mac.

Note | Chooser displays all servers running Services for Macintosh, regardless of the domain the user is logged on to. Mac users see server names, but aren't exposed to domains or workgroups.

Later Connections

After you have copied the AppleShare Folder to the Mac, you will be permitted to log on to the Windows NT Server using encrypted passwords, which enables you to access shared volumes that are unavailable to Guest.

To log on with a user account and password, follow these steps:

Logging on from a Macintosh Client

1. After restarting the Mac, open the Chooser. Select AppleTalk, and then open the desired server.

2. You will be asked to select a logon method from the following:

   ◆ Apple Standard UAMs

   ◆ Microsoft Authentication

   Select Microsoft Authentication and choose OK.

3. You will see the logon authentication window (see fig. 24.12). To log on with a user account:

   ◆ Select Registered User.

   ◆ Enter your user name in the Name box.

◆ Enter your password in the Password box. The password will not be displayed, and will be sent to Windows NT in encrypted form.

◆ Choose OK to log on and display the volume selection window.

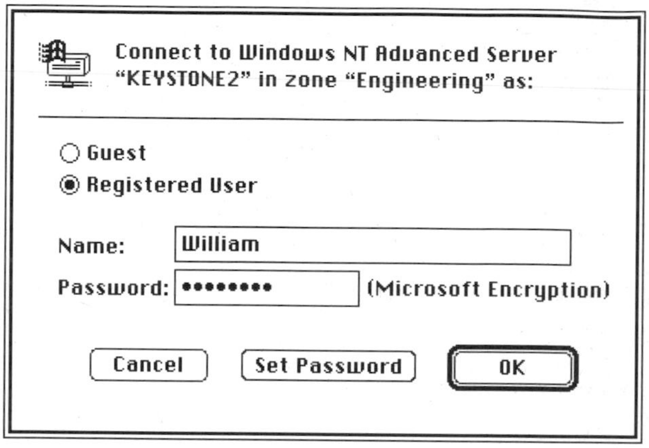

Figure 24.12

Logging on with a user account and password.

```
┌─────────────────────────────────────────────────┐
│  ▤▦   Connect to Windows NT Advanced Server      │
│  ▨▨   "KEYSTONE2" in zone "Engineering" as:      │
│  ─────────────────────────────────────────────── │
│                                                   │
│   ○ Guest                                         │
│   ◉ Registered User                               │
│                                                   │
│   Name:     │William                          │   │
│                                                   │
│   Password: │••••••••│    (Microsoft Encryption)  │
│                                                   │
│      ( Cancel )   ( Set Password )   (( OK ))     │
└─────────────────────────────────────────────────┘
```

4. In the volume selection window, additional directories may now be available depending on the permissions assigned to your user account. Check the volumes you want to mount and choose OK.

Managing Printing

Macintosh users can be given access to any printer that is directly attached to a Windows NT Server computer running Services for Macintosh. Interestingly, this feature enables Mac users to print PostScript jobs to non-PostScript printers supported by Windows NT. The Macintosh print service takes care of the necessary translations between PostScript and the printer's native command language.

Mac users can also use Services for Macintosh as an efficient way to share LaserWriter printers that are attached to the AppleTalk network. As discussed earlier, Services for Macintosh adds print spooling to the Macintosh printing process and also provides a way to sidestep LaserPrep wars.

Printing to Printers Shared by Windows NT

Before Mac users can access printers shared by Services for Macintosh, you must configure the Print Server for Macintosh service. After that, printer sharing is managed using Print Manager in exactly the same manner as conventional Windows NT printing.

To configure Print Server for Macintosh, follow these steps:

Configuring a Print Server for Macintosh

1. Create a user account that can be associated with the Print Server for Macintosh service. This account should have access to all printers your users will use.

2. In the Services utility in the Control Panel, configure the Print Server for Macintosh service, as shown in figure 24.13.

3. Stop and restart the Print Server for Macintosh service.

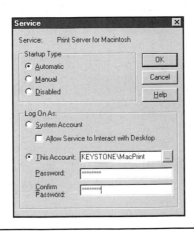

Figure 24.13

Configuring the Print Server for Macintosh service.

Creating the Printers

To make printers available to Macintosh users, they must be directly connected to the computer that is supporting Services for Macintosh. Simply create the printers, making sure that the Macintosh printer user has access to them.

Sharing Printers on the AppleTalk Network

Both Macintosh and PC users can share printers that are attached to the AppleTalk network. Macintosh users benefit because Windows NT Server functions as a print spooler, quickly spooling jobs and enabling the Mac users to get back to work while printing is completed.

To support an AppleTalk network printer through Windows NT Server, make the following decisions during printer creation:

1. Select **M**y Computer to specify how the printer will be managed.

2. In the **A**vailable Ports box, select Add P**o**rt to open the Printer Ports box.

3. Select AppleTalk Printing Devices and choose OK.

4. In the Available AppleTalk Printing Devices box, browse the zones and locate the desired printer.

5. Select the printer driver to be installed.

6. Supply the printer name.

7. Finish the installation.

Macintosh and PC users can now print to the newly created printer. PC users will need to configure their printers with appropriate printer drivers.

Using the MacFile Utility

When Services for Macintosh is installed, a MacFile utility is added to the Control Panel. This utility is used to observe the operation of the Macintosh services and to configure Macintosh security. The MacFile utility is shown in figure 24.14. The four buttons open windows with different sets of management information.

| **Tip** | You can also access the MacFile utility using the **P**roperties command in the MacF**i**le menu that is added to Server Manager. |

Figure 24.14

The MacFile utility.

The **U**sers button opens the window shown in figure 24.15. This window lists connected users and the volumes that they have logged. You can also determine which users have files open and which volumes contain those files. You have several options in this window:

◆ Select a user and choose **D**isconnect to disconnect a single user.

◆ Choose Disconnect **A**ll to disconnect all users.

◆ Choose **S**end Message to open the window in figure 24.16. From this window, you can send a message to a selected user or to all Macintosh users.

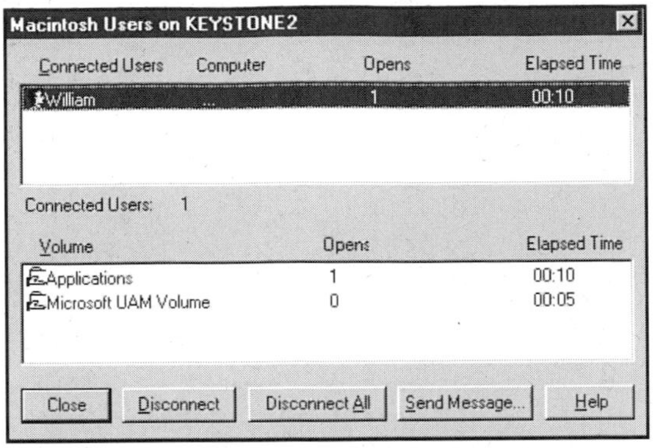

Figure 24.15

The Macintosh Users window.

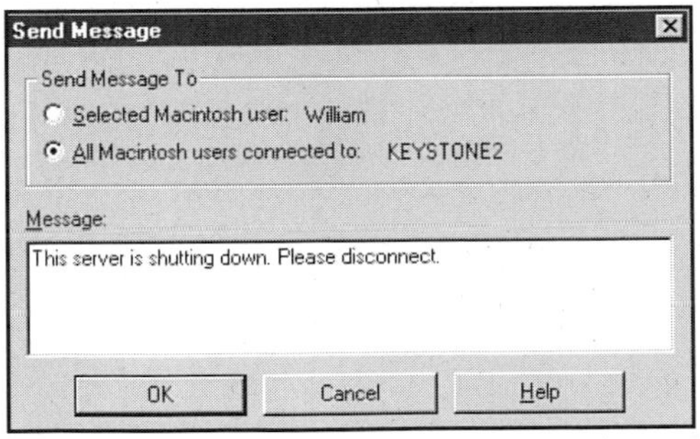

Figure 24.16

Sending a message to Macintosh users.

The **V**olumes button opens the Macintosh-Accessible Volumes window shown in figure 24.17. The information is much the same as in the users window, but is organized by volume.

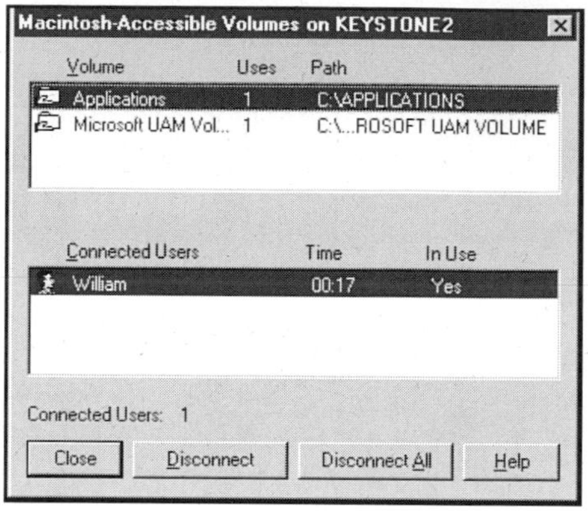

Figure 24.17

The Macintosh-Accessible Volumes window.

The **F**iles button opens the Files Opened window shown in figure 24.18. In this window, you can close files as follows:

◆ Select an open file and choose **C**lose Fork to close that file.

◆ Choose Close **A**ll Forks to close all files.

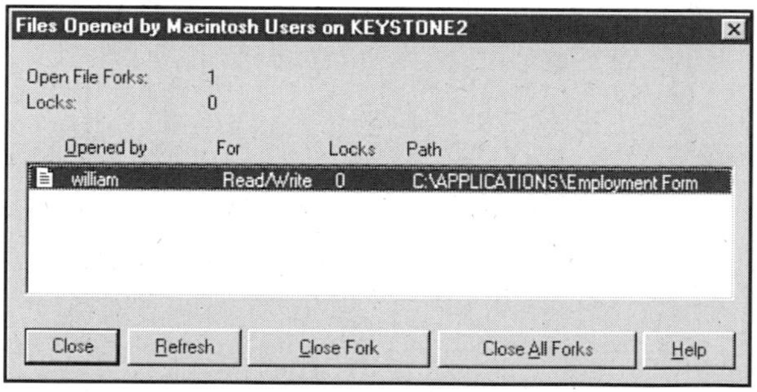

Figure 24.18

The open files window.

The **A**ttributes button opens the MacFile Attributes window shown in figure 24.19. Your options in this window are as follows:

◆ Choose **C**hange if you want to change the identification by which this server is known on the Macintosh network.

◆ Enter a message in the **L**ogon Message box if a logon message is desired.

◆ Remove the check from Allow **G**uests to Logon to disable guest logons.

◆ Check Allow **W**orkstations to Save Password if users are to be permitted to save their passwords in their logon configurations. (A very questionable practice in my opinion.)

◆ Check **R**equire Microsoft Authentication if clear text logons will not be permitted.

◆ If desired, limit the number of Macintosh sessions that will be permitted.

After you have configured options in MacFile Attributes window, initial configuration of the Services for Macintosh is complete.

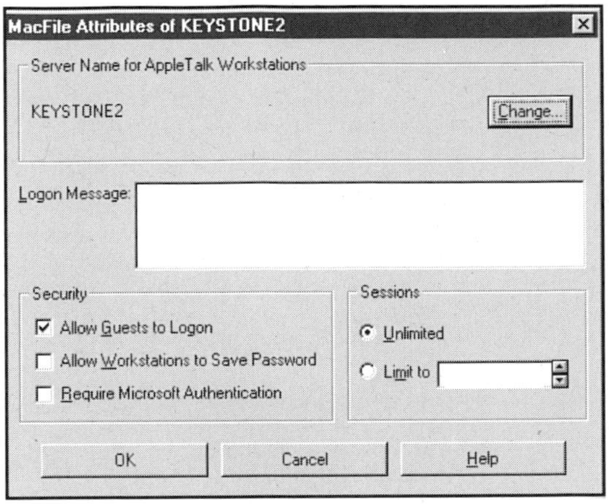

Figure 24.19

The MacFile Attributes window.

Testing Your Knowledge

1. What is the term for the Macintosh proprietary network?

2. How many devices are supported on a phase 1 AppleTalk network?

    A. 256

    B. 255

    C. 254

    D. 128

3. What is the term that signifies AppleTalk protocols running over Ethernet?

4. LocalTalk networks can have multiple zones.

    A. True

    B. False

5. AppleTalk supports routing among multiple zones.

    A. True

    B. False

6. Macintosh files are stored with two components called _____.

7. What are the two types of forks?

    A. Data

    B. Header

    C. Resource

    D. Attribute

8. How many characters in length can a Macintosh file be?

    A. 64

    B. 56

    C. 32

    D. 31

9. Under the Macintosh file system, what character serves the same purpose as the backslash (\) does in FAT and NTFS file systems?

    A. |

    B. ~

    C. :

    D. /

10. On the NT Server, the first volume that is shared is named _____ _____ VOLUME.

11. Macintosh volume security is applied to three entities: Owner, Primary Group, and Everyone. To each of these entities, you can assign the following three permissions: See Files, See Folders, and _____?

12. Macintosh files that are stored on Windows NT Server computers lose the type and creator information that is normally stored in the resource fork. How can Macintosh files that are stored on an NT Server be associated with applications?

    A. The Macintosh user must save the resource fork information locally.

    B. Macintosh users can include extensions in their file names, just as MS-DOS and Windows NT users are used to doing.

    C. There is no available method to permit file association under these circumstances.

13. With Services for Macintosh running, all Macintosh users can access which of the printer types listed?

    A. Printers attached directly to the NT Server with a serial or parallel port.

    B. Printers attached to MS-DOS, and Windows clients.

    C. Printing devices, such as the Apple LaserWriter, that can be attached directly to a LocalTalk network.

    D. Printing devices that are connected to the network through Ethernet or token-ring attachments.

14. Any Windows NT Server that is equipped with Services for Macintosh can function as an AppleTalk router.

    A. True

    B. False

15. What is the minimum version of the Macintosh operating system that Macintosh clients must be running before they can connect to the NT Server?

    A. 6.0.5

    B. 6.0.7

    C. 7.0.1

    D. 7.0.2

Review Answers

1. AppleTalk

2. C

3. EtherTalk

4. B

5. B

6. forks

7. A, C

8. D

9. C

10. MICROSOFT UAM

11. Make Changes

12. B

13. A, C, D

14. A

15. B

CHAPTER 25

Planning a Windows NT Clustering Strategy

Networked computing technology is changing right before our eyes; each new step in routing, architecture, cabling, and server capacity strengthens our ability to do more in less time. A network administrator's main task is to make the server run fast and efficiently, with little or no downtime, and although each upgrade of a particular product offers help to that end, you don't have to just wait for the next release for solutions. Skilled administrators can combine existing technologies to achieve their ends. Although these solutions do require testing, the administrator usually achieves them without the help of second-party software, by relying on his networking expertise.

Clustering is one of the many ways in which administrators achieve these ends without suffering the rigors of switching hardware and placing undue output demands on the existing system.

Clustering is best defined as a group of independent servers working together as a single unified networking system. When you cluster, so to speak, you are linking hardware together into a unified whole so that each independent system becomes a contributing portion of a single unified scenario, both sharing system resources and compensating for individual network deficits. A typical example of clustering would be the VAX-based systems utilized on many college campuses for e-mail service and campus-wide allocation of resources. Many individuals and vendors have used clustering as a means of coping with the issues of availability and scalability. (The next section defines and addresses these two concepts.)

This idea of bringing together server components did not just originate with Microsoft; many producers of large server hardware have previously used clustering for many tasks critical to sustaining an organization. The problem with many of the solutions that clustering has availed has been that they have often been difficult to figure out, problematic to install and configure, and usually have required expensive customized hardware.

Microsoft plans to bring a fail-safe, glitch-free clustering strategy to the *average* client/server professional. They plan to initialize this vision not with big, expensive hardware that is difficult to administer, but rather, utilizing open specs, with hardware that is readily available throughout the industry, and, hopefully, easy to use from an administrative standpoint.

Designing a clustering strategy with Windows NT is most likely to reduce undue stress on the network, and, thus, reduce server downtime. Server downtime, of course, not only puts industries at extreme security risk, but also damages their profitability.

If you have an appropriate Windows NT clustering architecture in place, systems can continue to run even if a single system goes belly-up. This *fail-over* strategy is discussed later in the chapter.

To familiarize you with the plan that Microsoft has for clustering, the following topics are discussed:

- ◆ Clustering architecture
- ◆ Clustering models
- ◆ Clustering's role in Windows NT
- ◆ What clustering offers
- ◆ Initiating a clustering strategy
- ◆ Clustering security
- ◆ Examples of clustering
- ◆ Application development for NT clusters
- ◆ Microsoft, NT, and clustering: a plan for the future

This chapter reviews and explains these and other issues concerning Windows NT clustering.

Clustering Architecture

Clustering consists of independent computer systems married together into a unified system. It can be done in a variety of ways; for example, by networking together, using either twisted-pair cabling or Ethernet, a set of desktop machines all running NT Server.

Traditional Architecture and SMP

In traditional architecture, such as on token ring or a star topography, achieving a greater server load capacity than is possible using one single processor entailed implementing the symmetric multiprocessor (SMP) system. In an SMP system, several boxes share an I/O subsystem and global memory, and this *shared memory model* (discussed later) runs the operating system singularly, with the applications running as if on a single system.

Such an architecture sometimes can prove a plausible solution, but one major drawback that it poses is that as microprocessor speeds continue to increase, shared memory processors become outrageously expensive. Also, increasing from a single server to two, four, or even eight servers can send your costs screaming, not to mention generate loads of frustration and eat away invaluable amounts of time to configure and maintain. Finally, neither traditional software nor an SMP system provides the relative simplicity and dependability of a single processor system. The one architecture that *can* provide the solution is the cluster.

The Cluster Remedy

At the high end of the range of possibilities, a cluster can be an amalgamation of high-performance SMP systems linked together via a high-speed networking strategy, such as 10BASE-T or 100VGAnyLan, and an I/O bus.

The beauty of such a system is that from the client end, it provides the illusion (known as a *single-system image*) that a single server acting on its own is furnishing the processing power. Even though this "server" *is* acting and being accessed as if it were a single server, it is actually a group of machines in concert.

Clustering is an architecture strategy for dealing with the factors of *availability* and *scalability*, which are defined and conceptualized as follows:

◆ **Availability.** Availability refers to the responsiveness of the server to disperse work over the range of the server. In clustering, when one system fails, the other systems within the cluster become "available" to assume the additional workload.

◆ **Scalability.** Scalability refers to the need for increased speed and memory within a particular system; in other words, the "scale" of the system needs to equal the demands on it. In the past, when users needed to "upscale" their network, they often needed an expensive hardware swap-out to accommodate additional drives and memory. With clustering, they can add on systems as needed to meet those requirements.

The benefit to administrators here is that they can add server power and memory incrementally by adding other commodity systems. As clients continually request more power for more complex end tasks, administrators can handle these additions without having to bring down and reconfigure the entire system, and without swapping out large capacity drives or hardware. As an organization grows and continues to take advantage of more powerful applications that deal with graphical and web technologies, therefore, you can set up the server to handle the increased workload capacity without having to more or less reinvent the wheel.

Note Are some of these capabilities starting to sound familiar? They might, if you've been following Microsoft's progress with dCOM. dCOM and clustering fit together in ways that can prove to be quite interesting when you understand the premise behind them. More on that later in the chapter.

More importantly, regarding client output and performance, and therefore server performance, if one system in a cluster fails, the workload can be rerouted among the still-operating systems. Your clients probably will not even suffer anything remotely like symptoms suggesting any kind of problem. To further break down the issue of clustering, the following section discusses the integral software models used in Windows NT clustering. Think of these software models as tools that, once you get a handle on them, can provide you with a blueprint that you can follow when you get into clustering with NT Server.

Clustering Models

This section focuses on illustrating two different models commonly used in clustering. *Model*, in this case, refers basically to the form that your clustering strategy takes. You want to get a firm grasp of the types of models available to you so that, as an administrator, you can see which one clearly would work best according to your particular circumstances. Understanding how these models fit into the NT framework ultimately enables you to implement the process with considerably less hassle. The two models discussed here are the shared disk and the shared nothing model.

Shared Disk Model

One way to configure software is to use the shared disk model. In the shared disk system, any application running on any component of the cluster can access any resource on any other part of the cluster.

Imagine that you are using Microsoft Access on your machine, for example, and are working from a publicly accessed drive. After you finish your task, you want to dump that latest document change, perhaps using your intranet, into a larger database that is available company-wide. Before you can complete this task, the document must be read twice from the disk, and replicated from one system to the next—and for that to happen, Microsoft Access must synchronize and serialize via the help of a Distributed Lock Manager (DLM). Through the DLM, the applications can track references to resources throughout the clustered network. If more than one server attempts to reference a single destination, the Lock Manager recognizes it and distributes a potential error.

One problem with DLM coordination is that it creates greater network traffic and causes undue strains on memory. Another remedy for these problems is the *shared nothing model* of software clustering.

Shared Nothing Model

In contrast to the shared disk model, the shared nothing model does exactly what its name suggests it might do: it controls ownership over a subset of server resources. In the shared nothing model, only one system may support, own, and have access privileges to one resource at a time. You can configure the cluster to take ownership of the failed resource in the event of a failure, in which case the end user makes a request from a particular system and the request automatically routes to the system that owns the application or resource.

Suppose, for example, that the end client is a designer using LightWave to create animated characters. After he finishes designing this particular character, he intends to use LightWave to render an image of it so that he can see his changes. In a clustered situation utilizing the shared nothing model, the request goes to whichever system has been selected to host the request. When the system recognizes that it needs to render an image generated in LightWave, it ships this subrequest to the system that can appropriately handle it. After the subsystem renders the image, it ships it back to the host system, which in turn, fires it back to the designer. And voilà—dancing animated popcorn box bands the next time you go see a movie.

A Windows NT clustering environment can support both the shared disk and the shared nothing models. Many applications can take advantage of clustering via use of the shared disk model. Applications that require a higher degree of scalability probably will utilize the advantages of the shared nothing paradigm. To give you a conceptualization of this information, the next section overviews how servers today stand in relation to clustering, and features Microsoft's vision for NT cluster support.

Where Clustering Fits into Windows NT

If you have read most of this book, you probably have already been compelled to utilize Windows NT Server 4. This server technology is very useful, and available to cluster, for several reasons. NT Server is built on a full 32-bit foundation and is multithreaded, offers true preemptive multitasking, and provides protection for both the applications running on NT and the operation system itself.

Before you take steps to further enhance Windows NT Server's clustering capacity, and before you begin to plan for NT Server clustering architecture, you need to know which aspects of Windows NT Server make it cluster-friendly. Consider the following:

◆ **Hardware support.** One hurdle you used to have to jump if you wanted to use clustering was its requirement of high-end expensive hardware. Windows NT Server clustering uses standard networking technology and PC platforms. Windows NT's layered driver component will allow Microsoft to add support for any specialized clustering technology strategy.

◆ **Server application support.** Given the server technologies now available as a part of an entire BackOffice strategy, other Microsoft products, such as Apache Server, Merchant Server, and Systems Management Server, can take advantage of clustering characteristics, and you can expect third parties to make contributions to support clustering APIs soon enough.

◆ **Non-disruptive cluster enhancement.** Because Windows NT Server is already cluster-compatible in terms of security and user administration, you can implement installation with clustering without disrupting the end user, which is a major boon. You don't have to throw a monkey wrench into organizational productivity by taking systems offline to perform major upgrades or additions (which administrators often are forced to do).

◆ **Application Programming Interfaces (APIs).** Microsoft currently is establishing industry standards for clustering APIs, which means software developers and programmers will be able to create applications that can take advantage of high-availability and scalability. Software such as database and print servers will be able to utilize APIs to exploit the potentials of clustering in Windows NT.

◆ **Understandable maintenance and configuration.** As previously mentioned, clustering can end up utilizing seemingly incompatible hardware, instigating long processes, and, in the end, providing insubstantial gains at best in actual system performance. Windows NT Server's already existing central management capabilities, however, make clustering much simpler to configure and maintain than in previously customized systems. Windows NT includes a range of graphical cluster and network management tools that make clustering easier and virtually problem-free.

The core components for constructing a clustered system actually shipped as a part of Windows NT Server 3.51, but Microsoft did not publicize them much. Some of the earlier features of clustering found in 3.51 include the capability to route requests with the redirector, the single-logon capability that is a part of NT domains, Performance Monitor, and the monitoring capabilities of the administration tools. These clustering components have all been updated with 4 to include the new features of NT 4. Microsoft reportedly is prioritizing clustering components for the next version of NT, to meet the demands of those who are initiating such network strategies.

Cluster Management

Microsoft's contributions to clustering amount primarily to its Wolfpack clustering software. The first phase of the Wolfpack scenario is for the network support two-node fail-over and fail-back capabilities. The second phase is the implementation of other vendors to have other clustering platforms and applications tested by Microsoft. Cluster management is performed via utilizing Microsoft Cluster Manager for Windows NT Server.

The Cluster Manager utilizes conventional hardware and an open specification to control the interactions within a cluster. Each individual node within a cluster runs a single instance of the cluster service software component. The cluster service breaks down into multiple subcomponents, which the following sections define in turn. The cluster service is the main application and controls all server processes within the cluster.

Resource Manager and Failover Manager

Managing resources within a group is the Resource Manager's main job. The Resource Manager receives group updates from the Node Manager and the Resource Monitor. The Resource Manager does in some ways what its name purports. It monitors server usage levels and allocates different jobs to parts of the cluster that contain unexploited memory and power. If it is unsuccessful in its attempt, the Failover Manager steps in and directs the group to another section of the network node.

Node Manager

The Node Manager serves to keep each of the individual nodes in synchronization with one another. It communicates with each individual node in the cluster to determine its performance and status. If a message is sent to another node asking for status and the node does not communicate a reply, the Resource Manager is notified in order to analyze the individual node error.

Event Processor

The event processor is pretty much the brain of the clustered network. It mainly handles event notification for the cluster. It also handles the network traffic, routing it to the proper subcomponents or to the cluster-based applications running within the cluster.

Communication Manager

The Communication Manager is a tool that ensures that communications between clustered nodes are established and maintained. The Communication Manager is notified in the event of node failure, and will cease communications and resource allocation at such time.

Database Manager

The Database Manager handles management of the clusters configuration database. It allows for consistent database communication between the individual servers that manage components of the cluster database.

Software Support for NT Clustering

The cluster service software supports applications running in a Wolfpack cluster. This service is the core component in Wolfpack and runs as an NT service. The cluster service supports fail-over capabilities on non-cluster–aware NT Server applications by first launching the application in a protected cluster and notifying the Resource Manager that the application has been assimilated into the cluster. Thereafter, normal cluster management functions monitor the application as it runs.

What Clustering Offers

Of the many potentials that clustering promises, the most important probably is the capability to aggregate separate servers into a single computing facility; by utilizing this capability, information technology organizations can decrease system downtime and can improve the flexibility of installations.

Decreased Downtime

Estimates report that system downtime incurs costs for businesses in the United States alone in the neighborhood of five billion dollars per year. The most likely cause of system downtime is the use of single system hardware in traditional networked systems. When you have multiple servers working in accord, however, to deliver functionality to the organization, the possibility of complete system failure is quite low. Multiple servers working in accord also allows certain areas of the network to experience problems without forcing the administrator to shut down the whole system to fix them.

Flexible Growth

The flexibility to grow installations beyond a single machine is one of the most compelling reasons to make clustering a part of an IT strategy. At some point, most organizations must face the fact that networked systems often grow exponentially compared to the budget allotted for them. Clustering enables the network administrator to create strategies that do not entail such stringent hardware demands; for example, clustering would make possible a strategy that could allow for the rerouting of hardware to lesser roles in the system as better hardware comes along instead of simply discarding it after a few years of use.

Initiating a Clustering Strategy

Although the idea of getting a clustering strategy started might sound tedious—indeed, you might have heard horror stories concerning incompatible hardware, or other problems—rest assured that with the future development of APIs for the NT clustering strategy, administrators will face few difficulties in configuring and maintaining a clustering profile. Microsoft offers two different clustering solutions, a fail-over solution and a multiple-node solution:

◆ **Fail-over solution.** Fail-over allows two servers to utilize the same hard disk within the original cluster, which provides an improvement in the area of available data for the end user. When one aspect of the system fails, the cluster software (for example, Wolfpack) "catches" the work and distributes it to another section of the system that exists within the cluster.

  For a good secondary example of this solution, consider the system of processors utilized on the space shuttle. If you have ever listened to the mission specialists talk about the five processors, you probably have heard hear them mention that if they "argue about a solution," so to speak, the arbitrating machine will turn itself off to let the others make a decision. When this fifth machine turns itself off, the others easily take up the slack because the computations from the disabled machine "fail-over" into the remaining ones. Within the NT model as well, the failure of one system does not affect the performance of the others.

◆ **Multiple-node solution.** A multiple-node solution essentially is what it sounds like; with multiple-node support built directly into NT, you can connect two or more servers together for increased reliability and performance. This process is considerably more proactive and cost-effective than a fail-over solution, in that you add processing power as the need arises, in incremental steps, instead of adding it in large, needless upgrades. In the past, administrators had to make large up-front commitments regarding hardware, without really knowing for sure how the organization might grow—often leading to expensive hardware that became obsolete all too soon. Multiple nodes let the administrator create additional drives, memory, and even CPUs with little hassle.

Windows NT 4 comes configured with base operating system support for clusters. This configuration includes components with which you can configure, maintain, and monitor system membership within the cluster, overall cluster name-space support, communication and fail-over support. Microsoft expects ease of setup and reliable management tools to be a high priority with the end customer in this arena.

Clustering Security

One issue that probably has already crossed your mind is security. If you implement clustering under a shared disk model, you have to wonder whether certain users might not be able to access certain files owing to the high rate of transfer between servers within the cluster. Known as *internode security*, you must determine whether you need to make communication between nodes secure so that (1) the system may function correctly, and (2) certain users may not gain unwarranted access to certain files contained within.

In contrast to clustering, with distributed computing, this type of server communication usually is exposed to external view, so barriers against unwanted violations are required.

One of the nice things about clustering is that the architecture may not require internal security measures, depending on whether the cluster is an exposed or enclosed system.

Exposed Cluster System

An *exposed cluster* (fig. 25.1 depicts an exposed system) is a system that shares public communication facilities with other systems that aren't part of the cluster. An example of an exposed cluster system would be a business that has a telephonic component. Although the administrator might be utilizing MAPI or another standard to integrate its telephone and network system, it might be running on a box that exists outside of the traditional network (the telephone system warrants that size of a processor). Under such a scenario, the cluster is being shared with an external component.

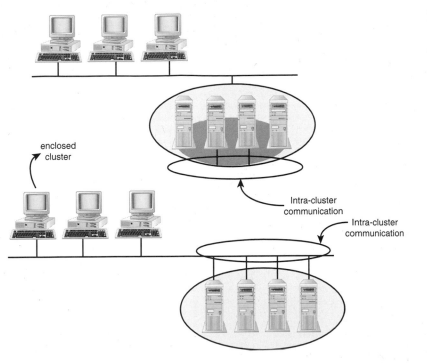

Figure 25.1

Exposed and enclosed clusters.

Several factors always apply when you have an exposed system:

◆ When you have a network channel that runs outside of the cluster, you always run the risk of a security breach; therefore, you need to have more security strategies in place to ensure that highly important and confidential data receives strong protection.

◆ You need to use standard protocols (that is, robust systems such as TCP/IP) to weather network tantrums, so naturally, a high cost accompanies this breadth of communication.

◆ Because most public access, standardized communication is message-based, your cluster nodes will need to utilize a message-based system to communicate.

◆ Because an exposed system incorporates the deluge of workstations that utilize widespread communication channels, the openness of such a system leaves it vulnerable to scavenging (or, the utilizing of unused cycles).

Enclosed Cluster System

In contrast to an exposed system, an enclosed cluster has communication facilities that are largely private (refer to fig. 25.1). An enclosed cluster system does not necessarily have to be exotic; the key is that it be private. The possibilities in a private system are broader, however, than in conventional communication practices:

◆ In an enclosed system, network traffic can utilize shared-disk, shared memory, messaging, and other means.

◆ Networked communication in an enclosed system doesn't have a huge overhead because administrators aren't stifled by standard protocols. If you are creating links within your own self-contained system, you can write it based purely on its needs instead of having to worry about open standards.

◆ In an enclosed system, security is implicit, so information can be transported across the wire, utilizing the same security provisions. For example, in Windows NT Server, because the same security provisions are used in separate sections of the operation system, you have a secure channel—consequently, adequate security doesn't cost that much in the long run.

As you would expect, there are advantages of an enclosed system over an exposed one, and advantages of an exposed one over an enclosed one. As in most cases, the best solution is the one that offers you the greatest performance while at the same time not jeopardizing security or eating up the IT manager's budget.

Examples of Clustering

This section offers and examines two examples of clustering that are used in a general organizational format. One takes place in a retail/point-of-sale scenario (an arena in which Windows NT Server is employed frequently) and focuses on the issue of data availability, and the other takes place in a mutual funds company and focuses on the issue of scalability. Hopefully, these two illustrations can help you come to an understanding of how clustering might fit into your existing network architecture.

Example One—Data Availability

In any retail chain, what brings in the revenue is keeping the point-of-sale terminals active and functioning.

In addition to simply checking out customers, employees must have access to a database that includes product, SKU codes, names, quantities, and availability of products, and, of course, the prices. If the terminals decide to go offline, the organization has no way of conducting business, bringing new shipments into the facility correctly, or tracking the movements of product.

With a clustering solution, you could have two separate servers, both of which have access to the disk array on which the database is located. In the event that you have a single server failure, the backup system is automatically brought up-to-speed, and the employees are automatically switched over to the remaining server without any notice (see fig. 25.2 and fig. 25.3).

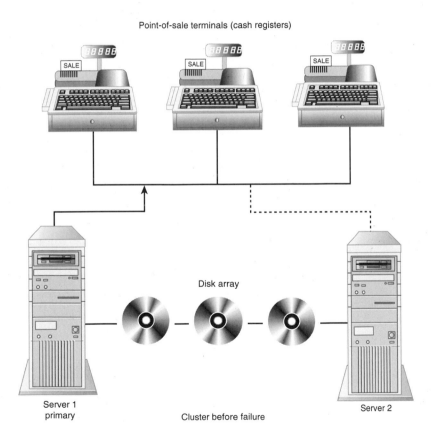

Point-of-sale terminals (cash registers)

Disk array

Server 1
primary

Cluster before failure

Server 2

Figure 25.2

The cluster before failure.

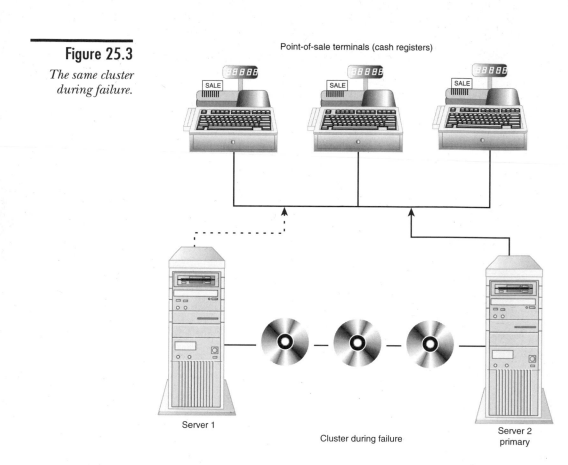

Figure 25.3

The same cluster during failure.

Point-of-sale terminals (cash registers)

Server 1

Cluster during failure

Server 2
primary

Because Windows NT Server 4 utilizes fault-tolerant disk architecture in the form of striping and duplexing, the disk array is protected. To complete this protection process, with the addition of the cluster, the system would continually stay online without any notice of problems out on the front end where business is being done.

Another example in which cluster availability is important is in the area of building security. Often, modern edifices utilize timed locks to secure a building after hours. In the event of a server failure, the building could be prematurely locked down, or, worse, could be completely unlocked. A clustered strategy in which one system automatically fails over to another would minimize this potential hazard.

Example Two—General Scalability

In standard networked computing, success and failure can be somewhat of a double-edged sword. If you have the task of managing a large network, the last thing you want is for server failure to become so routine that your phone is ringing off the hook with complaints. On the other hand, if a system runs smoothly and is administered correctly, the demands on it tend to increase over time as users come up with new ways to utilize the capabilities available to them, with either better workstation-based hardware or applications that require more processing power from the server to run adequately. The inundation of web-based technologies and huge multimedia software platforms makes this issue one continually being stressed.

One good example of the benefit of scalability exists in larger investment firms around the country. As more individuals take it upon themselves to invest for their future, investment firms have become larger and more complex. As firms of this nature grow steadily, information management people are forced to continually make changes to compensate for the increased demands on the system. These continual alterations can wreak havoc on an IT budget, as the timing for purchasing the technology is poor and it soon becomes outdated.

Certain inherent paradigms exist with Windows NT Server clustering that allow automatic re-tasking, easier configuration and troubleshooting with smaller staffs, and faster system deployment. All these things are possible with hardware from multiple NT-supported vendors, too, thus decreasing the chance for single-supplier shortage of availability of a particular product. As business booms, you can add components from time to time; you do not have to make one giant hardware purchase that could easily overshoot your needs if business tapers off. NT clustering lets a system administrator enjoy a cheap, usable platform for upgrading his network without requiring a complete system overhaul.

Application Development for NT Clusters

As Microsoft continues to churn out their strategy to make their server technology "cluster-enabled," development tools will be enhanced so that applications will become "cluster-intelligent." Microsoft plans to incorporate facilities that deal comfortably with automatic fail-over into their server-based programs. Although many applications will have the cluster-proficient strategies built into their subsystems, it will not be necessary for all programs to be cluster-intelligent to gain the advantages of clustering Windows NT servers. If generic applications are piggy-backed on top of cluster-intelligent applications running within a BackOffice architecture, they need not be cluster-enabled.

For example, an accounting firm could keep a large database of clients in either Access or Symantec's Act 32 database, or perhaps even in an old DOS version of Q&A, another formerly popular database system. Regardless of whether the firm is running one or, for some reason, all of these applications, if they are all running on top of something like SQL, then the clustering aspect is safe, because of clustering enhancements that have been integrated into SQL on versions 6.5 and beyond. Whether server applications perform such tasks as client/server connection interaction, the leveraging of database services, or file and print services, they will all benefit from clustering technology without any inherent changes to the application.

Microsoft, NT, and Clustering: A Plan for the Future

The biggest step forward that Microsoft has made in the last year is the implementation of its Wolfpack software, which is touted as the first-generation software for true clustering within Windows NT. Hewlett-Packard, Tandem, Compaq, NCR, Digital, Intel, and Sequent are just some of the companies that have set their sights on having products available to take advantage of the Wolfpack initiative. Within the framework of Wolfpack, as of this writing, all these organizations are in the process of defining industry standards for clustering APIs.

Within the release of NT 4, the individual server itself is already tackling the question of performance with such aspects as redundancy built into power suppliers, network cards, disk drives, and early warning mechanisms.

Besides the capability to balance workloads between systems, clustering also affords savings in systems management owing to its provision of a simple multiple server architecture that enables administrators to manage and share peripherals, as well as manage and replicate data. In the end, though, the most important aspect of clustering is the improved system resilience it provides. The following sections look at some of those products that embrace the Wolfpack capabilities of Windows NT Server.

Online Recovery Server

Compaq has recently come up with a way to network two inherently separate systems, through redundant linking. Using their product, Online Recovery Server, one server takes on the other's disk storage system through the use of an SCSI switch in the event of a single server failure. Using this clustering application, some downtime and data loss might occur, but if so, most likely only at a minimum.

ServerNet

Tandem, Inc., has taken up where Compaq leaves off, with a new technology embedded in their NonStopKernal component. This product, called ServerNet, provides a mesh that is redundant, switched, and routed, which also operates at high speed. In this model, when one server fails, there is a continual route to the next server in the cluster without a loss of the session that is current. This type of clustering package will provide Windows NT Server 4 and 5 support on its own specific server platform.

Digital Clusters

From the team over at Digital Equipment comes a clustering strategy they have been shipping since June of 1996, Digital Clusters for Windows NT. This product is aimed at IT managers, who (like the rest of the free world) are looking to Windows NT as the next step in the growth of their organizational PC LAN. Their vision for this product is a simplified, low-cost product that delivers significant availability based around industry standards. In version 1.0, two separate Windows NT systems can be linked via a shared SCSI bus, to create a single solution. As in generic models mentioned earlier, clients have access to shared disk drives, databases, and other applications. This is a clean-running product in that in the event of failure, an opposing server will reinitiate all clients, automatically assume the workload, and migrate shared storage and file storage.

Digital Clusters is an extremely well thought-out solution. In addition to already supporting Oracle 7 WorkGroup Server, NTFS file services and network shares, and SQL Server, it is economical, and with Windows NT, can run on Intel-based Prioris servers or even Digital's turbo-charged AlphaServers. Although Digital Clusters does not provide complete fault-tolerance, it does allow for users to partition workloads, thus making use out of both servers.

As Wolfpack standards continue to roll out, Digital plans to move in that direction, if they end up varying greatly from what is currently being utilized. With multiple-node support, Digital is seeking to add value and stay on top of the base clustering platform.

Another product not really robust enough to warrant a complete section of its own is LifeKeeper, from NCR. It shares many of Online Recovery Server's features; however, at the time of this writing, NCR is making sketchy promises regarding a complete move to future Wolfpack standards.

Testing Your Knowledge

1. Clustering is an architecture strategy for dealing with the factors of availability and _____.

2. What are two different models commonly used in clustering?

    A. Shared disk model

    B. Shared processor model

    C. Shared nothing model

    D. Star cluster model

3. What is the code name for Microsoft's current NT clustering technology?
4. The two types of clustering security systems are called exposed cluster and _____.

Review Answers

1. scalability
2. A, C
3. Wolfpack
4. Enclosed cluster system

PART V

Exploring the BackOffice Suite

CHAPTER 26

Introducing BackOffice

Microsoft *BackOffice* is a suite of client/server network applications, sold as a bundle or application suite, that runs on Windows NT Server. Windows NT provides the operating system on which all the components of BackOffice run. These applications provide an easy means for organizations to deploy client/server technology without having to resolve the painful incompatibilities that arise from integrating solutions from multiple vendors. This chapter talks all about BackOffice's major components and how you can use them to create and manage an enterprise's networked computing needs.

Components of BackOffice enable you to create a rich range of network applications for companies as small as the smallest workgroup using a single server, or as large as a worldwide enterprise using hundreds of servers and more than 100,000 clients. Support of networked applications is a particular strength of NT Server, and add to that the range of application services, scalability, and low cost relative to other client/server technologies of BackOffice, and you can see that BackOffice is a unique product offering.

The major components of BackOffice are the Internet Information Server and related support services (Index Proxy), Exchange Server, SQL Server, Systems Management Server, and SNA Server. These components provide Internet/intranet publishing services, mail and other messaging services, database and information management activities, remote system configuration, and mainframe host connectivity.

The compelling aspect of these technologies is their capability to piggyback NT Server's security system and provide access and privileges based on a unified security directory scheme. Additionally, you can deploy these applications in a distributed fashion, making it possible for you to employ multiple servers to balance the load of network activities and provide for fault tolerance. Usually, the underlying information that these services manage can be replicated across the network in the same manner that a primary domain server replicates the SAM security database between backup domain servers.

BackOffice Components

Version 2.5 of BackOffice includes the following applications:

◆ A web server, the Internet Information Server (IIS) 2.0

◆ A web site indexing tool, the Index Server (IIS) 2.0

◆ A web firewall, the Proxy Server (IIS) 2.0

◆ A messaging platform, Microsoft Exchange 4.0

◆ A database, Microsoft SQL Server 6.5

◆ A network configuration tool, Microsoft Systems Management Server (SMS) 1.2

◆ A mainframe/PC connection tool, SNA Server 3.0

◆ A common installer program, Setup

A few of the more important elements in the preceding list are discussed in greater detail in the section, "Exploring the Components of BackOffice," later in this chapter.

BackOffice was first introduced in the fall of 1995, and versions 1.0, 1.5, 2.0, and 2.5 have been released. A version 3.0 is planned for 1997; BackOffice is truly a work in progress.

The future additions to BackOffice servers will include the following components:

◆ **Internet Merchant Server.** A web server that contains software for electronic commerce on the Internet. Among the services that this server provides is secure transaction communication, and connection to banks and credit card companies for transaction verification.

◆ **Media Server.** Provides a system for storing and accessing rich data types, such as images, sound, and video.

Figure 26.1 shows you the relationship of Windows NT Server to the components of BackOffice, and to clients on a network.

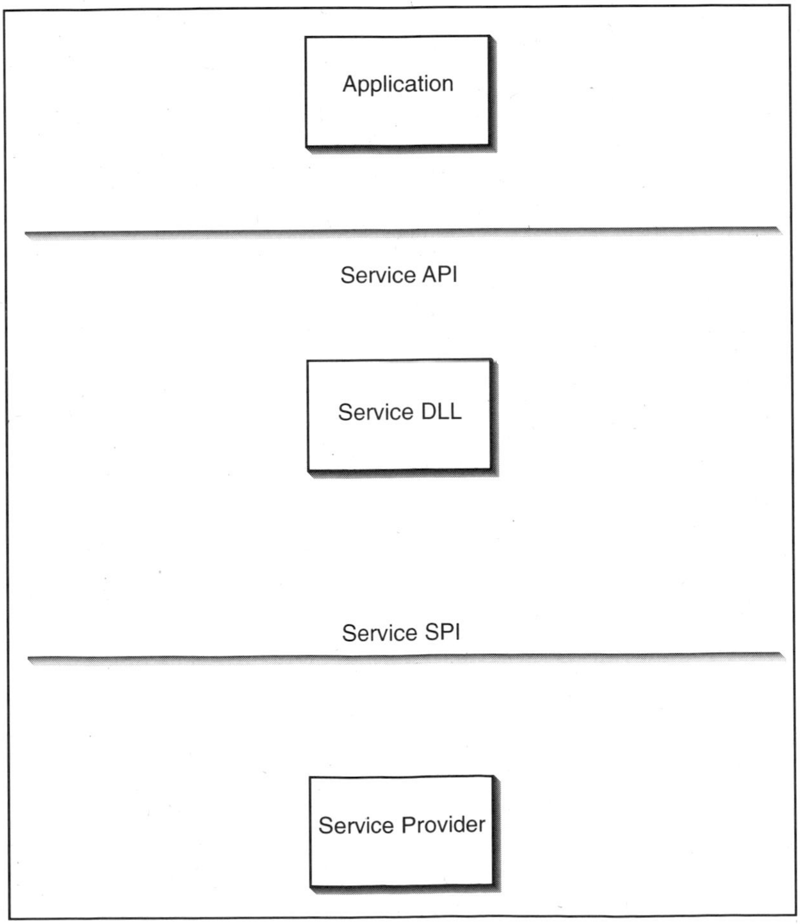

Figure 26.1

The components of BackOffice integrate with Windows NT Server to provide networked application services.

The Advantage of a Homogeneous Enterprise Solution

BackOffice gives you the chance to create an enterprise networking solution from a single vendor source. In that sense, it provides you with a homogeneous solution of applications and services that are designed or at least tested and meant to work together as a unit.

Each of the aforementioned BackOffice applications is the server side of a client/ server application that can be run on one or more NT Servers in an enterprise. The advantage that BackOffice offers to a network administrator is not only its low overall cost, but its tight integration of these applications as NT Server services, not to mention its high interapplication compatibility. This last benefit is particularly hard to achieve in client/server technology obtained from multiple vendors.

BackOffice applications run as threads on Windows NT Server, and inherit the multiprocessing and fault tolerance features that NT Server offers. Applications running as NT services can take advantage of both multiprocessor servers as well as be distributed in many cases over multiserver networked systems. Therefore, a network administrator can distribute the load of any application (such as Microsoft Exchange or SQL Server) across the network by adding additional servers running that application.

And most important, administrators can apply NT's built-in challenge response security system to BackOffice applications automatically as they are installed. There is no need for users in an enterprise to remember multiple passwords, because most BackOffice applications use the NT SAM security database for their security scheme. The one exception to this rule in the current BackOffice suite is SQL Server, which allows a network administrator to either accept the NT security database with its groups and users, or to define a new security scheme with appropriate access and privileges.

The NT security model allows for unique and secure client connections in the form of machine accounts and user accounts, each with unique permissions. Each user account lets a user log into a domain from any client in the domain or from any client in a trusted domain. Each user account belongs to one or more groups (everyone is a member of the user group at a minimum), thus providing a method for the assignments of a common set of privileges. BackOffice forms the basis for a network operating system and platform for LAN, Internet, and WAN topologies. By applying the NT security model to the applications in the BackOffice suite, you make administration of these C/S applications considerably easier.

This chapter briefly introduces you to each of the major components of BackOffice. It also briefly describes issues pertaining generally to BackOffice, such as the Setup program, licensing, application development, and the Microsoft Developers Program.

Client/Server Technology and Business Process Reengineering

In order to be competitive, many businesses are downsizing their operations, streamlining their information systems, and flattening their reporting structure. This process is often referred to as business process reengineering. One way to do this from an information technology (IT) point of view is to install client/server (C/S) systems in place of centralized computing departments organized around mainframe or minicomputers and "dumb" terminals. In C/S technology, each client is a single personal computer, and network services also run on server PCs. In this scheme, servers are almost atomic in nature, in that servers and services are added one computer at a time, and any number of additional servers can be added as network demands require.

When you compare the cost/processing power ratio of PC LANs running C/S applications to that of older legacy applications running on centralized systems (mainframes or minicomputers), you can easily see the potential for considerable savings. C/S applications are no less complex than mainframe applications, but they are much more flexible and scalable.

Although the BackOffice applications run exclusively on Windows NT, Windows NT can run on several different processor types such as Intel X86-, Alpha-, and MIPS-based computers. As you already have seen, NT Server supports an even wider variety of industry standard interfaces, such as ANSI SQL, ODBC, X.400, SMPT, HTTP, SNMP, and DMTF, and also supports networking protocols such as IPX/SPX, TCP/IP, and AppleTalk, that can run concurrently as part of a network stack. So, you can implement BackOffice applications as either homogeneous NT-only network solutions, or you can introduce BackOffice applications into a NetWare network or into an intranet where a wide variety of equipment types and client platforms are supported. These factors let you implement BackOffice on a wide variety of equipment and network types.

Windows Open Systems Architecture

While C/S technology offers great promise for all of the reasons mentioned in the previous section, implementation of C/S applications has been a nightmare for many companies. To implement C/S applications, developers have been forced to learn proprietary application programming interfaces (APIs) in order to deploy their technology across different network resources. Most of the effort involved in C/S technologies focuses on simply making one application co-exist and communicate with another. Consequently, developers must devote time to supplying robust middleware systems, working on distributed object services, and embedding many network services within their applications simply to get their business application to function correctly, which leaves them little time for developing the application itself and its user interface, and for embedding the correct business logic into it after developing it. BackOffice addresses this problem by using a common set of programming interfaces for application development. This section briefly describes the major components of this programming architecture.

Underpinning BackOffice's philosophy is the idea that a common set of APIs will lead to more sophisticated business applications with less effort and fewer conflicts.

In BackOffice enterprises, applications use two important programming interfaces: Windows Open Systems Architecture (WOSA) and Object Linking and Embedding (OLE). These two APIs shield the application developer from having to know or care about the network or client type, or about the other back-end services in use. These APIs provide the necessary network operating system functionality on which the BackOffice applications and services are built. The following sections describe WOSA, and another section a little later on overviews OLE.

WOSA is a three-level architecture, as shown in figure 26.2. The Server Provider Interface (SPI) translates server services into operating system requests, isolating them from whatever other services might be running. The middle layer of WOSA is a set of Dynamic Link Libraries (DLLs) that manages applications requests and device replies. So an application developer is presented with an API that accesses a consistent set of back-end services, such as mail services, databases, or PBXs, without giving any special consideration as to how each service implements or controls a particular device.

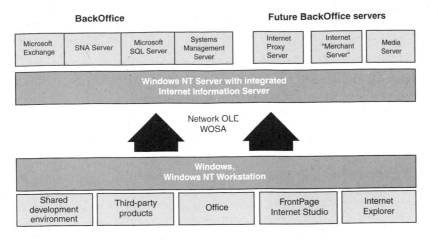

Figure 26.2

WOSA lets a developer create applications by accessing a standard set of APIs.

WOSA includes three types of services: common application services, connectivity services, and vertical market services. Examples of application services include the following:

◆ **Open Database Connectivity (ODBC).** Provides a specification for the creation of database data translation services that can connect a client database, such as Access, to a server database, such as SQL Server.

◆ **Message Application Programming Interface (MAPI).** The mail format and translation service used by Microsoft Exchange.

◆ **Windows Telephony Interface (TAPI).** Provides a range of digital/analog conversion routines that provide the necessary structure for telecommunication on computer.

◆ **License Service Application Programming Interface (LSAPI).** A system for centralized software license management.

LSAPI provides a set of program calls that allows a developer to create centralized software licensing applications. You see LSAPI in action when you run the Microsoft administration utilities that determine BackOffice license compliance.

What may not be obvious, but is very important to understand, is that NT Server's architecture is extensible. Additional APIs can be added, as program modules in future versions of NT Server, as new technology is developed. These services access a small program kernel that remains stable and unchanged by their addition, so that as new application types are developed, they are easily added to NT Server to support C/S application development.

Three examples of WOSA communication services are:

◆ Windows Sockets (Winsock), which allows for network access using different NT networking protocols

◆ Remote Procedure Calls (RPC)

◆ SNA API

Winsock provides for a named channel of communication between networked computers running the same or different network protocols. Therefore, Winsock provides a transport mechanism for network communications that isolates the transmitted data from the nature of the data source type. TCP/IP network communication can therefore communicate transparently with other protocols in the network stack, such as IPX/SPX.

Windows Sockets is a network programming interface for Microsoft Windows that translates network communications formatted for other protocols into a form that the TCP/IP can accept, and accepts communications back from TCP/IP. Windows Sockets eliminates the need to worry about TCP/IP conventions, and makes for easy connections to IPX/SPX, AppleTalk, DECnet, and XNS protocols from TCP/IP.

Both RPC and SNA allow NT services to communicate with other types of computers on heterogeneous networks. RPC is the foundation technology that provides for distributed applications running in an NT Server environment; its routines automatically generate network-related source code, and its runtime takes care of the networking, security, and naming services necessary to run the remote procedure call. RPC gives developers a means to modularize and distribute applications in a distributed network application. It is, in fact, RPC specifically that provides the necessary services that allow SQL Server applications to span multiple computers, or SQL Server database files to span multiple volumes on local or remote drives.

SNA is used either with IBM mainframe computers or with AS400 computers compatible with the SNA standard to provide a means to view and modify data residing on a mainframe, using PC technologies in a very cost-effective method. SNA Server is a unique application in the BackOffice technology suite, so that while very few companies employ SNA to access legacy data, nearly all companies that do so employ BackOffice as their enterprise foundation applications.

Finally, WOSA vertical market services includes:

◆ Extensions for Financial Services

◆ Extensions for Real Time Market Data

WOSA is an extensible architecture, so additional APIs can be added to improve the range of services provided. This characteristic is obvious, from the appearance of the vertical market services previously described. Also, since the architecture relies on the use of APIs, Microsoft can improve the internal workings of the services while keeping the program calls for services unchanged. Upcoming sections describe data transfer, the communications technology in WOSA, interapplication communications mechanisms, and PC/host connectivity communications. All of these programming modules find expression in BackOffice applications.

ODBC

The Open Database Connectivity (ODBC) specification is an industry standard that Microsoft was instrumental in defining and implementing. ODBC allows different databases to request data and services using the Standard Query Language (SQL), and to receive data. A wide variety of front-end databases, such as Access, FoxPro, Paradox, and dBASE, can communicate with server databases, such as Microsoft SQL Server, Oracle, Sybase, Informix, and others. IIS can use ODBC to communicate with SQL Server, both of which are central BackOffice components.

ODBC connectors may be thought of in terms of being the data equivalent of a device driver; each specific connection is a data pipe that applies to one, and only one, database. The database does not have to be relational; it only has to understand basic SQL syntax. The ODBC protocol itself supports many advanced SQL features.

ODBC allows for the development of heterogeneous database solutions, letting front-end and back-end systems access data with vendor neutral SQL program calls. Among the operations that can be performed in addition to data access are database replication and database updates.

Any application written with the OBDC specification in mind can access any other ODBC compliant data source. Therefore, a corporation can substitute one data source, such as Oracle, with another data source, such as Sybase, with minimal application redesign. As such, database users can work with ODBC-compliant applications on a client system without concern for the underlying network topology, or the structure or language of the target DBMS.

MAPI

MAPI is Microsoft's messaging subsystem. Its architecture is not unlike the print subsystem in Windows, where applications submit print jobs to the Print Manager and print spooler, where a target printer is specified for output, and where the print job is specified based on the selected printer, and Print Manager formats the print output in the required format.

Similarly, MAPI lets different messaging applications communicate with other messaging applications or services. A target service must be first chosen, whereupon MAPI formats the message appropriately. The messaging subsystem routes messages in the background through the message spooler, and can direct incoming messages to a message store, or can block messages for which no recipient may be determined. MAPI provides store-and-forward capabilities.

Both Microsoft Mail and Microsoft Exchange are MAPI-compliant applications, as are a large number of other third-party messaging applications. Microsoft Office components, such as Word and Excel, are also MAPI-compliant in that they utilize Simple MAPI and Common Messaging Calls (CMC) to send or receive mail. All Microsoft applications that have a Send command on the File menu call this API. CMC is similar to the industry standard for messaging, the X.400 API.

Microsoft Exchange server uses Extended MAPI, a more recent superset of MAPI, to provide the API that allows for rich messaging, forms, and a variety of special messaging services that enable Exchange as a groupware application.

RPC

The Remote Procedure Call (RPC) specification is the key programming interface that allows for distributed applications in a BackOffice enterprise. Microsoft's RPC is a version of DCE, a more general heterogeneous communication service specified by the Open Systems Foundation. Under RPC, an NT Server (and in many cases an NT Workstation) can be either an RPC client or an RPC server in a distributed computing environment.

Consider a large database system built using SQL Server. As the load on a single server increases, either through more users requiring data access or through larger data stores being managed, multiple SQL Servers may be brought online. These multiple SQL Servers are controlled through RPCs so that it appears to the user that only a single instance of SQL Server is running the database. Using RPC, BackOffice applications such as Microsoft Exchange can contain 100,000 or more clients, serviced by many Exchange servers.

RPC is different than using a socket; whereas a socket must format data communications for a particular remote application, an RPC runtime module automatically creates network source code with all of the appropriate addressing and security already defined for the remote application.

SNA

System Network Architecture (SNA) is an IBM protocol for data communication between a wide range of computer types. The SNA API in BackOffice allows IBM mainframes and AS/400 minicomputers to communicate with desktop PCs directly through a service. Microsoft SNA Server supports LU (logical unit) protocols, PU (physical unit) protocols, and data link protocols.

The WOSA SNA API enables vendors to write software that can access legacy data as if the client PC were a terminal on that mainframe or minicomputer's network. APPC can, for example, provide a peer-to-peer connection between a PC acting as a 5250 terminal and an AS/400. Other protocols in SNA, such as CPI-C, CSV, LUA, and EHLLAPI provide different emulations.

The use of SNA Server in BackOffice installations is common for large companies or enterprises with mainframes and minicomputers, but rare otherwise. It is true, however, that companies installing SNA Server almost universally install the other components of BackOffice as well.

OLE

OLE is Microsoft's object model. Originally, this specification was described as object linking and embedding. Now, however, OLE has a broader context within the Component Object Model (COM) that allows for object descriptions, storage, and utilization. Essentially, OLE is now a specification for the code needed to provide these functions.

You see OLE in action whenever you insert or link to a data object in a file. The metaphor is what Microsoft calls "Paste Special," although this awkwardly named command will probably fade from use in time. In OLE specification version 2, Microsoft expanded OLE to provide for in-place activation. Essentially, an embedded object, when activated, runs the registered application for the data type inside the parent application for that document. An Excel spreadsheet object in a Word document would, for example, launch Excel when you double-click on it, with the Excel toolbars and menu command replacing (temporarily) the Word toolbars and menus. Deactivating the object by clicking elsewhere returns Word toolbars and menus to view.

In future versions of BackOffice, OLE will play a central role. This role is being expanded by the adoption of the Component Object Model that defines how objects may be distributed between different network clients and servers. At the moment, the specification applies only for localized objects, but much energy is going into extending this model in future versions of the NT operating system. Windows NT Server 4 introduced the Distributed Component Object Model (DCOM), which allows OLE object to work across a LAN or on a TCP/IP internetwork using RPC. Version 5 of NT Server provides a method for tracking objects in a rich directory service.

ActiveX

The ActiveX extension of OLE arises from the Microsoft slogan "Activate the Internet." OLE objects and OCX (OLE custom controls) are all automatically ActiveX objects, but the ActiveX specification adds additional capabilities to the DCOM model. These additional features include audio, video, and 3D animation that are specific to Internet or intranet publishing. Here the DCOM model is distributed over the heterogeneous systems of TCP/IP networks, and supported by RPC for remote activation through URL addressing.

Many ActiveX objects are referred to as "DocObjects." These objects may be manipulated through the interface by standard methods. Microsoft's Internet Explorer is a classic example of a container application in which in-place activation using ActiveX DocObjects is the norm. You can see this in operation when you install Mail and News into MS Internet Explorer and watch the interface change as you use those applications. You can also link to a Word document in a hyperlink and have later versions of Microsoft Word (7 and later) run within the Internet Explorer container.

ActiveX controls, formerly OCXs, are simpler than DocObjects to use because they don't require you to spawn external programs. But they are more complex often to program; when you launch an ActiveX control, all of the programming logic necessary to run it is contained in the object.

In web development, scripting languages such as Perl are more often used than programming languages such as C or C++. Future versions of ActiveX will connect scripting languages in future DCOM extensions. Whereas OCX objects can be operated programmatically using automation with scripting in things like Visual Basic, ActiveX works with other scripting languages such as PerlScript and JavaScript to manipulate OCXs.

Although OLE never made it to the Macintosh, Macromedia is porting ActiveX controls to the Macintosh for web applications.

Exploring the Components of BackOffice

BackOffice is a suite of network application services. Organizations installing components of BackOffice typically deploy one or two of these applications at a time. Larger organizations may employ several components across an enterprise. In the sections that follow, each of the components of BackOffice is overviewed, and its function and purpose described. These sections describe how the different components of BackOffice relate to and interact with one another, and also detail some of the future plans for development of BackOffice that exist. Chapters 27 through 30 will discuss in more detail each component of BackOffice.

The Systems Management Server

The *Systems Management Server* (SMS) is a software solution that enables an administrator to remotely view, control, and configure Windows NT Server, LAN Manager, IBM LAN Server, and Novell NetWare servers, not to mention MS-DOS, Windows 3.x, Windows 95, Macintosh, and OS/2 clients.

When an administrator logs on to SMS, he or she can remotely install new software across the network, or upgrade older software on clients on the network. SMS offers a set of tools called a Help Desk that enables an administrator to diagnose problems on client computers, and remotely control those workstations to remedy those problems.

SMS also contains tools for alert and event management. So a network administrator can define events to be monitored in order to define the nature of network problems through a logging activity.

SMS is organized around a hierarchy of network servers running the SMS service. A central server runs on the top level, primary SMS servers run at the second level, and logon servers and distribution servers run at the bottom level.

A central server running Windows NT controls other SMS servers designed to service other networks or remote sites. SMS is linked to an SQL Server database that maintains an inventory of corporate assets. Only a single database is required at the central site.

The central SMS server can be connected to other Windows NT Servers, called primary SMS servers, when SMS needs to be distributed to balance the load, to reduce network traffic, or to support remote sites. Primary SMS servers are not required, but can greatly reduce network traffic.

It is also not required that each Primary SMS server have a local copy of the SQL Server database that inventories the enterprise's software, but it is typically done. A site that has a primary SMS server and an SQL database is called a *primary site*; a site that does not have the database is referred to as a *secondary site*. A secondary site requires that the primary SMS server query the central database for many functions, so its performance is limited.

On the third level of the SMS hierarchy are the logon servers, distributions servers, and helper servers. Logon servers typically are distributed throughout an organization and run on top of Novell NetWare servers, LAN Manager, or Windows NT Server. A logon server is oftentimes a server running a file and print server onto which SMS has been added. Logon servers store SMS data files locally. It is a requirement of SMS that each domain have at least one logon server operating on it.

Distribution servers store the software that client computers in the domain can install. Common distribution software is either managed by a network administrator who installs the software for clients, or is placed in a shared application directory on the Distribution server that clients can access.

In the SMS hierarchy, the fourth and lowest level consists of the client desktop systems that SMS servers can serve to reach and manage.

The SQL Server database that SMS manages stores information about the hardware components of each machine in the inventory. Typically, information on the microprocessor type, the storage devices, network adapter or network interface cards, and installed memory is stored, as is a table of each computer's IRQ assignments. SMS conforms to the Desktop Management Interface (DMI), and any device or software for which the developer has written a Management Information File (MIF) will appear in that computer's inventory. DMI is an industry standard supported by not only Microsoft, but also IBM, Hewlett-Packard, Intel, Novell, and Digital Equipment Corporation.

SMS logs information on computer hardware and software into MIF files, the same format that it also uses to describe events, software specifications, print and other network jobs, and information about users on a network. MIF files also store attributes describing the group of each particular component in the inventory. Each SMS database stores MIF groups as SQL Server tables, and each attribute of an MIF group is a column in that table.

The SMS database defines each group as having particular attributes. When the MIF file is missing, and the table describing that group is not found, SMS assumes that the group does not exist or is not supported. As currently written, SMS can read any MIF tables as defined by the DMI standard. Some attributes in the MIF tables that are defined by DMI, however, are not implemented in SMS, and are ignored.

When an MIF table contains a group that is not recognized, SMS adds the description of that attribute to its main table. It is possible, therefore, to define custom MIF inventory files in SMS. You can extend SMS to describe a library of objects, organizational structures, new hardware or software types, and so forth. Custom MIF files are a powerful extension of SMS.

Note   For more detailed information on SMS, see Chapter 27, "Systems Management Server."

Internet Information Server

BackOffice is being positioned as a premier platform for Internet/intranet activities. It comes with the Internet Information Server 2.0, which is a web server that runs on Windows NT Server; or in a more limited way on NT Workstation as a Peer Web service. The first version of Microsoft *Internet Information Server* (IIS) was available for the price of a download. Version 1.2 shipped with BackOffice 1.5; version 2.0 appeared in BackOffice 2.0. When you buy NT Server, the package includes IIS, which is the component of BackOffice most organizations will choose to implement.

Once you configure your server to run the TCP/IP network protocol and then properly configure the address of your server, IIS is ready to run. During installation of NT Server, you are prompted to install IIS. If you do so, IIS installs and will start up with your server when it boots.

As configured at the moment, IIS can support three different Internet data transfer protocols:

◆ **FTP.** The File Transfer Protocol is used for transferring files from one computer to another. FTP is the fastest of the transfer protocols in terms of data throughput. You can use dedicated FTP utilities such as WS_FTP for both uploading and downloading files. Modern browsers such as Microsoft Internet Explorer and Netscape Navigator can access FTP sites and download files from them. An FTP site looks like a hierarchical file listing.

◆ **Gopher.** The Gopher protocol also organizes information in a hierarchy, but can in addition display a description of the file type when viewed. Gopher space can also be hyperlinked from one site to another so that you can navigate to related sites, files, or topics. Also, Gopher maintains a worldwide listing of content so that Gopherspace can be searched for content. Gopher, while popular, has been eclipsed by the activity on the World Wide Web.

◆ **HTTP.** The HyperText Transfer Protocol is a specification for transferring data in the HyperText Markup Language. HTML files can contain pointers or links to other HTML files at different addresses, or to image files, animation, sound, video, and so forth. When you view HTML files in a web browser it uses the pointers or links to compose pages that show those images. HTTP is the protocol of the World Wide Web, which forms a hypertext system of documents on servers worldwide.

If you examine the Internet Service Manager, the administrative tool that comes with IIS, you see each of these three services running on NT Server. These services also appear in the Services control panel. Figure 26.3 shows you the IIS with these services running.

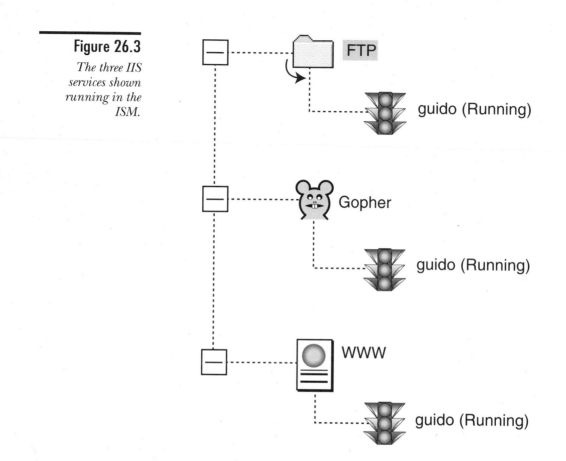

Figure 26.3

The three IIS services shown running in the ISM.

FTP

guido (Running)

Gopher

guido (Running)

WWW

guido (Running)

Additionally, Open Data Base Connectivity (ODBC) drivers can be installed with IIS to log web traffic to SQL Server files. IIS can therefore communicate with data sources to display web pages that are created "on demand." This database connection will become easier to use in future versions of BackOffice, as front-end tools are developed and introduced.

IIS functions either as an Internet or intranet service provider. You can configure IIS as a virtual server, so a single IIS server can appear to be multiple sites. Using this feature, you can host two or more domains on the same server, so a single server can appear to be several servers. Many Internet Service Providers (ISPs) rely on this feature to manage client domains on NT Server.

When you configure publishing services on IIS, you assign a default folder, and for web services, a default document. So if a reader navigates to your site, that folder and the default document are shown. IIS enables you to create virtual directories that let a site administrator or Webmaster distribute files across two or more volumes, either locally or remotely. What the reader sees is a virtual tree for any IIS request.

IIS has several features that make it one of the very best web server software solutions that you can adopt. First, IIS is a fast performer, because the software runs as a service of the operating system. IIS inherits all of the advantages that NT Server offers; that is, it can run on multiprocessor computers, it supports fault tolerance features such as disk mirroring and disk stripping with parity to protect your data, and it supports NT's security scheme (provided that you have installed IIS on an NTFS file system).

Microsoft views IIS as an extension of NT Server's file system, which is one of their justifications for distributing the web server software free, as part of the operating system. Whether you accept this logic, or just view this as Netscape busting, Microsoft does have this vision of web publishing for each and every server and client in a Microsoft enterprise. This vision applies equally well for both Internet web sites and publishing on an intranet.

You get IIS as part of NT Server, and you get Peer Web NT Workstation. (When you install the web page creation and site management tool, Microsoft FrontPage, on Windows 95, you get a much more limited web server, called the "Personal Web Server.") IIS essentially is the same software on NT Server as Peer Web on NT Workstation, but Server can manage a higher number of connections and is suitable for more active web sites. Peer Web service can only be used on an intranet.

Microsoft is building on IIS technology to offer a number of important extensions to the technology. For example, using a secure HTTP protocol, Microsoft is launching a version of IIS meant for commerce. A set of tools packaged with IIS for Internet Service Providers (ISPs), code named Normandy, has appeared to position NT Server as a complete solution for client Internet access, newsgroups, mail, and domain name services. IIS on Windows NT Server is rapidly becoming the most popular web server on the Internet, growing at a such a rate that it promises to overtake Unix boxes, which are the current market leader.

> **Note** For more detailed information on IIS, check out Chapter 28, "Internet Information Server."

Microsoft Mail and Exchange Server

Microsoft Mail was the first of the BackOffice applications to appear, and provided a message service with post office message stores, file transfers, forward and store capabilities, and directory synchronization. There are millions of Microsoft Mail clients installed worldwide today.

Microsoft Mail is not a true client/server application, because the mail transfer is accomplished by GUI client software and Message Transfer Agents (MTA). When introduced, Microsoft Mail was an efficient messaging service for small workgroups. As larger enterprises adopted mail, the lack of server software made it difficult to manage Mail installations.

In order to provide for more sophisticated messaging and groupware services, Microsoft introduced *Exchange Server*. Exchange was the result of a long development project called "Touchdown," the aim of which was to provide a client/server architecture for messaging. Exchange offers connectivity using X.400/X.500 messaging standards, and runs as a service on NT Server. There are organizations installing 100,000 or more Exchange clients using distributed Exchange servers. Exchange also is capable of integrating MS Mail clients, since both conform to the MAPI specification, with Exchange servicing Mail clients' messaging activities.

Exchange server enables you, not only to create post offices, but to create folders called information stores that Exchange clients can access. Information stores can be private or public. A public folder can be a container for both messages and files, and therefore takes on the characteristics of a bulletin board system. Access to these folders can be controlled based on user name and password.

Exchange also supports electronic forms and templates, a feature which enables an organization to create electronic forms (using Visual Basic as the forms builder) for both messaging and information submission and retrieval. Exchange can form the basis for an electronic document system that can be used for an organization's central business activities. Additionally, Exchange can manage an information tracking database, and has a scheduling component. Each Exchange client includes Schedule+ 7.0, allowing for group scheduling, contact management, and project management functions. Undoubtedly, Microsoft Outlook will replace Schedule+ in future versions of the software.

Because Exchange can be a distributed mail system, a database of X.500 objects is maintained. A directory that contains information on objects such as mail recipients, servers, folders, MTA configuration, and distribution lists is replicated between Exchange servers.

Exchange MTA has messaging components that enable it to connect to a wide variety of clients and services. Among the core messaging components are the following:

- Site connector
- Dynamic RAS connector
- Internet Mail connection
- Microsoft Mail connector
- X.400 connector

A connector is selected based on the recipient, entries in the Gateway Address Routing Table (GWART), and other defined preferences.

> **Note** For more detailed information on this subject, see Chapter 29, "Exchange Server."

SQL Server

Microsoft *SQL Server* is a relational database management system (RDBMS) that provides database services for client applications. Note that not only front-end databases such as Access or FoxPro, but also programs such as Microsoft Exchange, Systems Management Server (SMS), and the Microsoft Internet Information Server (IIS), each of which is a component of BackOffice in its own right, are all client applications. The logging of events to a SQL Server database is a major integration feature of BackOffice.

SQL Server is an outgrowth of a joint development project between Sybase and Microsoft based on Sybase SQL Server 10.x. In the several years now since Sybase and Microsoft stopped joint development, Microsoft has made numerous changes to SQL Server, including developing a different internal database engine that runs database processes as NT Server threads much more efficiently than Sybase's SQL Server does. Still, in many respects these products are similar.

SQL Server is a high-end relational database product with a full-featured programming language behind it. You can build and modify tables, select records, update data, and create new data using a standard variant of the Structured Query Language (SQL). The process of returning data is highly optimized for network traffic. For example, as a result set is fetched from the database, the first record or set of records are displayed while the remainder are collecting in the background. This gives the SQL Server client the appearance of participating in instantaneous transactions.

SQL Server is highly optimized for distributed computing in a client/server environment. The program enables you to store database files in one or more volumes with no restrictions that the database be local to the application running SQL Server. Additionally, SQL Server can be running as a distributed application on two or more computers, each accessing the same database file to process the same data request cooperatively. There are SQL Server installations with databases in the 100 GB range servicing thousands of users at a time.

By default, SQL Server inherits the domain properties of users and groups that are part of your security database. For example, administrators for your domain are automatically mapped to the system administrator in your SQL database. SQL Server also enables you to impose a different security scheme upon it, thus allowing a database administrator no additional privileges beyond their database ones. You can choose between the default and a custom security scheme when you first install SQL Server. Later on, you can use the SQL Security Manager to modify your security scheme.

A database stores data in a set of tables of related information. Tables are constructed around a common theme, or "object," the attributes of which form the columns or fields in that table. Each instance of the object is stored as a row in the table. For an example of table construction, consider a situation in which each purchase order is stored in a table with fields for PO#, date, and so forth. Database tables impose datatype restrictions on attributes of size and permissible data entry that make it easier to store uniform data, and help to organize data and perform calculations and other functions on them. As part of the table structure you can impose validation and autoentry rules for data entries into a field, and you can store rules for data entered into two or more fields. SQL Server will also store rules relating to records in related tables.

Each table can be related to a different table in the database, through either permanent or temporal relationships where the values in one column of a table can be matched to one or more values in another table. Through the use of these relationships, databases can provide information in many different ways. The design of the database is determined not only by the types of information that are to be stored in the system, but in the manner in which information is retrieved from the system.

For example, in a system storing purchase orders, it makes sense to store information common to each purchase described in a single file, and each line item information in a detail table. The relationship between the header file and the detail file is described as one-to-many (1:M), meaning that one or more records in the detail (child) table match the related value in the header (parent) table. SQL Server also supports one-to-one (1:1) and many-to-many (M:M) relationships, the latter being composed of three tables in a M:1:M relationship.

Underlying SQL Server and other RDBMS products is the logic of relational algebra, as devised by Codd and his associates in the late 1970s. RDMS allows you to store information in tables with little redundant information, and in a compact manner. The process of reducing data to its smallest representation is called *normalization*. When data storage is compact, data can be queried quickly and without expert knowledge of the details of how the database was constructed.

SQL Server 6.5 is the current version of this product, and was introduced as part of version 2.0 of BackOffice. A version 7.0 is slated for release in 1997.

When you install SQL Server, you typically define seven databases for use:

◆ **The master database.** Controls SQL Server database operations, checking user accounts, storage locations, stored procedures, configuration settings, and other system-wide settings.

◆ **The model database.** A template file for a user database.

◆ **The Tempdb database.** A temporary database used to write intermediate data sets to disk.

◆ **The msdb database.** Stores events managed by the scheduling utility of SQL Server, the SQL Executive. Things such as data replication, backups, alerts, event handling, history of performed tasks, and other automation is contained in this database.

◆ **The distribution database** (may take a different name). Created when you want to manage replication for a distributed database. This database stores transactions as they are being replicated in your system. If you aren't replicating a database, this database is not created.

◆ **The pubs database.** A sample database created for demonstration purposes. The documentation makes use of this database for training purposes.

◆ **The user-defined databases.** Contain tables that support different business applications.

SQL Server enables you to create up to 32,767 databases. You create databases, tables, objects, rules, and other features in the SQL Executive, which is the central management tool for SQL Server.

A very important feature of SQL Server is the logging of events and objects that BackOffice applications do to SQL Server databases. Besides NT Server, three important applications make use of SQL Server databases to manage their data:

◆ Event and activity files created by NT Server can be exported to SQL Server for analysis.

◆ SMS uses SQL Server tables to store an inventory of hardware and software contained in managed enterprises. This feature is described in the next section, and is required by SMS for SMS to operate.

◆ Exchange can accept data from SQL Server and publish it to a Public folder for access by connected users. This data can be presented in forms and views which not only display the data, but allow for querying the database based on stored procedures in SQL Server.

◆ The Internet Information Server can save its log files in SQL Server format for analysis of site traffic, and can manage data exported by SQL Server in HTML format.

SQL Server comes with a Web Assistant that can automatically create or modify web pages based on the data contained in your database. Using this tool you can control how often the output files in HTML format are updated. The scheduling feature offers you the following:

◆ Immediate update

◆ A later one-time update

◆ Regular updates on a particular day or so many times an hour

Using the Internet Database Connector, which is an ISAPI application, SQL Server can exchange data with web pages in response to a submitted request. IDC is a DLL (httpodbc.dll) that translates data requests via a web browser running the HTTP protocol. Data is returned from SQL Server in the form of an HTML document. IDC actually creates two different file types:

◆ **Internet Database Connector files (.idc).** Translates the data into a format used by SQL Server, and executes the SQL statement necessary to process them.

◆ **An HTML file (.htx).** The template for the HTML document that is returned by the database action to be viewed in the web browser.

As BackOffice continues to develop, SQL Server will undoubtedly play an increasingly important role in administering application transactions, maintaining system security, and providing network services.

> **Note** For more detailed information on this subject, check out Chapter 30, "SQL Server."

SNA Server

Mission-critical data is often stored on large host computers. For enterprises integrating BackOffice into existing information technology systems containing IBM mainframe and AS/400 minicomputers, Microsoft offers the *Microsoft SNA Server* to provide secure connectivity between those systems and desktop computers. SNA comes from the IBM standard Systems Network Architecture, specified to tie all of IBM's disparate computing platforms together. SNA Server provides the communications protocols necessary to send and receive data in an SNA environment, and runs as an application on Windows NT Server (as do other BackOffice components).

Any client that can connect to NT Server—that is, MS-DOS, Windows, Macintosh, and Unix—can use any one of NT's supported network protocols to connect to this legacy data. SNA Server connects to the mainframe or minicomputer using the SNA networking protocols (802.2, SDL X.25, DFT, Channel, or Twinax) and uses commands accessing the WOSA SNA API. SNA Server runs as a service on NT Server; version 3 can support 5,000 users and 15,000 host sessions through LAN or a variety of WAN connections.

SNA Server comes with ODBC drivers that enable it to access relational databases that reside on these legacy systems. Typically, users are interested in the data found in large distributed databases such as DB2 for MVS, SQL/DS for VM, and DBS/400 for the OS/400 operating system. File access is provided using the Advanced File Transfer Protocol. AFTP can transfer files from the host to an NT Server using SNA protocols. SNA, through its dial-up connectivity, enables a user to access host data from the Internet.

SNA arose out of a standard developed at IBM to tie together its different computer systems of all sizes. It has been adopted as an industry standard, and has been implemented as a method for data communication in heterogeneous computing environments. In an SNA network, a host system communicates with terminals. When PCs are the clients, terminal emulation is used for communication. Terminals and printers connect to cluster controllers, with communication controllers used to route network traffic. Terminals, printers, and the various controllers are referred to as *nodes* on the network.

An SNA Server connects through a controller to the mainframe or minicomputer. A user accessing the mainframe through SNA Server creates a session that is a network addressable unit.

In an SNA network, a Logical Unit (LU) is a session that either does batch transfers of data, emulates an IBM 3270 terminal or printer, provides interapplication communication, or emulates an IBM midrange computer session. Physical Units (PUs) are named communication links that SNA Server manages, with processing residing either in the cluster controller, the front-end processor, or in the host's communication software.

The SNA model uses two software modules to manage the resources of a network domain:

◆ **Systems Services Control Point (SSCP).** Runs on the host system and manages communications.

◆ **The Network Control Program (NCP).** Runs on the communications controller and manages network traffic and session management.

Two work architectures of SNA have been developed, one managed entirely by a single host system where subareas are assigned, and the other managed by a network of minicomputers called the Advanced Peer-to-Peer Networking (APPN) system. In subarea SNA, a hierarchy of network devices is established. The host is PU 5 and is unique. Front-end processors that manage connections are PU 4. Cluster controllers are PU 2, and connect to the various users and devices on the SNA network, which are LUs of various types.

When establishing SNA Server on an SNA network, this service acts as if it were a network gateway in the subarea SNA model. The gateway connects various LUs in the form of terminal and printer emulators on the PC LAN. Those PCs connect via standard LAN protocols supported by NT Server for its clients. SNA Server can also connect to the SNA network, emulating a cluster controller. SNA typically connects to a front-end processor and manages all of the LU devices connected to it.

When connected to a Peer-to-Peer SNA network, SNA Server still functions as a gateway device. It emulates a Low-Entry Network node.

SNA Server can be either a single-server service, or can be distributed as a group of servers across a network. When using multiple servers, the load may be balanced so that, should one server fail, there will still be host access through the other servers. Typically, host systems support many users, so it is rare to find single-server SNA Server systems. Although a small number of BackOffice installations install SNA Server, nearly all of the companies installing SNA Server do install several other components of BackOffice, as well.

The Admin utility of SNA Server is used to manage Servers and Connections, LU Pools, and Users and Groups. This utility can be run on either NT Server or Workstation to remotely configure an SNA Server. SNA Server can be remotely managed to provide the following functions:

◆ **Configuration setup.** Multiple configuration files can be managed, with one central SNA Server and replicated to backup servers, active at a time. In the case of an SNA Server failure, another SNA Server takes over.

◆ **LU and User configuration.** Users, groups, and sessions can be managed by the Admin utility, with services provided through the NT Server security scheme.

◆ **Remote Access Administration.** SNA Server can be accessed using the Remote Access Service (RAS), and administered through dial-up access.

◆ **Connection and link configuration.** Connections and links can be started, stopped, or removed; or started automatically at startup.

◆ **Link configuration.** SNA links can be installed or removed.

◆ **Troubleshooting.** SNA comes with a number of utilities to test and analyze network communication.

Typically, SNA Servers are placed in either a central location or in a branch location. A central location is typically closer to the host system, and provides better server performance, more secure communications, and better reliability. Branch locations are closer to users, and minimize network traffic over slower WAN lines. Many organizations install SNA Server in a distributed configuration with both a central SNA Server and a remote server to optimize their host as well as their user connections.

As Internet/intranet technology grows in popularity, many companies with IBM mainframe or AS/400 computers are installing TCP/IP networks in place of a hierarchical SNA network, or running both network protocols at the same time.

SNA Server can integrate with other components in the BackOffice suite to provide the following PC/host connectivity:

◆ **NT Server.** SNA Remote Access Service (RAS) can create a virtual WAN that links two NT Server networks together.

◆ **Mail and Exchange.** SNA RAS allows post offices to communicate with one another via SNA. Through third-party gateways SNA can link host e-mail and scheduling applications to Mail and Exchange servers.

◆ **SMS.** SNA RAS enables a network administrator to remotely control workstations and fully utilize all aspects of SMS.

◆ **SQL Server.** Through ODBC/DRDA, host data can be accessed in DB2, SQL/DS, and DB2/400 databases by SQL Server.

The Universal Installer

The "universal installer," which first appeared in BackOffice 2.0, theoretically speeds your installation of any or all BackOffice applications. BackOffice lets you click on a button for the application you want to install, whereby the Installer launches the setup program for that application.

If you would like to install two or more BackOffice applications, you will find yourself using the Setup programs for each of these applications one after the other. The universal installer does not install two or more BackOffice applications at the same time, so you will find that the Universal Installer is really just a minor convenience. One would expect that as the BackOffice suite continues to develop, someone will develop a truly integrated installer program.

With NT Server already installed on your system, you can run the Installer to set up SNA Server, SQL Server, Systems Management Server, Exchange Server, or the Internet Information Server. You can also use the Installer to run the NT Server installation again. You might do the operating system reinstallation to repair a corrupted system, or you may need to run the setup program to have NT Server add or remove components from your system.

To use the Installer program, follow the steps in the following exercise:

Using the Installer Program

1. Select the Run command from the Start menu, and run SETUP.EXE from the BackOffice CD.

   In Windows NT Server 4, a BackOffice folder in the Programs folder of the Start menu will appear.

2. If this is the first time you run the Installer, enter your name, company, and product serial number.

In its current form, the Installer does not transfer this information to the Setup programs of each BackOffice component.

3. Click on the check boxes next to the components of BackOffice that you want to install. Multiple components are installed consecutively.

4. Click on the OK button to initiate the installation of your selected component(s).

Typically, you will want to install each BackOffice component on a different computer, so that organizations dedicate one or more computers for each service. For smaller organizations and light network traffic, you can install two or more BackOffice components on a single machine. If you install two applications on a single server, be sure that the amount of memory on that server is sufficient to service both running applications. You can always move a service onto a dedicated computer at a later date.

Systems Management Server cannot be installed until SQL Server has been set up on your network and is running as a service. Although you can use the Installer to install two or more applications, you will find it easier to manage the installation of BackOffice components if you run the installations one at a time.

After you install a BackOffice component, you may be required to restart the computer on which you installed the service. You should note whether any error messages appear while that NT Server starts up. You may also see error messages appear after the log in. Many of the services enable you to configure NT Server so that they start up automatically. If they don't, you should start the installed application to see if any application errors are logged. Though this procedure might not be required in all cases, it is advisable to do so and will save you problems trying to figure out where the errors you are seeing arise from.

Pricing and Licensing

Microsoft makes each of the applications in the BackOffice suite available as stand-alone packages, but you can also buy all six applications together in a single box. There is no practical difference between purchasing BackOffice in these two different ways, but there is a major cost benefit to purchasing the suite if you want or need all the applications.

In early versions of BackOffice up to and including version 2.5, there was little additional information in the BackOffice package beyond documentation provided with each of the individual applications. Therefore, you get manuals for Mail, Exchange, SQL Server, and so on, but no integrated BackOffice manual. This situation is expected to change in the near future.

As with other Microsoft networked applications, BackOffice requires that you purchase both Client Access Licenses and Server Licenses. If you are installing three or more BackOffice server applications, a BackOffice Client Access License is a better value; it gives a desktop client access to a BackOffice application running on any server in your enterprise.

The BackOffice Server License applies to the installation of all BackOffice server components on a single server. Therefore, if you run three or more BackOffice applications on a single server, a Server License is a better value than Client Licenses. The BackOffice Server License is meant for small enterprises where a limited number of servers are in use.

Clearly, it is possible for your organization to start out small, with BackOffice Server Licenses, and then, as it adds additional servers, prefer to have BackOffice Client Licenses instead. There can also be borderline cases, or changes in the number of BackOffice applications deployed over time in your organization. Often the calculation of which licensing scheme is best is difficult to determine. Microsoft allows a one-time only conversion of Server Licenses into Client Licenses.

Table 26.1 lists typical prices for the server applications and client licenses in the BackOffice suite.

TABLE 26.1
Server and Client Licenses for BackOffice Applications

Application	Server License	Prices/# of Clients
BackOffice 2.0 Suite	$2,299	$3,799; 20-client pack
Windows NT Server 4	$649	$549; 20-client pack
SQL Server 6.5	$1,299	$2,299; 20-client pack
Exchange Server 4.0	$899	$25 Bundled with the Server License
Systems Management Server 1.2	$820	$819.95 for 5 licenses; add another 20-client pack for $849.95
Internet Information Server 1.0	$99 (free with NT 4)	Not applicable
SNA Server 3.0	$1,299	$1299.95 for five licenses; add another 20-client pack for $1995.00

The Microsoft Developer Program

In an effort to seed developers with BackOffice test beds for application development, Microsoft initiated a multitiered Microsoft Developer Network (MSDN) developer program. Of the programs in place, Level 3 of the Developer Program is specifically aimed at the companies or developers developing BackOffice solutions. The program provides license for five clients in a multiserver network environment.

At present, the Level 3 program's base cost is $1,295. If you sign up for an additional level of the program, you also receive Microsoft's Visual tools such as Visual C++ and Visual FoxPro. The version that comes with a copy of Microsoft Office 97 is priced at $1,695.

MSDN provides developers with programming information, software, driver toolkits, and quarterly BackOffice test platforms.

Table 26.2 lists the services provided to the three levels of MSDN membership. Note that Level 3 members are the only ones who get the BackOffice Test Platform with versions of the BackOffice server applications and the BackOffice SDK.

Table 26.2
MSDN Levels

MSDN Services	Level 1	Level 2	Level 3
Development Library (quarterly CD)	X	X	X
Developer Network News (bimonthly)	X	X	X
Two phone-support incidents	X	X	X
Microsoft Press discount	X	X	X
Access to online member forums	X	X	X
Development Platform (quarterly set of CDs)		X	X
Development Platform premium shipments		X	X
BackOffice Test Platform (quarterly set of CDs)			X

MSDN Services	Level 1	Level 2	Level 3
BackOffice Test Platform premium shipments			X
Two additional phone-support incidents			X

Those of us who are members of the Microsoft Level 3 program have been the recipient of a steady stream of developer CDs. The number of mailings (monthly), and their size and breadth has been impressive. Quarterly, you get the BackOffice Software Development Kit (SDK). The SDK lets C and C++ developers write products for BackOffice. The BackOffice SDK includes the Win32 SDK and SDKs for application in BackOffice. You also get the documentation for these SDKs and information on programming with them.

Mailings are monthly. Not only do you get copies of the operating systems, applications, and betas of applications, but you also get technical databases, documentation sets, foreign language versions, and many utility programs. The betas in the Level 3 program lag behind the betas released to the sites in the official beta programs by a month or two, but only users doing very active development work on a particular platform or application would notice this.

User Support

Microsoft provides priority technical support through a 24-hour 800 number for developers and end users alike. You get a couple of startup calls as part of your join-up fee for the developers program, and pay for additional support, if needed.

Any organization implementing BackOffice can purchase a support program at different support levels. The Comprehensive Service costs $3,995 per year and provides for up to 35 incidents a year. An incident is a problem that requires solution, no matter how many phone calls it takes. You can purchase additional incidents for $150 per incident. Comprehensive Service is appropriate for enterprises with internal support staff; it includes a server failure support with remote diagnostics, problem replication labs, and specified response times.

For large customers, Microsoft can provide a dedicated technical account manager. The Premier and Premier Global services provide a customer support plan, status reports, and reviews and analysis of the customer's information system technology. The Premier support service costs $25,000 per year and includes calls or services of up to 150 incidents per year.

For very large customers, the Premier Global account supports multinational corporations on an unlimited basis. This service costs $225,000 per year and includes 10 support contacts worldwide.

Testing Your Knowledge

1. Name at least three applications included with BackOffice Version 2.5.

2. What does the abbreviation WOSA stand for?

3. Three examples of WOSA communication services are:

   A. Windows sockets

   B. Remote procedure calls

   C. SNA API

   D. DHCP

4. Internet Information Server can utilize ODBC to communicate with SQL Server.

   A. True

   B. False

5. Currently, IIS can support which three Internet data transfer protocols?

   A. ActiveX

   B. FTP

   C. Gopher

   D. HTTP

6. Microsoft Mail provides a true client/server architecture for messaging.

   A. True

   B. False

7. Which of the listed SQL Server databases controls SQL Server database operations, user accounts, storage locations, stored procedures, configuration settings, and other system-wide settings?

   A. The model database

   B. The distribution database

   C. The user-defined database

   D. The master database

8. What BackOffice application provides enterprise integration with IBM mainframes and AS/400 minicomputers?

Review Answers

1. Internet Information Server, Exchange, SQL Server, System Management Server, SNA Server, Index Server, Proxy Server

2. Windows Open System Architecture

3. A, B, C

4. A

5. B, C, D

6. B

7. D

8. SNA Server (System Network Architecture)

CHAPTER 27

Systems Management Server

One of the largest software-related costs facing corporations today, often exceeding even the purchase of the software itself, are the costs incurred from installing and maintaining the broad range of software titles found in modern corporate computing environments. The majority of this work, being carried out manually by teams of overworked network administrators and support personnel, is tedious and time-consuming when you consider how large some of our modern corporations have become. Visiting each workstation and manually performing the necessary tasks has historically been how networked workstations and servers have kept their operating systems and software packages up-to-date.

Enter Microsoft Systems Management Server.

SMS is a robust and configurable solution that provides network support personnel with a method for centrally managing the hardware and software within their corporate networked environment. SMS can utilize the existing distributed network infrastructure to manage hardware and software for the company as a whole, including computers located across a WAN link. SMS currently is part of the Microsoft BackOffice suite and is designed to run on the Windows NT Server platform.

This chapter addresses the features, components, installation, and system flow of Systems Management Server. A familiarity with SMS terms and concepts is important in designing and troubleshooting an SMS system and in understanding how the SMS components relate to one another.

Systems Management Server Features

Using a hierarchical model (see fig. 27.1), based on a graded series of SMS sites, SMS offers the following features:

> **Note** This chapter takes an in-depth look at SMS installation, SMS services, NT Server changes, and the flow of data during several SMS processes. It is beyond the scope of this book to explain how each of the SMS features are used.

◆ **Hardware and software inventory collection and management.** SMS offers administrators methods for collecting and querying hardware and software configurations. Information is gathered at each site within the SMS infrastructure and forwarded up the site hierarchy until it reaches the Central site. Once gathered, this information can be queried, for example, to determine if the amount of hard disk space and RAM available on a particular client computer warrants an operating system upgrade for the workstation.

◆ **Software distribution and installation.** SMS Administrator can be used to create jobs that will install select software on clients and/or servers, distribute the package via a LAN or WAN link to the distribution servers, and share software that clients can run directly from the network servers.

> **Note** A *package* is an SMS object that tells the SMS system where the application software and configuration information files are located. A *job* is an SMS object that stores the instructions that the system is to perform; that is, to install a particular package onto a client computer. A job will deliver packages to the workstations or servers.

◆ **Network monitoring and troubleshooting.** SMS includes a powerful Network Diagnostic utility that gives the administrator the ability to capture and view network activity. With this tool, administrators can capture a stream of data from the network wire and use it to identify network traffic patterns and potential network problem spots.

◆ **Remote client control and troubleshooting.** SMS offers administrators diagnostic utilities and help desk utilities to remotely control and monitor supported SMS clients. Remote access can be individually controlled by the user of the remote client.

SMS Infrastructure

The SMS infrastructure is based on a hierarchical model composed of sites, domains, servers, and clients. Figure 27.1 illustrates a high-level overview of a typical SMS environment.

When designing your SMS system you can choose to use a single site setup or a multiple, hierarchical, site setup.

At the top of the hierarchy resides the central site. The central site is the main site in an SMS system. Parent sites and child sites, residing below the central site, eventually report their information up the hierarchy to the central site's site database. Under the central site, there could be multiple primary or secondary sites in the site hierarchy.

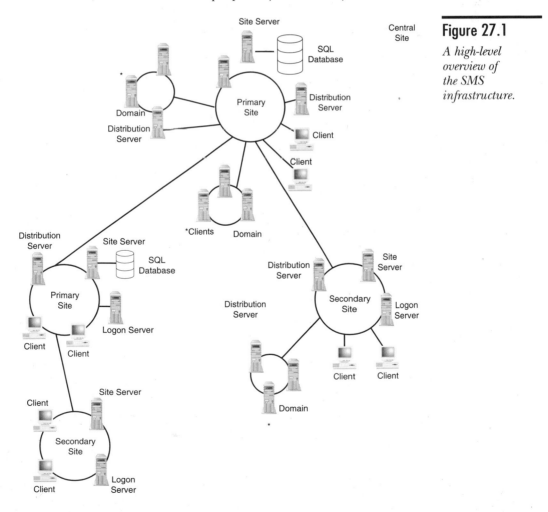

Figure 27.1

A high-level overview of the SMS infrastructure.

SMS Sites and Components

This section defines a site, then describes the different types of sites in an SMS system and the types of components that can be found in each site.

An *SMS site* is simply a collection of domains managed by a site server. The domains within each site are comprised of servers and workstations that have been grouped together to enable the administrator to manage them as a single entity. More on domains in the following section, "SMS Domains."

- **Central site.** The topmost primary site in the SMS hierarchy, the central site is the controlling entity for all subsites (child sites) beneath it, and is where all subsites report their inventory and events.

- **Child site.** Any primary or secondary site that was created by a primary site, or that has a parent site preceding it in the site hierarchy.

- **Parent site.** A site that has a primary or secondary site directly beneath it in the site hierarchy.

- **Primary site.** A site that has its own SQL Server database that stores the pertinent information for the site itself and all of the sites that fall below it in the SMS hierarchy. A primary site also has all of the site administration tools.

- **Secondary site.** A site that does not have its own SQL database, and forwards all site information to its parent site. Because a secondary site lacks any of the site administration tools, it depends on its parent or primary site for site administration.

Next, you are introduced to the individual components that form an SMS site. The following sections describe the types of domains, clients, services, and servers you are likely to find in an SMS site.

SMS Site Components

Each site in an SMS system shares common components. These components allow for software distribution, inventory collection, remote diagnostics, and Windows-based application management, a majority of which are shown in figure 27.1. First, let's define some terms and then we will take a much closer look at each component.

- **Services.** SMS services monitor the directories, system files, and databases for all domains within a site. By default, all SMS services are installed on the Site server. These services allow SMS to manage sites and communicate with other sites.

- **Server.** The SMS system includes four types of servers: site servers, logon servers, distribution servers, and helper servers.

◆ **Domain.** A set of servers and clients logically grouped to provide an organized approach to administering logon validation and inventory collection.

◆ **Client.** A client is any computer that has had the SMS software installed on it and is being managed by SMS. Clients are included in the SMS inventory process and are the receiving point for distributed software. Clients are addressed in greater detail in the section "Client Preparation."

◆ **Site.** An object representing a logical grouping of domains into a manageable administrative unit. There are two types of sites, primary and secondary. A primary site always serves as the central site.

SMS Services

Systems Management Server utilizes nine services in total: Inventory Agent (one service for both NT and LAN Manager), Package Command Manager for Windows NT, SMS Executive, Site Hierarchy Manager, Site Configuration Manager, Bootstrap, SNA Receiver, Client Configuration Manager, and the SNMP Trap Receiver.

The following section defines each service and discusses the role of each within SMS as well as each service's relationship to each other.

Inventory Agent

The Inventory Agent is the SMS component that creates and collects hardware and software information and reports the inventory to the SMS system. It performs inventory on servers running NT Server or LAN Manager (Inventory Agent for NT or Inventory Agent for OS/2). On clients, the inventory agent is launched from the logon servers from within the SMSLS batch file. The service runs by default every 1,440 minutes (24 hours).

> **Note** | NetWare logon servers have their inventory scanned by the Maintenance Manager. The Maintenance Manager logs in to the NetWare server and runs the INVDOS.EXE utility.

Package Command Manager for Windows NT

The Package Command Manager for Windows NT is an SMS component that is installed on all Logon Servers in the SMS infrastructure. It runs as an NT service and allows packages to be installed on machines running NT with little or no intervention from the user. Package Command Manager for Windows NT can also be used to install a package on an NT-based machine that is currently unattended.

SMS Executive

The SMS Executive service is an extremely important service, in that it acts as a management agent to determine which services to start on SMS site, logon, and helper servers. The SMS Executive reads the server's NT Registry to determine which services are required to be started on each particular server. These services (10 total) are:

◆ **Maintenance Manager.** Installed on each primary and secondary site server, the Maintenance Manager is responsible for installing and maintaining SMS client pieces on the site's logon servers. The Maintenance Manager replicates the required client configuration information to the logon servers and collects inventory information from them.

◆ **Inventory Processor.** Installed on each primary and secondary site server, the Inventory Processor creates, manages, and collects MIF files (Management Information Files) received from the various inventory agents. It creates a history file (a simple copy of the last RAW file received) that is used to compare existing data with new MIF files (or raw binary inventory information) as they are received from the inventory agents. If the information proves to indeed be new, only the differences are written to a Binary MIF known as a Delta MIF file, and are sent to the Inventory Data Loader.

◆ **Scheduler.** The Scheduler is the only component (actually a thread) that actively looks for pending jobs, and, when it finds them, schedules them for processing. It is responsible for compressing software before distribution and building the information files that go along with the compressed software packages. The Scheduler exists on each primary and secondary site.

◆ **Trap Filter.** Simply put, the Trap Filter filters Simple Network Management Protocol (SNMP) traps received from SNMP-managed devices, and either writes them to the database or drops them, depending on the conditions you have set. To minimize the hits to the database, Traps are dropped if they exceed a predetermined size (set to a maximum of the first 25 varbinds of the trap, with the varbinds also being limited in size).

> **Note** The term *varbind* is a SNMP Management Information Base (MIB) term that is a marriage of the terms "variable" and "binding." The term *variable* refers to a single instance of a managed device. Therefore, variable binding, or varbind, refers to the combination of the variables value with the name of the variable itself.

◆ **Site Reporter.** The Site Reporter exists in both primary and secondary sites (child sites) and is responsible for managing a queue of Delta MIFs that need to be reported to the parent site. The Site Reporter is responsible for creating a system job to transfer the MIFs on to the parent site.

◆ **Despooler.** The Despooler monitors the SITE.SRV\DESPOOLER\RECEIVE directory for compressed packages and information files built by the Scheduler. Using the instructions in the information file, the Despooler decompresses the software package files and manages their distribution.

◆ **Senders.** Senders are SMS components that actually move the data from one site to another. There are six types of SMS senders: one LAN Sender, two SNA Senders (interactive and batch), and three RAS Senders (X.25, Async, and ISDN). SMS Senders exist in both primary and secondary site servers and can be moved to a helper server to reduce the processing load on the site server.

◆ **Inventory Data Loader.** The Inventory Data Loader is a multithreaded process that uses information received from Delta MIFs to write changes to the SMS database. The change information is sent up from the Inventory Processor to the SITE.SRV\DATALOAD.BOX\DELTAMIF.COL\PROCESS subdirectory to be processed. Once processed, the Delta MIFs are placed in the Site Reporter outbox (SITE.SRV\SITEREP.BOX) to be sent to their parent site (if one exists).

◆ **Applications Manager.** The Applications Manager is responsible for monitoring the SMS site database for changes to packages, as well as for program group configuration information. If any changes are detected, the Applications Manager updates the information in the Program Control Group database for the site, and builds a system job to replicate the new information to its subsites.

◆ **Alerter.** The Alerter component exists only on primary sites; it processes alerts that have been triggered by a predetermined condition coming true.

Hierarchy Manager

The Hierarchy Manager exists only on primary sites, and monitors its site's database for configuration changes. When a change is detected, either within its own site or any of its subsites, the Hierarchy Manager creates a file called a site control file. The *site control file* contains all of the configuration information, current or proposed, for a site. These files are simple ASCII text and are used internally by SMS to report changes to the site database. There are three types of site control files:

◆ **sitectrl.ct0.** Resides in the SMS\Site.srv\Sitecfg.box directory. Contains a backup of the most recent site configuration. Also known as the *master site control file.*

◆ ***.ct1.** Temporary file that carries the proposed configuration changes from the Hierarchy Manager to the Site Configuration Manager. The Hierarchy Manager receives the proposed changes from either SMS Setup or the SMS Administrator.

◆ ***.ct2.** Temporary file sent from the Site Configuration Manager to the Hierarchy Manager, reporting the completion of the site configuration changes. Also known as a *site control response file.*

Figure 27.2 shows the flow of the files.

Figure 27.2

Flow of site control files.

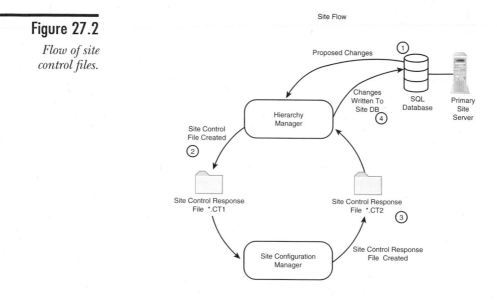

Site Configuration Manager

The Site Configuration Manager exists on both primary and secondary sites and is responsible for the installation and reconfiguration of sites, using information received from the Hierarchy Manager (site control file). The Site Configuration Manager is a service that starts when the site server is brought up; it is responsible for starting and monitoring all other SMS services on the site server and the logon servers.

You can adjust how often the Site Configuration Manager monitors the different pieces of the site by using the Windows NT Registry Editor to edit the Registry. The Registry key where the values are located is:

```
HKEY_LOCAL_MACHINE\SOFTWARE\Microsoft\SMS\Components\SMS_SITE_CONFIG_MANAGER
```

The values available for editing are:

◆ **Watchdogging Interval.** Default setting is 120 minutes. This setting controls how often the Site Configuration Manager checks for the availability of services or components, checks for new logon servers, and checks whether the other recording intervals are working.

◆ **Site Configuration Reporting Interval.** Default setting is 1,440 minutes (24 hours). This setting controls when the Site Configuration Manager creates a new site control file to report its current configuration. This interval is checked only at the next watchdog cycle and at the processing of a site control file.

◆ **Restart After Shutdown Delay.** Controls how long the Site Configuration Manager waits before starting SMS services once the Site server has been restarted. Default delay time is 5 minutes.

◆ **User Group Reporting Interval.** Default setting is 1,440 minutes. This setting controls how often the Site Configuration Manager gathers lists of all SMS user groups within a site. This information is written in the form of a management information format (MIF) file, and is used to report user groups to the site database. This interval is checked only at the next watchdog cycle or at the processing of a site control file.

◆ **Logon Script Configuration Interval.** Default setting is 1,440 minutes. This setting controls how often the Site Configuration Manager checks the logon script configuration for all of the domains within the site. This interval is checked only at the next watchdog cycle or at the processing of a site control file.

Bootstrap

The Bootstrap service is used to set up the Site server for a secondary site. Once the Hierarchy Manager at the primary site recognizes the request to install a secondary site, it sends a job to the new site to install the SMS installation directory and to start the bootstrap service in that directory on the secondary site server.

Once these tasks are complete, a package containing the necessary site components is built and sent to the new site. Once the package is received, the bootstrap service then executes the following steps:

1. The package is first decompressed.

2. The site directory structure is created, and components are placed in the appropriate directories on the site server.

3. Once the bootstrap detects the site control file sent by the primary site, the Site Configuration Manager is started, and the bootstrap service is removed.

SNA Receiver

Simply put, the SNA Receiver processes, at a remote site, data and instructions sent by an SNA Sender. After an SNA Sender (part of the SMS Executive service) is installed, the SNA Receiver is installed and activated by the Site Configuration Manager. The SNA Senders and Receivers are used in existing SNA environments and utilize

Microsoft SNA Servers Advanced Program to Program Communication (APPC) to communicate between sites.

Client Configuration Manager

The Client Configuration Manager is used by SMS Client Setup to make changes to computers running Windows NT when special access is required. The Client Configuration Manager utilizes the SMS service account to install the following SMS components:

- ◆ SNMP Event to Trap Translator
- ◆ SMS Client Inventory Service
- ◆ SMS Remote Control Agent

SNMP Trap Receiver

The SMS SNMP Trap Receiver enables SMS to capture, store, and view SNMP traps to the site database.

SMS Servers

The servers within an SMS system are responsible for the collection, distribution, and flow of information within an SMS infrastructure. When an SMS system is installed, Windows NT servers are utilized in different roles within an SMS site. One server within the site is designated as the site server which, if the site is small enough, may contain all of the SMS server components (that is, logon and distribution servers). If the site were quite large, you could have each server component running on its own NT server.

- ◆ **Site server.** A computer that contains all of the SMS service files and components required to manage the site. The site server must be a domain controller running NT Server 3.51 (with Service Pack 3 or later) or NT Server 4. Each site within the SMS Infrastructure must have a site server.

- ◆ **Logon server.** Any server within an SMS site that can validate a users' account information. There are no active components running on the logon servers, because they are mainly used for login authentication and as a gathering point for collected inventory information. Logon servers are the source for client installation code; they can be computers running NT Server 3.5 or higher, configured as domain controllers, LAN Manager 2.2 and LAN Server 3.x or 4.x domain controllers, or NetWare 3.x or 4.x servers (4.x servers in 3.x compatibility mode).

◆ **Distribution server.** Servers within an SMS site where files and applications, destined for client use, are sent and stored. From here, the clients can install the software to their local hard drive or run the software directly from the server as shared applications. Distribution servers can be computers running NT Workstation or Server 3.5 or later, LAN Manager or LAN Server servers, or NetWare servers.

◆ **Helper server.** Logon servers running NT 3.51 with Service Pack 3 or NT 4 as domain controllers. Helper Servers are rarely used. In a large SMS site, Helper servers can offload some of the site server's services, such as Scheduler, Despooler, and Inventory Data Loader. They can also be utilized to run a second instance of a sender to increase file transfer performance between sites.

SMS Domains

When you first install an SMS system you create a central site and a single SMS domain, known as the *site domain*. The site domain initially includes the first server that SMS was installed to. New domains added to the site must be on the same LAN as the site's site server.

Since a domain is a logical grouping of machines residing on the same LAN, you can create your SMS domains to match your administrative structure. For example, you could add existing Windows NT, LAN Manager, and IBM LAN Server domains to a site, create an SMS domain for your NetWare servers, and create an SMS domain for your clients. Depending on the size of your environment, you could even group your clients into individual SMS domains representing, for example, your sales department and your human resources department.

SMS Installation

Before you begin installing SMS, you need to spend some time to plan the type of site structure that is best suited to your current networked environment. Remember to plan ahead and include growth factors that will affect the overall design of your SMS site structure.

The design of your SMS system depends on how you set up your sites and which domains you choose to include in each site. Will you design one large site that contains all computers in your organization, or will you take a hierarchical approach and divide your domains among multiple sites? Your site structure can be designed to include your existing organizational requirements.

The installation process follows these general steps in the following exercise:

Installing SMS

1. Prepare the site server. Verify that the selected server meets all of the system requirements for an SMS site server.

2. Prepare the SQL server, which is required to hold the site database (primary site only). Verify that the selected server meets all of the system requirements for an SQL server.

3. Prepare the clients that will take part in the SMS site structure. Verify that the clients meet the client requirements.

4. Set up the SMS service account.

5. Establish time synchronization.

6. Install the site.

The following sections take a look at these steps in more detail.

Prepare the Site Server

The site server is the computer that is running the components and services needed to manage a site, and it must meet the following requirements:

◆ The computer it is being installed on must be on the NT 3.51 or 4 hardware compatibility list.

◆ It must have a 486/66 microprocessor.

◆ It must have 32 MB of RAM minimum if the computer is not running SQL server. If the computer is running SQL server, a minimum of 48 MB RAM is recommended.

◆ It must have a minimum of 100 MB of hard disk space is required for installation.

| Tip | These numbers should be considered the bare minimum. It is highly recommended you use a Pentium-based computer with as much RAM as your budget allows. I would also recommend at least 1 GB of disk space. |

Prepare the SQL Server

The next step in preparing for a site installation is to prepare the Microsoft SQL server. Although you can install the site server on the same server that is running SQL server, doing so is not recommended. The resources required to run SQL server usually place it on a dedicated NT server. The following list describes two steps that need to be accomplished on the SQL server prior to SMS installation.

◆ **SQL Server account creation.** SMS database creation and maintenance requires an account on the SQL server with Create Database, Dump Database, and Dump Transaction permissions on the master database. The SMS administrator utility is a SQL server client application, and will use this account to access the SMS database. The default sa account may also be used.

> **Tip**   Microsoft SQL server can be configured to use Integrated or Mixed security, which allows the user with a valid NT user account, who has been granted access to the SQL server, to log on to SQL server without supplying a user ID or password. See your SQL server documentation for further information.

◆ **Site database device and transaction log device creation.** The Site database device and Transaction log devices are required and must exist on separate devices. If the SQL server and site server are on the same physical computer, SMS setup will create the devices automatically. If they are not, these devices must be created before SMS installation begins. The administrator of the SQL server will use the SQL Enterprise Manager to create the required database devices.

> **Caution**   Existing SQL server devices may be used for the SMS database and log devices. Note that any databases in the existing devices will be deleted and the space within the device used for the new SMS database.

You need to remember some SQL Server parameters when setting up the SMS database. They can greatly affect the performance of SMS. Table 27.1 lists and explains these parameters.

TABLE 27.1
SQL Server Parameters

Parameter	Information to Properly Set Up Your SQL Server
Database and Transaction log device size	It is recommended that you allow 20 to 35 KB per computer in the SMS database for data. The transaction log device size should be at least 10 percent of the data size.
Temporary Database (tempdb) Size	The tempdb data device should be at least 20 percent of the site database device size.
Memory	The default size SQL Server allocates is 4,096 2 KB units (8 MB).
Open Objects	500 is default. This needs to be increased for very large sites. The number of open objects determines how many stored procedures, tables, and views can be opened simultaneously. 5,000 or greater is recommended.
User Connections	This is the maximum number of simultaneous user connections allowed on the SQL Server. A minimum of 20 connections is required during installation. Ten connections are recommended. Note that each connection takes up about 40 KB of memory, regardless of whether the connection is used.

SMS uses the SQL server's time to schedule tasks. It is very important to synchronize the time on the SQL server with the time on the site server.

Client Preparation

The next preinstallation step is to determine your client machine's capacity to run the SMS client software and to verify each client is supported under SMS. SMS will install between 1 MB and 4 MB of data to the client machines, depending on the client software running on the machine.

Because SMS supports such a wide variety of clients (MS-DOS, Windows 3.x, Windows for Workgroups 3.11, Windows 95, Windows NT 3.51 and up, OS/2 2.11, OS/2 Warp, and Macintosh System 7.x), it is a pretty safe bet that the majority of machines in your environment can be SMS clients. When preparing clients for SMS installation, follow these rules:

1. Make sure your clients are using one of these operating systems:

    ◆ Microsoft DOS version 3.3 or later

    ◆ Microsoft Windows version 3.1x

    ◆ Microsoft Windows for Workgroups version 3.11

    ◆ Microsoft Windows 95

    ◆ Microsoft Windows NT version 3.5x or later

    ◆ IBM OS/2 version 2.1x

    ◆ IBM OS/2 Warp

    ◆ Macintosh System 7.x

2. Make sure that the client's time is synchronized with that of the site server in the domain where the client is to be installed. Different clients have different methods for synchronizing time. Refer to your operating system manuals for the proper commands.

Create the SMS Service Account

The next preinstallation step is to create an SMS service account. The SMS service account is simply a user account used by the SMS services and clients to provide access to the servers in the site. The SMS service account must have administrator privileges and the Log On As A Service advanced user right. The service account must be a valid user account on all servers that interact with SMS, including the SQL server. You can choose between a Local Domain Account or a Trusted Domain Account for the SMS service account.

To create a Local Domain service, perform the steps in the following exercise:

Creating a Local Domain Service

1. Create a user account for the SMS service account in the NT domain where you are going to install the SMS system.

2. Add the newly created user account to the Administrators local group or to a global group that is a member of the Administrators local group.

3. Grant the user account the Log On As A Service advanced user right by following these steps:

    1. Click on **P**olicies, and then click on **U**ser Rights.

    2. Select the **S**how Advanced User Rights check box.

3. Click Log on as a service in the Right drop-down box, then click on Add.

4. Click on Show Users to display all users. Then, in the name box, select your newly created user account, and click on Add.

5. The SMS service account appears in the Add Names box. Click on OK.

6. The SMS service account appears in the Grant To box of the User Rights Policy dialog box. Click on OK to return to the User Manager for Domains window.

To create a Trusted Domain service perform the steps in the following exercise:

Creating a Trusted Domain Service

1. Make sure you have established a trust relationship between the NT domain that will hold the SMS service account and the NT domain that will trust the domain holding the SMS service account.

2. Create the SMS service account on the trusted domain.

3. Add the SMS service account to the Administrators local group on the trusted domain.

4. Grant the Logon as a service advanced user right to the trusted SMS service account on the trusted domain.

For more information on accomplishing each of the preceding steps, refer to your Windows NT Server documentation.

Caution If your environment uses LAN Manager 2.x servers as part of a Windows NT domain, you must use the domain user account setup procedures for setting up the local domain account. LAN Manager 2.x servers do not recognize local NT accounts, only global NT accounts.

In order to install SMS components on NetWare servers, you must create a user account with a user name and password that matches that of the SMS Service Account. This account must have SUPERVISOR/Admin privileges and must have all access permissions to all of the NetWare volumes.

Establish Time Synchronization

SMS uses date and time stamps for all of its scheduling and reporting functions. The computers running the SMS components must have time synchronization established for successful job scheduling, inventory information, and system status reporting.

Use a command such as the following one to synchronize time:

At the prompt, type **net time** *computername*/**set**/**y** to synchronize the time with a specific server, or type **net time**/**domain:** *domainname*/**set**/**yes** to synchronize the time with the Primary Domain Controller in the domain.

Install the Site

The first site installed in a new SMS system is a primary site that initially serves as a stand-alone central site. This is the site to which all the other sites in the SMS hierarchy report their inventory and events. Remember the reporting flow within an SMS system: The child sites report their inventory to their parent sites, which then report their inventory as well as their child sites' inventory to their parent sites, and on and on until all of this information reaches the central site. After the central site is in place, you can use the SMS Administrator program to tie the site to any existing SMS systems or begin to create a new SMS system.

Note The SMS setup program is used to install a primary site, and the SMS Administrator is used to install a secondary site.

To begin a site installation perform the steps in the following exercise:

Site Installation

1. Insert the SMS CD-ROM into the CD-ROM drive.

2. Change to the Smssetup directory, then change to the directory matching the type of processor in the site server (MIPS, x86, Alpha).

3. Type **setup.exe** and include any optional switches.

4. The Systems Management Server Setup window appears with available options. Click on **S**et up SMS 1.x.

5. The Systems Management Server Setup dialog box appears next (see fig. 27.3). Click on **C**ontinue.

6. If you do not have a previous version of SMS installed, the Registration dialog box appears. Enter your registration information and click on **C**ontinue.

7. The Registration dialog box appears again. Verify the information that you typed is correct and click on **C**ontinue. If you need to make any changes, click on the Ch**a**nge button.

8. Click on **I**nstall Primary Site in the Installation Options dialog box (see fig. 27.4).

9. Read the licensing information displayed and select the I agree that check box and click on **O**K.

Figure 27.3

*The Systems
Management
Server Setup
dialog box.*

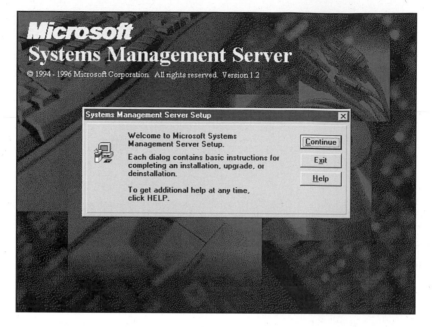

Figure 27.4

*The Installation
Options dia-
log box.*

10. Next you will see a Systems Management Server Setup Prerequisites message. Read through this information about preparing for an SMS installation.

11. The Installation Directory dialog box appears. By default, the setup utility will install the SMS directory at the root of the NTFS drive that has the most available

space. To select another location, type in the full path to an NTFS partition that has at least 100 MB available disk space.

12. The Setup Install Options dialog box appears, showing the options that will be installed by default (see fig. 27.5).

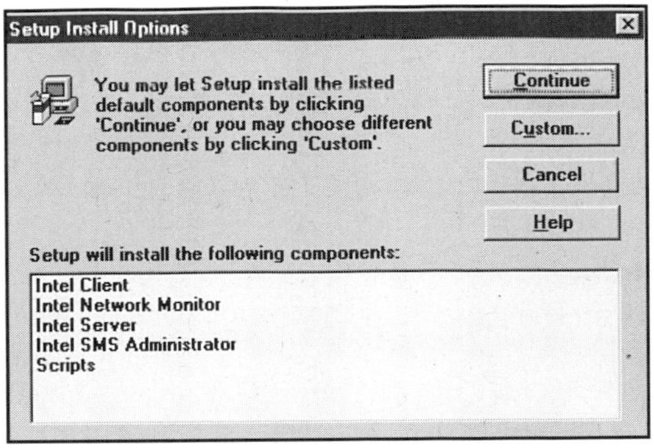

Figure 27.5

The Setup Install Options dialog box.

13. Choose **C**ontinue to accept the default options, or click on C**u**stom to choose additional components. If custom is selected, you will see a dialog box like the one shown in figure 27.6.

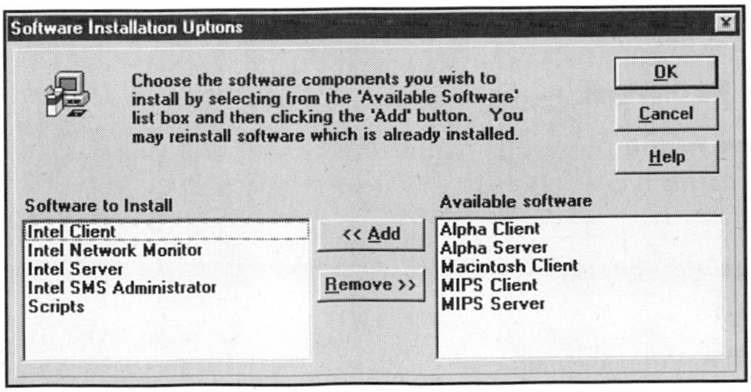

Figure 27.6

The Software Installation Options dialog box.

After you make your choices, click on **O**K. The Setup Install Options dialog box appears with your new choices. Verify that these choices are correct, and then click on **C**ontinue.

14. The SQL Database Configuration dialog box appears (see fig. 27.7).

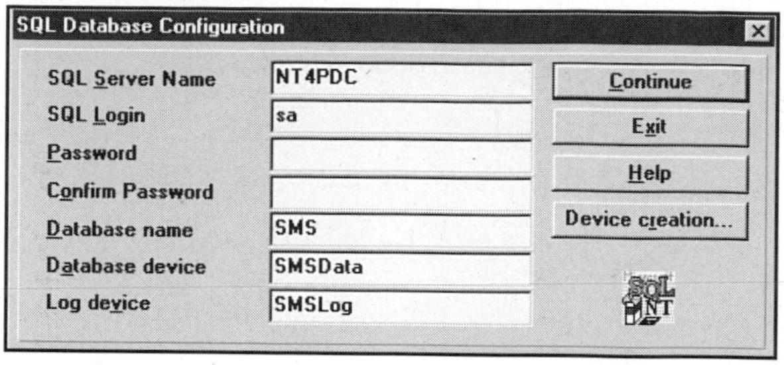

Figure 27.7

The SQL Database Configuration dialog box.

The following list describes each option and required responses in the SQL Database Configuration dialog box.

◆ **SQL Server Name.** Enter the name of the SQL Server where you want to place the SMS site database. If the SQL Server and the Site server are on the same computer, you can choose Device creation to have the setup utility create the devices for the database and transaction log automatically.

◆ **SQL Login.** Enter the account name of the SQL Server administrator, or else the name of an account that has Create Database, Dump Database, and Dump Transaction permissions on the master database. This account is used by SMS services that access the SMS site database.

◆ **Password.** Enter the password for the SMS Login ID you specified in the previous box.

◆ **Confirm Password.** Retype the password for verification.

◆ **Database name.** Enter the name of the site database (usually SMS). If you are creating a new database, you must follow the SQL Server identifier rules.

◆ **Database device.** Enter the name of the device that is to store the SMS site database.

◆ **Log device.** Enter the name of the device that is to store the SMS site database transaction log. The database and the transaction log must exist on separate devices.

15. Choose **C**ontinue. The Primary Site Configuration Information dialog box appears (see fig. 27.8).

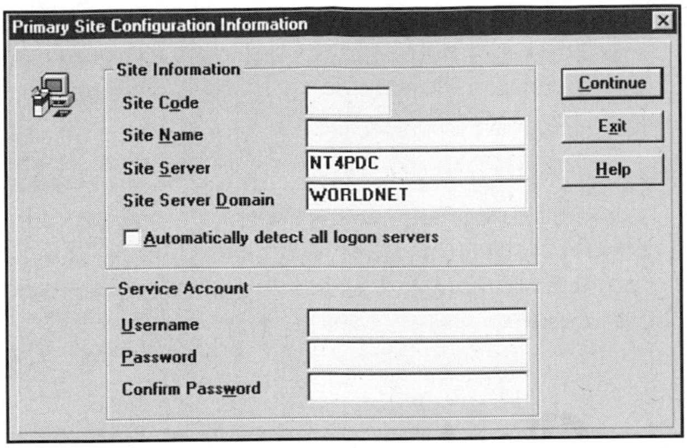

Figure 27.8

The Primary Site Configuration Information dialog box.

◆ **Site Code.** This three-character code is the unique name that identifies this site within the SMS hierarchy and is used for site-to-site communication.

◆ **Site Name.** This is the name that will appear in the Sites window of the SMS Administrator program.

◆ **Site Server.** This is the name of the current server.

◆ **Site Server Domain.** Enter the name of the domain where the NT server resides.

◆ **Automatically detect all logon servers.** Select this box to have the setup program detect all logon servers in the site domain. Once detected, the logon servers are added to the site database, and SMS components are installed on them. If this check box is not selected, you must manually add the logon servers after the installation process has completed.

◆ **Username.** Enter the SMS service account user name. As you may recall, the steps to create the service account are discussed earlier in the chapter.

◆ Enter the password for the SMS service account.

◆ Retype the SMS service account password for verification.

16. Click on **C**ontinue.

17. Next you are shown a progress dialog box. When all processes are complete, Setup launches the Hierarchy Manager and Site Configuration Manager services, and makes changes to the NT registry. Site Configuration Manager also starts Inventory Agent, Package Command Manager for Windows NT, and SMS Executive.

18. The SMS group and icons are created and installation is complete.

Remember that throughout most of the installation process, the setup program is verifying that you have enough disk space to install the selected components. If less than 100 MB is detected during setup, a warning box will appear telling you that you have insufficient disk space.

Also note that if you did not set the SQL Server Maximum User Connections to a number greater than 20, a dialog box will appear stating `Not Enough SQL Connections are available for correct execution of Systems Management Server`. Luckily, the folks at Microsoft saw this problem coming and added an option to, at this point, bump up the number of connections.

Adding a New Client

After a site is properly installed and configured, the next step is to add clients. The SMS Client Setup program (for Windows NT, it is CLI_NT.EXE; for MS-DOS, MS Windows, MS Windows for Workgroups or Win95, it is CLI_DOS.exe; for OS/2, it is CLI_OS2.exe) is launched from within the SMSLS and RUNSMS batch files after the client operating system has been determined. SMSLS is the batch file used to automatically run the Client Setup and Inventory Agent programs. Because SMSLS is configured to run from the login script, it will run each time the user logs on to the domain (NT or LAN Manager). Runsms is the manual version of SMSLS; it requires the user to connect to SMS_SHR on an SMS Logon server and manually run the batch file. If Runsms is used, the client is added to the SMS domain where the logon server that is supplying the batch file resides.

There are three options available when adding a new client to an SMS system:

◆ Use the Automatically Configure Workstation Logon Scripts option to have the Smsls.bat file run each time the user logs onto the network. This option will modify the logon scripts on all logon servers in the domain and add the Smsls.bat file. NetWare servers in the NetWare domains will have their system login scripts modified to run the Client Setup and the Inventory Agent programs.

◆ Add the Smsls.bat file manually to the user's logon scripts. NetWare servers in the NetWare domains can have their system login scripts modified to run the Smsls.scr script.

◆ Connect to *logonservername*\SMS_SHR, where *logonservername* is the name of a logon server residing within the domain where the client will be installed. Run the Runsms batch file—your two choices are Runsms.bat (DOS, Windows) and Runsms.cmd (OS/2)—to add the client to the SMS system and run an inventory scan.

Server Changes

When a site is first established, changes are made to the site server and the logon servers in several different ways. These changes are performed by the SMS installation process and vary depending on the type of server being installed. The next few sections discuss the changes that take place to the site and logon servers during the SMS installation process.

Note For those readers who are technically squeamish—Run! Flee! Scamper! These next few pages of information have been clinically proven to cause drowsiness and sometimes drooling on the part of the reader. Please use this information as a reference point and as an aid in troubleshooting your SMS environment.

The Registry

The NT Registry on each server in an SMS environment is modified to reflect its role within the SMS system. The Registry is automatically modified by the installation process and the modifications made are reflected in the following list.

Most of the SMS configuration information is placed in two locations within the NT Registry:

◆ **HKEY_LOCAL_MACHINE\System\CurrentControlSet\Services.** The information on which SMS services are installed and how they are configured for startup is placed here. This information is stored and managed by the NT Service Control Manager.

◆ **HKEY_LOCAL_MACHINE\Software\Microsoft\SMS.** This information, maintained and managed by SMS, is what controls the configuration information for the site and the services that are installed at the site.

Site Server Shares

Three shares are created by the Site Configuration Manager during the SMS installation process:

◆ **SMS_SITE.** Represents the SMS\Site.srv\Despooler.box\Receive directory and exists only on site servers. This share is used by the Bootstrap, Despooler, and Sender components. The SMS_SITE share is what a remote site connects to when transmitting packages and data to the local site.

- ◆ **SMS_SHRx.** Represents the root of the SMS installation location (c:\SMS would be SMS_SHRc). This share exists on site, logon, and helper servers running NT or LAN Manager. The SMS services use this share to communicate with one another.

- ◆ **SMS_SHR.** Represents the SMS\Logon.srv directory and exists on the site server and all logon servers running NT or LAN Manager. This share acts as the inventory collection point; it contains the files required for communication between SMS and its clients.

Logon Server Shares

The Logon server has three shares added to it during the SMS installation process. These new shares are very similar to the shares added to the site server and are described in the following list:

- ◆ **NETLOGON.** Points to the *x*:\WINNT\System32\Repl\Import\Scripts directory and is where the files required to utilize SMSLS.bat are placed when received from the site server.

- ◆ **SMS_SHRx.** Represents the root of the SMS installation location (that is, c:\SMS would be SMS_SHRc). This share exists on site, logon, and helper servers running NT or LAN Manager. The SMS services use this share to communicate with one another.

- ◆ **SMS_SHR.** Represents the SMS\Logon.srv directory and exists on the site server and on all logon servers running NT or LAN Manager. This share acts as the inventory collection point; it contains the files required for communication between SMS and its clients.

Site Server Directory Structure

A directory structure is created by the SMS installation utility on the site server when the site is first installed (primary or secondary site). What follows here are illustrations of the directory structure and explanations of what can be found in each directory and subdirectory. Figure 27.9 shows a site server's first level directory structure.

Figure 27.9

First level directory structure of an SMS site server.

Note You can determine what capacity a particular server is operating under by viewing the first-level directories in an SMS system. For example, *x*:\SMS\Logon.srv indicates that the server is operating as a logon server, and *x*:\sms\Site.srv indicates it is operating as a site server.

The following sections describe the subdirectories found in a site server's SMS directory structure. The subdirectories are listed here to give you an idea of the purpose of each directory and the files and/or subdirectories that each directory contains. We look first at the Site.srv subdirectories and then at the Primsite.srv subdirectories.

Site.srv

This SMS root level (*x*:\sms\Site.srv) directory Site.srv is the parent directory to the site server directories and subdirectories shown in figure 27.10. This directory structure is placed on each site server by the SMS installation utility at the time of installation.

Figure 27.10

Site.srv directory structure.

The Applications Manager component uses the appmgr.box directory to store program group and package information for the secondary sites.

The dataload.box directory is the storage location for binary .MIF inventory files. It contains the following subdirectories:

- ◆ **Deltamif.col.** Contains the collected binary .MIF files.

  - ◆ **badmifs.** Contains .MIF files that could not be processed by the Inventory Data Loader.

  - ◆ **Process.** Contains .MIF files the Inventory Data Loader is currently processing.

  - ◆ **Files.col.** Location of the collected files of the current site and its subsites.

The despoolr.box storage area is used by the Maintenance Manager to store job status MIF files for review by the Despooler component. It contains the following subdirectories:

- ◆ **store.** Contains compressed packages received by the Despooler.

- ◆ **receive.** Contains despooler instruction files (*.ins) received from senders.

The Inventory Processor monitors inventry.box, which is the directory that contains client inventory files (*.raw) that have been gathered from the logon servers and placed here by the Maintenance Manager. It contains the following subdirectories:

- ◆ **History.** Contains the history files maintained by the Inventory Processor.

- ◆ **Badraws.** Contains the *.raw files that could not be processed by the Inventory Processor.

The isvmif.box directory contains the MIF files generated by Independent Software Vendors (ISVs).

The Maintenance Manager and the Applications Manager use the Maincfg.box directory to store the following required subdirectories:

- ◆ **appctl.src.** Location for the directories used by the APPCTL program (Application Control program). The APPCTL program is the one responsible for creating the application groups within the client's program manager.

  - ◆ **inifiles.** The initialization files for the SMS network applications reside here.

  - ◆ **database.** The SMS network applications database resides here.

  - ◆ **scripts.** The SMS network application script files are stored here.

◆ **client.src.** This directory contains COPYLIST files and client component pieces for all of the supported SMS clients. It is used by the Maintenance Manager to build client configuration files for use by the SMS Client Setup utility and the Inventory Agent service. This information, along with the client components, is then replicated to all of the logon servers within the site.

◆ **invdom.box.** This directory is where resync.cfg, also known as the master inventory command file, is stored on each SMS domain. The resync.cfg file is located in the site.srv\maincfg.box\invdom.box*domain.000* directory.

◆ **mstest.** This directory contains the run-time version of MSTEST (Microsoft Test), as well as the utilities used when installing operating systems on SMS clients.

◆ **pcmdom.box.** This directory is where the Despooler places client information files for the clients that have been targeted for the Run Command on Workstation job. These information files are then picked up by the Maintenance Manager and replicated to all of the logon servers that serve the targeted clients.

◆ **pkgrule.** This directory is the location of the package.rul file.

The schedule.box directory is the drop-off location that SMS services use to store instruction files for system jobs. This directory is monitored by the Scheduler, which executes the system jobs based on the information contained in the instruction files.

The sender.box directory is where the sites senders are located. It contains two subdirectories:

◆ **requests.** The directory which is the location of the SMS sender's subdirectories (that is, Ras_asyn.000 and Lan_defa.000). Each sender monitors its directory (or outbox), looking for send requests from the Scheduler.

◆ **tosend.** The directory in which the compressed packages and despooler instruction files are placed to be sent to the remote target site.

Sitecfg.box is where the site control files used by the Site Configuration Manager for configuring a site are located.

The siterep.box directory is the holding area (queue) that the Site Reporter uses to collect and then distribute MIF files to the parent site.

platform.bin is where the SMS server components, including the SMS Administrator utility, are found. The server specific language subdirectory is located here, as is an event history subdirectory (errorhis).

Primsite.srv

This SMS root level directory (*x*:\sms\primsite.srv) is installed by the SMS installation utility and is located exclusively on primary site servers. The Primsite.srv directory contains secondary site configuration information and sample scripts for package installation and network application configuration. It contains the subdirectories found in figure 27.11.

Figure 27.11

Primsite.srv directory structure.

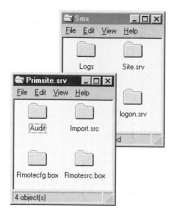

The following list explains each directory and subdirectory in detail:

- ◆ **Audit.** If the SMS Software Audit program runs as a Package Command Manager job, its inventory code is stored in this directory.

  - ◆ **package.** Otherwise, the inventory code is stored in this directory.

- ◆ **Import.src.** This directory is where the sample SMS scripts are stored.

- ◆ **Rmotecfg.box.** This directory is where the Site Hierarchy Manager places packages that have site control files destined for secondary sites.

- ◆ **Rmotesrc.box.** This directory is used to create a complete directory tree when the Site Hierarchy Manager is going to install a secondary site.

Logon Server Directory Structure

SMS logon servers have a similar, although much less complicated, directory structure than do site servers. This SMS root-level parent directory (*x*:\sms\logon.srv) contains all files and directories related to operating as a logon server and is installed by the SMS installation utility during installation. (see fig. 27.12). The following sections describe the logon servers directories, their files, and purpose.

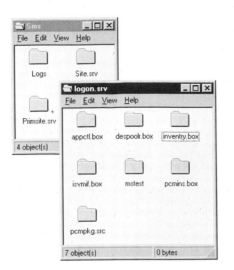

Figure 27.12

Logon server directory structure.

The appctl.box directory is the location of the network application database.

The despoolr.box directory is the subdirectory to which the Package Command Manager writes the application status MIF files after a package installation is complete, and from which the files are then picked up by the Maintenance Manager to be moved to the site server.

The inventry.box directory, monitored by the Maintenance Manager, contains client inventory files (*.raw) gathered from clients that the Maintenance Manager moves to the Site.srv\Inventry.box directory on the site server.

The isvmif.box is where the OS/2, Macintosh, and ISV MIF files are placed by the individual Inventory Agents. Once the Maintenance Manager detects new files in this directory, it will move them to the Site.srv\Inventry.box directory on the site server.

The mstest directory is the location of the run-time version of Microsoft Test.

The pcmins.box directory is where the Package Command Manager instruction files (*.ins) are replicated to from the site server.

The pcmpkg.src directory contains a subdirectory for each package the logon server has received. The packages are then decompressed and the subdirectories named with the same name as the SMS package ID for the package.

Smsid is the location of the *.uid file that is used to uniquely name each new client in the SMS domain.

platform.bin is where client executables used to install SMS clients are stored.

> **Note** SMS uses the Directory Replicator service to move the required batch and logon files from the primary domain controller (*pdcservername*\REPL$ share) to the logon servers (NETLOGON share). If the Directory Replicator service is not started, replication will not occur to the logon servers and an error will be logged by the primary domain controller.

System Flow Within SMS

Now that you have installed the sites, added the clients, and have an understanding of file and directory locations, you need to take a look at the heart of an SMS system.

Understanding the flow of information within and between sites is an integral part of successful SMS administration and troubleshooting. This next section is dedicated to broadening your understanding of the data flow by mapping a couple of the processes within SMS.

The first process mapped is Inventory Collection at a primary site. By default, inventory is collected every seven days, but this interval can be changed by invoking the SMS Administrator, Site properties, and clicking on the Inventory button.

Inventory Collection at Primary Sites

The inventory collection is handled by an inventory agent that runs on each client. This agent scans each client for software and hardware information and reports this data to the clients Logon server which is then gathered by the site server and added to the SMS database. Here are the steps:

1. The Inventory Agent scans a client for its hardware and software information.

   There are five variations of the Inventory Agent program:

   - **INVDOS.EXE**, for MS-DOS–based clients
   - **INV32CLI.EXE**, for Windows NT-based computers that are not running as SMS servers
   - **INV32WIN.EXE**, for SMS servers
   - **INVOS2.EXE**, for supported OS/2-based clients
   - **INVMAC**, for Macintosh clients

2. The Inventory Agent creates a RAW inventory file (*.raw) and writes it to LOGON.SRV\INVENTRY.BOX directory on the client's logon server.

If the client is a Macintosh or an OS/2 client, the inventory file that is created is a simple MIF (*.mif) text file and is written to the LOGON.SRV\ISVMIF directory on the client's logon server.

3. The inventory files (*.raw) are then collected from all of the logon servers and placed in the SITE.SRV\INVENTRY.BOX directory by the Maintenance Manager.

   The OS/2 and Macintosh .MIF files are moved to the SITE.SRV\ISVMIF directory on the site server.

4. The Inventory Processor then compares the new inventory information files with the history files kept in the SITE.SRV\INVENTRY.BOX\HISTORY directory. If changes are detected, the Inventory Processor processes the files, *.raw and *.mif, creating Delta MIF files, and places these binary MIF files into the SITE.SRV\DATALOAD.BOX\DELTAMIF.COL directory.

   If any of the .RAW files cannot be processed, the Inventory Processor places the files into the SITE.SRV\INVENTRY.BOX\BADRAWS directory.

   If any of the .MIF files cannot be processed, the Inventory Processor places the files into the SITE.SRV\INVENTRY.BOX\BADMIFS directory.

Note If the Inventory Processor does not detect any changes in the inventory data file, to minimize the information flowing to the Inventory Data Loader and to the parent sites, it will not create a Delta MIF file. If there has not been a Delta MIF file created after four days, however, SMS will create one.

5. The Inventory Data Loader then takes the binary Delta MIF files and places them into the SITE.SRV\DATALOAD.BOX\DELTAMIF.COL\PROCESS subdirectory. The Inventory Data Loader is a multi-threaded process that can spawn a new MIF processing thread if one is not available to process the Delta MIF files.

6. The MIF processing thread then renames the Delta MIF file by simply adding an "x" to the beginning of the file name, and begins to process it.

7. If the processing is successful, the thread then updates the site's database with information contained in the Delta MIF file.

   If the processing is not successful, the files are placed in the SITE.SRV\ DATALOAD.BOX\DELTAMIF.COL\BADMIFS subdirectory.

8. If there are no more Delta MIF files to process, the thread terminates.

9. The Delta MIF files are then placed in the SITE.SRV\SITEREP.BOX for transmission to the parent site, if one exists.

Inventory Collection at Secondary Sites

The main difference between collecting inventory at a primary site versus a secondary site is that since secondary sites do not have their own SQL database (and therefore do not have their own Inventory Data Loader), they store all of their inventory files in their parent's database.

The process of collecting inventory at secondary sites is as follows:

1. Same as collecting inventory at a primary site.

2. Same as primary site.

3. Same as primary site.

4. Same as primary site except that when the Inventory Processor processes the files to create the binary Delta MIF files, it writes the newly created Delta MIF files into the SITE.SRV\SITEREP.BOX directory on the secondary site's site server.

5. Once the Site Reporter detects that there have been MIF files added to the SITE.SRV\SITEREP.BOX directory, it places the files into the SITE.SRV\ SITEREP.BOX\sitecode subdirectory and creates a system job to transfer these files to the parent site.

Take a second here to look at the process that SMS uses to create, send, and receive a system job.

A system job is a job created by SMS to maintain or update a site by transferring SMS system instructions and files to other sites. This process includes sending inventory information from the secondary site to its parent site.

The steps are as follows:

◆ The Scheduler is responsible for starting the system job process by compressing the binary MIF files into a single file called *8-digit-job-id.p00* (the .p00 indicates a system job, the .s00 a sharing package, and the .w00 a workstation job). Once compressed, the package file is placed into the SITE.SRV\SENDER.BOX\TOSEND directory.

◆ The Scheduler also creates a despooler instruction file called *8-digit-job-id.i00*, which is also placed into the SITE.SRV\SENDER.BOX\TOSEND directory. The despooler instruction file (*.I00) contains information used by the destination site to decompress the package file.

◆ The Scheduler then creates a send request file (*.srq) that contains instructions used by the secondary site to connect to the destination site and send the files stored in the SITE.SRV\SENDER.BOX\TOSEND directory to it.

◆ This .SRQ file is then placed in the SITE.SRV\SENDER.BOX\REQUESTS\ *sender.000* directory. The sender is determined by the Scheduler, based on known senders at the destination site.

Note The Scheduler will always select the fastest sender from the list of available senders to transmit data from one site to another.

◆ Once the sender detects it has a pending .SRQ job in its outbox, it changes the file name to *.srs to indicate the job is in progress.

◆ The sender then connects to the remote site and transfers the package file (*.p00) from the SITE.SRV\SENDER.BOX\TOSEND directory to the remote site's SITE.SRV\DESPOOLER.BOX\RECEIVE directory.

◆ Once the package file has been completely received it is renamed to *.pck. The sender then transfers the *.i00 file from the SITE.SRV\ SENDER.BOX\TOSEND directory to the remote site's SITE.SRV\ DESPOOLER.BOX\RECEIVE directory.

◆ The instruction file is then renamed to *.ins to indicate that both files have been successfully sent.

◆ The Despooler decompresses and distributes the files following the instructions found in the instructions file. (In the case of inventory files, the Despooler places the binary Delta MIF files into the SITE.SRV\ DATALOAD\DELTAMIF.COL directory.)

6. The Inventory Data Loader then takes the binary Delta MIF files and places them into the SITE.SRV\DATALOAD.BOX\DELTAMIF.COL\PROCESS subdirectory.

And so on and so on, until the process is complete and the site database has been updated.

SMS Event Reporting

Another process flow that is important to know about is event (or error) reporting. SMS offers the capability to report events, forwarded by SMS components, by writing the events first to the Windows NT event log and then to the SMS database.

The steps by which it does so are as follows:

1. First the event is reported by an SMS component and written to the local Windows NT event log. If the component reporting the event is not running on the site server, an event is also written to the site server's NT event log.

2. The reporting component creates an .EMF (event MIF file) and places the file in one of the following directories:

   ◆ For primary site servers, SITE.SRV\DATALOAD.BOX\DELTAMIF.CO

   ◆ For secondary site servers, SITE.SRV\SITEREP.BO

3. If the site is a primary site, the Inventory Data Loader moves the binary MIF file into the SITE.SRV\DATALOAD.BOX\DELTAMIF.COL\PROCESS directory for processing.

4. If the Inventory Data Loader does not have an available thread for processing .EMF MIF files, it will spawn a new dedicated thread and begin processing the files.

5. If the .EMF MIF file processing is successful, the thread will then write the reported event information to the SMS database and move the .EMF file into the SITE.SRV\SITEREP.BOX directory for transmission to the parent site (if one exists).

6. Unsuccessful processing of the MIF files places them into the BADMIFS directory.

7. Once the Inventory Data Loader .EMF MIF thread has completed processing each of the .EMF files, the thread terminates.

This process continues with each site until the event information reaches the central site and is written to the central sites database.

> **Note** | SMS Administrator has an events window you can use to view events that have been reported to your local site or any site below you in the site hierarchy.

You can watch the files move from directory to directory by opening the related subdirectories, side by side, on your desktop, and waiting for the files to appear. The files are there only for a moment and then they are gone, so watch carefully.

This is also an excellent way to troubleshoot failed jobs. If you suspect a job has not reached its destination, go to the destination server and trace backward through the data flow until you find the file.

Unfortunately, this terminates the space available for the SMS chapter. This chapter is by no means a complete guide to the inner workings of SMS, nor does it cover the day-to-day administration of an SMS system. Those topics will have to be saved for another book.

Testing Your Knowledge

1. The System Management Server (SMS), is part of the Microsoft BackOffice suite.

    A. True

    B. False

2. What is the main, topmost primary site in an SMS system?

    A. Parent site

    B. Main site

    C. Child site

    D. Central site

3. Which SMS site is defined as any primary or secondary site that was created by a primary site, or that has a parent site preceding it in site hierarchy?

    A. Central site

    B. Parent site

    C. Child site

    D. Domain

4. The Inventory Agent is the SMS component that creates and collects hardware and software information, and reports the inventory to the SMS system. The SMS Agent can perform inventories on servers running which network operating systems?

    A. NT Server

    B. LAN Manager

    C. Netware 3.x

    D. Netware 4.x

5. Name at least four services that the SMS Executive starts.

6. You can adjust how often the site configuration manager monitors the different pieces of the site by using the Windows NT Registry Editor to edit the Registry. Which key contains the Registry values?

    A. KEY_LOCAL_MACHINE\SOFTWARE\Microsoft\SMS_SITE_CONFIG_MANAGER

    B. HKEY_LOCAL_MACHINE\Microsoft\SMS_SITE_CONFIG_MANAGER

    C. HKEY_LOCAL_MACHINE\SOFTWARE\SMS_SITE_CONFIG_MANAGER

    D. HKEY_LOCAL_MACHINE\SMS_SITE_CONFIG_MANAGER7.

7. When you first install an SMS system you create a central site and a single SMS domain, known as the _____ _____.

8. When installing SMS on an NT Server that is also running SQL Server, what is the minimum amount of RAM required?

   A. 24 MB

   B. 32 MB

   C. 64 MB

   D. 48 MB

9. What is the SMS root level directory?

   A. \sms\Site

   B. \sms\Site.srv

   C. \sms\root\Site.srv

   D. \sms\Sitesrv

Review Answers

1. A

2. D

3. C

4. A, B

5. Maintenance Manager, Inventory Processor, Scheduler, Trap Filter, Site Reporter, Despooler, Senders, Inventory Data Loader, Applications Manager, Alerter

6. A

7. site domain

8. D

9. B

CHAPTER 28

Internet Information Server

Windows NT Server version 4 includes the Internet Information Server (IIS). IIS is web server software that enables you to display and publish data on TCP/IP networks. IIS is a terrific quick start for organizations that want to start using the following technologies for Internet/intranet publishing:

◆ World Wide Web server

◆ File Transfer Process (FTP) server

◆ Gopher server

IIS works as well on the Internet as it does on private networks running the TCP/IP protocol, and on intranets, with just a few differences involved in its setup, as noted here:

◆ A secure Internet connection requires isolation of IIS from your network in some manner, either via a proxy server or behind a firewall.

Intranets can rely on NT Server's security scheme because users are known to you.

◆ With IIS on the Internet, you must obtain a domain name and become registered on a DNS name server.

On an intranet you have more freedom about how you assign TCP/IP addresses to your server and clients.

You will probably work with an Internet Service Provider (ISP) to accomplish both tasks. Most ISPs will maintain your Internet domain name space for you, freeing you of the responsibility of running a DNS name server. You can, if you want, run your own DNS server. In fact, a nice one is included with Windows NT Server 4.

IIS running on NT Server is becoming one of the most popular web server solutions in the marketplace. The program runs quickly, offers you NT Server's security scheme, and has many features that enable you to both scale up your web site and utilize your computer resources efficiently. This chapter touches on some of the highlights.

Preparing for Installation

Very little preparation is required to install IIS. Do the following exercise to get ready:

Preparing for IIS Installation

1. Configure TCP/IP in the computers that will be participating.

2. Identify a Windows NT Server computer that will host IIS. If you expect IIS to be heavily used, this server should be dedicated to the task of providing IIS services.

3. Disable any WWW, FTP, or Gopher servers that may be running on the IIS server.

4. Format the volumes on the server with NTFS to ensure the highest possible level of security.

5. Enable auditing, if you feel you need to closely monitor the server for security breaches.

6. Set up a name resolution method. You have several choices:

   DNS is best if you are going to be connected to the Internet, or if your network includes non-Microsoft hosts.

   WINS is probably easiest to maintain because it copes with network changes automatically, particularly if IP addresses are assigned by DHCP; however, it cannot supply names to non-Microsoft hosts unless it is configured to work in conjunction with the Windows NT DNS server.

   HOSTS files can be used to support Microsoft and non-Microsoft hosts, but they are static, and any change to the network means updating everyone's HOSTS files.

   LMHOSTS files can provide static naming for Microsoft hosts.

Installing the Internet Information Server

Installing the Internet Information Server is even easier than the preparing to install. To install IIS, follow the steps in the following exercise:

Installing IIS

◆ Select the Install Microsoft Internet Information Server box when you are installing Windows NT Server 4.

◆ Select the Install Internet Information Server icon on the Windows NT Server 4 desktop.

◆ Install the Internet Information Server as a service, using the Network utility on the Control Panel.

Only a few decisions are required during installation:

1. You must accept the license agreement.

2. You must determine which products from the first window, shown in figure 28.1, you want to install.

   The Internet Service Manager is the IIS administration application.

   You can elect to install any or all of the World Wide Web, FTP, and Gopher services.

   The ODBC Drivers and Administration option installs Open Data Base Connectivity support that in turn enables the server to log ODBC files, and enables ODBC access to the WWW service.

   If this is your first IIS server, be sure to install the Help and Sample Files option.

3. Also in the first window, you can change the installation directory by choosing Change **D**irectory.

4. The next window specifies the directories to which services will be installed. As figure 28.2 shows, you can customize the directories by choosing the appropriate Browse button.

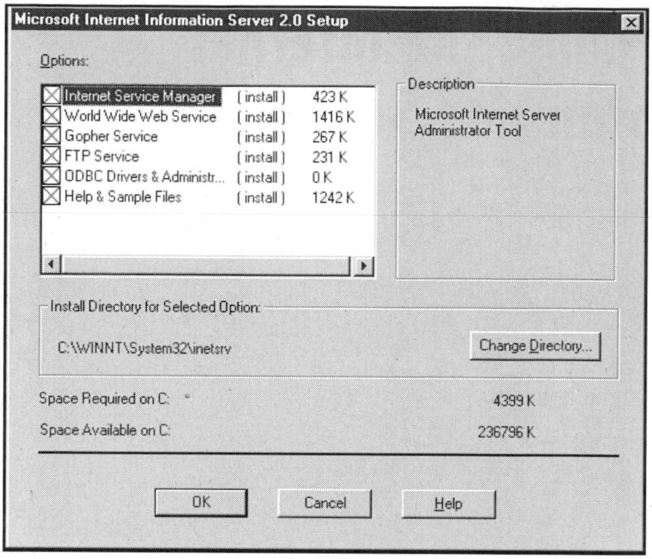

Figure 28.1

Selecting the IIS services to be installed.

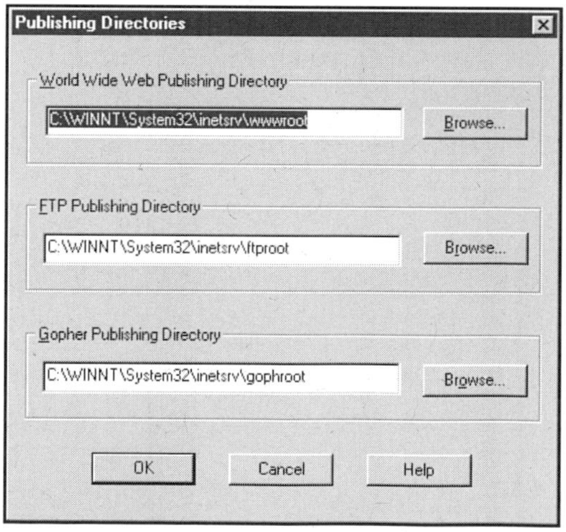

Figure 28.2

Specifying the service directories.

5. Next, you create the account that will be used by users to access resources on the server. The account is named IUSR_*computername*, where *computername* is the name of the computer running IIS. You will be asked to assign a password to this account.

6. Next, you are asked to select the ODBC drivers to be installed. For now, the only option is to install drivers for Microsoft SQL Server.

7. Now files are copied and the services are started. Installation is complete.

A new common program group is added to the Start menu. Look for the Microsoft Internet Server program group in the Programs menu. This program group contains four options:

◆ Internet Information Server Setup

◆ Internet Service Manager

◆ Key Manager

◆ Product Documentation

Using the Product Documentation

All of the online documentation is contained in HyperText Markup Language (HTML) files that you can read using a WWW browser. The Microsoft Internet Explorer is included with Windows NT Server 4 and appears on the desktop as an icon called "The Internet." You could start the Internet Explorer and locate the document files by entering the URL **file:C:\WINNT\system32\inetsrv\admin\htmldocs\inetdocs.htm**, but it is easier to simply select the Product Documentation option in the Microsoft Internet Server program group. Doing so starts the Internet Explorer with the appropriate URL, as shown in figure 28.3. In the figure, the user has browsed a bit to locate the main documentation table of contents in the *Microsoft Internet Information Server Installation and Administration Guide*. Moving around is simply a matter of clicking on the highlighted text.

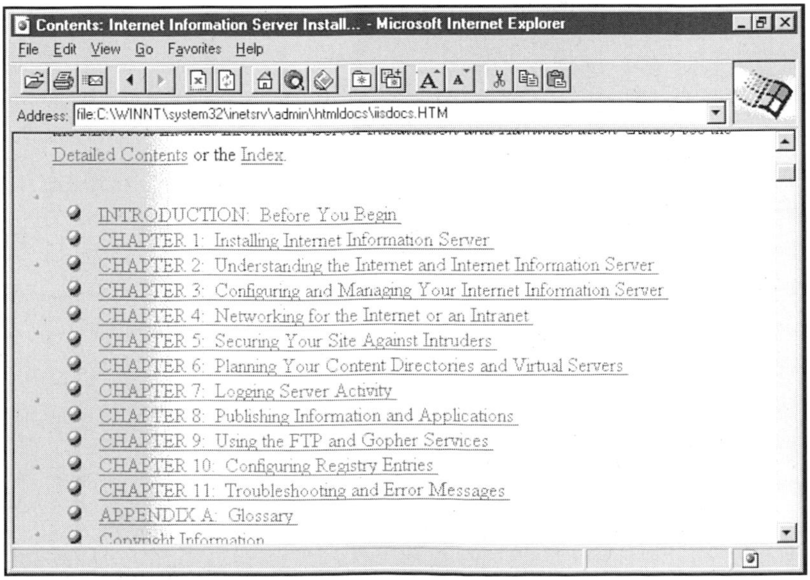

Figure 28.3

The table of contents in the online documentation.

Testing the Installation

Testing the WWW server is quite easy. The default root directory for the WWW server is C:\Winnt\system32\inetsrv\wwwroot. In that directory is a file named DEFAULT.HTM. This is the default file that users will view when they connect to the server.

To test the server, start Internet Explorer on a network computer (a client) and enter the URL **http://*computername***, where *computername* is the computer running the WWW server. Figure 28.4 shows the sample page that is displayed. In this example, with the user working on the local Microsoft network, the computer name is its NetBIOS name. It is possible to use a computer name because WINS is running on the network.

Figure 28.4

Testing the WWW server.

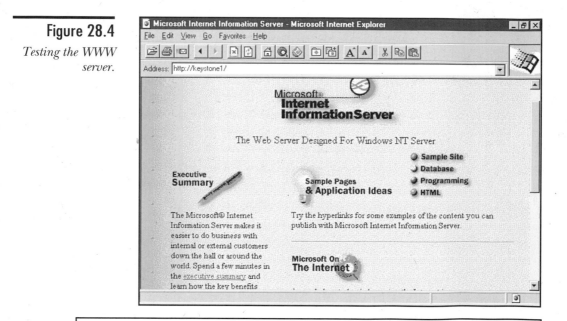

Universal Resource Locators

Universal Resource Locators, or URLs, are used to request access to directories, files, and services on the World Wide Web. A URL specifies three categories of information:

◆ The *protocol* to be used. The protocol name is followed by the characters ://. Protocol specifiers you will encounter in this chapter are

http:// HyperText Transport Protocol, the protocol used to display WWW documents formatted with HyperText Markup Language.

ftp:// File Transfer Protocol, a protocol that enables users to receive files from and send files to the server.

gopher:// Gopher, a protocol that supports a directory service that describes files that are available for user retrieval. Gopher is much like ftp, but identifies the files in a directory rather than presenting a raw directory listing.

◆ The *domain name* or *IP address* that the user wishes to access. Typically, users specify a domain name.

◆ The *path* to the information the user wishes to retrieve. A path can specify directories and subdirectories, and can specify a file to be accessed. The path is optional. If a path is not specified, the WWW server opens its root directory.

The following URL accesses the root directory of the WWW server at www.microsoft.com:

http://www.microsoft.com

Here is a URL that opens a specific subdirectory for FTP transfer:

ftp://www.widgets.com/public

Finally, this URL opens a specific file on a WWW server:

www://www.keystone.com/public/information/goodstuf.htm

Managing the IIS

All IIS services are managed from the Internet Service Manager shown in figure 28.5. You can open the Internet Service Manager by selecting its command from the IIS folder on the **P**rograms submenu of the Start menu. The window lists the services that are installed on a computer and indicates the state of the service. You can put any service in one of three states:

◆ **Running.** A Running service is started and operated normally. Start a service by selecting the service and choosing the S**t**art Service command in the **P**roperties menu, or by pressing the Start button on the toolbar.

◆ **Paused.** A Paused service continues to operate but will not permit new users to connect. Pause a service by selecting the service and choosing the **P**ause Service command in the **P**roperties menu, or by pressing the Pause button on the toolbar.

◆ **Stopped.** A Stopped service is no longer operating. Stop a service by using the Stop Service command in the **P**roperties menu, or by pressing the Stop button on the toolbar.

> **Tip** You can also start and stop IIS services by using the Services utility in the Control Panel.

Figure 28.5 shows the buttons on the toolbar. The functions of the buttons are as follows:

◆ **Connect to a server.** Connects the Internet Service Manager to a specific IIS server. Once connected, the services running on that server can be observed.

◆ **Find all servers.** Searches the network to identify all running servers. This search can take considerable time. Servers that are identified are displayed in the Internet Service Manager. In figure 28.5, two servers have been found.

◆ **Properties.** Opens the properties dialog box for a service.

◆ **Start service.** Starts the selected service.

◆ **Stop service.** Stops the selected service.

◆ **Pause service.** Pauses the selected service.

◆ **FTP services.** When this button is latched down, FTP servers are listed.

◆ **Gopher services.** When this button is latched down, Gopher servers are listed.

◆ **WWW services.** When this button is latched down, WWW servers are listed.

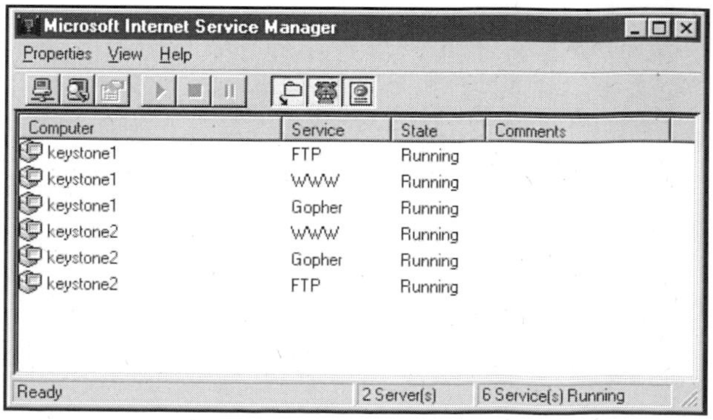

Figure 28.5

The Internet Service Manager, report view.

When IIS runs as a service on NT Server (or Workstation), you also see these services in the Service control panel. An administrator can configure an Internet service to start up automatically when the server boots, and to alter the security settings that the service should have. From the Services control panel you can start, pause, or stop a service, and see which services are running on the computer you are on. This method is an alternative to using the Internet Service Manager.

Selecting IIS Views

Besides the Report View shown in figure 28.5, you can also elect two other formats for display. To select the servers view (see fig. 28.6), choose Ser**v**ers View in the **V**iew menu. You can open the servers as shown to view the status for each service. A traffic signal specifies whether the service is running (green), paused (yellow), or stopped (red).

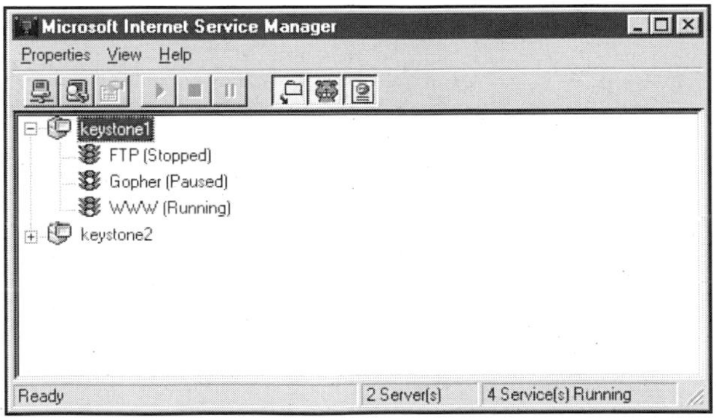

Figure 28.6

The Internet Service Manager, services view.

The services view lists all servers under the services they offer. Open this view by choosing Ser**v**ices View in the **V**iew menu (see fig. 28.7).

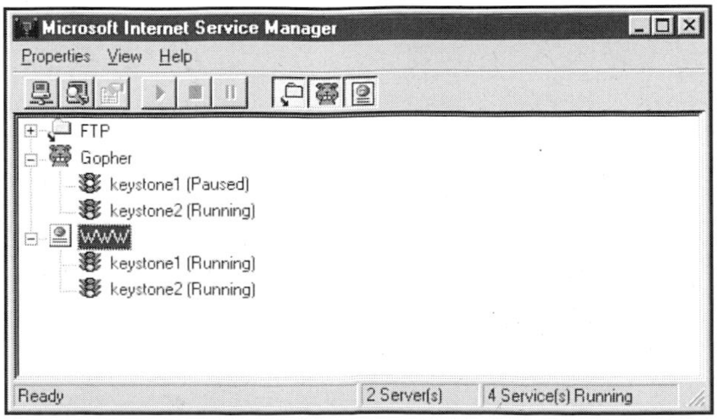

Figure 28.7

The Internet Service Manager, services view.

| Note | Other Windows NT Server management utilities can be used to supplement the Internet Service Manager: |

- ◆ Examine the logs in the Event Viewer to monitor operation.

- ◆ Use the Performance Monitor to keep track of resource utilization. An HTTP service object is added with counters to monitor many aspects of IIS operation.

Setting Up the WWW Service

Setting up a WWW Server is not especially difficult. Most of the work involved is creating the HTML pages to be displayed on the server. HTML, as well as other page creation technologies, are outside the scope of this book. Any bookstore will have dozens of books to choose from. Here are a couple from Macmillan:

- ◆ *Inside the World Wide Web,* from New Riders Publishing

- ◆ *Using HTML Special Edition,* from Que

You may want to check out some of the sample web pages that Microsoft has included with IIS for your use; they are a good starting place for corporate web pages.

The actual setup of a web site is rather straightforward, involving the following general steps:

- ◆ Verify that the IUSR_*servername* account has Read permissions for the WWW directory tree.

- ◆ Review the WWW server properties.

- ◆ Set up the directory tree.

- ◆ Add files to the directory.

If you have developed a site structure and content using a tool like Microsoft FrontPage, you need only to deploy your files on the server by either copying them to the appropriate directory on the server or by replicating that directory structure.

Setting Up the IUSR_*servername* Account

All users who access your WWW server inherit the permissions that are given to the IUSR_*servername* account. These permissions are typically limited to Read permissions in the WWW directory tree. By default, WWW files are stored in a directory starting at C:\Winnt\system32\inetpub\wwwroot. (The root directory of a WWW server is most commonly referred to as the *home* directory.) Use Windows NT Explorer to review the permissions assigned to the IUSR_*servername* account.

The root directory is where a reader seeking your domain without a specified folder or document would be directed. When you enter http://www.microsoft.com into your browser, for example, you are shown the default document in the root directory. See the discussion on the setup of the Directories tab in the "Directories" section soon hereafter.

Managing WWW Server Properties

Configure a WWW server by selecting the server and choosing **S**ervice Properties in the **P**roperties menu, or by pressing the Properties button on the toolbar. The properties sheet for a WWW server is shown in figure 28.8. Four tabs are used to configure the WWW server.

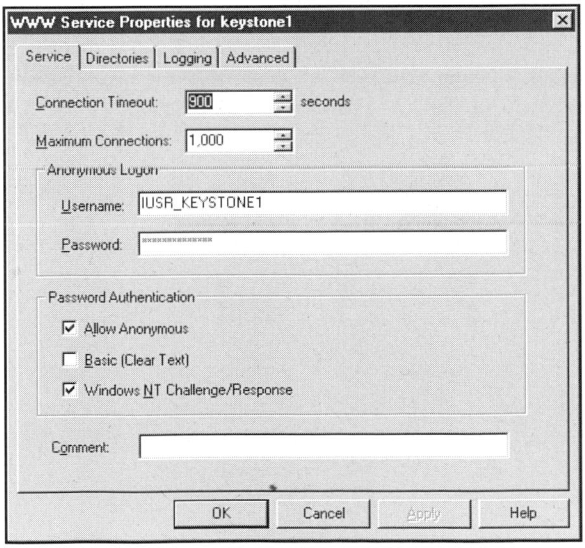

Figure 28.8

Configuring the WWW server service properties.

WWW Service Properties for keystone1

Service | Directories | Logging | Advanced

Connection Timeout: 900 seconds

Maximum Connections: 1,000

Anonymous Logon
Username: IUSR_KEYSTONE1
Password: ***********

Password Authentication
☑ Allow Anonymous
☐ Basic (Clear Text)
☑ Windows NT Challenge/Response

Comment:

OK | Cancel | Apply | Help

Services

The Service tab (refer to fig. 28.8) includes basic service settings. The fields in this tab are as follows:

◆ **Connection Timeout.** The value in this field determines how long the server will permit a connection to remain idle (no traffic) before the connection is broken at the server. This timeout ensures that improperly closed connections are eventually released.

◆ **Maximum Connections.** This value determines the number of users who can connect at a given time. Decrease this number if users begin to experience performance problems. (Take note of the bandwidth throttling feature of IIS on the Advanced tab; it lets you control the behavior of your web server when the maximum connections have been reached.)

◆ **Anonymous Logon Username.** The normal mode for using a WWW server is to permit users to log on anonymously (that is, without entering a user name and password). Users who connect anonymously gain the access that is permitted to the anonymous user. The default user name is IUSR_*servername*. The password you specify for access is for use within Windows NT only, and enables you to access volumes and folders that are protected by the NT challenge-response scheme. The Allow Anonymous box must be checked to permit anonymous logons.

◆ **Allow Anonymous.** When this box is checked, users can connect to the server without entering a user name or password. If you do not permit anonymous logons, users must log on using an account that is configured under User Manager for Domains.

◆ **Basic (Clear Text).** Check this box to enable users to log on with a user name and a password. Clear text logon enables users to log on with any WWW browser, but provides no security from users who snoop the network with protocol analyzers.

◆ **Windows NT Challenge/Response.** Check this box to force users to log on with a secure Windows NT logon. Passwords are encrypted. This feature is supported by Microsoft Internet Explorer 2.0 and later versions.

Directories

Setup installs a set of home directories for each of your services in the C:/WINNT/INETSRV folder. You can begin publishing your web pages in HTML format by adding them to the \WWWROOT folder.

> **Note** With FTP services, users can share files by navigating those folders they have access to the same way they would the file system in the Windows Explorer. Gopher, on the other hand, requires that directories and files be customized, and that links be included to other servers in your files.

You are free to modify these default directory assignments in the Directories tab of the Properties sheet of any service. The home directory for a service is also called its root directory. If no default document is given, a viewer will get an error if they connect to your site. Default documents are generally given the names DEFAULT.HTM or INDEX.HTM, and are what the user sees when no document is specified. Each folder in a WWW service can have and should have a default document for viewing. FTP doesn't require a default document, although it is customary to place a text file describing the contents of the folder in that server.

To specify a home directory, follow the steps in the following exercise:

Specifying a Home Directory

1. Double-click on the service in Internet Service Manager you want to modify. The Directories tab appears (see fig. 28.9).

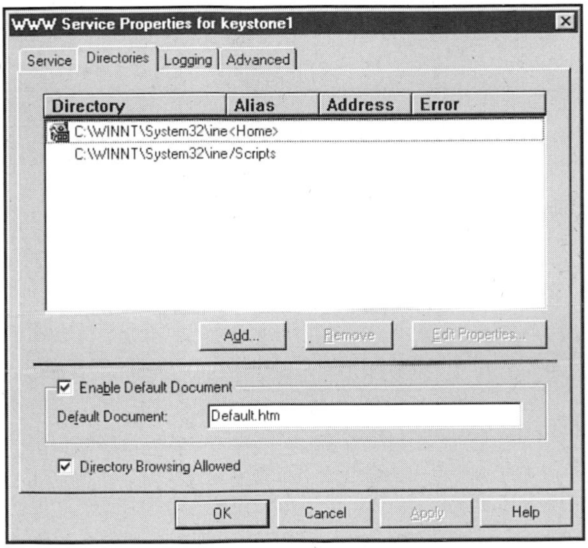

Figure 28.9

Directory tab for the WWW server.

2. Click on the Directories tab, and then click on the particular directory in the Directory list box.

   Any directory with a <Home> alias or a home icon to the left of the name can be modified.

3. Click on the **E**dit Properties button.

4. Enter the name of the new directory in the Directory Properties dialog box (see fig. 28.10).

   Or, click on the **B**rowse button and select a new home directory.

5. Set the options you want in the Access section.

Figure 28.10

The Directory properties dialog box for the WWW server.

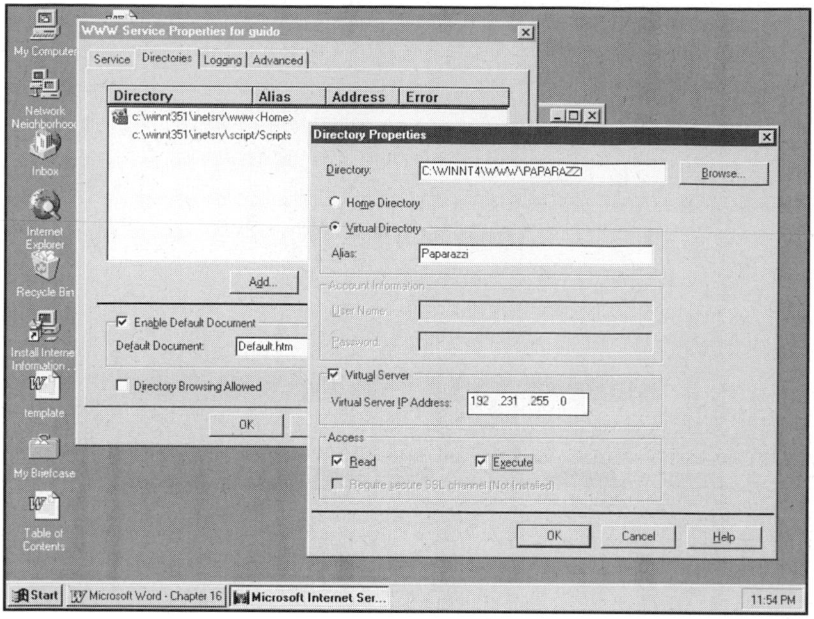

6. Click on the OK button.

7. Choose **A**pply, and then, finally, click on OK in the Properties sheet.

Two settings on this tab can be discussed briefly here.

Users can request a specific file by specifying the file name in a URL. In many cases, however, the user will simply specify a directory to be accessed. You can create a *default document* that will be displayed when a user accesses a WWW directory without specifying a file name. Two options on the Directory tab relate to default document support:

◆ **Ena**b**le Default Document.** Default documents will be automatically displayed only if this box is checked.

◆ **De**f**ault Document.** If you want to change the file name for your default document files, edit this field.

When a user accesses a directory offered by a WWW server, one of three things can happen:

◆ If the user has not specified an HTML file name in the URL and a default document file resides in the directory, the default document will be sent to the user.

◆ If the user has not specified an HTML file name in the URL and a default document is not found, the WWW server can send a *directory browsing document* that enables the user to browse the directories supported by the WWW server.

◆ If the user has not specified an HTML file name in the URL, a default document is not found, and directory browsing is not enabled, an error is returned to the user informing the user, You do not have permission to open this item. Access Forbidden.

Figure 28.11 shows an example of a browsing document that contains four HTML documents and two directories. The user clicks an entry to access a file or directory. To enable the WWW server to generate browsing documents, you must check Directory Browsing Allowed, in the Directories tab.

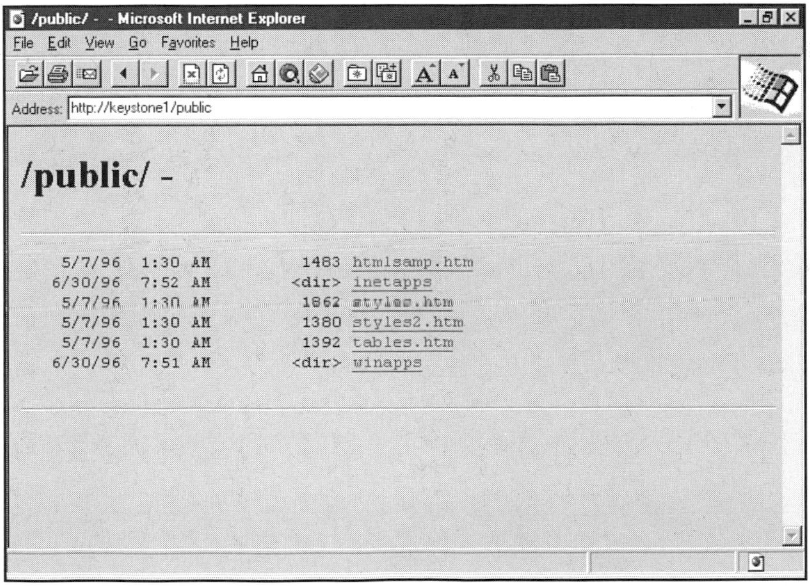

Figure 28.11

An HTML browsing document.

Directory browsing will show a hierarchical listing of files and directories as a set of folders and hypertext links. Directory browsing looks very much like the display seen in an FTP service. Directory browsing is useful when you have folders with lots of documents that aren't in HTML format, in which case a viewer can download those files and save them to disk without having to view them first.

Virtual Directories

WWW browsers are essentially a way of viewing HTML document files stored in content directories on the WWW server. Most web sites start out as a single folder of content, and although you can place all of your HTML files in a single content directory, it is often advantageous to configure multiple content directories (refer to fig. 28.9). IIS enables you to define virtual directories that span two or more directories, directories on different volumes, and even directories on remote volumes. This is a feature that enables you to maximize the use of your computer resources and to outgrow a partition, should that become necessary.

You can specify additional content directories for a site by adding them from within the Directories tab of the Properties sheet for that server. Each content directory can have a default document assigned to it.

To add or remove a directory from your service, follow the steps in the following exercise:

Adding and Removing a Directory from Your Service

1. In the Internet Service Manager, double-click on the service to which you want to add a directory or from which you want to delete one.

2. Click on the Directories tab.

3. Click A**d**d to add a directory.

   Or, click on a directory and then click on the **R**emove button to delete it.

4. Enter the name of the new directory in the Directory Properties dialog box.

   Or, use the **B**rowse button to specify a directory.

5. Set the Access options.

6. Click on the OK button.

7. Click on the **A**pply button, and then click on the OK button.

When a viewer specifies your domain, the web server serves up the default document in your home directory. A list of files appears for document browsing. If there is not a default document, and document browsing is not enabled, an error is returned and no other directories are searched.

With FTP access, the service searches inside the home directory for a subdirectory with the name of the user who is logging on. FTP also offers "anonymous FTP," or no-password access. For anonymous FTP, the service searches for the "anonymous" subdirectory. If in either search the directory does not exist, the current directory is used as the home directory.

Subdirectories of the home directory are accessible to clients in all three types of IIS services.

Virtual Servers

It also is possible to configure *virtual servers* that enable a single WWW server to have multiple personalities. This feature is called *multihoming,* and it lets your server service multiple domains, if needed. A single WWW server could support virtual WWW sites for several companies, for example. Virtual servers must work with DNS, which goes beyond the scope of this chapter. Both virtual directories and multi-homing are features that ISPs set up when using IIS on Windows NT Server to manage the web activities of their clients.

Virtual servers are particularly useful when you want to separate sections of an organization from each other. You might assign department addresses, for example, so that sales.microsoft.com and finance.microsoft.com are mapped to different virtual servers.

Keep in mind that for multihoming, each domain requires its own Internet Protocol (IP) address. To set up a virtual server(s), you either get

◆ Additional IP addresses for each domain from your ISP

◆ The DNS server, to create additional IP addresses for the virtual servers

To set up a virtual server, follow the steps in the following exercise:

Setting Up a Virtual Server

1. Double-click on a WWW service in Internet Service Manager to open the Properties sheet.

2. Click on the Directories tab, then click the A**d**d button.

3. Click on the **B**rowse button in the Directory list box of the Directory Properties dialog box.

4. Enter the alias name in the A**l**ias text box for the virtual server.

5. Click in the Virtu**a**l Server check box.

6. Enter the IP address for the virtual server.

7. Click in the E**x**ecute check box to allow users to execute applications at your site.

8. Close all dialog boxes.

If there are two or more IP addresses, specify which IP address applies to the directory you just created. If there are no IP addresses, the directory will be viewable by all virtual servers. The default directories created by the Setup program do not have associated IP addresses; you might want to supply them when you set up virtual servers.

Logging

The Logging tab enables you to manage logging for the WWW server (see fig. 28.12). Particularly if your server is connected to the Internet, you need to enable logging to assist you to maintain tight security. The options in this tab are as follows:

◆ **Enable Logging.** This box is checked by default.

◆ **Automatically open new log.** When this box is checked, new log files will be opened when the specified conditions are met. The option you choose will depend on the rate at which your log files grow.

◆ **Log file directory.** In this field, specify the directory in which log files are to be stored. The log file is named by date with the format IN*yymmdd*.LOG.

◆ **Log to SQL/ODBC Database.** If ODBC support is installed, you can direct logs to a SQL database. If this option is enabled, complete the remaining fields as required.

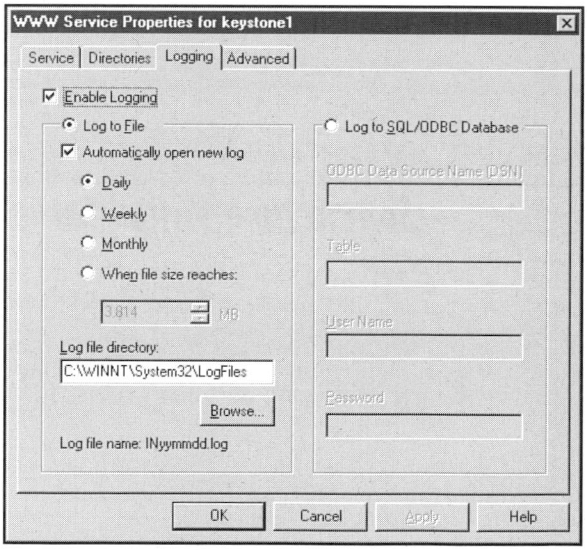

Figure 28.12

Configuring logging.

You can monitor the activities of any user who logs on to your web server, whether they log on from the Internet or on your intranet. Each of your running services can track events in its log. A wide variety of data may be saved, including the TCP/IP address of a computer requesting service, the service requested, the duration of the connection, amount of information transferred, and so on.

This information enables you to manage your site for performance, configure and optimize your site, do capacity planning, assess the popularity of particular resources, and do security auditing. You can set up the log as a standard Windows NT Event Log, or you can set it up as an SQL Server database, in which case the site could provide automated report generation. The IIS online help system contains information that will help you link an SQL Server database table through an ODBC connection to IIS and the SQL service log.

If you are logging activities, you should be aware that extensive log entries for web, FTP, and Gopher services will require a great deal of I/O activity. If the performance of IIS lags when IIS is busy, you might want to consider either adding additional memory or a faster computer to handle the load. You can also remove less necessary logged events.

The following is an example of a log entry that corresponds to the parameters client IP Address, client user name, date, time, service, computer Name, IP address of server, processing time (ms), bytes received, bytes sent, service status code, Windows NT status code, name of operation, and target of operation:

```
155.53.94.24, -, 12/10/96, 18:23:59, W3SVC, INETSRV12, 159.53.82.2, 220, 250,
➥1492, 200, 0, GET, /Guido/home/index.htm, -,
```

You can read this log entry as: an anonymous client at 155.53.94.24 gave a GET command for index.htm at 6:23 PM on December 10, 1996, from the virtual server at 159.53.82.2.

IIS ships with a log conversion utility that converts a log from the default format into the NCSA Common Log File or EMWAC format. The utility also provides DNS replacement of IP addresses with domain names.

The Windows NT Performance Monitor (perfmon) can also be used to track events relating to IIS. You can use the counters that are applicable to IIS services to tune and optimize IIS on your NT Server. Counters for the various services appear in the log, and events can be monitored in real time, historically, or viewed as a report. You can even set up the Performance Monitor to provide alerts when a threshold is violated. IIS provides HTTP (web), FTP, and Gopher counters to the Performance Monitor, but you can also define your own custom counters. The IIS online help system documents standard counters that can be monitors. These counters are in addition to the standard counters that Windows NT Server generates on its own, and the careful reading of these particular "tea leaves" are one good method of debugging a performance problem on IIS.

Advanced Access

The Advanced tab, shown in figure 28.13, enables you to set some access and network traffic limits. The settings are as follows:

◆ **Granted Access.** If this button is selected, computers with all IP addresses will be permitted access. Exceptions can be specified in the Access list.

◆ **De̲nied Access.** If this button is selected, computers with all IP addresses will be denied access. Exceptions can be specified in the A̲ccess list.

◆ **A̲ccess.** Computers listed in this box are exceptions to the normal access limit. You can add addresses to this list by choosing A̲dd.

◆ **Limit Network Use by all Internet Services on this computer.** An Internet server can get very busy and can affect the performance of an entire network. If you want to limit the network traffic generated by this server, check this box and adjust the value of the Ma̲ximum network use field.

Caution The only limitations supported by the Advanced tab are based on the IP address of the sender. Unfortunately, a Technique called IP address spoofing enables knowledgeable users to fake an IP address that can slip around address-based security. Don't ever trust a security system that depends on IP addresses; rather, be sure to get a good firewall if you are connecting critical systems to the Internet.

IIS offers you a feature that lets you limit the number of channels or connections that your Internet server provides. This feature, called *bandwidth throttling*, enables you to control access to your site and prevents your services from becoming overwhelmed, should a resource become popular.

When the connection limit is met, any additional request for service is met with a server unavailable message until the traffic decreases below the threshold. The setting lets you delay requests when your volume is close to the threshold, so that you balance a small delay for some users against maximizing your number of connections for your allowed connection limit.

To set the connection limit, click on the <u>L</u>imit Network Use by all Internet Services on this computer check box and enter the number of connections in the Ma<u>x</u>imum network use text box. Bandwidth throttling is an important setting that you should revisit whenever a site becomes more active.

Setting Up the FTP Service

To set up FTP, simply do these four basic steps:

◆ Review the FTP server properties.

◆ Verify that the IUSR_*servername* account has Read permissions for the FTP directories.

◆ Set up the directory structure.

◆ Add files to the directory.

No ongoing maintenance is required. Simply add and remove files from the directories as required.

Setting Up File Permissions

If users log on with a personal user name and password, the permissions they have are determined by the permissions given to their user accounts.

If users log on anonymously, they have the permissions assigned to the IUSR_ *servername* account. Typically, this account has Read permissions for the FTP directories. Write permissions may be given to specific directories to enable users to upload files. In some cases, an administrator will grant the Write permission but not the Read permission, preventing users from examining files that other users have uploaded until the administrator can review the files.

Configuring FTP Server Properties

The Properties window for the FTP server is similar to what you have seen for the WWW server, but it has several distinctive features.

FTP Services

On the Service tab is the check box A**l**low only anonymous connections (see fig. 28.14). FTP does not encrypt passwords when users establish connections, rendering passwords susceptible to discovery by anyone snooping about the network using a protocol analyzer. When users log on to FTP using their regular network user names and passwords, the passwords becomes vulnerable. It is common practice, therefore, to require anonymous connections from all users. Just be sure to apply proper security to the IUSR_*servername* account to ensure that users don't receive inappropriate access to network resources.

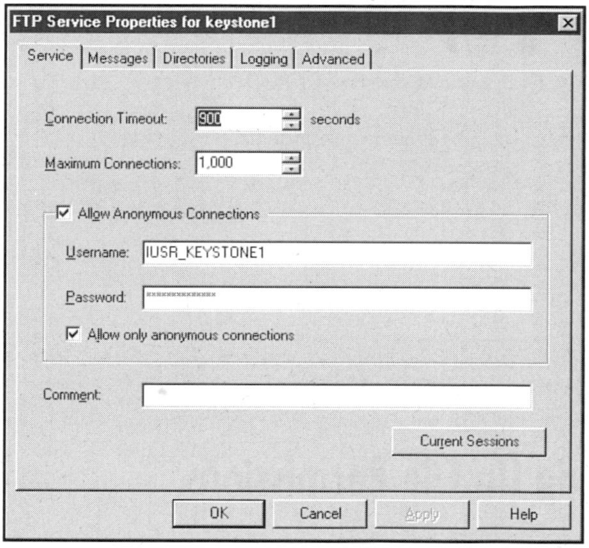

Figure 28.14

Configuring FTP service properties.

FTP Service Properties for keystone1

Service | Messages | Directories | Logging | Advanced

Connection Timeout: 900 seconds

Maximum Connections: 1,000

☑ Allow Anonymous Connections

Username: IUSR_KEYSTONE1

Password: *************

☑ Allow only anonymous connections

Comment:

Current Sessions

OK | Cancel | Apply | Help

Messages

The Messages tab (see fig. 28.15) can be used to specify three messages:

◆ A **W**elcome message that is displayed when users first connect. This message can be quite extensive.

◆ An E**x**it message that is displayed when users disconnect.

◆ A **M**aximum connections message that appears when the number of users has reached the value specified in the **M**aximum Connections field of the Service tab.

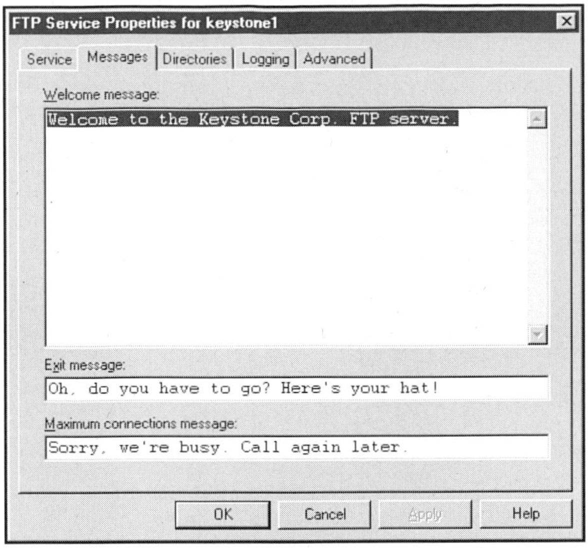

Figure 28.15

Configuring FTP server messages.

FTP Directories

A setting on this tab determines whether users will see a Unix-style directory or an MS-DOS–style directory (see fig. 28.16). Some browsers require directories with a Unix format, and Unix is the best choice unless the MS-DOS format is supported for all your WWW clients.

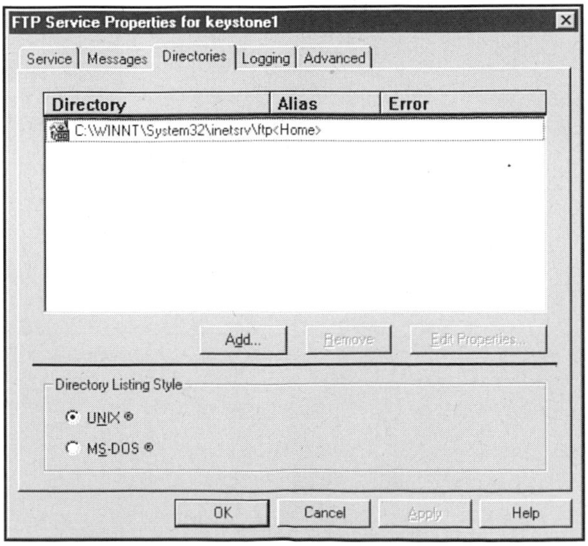

Figure 28.16

Selecting a directory style.

Using Internet Explorer to Access FTP Servers

Internet Explorer can access FTP servers using the FTP protocol. Figure 28.17 shows an example. The URL ftp://keystone1/ accessed the FTP service on the KEYSTONE1 server. The FTP root directory contains three files and one directory.

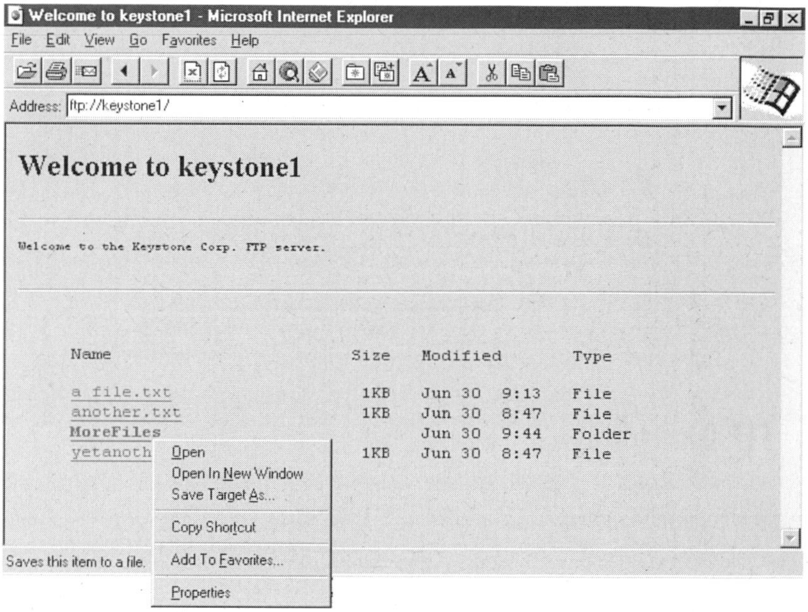

Figure 28.17

*Right-click a file
to open an
options menu.*

Welcome to keystone1

Welcome to the Keystone Corp. FTP server.

Name	Size	Modified	Type
a file.txt	1KB	Jun 30 9:13	File
another.txt	1KB	Jun 30 8:47	File
MoreFiles		Jun 30 9:44	Folder
yetanoth	1KB	Jun 30 8:47	File

In the figure, the user has right-clicked the file YETANOTHER.TXT, opening an options menu. To download the file, choose Save Target **A**s and specify a download location in the Save As dialog box.

Setting Up the Gopher Service

Gopher is nearly as easy to set up as FTP is, but you do need to create tag files and, optionally, indexes. The actual setup is straightforward, involving the following general steps:

◆ Verify that the IUSR_*servername* account has Read permissions for the FTP directories.

◆ Review the FTP server properties.

◆ Set up the directory structure.

◆ Add files to the directory.

◆ Create the tag files.

Setting Up File Permissions

All users log on anonymously, and, as such, have the permissions assigned to the IUSR_*servername* account. Be sure to give this account Read permissions to the gopher directories.

Configuring Gopher Service Properties

Gopher has some distinctive settings that you need to configure in the service properties. The Service tab is the only tab with properties that are distinct to gopher.

The Service tab contains fields that identify the service administrator (see fig. 28.18). These entries are defaults that appear in Gopher listings when other entries are not specified. Complete the following fields to identify the administrator of this server:

◆ **Name.** The name of the administrator.

◆ **Email.** The e-mail address of the administrator.

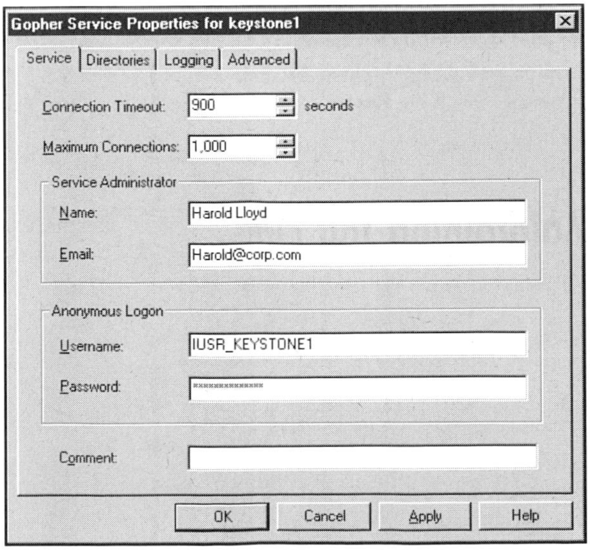

Figure 28.18

Configuring service properties for the gopher server.

Tag Files

A *tag file* is a special file that is associated with a file that will be advertised on the Gopher server. The tag file contains information describing the file and the administrator responsible for the file or the Gopher server.

The format of a tag file depends on whether the Gopher directories are stored on FAT or NTFS volumes.

- ◆ On a FAT volume, the tag file name is the same as the file name it describes, with the extension .GTG appended to it. For the file THISFILE.TXT, the corresponding tag file would be assigned the name THISFILE.TXT.GTG.

- ◆ On an NTFS volume, the tag file name is the same as the file name it describes, with the extension :GTG appended to it. For the file THISFILE.TXT, the corresponding tag file would be assigned the name THISFILE.TXT:GTG.

Tag files residing on FAT volumes can be directly edited with a conventional text editor. Tag files must be hidden in normal operation and must be unhidden for editing. You can manage the hidden file attribute with Windows NT Explorer.

Tag files residing on NTFS volumes are stored in an alternate data stream and cannot be edited with most text editors. These files are maintained with the gdsset utility described below.

> **Note**　If you move files to a different directory on a Gopher server, you must be sure to move the tag files as well. Use Windows NT Explorer to remove the hidden attribute. After the tag files have been moved, reassign the hidden attribute to the files.

Creating and Maintaining Tag Files

The gdsset utility is used to create and edit tag files. The syntax for gdsset is as follows:

```
gdsset -c -gn -f "friendly name" -a "administrator's name" -e e-mail address -h
➥hostname -d filename
```

The parameters for the gdsset command are as follows:

-c	Include this flag to change a file. Omit this flag to create a new file.
-g*n*	This parameter describes the file type *n* described by the entry. File types are described in the sidebar "Gopher File Types." (No space separates -g from the file type.)

-f "*friendly name*"	Specifies the Friendly Name, a freeform text name that is displayed instead of the file name. The quotation marks enable the friendly name to contain spaces.
-a "*administrator's name*"	The name appearing between the quote marks identifies the person responsible for maintaining the file. The quotation marks enable the name to contain spaces.
-e *e-mail address*	Specifies the administrator's e-mail address.
-h *hostname*	Specifies the name of the computer to link to.
-d *filename*	Specifies the name of the file for which the tag is being created.

The following syntax, for example, creates a tag file for the file INFOFILE.TXT:

```
gdsset -g0 -f "Interesting information" -a "Harold Lloyd"
-e harold@mail.keystone.com -d infofile.txt
```

Gopher File Types

The following list describes the available Gopher file types:

0	A file, typically a flat text file
1	A Gopher directory
2	A CSO phone-book server
3	An error
4	A Macintosh Binhex format file
5	An MS-DOS binary archive
6	A Unix uuencode format file
7	An index-search server
8	A Telnet session
9	A binary file
c	A calendar

continues

g	A GIF (graphic interchange file) graphic file
h	An HTML (World Wide Web) page
i	An in-line text that is not an item
I	An image file
m	A BSD format mbox file
P	A PDF document
T	A TN3270 mainframe session
:	A bitmap image

Using Internet Explorer to Access Gopher

Figure 28.19 shows the Internet Explorer browsing a gopher directory. This directory contains three files. Notice that the descriptions can be quite extensive, and can be made much more informative than a standard file name. Yes, you could use long standard file names, but they would not be usable by MS-DOS clients. Gopher descriptions can be viewed by all types of clients.

Right-click on a gopher entry to open an options menu where you can view properties or download the file.

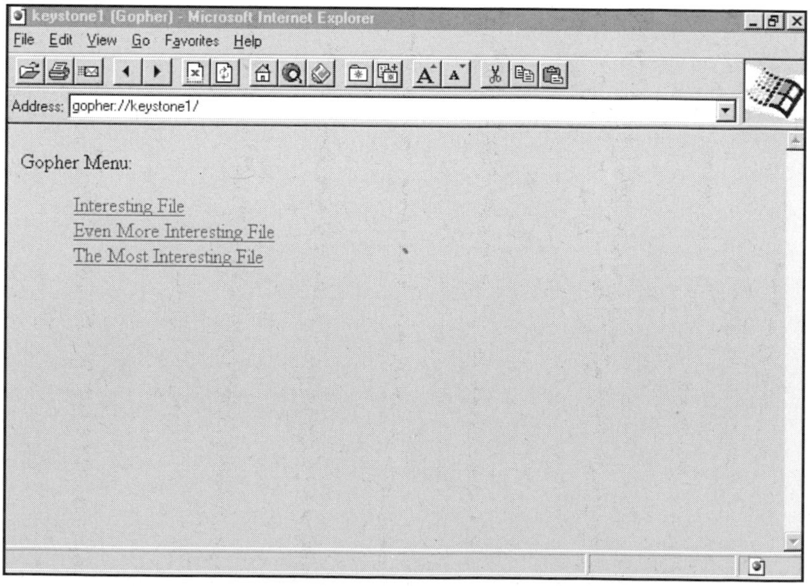

Figure 28.19

Browsing a gopher directory with Internet Explorer.

Internet Connections

If you are connecting your web server to the Internet, one of your first concerns is the type of connection to use. The best connection type for you depends on your budget, the amount of web traffic you expect to your site, and the web server's physical connection. You can connect to the Internet directly with connections that are the data equivalent of anything from a straw up to a fat pipe—a factor known in the trade as *bandwidth*. Bandwidth describes the data throughput that you can achieve (usually expressed in bits per second, or *bps*) with your connection.

You can also connect your web server to an Internet Service Provider (ISP) and piggyback that connection. For occasional users or small enterprises, an ISP connection is a cost-effective method for connecting to the web. More active web sites or large enterprises are more likely to need and want a direct Internet connection.

There are hundreds of ISPs that you can work with. Any computer magazine contains ads for them, as do the yellow pages (check the Computer Bulletin Boards, Internet, Computer Services, ISDN, or Telephone Installers sections) and books on the Internet. ISPs can be small startups or national organizations such as MCI or AT&T. The quality of rates and services vary widely, so it pays to investigate and shop around.

Connection costs generally fall into the following ranges:

Connection	Cost (per month)
PPP dial-up	$20 to $40
SLIP dial-up	$20 to $30
Dedicated (unlimited usage) PPP/SLIP	$200 to $300
56 K at 56 Kbps	$150 to $300
PPP ISDN at 128 Kbps	$70 to $100, plus equipment
T1 at 1.5 Mbps	$1,500 to $2,000
T3 at 45 Mbps	$65,000 to $80,000

Some services are based on a maximum connection time per month, others are based on hourly charges, and still others are permanent connections.

You probably would not want a dial-up connection for an IIS server; chances are that you would be looking for a permanent connection. Therefore, to the costs in the preceding table, you need to add the cost of a dedicated phone line at your location, and the cost of a dedicated phone line at your service provider's location. If you have a direct connection to the Internet, only your dedicated phone line is required.

For an IIS server that services 50 simultaneous connections, you may find that Frame Relay or ISDN is sufficient for your needs. T1 connections support between 100 and 500 simultaneous connections. ISPs often split a T1 line between clients, and split their cost. If you have a really active web site typical of a large enterprise that handles more connections, you can either install multiple T1 lines, or for service of up to 5,000 or more connections, a T3 line. Enterprises that have that many connected users require multiple IIS servers to distribute the load.

> | **Tip** | Getting connected is one of those decisions where bringing in a consultant can really save you money and reduce your stress level.

Most high-speed Internet connections use a lease line. To install a lease line, you should call your local phone company (not all local phone companies offer them) or an Interexchange carrier. A lease line is a direct connection, with transfer rates of from 56 kilobits per second up to those for T1 through T3 lines.

Few communication technologies are undergoing more rapid transformation than Internet connections. Many TV cable companies are experimenting with high-speed Internet access to their subscribers, as are other members of the telecommunications industry.

The following list describes some interesting direct Internet connection technologies:

◆ **Direct-broadcast satellite.** Satellite is a high-speed service using standard dish technology. Hughes Network Systems (800/347-3272) has a service called DirecPC for which a $699 add-in card is connected to a satellite dish. Speeds can reach 400 kilobits per second for received data; for outgoing communication, dial-up speeds are all that is possible.

◆ **Asymmetric Digital Subscriber Line (ADSL).** This technology delivers incoming data at 1.6 to 6 Mbps on a telephone wire connection. AT&T developed ADSL for interactive TV. Outgoing speed is moderate, about 64 Kbps, which is slightly faster than ISDN.

◆ **Cable modem.** A number of equipment vendors offer cable modem service. A cable modem is a router with a 10Base-T Ethernet connection that attaches to a proprietary cable. You can buy routers of this type from AT&T, Digital, General Instrument, Hewlett-Packard, Intel, LANCity, Motorola, and Zenith, for between $300 and $500. Ethernet type speeds of 10 Mbps are realized for incoming data.

Table 28.1 summarizes some of the fast connections just mentioned.

TABLE 28.1
Fast Web Connection Technologies

Issues	ISDN	Direct-broadcast Satellite	ADSL	Cable Modem
Signaling speeds	56 Kbps to 128 Kbps	400 Kbps downloading; 28.8 uploading (modem)	1.6 to 6 Mbps downloading; 64 Kbps uploading	10 Mbps downloading; 28.8 to 768 Kbps uploading
Costs	$350 to $500 up front; $24 per minute; $60 per month for ISDN (plus ISP charges)	$700 up front; $16 to $40 per month for Internet service	$300 to $500 up front (est.); monthly subscription and ISP charges	$300 to $500 up front; monthly subscription and ISP charges
Service providers	Local telephone companies	One vendor	Local telephone companies; long distance carriers	Local cable companies and long distance carriers
Availability	Good and getting better	Widely available once offered	Will be slowly adopted, community by community	Will be slowly adopted, community by community
Barriers to success	Lack of telephone company initiative; tariff problems	Lack of competitive pricing	Must be within 2.3 miles of central office; investment in new technology; telephone company must partner with ISP	Investment in two-way cable technology; cable company will probably partner with ISP

continues

TABLE 28.1, CONTINUED
Fast Web Connection Technologies

Issues	ISDN	Direct-broadcast Satellite	ADSL	Cable Modem
Subscriber equipment needed	ISDN adapter	Satellite terminal and receiver	ADSL modem	Cable modem with 10Base-T connection
Suitability for Internet access	Excellent service from ISPs	Excellent, but probably no choice of ISP	Excellent, but probably little choice of ISP	Excellent, but probably little choice of ISP
Suitability for remote-LAN access	Excellent, getting more practical	Poor	Poor, except between nearby premises with dedicated copper cables	Excellent within the same community, otherwise poor

From "Fast Connections," by Les Freed, *PC Magazine,* June 11, 1996, p. 145.

Security

When you have a dial-up connection, you control and monitor the connection. Typically, security in this situation is not a major issue. For direct and persistent Internet connections, however, security can be a major concern. There are several methods used to secure a web server that are worth your consideration; some are hardware solutions, others are software solutions. They include the use of firewalls, password access, secure protocols, and network isolation of web servers.

When you connect through an ISP, they will almost certainly have a firewall installed to protect users. A firewall is a computer that examines the incoming packets and filters them appropriately. A firewall may be a single computer with a direct Internet connection, which typically costs from $10,000 to $25,000. A firewall may be all the security you need when coupled with IIS' use of the NT challenge response security scheme.

If you are running IIS and can't afford a firewall, you can run TCP/IP on your web server alone. Packets must be translated into NetBEUI or IPX/SPX, a method called protocol isolation. This method works well, but isolates your server from internal clients.

A number of vendors, including Microsoft, have introduced proxy servers. A *proxy server* is a server that contains two or more network interface cards (NIC), one used for the Internet connection, the other to communicate with your internal network. Proxy servers are less effective than a firewall or protocol isolation, but provide better performance; they are a good compromise.

Turning off the IP Routing setting in the Network Control Panel when you configure Windows NT Server for TCP/IP gives you one way TCP/IP access incoming from the Internet and one way access outgoing to your LAN clients. The router device between your server and the Internet can also come with software that lets you filter packets, so check its documentation during setup. This method is the least secure of all of the methods mentioned.

When you install IIS, you are well advised to do so on an NTFS volume because doing so enables you to avail yourself of NT Server's C2 security scheme. In this scheme, passwords are double-encrypted. You can control access to resources on an NTFS volume down to the folder or file level on each and every network share. You can further monitor the event logs for an NTFS file system to see if sensitive information is being accessed. The FAT file system only lets you set overall execute permissions for WWW access, and overall read and write permission for FTP access from within the Internet Service Manager.

Secure Transactions

In order to establish IIS as a secure Internet platform, Microsoft has been active in the standards committees that are developing the technologies that will be used for secure transactions. A number of secure HTTP protocols have been developed, and Microsoft has long been engaged in developing secure Internet transaction servers. The impending release of the Microsoft Commerce Server, a version of IIS meant for cash and credit card transactions, is an outgrowth of this work.

One of the utilities that ships with IIS is the Key Manager. This application creates a digital key for Secure Sockets Layers (SSL) security. You generate a key pair, apply for an SSL certificate from a registration authority, and install the SSL certificate on your web server. Any communication you engage in is accompanied by the certificate indicating that the transmission originated from your server, and that the server is a secure site with a registered certificate.

A digital signature can be applied to a single server (IP address), or to all virtual servers on your network. With the digital signature enabled, the SSL feature in the Internet Service Manager applies to all web services. That is, SSL can be applied to any viewed directory.

Normandy

Microsoft is about to release a suite of products that it has called Normandy. Normandy will be part of the BackOffice suite of products, and will contain a set of connectors to Microsoft Exchange.

Here are the components slated to be part of Normandy:

◆ Internet Mail with SMTP/POP3 e-mail support and MIME encoding

◆ An NNTP USENET news service server

◆ An Internet Rely Chat (IRC) service

◆ An Internet directory or white pages

◆ A new security system using the Microsoft Internet Security Framework

◆ Customization through ActiveX components

◆ A search and retrieval utility for HTML content, Microsoft Office, and NNTP newsfeed documents

◆ Replication of information stores locally or remotely

Clearly, Normandy is aimed at ISPs, but many larger organizations might choose to adopt Normandy as part of the enterprise services. We will see whether Normandy really does hit the beaches running in 1997.

Testing Your Knowledge

1. Windows NT Server 3.5x and above come packaged with Internet Information Server (IIS).

   A. True

   B. False

2. Which name resolution is best if you are going to be connected to the Internet, or if your network includes non-Microsoft hosts?

   A. HOSTS files

   B. WINS

   C. LMHOSTS files

   D. DNS

3. After the installation of IIS, a new common program group is added to the Start menu entitled Internet Server. Which one of the following icons does not get installed into this new group?

    A. Internet Information Server Setup

    B. Internet Server Manager

    C. Key Manager

    D. Product Documentation

    E. Microsoft Internet Explorer

4. What does the abbreviation http stand for?

5. What does the abbreviation ftp stand for?

6. Universal Resource Locators (URLs) are used to request access to directories, files, and servers on the World Wide Web. What three categories of information does the URL specify?

    A. The protocol

    B. The domain name or IP address

    C. The server UNC name

    D. The path to the information the user wishes to retrieve

7. The IIS service can not be started, stopped, or paused from the Services utility in the Control Panel.

    A. True

    B. False

8. The installation of the IIS service adds an HTTP service object with counters, which enables you to monitor many aspects of IIS operations with the Performance Monitor.

    A. True

    B. False

9. What is the default root or home directory of the WWW server?

    A. C:\Winnt\system\inetsvr\wwwroot

    B. C:\Winnt\system32\wwwroot

    C. C:\Winnt\system32\inetpub\wwwroot

    D. C:\Winnt\inetsvr\wwwroot

10. When setting WWW service properties, what does the Connection Timeout option determine?

11. It is possible to configure virtual servers that enable a single WWW server to have multiple personalities. This lets your server service multiple domains, if needed. What is this feature called?

    A. multiservers

    B. virtual servers

    C. virtual homing

    D. multihoming

12. Before setting up the FTP service, you need to verify that the IUSR_*servername* account has which permission for the FTP directories?

    A. Read

    B. Delete

    C. Write

    D. Change

13. A _____ file is a special file associated with a file that will be advertised on the Gopher server. This special file contains information describing the file and the administrator responsible for the file or Gopher server.

14. Which connection type provides the greatest bandwidth?

    A. PPP ISDN

    B. T1

    C. T3

    D. 56 K

Review Answers

1. B

2. D

3. E

4. HyperText Transport Protocol

5. File Transfer Protocol

6. A, B, D

7. B

8. A

9. C

10. How long the server will permit a connection to remain idle before disconnecting.

11. D

12. A

13. tag

14. C

CHAPTER 29

Exchange Server

Microsoft Exchange Server offers an easy administration interface through graphical presentation of the system's components. Some of the graphical elements might be new to you, such as objects and containers. This chapter takes a look at these elements to present an overview.

Understanding Exchange Objects

An *object* is a record in the Microsoft Exchange Server directory. A site, a server, a mailbox, a folder, and a file are all objects, for example. When you view your system hierarchy, the objects are displayed (see fig. 29.1).

Figure 29.1

The display of your Microsoft Exchange Server system is a series of objects that you can manipulate and configure. It resembles the two-pane system familiar from Windows File Manager and Windows 95 Explorer.

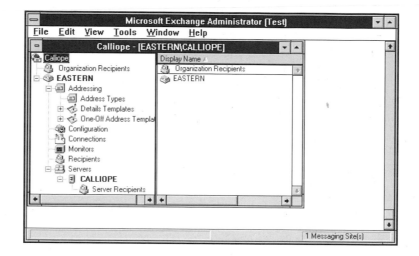

You can configure the properties of an object with the Properties dialog box for that object. The properties vary depending upon the object type, and can include permissions, object names, and choices about object behavior.

Details about setting properties and configuring objects are found throughout this book.

Containers

A *container* is a Microsoft Exchange Server object that holds other objects. All the mailbox objects, for example, are usually placed in a recipient's object, making the recipient's object a container.

Containers and the objects within them have a parent-child hierarchical structure that controls permissions. *Permissions* are the rules that determine which users can access the object and what manipulations they can perform upon it.

Parent objects are any objects that are superior to another object (the child object). A container object is a parent to all the objects within it (which could include other containers that become parents to the objects they contain). Permissions granted to the parent object are automatically inherited by every child object.

Child objects are any objects that are subordinate to another object (the parent).
Objects in a container are child objects because they are subordinate to the container
itself. The permissions granted to each child object are inherited from its parent.

Connectors

A *connector* is an object that sets the properties for a particular connection. Each type
of connection you establish has connectors (see fig. 29.2). Connectors also exist for
directory exchanges (used to update addresses and other recipient information), and
you can establish connectors between sites.

Figure 29.2

*Click on the
Connections object
to see the
connectors
installed on a
server.*

Object Types

Your Microsoft Exchange Server system has a variety of object types, and configuration options vary by object type. Here are some of the object types you will encounter:

- ◆ Site (container object)

- ◆ Connections (container object)

- ◆ Connectors

- ◆ Monitors (container object)

- ◆ Recipients (container object)

- ◆ Mailboxes

- ◆ Messages

◆ Distribution lists

◆ Public folders

◆ Servers (container object)

Understanding Server Components

Each server you establish in your system runs components of Microsoft Exchange Server. The specific services run by a specific server vary depending upon the installation and configuration choices you make. Recall that the server components are also referred to as the back-end components (the client components are the front-end components).

Microsoft Exchange Server has both core services and optional services. *Core services* are the directory and messaging services. *Optional services* enhance the power and flexibility of your system by adding connectivity as well as directory exchange with other systems. Most of the optional components are provided with your Microsoft Exchange Server disks. Some optional services, however, need to be purchased separately.

Directory

A server's *directory* holds information about the organization's resources and users, such as servers, mailboxes, public folders, and distribution lists. It is automatically replicated to all servers in the same site, and you can configure your system to replicate the server's directory to servers in other sites.

Information Stores

Recall that the information stores hold the data that move through your system via Microsoft Exchange Server's messaging functions. The public information store and the private information store are the components of the information stores. The information stores also maintain and enforce data security.

The public information store holds public folders, which can contain files or public messages. The public folder can be replicated on multiple servers. Microsoft Exchange Server ensures that the replication is ongoing so that whenever a public folder changes, the changes are replicated on every selected server. The private information store holds mailboxes and individual, personal messages.

Information Store Databases

The *public database* and the *private database* are databases that track the information in your public information stores and private information stores. The databases are part of the information store structure.

When an item is placed in a public folder, it is analogous to adding a record in a database. If it changes, the database record changes accordingly. To keep performance at an optimum level, Microsoft Exchange Server keeps a separate transaction log to record additions, deletions, and changes in the database. Everything is recorded in the transaction log and periodically saved to the database.

Message Transfer Agent (MTA)

The Message Transfer Agent (MTA) is your Microsoft Exchange Server postal service. MTA routes messages throughout your system and to gateways that connect to outside e-mail systems. When necessary, it handles the conversion of message formats and addresses for external systems.

The MTA is an object in a server container, and it moves messages from one server to another in order to deposit them in the correct mailbox or gateway location (using each server's MTA).

You can set the properties for an MTA object to limit the size of messages, enable log files, and rebuild the routing tables. Specific information about configuring and administering the MTA is found throughout this book.

The MTA engine uses three Microsoft Exchange Server core components to route and transfer data to other servers (or to foreign e-mail systems):

◆ Microsoft Exchange Server site connector

◆ Remote Access Service (RAS) connector

◆ X.400 connector

Site Connector

A *site connector* connects two sites using remote procedure calls (RPCs). The sites must be linked with permanent connections. Site connectors are easy to set up and configure because using RPCs means you do not need to worry about configuring a network transport—the connector uses the existing transport. This transparency means you can use multiple network platforms in your system.

RAS Connector

The *Remote Access Service* (RAS) connector also is a site connector, except it is used between sites where you do not have a permanent connection. It is an asynchronous communications connector that you can configure for regular, automatic initiation of the connection process.

X.400 Connector

You usually use the X.400 connector because you want to do the following:

◆ Connect sites that have low-bandwidth network connections.

◆ Take advantage of an existing X.400 backbone.

◆ Access a public X.400 system.

The connector can be configured to match your needs. You are able to schedule the times for initiating connections, control the size of messages that use the connector, and control the routes messages take.

Microsoft Exchange Server supports X.400 over the following OSI transports:

◆ Transport Protocol, Class 0 (TP0)/X.25

◆ Transport Protocol, Class 4 (TP4)/Connectionless Network Protocol (CLNP)

◆ TP0/RFC 1006 to Transmission Control Protocol/Internet Protocol (TCP/IP)

The X.400 connector supports all the standard binary message body parts (such as ASCII text, fax image, or a spreadsheet attachment) so that embedding and transferring binary data is supported for most messaging needs.

Other Connectors

Other connectors are built into Microsoft Exchange Server so that users have a wide variety of message targets:

◆ The Internet Mail Connector permits users to communicate with Internet users through the Simple Mail Transfer Protocol (SMTP). Because this connector is built into Microsoft Exchange Server, messages received from an Internet system are indistinguishable from internal messages.

◆ The Microsoft Mail connector gives users seamless connectivity to Microsoft Mail for PC Networks, Microsoft Mail for PC Networks gateways, and Microsoft Mail for AppleTalk Networks.

System Attendant

The *System Attendant* is an ongoing service that runs in the background, but it must be running in order for the Microsoft Exchange Server messaging processes to run.

The System Attendant performs several basic, important functions that enable messaging:

◆ It monitors the connections between servers to make sure that messages sent from one server are received at the target server.

◆ It runs any monitor tools you establish in the system (you can create monitors to check specific links between servers or to monitor specific server functions).

◆ It generates e-mail addresses for new message recipients so that mail gets to the right mailbox on the right server.

◆ It logs the information needed to track messages if you opt to enable the message tracking features.

The System Attendant also communicates with other components of Microsoft Exchange Server to perform some of its functions. Communication with the Directory is established by the System Attendant for the following:

◆ Looking up addresses

◆ Building routing tables

◆ Checking the uniformity of directory replication

Communication with the Key Management Component is established by the System Attendant to manage digital signatures and encryption information for mailboxes.

Communication with the System Attendant is initiated by the MTA when there is a message sent or received between a site and another site or system. The System Attendant logs the event in order to track the messaging activities.

The information store initiates communication with the System Attendant to notify the SA when the messaging is local.

Learning About Optional Components

Optional components are included in your Microsoft Exchange Server system that you can install on an as-needed basis. Some optional components, however, need to be purchased separately.

Directory Synchronization

The *directory synchronization component* exchanges directory information between Exchange Server and Microsoft Mail 3.x, as well as other messaging systems that use the Mail 3.x protocol.

The directory synchronization component works with the Directory (to add, modify, or delete custom recipients) and the MTA (to deliver directory-related messages bound for foreign e-mail systems). There is no communication between this component and any other components of Microsoft Exchange Server.

Key Management

The *Key Management component* manages all the security information that is used for digitally signing and sealing messages with Microsoft Exchange Server.

It sends communications to the Directory in order to store digital signatures and encryption information. It receives communication from the Administrator Program and the System Attendant to set up and manage the digital signatures and encryptions for mailboxes.

Microsoft Schedule+ Free/Busy Connector

The optional Schedule+ Free/Busy connector is used if the Schedule+ program is installed. It is the vehicle through which Microsoft Exchange Server exchanges Microsoft Schedule+ free and busy information with Microsoft Mail for PC Networks. It is actually an extension to the Microsoft Mail connector.

Free and busy information is collected in order to facilitate group scheduling. Schedule+ users are able to view each other's free and busy times in order to ascertain the most productive schedules for meetings (picking a time when all or most of the attendees are free).

The Schedule+ Free/Busy connector communicates with other components of Microsoft Exchange Server:

◆ It initiates communication to the Microsoft Mail connector in order to send information about free and busy times to post offices on Microsoft Mail for PC Networks.

◆ It initiates communication to the information store to send data about free and busy times for Microsoft Mail for PC Networks users. Once the data is in the information store, it can be accessed by Microsoft Exchange users.

◆ It initiates communication to the Directory in order to get address book information.

The Schedule+ Free/Busy connector is not on the receiving end of any communication from any other Microsoft Exchange Server components.

Third-Party Gateways

An optional, separate purchase, the Third-Party Gateways component is used to exchange messages to foreign e-mail systems, such as IBM's Professional Office System (PROFS) and System Network Architecture Distribution Services (SNADS). This component performs message translation in both directions so that users have no difficulty using the system.

Understanding Client Components

The Microsoft Exchange client components, which are installed on the workstations, comprise the front end of your Microsoft Exchange Server software:

◆ Microsoft Exchange component, which provides the messaging services to users

◆ Forms Designer component, which permits users to develop forms for messaging in a graphical environment

◆ Schedule+ component, which manages users' schedules and to-do lists, and provides a personal information manager

Let's look at the concepts and issues that have to be considered before deciding what to install. This should give you an edge in your planning.

In order to install the Microsoft Exchange client software, you must already have set up Windows NT user accounts and Microsoft Exchange Server mailboxes for users. An NT user account is configured with all the information that creates a user for Windows NT, including a name and password. For Microsoft Exchange Server, all users must have an NT user account in order to access a mailbox.

Client Components Options

You should consider two major decisions before you begin installation of the client components:

◆ The method of installation

◆ The location of the client files

Client Components Installation Methods

You can install the client components on client workstations directly from the Microsoft Exchange Server disks or CD-ROM.

You also can install the client components directly from the server once a workstation is connected to the server. In order to accomplish this, you must make sure you install the client software when you install Microsoft Exchange Server. The client software will be placed in a subdirectory called Clients, and there will be subdirectories named DOS, Ntx86, Win16, and Win95upg.

Each workstation will install the appropriate client files from the server as if they were connected to a CD-ROM.

Figure 29.3 shows the opening screen for installation via the network for a Windows for Workgroups client. Figure 29.4 is the opening screen for the same process being run on a Windows 95 client. Note that for Windows 95, this is an installation upgrade, because Exchange is an application included in Windows 95.

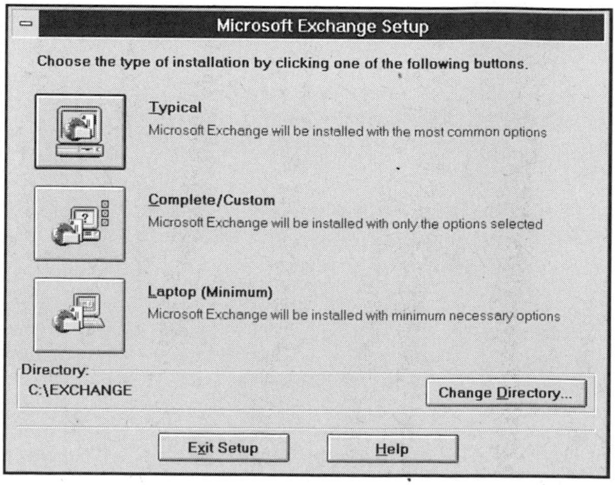

Figure 29.3

A Windows for Workgroups Client is installing the client components after logging on to the NT server.

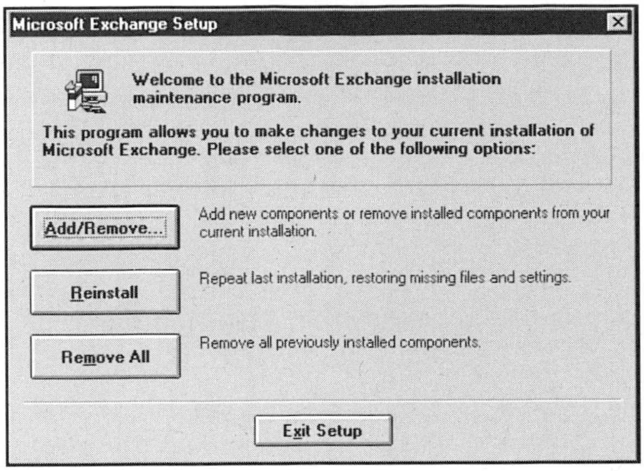

Figure 29.4

A Windows 95 client is upgrading Exchange from the NT server.

Using an Installation Point on a Different Server

By default, when the Clients directory is installed on an NT server, it is a shared directory and becomes an installation point for client machines. Clients can access the installation point and begin the installation of the client software.

As an alternative, you can copy the client files to another server, even a server that is not running NT, and use that server as the installation point for the client components. You must make sure that user access and permissions for the directory are established appropriately.

Exchange Software Location

You can configure Microsoft Exchange Server so that the client components run from either local hard drives or from the network. After you establish a shared directory, the Setup program for client components can designate the directory as the target drive and path.

User Profiles

Users can establish profiles that contain the configuration for their Microsoft Exchange sessions. In fact, they can have multiple profiles and direct the software to ask for a profile when Microsoft Exchange is launched. Multiple user profiles are useful for companies where users might find themselves at different computers occasionally.

Mobile Users

Mobile users who dial in to get their mail and messages need a bit of special handling, but all the necessary functions are available. The dial-in protocols differ by platform:

◆ MS-DOS clients can use ShivaRemote, which is included in Microsoft Exchange Server.

◆ WIN 3.x clients can also use ShivaRemote.

◆ Windows 95 clients use Microsoft Dial-Up Networking, which is included in Windows 95.

◆ Windows NT clients use Remote Access Service (RAS), which is included in Windows NT (Server and Workstation).

> **Caution**
>
> During installation of the client components, the Setup program provides an option to copy the ShivaRemote files to the \EXCHANGE\SHIVA directory on the local disk. Once the files are copied to the client computer, the ShivaRemote Setup program must be run to finish the installation and configuration of ShivaRemote.
>
> After installation and configuration, MS-DOS clients using ShivaRemote have to connect to the network, launch the software, and then disconnect from the network. For all other platforms, invoking the software makes connection and disconnection an automatic process.
>
> If your users have dial-up software that they prefer to use to access Microsoft Exchange Server to pick up their mail and messages, it is likely that the software is supported (almost all of them are). The connection and disconnection, however, must be made manually; the third-party software will not process the instructions needed to log on, get through the password processes, and reach the mailbox. Once there is a third-party connection, all the steps to open the Inbox, fetch any received messages, and so on, are taken one at a time as if the user were in front of the client workstation.

The Microsoft Exchange Server Setup Editor

One of the handy tools you will find in your Microsoft Exchange Server software is the Setup Editor (see fig. 29.5). You can use this program to establish default setup conditions for various platforms. Each platform can have specific configuration information regarding the location of files, how the notification of mail arrival is handled, and so forth.

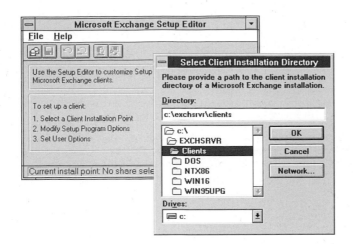

Figure 29.5

The Setup Editor enables you to program the configuration for each of the client installation points.

To jump-start your grey cells when considering the use of the Setup Editor, review the following scenario.

You have several hundred users and most of them work in your company's office, some are on the road most of the time, and some work from home. The office workstations are running various platforms:

◆ The accounting department is connected to two servers: one runs NetWare and contains the accounting software, and the other is an NT server running Microsoft Exchange Server and has each user's mailbox. All users are running DOS machines to get the speed and productivity they want from their text-based accounting programs.

◆ The executive suite and clerical staff are using computers that are running Windows of varying flavors. They are connected to NT server for their mail, and specific individuals are also connected to specific servers (some NetWare, some NT, maybe even some peer-to-peer) for software access.

◆ Salespeople are working from laptops as they rove the world servicing customers. The laptops run various operating systems, depending upon the comfort level of the individual users.

◆ The public relations people work from home, and their computers run whatever platform they find comfortable (or their children demand).

You need to decide how they will access the NT server running Microsoft Exchange Server to get their mail. You have several options for configuring all these client workstations:

◆ Software installed on local drives for every machine

◆ Software installed on local drives for the in-office machines only

◆ Software installed on local drives for mobile laptop users only

◆ Software installed on local drives for home users only

◆ Software installed on the server for every platform

◆ Repeat choices on local drives here, substituting server for local drives

You can remove all the installation choices except the one you want from any setup file. You can create a setup file for your mobile users, for example, so that the only choice they see is the setup for a portable computer.

You also have to set up a mail notification system:

◆ Do you want individuals in the office to be notified every time messages arrive in their mailboxes?

◆ Do you want individuals in the office to learn about their mail when they log on to check their mailboxes?

◆ For the remote users, do you want to notify somebody in the office every time mail is placed in the mailbox so a telephone call can be made to the remote user?

Okay, that last suggestion is silly, but this is just an example of the decisions you will have to make. You can control these options by using the features available in the Setup Editor.

> **Tip**   The Setup Editor creates default configurations, and you can use them as the basis of specific configurations if an individual user's needs do not match the original defaults. Nothing is etched in cement.

Understanding Mail Component Concepts

The Exchange component for clients is used for e-mail and information sharing. It is available for the following client platforms:

◆ Windows 3.x

◆ Windows for Workgroups 3.11

◆ Windows NT Workstation 3.51 and higher

◆ Windows NT Server 3.51 and higher

◆ Windows 95

◆ MS-DOS 5.0 and higher

Note that at the time of this writing, the Macintosh and Unix client software had not yet been released.

The messages and shared files that are sent and received by the client users all pass through the public and private folders located on a server running Microsoft Exchange Server. During your planning and installation, be sure that all users have a connection to the nearest, easiest-to-access server.

The Inbox

The client Inbox holds mail, messages, files, and whatever else has been sent to the client. It is a universal container that saves clients the trouble of fetching mail and then switching to another container to retrieve other items.

The Inbox appears as a folder in the graphical hierarchy of the client's mailbox configuration (see fig. 29.6). Users can arrange, sort, select, design, and otherwise customize their view of the Inbox.

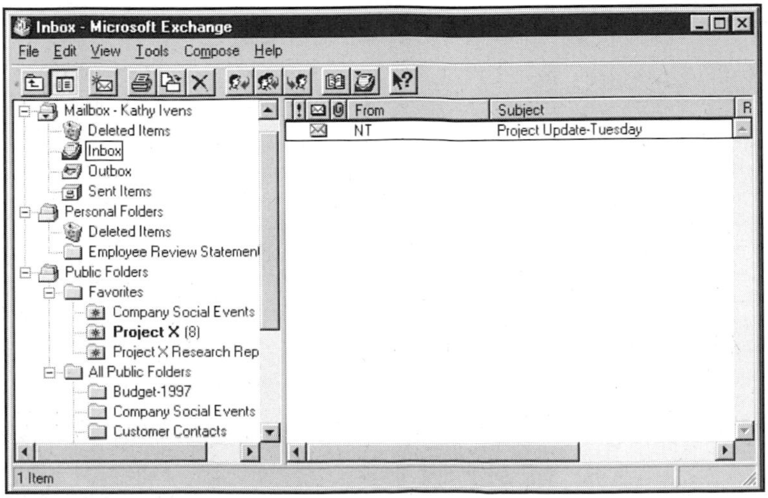

Figure 29.6

When a user checks mail on the server, the graphical display is easy to use, and there are lots of ways to customize the display and use of the mailbox.

Client Mail Assistants

Intelligent Mail Assistants can be established by each user on the server so that certain procedures are implemented even when the user is not logged on. The design and configuration of these Assistants are executed easily by using dialog boxes, and no programming or other special computer skills are necessary in order to get the full power of the Mail Assistants.

With the Inbox Assistant, users can configure their Inboxes so that the contents are reported back with a priority and selection scheme suiting each user. Incoming messages can be sorted and filed in specific folders automatically, so when a user does check the Inbox, everything is set up conveniently.

Users can establish procedures for being notified when a message arrives in the Inbox, or, when circumstances require it, set up an Out Of Office Assistant to handle mail while the user is away on vacation or a business trip, or is otherwise unavailable. This could be implemented either as forcing an immediate response to messages by generating an automatic reply to the sender (such as I'm away on vacation, will return on Monday), or forwarding the mail to someone else.

E-Mail with Personality

The Microsoft Exchange client Mail Component supports rich text formatting (RTF) and provides a full range of editing features. The message environment is identical across all the supported platforms. RTF is preserved only across graphical platforms, however, and if a message is sent to an e-mail application that can't use RTF, it is converted to regular ASCII text. Note that this conversion to regular text may leave behind unreadable characters where the formatting codes were.

When e-mail is created, the formatting and document tools are robust. There are toolbars and formatting bars (see fig. 29.7), making the following elements available:

- ◆ Fonts that are installed and supported by the underlying operating system
- ◆ Paragraph alignment: left, right, and centered
- ◆ Bullets, which can be inserted automatically, giving the paragraph a hanging indent
- ◆ Character formatting, including bold, italic, underline, and color
- ◆ Tool tips, which are just like those in Microsoft Office—pointing the mouse at a button produces a tool tip that tells you that button's function
- ◆ AutoText, which enables you to store frequently used text, formatting, graphics, or messages for quick retrieval

◆ Drag and drop editing, including elements from other applications (spreadsheets and graphics)

◆ Spelling checker

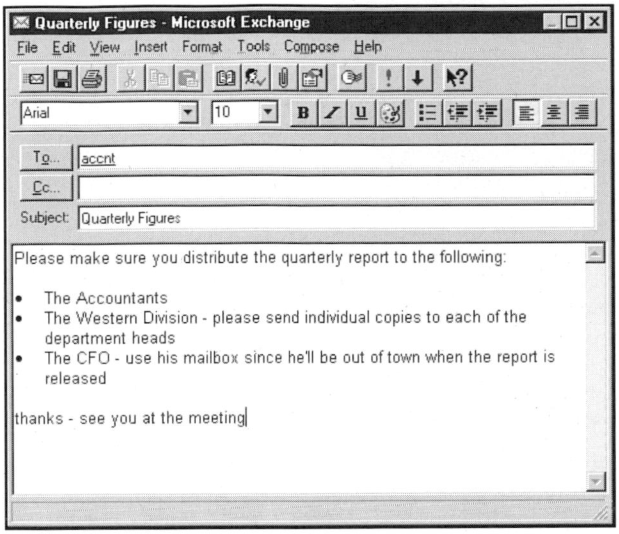

Figure 29.7

The window used to create a message is similar to that used by word processing applications, with plenty of configuration options, tools, and application features.

The Microsoft Exchange client mail component also supports incorporation of files as attachments. The attachments are in the form of icons, which can be placed in the body of a message (the icons include the file names). The message body supports object linking and embedding (OLE) 2.0, so users can edit any attached and embedded files they receive.

Understanding Form Designer Concepts

Sometimes it might be convenient or more productive to create a specific form to use when sending messages of a certain type. A predesigned form for all those messages that say "let's meet for lunch" or "where shall we meet for lunch?" makes sending such messages faster. A department head who likes to call meetings could create a form that requires very little data entry to complete.

Throughout the enterprise, forms for administration of the company can be designed for quick distribution—a vacation schedule form, announcements of the annual company picnic, and so on.

Once the Forms Designer is installed, it can be accessed during an Exchange session. Just choose Application **D**esign, **F**orms Designer from the **T**ools menu. When the program launches, you see the window shown in figure 29.8.

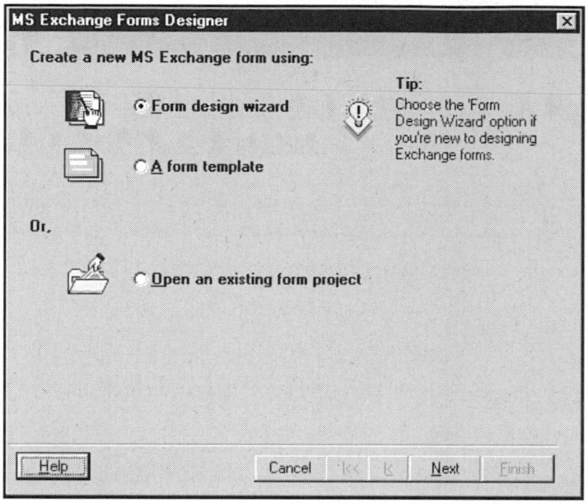

Figure 29.8

To create a new form, you can use the wizard for step-by-step help, or open a form as the starting point to creating a new custom form.

The Form Designer Wizard

Using the wizard is a simple process of answering questions about the type of form you want to create and the way you want it to look. You can create forms for messages (e-mail sent to one or more users) or for postings (items that are placed in folders for public access through the enterprise).

The process includes the capability of designing the method used to display your form to users (see fig. 29.9). You can change the fields that are displayed so that one set of fields is available during message creation and a different set displays when a user reads the data in the form.

Using Templates

If you choose Select Form Template, the dialog box displays a list of all the existing form templates (see fig. 29.10).

Design Elements

Once you create the basic layout for your form through the wizard, or by choosing a template, you can customize the form.

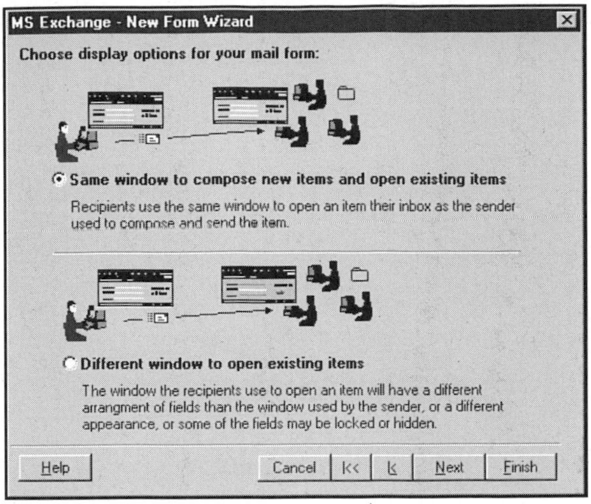

Figure 29.9

You can decide to have two formats for your new form, one for entering the data and a different one for reading it.

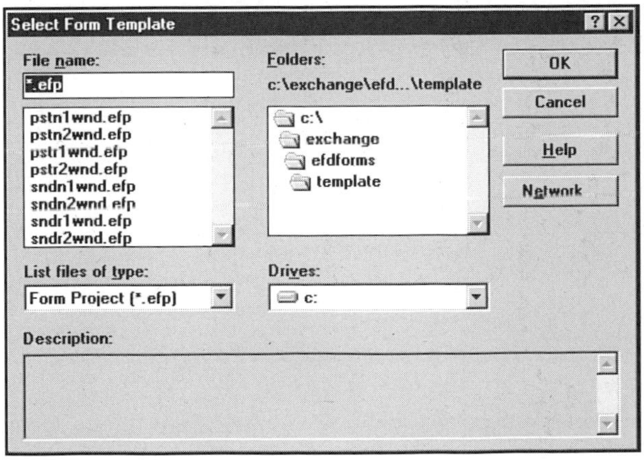

Figure 29.10

You can choose a form that approximates the form you want to create as a starting point for your design.

On the left side of your workspace is a toolbar that lists the fields that generally go into a message header (From, To, Date, and so on) as well as buttons that enable you to create other fields as needed. You can add any of the following field types and label them as you want:

◆ Text entry field

◆ Check box field

◆ Option button field

◆ List box or Combo box field

◆ Group box field (used for holding multiple options and selection buttons)

◆ Tabbed panel field (choices on separate windows, accessed by clicking on tabs)

◆ Picture field, in which you can insert a graphic

Field Properties

Once you drag a field to your form and position it where you want it, double-click on it to bring up its Properties dialog box (see fig. 29.11) and configure the way the field is used and displayed.

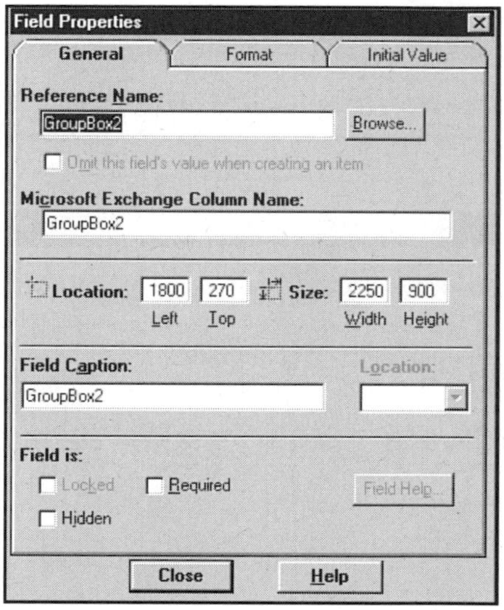

Figure 29.11

Once you insert a field in a form, you get to write the rules about its use.

You can format the location, size, font, alignment, and attributes for each field. If appropriate, you can also enter an initial value for certain fields.

Saving and Installing the Form

When you are happy with the new form, you can save it by choosing **S**ave or Save **A**s from the **F**ile menu. This saves the contents of the window as if you were saving a document, and, in effect, you have a new template.

Installing a form is a separate step. The form is compiled (it is a Visual Basic program that is so easy to use, you don't need to have any programming experience), and then is placed in a Form Registry for use (see fig. 29.12).

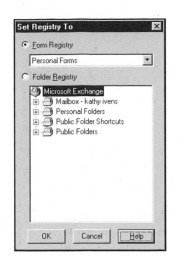

Figure 29.12

*You can install
a form into a
Registry or a
folder so it can be
used by you or
everyone in your
organization.*

A *Form Registry* is a container for forms that can be used by you (if it is a Personal Registry) or everyone (if it is a Global Registry).

A *Folder Registry* is a folder that contains forms and is usually a public folder dedicated to a particular topic. All the files and forms in the folder are connected to the topic. You might have a Personnel Policy folder, for instance, that contains memos, the company's employee policy handbook, and various forms for employees to fill out.

Caution You cannot install a form in the Global Registry unless you have the appropriate permissions on the network.

Before it is sent to the Registry, the form's properties have to be established (see fig. 29.13).

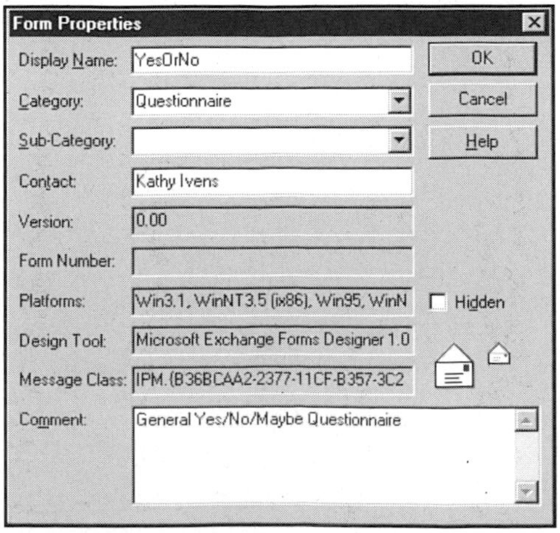

Figure 29.13

*As with all objects
in Microsoft
Exchange Server,
your form has to
have Properties.*

Application Design

Once a form has been designed, compiled, and put into general use, it is really an application. In fact, there is an executable file on your system that is the compiled runtime program you wrote. It has the same information in its Properties as any other executable file in your system.

Besides the capability to design the way the form looks, you can program the form's behavior. You can cause specific instructions (written by you) to appear any time Help is clicked, for instance. Your custom Help statements can be about the form or any specific field in the form.

You can cause specific actions to occur as a result of the data that is placed in the form. This means you can define an event (or a series of events) that should take place in response to an entry. The response might be that a new form is opened or some data is sent to a folder.

Your Microsoft Exchange Server client component has a number of sample applications you can use to help you understand how all this power can be used.

Although you can use all the features and power of Microsoft Exchange Server application design without any knowledge of programming, if you are comfortable with programming in Visual Basic, you can expand and strengthen the scope of your applications. You could, for example, create a form, have it automatically sent to specified recipients, make sure the replies are received, gather the replies, and create some sort of new file format from the data.

Understanding Schedule+ Concepts

Schedule+ is a dual-purpose program—it provides tools for individuals and also provides important services for the entire organization.

For an individual user, it is an easy-to-use application that helps you manage your time and provides the functions available in a personal information manager.

You can use Schedule+ to do the following:

◆ Display your schedule in a variety of formats (daily, weekly, monthly, or yearly).

◆ Track your projects with a task list.

◆ Combine your appointments and your task list to see everything you need to do in a specific day, week, or month.

◆ Keep a list of all your contacts.

For the organization, each individual user's schedule can be centrally collected in order to provide group scheduling:

◆ Choose a meeting time by determining the availability of the attendees.

◆ Send a notice to all the necessary people and collect their responses.

You also can schedule resources, such as conference rooms, and factor in their availability when you are scheduling events.

To understand the concepts and features in Schedule+, take a brief look at its functions. Examine the configuration options to get an idea of their breadth and explore some of the functional parts and how they work.

The Schedule+ Window

When you launch Schedule+, the window that displays is chock-full of information (see fig. 29.14).

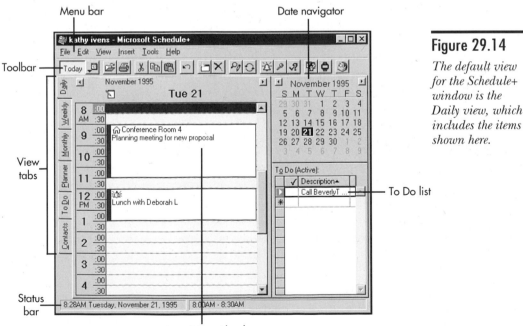

Figure 29.14

The default view for the Schedule+ window is the Daily view, which includes the items shown here.

Configuring Schedule+

The appearance and settings of Schedule+ can be configured to match your work habits. Most of the configuration options are controlled through the dialog box that displays when you choose **O**ptions from the **T**ools menu (see fig. 29.15).

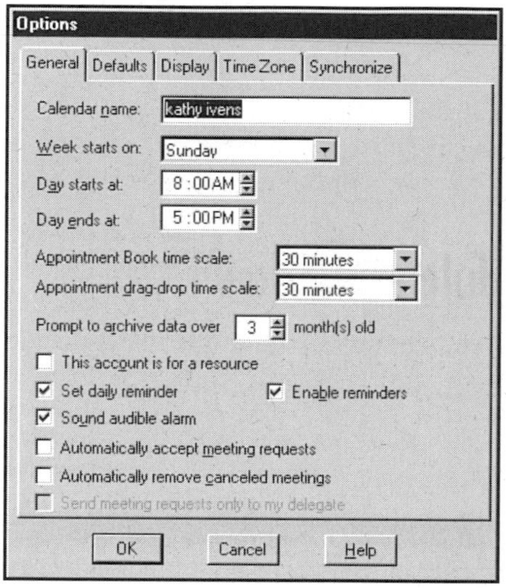

Figure 29.15

Having a wide choice of configuration options makes it easy to use Schedule+ in a way that exactly matches your needs.

Setting General Options

The following list takes a brief look at the variations available, starting with the General tab:

◆ Calendar **n**ame sets the active appointment book—you can have multiple appointment books.

◆ **W**eek starts on enables you to decide which day is the first day of the week (usually a choice between Sunday and Monday).

◆ D**a**y starts at specifies the hour that displays at the top of the appointment book.

◆ Day **e**nds at specifies the last hour that displays. Hours later than that time are still available for entry—but they are shaded.

◆ A**p**pointment Book time scale specifies the size of the time block in which you want to work. Some people prefer 15-minute blocks, for example, while others prefer 30-minute blocks.

◆ Appointment **d**rag-drop time scale specifies the time duration that changes when you drag the handles of an appointment block. If you choose 15 minutes, as you drag an appointment block to make it longer, the appointment becomes 15 minutes longer, then 30 minutes longer, and so forth. To change an appointment to a duration that does not match these multiples, you have to enter data instead of using drag and drop.

◆ Prompt to a**r**chive data over specifies the number of months that will elapse before you are prompted to archive the information in your schedule. Archiving removes the data from the current files and saves it in special archive files. This keeps your file sizes manageable, and you can still answer a question about where you were a year ago last Thursday.

◆ This acc**o**unt is for a resource, if selected, indicates that you are tracking the use of a room or another resource rather than a person.

◆ Set dai**l**y reminder, if selected, causes your To Do list for the current day to display when you first launch Schedule+ (see fig. 29.16).

◆ Ena**b**le reminders specifies that a pop-up appears to remind you about some task, event, or appointment that is imminent (see fig. 29.17).

◆ So**u**nd audible alarm, when selected, causes a noise to be sounded when a Reminder pops up.

◆ Automatically accept **m**eeting requests specifies that when any meeting request form comes to your mailbox, an acceptance is sent back and the meeting is scheduled in your appointment book.

◆ Automatically remove **c**anceled meetings causes meetings to be deleted from your appointment book when a cancellation notice is received in your mailbox.

◆ Send meeting requests only to my delegate, when selected, diverts meeting requests to another user who is acting as your delegate (usually an administrative assistant).

Understanding Access Permissions

If the Send meeting requests only to my delegate check box is greyed out, it means you have not created any delegates.

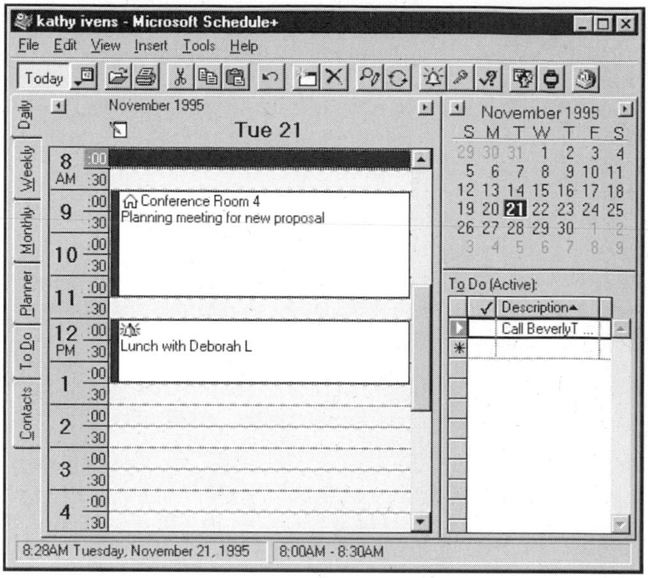

Figure 29.16

You can configure Schedule+ so that when you start the software at the beginning of your work day, today's list of things to do appears automatically.

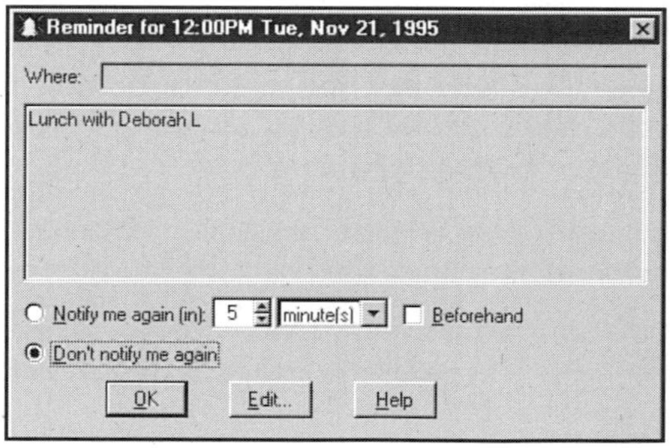

Figure 29.17

It's almost lunch time and you've been reminded of your lunch appointment. You can ask to be notified again in a specified number of minutes, ask to be notified at a certain interval before the actual date, or choose not to be reminded again.

Besides assigning a delegate, you can establish permissions for access to your schedule, giving others the right to change or add items. The sender does not need to be notified whether someone else is receiving your meeting notifications because your configuration options cause this to happen automatically. (Don't worry, you can restrict people with access from seeing your private appointments and notes.)

To give other users specific access to your schedule, follow the steps in the following exercise:

Assigning User Permissions to Your Schedule

1. From the **T**ools menu, choose Set A**c**cess Permissions.

2. To give a user permissions in your schedule, choose **A**dd to bring up the Add Users dialog box.

3. Click the arrow to the right of the box labeled **S**how Names from the to select the source of a users list (see fig. 29.18).

4. Highlight each user to whom you want to give access to your data, then choose **U**sers to move the name to the right panel. You can select multiple users. Click OK when you finish selecting users.

5. From the Users tab of the dialog box, highlight a user name and click the arrow next to the User r**o**le text box to choose a role for this user (see fig. 29.19).

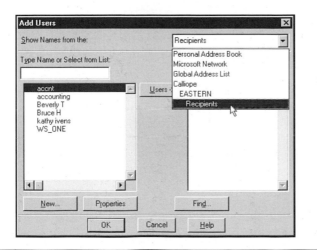

Figure 29.18

Because your mail comes to your Domain Server, you can choose a name from the users who have mailboxes and access to that Domain.

The user roles are connected to the four item types shown on the dialog box (see fig. 29.20). Each of the user roles has specific permissions for the four item types (except Custom, in which you can select permissions for each item type). The following are the available user roles:

◆ Read, which gives the user read-only access to all items except those you've marked as private.

◆ Create, which permits the user to read all items not marked private and to create new items.

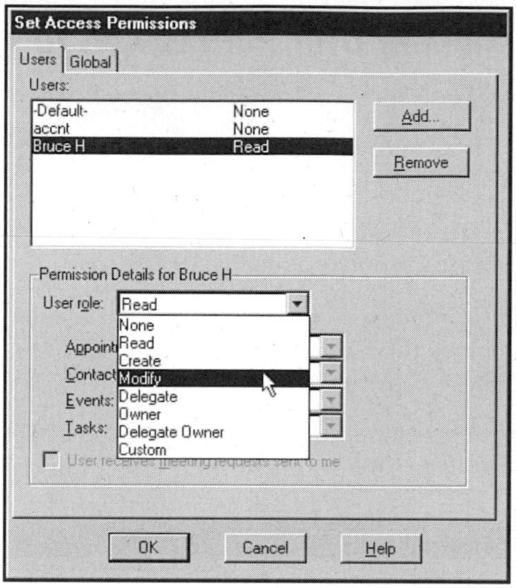

Figure 29.19

Giving another user permission to access or change your schedule data is a one-click operation.

◆ Modify, which enables the user to read and modify all items except those classified as private.

◆ Delegate, which permits the user to read and modify items. Private items are included in these permissions. A Delegate can also receive meeting requests sent to you.

◆ Owner, which enables the user to read and modify all items, including private items.

◆ Delegate Owner, which permits the user to read and modify all items and also receive and send meeting messages for you.

◆ Custom, which enables you to specify access for each particular item type.

Setting Defaults

The Defaults tab of the Options dialog box is where you set the default specifications for the events, tasks, and appointments you enter. Items such as priorities, reminder intervals, and so on, are configurable.

Configuring Display and Time Zone

Use the Display tab to control the colors and features of your Schedule+ windows. Then move to the Time Zone tab to choose a primary time zone and secondary time zone (to keep track of an office in a different time zone, or for your own schedule if you travel a lot).

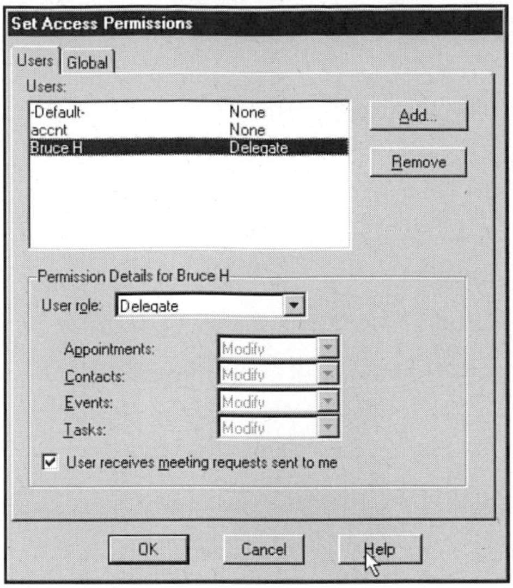

Figure 29.20

The level of access to each of the four types of items in your schedule is determined by the role of the user to whom you're giving permissions.

Synchronizing Schedules

Because you can keep multiple files in Schedule+, perhaps establishing a personal schedule and a business schedule, you can set up the configuration for synchronizing the items on the schedules. This helps you avoid scheduling yourself in two places at the same time.

Understanding Tab Views

Each tab view has a particular display configuration, and you can switch views as you need to. In addition, you can invent your own tab views and add them to your Schedule+ window.

The following are the default tab views:

◆ Daily, which displays a single day's appointments, the Date Navigator, and any active tasks in your To Do List

◆ Weekly, which displays the Appointment Book for a week (or as many days as you want it to) and the Date Navigator

◆ Monthly, which displays a monthly calendar with your appointments showing

◆ Planner, which shows your free/busy times

◆ To Do, which displays the To Do List

◆ Contacts, which shows a list of contacts and a business card display of those contacts

Changing Tabs

You can remove, edit, or create tabs to suit yourself as detailed in the following exercise:

Changing Tabs

1. Choose T**a**b Gallery from the **V**iew menu to see the Tab Gallery dialog box (see fig. 29.21).

2. To remove a current tab, highlight it and select **R**emove.

3. To change the position of a tab, highlight it and then choose Move **U**p or Move **D**own.

4. To add a new tab, select it and choose **A**dd. You can change the title of the tab if you want.

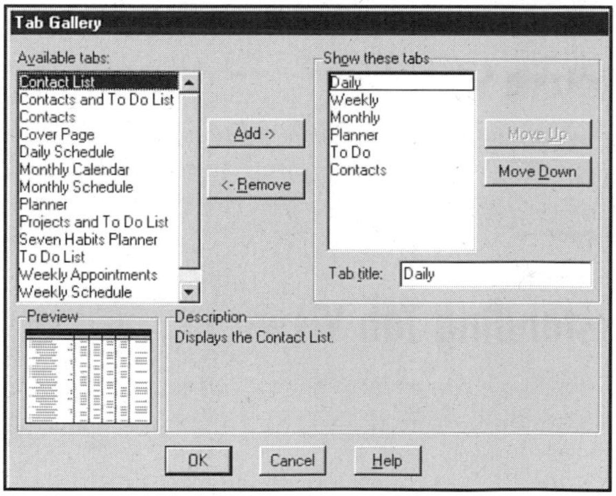

Figure 29.21

The Tab Gallery shows all available tabs in the left pane and the tabs currently being used in the right pane.

Putting Items into Your Schedule+ System

After you configure the look and settings of your Schedule+ software, it is time to enter items. All the items are available from the **I**nsert menu.

Appointments

Choose **A**ppointment to place an item into your calendar. The Appointment dialog box offers a host of options and places in which to store reference information (see fig. 29.22).

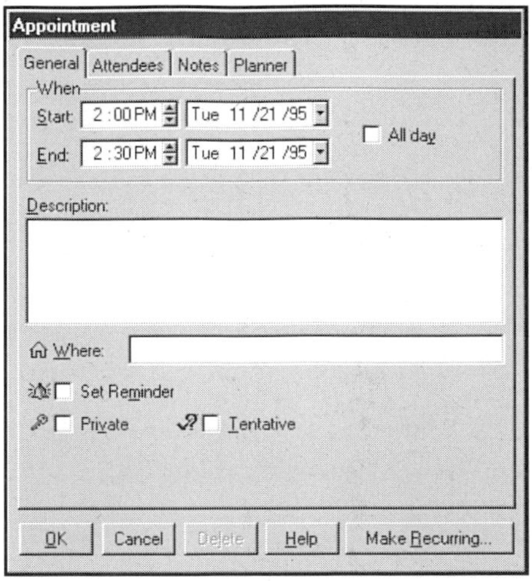

Figure 29.22

Set up an appointment, make it private if you want, and decide whether you need a reminder.

The Attendees tab displays the names of the other people expected to attend this appointment. You can issue an invitation to other users by choosing **I**nvite Others. This displays a dialog box into which you can insert names from any user list (see fig. 29.23).

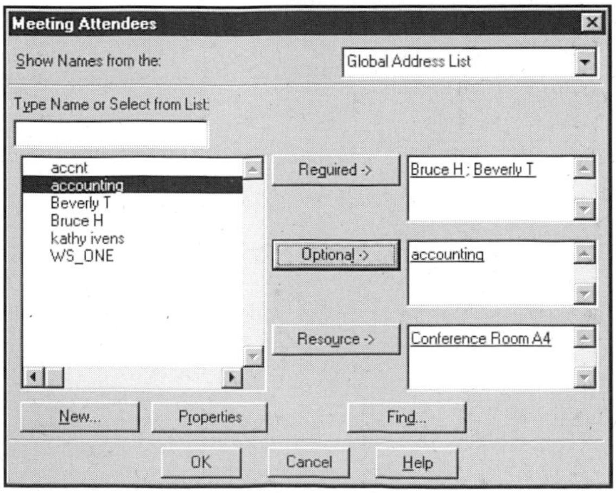

Figure 29.23

When you invite people to attend a meeting, their schedules are compared to yours. If there's a conflict with a required attendee, one schedule has to be changed.

The Notes tab is a place for you to make notes to yourself about this appointment.

The Planner tab displays a graphical indication of the meeting time, and it indicates the current status of responses from the other attendees (see fig. 29.24).

Figure 29.24

The meeting time is blocked on the calendar, and the attendees' status shows they have not yet responded.

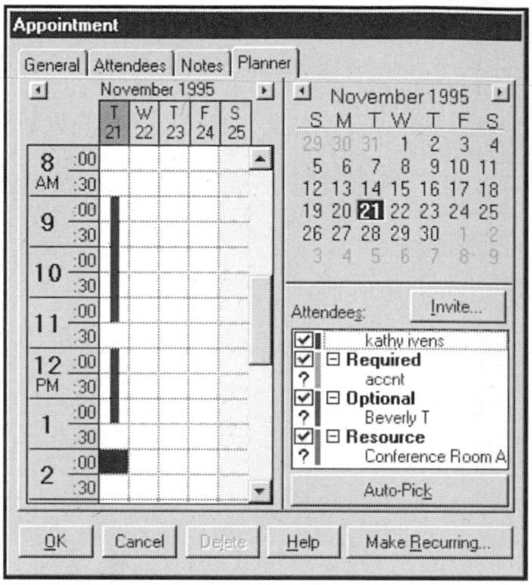

When you finish filling out the fields you need in the dialog box, choose OK. A Meeting Request form automatically appears so that you can send the meeting notice to the list of attendees.

Tasks

Choose **T**ask from the **I**nsert menu to enter a task in the To Do list:

◆ The General tab of the Task dialog box enables you to set a date range for the task and to specify whether you want to be reminded.

◆ The Status tab enables you to track the number of hours or days you have spent on the task (and reports back the percentage complete by using the number of estimated hours or days). The Status tab also provides fields for billing information.

◆ The Notes tab enables you to keep a diary of the progress or jot down any other kind of notes you'd like to amass about this task.

Projects

Choose **P**roject from the **I**nsert menu to establish a project in your system. A project is a way to link tasks that are related under one umbrella. Each project is named and given a priority. You can make a project private if you want.

After you create a project, when you insert any item, you can attach it to the project.

Contacts

In addition to handling your schedule and your list of things to do, Schedule+ has a built-in link to a personal information management system. Choose **C**ontact from the **I**nsert menu to begin (see fig. 29.25).

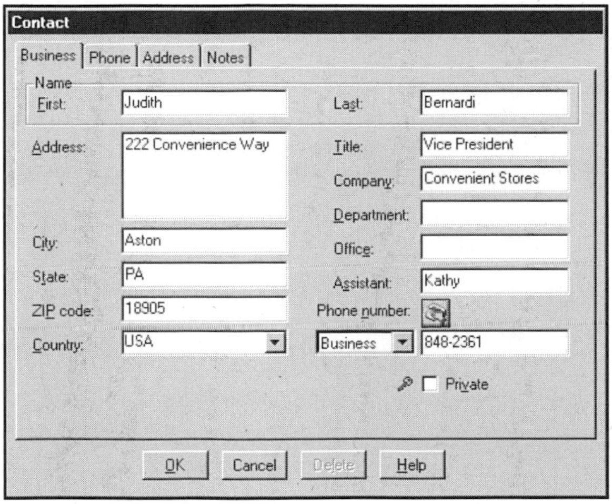

Figure 29.25

The Contact record holds information about people you want to keep track of— click on the telephone icon above the phone number to have Schedule+ dial the number.

Move to the Phone tab to insert additional telephone, fax, or pager numbers, and so forth.

Move to the Address tab to fill in a home address and other personal information (birthday, spouse's name, and so forth).

The Notes tab, of course, is for any comments or notes you want to keep on this contact.

Events

An event is something you want to remember to do or attend, but does not occupy any specific time block in your schedule. You might use the feature to track trade shows or conventions you'll probably want to attend and other miscellaneous reminders. When you choose **E**vent from the **I**nsert menu, the dialog box asks for an event day and start and end dates, and offers an opportunity to make the event private.

Permanent Items

You can also use Schedule+ to track permanent or recurring items. When you designate an item as recurring, you enter it only once. Schedule+ automatically fills in the future occurrences, and you can change or cancel any individual occurrence:

◆ Recurring appointments occur regularly (your Monday morning sales meeting, your monthly sales meeting). They are indicated in the appointment by a circular-arrow symbol.

◆ Recurring tasks are items for your To Do list that occur regularly.

◆ Annual events are events that occur every year on the same date, such as birthdays, anniversaries, and so forth.

This chapter is an overview to give you an idea of what to expect as you install and use Microsoft Exchange Server. The details you'll need for completing the installation and implementing the services are found throughout this book.

Testing Your Knowledge

1. What is the term that denotes a record in the Microsoft Exchange Server directory? A site, a server, a mailbox, a folder, and a file are all considered to be examples of this.

   A. Object

   B. Container

   C. Connector

   D. Directory hierarchy

2. What is the term for a Microsoft Exchange object that holds other objects? All the mailbox objects, for example, are usually placed in a recipient's object, making the recipient's object a container.

   A. Object

   B. Container

   C. Connector

   D. Directory hierarchy

3. Which one of the following is an object that sets the properties for a particular connection?

    A. Object

    B. Container

    C. Connector

    D. Directory hierarchy

4. What does the abbreviation MTA stand for?

5. What does a site connector do?

    A. It connects multiple sites into a manageable object.

    B. It is used as a container for multiple linked sites.

    C. It connects two sites using remote procedure calls.

    D. It establishes a link between two or more sites using APIs.

6. What does the abbreviation SMTP stand for?

7. What does the directory synchronization component do?

    A. Exchanges directory information between Exchange Server and Microsoft Mail 3.x.

    B. Synchronizes directory information in an environment using a site connector.

    C. Maintains a backup copy of the Exchange objects.

    D. Is used with Microsoft Exchange in conjunction with the replication service, as messaging can be very time-critical.

Review Answers

1. A

2. B

3. C

4. Message Transfer Agent

5. C

6. Simple Mail Transfer Protocol

7. A

CHAPTER 30

SQL Server

O ne of the major forces behind NT Server's success is its unique capability to act as a great file and print server *and* as an applications server. NT Server's capability to run 32-bit programs, use virtual memory, run multiple threads, and take full advantage of multiprocessors makes it a great platform for running client/server applications.

Many organizations' database of choice for handling departmental and enterprise-wide information needs is Microsoft's SQL Server. SQL Server is a robust relational database system that enables developers to create enterprise-wide client/server database applications.

SQL Server is a part of Microsoft's BackOffice, which means that it is tightly integrated with NT Server. Consequently, network administrators should find learning and using it similar to learning and using NT Server and other BackOffice applications. SQL Server uses NT Server's Event Viewer and Performance Monitor tools, for example, with which NT administrators already are familiar. As administrators all know, anything that makes their jobs even a little less hectic and a little less complex is certainly beneficial. SQL Server, and its close integration with NT Server, does just that.

This chapter introduces SQL Server, discusses how it works, and describes the responsibilities of the network administrator. It also describes how SQL Server integrates not only with NT Server, but with Microsoft Exchange, Systems Management Server, and the Internet Information Server. To learn all the steps necessary to install and use SQL Server in your network, you will need additional information, which you can find either in the SQL Server manuals, or from some of the resources listed at the end of this chapter.

What Makes SQL Server so Special?

SQL-style database management systems have tended toward being difficult to use and administer. Administrators traditionally have faced an array of problems, including the following hindrances and obstacles:

◆ They have had to type most, if not all, commands at a command prompt, forcing them to learn an arcane syntax. Only true die-hard DOS and Unix administrators love this approach to database management.

◆ They have had to perform virtually all tasks manually; no easy way to schedule common events, such as backing up data, has been available to them. Thus, administrators have had to stay late to make backups after hours.

◆ They have had to manage individual database servers separately because no means for centrally managing all the database servers in an enterprise have been available.

◆ Little, if any, integration has existed between the database servers and other applications. Databases have been, for the most part, isolated resources. To bridge this gap, administrators have had to tediously export the data to a common format and import it into other applications for use.

◆ Purchasing and managing the servers has been very expensive; only larger organizations have been able to afford them.

Microsoft's implementation of SQL Server has alleviated many of these problems. SQL Server offers many features not previously available for any database management system, including:

◆ Microsoft SQL Server is a complete distributed client/server relational database system.

◆ SQL Server has been optimized for high speed, supports multiple processors, and is scalable to meet the needs of large enterprises.

◆ SQL Server supports very large databases, data marts, and data warehousing.

◆ Administration has been simplified by the inclusion of many visual tools that relieve administrators from having to remember obscure commands. This inclusion greatly reduces the amount administrators have to take the time to learn. Of course, if you prefer commands over a GUI interface, you can still use them.

◆ All SQL Servers, no matter where they are located, can be managed from a single location.

◆ A built-in scheduler enables the administrator to schedule virtually any event for any time.

◆ Built-in data replication makes it easy to distribute data throughout the enterprise, and also helps to reduce user downtime and to distribute heavy database loads over many servers.

◆ Database backup and restoration is high speed, and backup can occur while a database is being used.

◆ Although SQL Server runs only on NT Server, client software can run on virtually any network, such as NetWare.

◆ SQL Server has been designed to integrate perfectly with NT Server. SQL Server even uses many of the NT Server tools you are already familiar with.

◆ SQL Server is designed to run on Intel, Alpha, MIPS, and Power-PC platforms, so administrators are able to choose the optimum platform on which to run their particular applications. This versatility saves money because administrators can run their applications on off-the-shelf servers, which are much less expensive than the older mini- and mainframes that were once required to run SQL databases.

◆ SQL integrates well with many of Microsoft's other BackOffice products, including Exchange, Systems Management Software, and Internet Information Server. It also integrates well with Microsoft Office applications.

What Is SQL Server?

Microsoft's SQL Server is a client/server relational database system. What, then, exactly is a client/server relational database system? The best way to explain it is to define it in two parts: the *client/server* part and the *relational database system* part.

What Does Client/Server Mean?

Client/server, also called *distributing computing*, means that all of the data processing of a program does not occur on a single computer, as it does on mini- or mainframe-based computer systems. Instead, different parts of the program run on more than one computer. With SQL Server, for example, the database engine part of the program resides on a server computer, while the other part of the program, the user interface, resides on a client workstation. Hence the term client/server. Instead of the entire program running on the server, part runs on the server and part runs on the client workstation.

Need an example of how a client/server database application might work? Consider a user who wants to query a database to find all customers living in Hawaii. He loads the client part of the program on his workstation, which provides the user-interface and perhaps some of the business logic for the application. The client program checks the query for accuracy, then sends the request for the data to the server. At the server, the server part of the application receives the request from the client, processes the request by running the query, and then sends the results back to the client. The user then uses the client program to format and view the data on-screen or to print it.

Client/server database applications have become very popular because of the many benefits they bring to organizations, including the following:

◆ **Cost.** Instead of relying on expensive proprietary mainframe systems, you can use off-the-shelf servers and client workstations, which are not only less expensive to buy, but much less expensive to operate and maintain.

◆ **Flexibility.** Client/server systems often can be created with off-the-shelf software, or with minimal programming. Microsoft's SQL Server can run on the server, for example, and Microsoft's Excel can run as the client interface.

◆ **Speed.** With the processing load distributed among multiple computers, the overall system can be faster, accommodate more users, and offer greater fault tolerance.

◆ **Data Accessibility.** Mainframe data is often hard, if not next to impossible, for the average user to retrieve. More often than not, a programmer must write a special program to extract the necessary data. Client/server databases generally enable users to access the data they need when they need it, far more easily. Many organizations, for example, are creating intranets that enable users to access data from SQL Server using a simple web browser.

SQL Server is a true client/server database that enables enterprises to design a distributed database system to meet their ever-changing needs.

What Is a Relational Database System?

A *relational database system* is a type of database architecture that has been widely adapted by software vendors (including Microsoft, for SQL Server). A relational database is divided into tables of data, each of which is further divided into rows (records) and columns (fields). Think of a table as a spreadsheet, with rows for records and fields for columns. Most databases include multiple tables, which can be combined to create new tables on the fly. Some other characteristics of relational database systems are listed and described here:

◆ **They use SQL (Structured Query Language).** Virtually all modern relational database systems use the SQL language to manipulate the data in a database. IBM developed SQL in the 1970s (and SQL is the name they gave it; pronounced "ess-que-ell"), and it has since become an industry standard. Most database programming done today involves the use of SQL, and SQL Server administrators must become familiar with the basics of SQL.

◆ **They are customizable.** In many ways, a relational database system resembles a high-level programming language. Although using it for creating a specific application is not always done quickly, it can be used to create virtually any type of application to meet an organization's needs.

◆ **They promote good data integrity.** Data integrity is critical; otherwise, the data in a database is worthless. Relational database systems include many features to help prevent bad data from being entered.

◆ **They can be easily changed.** The needs of businesses change almost daily, and relational databases are designed for easy modification.

◆ **They waste no space.** Unlike flat-file databases, where data is often repeated in many different records, relational databases, by eliminating most redundant data, waste very little precious space. This feature not only reduces disk space requirements, but can speed up data access.

◆ **They enable data security.** Access to data can be limited by the application itself, permitting many levels of security, if desired.

SQL Server includes all of the preceding characteristics, and many more.

Creating an SQL Server Application

SQL Server does not come with any off-the-shelf database applications for your organization. You have to buy them from companies who create SQL applications that run under SQL Server, or else write your own using the SQL language. Keep in mind that SQL Server is a development environment, not an end-user product like Microsoft Access. SQL Server is only a tool. You, or a developer, must write the code to make it perform the way you want.

SQL Server Clients

Included with SQL Server are several client-side tools that enable users to view and manipulate data in preexisting databases stored on a SQL Server. They include ISQL/w (GUI interface), ISQL (command-line–based), and MS-Query (see fig. 30.1). Unfortunately, these tools are designed primarily for use by administrators or developers, so none of them are easy to use for the typical user.

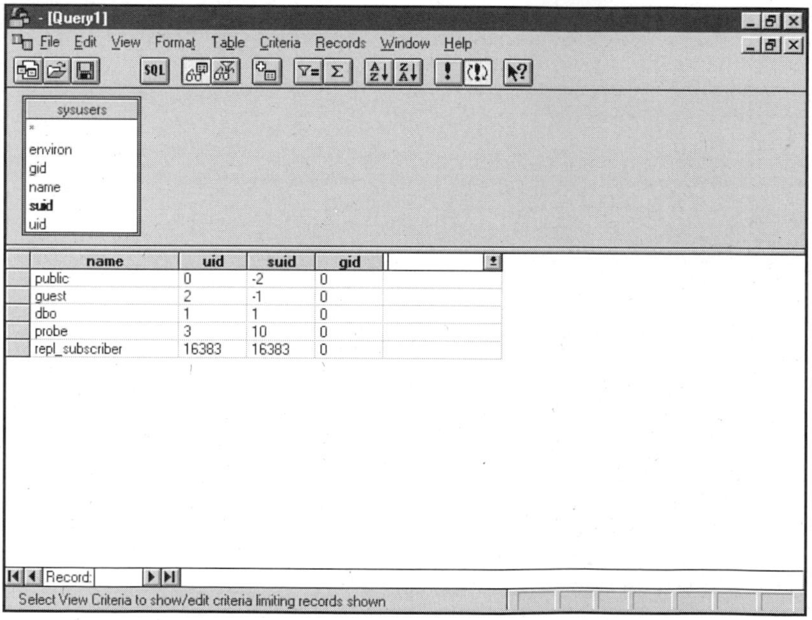

Figure 30.1

MS-Query is one of the several client tools included with SQL Server.

Other off-the-shelf software, including Microsoft Access and Microsoft Excel, can be used to view and manipulate data on SQL Server. Although these tools are friendlier than the tools included with SQL Server, they still demand an above average knowledge of SQL databases if you want to use it to view or manipulate data.

To make it easier for the casual user to access a SQL Server database, most organizations develop their own front-ends, or user-interface software, generally customized to meet the specific needs of the users.

Although any programming language can be used to create a client user-interface for SQL Server, one of the most popular ones is Microsoft's Visual BASIC, because it enables developers to quickly create user-interfaces that hide the complexity of SQL Server databases from end users.

Knowledge Necessary to Administer SQL Server

SQL Server does run under NT Server, but administering it is quite different from administering a standard file and print server. Consequently, many organizations assign an individual as a Database Administrator (DBA) to handle this responsibility.

A good DBA generally has these skills:

◆ Has a good background in NT and SQL Server

◆ Is very familiar with how to back up and restore data from a server

◆ Understands the business processes being modeled by the database management system

◆ Understands relational database design

◆ Understands SQL basics

Some of the tasks a DBA is responsible for include:

◆ Installing and/or upgrading SQL Server

◆ Creating and managing devices and databases

◆ Monitoring and tuning databases

◆ Backing up and restoring databases

◆ Managing database users and security

◆ Transferring data between SQL Server and other applications

◆ Replicating data

◆ Scheduling events

◆ Working with SQL developers

◆ Working with network administrators

Most organizations that use SQL Server are large enough to be able to separate the duties of the Network Administrator and the DBA, but not all. If you are a Network Administrator and are asked to be a DBA, do not pass up the opportunity. Generally, a DBA earns a higher salary, but not always. It also can broaden the scope of your career choices—and you might find it interesting.

How SQL Server Integrates with NT Server

One of the best reasons to choose SQL Server as an organization's enterprise database is its close integration with NT Server. Much of the integration is hidden below the surface, but many of the tools available in NT Server are used to administer SQL Server, including the following ones:

◆ **Registry Editor.** SQL Server stores its configuration data in NT's Registry, allowing direct access to SQL Server settings.

◆ **Control Panel.** SQL Server runs as three services, for all of which you can use the Services icon in NT's Control Panel to configure, stop, or start.

◆ **Disk Administrator.** SQL databases often contain mission-critical information. To help ensure that you do not lose important data, you can use NT Server's Disk Administrator tool to create fault tolerant drives to store SQL databases.

◆ **User Manager for Domains.** If you choose to use SQL Server's integrated security feature, SQL Server also uses the user accounts (created using User Manager for Domains) to control database access. Users, therefore, need have only one user account and password to log on to both NT Server and SQL Server.

◆ **Event Viewer.** SQL Server writes its events to NT Server's Event Viewer Applications log. You can use the Event Viewer to filter SQL events from other events, making it easy to view SQL Server messages (see fig. 30.2).

◆ **Performance Monitor.** Loading SQL Server on NT Server adds several new objects to Performance Monitor, enabling you to monitor and view SQL Server activity (see fig. 30.3). You should always monitor SQL Server to obtain optimal results.

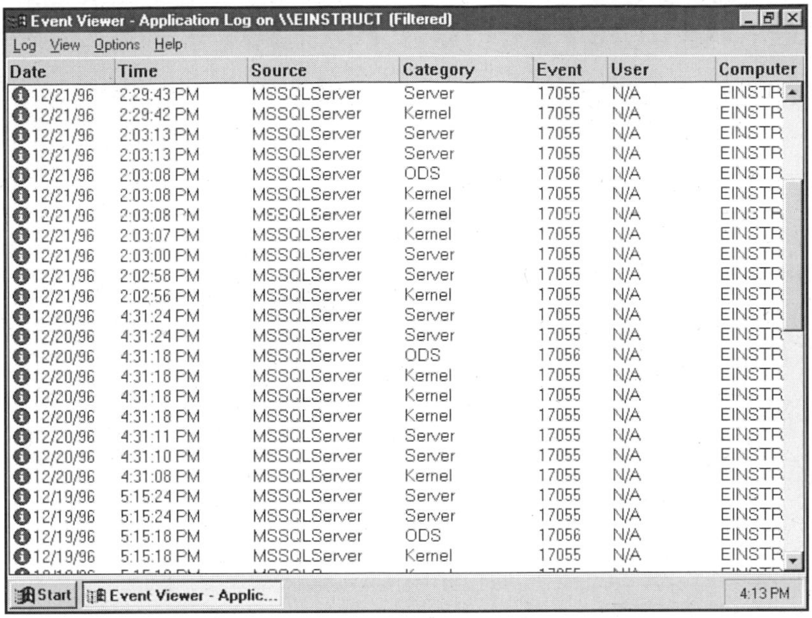

Figure 30.2

NT Server's Event Viewer is an integral part of SQL Server.

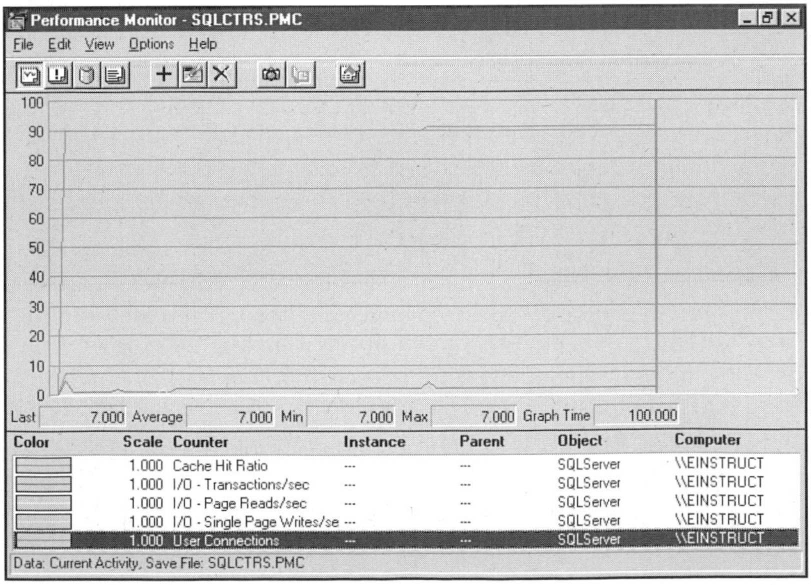

Figure 30.3

The Performance Monitor includes many counters to help the administrator monitor SQL Server's performance.

Fortunately, integrating SQL Server with NT Server is easy; you just load SQL Server onto NT Server, and all the integration features are automatically set up for you.

Installing SQL Server on NT Server

SQL Server comes on a CD from Microsoft and includes versions for the Intel, Alpha AXP, Power-PC, and MIPS platforms. Installation is easy, but like any software installation, the more you know your business needs and take the time to plan the installation, the smoother the installation will go.

Requirements for Installing SQL Server

The hardware requirements to run SQL in a production environment are a hardware manufacturer's dream come true.

Microsoft recommends the following minimal hardware for running SQL Server on NT Server:

CPU	Intel-based 80486, Pentium, Pentium Pro, Power-PC, Alpha AXP, MIPS
RAM	16 MB RAM minimum (32 MB RAM minimum if using replication)
Disk	60 MB minimum, 15 MB additional for SQL Server Books Online (optional)
CD-ROM	For installing SQL Server
NIC	NT-compatible

Microsoft's recommendations are pretty idealistic. The following list offers some more realistic hardware requirements and discusses why these requirements are more reasonable:

◆ **CPU.** Yes, SQL Server *will run* on any of the CPUs that Microsoft includes, but you specifically want to choose *the fastest* one you can afford. If you are running an Intel-based server, go directly to the Pentium Pro, which is optimized to run 32-bit code. Depending on your expected load, consider purchasing a multiprocessor server. SQL takes full advantage of multiple CPUs, and they can make a significant difference in performance, especially in decision-support environments.

◆ **RAM.** Consider 32 MB the absolute minimum, but seriously consider 64 MB or more, depending on the number of people accessing the server. SQL Server uses RAM very efficiently, and the more you give it, the faster it performs. It is not unusual to see SQL Server running on 512 MB or more of RAM.

◆ **Disk.** SQL Server is very I/O intensive, and which controllers and drives you use significantly affects performance. At the very least, choose a server that has two SCSI Fast/Wide controllers and enough disk space to meet your current and near-term needs. Also, seriously consider implementing hardware-based RAID for fault tolerance, because it provides much better performance than NT Server's built-in software-based RAID.

◆ **CD-ROM.** Go ahead and choose a SCSI CD-ROM; speed is not important.

◆ **NIC.** At the very minimum, select a 10-MB, PCI-based network interface card (NIC); PCI-based NICs have a 32-bit data path, and are significantly faster than 16-bit NICs. At the additional expense of just a few dollars, you can get a 10/100 NIC, which you can probably put to good use in the near future if you plan on upgrading to Fast Ethernet.

Sizing a server to run SQL server is not easy. When speccing a new server, seek the advice of an experienced SQL Server DBA. Once the server is in production, use the Performance Monitor to monitor performance and tune the hardware.

A couple of other additional installation issues to consider include operating system and file system. SQL Server requires the Microsoft Windows NT operating system, either version 3.51 or 4. Although you can use the FAT or NTFS file systems, NTFS provides additional fault tolerance, making it a substantially wiser choice.

| Tip | Microsoft regularly releases Service Packs for NT Server and SQL Server. These files fix bugs or enhance features. Check out Microsoft's WWW site for the latest Service Packs, download them, and install them to ensure your system is as up to date as possible. |

You can run SQL Server on any NT Server, including a Primary Domain Controller (PDC), Backup Domain Controller (BDC), or member server. You also can run it along with other BackOffice applications on the same NT server, or on an NT Server designated for file and print services. Just because something is possible, however, does not mean you want to do it. Most SQL applications require all the power a server can muster, so you should run SQL Server only on a member server, and devote all of this server's power to serving the needs of your database applications.

Installing SQL Server

If you find you would like to play around some with SQL Server, the general procedure for loading it is presented in the following exercise. Experienced NT administrators should find the information provided in these steps sufficient for the task, but more inexperienced readers might do better to find an administrator, or to skip on to the next section until a later date when they are more experienced.

Installing SQL Server

1. Be sure NT Server is properly installed and configured on the server, and that you are logged on to NT Server as a member of the Domain Administrators global group.

Note   You may install SQL Server only from an account that has Administrative rights.

2. From the User Manager for Domains, create a SQL Executive service account. SQL Server runs as three different services, one of which—the SQL Executive service, because it can span SQL servers—requires that it log on using a domain user account rather than the default LocalSystem account. Give the account a name that you will remember, add a password, specify that the password never expires, and make it a member of the Domain Administrators global group (see fig. 30.4). After you create the account, grant it the Log On As A Service right. This account comes into play later in the installation process.

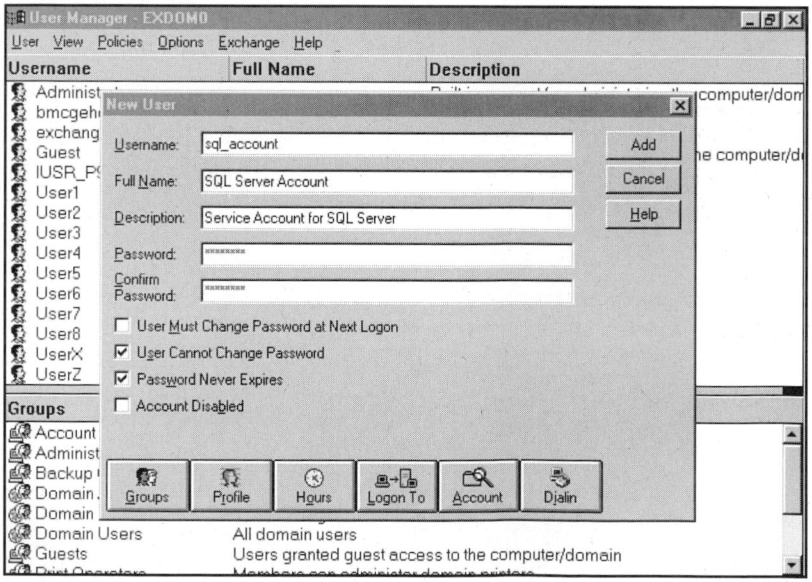

Figure 30.4

A SQL Server service account must be created using the User Manager for Domains before installing SQL Server.

3. Run Setup from the folder on the CD that contains the version of SQL Server for your platform. Use the \I386 folder for the Intel platform. The Welcome dialog box appears. Choose Continue.

What Is a Service Account?

A *service account* is a special user account that an NT service (a *service* is a program that runs on NT Server in the background) uses to log on and receive validation by NT's security system before beginning to run. Forcing authentication of services before they can run prevents malicious individuals from writing unauthorized programs that secretly run in the background, potentially causing havoc. Since SQL Server runs as a service, it must have its own service account before it can run.

NT has a built-in service account called LocalSystem, but it works only if the service runs exclusively on a single NT Server. SQL Server, on the other hand, can cross NT Server boundaries. Thus, you must manually create a special account, using the User Manager for Domains.

4. The Name and Organization dialog box appears. Enter the requested information and choose C<u>o</u>ntinue. The Verify Name and Organization dialog box appears. If the information is correct, choose C<u>o</u>ntinue.

5. The SQL Server Options dialog box appears. Choose the <u>I</u>nstall SQL Server and Utilities option, then choose C<u>o</u>ntinue (see fig. 30.5).

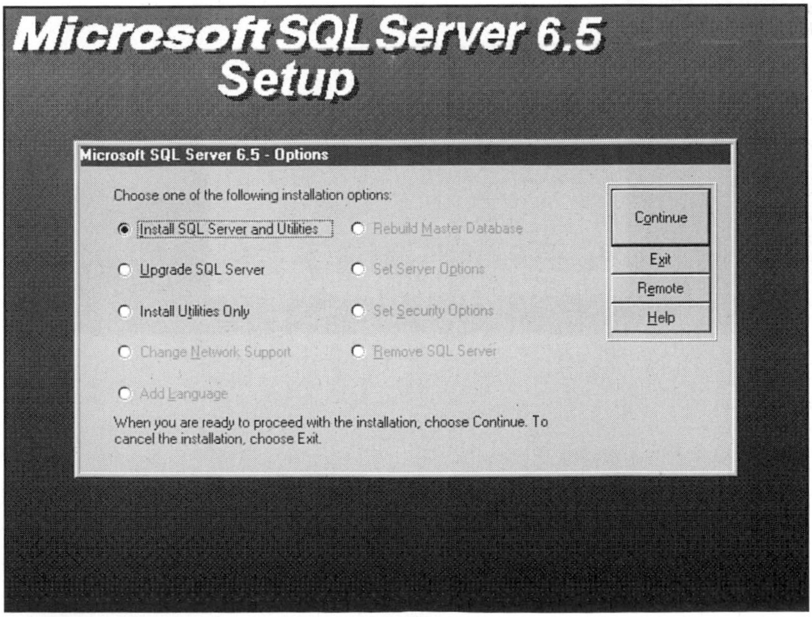

Figure 30.5

Choose the screen defaults when installing SQL Server for the first time.

6. The Licensing Options dialog box appears. Choose Per Ser**v**er or Per **S**eat licensing, as appropriate, then choose C**o**ntinue.

7. The SQL Server Installation Path dialog box appears. Choose the default, or another drive or directory, then choose C**o**ntinue.

8. The MASTER Device Creation dialog box appears. The MASTER device serves as the storage location for the MASTER database and its transaction log. The MASTER database is used to store configuration information for all the databases located on SQL Server. The minimum size is 25 MB, but Microsoft recommends making it at least 30 MB, if you have the available disk space. Choose the drive and directory where you want the MASTER device to be stored, and choose the size of the device. Choose C**o**ntinue to continue (see fig. 30.6).

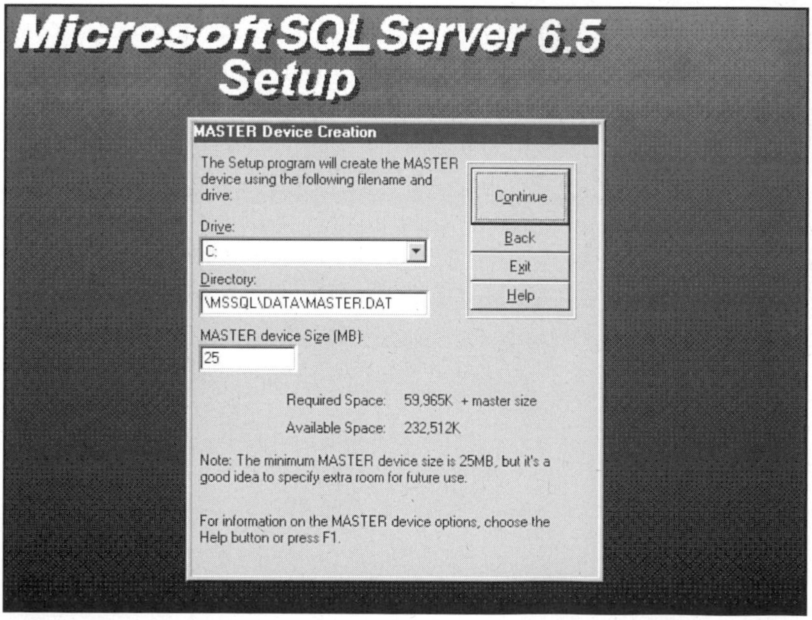

Figure 30.6

You must specify the size and location of the MASTER device during installation.

9. The SQL Server Books Online dialog box appears. Choose whether you want to load Books Online onto the server, to run it from a CD-ROM, or not to install it, then choose C**o**ntinue. If you have the space (15 MB), it is a good idea to load it because it makes looking up information, such as error messages, much easier.

10. The Installation Options dialog box, which appears next (see fig. 30.7), offers a wide number of options. Generally, the defaults work satisfactorily.

   The Character Set option enables you to choose which character set you want SQL Server to use. The default is the ISO Character Set.

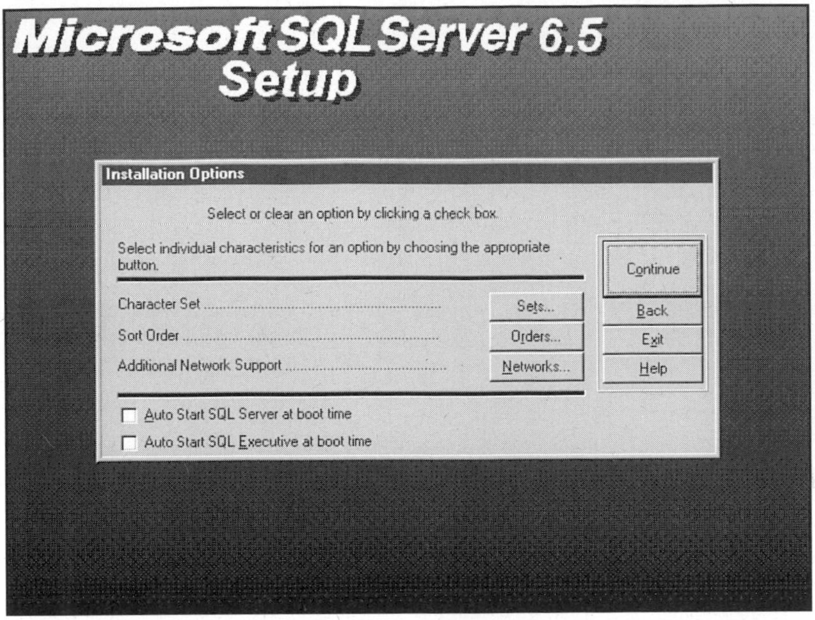

Figure 30.7

*Generally, the
default SQL
Server installation
options work fine
for most networks.*

The Sort Order option lets you determine how you want SQL Server to sort data
in databases. The default is Dictionary Order, Case-Insensitive sort order.

The Additional Network Support enables you to choose the network files
necessary for SQL Server to communicate over a network. The default, Named
Pipes, should work for most networks. Carefully review all of the network options
to determine if you need any of the others; more than one can be selected to
work on your network, if necessary.

If you want SQL Server and SQL Executive to start automatically at boot time,
click on the appropriate boxes. After you specify all the options, choose Continue.

11. The SQL Executive Log On Account dialog box appears next. For SQL Server's
    service account, enter the name of the account you used the User Manager for
    Domains to create, then enter its password. Choose Continue.

SQL Server then copies from the CD onto your server, and the MASTER device and
several databases are created, completing installation of SQL Server. Expect installation to take some time, proportionate to the size of the MASTER device.

SQL Server Administration Tools

One of the major factors contributing to SQL Server's ever-increasing popularity is the many visual administration tools it provides. This might not sound like a big deal, but managing SQL database programs traditionally has required administrators to type commands at command prompts. Most of SQL Server's tools are visual, making your job much easier. The following list introduces you to some of the more important SQL Server administrative tools:

◆ **SQL Server Setup.** In addition to its use during the initial installation of SQL Server, SQL Server Setup also serves you in changing a SQL Server installation, rebuilding the SQL Server MASTER Database, and removing SQL Server.

◆ **SQL Service Manager.** Similar in function to the Services Icon under NT's Control Panel, this program lets you stop and start SQL Server services (see fig. 30.8).

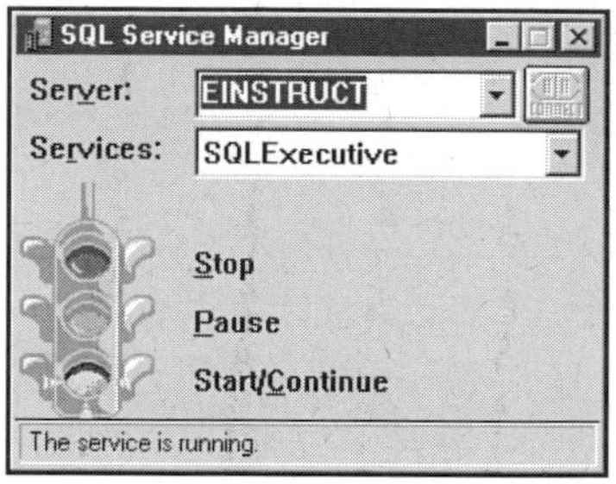

Figure 30.8

The SQL Service Manager turns SQL services off and on.

◆ **Enterprise Manager.** This program is the most important SQL Server management tool; it lets you manage both local and remote SQL Server systems from the same screen. Consider it SQL Server's management workstation (see fig. 30.9). Many features of the Enterprise Manager are covered later in this chapter.

◆ **SQL Security Manager.** This tool enables you to set up SQL Server's integrated and mixed security.

◆ **SQL Client Configuration Manager.** This tool serves you in configuring SQL Server client connections.

◆ **ISQL/w and ISQL.** Both of these programs are designed for running database queries and administering SQL Server using manually entered SQL statements. ISQL/w (see fig. 30.10) uses a visual interface, whereas ISQL provides a text-based version of the program. Most of what administrators can do by entering SQL commands here they also can accomplish by using the Enterprise Manager.

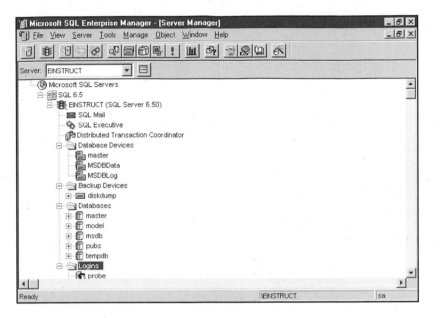

Figure 30.9

The Enterprise Manager is where most administrators spend their time to administer SQL Server.

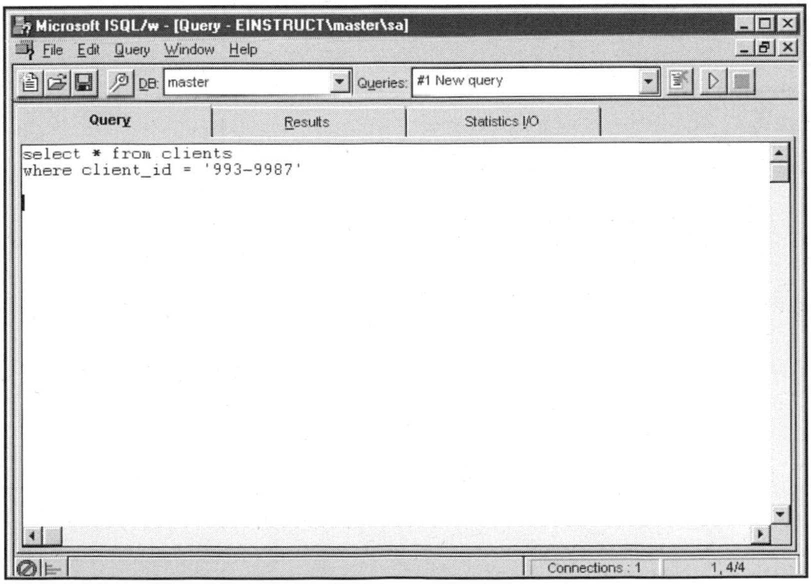

Figure 30.10

ISQL/w can be used to manually enter database queries using SQL statements.

◆ **Database Maintenance Plan Wizard.** SQL Server requires regular maintenance, and the Database Maintenance Plan Wizard makes these tasks less mundane by performing them for you. The wizard steps you through a majority of the important maintenance tasks required and automates them, saving you much time. This tool is explored in more depth later in this chapter (see fig. 30.11).

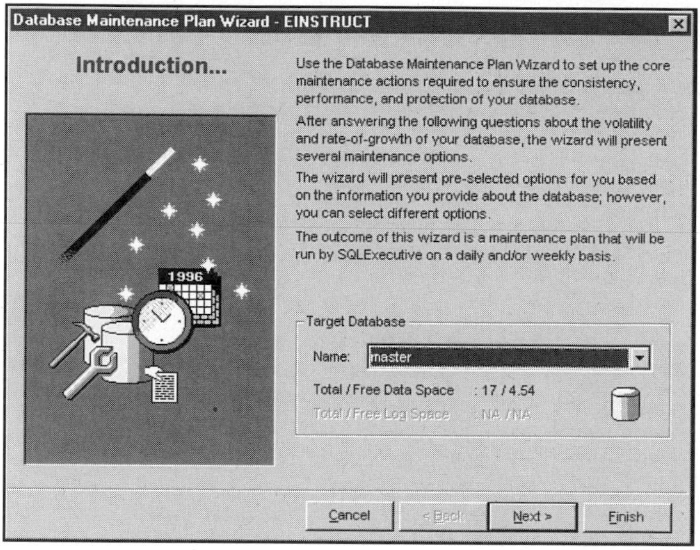

Figure 30.11

*The Database
Maintenance Plan
Wizard makes
SQL Server easy to
administer.*

◆ **SQL Server Web Assistant.** This great new tool automates the creation of HyperText Markup Language (HTML) web pages from data found in an SQL database. It is discussed later, in the context of its involvement in SQL Server's integration with Microsoft's Internet Information Server.

◆ **BCP.** Bulk Copy Program (BCP) is a command-line utility you can use to import and export data to and from SQL Server.

◆ **Stored and extended procedures.** SQL Server includes many predefined procedures (entered as commands into ISQL/w or ISQL) that perform a variety of administrative tasks. A *stored procedure* is a compiled SQL program. An *extended procedure* is a function stored as part of a DLL (Dynamic Link Library). SQL Server programmers often write stored procedures to accomplish specific database tasks, such as perform predefined queries.

◆ **DBCC Commands.** DBCC (Database Consistency Checker) commands are manually typed into ISQL/w or ISQL to perform database maintenance, or to run as a scheduled task.

Administrators must master these features, along with several others, in order to administer SQL Server.

Common SQL Server Management Tasks

Compared to many other server applications, an SQL Server needs regular care and feeding (that is, proactive management). SQL Server databases are dynamic, always changing, which can lead to many potential problems. A server might run out of disk space, for example, or might become corrupted when data is changed or deleted improperly. Unless the administrator watches carefully after an SQL Server, small problems can quickly become big problems, incurring, in the case of a mission-critical database (which most are), heavy expenses—disaster preys without mercy on the dilatory administrator.

This section looks at the many routine SQL Server management tasks for which administrators are responsible. These tasks can include configuring a server for optimum performance, creating and managing devices and databases, setting up database replication, backing up and restoring data, implementing fault tolerance, managing security, executing queries, and much more. For specific information on how to perform the tasks described in the following sections, refer to the SQL Server documentation or the resources listed at the end of this chapter.

Managing SQL Server Configuration

Administrators do most SQL Server configuration via the Enterprise Manager, including registering SQL Servers (you can manage more than one SQL Server from the Enterprise Manager) and making changes to SQL Server settings that can directly affect performance. The Enterprise Manager includes a handy configuration screen to make it easy to view current settings, and to change them. Generally, you must change many of these settings after installing SQL Server in order for it to perform optimally (see fig. 30.12).

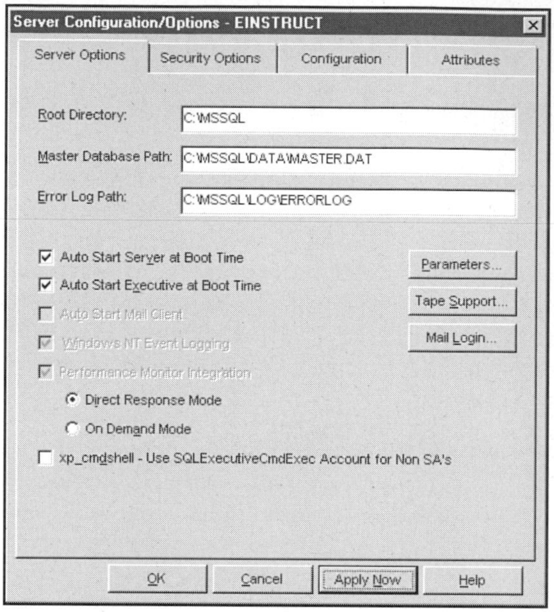

Figure 30.12

*SQL Server's
configuration
screen makes it
easy to configure
SQL Server.*

Creating and Managing Devices

Before the administrator can create a database, he must create a database device (see fig. 30.13). A *database device* is a disk file used to store SQL databases and their affiliated transaction logs. Think of it as a pre-allocated storage area reserved for future use by a database. A single database may be stored on a single device, multiple databases may be stored on a single device, or a single database may be stored on multiple devices.

What Is a Transaction Log?

A *transaction log* is a listing, or history, of all the data changes to a database. Whenever a database is created on a database device, SQL Server creates a corresponding transaction log, which it uses to help ensure database integrity if the server fails during access or usage of the database.

Database transactions all have beginning and ending points, written one at a time to the transaction log. Periodically, these completed transactions are applied to the actual database. If the server should fail when the transaction log is updating the database, it may well mean that the transaction was not completely written to the database. When SQL Server restarts, it checks the database to see if the database contains any incompletely entered transactions. If so, it uses the transaction log to rollback the incomplete part of the transaction. This process also helps to ensure database integrity.

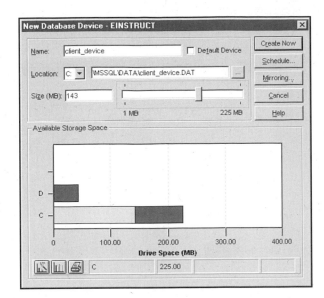

Figure 30.13

Devices must be created before databases can be created.

When SQL Server is installed, the setup process creates three special database devices that SQL Server uses for its own purposes, MASTER.DAT, MSDB.DAT, and MSDBLOG.DAT. MASTER.DAT stores the MASTER database required to run and manage the server, and also stores its transaction log, along with several other databases and logs necessary for SQL server to operate. SQL Server uses MSDB.DAT and MSDBLOG.DAT together to store the database and transaction log for its scheduler.

Besides creating database devices, the administrator is responsible for creating backup (or dump) devices. A *backup device* is used to backup SQL Server databases and transaction logs. Unlike database devices, backup devices are not used to pre-allocate disk space. A backup device can be a hard disk, floppy disk, tape device, or named pipe (for use by special programs).

Database devices generally are created using the Enterprise Manager. Once created, they can be used to store databases created by the administrator. Database devices can also be expanded if necessary, or deleted.

Creating and Managing Databases

After at least one database device has been created, a database can be created within it. Creating a database dedicates a predefined amount of space for a database within a database device, and generates several database tables that describe the database's structure. For every database created, a transaction log is also created. Generally, to make backing up (dumping) a database much easier, you should put a single database in a single database device and the database's transaction log into a separate database device.

Most of the time, databases are created using the Enterprise Manager. After a database is created, it may be reduced or expanded in size, or deleted (see fig. 30.14).

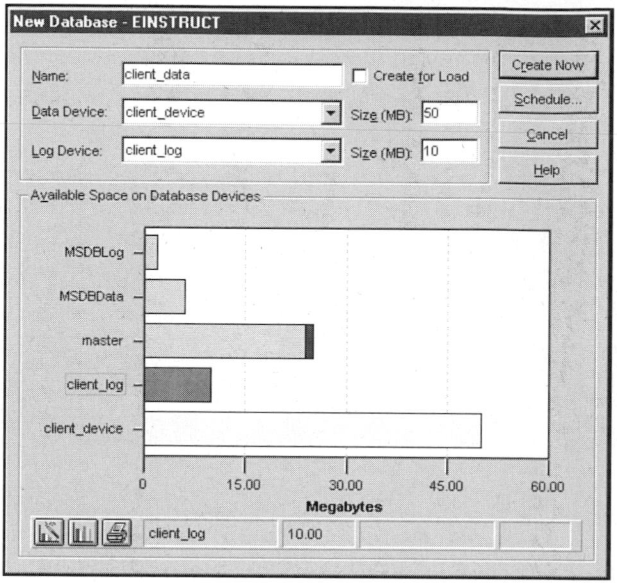

Figure 30.14

Databases and their log files must be created on preexisting devices.

Implementing Fault Tolerance

Most SQL Server database information is mission critical; it must be available 24 hours a day, seven days a week. To help ensure that it is, most administrators incorporate some type of disk fault tolerance into their physical server. The preferred method of doing so is to store SQL Server databases using disk mirroring or RAID-level 5. This can be accomplished through hardware, or by using NT Server's Disk Administrator.

If physical disk fault tolerance is not possible, SQL Server enables you to mirror database devices to other database devices located on other hard disks, enabling, therefore, a duplicate copy of the database device to be immediately available to take over in the event of failure of the original database device.

Whether you use RAID or SQL Server's database mirroring, it is still critical that your database data be backed up. Even the best fault tolerant systems fail.

Establishing and Managing Security

The SQL Server administrator is responsible for establishing security for the server itself, as well as the databases stored on the server. The following list describes the possible security types:

◆ **Standard.** Standard security uses SQL Server's built-in security, and stores a SQL Server user's logon name and password. This mode works with any network configuration, although users must log on twice, to NT (or another network operating system), and to SQL Server.

◆ **Integrated.** Integrated security uses NT Server's built-in security, which enables users to use their NT user accounts and passwords to gain access to SQL Server. Integrated security requires that a users' accounts be in a trusted NT domain. Using this option, users have to log on only once.

◆ **Mixed.** Mixed security combines the best of both standard and integrated security.

No matter what security model you choose, users may log on only to SQL Server; they do not automatically receive access to any of the databases stored on the SQL Server. Users must have a *user logon ID* (using either Standard or Integrated security) to gain access to SQL Server, but to gain access a specific SQL Server database, they must also have a *database user name*.

Database user names are assigned to a database after the database is created. Associated with this name are the permissions that each user has to the database. Before a user can view the data in a particular database, therefore, the user's database name must be included in the database, and the associated database permissions must allow the user to view the database data.

To ease the management burden of tracking two types of IDs, database user names are automatically associated with users' logon IDs. So, when users log on to SQL Server, they not only are approved to log on to SQL Server, but to any database on that SQL Server that has their database user names associated with it. Users do not have to log on separately to each database that they need to access.

What Is a SQL Server Permission?

A SQL Server permission varies somewhat from a file or directory permission under NT Server. There are two types of permissions; statement and object. *Statement permissions* determine who can delete or create objects within a database. *Object permissions* determine who can access or change database data.

Running Queries

Using SQL, both ISQL/w and ISQL can be used to run queries by entering SQL statements. Before doing so, the administrator needs to know the basics of the SQL language. Running queries against a database enables the administrator, or others, to quickly find out the answers to a wide variety of questions. A query could be written to count the number of clients from the zip code area 66212 who purchased a particular item in the past three months, for example.

One of the administrator's most important tasks is to make sure queries run as efficiently as possible. To help speed up query processing, SQL Server includes a query optimizer that attempts to run a query as efficiently as possible. The query optimizer cannot always do its task as well as it should, however, and it is up to the administrator to manually "tune" queries to run as optimally as possible. The administrator can use ISQL/w's showplan tool to provide the necessary information to help optimize queries.

Backing Up and Restoring Data

Although the administrator is responsible for many important tasks, the most important task is backing up (dumping) databases and their logs. Even the most fault tolerance disk systems fail, and a ready backup must be available to restore the databases and their logs to new hardware. Database backups and restoration normally is done using the Enterprise Manager.

The two common ways of backing up database data are (1) performing a *database backup,* and, (2) performing a *transaction log backup.* A database backup is a full backup of a database and its transaction log to a backup device (a storage device, such as a tape backup or another disk). Conducting a database backup does not truncate (clear out) the transaction log.

To keep the transaction log from filling up with applied transactions, it must be truncated periodically (the applied transaction must be removed) by performing a transaction log backup (see fig. 30.15).

A transaction log backup is like an incremental backup; all the transactions that have occurred since the last transaction log backup are backed up, usually to a tape backup device. A transaction log backup is used to truncate the inactive part (the applied transactions) of the transaction log, and copy it to a backup device. A common way to back up a database is to do a full database backup once a week and do an incremental transaction log backup daily.

A database and its transaction log can be backed up while it is being used, although user performance suffers during the backup. This capability is an important feature, owing to the fact that many SQL Server databases must be available all hours of the day.

The capability to restore a backup is just as important as the capability to back it up. Database restoration can be very complicated, and requires careful planning and testing. Naturally, you want to be able to restore data as quickly as possible, so you should practice restore procedures to ensure that you know every precise step that must be taken.

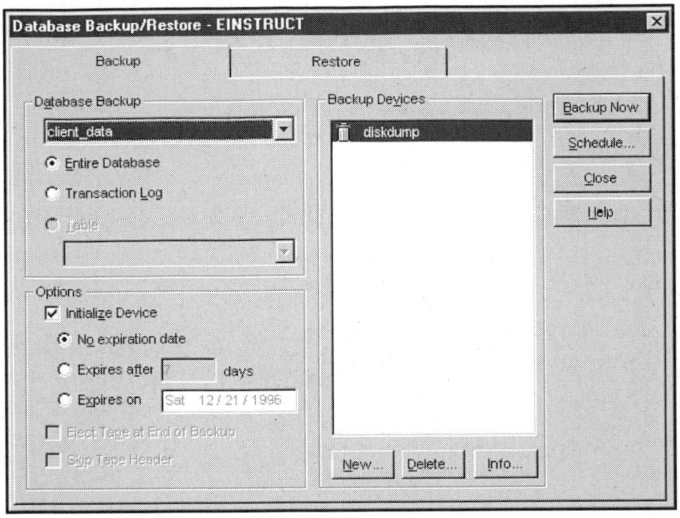

Figure 30.15

To back up a database, it is "dumped" to a "dump device," generally a tape device.

Creating and Monitoring Alerts

The Alert Manager, part of the Enterprise Manager, enables the administrator to create alerts that occur automatically under a particular circumstance, and carry out predefined actions, such as e-mailing or paging the administrator. You can create three types of alerts using Alert Manager: Standard alerts, Performance Monitor alerts, and Business alerts.

◆ **Standard alerts.** Standard alerts let the administrator know if a particular error occurs, such as if a database is out of space or a table has become corrupted (see fig. 30.16).

◆ **Performance Monitor alerts.** Performance Monitor alerts use the Performance Monitor alert function to send an alert to the administrator when a particular counter reaches a preset number. An administrator would probably want to know when NT Server's PAGEFILE.SYS is almost full, for example.

◆ **Business alerts.** Business alerts are a powerful tool that allow SQL Server to notify the administrator when a particular event has occurred in a database. If you want to know when the number of customers in a database has exceeded a certain number, for example, you can be notified. If you want to know if sales at a particular store are not meeting a predetermined amount for the month, a designated individual can be notified by e-mail automatically.

Figure 30.16

Figure 30.16

*Standard alerts are
created using the
SQL Enterprise
Manager.*

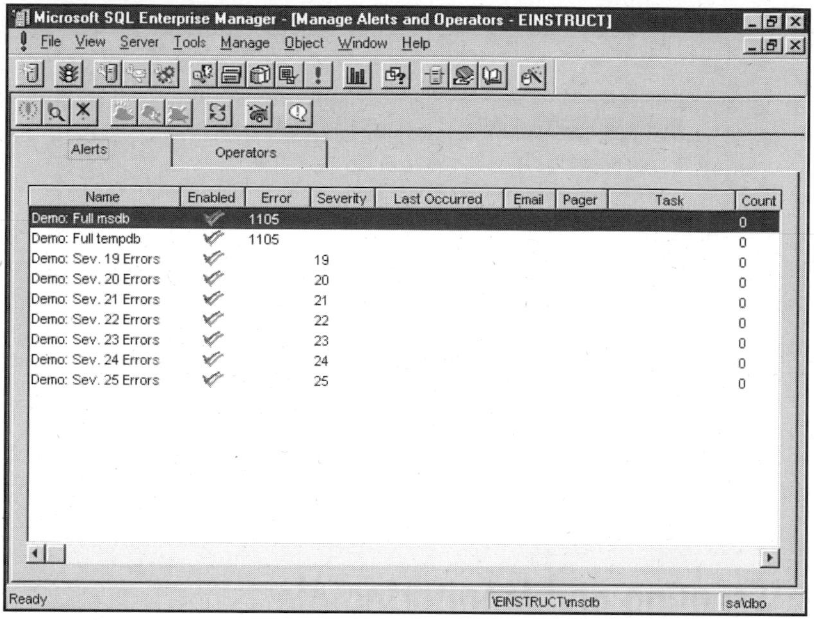

Scheduling Events

You can automate nearly any SQL Server task using the Task Scheduler. It enables the administrator to schedule events, such as backing up a database or transaction log, or to automatically run DBCC commands to check for corrupt data. You also can arrange for the Task Manager to send an e-mail or page to the administrator upon the successful or unsuccessful completion of a scheduled task (see fig. 30.17).

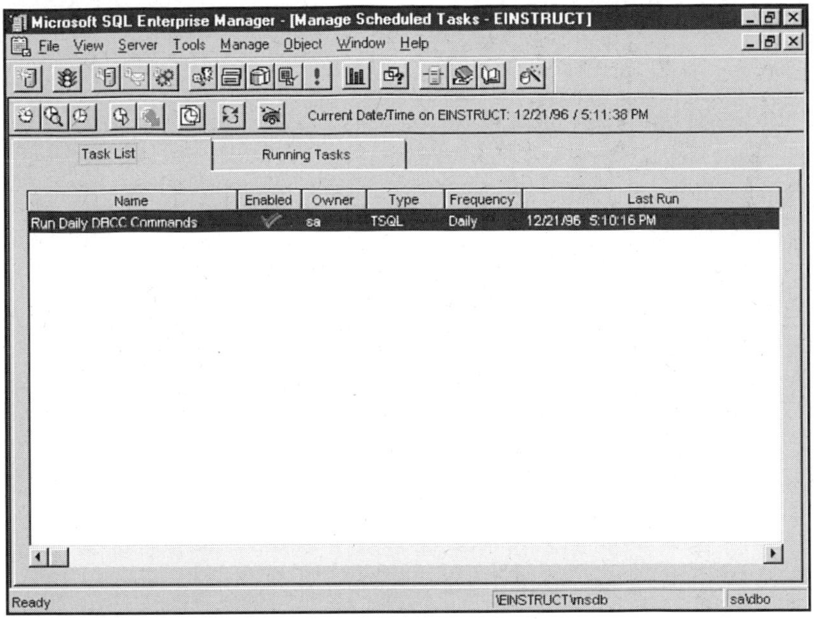

Figure 30.17

Virtually every management task can be scheduled using SQL Server's Task Scheduler.

Managing Replication

One of the most powerful features of SQL Server is its capability to replicate data. *Data replication* refers to SQL Server's capability for duplicating databases or tables onto one or more other SQL servers. The replicated data is read-only, and so it cannot be modified.

You use can replication in many ways. If a group of users needs to query a particular database, for example, the server slows down during processing of the query. Querying the database often can pose a problem if the database also is actively being used to store transaction-based data. Using replication enables automatic duplication of a database to another SQL Server that can be used for running the queries. The original SQL Server database then can be used for heavy-duty data entry without having to suffer the speed degradation that tends to happen under the duress of extensive querying. Proper use of data replication helps balance the load on database servers.

To set up replication, you designate one server as the *publisher*, which holds the data to be replicated. Every server that receives the replicated data is referred to as a *subscriber*. Either the publishing server, or another server acting in its place, is designated the role of a *distributor*. The distributor contains the replication distribution database, which has the job of storing and forwarding the replicated data from the publisher to one or more subscribers.

Setting up replication can be complex, depending on your business needs. Careful planning is required to ensure that everything works as expected and that server performance does not suffer. Replication is set up using the Enterprise Manager.

Importing and Exporting Data

If you want to import data into a SQL Server database from another database program, or to export data from a SQL Server database to be used by another program, use the Bulk Copy Program (BCP) tool. BCP is a command-line utility that requires the administrator to type in obscure options and switches. To avoid having to retype the same complex syntax every time BCP needs to run to perform a specific task, you should create a batch file to store the command and its parameters. Often the Task Scheduler is used to run a BCP operation at night.

Troubleshooting

Troubleshooting is never fun, but SQL Server tries to help you as much as possible, although it has a long way to go before it can be considered user-friendly. SQL Server has many predefined error messages, which consist of a message number and severity level. This information can be looked up in SQL Server's Books Online, which is SQL Server's user manual in help format. This makes it relatively painless to look up an error message.

Errors are logged in both the Error Log and the NT Server Event Viewer. The Error Log (see fig. 30.18) is a text file that lists every error message along with the time it occurred. The same errors logged in the Error Log are also placed in the application's window of Event Viewer. Generally, using the Event Viewer to view messages is easier, owing to its superior interface.

Another troubleshooting tool included with SQL Server is the Detail Activity Page of the Current Activity dialog box, found in the Enterprise Manager. It allows the administrator to view current SQL Server activity, thus helping him decipher the system's internal goings on.

You can use a visual tool called SQL Trace to display SQL activity for a server. Administrators can use this information to see who is doing what on the server, and it often helps in tracking down problems.

Administrators also can use DBCC (Database Consistency Checker) commands to troubleshoot SQL Server problems.

Like any network application, troubleshooting often is more of an art than a science. Only through experience using the preceding tools will the administrator learn how to best diagnose problems.

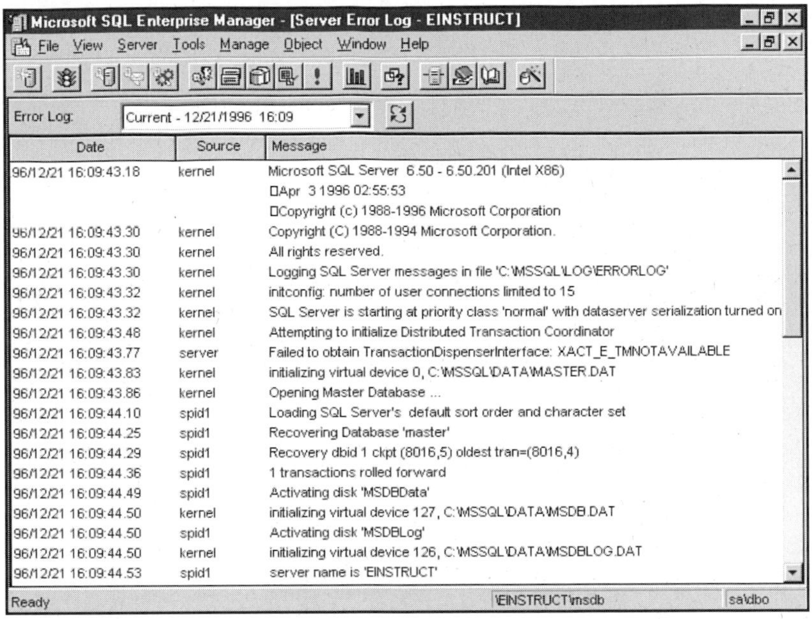

Figure 30.18

The Enterprise Manager can be used to display the Error Log.

Monitoring Activity (User and Server)

You can view current user activity from the User Activity window in the Enterprise Manager. This feature enables administrators to view each user's activity, stop a process users are running, and even directly send users e-mail messages.

You can use NT Server's Performance Monitor tool to monitor SQL Server's performance. SQL Server adds several new objects to Performance Monitor, enabling administrators to monitor server performance. You can track real-time events or log events to create a baseline of SQL Server activity, for example. Some of the key areas to track when monitoring an SQL Server include memory usage, processor activity, disk I/O, number of user connections, and table locks.

Optimizing SQL Server Under NT Server

Tuning SQL Server is a never-ending task unless your data never changes. If your data changes, however, or the number of people who access databases increase, you are responsible for monitoring SQL Server's performance, and making the necessary changes to keep it humming smoothly along. SQL Server optimization tips could fill an entire book, but here are several to help you keep SQL running as efficiently as possible:

◆ **Use the right hardware.** SQL Server is a very smart program; it will take advantage of the hardware you give it. Use NT Server's Performance Monitor to find out where your bottlenecks are, and correct the problems. If your database is used mostly for transaction processing, your bottlenecks are most likely in the areas of RAM and disk I/O. If your database is used mostly for decision support analysis, the CPU may be the bottleneck. Do not forget to take future growth into account. Databases tend to grow quickly, and you do not want to find out your server is under-powered after it is in production for three months.

◆ **Choose the correct NT Server role.** When installing NT Server on the server that will run SQL Server, configure NT as a member server rather than as a Primary Domain Controller (PDC) or Backup Domain Controller (BDC) to give SQL Server more resources to draw from.

◆ **Limit non-database use.** For optimum performance, SQL Server should be the only application running on the NT Server. SQL Server can coexist with other network applications, but forcing it to share resources diminishes its performance.

◆ **Designate NT Server as an applications server.** When configuring NT Server to run SQL Server, be sure you have specified NT Server to run as an applications server. To do so, just select Server Properties from the Network Properties in the Control Panel.

◆ **Optimize queries.** Use the Showplan, Statistics I/O, No Execute, and Stats Time tools (available from ISQL/w) to help you optimize query performance.

◆ **Regularly run DBCC commands.** You need to run many DBCC commands regularly to check for potential database corruption, but you need to run one in particular, called the UPDATE STATISTICS command, in order to update outdated table indexes. Outdated table indexes can cause queries to run much more slowly than they should.

◆ **Tune SQL Server configuration.** SQL Server offers many configuration options that directly affect server performance. They are located under the Server Configuration/Option dialog box in the Enterprise Manager. You usually need to change many of the default memory settings that this dialog box contains before SQL Server will run efficiently. Take the time to learn about these options. Search SQL Server's Books Online for advice on how to configure SQL Server for optimum performance.

SQL Server is a powerful tool in its own right, but you can combine its power with other Microsoft BackOffice products for even better results. The following section looks at how you can integrate SQL Server with Microsoft Exchange, Internet Information Server, and Systems Management Software. For more specific information on how to integrate these products, see the specific product's documentation or the resources at the end of this chapter.

Integrating SQL Server with Microsoft Exchange

Microsoft Exchange is an enterprise-wide messaging system that offers organizations electronic mail, scheduling, and groupware functions. Like all Microsoft BackOffice applications, Microsoft Exchange is closely integrated with NT Server. If you are thinking about using Exchange, or are currently using it, you can take advantage of the many ways SQL Server integrates with it.

SQL Server and Exchange integrate on two different levels. First, SQL Server can easily use Exchange as the messaging system to send a variety of status or alert messages to the SQL administrator, or to other SQL users. This feature is built into SQL Server. On a different level, Exchange users can view or change SQL data by sending mail messages directly to SQL, whereby the results, if any, can be sent back to the sender via e-mail. This feature requires some customized programming, but offers great flexibility.

Sending Messages to Exchange Server Using SQL Server

As the SQL administrator, you can have SQL Server send you, someone else, or a group a message to alert you or them about important SQL Server events. For example, you would want to be notified if a database ran out of disk space. Five types of events where you can specify that a message be sent via Microsoft Exchange can occur within SQL Server, as follow:

◆ **SQL Server alerts.** SQL Server's Alert Manager allows the administrator to send a message, via Exchange, to Exchange users, should the Alert Manager detect a particular condition on the SQL Server. If a database is out of space or becomes corrupt, for example, the Alert Manager can send out a message immediately, so the problem can be fixed quickly. Figure 30.19 shows the Edit Alert dialog box, where operators are specified to receive e-mail messages.

◆ **SQL Performance Monitor threshold.** You can set up NT Server's Performance Monitor tool to send e-mail messages when a particular SQL counter threshold is exceeded. An SQL administrator might want to know if the transaction log were too full, for example, or if too many locks were being used, or perhaps if some other condition that also might affect the database's performance were being met.

◆ **Scheduled task performance.** SQL Server's Task Scheduler tool can send anyone messages specifying whether a particular scheduled event was successful.

A message might be sent if a database backup failed, for example, or if the nightly data export failed.

◆ **Database Maintenance Wizard reports.** If you use the Database Maintenance Wizard to automate some of your routine SQL Server maintenance tasks, you can have it e-mail you a report describing what tasks the wizard did and their results.

◆ **Business Rule alert.** This is one of SQL Server's most powerful "secrets." It allows you to define virtually any condition within any database and have a message automatically sent to anyone when the condition occurs. If the sales manager wants to know when a very important customer places an order, for example, SQL Server can identify that the order was placed and send an e-mail message to the sales manager.

Creating a Business Rule alert requires that the administrator use the Alert Manager tool, and know how to write SQL statements. By taking advantage of this feature, the managers of an organization can be kept up-to-date on all important events, just by automatically receiving e-mail messages.

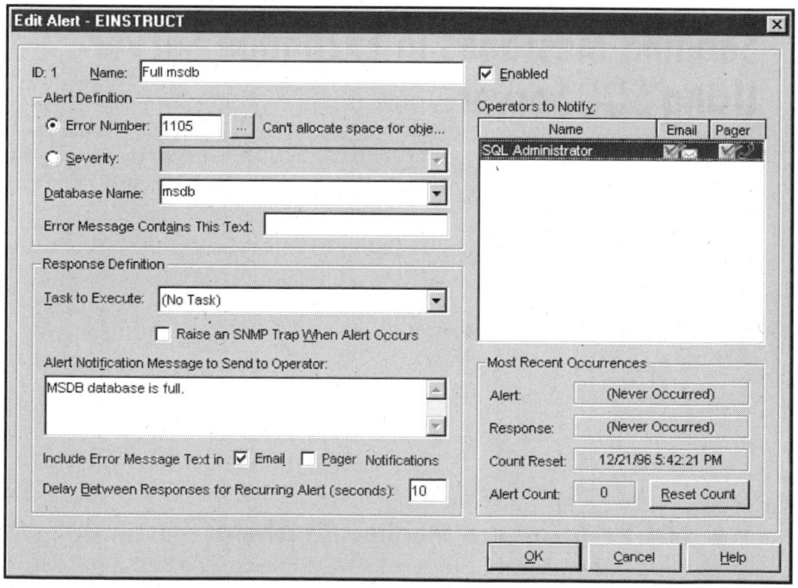

Figure 30.19

Any database administrator can be notified when an alert is triggered.

What Is SQLMail?

SQLMail is the part of SQL Server that handles MAPI messaging. By using built-in stored or extended procedures, SQL Server can communicate with any other MAPI-enabled program. SQLMail messages can include text, attached files, and even output from a database query.

SQLMail is automatically installed when SQL Server is installed, but it must be configured before it can begin to receive or send e-mail messages via Exchange.

To configure SQLMail, first create an Exchange mail account for the exclusive use of SQL Server. Next, run SQL Server's Setup program, and tell it that you want SQLMail enabled. After these steps are completed, SQLMail can send and receive messages from Exchange.

MAPI, or Messaging Applications Programming Interface, is a set of messaging functions for programmers who want to send e-mail messages from a MAPI-enabled application to another MAPI-enabled application, no matter which software company wrote the programs. It is an industry-standard messaging API developed and made popular by Microsoft.

Programs can have various levels of MAPI compliance. They include:

- **MAPI-Aware.** A program knows how to communicate using MAPI, but it is not a required feature of the program. Microsoft Office applications are MAPI-aware, for example.

- **MAPI-Enabled.** Communicating via MAPI is one of the main functions of the program. An example of a MAPI-enabled program is Microsoft Mail.

- **MAPI-Based Workgroup Application.** An advanced MAPI program designed to work over a network without user or administrator intervention. An example of a MAPI-based workgroup application is Microsoft Exchange.

Communicating with a SQL Server

A powerful but often under-used feature of Exchange is its electronic forms feature. By using Exchange's Forms Designer, or by custom programming in a language such as Visual BASIC, electronic forms can be created that allow an e-mail user to view, query, and change data in a SQL Server database. A user could send a help desk request via an e-mail message, for example. The message could be posted to a SQL database where the Help Desk staff would keep track of the request (see fig. 30.20). Also, a user could send a database query to a SQL database, where the query would be run and the results e-mailed back to the user.

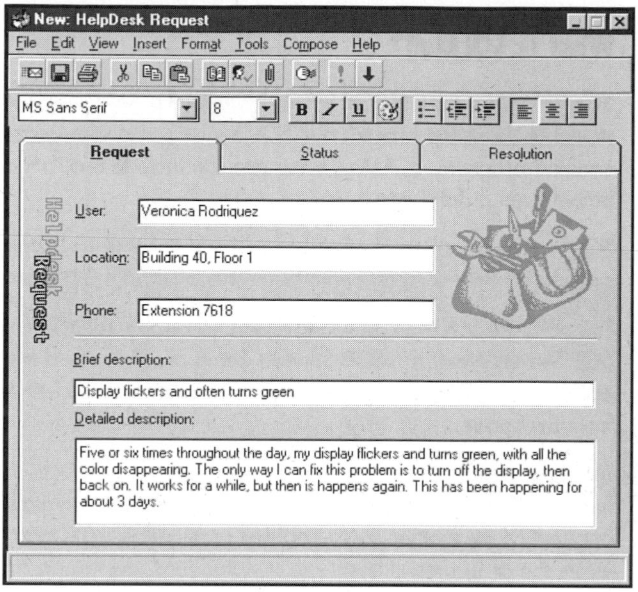

Figure 30.20

This sample electronic form, which comes with Microsoft Exchange, shows the type of forms that can be created and integrated with an SQL Server database.

Unfortunately, because custom applications have to be written to produce whatever results are desired, this ability requires the expertise of a programmer well-versed in Visual BASIC, MAPI, and SQL Server.

Integrating SQL Server with Internet Information Server

Microsoft's Internet Information Server (IIS) is a powerful and flexible World Wide Web (WWW), Gopher, and File Transfer Protocol (FTP) server. It comes free with NT Server and can handle virtually any organization's Internet and intranet needs. Microsoft has done a great job of integrating IIS with SQL Server. The integration of these two BackOffice products can go in three different directions:

◆ SQL Server Web Assistant

◆ Advanced Data Connector

◆ Using SQL Server to store IIS log files

The SQL Server Web Assistant

The SQL Server Web Assistant is a clever utility that has SQL Server automatically generate standard web pages using the HyperText Markup Language (HTML). Using this utility, then, you can publish virtually any kind of database information as web pages that can be viewed by any web browser. Databases can be connected to web servers on both the Internet and internal intranets.

You might create a product inventory database that allows potential customers to view current stock-on-hand, for example, or you might create a database that allows your employees to view an up-to-date employee list, complete with phone numbers and related information. You also might publish an internal database that show sales for all the branch offices for the month. Virtually all data stored in an SQL Server database can be published in web pages, using the Web Assistant (see figure 30.21).

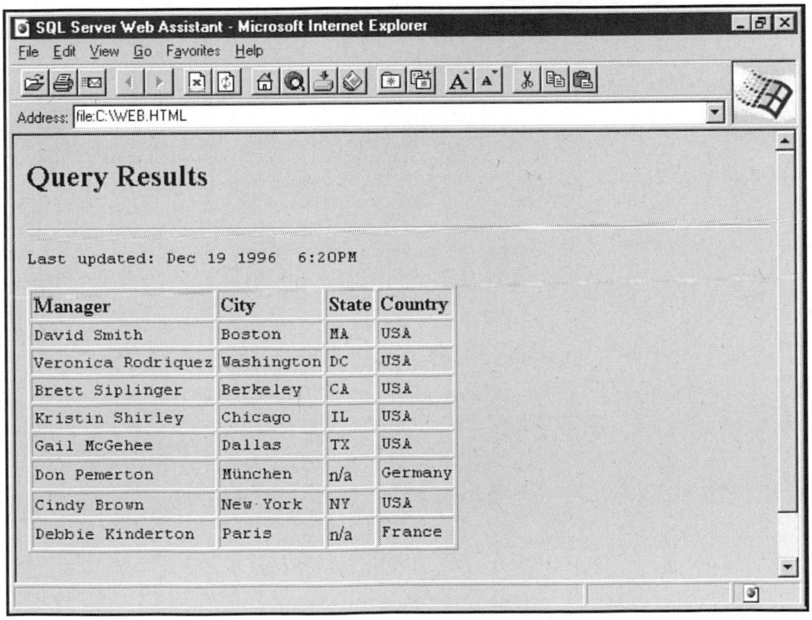

Figure 30.21

A sample web page created using the Web Assistant.

Whenever data in a database changes, SQL Server can automatically create web pages that contain whatever predefined database data you want. The web pages created are stored on the web server like any other HTML document. Whenever a user from a web browser accesses the Universal Resource Locator (URL) for the page, their browser displays it. If you have specified that the web page be updated (re-created) whenever data in the database changes, the web pages that your users view will be as up to date as the data in your database.

The Web Assistant is a program separate from SQL Server that is found in the SQL Server program group. Once the Web Assistant is run, a wizard appears on-screen, leading you through the steps in the following exercise:

SQL Server Web Assistant Wizard

1. You must specify the name of the SQL Server you want to access.

2. Next, you have to tell the Web Assistant what data you want it to extract from the database and display as web pages. The easiest way to do this is to use the graphical database hierarchy on the screen that enables you to click on the database, table, and fields you want to include (see fig. 30.22). You may also specify a query or a stored procedure with which to extract the data.

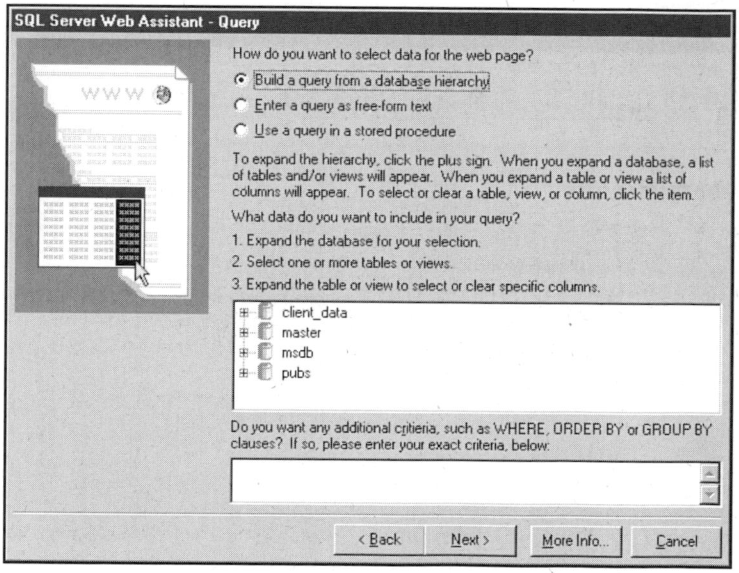

Figure 30.22

The Web Assistant enables you to specify exactly what database information you want to publish as web pages.

3. Next, you must schedule how often a web page should be updated. You have several options, including to have SQL Server automatically update the page anytime any of the data in the database changes, or to update at specific time intervals, such as once a day.

4. Next, you must specify the name of the file and the location at which to store the web page. You may also specify that when the web page is created, it follow the design of a particular web page template. If you do not specify a template, Web Assistant creates a default web page format for you.

5. Last, you have some limited options on how to format the type on the web page, along with a few other options that affect the final appearance of the web page.

After you specify formatting options to your satisfaction, select Finish. At that point, the web page will be created.

By repeatedly using the Web Assistant, you can create as many web pages as you need that provide the data you want viewed from your web site.

Advanced Data Connector

The Web Assistant goes a long way toward making data more easily available to web users. Although the data is kept up-to-date for display as a web page, the Web Assistant requires that all queries be predefined, which, unfortunately, prevents users from creating their own queries.

To let users create their own queries, the use of Microsoft's Advanced Data Connector (ADC) and custom programming is required. The ADC allows web developers to create database-related applications within ActiveX-enabled browsers. The ADC is an application that works with IIS to allow easy transfer of data between a web browser on a workstation and SQL Server (or any ODBC-compliant) database.

A user at a web browser might enter a query into a form, for example. The query would then be transmitted to an IIS server, where, through the use of the Advanced Data Connector, it would be transmitted to a SQL Server Database. The results of the query would then immediately be transmitted to the web browser. At that point, the user could view, change, or add to the data displayed, and then have these changes send back to the SQL Server database by way of IIS and the ADC.

This capability opens up endless possibilities for organizations to use web browsers as database clients, whether a user is accessing the database via the Internet or an employee is accessing the database via an intranet.

Web developers familiar with Microsoft's Visual BASIC can develop ActiveX applications that are automatically downloaded to a web browser, which acts as the "engine" that allows database information to be easily accessed by users.

Using SQL Server to Store IIS Log Files

Whenever IIS is accessed, it records the IP address of whoever requested the information, what they requested, the date, time of the request, and several other pieces of information. By default, this information is stored in ASCII files for viewing by the Webmaster. Unless you have purchased a specialized analysis tool that can read and analyze these logs, it is very difficult to make much sense out of them.

Most Webmasters need to know who is viewing their site, along with what they are looking at, and when. This information is important to establishing the success and value of the site.

Fortunately, Microsoft included an additional logging feature in IIS that allows the log files to be directly written to a SQL Server database. By choosing this option, anyone can run queries against the data, making it much easier to analyze the log's data (see fig. 30.23). It is very easy to write a query to find which IP addresses have been accessing the site, for example, and to sort them in the order of highest hits to lowest hits.

Setting up IIS to log to SQL Server is very easy. First, you create a database on a SQL Server. Next, on IIS, you specify an ODBC data source, along with the name of the table to store the data. Once this is configured, all hits on IIS are automatically logged in the SQL Server database.

Integrating SQL Server with Systems Management Server

Microsoft's Systems Management Server (SMS), another component of BackOffice, is a powerful network administrative tool that includes these features:

◆ **Inventory management.** As directed by the administrator, SMS collects an inventory list of all the hardware for each of the computers attached to a network.

◆ **Software distribution.** Software can be automatically distributed to, and set up on, most computers attached to a network.

◆ **Shared application management.** Shared network software can be automatically distributed and managed.

◆ **Remote control and diagnostics.** SMS allows an administrator to remotely attach to most computers in a network and then take control of their screens, and to gather diagnostic information, if needed.

◆ **Network Monitor.** A software-based protocol analyzer used to capture and analyze network packets.

Before SMS can perform most of the preceding features, it must first collect hardware information on the computers. All the inventory information must be stored in a SQL server database, which means that if you purchase SMS, you must also purchase SQL Server.

SQL Server and SMS Installation Issues

Before SMS can be installed on an NT Server, SQL Server must already be installed, configured, and working correctly. Before you install SMS, you should consider the following:

◆ How many SMS sites are you going to install? SMS allows the administrator to create different sites. Generally a separate site is created for each separate geographic area into which the network extends. If an organization has offices in Kansas City and Seattle, for example, a separate site would be created for each physical location where the network extends.

◆ Will each separate SMS site have its own SQL Server database or will it share the same SQL Server database (via a LAN or WAN link)? The answer to this question depends on the particular circumstances the administrator faces (a discussion of these goes beyond the scope of this chapter). This is important to determine before SMS is installed, because SQL Server has to be installed first at each site, assuming that SQL Server will be at each site.

◆ Where should you locate SQL Server? Will it be on the same server as SMS? Not a good idea if you have many clients attached to the network. Or will it be on a separate physical server? And if so, how big should the server hardware be? Again, the answers to these questions depend on the organization's particular circumstances.

◆ How do you want to optimize SQL Server to work with SMS? Microsoft has made some very specific recommendations on how SQL Server should be configured for optimum performance. You can find this information in the SMS manual, and in Books Online. The exact settings will depend on the number of computers in your network and the capability of your server hardware.

◆ Do you want to use SQL Server to manage other databases on the same physical server as SMS? The answer to this question depends on the projected load on the SQL Server, and the organization's particular circumstances.

Only after you answer all these questions are you in a good position to install SQL Server and SMS.

Integrating SMS with SQL Server

After you answer these questions and install SQL Server properly configured for SMS, you're ready to install SMS. The actual steps to integrate SMS with SQL Server depend on the location of SQL Server. If SQL Server is on the same physical server as SMS, the SMS setup program will automatically create the necessary devices and databases within SQL Server. If SQL Server is located on a separate server, however, the required SMS devices and databases will not be created automatically, so you will have to manually create them, following the guidelines in the SMS manual or Books Online. Once the devices and databases are created, you point to them during the SMS setup process, and SMS will take over from there.

Retrieving SMS Data from a SQL Server Database

SMS has a built-in capability to query SMS data stored in a SQL Server database. The provided options, however, are not the most flexible. If you want to, and have the time, you can use SQL statements to extract data from the SMS database just like you would from any SQL Server database. You also can use another front end program, such as Microsoft Access, or a custom Visual BASIC program, to extract data into any form you desire.

Ongoing SQL Server Maintenance

After installing SMS, the ongoing maintenance to the SMS database is the same as to any database, including regularly running DBCC commands and making backups.

Learning More About SQL Server

Learning how to administer SQL Server is no small task. Not only is it an overwhelming program, SQL terminology is not always intuitive, and SQL databases require constant attention. (No wonder SQL Server DBAs generally earn more than regular network administrators.)

If you want to learn more about SQL Server, you can do some research in many different areas, including the following:

◆ Books

◆ Magazines

◆ Web sites

◆ CD subscriptions

Books

Explore the following books for helpful information:

◆ *Microsoft SQL Server 6.5 DBA Survival Guide* by Mark Spenik and Orryn Sledge, Sams Publishing, 1996.

◆ *Microsoft SQL Server 6.5 Unleashed* by David Solomon and Ray Rankins, Sams Publishing, 1996.

◆ *Microsoft SQL Server Training*, Microsoft Official Curriculum, Microsoft Press, 1996.

◆ *Special Edition Using MS SQL Server 6.5* by Bob Branchek, Steve Wynkoop, and Peter Hazlehurst, QUE Publishing, 1996.

Magazines

Explore the following magazines for helpful information:

◆ *BackOffice Magazine*

◆ *Microsoft SQL Server Professional*

◆ *Windows NT Magazine*

◆ *NT Systems Magazine*

Web Sites

Explore the following web sites for helpful information:

◆ *BackOffice Magazine* (www.backoffice.com)

◆ Beverly Hills Software (www.bhs.com)

◆ Microsoft Corporation (www.microsoft.com)

◆ *Windows NT Magazine* (www.winntmag.com)

CD Subscriptions

Explore the following CD subscriptions for helpful information:

◆ *Microsoft Technet*, Microsoft Corporation

◆ *Microsoft Developers Network*, Microsoft Corporation

 Tip   To find the latest information on SQL Server, search the web using your favorite search engine.

Testing Your Knowledge

1. What does the abbreviation SQL stand for?

2. Microsoft SQL Server is an end-user product like Microsoft Access.

   A. True

   B. False

3. Microsoft SQL Server is not processor-dependent, because it runs on top of NT Server's HAL layer.

   A. True

   B. False

4. What is the minimum hard disk space required for Microsoft SQL Server, not including the 15 MB additional space needed for the optional SQL Server books online?

   A. 16 MB

   B. 32 MB

   C. 60 MB

   D. 64 MB

5. SQL Server is processor-intensive, thus it can take full advantage of fast, high-end CPUs and multiple CPUs.

   A. True

   B. False

6. Microsoft SQL Server must be run on a PDC.

   A. True

   B. False

7. The minimum size of the MASTER database is 25 MB, but Microsoft recommends making it at least what size?

   A. 32 MB

   B. 30 MB

   C. 60 MB

   D. 64 MB

8. Name at least four SQL Server administration tools.

9. Before the administrator can create a database, he must create a database device. A database device is a disk file used to store SQL databases and their affiliated transaction logs. What is the purpose of the transaction logs?

   A. A transaction log is a virtual, logical database listing of key database device components such as keys and indexes, which is used exclusively by the Event Viewer to track changes of such components.

   B. A transaction log is a historical listing of all the data changes to a database, which is used to ensure database integrity if the server fails during access or usage of the database.

   C. A transaction log is used as a fault tolerance method for the databases by keeping the essential database components replicated.

10. When SQL Server is installed, the setup process creates which three special database devices that SQL Server uses for its own purposes?

    A. MSSQLDB.DAT

    B. MSDB.DAT

    C. MASTER.DAT

    D. MSDBLOG.DAT

11. A SQL Server permission varies somewhat from a file or directory permission under NT Server. There are two types of permissions: statement and object. Statement permissions determine who can delete or create objects within a database. What do object permissions determine?

    A. Who can access or change database data.

    B. Who can replicate or backup database data.

    C. Who can perform indexing on database data.

12. The two common ways of backing up database data are performing a database backup, and performing a _____ _____ backup.

13. What are the three types of alerts that can be created using the Alert Manager?

    A. Standard alerts

    B. Performance Monitor alerts

    C. SQL Admin alerts

    D. Business alerts

Review Answers

1. Structured Query Language

2. B

3. B

4. C

5. A

6. B

7. B

8. SQL Server Setup, SQL Server Manager, Enterprise Manager, SQL Security Manager, SQL Client Configuration Manager, ISQL/w and ISQL, Database Maintenance Plan Wizard, SQL Server Web Assistant, BCP, Stored and extended procedures, DBCC Commands

9. B

10. B, C, D

11. A

12. transaction log

13. A, B, D

APPENDIX A

Overview of the Certification Process

To become a Microsoft Certified Professional, candidates must pass rigorous certification exams that provide a valid and reliable measure of their technical proficiency and expertise. These closed-book exams have on-the-job relevance because they are developed with the input of professionals in the computer industry and reflect how Microsoft products are actually used in the workplace. The exams are conducted by an independent organization—Sylvan Prometric—at more than 700 Sylvan Authorized Testing Centers around the world.

Currently Microsoft offers four types of certification, based on specific areas of expertise:

◆ **Microsoft Certified Product Specialist (MCPS).** Qualified to provide installation, configuration, and support for users of at least one Microsoft desktop operating system, such as Windows 95. In addition, candidates may take additional elective exams to add areas of specialization. MCPS is the first level of expertise.

◆ **Microsoft Certified Systems Engineer (MCSE).** Qualified to effectively plan, implement, maintain, and support information systems with Microsoft Windows NT and other Microsoft advanced systems and workgroup products, such as Microsoft Office and Microsoft BackOffice. The Windows NT Server 4.0 exam can be used as one of the four core operating systems exams. MCSE is the second level of expertise.

◆ **Microsoft Certified Solution Developer (MCSD).** Qualified to design and develop custom business solutions using Microsoft development tools, technologies, and platforms, including Microsoft Office and Microsoft BackOffice. MCSD also is a second level of expertise, but in the area of software development.

◆ **Microsoft Certified Trainer (MCT).** Instructionally and technically qualified by Microsoft to deliver Microsoft Education Courses at Microsoft authorized sites. An MCT must be employed by a Microsoft Solution Provider Authorized Technical Education Center or a Microsoft Authorized Academic Training site.

The following sections describe the requirements for each type of certification.

Note	For up-to-date information about each type of certification, visit the Microsoft Training and Certification World Wide Web site at http://www.microsoft.com/tran_cert. You must have an Internet account and a WWW browser to access this information. You also can call the following sources:

   ◆ Microsoft Certified Professional Program: 800-636-7544

   ◆ Sylvan Prometric Testing Centers: 800-755-EXAM

   ◆ Microsoft Online Institute (MOLI): 800-449-9333

How to Become a Microsoft Certified Product Specialist (MCPS)

Becoming an MCPS requires you pass one operating system exam. Passing the "Implementing and Supporting Microsoft Windows NT Server 4.0" exam (#70-67), which this book covers, satisfies the MCPS requirement.

Windows NT Server 4.0 is not the only operating system you can be tested on to get your MCSP certification. The following list shows the names and exam numbers of all the operating systems from which you can choose to get your MCPS certification:

   ◆ Implementing and Supporting Microsoft Windows 95 #70-63

   ◆ Implementing and Supporting Microsoft Windows NT Workstation 4.02 #70-73

- ◆ Implementing and Supporting Microsoft Windows NT Workstation 3.51 #70-42

- ◆ Implementing and Supporting Microsoft Windows NT Server 4.0 #70-67

- ◆ Implementing and Supporting Microsoft Windows NT Server 3.51 #70-43

- ◆ Microsoft Windows for Workgroups 3.11–Desktop #70-48

- ◆ Microsoft Windows 3.1 #70-30

- ◆ Microsoft Windows Operating Systems and Services Architecture I #70-150

- ◆ Microsoft Windows Operating Systems and Services Architecture II #70-151

How to Become a Microsoft Certified Systems Engineer (MCSE)

MCSE candidates need to pass four operating system exams and two elective exams. The MCSE certification path is divided into two tracks: the Windows NT 3.51 track and the Windows NT 4.0 track.

Table A.1 shows the core requirements (four operating system exams) and the elective courses (two exams) for the Windows NT 3.51 track.

TABLE A.1
Windows NT 3.51 MCSE Track

Take These Two Required Exams (Core Requirements)	Plus, Pick One of the Following Operating System Exams (Core Requirement)	Plus, Pick One of the Following Networking Exams (Core Requirement)	Plus, Pick Two of the Following Elective Exams (Elective Requirements)
Implementing and Supporting Microsoft Windows NT Server 3.51 #70-43	Implementing and Supporting Microsoft Windows 95 #70-63	Networking Microsoft Windows for Workgroups 3.11 #70-46	Microsoft SNA Server #70-12

continues

TABLE A.1, CONTINUED
Windows NT 3.51 MCSE Track

Take These Two Required Exams (Core Requirements)	Plus, Pick One of the Following Operating System Exams (Core Requirement)	Plus, Pick One of the Following Networking Exams (Core Requirement)	Plus, Pick Two of the Following Elective Exams (Elective Requirements)
AND Implementing and Supporting Microsoft Windows NT Workstation 3.51 #70-42	*OR* Microsoft Windows for Workgroups 3.11–Desktop #70-48	*OR* Networking with Microsoft Windows 3.1 #70-47	*OR* Implementing and Supporting Microsoft Systems Management Server 1.0 #70-14
	OR Microsoft Windows 3.1 #70-30	*OR* Networking Essentials #70-58	*OR* Microsoft SQL Server 4.2 Database Implementation #70-21
			OR Microsoft SQL Server 4.2 Database Administration for Microsoft Windows NT #70-22
			OR System Administration for Microsoft SQL Server 6 #70-26
			OR Implementing a Database Design on Microsoft SQL Server 6 #70-27
			OR Microsoft Mail for PC Networks 3.2-Enterprise #70-37

Take These Two Required Exams (Core Requirements)	Plus, Pick One of the Following Operating System Exams (Core Requirement)	Plus, Pick One of the Following Networking Exams (Core Requirement)	Plus, Pick Two of the Following Elective Exams (Elective Requirements)
			OR Internetworking Microsoft TCP/IP on Microsoft Windows NT (3.5–3.51) #70-53
			OR Internetworking Microsoft TCP/IP on Microsoft Windows NT 4.0 #70-59
			OR Implementing and Supporting Microsoft Exchange Server 4.0 #70-75
			OR Implementing and Supporting Microsoft Internet Information Server #70-77
			OR Implementing and Supporting Microsoft Proxy Server 1.0 #70-78

Table A.2 shows the core requirements (four operating system exams) and elective courses (two exams) for the Windows NT 4.0 track. Tables A.1 and A.2 have many of the same exams listed, but there are distinct differences between the two. Make sure you read each track's requirements carefully.

TABLE A.2
Windows NT 4.0 MCSE Track

Take These Two Required Exams (Core Requirements)	Plus, Pick One of the Following Operating System Exams (Core Requirement)	Plus, Pick One of the Following Networking Exams (Core Requirement)	Plus, Pick Two of the Following Elective Exams (Elective Requirements)
Implementing and Supporting Microsoft Windows NT Server 4.0 #70-67	Implementing and Supporting Microsoft Windows 95 #70-63	Networking Microsoft Windows for Workgroups 3.11 #70-46	Microsoft SNA Server #70-12
AND Implementing and Support-Microsoft Windows NT Server in the Enterprise #70-68	*OR* Microsoft Windows for Workgroups 3.11-Desktop	*OR* Networking with Microsoft Windows 3.1 #70-47	*OR* Implementing and Supporting Microsoft Systems Management Server 1.0 #70-14
	OR Microsoft Windows 3.1 #70-30	*OR* Networking Essentials #70-58	*OR* Microsoft SQL Server 4.2 Database Implementation #70-21
	OR Implementing and Supporting Microsoft Windows NT Workstation 4.02 #70-73		*OR* Microsoft SQL Server 4.2 Database Administration Microsoft Windows NT #70-22
			OR System Administration for Microsoft SQL Server 6 #70-26
			OR Implementing a Database Design on Microsoft SQL Server 6 #70-27

Take These Two Required Exams (Core Requirements)	Plus, Pick One of the Following Operating System Exams (Core Requirement)	Plus, Pick One of the Following Networking Exams (Core Requirement)	Plus, Pick Two of the Following Elective Exams (Elective Requirements)
			OR Microsoft Mail for PC Networks 3.2–Enterprise #70-37
			OR Internetworking Microsoft TCP/IP on Microsoft Windows NT (3.5–3.51) #70-53
			OR Internetworking Microsoft TCP/IP on Microsoft Windows NT 4.0 #70-59
			OR Implementing and Supporting Microsoft Exchange Server 4.0 #70-75
			OR Implementing and Supporting Microsoft Internet Information Server #70-77
			OR Implementing and Supporting Microsoft Proxy Server 1.0 #70-78

How to Become a Microsoft Certified Solution Developer (MCSD)

MCSD candidates need to pass two core technology exams and two elective exams. Unfortunately, the "Implementing and Supporting Microsoft Windows NT Server 4.0"

(#70-67) exam does NOT apply toward any of these requirements. Table A.3 shows the required technology exams, plus the elective exams that apply toward obtaining the MCSD.

Caution The "Implementing and Supporting Microsoft Windows NT Server 4.0" (#70-67) exam does NOT apply toward any of the MCSD requirements.

TABLE A.3
MCSD Exams and Requirements

Take These Two Core Technology Exams	Plus, Choose from Two of the Following Elective Exams
Microsoft Windows Operating Systems and Services Architecture I #70-150	Microsoft SQL Server 4.2 Database Implementation #70-21
AND Microsoft Windows Operating Systems and Services Architecture II #70-151	*OR* Developing Applications with C++ Using the Microsoft Foundation Class Library #70-24
	OR Implementing a Database Design on Microsoft SQL Server 6 #70-27
	OR Microsoft Visual Basic 3.0 for Windows–Application Development #70-50
	OR Microsoft Access 2.0 for Windows–Application Development #70-51
	OR Developing Applications with Microsoft Excel 5.0 Using Visual Basic for Applications #70-52
	OR Programming in Microsoft Visual FoxPro 3.0 for Windows #70-54
	OR Programming with Microsoft Visual Basic 4.0 #70-65

Take These Two Core Technology Exams	Plus, Choose from Two of the Following Elective Exams
	OR Microsoft Access for Windows 95 and the Microsoft Access Development Toolkit #70-69
	OR Implementing OLE in Microsoft Foundation Class Applications #70-25

Becoming a Microsoft Certified Trainer (MCT)

To understand the requirements and process for becoming a Microsoft Certified Trainer (MCT), you need to obtain the Microsoft Certified Trainer Guide document (MCTGUIDE.DOC) from the following WWW site:

http://www.microsoft.com/train_cert/download.htm

On this page, click on the hyperlink MCT GUIDE (mctguide.doc) (117 KB). If your WWW browser can display DOC files (Word for Windows native file format), the MCT Guide displays in the browser window. Otherwise, you need to download it and open it in Word for Windows or Windows 95 WordPad. The MCT Guide explains the four-step process to becoming an MCT. The general steps for the MCT certification are as follows:

1. Complete and mail a Microsoft Certified Trainer application to Microsoft. You must include proof of your skills for presenting instructional material. The options for doing so are described in the MCT Guide.

2. Obtain and study the Microsoft Trainer Kit for the Microsoft Official Curricula (MOC) course(s) for which you want to be certified. You can order Microsoft Trainer Kits by calling 800-688-0496 in North America. Other regions should review the MCT Guide for information on how to order a Microsoft Trainer Kit.

3. Pass the Microsoft certification exam for the product for which you want to be certified to teach.

4. Attend the MOC course for which you want to be certified. This is done so you can understand how the course is structured, how labs are completed, and how the course flows.

Caution You should use the preceding steps as a general overview of the MCT certification process. The actual steps you need to take are described in detail in the MCTGUIDE.DOC file on the WWW site mentioned earlier. Do not misconstrue the preceding steps as the actual process you need to take.

If you are interested in becoming an MCT, you can receive more information by visiting the Microsoft Certified Training (MCT) WWW site at http://www.microsoft.com/train_cert/mctint.htm; or by calling 800-688-0496.

All About TestPrep

The electronic TestPrep utility included on the CD-ROM accompanying this book enables you to test your Windows NT Server 4 knowledge in a manner similar to that employed by the actual Microsoft exam. When you first start the TestPrep exam, select the number of questions you want to be asked and the objective categories in which you want to be tested. You can choose anywhere from one to 70 questions, and from one to six categories, of which the real exam consists.

Although it is possible to maximize the TestPrep application, the default is for it to run in smaller mode so you can refer to your Windows NT Desktop while answering questions. TestPrep uses a unique randomization sequence to ensure that each time you run the program you are presented with a different sequence of questions—this enhances your learning and prevents you from merely learning the expected answers over time without reading the question each and every time.

Question Presentation

TestPrep emulates the actual Microsoft "Implementing and Supporting Microsoft Windows NT Server 4" exam (#70-67), in that radial (circle) buttons are used to signify only one correct choice, while check boxes (squares) are used to signify multiple correct answers. Whenever more than one answer is correct, the number you should select is given in the wording of the question.

You can exit the program at any time by choosing the Exit key, or you can continue to the next question by choosing the Next key.

Scoring

The TestPrep Score Report uses actual numbers from the "Implementing and Supporting Microsoft Windows NT Server 4" exam. For Windows NT Server, a score of 764 or higher is considered passing; the same parameters apply to TestPrep. Each objective category is broken into categories with a percentage correct given for each of the six categories.

Choose Show Me What I Missed to go back through the questions you answered incorrectly and see what the correct answers are. Choose Exit to return to the beginning of the testing routine and start over.

Non-Random Mode

You can run TestPrep in Non-Random mode, which enables you to see the same set of questions each time, or on each machine. To run TestPrep in this manner, you need to create a shortcut to the executable file, and place the CLASS parameter on the command line calling the application, after the application's name. For example:

```
C:\TESTENG\70_67.EXE CLASS
```

Now, when you run TestPrep, the same sequence of questions will appear each and every time. To change the sequence but stay in Non-Random mode (for example, if you're in a classroom setting, where it is important that everyone see the same questions), choose Help, Class Mode on the main screen. This lets you enter a number from 1 to 8 to select a predefined sequence of questions.

Instructor Mode

To run TestPrep in Instructor mode (seeing the same set of questions each time, or on each machine), create a shortcut to the executable file, and place the INSTR parameter following CLASS on the command line calling the application, after the application's name. For example:

```
C:\TESTENG\70_67.EXE CLASS INSTR
```

Now, when you run TestPrep, the same sequence of questions will appear each and every time. Additionally, the correct answer will be marked already, and the objective category from which the question is coming will be given in the question. To change the sequence of questions that appear, choose Help, Class Mode on the main screen. This prompts you to enter a number from 1 to 8 to select a predefined sequence of questions; increment that by 100 and the sequence will be presented in Instructor mode.

Flash Cards

As a further learning aid, you can use the FLASH! Electronic Flash Cards program to convert some of the questions in the database into a fill-in-the-blank format. Run the FLASH! program and select the categories on which you want to be tested. The engine then goes through the database in sequential order and tests your knowledge without multiple choice possibilities.

INDEX I